Human Development

eighth edition

Diane E. Papalia
Sally Wendkos Olds
Ruth Duskin Feldman
in consultation with
Dana Gross

Boston Burr Ridge, IL Dubuque, IA Madison, WI New York San Francisco St. Louis
Bangkok Bogotá Caracas Lisbon London Madrid
Mexico City Milan New Delhi Seoul Singapore Sydney Taipei Toronto

McGraw-Hill Higher Education

A Division of The McGraw-Hill Companies

HUMAN DEVELOPMENT, EIGHTH EDITION

Published by McGraw-Hill, an imprint of The McGraw-Hill Companies, Inc., 1221 Avenue of the Americas, New York, NY 10020.

This book is printed on acid-free paper.

1 2 3 4 5 6 7 8 9 0 VNH/VNH 0 9 8 7 6 5 4 3 2 1 0

ISBN 0–07–232139–3
ISBN 0–07–118005–2 (ISE)

Vice president and editor-in-chief: *Thalia Dorwick*
Editorial director: *Jane E. Vaicunas*
Senior sponsoring editor: *Rebecca H. Hope*
Senior developmental editor: *Sharon Geary*
Marketing manager: *Chris Hall*
Project manager: *Vicki Krug*
Lead media producer: *David Edwards*
Senior production supervisor: *Sandra Hahn*
Design manager: *Stuart D. Paterson*
Cover/interior designer: *Elise Lansdon*
Cover photos: *©PhotoDisc*
Senior photo research coordinator: *Carrie K. Burger*
Photo research: *Inge King*
Supplement coordinator: *Stacy A. Patch*
Compositor: *York Graphic Services, Inc.*
Typeface: *10/12 Palatino*
Printer: *Von Hoffmann Press, Inc.*

The credits section for this book begins on page A1 and is considered an extension of the copyright page.

Library of Congress Cataloging-in-Publication Data

Papalia, Diane E.
Human development / Diane E. Papalia, Sally Wendkos Olds, Ruth Duskin Feldman.—8th ed.
p. cm.
Includes bibliographical references and index.
ISBN 0–07–232139–3 (alk. paper)
1. Developmental psychology. 2. Developmental psychobiology. I. Olds, Sally Wendkos. II. Feldman, Ruth Duskin.

BF713 .P35 2001
914.7′210486—dc21 00–032902
CIP

INTERNATIONAL EDITION ISBN 0-07-118005-2

www.mhhe.com

About the Authors

As a professor, **Diane E. Papalia** taught thousands of undergraduates at the University of Wisconsin-Madison. She received her bachelor's degree, majoring in psychology, from Vassar College and both her master's degree in child development and family relations and her Ph.D. in life-span developmental psychology from West Virginia University. She has published numerous articles in such professional journals as *Human Development, International Journal of Aging and Human Development, Sex Roles, Journal of Experimental Child Psychology,* and *Journal of Gerontology.* Most of these papers have dealt with her major research focus, cognitive development from childhood through old age. She is especially interested in intelligence in old age and factors that contribute to the maintenance of intellectual functioning in late adulthood. She is a Fellow in the Gerontological Society of America. She is the coauthor, with Sally Wendkos Olds and Ruth Duskin Feldman, of *A Child's World,* now in its eighth edition; of *Psychology* with Sally Wendkos Olds; and of *Adult Development and Aging,* with Cameron J. Camp and Ruth Duskin Feldman.

Sally Wendkos Olds is an award-winning professional writer who has written more than 200 articles in leading magazines and is the author or coauthor of six books addressed to general readers, in addition to the three textbooks she has coauthored with Dr. Papalia. Her book *The Complete Book of Breastfeeding,* a classic since its publication in 1972, was reissued in 1999 in a completely updated and expanded edition; more than 2 million copies are in print. She is also the author of *The Working Parents' Survival Guide* and *The Eternal Garden: Seasons of Our Sexuality* and the coauthor of *Raising a Hyperactive Child* (winner of the Family Service Association of America National Media Award) and *Helping Your Child Find Values to Live By.* She has spoken widely on the topics of her books and articles to both professional and lay audiences, in person and on television and radio. She received her bachelor's degree from the University of Pennsylvania, where she majored in English literature and minored in psychology. She was elected to Phi Beta Kappa and was graduated summa cum laude.

Ruth Duskin Feldman is an award-winning writer and educator. With Diane E. Papalia and Sally Wendkos Olds, she coauthored the fourth and seventh editions of *Human Development* and the eighth edition of *A Child's World.* She also is coauthor, with Dr. Papalia and Cameron J. Camp, of *Adult Development and Aging.* A former teacher, she has developed educational materials for all levels from elementary school through college and has prepared ancillaries to accompany the Papalia-Olds books. She is author or coauthor of four books addressed to general readers, including *Whatever Happened to the Quiz Kids? Perils and Profits of Growing Up Gifted.* She has written for numerous newspapers and magazines and has lectured extensively and made national and local media appearances throughout the United States on education and gifted children. She received her bachelor's degree from Northwestern University, where she was graduated with highest distinction and was elected to Phi Beta Kappa.

To all those who have had an impact on our own

development—our families and friends and teachers

who have nurtured us, challenged us,

taught us by their example,

provided support and companionship,

and been there for us over the years.

Dana Gross, chief consultant to this edition, received her Ph.D. in child psychology from the Institute of Child Development at the University of Minnesota. Since 1988 she has been at St. Olaf College, where she is an associate professor of psychology, Director of Linguistic Studies, and an affiliate faculty member of the Asian Studies department. Her broad teaching and research interests include perception, language, cognition, and social cognition, as well as cross-cultural child development. She has published in several professional journals, has presented her work at numerous conferences, and coauthored a chapter in *Developing Theories of Mind,* edited by Astington, Harris, and Olson. Dr. Gross has prepared instructors' manuals and test banks for several McGraw-Hill textbooks and served as chief consultant on Papalia, Olds, and Feldman's recent publication of *A Child's World,* eighth edition.

Contents in Brief

Contents

Chapter 4

Physical Development During the First Three Years

Chapter 5

Cognitive Development During the First Three Years

Chapter 6

Psychosocial Development During the First Three Years

Part Three
Early Childhood

Chapter 7
Physical and Cognitive Development in Early Childhood

Physical Development

Cognitive Development

Chapter 8
Psychosocial Development in Early Childhood

Part Four
Middle Childhood

Chapter 9
Physical and Cognitive Development in Middle Childhood

Chapter 10
Psychosocial Development in Middle Childhood

Part Five
Adolescence

Chapter 11
Physical and Cognitive Development in Adolescence

Chapter 14

Psychosocial Development in Young Adulthood

Part Seven
Middle Adulthood

Chapter 15

Physical and Cognitive Development in Middle Adulthood

Physical Development

Cognitive Development

Chapter 16

Psychosocial Development in Middle Adulthood

Part Eight
Late Adulthood

Chapter 17
Physical and Cognitive Development in Late Adulthood

Physical Development

Cognitive Development

Chapter 18
Psychosocial Development in Late Adulthood

Epilogue The End of Life

Preface

With the publication of the previous, seventh edition, *Human Development* celebrated its twentieth birthday. Just as human beings continue to grow and develop after reaching the age of maturity, so should a good textbook. With this eighth edition, virtually the entire book has been revamped—its design, content, and pedagogical features. At the same time, we have sought to retain the engaging qualities of tone, style, and substance that have contributed to this book's popularity over the years.

Dana Gross, Ph.D., associate professor of psychology at St. Olaf College in Northfield, Minnesota, has served as consultant for this edition, helping us to keep up with the latest findings in a rapidly expanding field. Dr. Gross not only uncovered hundreds of new references but also participated in the planning of this revision and read and commented on the entire manuscript during its formative stages. She also prepared the innovative new Independent Study Projects, to be found in the *Instructor's Manual.* Her current classroom experience provides a valuable perspective on the needs of students today. In addition, as a parent of two preschoolers, she rounds out an author team that consists of the parent of an early adolescent and two grandparents whose children are now young and middle-aged adults.

Our Aims for This Edition 

The primary aims of this eighth edition are the same as those of the first seven: to emphasize the continuity of development throughout the life span; to highlight the interrelationships among the physical, cognitive, and psychosocial realms of development; and to integrate theoretical, research-related, and practical concerns.

The Eighth Edition: What's New? 

Pedagogical Features

The most obvious change in this edition is the switch to a single-column format. This has enabled us to introduce a new, comprehensive Learning System consisting of a coordinated set of marginal features to guide and check students' learning. The Visual Walk-Through following this Preface previews the Learning System and other pedagogical features in detail.

Organizational Changes

There are two major approaches to the study of human development: the chronological approach (describing all aspects of development at each period of life) and the topical approach (focusing on one aspect of development at a time). We have chosen the chronological approach, which provides a sense of the multifaceted sweep of human development, as we get to know first the developing person-to-be in the womb, then the infant and toddler, then the young child, the schoolchild, the adolescent, the young adult, the adult at midlife, and the person in late adulthood.

In line with our chronological approach, we have divided this book into eight parts and an epilogue. After Part 1, which introduces the study of human development, Parts Two through Eight discuss physical, cognitive, and psychosocial development during each of the periods of the life span, concluding with the Epilogue, the end of life.

To initiate students into the dynamic discipline of human development, we have given special attention to the opening section. In Part 1, the material formerly covered in a single introductory chapter has been both streamlined and enhanced by dividing it into three shorter, more easily digestible segments:

- A new Prologue sets the stage for the exciting study of human development. It sums up recent methodological advances and thematic shifts, as well as fundamental points on which consensus has emerged.
- Chapter 1 provides a thumbnail sketch of how the study of the life span developed and of its goals and basic concepts. This first chapter includes a new section on the influences of family type, socioeconomic status, ethnicity, and culture.
- A thorough introduction to theory and research has been moved to the new Chapter 2. The expanded discussion of theoretical perspectives begins by highlighting three key issues: the relative importance of heredity and environment, whether development is active or passive, and whether development is continuous or occurs in stages. We also present an expanded description of research methods and designs and, as before, a discussion of the ethics of research.

The organization of material within and among chapters has been carefully assessed and improved throughout. For example:

- The humanistic perspective and an expanded discussion of Bronfenbrenner's bioecological theory have been moved to Chapter 2.
- Sternberg's triarchic theory of intelligence has been moved to Chapter 9.
- In Chapter 5, the material on early cognitive development has been reorganized under classic approaches (behaviorist, psychometric, and Piagetian) and newer approaches (information processing, cognitive neuroscience, and social-contextual).
- Chapter 13 contains a newly consolidated section on sexual and reproductive issues, including sexual dysfunction, sexually transmitted diseases, menstrual problems, and infertility.
- The sections on education and work in adulthood have been reorganized for greater emphasis on cognitive growth.

Content Changes

Because we believe that all parts of life are important, challenging, and full of opportunities for growth and change, we provide evenhanded treatment of all periods of the life span, taking care not to overemphasize some and slight others. In this revision, we have taken special pains to draw on the most recent information available. In line with the growing recognition of human development as a rigorous scientific enterprise, we have broadened the research base of each chapter more extensively than ever before. We have added many tables and figures and have updated statistics throughout. We have striven to make our coverage as concise and readable as possible, while still doing justice to the vast scope and significance of current theoretical and research work.

This edition continues to expand our cultural coverage, reflecting the diversity of the population in the United States and in other countries around the world. Our photo illustrations show an ever greater commitment to depicting this diversity. The text provides new or enhanced discussions of such topics as cultural differences in temperament, parenting styles, and goals of preschool education; the role of culture in cognitive development; and cultural influences on aggression and school achievement.

Among the important topics given new or greatly revised coverage, chapter by chapter, are the following:

Chapter 1

- Digging Deeper box on children of the Great Depression
- Practically Speaking box on critical periods in language development
- Concept of social construction
- Major contextual influences (family, socioeconomic status, neighborhood, culture, ethnicity)

Chapter 2

- Three basic theoretical issues; theories now discussed before methods
- Bronfenbrenner's theory included under contextual theoretical perspective
- Digging Deeper box on adaptive value of immaturity
- Microgenetic studies
- Cognitive neuroscience approach
- Ethnographic studies
- Ethics discussed in text rather than box
- Critiques of theories streamlined

Chapter 3

- Digging Deeper box on human cloning
- Concept of quantitative trait loci (QTL)
- Co-twin control and chorion control studies
- Figure on reaction range
- Gene-environment interaction and gene-environment correlation
- Genetic counseling moved from box to text
- Multiple births
- Fetal development
- Prenatal environment and prenatal care

Chapter 4

- Historical changes in birth practices
- Concept of parturition
- Methods of delivery, including epidurals
- Effects of favorable environment in overcoming impact of birth complications
- Infant mortality rate and sudden infant death syndrome (SIDS)
- Brain development, including several new figures
- Revised table on reflexes
- Motor development

Chapter 5

- Digging Deeper box on whether toddlers can "read" others' wishes
- Material on cognitive development organized into classic and newer approaches
- Cognitive neuroscience approach
- Social-contextual approach

- Early intervention
- Table on key developments of sensorimotor stage
- Infant memory
- Development of knowledge about objects and space
- Early perceptual and processing abilities
- Language development

Chapter 6

- Window on the World box on fatherhood in three cultures
- Practically Speaking box on maternal depression (new section on brain growth and emotional development)
- Figure on timetable of emotional development
- Still-face paradigm
- Cross-cultural differences in temperament
- Children of working parents section with much revised material, especially on effects of child care on various aspects of development
- National Institute of Child Health and Human Development (NICHD) study, including new tables on choosing child care and effects of early child care
- Social referencing

Chapter 7

- Handedness
- Artistic development
- Figure on leading causes of death for children in the developing world
- Exposure to smoking
- Table on health outcomes for poor children
- Spatial thinking
- Biological understanding
- Concept of Flynn effect
- Digging Deeper box on imaginary playmates
- Causality
- Theory of mind
- Language development
- Practically Speaking box on eyewitness testimony
- Goals of preschools—a cross-cultural comparison

Chapter 8

- Digging Deeper box on children's beliefs about gender
- Cultural differences in parenting styles
- Concept of self-efficacy
- Biological approaches to gender
- Section on play revised and moved to follow gender
- Gender differences in play moved to play section
- Spanking, power assertion, induction, and withdrawal of love
- Aggression, with new sections on cultural influences
- Prosocial behavior
- Maltreatment
- Window on the World box on nation of only children

Chapter 9

- Obesity
- Rough-and-tumble play
- Gender differences in play
- Medical problems and accidents
- Categorization—containing material on seriation, transitive inference, and class inclusion
- Causality
- Influences of neurological development and culture on cognitive development
- Information-processing approach
- Memory and other processing skills

- Gardner's Theory of Multiple Intelligences
- Sternberg's Triarchic Theory of Intelligence—moved from Chapter 13
- Alternative directions in intelligence testing—K-ABC and Sternberg's Triarchic Abilities Test
- The child in school
- Importance of first grade
- Controversial issues: homework and social promotion
- Cultural influences on achievement
- Practically Speaking box on teaching reading
- Learning disabilities
- Attention deficit/hyperactivity disorder (ADHD)

Chapter 10

- Emotional growth
- Aggression—including new section on bullies and victims
- Disruptive behavior disorders
- Table on characteristics of resilient children
- Effect of parents' work
- Adoptive families—moved from Chapter 14
- Effects of divorce
- Digging Deeper box on parents staying together for the children
- Living in a one-parent family
- Living in a stepfamily
- Sibling relations
- Friendships, including table on Selman's stages
- Depression

Chapter 11

- Physical fitness
- Sleep needs
- Drug use
- Figure on formal operations tasks
- Self-efficacy beliefs and academic motivation, with table
- Table on social capital
- Practically Speaking box on teenagers working part time

Chapter 12

- Digging Deeper box on youth violence epidemic
- Elkind's concept of patchwork self
- Sexually transmitted diseases (STDs) revised and moved from Chapter 11
- Adolescent rebellion
- How adolescents spend their time
- Preventing juvenile delinquency

Chapter 13

- Sexual and reproductive issues, with new sections including sexual dysfunction, STDs, problems related to menstruation, and infertility
- Assisted reproduction moved from Chapter 14 and into a Practically Speaking box
- Obesity
- Physical activity
- Smoking
- Schaie's model of cognitive development, including new figure
- Development of faith moved to Digging Deeper box
- Education and work: reorganized section, including cognitive growth in college, cognitive complexity of work, work and age, workplace education and adult literacy, and equal opportunity issues

Chapter 14

- Integrating approaches to psychosocial development
- Normative-crisis models

- Friendships
- Marital and nonmarital lifestyle types
- Practically Speaking box on domestic violence

Chapter 15

- Middle age: a cultural construct
- Physical changes
- Health
- Burnout and unemployment as stressors
- Table on benefits and risks of estrogen-replacement therapy (ERT)
- Table on lifestyle factors in selected diseases
- Schaie's Seattle Longitudinal Study
- Combined work and education coverage, including age-based roles, occupational patterns, work and cognitive development, and the mature learner

Chapter 16

- Looking at the life course in middle age
- Psychological well-being and mental health
- Gender identity
- Narrative psychology
- Identity styles, socioemotional selectivity theory, and social convoys moved from Chapter 18
- Theories updated and new table on generativity added
- Midlife divorce
- Friendships at midlife
- Grandparenthood

Chapter 17

- Digging Deeper box on centenarians
- Regional and ethnic differences in life expectancy
- Gender differences in aging
- Theories of why people age, with new figure
- Aging brain
- Alcohol and aging
- Depression and aging
- Health status
- Physical activity
- Alzheimer's disease
- Change in processing abilities
- Neurological changes and memory

Chapter 18

- Window on the World box on aging in Japan
- Table on alternative living arrangements
- Table on United Nations Principles for Older Persons
- Personal relationships

Epilogue

- Streamlined discussion of death, dying, and bereavement
- Suicide
- Euthanasia and assisted suicide

Supplementary Materials

Human Development, eighth edition, is accompanied by a comprehensive learning and teaching package, keyed into the new Learning System. Each component of this package has been thoroughly revised and expanded to include important new course material. The supplements listed here may accompany Human Development, Eighth Edition. Please contact your local McGraw-Hill representative for details concerning policies, prices, and availability as some restrictions may apply.

For the Instructor

Instructor's Manual

Peggy J. Skinner, Ph.D., and Wanda M. Clark, Ph.D.
South Plains College, Levelland, TX

This comprehensive revision provides a variety of new as well as retained tools for both seasoned instructors and those new to the Human Development course. New features include a chapter introduction, suggested lecture openers, essay questions and possible answers, as well as critical thinking exercises and possible answers. Additionally, a new innovative annotated outline called the Total Teaching Reference Package has been added to each chapter. Building on a traditional chapter outline, all the MGH resources available to the instructor have been correlated to the main concepts in each chapter. As well as revising learning objectives and key terms, significant new material has been added to classroom activities and projects. The latter now takes account of varied group size and provides a helpful completion time estimate. The end matter section offers tips on study skills, learning styles, APA style, using the Internet in teaching, and an updated transparency list.

Test Bank

By Earl Wade Gladin, Bob Jones University

This comprehensive test bank has been extensively revised to include a wide range of multiple-choice, fill-in-the-blank, critical thinking, and essay questions from which instructors can create their test material. Text box questions linked closely to the main text have been added. Each item is designated as factual, conceptual, or applied, as defined by Benjamin Bloom's Taxonomy of Educational Objectives.

Computerized Test Bank

By Earl Wade Gladin, Bob Jones University

This computerized test bank contains all of the questions in the print version and is available in both Macintosh and Windows platforms.

The McGraw-Hill Developmental Psychology Image Database

Overhead Transparencies and CD-ROM

This set of 200 full-color images was developed using the best selection of our human development illustrations and tables and is available both in a print overhead transparency set and on a CD-ROM with a fully functioning editing feature. Instructors can add their own lecture notes to the CD-ROM and can organize the images to correspond to their particular classroom needs. The author also has selected key images for each chapter, which are available via the text's website.

Instructor's Resources CD-ROM

This resourceful tool offers instructors the opportunity to customize McGraw-Hill materials to create their lecture presentations. Resources included for instructors include the Instructor's Manual materials, PowerPoint presentation slides, and the Image Database for Human Development.

Online Learning Center website

This extensive website, designed specifically to accompany Papalia, Olds, and Feldman's *Human Development* (8/e), offers an array of resources for both instructor and student. PowerPoint presentations, author-selected images from the database, Web links, and more resources can be found by logging on to the text site at http://www.mhhe.com/papaliah8.

Interactive Text Bibliography

The *New! Interactive Bibliography* to accompany Papalia, *Human Development*, Eighth Edition. Announcing the first truly interactive text bibliography, giving you and your students the opportunity to learn more about this text's references and researchers. This comprehensive bibliography has been greatly enhanced and expanded to offer the most up-to-date listing of reference citations in developmental psychology. Now located on the text's Online Learning Center, this interactive resource for instructors and students of *Human Development*, Eighth Edition, contains website links to many important sites highlighting key researchers, research organizations, and groups (both government and independent) actively supporting issues related to human development. Instructors can supplement their lectures by quickly researching additional information for further in-depth study or for gathering topical and interesting ideas for classroom discussion. Students can use this resource for investigating key topics and people for research projects, exams, or for career or personal interest. We invite you to try this exciting new resource at http://www.mhhe.com/papaliah8

Printed copies of the bibliography are available upon request.

The AIDS Booklet

Frank D. Cox

This brief but comprehensive text has recently been revised to provide the most up-to-date information about Acquired Immune Deficiency Syndrome (AIDS).

The Critical Thinker

Richard Mayer and Fiona Goodchild of the University of California, Santa Barbara, use excerpts from introductory psychology textbooks to show students how to think critically about psychology.

Annual Editions—Human Development

Published by Dushkin/McGraw-Hill, this is a collection of articles on topics related to the latest research and thinking in human development.

PageOut-Build your own course website in less than an hour.

You don't have to be a **computer whiz** to create a website. Especially with an exclusive McGraw-Hill product called **PageOut**™. It requires no prior knowledge of HTML. No long hours of coding. And no design skills on your part. www.pageout.net

PowerPoint™ Lecture

Available on the Internet, these presentations cover the key points of the chapter and include charts and graphs from the text where relevant. They can be used as is or modified to meet your personal needs. www.mhhe.com/papaliah8

For the Student

Student Study Guide

By Leilani Brown, University of Hawaii, Hilo.

This revised *Student Study Guide* includes such new features as a short chapter introduction, essay questions with possible answers, and an innovative annotated outline similar to that in the *Instructor's Manual*. Learning objectives, self-tests, key terms, and supplemental readings have been considerably revised in this new edition. The preface provides extensive tips for students on how to study, manage time, and target their learning more effectively.

Making the Grade CD-ROM

This user-friendly CD-ROM gives students an opportunity to test their comprehension of the course material. The CD-ROM contains a Learning Assessment questionnaire that the student can complete to find out what type of learner he/she is. Once the student's learning style is identified, he/she can go to the testing component included specifically for that learning style.

Guide to Life-Span Development for Future Educators

Guide to Life-Span Development for Future Nurses

These useful student tools help students apply the concepts of human development to their professional education. These two brief supplements contain information, exercises, and sample tests designed to help students prepare for certification and understand human development from a professional perspective.

Online Learning Center website

The official website for the text contains Chapter Outlines, Practice Quizzes that can be e-mailed to the professor, Links to Relevant Internet sites, Internet Primer, Career Appendix, and a Statistics Primer. www.mhhe.com/papaliah8

Interactive Text Bibliography

Announcing the first truly interactive text bibliography, giving you and your students the opportunity to learn more about this text's references and researchers. This comprehensive bibliography has been greatly enhanced and expanded to offer the most up-to-date listing of reference citations in developmental psychology. Now located on the text's Online Learning Center, this interactive resource for instructors and students of *Human Development,* Eighth Edition, contains website links to many important sites highlighting key researchers, research organizations, and groups (both government and independent) actively supporting issues related to human development. Instructors can supplement their lectures by quickly researching additional information for further in-depth study or for gathering topical and interesting ideas for classroom discussion. Students can use this resource for investigating key topics and people for research projects, exams, or for career or personal interest. We invite you to try this exciting new resource at http://www.mhhe.com/papaliah8

Printed copies of the bibliography are available upon request.

The Resource Guide on the McGraw-Hill website

http://www.mhhe.com/papaliah8 helps interested readers seek information and assistance with regard to practical concerns related to topics discussed in the book. Hotlinks are provided when available to make contacting agencies and organizations easier.

Student and Instructor Supplements Users–We want to hear from you!

If you are currently using a McGraw-Hill supplement, we'd like to hear from you. In an effort to improve the quality of future supplements, we invite you to visit our text website and complete an evaluation form. This completed form will be e-mailed directly to the editors and will be considered as we develop future supplements for human sexuality. This form can be found at www.mhhe.com/papaliah8

Acknowledgments

We would like to express our gratitude to the many friends and colleagues who, through their work and their interest, helped us clarify our thinking about human development. We are especially grateful for the valuable help given by those who reviewed the seventh edition of *Human Development,* provided user diaries of the seventh edition, and reviewed the manuscript drafts of this eighth edition. Their evaluations and suggestions helped greatly in the preparation of this new edition. These reviewers, who are affiliated with both two- and four-year institutions, are as follows.

Reviewers of the Seventh Edition in Preparation for the Revision

Martin L. Harris,
Southern California College

Feleccia R. Moore-Davis,
Houston Community College–Central College

Jane Bock,
University of Wisconsin–Green Bay

Peter J. Caprioglio,
Middlesex Community-Technical College

John Phelan,
Western Oklahoma State College

Jean L. Edwards,
Jones County Junior College

Stephen Burgess,
Southwest Oklahoma State University

Saundra K. Ciccarelli,
Gulf Coast Community College

Mel Ciena,
University of San Francisco

Cynthia Calhoun,
State Technical Institute at Memphis

Sheldon Brown,
North Shore Community College

User Diary Reviewers

Lynn Gillikin,
College of William & Mary

Ursula Flint,
Sierra College

Allyssa McCabe,
University of Massachusetts, Lowell

Focus Group Participants

Robert D. Kavanaugh,
Williams College

Jean Berko Gleason,
Boston University

Eleonara Villegas-Reimers,
Wheelock College

Trudi Feinstein,
Emerson College

Nancy B. Blackman,
Endicott College

Shirley Cassara,
Bunker Hill Community College

Peter V. Correa,
Emerson College

Reviewers of Eighth Edition Manuscript

Steven C. Funk,
Northern Arizona University

Michele J. Eliason,
The University of Iowa

Molly E. Lynch,
University of Texas at San Antonio

Patricia Guth,
Westmoreland County Community College

Anne C. Watson,
West Virginia University

Wendy J. Micham,
Victor Valley College

Stephen J. Houseworth,
The College of William & Mary

Bill Fisk,
Clemson University

Rosemary T. Hornak,
Meredith College

Janet Gregory,
Massey University

Kim Shifren,
Towson University

Joe M. Price,
San Diego State University

Yo Jackson,
University of Kansas

Earl Wade Gladin,
Bob Jones University

We would like to thank the more than 650 professors who participated in our *Human Development* market survey last fall and whose input contributed substantially to the revision of the text. And finally, we would like to acknowledge those instructors using *Human Development* who have contacted us directly through our website. By taking the time to send us their comments about their experiences using the text, they have helped to strengthen it more.

We appreciate the strong support we have had from our publisher. We would like to express our special thanks to Jane Vaicunas, editorial director; Rebecca Hope, senior sponsoring editor; Sharon Geary, senior developmental editor; Vicki Krug, project manager; Laurie McGee, copy editor; Stuart Paterson, design manager; Carrie Burger, photo research coordinator; Rita Lombard, supplement development editor; and our research assistants, Amanda Fingarson, Jessica Shryack, Molly Middlecamp, and Loran Nordgren. Keri Toksu coordinated the preparation of the bibliography. Inge King, photo editor of all previous editions of *Human Development,* again used her sensitivity, her interest, and her good eye to find outstanding photographs. Elise Lansdon produced a strikingly new and attractive book design.

As always, we welcome and appreciate comments from readers, which help us continue to improve *Human Development.*

Diane E. Papalia
Sally Wendkos Olds
Ruth Duskin Feldman

Visual Walk-Through

A special goal for this edition has been to increase its pedagogical value. The shift to a single-column format has made it possible to introduce a comprehensive, unified Learning System, which will help students focus their reading and review and retain what they learn.

As always, we seek to make the study of human development come alive by telling illustrative stories about actual incidents in the lives of real people. In this edition, each chapter opens with a fascinating biographical vignette from a period in the life of a well-known person (such as Elvis Presley, Eva Perón, Anne Frank, Jackie Robinson, John Glenn, and Mahatma Gandhi) or a classic case (such as the Wild Boy of Aveyron and Charles Darwin's diary of his son's first year). The subjects of these vignettes are people of diverse national and ethnic origins, whose experiences dramatize important themes in the chapter. We believe students will enjoy and identify with these stories, which lead directly into the body of the chapter and are woven into its fabric. These vignettes, along with the shorter true anecdotes that appear throughout the book—some of them about the author's own children and grandchildren—underline the fact that there is no "average" or "typical" human being, that each person is an individual with a unique personality and a unique set of life circumstances. They are reminders that whenever we talk about human development, we talk about real people in a real world.

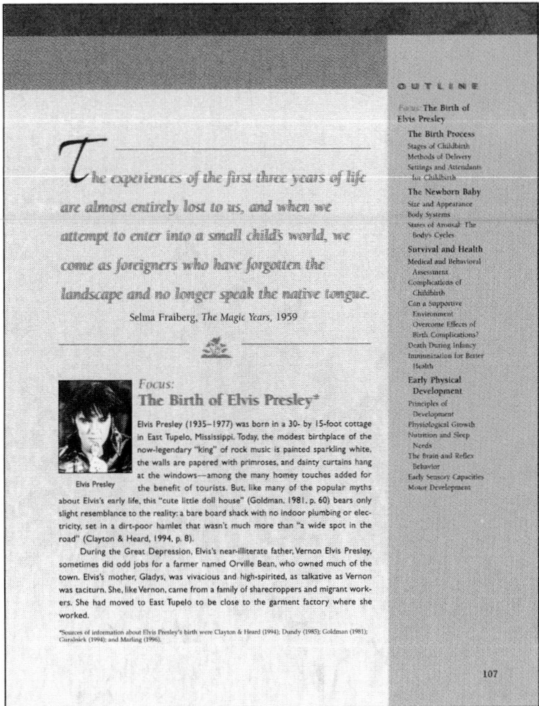

The experiences of the first three years of life are almost entirely lost to us, and when we attempt to enter into a small child's world, we come as foreigners who have forgotten the landscape and no longer speak the native tongue.

Selma Fraiberg, *The Magic Years*, 1959

Focus:
The Birth of Elvis Presley*

Elvis Presley

Elvis Presley (1935–1977) was born in a 30- by 15-foot cottage in East Tupelo, Mississippi. Today, the modest birthplace of the now-legendary "king" of rock music is painted sparkling white, the walls are papered with primroses, and dainty curtains hang at the windows—among the many homey touches added for the benefit of tourists. But, like many of the popular myths about Elvis's early life, this "cute little doll house" (Goldman, 1981, p. 60) bears only slight resemblance to the reality: a bare board shack with no indoor plumbing or electricity, set in a dirt-poor hamlet that wasn't much more than "a wide spot in the road" (Clayton & Heard, 1994, p. 8).

During the Great Depression, Elvis's near-illiterate father, Vernon Elvis Presley, sometimes did odd jobs for a farmer named Orville Bean, who owned much of the town. Elvis's mother, Gladys, was vivacious and high-spirited, as talkative as Vernon was taciturn. She, like Vernon, came from a family of sharecroppers and migrant workers. She had moved to East Tupelo to be close to the garment factory where she worked.

*Sources of information about Elvis Presley's birth were Clayton & Heard (1994); Dundy (1985); Goldman (1981); Guralnick (1994); and Marling (1996).

OUTLINE

107

New Learning System

The new Learning System forms the conceptual framework of each chapter and is carried through all text supplements. It has the following four parts.

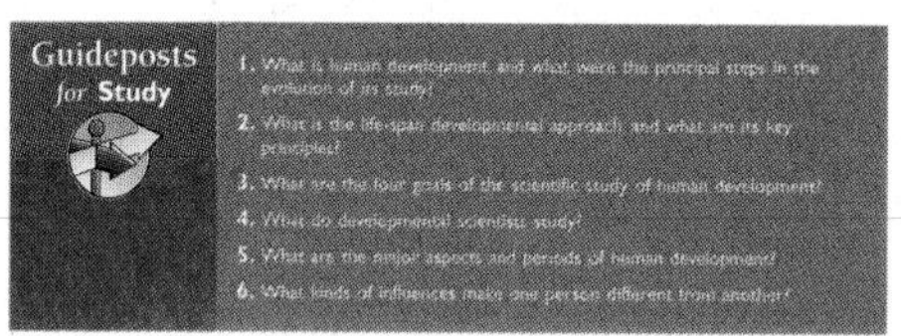

How the Study of Human Development Evolved

The field of **human development** is the scientific study of ways in which people change, as well as of characteristics that remain fairly stable throughout life. Human development has, of course, been going on as long as human beings have existed, but its formal scientific study is relatively new. Since the early nineteenth century, when Itard studied Victor, efforts to understand children's development have gradually expanded to studies of the whole life span.

Guidepost
1.

human development
Scientific study of change and continuity throughout the human life span.

By the end of the nineteenth century, several important trends were preparing the way for the scientific study of child development. Scientists had unlocked the mystery of conception and (as in the case of Victor) were arguing about "nature versus nurture," that is, about the relative importance of inborn characteristics and external influences. The discovery of germs and immunization made it possible for many more children to survive infancy. Because of an abundance of cheap labor, children were less needed as workers. Laws protecting them from long workdays let them spend more time in school, and parents and teachers became more concerned with identifying and meeting children's developmental needs. The new science of psychology taught that people could understand themselves by learning what had influenced them as children.

The idea that development continues beyond childhood is a relatively new one. Adolescence was not considered a separate period of development until the early twentieth century, when G. Stanley Hall, a pioneer in child study, published a popular (though unscientific) book called *Adolescence* (1904–1916). Hall also was one of the first psychologists to become interested in aging. In 1922, at age 78, he published *Sensescence: The Last Half of Life.* Six years later, Stanford University opened the first major scientific research unit devoted to aging. But not until a generation later did the study of aging blossom. Since the late 1930s, a number of important long-term studies discussed in the second half of this book, such as those of K. Warner Schaie, George Vaillant, Daniel Levinson, and Ravenna Helson, have focused on intelligence and personality development in adulthood and old age.

Life-span studies in the United States grew out of programs designed to follow children through adulthood. The Stanford Studies of Gifted Children (begun in 1921 under the direction of Lewis M. Terman) trace the development of people (now in old age) who were identified as unusually intelligent in childhood. Other major studies that began around 1930—the Fels Research Institute Study, the Berkeley Growth and Guidance Studies, and the Oakland (Adolescent) Growth Study—have given us much information on long-term development.

As these studies extended into the adult years, developmental scientists began to focus on how particular experiences, tied to time and place, affect the

Chapter One The Study of Human Development 9

Guideposts for Study

These topical questions, similar to Learning Objectives, are first posted near the beginning of each chapter to capture students' interest and motivate them to look for answers as they read. The questions are broad enough to form a coherent outline of each chapter's content, but specific enough to invite careful study. Each Guidepost is repeated in the margin at the beginning of the section that deals with the topic in question and is repeated in the Chapter Summary to facilitate study.

Checkpoints

These more detailed marginal questions, placed at or near the end of major sections of text, enable students to test their understanding of what they have read. Students should be encouraged to stop and review any section for which they cannot answer one or more Checkpoints.

Infants, for example, are dependent on adults to meet their basic needs for food, clothing, and shelter, as well as for human contact and affection. They form attachments to parents or caregivers, who also become attached to them. With the development of speech and self-locomotion, toddlers become more self-reliant; they need to assert their autonomy but also need parents to help them keep their impulses in check. During early childhood, children develop more self-control and more interest in other children. During middle childhood, control over behavior gradually shifts from parent to child, and the peer group becomes increasingly important. A main task of adolescence is the search for identity—personal, sexual, and occupational. As adolescents become physically mature, they deal with sometimes conflicting needs and emotions as they prepare to separate from the security of the parental nest.

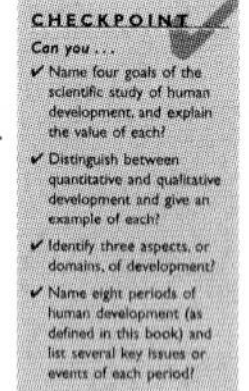

The developmental tasks of young adulthood include the establishment of independent lifestyles, occupations, and, usually, families. During middle adulthood, most people need to deal with some decline in physical capabilities, and women with the loss of reproductive capacity. At the same time, many middle-aged people find excitement and challenge in life changes—launching new careers and adult children—while some face the need to care for elderly parents. In late adulthood, people cope with losses in their own faculties, the loss of loved ones, and preparations for their own death. If they retire, they must deal with the loss of work-based relationships but may get increased pleasure out of friendships, family, and volunteer work and the opportunity to explore previously neglected interests. Many older people become more introspective, searching out the meaning of their lives.

Influences on Development

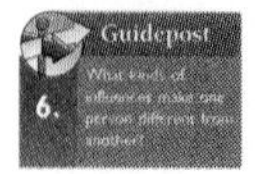

Students of development are interested in processes of development that affect every normal person, but they also want to know about **individual differences,** both in influences on development and in its outcome. People differ in sex, height, weight, and body build; in constitutional factors such as health and energy level; in intelligence; and in personality characteristics and emotional reactions. The contexts of their lives and lifestyles differ, too: the homes, communities, and societies they live in, the relationships they have, the kinds of schools they go to (or whether they go to school at all), their occupations, and how they spend their leisure time.

individual differences
Variations in characteristics or developmental outcomes between one child and another.

Some basic differences are obvious, such as whether a person is male or female. Other differences, such as variations in talent and temperament, may be subtle. All of these differences, and more, may help explain why one person turns out unlike another. Because development is complex, and the factors that affect it cannot always be measured precisely, scientists cannot answer that question fully. However, they have learned much about what people need to develop normally, how they react to the many influences upon and within them, and how they can best fulfill their potential.

Heredity, Environment, and Maturation

Some influences on development originate with **heredity:** the inborn genetic endowment from a person's biological parents. Others come from the external **environment:** the world outside the self, beginning in the womb. Individual differences increase as people grow older. Many typical changes of infancy and early childhood seem to be tied to **maturation** of the body and brain—the unfolding of a natural, genetically influenced sequence of physical changes and behavior patterns, including readiness to master new abilities such as walking and talking. As children grow into adolescents and then into adults, differences in innate characteristics and life experience play a greater role.

heredity
Inborn influences on development, carried on the genes inherited from the biological parents.

environment
Totality of nongenetic influences on development, external to the self.

maturation
Unfolding of a genetically influenced, often age-related, sequence of physical changes and behavior patterns, including the readiness to master new abilities.

16 Part One The Study of Human Development

Which characteristics are most likely to endure? Which are likely to change, and why? These are among the basic questions that the study of human development seeks to answer.

Aspects of Development

The study of human development is complicated by the fact that change and stability occur in various aspects of the self. To simplify discussion, developmental scientists talk separately about *physical development*, *cognitive development*, and *psychosocial development*. Actually, though, these aspects, or domains, of development are intertwined. Throughout life, each affects the others.

Growth of the body and brain, sensory capacities, motor skills, and health are part of *physical development* and may influence other aspects of development. For example, a child with frequent ear infections may develop language more slowly than a child without this problem. During puberty, dramatic physiological and hormonal changes affect the developing sense of self. In some older adults, physical changes in the brain may lead to intellectual and personality deterioration.

Change and stability in mental abilities, such as learning, memory, language, thinking, moral reasoning, and creativity constitute *cognitive development*. They are closely related to physical and emotional growth. The ability to speak depends on the physical development of the mouth and brain. A child who has difficulty expressing herself in words may evoke negative reactions in others, influencing her popularity and sense of self-worth.

Change and stability in personality and social relationships together constitute *psychosocial development*, and this can affect cognitive and physical functioning. For example, anxiety about taking a test can impair performance. Social support can help people cope with the potentially negative effects of stress on physical and mental health. Conversely, physical and cognitive capacities can affect psychosocial development. They contribute greatly to self-esteem and can affect social acceptance and choice of occupation.

Although we will be looking separately at physical, cognitive, and psychosocial development, a person is more than a bundle of isolated parts. Development is a unified process. In this book, at the opening of each part and throughout the text, we will highlight links among the three major domains of development.

Guidepost 5. What are the major aspects and periods of development?

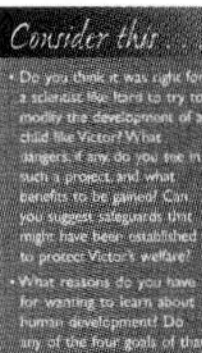

Consider this . . .

- Do you think it was right for a scientist like Itard to try to modify the development of a child like Victor? What dangers, if any, do you see in such a project, and what benefits to be gained? Can you suggest safeguards that might have been established to protect Victor's welfare?
- What reasons do you have for wanting to learn about human development? Do any of the four goals of that study seem more important to you than others?
- Can you identify ways in which one aspect of your development has affected other aspects?

Periods of the Life Span

The concept of periods of the life span is a **social construction:** an idea about the nature of reality accepted by members of a particular society at a particular time on the basis of shared subjective perceptions or assumptions. There is no objectively definable moment when a child becomes an adult, or a young person becomes old. Societies the world over recognize differences in the way people of different ages think, feel, and act, but they divide the life span in varying ways. In industrial societies, as we have already mentioned, the concept of adolescence as a period of development is quite recent. Middle age, too, was not seen as a separate stage of life in earlier times, when life was shorter. Nor is it considered a separate stage in some preindustrial societies, in which social roles do not change appreciably between young adulthood and old age.

The Chippewa Indians have only two periods of childhood: from birth until the child walks, and from walking to puberty. Adolescence is part of adulthood, which lasts until the coming of the first grandchild; a later period of adulthood begins with the birth of the first great-grandchild. The African Swazi define eight periods of life and mark each with a ceremony. Babyhood begins at 3 months, when an infant is considered likely to survive. Then come toddlerhood (which

social construction
Concept about the nature of reality, based on societally shared subjective perceptions or assumptions.

Chapter One The Study of Human Development 13

Consider this . . .

These periodic marginal questions challenge students to interpret, apply, or critically evaluate information presented in the text.

Now that you have had a brief overview of the field of human development and some of its basic concepts, it's time to look more closely at the issues developmental scientists think about and how they do their work. In Chapter 2, we will introduce you to some influential theories of how development takes place and to the methods investigators commonly use to study it.

Summary

How the Study of Human Development Evolved

Guidepost 1. What is human development, and what were the principal steps in the evolution of its study?

- **Human development** is the study of change and stability throughout life. The study of human development began with studies of childhood during the nineteenth century. Adolescence was not considered a separate phase of development until the twentieth century.
- As researchers became interested in following development throughout adulthood, **life-span development** became a field of study.

Guidepost 2. What is the life-span developmental approach, and what are its key principles?

- Baltes's life-span developmental approach is a framework for the study of life-span development. Its key principles include the idea that development is lifelong, the importance of history and context, multidimensionality, multidirectionality, and **plasticity.**

Human Development Today: An Introduction to the Field

Guidepost 3. What are the four goals of the scientific study of human development?

- The study of human development seeks to describe, explain, predict, and modify development.

Guidepost 4. What do developmental scientists study?

- Developmental scientists study developmental change. They are concerned with both **quantitative change** and **qualitative change,** as well as with stability of personality and behavior.

Guidepost 5. What are the major aspects and periods of human development?

- The three major aspects of development are physical, cognitive, and psychosocial. These forms of development do not occur in isolation; each affects the others.
- The concept of periods of development is a **social construction.** All societies recognize such periods, but the precise divisions vary. In this book, the life span is divided into eight periods: the prenatal period, infancy and toddlerhood, early childhood, middle childhood, adolescence, young adulthood, middle adulthood, and late adulthood. At each period of the life span, people have characteristic developmental needs and tasks.

Influences on Development

Guidepost 6. What kinds of influences make one person different from another?

- Influences on development come from both **heredity** and **environment.** Many typical changes during childhood are related to **maturation. Individual differences** increase with age.
- One important environmental, or contextual, influence is the family. In different societies, either the **nuclear family** or **extended family** predominates.
- **Socioeconomic status (SES)** is often related to developmental processes and outcomes through such factors as the quality of home and neighborhood environments, of medical care, and of schooling. The most powerful neighborhood influences on outcomes of development seem to be neighborhood income and human capital. Multiple *risk factors* increase the likelihood of poor outcomes.
- Other important environmental influences stem from **ethnic groups** and **culture.** In large, multiethnic societies, immigrant groups often acculturate, or adapt, to the majority culture while preserving aspects of their own.
- Influences on individuals may be **normative** or nonnormative. Normative age-graded influences affect people of the same age. Normative history-graded influences affect a particular **cohort.** Nonnormative life events are unusual in themselves or in their timing.
- There is strong evidence of **critical periods** for certain kinds of early physical development. For cognitive and psychosocial development, there appears to be more plasticity.

Key Terms

human development (9)
life-span development (10)
plasticity (11)
quantitative change (12)
qualitative change (12)
social construction (13)
individual differences (16)
heredity (16)
environment (16)
maturation (16)
nuclear family (17)
extended family (18)
socioeconomic status (SES) (18)
risk factors (19)
culture (19)
ethnic group (19)
normative (20)
cohort (20)
critical period (21)

Chapter One The Study of Human Development 23

Chapter Summaries

As in previous editions, the Chapter Summaries are organized by the major topics in the chapter. In this edition, the Guidepost questions appear under the appropriate major topics. Each Guidepost is followed by a series of brief statements restating the most important points that fall under it, thus creating a self-testing question-answer format. Students should be encouraged to try to answer each Guidepost question before reading the summary material that follows.

Other Special Features in This Edition

This edition includes three kinds of boxed material.

Digging Deeper **Box 3-1**

Human Cloning: Issues and Implications

Now that scientists have successfully cloned sheep and mice, cloning human beings seems the likely next step. Will we soon be able to duplicate a Mozart or an Einstein? Do scientists have the right to "play God" with human life and personality?

Perhaps the most familiar use of cloning is in horticulture: gardeners reproduce a plant specimen valued for its vigor or beauty by taking cuttings from the mature plant and letting them take root. Cloning human beings would be much more complicated. An ovum would have to be removed from a woman's body and placed in a test tube. Its nucleus would be replaced by the nucleus of a body cell from the person to be cloned—a cell that contains all the paired chromosomes present in a zygote. After cell division begins, the resulting blastula would be implanted in the uterus of a woman, who would, in due time, give birth to an infant endowed with the same genetic makeup as the donor of the nucleus.

The ability to replicate human beings offers intriguing possibilities. In the broadest terms, the conscious selection of individuals for cloning might raise the genetic level of the human species. On a personal level, it could give infertile couples, or those in which one partner has a risky genetic profile, an additional option for producing a child genetically related to at least one of them. Or a couple might choose to clone existing offspring, a dead or dying parent or child, or one who needs a tissue or organ transplant but lacks a suitable donor.

These potential uses raise concerns so troubling to some people that the U.S. Congress has debated proposals to ban human cloning. The chief ethical issues involve the sanctity and dignity of human life. Opponents of cloning argue that it would devalue human beings by depriving them of their uniqueness and treating them as "interchangeable commodities" (Annas, 1998, p. 123).

Actually, a clone is not much different from a laterborn "identical" twin, raised by the older "twin" and his or her spouse. Such relationships might involve novel challenges, but it is argued that these challenges could be met through regulations requiring informed consent and counseling for the couple, guarantees of parental rights and responsibilities, and—to discourage commercial uses of cloning—a limit on the number of clones derived from any particular individual (Robertson, 1998).

Both the potential motives for cloning and the arguments against it may reflect a misunderstanding of the role of genes in human development. Although cloning can produce identical genotypes, it cannot produce identical phenotypes. Like monozygotic twins, clones would not look, feel, be, or act exactly like their genetic donors—in fact, even less so, since they would develop in different uterine environments and would grow up in different circumstances. Even physical appearance can be affected by prenatal experiences, such as the way a fetus is attached to the placenta and the substances it absorbs from the mother's blood (Eisenberg, 1999). Brain development, both before and after birth, is highly dependent on a combination of maturation and experience. And such complex characteristics as intelligence and personality hinge on a virtually inseparable intertwining of nature and nurture.

Thus, "to produce another Wolfgang Amadeus Mozart, we would need not only Wolfgang's genome [genetic makeup] but his mother's uterus, his father's music lessons, his parents' friends and his own, the state of music in 18th century Austria, Haydn's patronage, and on and on. . . . We [cannot assume] that his genome, cultivated in another world at another time, would result in the same musical genius. If a particular strain of wheat yields different harvests under different conditions of climate, soil, and cultivation, how can we assume that so much more complex a genome as that of a human being would yield its desired crop of operas, symphonies, and chamber music under different circumstances of nurture?" (Eisenberg, 1999, p. 474).

Indeed, instead of improving the human species, widespread cloning might have a *negative* effect. It might limit the adaptability of the human gene pool by emphasizing characteristics (such as Mozart's musical ability) that have been successful in particular environments but might turn out to be less successful in other, unforeseen circumstances. "Social evolution demands new types of men and women. Cloning would condemn us always to plan the future on the basis of the past" (Eisenberg, 1999, p. 473).

the vertebral canal) and cleft palate (a fissure in the roof of the mouth) probably result from multifactorial transmission. Attention deficit disorder with hyperactivity (ADDH) is one of a number of behavioral disorders thought to be transmitted multifactorially.

Defects Transmitted by Dominant Inheritance

Most of the time, normal genes are dominant over those carrying abnormal traits, but sometimes the gene for an abnormal trait is dominant. When one parent has a dominant abnormal gene and one recessive normal gene and the other parent

Chapter Three Forming a New Life 71

New "Digging Deeper" Boxes

These boxes explore in depth important, cutting-edge, or controversial research-related issues mentioned more briefly in the text. Some of these include new or significantly expanded or updated discussions of Elder's work on children of the Great Depression; the adaptive value of immaturity; human cloning; effects of maternal depression on infants; toddlers' ability to "read" others' wishes; children's beliefs about gender; whether parents should stay together for the sake of the children; the youth violence epidemic; and centenarians.

"Window on the World" Boxes

This boxed feature offers focused glimpses of human development in societies other than our own (in addition to the cultural coverage in the main body of the text). These boxes highlight the fact that people grow up, live, and thrive in many different kinds of cultures, under many different influences. Among the new, significantly updated, or expanded topics are: purposes of cross-cultural research; fatherhood in three cultures; China's one-child policy; and aging in Japan.

Window on the World **Box 2-2**

Purposes of Cross-Cultural Research

By looking at people from different cultural groups, researchers can learn in what ways development is universal (and thus intrinsic to the human condition) and in what ways it is culturally determined. For example, children everywhere learn to speak in the same sequence, advancing from cooing and babbling to single words and then to simple combinations of words. The words vary from culture to culture, but around the world toddlers put them together to form sentences similar in structure. Such findings suggest that the capacity for learning language is universal and inborn.

On the other hand, culture can exert a surprisingly large influence on early motor development. African babies, whose parents often prop them in a sitting position and bounce them on their feet, tend to sit and walk earlier than U.S. babies (Rogoff & Morelli, 1989).

One hundred years ago, most developmentalists assumed that the fundamental processes of development were universal. Cross-cultural research, when done, was seen as a way to highlight the workings of these universal processes under contrasting environmental conditions. Today it is becoming clear that the cultural context can make a critical difference in the timing and expression of many aspects of development (Parke et al., 1994).

The society people grow up in influences the skills they learn. In the United States, children learn to read, write, and, increasingly, to operate computers. In rural Nepal, they learn how to drive water buffalo and find their way along mountain paths.

One important reason to conduct research among different cultural groups is to recognize biases in traditional western theories and research that often go unquestioned until they are shown to be a product of cultural influences. "Working with people from a quite different background can make one aware of aspects of human activity that are not noticeable until they are missing or differently arranged, as with the fish who reputedly is unaware of water until removed from it" (Rogoff & Morelli, 1989, p. 343).

Since so much research in human development has focused on western industrialized societies, many people have defined typical development in these societies as the norm, or standard of behavior. Measuring against this "norm" leads to narrow—and often, wrong—ideas about development. Pushed to its extreme, this belief can cause the development of people in other ethnic and cultural groups to be seen as deviant (Rogoff & Morelli, 1989).

In this book we discuss several influential theories developed from research in western societies that do not hold up when tested on people from other cultures—theories about gender roles, abstract thinking, moral reasoning, and a number of other aspects of human development. Throughout this book, we consistently look at children in cultures and subcultures other than the dominant one in the United States to show how closely development is tied to society and culture and to add to our understanding of normal development in many settings.

babies being born, regard death as natural, do important work, be assertive, and know precisely what they will be expected to do as adults. Her findings have been debated (D. Freeman, 1983; L. D. Holmes, 1987), in part on the ground that her Samoan sample was not representative of the island's population. Still, "Mead's basic message to the child development field remains as valid today as in 1930: To understand how children grow up under varied environmental conditions, one must be willing to go to where those conditions already exist, to examine them with respect and in detail, and to change one's assumptions in the face of new observations" (LeVine et al., 1994, p. 9).

Correlational Studies

correlational study Research design intended to discover whether a statistical relationship between variables exists, either in direction or in magnitude.

A **correlational study** is an attempt to find a *correlation,* or statistical relationship, between *variables,* phenomena that change or vary among people or can be varied for purposes of research. Correlations are expressed in terms of direction (positive or negative) and magnitude (degree). Two variables that are related *positively* increase or decrease together. A positive, or direct, correlation between televised violence and aggressiveness would exist if children who watched more violent television hit, bit, or kicked more than children who watched less violent television. Two variables have a *negative,* or inverse, correlation if, as one increases, the other decreases. Studies show a negative correlation between amount of school-

50 Part One About Human Development

Box 1-2
Is There a Critical Period for Language Acquisition?

In 1970, a 13½-year-old girl named Genie (not her real name) was discovered in a suburb of Los Angeles (Curtiss, 1977; Fromkin, Krashen, Curtiss, Rigler & Rigler, 1974; Pines, 1981; Rymer, 1993). The victim of an abusive father, she had been confined for nearly twelve years to a small room in her parents' home, tied to a potty chair and cut off from normal human contact. She weighed only 59 pounds, could not straighten her arms or legs, could not chew, had no bladder or bowel control, and did not speak. She recognized only her own name and the word *sorry*.

Only three years before, Eric Lenneberg (1967, 1969) had proposed that there is a critical period for language acquisition, beginning in early infancy and ending around puberty. Lenneberg argued that it would be difficult, if not impossible, for a child who had not yet acquired language to do so after that age. But Lenneberg could offer only indirect evidence for his hypothesis. He pointed out that deaf children who had heard speech early in life could more easily learn to talk than those who had not. He noted that both deaf and retarded children stop acquiring language skills at puberty. Furthermore, a child who suffers brain injury before the early teens may recover linguistic ability if other parts of the brain remain intact, whereas if the injury occurs during adolescence or adulthood, loss of language is likely to be irreversible.

The discovery of Genie offered the opportunity for a test of Lenneberg's hypothesis. Could Genie be taught to speak, or was it too late? The National Institute of Mental Health (NIMH) funded a study, and a series of researchers took over Genie's care and gave her intensive testing and language training.

Genie's progress during the next few years (before the NIMH withdrew funding and her mother regained custody and cut her off from contact with the professionals who had been teaching her) both challenges and supports the idea of a critical period for language acquisition. Genie did learn some simple words and could string them together into primitive, but rule-governed, sentences. She also learned the fundamentals of sign language. But she never used language normally, and "her speech remained, for the most part, like a somewhat garbled telegram" (Pines, 1981, p. 29). When her mother, unable to care for her, turned her over to a series of abusive foster homes, she regressed into total silence.

What explains Genie's initial progress and her inability to sustain it? The fact that she was just beginning to show signs of puberty at age 13½ may indicate that she was still in the critical period, though near its end. The fact that she apparently had learned a few words before being locked up at the age of 20 months may mean that her language-learning mechanisms may have been triggered early in the critical period, allowing later learning to occur. On the other hand, the fact that she was so abused and neglected may have retarded her so much—emotionally, socially, and cognitively—that, like Victor, the wild boy of Aveyron, she cannot be considered a true test of the critical period (Curtiss, 1977). The competition and lack of continuity among the researchers who were studying and teaching her also confused the issue (Rymer, 1993).

Case studies like those of Genie and Victor dramatize the difficulty of acquiring language after the early years of life, but they do not permit conclusive judgments because there are too many complicating factors. Researchers seeking study participants who lack early exposure to language, but whose environment and development are otherwise normal, have therefore turned to deaf persons for whom American Sign Language (ASL) is the primary language. More than nine out of ten deaf children are born to hearing parents. They typically are first exposed to ASL when they enter residential schools for the deaf, efforts to expose them to English having been unsuccessful (Newport, 1991).

One cross-sectional study compared three groups of ASL users at a residential school for the deaf: *native learners*, who had been exposed to ASL from birth by deaf, signing parents; *early learners*, who were first exposed to ASL between ages 4 and 6 by deaf peers upon entering the residential school; and *late learners*, who were first exposed after age 12, having previously attended nonresidential schools that used strictly oral methods. All three groups had mastered the basic word order of their language (as Genie did), but their proficiency varied dramatically. The older a person had been when first exposed to ASL, the more likely that person was to sign ungrammatically and inconsistently. This was true despite the fact that all of the participants had been using ASL for at least thirty years. These findings suggest that it is the initial maturational level of the learner that determines how well a language will be learned (Newport, 1991).

A cross-sectional study of Chinese and Korean immigrants' use of English supports a critical period for second-language learning as well. The participants, all of them college students or faculty, had entered the United States at least five years before, at ages ranging from 3 to 39. Their English performance showed a striking pattern, which conformed to the maturational curve: the later the age of arrival, up to late adolescence, the worse the performance, which then held steady at a low level among those who had arrived as adults (Newport, 1991).

If a critical period for language learning exists, what explains it? Do the brain's mechanisms for acquiring language decay as the brain matures? That would seem strange, since other cognitive abilities improve. An alternative hypothesis is that this very increase in cognitive sophistication interferes with an adolescent's or adult's ability to learn a language. Young children acquire language in small chunks that can be readily digested. Older learners, when they first begin learning a language, tend to absorb a great deal at once and then may have trouble analyzing and interpreting it (Newport, 1991).

22 Part One The Study of Human Development

"Practically Speaking" Boxes

These boxes build bridges between academic study and everyday life by showing ways to apply research findings on various aspects of human development. Among the new, expanded, or substantially updated topics are: reliability of young children's eyewitness testimony; methods of teaching reading; effects of part-time work on adolescents' school achievement; and dealing with domestic violence.

We also provide a number of other new and/or enhanced teaching and learning aids:

Part Overviews

At the beginning of each part, an overview introduces the period of life discussed in the chapters that follow.

Linkups to Look For

New to the part overviews are bulleted lists that point to examples of the interaction of physical, cognitive, and psychosocial aspects of development.

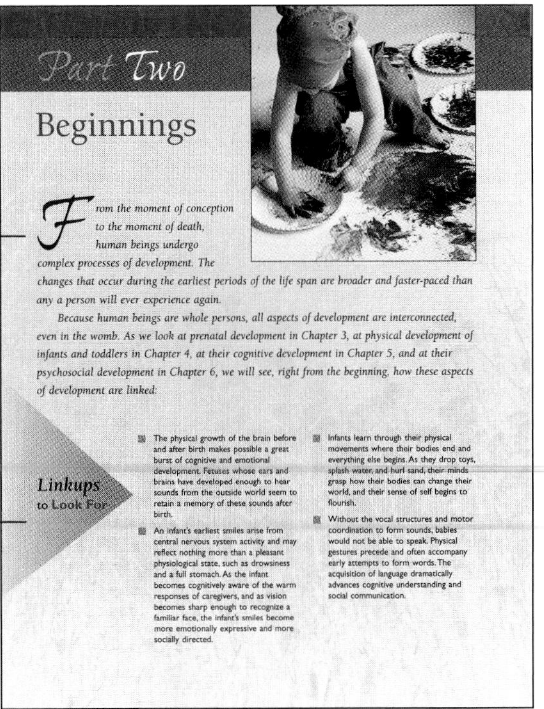

Part Two

Beginnings

From the moment of conception to the moment of death, human beings undergo complex processes of development. The changes that occur during the earliest periods of the life span are broader and faster-paced than any a person will ever experience again.

Because human beings are whole persons, all aspects of development are interconnected, even in the womb. As we look at prenatal development in Chapter 3, at physical development of infants and toddlers in Chapter 4, at their cognitive development in Chapter 5, and at their psychosocial development in Chapter 6, we will see, right from the beginning, how these aspects of development are linked:

Linkups to Look For

- The physical growth of the brain before and after birth makes possible a great burst of cognitive and emotional development. Fetuses whose ears and brains have developed enough to hear sounds from the outside world seem to retain a memory of these sounds after birth.
- An infant's earliest smiles arise from central nervous system activity and may reflect nothing more than a pleasant physiological state, such as drowsiness and a full stomach. As the infant becomes cognitively aware of the warm responses of caregivers, and as vision becomes sharp enough to recognize a familiar face, the infant's smiles become more emotionally expressive and more socially directed.
- Infants learn through their physical movements where their bodies end and everything else begins. As they drop toys, splash water, and hurl sand, their minds grasp how their bodies can change their world, and their sense of self begins to flourish.
- Without the vocal structures and motor coordination to form sounds, babies would not be able to speak. Physical gestures precede and often accompany early attempts to form words. The acquisition of language dramatically advances cognitive understanding and social communication.

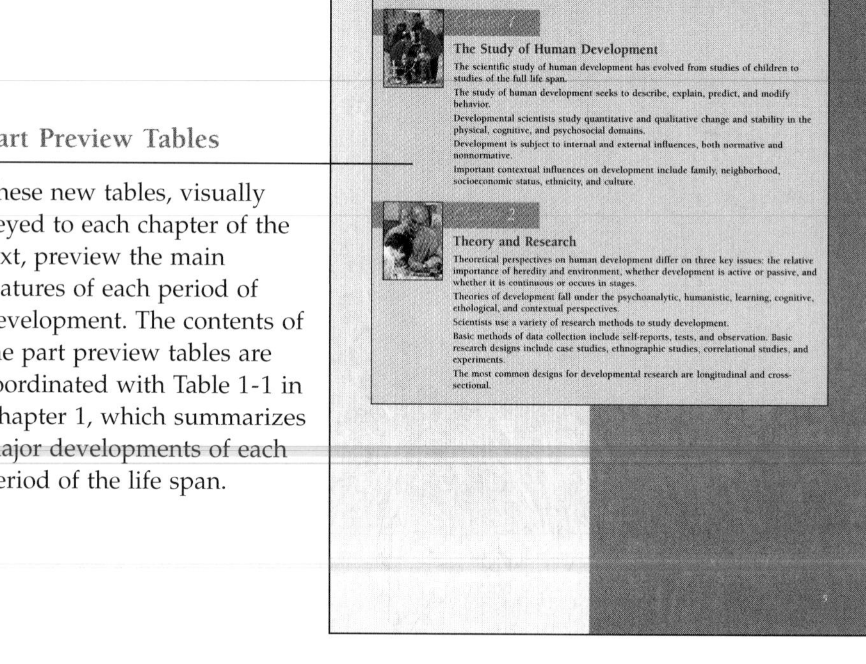

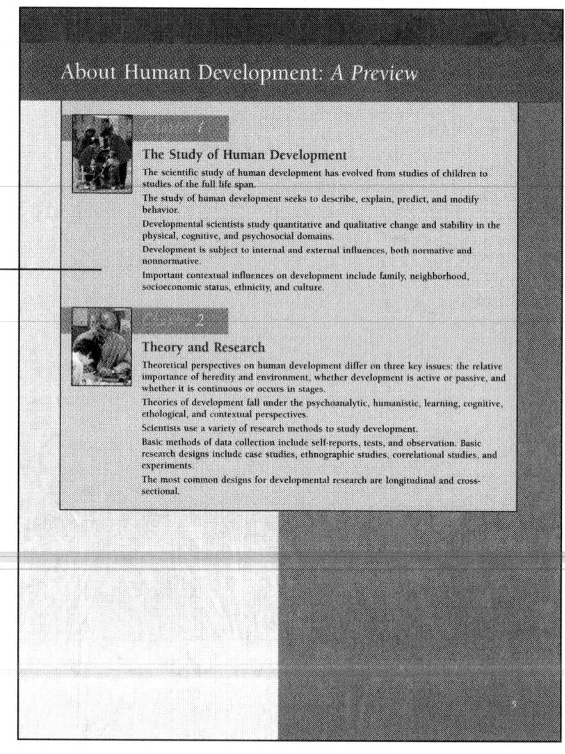

About Human Development: *A Preview*

Chapter 1

The Study of Human Development

The scientific study of human development has evolved from studies of children to studies of the full life span.

The study of human development seeks to describe, explain, predict, and modify behavior.

Developmental scientists study quantitative and qualitative change and stability in the physical, cognitive, and psychosocial domains.

Development is subject to internal and external influences, both normative and nonnormative.

Important contextual influences on development include family, neighborhood, socioeconomic status, ethnicity, and culture.

Chapter 2

Theory and Research

Theoretical perspectives on human development differ on three key issues: the relative importance of heredity and environment, whether development is active or passive, and whether it is continuous or occurs in stages.

Theories of development fall under the psychoanalytic, humanistic, learning, cognitive, ethological, and contextual perspectives.

Scientists use a variety of research methods to study development.

Basic methods of data collection include self-reports, tests, and observation. Basic research designs include case studies, ethnographic studies, correlational studies, and experiments.

The most common designs for developmental research are longitudinal and cross-sectional.

5

Part Preview Tables

These new tables, visually keyed to each chapter of the text, preview the main features of each period of development. The contents of the part preview tables are coordinated with Table 1-1 in Chapter 1, which summarizes major developments of each period of the life span.

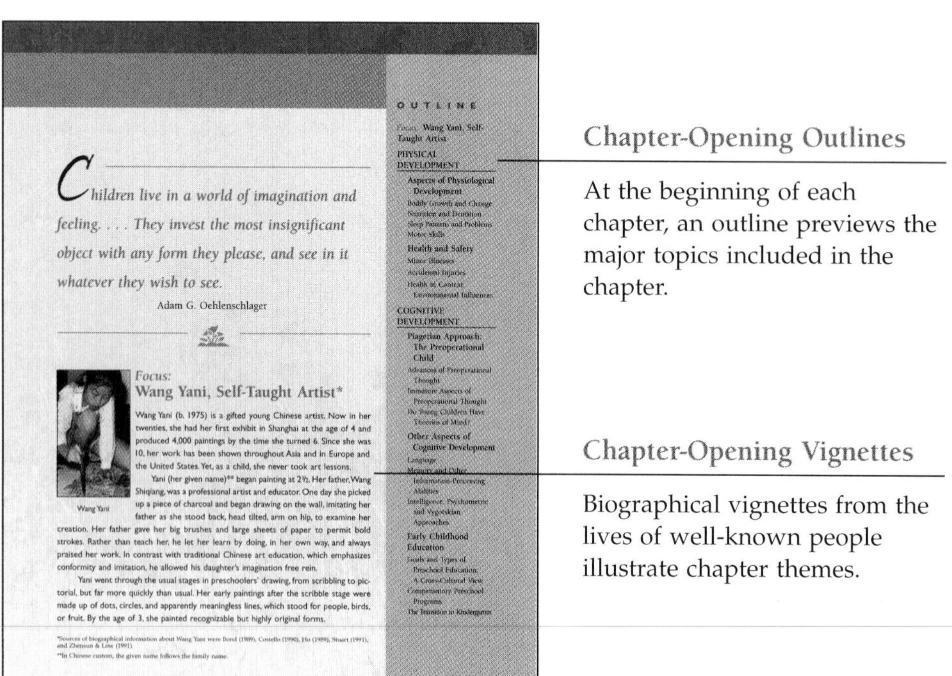

Children live in a world of imagination and feeling. . . . They invest the most insignificant object with any form they please, and see in it whatever they wish to see.

Adam G. Oehlenschlager

Focus:
Wang Yani, Self-Taught Artist*

Wang Yani

Wang Yani (b. 1975) is a gifted young Chinese artist. Now in her twenties, she had her first exhibit in Shanghai at the age of 4 and produced 4,000 paintings by the time she turned 6. Since she was 10, her work has been shown throughout Asia and in Europe and the United States. Yet, as a child, she never took art lessons.

Yani (her given name)** began painting at 2½. Her father, Wang Shiqiang, was a professional artist and educator. One day she picked up a piece of charcoal and began drawing on the wall, imitating her father as she stood back, head tilted, arm on hip, to examine her creation. Her father gave her big brushes and large sheets of paper to permit bold strokes. Rather than teach her, he let her learn by doing, in her own way, and always praised her work. In contrast with traditional Chinese art education, which emphasizes conformity and imitation, he allowed his daughter's imagination free rein.

Yani went through the usual stages in preschoolers' drawing, from scribbling to pictorial, but far more quickly than usual. Her early paintings after the scribble stage were made up of dots, circles, and apparently meaningless lines, which stood for people, birds, or fruit. By the age of 3, she painted recognizable but highly original forms.

*Sources of biographical information about Wang Yani were Bond (1989), Costello (1990), Ho (1989), Stuart (1991), and Zhensun & Low (1991).

**In Chinese custom, the given name follows the family name.

OUTLINE

Focus: Wang Yani, Self-Taught Artist

PHYSICAL DEVELOPMENT

- **Aspects of Physiological Development**
  - Bodily Growth and Change
  - Nutrition and Dentition
  - Sleep Patterns and Problems
  - Motor Skills
- **Health and Safety**
  - Minor Illnesses
  - Accidental Injuries
  - Health in Context: Environmental Influences

COGNITIVE DEVELOPMENT

- **Piagetian Approach: The Preoperational Child**
  - Advances of Preoperational Thought
  - Immature Aspects of Preoperational Thought
  - Do Young Children Have Theories of Mind?
- **Other Aspects of Cognitive Development**
  - Language
  - Memory and Other Information-Processing Abilities
  - Intelligence: Psychometric and Vygotskian Approaches
- **Early Childhood Education**
  - Goals and Types of Preschool Education: A Cross-Cultural View
  - Compensatory Preschool Programs
  - The Transition to Kindergarten

237

Chapter-Opening Outlines

At the beginning of each chapter, an outline previews the major topics included in the chapter.

Chapter-Opening Vignettes

Biographical vignettes from the lives of well-known people illustrate chapter themes.

Yani's father encouraged her to paint what she saw outdoors near their home in the scenic riverside town of Gongcheng. Like traditional Chinese artists, she did not paint from life but constructed her brightly colored compositions from mental images—vivid memories of what she had seen. Her visual memory has been called astounding. When she was only 4, her father taught her Chinese characters (letters) of as many as 25 strokes by "writing" them in the air with his finger. Yani immediately put them down on paper.

Her father helped develop her powers of observation and imagery by carrying her on his shoulders as he hiked in the fields and mountains or lying with her in the grass and telling stories about the passing clouds. The pebbles along the riverbank reminded her of the monkeys at the zoo, which she painted over and over between the ages of 3 and 6. Yani made up stories about the monkeys she created. They often represented Yani herself—eating a snack, refereeing an argument among friends, or trying to conquer her fear of her first shot at the doctor's office. Painting, to Yani, was not an objective representation of reality; it was a mirror of her mind, a way to transform her sensory impressions into simple but powerful semiabstract images onto which she projected her thoughts, feelings, and dreams.

Because of her short arms, Yani's brush strokes at first were short. Her father trained her to hold her brush tightly, by trying to grab it from behind when she was not looking. She learned to paint with her whole arm, twisting her wrist to produce the effect she wanted. As her physical dexterity and experience grew, her strokes became more forceful, varied, and precise: broad, wet strokes to define an animal's shape; fuzzy, nearly dry ones to suggest feathers, fur, or tree bark.

As she grew older, Yani's subjects expanded to include landscapes, pine trees, and lotus flowers. The materials she used—bamboo brushes, ink sticks, and rice paper—were traditional, but her style—popularly called *xieyi*, "idea writing"—was not. It was, and remains, playful, free, and spontaneous.

With quick reflexes, a fertile imagination, remarkable visual abilities, strong motivation, and her father's sensitive guidance, Yani's artistic progress has been swift. As a young adult, she is considered an artist of great promise. Yet she herself finds painting very simple: "You just paint what you think about. You don't have to follow any instruction. Everybody can paint" (Zhensun & Low, 1991, p. 9).

Although Wang Yani's artistic growth has been unusual, it rested on typical developments of early childhood: rapid improvement in muscular control and eye-hand coordination, accompanied by a growing understanding of the world around her—an understanding guided by her powers of observation and memory and her verbal interactions with her father. Together these physical, cognitive, and social influences helped her express her thoughts and emotions through art.

In this chapter, we look at physical and cognitive development during the years from 3 to 6. Youngsters in this age group grow more slowly than before, but still at a fast pace; and they make so much progress in muscle development and coordination that they can do much more. Children also make enormous advances in the abilities to think, speak, and remember. In this chapter, we trace all these developing capabilities and consider several important concerns. We also assess the increasingly common experience of early childhood education.

After you have read and studied this chapter, you should be able to answer the following questions:

238 Part Three Early Childhood

Chapter Overviews

Near the beginning of each chapter, a brief overview of topics to be covered leads the reader smoothly from the opening vignette into the body of the chapter.

identify children who could not handle academic work and who should be removed from regular classes and given special training. The test that Binet and his colleague Theodore Simon developed was the forerunner of psychometric tests, used for children of all levels of ability, which score intelligence by numbers. One is the Stanford-Binet Intelligence Scale, an American version of the traditional Binet-Simon tests (see Chapter 7).

The goals of psychometric testing are to measure quantitatively the factors that are thought to make up intelligence (such as comprehension and reasoning), and, from the results of that measurement, to predict future performance (such as school achievement). **IQ (intelligence quotient) tests** consist of questions or tasks that are supposed to show how much of the measured abilities a person has, by comparing her or his performance with that of other test-takers. A child's score is compared with **standardized norms:** standards obtained from the scores of a large, representative sample of children the same age who were given the test while it was being developed.

IQ (intelligence quotient) tests
Psychometric tests that seek to measure how much intelligence a person has by comparing her or his performance with standardized norms.

standardized norms
Standards for evaluating performance of persons who take an intelligence test, obtained from scores of a large, representative sample who took the test while it was in preparation.

Test developers devise techniques to try to ensure that tests have high **validity** (the tests measure the abilities they claim to measure) and **reliability** (the test results are reasonably consistent from one time to another). Tests can be meaningful and useful only if they are both valid and reliable. For school-age children, intelligence test scores can predict school performance fairly accurately and reliably. Testing infants' and toddlers' intelligence is another matter.

validity
Capacity of a test to measure what it is intended to measure.

reliability
Consistency of a test in measuring performance.

Testing Infants' and Toddlers' Intelligence

Infants are intelligent from birth, but measuring their intelligence is not easy. Since babies cannot tell us what they know and how they think, the most obvious way to gauge their intelligence is by assessing what they can do. But if they do not grasp a rattle, it is hard to tell whether they do not know how, do not feel like doing it, do not realize what is expected of them, or have simply lost interest.

Still, sometimes there are reasons to test an infant's intelligence. If parents are worried because a baby is not doing the same things as other babies the same age, developmental testing may reassure them that development is normal—or may alert them to a problem. Developmental tests compare a baby's performance on a series of tasks with norms established by observing what large numbers of infants and toddlers can do at particular ages.

The **Bayley Scales of Infant Development** (Bayley, 1969, 1993; see Table 5-1) are widely used for these purposes. The Bayley-II, revised in 1993, is designed to assess the developmental status of children from 1 month to $3^1/_2$ years. It is used primarily with children suspected of being at risk for abnormal development (B. Thompson et al., 1994). The Bayley-II has three sections: a *mental scale,* which measures such abilities as perception, memory, learning, and vocalization; a *motor scale,* which measures gross (large-muscle) and fine (manipulative) motor skills, including sensorimotor coordination; and a *behavior rating scale* to be completed by the examiner. Separate scores, called *developmental quotients (DQs),* are calculated for each scale. DQs are most useful for early detection of emotional disturbances, learning problems, and sensory, neurological, and environmental deficits.

Bayley Scales of Infant Development
Standardized test of infants' mental and motor development.

Although these scores give a reasonably accurate picture of a child's current developmental status, they have little value in predicting future functioning (Anastasi & Urbina, 1997). One reason, as we'll see, is that environmental influences affect cognitive development, especially as children approach age 3 (Klebanov, Brooks-Gunn, McCarton, & McCormick, 1998). Another reason is that the developmental tests traditionally used for babies measure mostly sensory and motor abilities, whereas intelligence tests for older children place more emphasis on verbal abilities (Bornstein & Sigman, 1986; Colombo, 1993; McCall & Carriger, 1993). Not until at least the third year of life, when children may be tested with

Chapter Five Cognitive Development During the First Three Years 157

Key Terms

Whenever an important new term is introduced in the text, it is highlighted in boldface and defined, both in the text and, sometimes more formally, in the end-of-book glossary. For the first time in this edition, key terms and their definitions appear in the margins near the place where they are introduced in the text, and all key terms appear in boldface in the Chapter Summaries and subject index.

Art Program

Many points in the text are underscored pictorially through carefully selected drawings, graphs, and photographs. The illustration program includes new figures and many full-color photographs.

Nonetheless, infants themselves prefer simplified speech. This preference is clear before 1 month of age, and it does not seem to depend on any specific experience (Cooper & Aslin, 1990; Kuhl et al., 1997).

Infants' preference for CDS crosses language barriers. In one experiment, $4\frac{1}{2}$- and 9-month-old babies of immigrants to Canada from Hong Kong, whose native tongue was Cantonese, were more attentive, happy, and excited when shown a videotape of a Cantonese-speaking woman using CDS than when the woman used normal adult speech—and so were the babies of English-speaking parents (Werker, Pegg, & McLeod, 1994). The preference for CDS is not limited to spoken language. In an observational study in Japan, deaf mothers were videotaped reciting everyday sentences in sign language, first to their deaf 6-month-old infants and then to deaf adult friends. The mothers signed more slowly and with more repetition and exaggerated movements when directing the sentences to the infants, and other infants the same age paid more attention and appeared more responsive when shown these tapes (Masataka, 1996). What's more, 6-month-old *hearing* infants who had never been exposed to sign language also showed a preference for infant-directed sign. This is powerful evidence that infants, whether hearing or deaf, are universally attracted to CDS (Masataka, 1998).

Preparing for Literacy: The Benefits of Reading Aloud

Most babies love to be read to, and the frequency with which parents or caregivers read to them, as well as the way they do it, can influence how well children speak and eventually how well and how soon they read. Children who learn to read early are generally those whose parents read to them very frequently when they were very young.

Reading to an infant or toddler offers opportunities for emotional intimacy and fosters parent-child communication. Adults help a child's language development when they paraphrase what the child says, expand on it, talk about what interests the child, remain quiet long enough to give the child a chance to respond, and ask specific questions (Rice, 1989). Read-aloud sessions offer a perfect opportunity for this kind of interaction.

A child will get more out of such sessions if adults ask challenging, open-ended questions rather than those calling for a simple yes or no ("What is the cat doing?" instead of "Is the cat asleep?"). In one study, 21- to 35-month-olds whose parents did this—and who added to the child's answers, corrected wrong ones, gave alternative possibilities, encouraged the child to tell the story, and bestowed

By reading aloud to his 2-year-old son and asking questions about the pictures in the book, this father is helping the boy build language skills and prepare to become a good reader.

Chapter Five Cognitive Development During the First Three Years 189

Key Terms

intelligent behavior (157)
behaviorist approach (157)
psychometric approach (157)
Piagetian approach (157)
classical conditioning (158)
operant conditioning (158)
time window (161)
IQ (intelligence quotient) tests (161)
standardized norms (161)
validity (161)
reliability (161)
Bayley Scales of Infant Development (162)
Home Observation for Measurement of the Environment (HOME) (163)
developmental priming mechanisms (164)
early intervention (164)
sensorimotor stage (165)
schemes (166)
circular reactions (166)
representational ability (168)
deferred imitation (168)
object permanence (168)
A, not-B, error (169)
invisible imitation (170)
visible imitation (170)
information-processing approach (172)
cognitive neuroscience approach (172)
social-contextual approach (172)
habituation (173)
dishabituation (173)
visual preference (174)
cross-modal transfer (174)
visual recognition memory (175)
violation-of-expectations (176)
explicit memory (181)
implicit memory (181)
working memory (181)
guided participation (182)
language (182)
literacy (183)
prelinguistic speech (183)
linguistic speech (185)
holophrase (185)
telegraphic speech (186)
syntax (187)
nativism (189)
language acquisition device (LAD) (189)
code mixing (192)

192 Part Two Beginnings

End-of-Chapter Lists of Key Terms

At the end of every chapter, key terms are listed in the order in which they first appear and are cross-referenced to pages where they are defined.

Human Development

Prologue

When you look through your family photo album, do you wonder about the people whose images are frozen there at a succession of moments in time? When you see that snapshot of your mother on her first bicycle, do you suppose that she had trouble learning to ride? Did she take a lot of spills? And why is she smiling shyly in that photo of her taken on the first day of school? Was she nervous about meeting her teacher? There she is with your father on their wedding day. Did their lives turn out as they hoped? There is your mother, holding you as a baby. How did that little girl on a bike turn into the woman with an infant in her arms? How did *you* become the person you are today? How will you become the person you will be tomorrow?

Snapshots tell us little about the processes of inward and outward change that make up a human life. Even a series of home movies or videotapes, which can follow people from moment to moment as they grow older, will not capture a progression of changes so subtle that we often cannot detect them until after they have occurred. The processes that produce those changes—the processes by which human beings develop across time—are the subject of this book.

Human Development: An Exciting, Evolving Field

Human beings have been the focus of scientific study for more than one hundred years. This exploration is an ever-evolving endeavor. The questions that developmental scientists—people engaged in the professional study of human development—seek to answer, the methods they use, and the explanations they propose are not the same today as they were even twenty-five years ago. These shifts reflect progress in understanding, as new investigations build on or challenge earlier ones. They also reflect the changing cultural and technological context, which influences the goals, attitudes, and tools that scientists bring to their work.

Advances in neuroscience and brain imaging are making it possible to probe the mysteries of temperament—tracing overanxiety, for example, to the chemistry of the brain. Advances in behavioral genetics enable scientists to assess more precisely the relative influences of inheritance and experience. Cameras, videocassette recorders, and computers allow investigators to scan infants' facial expressions for early signs of emotions or to analyze how mothers and babies communicate. Sensitive instruments that measure eye movements, heart rate, blood pressure, muscle tension, and the like are turning up intriguing connections between biological functions and psychological or social ones: between infant visual attentiveness and childhood intelligence, between electrical brain wave patterns and the emergence of logical thought, and between the chemical content of blood plasma and the likelihood of delinquency. Other instruments give us a picture of the normally aging brain as compared with the brain of a person afflicted with Alzheimer's disease.

Human Development: Basic Themes

As the study of human development has matured, a consensus has emerged on several fundamental themes, which will come up repeatedly in this book:

1. *All domains of development are interrelated.* Although developmental scientists often look separately at various aspects of development, each affects the others. For example, increasing physical mobility helps a baby learn about the world. The hormonal and physical changes of puberty influence emotional development. Sleep habits and nutrition in adulthood can affect memory. Researchers even have identified possible links between personality traits and length of life.
2. *Normal development includes a wide range of individual differences.* Each person is a distinct individual. One is outgoing, another shy. One is agile, another awkward. How those differences, and a multitude of others, come about is among the fascinating questions that developmental scientists address. Some influences on individual differences are inborn. Others come from experience. Family characteristics, the effects of gender, social class, race, and ethnicity, and the presence or absence of physical, mental, or emotional disability all affect the way a person develops.
3. *People help shape their own development and influence others' responses to them.* Right from the start, through the responses they evoke in others, infants influence their environment and then respond to the environment they have helped create. Influence is *bidirectional* (two-way). When babies babble and coo, adults talk back, encouraging the baby to "talk" more. Teenagers' budding sexuality may remind parents that they are not as young as they once were; and the parents' reactions, in turn, may affect how teenagers respond to the changes they are undergoing. Older adults shape their own development by deciding when—or whether—to retire from paid work.
4. *Historical and cultural contexts strongly influence development.* Each person develops within a specific environment, or context, bounded by time and place. Major historical events such as wars, depressions, and famines profoundly affect the development of entire generations. So do revolutionary new technologies, such as the computer. In western industrial societies, medical advances, as well as improvements in nutrition and sanitation, have dramatically reduced infant and child mortality as well as deaths of women in childbirth; and social changes, such as the increasing number of mothers in the workplace, have greatly altered family life. In studying human beings, we need to be aware of contextual patterns specific to a given culture. For example, among the Efe people of the African country of Zaire, infants have as many as five caregivers from birth and are breast-fed by women other than their mothers; and the Gusii of western Kenya have no recognized stage of life comparable to middle age.
5. *Early experience is important, but people can be remarkably resilient.* A traumatic incident or a severely deprived childhood can have grave emotional consequences, but the life histories of countless people show that the effects of painful experience, such as growing up in poverty or the death of a parent, can be overcome.
6. *Development continues throughout the life span.* At one time, it was believed that growth and development ended with adolescence. Today most developmental scientists agree that people have the potential to change as long as they live. The changes of early life are especially dramatic, as almost helpless newborns transform themselves into competent, exploring children. But change during adulthood can be striking, too. Even very old people can show growth, and the experience of dying can be a final attempt to come to terms with one's life—in short, to develop.

Studying Real People in the Real World

The scientific study of human development is founded on the belief that knowledge is useful. The classic distinction between *basic research,* the kind undertaken purely in a spirit of intellectual inquiry, and *applied research,* which addresses a practical problem, is becoming less meaningful. Increasingly, research findings have direct application to child rearing, education, health, and social policy. For example, memory research can help determine the weight to be given children's courtroom testimony. Research on factors that increase the risks of antisocial behavior can suggest ways to prevent it. Research into the understanding of death across the life span can enable professionals to help children and adults deal with bereavement.

Ultimately, *you* are the one who will apply what you learn from this book. Real people are not abstractions; they are living, working, loving, laughing, weeping, question-asking, decision-making human beings. Observe the adults and children about you. Pay attention as they confront the challenges of everyday life. Think about your own experiences and how they relate to what you read in this book. With the insights you gain, you will be able to look at yourself and at other people with new eyes.

How to Use This Book

To aid in your study of human development, we have organized this book around a learning system designed to engage your interest, focus your attention, and help you review and retain what you learn.

Each chapter starts with a vignette about a well-known person whose life story introduces important chapter themes. Next come broad overview questions called "Guideposts for Study." Think about these questions as you read; you will find each "Guidepost" repeated in the margin at the point where you can begin to find the answer in the text. Throughout each chapter are marginal "Checkpoints": more detailed questions to help you assess your mastery of what you have learned. If you cannot answer some of these questions, you should go back over the relevant sections of text. The "Guideposts" are repeated again in the Summary at the end of the chapter, where you can use them as questions for review. Try to answer each question *before* reading the points summarized below it.

Throughout this book, you will find additional aids to learning:

- The opening of each part, except the first, highlights "Linkups to Look For": examples of interrelationships among various aspects of development. Preview tables, keyed to chapter-opening photos, summarize the main points to be covered for each period of life.
- Key terms are highlighted in **boldface** and defined in the margins, as well as in the Glossary at the end of the book. Key terms are also listed at the end of each chapter, with the page numbers where they first appear, and are incorporated in **boldface** into the Summary.
- "Consider this . . . " questions, also in the margins, have no "right" answer; they ask for your own responses to what you read.
- "Digging Deeper" boxes explore more deeply topics mentioned in the text. "Window on the World" boxes highlight cross-cultural material. "Practically Speaking" boxes illustrate real-world applications of research.
- A Bibliography at the end of the book lists all sources cited in the text, so you can look them up for further study.
- A Resource Guide on the McGraw-Hill website (http://www.mhhe.com/papaliahd8) lists organizations that provide information and assistance on such practical problems as adoption, drug abuse, divorce, and aging.

We hope this learning system will help make your study of human development more thorough, efficient, and rewarding.

Part One

About Human Development

Part I of this book is a guide map to the field of human development. It traces routes that investigators have followed in the quest for information about what makes children grow up the way they do; presents guideposts for studying how people continue to develop; points out the main directions students of development follow today; and poses questions about the best way to reach the destination: knowledge.

In Chapter 1, we describe how the study of human development has evolved and introduce its goals and basic concepts. We look at the many influences that help make each person a unique individual.

In Chapter 2, we introduce some of the most prominent theories about human development—theories that will come up in more detail later in this book. We explain how developmental scientists study people, what research methods they use, and what ethical standards govern their work.

About Human Development: *A Preview*

Chapter 1

The Study of Human Development

The scientific study of human development has evolved from studies of children to studies of the full life span.

The study of human development seeks to describe, explain, predict, and modify behavior.

Developmental scientists study quantitative and qualitative change and stability in the physical, cognitive, and psychosocial domains.

Development is subject to internal and external influences, both normative and nonnormative.

Important contextual influences on development include family, neighborhood, socioeconomic status, ethnicity, and culture.

Chapter 2

Theory and Research

Theoretical perspectives on human development differ on three key issues: the relative importance of heredity and environment, whether development is active or passive, and whether it is continuous or occurs in stages.

Theories of development fall under the psychoanalytic, humanistic, learning, cognitive, ethological, and contextual perspectives.

Scientists use a variety of research methods to study development.

Basic methods of data collection include self-reports, tests, and observation. Basic research designs include case studies, ethnographic studies, correlational studies, and experiments.

The most common designs for developmental research are longitudinal and cross-sectional.

Chapter 1

The Study of Human Development

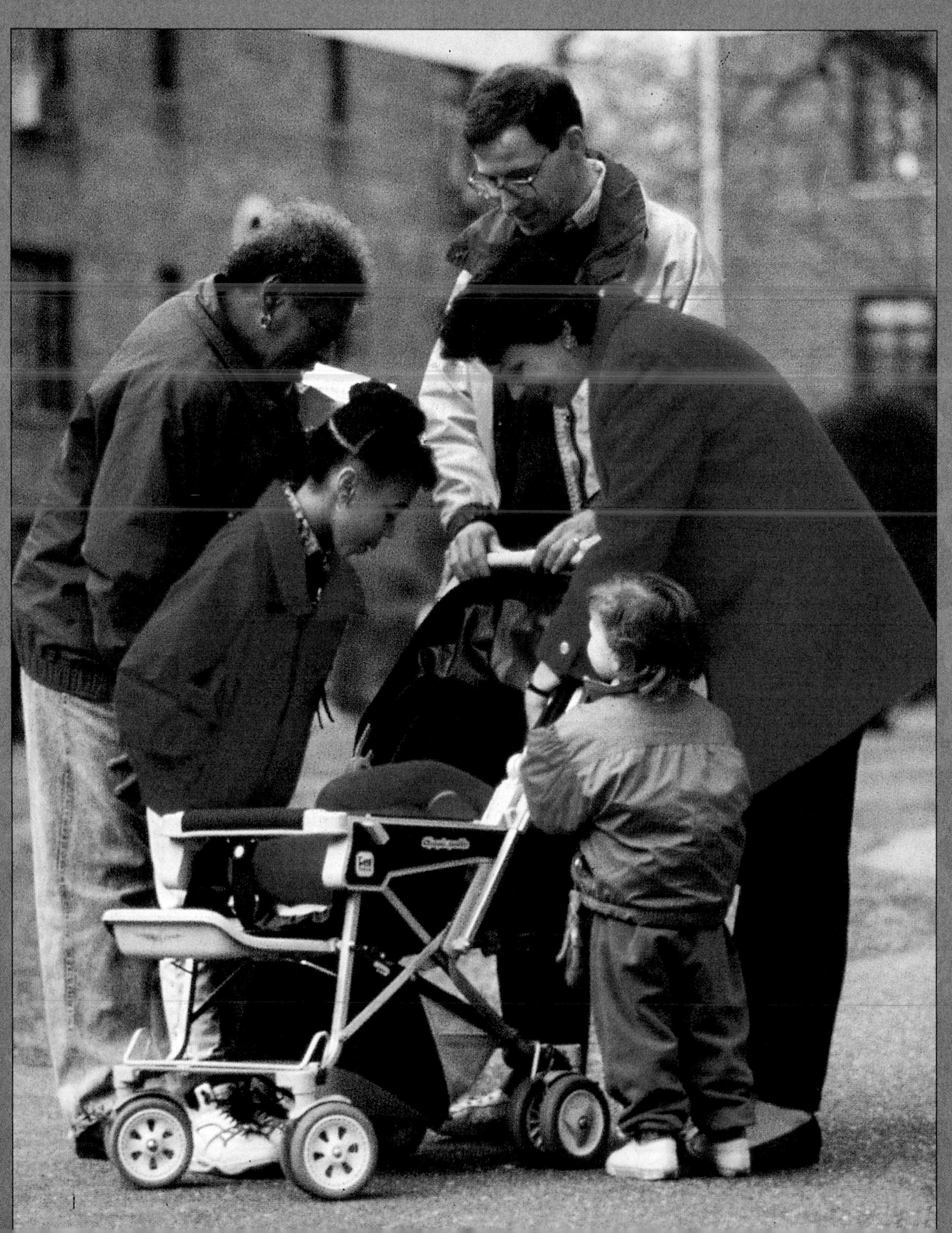

OUTLINE

There is nothing permanent except change.

Heraclitus, fragment (sixth century B.C.)

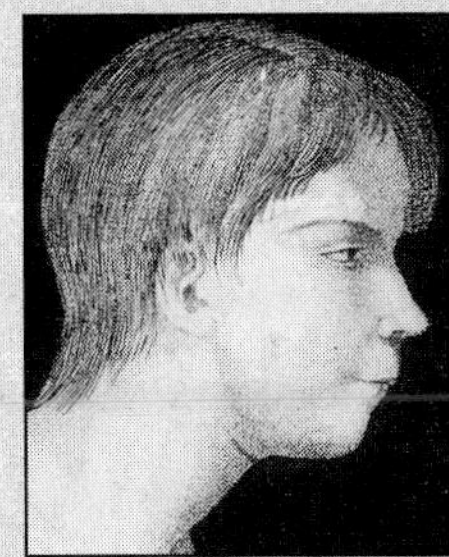

Victor

Focus: Victor, the Wild Boy of Aveyron*

On January 8, 1800, a naked boy, his face and neck heavily scarred, appeared on the outskirts of the village of Saint-Sernin in the sparsely populated province of Aveyron in south central France. The boy, who was only four and a half feet tall but looked about 12 years old, had been spotted several times during the previous two and a half years, climbing trees, running on all fours, drinking from streams, and foraging for acorns and roots.

When the dark-eyed boy came to Saint-Sernin, he neither spoke nor responded to speech. Like an animal accustomed to living in the wild, he spurned prepared foods and tore off the clothing people tried to put on him. It seemed clear that he had either lost his parents or been abandoned by them, but how long ago this had occurred was impossible to tell.

The boy appeared during a time of intellectual and social ferment, when a new, scientific outlook was beginning to replace mystical speculation. Philosophers debated questions about the nature of human beings—questions that would become central to the study of human development. Are the qualities, behavior, and ideas that define what it means to be human innate or acquired? How important is social contact during the formative years? Can its lack be overcome? A study of a child who had grown up in isolation might provide evidence of the relative impact of "nature" (a child's inborn characteristics) and "nurture" (upbringing, schooling, and other societal influences).

After initial observation, the boy, who came to be called Victor, was sent to a school for deaf-mutes in Paris. There, he was turned over to Jean-Marc-Gaspard Itard, an ambitious 26-year-old practitioner of the emerging science of "mental medicine," or psychiatry. Itard believed that Victor's development had been limited by isolation and that he simply needed to be taught the skills that children in civilized society normally acquire.

*Sources of information about the wild boy of Aveyron were Frith (1989) and Lane (1976).

Itard took Victor into his home and, during the next five years, gradually "tamed" him. Itard first awakened his pupil's ability to discriminate sensory experience through hot baths and dry rubs. He then moved on to painstaking, step-by-step training of emotional responses and instruction in moral and social behavior, language, and thought. The methods Itard used—based on principles of imitation, conditioning, and behavioral modification, all of which we discuss in Chapter 2—were far ahead of their time, and he invented many teaching devices used today.

But the education of Victor (which was dramatized in Francois Truffaut's film *The Wild Child*) was not an unqualified success. The boy did make remarkable progress: he learned the names of many objects and could read and write simple sentences; he could express desires, obey commands, and exchange ideas. He showed affection, especially for Itard's housekeeper, Madame Guérin, as well as such emotions as pride, shame, remorse, and the desire to please. However, aside from uttering some vowel and consonant sounds, he never learned to speak. Furthermore, he remained totally focused on his own wants and needs and never seemed to lose his yearning "for the freedom of the open country and his indifference to most of the pleasures of social life"(Lane, 1976, p. 160). When the study ended, Victor—no longer able to fend for himself, as he had done in the wild—went to live with Madame Guérin until his death in his early forties in 1828.

Why did Victor fail to fulfill Itard's hopes for him? It has been suggested that the boy was a victim of brain damage, autism (a disorder involving lack of social responsiveness), or severe early maltreatment. Itard's instructional methods, advanced as they were, may have been inadequate. Itard himself came to believe that the effects of long isolation could not be fully overcome, and that Victor may have been too old, especially for language learning.

Although Victor's story does not yield definitive answers to the questions Itard set out to explore, it is important because it was one of the first systematic attempts to study human development. Since Victor's time, we have learned much about how people develop, but developmental scientists are still investigating such fundamental questions as the relative importance of nature and nurture. Victor's story dramatizes the challenges and complexities of the scientific study of human development — the study on which you are about to embark.

In this chapter, we describe how the field of human development has itself developed as scientists have learned more about infants, children, adolescents, and adults. We present the goals and basic concepts of the field today. We identify aspects of development and show how they interrelate. We summarize major developments during each part of the life span. We look at influences on development and the contexts in which it occurs, including the influences of family, neighborhood, socioeconomic status, ethnicity, and culture, and of the time in which a person lives.

After you have read and studied this chapter, you should be able to answer the following questions:

Guideposts *for* **Study**

1. What is human development, and what were the principal steps in the evolution of its study?
2. What is the life-span developmental approach, and what are its key principles?
3. What are the four goals of the scientific study of human development?
4. What do developmental scientists study?
5. What are the major aspects and periods of human development?
6. What kinds of influences make one person different from another?

How the Study of Human Development Evolved 

The field of **human development** is the scientific study of ways in which people change, as well as of characteristics that remain fairly stable throughout life. Human development has, of course, been going on as long as human beings have existed, but its formal scientific study is relatively new. Since the early nineteenth century, when Itard studied Victor, efforts to understand children's development have gradually expanded to studies of the whole life span.

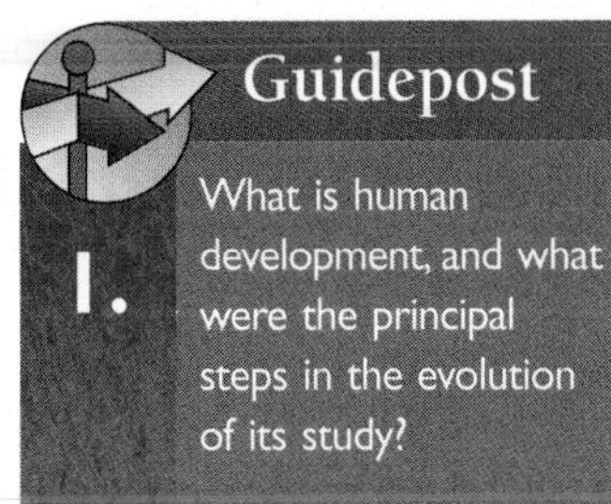
Guidepost
1.
What is human development, and what were the principal steps in the evolution of its study?

human development Scientific study of change and continuity throughout the human life span.

By the end of the nineteenth century, several important trends were preparing the way for the scientific study of child development. Scientists had unlocked the mystery of conception and (as in the case of Victor) were arguing about "nature versus nurture," that is, about the relative importance of inborn characteristics and external influences. The discovery of germs and immunization made it possible for many more children to survive infancy. Because of an abundance of cheap labor, children were less needed as workers. Laws protecting them from long workdays let them spend more time in school, and parents and teachers became more concerned with identifying and meeting children's developmental needs. The new science of psychology taught that people could understand themselves by learning what had influenced them as children.

The idea that development continues beyond childhood is a relatively new one. Adolescence was not considered a separate period of development until the early twentieth century, when G. Stanley Hall, a pioneer in child study, published a popular (though unscientific) book called *Adolescence* (1904–1916). Hall also was one of the first psychologists to become interested in aging. In 1922, at age 78, he published *Sensescence: The Last Half of Life.* Six years later, Stanford University opened the first major scientific research unit devoted to aging. But not until a generation later did the study of aging blossom. Since the late 1930s, a number of important long-term studies discussed in the second half of this book, such as those of K. Warner Schaie, George Vaillant, Daniel Levinson, and Ravenna Helson, have focused on intelligence and personality development in adulthood and old age.

Life-span studies in the United States grew out of programs designed to follow children through adulthood. The Stanford Studies of Gifted Children (begun in 1921 under the direction of Lewis M. Terman) trace the development of people (now in old age) who were identified as unusually intelligent in childhood. Other major studies that began around 1930—the Fels Research Institute Study, the Berkeley Growth and Guidance Studies, and the Oakland (Adolescent) Growth Study—have given us much information on long-term development.

As these studies extended into the adult years, developmental scientists began to focus on how particular experiences, tied to time and place, affect the course of people's lives. The Terman sample, for example, reached adulthood in the 1930s, during the Great Depression; the Oakland sample, during World War II; and the Berkeley sample around 1950, the postwar boom period. What did it mean to be a child in each of these periods? To be an adolescent? To become an adult? The answers differ in important ways (Modell, 1989; see Box 1-1).

life-span development Concept of development as a lifelong process, which can be studied scientifically.

Today most developmental scientists recognize that development goes on throughout life. This concept of a lifelong process of development that can be studied scientifically is known as **life-span development.**

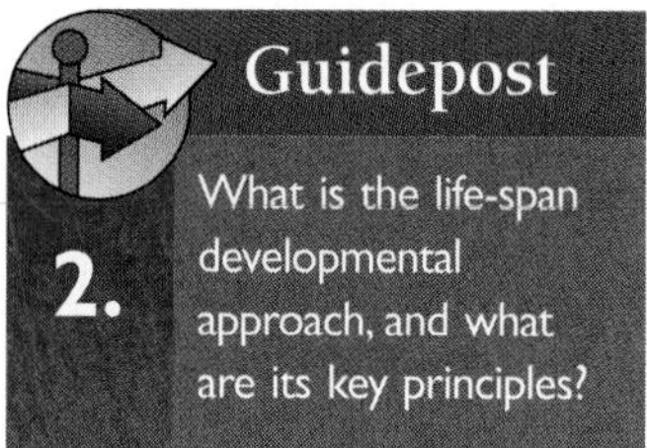

Guidepost
2.
What is the life-span developmental approach, and what are its key principles?

Paul B. Baltes (1987; Baltes, Lindenberger, & Staudinger, 1998), a leader in the study of life-span developmental psychology, has identified key principles of a life-span developmental approach, a framework for the study of life-span development. Among them are:

- *Development is lifelong.* Each period of the life span is influenced by what happened before and will affect what is to come. Each period has its own unique characteristics and value; none is more or less important than any other.

Digging Deeper

Box 1-1

Studying the Life Course: Growing Up in Hard Times

As recently as the 1960s, "human lives were an uncommon subject of study, particularly in their social and historical context" (Elder, 1998, p. 939), and researchers did not connect child development with what happens beyond childhood. Life-span studies have changed all that.

Current awareness of the need to look at the life course in its social and historical context is indebted in part to Glen H. Elder, Jr. In 1962, Elder arrived on the campus of the University of California at Berkeley to work on the Oakland Growth Study, a longitudinal study of social and emotional development in 167 urban young people born around 1920, about half of them from middle-class homes. The study had begun at the beginning of the Great Depression of the 1930s, when the youngsters, who had spent their childhoods in the boom years of the Roaring '20s, were entering adolescence. Comparing data on two groups of participants—those from severely deprived families and those whose families had suffered relatively little hardship after the economy's collapse—Elder observed how societal disruption can alter family processes, and through them, children's development (Elder, 1974).

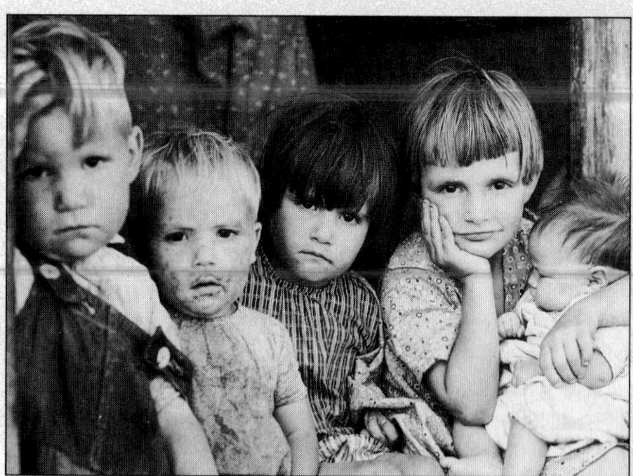

Glen Elder's studies of children growing up during the Great Depression showed how a major sociohistorical event can affect children's current and future development.

As economic stress changed parents' lives, it changed children's lives, too. Deprived families (those that had lost more than 35 percent of their income) reassigned economic roles. Mothers got outside jobs. Girls took over many household chores, and many boys looked for part-time work. Mothers took on more parental authority. Fathers, preoccupied with their job losses and irritable about their loss of status within the family, sometimes drank heavily. Parents argued more. The adolescent children, in turn, tended to show developmental difficulties. This was less true of youngsters whose parents were able to control their emotions and weather the economic storm with less family discord.

For the boys, particularly, the long-term effects of the ordeal were not entirely negative. Boys who got jobs to help out became more independent and were better able to escape the stressful family atmosphere than girls, who focused their helping efforts at home. As adolescents, the deprived Oakland boys showed somewhat worse self-

- *Development depends on history and context.* Each person develops within a specific set of circumstances or conditions defined by time and place. Human beings influence, and are influenced by, their historical and social context. They not only respond to their physical and social environments but also interact with and change them.
- *Development is multidimensional and multidirectional.* Development throughout life involves a balance of growth and decline. As people gain in one area, they may lose in another, and at varying rates. Children grow mostly in one direction—up—both in size and in abilities. In adulthood the balance gradually shifts. Some capacities, such as vocabulary, continue to increase; others, such as the ability to solve unfamiliar problems, may diminish; and some new attributes, such as expertise, may emerge. People seek to maximize gains and to minimize losses by learning to manage or compensate for them.
- *Development is pliable, or plastic:* **Plasticity** means modifiability of performance. Many abilities, such as memory, strength, and endurance, can

Can you . . .

✔ Trace highlights in the evolution of the study of human development?

✔ Summarize five central principles of Baltes's life-span developmental approach?

plasticity
Modifiability of performance.

—Continued

image problems (self-consciousness, emotional vulnerability, and desire to "fit in") than nondeprived youngsters but outgrew those problems without lasting effects. Having been prematurely pressed into adultlike roles, they entered real adult roles of marriage and work at early ages. As adults, they were strongly work-oriented but also valued family activities and cultivated dependability in their children.

Elder noted that effects of a major economic crisis depend on a child's stage of development. The children in the Oakland sample were already teenagers during the 1930s. They could draw on their own emotional, cognitive, and economic resources. A child born in 1929 would have been entirely dependent on the family. On the other hand, the parents of the Oakland children, being older, may have been less resilient in dealing with the loss of a job, and their emotional vulnerability may well have affected the tone of family life and their treatment of their children.

Fifty years after the Great Depression, in the early 1980s, a precipitous drop in the value of midwestern agricultural land pushed many farm families into debt or off the land and into an uncertain future. This Farm Crisis gave Elder the opportunity to replicate his earlier research, this time in a rural setting. In 1989, he and his colleagues (Conger & Elder, 1994; Conger et al., 1993) interviewed 451 farm and small-town families in north central Iowa. The researchers also videotaped family interactions.

Each family included two parents, a seventh-grade son or daughter, and a sibling up to four years older or younger. Thus the researchers were able to assess the impact of drastic income loss on family members at varying stages of life. The study design also gave researchers a glimpse of the complex dynamics of family relationships and how these relationships link "broad socioeconomic changes to the experiences and well-being of individual family members" (Conger & Elder, 1994, p. 7).

As in the depression-era study, many of these rural parents, under pressure of economic hardship, developed emotional problems. Depressed parents were more likely to fight with each other and to mistreat or withdraw from their children. The children, in turn, tended to lose self-confidence, to be unpopular, and to do poorly in school. One difference between the findings of the two studies reflects societal change between the 1930s and 1980s. In the 1980s this pattern of parental behavior fit both mothers and fathers, whereas in the 1930s it was less true of mothers, whose economic role before the collapse had been more marginal. The Iowa findings also show bidirectionality of influence. The rural preadolescents were not just the passive recipients of their parents' attitudes and behavior. When the farm boys, in particular, worked hard to contribute to the family's economic survival, their parents felt more positively about them (Conger & Elder, 1994; Conger et al., 1993; Elder, 1998).

Elder's work, like other studies of the life course, gives researchers a window into processes of development that previous approaches could not have revealed. The Farm Crisis study continues, with the families being reinterviewed yearly. Eventually it may enable us to see long-term effects of early hardship on the later lives of people who experienced it at different ages and in varying family situations.

(Source: Unless otherwise referenced, this discussion is based on Elder, 1998.)

be significantly improved with training and practice, even late in life. However, as Itard learned, even children are not infinitely pliable; the potential for change has limits.

Because human development is so complex, its study requires a partnership of scholars from many disciplines, including psychology, psychiatry, sociology, anthropology, biology, genetics (the study of inherited characteristics), family science (the interdisciplinary study of family relations), education, history, philosophy, and medicine. This book draws on research in all these fields.

Human Development Today: An Introduction to the Field

From the moment of conception, people undergo processes of development. The field of human development is the scientific study of those processes.

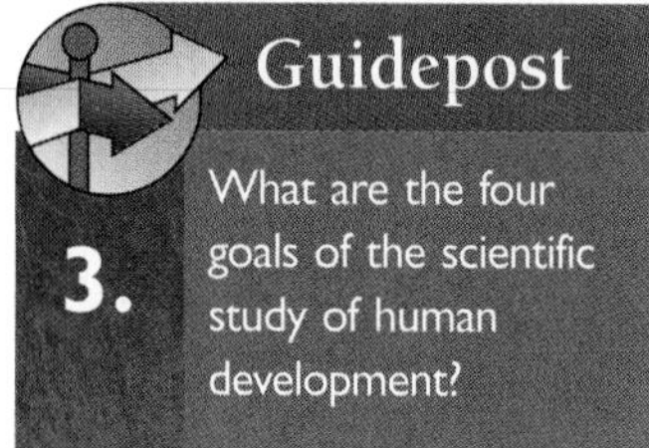

Guidepost

3. What are the four goals of the scientific study of human development?

The Science and Its Goals

As the field of human development became a scientific discipline, its goals evolved to include *description, explanation, prediction,* and *modification* of behavior. *Description* is an attempt to accurately portray behavior. *Explanation* is the uncovering of possible causes of behavior. *Prediction* is forecasting later development on the basis of earlier or present development. *Modification* is intervention to promote optimal development.

By looking at language development as an example, we can see how these four goals work together. For example, to *describe* when most normal children say their first word or how large their vocabulary typically is at a certain age, developmental scientists observe large groups of children and establish norms, or averages, for behavior at various ages. They then attempt to *explain* what causes or influences the observed behavior—for example, how children acquire and learn to use language, and why a child like Victor, who may have lacked early exposure to language, did not learn to speak. This knowledge may make it possible to *predict* what language ability at a given age can tell about later behavior—for example, about the likelihood that a child like Victor could still be taught to speak. Finally, awareness of how language develops may be used to *modify* behavior, as Itard attempted to do in tutoring Victor.

An understanding of adult development, too, has practical implications. It can help people deal with life's transitions: a woman returning to work after maternity leave, a person making a career change or about to retire, a widow or widower dealing with loss, someone coping with a terminal illness.

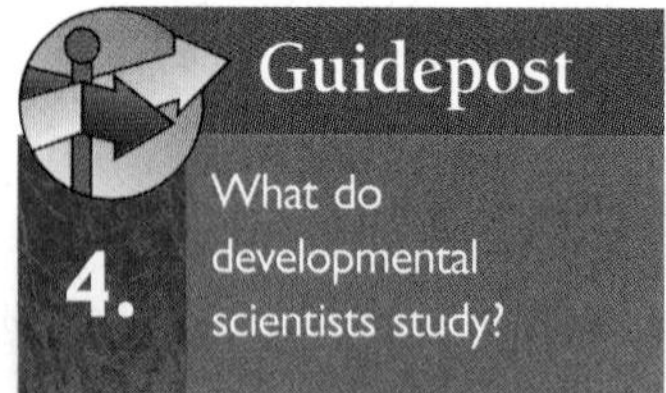

Guidepost

4. What do developmental scientists study?

quantitative change Change in number or amount, such as in height, weight, or size of vocabulary.

qualitative change Change in kind, structure, or organization, such as the change from nonverbal to verbal communication.

Developmental Processes: Change and Stability

Developmental scientists study two kinds of developmental change: *quantitative* and *qualitative.* **Quantitative change** is a change in number or amount, such as growth in height, weight, vocabulary, or frequency of communication. **Qualitative change** is a change in kind, structure, or organization. It is marked by the emergence of new phenomena that cannot easily be anticipated on the basis of earlier functioning, such as the change from a nonverbal child to one who understands words and can communicate verbally.

Despite these changes, most people show an underlying *stability,* or constancy, of personality and behavior. For example, about 10 to 15 percent of children are consistently shy, and another 10 to 15 percent are very bold. Although various influences can modify these traits somewhat, they seem to persist to a moderate degree, especially in children at one extreme or the other (see Chapter 3). Broad dimensions of personality, such as conscientiousness and openness to new experience, seem to stabilize before or during young adulthood (see Chapter 14).

Which characteristics are most likely to endure? Which are likely to change, and why? These are among the basic questions that the study of human development seeks to answer.

Aspects of Development

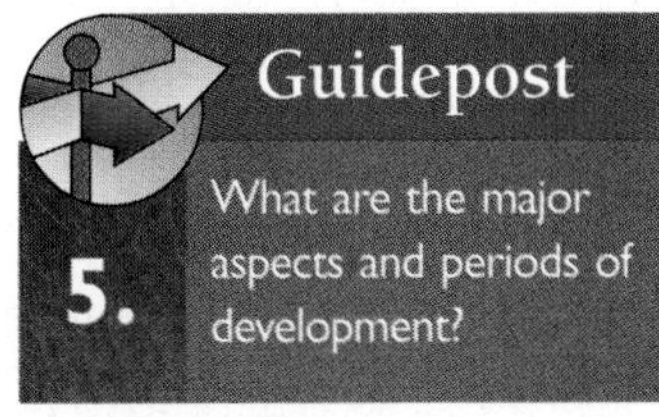

Guidepost
5.
What are the major aspects and periods of development?

The study of human development is complicated by the fact that change and stability occur in various aspects of the self. To simplify discussion, developmental scientists talk separately about *physical development, cognitive development,* and *psychosocial development.* Actually, though, these aspects, or domains, of development are intertwined. Throughout life, each affects the others.

Growth of the body and brain, sensory capacities, motor skills, and health are part of *physical development* and may influence other aspects of development. For example, a child with frequent ear infections may develop language more slowly than a child without this problem. During puberty, dramatic physiological and hormonal changes affect the developing sense of self. In some older adults, physical changes in the brain may lead to intellectual and personality deterioration.

Change and stability in mental abilities, such as learning, memory, language, thinking, moral reasoning, and creativity constitute *cognitive development.* They are closely related to physical and emotional growth. The ability to speak depends on the physical development of the mouth and brain. A child who has difficulty expressing herself in words may evoke negative reactions in others, influencing her popularity and sense of self-worth.

Change and stability in personality and social relationships together constitute *psychosocial development,* and this can affect cognitive and physical functioning. For example, anxiety about taking a test can impair performance. Social support can help people cope with the potentially negative effects of stress on physical and mental health. Conversely, physical and cognitive capacities can affect psychosocial development. They contribute greatly to self-esteem and can affect social acceptance and choice of occupation.

Although we will be looking separately at physical, cognitive, and psychosocial development, a person is more than a bundle of isolated parts. Development is a unified process. In this book, at the opening of each part and throughout the text, we will highlight links among the three major domains of development.

Consider this . . .

- Do you think it was right for a scientist like Itard to try to modify the development of a child like Victor? What dangers, if any, do you see in such a project, and what benefits to be gained? Can you suggest safeguards that might have been established to protect Victor's welfare?
- What reasons do you have for wanting to learn about human development? Do any of the four goals of that study seem more important to you than others?
- Can you identify ways in which one aspect of your development has affected other aspects?

Periods of the Life Span

The concept of periods of the life span is a **social construction:** an idea about the nature of reality accepted by members of a particular society at a particular time on the basis of shared subjective perceptions or assumptions. There is no objectively definable moment when a child becomes an adult, or a young person becomes old. Societies the world over recognize differences in the way people of different ages think, feel, and act, but they divide the life span in varying ways. In industrial societies, as we have already mentioned, the concept of adolescence as a period of development is quite recent. Middle age, too, was not seen as a separate stage of life in earlier times, when life was shorter. Nor is it considered a separate stage in some preindustrial societies, in which social roles do not change appreciably between young adulthood and old age.

social construction
Concept about the nature of reality, based on societally shared subjective perceptions or assumptions.

The Chippewa Indians have only two periods of childhood: from birth until the child walks, and from walking to puberty. Adolescence is part of adulthood, which lasts until the coming of the first grandchild; a later period of adulthood begins with the birth of the first great-grandchild. The African Swazi define eight periods of life and mark each with a ceremony. Babyhood begins at 3 months, when an infant is considered likely to survive. Then come toddlerhood (which

Consider this . . .

- Why do you think different societies divide the periods of the life span in different ways?

begins when the baby can walk), childhood (which begins at age 6), puberty, and marriage. For a woman, the next stages come when her first child is born and when she goes to live with a married son. In the final stage, a person is respected as "almost an ancestor," leads community rituals, and supervises children's education (Broude, 1995, p. 113).

In this book, we follow a sequence of eight periods generally accepted in western industrial societies. After describing the crucial changes that occur in the first period, before birth, we trace all three aspects of development through infancy and toddlerhood, early childhood, middle childhood, adolescence, young adulthood, middle adulthood, and late adulthood (see Table 1-1). For space reasons, we have combined physical and cognitive development at each

Table 1-1 Typical Major Developments in Eight Periods of the Life Span

Age Period	Physical Developments	Cognitive Developments	Psychosocial Developments
Prenatal Period (conception to birth)	Conception occurs. The genetic endowment interacts with environmental influences from the start. Basic body structures and organs form. Brain growth spurt begins. Physical growth is the most rapid in the life span. Fetus hears and responds to sensory stimuli. Vulnerability to environmental influences is great.	Abilities to learn and remember are present during fetal stage.	Fetus responds to mother's voice and develops a preference for it.
Infancy and Toddlerhood (birth to age 3)	All senses operate at birth to varying degrees. The brain grows in complexity and is highly sensitive to environmental influence. Physical growth and development of motor skills are rapid.	Abilities to learn and remember are present, even in early weeks. Use of symbols and ability to solve problems develop by end of second year. Comprehension and use of language develop rapidly.	Attachments to parents and others form. Self-awareness develops. Shift from dependence to autonomy occurs. Interest in other children increases.
Early Childhood (3 to 6 years)	Growth is steady; appearance becomes more slender and proportions more adultlike. Appetite diminishes, and sleep problems are common. Handedness appears; fine and gross motor skills and strength improve.	Thinking is somewhat egocentric, but understanding of other people's perspectives grows. Cognitive immaturity leads to some illogical ideas about the world. Memory and language improve. Intelligence becomes more predictable.	Self-concept and understanding of emotions become more complex; self-esteem is global. Independence, initiative, self-control, and self-care increase. Gender identity develops. Play becomes more imaginative, more elaborate, and more social. Altruism, aggression, and fearfulness are common. Family is still focus of social life, but other children become more important. Attending preschool is common.
Middle Childhood (6 to 11 years)	Growth slows. Strength and athletic skills improve.	Egocentrism diminishes. Children begin to think logically but concretely. Memory and language skills increase.	Self-concept becomes more complex, affecting self-esteem.

(Continued)

period after infancy and toddlerhood (when change is most dramatic) into a single chapter.

The age divisions shown in Table 1-1 are approximate and somewhat arbitrary. This is especially true of adulthood, when there are no clear-cut social or physical landmarks, such as starting school and entering puberty, to signal a shift from one period to another. Also, individual differences exist in the way people deal with the characteristic events and issues of each period. One toddler may be toilet trained by 18 months; another, not until 3 years. Despite these differences, however, developmental scientists believe that certain basic developmental needs must be met and certain developmental tasks must be mastered during each period for normal development to occur.

Age Period	Physical Developments	Cognitive Developments	Psychosocial Developments
	Respiratory illnesses are common, but health is generally better than at any other time in life span.	Cognitive gains permit children to benefit from formal schooling. Some children show special educational needs and strengths.	Coregulation reflects gradual shift in control from parents to child. Peers assume central importance.
Adolescence *(11 to about 20 years)*	Physical growth and other changes are rapid and profound. Reproductive maturity occurs. Major health risks arise from behavioral issues, such as eating disorders and drug abuse.	Ability to think abstractly and use scientific reasoning develops. Immature thinking persists in some attitudes and behaviors. Education focuses on preparation for college or vocation.	Search for identity, including sexual identity, becomes central. Relationships with parents are generally good. Peer groups help develop and test self-concept but also may exert an antisocial influence.
Young Adulthood *(20 to 40 years)*	Physical condition peaks, then declines slightly. Lifestyle choices influence health.	Cognitive abilities and moral judgments assume more complexity. Educational and career choices are made.	Personality traits and styles become relatively stable, but changes in personality may be influenced by life stages and events. Decisions are made about intimate relationships and personal lifestyles. Most people marry, and most become parents.
Middle Adulthood *(40 to 65 years)*	Some deterioration of sensory abilities, health, stamina, and prowess may take place. Women experience menopause.	Most basic mental abilities peak; expertise and practical problem-solving skills are high. Creative output may decline but improve in quality. For some, career success and earning powers peak; for others, burnout or career change may occur.	Sense of identity continues to develop; stressful midlife transition may occur. Double responsibilities of caring for children and elderly parents may cause stress. Launching of children leaves empty nest.
Late Adulthood *(65 years and over)*	Most people are healthy and active, although health and physical abilities decline somewhat. Slowing of reaction time affects some aspects of functioning.	Most people are mentally alert. Although intelligence and memory may deteriorate in some areas, most people find ways to compensate.	Retirement from workforce may offer new options for use of time. People need to cope with personal losses and impending death. Relationships with family and close friends can provide important support. Search for meaning in life assumes central importance.

Infants, for example, are dependent on adults to meet their basic needs for food, clothing, and shelter, as well as for human contact and affection. They form attachments to parents or caregivers, who also become attached to them. With the development of speech and self-locomotion, toddlers become more self-reliant; they need to assert their autonomy but also need parents to help them keep their impulses in check. During early childhood, children develop more self-control and more interest in other children. During middle childhood, control over behavior gradually shifts from parent to child, and the peer group becomes increasingly important. A main task of adolescence is the search for identity—personal, sexual, and occupational. As adolescents become physically mature, they deal with sometimes conflicting needs and emotions as they prepare to separate from the security of the parental nest.

The developmental tasks of young adulthood include the establishment of independent lifestyles, occupations, and, usually, families. During middle adulthood, most people need to deal with some decline in physical capabilities, and women with the loss of reproductive capacity. At the same time, many middle-aged people find excitement and challenge in life changes—launching new careers and adult children—while some face the need to care for elderly parents. In late adulthood, people cope with losses in their own faculties, the loss of loved ones, and preparations for their own death. If they retire, they must deal with the loss of work-based relationships but may get increased pleasure out of friendships, family, and volunteer work and the opportunity to explore previously neglected interests. Many older people become more introspective, searching out the meaning of their lives.

CHECKPOINT

Can you . . .

- ✔ Name four goals of the scientific study of human development, and explain the value of each?
- ✔ Distinguish between quantitative and qualitative development and give an example of each?
- ✔ Identify three aspects, or domains, of development?
- ✔ Name eight periods of human development (as defined in this book) and list several key issues or events of each period?

Influences on Development

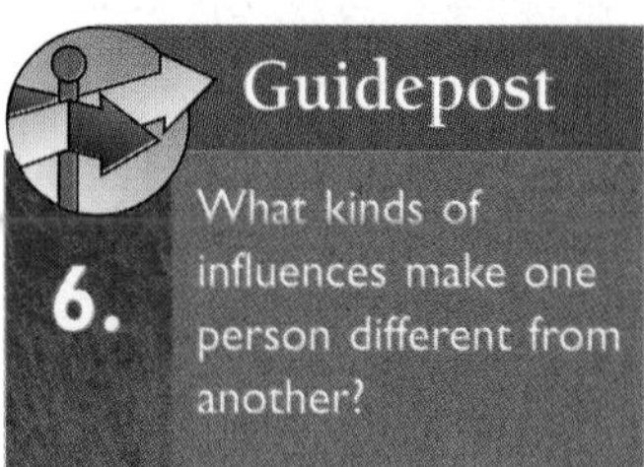

Guidepost
6.
What kinds of influences make one person different from another?

Students of development are interested in processes of development that affect every normal person, but they also want to know about **individual differences,** both in influences on development and in its outcome. People differ in sex, height, weight, and body build; in constitutional factors such as health and energy level; in intelligence; and in personality characteristics and emotional reactions. The contexts of their lives and lifestyles differ, too: the homes, communities, and societies they live in, the relationships they have, the kinds of schools they go to (or whether they go to school at all), their occupations, and how they spend their leisure time.

individual differences
Variations in characteristics or developmental outcomes between one child and another.

Some basic differences are obvious, such as whether a person is male or female. Other differences, such as variations in talent and temperament, may be subtle. All of these differences, and more, may help explain why one person turns out unlike another. Because development is complex, and the factors that affect it cannot always be measured precisely, scientists cannot answer that question fully. However, they have learned much about what people need to develop normally, how they react to the many influences upon and within them, and how they can best fulfill their potential.

Heredity, Environment, and Maturation

Some influences on development originate with **heredity:** the inborn genetic endowment from a person's biological parents. Others come from the external **environment:** the world outside the self, beginning in the womb. Individual differences increase as people grow older. Many typical changes of infancy and early childhood seem to be tied to **maturation** of the body and brain—the unfolding of a natural, genetically influenced sequence of physical changes and behavior patterns, including readiness to master new abilities such as walking and talking. As children grow into adolescents and then into adults, differences in innate characteristics and life experience play a greater role.

heredity
Inborn influences on development, carried on the genes inherited from the biological parents.

environment
Totality of nongenetic influences on development, external to the self.

maturation
Unfolding of a genetically influenced, often age-related, sequence of physical changes and behavior patterns, including the readiness to master new abilities.

Even in processes that everyone goes through, rates and timing of development vary. Throughout this book, we talk about average ages for the occurrence of certain behaviors: the first word, the first step, the first menstruation or "wet dream," the development of logical thought. But these ages are *merely* averages. Only when deviation from the average is extreme should we consider development exceptionally advanced or delayed.

In trying to understand the similarities and differences in development, then, we need to look at the *inherited* characteristics that give each person a special start in life. We also need to consider the many *environmental* factors that affect people, especially such major contexts as family, neighborhood, socioeconomic status, ethnicity, and culture. We need to look at influences that affect many or most people at a certain age or a certain time in history, and also at those that affect only certain individuals. Finally, we need to look at how timing can affect the impact of certain influences.

Major Contextual Influences

As Baltes's life-span developmental approach reminds us, human beings are social beings. Right from the start, they develop within a social and historical context. For an infant, the immediate context normally is the family; but the family in turn is subject to the wider and ever-changing influences of neighborhood, community, and society. In Chapter 2, we'll discuss Urie Bronfenbrenner's theory of development, which focuses on the interconnections among the many contexts that affect a developing person. For now, let's start with some basic definitions.

Family

Family may mean something different in different times and places. Its attributes have changed greatly during the past 150 years.

Historically, the **nuclear family,** a two-generational kinship, economic, and household unit consisting of two parents and their biological or adopted children, was the dominant form in the United States and other western industrial societies. Parents and children typically worked side by side on the family farm. Large families provided many hands to share the work, and children's activities and education revolved around the priorities of agricultural production. By the mid–twentieth century, most U.S. families had moved off the farm. Most children grew up in cities, had only one or two siblings, and spent much of their time in

nuclear family
Two-generational economic, kinship, and living unit made up of parents and their biological or adopted children.

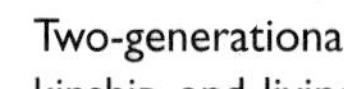

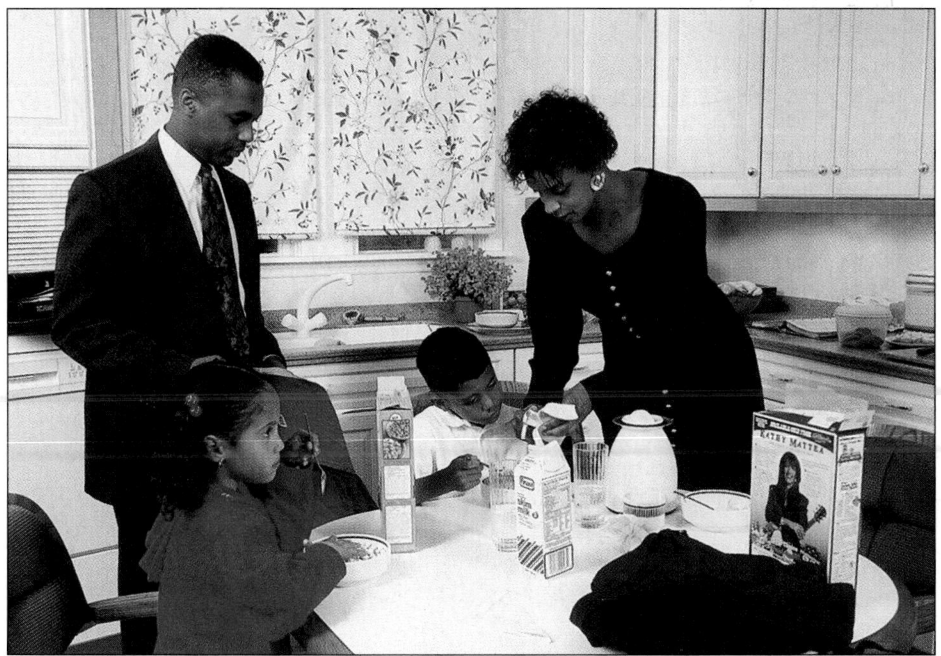

In today's nuclear family, unlike the typical U.S. family of 150 years ago, both parents are likely to work outside the home. Families are smaller than in the past, and children spend more of their time in school.

school. Adults were better educated than in earlier generations, and men were away at work for much of the day (Hernandez, 1997).

During the past fifty years, change has accelerated. Today both parents are likely to work outside the home. A child is likely to receive a considerable amount of care from relatives or nonrelatives. If a couple are divorced, their children may live with one or the other parent or may move back and forth between their homes. The household may include a stepparent and stepsiblings, or a parent's live-in partner. There are increasing numbers of single and childless adults, unmarried parents, and gay and lesbian households (Hernandez, 1997).

extended family Multigenerational kinship network of parents, children, and more distant relatives, sometimes living together in an *extended-family household.*

In many societies, such of those of Asia and Latin America, and among some minority groups in the United States, the **extended family**—a multigenerational kinship network of grandparents, aunts, uncles, cousins, and more distant relatives—is the basic pattern of social organization, and many or most people live in *extended-family households.* However, that pattern is now eroding in developing countries, due to industrialization and migration to urban centers (N. M. Brown, 1990; Gorman, 1993).

Socioeconomic Status and Neighborhood

socioeconomic status (SES) Combination of economic and social factors describing an individual or family, including income, education, and occupation.

Socioeconomic status (SES) combines several related factors, including income, education, and occupation. Throughout this book, we describe many studies that relate SES to developmental processes (such as differences in mothers' verbal interaction with their children) and to developmental outcomes (such as health and cognitive performance; see Table 1-2). It is generally not SES itself that affects these outcomes, but factors associated with SES, such as the kinds of homes and neighborhoods people live in and the quality of medical care, schooling, and other opportunities available to them. Poor children, for example, are more likely than other children to have emotional or behavioral problems, and their cognitive potential and school performance suffer even more (Brooks-Gunn, Britto, & Brady, in press; Brooks-Gunn & Duncan, 1997; Duncan & Brooks-Gunn, 1997; McLoyd, 1998). But the harm done by poverty may be indirect, through its impact on par-

Table 1-2 Poor Outcomes for Poor Children

Outcome	Poor Children's Higher Risk Relative to Nonpoor Children
Health	
Death in childhood	1.5 to 3 times more likely
Stunted growth	2.7 times more likely
Iron deficiency in preschool years	3 to 4 times more likely
Partial or complete deafness	1.5 to 2 times more likely
Partial or complete blindness	1.2 to 1.8 times more likely
Serious physical or mental disabilities	About 2 times more likely
Fatal accidental injuries	2 to 3 times more likely
Pneumonia	1.6 times more likely
Education	
Average IQ score at age 5	9 points lower
Average achievement scores at age 3 and above	11 to 25 percentiles lower
Learning disabilities	1.3 times more likely
Placement in special education	2 or 3 percentage points more likely
Below-usual grade for child's age	2 percentage points more likely for each year of childhood spent in poverty
Dropping out between ages 16 and 24	2 times more likely than middle-income youths; 11 times more likely than wealthy youths

Source: Children's Defense Fund, 1998, p. xiv; from Sherman, 1997, p. 4.

ents' emotional state and parenting practices and on the home environment they create. (In Chapter 10 we'll look more closely at indirect effects of poverty.)

SES limits people's choices of where to live. Recently researchers have begun to study how the composition of a neighborhood affects the way children turn out. So far, the most powerful factors seem to be average neighborhood *income* and *human capital*—the presence of educated, employed adults who can build the community's economic base and provide models of what a child can hope to achieve (Brooks-Gunn et al., 1997; Leventhal & Brooks-Gunn, in press). Threats to children's well-being multiply if several **risk factors**—conditions that increase the likelihood of a negative outcome—coexist, as they often do. Living in a poor neighborhood with large numbers of people who are unemployed and on welfare makes it less likely that effective social support will be available (Black & Kirshnakumar, 1998). The percentage of children living in such neighborhoods grew from 3 percent in 1970 to 17 percent in 1990 (Annie E. Casey Foundation, 1997).

risk factors
Conditions that increase the likelihood of a negative developmental outcome.

Culture and Ethnicity

Culture refers to a society's or group's total way of life, including customs, traditions, beliefs, values, language, and physical products, from tools to artworks—all of the learned behavior that is passed on from parents to children. Culture is not static; it is constantly changing, often through contact with other cultures.

culture
A society's or group's total way of life, including customs, traditions, beliefs, values, language, and physical products—all learned behavior passed on from parents to children.

Some cultures have variations, or *subcultures,* associated with certain groups, usually ethnic groups, within a society. An **ethnic group** consists of people united by ancestry, race, religion, language, and/or national origin, which contribute to a sense of shared identity and shared attitudes, beliefs, and values. Most ethnic groups trace their roots to a country of origin, where they or their forebears had a common culture that continues to influence their way of life.

ethnic group
Group united by ancestry, race, religion, language, and/or national origins, which contribute to a sense of shared identity.

The United States has always been a nation of immigrants and ethnic groups. The European-descended "majority" actually consists of many distinct ethnic groups—German, Belgian, Irish, French, Italian, and so forth. There also is diversity within the Hispanic (or Latino) and African American communities, the largest minority groups. Cubans, Puerto Ricans, and Mexican Americans—all Hispanic Americans—have different histories and cultures and varying socio-economic status. Similarly, African Americans from the rural South differ from those of Caribbean ancestry. Asian Americans, too, hail from a variety of countries with distinct cultures, from modern, industrial Japan to communist China to the remote mountains of Nepal, where many people still practice their ancient way of life. If current immigration levels continue, by the year 2030 what are today called minorities are projected to total half of the population, and by 2050 well over half (Hernandez, 1997). In addition, intermarriage among members of ethnic groups is producing a rising number of offspring of mixed ethnicity (Phinney & Alipuria, 1998).

In large, multiethnic societies such as the United States, immigrant or minority groups adapt, or *acculturate,* to the majority culture by learning the language and customs needed to get along in the dominant culture while trying to preserve some of their own cultural practices and values. (Acculturation is not the same as cultural *assimilation,* in which the minority simply adopts the ways of the majority.) People often live in neighborhoods with other members of their own ethnic group, reinforcing shared cultural patterns. These cultural patterns may influence the composition of the household, its economic and social resources, the way its members act toward one another, the foods they eat, the games children play, the way they learn, and how well they do in school.

Different ethnic groups have distinct adaptive strategies that promote group survival and well-being and govern the upbringing of children. African American, American Indian, Asian-Pacific American, and Hispanic American families emphasize group values (such as loyalty) more than the individualistic ones (autonomy, competition, and self-reliance) stressed in western cultures. Children in these minority families are encouraged to cooperate with and depend on each other. Because of economic need, social roles tend to be flexible: adults often share breadwinning, and children are given responsibility for younger brothers and sisters. The extended family provides close ties and strong support systems. People are more likely than in white families to live in extended-family households where they have daily contact with kinfolk, and school-age children are more likely to include extended family in their inner circle of support (Harrison, Wilson, Pine, Chan, & Buriel, 1990; Levitt, Guacci-Franco, & Levitt, 1993).

Consider this . . .

- Looking back, what were some of the most important influences on your development? What influences affect you most strongly today?
- How might you be different if you had grown up in a culture other than your own?
- In view of poverty's long-term effects on children's development, what can and should be done to combat it?

When we talk about influences of ethnicity and culture, especially on members of minority groups, it is important to distinguish effects of shared biological traits, of socioeconomic status (which may result from prejudice or lack of educational and employment opportunity), and of cultural attitudes that help shape development. The prejudice and discrimination that limit opportunity for many African Americans and other minorities intensify the bonds of mutual support within their families and communities. When African Americans move into the middle class, they tend to retain their distinctive ethnic and cultural patterns, along with their shared bonds with other African Americans who are less financially successful. Thus the behavior and attitudes of middle-class African Americans may differ substantially from those of middle-class white Americans. *How long* a family has been middle class makes a difference. African Americans who grew up poor and worked their way into middle-class status are likely to feel and act different from African Americans whose families have been middle class for four generations. This also holds true for Mexican Americans and Puerto Rican Americans (Banks, 1998).

Normative and Nonnormative Influences

As Baltes's life-span developmental approach points out, development has many roots. To understand similarities and differences in development, we must look at influences that impinge on many or most people and at those that touch only certain individuals. We also need to consider influences of time and place (Baltes, Reese, & Lipsitt, 1980).

normative
Characteristic of an event that occurs in a similar way for most people in a group.

A **normative** event is experienced in a similar way by most people in a group. *Normative age-graded influences* are highly similar for people in a particular age group. They include biological events (such as puberty and menopause) and social events (such as entry into formal education, marriage, parenthood, and retirement). The timing of biological events is fixed, within a normal range. (People don't experience puberty at age 35, or menopause at 12.) The timing of social events is more flexible and varies in different times and places, though within maturational limits. A woman normally may conceive and bear a child any time between puberty and menopause. Children in western industrial societies generally begin formal education around age 5 or 6; but in some developing countries, schooling begins much later, if at all.

cohort
Group of people who share a similar experience, such as growing up at the same time and in the same place.

Normative history-graded influences are common to a particular **cohort:** a group of people who share a similar experience, in this case growing up at the same time in the same place. Examples of such influences are the Great Depression of the 1930s (refer back to Box 1-1), the massive famines in Africa during the 1980s and 1990s, and the violent conflicts in eastern Europe in the 1990s. Also in this category are such cultural and technological developments as the changing roles of women and the impact of television and computers.

Nonnormative influences are unusual events that have a major impact on individual lives. They are either typical events that happen at an atypical time of life (such as marriage in the early teens, or the death of a parent when a child is young) or atypical events (such as having a birth defect or being in an automobile crash). They can also, of course, be happy events (such as winning a scholarship or an unexpected promotion). People often help create their own nonnormative life events—say, by applying for a new job or taking up a risky hobby such as skydiving—and thus participate actively in their own development. (Normative and nonnormative events are further discussed in Chapter 14.)

Widespread use of computers is a normative history-graded influence on children's development, which did not exist in earlier generations.

Timing of Influences: Critical or Sensitive Periods

A **critical period** is a specific time when a given event, or its absence, has the greatest impact on development. For example, if a woman receives X rays, takes certain drugs, or contracts certain diseases at certain times during pregnancy, the fetus may show specific ill effects. The amount and kind of damage will vary, depending on the nature of the "shock" and on its timing.

A child deprived of certain kinds of experience during a critical period is likely to show permanent stunting of physical development. Undernourishment during the critical period of brain growth just after birth can result in brain damage. Also, if a physical problem interfering with the ability to focus the eyes is not corrected early in life, the brain mechanisms necessary for depth perception will not develop (Bushnell & Boudreau, 1993).

The concept of critical periods is more controversial when applied to cognitive and psychosocial development. For these aspects of development there seems to be greater plasticity. Although the human organism may be particular *sensitive* to certain psychological experiences at certain times of life, later events often can reverse the effects of early ones. One investigator (Lennenberg, 1967, 1969) did propose a critical period for language development, before puberty, and this concept has been advanced as one explanation for the "wild child's" limited progress in learning to talk (Lane, 1976; see Box 1-2). Newer research suggests, however, that the capacity for language acquisition may be fairly resilient. Even if the parts of the brain best suited to language processing are damaged, nearly normal language development can occur—though the child may have to keep playing catch-up with normal children at each new stage of language development (M. H. Johnson, 1998). Further research may help delineate which aspects of development are decisively formed during critical periods and which aspects remain modifiable.

critical period
Specific time when a given event, or its absence, has the greatest impact on development.

CHECKPOINT

Can you . . .

- ✔ Explain why individual differences tend to increase with age?
- ✔ Discuss the influence of family and neighborhood composition, socioeconomic status, culture, and ethnicity?
- ✔ Give examples of normative age-graded, normative history-graded, and nonnormative influences? (Include some normative history-graded influences that impacted different generations.)
- ✔ Explain why the concept of "critical" periods may more accurately apply to physical than to cognitive development?

Practically Speaking

Box 1-2
Is There a Critical Period for Language Acquisition?

In 1970, a 13½-year-old girl named Genie (not her real name) was discovered in a suburb of Los Angeles (Curtiss, 1977; Fromkin, Krashen, Curtiss, Rigler & Rigler, 1974; Pines, 1981; Rymer, 1993). The victim of an abusive father, she had been confined for nearly twelve years to a small room in her parents' home, tied to a potty chair and cut off from normal human contact. She weighed only 59 pounds, could not straighten her arms or legs, could not chew, had no bladder or bowel control, and did not speak. She recognized only her own name and the word *sorry*.

Only three years before, Eric Lenneberg (1967, 1969) had proposed that there is a critical period for language acquisition, beginning in early infancy and ending around puberty. Lenneberg argued that it would be difficult, if not impossible, for a child who had not yet acquired language to do so after that age. But Lenneberg could offer only indirect evidence for his hypothesis. He pointed out that deaf children who had heard speech early in life could more easily learn to talk than those who had not. He noted that both deaf and retarded children stop acquiring language skills at puberty. Furthermore, a child who suffers brain injury before the early teens may recover linguistic ability if other parts of the brain remain intact, whereas if the injury occurs during adolescence or adulthood, loss of language is likely to be irreversible.

The discovery of Genie offered the opportunity for a test of Lenneberg's hypothesis. Could Genie be taught to speak, or was it too late? The National Institute of Mental Health (NIMH) funded a study, and a series of researchers took over Genie's care and gave her intensive testing and language training.

Genie's progress during the next few years (before the NIMH withdrew funding and her mother regained custody and cut her off from contact with the professionals who had been teaching her) both challenges and supports the idea of a critical period for language acquisition. Genie did learn some simple words and could string them together into primitive, but rule-governed, sentences. She also learned the fundamentals of sign language. But she never used language normally, and "her speech remained, for the most part, like a somewhat garbled telegram" (Pines, 1981, p. 29). When her mother, unable to care for her, turned her over to a series of abusive foster homes, she regressed into total silence.

What explains Genie's initial progress and her inability to sustain it? The fact that she was just beginning to show signs of puberty at age 13½ may indicate that she was still in the critical period, though near its end. The fact that she apparently had learned a few words before being locked up at the age of 20 months may mean that her language-learning mechanisms may have been triggered early in the critical period, allowing later learning to occur. On the other hand, the fact that she was so abused and neglected may have retarded her so much—emotionally, socially, and cognitively—that, like Victor, the wild boy of Aveyron, she cannot be considered a true test of the critical period (Curtiss, 1977). The competition and lack of continuity among the researchers who were studying and teaching her also confused the issue (Rymer, 1993).

Case studies like those of Genie and Victor dramatize the difficulty of acquiring language after the early years of life, but they do not permit conclusive judgments because there are too many complicating factors. Researchers seeking study participants who lack early exposure to language, but whose environment and development are otherwise normal, have therefore turned to deaf persons for whom American Sign Language (ASL) is the primary language. More than nine out of ten deaf children are born to hearing parents. They typically are first exposed to ASL when they enter residential schools for the deaf, efforts to expose them to English having been unsuccessful (Newport, 1991).

One cross-sectional study compared three groups of ASL users at a residential school for the deaf: *native learners,* who had been exposed to ASL from birth by deaf, signing parents; *early learners,* who were first exposed to ASL between ages 4 and 6 by deaf peers upon entering the residential school; and *late learners,* who were first exposed after age 12, having previously attended nonresidential schools that used strictly oral methods. All three groups had mastered the basic word order of their language (as Genie did), but their proficiency varied dramatically. The older a person had been when first exposed to ASL, the more likely that person was to sign ungrammatically and inconsistently. This was true despite the fact that all of the participants had been using ASL for at least thirty years. These findings suggest that it is the initial maturational level of the learner that determines how well a language will be learned (Newport, 1991).

A cross-sectional study of Chinese and Korean immigrants' use of English supports a critical period for second-language learning as well. The participants, all of them college students or faculty, had entered the United States at least five years before, at ages ranging from 3 to 39. Their English performance showed a striking pattern, which conformed to the maturational curve: the later the age of arrival, up to late adolescence, the worse the performance, which then held steady at a low level among those who had arrived as adults (Newport, 1991).

If a critical period for language learning exists, what explains it? Do the brain's mechanisms for acquiring language decay as the brain matures? That would seem strange, since other cognitive abilities improve. An alternative hypothesis is that this very increase in cognitive sophistication interferes with an adolescent's or adult's ability to learn a language. Young children acquire language in small chunks that can be readily digested. Older learners, when they first begin learning a language, tend to absorb a great deal at once and then may have trouble analyzing and interpreting it (Newport, 1991).

Now that you have had a brief overview of the field of human development and some of its basic concepts, it's time to look more closely at the issues developmental scientists think about and how they do their work. In Chapter 2, we will introduce you to some influential theories of how development takes place and to the methods investigators commonly use to study it.

Summary

How the Study of Human Development Evolved

Guidepost 1. What is human development, and what were the principal steps in the evolution of its study?

- **Human development** is the study of change and stability throughout life. The study of human development began with studies of childhood during the nineteenth century. Adolescence was not considered a separate phase of development until the twentieth century.
- As researchers became interested in following development throughout adulthood, **life-span development** became a field of study.

Guidepost 2. What is the life-span developmental approach, and what are its key principles?

- Baltes's life-span developmental approach is a framework for the study of life-span development. Its key principles include the idea that development is lifelong, the importance of history and context, multidimensionality, multidirectionality, and **plasticity.**

Human Development Today: An Introduction to the Field

Guidepost 3. What are the four goals of the scientific study of human development?

- The study of human development seeks to describe, explain, predict, and modify development.

Guidepost 4. What do developmental scientists study?

- Developmental scientists study developmental change. They are concerned with both **quantitative change** and **qualitative change,** as well as with stability of personality and behavior.

Guidepost 5. What are the major aspects and periods of human development?

- The three major aspects of development are physical, cognitive, and psychosocial. These forms of development do not occur in isolation; each affects the others.
- The concept of periods of development is a **social construction.** All societies recognize such periods, but the precise divisions vary. In this book, the life span is divided into eight periods: the prenatal period, infancy and toddlerhood, early childhood, middle childhood, adolescence, young adulthood, middle adulthood, and late adulthood. At each period of the life span, people have characteristic developmental needs and tasks.

Influences on Development

Guidepost 6. What kinds of influences make one person different from another?

- Influences on development come from both **heredity** and **environment.** Many typical changes during childhood are related to **maturation. Individual differences** increase with age.
- One important environmental, or contextual, influence is the family. In different societies, either the **nuclear family** or **extended family** predominates.
- **Socioeconomic status (SES)** is often related to developmental processes and outcomes through such factors as the quality of home and neighborhood environments, of medical care, and of schooling. The most powerful neighborhood influences on outcomes of development seem to be neighborhood income and human capital. Multiple *risk factors* increase the likelihood of poor outcomes.
- Other important environmental influences stem from **ethnic groups** and **culture.** In large, multiethnic societies, immigrant groups often acculturate, or adapt, to the majority culture while preserving aspects of their own.
- Influences on individuals may be **normative** or nonnormative. Normative age-graded influences affect people of the same age. Normative history-graded influences affect a particular **cohort.** Nonnormative life events are unusual in themselves or in their timing.
- There is strong evidence of **critical periods** for certain kinds of early physical development. For cognitive and psychosocial development, there appears to be more plasticity.

Key Terms

human development (9)
life-span development (10)
plasticity (11)
quantitative change (12)
qualitative change (12)
social construction (13)
individual differences (16)
heredity (16)
environment (16)
maturation (16)
nuclear family (17)
extended family (18)
socioeconomic status (SES) (18)
risk factors (19)
culture (19)
ethnic group (19)
normative (20)
cohort (20)
critical period (21)

Chapter 2

Theory and Research

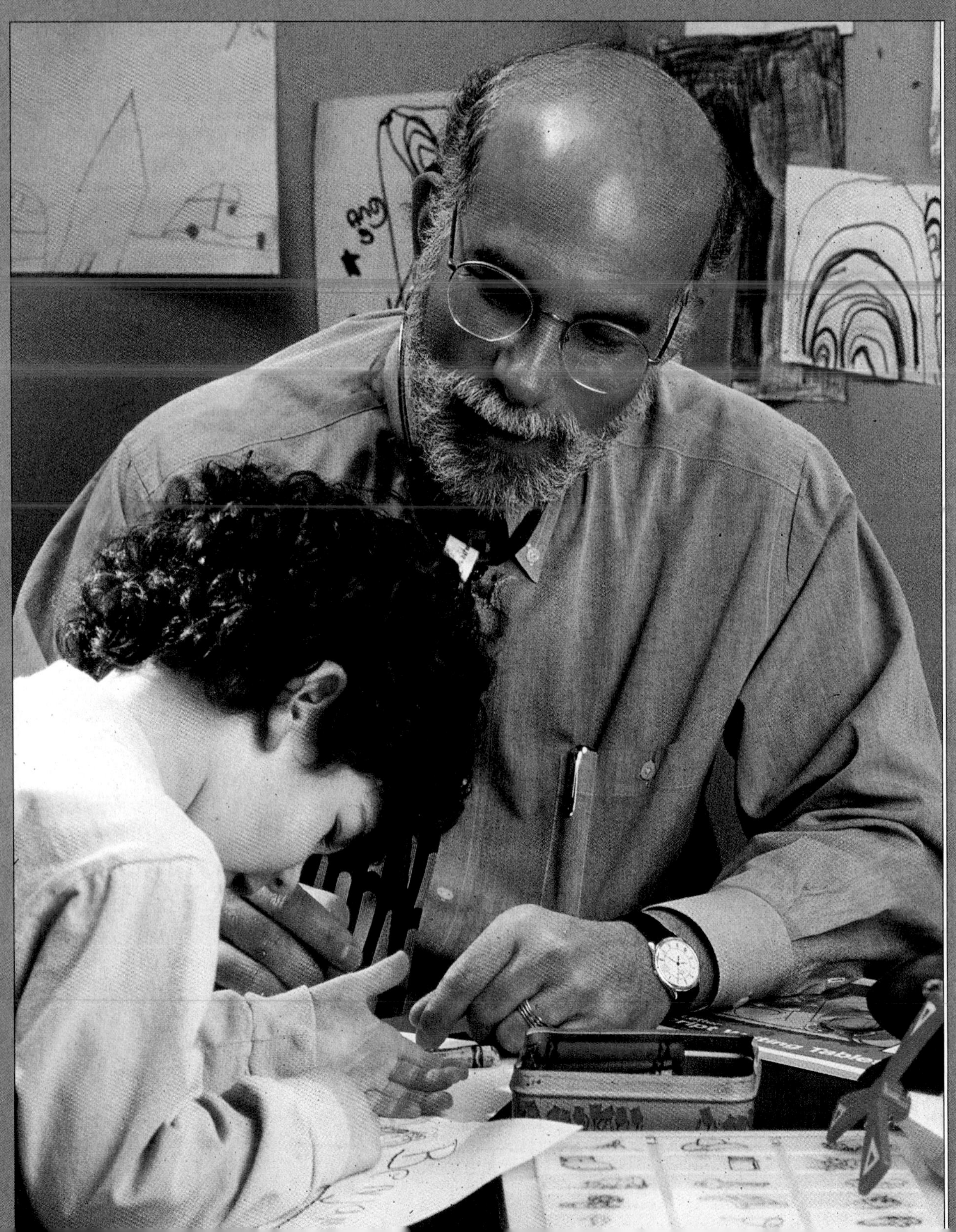

There is one thing even more vital to science than intelligent methods; and that is, the sincere desire to find out the truth, whatever it may be.

Charles Sanders Peirce, *Collected Papers*, vol. 5

Margaret Mead

Focus: Margaret Mead, Pioneer in Cross-Cultural Research

Margaret Mead (1901–1978) was a world-famous American anthropologist. In the 1920s, at a time when it was rare for a woman to expose herself to the rigors of fieldwork with remote, preliterate peoples, Mead spent nine months on the South Pacific island of Samoa, studying girls' adjustment to adolescence. Her best-selling first book, *Coming of Age in Samoa* (1928), challenged accepted views about the inevitability of adolescent rebellion.

An itinerant childhood built around her parents' academic pursuits prepared Mead for a life of roving research. In New Jersey, her mother, who was working on her doctoral thesis in sociology, took Margaret along on interviews with recent Italian immigrants—the child's first exposure to fieldwork. Her father, a professor at the University of Pennsylvania's Wharton business school, taught her respect for facts and "the importance of thinking clearly" (Mead, 1972, p. 40). He stressed the link between theory and application—as Margaret did when, years later, she tested her theories of child rearing on her daughter. Margaret's grandmother, a former schoolteacher, sent her out in the woods to collect and analyze mint specimens. "I was not well drilled in geography or spelling," Mead wrote in her memoir, *Blackberry Winter* (1972, p. 47). "But I learned to observe the world around me and to note what I saw."

Margaret took copious notes on the development of her younger brother and two younger sisters. Her curiosity about why one child in a family behaved so differently from another led to her later interest in temperamental variations within a culture.

OUTLINE

How cultures define male and female roles was another research focus. Margaret saw her mother and her grandmother as educated women who had managed to have husbands, children, and professional careers; and she expected to do the same. She was dismayed when, at the outset of her career, the distinguished anthropologist Edward Sapir told her she "would do better to stay at home and have children than to go off to the South Seas to study adolescent girls" (Mead, 1972, p. 11).

Margaret's choice of anthropology as a career was consistent with her homebred respect for the value of all human beings and their cultures. Recalling her father's insistence that the only thing worth doing is to add to the store of knowledge, she saw an urgent need to document once-isolated cultures now "vanishing before the onslaught of modern civilization" (Mead, 1972, p. 137).

"I went to Samoa—as, later, I went to the other societies on which I have worked—to find out more about human beings, human beings like ourselves in everything except their culture," she wrote. "Through the accidents of history, these cultures had developed so differently from ours that knowledge of them could shed a kind of light upon us, upon our potentialities and our limitations" (Mead, 1972, p. 293). The ongoing quest to illuminate those "potentialities and limitations" is the business of theorists and researchers in human development.

Margaret Mead's life was all of a piece. The young girl who filled notebooks with observations about her siblings became the scientist who traveled to distant lands and studied cultures very different from her own.

Mead's story underlines several important points about the study of human development. First, the study of people is not dry, abstract, or esoteric. It deals with the substance of real life.

Second, a cross-cultural perspective can reveal which patterns of behavior, if any, are universal and which are not. Most studies of human development have been done in western, developed societies, using white, middle-class participants. Today developmental scientists are increasingly conscious of the need to expand the research base, as Mead and her colleagues sought to do.

Third, theory and research are two sides of the same coin. As Mead reflected on her own experiences and observed the behavior of others, she constantly formed tentative explanations to be tested by later research.

Fourth, although the goal of science is to obtain verifiable knowledge through open-minded, impartial investigation, developmental science cannot be completely objective. Observations about human behavior are products of very human individuals whose inquiries and interpretations are inevitably influenced by their own background, values, and experiences. As Mead's daughter, Mary Catherine Bateson (1984), herself an anthropologist, noted in response to methodological criticism of Mead's early work in Samoa, a scientific observer is like a lens, which inevitably introduces some distortion into what is observed. A different lens (that is, a different observer) might change the focus and thus get different results. In striving for greater objectivity, investigators must scrutinize how they and their colleagues conduct their work, the assumptions on which it is based, and how they arrive at their conclusions.

In the first part of this chapter, we present major issues and theoretical perspectives that underlie much research in human development. In the remainder of the chapter, we look at how researchers gather and assess information, so that you will be better able to judge whether their conclusions rest on solid ground.

After you have read and studied this chapter, you should be able to answer the following questions:

Guideposts *for* Study

1. What purposes do theories serve?
2. What are three basic theoretical issues on which developmental scientists differ?
3. What are six theoretical perspectives on human development, and what are some theories representative of each?
4. How do developmental scientists study people, and what are some advantages and disadvantages of each research method?
5. What ethical problems may arise in research on human beings, and how can they best be resolved?

Basic Theoretical Issues

As we noted in Chapter 1, the goals of the study of human development are to describe, explain, predict, and modify human behavior. In keeping with these goals, developmental scientists have come up with many, sometimes conflicting, theories about why people develop as they do. A **theory** is a set of logically related concepts or statements, which seeks to describe and explain development and to predict what kinds of behavior might occur under certain conditions. Theories organize data, the information gathered by research, and are a rich source of **hypotheses**—tentative explanations or predictions that can be tested by further research.

theory
Coherent set of logically related concepts that seeks to organize, explain, and predict data.

hypotheses
Possible explanations for phenomena, used to predict the outcome of research.

Theories change to incorporate new findings. Sometimes research supports a hypothesis and the theory on which it was based. At other times, as with Mead's findings on adolescence, scientists must modify their theories to account for unexpected data. Research findings often suggest additional questions and hypotheses to be examined and provide direction for dealing with practical issues.

The way theorists explain development depends in part on the way they view three basic issues: (1) the relative weight given to heredity and environment; (2) whether people are active or passive in their own development; and (3) whether development is continuous or occurs in stages.

Which Is More Important: Heredity or Environment?

Which has more impact on development: heredity or environment? This issue has aroused intense debate. Theorists differ in the relative importance they give to *nature* (the inborn traits and characteristics inherited from the biological parents) and *nurture* (environmental influences, both before and after birth, including influences of family, peers, schools, neighborhoods, society, and culture).

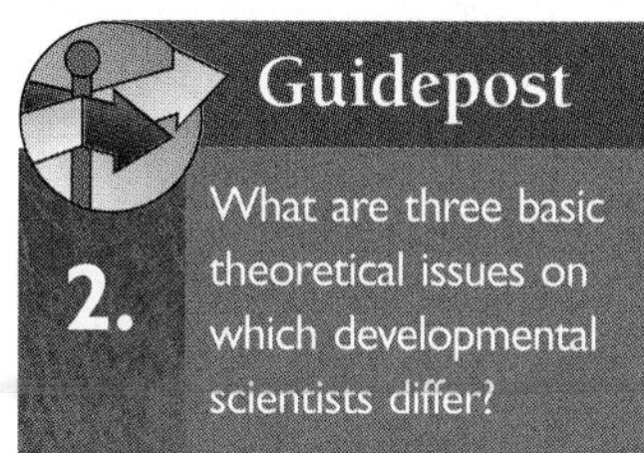

How much is inherited? How much is environmentally influenced? These questions matter. If parents believe that intelligence can be strongly influenced by experience, they may make special efforts to talk to and read to their children and offer them toys that help them learn. If parents believe that intelligence is inborn and unchangeable, they may be less likely to make such efforts.

Today, scientists have found ways to measure more precisely the roles of heredity and environment in the development of specific traits within a population (Neisser et al., 1996). When we look at a particular person, however, research with regard to almost all characteristics points to a blend of inheritance and

Does golf champion Tiger Woods owe his prowess to inborn talent or to his father's tough training? Most developmental scientists today would say, "Both."

experience. Thus, even though intelligence has a strong hereditary component, parental stimulation, education, peer influence, and other variables make a difference. As children grow up, their natural tendencies to, say, music or sports lead them into activities that strengthen those tendencies. While there is still considerable dispute about the relative importance of nature and nurture, many contemporary theorists and researchers are more interested in finding ways to explain how they interact, or work together.

Is Development Active or Passive?

The second issue hinges on one's view of the nature of human beings: are people active or passive in their own development? Many theorists subscribe to one of two contrasting models, or images, of development: *mechanistic* and *organismic.*

mechanistic model
Model, based on the machine as a metaphor, that views development as a passive, predictable response to internal and external stimuli; focuses on quantitative development; and studies phenomena by analyzing the operation of their component parts.

organismic model
Model that views development as internally initiated by an active person, or organism, and as occurring in a universal sequence of qualitatively different stages of maturation.

In the **mechanistic model,** people are like machines that react to environmental input (Pepper, 1942, 1961). Fill a car with gas, turn the ignition key, press the accelerator, and the vehicle will move. In the mechanistic view, human behavior is much the same. If we know enough about how the human "machine" is put together and about the internal and external forces impinging on it, we can predict what the person will do. Mechanistic research seeks to identify and isolate the factors that make people behave—or react—as they do.

The **organismic model** sees people as active, growing organisms that set their own development in motion (Pepper, 1942, 1961). They initiate events; they do not just react. The impetus for change is internal. Environmental influences do not cause development, though they can speed or slow it. The whole of a human being's behavior is greater than the sum of the parts that make it up. Thus, say organismic theorists, we cannot predict behavior by breaking it down into simple responses to environmental stimulation, as the mechanistic model suggests.

Is Development Continuous, or Does It Occur in Stages?

The two basic theoretical models also differ on the third issue: Is development continuous, or does it occur in stages?

Mechanistic theorists see development as continuous—always governed by the same processes, allowing prediction of earlier behaviors from later ones. These theorists focus on *quantitative* change: for example, changes in the frequency with which a response is made, rather than changes in the kind of response.

Organismic theorists emphasize *qualitative* change (Looft, 1973). They see development as occurring in a series of distinct stages. At each stage, people cope with different kinds of problems and develop different kinds of abilities. Each stage builds on the previous one and prepares the way for the next.

CHECKPOINT

Can you . . .

- ✔ State three basic issues regarding the nature of human development?
- ✔ Contrast the mechanistic and organismic models of development?

An Emerging Consensus

As the study of human development has evolved, the mechanistic and organismic models have shifted in influence and support (Parke et al., 1994). Most of the early pioneers in the field, including Sigmund Freud, Erik Erikson, and Jean Piaget, favored organismic, or stage, approaches. The mechanistic view gained adherents during the 1960s, with the popularity of learning theories derived from the work of John B. Watson. (We discuss all these theorists in the next section.)

Today the pendulum has swung back—but not all the way. Quasi-organismic approaches centered on the biological bases of behavior are on the rise; but instead of an emphasis on broad stages, there is an effort to discover what specific kinds of behavior show continuity or lack of continuity and what processes are involved in each.

Just as a consensus is emerging about how heredity and environment work together, many developmental scientists are coming to a more balanced view of active versus passive development. There is wide agreement that influence is *bidirectional:* people change their world even as it changes them (Parke et al., 1994).

Theoretical Perspectives

Theories generally fall within several broad theoretical perspectives. Each of these perspectives emphasizes different kinds of developmental processes and takes differing views on such issues as those we've just discussed. These perspectives influence the questions researchers ask, the methods they use, and the ways they interpret data. Therefore, to evaluate and interpret research, it is important to recognize the theoretical perspective on which it is based.

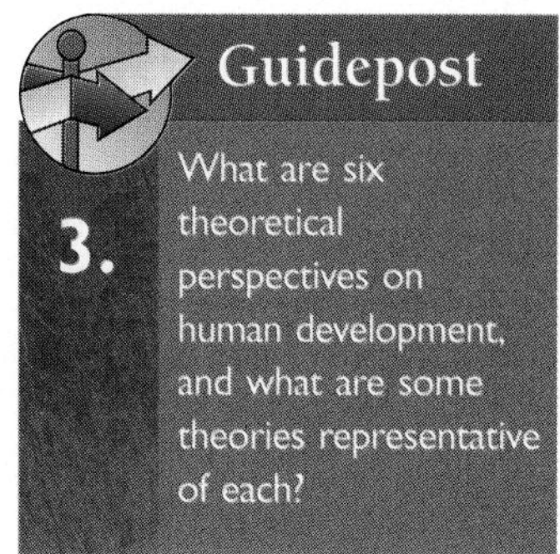

Guidepost
3.
What are six theoretical perspectives on human development, and what are some theories representative of each?

Let's look at six perspectives (summarized in Table 2-1) that underlie influential theories and research on human development: (1) *psychoanalytic* (which focuses on unconscious emotions and drives); (2) *learning* (which studies observable behavior); (3) *humanistic* (which stresses people's control over their own development); (4) *cognitive* (which analyzes thought processes); (5) *ethological* (which considers evolutionary underpinnings of behavior); and (6) *contextual* (which emphasizes the impact of the historical, social, and cultural context). None of these theoretical perspectives has all the answers; each has something to contribute to our understanding of human development.

Psychoanalytic Perspective

The **psychoanalytic perspective** is concerned with unconscious forces that motivate human behavior. At the beginning of the twentieth century, Sigmund Freud (1856–1939), a Viennese physician, developed *psychoanalysis,* a therapeutic approach aimed at giving patients insight into unconscious emotional conflicts. By asking questions designed to summon up long-buried memories, Freud concluded that the source of emotional disturbances lay in repressed traumatic experiences of early childhood. The psychoanalytic perspective has been expanded and modified by other theorists and practitioners, including Erik H. Erikson.

psychoanalytic perspective View of development concerned with unconscious forces motivating behavior.

Sigmund Freud: Psychosexual Development

Freud (1953, 1964a, 1964b) believed that personality is formed in the first few years of life, as children deal with unconscious conflicts between their inborn biological urges and the requirements of society. He proposed that these conflicts occur in an unvarying sequence of maturationally based stages of **psychosexual development,** in which pleasure shifts from one body zone to another—from the mouth to the anus and then to the genitals. At each stage, the behavior that is the chief source of gratification changes—from feeding to elimination and eventually to sexual activity.

psychosexual development In Freudian theory, an unvarying sequence of stages of personality development during infancy, childhood, and adolescence, in which gratification shifts from the mouth to the anus and then to the genitals.

Of the five stages of personality development that Freud described (see Table 2-2), he considered the first three—those of the first few years of life—crucial. He suggested that if children receive too little or too much gratification in any of these stages, they are at risk of *fixation*—an arrest in development that can show up in adult personality. For example, babies whose needs are not met during the *oral stage,* when feeding is the main source of sensual pleasure, may grow up to become nail-biters or develop "bitingly" critical personalities. Babies who receive so *much* oral pleasure that they do not want to abandon this stage may become compulsive eaters or smokers. A person who, as a toddler, had too-strict toilet training may be fixated at the *anal stage,* when the chief source of pleasure was moving the bowels. Such a person may be obsessively clean and neat, rigidly tied to schedules and routines, or defiantly messy.

Table 2-1 Six Perspectives on Human Development

Perspective	Important Theories	Basic Beliefs
Psychoanalytic	Freud's psychosexual theory	Behavior is controlled by powerful unconscious urges.
	Erikson's psychosocial theory	Personality is influenced by society and develops through a series of crises.
Learning	Behaviorism, or traditional learning theory (Pavlov, Skinner, Watson)	People are responders; the environment controls behavior.
	Social-learning (social-cognitive) theory (Bandura)	Children learn in a social context by observing and imitating models; person is an active contributor to learning.
Humanistic	Maslow's self-actualization theory	People have the ability to take charge of their lives and foster their own development.
Cognitive	Piaget's cognitive-stage theory	Qualitative changes in thought occur between infancy and adolescence. Person is active initiator of development.
	Information-processing theory	Human beings are processors of symbols.
Ethological	Bowlby's and Ainsworth's attachment theory	Human beings have the adaptive mechanisms to survive; critical or sensitive periods are stressed; biological and evolutionary bases for behavior and predisposition toward learning are important
Contextual	Bronfenbrenner's bioecological theory	Development occurs through interaction between a developing person and five surrounding, interlocking contextual systems of influences, from microsystem to chronosystem.
	Vygotsky's sociocultural theory	Child's sociocultural context has an important impact on development.

According to Freud, a key event in psychosexual development occurs during the *phallic stage* of early childhood, when the site of pleasure shifts to the genitals. Boys develop sexual attachment to their mothers (the *Oedipus complex*) and girls to their fathers (the *Electra complex*), and they have aggressive urges toward the same-sex parent, whom they regard as a rival. The boy learns that a girl does not have a penis, assumes that it was cut off, and worries that his father will castrate him too. The girl experiences what Freud called *penis envy* and blames her mother for not having given her a penis.

Children eventually resolve this anxiety by identifying with the same-sex parent and move into the relatively calm *latency stage* of middle childhood. They become socialized, develop skills, and learn about themselves and society. The *genital stage,* the final one, lasts throughout adulthood. The physical changes of puberty reawaken the *libido,* the energy that fuels the sex drive. The sexual urges

Technique Used	Stage-Oriented	Causal Emphasis	Active or Passive Individual
Clinical observation	Yes	Innate factors modified by experience	Passive
Clinical observation	Yes	Interaction of innate and experiential factors	Active
Rigorous scientific (experimental) procedures	No	Experience	Passive
Rigorous scientific (experimental) procedures	No	Experience modified by innate factors	Active and passive
Discussion of feelings	No	Interaction of innate and experiential factors	Active
Flexible interviews; meticulous observation	Yes	Interaction of innate and experiential factors	Active
Laboratory research; technological monitoring of physiologic responses	No	Interaction of innate and experiental factors	Active and passive
Naturalistic and laboratory observation	No	Interaction of innate and experiential factors	Active or passive (theorists vary)
Naturalistic observation and analysis	No	Interaction of innate and experiential factors	Active
Cross-cultural research; observation of child interacting with more competent person	No	Experience	Active

of the phallic stage, repressed during latency, now resurface to flow in socially approved channels, which Freud defined as heterosexual relations with persons outside the family of origin.

Freud proposed three hypothetical parts of the personality: the *id,* the *ego,* and the *superego.* Newborns are governed by the *id,* a source of motives and desires that is present at birth. The id seeks immediate satisfaction. When gratification is delayed, as it is when they have to wait to be fed, infants begin to see themselves as separate from the outside world. The *ego,* which represents reason or common sense, develops during the first year of life; its aim is to find realistic ways to gratify the id that are acceptable to the *superego,* which develops at about age 5 or 6. The *superego* includes the conscience and incorporates socially approved "shoulds" and "should nots" into the child's own value system. The superego is highly demanding; if its demands are not met, a child may feel guilty and anxious.

The Viennese physician Sigmund Freud developed an original, influential, and controversial theory of psychosexual development in childhood, based on his adult patients' recollections. His daughter, Anna, shown here with her father, followed in his professional footsteps and constructed her own theories of personality development.

Table 2-2 Developmental Stages According to Various Theories

Psychosexual Stages (Freud)	Psychosocial Stages (Erikson)	Cognitive Stages (Piaget)
Oral (birth to 12–18 months). Baby's chief source of pleasure involves mouth-oriented activities (sucking and feeding).	*Basic trust versus mistrust (birth to 12–18 months).* Baby develops sense of whether world is a good and safe place. Virtue: hope.	*Sensorimotor (birth to 2 years).* Infant gradually becomes able to organize activities in relation to the environment through sensory and motor activity.
Anal (12–18 months to 3 years). Child derives sensual gratification from withholding and expelling feces. Zone of gratification is anal region, and toilet training is important activity.	*Autonomy versus shame and doubt (12–18 months to 3 years).* Child develops a balance of independence and self-sufficiency over shame and doubt. Virtue: will.	*Preoperational (2 to 7 years).* Child develops a representational system and uses symbols to represent people, places, and events. Language and imaginative play are important manifestations of this stage. Thinking is still not logical.
Phallic (3 to 6 years). Child becomes attached to parent of the other sex and later identifies with same-sex parent. Superego develops. Zone of gratification shifts to genital region.	*Initiative versus guilt (3 to 6 years).* Child develops initiative when trying out new activities and is not overwhelmed by guilt. Virtue: purpose.	
Latency (6 years to puberty). Time of relative calm between more turbulent stages.	*Industry versus inferiority (6 years to puberty).* Child must learn skills of the culture or face feelings of incompetence. Virtue: skill.	*Concrete operations (7 to 11 years).* Child can solve problems logically if they are focused on the here and now, but cannot think abstractly.
Genital (puberty through adulthood). Reemergence of sexual impulses of phallic stage, channeled into mature adult sexuality.	*Identity versus identity confusion (puberty to young adulthood).* Adolescent must determine own sense of self ("Who am I?") or experience confusion about roles. Virtue: fidelity.	*Formal operations (11 years through adulthood).* Person can think abstractly, deal with hypothetical situations, and think about possibilities.
	Intimacy versus isolation (young adulthood). Person seeks to make commitments to others; if unsuccessful, may suffer from isolation and self-absorption. Virtue: love.	
	Generativity versus stagnation (middle adulthood). Mature adult is concerned with establishing and guiding the next generation or else feels personal impoverishment. Virtue: care.	
	Integrity versus despair (late adulthood). Elderly person achieves acceptance of own life, allowing acceptance of death, or else despairs over inability to relive life. Virtue: wisdom.	

Note: All ages are approximate.

Freud described a number of *defense mechanisms,* ways in which people unconsciously deal with anxiety by distorting reality. For example, a child may *repress* (block from consciousness and memory) feelings or experiences that cause anxiety. Or a child dealing with a worrisome event, such as the birth of a sibling or entrance into school, may *regress*—revert to earlier behavior, such as sucking a thumb or wetting the bed.

Freud's theory made historic contributions, and several of his central themes have been validated by research. Freud made us aware of the importance of unconscious thoughts, feelings, and motivations; the role of childhood experiences in forming personality; the ambivalence of emotional responses, especially to parents; and ways in which mental images of early relationships affect later ones (Westen, 1998). He also opened our eyes to the presence from birth of sexual urges. Although many psychoanalysts today reject his narrow emphasis on sexual and aggressive drives, his psychoanalytic method greatly influenced modern-day psychotherapy.

Some aspects of Freud's theories are hard to test. Research has questioned or invalidated many of his concepts—for example, his idea that the superego and *gender identity* (awareness of being male or female) are outcomes of conflicts during the phallic stage (Emde, 1992). On the other hand, the concepts of oral and anal personalities and of oedipal feelings in early childhood have substantial research support (Westen, 1998).

In some respects, Freud's theory grew out of his place in history and in society. Much of it, such as the concept of penis envy, seems to demean women, no doubt because of its roots in the male-dominated social system of a Victorian-era European culture. Also, Freud based his theories about normal development, not on a population of average children, but on a clientele of upper-middle-class adults, mostly women, in therapy. His concentration on biological and maturational factors and on early experience does not take into account other, and later, influences on personality. Many of Freud's followers, including Erik Erikson, have broadened Freud's focus, stressing social influences and the evolution from immature, self-gratifying relationships to mature, interdependent ones (Westen, 1998).

The psychoanalyst Erik H. Erikson departed from Freudian theory in emphasizing societal, rather than chiefly biological, influences on personality. Erikson described development as proceeding through eight crises, or turning points, throughout the life span.

psychosocial development In Erikson's theory, the socially and culturally influenced process of development of the ego, or self; it consists of eight stages throughout the life span, each revolving around a crisis that can be resolved by achieving a healthy balance between alternative positive and negative traits.

Erik Erikson: Psychosocial Development

Erik Erikson (1902–1994), a German-born psychoanalyst, was part of Freud's inner circle in Vienna until he fled the threat of Nazism and came to the United States in 1933. His broad personal and professional experience led him to modify and extend Freudian theory by emphasizing the influence of society on the developing personality.

Whereas Freud maintained that early childhood experiences permanently shape personality, Erikson contended that ego development is lifelong. Erikson's (1950, 1982; Erikson, Erikson, & Kivnick, 1986) theory of **psychosocial development** covers eight stages across the life span (refer back to Table 2-2), which we will discuss in the appropriate chapters. Each stage involves a "crisis" in personality—a major developmental issue that is particularly important at that time and will remain an issue to some degree throughout the rest of life. The crises, which emerge according to a maturational timetable, must be satisfactorily resolved for healthy ego development.

Successful resolution of each of the eight crises requires the balancing of a positive trait and a corresponding negative one. Although the positive quality should predominate, some degree of the negative is needed as well. The crisis of infancy, for example, is *basic trust versus basic mistrust.* People need to trust the world and the people in it, but they also need to learn some mistrust to protect themselves from danger. The successful outcome of each crisis is the development of a particular "virtue" or strength—in this first crisis, the "virtue" of *hope.*

Erikson's theory has held up better than Freud's, especially in its emphasis on social and cultural influences and on development beyond adolescence. However, some of Erikson's concepts, like Freud's, are difficult to test.

CHECKPOINT

Can you . . .

- ✔ Identify the chief concern of the psychoanalytic perspective?
- ✔ Name Freud's five stages of development and three parts of the personality?
- ✔ State Freud's contributions to the study of human development?
- ✔ Tell two ways in which Erikson's theory differs from Freud's?
- ✔ Explain Erikson's concept of crises in development?

learning perspective
View of development that holds that changes in behavior result from experience, or adaptation to the environment; the two major branches are behaviorism and social-learning theory.

learning
Long-lasting change in behavior that occurs as a result of experience.

behaviorism
Learning theory that emphasizes the study of observable behaviors and events and the predictable role of environment in causing behavior.

classical conditioning
Kind of learning in which a previously neutral stimulus (one that does not originally elicit a particular response) acquires the power to elicit the response after the stimulus is repeatedly associated with another stimulus that ordinarily does elicit the response.

Learning Perspective

The **learning perspective** is concerned with finding out the objective laws that govern observable behavior. Learning theorists maintain that development results from **learning,** a long-lasting change in behavior based on experience, or adaptation to the environment. Learning theorists see development as continuous (not in stages) and emphasize quantitative change.

Learning theorists have helped to make the study of human development more scientific. Their terms are defined precisely, and their theories can be tested in the laboratory. By stressing environmental influences, they help explain cultural differences in behavior (Horowitz, 1992).

Two important learning theories are *behaviorism* and *social-learning theory.*

Behaviorism

Behaviorism is a mechanistic theory, which describes observed behavior as a predictable response to experience. Although biology sets limits on what people do, behaviorists view the environment as much more influential. They hold that human beings at all ages learn about the world the same way other organisms do: by reacting to conditions, or aspects of their environment, that they find pleasing, painful, or threatening. Behaviorists look for events that determine whether or not a particular behavior will be repeated. Behavioral research focuses on *associative learning,* in which a mental link is formed between two events. Two kinds of associative learning are *classical conditioning* and *operant conditioning.*

Classical Conditioning Eager to capture Anna's memorable moments on film, her father took pictures of the infant smiling, crawling, and showing off her other achievements. Whenever the flash went off, Anna blinked. One evening when Anna was 11 months old, she saw her father hold the camera up to his eye—and she blinked *before* the flash. She had learned to associate the camera with the bright light, so that the sight of the camera alone activated her blinking reflex.

Anna's blinking is an example of **classical conditioning,** in which a person or animal learns a reflexive response to a stimulus that did not originally evoke it, after the stimulus is repeatedly associated with a stimulus that *does* elicit the response.

The principles of classical conditioning were developed by the Russian physiologist Ivan Pavlov (1849–1936), who devised experiments in which dogs learned to salivate at the sound of a bell that rang at feeding time. The American behaviorist John B. Watson (1878–1958) applied stimulus-response theories to children, claiming that he could mold any infant in any way he chose. In one of the earliest and most famous demonstrations of classical conditioning in human beings (Watson & Rayner, 1920), he taught an 11-month-old baby known as "Little Albert" to fear furry white objects.

In this study, Albert was exposed to a loud noise just as he was about to stroke a furry white rat. The noise frightened him, and he began to cry. After repeated pairings of the rat with the loud noise, Albert whimpered with fear whenever he saw the rat. Although the ethics of this research are highly dubious, the study did show that a baby could be conditioned to fear things he had not been afraid of before.

Critics of such methods sometimes associate conditioning with thought control and manipulation. Actually, as we saw in Anna's example, classical conditioning is a natural form of learning that occurs even without intervention. By learning what events go together, children can anticipate what is going to happen, and this knowledge makes their world a more orderly, predictable place.

Consider this . . .

- Watson and Rayner's experiment that conditioned fear in "Little Albert" would violate today's ethical standards for research, yet it provided valuable information about human behavior. In an experiment such as this, where would you draw the line between society's need to learn and an infant's rights?
- Some people have raised ethical objections to behaviorists' goal of controlling or shaping behavior. If developmentalists *could* mold people so as to eliminate antisocial behavior, *should* they?

Operant Conditioning Baby Terrell lies peacefully in his crib. When he happens to smile, his mother goes over to the crib and plays with him. Later his father does the same thing. As this sequence is repeated, Terrell learns that something he does (smiling) can produce something he likes (loving attention from a parent); and so he keeps smiling to attract his parents' attention. An originally accidental behavior (smiling) has become a conditioned response.

operant conditioning
Kind of learning in which a person tends to repeat a behavior that has been reinforced or to cease a behavior that has been punished.

reinforcement
In operant conditioning, a stimulus experienced following a behavior, which increases the probability that the behavior will be repeated.

punishment
In operant conditioning, a stimulus experienced following a behavior, which decreases the probability that the behavior will be repeated.

This kind of learning is called **operant conditioning** because the individual learns from the consequences of "operating" on the environment. The American psychologist B. F. Skinner (1904–1990), who formulated the principles of operant conditioning, worked primarily with rats and pigeons, but Skinner (1938) maintained that the same principles apply to human beings. He found that an organism will tend to repeat a response that has been reinforced and will suppress a response that has been punished. **Reinforcement** is a consequence of behavior that increases the likelihood that the behavior will be repeated; in Terrell's case, his parents' attention reinforces his smiling. **Punishment** is a consequence of behavior that *decreases* the likelihood of repetition. Whether a consequence is reinforcing or punishing depends on the person. What is reinforcing for one person may be punishing for another.

Reinforcement can be either positive or negative. *Positive reinforcement* consists of *giving* a reward, such as food, gold stars, money, or praise—or playing with a baby. *Negative reinforcement* consists of *taking away* something the individual does not like (known as an *aversive event*), such as a loud noise. Negative reinforcement is sometimes confused with punishment. However, they are different. Punishment suppresses a behavior by *bringing on* an aversive event (such as spanking a child or giving an electric shock to an animal), or by *withdrawing* a positive event (such as watching television). Negative reinforcement encourages repetition of a behavior by *removing* an aversive event.

The psychologist Albert Bandura is a leading advocate of social-learning, or social cognitive, theory, which emphasizes learning through observation and imitation.

Reinforcement is most effective when it immediately follows a behavior. If a response is no longer reinforced, it will eventually return to its original (baseline) level. This is called *extinction.* If, after a while, no one plays with Terrell when he smiles, he may not stop smiling but will smile far less than if his smiles still brought reinforcement.

Behavior modification, or behavior therapy, is a form of operant conditioning used to eliminate undesirable behavior or to instill positive behavior. This may be done by *shaping:* reinforcing responses that are more and more like the desired one. Behavior modification is particularly effective among children with special needs, such as youngsters with mental or emotional disabilities.

Social-Learning (Social Cognitive) Theory

social-learning theory
Theory, proposed by Bandura, that behaviors are learned by observing and imitating models. Also called *social cognitive theory.*

Social-learning theory maintains that children, in particular, learn social behaviors by observing and imitating models. The American psychologist Albert Bandura (b. 1925) developed many of the principles of social-learning theory, also known as *social cognitive theory,* which today is more influential than behaviorism.

Unlike behaviorism, social-learning theory (Bandura, 1977, 1989) regards the learner as active. Whereas behaviorists see the environment as molding the person, social-learning theorists believe that the person also acts upon the environment—in fact, *creates* the environment to some extent. Although social-learning theorists, like behaviorists, emphasize laboratory experimentation, they believe that theories based on animal research cannot explain human behavior. People learn in a social context, and human learning is more complex than simple conditioning. Social-learning theorists acknowledge the importance of cognition; they see cognitive responses to perceptions, rather than largely automatic responses to reinforcement or punishment, as central to development. Thus, social-learning theory is a bridge between classical learning theory and the cognitive perspective.

observational learning
In social-learning theory, learning that occurs through watching the behavior of others.

CHECKPOINT

Can you . . .

- ✔ Identify the chief concerns, strengths, and weaknesses of the learning perspective?
- ✔ List the steps in classical conditioning, and give an example?
- ✔ Tell how operant conditioning differs from classical conditioning?
- ✔ Distinguish among positive reinforcement, negative reinforcement, and punishment, and give an example of each?
- ✔ Tell how behavior modification works?
- ✔ Compare behaviorism and social-learning (social cognitive) theory?
- ✔ Give examples of observational learning?

Of particular importance in social-learning theory is observation and imitation of models. People acquire new abilities through **observational learning**—by watching others. They demonstrate their learning by imitating the model, sometimes when the model is no longer present. According to social-learning theory, imitation of models is the most important element in how children learn a language, deal with aggression, develop a moral sense, and learn gender-appropriate behaviors. However, observational learning can occur even if the child does not imitate the observed behavior.

Children actively advance their own social learning by choosing models to imitate. The choice is influenced by characteristics of the model, the child, and the environment. A child may choose one parent over the other. Or the child may choose another adult (say, a teacher, a television personality, a sports figure, or a drug dealer) or an admired peer in addition to—or instead of—either parent.

The specific behavior children imitate depends on what they perceive as valued in their culture. If all the teachers in Carlos's school are women, he probably will not copy their behavior, which he probably considers "unmanly." However, if he meets a male teacher he likes, he may change his mind about the value of teachers as models.

Cognitive factors, such as the abilities to pay attention and to mentally organize sensory information, affect the way people incorporate observed behavior into their own. Cognitive processes are at work as people observe models, learn "chunks" of behavior, and mentally put the chunks together into complex new behavior patterns. Rita, for example, imitates the toes-out walk of her dance teacher but models her dance steps after those of Carmen, a slightly more advanced student. Even so, she develops her own style of dancing by putting her observations together into a new pattern. Children's developing ability to use mental symbols to stand for a model's behavior enables them to form standards for judging their own behavior.

Humanistic Perspective

humanistic perspective
View of personality development that sees people as having the ability to foster their own positive, healthy development through the distinctively human capacities for choice, creativity, and self-realization.

hierarchy of needs
In Maslow's terminology, a rank-order of needs that motivate human behavior.

self-actualization
In Maslow's terminology, the highest in the hierarchy of human needs (which can be achieved only after other needs are met): the need to fully realize one's potential.

The **humanistic perspective** developed in the 1950s and 1960s in response to what some psychologists saw as negative beliefs about human nature underlying psychoanalytic and behavioral theories. Humanistic psychologists, such as Abraham Maslow and Carl Rogers, reject the idea that people are largely captives of early unconscious experiences, instinctual urges, or environmental forces. Unlike Freud, who saw personality as set early in childhood, or behaviorists, who view people as automatic reactors to events, humanistic theorists emphasize people's ability—regardless of age or circumstances—to take charge of their lives.

Humanistic psychologists give special attention to internal factors in personality: feelings, values, and hopes. They seek to help people foster their own development through the distinctively human capacities of choice, creativity, and self-realization. They stress the potential for positive, healthy development; any negative characteristics, they say, are the result of damage inflicted on the developing person.

Maslow (1908–1970) identified a **hierarchy of needs:** a rank-order of needs that motivate human behavior (see Figure 2-1). According to Maslow (1954), only when people have satisfied basic needs can they strive to meet higher needs. The most basic need is physiological survival. Starving persons will take great risks to get food; only when they have obtained it can they worry about the next level of needs, those concerning personal security. These needs, in turn, must be substantially met before people can freely seek love and acceptance, esteem and achievment, and finally **self-actualization,** the full realization of potential.

Self-actualized people, said Maslow (1968), have a keen perception of reality, accept themselves and others, and appreciate nature. They are spontaneous, highly creative, and self-directed and are good problem solvers. They have satisfying re-

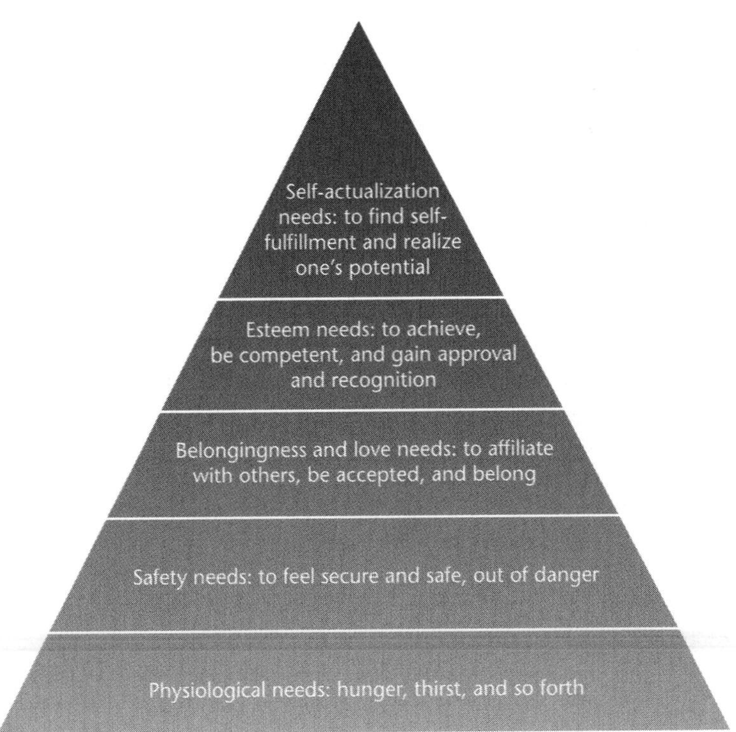

Figure 2-1
Maslow's hierarchy of needs. According to Maslow, human needs have different priorities. As each level of needs is met, a person can look to the needs of the next higher level.
(Source: Maslow, 1954.)

lationships, but they also have a desire for privacy. They have a strong sense of values and a nonauthoritarian character. They respond to experience with fresh appreciation and rich emotion. Most of them have profound mystical or spiritual experiences, called *peak experiences,* which can lead to a sense of self-transcendence, or oneness with something beyond the self. No one is ever completely self-actualized; a healthy person is continually moving up to more fulfilling levels.

Maslow's hierarchy of needs seems to be grounded in human experience, but it does not invariably hold true. History is full of accounts of self-sacrifice, in which people gave up what they needed for survival so that someone else (a loved one or even a stranger) might live.

Still, humanistic theories such as Maslow's have made a valuable contribution by promoting approaches, both to child rearing and to adult self-improvement, that respect the individual's uniqueness. Their limitations as scientific theories have to do largely with subjectivity; their concepts are not clearly defined and so are hard to test.

CHECKPOINT

Can you . . .

- ✔ Identify the central concerns and assumptions of the humanistic perspective?
- ✔ Explain Maslow's hierarchy of needs?
- ✔ State the contributions and limitations of humanistic theories?

Cognitive Perspective

The **cognitive perspective** is concerned with thought processes and the behavior that reflects those processes. This perspective encompasses both organismic and mechanistically influenced theories. It includes the cognitive-stage theory of Piaget, the newer information-processing approach, and neo-Piagetian theories, which combine elements of both. It also includes contemporary efforts to apply findings of brain research to the understanding of cognitive processes.

cognitive perspective
View of development that is concerned with thought processes and the behavior that reflects those processes.

Jean Piaget's Cognitive-Stage Theory

Much of what we know about how children think is due to the Swiss theoretician Jean Piaget (1896–1980). Piaget was the forerunner of today's "cognitive revolution" with its emphasis on mental processes. Piaget viewed children organismically, as active, growing beings with their own internal impulses and patterns of development. He saw cognitive development as the product of children's efforts to understand and act on their world.

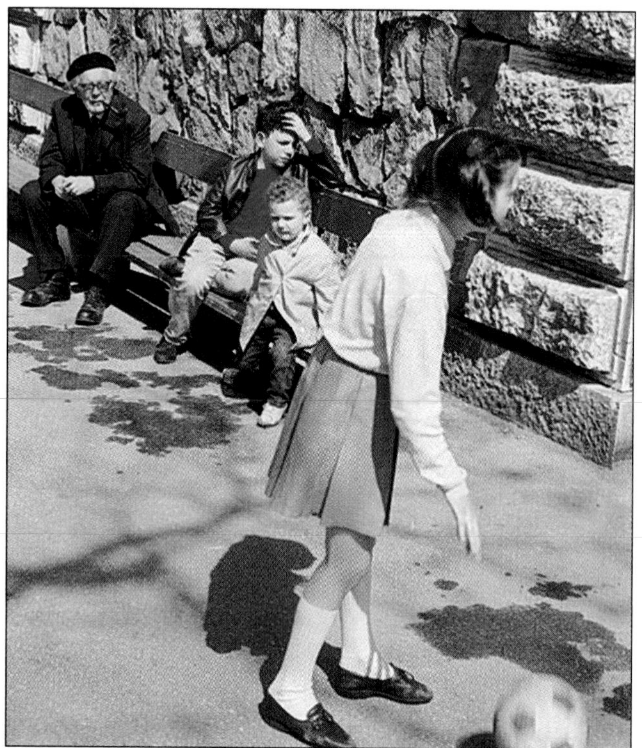

The Swiss psychologist Jean Piaget studied children's cognitive development by observing and talking with his own youngsters and others.

Piaget's *clinical method* combined observation with flexible questioning. To find out how children think, Piaget followed up their answers with more questions. In this way he discovered that a typical 4-year-old believed that pennies or flowers were more numerous when arranged in a line than when heaped or piled up. From his observations of his own and other children, Piaget created a comprehensive theory of cognitive development.

Piaget believed that cognitive development begins with an inborn ability to adapt to the environment. By rooting for a nipple, feeling a pebble, or exploring the boundaries of a room, young children develop a more accurate picture of their surroundings and greater competence in dealing with them.

Piaget described cognitive development as occurring in a series of qualitatively different stages (listed in Table 2-2 and discussed in detail in later chapters). At each stage a child's mind develops a new way of operating. From infancy through adolescence, mental operations evolve from learning based on simple sensory and motor activity to logical, abstract thought. This gradual development occurs through three interrelated principles: *organization, adaptation,* and *equilibration.*

organization
In Piaget's terminology, integration of knowledge into a system to make sense of the environment.

schemes
In Piaget's terminology, basic cognitive structures consisting of organized patterns of behavior used in different kinds of situations.

adaptation
In Piaget's terminology, adjustment to new information about the environment through the complementary processes of assimilation and accommodation.

assimilation
In Piaget's terminology, incorporation of new information into an existing cognitive structure.

accommodation
In Piaget's terminology, changes in an existing cognitive structure to include new information.

equilibration
In Piaget's terminology, the tendency to strive for equilibrium (balance) among cognitive elements within the organism and between the organism and the outside world.

Organization is the tendency to create increasingly complex cognitive structures: systems of knowledge or ways of thinking that incorporate more and more accurate images of reality. These structures, called **schemes,** are organized patterns of behavior that a person uses to think about and act in a situation. As children acquire more information, their schemes become more and more complex. An infant has a simple scheme for sucking but soon develops varied schemes for how to suck at the breast, a bottle, or a thumb. At first schemes for looking and grasping operate independently. Later, infants integrate these separate schemes into a single scheme that allows them to look at an object while holding it.

Adaptation is Piaget's term for how a child handles new information that seems to conflict with what the child already knows. Adaptation involves two steps: (1) **assimilation,** taking in information and incorporating it into existing cognitive structures, and (2) **accommodation,** changing one's cognitive structures to include the new knowledge. **Equilibration**—a constant striving for a stable balance, or equilibrium—dictates the shift from assimilation to accommodation. When children cannot handle new experiences within their existing structures, they organize new mental patterns that integrate the new experience, thus restoring equilibrium. A breast- or bottle-fed baby who begins to suck on the spout of a "sippy" cup is showing assimilation—using an old scheme to deal with a new object or situation. When the infant discovers that sipping from a cup requires somewhat different tongue and mouth movements from those used to suck on a breast or bottle, she accommodates by modifying the old scheme. She has adapted her original sucking scheme to deal with a new experience: the cup. Thus, assimilation and accommodation work together to produce equilibrium and cognitive growth.

Piaget's careful observations have yielded a wealth of information, including some surprising insights. Who, for example, would have thought that not until about age 7 do children realize that a ball of clay that has been rolled into a "worm" before their eyes still contains the same amount of clay? Or that an infant might think that a person who has moved out of sight may no longer exist? Piaget has shown us that children's minds are not miniature adult minds. Understanding how children think makes it easier for parents and teachers to teach them.

Yet, as we discuss in Chapters 5 and 7, Piaget seriously underestimated the abilities of infants and young children. Some contemporary psychologists question his clearly demarcated stages; they point to evidence that cognitive development is more gradual and continuous (Flavell, 1992). Furthermore, research beginning in the late 1960s has challenged Piaget's basic idea that children's thinking develops in a single, universal progression leading to formal thought. Instead, children's cognitive processes seem closely tied to specific content (what they are thinking *about*), as well as to the context of a problem and the kinds of information and thought a culture considers important (Case & Okamoto, 1996). Finally, research on adult cognition suggests that Piaget's focus on formal logic as the apex of cognitive development is too narrow. It does not account for the emergence of such mature abilities as practical problem solving, wisdom, and the capacity to deal with ambiguous situations and competing truths.

The Information-Processing Approach

The newer **information-processing approach** attempts to explain cognitive development by observing and analyzing the mental processes involved in perceiving and handling information. Scientists who take this approach study how people acquire, remember, and use information through manipulation of symbols or mental images. The information-processing approach is not a single theory but a framework, or set of assumptions, that underlies a wide range of theories and research.

information-processing approach
Approach to the study of cognitive development by observing and analyzing the mental processes involved in perceiving and handling information.

Information-processing theorists compare the brain to a computer. Sensory impressions go in; behavior comes out. But what happens in between? How does the brain transform sensation and perception (say, of an unfamiliar face) into usable information (the ability to recognize that face again)?

Information-processing researchers infer what goes on in the mind. For example, they may ask a child to recall a list of words and then observe any difference in performance if the child repeats the list over and over before being asked to recall the words. Through such studies, some information-processing researchers have developed *computational models* or flow charts analyzing the specific steps the brain appears to go through in gathering, storing, retrieving, and using information.

Despite the use of the "passive" computer model, information-processing theorists see people as active thinkers about their world. Unlike Piaget, they generally do not propose stages of development, but they do note age-related increases in the speed, complexity, and efficiency of mental processing and in the amount and variety of material that can be stored in memory.

The information-processing approach provides a valuable way to gather information about the development of memory and other cognitive processes. It has at least three practical applications. First, it enables researchers to estimate an infant's later intelligence from the efficiency of sensory perception and processing. Second, by understanding how children gain, recall, and use information, parents and teachers can help them become more aware of their own mental processes and of strategies to enhance them. Finally, psychologists can use information-processing models to test, diagnose, and treat learning problems. By pinpointing the weakness in the information-processing system, they can tell whether the difficulty is with vision or hearing, attentiveness, or getting information into memory (R. M. Thomas, 1996).

Neo-Piagetian Theories

During the 1980s, in response to criticisms of Piaget's theory, neo-Piagetian developmental psychologists began to integrate some elements of his theory with the information-processing approach. Instead of describing a single, general system of increasingly logical mental operations, neo-Piagetians focus on *specific* concepts, strategies, and skills. They believe that children develop cognitively by

CHECKPOINT

Can you . . .

- ✔ Contrast Piaget's assumptions and methods with those of classical learning theory and of the information-processing approach?
- ✔ List three interrelated principles that bring about cognitive growth, according to Piaget, and give an example of each?
- ✔ State contributions and criticisms of Piaget's theory?
- ✔ Describe what information-processing researchers do, and tell three ways in which such research can be applied?
- ✔ Tell how Case's theory draws from both Piaget and the information-processing approach?
- ✔ Explain how brain research can contribute to the understanding of cognitive processes?

cognitive neuroscience approach
Approach to the study of cognitive development that links brain processes with cognitive ones.

ethological perspective
View of development that focuses on the biological and evolutionary bases of behavior.

becoming more efficient at processing information. According to Robbie Case (1985, 1992), there is a limit to the amount of information a child can keep in mind. By practicing a skill, such as counting or reading, the child can become faster and more proficient, freeing mental "space" for additional information and more complex problem solving. Maturation of neurological processes also expands available memory capacity.

Recently Case (Case & Okamoto, 1996) has been testing a model that modifies Piaget's idea of cognitive structures. Unlike Piaget's *operational* structures, such as concrete and formal operations, which apply to any domain of thought, Case's are *conceptual* structures within specific domains such as number, story understanding, and spatial relations. In Case's model, children, as they acquire knowledge, go through stages in which their conceptual structures become more complex, better coordinated, and multidimensional. For example, a child's understanding of spatial concepts begins with a recognition of shapes of objects, moves on to a sense of their relative size and location, and then to an understanding of perspective.

The neo-Piagetian approach is a promising effort to explain the processes by which qualitative changes in cognition occur and the constraints on learning at any given stage. Because of its emphasis on efficiency of processing, it helps account for individual differences in cognitive ability and for uneven development in various domains.

The Cognitive Neuroscience Approach

For most of the history of psychology, theorists and researchers studied cognitive processes apart from the physical workings of the brain in which these processes occur. Today, when new instruments make it possible to see the brain in action, adherents of the **cognitive neuroscience approach** argue that an accurate understanding of cognitive functioning must be linked to processes that take place in the brain.

Brain research supports important aspects of information-processing models, such as the existence of separate structures to handle conscious and unconscious memory. Neurological research also may be able to shed light on such issues as whether intelligence is general or specialized and what influences a young child's readiness for formal learning (Byrnes & Fox, 1998).

Ethological Perspective

The **ethological perspective** focuses on biological and evolutionary bases of behavior. It looks beyond the immediate adaptive value of behavior for an individual to its function in promoting the survival of the group or species.

In the 1930s, two European zoologists, Konrad Lorenz and Niko Tinbergen, developed the scientific discipline of *ethology*, the study of the behavior of species of animals, by observing them, usually in their natural surroundings. In the 1950s, the British psychologist John Bowlby extended ethological principles to human development.

Ethologists believe that, for each species, a variety of innate, species-specific behaviors have evolved to increase its odds of survival. They do comparative research to identify which behaviors are universal and which are specific to a particular species or are modified by culture. They also identify behaviors that are adaptive at different parts of the life span; for example, an infant needs to stay close to the mother, but for an older child more independent exploration is important. (Box 2-1 looks more deeply at the adaptiveness of immaturity from an evolutionary perspective.)

Bowlby (1951) was convinced of the importance of the mother-baby bond and warned against separating mother and baby without providing good substitute caregiving. His conviction arose partly from examining ethological studies of bonding in animals and partly from seeing disturbed children in a psychoanalytic clinic in London. Mary Ainsworth, originally a junior colleague of Bowlby, studied African and American babies and devised the now-famous "Strange Situation" (see Chapter 6) to measure attachment to parents. Research on attachment is based on the belief that infant and parent are biologically predisposed to becoming attached to each other and that such attachment promotes the baby's survival.

So far, the ethological approach has been applied chiefly to a few specific developmental issues, such as attachment, dominance and aggression among peers, and everyday problem-solving skills. It points up the value of careful observation of children in their natural settings. Its methods can fruitfully be combined with other techniques, such as verbal questioning (P. H. Miller, 1993).

CHECKPOINT

Can you . . .

✔ Identify the chief concern and assumptions of the ethological perspective?

✔ Tell what kinds of topics ethological researchers study, and point out the uses of their methods?

Contextual Perspective

According to the **contextual perspective,** development can be understood only in its social context. Contextualists see the individual, not as a separate entity interacting with the environment, but as an inseparable part of it. (Baltes's life-span developmental approach, introduced in Chapter 1, is heavily influenced by contextual thinking.)

contextual perspective View of development that sees the individual as inseparable from the social context.

Urie Bronfenbrenner's Bioecological Theory

The American psychologist Urie Bronfenbrenner's (1979, 1986, 1994; Bronfenbrenner & Morris, 1998) currently influential **bioecological theory** describes the

bioecological theory Bronfenbrenner's approach to understanding processes and contexts of development.

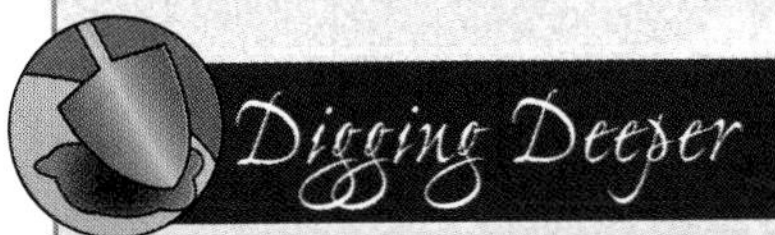

Box 2-1

The Adaptive Value of Immaturity

In comparison with other animals, and even with other primates, human beings take a long time to grow up. For example, it takes chimpanzees about eight years to reach reproductive maturity, rhesus monkeys about four years, and lemurs only about two years. Human beings, by contrast, do not mature physically until early in the teenage years and, at least in modern industrialized societies, typically reach cognitive and psychosocial maturity even later.

From the point of view of Darwinian evolutionary theory, this prolonged period of immaturity is essential to the survival and well-being of the species. Human beings, more than any other animal, live by their intelligence. Human communities and cultures are highly complex, and there is much to learn in order to "know the ropes." A long childhood serves as essential preparation for adulthood.

Apart from their long-term value, some aspects of immaturity (discussed in more detail later in this book) serve immediate adaptive purposes. For example, some primitive reflexes, such as rooting for the nipple, are protective for newborns and disappear when no longer needed. The development of the human brain, despite its rapid prenatal growth, is much less complete at birth than that of the brains of other primates; if the fetus's brain attained full human size before birth, its head would be too big to go through the birth canal. Instead, the human brain continues to grow throughout childhood, eventually far surpassing the brains of our simian cousins in the capacities for language and thought.

The human brain's slower development gives it greater flexibility, or *plasticity,* as not all connections are "hard wired" at an early age. "This behavioral and cognitive flexibility is perhaps the human species's greatest adaptive advantage" (Bjorklund, 1997, p. 157). It helps account for the resiliency of children who are victims of war,

From an evolutionary perspective, the prolonged period of immaturity known as *childhood* permits human beings to develop adaptive skills. One important way this happens is through "pretend" play. This girl playing "doctor" with her teddy bear is developing her imagination and experimenting with social roles.

—*Continued*

malnourishment, or abuse, yet manage to overcome the effects of early environmental deprivation.

The extended period of immaturity and dependency during infancy and childhood allows children to spend much of their time in play; and, as Piaget maintained, it is largely through play that cognitive development occurs. Play also enables children to develop motor skills and experiment with social roles. It is a vehicle for creative imagination and intellectual curiosity, the hallmarks of the human spirit.

Research on animals suggests that the immaturity of early sensory and motor functioning may protect infants from overstimulation. By limiting the amount of information they have to deal with, it may help them make sense of their world and focus on experiences essential to survival, such as feeding and attachment to the mother. Later, infants' limited memory capacity may simplify the processing of linguistic sounds and thus facilitate early language learning.

The differing rates of development of the various senses may minimize competition among them. In many species the sense of sight is the last to develop. Studies have found that premature visual stimulation can interfere with newborn rats' ability to smell (Kenny & Turkewitz, 1986); and quail chicks that have received prenatal visual stimulation cannot tell their mother's call from that of another quail (Lickliter & Hellewell, 1992). On the other hand, much research supports the value of early sensory stimulation for human infants. The animal studies reported in the preceding sentence merely provide a warning that such stimulation should be within a normal range, and that extraordinary stimulation can have unintended negative effects.

Limitations on young children's thought may have adaptive value. For example, Piaget observed that young children are *egocentric;* they tend to see things from their own point of view. Some research suggests that a tendency toward egocentrism may actually help children learn. In one study (Ratner & Foley, 1997), 5-year-olds took turns with an adult in placing furniture in a doll house. In a control group, the adult had already placed half of the items, and the children were then asked to place the other half. When questioned afterward, the children who had taken turns with the adult were more likely than those in the control group to claim that they had placed pieces of furniture the adult had actually placed, but they also remembered more about the task and were better able to repeat it. It may be that an "I did it!" bias helps young children's recall by avoiding the need to distinguish between their own actions and the actions of others. Young children also tend to be unrealistic in their assessment of their abilities, believing they can do more than they actually can. This immature self-judgment can be beneficial in that it encourages children to try new things and reduces their fear of failure.

All in all, evolutionary theory and research suggest that immaturity is not necessarily equivalent to deficiency, and that some attributes of infancy and childhood have persisted because they are appropriate to the tasks of a particular time of life. That does not mean, of course, that *all* early behavior is adaptive, or that children should be "babied" indefinitely; "maturity is still the goal of development" (Bjorklund, 1997, p. 166). What it does mean is that each phase of development is entitled to respect and understanding in its own right, and not just as a pathway to a later phase.

Source: Bjorklund, 1997.

range of interacting influences that affect a developing person. Every biological organism develops within the context of ecological systems that support or stifle its growth. Just as we need to understand the ecology of the ocean or the forest if we wish to understand the development of a fish or a fossil, we need to understand the ecology of the human environment if we wish to understand how people develop.

According to Bronfenbrenner, development occurs through increasingly complex processes of regular, active, two-way interaction between a developing person and the immediate, everyday environment—processes that are affected by more remote contexts of which the person may not even be aware. To understand these processes, we must study the multiple contexts in which they occur. These begin with the home, classroom, workplace, and neighborhood; connect outward to societal institutions, such as educational and transportation systems; and finally encompass cultural and historical patterns that affect the family, the school, and virtually everything else in a person's life. Bronfenbrenner identifies five interlocking contextual systems, from the most intimate to the broadest: the *microsystem, mesosystem, exosystem, macrosystem,* and *chronosystem* (see Figure 2-2). Although we separate the various levels of influence for purposes of illustration, in reality they continually interact.

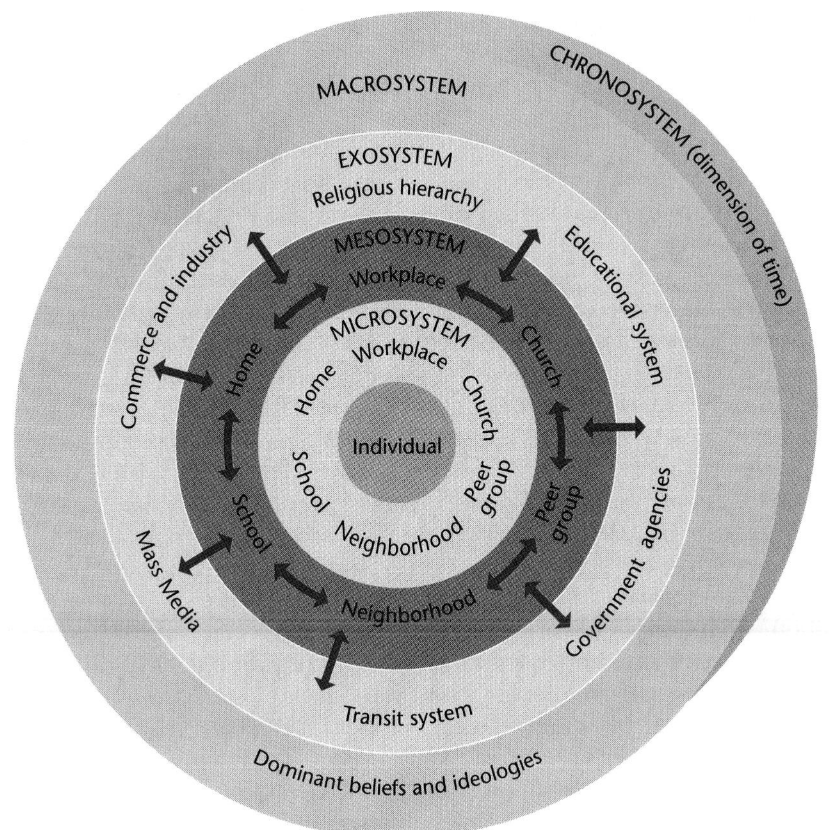

Figure 2-2
Bronfenbrenner's bioecological theory. Concentric circles show five levels of environmental influence, from the most intimate environment (innermost circle) to the broadest—all within the dimension of time. The circles form a set of nested influences, like egg-shaped boxes that fit inside one another, encasing the developing person. The figure shows what we would see if we sliced the nested "boxes" across the middle and looked inside. Keep in mind that the boundaries between the "boxes" are fluid, and the "boxes" are interconnected.
(Source: Adapted from Cole & Cole, 1989.)

A **microsystem** is a pattern of activities, roles, and relationships within a setting, such as the home, school, workplace, or neighborhood, in which a person functions on a firsthand, day-to-day basis. It is through the microsystem that more distant influences, such as social institutions and cultural values, reach the developing person.

microsystem
In Bronfenbrenner's terminology, a setting in which a person interacts bidirectionally with others on an everyday, face-to-face basis.

A microsystem involves personal, face-to-face relationships, and bidirectional influences flow back and forth. How, for example, does a new baby affect the parents' lives? How do their feelings and attitudes affect the baby? By looking at the family as a functional system, researchers have come up with some surprises: for example, the extent to which siblings' environment differs within the same household (see Chapter 3). A person's workplace is another important microsystem. How does an employer's treatment of employees affect their productivity, and how does their productivity affect the employer's treatment of them?

A **mesosystem** is the interaction of two or more microsystems that contain the developing person. It may include linkages between home and school (such as parent-teacher conferences), between home and workplace (such as conflicts between parental and job responsibilities), or between the family and the peer group. Attention to mesosystems can alert us to differences in the ways the same person acts in different settings. For example, a child who can satisfactorily complete a school assignment at home may become tongue-tied when asked a question about the assignment in class.

mesosystem
In Bronfenbrenner's terminology, a system of linkages of two or more microsystems of which a person is a part.

An **exosystem,** like a mesosystem, consists of linkages between two or more settings; but in an exosystem, unlike a mesosystem, at least one of these settings does *not* contain the developing person and thus affects him or her only indirectly. Exosystem influences on children's development include parents'

exosystem
In Bronfenbrenner's terminology, a system of linkages between two or more settings, one of which does not contain the developing person.

workplaces and parents' social networks. A man who is frustrated on the job may mistreat his child. A woman whose employer encourages breast-feeding by providing pumping and milk storage facilities may be more likely to continue nursing her baby.

macrosystem
In Bronfenbrenner's terminology, the system of overall cultural patterns that embraces all of a society's microsystems, mesosystems, and exosystems.

The **macrosystem** consists of overall cultural patterns, like those Margaret Mead studied: dominant values, beliefs, customs, and economic and social systems of a culture or subculture (such as capitalism and socialism), which filter down in countless ways to individuals' daily lives. For example, whether a person lives in a nuclear or extended-family household is strongly influenced by a culture's macrosystem. We can see a more subtle macrosystem influence in the individualistic values stressed in the United States, as contrasted with the predominant value of group harmony in Chinese culture.

chronosystem
In Bronfenbrenner's terminology, a system that shows effects of time on the microsystem, mesosystem, exosystem, and macrosystem.

The **chronosystem** adds the dimension of time: the degree of stability or change in a person's world. This can include changes in family composition, place of residence, or employment, as well as larger events such as wars, economic cycles (refer back to Box 1-1), and waves of immigration. Changes in family patterns (such as the increase in working mothers in western industrial societies and the decline of the extended-family household in some developing countries) are chronosystem factors. So are mobility between social classes and acculturation of immigrant groups (refer back to Chapter 1).

According to Bronfenbrenner, a person is not merely an outcome of development, but a shaper of it. People affect their own development through their biological and psychological characteristics, talents and skills, disabilities, and temperament.

Bronfenbrenner reminds us that people do not develop in isolation. By highlighting the interrelated contexts of, and influences on, development, his theory provides a key to analysis of the developmental processes that underlie such diverse phenomena as antisocial behavior and academic achievement. At the same time, the theory calls attention to the complexity of studying and describing these influences and processes.

According to the Russian psychologist Lev Semenovich Vygotsky, children learn through social interaction.

Lev Vygotsky's Sociocultural Theory

The Russian psychologist Lev Semenovich Vygotsky (1896–1934) was a prominent proponent of the contextual perspective, particularly as it applies to children's cognitive development.

In contrast with Bronfenbrenner, who sees contextual systems as centered around the individual person, Vygotsky's central focus is the social, cultural, and historical complex of which a child is a part. To understand cognitive development, he maintained, one must look to the social processes from which a child's thinking is derived.

sociocultural theory
Vygotsky's theory, which analyzes how specific cultural practices, particularly social interaction with adults, affect children's development.

Vygotsky's (1978) **sociocultural theory,** like Piaget's theory of cognitive development, stresses children's active engagement with their environment. But whereas Piaget described the solo mind taking in and interpreting information about the world, Vygotsky saw cognitive growth as a *collaborative* process. Children, according to Vygotsky, learn through social interaction. They acquire cognitive skills as part of their induction into a way of life. Shared activities help children to internalize their society's ways of thinking and behaving and to make those ways their own.

zone of proximal development (ZPD)
Vygotsky's term for the difference between what a child can do alone and what the child can do with help.

According to Vygotsky, adults (or more advanced peers) must help direct and organize a child's learning before the child can master and internalize it. This guidance is most effective in helping children cross the **zone of proximal development (ZPD),** the gap between what they are already able to do and what they are not quite ready to accomplish by themselves. (*Proximal* means "nearby.") Children in the ZPD for a particular task can almost, but not quite, perform the task on their own. With the right kind of guidance, however, they can do it successfully. In the course of the collaboration, responsibility for directing and monitoring learning gradually shifts to the child.

A similar principle applies when teaching a child to float. The mentor first supports the child in the water, letting go gradually as the child's body relaxes into a horizontal position. When the child seems ready, the mentor withdraws all but one finger and finally lets the child float freely. Some researchers (Wood, 1980; Wood, Bruner, & Ross, 1976) have applied the metaphor of scaffolds—the temporary platforms on which construction workers stand—to this way of teaching. **Scaffolding** is the temporary support that parents, teachers, or others give a child to do a task until the child can do it alone.

scaffolding
Temporary support given to a child who is mastering a task.

Vygotsky's theory has important implications for education and cognitive testing. Tests based on the ZPD, which focus on a child's potential, provide a valuable alternative to standard intelligence tests that assess what the child has already learned; and many children may benefit from the sort of expert guidance Vygotsky prescribes.

Overall, a major contribution of the contextual perspective has been its emphasis on the social component in development. The contextual perspective also reminds us that the development of children in one culture or one group within a culture (such as white, middle-class Americans) may not be an appropriate norm for children in other societies or cultural groups.

No one theory of human development is universally accepted, and no one theoretical perspective explains all facets of development. Indeed, the trend today is away from "grand" theories (such as those of Freud and Piaget) and toward smaller, more limited "minitheories" aimed at explaining specific phenomena, such as how poverty influences family relations. At the same time, there is increasing recognition of the interplay among the physical, cognitive, and psychosocial domains—for example, in the relationship between motor development and perception, or between social interaction and the acquisition of cognitive skills. There also is growing awareness of the importance of historical change and of the need to explore cultural diversity in a rigorous, disciplined way.

CHECKPOINT

Can you . . .

- ✔ Identify the chief assumptions of the contextual perspective?
- ✔ Name Bronfenbrenner's five systems of contextual influence and give examples of each?
- ✔ Explain how Vygotsky's central focus differs from Bronfenbrenner's and Piaget's?
- ✔ Tell how Vygotsky's theory applies to educational teaching and testing?

Consider this . . .

- From what you have read so far, which, if any, of the theoretical perspectives presented in this chapter seems to you most useful?

Research Methods

Guidepost

4. How do developmental scientists study people, and what are some advantages and disadvantages of each research method?

Theories of human development often grow out of, and are tested by, research. Researchers coming from various theoretical perspectives use a variety of methods to study people in a variety of settings, but the **scientific method** refers to an overall process that characterizes scientific inquiry in any field. Following the scientific method enables researchers to come to sound conclusions about human development. The steps in the method are:

- *Identifying a problem* to be studied, often on the basis of a theory or of previous research.
- *Formulating hypotheses* to be tested by research.
- *Collecting data.*
- *Analyzing the data* to determine whether they support the hypothesis.
- *Disseminating findings* so that other observers can check, learn from, analyze, repeat, and build on the results.

scientific method
System of scientific inquiry, including identification of a problem, formulation and testing of alternative hypotheses, collection and analysis of data, and public dissemination of findings.

Because hypotheses are derived from theories, research questions and methods reflect the theoretical orientation of the researcher. For example, in trying to understand how a child develops a sense of right and wrong, a behaviorist would examine the way parents have responded to the child's behavior in the past, that is, what kinds of behavior they have punished or praised; a social-learning theorist would focus on imitation of moral examples, possibly in stories children read or in movies; and an information-processing researcher might do a task analysis to identify the steps a child goes through in determining the range of moral options available and then in deciding which option to pursue.

Two key issues at the outset of any investigation are how the participants will be chosen—the sampling method—and how the data will be collected. These decisions often depend on what questions the research is intended to answer. All these issues play a part in a research design, or plan.

Sampling

sample
Group of participants chosen to represent the entire population under study.

random selection
Sampling method that ensures representativeness because each member of the population has an equal and independent chance to be selected.

How can we be sure that the results of research are true generally, and not just for the participants? First, we need to determine who gets into the study. Because studying an entire *population* (a group to which we want to apply the findings) is usually too costly and time-consuming, investigators select a **sample,** a smaller group within the population. The sample should adequately represent the population under study—that is, it should show relevant characteristics in the same proportions as in the entire population. Otherwise the results cannot properly be *generalized,* or applied to the population as a whole.

Often researchers seek to achieve representativeness through **random selection,** in which each person in a population has an equal and independent chance of being chosen. If we wanted to study the effects of a pilot educational program, one way to select a random sample would be to put all the names of participating children into a large bowl, stir it, and then draw out a certain number of names. A random sample, especially a large one, is likely to represent the population well.

Unfortunately, a random sample of a large population is often difficult to obtain. Instead, many studies use samples selected for convenience or accessibility (for example, children born in a particular hospital or attending a particular day care center). The findings of such studies may not apply to the population as a whole.

Forms of Data Collection

Common ways of gathering data (see Table 2-3) include self-reports (verbal reports by study participants), tests and other behavioral measures, and observation. Depending in part on time and financial constraints, researchers may use one or more of these data collection techniques in any research design. Currently there is a trend toward increased use of self-reports and observation in combination with more objective measures.

Self-Reports: Diaries, Interviews, Questionnaires

The simplest form of self-report is a *diary* or log. Adolescents may be asked, for example, to record what they eat each day, or the times when they feel depressed. In studying young children, *parental self-reports*—diaries, journals, interviews, or questionnaires—are commonly used, often together with other methods, such as videotaping or recording. Parents may be videotaped playing with their babies and then may be shown the tapes and asked to explain why they reacted as they did.

In a face-to-face or telephone *interview,* researchers ask questions about attitudes, opinions, or behavior. Interviews may cover such topics as parent-child relationships, sexual activities, and occupational goals. In a *structured* interview, each participant is asked the same set of questions. An *open-ended* interview is more flexible; as in Piaget's clinical method, the interviewer can vary the topics and order of questions and can ask follow-up questions based on the responses. To reach more people and protect their privacy, researchers sometimes distribute a printed *questionnaire,* which participants fill out and return.

Table 2-3 Characteristics of Major Methods of Data Collection

Type	Main Characteristics	Advantages	Disadvantages
Self-report: diary, interview, or questionnaire	Participants are asked about some aspect of their lives; questioning may be highly structured or more flexible.	Can provide firsthand information about a person's life, attitudes, or opinions.	Participant may not remember information accurately or may distort responses in a socially desirable way; how question is asked or by whom may affect answer.
Behavioral measures	Participants are tested on abilities, skills, knowledge, competencies, or physical responses.	Provides objectively measurable information; avoids subjective distortions.	Cannot measure attitudes or other nonbehavioral phenomena; results may be affected by extraneous factors.
Naturalistic observation	People are observed in their normal setting, with no attempt to manipulate behavior.	Provides good description of behavior; does not subject people to unnatural settings that may distort behavior.	Lack of control; observer bias.
Laboratory observation	Participants are observed in the laboratory, with no attempt to manipulate behavior.	Provides good descriptions; greater control than naturalistic observation, since all participants are observed under same conditions.	Observer bias; controlled situation can be artificial.

By questioning a large number of people, investigators get a broad picture—at least of what the respondents *say* they believe or do or did. However, heavy reliance on self-reports may be unwise, since much of what people feel and think is on an unconscious level (Westen, 1998). Some people forget when and how events actually took place, and others consciously or unconsciously distort their replies to fit what is considered socially desirable. How a question is asked, and by whom, can affect the answer. When questioned about risky or socially disapproved behavior, such as sexual habits and drug use, respondents may be more candid in responding to a computerized survey than to a paper-and-pencil one (Turner et al., 1998). In any event, people willing to participate in interviews or fill out questionnaires tend to be an unrepresentative sample.

Behavioral and Performance Measures

For many kinds of research, investigators use more objective measures instead of, or in addition to, self-reports. A behavioral or performance measure *shows* something about a person rather than asking the person or someone else, such as a parent, to *tell* about it. Tests and other behavioral and neuropsychological measures, including mechanical and electronic devices, may be used to assess abilities, skills, knowledge, competencies, or physiological responses, such as heart rate and brain activity. Although these measures are less subjective than self-reports, results can be affected by such factors as fatigue and self-confidence.

Some tests, such as intelligence tests, measure abilities by comparing performance with that of other test-takers. Tests can be meaningful and useful only if they are both *valid* (that is, the tests measure the abilities they claim to measure) and *reliable* (that is, the results are reasonably consistent from one time to another). To avoid bias, intelligence tests must be *standardized,* that is, given and scored by the same methods and criteria for all test takers. (Intelligence testing is further discussed in Chapters 7 and 9.)

naturalistic observation Research method in which behavior is studied in natural settings without the observer's intervention or manipulation.

laboratory observation Research method in which the behavior of all participants is noted and recorded in the same situation, under controlled conditions.

Naturalistic and Laboratory Observation

Observation can take two forms: *naturalistic observation* and *laboratory observation.* In **naturalistic observation,** researchers look at people in real-life settings. The researchers do not try to alter behavior or the environment; they simply record what they see. In **laboratory observation,** researchers observe and record behavior in a controlled situation, such as a laboratory. By observing all participants under the same conditions, investigators can more clearly identify any differences in behavior not attributable to the environment.

Both kinds of observation can provide valuable descriptions of behavior, but they have limitations. For one, they do not explain *why* people behave as they do, though they may suggest interpretations. Then, too, an observer's presence can alter behavior. Even when observers stay behind one-way mirrors, where they can see but cannot be seen, children or adults may know that they are being watched and may act differently. Finally, there is a risk of *observer bias:* the researcher's tendency to interpret data to fit expectations, or to emphasize some aspects and minimize others. During the 1960s, laboratory observation was most commonly used so as to achieve more rigorous control. Currently, there is growing use of naturalistic observation supplemented by such technological devices as portable videotape recorders and computers, which increase objectivity and enable researchers to analyze moment-by-moment changes in facial expressions or other behavior.

CHECKPOINT

Can you . . .

- ✔ Summarize the five steps in the scientific method and tell why each is important?
- ✔ Explain the purpose of random selection and tell how it can be achieved?
- ✔ Compare the advantages and disadvantages of various forms of data collection?

Basic Research Designs

A research design is a plan for conducting a scientific investigation: what questions are to be answered, how participants are to be selected, how data are to be collected and interpreted, and how valid conclusions can be drawn. Four of the basic designs used in developmental research are case studies, ethnographic studies, correlational studies, and experiments. Each design has advantages and drawbacks, and each is appropriate for certain kinds of research problems (see Table 2-4).

Case Studies

case study Scientific study covering a single case or life.

A **case study** is a study of a single case or individual, such as Victor, the wild boy of Aveyron (refer back to Chapter 1). A number of theories, especially psychoanalytic ones, have grown out of clinical case studies, which include careful obser-

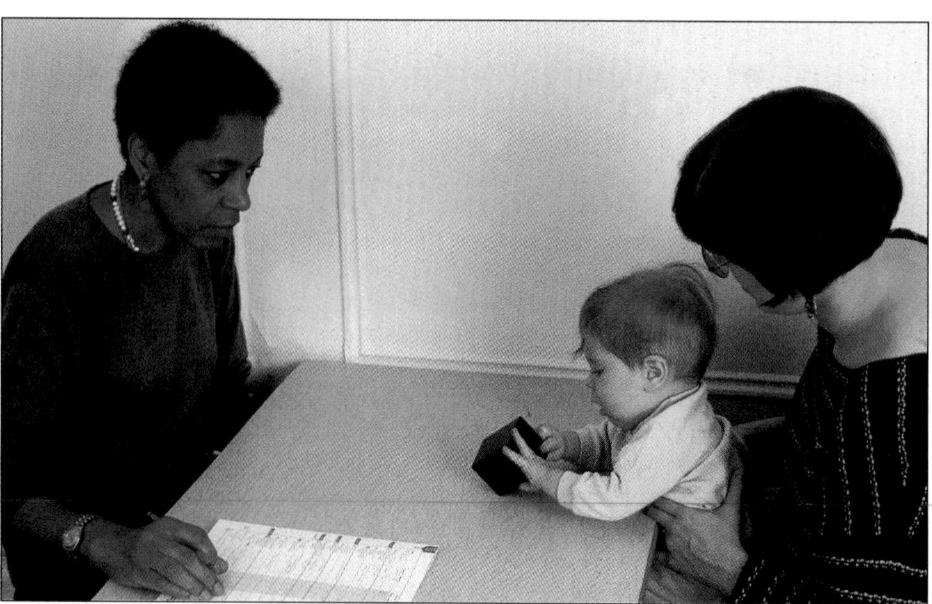

A child under laboratory observation may or may not behave the same way as in a naturalistic setting, such as at home or at school, but both kinds of observation can provide valuable information.

Table 2-4 Basic Research Designs

Type	Main Characteristics	Advantages	Disadvantages
Case study	Study of single individual in depth.	Flexibility; provides detailed picture of one person's behavior and development; can generate hypotheses.	May not generalize to others; conclusions not directly testable; cannot establish cause and effect.
Ethnographic study	In-depth study of a culture or subculture.	Can help overcome culturally based biases in theory and research; can test universality of developmental phenomena.	Subject to observer bias.
Correlational study	Attempt to find positive or negative relationship between variables.	Allows prediction of one variable on basis of another; can suggest hypotheses about causal relationships.	Cannot establish cause and effect.
Experiment	Controlled procedure in which an experimenter manipulates the independent variable to determine its effect on the dependent variable; may be conducted in the laboratory or field.	Establishes cause-and-effect relationships; highly controlled procedure that can be repeated by another investigator. Degree of control is greatest in the laboratory experiment.	Findings, especially when derived from laboratory experiments, may not generalize to situations outside the laboratory.

vation and interpretation of what patients say and do. Case studies also may use behavioral or neuropsychological measures and biographical, autobiographical, or documentary materials.

Case studies offer useful, in-depth information. They can explore sources of behavior and can test treatments. They also can suggest a need for other research. Another important advantage is flexibility: the researcher is free to explore avenues of inquiry that arise during the course of the study. However, case studies have shortcomings. From studying Victor, for instance, we learn much about the development of a single child, especially a child with a rare or unusual condition, but not how the information applies to children in general. Furthermore, case studies cannot explain behavior with certainty, because there is no way to test their conclusions. Even though it seems reasonable that Victor's severely deprived environment caused or contributed to his language deficiency, it is impossible to know whether he would have developed normally with a normal upbringing.

Ethnographic Studies

An **ethnographic study** can be thought of as a case study of a culture or subculture. It is an in-depth study that seeks to describe the pattern of relationships, customs, beliefs, technology, arts, and traditions that make up a society's way of life.

Ethnographic research can be qualitative, quantitative, or both. It uses a combination of methods, including **participant observation.** Participant observation is a form of naturalistic observation in which researchers live or participate in the societies or groups they observe, often for long periods of time; thus their findings are especially open to observer bias. On the other hand, ethnographic research can help overcome cultural biases in theory and research (see Box 2-2). Ethnography demonstrates the error of assuming that principles developed from research in western cultures are universally applicable.

An early example was the work of Margaret Mead (1928, 1930, 1935). In Samoa, she observed none of the emotional tumult, or "storm and stress," then believed by western psychologists to be typical of adolescence. Rather, she saw a serene, gradual transition from childhood to adulthood and an easy acceptance of adult roles. Mead suggested that adolescence is relatively stress-free in a society that lets children see adult sexual activity, engage in their own sex play, watch

ethnographic study
In-depth study of a culture, which uses a combination of methods including participant observation.

participant observation
Research method in which the observer lives with the people or participates in the activity under observation.

Window on the World

Box 2-2
Purposes of Cross-Cultural Research

By looking at people from different cultural groups, researchers can learn in what ways development is universal (and thus intrinsic to the human condition) and in what ways it is culturally determined. For example, children everywhere learn to speak in the same sequence, advancing from cooing and babbling to single words and then to simple combinations of words. The words vary from culture to culture, but around the world toddlers put them together to form sentences similar in structure. Such findings suggest that the capacity for learning language is universal and inborn.

On the other hand, culture can exert a surprisingly large influence on early motor development. African babies, whose parents often prop them in a sitting position and bounce them on their feet, tend to sit and walk earlier than U.S. babies (Rogoff & Morelli, 1989).

One hundred years ago, most developmentalists assumed that the fundamental processes of development were universal. Cross-cultural research, when done, was seen as a way to highlight the workings of these universal processes under contrasting environmental conditions. Today it is becoming clear that the cultural context can make a critical difference in the timing and expression of many aspects of development (Parke et al., 1994).

The society people grow up in influences the skills they learn. In the United States, children learn to read, write, and, increasingly, to operate computers. In rural Nepal, they learn how to drive water buffalo and find their way along mountain paths.

One important reason to conduct research among different cultural groups is to recognize biases in traditional western theories and research that often go unquestioned until they are shown to be a product of cultural influences. "Working with people from a quite different background can make one aware of aspects of human activity that are not noticeable until they are missing or differently arranged, as with the fish who reputedly is unaware of water until removed from it" (Rogoff & Morelli, 1989, p. 343).

Since so much research in human development has focused on western industrialized societies, many people have defined typical development in these societies as the norm, or standard of behavior. Measuring against this "norm" leads to narrow—and often, wrong—ideas about development. Pushed to its extreme, this belief can cause the development of people in other ethnic and cultural groups to be seen as deviant (Rogoff & Morelli, 1989).

In this book we discuss several influential theories developed from research in western societies that do not hold up when tested on people from other cultures—theories about gender roles, abstract thinking, moral reasoning, and a number of other aspects of human development. Throughout this book, we consistently look at children in cultures and subcultures other than the dominant one in the United States to show how closely development is tied to society and culture and to add to our understanding of normal development in many settings.

babies being born, regard death as natural, do important work, be assertive, and know precisely what they will be expected to do as adults. Her findings have been debated (D. Freeman, 1983; L. D. Holmes, 1987), in part on the ground that her Samoan sample was not representative of the island's population. Still, "Mead's basic message to the child development field remains as valid today as in 1930: To understand how children grow up under varied environmental conditions, one must be willing to go to where those conditions already exist, to examine them with respect and in detail, and to change one's assumptions in the face of new observations" (LeVine et al., 1994, p. 9).

Correlational Studies

correlational study Research design intended to discover whether a statistical relationship between variables exists, either in direction or in magnitude.

A **correlational study** is an attempt to find a *correlation,* or statistical relationship, between *variables,* phenomena that change or vary among people or can be varied for purposes of research. Correlations are expressed in terms of direction (positive or negative) and magnitude (degree). Two variables that are related *positively* increase or decrease together. A positive, or direct, correlation between televised violence and aggressiveness would exist if children who watched more violent television hit, bit, or kicked more than children who watched less violent television. Two variables have a *negative,* or inverse, correlation if, as one increases, the other decreases. Studies show a negative correlation between amount of schooling and the risk of developing dementia due to Alzheimer's disease in old age. In other words, the less schooling, the more dementia (Katzman, 1993).

Correlations are reported as numbers ranging from –1.0 (a perfect negative relationship) to +1.0 (a perfect positive relationship). Perfect correlations are rare. The closer a correlation comes to +1.0 or –1.0, the stronger the relationship, either positive or negative. A correlation of zero means that the variables have no relationship.

Correlations allow us to predict one variable on the basis of another. If, for example, we found a positive correlation between watching televised violence and fighting, we would predict that children who watch violent shows are more likely to get into fights. The greater the magnitude of the correlation between two variables, the greater the ability to predict one from the other.

Although correlations may indicate possible causes, the causal relations they suggest need to be examined critically. We cannot be sure from a positive correlation between televised violence and aggressiveness that watching televised violence *causes* aggressive play; we can conclude only that the two variables are related. It is possible that the causation goes the other way: aggressive play may lead children to watch more violent programs. Or a third variable—perhaps an inborn predisposition toward aggressiveness—may cause a child both to watch violent programs and to act aggressively. Similarly, we cannot be sure that schooling protects against dementia; it may be that another variable, such as socioeconomic status, might explain both lower levels of schooling and higher levels of dementia. To be certain that one variable causes another, we would need to design a controlled experiment—something that, in studying human beings, is not always possible for practical or ethical reasons.

Experiments

An **experiment** is a controlled procedure in which the experimenter manipulates variables to learn how one affects another. Scientific experiments must be conducted and reported in such a way that another experimenter can *replicate* them, that is, repeat them in exactly the same way with different participants to verify the results and conclusions.

experiment
Rigorously controlled, replicable (repeatable) procedure in which the researcher manipulates variables to assess the effect of one on the other.

Groups and Variables To do an experiment, the experimenter may divide the participants into two kinds of groups. An **experimental group** is composed of people who are to be exposed to the experimental manipulation or *treatment*—the phenomenon the researcher wants to study. Afterward, the effect of the treatment will be measured one or more times. A **control group** is composed of people who are similar to the experimental group but do not receive the treatment, or receive a different treatment. An experiment may include one or more of each type of group. Or, if the experimenter wants to compare the effects of different treatments (say, of the lecture method versus the discussion method of teaching), the overall sample may be divided into *treatment groups,* each of which receives one of the treatments under study.

experimental group
In an experiment, the group receiving the treatment under study; any changes in these people are compared with changes in the control group.

control group
In an experiment, a group of people who are similar to the people in the experimental group but who do not receive the treatment whose effects are to be measured; the results obtained with this group are compared with the results obtained with the experimental group.

Let's look at how one team of researchers (Whitehurst, Falco, et al., 1988) performed an experiment to find out what effect a special method of reading picture books to very young children might have on their language and vocabulary skills. The researchers compared two groups of middle-class children ages 21 to 35 months. In the *experimental group,* the parents adopted the new read-aloud method (the treatment), which involved encouraging children's active participation and giving frequent, age-based feedback. In the *control group,* parents simply read aloud as they usually did. The parents of the children in the experimental group asked the children challenging open-ended questions rather than questions calling for simple yes-no answers. (Instead of asking, "Is the cat asleep?", they would ask, "What is the cat doing?") They expanded on the children's answers, corrected wrong answers, gave alternative possibilities, and bestowed praise. After 1 month of the program, the children in the experimental group were 8.5 months ahead of the control group in level of speech and 6 months ahead in vocabulary; 9 months later, the experimental group was still 6 months ahead of the controls. It is fair to conclude, then, that this read-aloud method improved the children's language and vocabulary skills.

In the experiment just described, the type of reading approach was the *independent variable,* and the children's language skills were the *dependent variable.* An **independent variable** is something over which the experimenter has direct control. A **dependent variable** is something that may or may not change as a result of changes in the independent variable; in other words, it *depends* on the independent variable. In an experiment, a researcher manipulates the independent variable to see how changes in it will affect the dependent variable.

independent variable
In an experiment, the condition over which the experimenter has direct control.

dependent variable
In an experiment, the condition that may or may not change as a result of changes in the independent variable.

random assignment
Technique used in assigning members of a study sample to experimental and control groups, in which each member of the sample has an equal chance to be assigned to each group and to receive or not receive the treatment.

If an experiment finds a significant difference in the performance of the experimental and control groups, how do we know that the cause was the independent variable? For example, in the read-aloud experiment, how can we be sure that the reading method and not some other factor (such as intelligence) caused the difference in language development of the two groups? The experimenter must control for effects of such extraneous factors through **random assignment:** assigning the participants to groups in such a way that each person has an equal chance of being placed in any group.

If assignment is random and the sample is large enough, differences in such factors as age, sex, race, IQ, and socioeconomic status will be evenly distributed so that the groups initially are as alike as possible in every respect except for the variable to be tested. Otherwise, unintended differences between the groups might confound, or contaminate, the results, and any conclusions drawn from the experiment would have to be viewed with great suspicion. Also, during the course of the experiment, the experimenter must make sure that everything except the independent variable is held constant. For example, in the read-aloud study, parents of the experimental and control groups must spend the same amount of time reading to their children. In that way, the experimenter can be sure that any differences between the reading skills of the two groups are due to the reading method, and not some other factor.

Laboratory, Field, and Natural Experiments The control necessary for establishing cause and effect is most easily achieved in *laboratory experiments.* In a laboratory experiment the participants are brought to a special place where they experience conditions manipulated by the experimenter. The experimenter records the participants' reactions to these conditions, perhaps comparing them with their own or other participants' behavior under different conditions.

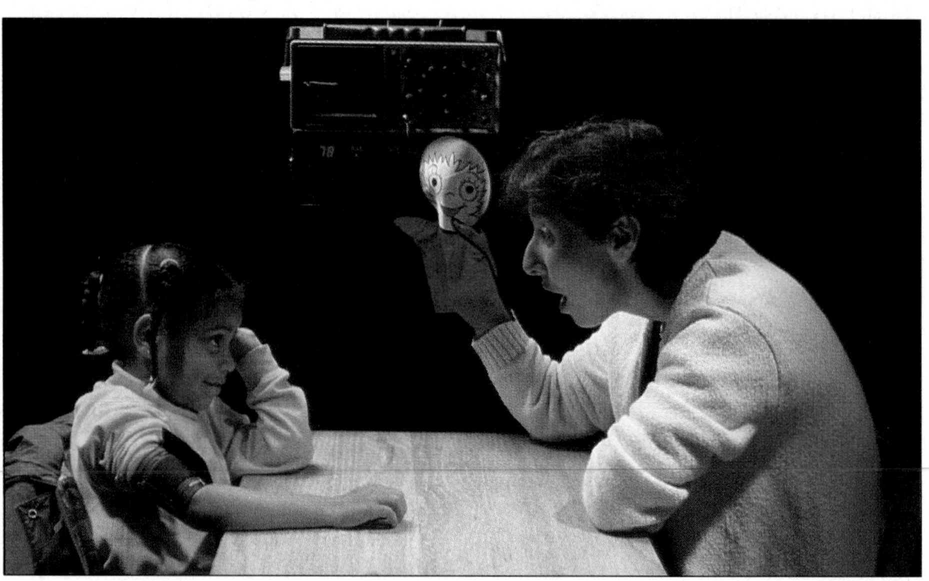

Experiments use strictly controlled procedures that manipulate variables to determine how one affects another. To study emotional resiliency, this research project at the University of California at San Francisco monitors the heart rate and blood pressure of young children as they explain their feelings in response to a hand puppet's happy or angry face.

However, not all experiments can be readily done in the laboratory. A *field experiment* is a controlled study conducted in a setting that is part of everyday life, such as a child's home or school. The experiment in which parents tried out a new way of reading aloud was a field experiment.

Laboratory and field experiments differ in two important respects. One is the *degree of control* exerted by the experimenter; the other is the degree to which findings can be *generalized* beyond the study situation. Laboratory experiments can be more rigidly controlled and thus easier to replicate. However, the results may be less generalizable to real life; because of the artificiality of the situation, participants may not act as they normally would.

When, for practical or ethical reasons, it is impossible to conduct a true experiment, a *natural experiment* may provide a way of studying certain events. A natural experiment compares people who have been accidentally "assigned" to separate groups by circumstances of life—one group of children who were exposed, say, to famine or AIDS or a birth defect or superior education, and another group who were not. A natural experiment, despite its name, is actually a correlational study, since controlled manipulation of variables and random assignment to treatment groups are not possible.

CHECKPOINT

Can you . . .

- ✔ Compare the uses and drawbacks of case studies, ethnographic studies, correlational studies, and experiments?
- ✔ Explain why and how a controlled experiment can establish casual relationships?
- ✔ Distinguish among laboratory, field, and natural experiments?

There is no one "right" way to study human beings. Many questions can be approached from several angles, each yielding different kinds of information. Experiments have important advantages over other research designs: the ability to establish cause-and-effect relationships and to permit replication. However, experiments can be too artificial and too narrowly focused. In recent decades, therefore, many researchers have concentrated less on laboratory experimentation or have supplemented it with a wider array of methods. In addition, some questions do not lend themselves to experimentation because some variables, such as age, gender, and race, cannot be manipulated. When studying such variables—for example, the relationship between memory loss and aging—researchers must rely on correlative studies, even though they cannot conclusively determine causation.

Consider this . . .

- What do you think Margaret Mead meant when she wrote that research in foreign cultures "could shed a kind of light upon us, upon our potentialities and our limitations"? How can ethnographic studies do that? What are some potential difficulties with this kind of research?
- Because of ethical limitations on experimentation with humans, researchers often must rely on correlational studies to suggest links, for example, between televised violence and aggression. How would you evaluate the usefulness of information gained from such studies?
- What kinds of research seem most suitable to a laboratory setting and what kinds to a field setting? Give examples.

Developmental Research Designs

The two most common research strategies used to study human development are *longitudinal* and *cross-sectional* studies (see Figure 2-3). Longitudinal studies reveal how people change or stay the same as they grow older; cross-sectional studies show similarities and differences among age groups. Because each of these designs has drawbacks, researchers have also devised *sequential* designs. To directly observe change, *microgenetic studies* can be used.

Longitudinal, Cross-Sectional, and Sequential Studies

In a **longitudinal study,** researchers study the same person or persons more than once, sometimes years apart. They may measure a single characteristic, such as vocabulary size, height, or aggressiveness, or they may look at several aspects of development to find relationships among them. The Oakland (Adolescent) Growth Study (see Chapter 1), which began in 1932, was initially designed to assess social and emotional development from the preteens through the senior high school years; ultimately, many of the participants were followed into old age. Eventually the research began to focus on *planful competence,* a combination of self-confidence, intellectual commitment, and dependable effectiveness, which helps people mobilize resources and cope with difficulties. Participants who as teenagers showed planful competence made good choices in adolescence and early adulthood, which often led to promising opportunities (scholarships, good jobs, and competent spouses). Less competent teenagers made poorer early decisions and tended to lead crisis-ridden lives (Clausen, 1993).

longitudinal study
Study design in which data are collected about the same people over a period of time, to assess developmental changes that occur with age.

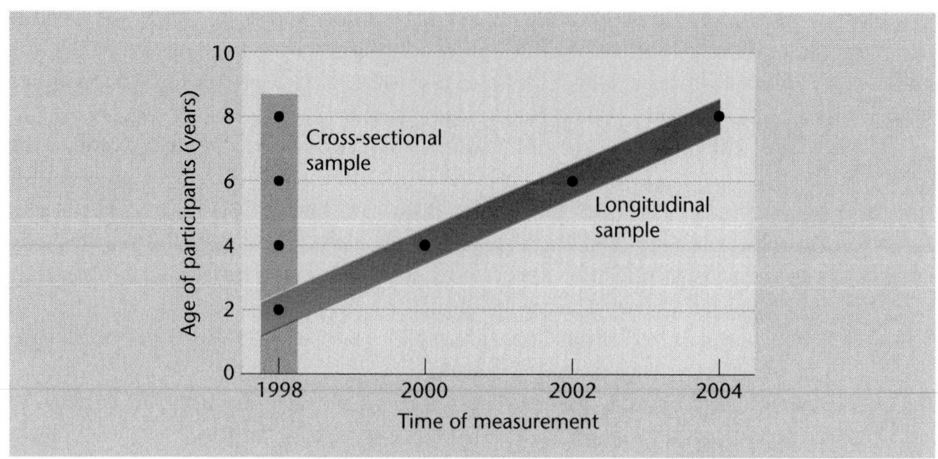

Figure 2-3

The two most common ways to obtain data about age-related development. In a *cross-sectional* study, people of different ages are measured at one time. Here, groups of 2-, 4-, 6-, and 8-year-olds were tested in 1998 to obtain data about age differences in performance. In a *longitudinal* study, the same people are measured more than once. Here, a sample of children were first measured in 1998, when they were 2 years old; follow-up testing is done in 2000, 2002, and 2004, when the children are 4, 6, and 8, respectively. This technique shows age changes in performance. (*Note:* Dots indicate times of measurement.)

cross-sectional study
Study design in which people of different ages are assessed on one occasion, providing comparative information about different age cohorts.

In a **cross-sectional study,** people of different ages are assessed at one time. In one cross-sectional study, researchers asked 3-, 4-, 6-, and 7-year-olds about what a pensive-looking woman was doing, or about the state of someone's mind. There was a striking increase with age in children's awareness of mental activity (J. H. Flavell, Green, & Flavell, 1995). These findings strongly suggest that as children become older, their understanding of mental processes improves. However, we cannot draw such a conclusion with certainty. We don't know whether the 7-year-olds' awareness of mental activity when they were 3 years old was the same as that of the current 3-year-olds in the study. The only way to see whether change occurs with age is to conduct a longitudinal study of a particular person or group.

Both cross-sectional and longitudinal designs have strengths and weaknesses (see Table 2-5). Longitudinal research, by repeatedly studying the same people, can track individual patterns of continuity and change. It avoids confounding developmental effects with effects of cohort membership (the differing experiences of children born, for example, before and after the advent of the Internet). However, a longitudinal study done on a particular cohort may not apply to a different cohort. (In other words, the results of a study of people born in the 1920s, such as the Oakland Growth Study, may not apply to people born in the 1990s.) Furthermore, longitudinal studies generally are more time-consuming and expensive than cross-sectional studies; it is hard to keep track of a large group of participants over the years, to keep records, and to keep the study going despite turnover in research personnel. Then there is the problem of attrition: participants may die or drop out. Another likely difficulty is bias in the sample: people who volunteer for such studies, and especially those who stay with them, tend to be above average in intelligence and socioeconomic status. Also, results can be affected by repeated testing: people may do better in later tests because of familiarity with test materials and procedures.

Advantages of cross-sectional research include speed and economy; data can be gathered fairly quickly from large numbers of people. And, since participants are assessed only once, there is no problem of attrition or repeated testing. A drawback of cross-sectional studies is that they may overlook individual differences by focusing on group averages. Their major disadvantage, however, is that the results may be affected by cohort differences. Cross-sectional studies are sometimes interpreted as yielding information about developmental changes in groups or individuals, but such information is often misleading. Thus, although cross-sectional studies still dominate the field—no doubt because they are so much easier to do—the proportion of research devoted to longitudinal studies, especially short-term ones, is increasing (Parke et al., 1994).

Table 2-5 Longitudinal and Cross-Sectional Research: Pros and Cons

Type of study	Procedure	Advantages	Disadvantages
Longitudinal	Data are collected on same person or persons over a period of time.	Can show age-related change or continuity; avoids confounding cohort effects.	Time-consuming, expensive; problems of attrition, bias in sample, and effects of repeated testing; results may be valid only for cohort tested.
Cross-sectional	Data are collected on people of different ages at the same time.	Can show similarities and differences among age groups; speedy, economical; no problem of attrition or repeated testing.	Cannot establish age effects; masks individual differences; can be confounded by cohort effects.

The **cross-sequential study** is one of several strategies designed to overcome the drawbacks of longitudinal and cross-sectional studies. This method combines the other two: researchers assess a cross-sectional sample more than once to determine how members of each age cohort have changed. This procedure permits researchers to separate age-related changes from cohort effects. The major drawbacks of sequential studies involve time, effort, and complexity. Sequential designs require large numbers of participants and the collection and analysis of huge amounts of data over a period of years. Interpreting their findings and conclusions can demand a high degree of sophistication.

cross-sequential study Study design that combines cross-sectional and longitudinal techniques by assessing people in a cross-sectional sample more than once.

Microgenetic Studies

Although developmentalists study change, they rarely can observe it directly in everyday life because it usually happens so slowly. But what if the process could be compressed into a very short time frame? A **microgenetic study** does just that, by repeatedly exposing participants to a stimulus for change, or opportunity for learning, over a short period of time, enabling researchers to see and analyze the processes by which change occurs.

microgenetic study Study design that allows researchers to directly observe change by exposing participants to stimuli repeatedly over a short period of time.

In one series of experiments using operant conditioning (Rovee-Collier & Boller, 1995; see Chapter 5), infants as young as 2 months old learned to kick to set in motion a brightly colored mobile to which one leg was attached—if the infants were exposed to a similar situation repeatedly within a few days or weeks. Building on this work, Esther Thelen (1994) tied 3-month-olds' left and right legs together with soft elastic fabric. Would they learn to kick with both legs at once to activate the mobile? The infants' movements were videotaped, and the frequency and speed of kicks, using one or both legs, were then analyzed with the help of a computer. The results showed that the infants gradually switched to kicking with both legs when it proved more effective, and observers were able to chart exactly how and when this change occurred.

CHECKPOINT

Can you . . .

- ✔ List advantages and disadvantages of longitudinal, cross-sectional, and cross-sequential research?
- ✔ Explain how microgenetic studies are done and what kinds of data they can reveal?

Ethics of Research

Should research that might harm its participants ever be undertaken? How can we balance the possible benefits against the risk of mental, emotional, or physical injury to individuals?

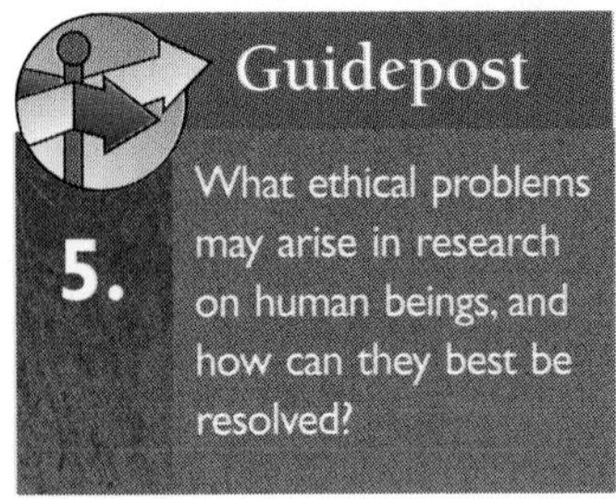

5. What ethical problems may arise in research on human beings, and how can they best be resolved?

In resolving such ethical dilemmas, researchers are supposed to be guided by three principles: (1) *beneficence:* the obligation to maximize potential benefits to participants and minimize possible harm; (2) *respect* for participants' autonomy and protection of those who are unable to exercise their own judgment; and (3) *justice:* inclusion of diverse groups while being sensitive to any special impact the research situation may have on them.

Objections to Watson and Rayner's study of "Little Albert," described earlier in this chapter, helped give rise to today's more stringent ethical standards. Federally mandated committees at colleges, universities, and other institutions review proposed research from an ethical standpoint. Guidelines of the American Psychological Association (1992) and the Society for Research in Child Development (1996) cover such issues as protection of participants from harm and loss of dignity; guarantees of privacy and confidentiality, informed consent, avoidance of deception, and the right to decline or withdraw from an experiment at any time; and the responsibility of investigators to correct any undesirable effects. Still, specific situations often call for hard judgments.

Right to Informed Consent

Informed consent exists when participants voluntarily agree to be in a study, are competent to give consent, are fully aware of the risks as well as the potential benefits, and are not being exploited. The National Commission for the Protection of Human Subjects of Biomedical and Behavioral Research (1978) recommends that children age 7 or over be asked to give their own consent to take part in research and that children's objections should be overruled only if the research promises direct benefit to the child, as in the use of a new experimental drug.

Consider this . . .

- What steps should be taken to protect children and other vulnerable persons from harm due to involvement in research?
- At what age do you think a child becomes capable of giving informed consent to participate in research? (You may want to return to this question after you have read the parts of this book dealing with young children's cognitive and emotional development.)
- If deception is to be used in a study, is it possible to obtain informed consent? If not, does that mean that studies using deception should not be done?
- Behavioral, ethological, neurological, and medical research is often done with animals. What contributions can animal research make to the study of people? What might be some ethical or other limitations of such research?

However, some ethicists argue that young children cannot give meaningful, voluntary *consent,* since they cannot fully understand what is involved; they can merely *assent,* that is, agree to participate. The usual procedure, therefore, when children under 18 are involved, is to ask the parents or legal guardians, and sometimes school personnel, to give consent. But can we be sure that they are acting in the child's best interests? Parents may think that participation in a study of a promising new treatment will benefit a child, even though the child may be assigned to a control group that does not receive the treatment (Fisher, 1993).

Some studies rely on participants who may be especially vulnerable. For example, studies that seek the causes and treatments for Alzheimer's disease need participants whose mental status may preclude their being fully or even partially aware of what is involved. What if a person gives consent and later forgets having done so? Current practice, to be on the safe side, is to ask both participants and caregivers for consent.

Can informed consent exist if participants are deceived about the nature or purpose of a study, or about the procedures they will be subjected to? Suppose that children are told they are trying out a new game when they are actually being tested on their reactions to success or failure? Suppose that adults are told they are participating in a study on learning when they are really being tested on their willingness to inflict pain? Experiments like these, which cannot be carried out without deception, have been done—and they have added significantly to our knowledge, but at the cost of the participants' right to know what they were getting involved in. Ethical guidelines call for withholding information *only* when it is essential to the study; and then, investigators should avoid methods that could cause pain, anxiety, or harm. The participants should be debriefed afterwards to let them know why the deception was necessary and to make sure they have not suffered as a result.

Right to Self-Esteem

Should people be subjected to research that may damage their self-esteem? Studies on limits of memory, for example, have a built-in "failure factor": the researcher keeps asking questions until the participant is unable to answer. Might this inevitable failure affect a participant's self-confidence? Similarly, when researchers publish findings that middle-class children are academically superior to poor children, unintentional harm may be done to the latter's self-esteem. Such studies also may affect teachers' expectations and students' performance.

Right to Privacy and Confidentiality

Is it ethical to use one-way mirrors and hidden cameras to observe people without their knowledge? How can we protect the confidentiality of personal information that participants may reveal in interviews or questionnaires?

What if, during the course of research, an investigator notices that a child seems to have a learning disability or some other treatable condition? Is the researcher obliged to share such information with parents or guardians, or to recommend services that may help the child, when sharing the information might contaminate the research findings? Such a decision should not be made lightly, since sharing information of uncertain validity may create damaging misconceptions about a child. Furthermore, researchers should not overstep the bounds of their own competence in making diagnoses and referrals. On the other hand, researchers need to know, and inform participants of, their legal responsibility to report child abuse or neglect or any other illegal activity of which they become aware.

CHECKPOINT

Can you . . .

- ✔ Name three principles that govern decisions about inclusion of participants in research?
- ✔ Name three rights of participants in research and discuss their implications?

Our final word in these introductory chapters is that this entire book is far from the final word. While we have tried to incorporate the most important and the most up-to-date information about how people develop, developmental scientists are constantly learning more. As you read this book, you are certain to come up with your own questions. By thinking about them, and perhaps eventually conducting research to find answers, it is possible that you yourself, now just embarking on the study of human development, will someday add to our knowledge about the interesting species to which we all belong.

Summary

Basic Theoretical Issues

Guidepost 1. What purposes do theories serve?

- A **theory** is used to explain data and to generate **hypotheses** that can be tested by research.

Guidepost 2. What are three basic theoretical issues on which developmental scientists differ?

- Developmental theories vary in their positions on three basic issues: the relative importance of heredity and environment, the active or passive character of development, and the existence of stages of development.
- Some theorists are influenced by a **mechanistic model** of development; others by an **organismic model.**

Theoretical Perspectives

Guidepost 3. What are six theoretical perspectives on human development, and what are some theories representative of each?

- The **psychoanalytic perspective** sees development as motivated by unconscious emotional conflicts. Leading examples are: (1) Freud's theory of **psychosexual development,** and (2) Erikson's theory of **psychosocial development.**
- The **learning perspective** views development as a result of **learning,** a response to external events. Leading examples are: (1) Watson's and Skinner's **behaviorism,** which asserts that behavior can be predictably altered by **classical conditioning** or **operant conditioning** (use of **reinforcement** and **punishment**) and (2) Bandura's **social-learning theory,** which stresses **observational learning.**
- The **humanistic perspective** views people as consciously choosing their own developmental goals. An example is Maslow's **hierarchy of needs,** culminating in **self-actualization.**
- The **cognitive perspective** describes people as active initiators of development in response to experience. Leading examples are: (1) Piaget's cognitive-stage theory, based on **organization** of **schemes, adaptation**

(a combination of **assimilation** and **accommodation**), and **equilibration;** (2) the **information-processing approach,** which analyzes the mental processes; and (3) the **cognitive neuroscience approach,** based on brain research.
- The **ethological perspective,** represented by Bowlby and Ainsworth, describes adaptive behaviors that promote group survival.
- The **contextual perspective** focuses on interaction between the individual and the social context. Leading examples are: (1) Bronfenbrenner's **bioecological theory,** based on five interlocking levels of environmental influence (the **microsystem, mesosystem, exosystem, macrosystem,** and **chronosystem**) and (2) Vygotsky's **sociocultural theory,** which focuses on how adults guide children's learning through the **zone of proximal development (ZPD),** a concept that gave rise to the technique of **scaffolding.**

Research Methods

Guidepost 4. How do developmental scientists study people, and what are some advantages and disadvantages of each research method?

- To arrive at sound conclusions, researchers use the **scientific method.**
- **Random selection** of a research **sample** can ensure generalizability.
- Forms of data collection include self-reports (diaries, interviews, and questionnaires); behavioral and performance measures; and observation. Observation may take the form of **naturalistic observation, laboratory observation,** or **participant observation.**
- Four basic designs used in developmental research are the **case study, ethnographic study, correlational study,** and **experiment.** Only experiments can firmly establish causal relationships. Cross-cultural research can indicate whether certain aspects of development are universal or culturally influenced.
- In an experiment, the experimenter manipulates the **independent variable** to see its effect on the **dependent variable.** Experiments must be rigorously controlled so as to be valid and replicable. **Random assignment** of participants to the **experimental group** and **control group** is necessary to make sure that the effect of the independent variable, and not some other factor, is being tested.
- Laboratory experiments are easiest to control and replicate, but findings of field experiments may be more generalizable beyond the study situation. Natural experiments may be useful in situations in which true experiments would be impractical or unethical.
- The two most common designs used to study age-related development are the **longitudinal study** and the **cross-sectional study.** Cross-sectional studies compare age groups; longitudinal studies describe continuity or change in the same participants. The **cross-sequential study** is intended to overcome the weaknesses of the other two designs. A **microgenetic study** allows direct observation of change over a short period of time.

Guidepost 5. What ethical problems may arise in research on human beings, and how can they best be resolved?

- Difficult ethical issues in research on human development involve the rights of participants to informed consent, self-esteem, privacy, and confidentiality.
- Researchers seek to resolve ethical issues on the basis of principles of beneficence, respect, and justice.

Key Terms

theory (27)
hypotheses (27)
mechanistic model (28)
organismic model (28)
psychoanalytic perspective (29)
psychosexual development (29)
psychosocial development (33)
learning perspective (34)
learning (34)
behaviorism (34)
classical conditioning (34)
operant conditioning (35)
reinforcement (35)
punishment (35)
social-learning theory (35)
observational learning (36)
humanistic perspective (36)
hierarchy of needs (36)
self-actualization (36)
cognitive perspective (37)
organization (38)
schemes (38)
adaptation (38)
assimilation (38)
accommodation (38)
equilibration (38)
information-processing approach (39)
cognitive neuroscience approach (40)
ethological perspective (40)
contextual perspective (41)
bioecological theory (41)
microsystem (43)
mesosystem (43)
exosystem (43)
macrosystem (44)
chronosystem (44)
sociocultural theory (44)
zone of proximal development (ZPD) (44)
scaffolding (45)
scientific method (45)
sample (46)
random selection (46)
naturalistic observation (48)
laboratory observation (48)
case study (48)
ethnographic study (49)
participant observation (49)
correlational study (50)
experiment (51)
experimental group (51)
control group (51)
independent variable (52)
dependent variable (52)
random assignment (52)
longitudinal study (53)
cross-sectional study (54)
cross-sequential study (55)
microgenetic study (55)

Part Two

Beginnings

From the moment of conception to the moment of death, human beings undergo complex processes of development. The changes that occur during the earliest periods of the life span are broader and faster-paced than any a person will ever experience again.

Because human beings are whole persons, all aspects of development are interconnected, even in the womb. As we look at prenatal development in Chapter 3, at physical development of infants and toddlers in Chapter 4, at their cognitive development in Chapter 5, and at their psychosocial development in Chapter 6, we will see, right from the beginning, how these aspects of development are linked:

Linkups to Look For

- The physical growth of the brain before and after birth makes possible a great burst of cognitive and emotional development. Fetuses whose ears and brains have developed enough to hear sounds from the outside world seem to retain a memory of these sounds after birth.
- An infant's earliest smiles arise from central nervous system activity and may reflect nothing more than a pleasant physiological state, such as drowsiness and a full stomach. As the infant becomes cognitively aware of the warm responses of caregivers, and as vision becomes sharp enough to recognize a familiar face, the infant's smiles become more emotionally expressive and more socially directed.
- Infants learn through their physical movements where their bodies end and everything else begins. As they drop toys, splash water, and hurl sand, their minds grasp how their bodies can change their world, and their sense of self begins to flourish.
- Without the vocal structures and motor coordination to form sounds, babies would not be able to speak. Physical gestures precede and often accompany early attempts to form words. The acquisition of language dramatically advances cognitive understanding and social communication.

Beginnings: *A Preview*

Chapter 3

Forming a New Life

Conception occurs.

The genetic endowment interacts with environmental influences from the start.

Basic body structures and organs form.

Brain growth spurt begins.

Physical growth is the most rapid in the life span.

Fetus hears and responds to sensory stimuli; abilities to learn and remember are present.

Vulnerability to environmental influences is great.

Chapter 4

Physical Development During the First Three Years

A method and setting for childbirth are chosen, and the progress of the birth is monitored.

The newborn emerges and is assessed for immediate health, developmental status, and any complications of childbirth.

All body systems operate at birth.

All senses operate at birth to varying degrees.

The brain grows in complexity and is highly sensitive to environmental influence.

Physical growth and development of motor skills are rapid.

Chapter 5

Cognitive Development During the First Three Years

Abilities to learn and remember are present, even in early weeks.

Use of symbols and ability to solve problems develop by the end of the second year.

Comprehension and use of language develop rapidly.

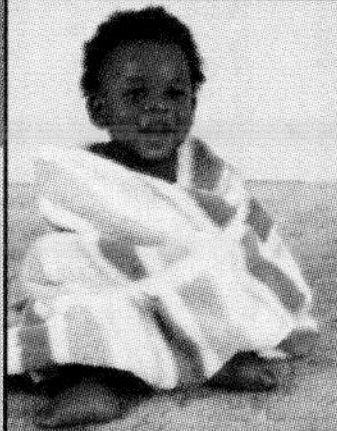

Chapter 6

Psychosocial Development During the First Three Years

Attachments to parents and others form.

Self-awareness develops.

Shift from dependence to autonomy occurs.

Interest in other children increases.

Chapter 3

Forming a New Life

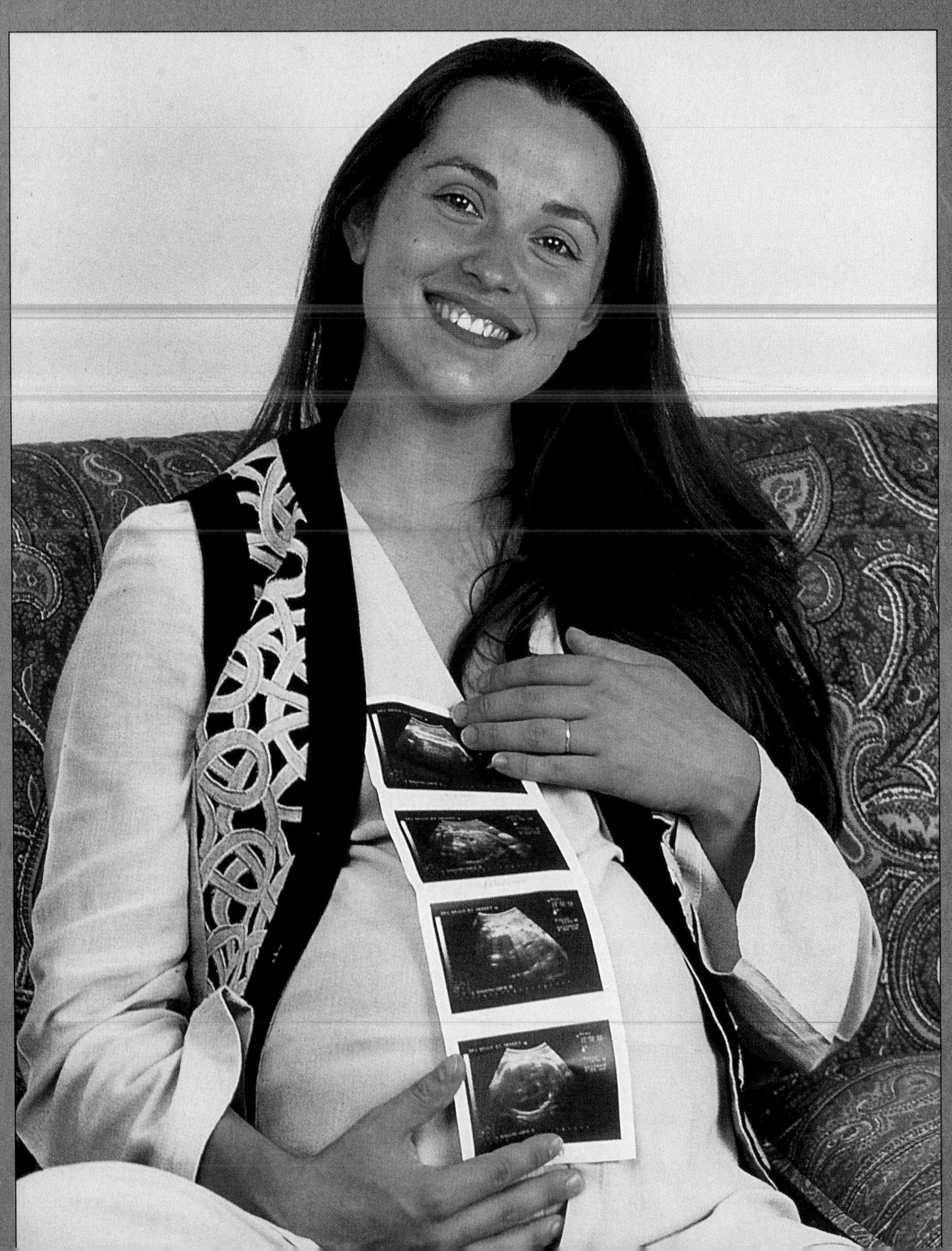

If I could have watched you grow as a magical mother might, if I could have seen through my magical transparent belly, there would have been such ripening within. . . .

Anne Sexton, 1966

OUTLINE

Abel Dorris

Focus: Abel Dorris and Fetal Alcohol Syndrome

Fetal alcohol syndrome (FAS), a cluster of abnormalities shown by children whose mothers drank during pregnancy, is a leading cause of mental retardation. But in 1971, when the writer Michael Dorris adopted a 3-year-old Sioux boy whose mother had been a heavy drinker, the facts about FAS were not yet widely publicized or scientifically investigated. Not until eleven years later, as Dorris relates in *The Broken Cord* (1989), did he discover the source of his adopted son's developmental problems.

The boy, named Abel ("Adam" in the book), had been born almost seven weeks premature, with low birthweight, and had been abused and malnourished before being removed to a foster home. His mother had died at 35 of alcohol poisoning. His father had been beaten to death in an alley after a string of arrests. The boy was small for his age, was not toilet-trained, and could speak only about twenty words. Although he had been diagnosed as mildly retarded, Dorris was certain that with a positive environment the boy would catch up.

Abel did not catch up. When he turned 4, he was still in diapers and weighed only 27 pounds. He had trouble remembering names of playmates. His activity level was unusually high, and the circumference of his skull was unusually small. He suffered severe, unexplained seizures.

As the months went by, Abel had trouble learning to count, identify primary colors, and tie his shoes. Before entering school, he was labeled "learning disabled." His IQ was, and remained, in the mid-60s. Thanks to the efforts of a devoted first-grade teacher, Abel did learn to read and write, but his comprehension was low. When the boy finished elementary school in 1983, he "still could not add, subtract, count money, or consistently identify the town, state, country, or planet of his residence" (Dorris, 1989, pp. 127–128).

By then, Michael Dorris had solved the puzzle of what was wrong with his son. As an associate professor of Native American studies at Dartmouth College, he was acquainted with the cultural pressures that make drinking prevalent among American Indians. In 1982, the year before Abel's graduation, Michael visited a treatment center for chemically dependent teenagers at a Sioux reservation in South Dakota. There he was astonished to see three boys who "could have been [Abel's] twin brothers" (Dorris, 1989, p. 137). They not only looked like Abel but acted like him.

Fetal alcohol syndrome had been identified during the 1970s, while Abel was growing up. Once alcohol enters a fetus's bloodstream, it remains there in high concentrations for long periods of time, causing brain damage and harming other body organs. There is no cure. As one medical expert wrote, "for the fetus the hangover may last a lifetime" (Enloe, 1980, p. 15).

For the family, too, the effects of FAS can be devastating. The years of constant attempts first to restore Abel to normality and then to come to terms with the damage irrevocably done in the womb may well have been a factor in the later problems in Dorris's marriage to the writer Louise Erdrich, which culminated in divorce proceedings and his suicide in 1997 at age 52. According to Erdrich, Dorris suffered from extreme depression, possibly exacerbated by the difficulties he faced as a father (L. Erdrich, personal communication, March 1, 2000).

As for Abel Dorris, at the age of 20 he had entered a vocational training program and had moved into a supervised home, taking along his collections of stuffed animals, paper dolls, newspaper cartoons, family photographs, and old birthday cards. At 23, five years before his father's death, he was hit by a car and killed (Lyman, 1997).

The story of Abel Dorris is a devastating reminder of the awesome responsibility prospective parents have for the development of the new life they have set in motion. First comes the hereditary endowment they provide. Then come environmental influences—starting with the mother's body. In addition to what the mother does and what happens to her, there are other environmental influences, from those that affect the father's sperm to the technological, social, and cultural environment, which may affect the kind of care a woman gets in the months before giving birth.

In this chapter, we describe how conception normally occurs, how the mechanisms of heredity operate, and how the biological inheritance interacts with environmental influences within and outside the womb. We trace the course of prenatal development (development before birth), describe influences upon it, and report on ways to monitor and intervene in it. (In Chapter 14, we'll discuss techniques of artificially assisted reproduction often used when one or both prospective parents are infertile.)

After you have read and studied this chapter, you should be able to answer the following questions:

Guideposts *for* Study

1. How does conception normally occur?

2. What causes multiple births?

3. How does heredity operate in determining sex and transmitting normal and abnormal traits?

4. How do scientists study the relative influences of heredity and environment, and how do heredity and environment work together?

5. What role do heredity and environment play in physical health, intelligence, and personality?

6. What are the three stages of prenatal development, and what happens during each stage?

7. What can fetuses do?

8. What environmental influences can affect prenatal development?

9. What techniques can assess a fetus's health and well-being, and what is the importance of prenatal care?

Conceiving New Life

Some day scientists may find it possible to **clone** (make a genetic copy of) a human being. Until then, every person's biological beginning will continue to be a split-second event when a single spermatozoon, one of millions of sperm cells from the biological father, joins an ovum, one of the several hundred thousand ova produced by the biological mother's body. As we will see, which sperm meets which ovum has tremendous implications for the new person.

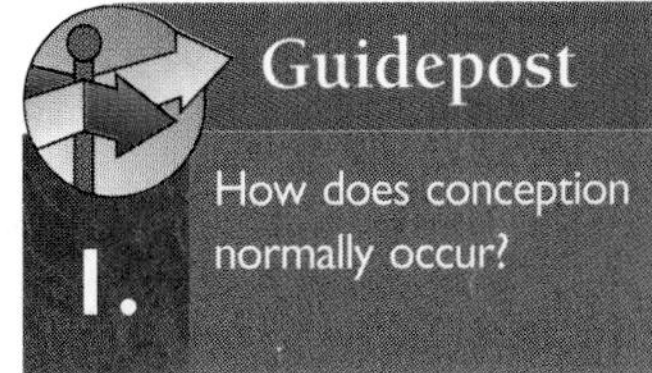

Guidepost

1. How does conception normally occur?

How Fertilization Takes Place

Fertilization, or conception, is the process by which sperm and ovum—the male and female *gametes,* or sex cells—combine to create a single cell called a **zygote,** which then duplicates itself again and again by cell division to become a baby. A

clone
(verb) To make a genetic copy of an individual; (noun) a genetic copy of an individual.

fertilization
Union of sperm and ovum fuse to produce a zygote; also called *conception.*

zygote
One-celled organism resulting from fertilization.

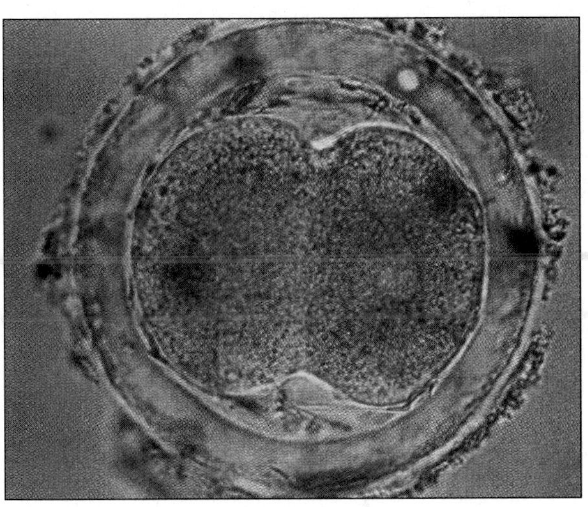

Fertilization takes place when a sperm cell unites with an ovum to form a single new cell. The fertilized ovum shown here has begun to grow by cell division. It will eventually differentiate into 800 billion or more cells with specialized functions.

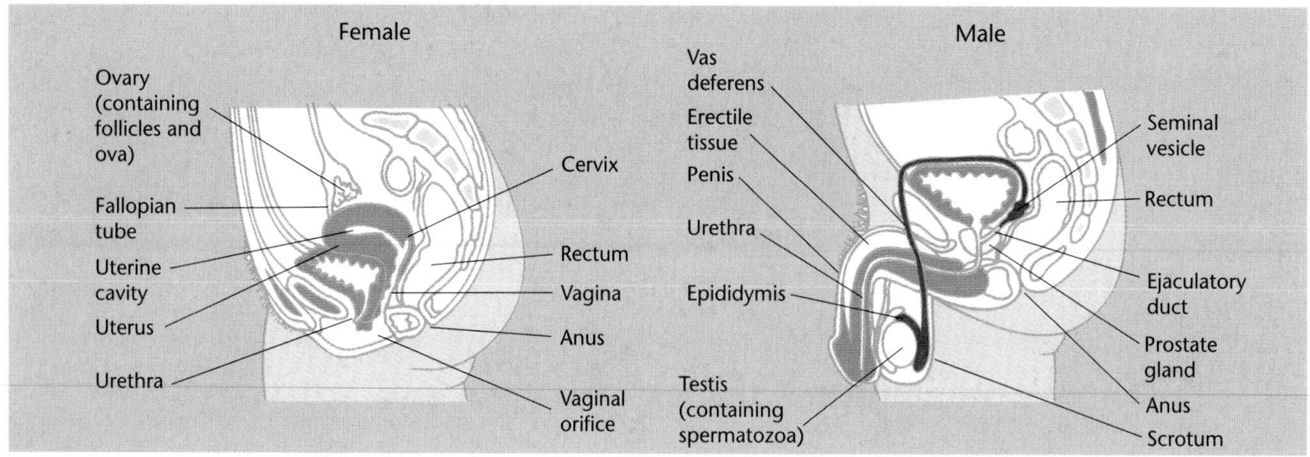

Figure 3-1
Human reproductive systems.

girl is born with all the ova she will ever have—about 400,000. At birth, these immature ova are in her two ovaries (see Figure 3-1), each ovum in its own small sac, or *follicle.*

In a sexually mature woman, *ovulation*—rupture of a mature follicle in either ovary and expulsion of its ovum—occurs about once every 28 days until menopause. The ovum is swept along through the fallopian tube by tiny hair cells, called *cilia,* toward the uterus, or womb. Fertilization normally occurs during the brief time the ovum is passing through the fallopian tube.

Sperm are produced in the testicles (testes), or reproductive glands, of a mature male (refer back to Figure 3-1) at a rate of several hundred million a day and are ejaculated in the semen at sexual climax. They enter the vagina and try to swim through the cervix (the opening of the uterus) and into the fallopian tubes, but only a tiny fraction make it that far.

Fertilization is most likely if intercourse occurs on the day of ovulation or during the five days before (Wilcox, Weinberg, & Baird, 1995). If fertilization does not occur, the ovum and any sperm cells in the woman's body die. The sperm are absorbed by the woman's white blood cells, and the ovum passes through the uterus and exits through the vagina.

Guidepost

2. What causes multiple births?

What Causes Multiple Births?

Multiple births are thought to occur in two ways. Most commonly, the mother's body releases two ova within a short time (or sometimes, perhaps, a single ovum splits) and then both are fertilized. The resulting babies are **dizygotic (two-egg) twins,** commonly called *fraternal twins.* The second way is for a single fertilized ovum to split into two. The babies that result from this cell division are **monozygotic (one-egg) twins,** commonly called *identical twins.* Triplets, quadruplets, and other multiple births can result from either of these processes or a combination of both.

dizygotic (two-egg) twins
Twins conceived by the union of two different ova (or a single ovum that has split) with two different sperm cells within a brief period of time; also called *fraternal twins.*

monozygotic (one-egg) twins
Twins resulting from the division of a single zygote after fertilization; also called *identical twins.*

temperament
Person's characteristic disposition, or style of approaching and reacting to situations.

Monozygotic twins have the same hereditary makeup and are the same sex, but—in part because of differences in prenatal as well as postnatal experience—they differ in some respects. They may not be identical in **temperament** (disposition, or style of approaching and reacting to situations). In some physical characteristics, such as hair whorls, dental patterns, and handedness, they may be mirror images of each other; one may be left-handed and the other right-handed. Dizygotic twins, who are created from different sperm cells and usually from different ova, are no more alike in hereditary makeup than any other siblings and may be the same sex or different sexes.

Monozygotic twins—about one-third of all twins—seem to be the result of an "accident" of prenatal development; their incidence is about the same in all ethnic groups. Dizygotic twins are most common among African Americans, white northern Europeans, and east Indians and are least common among other Asians (Behrman, 1992). These differences may be due to hormonal tendencies that may make women of some ethnic groups more likely to release more than one ovum at the same time.

The incidence of multiple births in the United States has grown rapidly. Between 1980 and 1997, live twin births (which in 1997 accounted for 94 percent of multiple births) increased by 52 percent from 68,339 to 104,137, and the number of triplets and larger multiples quadrupled from 1,337 to 6,737. Meanwhile, the number of single births rose only 6 percent. The rise in multiple births is due in part to delayed childbearing, since such births are more likely to happen to older women. Twin birth rates for women in their late forties have multiplied a thousandfold; two and a half times more twins (444) were born to women ages 45 to 49 in 1997 than during the entire decade of the 1980s. A more important factor in the multiple birth rate is the increased use of fertility drugs, which spur ovulation, and of such techniques as in vitro fertilization (see Chapter 14). This is of concern, since multiple births are more likely to lead to disability or death in infancy (Martin & Park, 1999).

CHECKPOINT

Can you . . .

✔ Explain how and when fertilization normally takes place?

✔ Distinguish between monozygotic and dizygotic twins, and tell how each comes about?

Mechanisms of Heredity

The science of genetics is the study of *heredity*—the inborn factors, inherited from the biological parents, that affect development. When ovum and sperm unite, they endow the baby-to-be with a genetic makeup that influences a wide range of characteristics from color of eyes and hair to health, intellect, and personality.

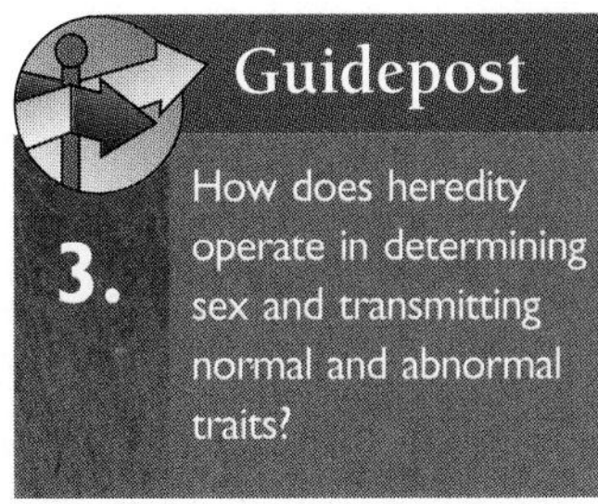

Guidepost
3.
How does heredity operate in determining sex and transmitting normal and abnormal traits?

Genes and Chromosomes

The basic unit of heredity is the **gene.** Genes contain all the hereditary material passed from biological parents to children. Each cell in the human body contains an estimated 60,000 to 100,000 genes, which are made of the chemical **deoxyribonucleic acid (DNA).** DNA carries the biochemical instructions that tell the cells how to make the proteins that enable them to carry out each specific body function. Each gene seems to be located by function in a definite position on a rod-shaped structure called a **chromosome.**

Every cell in the human body except the sex cells has 23 pairs of chromosomes—46 in all. Through a complex process of cell division called *meiosis,* each sex cell, or gamete (sperm or ovum) ends up with only 23 chromosomes—one from each pair. Thus, when sperm and ovum fuse at conception, they produce a zygote with 46 chromosomes, half from the father and half from the mother.

Three-quarters of the genes every child receives are identical to those received by every other child; they are called *monomorphic genes,* and they define characteristics that make a person recognizably human. The other one-quarter of a child's genes are *polymorphic genes,* which define each person as an individual. Since there are about 20,000 or more polymorphic genes, many of which come in several variations, and since meiotic division is random, it is virtually impossible for any two children (other than monozygotic twins) to receive exactly the same combination of genes.

At conception, then, the single-celled zygote has all the biological information needed to guide its development into a human baby. This happens through *mitosis,* a process by which the cells divide in half over and over again. Each

gene
Basic functional unit of heredity, which contains all inherited material passed from biological parents to children.

deoxyribonucleic acid (DNA)
Chemical of which genes are composed, which controls the functions of body cells.

chromosome
One of 46 rod-shaped structures that carry the genes.

division creates a duplicate of the original cell, with the same hereditary information. When development is normal, each cell (except the gametes) continues to have 46 chromosomes identical to those in the original zygote.

What Determines Sex?

In some societies, a woman's failure to produce sons is justification for divorce. The irony in this custom is that it is the father's sperm that determines a child's sex.

autosomes
The 22 pairs of chromosomes not related to sexual expression.

sex chromosomes
Pair of chromosomes that determines sex: XX in the normal female, XY in the normal male.

At the moment of conception, the 23 chromosomes from the sperm and the 23 from the mother's ovum form 23 pairs. Twenty-two pairs are **autosomes,** chromosomes that are not related to sexual expression. The twenty-third pair are **sex chromosomes**—one from the father and one from the mother—which govern the baby's sex.

Sex chromosomes are either *X chromosomes* or *Y chromosomes.* The sex chromosome of every ovum is an X chromosome, but the sperm may contain either an X or a Y chromosome. The Y chromosome contains the gene for maleness, the SRY gene. When an ovum (X) is fertilized by an X-carrying sperm, the zygote formed is XX, a female. When an ovum (X) is fertilized by a Y-carrying sperm, the resulting zygote is XY, a male (see Figure 3-2).

Initially, the embryo's rudimentary reproductive system is no different in males than in females. About 6 to 8 weeks after conception, male embryos normally start producing the male hormone testosterone. Exposure to steady, high levels of testosterone results in the development of a male body with male sexual organs.

Until recently, then, it was assumed that femaleness is a genetic "default setting," which will be operative unless a gene for maleness and a resulting exposure to male hormones overrides it. Now, however, it appears that the development of female characteristics is controlled by a signaling molecule called *Wnt-4,* a mutation of which can "masculinize" a genetically female fetus (Vainio, Heikkiia, Kispert, Chin, & McMahon, 1999). Also, an extra copy of the DDS gene on the X chromosome in a genetically male fetus seems able to override the SRY gene on the Y chromosome, which normally triggers male sexual development (Bardoni et al., 1994). Thus, sexual differentiation appears to be a more complex process than was previously thought.

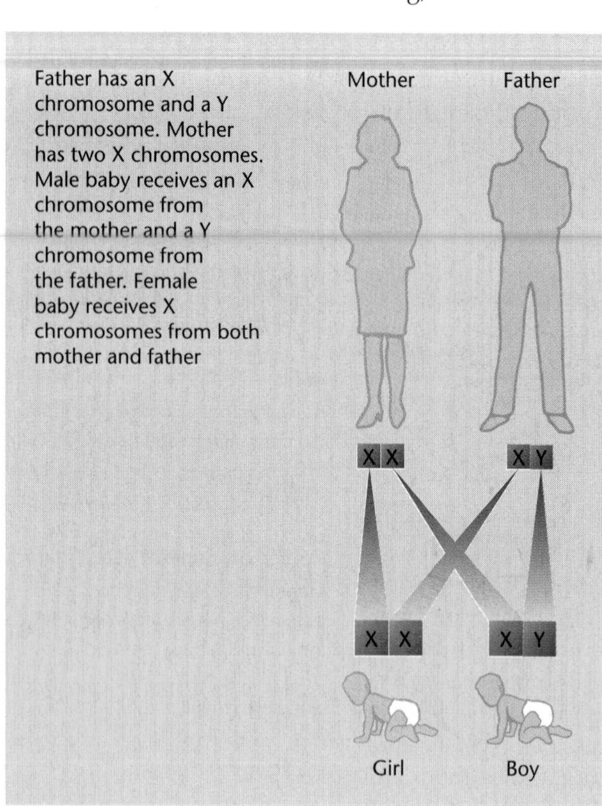

Father has an X chromosome and a Y chromosome. Mother has two X chromosomes. Male baby receives an X chromosome from the mother and a Y chromosome from the father. Female baby receives X chromosomes from both mother and father
Mother
Father
X X
X Y
X X
X Y
Girl
Boy

Figure 3-2
Determination of sex. Females have two X chromosomes; males have an X chromosome and a Y chromosome. Since all babies receive an X chromosome from the mother, sex is determined by whether an X or Y chromosome is received from the father.

Patterns of Genetic Transmission

During the 1860s, Gregor Mendel, an Austrian monk, laid the foundation for our understanding of patterns of inheritance. He cross-bred pea plants that produced only yellow seeds with pea plants that produced only green seeds. The resulting hybrid plants produced yellow seeds, meaning, he said, that yellow was *dominant* over green. Yet when he bred the yellow-seeded hybrids with each other, only 75 percent of their offspring had yellow seeds, and the other 25 percent had green seeds. This proved, Mendel said, that a hereditary characteristic (in this case, the color green) can be *recessive,* that is, carried by an organism that does not express, or show, it.

Mendel also tried breeding for two traits at once. Crossing pea plants that produced round yellow seeds with plants that produced wrinkled green seeds, he found that color and shape were independent of each other. Mendel thus showed that hereditary traits are transmitted separately.

Today we know that the genetic picture in humans is far more complex than Mendel imagined. Most human traits fall along a continuous spectrum (for example, from light skin to dark). It is hard to find a single normal trait that people inherit through simple dominant transmission other than the ability to curl the tongue lengthwise. Let's look at various forms of inheritance.

Dominant and Recessive Inheritance

If you are a "tongue curler," you inherited this ability through *dominant inheritance.* If you are a redhead but both your parents have dark hair, *recessive inheritance* occurred. How do these two types of inheritance work?

Genes that can produce alternative expressions of a characteristic (such as ability or inability to curl the tongue) are called **alleles.** Every person receives a pair of alleles for a given characteristic, one from each biological parent. When both alleles are the same, the person is **homozygous** for the characteristic; when they are different, the person is **heterozygous.** In **dominant inheritance,** when a person is heterozygous for a particular trait, the dominant allele governs. In other words, when an offspring receives alleles for two contradictory traits, only one of them, the dominant one, will be expressed. **Recessive inheritance,** the expression of a recessive trait, occurs only when a person receives the recessive allele from both parents.

If you inherited one allele for tongue-curling ability from each parent (see Figure 3-3), you are homozygous for tongue curling and can curl your tongue. If, say, your mother passed on an allele for the ability and your father passed on an allele lacking it, you are heterozygous. Since the ability is dominant (D) and its lack is recessive (d), you, again, can curl your tongue. But if you received the recessive allele from both parents, you would not be a tongue-curler.

Most traits seem to be transmitted by the interaction of several genes with effects of varying sizes, or **quantitative trait loci (QTL).** QTL is one reason that simple dominance and recessiveness cannot explain the inheritance of such complex human traits as intelligence, which may be affected by 50 or more genes. Indeed, whereas there are more than 1,000 rare genes that individually determine abnormal traits, there is no known single gene that, by itself, significantly accounts for individual differences in any complex normal behavior. Instead, such behaviors are likely to be influenced by many genes with small but sometimes identifiable effects (Plomin, 1995).

In addition, **multifactorial transmission,** a combination of genetic and environmental factors, plays a role in the expression of most traits. Let's see how.

Genotypes and Phenotypes: Multifactorial Transmission

If you can curl your tongue, that ability is part of your **phenotype,** the array of observable characteristics through which your **genotype,** or underlying genetic makeup, is expressed. Except for monozygotic twins, no two people have the same genotype. The phenotype is the product of the genotype plus any relevant environmental influences.

As Figure 3-3 shows, the same phenotypical characteristic may arise from different genotypes: either a homozygous combination of two dominant alleles or a heterozygous combination of one dominant allele and one recessive allele. If you are heterozygous for tongue curling and you and a mate who is also heterozygous for the trait have four children, the statistical probability is that one child will be homozygous for the ability, one will be homozygous lacking it, and the other two will be heterozygous. Thus, three of your children will have phenotypes that include tongue curling (they will be able to curl their tongues), but this ability will arise from two different genotypical patterns (homozygous and heterozygous).

Tongue curling has a strong genetic base; but for most traits, experience modifies the expression of the genotype. Let's say that Steven has inherited musical talent. If he takes music lessons and practices regularly, he may delight his

alleles
Paired genes (alike or different) that affect a particular trait.

homozygous
Possessing two identical alleles for a trait.

heterozygous
Possessing differing alleles for a trait.

dominant inheritance
Pattern of inheritance in which, when an individual receives contradictory alleles for a trait, only the dominant one is expressed.

recessive inheritance
Pattern of inheritance in which an individual receives identical recessive alleles from both parents, resulting in expression of a recessive (nondominant) trait.

quantitative trait loci (QTL)
Interaction of multiple genes, each with effects of varying size, to produce a complex trait.

multifactorial transmission
Combination of genetic and environmental factors to produce certain complex traits.

phenotype
Observable characteristics of a person.

genotype
Genetic makeup of a person, containing both expressed and unexpressed characteristics.

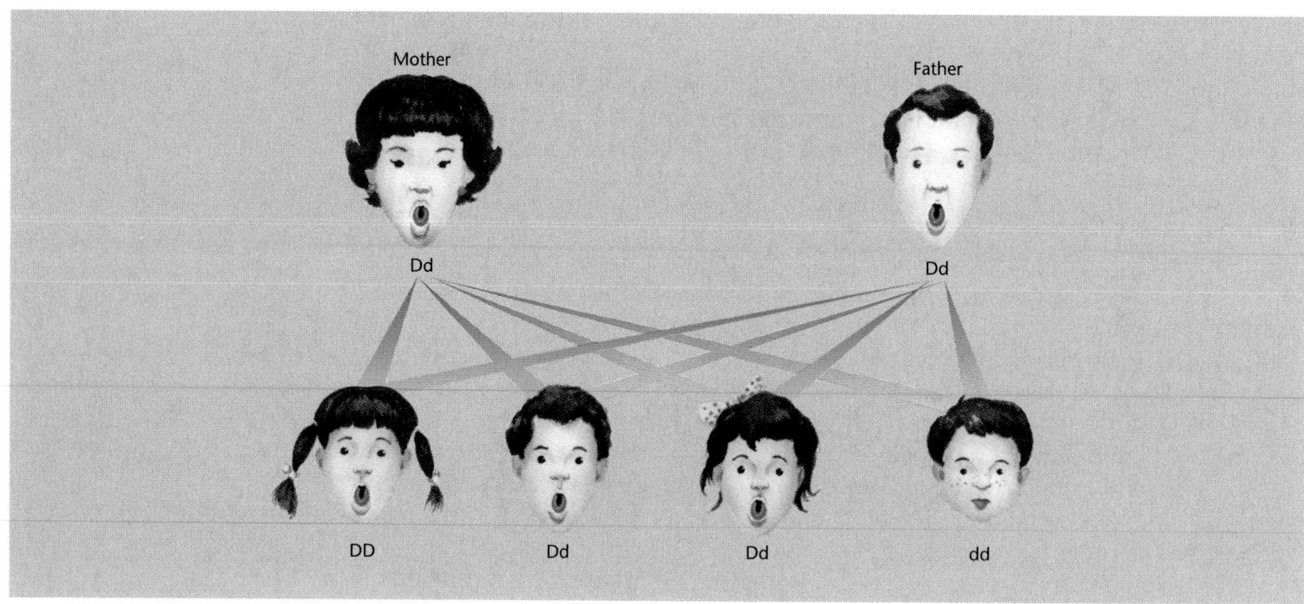

Figure 3-3
Phenotypes and genotypes. Because of dominant inheritance, the same observable phenotype (in this case, the ability to curl the tongue lengthwise) can result from two different genotypes (genetic patterns). This mother's and father's genotypes are heterozygous; each has one dominant gene (D) for the ability and one recessive gene (d) lacking the ability. Since the ability is dominant, both can curl their tongues. Each child receives one gene for this trait from each parent. Statistical averages predict that three out of four children in this family will express the trait in their phenotypes (that is, be able to curl their tongues). Two of these three children *(center)* will have heterozygous genotypes (Dd), like the parents; the third child *(left)* with the same phenotype will have a homozygous genotype (DD). The fourth child *(right)* will receive recessive genes from both parents and will be unable to curl the tongue. A phenotype expressing a recessive characteristic (such as inability to curl the tongue) must have a homozygous genotype (dd).

CHECKPOINT

Can you . . .

- ✔ Explain why no two people, other than monozygotic twins, have the same genetic heritage?
- ✔ Explain why it is the sperm that determines a baby's sex?
- ✔ Tell how dominant inheritance and recessive inheritance work, and why most normal traits are not the products of simple dominant or recessive transmission?

family with his performances. If his family likes and encourages classical music, he may play Bach preludes; if the other children on his block influence him to prefer popular music, he may eventually form a rock group. However, if from early childhood he is not encouraged and not motivated to play music, and if he has no access to a musical instrument or to music lessons, his genotype for musical ability may not be expressed (or may be expressed to a lesser extent) in his phenotype. Some physical characteristics (including height and weight) and most psychological characteristics (such as intelligence and personality traits, as well as musical ability) are products of multifactorial transmission.

The difference between genotype and phenotype helps explain why even a clone can never be an exact duplicate of another human being (see Box 3-1). Later in this chapter we discuss in more detail how environmental influences work together with the genetic endowment to influence development.

Genetic and Chromosomal Abnormalities

Birth disorders accounted for 22 percent of infant deaths in 1997 (Hoyert, Kochanek, & Murphy, 1999). Most of the serious malformations involve the circulatory or central nervous systems (see Table 3-1).

It is in genetic defects and diseases that we see most clearly the operation of dominant and recessive transmission in humans, and also of a variation, *sex-linked inheritance.* Some defects are due to abnormalities in genes or chromosomes. Some are due to *mutations:* permanent alterations in genes or chromosomes that often produce harmful characteristics. Mutations can occur spontaneously or can be induced by environmental hazards, such as radiation. Many disorders arise when an inherited predisposition interacts with an environmental factor, either before or after birth. Spina bifida (incomplete closure of

Box 3-1

Human Cloning: Issues and Implications

Now that scientists have successfully cloned sheep and mice, cloning human beings seems the likely next step. Will we soon be able to duplicate a Mozart or an Einstein? Do scientists have the right to "play God" with human life and personality?

Perhaps the most familiar use of cloning is in horticulture: gardeners reproduce a plant specimen valued for its vigor or beauty by taking cuttings from the mature plant and letting them take root. Cloning human beings would be much more complicated. An ovum would have to be removed from a woman's body and placed in a test tube. Its nucleus would be replaced by the nucleus of a body cell from the person to be cloned—a cell that contains all the paired chromosomes present in a zygote. After cell division begins, the resulting blastula would be implanted in the uterus of a woman, who would, in due time, give birth to an infant endowed with the same genetic makeup as the donor of the nucleus.

The ability to replicate human beings offers intriguing possibilities. In the broadest terms, the conscious selection of individuals for cloning might raise the genetic level of the human species. On a personal level, it could give infertile couples, or those in which one partner has a risky genetic profile, an additional option for producing a child genetically related to at least one of them. Or a couple might choose to clone existing offspring, a dead or dying parent or child, or one who needs a tissue or organ transplant but lacks a suitable donor.

These potential uses raise concerns so troubling to some people that the U.S. Congress has debated proposals to ban human cloning. The chief ethical issues involve the sanctity and dignity of human life. Opponents of cloning argue that it would devalue human beings by depriving them of their uniqueness and treating them as "interchangeable commodities" (Annas, 1998, p. 123).

Actually, a clone is not much different from a later-born "identical" twin, raised by the older "twin" and his or her spouse. Such relationships might involve novel challenges, but it is argued that these challenges could be met through regulations requiring informed consent and counseling for the couple, guarantees of parental rights and responsibilities, and—to discourage commercial uses of cloning—a limit on the number of clones derived from any particular individual (Robertson, 1998).

Both the potential motives for cloning and the arguments against it may reflect a misunderstanding of the role of genes in human development. Although cloning can produce identical genotypes, it cannot produce identical phenotypes. Like monozygotic twins, clones would not look, feel, be, or act exactly like their genetic donors—in fact, even less so, since they would develop in different uterine environments and would grow up in different circumstances. Even physical appearance can be affected by prenatal experiences, such as the way a fetus is attached to the placenta and the substances it absorbs from the mother's blood (Eisenberg, 1999). Brain development, both before and after birth, is highly dependent on a combination of maturation and experience. And such complex characteristics as intelligence and personality hinge on a virtually inseparable intertwining of nature and nurture.

Thus, "to produce another Wolfgang Amadeus Mozart, we would need not only Wolfgang's genome [genetic makeup] but his mother's uterus, his father's music lessons, his parents' friends and his own, the state of music in 18th century Austria, Haydn's patronage, and on and on. . . . We [cannot assume] that his genome, cultivated in another world at another time, would result in the same musical genius. If a particular strain of wheat yields different harvests under different conditions of climate, soil, and cultivation, how can we assume that so much more complex a genome as that of a human being would yield its desired crop of operas, symphonies, and chamber music under different circumstances of nurture?" (Eisenberg, 1999, p. 474).

Indeed, instead of improving the human species, widespread cloning might have a *negative* effect. It might limit the adaptability of the human gene pool by emphasizing characteristics (such as Mozart's musical ability) that have been successful in particular environments but might turn out to be less successful in other, unforeseen circumstances. "Social evolution demands new types of men and women. Cloning would condemn us always to plan the future on the basis of the past" (Eisenberg, 1999, p. 473).

the vertebral canal) and cleft palate (a fissure in the roof of the mouth) probably result from multifactorial transmission. Attention deficit disorder with hyperactivity (ADDH) is one of a number of behavioral disorders thought to be transmitted multifactorially.

Defects Transmitted by Dominant Inheritance

Most of the time, normal genes are dominant over those carrying abnormal traits, but sometimes the gene for an abnormal trait is dominant. When one parent has a dominant abnormal gene and one recessive normal gene and the other parent

Table 3-1 Some Birth Defects

Problem	Characteristics of Condition	Who Is at Risk	What Can Be Done
Alpha$_1$ antitrypsin deficiency	Enzyme deficiency that can lead to cirrhosis of the liver in early infancy and emphysema and degenerative lung disease in middle age.	1 in 1,000 white births	No treatment.
Alpha thalassemia	Severe anemia that reduces ability of the blood to carry oxygen; nearly all affected infants are stillborn or die soon after birth.	Primarily families of Malaysian, African, and southeast Asian descent	Frequent blood transfusions.
Beta thalassemia (Cooley's anemia)	Severe anemia resulting in weakness, fatigue, and frequent illness; usually fatal in adolescence or young adulthood.	Primarily families of Mediterranean descent	Frequent blood transfusions.
Cystic fibrosis	Body makes too much mucus, which collects in the lung and digestive tract; children do not grow normally and usually do not live beyond age 30; the most common inherited *lethal* defect among white people.	1 in 2,000 white births	Daily physical therapy to loosen mucus; antibiotics for lung infections; enzymes to improve digestion; gene therapy (in experimental stage).
Duchenne's muscular dystrophy	Fatal disease usually found in males, marked by muscle weakness; minor mental retardation is common; respiratory failure and death usually occur in young adulthood.	1 in 3,000 to 5,000 male births	No treatment.
Hemophilia	Excessive bleeding, usually affecting males rather than females; in its most severe form, can lead to crippling arthritis in adulthood.	1 in 10,000 families with a history of hemophilia	Frequent transfusions of blood with clotting factors.
Neural-tube defects:			
Anencephaly	Absence of brain tissues; infants are stillborn or die soon after birth.	1 in 1,000	No treatment.
Spina bifida	Incompletely closed spinal canal, resulting in muscle weakness or paralysis and loss of bladder and bowel control; often accompanied by hydrocephalus, an accumulation of spinal fluid in the brain, which can lead to mental retardation.	1 in 1,000	Surgery to close spinal canal prevents further injury; shunt placed in brain drains excess fluid and prevents mental retardation.
Phenylketonuria (PKU)	Metabolic disorder resulting in mental retardation.	1 in 10,000 to 25,000 births	Special diet begun in first few weeks of life can offset mental retardation.
Polycystic kidney disease	*Infantile form;* enlarged kidneys, leading to respiratory problems and congestive heart failure. *Adult form;* kidney pain, kidney stones, and hypertension resulting in chronic kidney failure.	1 in 1,000	Kidney transplants.
Sickle-cell anemia	Deformed, fragile red blood cells that can clog the blood vessels, depriving the body of oxygen; symptoms include severe pain, stunted growth, frequent infections, leg ulcers, gallstones, susceptibility to pneumonia, and stroke.	1 in 500 African Americans	Painkillers, transfusions for anemia and to prevent stroke, antibiotics for infections.
Tay-Sachs disease	Degenerative disease of the brain and nerve cells, resulting in death before age 5.	1 in 3,000 eastern European Jews, rarer in other groups	No treatment.

Source: Adapted from AAP Committee on Genetics, 1996; Tisdale, 1988, pp 68–69.

has two recessive normal genes, each of their children has a 50-50 chance of inheriting the abnormal gene (see Figure 3-4). Because the abnormal gene is dominant, every child who receives it will have the defect. (Of course, if one parent has *two* dominant abnormal genes, that is, if one parent is homozygous for the condition, *all* the children will be affected.) Among the 1,800 disorders known to be transmitted by dominant inheritance are achondroplasia (a type of dwarfism) and Huntington's disease.

Defects Transmitted by Recessive Inheritance

Recessive defects are expressed only if a child receives the same recessive gene from each biological parent. Suppose that only one parent, say, the father, has a faulty recessive gene. If he is homozygous for the trait (has two alleles for it), he has the disorder; if he is heterozygous (has one normal and one defective allele), he is a *carrier* for the defect but does not suffer from it. In either case, none of his children will have it, because the mother does not carry the faulty gene. However, the father can pass on the defective gene to the children, and they have a 50-50 chance of being carriers and passing it on to future generations. If *both* parents are carriers (see Figure 3-5), although *they* are unaffected, each child has 1 chance in 4 of inheriting the abnormal gene from both of them and suffering the disorder, as well as 1 chance in 2 of being a carrier. Some defects transmitted recessively, such as Tay-Sachs disease and sickle-cell anemia, are more common among certain ethnic groups, which, through inbreeding (marriage and reproduction within the group) have passed down recessive characteristics (see Table 3-2).

Defects transmitted by recessive inheritance are more likely to be lethal at an early age than those transmitted by dominant inheritance. If a dominantly

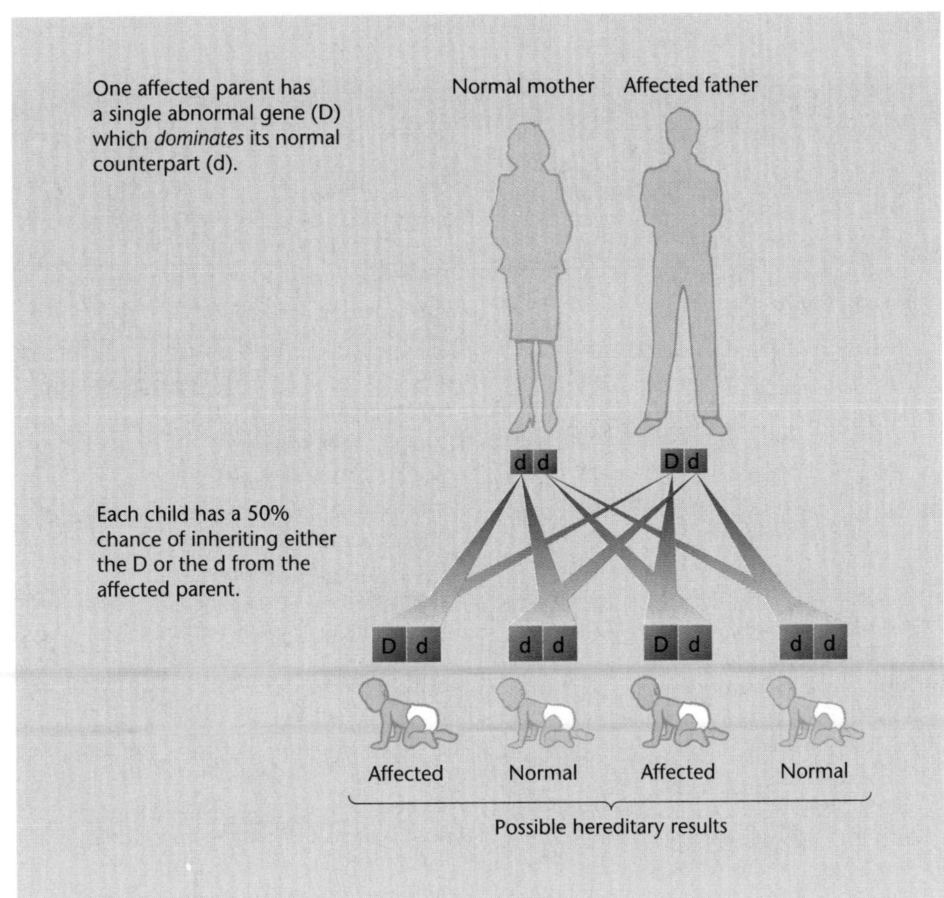
One affected parent has a single abnormal gene (D) which *dominates* its normal counterpart (d).
Normal mother
Affected father
d d
D d
Each child has a 50% chance of inheriting either the D or the d from the affected parent.
D d
d d
D d
d d
Affected
Normal
Affected
Normal
Possible hereditary results

Figure 3-4
Dominant inheritance of a birth defect.

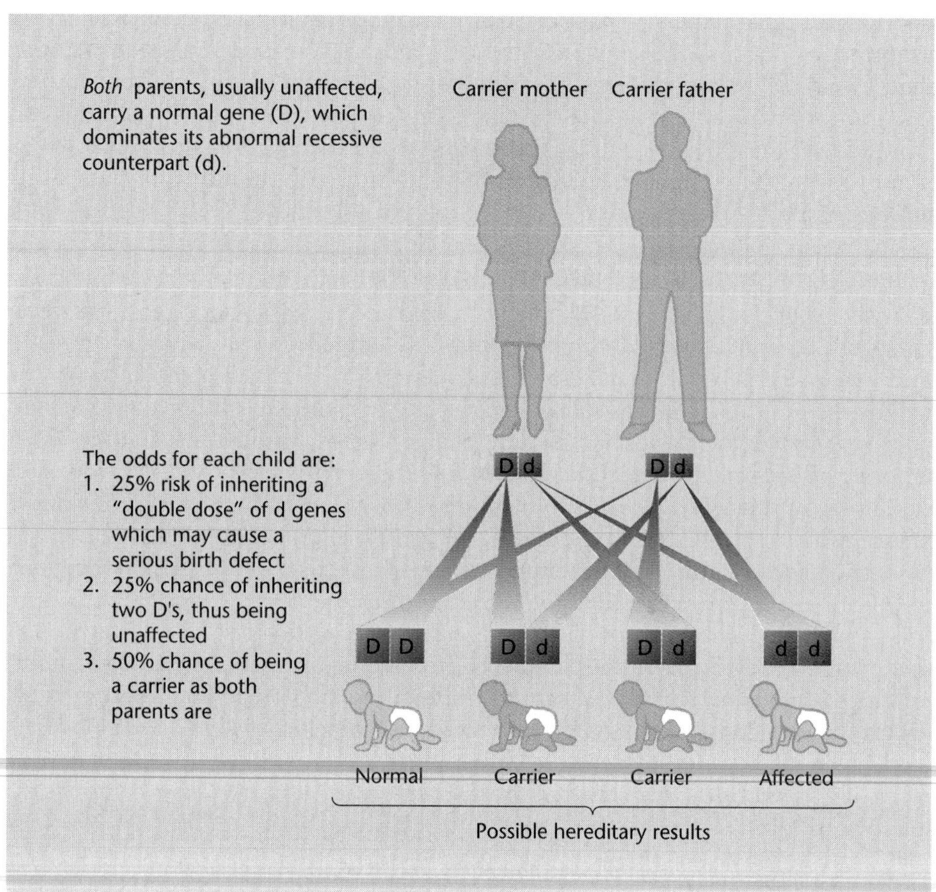
Both parents, usually unaffected, carry a normal gene (D), which dominates its abnormal recessive counterpart (d).
Carrier mother
Carrier father
D d
D d
The odds for each child are:
1. 25% risk of inheriting a "double dose" of d genes which may cause a serious birth defect
2. 25% chance of inheriting two D's, thus being unaffected
3. 50% chance of being a carrier as both parents are
D D
D d
D d
d d
Normal
Carrier
Carrier
Affected
Possible hereditary results

Figure 3-5
Recessive inheritance of a birth defect.

Table 3-2 Chances of Genetic Disorders for Various Ethnic Groups

If You Are	The Chance Is About	That
African American	1 in 12	You are a carrier of sickle-cell anemia.
	7 in 10	You will have milk intolerance as an adult.
African American and male	1 in 10	You have a hereditary predisposition to develop hemolytic anemia after taking sulfa or other drugs.
African American and female	1 in 50	You have a hereditary predisposition to develop hemolytic anemia after taking sulfa or other drugs.
White	1 in 25	You are a carrier of cystic fibrosis.
	1 in 80	You are a carrier of phenylketonuria (PKU).
Jewish (Ashkenazic)	1 in 30	You are a carrier of Tay-Sachs disease.
	1 in 100	You are a carrier of familial dysautonomia.
Italian American or Greek American	1 in 10	You are a carrier of beta thalassemia.
Armenian or Jewish (Sephardic)	1 in 45	You are a carrier of familial Mediterranean fever.
Afrikaner (white South African)	1 in 330	You have porphyria.
Asian	almost 100%	You will have milk intolerance as an adult.

Source: Adapted from Milunsky, 1992, p. 122.

transmitted defect killed a person before the age of reproduction, it could not be passed on to the next generation and therefore would soon disappear. A recessive defect can be transmitted by carriers who do not have the disorder and thus may live to reproduce.

Defects Transmitted by Sex-Linked Inheritance

In **sex-linked inheritance,** certain recessive disorders linked to genes on the sex chromosomes show up differently in male and female children. Red-green color-blindness is one of these sex-linked conditions. Another is hemophilia, a disorder in which blood does not clot when it should.

sex-linked inheritance Pattern of inheritance in which certain characteristics carried on the X chromosome inherited from the mother are transmitted differently to her male and female offspring.

Sex-linked recessive traits are carried on one of the X chromosomes of an unaffected mother. Sex-linked disorders almost always appear only in male children; in females, a normal dominant gene on the X chromosome from the father overrides the defective gene on the X chromosome from the mother. Boys are more vulnerable to these disorders because there is no opposite dominant gene on the shorter Y chromosome from the father to override a defect on the X chromosome from the mother.

Each son of a normal man and a woman who is a carrier has a 50 percent chance of inheriting the mother's harmful gene—and the disorder—and a 50 percent chance of receiving the mother's normal X chromosome and being unaffected (see Figure 3-6). Daughters have a 50 percent chance of being carriers. An affected father cannot pass on such a gene to his sons, since he contributes a Y chromosome to them; but he can pass on the gene to his daughters, who then become carriers.

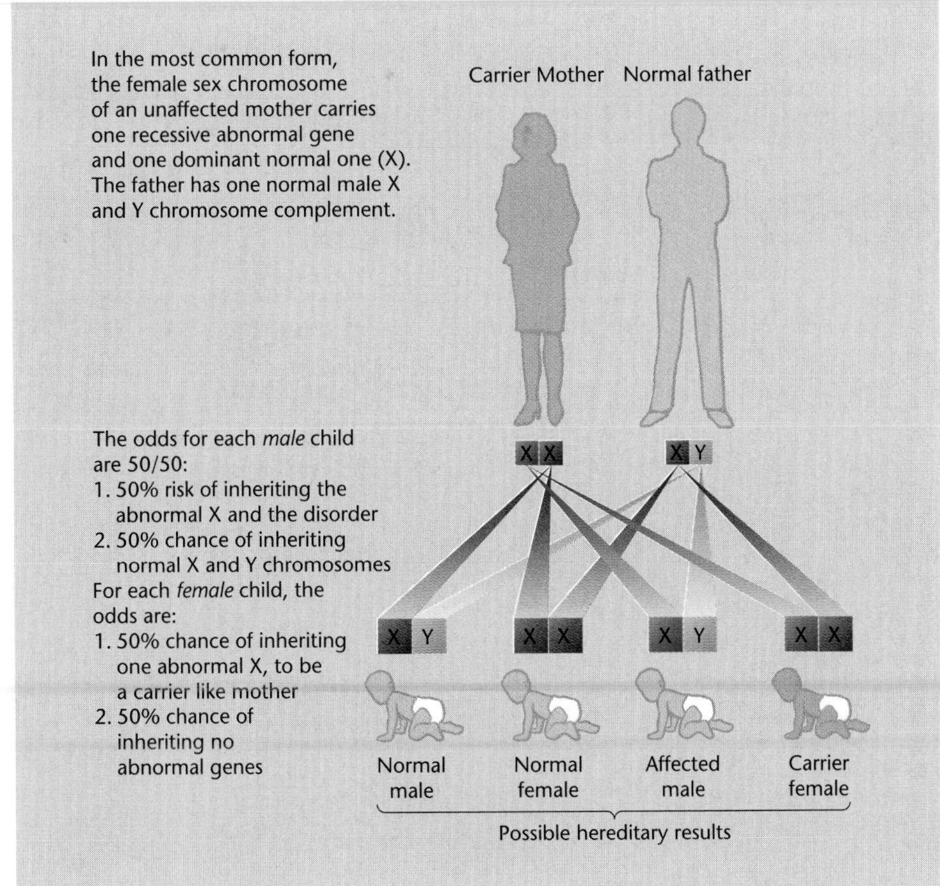
In the most common form, the female sex chromosome of an unaffected mother carries one recessive abnormal gene and one dominant normal one (X). The father has one normal male X and Y chromosome complement.
Carrier Mother
Normal father
X X
X Y
The odds for each *male* child are 50/50:
1. 50% risk of inheriting the abnormal X and the disorder
2. 50% chance of inheriting normal X and Y chromosomes
For each *female* child, the odds are:
1. 50% chance of inheriting one abnormal X, to be a carrier like mother
2. 50% chance of inheriting no abnormal genes
X Y
X X
X Y
X X
Normal male
Normal female
Affected male
Carrier female
Possible hereditary results

Figure 3-6
Sex-linked inheritance of a birth defect.

Down syndrome
Chromosomal disorder characterized by moderate-to-severe mental retardation and by such physical signs as a downward-sloping skin fold at the inner corners of the eyes.

This boy shows the chief identifying characteristic of Down syndrome: a downward sloping skinfold at the inner corner of the eye. Although Down syndrome is a major cause of mental retardation, children with this chromosomal abnormality have a good chance of living productive lives.

Occasionally, a female does inherit a sex-linked condition. For example, if her father is a hemophiliac and her mother happens to be a carrier for the disorder, the daughter has a 50 percent chance of receiving the abnormal X chromosome from each parent and having the disease.

Chromosomal Abnormalities

About 1 in every 156 children born in western countries is estimated to have a chromosomal abnormality (Milunsky, 1992). Some of these abnormalities are inherited; others result from accidents during prenatal development and are not likely to recur in the same family.

Some chromosomal disorders, such as Klinefelter syndrome, are caused by an extra sex chromosome (shown by the pattern XXY). Others, such as Turner syndrome, result from a missing sex chromosome (XO). Characteristics of the most common sex chromosome disorders are shown in Table 3-3.

Other chromosomal abnormalities occur in the autosomes. **Down syndrome,** the most common of these, is responsible for about one-third of all cases of moderate-to-severe mental retardation. The condition is also called *trisomy-21,* because it is usually caused by an extra twenty-first chromosome or the translocation of part of the twenty-first chromosome onto another chromosome. The most obvious physical characteristic associated with the disorder is a downward-sloping skin fold at the inner corners of the eyes.

More than 90 percent of cases of Down syndrome are caused by a mistake in chromosomal distribution during development of the ovum, sperm, or zygote. (One of two identical twins may have the disorder, since such an accident can happen in the development of one twin and not the other.) When the mother is under age 35, the disorder is more likely to be hereditary. A clue to its genetic basis is the discovery of a gene on chromosome 21 responsible for a brain protein that seems to lead to Down syndrome (Allore et al., 1988).

About 1 in every 700 babies born alive has Down syndrome (Hayes & Batshaw, 1993). The risk is greatest with older parents. The chances rise from 1 such birth in 2,000 among 25-year-old mothers to 1 in 40 for women over 45. The risk also

Table 3-3 Sex Chromosome Abnormalities

Pattern/Name	Characteristic*	Incidence	Treatment
XYY	Male; tall stature; tendency to low IQ, especially verbal.	1 in 1,000 male births	No special treatment
XXX (triple X)	Female, normal appearance, menstrual irregularities, learning disorders, mental retardation.	1 in 1,000 female births	Special education
XXY (Kleinfelter)	Male, sterility, underdeveloped secondary sex characteristics, small testes, learning disorders.	1 in 1,000 male births	Hormone therapy, special education
XO (Turner)	Female, short stature, webbed neck, impaired spatial abilities, no menstruation, infertility, underdeveloped sex organs, incomplete development of secondary sex characteristics.	1 in 1,500 to 2,500 female births	Hormone therapy, special education
Fragile X	Minor-to-severe mental retardation; symptoms, which are more severe in males, include delayed speech and motor development, speech impairments, and hyperactivity; the most common *inherited* form of mental retardation.	1 in 1,200 male births; 1 in 2,000 female births	Educational and behavioral therapies when needed

*Not every affected person has every characteristic.

increases with the father's age, especially among men over 50 (Abroms & Bennett, 1981). DNA analysis has shown that the extra chromosome seems to come from the mother's ovum in 95 percent of cases (Antonarakis & Down Syndrome Collaborative Group, 1991); the other 5 percent of cases seem to be related to the father.

The prognosis for children with Down syndrome is brighter than was once thought. Many live at home until adulthood and then enter small group homes. Many can support themselves; they tend to do well in structured job situations. More than 70 percent of people with Down syndrome live into their sixties, but they are at special risk of developing Alzheimer's disease (Hayes & Batshaw, 1993).

Genome Imprinting

genome imprinting Process by which genes that temporarily have been chemically altered in the mother or father have differing effects when transmitted to offspring.

Through **genome imprinting,** some genes seem to be temporarily imprinted, or chemically altered, in either the mother or the father. These genes, when transmitted to offspring, have different effects than do comparable genes from the other parent. An imprinted gene will dominate one that has not been imprinted. Genome imprinting may explain why, for example, children who inherit Huntington's disease from their fathers are far more likely to be affected at an early age than children who inherit the Huntington's gene from their mothers (Sapienza, 1990).

A particularly dramatic example of genome imprinting appea[r...] girls and young women with Turner syndrome, in which an X ch[...] missing (refer back to Table 3-3). Those who had received their sing[...] some from their fathers were better adjusted socially and had strong[...] cognitive skills than those who had received the X chromosome fro[...] ers. This suggests that social competence is influenced by an impr[...] genes on the X chromosome, which is "turned off" when that chrom[...] from the mother (Skuse et al., 1997).

Genetic Counseling

Genetic counseling can help prospective parents assess their risk o[...] dren with genetic or chromosomal defects. People who have alreac[...] with a genetic defect, who have a family history of hereditary illne[...] from conditions known or suspected to be inherited, or who com[...] groups at higher-than-average risk of passing on genes for certair[...] get information about their likelihood of producing affected childr[...]

A genetic counselor may be a pediatrician, an obstetrician, a family doctor, a nurse, or a genetic specialist. She or he takes a family history and gives the prospective parents and any biological children physical examinations. Laboratory investigations of blood, skin, urine, or fingerprints may be performed. Chromosomes from body tissues may be analyzed and photographed, and the photographs enlarged and arranged according to size and structure on a chart called a *karyotype.* This chart can show chromosomal abnormalities and can indicate whether a person who appears normal might transmit genetic defects to a child (see Figure 3-7). The counselor tries to help clients understand the mathematical risk of a particular condition, explains its implications, and presents information about alternative courses of action.

Geneticists have made great contributions to avoidance of birth defects. For example, since so many Jewish couples have been tested for Tay-Sachs genes, far fewer Jewish babies have been born with the disease; in fact, it is now far more likely to affect non-Jewish babies (Kaback et al., 1993). Similarly, screening and counseling of women of childbearing age from Mediterranean countries, where beta thalassemia (refer back to Table 3-1) is common, has brought a decline in births of affected babies and greater knowledge of the risks of being a carrier (Cao, Saba, Galanello, & Rosatelli, 1997).

CHECKPOINT

Can you . . .

- ✔ Compare the operation of dominant inheritance, recessive inheritance, sex-linked inheritance, and genome imprinting in transmission of birth defects?
- ✔ Tell at least three ways in which chromosomal disorders can occur?
- ✔ Explain the purposes of genetic counseling?

Consider this . . .

- Should genetic counseling be made compulsory for all people wanting to get married or for people in certain categories? Give reasons.
- Would you want to know that you had a gene predisposing you to lung cancer? To Alzheimer's disease? Would you want your child to be tested for these genes?
- If you or your partner were pregnant and either of you had a family history of a birth disorder, would you want to know your baby's chances of being born with it?

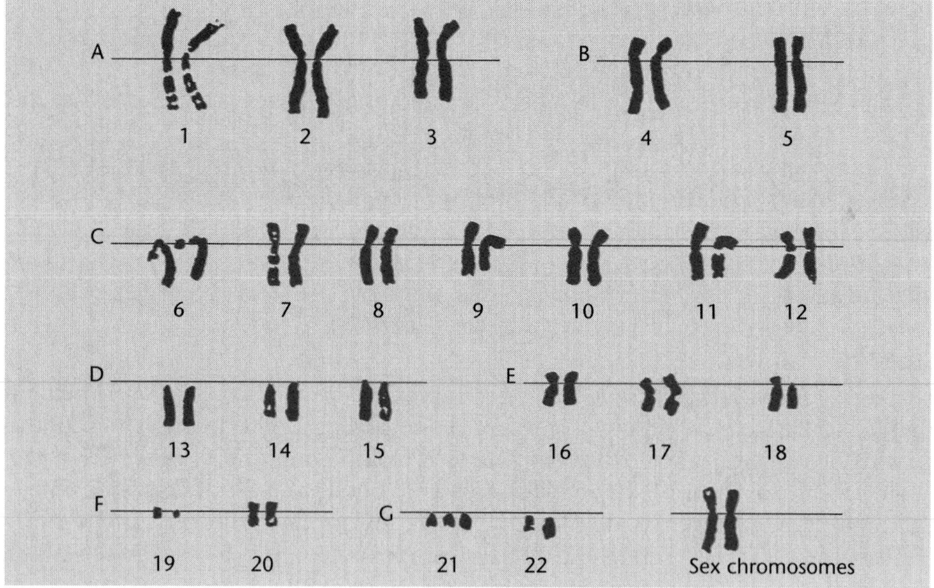

Figure 3-7

A karyotype is a chart that shows the chromosomes when they are separated and aligned for cell division. We know that this is a karyotype of a person with Down syndrome, because there are three chromosomes instead of the usual two on chromosome 21. Since pair 23 consists of two X's, we know that this is the karyotype of a female.

Source: Babu & Hirschhorn, 1992; March of Dimes Birth Defects Foundation, 1987.

genetic testing
Procedure for ascertaining a person's genetic makeup for purposes of identifying predispositions to specific hereditary diseases or disorders.

Today, researchers are rapidly identifying genes that contribute to many serious diseases and disorders, as well as those that influence normal traits. Their work is likely to lead to widespread **genetic testing** to reveal genetic profiles—a prospect that involves dangers as well as benefits (see Box 3-2).

Nature and Nurture: Influences of Heredity and Environment

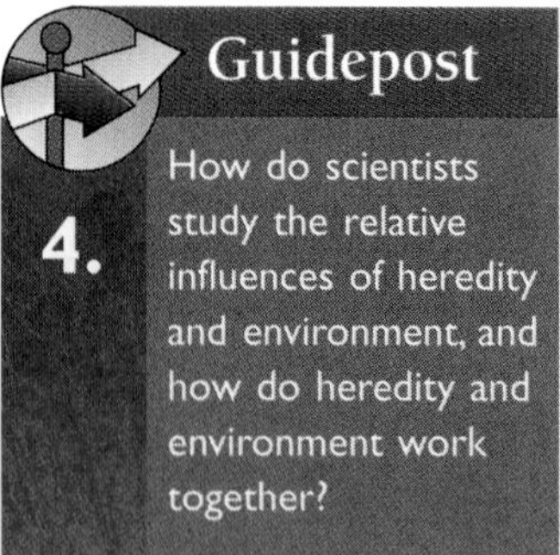

Guidepost

4. How do scientists study the relative influences of heredity and environment, and how do heredity and environment work together?

Which is more important, nature or nurture? The answer varies. While certain rare physical disorders are virtually 100 percent inherited, phenotypes for most complex normal traits having to do with health, intelligence, and personality are subject to both hereditary and environmental forces. Let's see how scientists study and explain the influences of heredity and environment.

Studying Heredity and Environment

As genes that govern specific traits are identified, it becomes possible to observe and measure their effects (Plomin & Rutter, 1998). Meanwhile, researchers in **behavioral genetics,** the quantitative study of relative hereditary and environmental influences, rely chiefly on three types of correlational research: family, adoption, and twin studies.

behavioral genetics
Quantitative study of relative hereditary and environmental influences.

heritability
Statistical estimate of contribution of heredity to individual differences in a specific trait within a given population.

Heritability is a statistical estimate of how great a contribution heredity makes toward individual differences in a specific trait at a certain time *within a given population.* Heritability does *not* refer to the relative influence of heredity and environment in a particular individual; those influences may be virtually impossible to separate. Nor does heritability tell us how traits develop. It merely indicates the statistical extent to which genes contribute to a trait.

Heritability is expressed as a percentage ranging from zero to 100 percent; the greater the percentage, the greater the heritability of a trait. Researchers usually measure heritability by calculating the incidence of a trait, or the degree of similarity for that trait, in members of the same family, in monozygotic twins as

Box 3-2

Genetic Testing and Genetic Engineering

What are your chances of developing colon cancer or Alzheimer's disease, or another genetically influenced condition? Genetic testing is becoming more common as scientists find ways to identify people genetically at risk to develop a variety of diseases and disorders.

The Human Genome Project, a $3 billion research effort under the joint leadership of the National Institutes of Health and the U.S. Department of Energy, is designed to map the chromosomal locations of all the estimated 60,000 to 100,000 human genes and identify those that cause or trigger particular disorders. The project is expected to be completed by 2003.

The genetic information gained from such research could save many lives and improve the quality of many others by increasing our ability to predict, control, treat, and cure disease. A person who learns of a genetic predisposition to lung cancer might be motivated to stop smoking. A woman who has a genetic tendency to breast cancer might be advised to undergo earlier and more frequent breast examinations. Already, genetic screening of newborns is saving lives and preventing mental retardation by permitting identification and treatment of infants with sickle cell anemia or phenylketonuria (Holtzman, Murphy, Watson, & Barr, 1997). Genetic information can help people decide whether to have children and with whom. It also may allow more time to plan what to do in the event of illness or death (Post, 1994).

Gene therapy (repairing or replacing abnormal genes) is already an option for some rare genetic disorders and eventually will be possible *in utero* (Anderson, 1998). In utero gene therapy could head off a disorder and might prove more efficient than starting treatment after birth, when symptoms appear (Zanjani & Anderson, 1999). However, the prospect of human gene transfer experiments raises ethical concerns about safety, benefit to participants, and the difficulty of obtaining meaningful informed consent (Sugarman, 1999).

Genetic testing itself involves ethical issues. For one thing, predictions are imperfect; a false positive result may cause needless anxiety, while a false negative result may delude a person into complacency. And what if a genetic condition is incurable? Is there any point in knowing you have the gene for a potentially debilitating condition if you cannot do anything about it (Holtzman et al., 1997)? A panel of experts has recommended against genetic testing for diseases for which there is no known cure (Institute of Medicine [IOM], 1993). On the other hand, some people who have family histories of a disease might be relieved once they know the worst that is likely to happen (Wiggins et al., 1992).

What about privacy? Although medical data are supposed to be confidential, it is almost impossible to keep such information private. And do parents, children, or siblings have a legitimate claim to information about a patient that may affect them? (Plomin & Rutter, 1998; Rennie, 1994).

A major concern is *genetic determinism:* the misconception that a person with a gene for a disease is bound to get the disease. All that genetic testing can tell us is the likelihood that a person will get a disease. Most diseases involve a complex combination of genes or depend in part on lifestyle or other environmental factors (Plomin & Rutter, 1998). Is it fair to use a genetic profile to deny employment to a currently healthy person? Job and insurance discrimination on the basis of genetic information has already occurred—even though tests may be imprecise and unreliable and people deemed at risk of a disease may never develop it (Lapham, Kozma, & Weiss, 1996).

Some states have passed laws prohibiting job or insurance discrimination on the basis of genetic information and/or denying employers access to such information. The federal Equal Employment Opportunity Commission (EEOC) has stated that genetically based job discrimination violates the Americans with Disabilities Act. The Health Insurance Portability and Accountability Act of 1996 prohibits group health insurance plans from using genetic information to establish eligibility or from treating such information as a preexisting condition, in the absence of a diagnosis. However, existing federal laws do not protect privacy or restrict access to genetic information (Rothenberg et al., 1997).

Specific issues have to do with testing of children. Whose decision should it be to have a child tested—the parent's or the child's? Should a child be tested to benefit a sibling or someone else? How will a child be affected by learning that he or she is likely to develop a disease twenty, thirty, or fifty years later? Will the child grow up thinking "There's something wrong with me"? Will parents who learn that a child has a gene for an incurable disease become overprotective? (Wertz, Fanos, & Reilly, 1994) Or will they be afraid to become too attached to a child who may die young (Marshall, 1993)? If testing shows that a presumed biological father is not really the father of the child, should that information be disclosed? To whom, and with what results? (Plomin & Rutter, 1998; Voelker, 1993).

A particularly chilling prospect is that results of genetic testing could be misused to justify sterilization of people with "undesirable" genes. Prospective parents might decide to abort a normal fetus with the "wrong" genetic makeup (Plomin & Rutter, 1998). Gene therapy, for all its prospective benefits, also has the potential for abuse. Should such therapy be used to reverse baldness? To make a short child taller, or a chubby child thinner? To improve an unborn baby's appearance or intelligence? The path from therapeutic correction of defects to genetic engineering for cosmetic or functional purposes may well be a slippery slope (Anderson, 1998), leading to a society in which some parents could afford to provide the "best" genes for their children while others could not (Rifkin, 1998).

Within the next fifteen years, genetic testing and gene therapy "will almost certainly revolutionize the practice of medicine" (Anderson, 1998, p. 30). It is not yet clear whether the benefits of these new biotechnologies will outweigh the risks.

Monozygotic twins separated at birth are sought after by researchers who want to study the impact of genes on personality. These twins, adopted by different families and not reunited till age 31, both became firefighters. Was this a coincidence, or did it reflect the influence of heredity?

compared with dizygotic twins, or in adopted children as compared with their adoptive and biological parents or siblings.

Such studies are based on the assumption that immediate family members are more genetically similar than more distant relatives, monozygotic twins are more genetically similar than dizygotic twins, and children are genetically more like their biological families than their adoptive families. Thus, if heredity is an important influence on a particular trait, siblings should be more alike than cousins with regard to that trait, monozygotic twins should be more alike than dizygotic twins, and adoptive children should be more like their biological parents than their adoptive parents. By the same token, if a shared environment exerts an important influence on a trait, persons who live together should be more similar than persons who do *not* live together.

In *family studies,* researchers measure the degree to which biological relatives share certain traits and whether the closeness of the familial relationship is associated with the degree of similarity. If the correlation is strong, the researchers can infer a genetic influence. However, family studies cannot rule out environmental influences. A family study alone cannot tell us whether obese children of obese parents inherited the tendency or whether they are fat because their diet is like that of their parents. For that reason, researchers do adoption studies, which can separate the effects of heredity from those of a shared environment.

Adoption studies look at similarities between adopted children and their adoptive families and also between adopted children and their biological families. When adopted children are more like their biological parents and siblings in a particular trait (say, obesity), we see the influence of heredity. When they resemble their adoptive families more, we see the influence of environment.

Studies of twins compare pairs of monozygotic twins and same-sex dizygotic twins. (Same-sex twins are used so as to avoid any confounding effects of gender.) Monozygotic twins are twice as genetically similar, on average, as dizygotic twins, who are no more genetically similar than other same-sex siblings. When monozygotic twins are more **concordant** (that is, have a statistically greater tendency to show the same trait) than dizygotic twins, we see the likely effects of heredity. Concordance rates, which may range from zero to 100 percent, tell what percentage of pairs of twins in a sample are concordant, or similar.

When monozygotic twins show higher concordance for a trait than dizygotic twins, the likelihood of a genetic factor can be studied further through adoption studies. Studies of monozygotic twins separated in infancy and reared apart have found strong resemblances between the twins. Such findings support a hereditary basis for many physical and psychological characteristics.

Consider this . . .

- In what ways are you more like your mother and in what ways like your father? How are you similar and dissimilar to your siblings? Which differences would you guess come chiefly from heredity and which from environment?

concordant
Term describing twins who share the same trait or disorder.

Still, the effects of genetic influences, especially on behavioral traits, are rarely inevitable: even in a trait strongly influenced by heredity, the environment can have substantial impact. As we'll see in the next section, behavioral genetics has thrown a spotlight on the *kinds* of environmental factors that make the most difference.

Two newer types of twin studies—*co-twin control* and *chorion control* studies—allow researchers to look at the nature and timing of nongenetic influences in the womb (Phelps, Davis, & Schartz, 1997). *Co-twin control studies* compare the prenatal (or postnatal) development and experiences of one monozygotic twin with those of the other, who serves as a one-person "control group." *Chorion control studies* focus on prenatal influences by comparing two types of monozygotic twins: (1) *monochorionic* twins, who developed within the same fluid-filled sac and thus had a similar prenatal environment, and (2) *dichorionic* twins, who grew within separate sacs, as about one-third of monozygotic twins, like all dizygotic twins, do.

Monochorionic twins normally share blood and have similar hormonal levels, which affect brain development. They also share exposure to any infectious agents that come from the mother's body. Because dichorionic twins are attached to different parts of the uterine wall, one twin may be better nourished than the other and better protected against infection. Twin studies that do not take account of these factors may either underestimate or overestimate genetic influences. Monochorionic twins tend to be more concordant than dichorionic twins in IQ, certain personality patterns, and cholesterol levels.

CHECKPOINT

Can you . . .

- ✔ State the basic assumption underlying studies of behavioral genetics and how it applies to family studies, twin studies, and adoption studies?
- ✔ Identify two types of twin studies that focus on environmental influences in the womb?

How Heredity and Environment Work Together

In contrast to the classic nature-versus-nurture argument, most developmental scientists today see the relationship between genetic and environmental factors as fundamentally intertwined. Let's consider several ways in which heredity and environment work together.

Reaction Range and Canalization

Many characteristics vary, within genetic limits, under varying environmental conditions. The concepts of *reaction range* and *canalization* can help us visualize how this happens.

Reaction range is a range of potential expressions of a hereditary trait. Body size, for example, depends largely on biological processes, which are genetically regulated. Even so, a range of sizes is possible, depending on environmental opportunities and constraints and a person's own behavior. In societies in which nutrition has dramatically improved, an entire generation has grown up to tower over the generation before. The better-fed children share their parents' genes but have responded to a healthier world. Once a society's average diet becomes adequate for more than one generation, however, children tend to grow to heights similar to their parents'. Ultimately, height has genetic limits: we don't see people who are only a foot tall, or any who are 10 feet tall.

reaction range
Potential variability, depending on environmental conditions, in the expression of a hereditary trait.

Heredity can influence whether a reaction range is wide or narrow. For example, a child born with a defect producing mild retardation is more able to respond to a favorable environment than a child born with severe limitations. A child of normal native intelligence is likely to have a higher IQ if raised in an enriched home and school environment than if raised in a more restrictive environment; but a child with more native ability will probably have a much wider reaction range (see Figure 3-8).

The metaphor of **canalization** illustrates how heredity restricts the range of development for some traits. After a heavy storm, the rainwater that has fallen on a pavement has to go somewhere. If the street has potholes, the water will fill them. If deep canals have been dug along the edges of the street, the water will flow into the canals instead. Some human characteristics, such as eye color, are so strongly programmed by the genes that they are said to be highly canalized: there is little opportunity for variance in their expression.

canalization
Limitation on variance of expression of certain inherited characteristics.

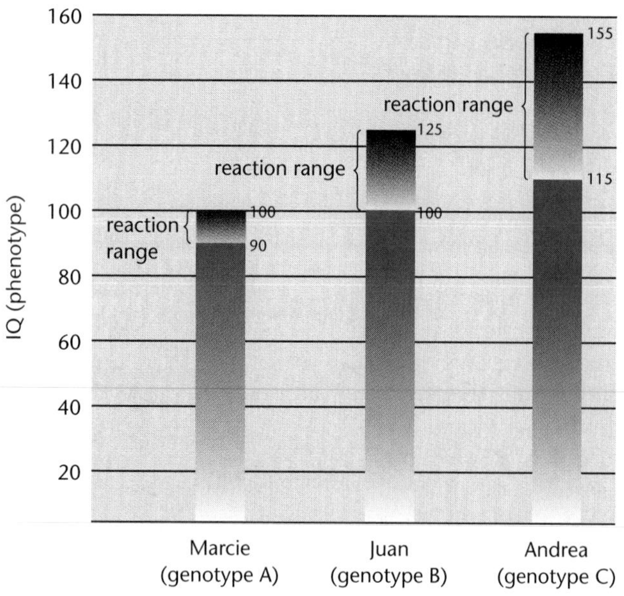

Figure 3-8

Intelligence and reaction range. Children with different genotypes for intelligence will show varying reaction ranges when exposed to a restricted (blue portion of bar) or enriched (entire bar) environment.

Certain behaviors also develop along genetically "dug" channels; it takes an extreme change in environment to alter their course. Behaviors that depend largely on maturation seem to appear when a child is ready. Normal babies follow a typical sequence of motor development: crawling, walking, and running, in that order, at certain approximate ages. Still, this development is not completely canalized; experience can affect its pace and timing.

Cognition and personality are more subject to variations in experience: the kinds of families children grow up in, the schools they attend, and the people they encounter. Consider language. Before children can talk, they must reach a certain level of neurological and muscular maturation. No 6-month-old could speak this sentence, no matter how enriched the infant's home life might be. Yet environment does play a large part in language development. If parents encourage babies' first sounds by talking back to them, children are likely to start to speak earlier than if their early vocalizing is ignored. Heredity, then, lays the foundation for development, but environment affects the form of the structure and the pace at which construction proceeds.

Genotype-Environment Interaction

genotype-environment interaction
The portion of phenotypic variation that results from the reactions of genetically different individuals to similar environmental conditions.

Whereas reaction range and canalization affect the expression of the same *hereditary* trait under varying environmental conditions, **genotype-environment interaction** refers to the effects of similar *environmental* conditions on genetically different individuals. To take a familiar example, many people are exposed to pollen and dust, but people with a genetic predisposition are more likely to develop allergic reactions. Thus it may take the interaction of hereditary and environmental factors, not just one or the other, to produce certain conditions.

Genotype-Environment Correlation

genotype-environment correlation
Tendency of certain genetic and environmental influences to reinforce each other; may be passive, reactive (evocative), or active. Also called *genotype-environment covariance.*

The environment often reflects or reinforces genetic differences. That is, certain genetic and environmental influences tend to act in the same direction. This is called **genotype-environment correlation,** or *genotype-environment covariance,* and it works in three ways to strengthen the phenotypic expression of a genotypic tendency (Bergeman & Plomin, 1989; Scarr, 1992; Scarr & McCartney, 1983):

- *Passive correlations:* Generally parents, who provide the genes that predispose a child toward a trait, also provide an environment that encourages the development of that trait. For example, a musical parent is likely to create a home environment in which music is heard regularly, to give a child music lessons, and to take the child to musical events. If the child inherited the parent's musical talent, the child's musicality will reflect a combination of genetic and environmental influences. This type of correlation is called *passive* because the child does not control it; it is most applicable to young children, whose parents, the source of their genetic legacy, also have a great deal of control over their early experiences.

- *Reactive, or evocative, correlations:* Children with differing genetic makeups evoke different responses from adults. Parents may make a special effort to provide musical experiences to a child who shows interest and ability in music. This response, in turn, strengthens the child's genetic inclination toward music.

Musical ability is one of many characteristics passed on from parents to children through a combination of genetic and environmental influences. This father playing the guitar with his daughter may be more motivated to do so because she shows interest and ability in music. In turn, the enjoyable experience with her father is likely to strengthen the little girl's natural inclination toward music.

- *Active correlations:* As children get older and have more freedom to choose their own activities and environments, they actively select or create experiences consistent with their genetic tendencies. A child with a talent for music will probably seek out musical friends, take music classes, and go to concerts. A shy child is likely to spend more time in solitary pursuits than an outgoing youngster. This tendency to seek out environments compatible with one's genotype is called **niche-picking;** it helps explain why identical twins reared apart tend to be quite similar.

niche-picking
Tendency of a person, especially after early childhood, to seek out environments compatible with his or her genotype.

What Makes Siblings So Different? The Nonshared Environment

Although two children in the same family may bear a striking physical resemblance to each other, siblings tend to be more different than alike in intellect and especially in personality (Plomin, 1989). One reason, of course, may be genetic differences, which lead children to respond differently to a similar environment. A child with a high IQ may be more stimulated by a roomful of books and puzzles than a child with a markedly lower IQ—an example of genotype-environment interaction. Surprisingly, though, the family environment itself seems to make siblings more different—as different, in fact, as any two unrelated children! Apparently, the experiences that strongly affect development are not those that are similar for all children in a family, but those that are different (Plomin & Daniels, 1987).

These **nonshared environmental effects** result from the unique environment in which each child in a family grows up. What factors contribute to this nonshared environment? One is family composition—the differences between boys' and girls' experiences, or between those of firstborns and laterborns. Another is the way parents and siblings treat each child. Certain events, such as illnesses and accidents, and experiences outside the home (for example, with teachers and peers) affect one child and not another. While heredity accounts for most of the similarity between siblings, the nonshared environment accounts for most of the difference. Indeed, a great deal of research across the life span suggests that most of the variability in behavioral traits in the population as a whole is environmental, but of the nonshared type (McClearn et al., 1997; Plomin, 1996; Plomin & Daniels, 1987; Plomin, Owen, & McGuffin, 1994).

nonshared environmental effects
The unique environment in which each child grows up, consisting of distinctive influences or influences that affect one child differently than another.

CHECKPOINT

Can you . . .

- ✔ Explain and give at least one example of reaction range, canalization, genotype-environment interaction, and genotype-environment correlation?
- ✔ List three kinds of influences that contribute to nonshared environmental effects?
- ✔ Explain the meaning of the phrase, "genes drive experience"?

Genotype-environment correlations may play an important role in the nonshared environment. Children's genetic differences may lead parents and siblings to react to them differently and treat them differently; and genes may influence how children perceive and respond to that treatment, and what its outcome will be. Children also mold their own environments by the choices they make—what they do and with whom—and their genetic makeup influences these choices. In other words, "genes drive experience" (Scarr & McCartney, 1983, p. 425). A child who has inherited artistic talent may spend a great deal of time creating "masterpieces" in solitude, while a sibling who is athletically inclined spends more time playing ball with others. Thus, not only will the children's abilities (in, say, painting or soccer) develop differently, but their social lives will be different as well. These differences tend to be accentuated as children grow older and have more experiences outside the family (Bergeman & Plomin, 1989; Bouchard, 1994; Plomin, 1990, 1996; Plomin et al., 1994; Scarr, 1992; Scarr & McCartney, 1983).

Some Characteristics Influenced by Heredity and Environment

Keeping in mind the complexity of unraveling the influences of heredity and environment, let's look more closely at their roles in producing certain characteristics.

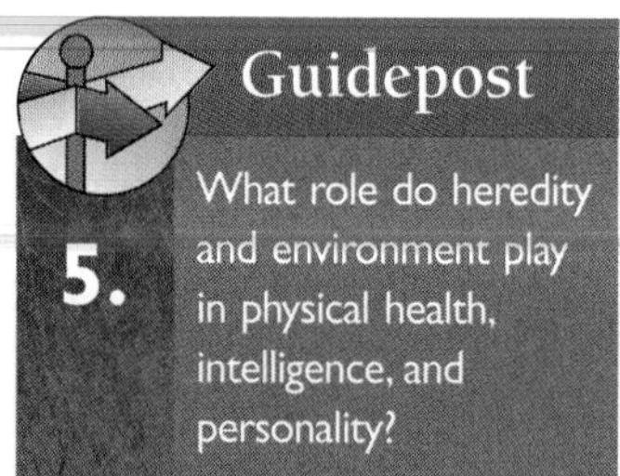

Guidepost
5.
What role do heredity and environment play in physical health, intelligence, and personality?

Physical and Physiological Traits

Not only do monozygotic twins generally look alike; they are also more concordant than dizygotic twins in their risk for such medical disorders as hypertension (high blood pressure), heart disease, stroke, rheumatoid arthritis, peptic ulcers, and epilepsy (Brass, Isaacsohn, Merikangas, & Robinette, 1992; Plomin et al., 1994).

obesity
Extreme overweight in relation to age, sex, height, and body type; sometimes defined as having a body mass index (weight-for-height) at or above the 85th or 95th percentile of growth curves for children of the same age and sex.

Obesity—extreme overweight, variously defined in childhood as having a body mass index (comparison of weight to height) at or above the 85th or 95th percentile for age and sex—is a multifactorial condition. Twin studies, adoption studies, and other research suggest that as much as 80 percent of the risk of obesity is genetic (Leibel, 1997). In genetic mapping, as many as 200 genes and other genetic markers have been linked with obesity so far (Pérusse, Chagnon, Weisnagel, & Bouchard, 1999). However, the kind and amount of food eaten in a particular home or in a particular social or ethnic group, and the amount of exercise that is encouraged, can increase or decrease the likelihood that a person will become obese. The rapid rise in the prevalence of obesity in western countries seems to result from the interaction of a genetic predisposition with inadequate exercise (Leibel, 1997; see chapter 9).

Our days on earth seem to be greatly affected by our genes. In one study, adopted children whose biological parents had died before age 50 were twice as likely to have died young themselves as adopted children whose biological parents had lived past 49 (Sorensen, Nielsen, Andersen, & Teasdale, 1988). Still, sound health and fitness practices can increase longevity by tempering predispositions toward certain illnesses, such as cancer and heart disease.

Intelligence

Heredity seems to exert a strong influence on general intelligence and also on specific abilities (McClearn et al., 1997; Plomin et al., 1994). Heritability of IQ is generally estimated at .50, meaning that genes account for about half of the measured variation in intelligence within a population. Still, experience counts, too; an enriched or impoverished environment can substantially affect the development and expression of innate ability (Neisser et al., 1996). Apparently, many genes, each with its own small effect, combine to establish a range of possible reactions to a range of possible experiences (Scarr, 1997a; Weinberg, 1989; refer back to Figure 3-8).

An analysis of 212 studies (Devlin, Daniels, & Roeder, 1997) points to the impact of the earliest environment: the womb. According to this analysis, the prenatal environment may account for 20 percent of the similarity in IQ between twins and 5 percent of the similarity in nontwin siblings (who occupy the same womb at different times), bringing heritability of IQ down to *below* 50 percent. These findings suggest that the influence of genes on intelligence may be weaker, and the influence of the prenatal environment stronger, than was previously thought, underlining the importance of a healthy prenatal environment. The possibility that prenatal intervention could raise the average IQ of the population is a fascinating one. However, just what aspects of the prenatal environment are most influential is as yet unclear.

Personality

Specific aspects of personality appear to be inherited, at least in part. Analyses of five major groupings of traits discussed in Chapter 14—extraversion, neuroticism, conscientiousness, agreeableness, and openness to experience—suggest a heritability of about 40 percent. Setting aside variances attributable to measurement error brings heritability closer to 66 percent for these trait groupings (Bouchard, 1994).

Temperament (discussed in detail in Chapter 6) appears to be largely inborn and is often consistent over the years, though it may respond to special experiences or parental handling (A. Thomas & Chess, 1984; A. Thomas, Chess, & Birch, 1968). An observational study of 100 pairs of 7-year-old siblings (half of them adoptive siblings and half siblings by birth) found significant genetic influences on activity, sociability, and emotionality (Schmitz, Saudino, Plomin, Fulker, & DeFries, 1996).

A large body of research strongly suggests that shyness and its opposite, boldness, are largely inborn and tend to stay with a person throughout life. Jerome Kagan, a professor of psychology at Harvard University, and his colleagues have studied about 400 children longitudinally, starting in infancy (Arcus & Kagan, 1995; DiLalla, Kagan, & Reznick, 1994; Garcia-Coll, Kagan, & Reznick, 1984; Kagan, 1989, 1997; Kagan, Reznick, Clarke, Snidman, & Garcia-Coll, 1984; Kagan, Reznick, & Gibbons, 1989; Reznick et al., 1986; Robinson, Kagan, Reznick, & Corley, 1992). Shyness, or what these researchers call "inhibition to the unfamiliar," was present to a marked degree in about 15 percent of the children, first showing up in infancy and persisting in most cases until at least early adolescence. Another 10 to 15 percent were uncommonly bold (comfortable in strange situations). These personality characteristics were associated with physiological signs, such as hormonal and brain activity, which may give clues to the heritability of the traits.

Although the research discussed so far provides strong evidence of genetic influences on personality, this evidence is indirect. Now scientists have begun to identify genes directly linked with specific personality traits. One of these genes has been found to play a part in *neuroticism,* a group of traits involving anxiety, which may contribute to depression. An estimated 10 to 15 other genes also may be involved in anxiety (Lesch et al., 1996).

Consider this . . .

- What practical difference does it make whether a trait such as obesity, intelligence, or shyness is influenced more by heredity or by environment, since heritability can be measured only for a population, not for an individual?

Psychopathology

There is evidence for a strong hereditary influence on schizophrenia, autism, alcoholism, and depression. (The latter two are discussed later in this book.) All tend to run in families and to show greater concordance between monozygotic twins than between dizygotic twins. However, heredity alone does not produce such disorders; an inherited tendency can be triggered by environmental factors.

schizophrenia
Mental disorder marked by loss of contact with reality; symptoms include hallucinations and delusions.

Schizophrenia, a disorder marked by loss of contact with reality and by such symptoms as hallucinations and delusions, seems to have a strong genetic component. The risk of schizophrenia is ten times as great among siblings and offspring of schizophrenics as among the general population; and twin and adoption studies suggest that this increased risk comes from shared genes, not shared environments. The estimated genetic contribution is between 63 and 85 percent (McGuffin, Owen, & Farmer, 1995).

However, since not all monozygotic twins are concordant for the illness, its cause cannot be purely genetic. Co-twin studies suggest that a prenatal viral infection, carried in the blood shared by monochorionic twins, may play a part (Phelps et al., 1997). In a study of the incidence of schizophrenia among all persons born in Denmark between 1935 and 1978, family history was associated with the highest risk of having the illness, but place of birth also made a difference. People born in urban areas were more likely to be schizophrenic than those born in rural areas, perhaps because of greater likelihood of birth complications and of exposure to infections during pregnancy and childhood (Mortenson et al., 1999).

autism
Pervasive developmental disorder characterized by lack of normal sociability, impaired communication, and repetitive, obsessive behaviors.

Autism is one of a group of severe *pervasive developmental disorders;* it is characterized by lack of normal sociability, impaired communication, and a restricted, narrow range of repetitive, often obsessive behaviors, such as spinning, rocking, hand-flapping, and head-banging. It develops within the first $2^1/_2$ years, mostly in boys, and it continues to varying degrees throughout life (American Psychiatric Association [APA], 1994).

An autistic baby may fail to notice the emotional signals of others (Sigman, Kasari, Kwon, & Yirmiya, 1992) and may refuse to cuddle or make eye contact. About 3 out of 4 autistic children are mentally retarded (APA, 1994), but they often do well on tests of manipulative or visual-spatial skill and may perform unusual mental feats, such as memorizing entire train schedules.

Autism is a biological disorder of brain functioning (Rapin, 1997). It seems to have a strong genetic basis; concordance between monozygotic twins is more than 90 percent, as compared with 5 to 10 percent among same-sex dizygotic twins (Bailey, Le Couteur, Gottesman, & Bolton, 1995). A gene that regulates serotonin, a brain chemical, seems to be related to autism (Cook et al., 1997).

Autism has no known cure, but improvement, sometimes substantial, does occur. Some autistic children can be taught to speak, read, and write. Behavior therapy (see Chapter 2) can help autistic children learn such basic social skills as paying attention, sustaining eye contact, and feeding and dressing themselves and can help control problem behaviors. Drugs may help to manage specific symptoms, but their usefulness is limited. Only about 5 to 10 percent of autistic children grow up to live independently; most need some degree of care throughout life ("Autism–Part II," 1997; Rapin, 1997).

CHECKPOINT

Can you . . .

✔ Assess the evidence for genetic and environmental influences on obesity, intelligence, and temperament?

✔ Name and describe two mental disorders that show a strong genetic influence?

Prenatal Development

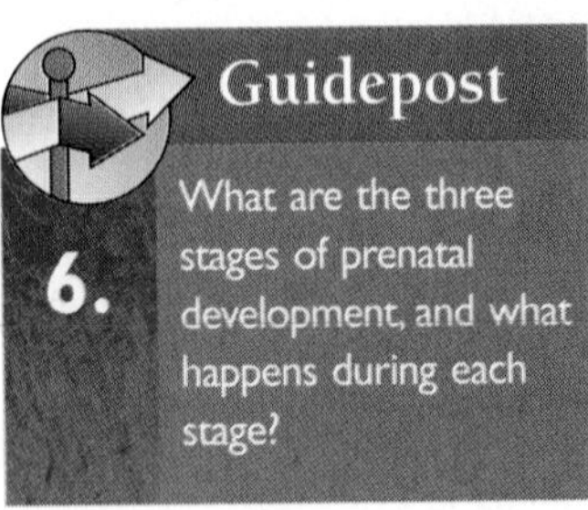

Guidepost
6.
What are the three stages of prenatal development, and what happens during each stage?

If you had been born in China, you would probably celebrate your birthday on your estimated date of conception rather than your date of birth. This Chinese custom recognizes the importance of *gestation,* the approximately 9-month (or 266-day) period of development between conception and birth. Scientists, too, date *gestational age* from conception.

What turns a fertilized ovum, or *zygote,* into a creature with a specific shape and pattern? Research suggests that an identifiable group of genes is responsible for this transformation in vertebrates, presumably including human beings. These genes produce molecules called *morphogens,* which are switched on after fertilization and begin sculpting arms, hands, fingers, vertebrae, ribs, a brain, and other body parts (Echeland et al., 1993; Kraus, Concordet, & Ingham, 1993; Riddle,

Johnson, Laufer, & Tabin, 1993). Scientists are also learning about the environment inside the womb and how it affects the developing person.

In this section we trace the course of gestation, or prenatal development. We discuss environmental factors that can affect the developing person-to-be, assess techniques for determining whether development is proceeding normally, and explain the importance of prenatal care.

Stages of Prenatal Development

Prenatal development takes place in three stages: *germinal, embryonic,* and *fetal.* (Table 3-4 gives a month-by-month description.) During these three stages of gestation, the original single-celled zygote grows into an *embryo* and then a *fetus.* Both before and after birth, development proceeds according to two fundamental principles. Growth and motor development occur from top down and from the center of the body outward.

cephalocaudal principle
Principle that development proceeds in a head-to-tail direction; that is, that upper parts of the body develop before lower parts.

The **cephalocaudal principle** (from Latin, meaning "head to tail") dictates that development proceeds from the head to the lower part of the trunk. An embryo's head, brain, and eyes develop earliest and are disproportionately large until the other parts catch up. At 2 months of gestation, the embryo's head is half the length of the body. By the time of birth, the head is only one-fourth the length of the body but is still disproportionately large. According to the **proximodistal principle** (from Latin, "near to far"), development proceeds from parts near the center of the body to outer ones. The embryo's head and trunk develop before the limbs, and the arms and legs before the fingers and toes.

proximodistal principle
Principle that development proceeds from within to without; that is, that parts of the body near the center develop before the extremities.

Germinal Stage (Fertilization to 2 Weeks)

During the **germinal stage,** from fertilization to about 2 weeks of gestational age, the zygote divides, becomes more complex, and is implanted in the wall of the uterus (see Figure 3-9).

germinal stage
First 2 weeks of prenatal development, characterized by rapid cell division, increasing complexity and differentiation, and implantation in the wall of the uterus.

Within 36 hours after fertilization, the zygote enters a period of rapid cell division and duplication, or mitosis. Seventy-two hours after fertilization, it has divided into 16 to 32 cells; a day later it has 64 cells. This division continues until the original single cell has developed into the 800 billion or more specialized cells that make up the human body.

While the fertilized ovum is dividing, it is also making its way down the fallopian tube to the uterus, a journey of 3 or 4 days. Its form changes into a fluid-filled sphere, a *blastocyst,* which floats freely in the uterus for a day or two and then begins to implant itself in the uterine wall. As cell differentiation begins, some cells around the edge of the blastocyst cluster on one side to form the *embryonic disk,* a thickened cell mass from which the embryo begins to develop. This mass is already differentiating into two layers. The upper layer, the *ectoderm,* will become the outer layer of skin, the nails, hair, teeth, sensory organs, and the nervous system, including the brain and spinal cord. The lower layer, the *endoderm,* will become the digestive system, liver, pancreas, salivary glands, and respiratory system. Later a middle layer, the *mesoderm,* will develop and differentiate into the inner layer of skin, muscles, skeleton, and excretory and circulatory systems.

Other parts of the blastocyst begin to develop into organs that will nurture and protect the unborn child: the *placenta,* the *umbilical cord,* and the *amniotic sac* with its outermost membrane, the *chorion.* The *placenta,* which has several important functions, will be connected to the embryo by the *umbilical cord.* Through this cord the placenta delivers oxygen and nourishment to the developing baby and removes its body wastes. The placenta also helps to combat internal infection and gives the unborn child immunity to various diseases. It produces the hormones that support pregnancy, prepare the mother's breasts for lactation, and eventually stimulate the uterine contractions that will expel the baby from the

Table 3-4 Prenatal Development

Month	Description 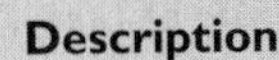
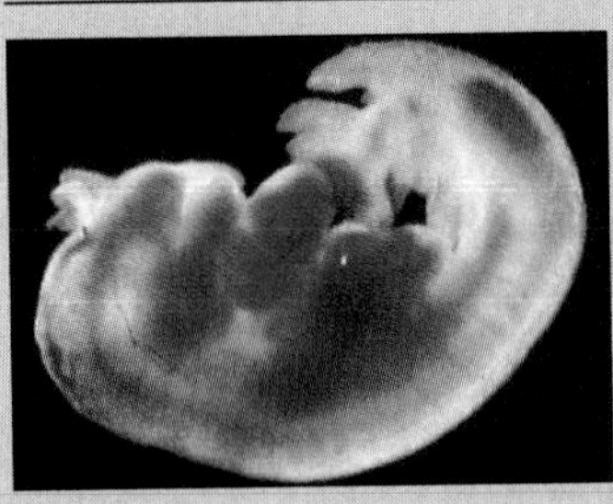 1 month	During the first month, growth is more rapid than at any other time during prenatal or postnatal life; the embryo reaches a size 10,000 times greater than the zygote. By the end of the first month, it measures about $1/2$ inch in length. Blood flows through its veins and arteries, which are very small. It has a miniscule heart, beating 65 times a minute. It already has the beginning of a brain, kidneys, liver, and digestive tract. The umbilical cord, its lifeline to the mother, is working. By looking very closely through a microscope, it is possible to see the swellings on the head that will eventually become eyes, ears, mouth, and nose. Its sex cannot yet be determined.
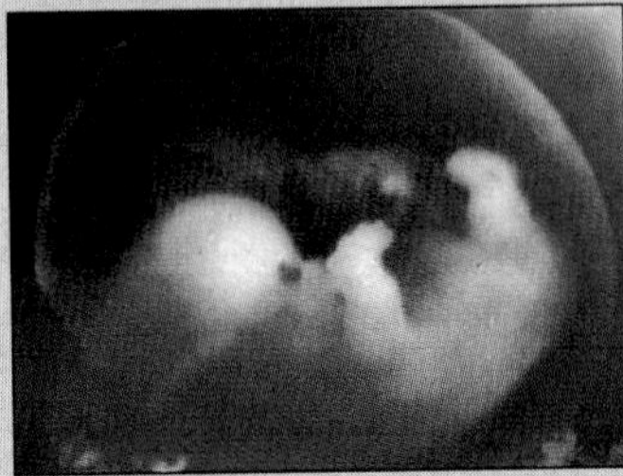 7 weeks	By the end of the second month, the organism is less than 1 inch long and weighs only $1/3$ ounce. Its head is half its total body length. Facial parts are clearly developed, with tongue and teeth buds. The arms have hands, fingers, and thumbs, and the legs have knees, ankles, and toes. It has a thin covering of skin and can make handprints and footprints. Bone cells appear at about 8 weeks. Brain impulses coordinate the function of the organ system. Sex organs are developing; the heartbeat is steady. The stomach produces digestive juices; the liver, blood cells. The kidneys remove uric acid from the blood. The skin is now sensitive enough to react to tactile stimulation. If an aborted 8-week-old fetus is stroked, it reacts by flexing its trunk, extending its head, and moving back its arms.
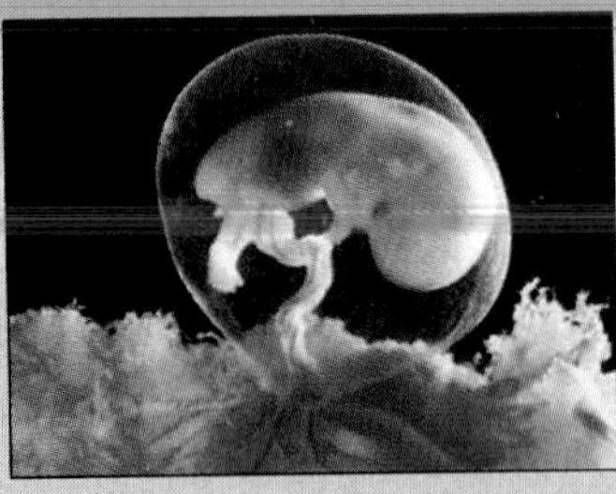 3 months	By the end of the third month, the fetus weighs about 1 ounce and measures about 3 inches in length. It has fingernails, toenails, eyelids (still closed), vocal cords, lips, and a prominent nose. Its head is still large—about one-third its total length—and its forehead is high. Sex can easily be determined. The organ systems are functioning, and so the fetus may now breathe, swallow amniotic fluid into the lungs and expel it, and occasionally urinate. Its ribs and vertebrae have turned into cartilage. The fetus can now make a variety of specialized responses; it can move its legs, feet, thumbs, and head; its mouth can open and close and swallow. If its eyelids are touched, it squints; if its palm is touched, it makes a partial fist; if its lip is touched, it will suck; and if the sole of the foot is stroked, the toes will fan out. These reflexes will be present at birth but will disappear during the first months of life.
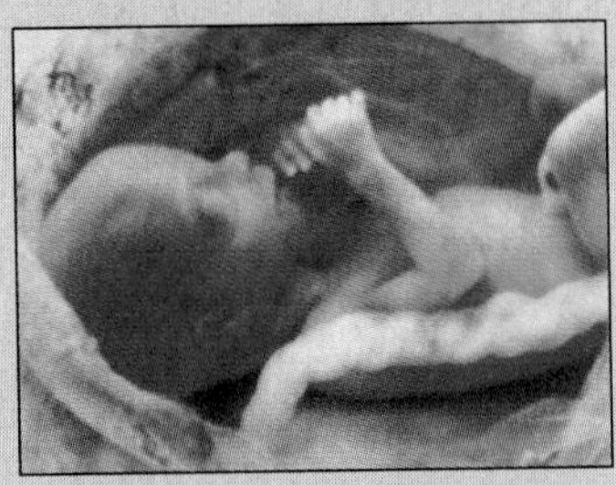 4 months	The body is catching up to the head, which is now only one-fourth the total body length, the same proportion it will be at birth. The fetus now measures 8 to 10 inches and weighs about 6 ounces. The umbilical cord is as long as the fetus and will continue to grow with it. The placenta is now fully developed. The mother may be able to feel the fetus kicking, a movement known as *quickening,* which some societies and religious groups consider the beginning of human life. The reflex activities that appeared in the third month are now brisker because of increased muscular development.
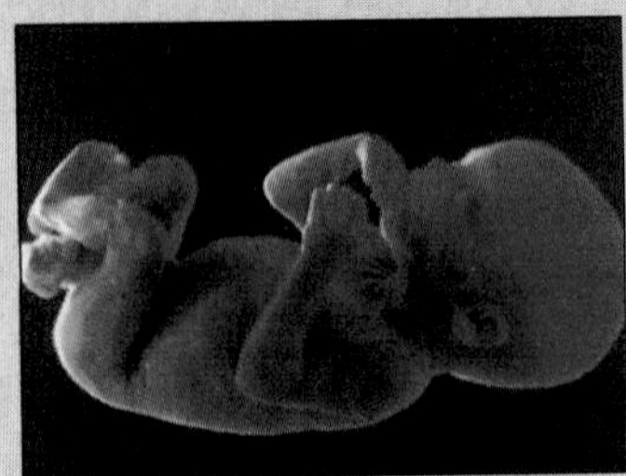 5 months	The fetus, now weighing about 12 ounces to 1 pound and measuring about 1 foot, begins to show signs of an individual personality. It has definite sleep-wake patterns, has a favorite position in the uterus (called its *lie*), and becomes more active—kicking, stretching, squirming, and even hiccuping. By putting an ear to the mother's abdomen, it is possible to hear the fetal heartbeat. The sweat and sebaceous glands are functioning. The respiratory system is not yet adequate to sustain life outside the womb; a baby born at this time does not usually survive. Coarse hair has begun to grow for eyebrows and eyelashes, fine hair is on the head, and a woolly hair called *lanugo* covers the body.

Month	Description
 6 months	The rate of fetal growth has slowed down a little—by the end of the sixth month, the fetus is about 14 inches long and weighs $1\frac{1}{4}$ pounds. It has fat pads under the skin; the eyes are complete, opening, closing, and looking in all directions. It can hear, and it can make a fist with a strong grip. A fetus born during the sixth month still has only a slight chance of survival, because the breathing apparatus has not matured. However, some fetuses of this age do survive outside the womb.
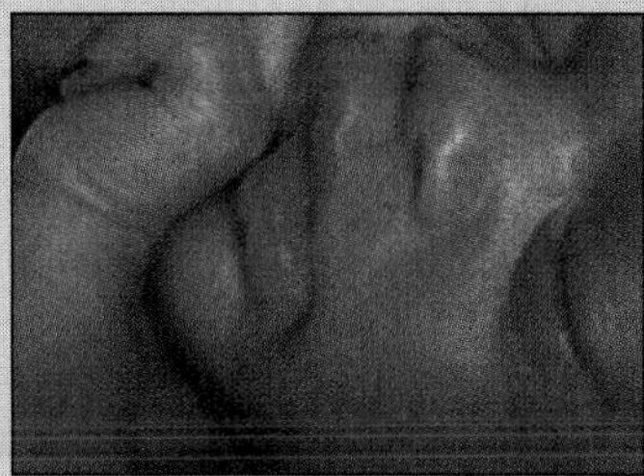 7 months	By the end of the seventh month, the fetus, about 16 inches long and weighing 3 to 5 pounds, now has fully developed reflex patterns. It cries, breathes, swallows, and may suck its thumb. The lanugo may disappear at about this time, or it may remain until shortly after birth. Head hair may continue to grow. The chances that a fetus weighing at least $3\frac{1}{2}$ pounds will survive are fairly good, provided it receives intensive medical attention. It will probably need to be kept in an isolette until a weight of 5 pounds is attained.
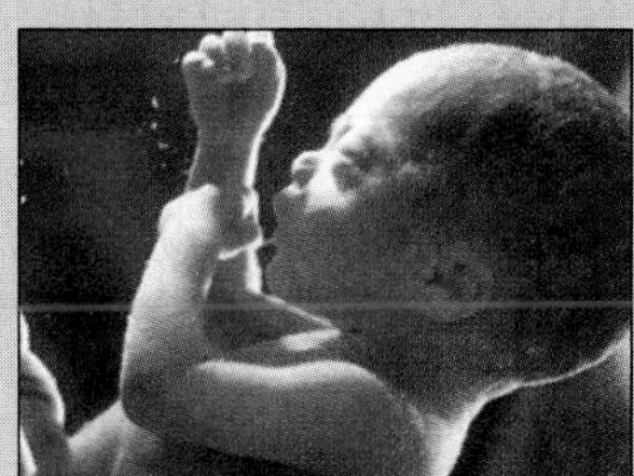 8 months	The 8-month-old fetus is 18 to 20 inches long and weighs between 5 and 7 pounds. Its living quarters are becoming cramped, and so its movements are curtailed. During this month and the next, a layer of fat is developing over the fetus's entire body, which will enable it to adjust to varying temperatures outside the womb.
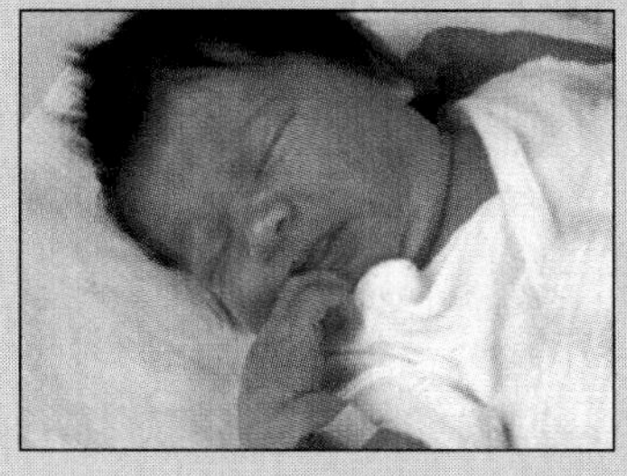 9 months–newborn	About a week before birth, the fetus stops growing, having reached an average weight of about $7\frac{1}{2}$ pounds and a length of about 20 inches, with boys tending to be a little longer and heavier than girls. Fat pads continue to form, the organ systems are operating more efficiently, the heart rate increases, and more wastes are expelled through the umbilical cord. The reddish color of the skin is fading. At birth, the fetus will have been in the womb for about 266 days, although gestational age is usually estimated at 280 days because most doctors date the pregnancy from the mother's last menstrual period.

Note: Even in these early stages, individuals differ. The figures and descriptions given here represent averages.

mother's body. The *amniotic sac* is a fluid-filled membrane that encases the developing baby, protecting it and giving it room to move. The *trophoblast,* the outer cell layer of the blastocyst (which becomes part of the placenta), produces tiny threadlike structures that penetrate the lining of the uterine wall and enable the developing organism to cling there until it is fully implanted in the uterine lining.

Only about 10 percent to 20 percent of fertilized eggs complete the crucial task of implantation and continue to develop. Researchers have now identified a gene called *Hoxa10,* which appears to control whether an embryo will be successfully implanted in the uterine wall (Taylor, Arici, Olive, & Igarashi, 1998).

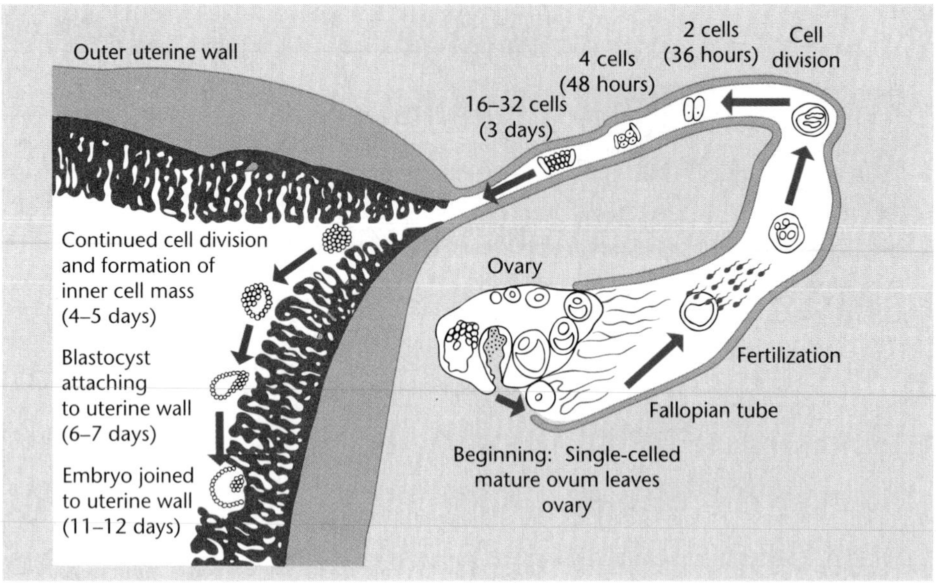

Figure 3-9
Early development of a human embryo. This simplified diagram shows the progress of the ovum as it leaves the ovary, is fertilized in the fallopian tube, and then divides while traveling to the lining of the uterus. Now a blastocyst, it is implanted in the uterus, where it will grow larger and more complex until it is ready to be born.

Embryonic Stage (2 to 8 Weeks)

embryonic stage
Second stage of gestation (2 to 8 weeks), characterized by rapid growth and development of major body systems and organs.

During the **embryonic stage,** the second stage of gestation, from about 2 to 8 weeks, the organs and major body systems—respiratory, digestive, and nervous—develop rapidly. This is a critical period, when the embryo is most vulnerable to destructive influences in the prenatal environment (see Figure 3-10). An organ system or structure that is still developing at the time of exposure is most likely to be affected. Defects that occur later in pregnancy are likely to be less serious.

spontaneous abortion
Natural expulsion from the uterus of a conceptus that cannot survive outside the womb; also called *miscarriage*.

The most severely defective embryos usually do not survive beyond the first *trimester,* or 3-month period, of pregnancy. A **spontaneous abortion,** commonly called a *miscarriage,* is the expulsion from the uterus of an embryo or fetus that is unable to survive outside the womb. Most miscarriages result from abnormal pregnancies; about 50 to 70 percent involve chromosomal abnormalities.

Males are more likely than females to be spontaneously aborted or *stillborn* (dead at birth). Thus, although about 125 males are conceived for every 100 females—a fact that has been attributed to the greater mobility of sperm carrying the smaller Y chromosome—only 106 boys are born for every 100 girls. Males' greater vulnerability continues after birth: more of them die early in life, and at

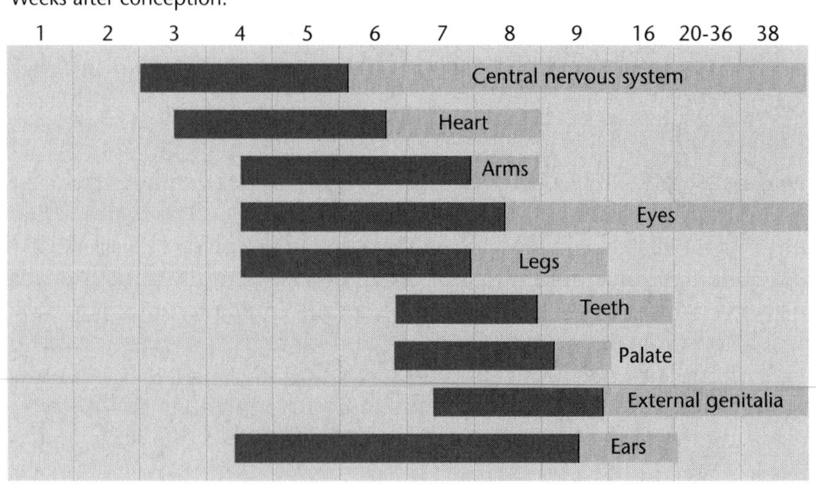

Figure 3-10
When birth defects occur. Body parts and systems are most vulnerable to damage when they are developing most rapidly (darkly shaded areas), generally within the first trimester of pregnancy. *Note:* Intervals of time are not all equal.
(Source: J. E. Brody, 1995; data from March of Dimes.)

every age they are more susceptible to many disorders. As a result, there are only 96 males for every 100 females in the United States (U.S. Department of Health and Human Services [USDHHS], 1996a). Furthermore, the proportion of male births appears to be falling in the United States, Canada, and several European countries, while the incidence of birth defects among males is rising, perhaps reflecting effects of environmental pollutants (Davis, Gottlieb, and Stampnitzky, 1998).

Fetal Stage (8 Weeks to Birth)

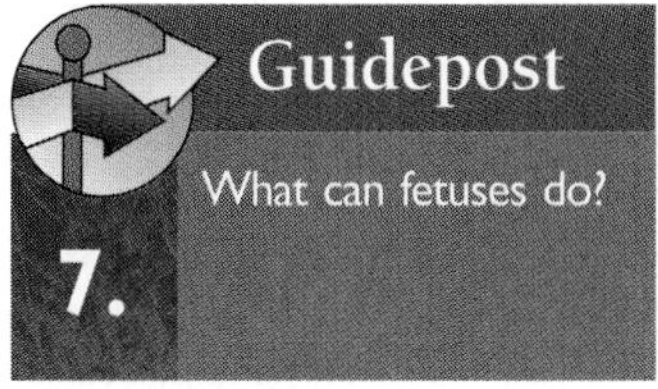
Guidepost
What can fetuses do?
7.

The appearance of the first bone cells at about 8 weeks signals the **fetal stage,** the final stage of gestation. During this period, the fetus grows rapidly to about 20 times its previous length, and organs and body systems become more complex. Right up to birth, "finishing touches" such as fingernails, toenails, and eyelids develop.

fetal stage
Final stage of gestation (from 8 weeks to birth), characterized by increased detail of body parts and greatly enlarged body size.

ultrasound
Prenatal medical procedure using high-frequency sound waves to detect the outline of a fetus and its movements, so as to determine whether a pregnancy is progressing normally.

Fetuses are not passive passengers in their mothers' wombs. They breathe, kick, turn, flex their bodies, do somersaults, squint, swallow, make fists, hiccup, and suck their thumbs. The flexible membranes of the uterine walls and amniotic sac, which surround the protective buffer of amniotic fluid, permit and even stimulate limited movement.

Scientists can observe fetal movement through **ultrasound,** using high-frequency sound waves to detect the outline of the fetus. Other instruments can monitor heart rate, changes in activity level, states of sleep and wakefulness, and cardiac reactivity. In one study, fetuses monitored from 20 weeks of gestation until term had increasingly slower but more variable heart rates—possibly in response to the increasing stress of the mother's pregnancy—and greater cardiac response to stimulation. They also showed less, but more vigorous, activity—perhaps a result of the increasing difficulty of movement for a growing fetus in a constricted environment, as well as of maturation of the nervous system. A significant "jump" in all these aspects of fetal development seems to occur between 28 and 32 weeks; it may help explain why infants born prematurely at this time are more likely to survive and flourish than those born earlier (DiPietro, Hodgson, Costigan, Hilton, & Johnson, 1996).

The movements and activity level of fetuses show marked individual differences, and their heart rates vary in regularity and speed. There also are differences between males and females. Male fetuses, regardless of size, are more active and tend to move more vigorously than female fetuses throughout gestation. Thus infant boys' tendency to be more active than girls may be at least partly inborn (DiPietro, Hodgson, Costigan, Hilton, & Johnson, 1996).

Beginning at about the 12th week of gestation, the fetus swallows and inhales some of the amniotic fluid in which it floats. The amniotic fluid contains substances that cross the placenta from the mother's bloodstream and enter the fetus's own bloodstream. Partaking of these substances may stimulate the budding senses of taste and smell and may contribute to the development of organs needed for breathing and digestion (Mennella & Beauchamp, 1996a; Ronca & Alberts, 1995; Smotherman & Robinson, 1995, 1996). Mature taste cells appear at about 14 weeks of gestation. The olfactory system, which controls the sense of smell, also is well developed before birth (Bartoshuk & Beauchamp, 1994; Mennella & Beauchamp, 1996a).

Fetuses respond to the mother's voice and heartbeat and the vibrations of her body, showing that they can hear and feel. Familiarity with the mother's voice may have a basic survival function: to help newborns locate the source of food. Hungry infants, no matter on which side they are held, turn toward the breast in the direction from which they hear the mother's voice (Noirot & Algeria, 1983, cited in Rovee-Collier, 1996). Responses to sound and vibration seem to begin at 26 weeks of gestation, rise, and then reach a plateau at about 32 weeks (Kisilevsky, Muir, & Low, 1992).

CHECKPOINT

Can you . . .

- ✔ Identify two principles that govern physical development and give examples of their application during the prenatal period?
- ✔ Describe how a zygote becomes an embryo?
- ✔ Explain why defects and miscarriages are most likely to occur during the embryonic stage?
- ✔ Describe findings about fetal activity, sensory development, and memory?

Fetuses seem to learn and remember. In one experiment, 3-day-old infants sucked more on a nipple that activated a recording of a story their mother had frequently read aloud during the last 6 weeks of pregnancy than on nipples that activated recordings of two other stories. Apparently, the infants recognized the story they had heard in the womb. A control group, whose mothers had not recited a story before birth, responded equally to all three recordings (DeCasper & Spence, 1986). Similar experiments have found that newborns 2 to 4 days old prefer musical and speech sequences heard before birth. They also prefer their mother's voice to those of other women, female voices to male voices, and their mother's native language to another language (DeCasper & Fifer, 1980; DeCasper & Spence, 1986; Fifer & Moon, 1995; Lecanuet et al., 1995; Moon, Cooper, & Fifer, 1993).

How do we know that these preferences develop before rather than after birth? Newborns were given the choice of sucking to turn on a recording of the mother's voice or a "filtered" version of her voice as it might sound in the womb. The newborns sucked more often to turn on the filtered version, suggesting that fetuses develop a preference for the kinds of sounds they hear before birth (Fifer & Moon, 1995; Moon & Fifer, 1990).

Environmental Influences: The Mother's Role

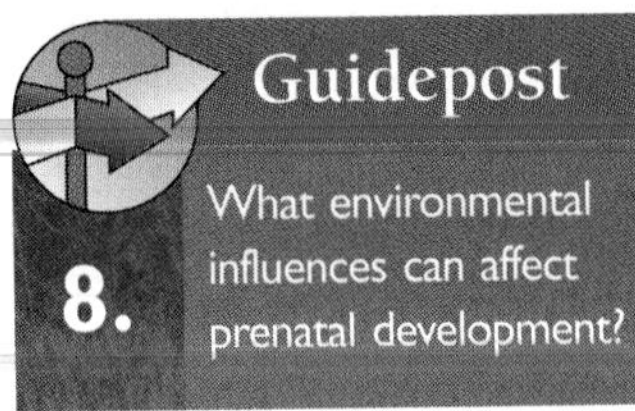
Guidepost
8.
What environmental influences can affect prenatal development?

teratogenic
Capable of causing birth defects.

Since the prenatal environment is the mother's body, virtually everything that impinges on her well-being, from her diet to her moods, may alter her unborn child's environment and affect its growth.

Not all environmental hazards are equally risky for all fetuses. Some factors that are **teratogenic** (birth defect-producing) in some cases have little or no effect in others. The timing of exposure to a teratogen, its intensity, and its interaction with other factors may be important (refer back to Figure 3-10).

Vulnerability may depend on a gene either in the fetus or in the mother. For example, fetuses with a particular variant of a growth gene, called *transforming growth factor alpha,* have six times more risk than other fetuses of developing a cleft palate if the mother smokes while pregnant, and almost nine times more risk if she smokes more than 10 cigarettes a day (Hwang et al., 1995). Women without the abnormal allele who smoke at least 20 cigarettes a day are at heightened risk of having babies with cleft palates, but their risk is even greater if the abnormal gene is present (Shaw, Wasserman, et al., 1996).

Nutrition

Women need to eat more than usual when pregnant: typically, 300 to 500 more calories a day, including extra protein (Winick, 1981). Pregnant women who gain between 22 and 46 pounds are less likely to miscarry or to bear babies who are stillborn or whose weight at birth is dangerously low (Abrams & Parker, 1990).

Malnutrition during fetal growth may have long-range effects. In rural Gambia, in western Africa, people born during the "hungry" season, when foods from the previous harvest are badly depleted, are ten times more likely to die in early adulthood than people born during other parts of the year (Moore et al., 1997). Psychiatric examinations of Dutch military recruits whose mothers had been exposed to wartime famine during pregnancy suggest that severe prenatal nutritional deficiencies in the first or second trimesters affect the developing brain, increasing the risk of antisocial personality disorders at age 18 (Neugebauer, Hoek, & Susser, 1999).

Malnourished women who take dietary supplements while pregnant tend to have bigger, healthier, more active, and more visually alert infants (J. L. Brown, 1987; Vuori et al., 1979); and women with low zinc levels who take daily zinc supplements are less likely to have babies with low birthweight and small head circumference (Goldenberg et al., 1995). However, certain vitamins (including A, B_6, C, D, and K) can be harmful in excessive amounts. Iodine deficiency, unless corrected before the third trimester of pregnancy, can cause cretinism, which may involve severe neurological abnormalities or thyroid problems (Cao et al., 1994; Hetzel, 1994).

Only recently have we learned of the critical importance of folic acid (a B vitamin) in a pregnant woman's diet. For some time, scientists have known that China has the highest incidence in the world of babies born with the neural-tube defects anencephaly and spina bifida (refer back to Table 3-1), but it was not until the 1980s that researchers linked that fact with the timing of the babies' conception. Traditionally, Chinese couples marry in January or February and try to conceive as soon as possible. That means pregnancies often begin in the winter, when rural women have little access to fresh fruits and vegetables, important sources of folic acid.

After medical detective work established the lack of folic acid as a cause of neural-tube defects, China embarked on a massive program to give folic acid supplements to prospective mothers (Tyler, 1994). In the United States, women of childbearing age are now urged to include this vitamin in their diets even before becoming pregnant, since damage from folic acid deficiency can occur during the early weeks of gestation (American Academy of Pediatrics [AAP] Committee on Genetics, 1993; "Wellness Facts," 1999). Increasing women's folic acid consumption by just four-tenths of a milligram each day would reduce the incidence of neural-tube defects by about one-half (Daly, Kirke, Molloy, Weir, & Scott, 1995).

Obese women also risk having children with neural-tube defects. Women who, before pregnancy, weigh more than 176 pounds or have an elevated body mass index (weight compared with height) are more likely to produce babies with such defects, regardless of folate intake. Obesity also increases the risk of other complications of pregnancy, including miscarriage, stillbirth, and *neonatal death* (death during the first month of life) (Goldenberg & Tamura, 1996; G. M. Shaw, Velie, & Schaffer, 1996; Werler, Louik, Shapiro, & Mitchell, 1996).

Physical Activity

Moderate exercise does not seem to endanger the fetuses of healthy women (Carpenter et al., 1988); an expectant mother normally can continue to jog, cycle, swim, or play tennis. Regular exercise prevents constipation and improves respiration, circulation, muscle tone, and skin elasticity, all of which contribute to a more comfortable pregnancy and an easier, safer delivery.

Employment during pregnancy generally entails no special hazards. However, strenuous working conditions, occupational fatigue, and long working hours may be associated with a greater risk of premature birth (Luke et al., 1995).

The American College of Obstetrics and Gynecology (1994) recommends that women in low-risk pregnancies be guided by their own abilities and stamina. The safest course seems to be for pregnant women to exercise moderately, not pushing themselves and not raising their heart rate above 150, and to taper off at the end of each session rather than stop abruptly.

CHECKPOINT

Can you . . .

✔ Summarize recommendations concerning an expectant mother's diet and physical activity?

Drug Intake

Practically everything an expectant mother takes in makes its way to the uterus. Drugs may cross the placenta, just as oxygen, carbon dioxide, and water do. Vulnerability is greatest in the first few months of gestation, when development is most rapid. Some problems resulting from prenatal exposure to drugs can be treated if the presence of a drug can be detected early.

What are the effects of the use of specific drugs during pregnancy? Let's look first at medical drugs; then at alcohol, nicotine, and caffeine; and finally at some illegal drugs: marijuana, opiates, and cocaine.

Consider this . . .

- Thousands of adults now alive suffered gross abnormalities because, during the 1950s, their mothers took the tranquilizer thalidomide during pregnancy. As a result, the use of thalidomide was banned in the United States and some other countries. Now thalidomide has been found to be effective in treating or controlling many illnesses, from mouth ulcers to brain cancer. Should its use for these purposes be permitted even though there is a risk that pregnant women might take it?

Medical Drugs It once was thought that the placenta protected the fetus against drugs the mother took during pregnancy—until the early 1960s, when a tranquilizer called *thalidomide* was banned after it was found to have caused stunted or missing limbs, severe facial deformities, and defective organs in some 12,000 babies. The thalidomide disaster sensitized medical professionals and the public to the potential dangers of taking drugs while pregnant. Today, nearly thirty drugs have been found to be teratogenic in clinically recommended doses (Koren, Pastuszak, & Ito, 1998). Among them are the antibiotic tetracycline; certain barbiturates, opiates, and other central nervous system depressants; several hormones, including diethylstilbestrol (DES) and androgens; certain anticancer drugs, such as methotrexate; Accutane, a drug often prescribed for severe acne; and aspirin and other nonsteroidal anti-inflammatory drugs, which should be avoided during the third trimester.

Effects may not be only physical and can be long-lasting. In one study, Danish men in their thirties whose mothers had taken phenobarbitol during pregnancy (especially during the last trimester) had significantly lower verbal intelligence scores than a control group. Coming from a lower socioeconomic background or having been the product of an unwanted pregnancy tended to magnify the negative outcome, showing an interaction of environmental factors before and after birth (Reinisch, Sanders, Mortensen, Psych, & Rubin, 1995).

The American Academy of Pediatrics (AAP) Committee on Drugs (1994) recommends that *no* medication be prescribed for a pregnant or breast-feeding woman unless it is essential for her health or her child's. Pregnant women should not take over-the-counter drugs without consulting a doctor (Koren et al., 1998).

fetal alcohol syndrome (FAS) Combination of mental, motor, and developmental abnormalities affecting the offspring of some women who drink heavily during pregnancy.

Alcohol Like Abel Dorris, about 1 infant in 750 suffers from **fetal alcohol syndrome (FAS),** a combination of slowed prenatal and postnatal growth, facial and bodily malformations, and disorders of the central nervous system. Problems related to the central nervous system can include, in infancy, poor sucking response, brain-wave abnormalities, and sleep disturbances; and, throughout childhood, slow information processing, short attention span, restlessness, irritability, hyperactivity, learning disabilities, and motor impairments.

The number of children known to have FAS has increased more than sixfold since 1979, to 6.7 per 10,000 births (Centers for Disease Control and Prevention [CDC], 1995). However, it is not clear whether this represents a real increase in the number of infants with FAS or merely an increase in awareness and reporting of the problem. For every child with FAS, as many as ten others may be born with *fetal alcohol effects.* This less severe condition can include mental retardation, retardation of intrauterine growth, and minor congenital abnormalities.

Even moderate drinking may harm a fetus, increasing the risk of retarded growth (Mills, Graubard, Harley, Rhoads, & Berendes, 1984) and slow information processing (Jacobson, Jacobson, Sokol, Martier, & Ager, 1993). The more the mother drinks, the greater the effect. Moderate or heavy drinking during pregnancy seems to alter the character of a newborn's cry, an index of neurobehavioral status. (So does moderate smoking during pregnancy.) Disturbed neurological and behavioral functioning may, in turn, affect early social interaction with the mother, which is vital to emotional development (Nugent et al., 1996).

Some FAS problems recede after birth; but others, such as retardation, behavioral and learning problems, and hyperactivity, tend to persist into adulthood. Unfortunately, enriching these children's education or general environment does not seem to enhance their cognitive development (Kerns, Don, Mateer, & Streissguth, 1997; Spohr, Willms, & Steinhausen, 1993; Streissguth et al., 1991; Strömland & Hellström, 1996).

Since there is no known safe level of drinking during pregnancy, it is best to avoid alcohol from the time a woman begins *thinking* about becoming pregnant until she stops breast-feeding (AAP Committee on Substance Abuse, 1993). Sadly, despite the known health risks, alcohol use during pregnancy has increased substantially; 16.3 percent of pregnant women were alcohol users in 1995, as compared with 12.4 percent in 1991, and the rate of frequent drinking increased fourfold from 0.8 to 3.5 percent (CDC, 1997).

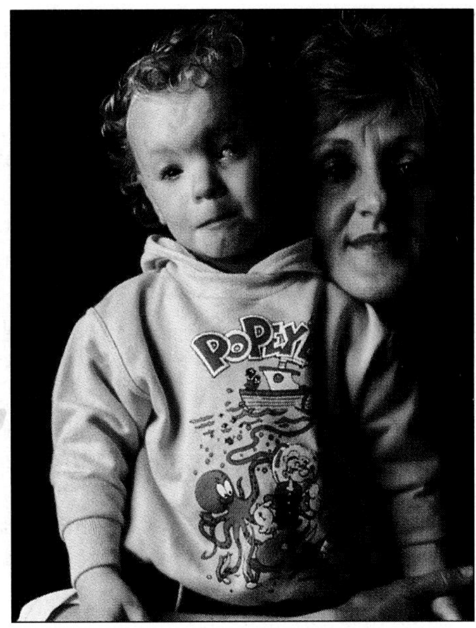

A mother who drinks during pregnancy risks having a child born with fetal alcohol syndrome, as this 4-year-old boy was.

Nicotine Cigarette smoking by pregnant women causes the deaths of an estimated 5,600 babies every year in the United States, as well as 115,000 miscarriages. Of the deaths, 1,900 are cases of *sudden infant death syndrome (SIDS),* in which an apparently healthy infant is unexpectedly found dead (see Chapter 4); the other 3,700 infants die by the age of 1 month, many of them because they are too small to survive. Smoking during pregnancy is estimated to contribute to the births of 53,000 low-birthweight babies (weighing less than 5½ pounds at birth) annually and 22,000 babies who need intensive care (DiFranza & Lew, 1995).

Since women who smoke during pregnancy also tend to smoke after giving birth, it is hard to separate the effects of prenatal and postnatal exposure. One study did this by examining 500 newborns about 48 hours after birth, while they were still in the hospital's nonsmoking maternity ward and thus had not been exposed to smoking outside the womb. Newborns whose mothers had smoked during pregnancy were shorter and lighter and had poorer respiratory functioning than babies of nonsmoking mothers (Stick, Burton, Gurrin, Sly, & LeSouëf, 1996).

A mother's smoking during pregnancy may increase her child's risk of cancer. Urine samples of infants in Düsseldorf, Germany, whose mothers had smoked while pregnant contained a cancer-causing chemical found only in tobacco; samples from infants of nonsmoking mothers did not (Lackmann et al., 1999).

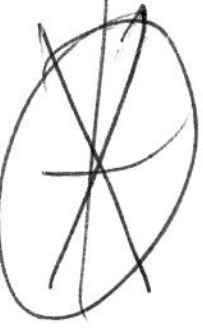

Smoking during pregnancy seems to have some of the same effects on children when they reach school age as drinking during pregnancy: poor attention span, hyperactivity, anxiety, learning and behavior problems, perceptual-motor and linguistic problems, poor IQ scores, low grade placement, and neurological problems (Landesman-Dwyer & Emanuel, 1979; Milberger, Biederman, Faraone, Chen, & Jones, 1996; Naeye & Peters, 1984; D. Olds, Henderson, & Tatelbaum, 1994a, 1994b; Streissguth et al., 1984; Wakschlag et al., 1997; Weitzman, Gortmaker, & Sobol, 1992; Wright et al., 1983). A ten-year longitudinal study of 6- to 23-year-old offspring of women who reported having smoked heavily during pregnancy found a fourfold increase in risk of conduct disorder in boys, beginning before puberty, and a fivefold increased risk of drug dependence in girls, beginning in adolescence, in comparison with young people whose mothers had not smoked during pregnancy (Weissman, Warner, Wickramaratne, & Kandel, 1999).

Unlike alcohol use, smoking during pregnancy is declining. Its prevalence fell by 26 percent between 1991 and 1996 (from almost 20 percent to 14 percent). However, for pregnant teenagers, ages 15 to 19, smoking increased to 17.2 percent in 1995 and 1996, reversing a previous decline (National Center for Health Statistics [NCHS], 1998b).

Caffeine Can the caffeine a pregnant woman swallows in coffee, tea, cola, or chocolate cause trouble for her fetus? For the most part, the answer is not clear. It does seem clear that caffeine is not a teratogen for human babies (Hinds, West, Knight, & Harland, 1996). A case-controlled study showed no effect of caffeine on low birthweight, premature birth, or retarded fetal growth (Santos, Victora, Huttly, & Carvalhal, 1998). However, caffeine consumption has been associated with spontaneous abortion (Dlugosz et al, 1996), and four or more cups of coffee a day may dramatically increase the risk of sudden infant death syndrome (Ford et al., 1998).

Marijuana Findings about marijuana use by pregnant women are mixed. Some evidence suggests that heavy use can lead to birth defects. A Canadian study found temporary neurological disturbances, such as tremors and startles, as well as higher rates of low birthweight in the infants of marijuana smokers (Fried, Watkinson, & Willan, 1984).

In Jamaica (West Indies), where marijuana use is common, an analysis of infants' cries concluded that a mother's heavy marijuana use affects her baby's nervous system (Lester & Dreher, 1989). However, in another study, 3-day-old infants of mothers who had used marijuana prenatally showed no difference from a control group of nonexposed newborns; and at 1 month, the exposed babies were more alert and sociable and less irritable (Dreher, Nugent, & Hudgins, 1994). The authors of this study suggest that rural Jamaican women who use marijuana are likely to be better educated than nonusers, to have higher income, and to have more adults living in the household and that these factors may combine to create a more favorable childrearing environment. Thus scientists cannot look at a single factor, such as marijuana use, in isolation, but must explore the cultural context in which it occurs. Still, the safest course for women of childbearing age is *not* to use marijuana.

Opiates Women addicted to morphine, heroin, and codeine are likely to bear premature, addicted babies who will be addicted to the same drugs and will suffer the effects until at least age 6. Addicted newborns are restless and irritable and often have tremors, convulsions, fever, vomiting, and breathing difficulties; they tend to die soon after birth (Cobrinick, Hood, & Chused, 1959; Henly & Fitch, 1966; Ostrea & Chavez, 1979). Those who survive cry often and are less alert and less responsive than other babies (Strauss, Lessen-Firestone, Starr, & Ostrea, 1975). In early childhood they weigh less, are shorter, are less well adjusted, and score lower on tests of perceptual and learning abilities (G. Wilson, McCreary, Kean, & Baxter, 1979). These children tend not to do well in school, to be unusually anxious in social situations, and to have trouble making friends (Householder, Hatcher, Burns, & Chasnoff, 1982).

Cocaine Official estimates of the number of cocaine-exposed infants born in the United States each year range from 45,000 to 375,000 (Lester, LaGasse, & Siefer, 1998). The effects may be more subtle than those of alcohol or some other drugs; many "cocaine babies" look like normal infants (Azar, 1997). Furthermore, cocaine's effects are difficult to isolate, since women who use it also tend to use other substances, such as alcohol and marijuana (Napiorkowski et al., 1996; Tronick, Frank, Cabral, Mirochnick, & Zuckerman, 1996).

A pregnant woman's use of cocaine is associated with a higher risk of spontaneous abortion, prematurity, low birthweight, and small head size. "Cocaine babies" are generally not as alert as other babies and not as responsive, either emotionally or cognitively; or they may be more excitable, more irritable, and less able to regulate their sleep-wake patterns (Alessandri, Sullivan, Imaizumi, & Lewis, 1993; Kliegman, Madura, Kiwi, Eisenberg, & Yamashita, 1994; Lester et al., 1991; Napiorkowski et al., 1996; Ness et al., 1999; Phillips, Sharma, Premachandra, Vaughn, & Reyes-Lee, 1996; Singer et al., 1994; Tronick et al., 1996; Zuckerman et al., 1989).

These infants may show impaired motor activity (Fetters & Tronick, 1996) or excessive activity, as well as extreme muscular tension, jerky movements, startles, tremors, and other signs of neurological stress (Napiorkowski et al., 1996). They tend to have trouble regulating attention (Mayes, Granger, Frank, Schottenfeld, & Bornstein, 1993) and emotional arousal. When interrupted, frustrated, or upset, it is hard for them to "regroup," recover, and move on. This and other evidence suggests that cocaine may affect specific regions of the developing brain that control these functions (Bendersky, Alessandri, & Lewis, 1996; Bendersky & Lewis, 1998). The more cocaine a woman takes while pregnant, the greater the odds of impaired fetal growth and neurological functioning (Chiriboga, Brust, Bateman, & Hauser, 1999).

Cocaine babies tend to have trouble participating in normal give-and-take with a caregiver. The baby's inactivity, lethargy, irritability, or unresponsiveness may frustrate the mother and prevent her from forming a close, caring relationship with her infant. On the other hand, it may be that cocaine-exposed infants do not learn to regulate and express their emotions because their cocaine-using mothers are less sensitive and responsive than other mothers (Alessandri, Sullivan, Bendersky, & Lewis, 1995; Bendersky et al., 1996; Bendersky & Lewis, 1998; Phillips et al., 1996).

Physically, some cocaine-exposed infants do recover. Especially if they had good prenatal care, they often catch up in weight, length, and head circumference by 1 year of age (Racine, Joyce, & Anderson, 1993; Weathers, Crane, Sauvain, & Blackhurst, 1993). However, deficiencies in motor control, especially hand use and eye-hand coordination, have been found at age 2 (Arendt, Angelopoulos, Salvator, & Singer, 1999). Psychosocial effects tend to last longer; cocaine-exposed children show a tendency toward such behavioral problems as aggressiveness and anxiety, especially when under stress (Azar, 1997).

Consider this . . .

- Does society's interest in protecting an unborn child justify coercive measures against pregnant women who ingest alcohol or other drugs that could harm the fetus? If so, what form should such measures take?

Exposure to *low* levels of cocaine seems to have little long-term effect on cognition, but exposure to *high* levels may lead to difficulties, especially in learning complex skills (Alessandri, Bendersky, & Lewis, 1998). Minor brain damage due to cocaine exposure may increase the number of children who fail in school and may raise special education costs in the United States by about $350 million a year (Lester, LaGasse, & Seifer, 1998).

acquired immune deficiency syndrome (AIDS)
Viral disease that undermines effective functioning of the immune system.

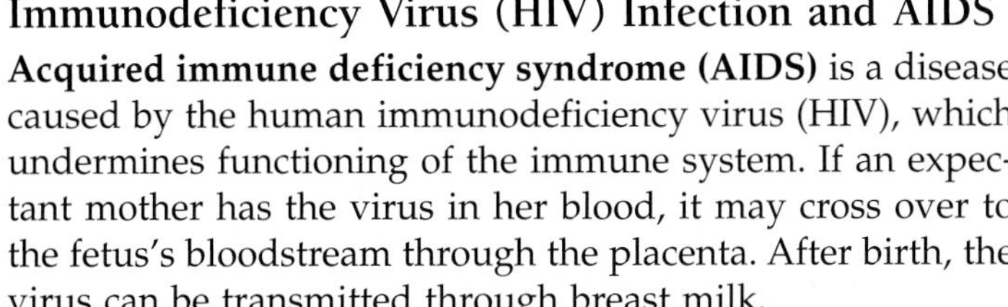

Immunodeficiency Virus (HIV) Infection and AIDS

Acquired immune deficiency syndrome (AIDS) is a disease caused by the human immunodeficiency virus (HIV), which undermines functioning of the immune system. If an expectant mother has the virus in her blood, it may cross over to the fetus's bloodstream through the placenta. After birth, the virus can be transmitted through breast milk.

Important advances have been made in the prevention, detection, and treatment of HIV infection in infants. These include the successful use of the drug zidovudine, commonly called AZT, to curtail transmission; the recognition that women with HIV should not breast-feed; and the availability of new drugs to treat AIDS-related pneumonia. Between 1992 and 1997, when zidovudine therapy became widespread, the number of babies who got AIDS from their mothers dropped by about two-thirds, raising the hope that mother-to-child transmission of the virus can be virtually eliminated (Lindegren et al., 1999). The treatment appears to have no adverse effects on uninfected children born to infected mothers (Culnane et al., 1999). The risk of transmission also can be reduced by choosing cesarean delivery (International Perinatal HIV Group, 1999).

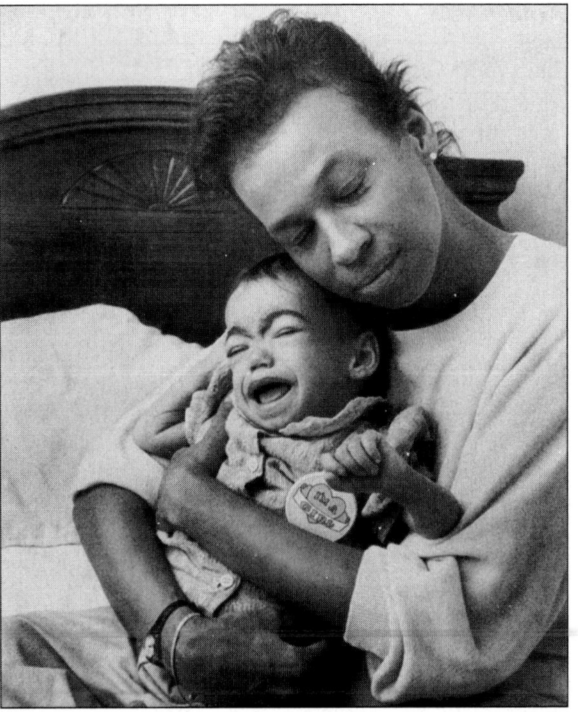

This 26-year-old mother contracted AIDS from her husband, who had gotten it from a former girlfriend, an intravenous drug user. The father died first of this modern plague, then the 21-month-old baby, and lastly the mother.

Prospects for children born with HIV infection have improved. The progress of the disease, at least in some children, seems slower than was previously thought. While some develop full-blown AIDS by their first or second birthday, others live for years without apparently being affected much, if at all (European Collaborative Study, 1994; Grubman et al., 1995; Nielsen et al., 1997; Nozyce et al., 1994). This also means, however, that infected children who appear healthy may not be diagnosed in the early stages.

Other Maternal Illnesses

Some illnesses contracted during pregnancy can have serious effects on the developing fetus. Rubella (German measles), if contracted by a woman before her 11th week of pregnancy, is almost certain to cause deafness and heart defects in her baby. Between 13 and 16 weeks of pregnancy, the chances of such effects are only about 1 in 3, and after 16 weeks, almost nil (E. Miller, Cradock-Watson, & Pollock, 1982). Such defects are rare these days, since most children are inoculated against rubella, making it unlikely that a pregnant woman will catch the disease.

Diabetes, tuberculosis, and syphilis can cause problems in fetal development, and gonorrhea and genital herpes can have harmful effects on the baby at the time of delivery. A diabetic mother's metabolic regulation, especially during the second and third trimesters of pregnancy, unless carefully managed, may affect her child's long-range neurobehavioral development and cognitive performance (Rizzo, Metzger, Dooley, & Cho, 1997). The incidence of genital herpes simplex virus (HSV) has increased among newborns. They may acquire the disease from the mother or father either at or soon after birth (Sullivan-Bolyai, Hull, Wilson, & Corey, 1983), causing blindness, other abnormalities, or death.

Both prospective parents should try to prevent all infections—common colds, flu, urinary tract and vaginal infections, and sexually transmitted diseases—whenever possible. The father can transmit an infection to the mother, which could have dire effects on the fetus. If the mother does contract an infection, she should have it treated promptly by a physician who knows she is pregnant. Pregnant women also should be screened for thyroid deficiency, which can affect their children's future cognitive performance (Haddow et al., 1999).

Maternal Age

After age 35 there is more chance of miscarriage or stillbirth, and more likelihood of premature delivery, retarded fetal growth, other birth-related complications, or birth defects. Older pregnant women are more likely to suffer complications and possibly even death due to diabetes, high blood pressure, or severe bleeding. However, the risks of delayed childbearing appear to be lower than was previously believed; most risks to the infant's health are not much greater than for babies born to younger mothers. Due to widespread screening for fetal defects among older expectant mothers, deliveries of malformed fetuses have decreased (Berkowitz, Skovron, Lapinski, & Berkowitz, 1990; P. Brown, 1993; Cunningham & Leveno, 1995; Fretts, Schmittdiel, McLean, Usher, & Goldman, 1995). (Risks of teenage pregnancy are discussed in Chapter 12.)

CHECKPOINT

Can you . . .

- ✔ Describe the short-term and long-term effects on the developing fetus of a mother's use of medical drugs, alcohol, tobacco, caffeine, marijuana, opiates, and cocaine during pregnancy?
- ✔ Summarize the risks of maternal illnesses, delayed childbearing, and exposure to chemicals and radiation?

Outside Environmental Hazards

Chemicals, radiation, extremes of heat and humidity, and other hazards of modern life can affect prenatal development. Women who work with chemicals used in manufacturing semiconductor chips have about twice the rate of miscarriage as other female workers (Markoff, 1992). Infants exposed prenatally to high levels of lead score lower on tests of cognitive abilities than those exposed to low or moderate levels (Bellinger, Leviton, Watermaux, Needleman, & Rabinowitz, 1987; Needleman & Gatsonis, 1990). Children exposed prenatally to heavy metals have higher rates of childhood illness and lower measured intelligence than children not exposed to these metals (Lewis, Worobey, Ramsay, & McCormack, 1992).

Radiation can cause genetic mutations. Nuclear radiation affected Japanese infants after the atomic bomb explosions in Hiroshima and Nagasaki (Yamazaki

& Schull, 1990) and German infants after the spill-out at the nuclear power plant at Chernobyl in the Soviet Union (West Berlin Human Genetics Institute, 1987). In utero exposure to radiation has been linked to greater risk of mental retardation, small head size, chromosomal malformations, Down syndrome, seizures, and poor performance on IQ tests and in school. The critical period seems to be 8 through 15 weeks after fertilization (Yamazaki & Schull, 1990).

Environmental Influences: The Father's Role

The father, too, can transmit environmentally caused defects. A man's exposure to lead, marijuana or tobacco smoke, large amounts of alcohol or radiation, DES, or certain pesticides may result in abnormal sperm (R. Lester & Van Theil, 1977). Fathers whose diet is low in vitamin C are more likely to have children with birth defects and certain types of cancer (Fraga et al., 1991).

A man's use of cocaine can cause birth defects in his children. The cocaine seems to attach itself to his sperm, and this cocaine-bearing sperm then enters the ovum at conception. Other toxins, such as lead and mercury, may "hitchhike" onto sperm in the same way (Yazigi, Odem, & Polakoski, 1991).

Older fathers may be a significant source of birth defects (Crow, 1993, 1995). A later paternal age (averaging in the late thirties) is associated with increases in the risk of several rare conditions, including Marfan's syndrome (deformities of the head and limbs) and dwarfism (G. Evans, 1976). Advanced age of the father may also be a factor in about 5 percent of cases of Down syndrome (Antonarakis & Down Syndrome Collaborative Group, 1991). More male cells than female ones undergo mutations, and mutations may increase with paternal age.

A father's smoking is a harmful environmental influence, which has been linked with low birthweight and an increased risk of cancer in adulthood (D. H. Rubin, Krasilnikoff, Leventhal, Weile, & Berget, 1986; Sandler, Everson, Wilcox, & Browder, 1985). In such studies, it is often hard to distinguish between prebirth and childhood exposure to smoke, and between a father's and a mother's smoking. To avoid the latter problem, researchers did a study in Shanghai, China, where many men smoke but few women do. The study found a strong connection between paternal cigarette smoking and the risk of childhood cancer, particularly acute leukemia and lymphoma (Ji et al., 1997).

Consider this . . .

- Since cocaine, marijuana, tobacco, and other substances can produce genetic abnormalities in a man's sperm, should men of childbearing age be forced to abstain from them? How could such a prohibition be enforced?

CHECKPOINT

Can you . . .

✔ Identify at least three ways in which environmentally caused defects can be influenced by the father?

Prenatal Assessment and Intervention

Not long ago, almost the only decision parents had to make about their babies before birth was the decision to conceive; most of what happened in the intervening months was beyond their control. Now we have an array of tools to assess an unborn baby's progress and well-being, and even to intervene to correct some abnormal conditions.

Guidepost 9. What techniques can assess a fetus's health and well-being, and what is the importance of prenatal care?

Ultrasound

Some parents see their baby for the first time in a *sonogram.* As we mentioned earlier, this picture of the uterus, fetus, and placenta is created by *ultrasound,* high-frequency sound waves directed into the mother's abdomen. Ultrasound provides the clearest images yet of a fetus in the womb, with little or no discomfort to the mother. Ultrasound is used to measure fetal growth, to judge gestational age, to detect multiple pregnancies, to evaluate uterine abnormalities, to detect major structural abnormalities in the fetus, and to determine whether a fetus has died, as well as to guide other procedures, such as amniocentesis. Results from ultrasound can suggest what other procedures may be needed. Ultrasound also can reveal the sex of the fetus.

The use of ultrasound is increasingly common; 64 percent of mothers who had live births used it in 1996, as compared with only 48 percent in 1989 (Ventura,

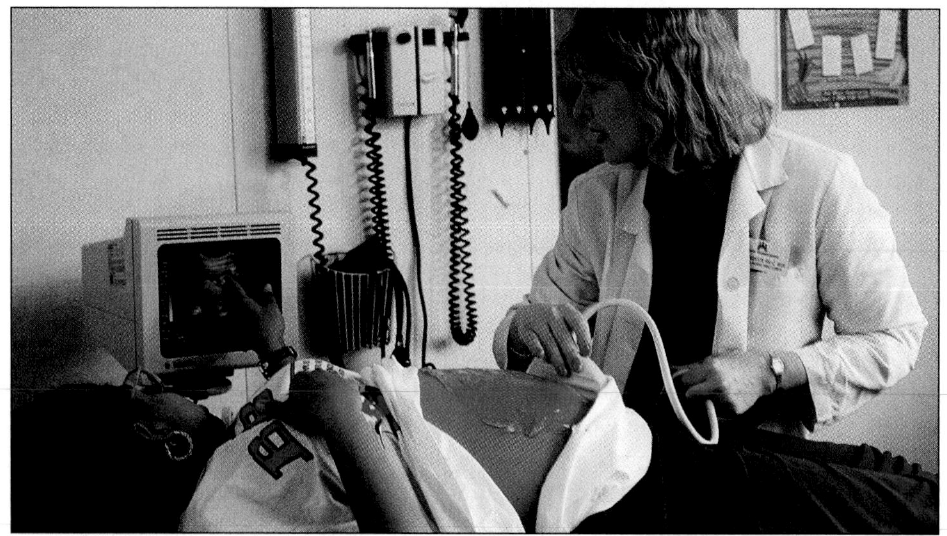

The most effective way to prevent birth complications is early prenatal care, which may include ultrasound checkups, such as this woman is having, to follow the fetus's development. Ultrasound is a diagnostic tool that presents an immediate image of the fetus in the womb.

Martin, Curtin, & Matthews, 1998). However, ultrasound screening does not appear to reduce fetal and neonatal death (Ewigman et al., 1993). Thus there seems to be no reason to use it in low-risk pregnancies, especially since some research suggests that frequently repeated ultrasound may affect fetal growth (Newnham, Evans, Michael, Stanley, & Landau, 1993).

Amniocentesis

amniocentesis
Prenatal diagnostic procedure in which a sample of amniotic fluid is withdrawn and analyzed to determine whether any of certain genetic defects are present.

In **amniocentesis,** a sample of the amniotic fluid that surrounds the fetus is withdrawn and analyzed. This fluid contains fetal cells, and its analysis enables physicians to detect the presence of certain genetic or multifactorial defects and all recognizable chromosomal disorders. Amniocentesis, like ultrasound, also can reveal the sex of the fetus, which may help in diagnosing sex-linked disorders. In some Asian countries in which sons are preferred, both procedures have been used (in some places, illegally) for "sex-screening" of unborn babies, with the result that in these populations males now predominate (Burns, 1994; Kristof, 1993; WuDunn, 1997).

Amniocentesis is much less common than ultrasound; only 3.2 percent of mothers with live births used it in 1996 (Ventura et al., 1998). It is recommended for pregnant women ages 35 and over. It is also recommended if the woman and her partner are both known carriers of such diseases as Tay-Sachs and sickle-cell anemia, or if they have a family history of such conditions as Down syndrome, spina bifida, Rh disease, and muscular dystrophy.

Amniocentesis is usually done between the 15th and 18th weeks of pregnancy. Women who have the test earlier may greatly increase their risk of miscarriage, which is more common during the first trimester. A randomized Canadian Study found a 7.6 percent rate of fetal loss when amniocentesis was done between the 11th and 12th weeks of gestation, as compared with 5.9 percent between the 15th and 16th weeks (Canadian Early and Mid-Trimester Amniocentesis Trial [CEMAT] Group, 1998).

Other Assessment Methods

chorionic villus sampling
Prenatal diagnostic procedure in which tissue from villi (hairlike projections of the membrane surrounding the fetus) is analyzed for birth defects.

In **chorionic villus sampling (CVS),** tissue from the ends of villi—hairlike projections of the chorion, the membrane surrounding the fetus, which are made up of fetal cells—are tested for the presence of birth defects and disorders. This procedure can be performed between 8 and 13 weeks of pregnancy (earlier than amniocentesis), and it yields results within about a week. However, one study found almost a 5 percent greater chance of miscarriage or neonatal death after CVS than after amniocentesis (D'Alton & DeCherney, 1993).

Embryoscopy, insertion of a tiny viewing scope into a pregnant woman's abdomen, can provide a clear look at embryos as young as 6 weeks. The procedure is promising for early diagnosis and treatment of embryonic and fetal abnormalities (Quintero, Abuhamad, Hobbins, & Mahoney, 1993).

Preimplantation genetic diagnosis can identify some genetic defects in embryos of four to eight cells, which were conceived by in vitro fertilization (see Chapter 14) and have not yet been implanted in the mother's uterus. In one study, researchers extracted and examined a single cell for cystic fibrosis (Handyside, Lesko, Tarín, Winston, & Hughes, 1992). Defective embryos were not implanted.

By inserting a needle into tiny blood vessels of the umbilical cord under the guidance of ultrasound, doctors can take samples of a fetus's blood. They can then get a blood count, examine liver function, and assess various other body functions. This procedure, called **umbilical cord sampling,** or *fetal blood sampling,* can test for infection, anemia, heart failure, and certain metabolic disorders and immunodeficiencies and seems to offer promise for identifying other conditions. However, the technique is associated with miscarriage, bleeding from the umbilical cord, early labor, and infection (Chervenak, Isaacson, & Mahoney, 1986; D'Alton & DeCherney, 1993; Kolata, 1988).

A blood sample taken from the mother between the 16th and 18th weeks of pregnancy can be tested for the amount of alpha fetoprotein (AFP) it contains. This **maternal blood test** is appropriate for women at risk of bearing children with defects in the formation of the brain or spinal cord, such as anencephaly or spina bifida, which may be detected by high AFP levels. To confirm or refute the presence of suspected conditions, ultrasound or amniocentesis, or both, may be performed.

Blood tests of samples taken between the 15th and 20th weeks of gestation can predict about 60 percent of cases of Down syndrome. The diagnosis can then be confirmed by amniocentesis. This blood test is particularly important for women under 35, who bear 80 percent of all Down syndrome babies but are not usually targeted to receive amniocentesis (Haddow et al., 1992).

The discovery that fetal cells that "leak" into the mother's blood early in pregnancy can be isolated and analyzed (Simpson & Elias, 1993) will make it possible to detect genetic as well as chromosomal disorders from a maternal blood test without using more invasive, risky procedures, such as amniocentesis, chorionic villus sampling, and fetal blood sampling. Already researchers have succeeded in screening fetal blood cells for single genes for sickle cell anemia and thalassemia (Cheung, Goldberg, & Kan, 1996).

preimplantation genetic embryoscopy
Prenatal medical procedure in which a scope is inserted in the abdomen of a pregnant woman to permit viewing of the embryo for diagnosis and treatment of abnormalities.

diagnosis
Medical procedure in which cells from an embryo conceived by in vitro fertilization are analyzed for genetic defects prior to implantation of the embryo in the mother's uterus.

umbilical cord sampling
Prenatal medical procedure in which samples of a fetus's blood are taken from the umbilical cord to assess body functioning; also called *fetal blood sampling.*

maternal blood test
Prenatal diagnostic procedure to detect the presence of fetal abnormalities, used particularly when the fetus is at risk of defects in the central nervous system.

Fetal Therapy

Conditions detected by prenatal assessment can be corrected before birth in three ways: administration of medicine, blood transfusion, and surgery. Fetuses can swallow and absorb medicines, nutrients, vitamins, and hormones that are injected into the amniotic fluid, and drugs that might not pass through the placenta can be injected through the umbilical cord. Blood can be transfused through the cord as early as the 18th week of gestation.

In 1996, surgeons successfully performed a bone marrow transplant in the womb to prevent the development of a rare, usually fatal disorder, severe combined immunodeficiency, in a fetus identified by chorionic villus sampling as having the mutant gene for it. The baby was born healthy by cesarean delivery and showed no sign of the disorder throughout infancy (Flake et al., 1996). Similar transplantation procedures may be effective in treating other congenital diseases.

CHECKPOINT

Can you . . .

- ✔ Describe seven techniques for identifying defects or disorders in an embryo or fetus and discuss their advantages and disadvantages?
- ✔ List three forms of fetal therapy?

Prenatal Care

Screening for treatable defects and diseases is only one reason for the importance of prenatal care. Early, high-quality prenatal care, which includes educational, social, and nutritional services, can help prevent maternal and infant death and other complications of birth. It can provide first-time mothers with information about pregnancy, childbirth, and infant care. Poor women who get prenatal care benefit by being put in touch with other needed services, and they are more likely to get medical care for their infants after birth (Shiono & Behrman, 1995).

Every pregnant woman in Belgium, Denmark, Germany, France, Ireland, Netherlands, Norway, Spain, Switzerland, Great Britain, and Israel is entitled to free or very low cost prenatal and postnatal care and paid maternity leave from work. In the United States, although prenatal care is widespread, its uniform national standards and guaranteed financial coverage are lacking. The percentage of pregnant women who start care during the first trimester of pregnancy and receive the recommended number of visits or more has grown steadily since the 1980s (Kogan et al., 1998; Ventura et al., 1998). Still, in 1996 almost 1 in 5 expectant mothers did not get care until after the first trimester, and 1 in 25 received no care until the last trimester or no care at all (NCHS, 1998a; Ventura et al., 1998).

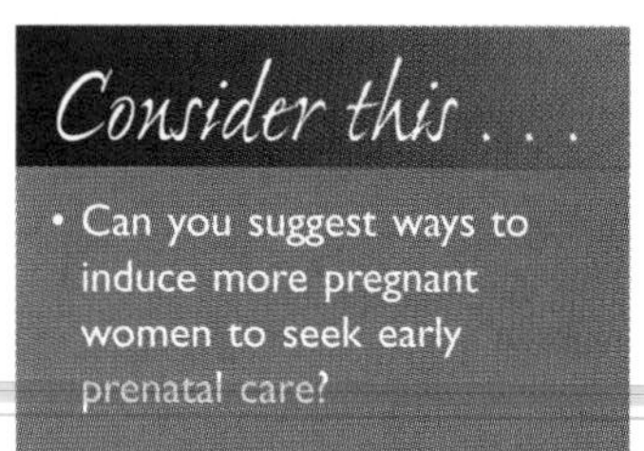

Consider this . . .
• Can you suggest ways to induce more pregnant women to seek early prenatal care?

Even as usage of prenatal care has increased, rates of low birthweight and premature birth have worsened (Kogan et al., 1998). Why? One answer is that the benefits of prenatal care are not evenly distributed. Women most at risk of bearing low-birthweight babies—teenage and unmarried women, those with little education, and some minority women—get the least prenatal care (S. S. Brown, 1985; Ingram, Makuc, & Kleinman, 1986; NCHS, 1994a, 1998a; Singh, Forrest, & Torres, 1989; USDHHS, 1996a; see Figure 3-11). And the underlying environmen-

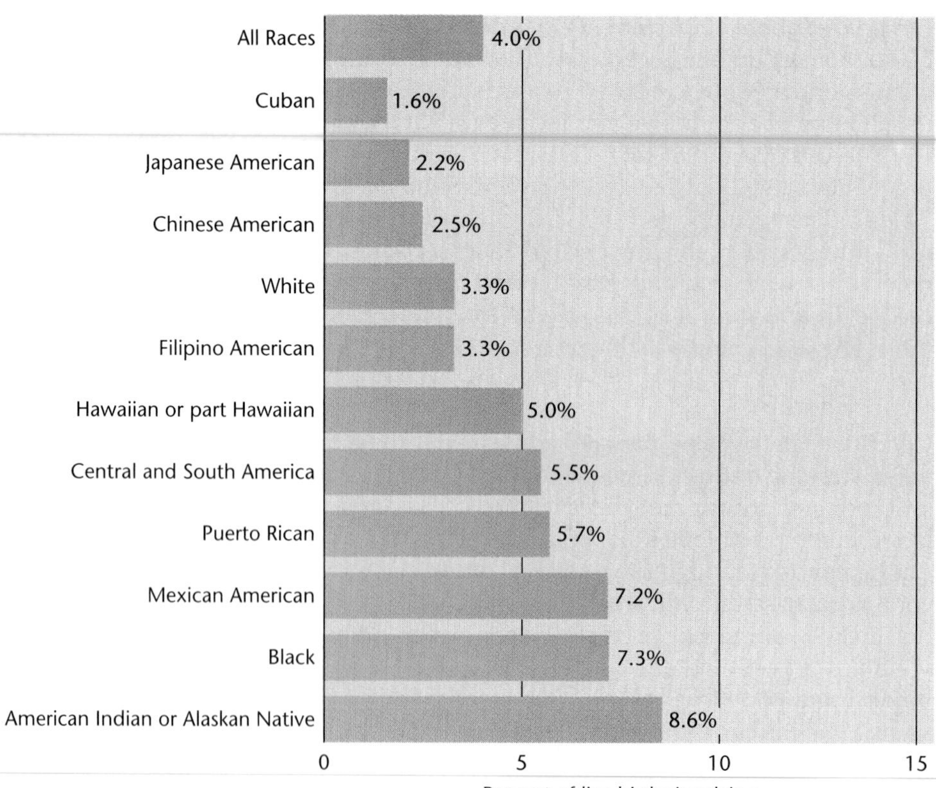

Figure 3-11
Proportion of U.S. mothers with late or no prenatal care, according to race or ethnicity, 1996. Late prenatal care begins in the last 3 months of pregnancy.
(Source: NCHS, 1998a.)

tal and lifestyle factors that put these women's babies at higher risk may not easily be addressed by prenatal care alone (Misra & Guyer, 1998).

Merely increasing the quantity of prenatal care does not address the *content* of care (Misra & Guyer, 1998). Most prenatal care programs in the United States focus on screening for major complications and are not designed to attack the causes of low birthweight. A national panel has recommended that prenatal care be restructured to provide more visits early in the pregnancy and fewer in the last trimester. In fact, care should begin *before* pregnancy. Prepregnancy counseling could make more women aware, for example, of the importance of getting enough folic acid in their diet and making sure that they are immune to rubella. In addition, care needs to be made more accessible to poor and minority women (Shiono & Behrman, 1995). Good prenatal care can give every child the best possible chance for entering the world in good condition to meet the challenges of life outside the womb—challenges we discuss in the next three chapters.

CHECKPOINT

Can you . . .

✔ Tell why early, high-quality prenatal care is important, and tell how prenatal care in the United States could be improved?

Summary

Conceiving New Life

Guidepost 1. How does conception normally occur?

- Until it becomes possible to **clone** a human being, the formation of a new human life will continue to require **fertilization,** the union of an ovum and a sperm. Fertilization results in the formation of a one-celled **zygote,** which then duplicates itself by cell division.

Guidepost 2. What causes multiple births?

- Twin births can occur either by the fertilization of two ova (or one ovum that has split) or by the splitting of one fertilized ovum. Larger multiple births result from either one of these processes or a combination of the two.
- **Dizygotic (two-egg) twins** (commonly called *fraternal twins*) have different genetic makeups and may be of different sexes; **monozygotic (one-egg) twins** (commonly called *identical twins*) have the same genetic makeup. Because of differences in prenatal and postnatal experience, "identical" twins may differ in some respects, for example, in **temperament.**

Mechanisms of Heredity

Guidepost 3. How does heredity operate in determining sex and transmitting normal and abnormal traits?

- The basic unit of heredity is the **gene,** which is made of **deoxyribonucleic acid (DNA).** DNA carries the biochemical instructions that govern bodily functions and determine inherited characteristics. Each gene seems to be located by function in a definite position on a **chromosome.**
- At conception, each normal human being receives 23 chromosomes from the mother and 23 from the father. These form 23 pairs of chromosomes—22 pairs of **autosomes** and 1 pair of **sex chromosomes.** A child who receives an X chromosome from each parent will be a female. If the child receives a Y chromosome from the father, a male will be conceived.
- The simplest patterns of genetic transmission are **dominant inheritance** and **recessive inheritance.** When a pair of **alleles** are the same, a person is **homoygous** for the trait; when they are different, the person is **heterozygous.**
- Most normal human characteristics are the result of **quantitative trait loci (QTL)** effects or **multifactorial transmission.** Except for monozygotic twins, each child inherits a unique **genotype,** or combination of genes. Dominant inheritance and multifactorial transmission explain why a person's **phenotype** does not always express the underlying genotype.
- Birth defects and diseases are generally transmitted through simple dominant, recessive, or **sex-linked inheritance,** or by **genome imprinting.** Chromosomal abnormalities also can result in birth defects; **Down syndrome** is the most common.
- Through **genetic counseling,** prospective parents can receive information about the mathematical odds of having children with certain birth defects.
- **Genetic testing** to identify people likely to develop certain diseases is likely to become more widespread as scientists complete the identification and location of all human genes; however, such testing involves risks as well as benefits.

Nature and Nurture: Influences of Heredity and Environment

Guidepost 4. How do scientists study the relative influences of heredity and environment, and how do heredity and environment work together?

- Research in **behavioral genetics** is based on the assumption that if heredity is an important influence on a trait, genetically closer persons will be more similar in that trait. Family studies, adoption studies, and studies of twins enable researchers to measure the **heritability**

of specific traits. Monozygotic twins tend to be more **concordant** for genetically influenced traits than dizygotic twins.
- The concepts of **reaction range, canalization, genotype-environment interaction, genotype-environment correlation** (or genotype-environment covariance), and **niche-picking** describe ways in which heredity and environment work together.
- Siblings tend to be more different than alike in intelligence and personality. Heredity accounts for most of the similarity; **nonshared environmental effects** account for most of the difference.

Guidepost 5. What role do heredity and environment play in physical health, intelligence, and personality?

- **Obesity,** longevity, intelligence, temperament, and shyness are examples of characteristics influenced by both heredity and environment. The relative influences of heredity and environment may vary across the life span.
- **Schizophrenia, autism,** alcoholism, and depression are examples of psychopathological disorders influenced by both heredity and environment.

Prenatal Development

Guidepost 6. What are the three stages of prenatal development, and what happens during each stage?

- Prenatal development is a genetically directed process that occurs in three stages of gestation: the **germinal stage,** the **embryonic stage,** and the **fetal stage.**
- Growth and development both before and after birth follow the **cephalocaudal principle** (head to tail) and the **proximodistal principle** (center outward).
- About one-third of all conceptions end in **spontaneous abortion,** usually in the first trimester of pregnancy.

Guidepost 7. What can fetuses do?

- Fetal activity can be observed by **ultrasound** and other means. As fetuses grow, they move less, but more vigorously. Swallowing amniotic fluid, which contains substances from the mother's body, stimulates taste and smell. Fetuses seem able to hear, exercise sensory discrimination, learn, and remember.

Guidepost 8. What environmental influences can affect prenatal development?

- The developing organism can be greatly affected by its prenatal environment. Some environmental factors are **teratogenic;** the likelihood of birth defects may depend on the timing and intensity of an environmental event and its interaction with genetic factors.
- Important environmental influences involving the mother include nutrition, physical activity, smoking, drinking (which can produce **fetal alcohol syndrome, [FAS]**), intake of other legal or illegal drugs, transmission of **acquired immune deficiency syndrome (AIDS),** other maternal illnesses or infections, maternal age, incompatibility of blood type, and external environmental hazards, such as chemicals and radiation. External influences also may affect the father's sperm.

Guidepost 9. What techniques can assess a fetus's health and well-being, and what is the importance of prenatal care?

- Ultrasound, **amniocentesis, chorionic villus sampling, embryoscopy, preimplantation genetic diagnosis, umbilical cord sampling,** and **maternal blood tests** are used to determine whether an unborn baby is developing normally. Some abnormal conditions can be corrected through fetal therapy.
- Early, high-quality prenatal care is essential for healthy development. It can lead to detection of defects and disorders and, especially if begun early and targeted to the needs of at-risk women, may help reduce maternal and infant death, low birthweight, and other birth complications.

Key Terms

clone (65)
fertilization (65)
zygote (65)
dizygotic (two-egg) twins (66)
monozygotic (one-egg) twins (66)
temperament (66)
gene (67)
deoxyribonucleic acid (DNA) (67)
chromosome (67)
autosomes (68)
sex chromosomes (68)
alleles (69)
homozygous (69)
heterozygous (69)
dominant inheritance (69)
recessive inheritance (69)
quantitative trait loci (QTL) (69)
multifactorial transmission (69)
phenotype (69)
genotype (69)
sex-linked inheritance (75)
Down syndrome (76)
genome imprinting (77)
genetic counseling (77)
genetic testing (78)
behavioral genetics (78)
heritability (78)
concordant (80)
reaction range (81)
canalization (81)
genotype-environment interaction (82)
genotype-environment correlation (82)
niche-picking (83)
nonshared environmental effects (83)
obesity (84)
schizophrenia (86)
autism (86)
cephalocaudal principle (87)
proximodistal principle (87)
germinal stage (87)
embryonic stage (90)
spontaneous abortion (90)
fetal stage (91)
ultrasound (91)
teratogenic (92)
fetal alcohol syndrome (FAS) (94)
acquired immune deficiency syndrome (AIDS) (97)
amniocentesis (100)
chorionic villus sampling (100)
embryoscopy (101)
preimplantation genetic diagnosis (101)
umbilical cord sampling (101)
maternal blood test (101)

Chapter 4

Physical Development During the First Three Years

The experiences of the first three years of life are almost entirely lost to us, and when we attempt to enter into a small child's world, we come as foreigners who have forgotten the landscape and no longer speak the native tongue.

Selma Fraiberg, *The Magic Years*, 1959

Elvis Presley

Focus: The Birth of Elvis Presley*

Elvis Presley (1935–1977) was born in a 30- by 15-foot cottage in East Tupelo, Mississippi. Today, the modest birthplace of the now-legendary "king" of rock music is painted sparkling white, the walls are papered with primroses, and dainty curtains hang at the windows—among the many homey touches added for the benefit of tourists. But, like many of the popular myths about Elvis's early life, this "cute little doll house" (Goldman, 1981, p. 60) bears only slight resemblance to the reality: a bare board shack with no indoor plumbing or electricity, set in a dirt-poor hamlet that wasn't much more than "a wide spot in the road" (Clayton & Heard, 1994, p. 8).

During the Great Depression, Elvis's near-illiterate father, Vernon Elvis Presley, sometimes did odd jobs for a farmer named Orville Bean, who owned much of the town. Elvis's mother, Gladys, was vivacious and high-spirited, as talkative as Vernon was taciturn. She, like Vernon, came from a family of sharecroppers and migrant workers. She had moved to East Tupelo to be close to the garment factory where she worked.

*Sources of information about Elvis Presley's birth were Clayton & Heard (1994); Dundy (1985); Goldman (1981); Guralnick (1994); and Marling (1996).

OUTLINE

Gladys first noticed handsome Vernon on the street and then, soon after, met him in church. They eloped on June 17, 1933. Vernon was 17 and Gladys, 21. They borrowed the three dollars for the license.

At first the young couple lived with friends and family. When Gladys became pregnant, Vernon borrowed $180 from his employer, Bean, to buy lumber and nails and, with the help of his father and older brother, built a two-room cabin next to his parents' house on Old Saltillo Road. Bean, who owned the land, was to hold title to the house until the loan was paid off.

Vernon and Gladys moved into their new home in December, 1934, about a month before she gave birth. Her pregnancy was a difficult one; her legs swelled, and she finally quit her job at the garment factory, where she had to stand on her feet all day pushing a heavy steam iron.

When Vernon got up for work in the wee hours of January 8, a bitterly cold morning, Gladys was hemorrhaging. The midwife told Vernon to get the doctor, Will Hunt. (His $15 fee was paid by welfare.) At about 4 o'clock in the morning, Dr. Hunt delivered a stillborn baby boy, Jesse Garon. The second twin, Elvis Aron, was born about 35 minutes later. Gladys—extremely weak and losing blood—was taken to the hospital charity ward with baby Elvis. They stayed there for more than 3 weeks.

Baby Jesse remained an important part of the family's life. Gladys frequently talked to Elvis about his brother. "When one twin died, the one that lived got the strength of both," she would say (Guralnick, 1994, p. 13). Elvis took his mother's words to heart. Throughout his life, his twin's imagined voice and presence were constantly with him.

As for Elvis's birthplace, he lived there only until the age of 3. Vernon, who sold a pig to Bean for $4, was accused of altering the check to $40. He was sent to prison, and when the payment on the house loan came due, Bean evicted Gladys and her son, who had to move in with family members. In later years, Elvis would drive back to East Tupelo (now Tupelo's suburban Presley Heights). He would sit in his car in the dark, looking at the cottage on what is now called Elvis Presley Drive and "thinking about the course his life had taken" (Marling, 1996, p. 20).

Elvis Presley is just one of many well-known people—including almost all the presidents of the United States—who were born at home. At one time, medical care during pregnancy was rare, and most births were attended by midwives. Birth complications and stillbirth were common, and many women died in childbirth. A rising standard of living, together with medical advances, have eased childbirth and reduced its risks. Today, the overwhelming majority of births in the United States occur in hospitals. However, there is a small but growing movement back to home birth, as is still the custom in many less developed countries.

In this chapter, we describe how babies come into the world, how newborn babies look, and how their body systems work. We discuss ways to safeguard their life and health. We see how infants, who spend most of their time sleeping and eating, become busy, active toddlers and how parents and other caregivers can foster healthy growth and development. We see how sensory perception goes hand in hand with motor skills and helps shape the astoundingly rapid development of the brain.

After you have read and studied this chapter, you should be able to answer the following questions:

CH. 4

Guideposts *for* **Study**

1. What happens during each of the four stages of childbirth?
2. What alternative methods and settings of delivery are available today?
3. How do newborn infants adjust to life outside the womb?
4. How can we tell whether a new baby is healthy and is developing normally?
5. What complications of childbirth can endanger newborn babies' adjustment or even their lives?
6. How can we enhance babies' chances of survival and health?
7. What influences the growth of body and brain?
8. How do the senses develop during infancy?
9. What are some early milestones in motor development, and what are some influences on it?

The Birth Process

For centuries, childbirth in Europe, and later in the United States, followed a familiar pattern, much as in some developing countries today. Birth was a female social ritual; the prospective father was nowhere in sight. The woman, surrounded by female relatives and neighbors, sat up in her own bed, modestly draped in a sheet. The midwife who presided over the event offered "advice, massages, potions, irrigations, and talismans," but "the cries of the mother during labor were considered to be as natural as those of the baby at birth" (Fontanel & d'Harcourt, 1997, p. 28).

The development of the science of obstetrics early in the nineteenth century professionalized childbirth for middle- and upper-class urban mothers. Maternity hospitals became the birth setting of choice for those who could afford them (but not for many country women, like Gladys Presley). A male physician was in charge, with surgical instruments ready in case of trouble.

Still, childbirth was "a struggle with death" (Fontanel & d'Harcourt, 1997, p. 34) for both mother and baby. At the end of the nineteenth century, in England and Wales, an expectant mother was almost fifty times as likely to die in childbirth as today (Saunders, 1997). A woman who conceived in 1950 in the United States was more than three times as likely as in 1993 to lose her baby either before or within one year after birth (USDHHS, 1996a). The dramatic reductions in risks surrounding pregnancy and childbirth, particularly during the past fifty years, are largely due to the availability of antibiotics, blood transfusions, safe anesthesia, improved hygiene, and drugs for inducing labor when necessary. In addition, improvements in prenatal assessment and care make it far more likely that a baby will be born healthy.

Stages of Childbirth

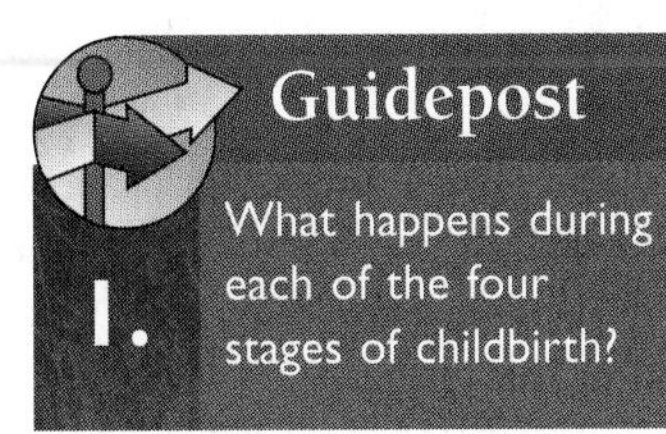
Guidepost
1.
What happens during each of the four stages of childbirth?

The uterine contractions that expel the fetus begin—typically, 266 days after conception—as mild tightenings of the uterus. A woman may have felt similar contractions at times during the final months of pregnancy, but she may recognize birth contractions as the "real thing" because of their greater regularity and intensity.

parturition Process of uterine, cervical, and other changes, usually lasting about two weeks, preceding childbirth.

Parturition—the process of uterine, cervical, and other changes that brings on labor—typically begins about two weeks before delivery, when the balance between progesterone and estrogen shifts. During most of gestation, progesterone keeps the uterine muscles relaxed and the cervix firm. During parturition, sharply rising estrogen levels stimulate the uterus to contract and the cervix to become more flexible. The timing of parturition seems to be determined by the rate at which the placenta produces a protein called *corticotropin-releasing hormone (CRH)*, which also promotes maturation of the fetal lungs to ready them for life outside the womb. The rate of CRH production as early as the fifth month of pregnancy may predict whether a baby will be born early, "on time," or late (Smith, 1999).

Normal vaginal childbirth, or labor, takes place in four overlapping stages (see Figure 4-1). The *first stage*, the longest, typically lasts 12 hours or more for a woman having her first child. In later births the first stage tends to be shorter. During this stage, regular and increasingly frequent uterine contractions cause the cervix to dilate, or widen.

The *second stage* typically lasts about $1^1/_2$ hours or less. It begins when the baby's head begins to move through the cervix into the vaginal canal, and it ends when the baby emerges completely from the mother's body. If this stage lasts longer than 2 hours, signaling that the baby needs more help, a doctor may grasp the baby's head with forceps or, more often, use vacuum extraction with a suction cup to pull it out of the mother's body (Curtin & Park, 1999). At the end of this stage, the baby is born; but it is still attached to the placenta in the mother's body by the umbilical cord, which must be cut and clamped.

During the *third stage*, which lasts about 5 to 30 minutes, the placenta and the remainder of the umbilical cord are expelled from the mother. The couple of hours after delivery constitute the *fourth stage*, when the mother rests in bed while her recovery is monitored.

electronic fetal monitoring Mechanical monitoring of fetal heartbeat during labor and delivery.

Electronic fetal monitoring was used in 83 percent of live births in the United States in 1996 to track the fetus's heartbeat during labor and delivery (Ventura et al., 1998). The procedure is intended to detect a lack of oxygen, which may lead to brain damage. It can provide valuable information in high-risk deliveries, including those in which the fetus is very small or seems to be in distress. Yet monitoring has drawbacks when used routinely in low-risk pregnancies. It is costly; it restricts the mother's movements during labor; and, most important, it has an extremely high "false positive" rate, suggesting that fetuses are in trouble when they are not. Such warnings may prompt doctors to deliver by the riskier cesarean method (described in the next section) rather than vaginally (Nelson, Dambrosia, Ting, & Grether, 1996).

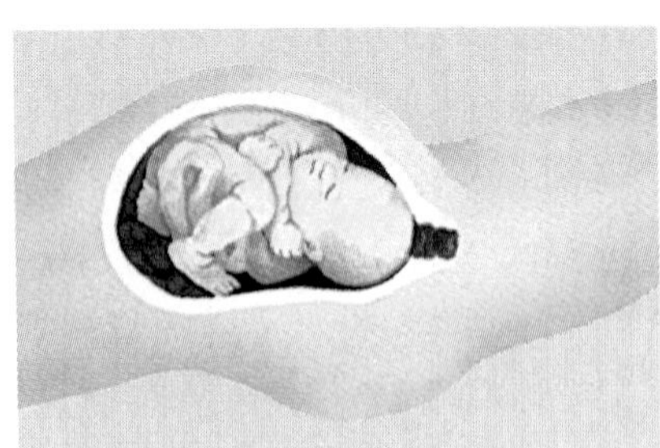

(a) First stage

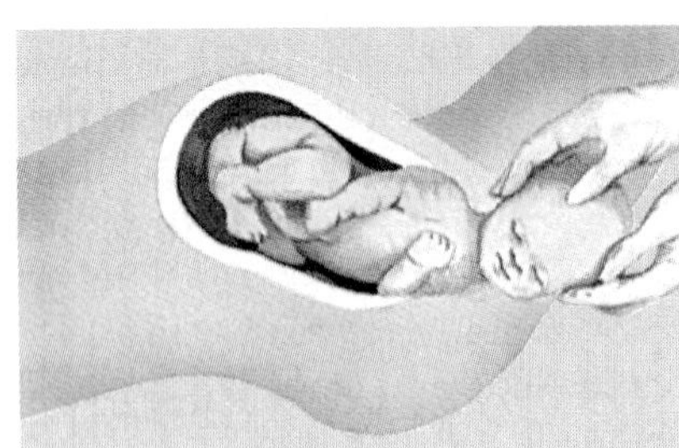

(b) Second stage

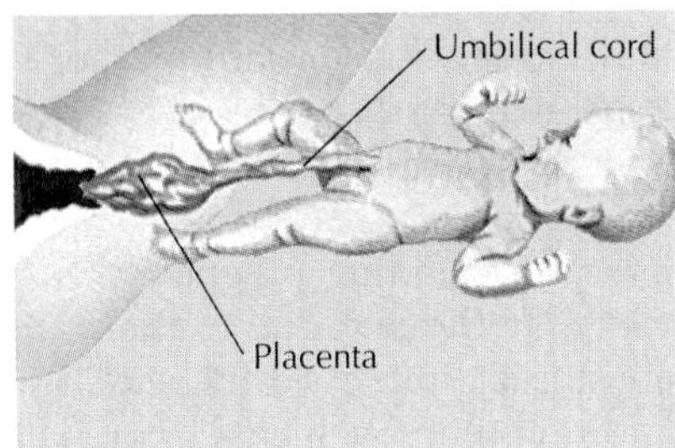

(c) Third stage

Figure 4-1

The first three stages of childbirth. (a) During the first stage of labor, a series of stronger and stronger contractions dilates the cervix, the opening to the mother's womb. (b) During the second stage, the baby's head moves down the birth canal and emerges from the vagina. (c) During the brief third stage, the placenta and umbilical cord are expelled from the womb. Then the cord is cut. During the fourth stage, recovery from delivery (not shown), the mother's uterus contracts.

(Source: Adapted from Lagercrantz & Slotkin, 1986.)

Methods of Delivery

The primary concern in choosing a method for delivering a baby is the safety of both mother and baby. Second is the comfort of the mother.

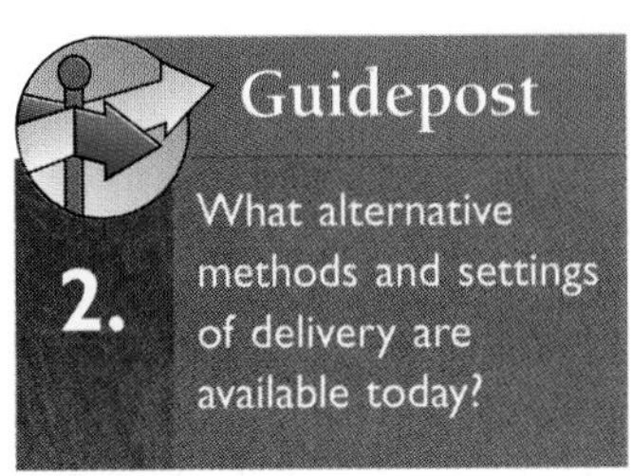

Guidepost
2.
What alternative methods and settings of delivery are available today?

Vaginal versus Cesarean Delivery

The normal method of childbirth, described above, is vaginal delivery. **Cesarean delivery** is a surgical procedure to remove the baby from the uterus by cutting through the abdomen. In 1997, 20.8 percent of U.S. births occurred this way, as compared with only 5.5 percent in 1970 (CDC, 1993; Curtin & Park, 1999). The operation is commonly performed when labor progresses too slowly, when the fetus seems to be in trouble, or when the mother is bleeding vaginally. Often a cesarean is needed when the fetus is in the breech position (feet first) or in the transverse position (lying crosswise in the uterus), or when its head is too big to pass through the mother's pelvis. Surgical deliveries are more likely when the birth involves a first baby, a large baby, or an older mother. Thus the increase in cesarean rates since 1970 is in part a reflection of a proportional increase in first births, a rise in average birth weight, and a trend toward later childbirth (Parrish, Holt, Easterling, Connell, & LoGerfo, 1994). Other suggested explanations include increased use of electronic fetal monitoring, physicians' fear of malpractice litigation, and the desire to avoid a difficult labor (Sachs, Kobelin, Castro, & Frigoletto, 1999).

cesarean delivery
Delivery of a baby by surgical removal from the uterus.

Cesarean birthrates in the United States are among the highest in the world, but rising rates in European countries during the past decade have narrowed the gap (Notzon, 1990; Sachs et al., 1999). Meanwhile, the U.S. rate of cesarean births decreased by 9 percent during the 1990s, and the percentage of vaginal births after a previous cesarean increased by about 50 percent (from 18.9 in 1989 to 27.4 in 1997), reflecting a growing belief that the procedure is unnecessary or harmful in many cases (Curtin & Park, 1999). About 4 percent of cesareans result in serious complications, such as bleeding and infections (Nelson, Dambrosia, Ting, & Grether, 1996). For the baby, there may be an important risk in bypassing the struggle to be born, which apparently stimulates the production of stress hormones that may aid in the adjustment to life outside the womb (Lagercrantz & Slotkin, 1986).

Still, some physicians argue that efforts to push for a further reduction in cesarean deliveries—through greater reliance on operative vaginal deliveries (use of forceps or suction) and encouragement of vaginal delivery for women who have had previous cesarean deliveries—may be misguided. Although these procedures are fairly safe, they do carry risks, which must be weighed against the risks of cesarean delivery (Sachs et al., 1999). The greatest risk is to women whose labor is unsuccessful and who therefore must undergo a cesarean after all (McMahon, Luther, Bowes, & Olshan, 1996). The chances of brain hemorrhage, for example, are higher either in an operative vaginal delivery or in a cesarean undertaken after labor has begun than in a normal vaginal delivery or a cesarean done before labor, suggesting that the risk is from abnormal labor (Towner, Castro, Eby-Wilkens, & Gilbert, 1999).

Medicated versus Unmedicated Delivery

In the mid–nineteenth century, England's Queen Victoria became the first woman in history to be sedated during delivery, that of her eighth child. Anesthesia became standard practice as more births took place in hospitals.

General anesthesia, which renders the woman completely unconscious, is rarely used today, even in cesarean births. The woman is given local anesthesia if she wants and needs it, but she can see and participate in the birth process and can hold her newborn immediately afterward. Regional (local) anesthesia blocks

In Lamaze classes for expectant parents, mothers learn breathing and muscular exercises to make labor easier, and fathers learn how to assist through labor and delivery.

the nerve pathways that would carry the sensation of pain to the brain, or the mother can receive a relaxing analgesic. All these drugs pass through the placenta to enter the fetal blood supply and tissues, and thus may potentially pose dangers to the baby.

Alternative methods of childbirth were developed to minimize the use of drugs while maximizing both parents' active involvement. In 1914 a British physician, Dr. Grantly Dick-Read, suggested that pain in childbirth was caused mostly by fear. To eliminate fear, he advocated **natural childbirth:** educating women about the physiology of reproduction and training them in physical fitness and in breathing and relaxation during labor and delivery. By midcentury, Dr. Fernand Lamaze was using the **prepared childbirth** method. This technique substitutes voluntary, or learned, physical responses to the sensations of uterine contractions for the old responses of fear and pain.

natural childbirth
Method of childbirth, developed by Dr. Grantly Dick-Read, that seeks to prevent pain by eliminating the mother's fear of childbirth through education about the physiology of reproduction and training in methods of breathing and relaxation during delivery.

prepared childbirth
Method of childbirth, developed by Dr. Ferdinand Lamaze, that uses instruction, breathing exercises, and social support to induce controlled physical responses to uterine contractions and reduce fear and pain.

In the Lamaze method, a woman learns about the anatomy and physiology involved in childbirth. She is trained to pant or breathe rapidly "in sync" with the contractions and to concentrate on other sensations. She learns to relax her muscles as a conditioned response to the voice of her "coach" (usually the father or a friend), who attends classes with her, takes part in the delivery, and helps with the exercises.

Advocates of natural methods argue that use of drugs poses risks for babies and deprives mothers of what can be an empowering and transforming experience. In some early studies, infants appeared to show immediate ill effects of obstetric medication in poorer motor and physiologic responses (A. D. Murray, Dolby, Nation, & Thomas, 1981) and, through the first year, in slower motor development (Brackbill & Broman, 1979). However, later research suggested that medicated delivery may *not* do measurable harm. When babies born to medicated and nonmedicated mothers were compared on strength, tactile sensitivity, activity, irritability, and sleep patterns, no evidence of any drug effect appeared (Kraemer, Korner, Anders, Jacklin, & Dimiceli, 1985).

CABOYER METHOD

Improvements in medicated delivery during the past two decades have led more and more mothers to choose pain relief. Spinal or epidural injections have become increasingly common as physicians have found effective ways to relieve pain with smaller doses of medication (Hawkins, 1999). "Walking epidurals" enable a woman to feel sensations, move her legs, and fully participate in the birth. In a recent analysis of ten studies involving 2,369 births in Europe, the United States, and Canada, women who had regional injections (epidurals) enjoyed more effective pain relief—but longer labor—than women who had narcotic injections, and their babies tended to arrive in healthier condition. There was no significant difference in the rate of cesarean deliveries (Halpern, Leighton, Ohlsson, Barrett, & Rice, 1998).

Settings and Attendants for Childbirth

Settings and attendants for childbirth tend to reflect the overall cultural system. In developing cultures, birthing is considered a normal part of family life; but there are cultural variations. A Mayan woman in Yucatan gives birth in the hammock in which she sleeps every night; the father-to-be is expected to be present, along with the midwife. To evade evil spirits, mother and child remain at home for a week (Jordan, 1993). By contrast, among the Ngoni in East Africa, men are excluded from the event. In rural Thailand, a new mother generally resumes normal activity within a few hours after giving birth (Broude, 1995; Gardiner, Mutter, & Kosmitzki, 1998).

In the United States, about 99 percent of babies are born in hospitals; 92 percent are attended by physicians and 7 percent by midwives (Curtin & Park, 1999). Most midwives are registered nurses with special training in midwifery; some have been trained by apprenticeship. A midwife may or may not work under a doctor's direction.

Women using nurse-midwives rather than doctors for low-risk hospital births tend to have equally good outcomes with less anesthesia. They are less likely to need episiotomies (incisions to enlarge the vaginal opening before birth), to have labor induced, or to end up having cesarean deliveries (Rosenblatt et al., 1997). Of course, these results may not be due to something the midwives did or did not do; rather, women who choose midwives may be more likely to take care of themselves during pregnancy, increasing their chances of normal delivery.

As safety in childbirth has become more assured, some women are opting for the more intimate, personal experience of home birth, which can involve the whole family. A home birth usually is attended by a trained nurse-midwife, with

> *Consider this . . .*
>
> - If you or your partner were expecting a baby, and the pregnancy seemed to be going smoothly, would you prefer (a) medicated or nonmedicated delivery, (b) hospital, birth center, or home birth, and (c) attendance by a physician or midwife? Give reasons. If you are a man, would you choose to be present at the birth? If you are a woman, would you want your partner present?

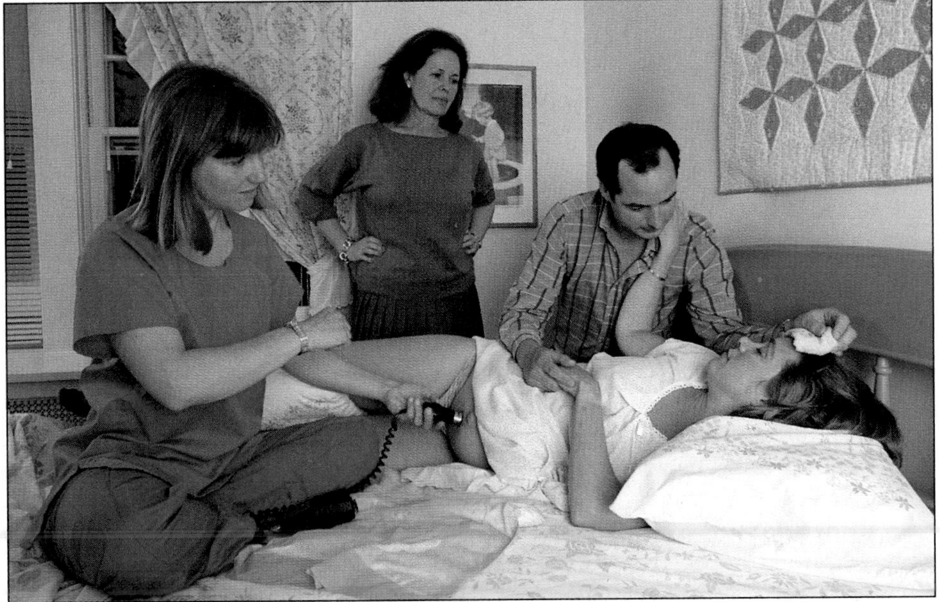

At a birth center in Princeton, New Jersey, a woman gives birth in a small house in a semiresidential area. Her husband and her mother give moral support as the midwife checks the fetal heartbeat. Informal, homelike settings for birth are growing in popularity for women with good medical histories and normal, uncomplicated pregnancies. However, it is essential to have arrangements with an ambulance service and a local hospital in case of emergency.

the resources of medical science close at hand. Studies suggest that home births can be at least as safe as hospital births in low-risk deliveries attended by skilled practitioners (Durand, 1992; Korte & Scaer, 1984).

In recent years, many hospitals have sought to humanize childbirth by establishing homelike birth centers, where labor and delivery can take place under soft lights while the father or other companion stays with the mother. Many hospitals also have rooming-in policies, which allow babies to stay in the mother's room much or all of the time.

Freestanding birth centers generally offer prenatal care and are staffed principally by nurse-midwives, with one or more physicians and nurse-assistants. They are designed for low-risk births with discharge the same day, and they appear to be a safe alternative to hospital delivery in such circumstances (Guyer, Strobino, Ventura, Singh, 1995).

CHECKPOINT

Can you . . .

- ✔ Describe the four stages of vaginal childbirth?
- ✔ Discuss the uses and disadvantages of cesarean births and electronic fetal monitoring?
- ✔ Compare medicated delivery, natural childbirth, and prepared childbirth?
- ✔ Weigh the comparative advantages of various types of settings and attendants for childbirth?

In many traditional cultures, childbearing women are attended by a *doula,* an experienced mother who can furnish emotional support and, unlike a doctor or midwife, can stay at a woman's bedside throughout labor. Although doulas attend only 1 percent of U.S. births, they are gaining wider acceptance (Gilbert, 1998).

In eleven randomized, controlled studies, women attended by doulas had shorter labor, less anesthesia, and fewer forceps and cesarean deliveries than mothers who had not had doulas. The benefits of the father's presence during labor and delivery were not as great. In one such study, six weeks after giving birth, mothers who had had doulas were more likely to be breast-feeding and reported higher self-esteem, less depression, and a more positive view of their babies and their own caregiving abilities (Klaus & Kennell, 1997). Perhaps, having had easier births, the doula-attended women recovered more quickly and felt more able to cope with mothering; or the emotional nurturing provided by the doulas may have served as a model for them. These findings remind us that social and psychological factors can have profound effects even on such a basic biological process as childbirth.

The Newborn Baby

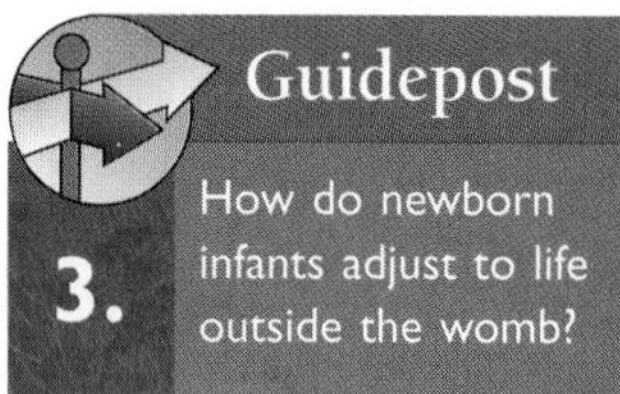

Guidepost

3. How do newborn infants adjust to life outside the womb?

neonatal period
First 4 weeks of life, a time of transition from intrauterine dependency to independent existence.

neonate
Newborn baby, up to 4 weeks old.

The first 4 weeks of life, the **neonatal period,** is a time of transition from the uterus, where a fetus is supported entirely by the mother, to an independent existence. What are the physical characteristics of newborn babies, and how are they equipped for this crucial transition?

Size and Appearance

An average newborn, or **neonate,** in the United States is about 20 inches long and weighs about $7\frac{1}{2}$ pounds. At birth, 95 percent of full-term babies weigh between $5\frac{1}{2}$ and 10 pounds and are between 18 and 22 inches long. Boys tend to be slightly longer and heavier than girls, and a firstborn child is likely to weigh less at birth than laterborns.

In their first few days, neonates lose as much as 10 percent of their body weight, primarily because of a loss of fluids. They begin to gain weight again at about the fifth day and are generally back to birthweight by the tenth to the fourteenth day.

New babies have distinctive features, including a large head (one-fourth the body length) and a receding chin (which makes it easier to nurse). At first, a neonate's head may be long and misshapen because of the "molding" that eased its passage through the mother's pelvis. This temporary molding was possible because an infant's skull bones are not yet fused; they will not be completely joined for 18 months. The places on the head where the bones have not yet grown together—the soft spots, or **fontanels**—are covered by a tough membrane. Since the cartilage in the baby's nose also is malleable, the trip through the birth canal may leave the nose looking squashed for a few days.

Many newborns have a pinkish cast; their skin is so thin that it barely covers the capillaries through which blood flows. During the first few days, some neonates are very hairy because some of the **lanugo,** a fuzzy prenatal hair, has not yet fallen off. All new babies are covered with **vernix caseosa** ("cheesy varnish"), an oily protection against infection that dries within the first few days.

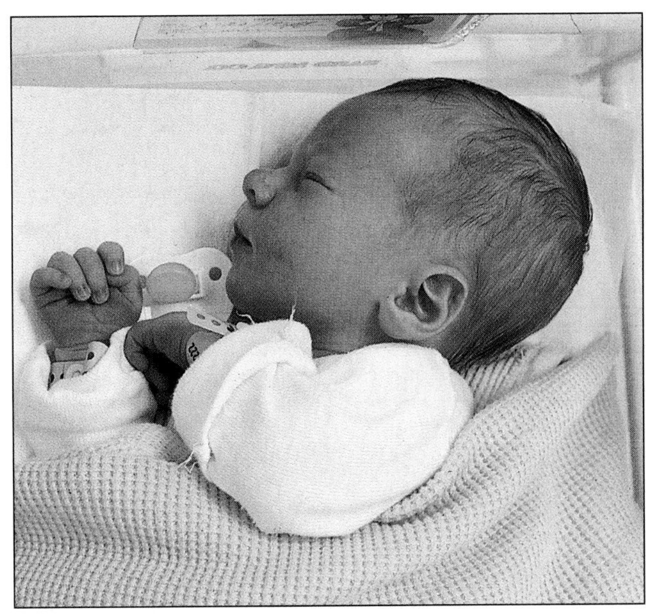

This 1-day-old boy's head is temporarily elongated from its passage through the birth canal. This "molding" of the head during birth occurs because the bones of the skull have not yet fused.

Body Systems

Before birth, blood circulation, respiration, nourishment, elimination of waste, and temperature regulation were accomplished through the mother's body. After birth, babies must do all of this themselves.

The fetus and mother have separate circulatory systems and separate heartbeats; the fetus's blood is cleansed through the umbilical cord, which carries "used" blood to the placenta and returns a fresh supply. After birth, the baby's circulatory system must operate on its own. A neonate's heartbeat is fast and irregular, and blood pressure does not stabilize until about the tenth day of life.

The fetus gets oxygen through the umbilical cord, which also carries away carbon dioxide. A newborn needs much more oxygen than before and must now get it alone. Most babies start to breathe as soon as they are exposed to air. If breathing has not begun within about 5 minutes, the baby may suffer permanent brain injury caused by **anoxia,** lack of oxygen. Because infants' lungs have only one-tenth as many air sacs as adults' do, infants (especially those born prematurely) are susceptible to respiratory problems.

In the uterus, the fetus relies on the umbilical cord to bring food from the mother and to carry fetal body wastes away. At birth, babies instinctively suck to take in milk, and their own gastrointestinal secretions digest it. During the first few days infants secrete **meconium,** a stringy, greenish-black waste matter formed in the fetal intestinal tract. When the bowels and bladder are full, the sphincter muscles open automatically; a baby will not be able to control these muscles for many months.

Three or four days after birth, about half of all babies (and a larger proportion of babies born prematurely) develop **neonatal jaundice:** their skin and eyeballs look yellow. This kind of jaundice is caused by the immaturity of the liver. Usually it is not serious, does not need treatment, and has no long-term effects. More severe jaundice is treated by putting the baby under fluorescent lights and sometimes by exchange transfusion of the baby's blood. Severe jaundice that is not monitored and treated promptly may result in brain damage (Gartner, 1994).

The layers of fat that develop during the last two months of fetal life enable healthy full-term infants to keep their body temperature constant after birth despite changes in air temperature. Newborn babies also maintain body temperature by increasing their activity when air temperature drops.

fontanels
Soft spots on head of young infant.

lanugo
Fuzzy prenatal body hair, which drops off within a few days after birth.

vernix caseosa
Oily substance on a neonate's skin that protects against infection.

anoxia
Lack of oxygen, which may cause brain damage.

meconium
Fetal waste matter, excreted during the first few days after birth.

neonatal jaundice
Condition, in many newborn babies, caused by immaturity of liver and evidenced by yellowish appearance; can cause brain damage if not treated promptly.

CHECKPOINT

Can you . . .

✔ Describe the normal size and appearance of a newborn baby?

✔ Name several distinctive features that change within the first few days of life?

Table 4-1 States of Arousal in Infancy

State	Eyes	Breathing	Movements	Responsiveness
Regular sleep	Closed; no eye movement	Regular and slow	None, except for sudden, generalized startles	Cannot be aroused by mild stimuli
Irregular sleep	Closed; occasional rapid eye movements	Irregular	Muscles twitch, but no major movements	Sounds or light bring smiles or grimaces in sleep.
Drowsiness	Open or closed	Irregular	Somewhat active	May smile, startle, suck, or have erections in response to stimuli
Alert inactivity	Open	Even	Quiet: may move head, limbs, and trunk while looking around	An interesting environment (with people or things to watch) may initiate or maintain this state
Waking activity and crying	Open	Irregular	Much activity	External stimuli (such as hunger, cold, pain, being restrained, or being put down) bring about more activity, perhaps starting with soft whimpering and gentle movements and turning into a rhythmic crescendo of crying or kicking, or perhaps beginning and enduring as uncoordinated thrashing and spasmodic screeching

Sources: Adapted from information in Prechtl & Beintema, 1964; P. H. Wolff, 1966.

States of Arousal

state of arousal
An infant's degree of alertness; his or her condition, at a given moment, in the periodic daily cycle of wakefulness, sleep, and activity.

Babies have an internal "clock," which regulates their daily cycles of eating, sleeping, and elimination, and perhaps even their moods. These periodic cycles of wakefulness, sleep, and activity, which govern an infant's **state of arousal,** or degree of alertness (see Table 4-1), seem to be inborn and highly individual. For example, newborn babies average about 16 hours of sleep a day, but one may sleep only 11 hours while another sleeps 21 hours (Parmelee, Wenner, & Schulz, 1964).

Most new babies wake up every 2 to 3 hours, day and night. Short stretches of sleep alternate with shorter periods of consciousness, which are devoted mainly to feeding. Newborns have about six to eight sleep periods, which vary between quiet and active sleep. Active sleep is probably the equivalent of rapid eye movement (REM) sleep, which in adults is associated with dreaming. Active sleep appears rhythmically in cycles of about 1 hour and accounts for 50 to 80 percent of a newborn's total sleep time.

Some new babies are more active than others. These activity levels reflect temperamental differences that continue throughout childhood, and often throughout life. Neonates' unique behavior patterns elicit varying responses from their caregivers. Adults react very differently to a placid baby than to an excitable one; to an infant they can quiet easily than to one who is often inconsolable; to a baby who is often awake and alert than to one who seems uninterested in the surroundings. Babies, in turn, respond to the way their caregivers treat them. This bidirectional influence can have far-reaching effects on what kind of person a baby turns out to be. Thus, from the start, children affect their own lives by molding the environment in which they grow.

CHECKPOINT

Can you . . .

- ✔ Compare the fetal and neonatal systems of circulation, respiration, digestion and excretion, and temperature regulation?
- ✔ Identify and describe two dangerous conditions that can occur when a newborn's body systems are not functioning normally?
- ✔ Describe typical early patterns of sleep and arousal?
- ✔ Explain the significance of differing activity levels.

Survival and Health

Although the great majority of births result in normal, healthy babies, some do not. How can we tell whether a newborn is at risk? What complications of birth can cause damage? How many babies die during infancy, and why? What can be done to prevent debilitating childhood diseases? How can we ensure that babies will live, grow, and develop as they should?

Medical and Behavioral Assessment

The first few minutes, days, and weeks after birth are crucial for development. It is important to know as soon as possible whether a baby has any problem that needs special care.

Guidepost 4. How can we tell whether a new baby is healthy and is developing normally?

The Apgar Scale

One minute after delivery, and then again 5 minutes after birth, most babies are assessed using the **Apgar scale** (see Table 4-2). Its name, after its developer, Dr. Virginia Apgar (1953), helps us remember its five subtests: *a*ppearance (color), *p*ulse (heart rate), *g*rimace (reflex irritability), *a*ctivity (muscle tone), and *r*espiration (breathing). The newborn is rated 0, 1, or 2 on each measure, for a maximum score of 10. A 5-minute score of 7 to 10—achieved by 98.6 percent of babies born in the United States in 1996—indicates that the baby is in good to excellent condition (Ventura, Martin, Curtin, & Mathews, 1998). A score below 7 means the baby needs help to establish breathing; a score below 4 means the baby needs immediate lifesaving treatment. If resuscitation is successful, bringing the baby's score to 4 or more, no long-term damage is likely to result (AAP Committee on Fetus and Newborn and American College of Obstetricians and Gynecologists [ACOG] Committee on Obstetric Practice, 1996).

Apgar scale Standard measurement of a newborn's condition; it assesses appearance, pulse, grimace, activity, and respiration.

A low Apgar score does not always mean that a baby is suffocating. An infant's score may be affected by the amount of medication the mother received; or neurological or cardiorespiratory conditions may interfere with one or more vital signs. Premature infants (those born before 37 weeks of gestation) may score low because of physiological immaturity. Scores of 0 to 3 at 10, 15, and 20 minutes after birth are increasingly associated with cerebral palsy (muscular impairment due to brain damage before or during birth) or other future neurological problems; such conditions may or may not be caused by oxygen deprivation (AAP Committee on Fetus and Newborn and ACOG Committee on Obstetric Practice, 1996).

Assessing Neurological Status: The Brazelton Scale

The **Brazelton Neonatal Behavioral Assessment Scale (NBAS)** is used to assess neonates' responsiveness to their physical and social environment, to identify problems in neurological functioning, and to predict future development. The test is named for its designer, Dr. T. Berry Brazelton (1973, 1984; Brazelton & Nugent,

Brazelton Neonatal Behavioral Assessment Scale Neurological and behavioral test to measure neonate's response to the environment.

Table 4-2 Apgar Scale

Sign*	0	1	2
Appearance (color)	Blue, pale	Body pink, extremities blue	Entirely pink
Pulse (heart rate)	Absent	Slow (below 100)	Rapid (over 100)
Grimace (reflex irritability)	No response	Grimace	Coughing, sneezing, crying
Activity (muscle tone)	Limp	Weak, inactive	Strong, active
Respiration (breathing)	Absent	Irregular, slow	Good, crying

*Each sign is rated in terms of absence or presence from 0 to 2; highest overall score is 10.

Source: Adapted from V. Apgar, 1953.

1995). It assesses *motor organization* as shown by such behaviors as activity level and the ability to bring a hand to the mouth; *reflexes; state changes,* such as irritability, excitability, and ability to quiet down after being upset; *attention and interactive capacities,* as shown by general alertness and response to visual and auditory stimuli; and indications of *central nervous system instability,* such as tremors and changes in skin color. The NBAS takes about 30 minutes, and scores are based on a baby's best performance.

Neonatal Screening for Medical Conditions

Children who inherit the enzyme disorder phenylketonuria, or PKU (refer back to Table 3-1), will become mentally retarded unless they are fed a special diet beginning in the first 3 to 6 weeks of life. Screening tests that can be administered soon after birth can often discover such correctable defects.

CHECKPOINT

Can you . . .

✔ Discuss the uses of the Apgar test, the Brazelton scale, and routine postbirth screening for rare disorders?

Routine screening of all newborn babies for such rare conditions as PKU (1 case in 10,000 to 25,000 births), congenital hypothyroidism (1 in 3,600 to 5,000), galactosemia (1 in 60,000 to 80,000), and other, even rarer disorders is expensive. Yet the cost of testing thousands of newborns to detect one case of a rare disease may be less than the cost of caring for one mentally retarded person for a lifetime. All states require routine screening for PKU and congenital hypothyroidism; states vary on requirements for other screening tests (AAP Committee on Genetics, 1996).

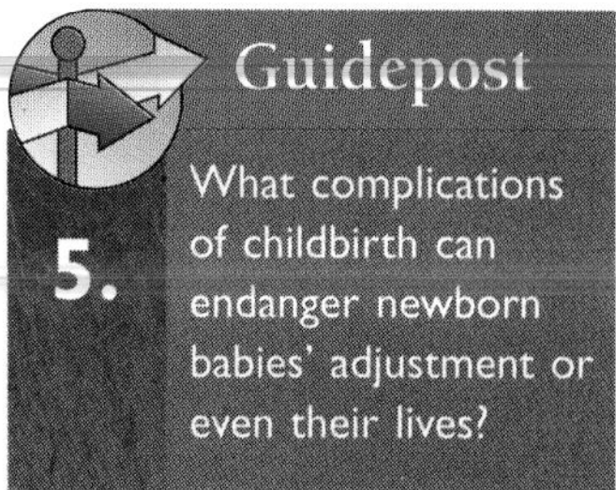

Guidepost
5.
What complications of childbirth can endanger newborn babies' adjustment or even their lives?

Complications of Childbirth

For a small minority of babies, the passage through the birth canal is a particularly harrowing journey. About 2 newborns in 1,000 are injured in the process (Wegman, 1994). **Birth trauma** (injury sustained at the time of birth) may be caused by anoxia (oxygen deprivation), diseases or infections, or mechanical injury. Sometimes the trauma leaves permanent brain damage, causing mental retardation, behavior problems, or even death. A larger proportion of infants are born very small or remain in the womb too long—complications that can impair their chances of survival and well-being.

birth trauma
Injury sustained at the time of birth due to oxygen deprivation, mechanical injury, infection, or disease.

low birthweight
Weight of less than $5^1/_2$ pounds at birth because of prematurity or being small for date.

preterm (premature) infants
Infants born before completing the thirty-seventh week of gestation.

small-for-date (small-for-gestational age) infants
Infants whose birthweight is less than that of 90 percent of babies of the same gestational age, as a result of slow fetal growth.

Low Birthweight

In 1998, according to preliminary data, 7.6 percent of babies born in the United States (up from 6.8 percent in 1986) had **low birthweight**—they weighed less than 2,500 grams ($5^1/_2$ pounds) at birth. Very-low-birthweight babies, who weigh less than 1,500 grams ($3^1/_3$ pounds), accounted for 1.45 percent of births. Low birthweight is the second leading cause of death in infancy, after birth defects (Martin, Smith, Mathews, & Ventura, 1999). Preventing and treating low birthweight can increase the number of babies who survive the first year of life.

Low-birthweight babies fall into two categories: *preterm* and *small-for-date.* Babies born before completing the 37th week of gestation are called **preterm (premature) infants;** they may or may not be the appropriate size for their gestational age. The increase in preterm births may in part reflect the rise in cesarean deliveries and induced labor and in births to unmarried and older women, ages 35 and up (Kramer et al., 1998). **Small-for-date (small-for-gestational age) infants,** who may or may not be preterm, weigh less than 90 percent of all babies of the same gestational age. Their small size is generally the result of inadequate prenatal nutrition, which slows fetal growth. Much of the increased prevalence of low birthweight is attributed to the rise in multiple births.

Who Is Likely to Have a Low-Birthweight Baby? Factors increasing the likelihood that a woman will have an underweight baby include: (1) *demographic and socioeconomic factors,* such as being African American, under age 17 or over 40, poor, unmarried, or undereducated; (2) *medical factors predating the pregnancy,* such as having no children or more than four, being short or thin, having had previous low-birthweight infants or multiple miscarriages, having had low birthweight herself, or having genital or urinary abnormalities or chronic hypertension; (3) *prenatal behavioral and environmental factors,* such as poor nutrition, inadequate prenatal care, smoking, use of alcohol or other drugs, or exposure to stress, high altitude, or toxic substances; and (4) *medical conditions associated with the pregnancy,* such as vaginal bleeding, infections, high or low blood pressure, anemia, too little weight gain, and having last given birth less than 6 months or 10 or more years before (S. S. Brown, 1985; Chomitz, Cheung, & Lieberman, 1995; Nathanielsz, 1995; Shiono & Behrman, 1995; Wegman, 1992; Zhu, Rolfs, Nangle, & Horan, 1999). The safest interval between pregnancies is 18 to 23 months (Zhu et al., 1999).

Many of these factors are interrelated, and socioeconomic status cuts across many of them. Teenagers' higher risk of having low-birthweight babies may stem more from malnutrition and inadequate prenatal care than from age, since teenagers who become pregnant are likely to be poor. At least one-fifth of all low birthweights are attributed to smoking. This proportion rises when a smoking mother is also underweight and does not gain enough during pregnancy—a combination that accounts for nearly two-thirds of cases of retarded fetal growth. Even before they become pregnant, women can cut down their chances of having a low-birthweight baby by eating well, not smoking or using drugs, drinking little or no alcohol, and getting good medical care (Chomitz et al., 1995; Shiono & Behrman, 1995).

Although the United States is more successful than any other country in the world in *saving* low-birthweight babies, the rate of such births to U.S. women is higher than in 21 European, Asian, and Middle Eastern nations (UNICEF, 1996). Worse still, the rates of low birthweight for African American babies are higher than the rates in 73 other countries, including a number of African, Asian, and South American nations (UNICEF, 1992). African American babies are more than twice as likely as white babies to be underweight, mostly because they are more likely to be preterm (Martin et al., 1999). Babies of Puerto Rican origin are almost one and a half times as likely as white babies to have low birthweight. Rates for most other minorities are about the same as for white births (NCHS, 1998a; Ventura et al., 1998).

The higher rates for African American women may in part reflect greater poverty, less education, less prenatal care, and a greater incidence of teenage and unwed pregnancy. However, even college-educated black women are more likely than white women to bear low-birthweight babies (S. S. Brown, 1985; Chomitz et al., 1995; Schoendorf, Hogue, Kleinman, & Rowley, 1992). This may be due to poorer general health, or it may stem from specific health problems that span generations. The cause does not seem to be primarily genetic, since birthweights of babies of African-born black women are more similar to birthweights of infants of U.S.-born white women than of U.S.-born black women (David & Collins, 1997). The high proportion of low-birthweight babies in the African American population is the major factor in the high mortality rates of black babies (see Table 4-3).

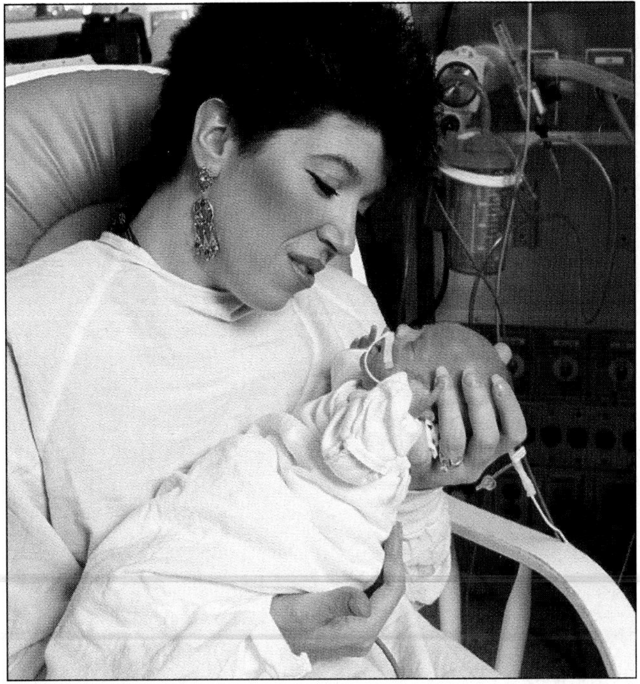

The tiniest babies thrive on human touch. This mother's holding and stroking of her low-birthweight baby girl will help establish a bond between mother and child, and will also help the baby grow and be more alert.

Treatment and Outcomes The most pressing fear for very small babies is that they will die in infancy. Because their immune systems are not fully developed, they are especially vulnerable to infection. Their

Table 4-3 Birthweight and Mortality: Black and White Infants

	Low Birthweight (less than $5^1/_2$ pounds, or 2,500 grams), % of births (1996)	Very Low Birthweight (less than 3.3 pounds, or 1,500 grams), % of births (1996)	Infant Mortality Rate per 1,000 (1996)	Neonatal Mortality Rate per 1,000 (1996)	Postneonatal Mortality Rate per 1,000 (1996)	Decline in Infant Mortality Rate, 1970–1996
Black infants	13.1	2.99	14.7	9.6	5.1	55%
White infants	6.34	1.09	6.1	4.0	2.1	66%

Note: Black infants are more likely than white infants to die in the first year from sudden infant death syndrome, respiratory distress syndrome, infections, injuries, disorders related to short gestation and low birthweight, pneumonia and influenza, and as a result of maternal complications of pregnancy.

Source: NCHS, 1998a.

nervous systems may not be mature enough for them to perform functions basic to survival, such as sucking, and they may need to be fed intravenously (through the veins). Because they have insufficient fat to insulate them and to generate heat, it is hard for them to stay warm enough. Respiratory distress syndrome, also called *hyaline membrane disease,* is common.

In a study of 122,754 live births at a Dallas hospital, full-term newborns who were severely undergrown—at or below the third percentile of weight for their gestational age—had significantly increased risk of endangered health shortly after birth and of neonatal death. For preterm infants, the risk of adverse outcomes increased continuously with decreasing weight (McIntire, Bloom, Casey, & Leveno, 1999).

Many preterm babies with very low birthweight lack surfactant, an essential lung-coating substance that keeps air sacs from collapsing; they may breathe irregularly or stop breathing altogether. Administering surfactant to high-risk preterm newborns has increased their survival rate (Corbet et al., 1995; Horbar et al., 1993), allowing significant numbers of infants who are born at 24 weeks of gestation and weigh as little as 500 grams (about 1 pound 2 ounces) to survive. However, these infants are likely to be in poor health and to have neurological deficits—at 20 months, a 20 percent rate of mental retardation and 10 percent likelihood of cerebral palsy (Hack, Friedman, & Fanaroff, 1996).

A low-birthweight baby is placed in an *isolette* (an antiseptic, temperature-controlled crib) and fed through tubes. To counteract the sensory impoverishment of life in an isolette, hospital workers and parents are encouraged to give these small babies special handling. Gentle massage seems to foster growth, behavioral organization, weight gain, motor activity, and alertness (T. M. Field, 1986, 1998; Schanberg & Field, 1987).

Even if low-birthweight babies survive the dangerous early days, there is concern about their long-term development. Most of these babies do fairly well, owing in part to follow-up support. An analysis of 80 studies showed only about a 6-point difference in average IQ after age 2 between children of low and normal birthweight, and both groups were in the normal range: 97.7 as compared with 103.78 (Aylward, Pfeiffer, Wright, & Verhulst, 1989).

Very-low-birthweight babies have a less promising prognosis. At school age, those who weighed the least at birth have the most behavioral, social, attention, and language problems (Klebanov, Brooks-Gunn, & McCormick, 1994). In one study, about half of a sample of eighty-eight 7-year-olds who had weighed less than 3.3 pounds at birth needed special education, compared with only 15 percent of a normal-weight, full-term comparison group (Ross, Lipper, & Auld, 1991). Small-for-gestational age infants are more likely to be neurologically and cognitively impaired during their first 6 years of life than equally premature infants whose weight was appropriate for their gestational age (McCarton, Wallace, Divon, & Vaughan, 1996).

Consider this . . .

- In view of the long-term outlook for very-low-birthweight babies and the expense involved in helping them survive, how much of society's resources should be put into rescuing these babies?

Birthweight alone does not necessarily determine the outcome. Boys are more likely than girls to have problems during childhood that interfere with everyday activities, and to need special education or other special help (Verloove-Vanhorick et al., 1994). Gender and other demographic factors, such as family income and the mother's educational level and marital status, seem to play a major role in whether or not a low-birthweight child will be emotionally handicapped or will suffer a speech and language impairment. Demographic factors also play some part in the prevalence of specific learning disabilities and in mild mental handicaps. Only the most severe educational disabilities are affected by medical factors alone (Resnick et al., 1998).

Postmaturity

Close to 9 percent of pregnant women have not gone into labor 2 weeks after the due date, or 42 weeks after the last menstrual period (Ventura, Martin, Curtin, & Mathews, 1998). At that point, a baby is considered **postmature.** Postmature babies tend to be long and thin, because they have kept growing in the womb but have had an insufficient blood supply toward the end of gestation. Possibly because the placenta has aged and become less efficient, it may provide less oxygen. The baby's greater size also complicates labor: the mother has to deliver a baby the size of a normal 1-month-old.

postmature
Referring to a fetus not yet born as of 2 weeks after the due date or 42 weeks after the mother's last menstrual period.

Since postmature fetuses are at risk of brain damage or even death, doctors sometimes induce labor with drugs or perform cesarean deliveries. However, if the due date has been miscalculated, a baby who is actually premature may be delivered. To help make the decision, doctors monitor the baby's status with ultrasound to see whether the heart rate speeds up when the fetus moves; if not, the baby may be short of oxygen. Another test involves examining the volume of amniotic fluid; a low level may mean the baby is not getting enough food.

CHECKPOINT

Can you . . .

✔ Discuss the risk factors, treatment, and outcomes for low-birthweight babies?

✔ Explain the risks of postmaturity?

Can a Supportive Environment Overcome Effects of Birth Complications?

A child's prospects for overcoming the early disadvantage of low birthweight depend on several interacting factors. One is the family's socioeconomic circumstances (Aylward et al., 1989; McGauhey, Starfield, Alexander, & Ensminget, 1991; Ross et al., 1991). Another is the quality of the early environment.

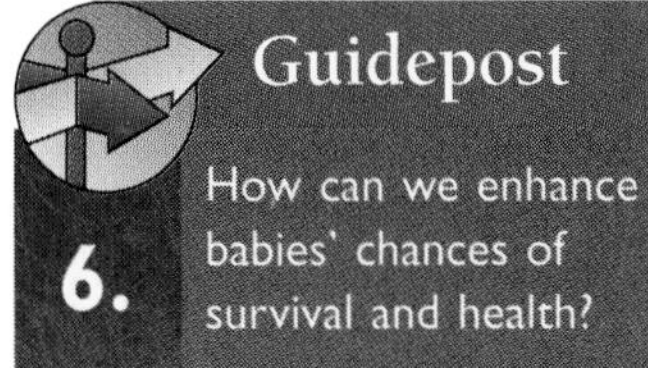

Guidepost
6.
How can we enhance babies' chances of survival and health?

The Infant Health and Development Studies

A large-scale study (Infant Health & Development Program [IHDP], 1990) followed 985 preterm, low-birthweight babies in eight parts of the United States—most of them from poor inner-city families—from birth to age 3. One-third of the heavier (but still low-birthweight) babies and one-third of the lighter ones were randomly assigned to "intervention" groups and the remaining two-thirds in each weight category to "follow-up" groups. The parents of the intervention groups received home visits that provided counseling, information about children's health and development, and instruction in children's games and activities; at 1 year, these babies entered an educational day care program. The children in all four groups received pediatric follow-up services.

When the program stopped, the 3-year-olds in both intervention groups were doing better on cognitive and social measures, were much less likely to show mental retardation, and had fewer behavioral problems than the groups that had received follow-up only (Brooks-Gunn, Klebanov, Liaw, & Spiker, 1993). However, two years later, at age 5, the children in the lower-birthweight intervention group no longer held a cognitive edge over the comparison group. Furthermore, having been in the intervention program made no difference in health or behavior (Brooks-Gunn et al., 1994). By age 8, the cognitive superiority of children in the higher-birthweight intervention group over their counterparts in the follow-up group had dwindled to 4 IQ points; and all four groups had substantially below-average IQs and vocabulary scores (McCarton et al., 1997; McCormick, McCarton, Brooks-Gunn, Belt, & Gross, in press). It seems, then, that for such an intervention to have lasting effects, it needs to continue beyond age 3.

Studies of the full IHDP sample underline the importance of what goes on in the home. Children who got little parental attention and care were more likely to be undersized and to do poorly on cognitive tests than children from more favorable home environments (Kelleher et al., 1993; McCormick et al., in press). Those whose cognitive performance stayed high had mothers who scored high themselves on cognitive tests and who were responsive and stimulating. Babies who had more than one risk factor (such as poor neonatal health combined with having a mother who did not receive counseling or was less well educated or less responsive) fared the worst (Liaw & Brooks-Gunn, 1993).

The Kauai Study

A longer-term study shows how a favorable environment can counteract effects of low birthweight, birth injuries, and other birth complications. For more than three decades, Emmy E. Werner (1987, 1995) and a research team of pediatricians, psychologists, public health workers, and social workers have followed 698 children born in 1955 on the Hawaiian island of Kauai—from the prenatal period through birth, and then into young adulthood. The researchers interviewed the mothers; recorded their personal, family, and reproductive histories; monitored the course of their pregnancies; and interviewed them again when the children were 1, 2, and 10 years old. They also observed the children interacting with their parents at home and gave them aptitude, achievement, and personality tests in elementary and high school. The children's teachers reported on their progress and their behavior. The young people themselves were interviewed at ages 18 and 30.

Among the children who had suffered problems at or before birth, physical and psychological development was seriously impaired *only* when they grew up in persistently poor environmental circumstances. From toddlerhood on, unless the early damage was so serious as to require institutionalization, those children who had a stable and enriching environment did well (E. E. Werner, 1985; 1987). In fact, they had fewer language, perceptual, emotional, and school problems than children who had *not* experienced unusual stress at birth but who had re-

Thanks to their own resilience, fully a third of the at-risk children studied by Emmy Werner and her colleagues developed into self-confident, successful adults. These children had a positive and active approach to problem solving, the abilities to see some useful aspects of even painful experiences and to attract positive responses from other people, and a strong tendency to use faith in maintaining an optimistic vision of a fulfilling life.

ceived little intellectual stimulation or emotional support at home (E. E. Werner, 1989; E. E. Werner et al., 1968). The children who had been exposed to *both* birth-related problems and later stressful experiences showed the worst health problems and the most retarded development (E. E. Werner, 1987).

Given a supportive environment, then, many children can overcome a poor start in life. Even more remarkable is the resilience of children who escape damage despite *multiple* sources of stress. Even when birth complications were combined with such environmental risks as chronic poverty, family discord, divorce, or parents who were mentally ill, many children came through relatively unscathed. Of the 276 children who at age 2 had been identified as having four or more risk factors, two-thirds developed serious learning or behavior problems by the age of 10 or, by age 18, had become pregnant, gotten in trouble with the law, or become emotionally troubled. Yet by age 30, one-third of these highly at-risk children had managed to become "competent, confident, and caring adults" (E. E. Werner, 1995, p. 82).

Protective factors, which tended to reduce the impact of early stress, fell into three categories: (1) individual attributes that may be largely genetic, such as energy, sociability, and intelligence; (2) affectionate ties with at least one supportive family member; and (3) rewards at school, work, or place of worship that provide a sense of meaning and control over one's life (E. E. Werner, 1987). While the home environment seemed to have the most marked effect in childhood, in adulthood the individuals' own qualities made a greater difference (E. E. Werner, 1995).

protective factors
Influences that reduce the impact of early stress and tend to predict positive outcomes.

These studies underline the need to look at child development in context. They show how biological and environmental influences interact, making resiliency possible even in babies born with serious complications.

CHECKPOINT

Can you . . .

- ✔ Discuss the effectiveness of the home environment and of intervention programs in overcoming effects of low birthweight and other birth complications?
- ✔ Name three protective factors identified by the Kauai study?

Death During Infancy

One of the most tragic losses is the death of an infant. Great strides have been made in protecting the lives of new babies, but these improvements are not evenly distributed throughout the population. Too many babies still die—some of them for no apparent reason, without warning or explanation.

Reducing Infant Mortality

In recent decades, prospects for surviving the early years of life have improved in all regions of the world. The improvement is especially dramatic in the developing regions of Africa, the Middle East, and Southeast Asia, where the threat of early death from such causes as birth complications, neonatal disorders, diarrhea, respiratory disease, and vaccine-preventable disease remains the greatest (Wegman, 1999). Worldwide, in 1998 an estimated 7.7 million children were expected to die before their first birthday, accounting for about 14 percent of all deaths. But while infant deaths represent as many as 25 percent of all deaths in developing countries, they account for only 1 percent of deaths in the developed world (U.S. Bureau of the Census, 1999c).

In the United States, the **infant mortality rate**—the proportion of babies who die within the first year—is the lowest ever. In 1998, according to preliminary data, there were 7.2 deaths in the first year for every 1,000 live births, compared with 20 per 1,000 in 1970, a 63.5 percent drop. *Neonatal mortality,* deaths during the first 4 weeks, plunged even further, by about 68 percent. Still, almost two-thirds of infant deaths take place during the neonatal period. *Postneonatal mortality* (death after the first 4 weeks) has declined by about 49 percent (Martin et al., 1999; NCHS, 1998a; Peters, Kochanek, & Murphy, 1998).

infant mortality rate
Proportion of babies born alive who die within the first year.

The continuing improvement in infant mortality rates during the 1990s, even at a time when more babies are born perilously small, has been due in part to effective treatment for respiratory distress and to prevention of sudden infant death syndrome (SIDS) (discussed in the next section), as well as to medical advances in keeping very small babies alive and treating sick newborns. Still, too many babies die—28,486 in 1998, according to preliminary data (Martin et al., 1999). Furthermore, U.S. babies have a poorer chance of reaching their first birthday than babies in many other industrialized countries (Wegman, 1996; see Figure 4-2). The higher survival rates of infants in western Europe and the Pacific Rim may be attributable to free pre- and postnatal health care and, in the Pacific Rim countries, to assistance from extended family members before and at birth (Gardiner et al., 1998).

Birth defects (congenital abnormalities) were the leading cause of infant deaths in the United States in 1998, according to preliminary data. Second was low birthweight, third was SIDS, and fourth was respiratory distress syndrome (Martin et al., 1999). Causes of death in white and Hispanic newborns and those descended from Asians and Pacific Islanders fit this pattern. Black neonates are most likely to die of disorders related to low birthweight, and SIDS is the leading cause of death for Native American babies (MacDorman & Atkinson, 1998; Martin et al., 1999).

Age of the mother is not a factor in neonatal mortality; pound for pound, babies born to teenagers and those born to adults have an equal chance of survival. What puts teenagers' babies at higher risk of dying in the first 4 weeks is the greater likelihood of low birthweight (Rees, Lederman, & Kiely, 1996). This is especially likely for African American babies.

Although infant mortality has declined for all races (Peters et al., 1998), the rates for white babies have fallen more than for black babies (refer back to Table 4-3). Black babies are nearly two and a half times as likely to die as white

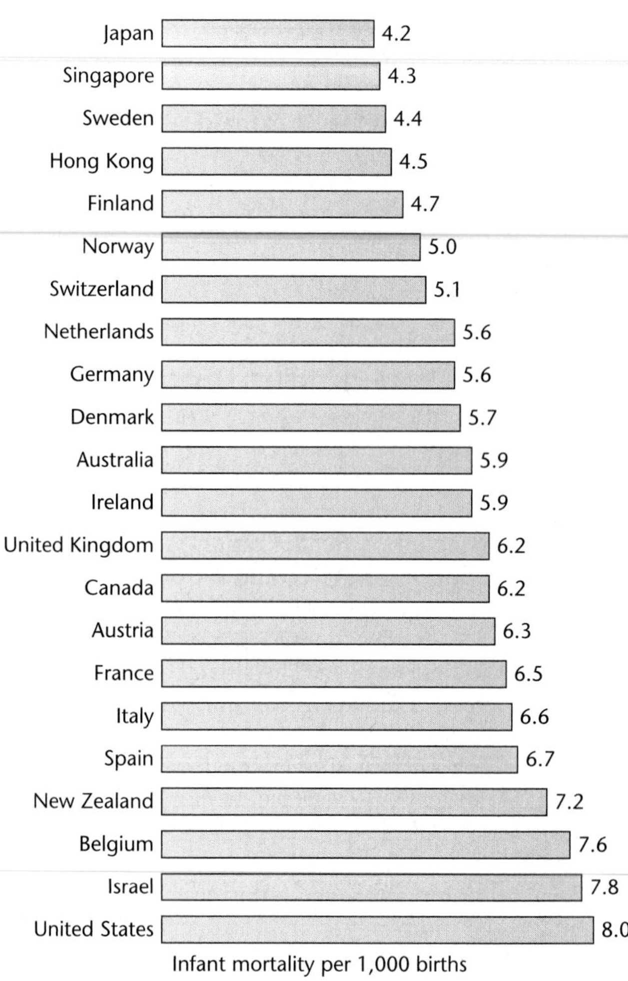

Figure 4-2

Infant mortality rates in industrialized countries. In 1994, the United States had a higher infant mortality rate than 21 other industrialized nations with populations of more than 1 million, largely because of its very high mortality rate for African American babies (see Table 4-3). In recent years most nations, including the United States, have shown dramatic improvement.

Note: Rates for Hong Kong, Norway, Denmark, France, Spain, New Zealand, and Israel are for 1993. Rates for Denmark and Canada are based on provisional data. (Source: Wegman, 1996, Table 2, p. 1022, based on data from United Nations Statistical Division.)

babies—14.1 as compared with 6 per 1,000 live births in 1998, according to preliminary data. This disparity is fairly comparable to the disparity in the prevalence of low birthweight. Hispanic infants, as a group, die at the same rate as white babies (6 per 1,000), though the rates are higher (7.8 per 1,000 in 1996) for Puerto Rican infants (Martin et al., 1999; NCHS, 1998a; Peters et al., 1998).

CHECKPOINT

Can you . . .

✔ Summarize trends in infant mortality, and explain why black infants are less likely to survive than white infants?

Sudden Infant Death Syndrome (SIDS)

Sudden infant death syndrome (SIDS), sometimes called "crib death," is the sudden death of an infant under 1 year of age in which the cause of death remains unexplained after a thorough investigation that includes an autopsy. In 1998, according to preliminary data, 2,529 U.S. babies were victims of SIDS (Martin et al., 1999). SIDS occurs most often between 2 and 4 months of age (Willinger, 1995).

sudden infant death syndrome (SIDS) Sudden and unexplained death of an apparently healthy infant.

A number of risk factors, such as being black, male, and of low birthweight, are associated with SIDS. Often SIDS mothers are young, unmarried, and poor; have received little or no prenatal care; have been ill during pregnancy; smoke or abuse drugs or both; and have had another baby less than a year before the one who died. The fathers, too, are likely to be young and to smoke (Babson & Clarke, 1983; C. E. Hunt & Brouillette, 1987; Kleinberg, 1984; Klonoff-Cohen et al., 1995; E. A. Mitchell et al., 1993; D. C. Shannon & Kelly, 1982a, 1982b; USDHHS, 1990). The risk of SIDS is worsened by poor socioeconomic circumstances, but SIDS also strikes infants in advantaged families.

What causes SIDS? The condition is not contagious, nor is it caused by choking or vomiting. One theory suggests a neurological anomaly, perhaps an abnormality in brain chemistry. Studies point to difficulties in the regulation of respiratory control (C. E. Hunt & Brouillette, 1987), in making the transition from sleep to wakefulness (Schechtman, Harper, Wilson, & Southall, 1992), and in arousal and ability to turn the head to avoid suffocation (K. A. Waters, Gonzalez, Jean, Morielli, & Brouillette, 1996). Researchers in Italy have found a strong correlation between SIDS and an unusual abnormality in the heartbeat, which can be identified by electrocardiogram screening (Schwartz, Stramba-Badiale, et al., 1998).

It seems likely that SIDS results from a combination of factors. An underlying biological defect may make some infants vulnerable, during a critical period in their development, to certain contributing or triggering experiences, such as exposure to smoke or sleeping on the stomach (Cutz, Perrin, Hackman, & Czegledy-Nagy, 1996).

Research strongly supports the connection with parental smoking (Aligne & Stoddard, 1997; AAP Committee on Environmental Health, 1997). Perhaps 30 percent of SIDS deaths could be prevented if pregnant women did not smoke (J. A. Taylor & Sanderson, 1995). Exposure to smoke, both before and after birth, seems related to brain and lung development (Cutz et al., 1996; Milerad & Sundell, 1993). Caffeine exposure also may be a risk factor. If a mother drank at least four cups of coffee a day while pregnant—or equivalent amounts of other caffeinated beverages—her baby has a 65 percent greater risk of SIDS (Ford et al., 1998).

A clue to what happens in SIDS has emerged from the discovery of defects in chemical receptors, or nerve endings, in the brain stem, which receive and send messages that control breathing. These defects may prevent SIDS babies from awakening when they are breathing too much stale air containing carbon dioxide trapped under their blankets (Kinney et al., 1995). This may be especially likely to happen when the baby is sleeping face down. SIDS babies may be deficient in a protective mechanism that allows an infant to become aroused enough to turn the head when breathing is restricted (K. A. Waters et al., 1996). Even in normal, healthy infants, prone sleeping inhibits the swallowing reflex, which protects the airways from choking due to infusion of nasal and digestive fluids (Jeffery, Megevand, & Page, 1999).

CHECKPOINT

Can you ...

✔ Discuss risk factors, causes, and prevention of sudden infant death syndrome?

Studies support the relationship between SIDS and sleeping on the stomach (Skadberg, Morild, & Markestad, 1998; J. A. Taylor et al., 1996). Side-sleeping is not safe either, because infants put to bed on their sides often turn onto their stomachs (Skadberg et al., 1998). SIDS rates fell by as much as 70 percent in some countries following recommendations by the American Academy of Pediatrics and international medical authorities that healthy babies be put to sleep on their backs (Dwyer, Ponsonby, Blizzard, Newman, & Cochrane, 1995; C.E. Hunt, 1996; Skadberg et al., 1998; Willinger, Hoffman, & Hartford, 1994). Infants should not sleep on soft surfaces, such as pillows, quilts, or sheepskin (AAP Task Force on Infant Positioning and SIDS, 1992, 1996, 1997; Dwyer, Ponsonby, Newman, & Gibbons, 1991; Kemp, Livne, White, & Arfken, 1998).

Consider this . . .

- What more do you think can and should be done to reduce the incidence of low birthweight and bring down the infant mortality rate?

Sleeping on the back does tend to result in a temporary delay in the development of motor skills requiring upper-body strength, such as rolling over, sitting, crawling, and standing. However, these milestones are still attained within the normal age range, and the age at which babies begin to walk is not significantly affected (Davis, Moon, Sachs, & Ottolini, 1998).

Immunization for Better Health

Such once-familiar and sometimes fatal childhood illnesses as measles, whooping cough, and infantile paralysis (polio) are now largely preventable, thanks to the development of vaccines that mobilize the body's natural defenses. Unfortunately, many children still are not adequately protected. In the developing world, 18 percent of deaths of children under age 5 are from vaccine-preventable diseases: measles, neonatal tetanus, pertussis, and tuberculosis (Wegman, 1999).

CHECKPOINT

Can you ...

✔ Explain why full immunization of all preschool children is important?

In the United States, since 1990, the prevalence of vaccine-preventable illnesses has dropped sharply. By 1998, disease and death rates for diphtheria, pertussis, tetanus, measles, mumps, rubella, and type B influenza were at or near all-time lows (CDC, 1999b). This dramatic improvement in child health followed a nationwide immunization initiative. In 1994 Congress appropriated more than $800 million to improve community education, to make vaccines more available and less costly, and to provide free vaccines to the uninsured and those on Medicaid. By 1998, the overall immunization rate for 19- to 35-month-olds had reached a record 80 percent. Still, many children lack one or more of the required shots, and there is substantial variation in coverage among states and cities (CDC, 1999b).

Consider this . . .

- Who should be primarily responsible for ensuring that children are immunized: parents, community agencies, or government?

One reason some parents hesitate to immunize their children is fear that vaccines (especially pertussis vaccine) may cause brain damage. However, the association between pertussis vaccine and neurologic illness appears very small (Gale et al., 1994). The potential damage from the diseases that this vaccine prevents is far greater than the risks of the vaccine.

Early Physical Development

Fortunately, most infants do survive, develop normally, and grow up healthy. What principles govern their development? What are the typical growth patterns of body and brain? How do babies' needs for nourishment and sleep change? How do their sensory and motor abilities develop?

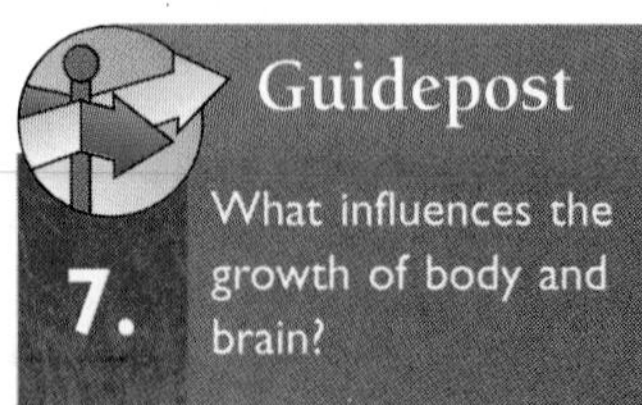

Guidepost

7. What influences the growth of body and brain?

Principles of Development

As before birth, physical growth and development follow the maturational principles introduced in Chapter 3: the *cephalocaudal principle* and *proximodistal principle.*

According to the *cephalocaudal principle,* growth occurs from head to tail. Because the brain grows so rapidly before birth, a newborn baby's head is disproportionately large. By 1 year, the brain is 70 percent of its adult weight, but the rest of the body is only about 10 to 20 percent of adult weight. The head becomes proportionately smaller as the child grows in height and the lower parts of the body develop (see Figure 4-3). Sensory and motor development proceed according to the same principle: infants learn to use the upper parts of the body before the lower parts. They see objects before they can control their trunk, and they learn to do many things with their hands long before they can crawl or walk.

According to the *proximodistal principle* (inner to outer), growth and motor development proceed from the center of the body outward. In the womb, the head and trunk develop before the arms and legs, then the hands and feet, and then the fingers and toes. During infancy and early childhood, the limbs continue to grow faster than the hands and feet. Similarly, children first develop the ability to use their upper arms and upper legs (which are closest to the center of the body), then the forearms and forelegs, then hands and feet, and finally, fingers and toes.

Physiological Growth

Children grow faster during the first 3 years, especially during the first few months, than they ever will again (see Figure 4-4). At 5 months, the average baby's birthweight has doubled from $7\frac{1}{2}$ pounds to about 15 pounds, and, by 1 year, has tripled to about 22 pounds. This rapid growth rate tapers off during the second year, when a child typically gains 5 or 6 pounds, quadrupling the birthweight by the second birthday. During the third year, the average gain is somewhat less, about 4 to 5 pounds. Height typically increases by about 10 to 12 inches during the first year (making the typical 1-year-old about 30 inches tall); by about 5 inches during the second year (so that the average 2-year-old is about 3 feet tall); and by 3 to 4 inches during the third year. As a baby grows, body shape and proportions change, too; a 3-year-old typically is slender compared with a chubby, potbellied 1-year-old.

Teething usually begins around 3 or 4 months, when infants begin grabbing almost everything in sight to put into their mouths; but the first tooth may not actually arrive until sometime between 5 and 9 months of age, or even later. By the first birthday, babies generally have 6 to 8 teeth; by age $2\frac{1}{2}$, they have a mouthful of 20.

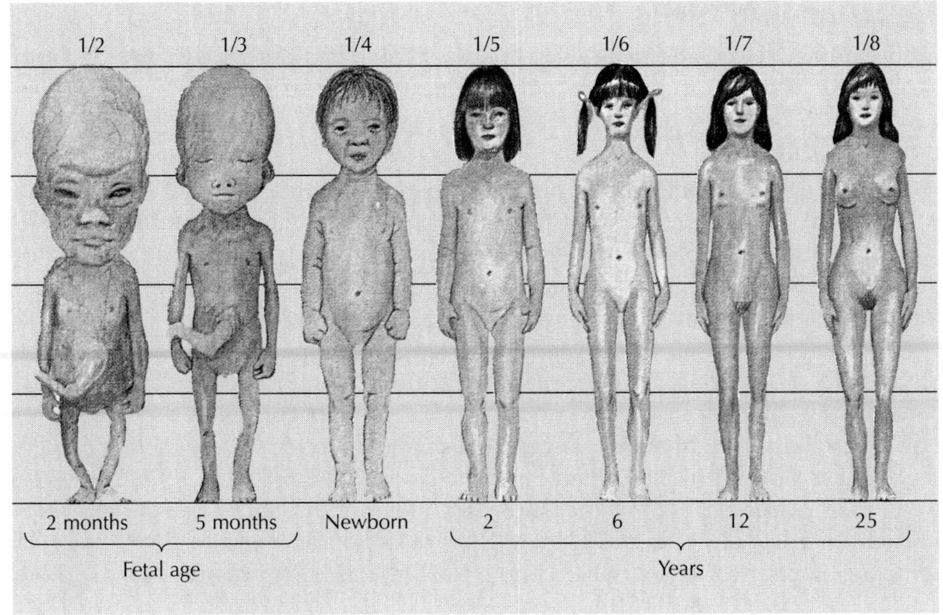

Figure 4-3
Changes in proportions of the human body during growth. The most striking change is that the head becomes smaller relative to the rest of the body. The fractions indicate head size as a proportion of total body length at several ages. More subtle is the stability of the trunk proportion (from neck to crotch). The increasing leg proportion is almost exactly the reverse of the decreasing head proportion.

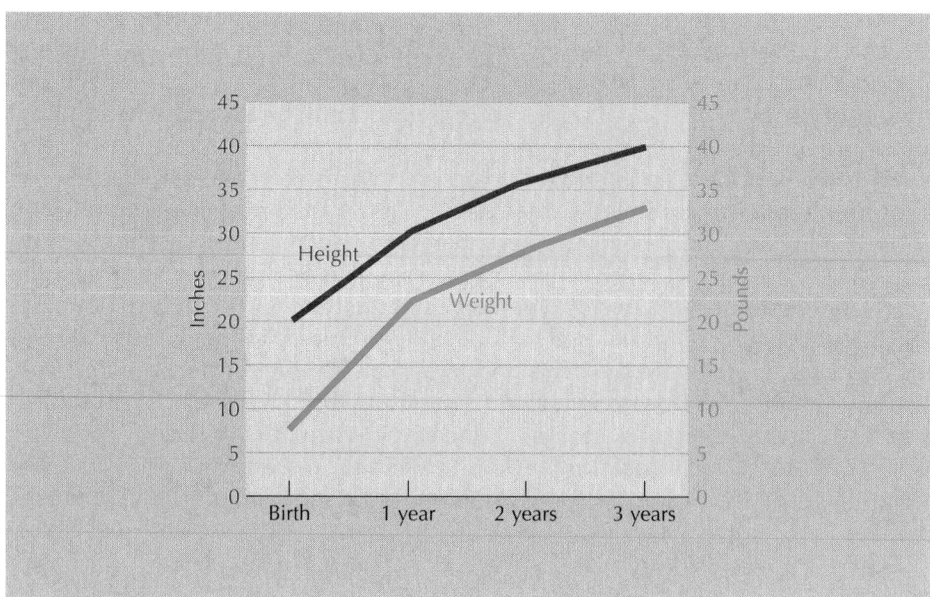

Figure 4-4
Growth in height and weight during infancy and toddlerhood. Babies grow most rapidly in both height and weight during the first few months of life, then taper off somewhat by age 3.

The genes an infant inherits have a strong influence on body type; they help determine whether the child will be tall or short, thin or stocky, or somewhere in between (Stunkard, Foch, & Hrubec, 1986; Stunkard, Harris, Pedersen, & McClearn, 1990). This genetic influence interacts with such environmental influences as nutrition and living conditions. For example, Japanese American children are taller and weigh more than children the same age in Japan, probably because of dietary differences (Broude, 1995). By the age of 4, some children in Africa and Asia weigh 13 pounds less and are 7 inches shorter than children the same age in Europe and the United States (Gardiner et al., 1998).

Today, with improved nutrition and sanitation, together with the decrease in child labor, children in western industrial countries are growing taller and maturing sexually at an earlier age than a century ago. Better medical care, especially immunization and antibiotics, also plays a part. Children who are ill for a long time may never achieve their genetically programmed stature because they may never make up for the loss of growth time while they were sick.

CHECKPOINT

Can you . . .

✔ Summarize typical patterns of growth during the first three years?

✔ Discuss factors that affect growth?

Nutrition and Sleep Needs

Proper nutrition and adequate sleep are essential to healthy growth. Feeding and sleep needs change rapidly, especially during the first year of life.

Early Feeding

From the beginnings of human history, babies were breast-fed. A woman who was either unable or unwilling to nurse her baby usually found another woman, a "wet nurse," to do it. Early in the twentieth century, with the advent of dependable refrigeration and pasteurization, manufacturers began to develop formulas to modify and enrich cow's milk for infant consumption.

During the next half-century, formula feeding became the norm in the United States and some other industrialized countries. By 1971, only 25 percent of American mothers even tried to nurse. Since then, recognition of the benefits of breast milk has brought about a reversal of this trend, so that today nearly 60 percent of new mothers in the United States breast-feed (A. S. Ryan, 1997). However, fewer than 22 percent are still breast-feeding at 6 months, and many of these supplement breast milk with formula (AAP Work Group on Breastfeeding, 1997). In some developing countries, where bottle-feeding has been promoted as the more modern method, some poor mothers dilute formula, unwittingly endangering their babies' health and lives (Gardiner et al., 1998).

Breast milk is almost always the best food for newborns and is recommended for at least the first 12 months. The only acceptable alternative is an iron-fortified formula based on either cow's milk or soy protein and containing supplemental vitamins and minerals. Breast milk is more digestible and more nutritious than formula and is less likely to produce allergic reactions (AAP, 1989a, 1996; AAP Work Group on Breastfeeding, 1997; Eiger & Olds, 1999). Human milk is a complete source of nutrients for at least the first 6 months; during this time breast-fed babies normally do not need any other food. Neither they nor formula-fed infants need additional water (AAP Work Group on Breastfeeding, 1997).

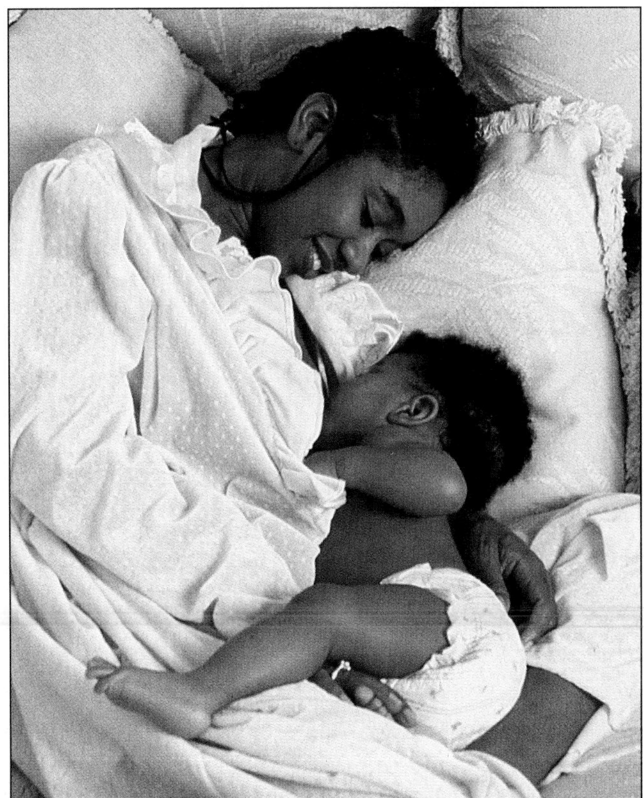

Breast milk can be called the "ultimate health food" because it offers so many benefits to babies—physical, cognitive, and emotional.

The health advantages of breast-feeding are striking during the first 2 years and even later in life (A. S. Cunningham, Jelliffe, & Jelliffe, 1991; J. Newman, 1995; A. L. Wright, Holberg, Taussig, & Martinez, 1995). Among the illnesses prevented or minimized by breast-feeding are diarrhea, respiratory infections (such as pneumonia and bronchitis), otitis media (an infection of the middle ear), and staphylococcal, bacterial, and urinary tract infections (AAP Work Group on Breastfeeding, 1997; A. S. Cunningham et al., 1991; Dewey, Heinig, & Nommsen-Rivers, 1995; J. Newman, 1995; Scariati, Grummer-Strawn, & Fein, 1997a). Breast-feeding also seems to have benefits for visual acuity (Makrides, Neumann, Simmer, Pater, & Gibson, 1995), neurological development (Lanting, Fidler, Huisman, Touwen, & Boersma, 1994), and cognitive development (AAP Work Group on Breastfeeding, 1997; Horwood & Fergusson, 1998).

Nursing mothers need to be as careful as pregnant women about what they take into their bodies. Breast-feeding is inadvisable if a mother is infected with the AIDS virus, which can be transmitted through her milk, especially during the early months; if she has another infectious illness; if she has untreated active tuberculosis; or if she is taking any drug that would not be safe for the baby (AAP Committee on Drugs, 1994; AAP Committee on Infectious Diseases, 1994; AAP Work Group on Breastfeeding, 1997; Eiger & Olds, 1999; Miotti et al., 1999; WHO/UNICEF Constitution on HIV Transmission and Breastfeeding, 1992).

Feeding a baby is an emotional as well as a physical act. Warm contact with the mother's body fosters emotional linkage between mother and baby. Such bonding can take place through either breast- or bottle-feeding and through many other caregiving activities, most of which can be performed by fathers as well as mothers. The quality of the relationship between parent and child and the provision of abundant affection and cuddling may be more important than the feeding method.

> *Consider this. . .*
>
> • "Every mother who is physically able should breast-feed." Do you agree or disagree? Give reasons.

Cow's Milk, Solid Foods, and Juice

Iron-deficiency anemia is the world's most common nutritional disorder, affecting as many as one-fourth of all 6- to 24-month-old babies in the United States. Infants with iron-deficiency anemia do more poorly on cognitive tests than other infants. They also tend to be less independent, joyful, attentive, and playful, and more wary, hesitant, and easily tired (Lozoff et al., 1998). Because infants fed plain cow's milk in the early months of life may suffer from iron deficiency (Sadowitz & Oski, 1983), the American Academy of Pediatrics (AAP, 1989b, 1996; AAP Committee on Nutrition, 1992b) recommends that babies receive breast milk or, alternatively, iron-fortified formula for at least the first year.

At 1 year, babies can switch to cow's milk if they are getting a balanced diet of supplementary solid foods that provide one-third of their caloric intake (AAP, 1989b). To promote proper growth, the milk should be homogenized whole milk fortified with vitamin D, not skim milk or reduced-fat (1 or 2 percent) milk (AAP, 1996).

Iron-enriched solid foods—usually beginning with cereal—should be gradually introduced during the second half of the first year (AAP Work Group on Breastfeeding, 1997). At this time, too, fruit juice may be introduced. A recent study based on mothers' reports of toddlers' diets (Skinner, Carruth, Moran, Houck, & Coletta, 1999) did not support earlier findings that large amounts of fruit juice interfere with growth (M. M. Smith & Lifshitz, 1994).

Changing Sleep Patterns

At about 3 months, most babies grow more wakeful in the late afternoon and early evening and start to sleep through the night. By 6 months, more than half their sleep occurs at night. The place where they do their sleeping may change, too—perhaps from the parents' bedroom to a room of their own (see Box 4-1). By this time, active sleep accounts for only 30 percent of sleep time, and the length of the cycle becomes more consistent (Coons & Guilleminault, 1982). The amount of REM sleep continues to decrease steadily throughout life.

Cultural variations in sleep patterns may be related to feeding practices. Many U.S. parents time the evening feeding, or start solid foods, so as to encourage nighttime sleep. Mothers in rural Kenya allow their babies to nurse as they please, and their 4-month-olds continue to sleep only four hours at a stretch (Broude, 1995).

CHECKPOINT

Can you . . .

- ✔ Summarize pediatric recommendations regarding breast-feeding versus formula and the introduction of cow's milk, solid foods, and fruit juices?
- ✔ Tell how sleep patterns change after the first few months, and how culture may influence these changes?

The Brain and Reflex Behavior

What makes newborns respond to a nipple? What tells them to start the sucking movements that allow them to control their intake of fluids? These are functions of the **central nervous system**—the brain and *spinal cord* (a bundle of nerves running through the backbone)—and of a growing peripheral network of nerves extending to every part of the body. Through this network, sensory messages travel to the brain, and motor commands travel back.

central nervous system Brain and spinal cord.

Building the Brain

The growth of the brain both before birth and during the childhood years is fundamental to future physical, cognitive, and emotional development. Through various brain-imaging tools, researchers are gaining a clearer picture of how that growth occurs (Behrman, 1992; Casaer, 1993; Gabbard, 1996).* For example, from positron emission tomography (PET) scans showing patterns of glucose metabolism, which are indicators of changes in functional activity, we have learned that the brain's maturation takes much longer than was previously thought (Chugani, 1998).

The brain at birth weighs only about 25 percent of its eventual adult weight of $3^1/_2$ pounds. It reaches nearly 90 percent of that weight by age 3. By age 6, it is almost adult size; but growth and functional development of specific parts of the brain continue into adulthood. Increases in brain weight and volume can be measured before birth by ultrasound and after birth by the circumference of the

*Unless otherwise referenced, the discussion in this section is largely based on Gabbard (1996).

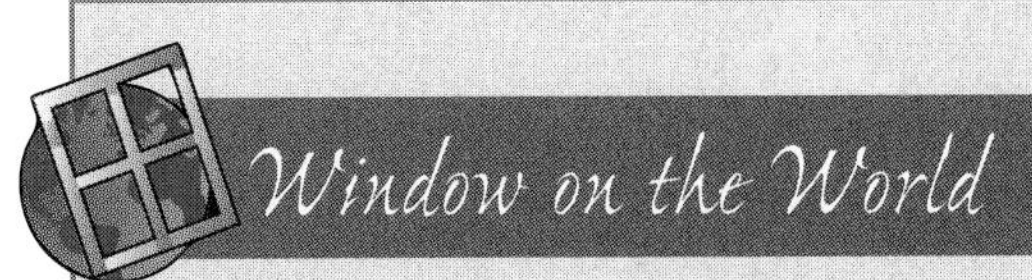

Box 4-1
Sleep Customs

There is considerable cultural variation in newborns' sleeping arrangements. In many cultures, infants sleep in the same room with their mothers for the first few years of life, and frequently in the same bed, making it easier to nurse at night (Broude, 1995). In the United States, it is common practice, reflecting the prevailing recommendations of child-care experts, to have a separate bed and a separate room for the infant.

Some experts find benefits in the shared sleeping pattern. One research team that has been monitoring sleep patterns of mothers and their 3-month-old infants found that those who sleep together tend to wake each other up during the night and suggested that this may prevent the baby from sleeping too long and too deeply and having long breathing pauses that might be fatal (McKenna & Mosko, 1993). However, the American Academy of Pediatrics Task Force on Infant Positioning and SIDS (1997) did not find this evidence persuasive; instead, the Task Force found that, under some conditions, such as the use of soft bedding, or maternal smoking or drug use, bed sharing can increase the risk of SIDS. This is far from a new concern: medieval church authorities forbade parents to sleep next to their newborns for fear of suffocation (Nakajima & Mayor, 1996). Yet modern-day Japan, where mothers and infants commonly sleep in the same bed, has one of the lowest SIDS rates in the world (Hoffman & Hillman, 1992).

One thing is clear: bed-sharing promotes breast-feeding. Infants who sleep with their mothers breast-feed about three times longer during the night than infants who sleep in separate beds (McKenna, Mosko, & Richard, 1997). By snuggling up together, mother and baby stay oriented toward each other's subtle bodily signals. Mothers can respond more quickly and easily to an infant's first whimpers of hunger, rather than having to wait until the baby's cries are loud enough to be heard from the next room.

In interviews, middle-class U.S. parents and Mayan mothers in rural Guatemala revealed their childrearing values and goals in their explanations about sleeping arrangements (Morelli, Rogoff, Oppenheim, & Goldsmith, 1992). The U.S. parents, many of whom kept their infants in the same room but not in the same bed for the first 3 to 6 months, said they moved the babies to separate rooms because they wanted to make them self-reliant and independent. The Mayan mothers kept infants and toddlers in their beds until the birth of a new baby, when the older child would sleep with another family member or in a bed in the mother's room. The Mayan mothers valued close parent-child relationships and expressed shock at the idea that anyone would put a baby to sleep in a room all alone.

Societal values influence parents' attitudes and behaviors. Throughout this book we will see many ways in which such culturally determined attitudes and behaviors affect children.

---

baby's head. These measurements provide a check on whether the brain is growing normally.

The brain's growth is not smooth and steady; it occurs in fits and starts. **Brain growth spurts,** periods of rapid growth and development, coincide with changes in cognitive behavior (Fischer & Rose, 1994, 1995). Different parts of the brain grow more rapidly at different times.

> *Consider this . . .*
>
> - How would you weigh the advantages and disadvantages of having an infant sleep in the parental bed?

brain growth spurts
Periods of rapid brain growth and development.

Major Parts of the Brain Beginning about two weeks after conception, the brain gradually develops from a long hollow tube into a spherical mass of cells (see Figure 4-5). By birth, the growth spurt of the spinal cord and *brain stem* (the part of the brain responsible for such basic bodily functions as breathing, heart rate, body temperature, and the sleep-wake cycle) has almost run its course. The *cerebellum* (the part of the brain that maintains balance and motor coordination) grows fastest during the first year of life (Casaer, 1993).

The *cerebrum,* the largest part of the brain, is divided into right and left halves, or hemispheres, each with specialized functions. This specialization of the hemispheres is called **lateralization.** The left hemisphere is mainly concerned with language and logical thinking, the right hemisphere with visual and spatial functions such as map reading and drawing. The two hemispheres are joined by a tough band of tissue called the *corpus callosum,* which allows them to share information and coordinate commands. The corpus callosum grows dramatically during childhood, reaching adult size by about age 10.

lateralization
Tendency of each of the brain's hemispheres to have specialized functions.

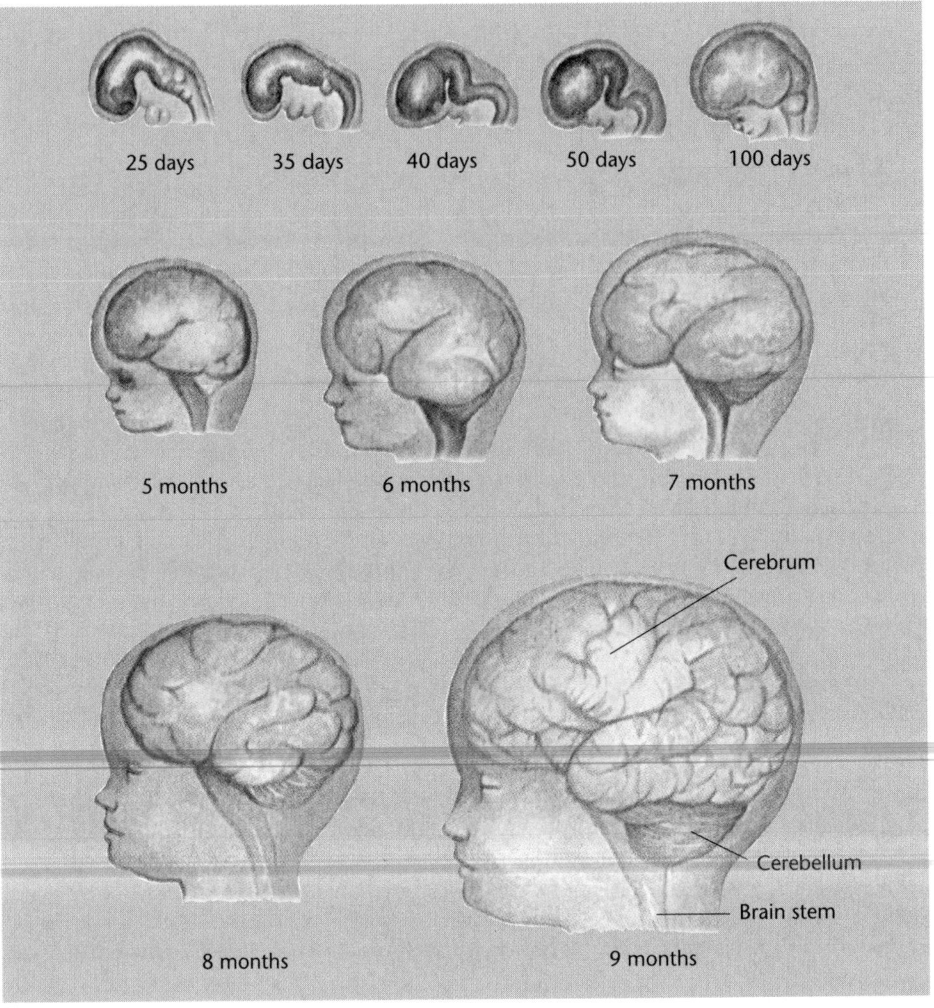

Figure 4-5
Fetal brain development from 25 days of gestation through birth. The brain stem, which controls basic biological functions such as breathing, develops first. As the brain grows, the front part expands greatly to form the cerebrum (the large, convoluted upper mass). Specific areas of the gray matter (the outer covering of the brain) have specific functions, such as sensory and motor activity; but large areas are "uncommitted" and thus are free for higher cognitive activity, such as thinking, remembering, and problem solving. The subcortex (the brain stem and other structures below the cortical layer) handles reflex behavior and other lower-level functions. The cerebellum, which maintains balance and motor coordination, grows most rapidly during the first year of life.
(Source: Casaer, 1993; Restak, 1984.)

Each cerebral hemisphere has four lobes, or sections: the *occipital, parietal, temporal,* and *frontal* lobes, which control different functions (see Figure 4-6) and develop at different rates. The regions of the *cerebral cortex* (the outer surface of the cerebrum) that govern vision and hearing are mature by 6 months of age, but the areas of the frontal lobe responsible for making mental associations, remembering, and producing deliberate motor responses remain immature for several years.

neurons
Nerve cells.

Brain Cells The brain is composed of *neurons* and *glial cells.* **Neurons,** or nerve cells, send and receive information. *Glial cells* support and protect the neurons.

Beginning in the second month of gestation, an estimated 250,000 immature neurons are produced every minute through cell division (mitosis). At birth, most of the more than 100 billion neurons in a mature brain are already formed but are not yet fully developed. The number of neurons increases most rapidly between the 25th week of gestation and the first few months after birth. This cell proliferation is accompanied by a dramatic growth in cell size.

Originally the neurons are simply cell bodies with a nucleus, or center, composed of deoxyribonucleic acid (DNA), which contains the cell's genetic programming. As the brain grows, these rudimentary cells migrate to various parts of it. There they sprout *axons* and *dendrites*—narrow, branching extensions. Axons send signals to other neurons, and dendrites receive incoming messages from them, through *synapses,* the nervous system's communication links. The synapses

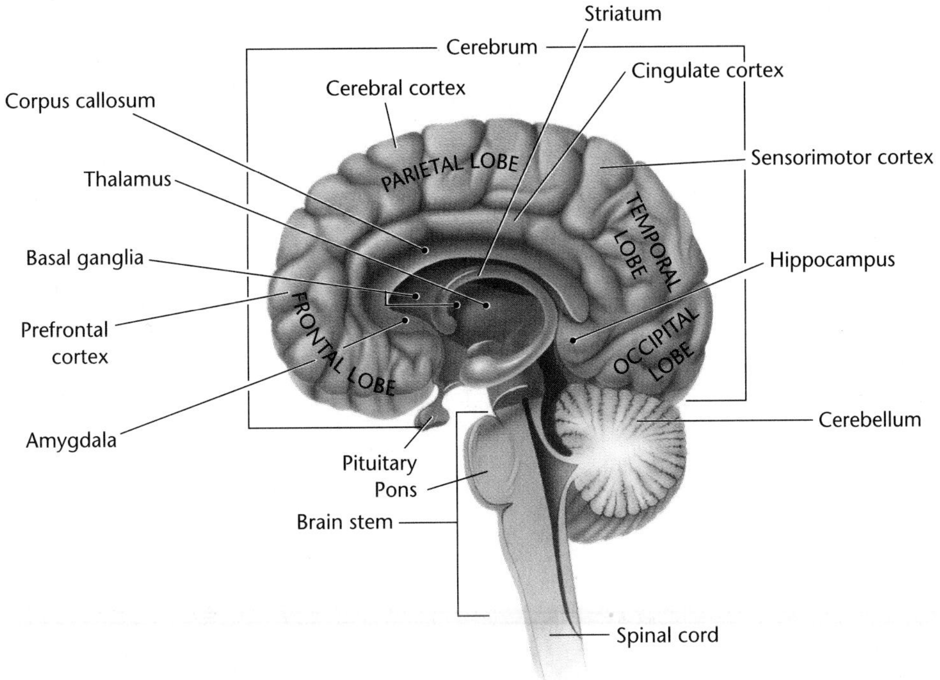

Figure 4-6
Parts of the brain, side view. The brain consists of three main parts: the brain stem, the cerebellum, and, above those, the large cerebrum. The brain stem, an extension of the spinal cord, is one of the regions of the brain most completely developed at birth. It controls such basic bodily functions as breathing, circulation, and reflexes. The cerebellum, at birth, begins to control balance and muscle tone; later it coordinates sensory and motor activity. The cerebrum constitutes almost 70 percent of the weight of the nervous system and handles thought, memory, language, and emotion. It is divided into two halves, or hemispheres, each of which has four sections, or lobes (right to left): (a) The occipital lobe processes visual information. (b) The temporal lobe helps with hearing and language. (c) The parietal lobe allows an infant to receive touch sensations and spatial information, which facilitates eye-hand coordination. (d) The frontal lobe develops gradually during the first year, permitting such higher-level functions as speech and reasoning. The cerebral cortex, the outer surface of the cerebrum, consists of gray matter; it is the seat of thought processes and mental activity. Parts of the cerebral cortex—the sensorimotor cortex and cingulate cortex—as well as several structures deep within the cerebrum, the thalamus, hippocampus, and basal ganglia, all of which control basic movements and functions, are largely developed at birth.

are tiny gaps, which are bridged with the help of chemicals called *neurotransmitters.* Eventually a particular neuron may have anywhere from 5,000 to 100,000 synaptic connections to and from the body's sensory receptors, its muscles, and other neurons within the central nervous system.

The multiplication of dendrites and synaptic connections, especially during the last $2^1/_2$ months of gestation and the first 6 months to 2 years of life (see Figure 4-7), accounts for much of the brain's growth in weight and permits the emergence of new perceptual, cognitive, and motor abilities. Most of the neurons in the cortex, which is responsible for complex, high-level functioning, are in place by 20 weeks of gestation, and its structure becomes fairly well defined during the next 12 weeks. Only after birth, however, do the cells begin to form connections that allow communication to take place.

As the neurons multiply, migrate to their assigned locations, and develop connections, they undergo the complementary processes of *integration* and *differentiation.* Through **integration,** the neurons that control various groups of muscles coordinate their activities. Through **differentiation,** each neuron takes on a specific, specialized structure and function.

At first the brain produces more neurons and synapses than it needs. Those that are not used or do not function well die out. This process of **cell death,** or pruning of excess cells, begins during the prenatal period and continues after birth (see Figure 4-8), helping to create an efficient nervous system. The number of synapses seems to peak at about age 2, and their elimination continues well into adolescence. Even as some neurons die out, new research suggests, others may continue to form during adult life (Eriksson et al., 1998; Gould, Reeves, Graziano, & Gross, 1999; see Chapter 17). Connections among cortical cells continue to improve into adulthood, allowing more flexible and more advanced motor and cognitive functioning.

integration
Process by which neurons coordinate the activities of muscle groups.

differentiation
Process by which neurons acquire specialized structure and function.

cell death
Elimination of excess brain cells to achieve more efficient functioning.

Myelination Much of the credit for improvement in efficiency of communication goes to the glial cells, which coat the neural pathways with a fatty substance

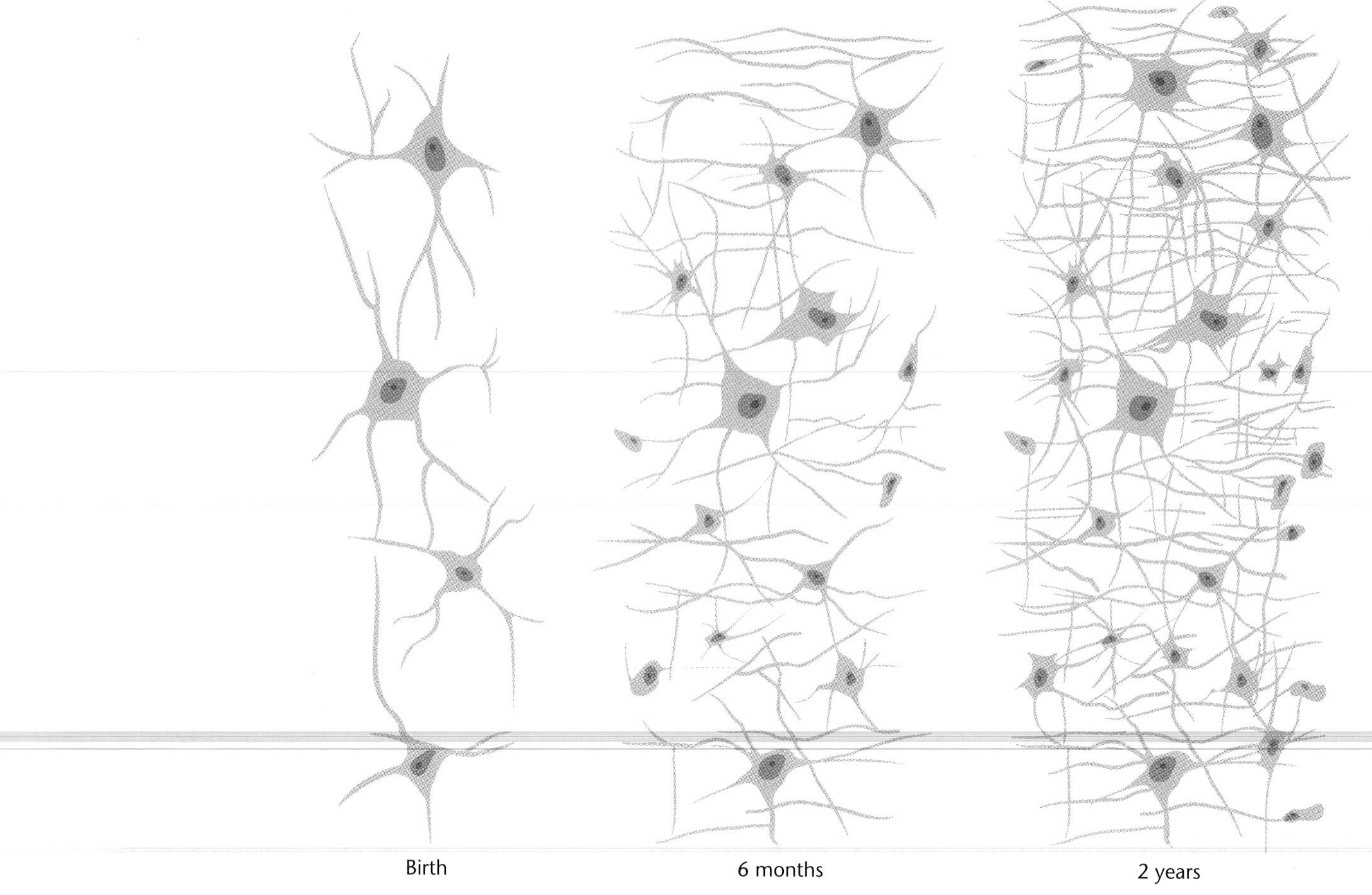

Figure 4-7

Growth of neural connections during first 2 years of life. The rapid increase in the brain's density and weight is due largely to the formation of dendrites, extension of nerve cell bodies, and the synapses that link them. This mushrooming communications network sprouts in response to environmental stimulation and makes possible impressive growth in every domain of development.
(Source: Conel, 1959.)

myelination
Process of coating neurons with a fatty substance (myelin) that enables faster communication between cells.

called *myelin.* This process of **myelination** enables signals to travel faster and more smoothly, permitting the achievement of mature functioning. Myelination begins about halfway through gestation in some parts of the brain and continues into adulthood in others. The pathways related to the sense of touch—the first sense to develop—are myelinated by birth. Myelination of visual pathways, which are slower to mature, begins at birth and continues during the first 5 months of life. Pathways related to hearing may begin to be myelinated as early as the fifth month of gestation, but the process is not complete until about age 4. The parts of the cortex that control attention and memory, which are slower to develop, are not fully myelinated until young adulthood. Myelination in an information relay zone of the *hippocampus,* a structure deep in the temporal lobe that plays a key role in memory, and related formations continues to increase until at least age 70 (Benes, Turtle, Kahn, & Farol, 1994).

Myelination of sensory and motor pathways, first in the fetus's spinal cord and later, after birth, in the cerebral cortex, may account for the appearance and disappearance of early reflexes.

reflex behaviors
Automatic, involuntary, innate responses to stimulation.

Early Reflex Behaviors

When babies (or adults) blink at a bright light, they are acting involuntarily. Such automatic, innate responses to stimulation are called **reflex behaviors.** They are

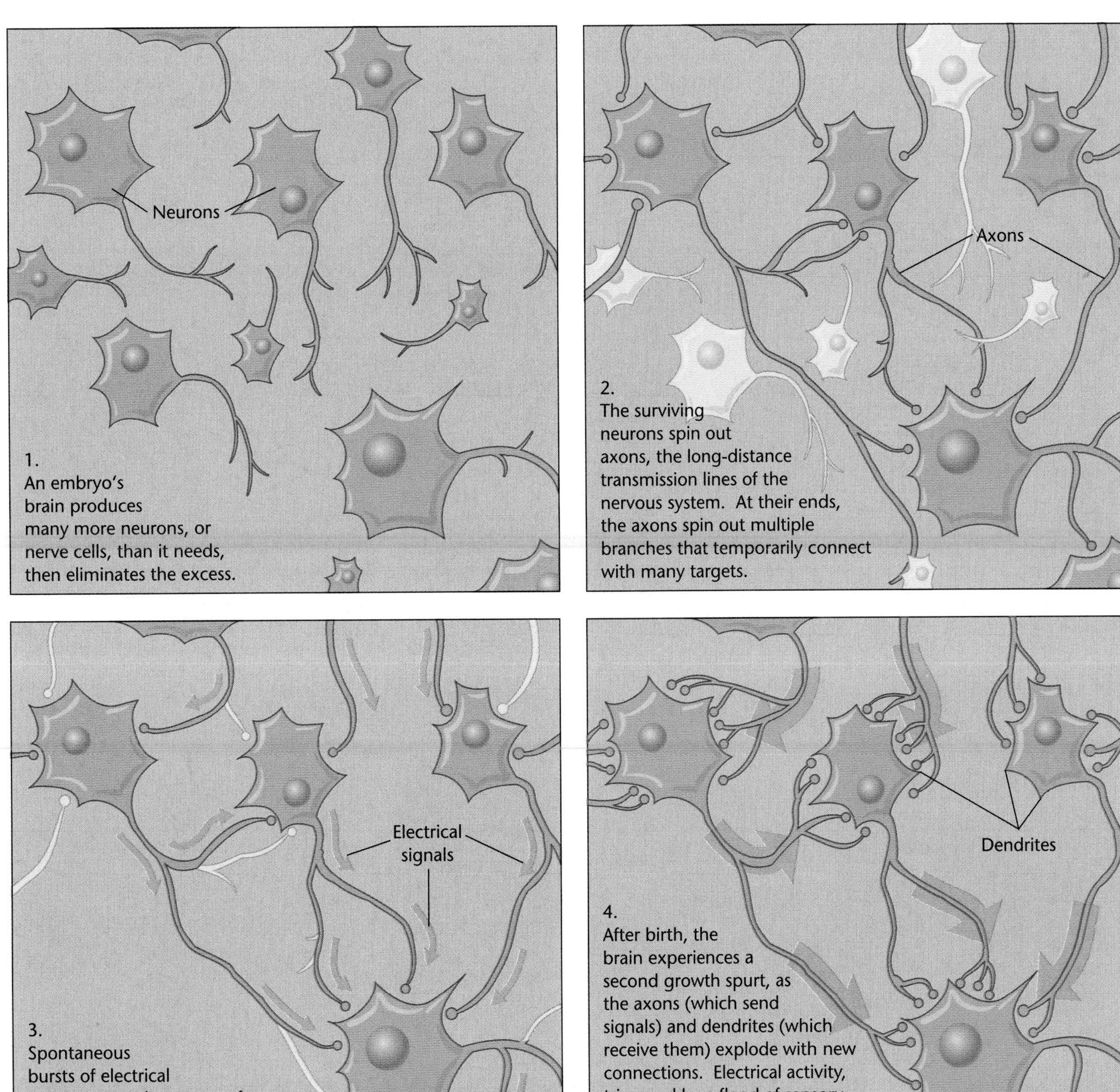

Figure 4-8

Wiring the brain: development of neural connections before and after birth.

(Source: Nash, 1997, p. 51.)

controlled by the lower brain centers that govern other involuntary processes, such as breathing and heart rate. These are the parts of the brain most fully myelinated at birth. Reflex behaviors play an important part in stimulating the early development of the central nervous system and muscles.

Human infants have an estimated 27 major reflexes, many of which are present at birth or soon after (Gabbard, 1996; see Table 4-4 for examples). *Primitive reflexes,* such as sucking, rooting for the nipple, and the Moro reflex (a response to being startled or beginning to fall), are related to instinctive needs for survival

Table 4-4 Early Human Reflexes

Reflex	Stimulation	Baby's Behavior	Typical Age of Appearance	Typical Age of Disappearance
Moro	Baby is dropped or hears loud noise.	Extends legs, arms, and fingers, arches back, draws back head.	7th month of gestation	3 months
Darwinian (grasping)	Palm of baby's hand is stroked.	Makes strong fist; can be raised to standing position if both fists are closed around a stick.	7th month of gestation	4 months
Tonic neck	Baby is laid down on back.	Turns head to one side, assumes "fencer" position, extends arms and legs on preferred side, flexes opposite limbs.	7th month of gestation	5 months
Babkin	Both of baby's palms are stroked at once.	Mouth opens, eyes close, neck flexes, head tilts forward.	Birth	3 months
Babinski	Sole of baby's foot is stroked.	Toes fan out; foot twists in.	Birth	4 months
Rooting	Baby's cheek or lower lip is stroked with finger or nipple.	Head turns; mouth opens; sucking movements begin.	Birth	9 months
Walking	Baby is held under arms, with bare feet touching flat surface.	Makes steplike motions that look like well-coordinated walking.	1 month	4 months
Swimming	Baby is put into water face down.	Makes well-coordinated swimming movements.	1 month	4 months

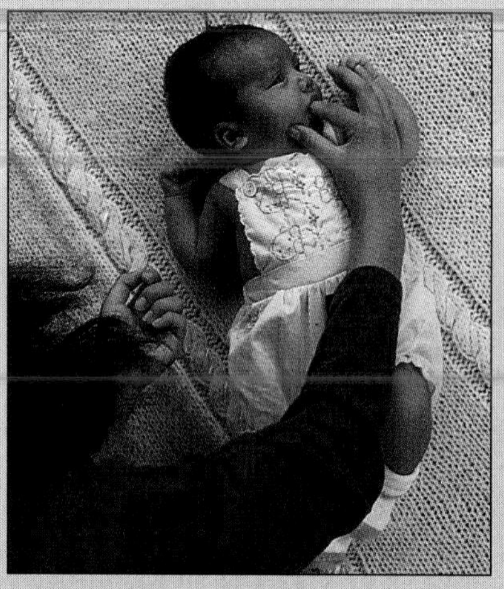

Rooting reflex

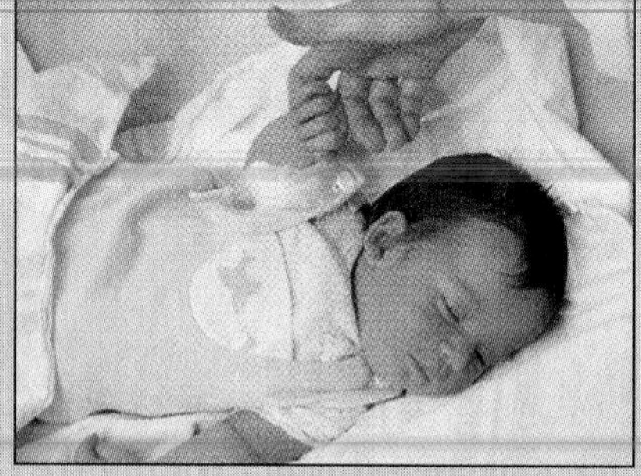

Darwinian reflex

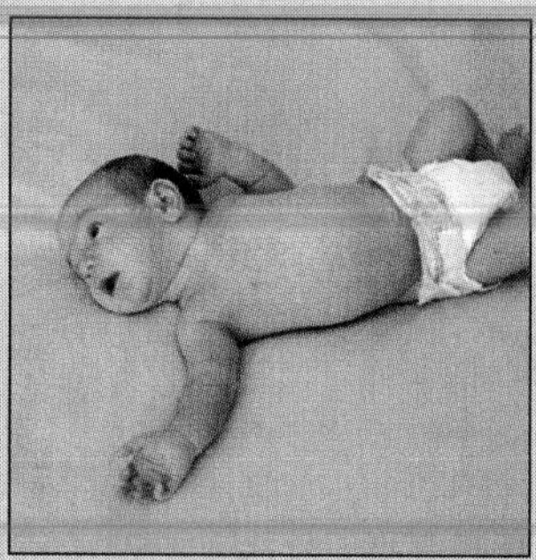

Tonic neck reflex

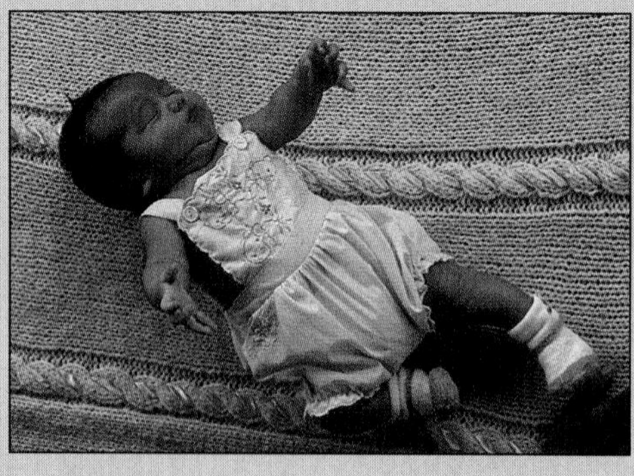

Moro reflex

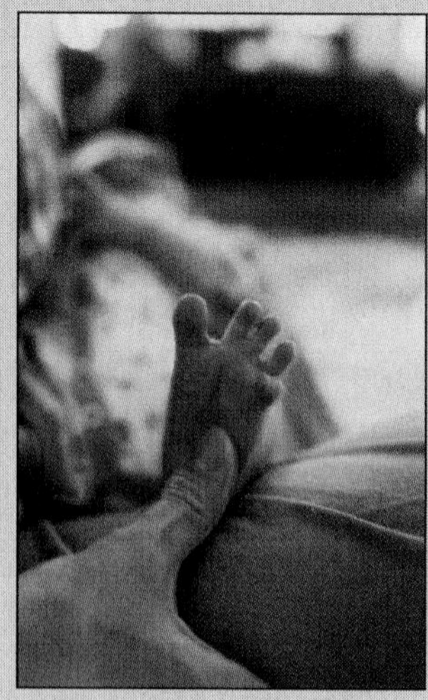

Babinski reflex

Walking reflex

Source: Adapted in part from Gabbard, 1996.

and protection. Some primitive reflexes may be part of humanity's evolutionary legacy. One example is the grasping reflex, by which infant monkeys hold on to the hair of their mothers' bodies. As the higher brain centers become active, during the first 2 to 4 months, infants begin to show *postural reflexes:* reactions to changes in position or balance. For example, infants who are tilted downward extend their arms in the parachute reflex, an instinctive attempt to break a fall.

Locomotor reflexes, such as the walking and swimming reflexes, resemble voluntary movements that do not appear until months after the reflexes have disappeared. As we'll see, there is debate about whether or not locomotor reflexes prepare the way for their later, voluntary counterparts.

Most of the early reflexes disappear during the first 6 months to 1 year. Reflexes that continue to serve protective functions—such as blinking, yawning, coughing, gagging, sneezing, shivering, and the pupillary reflex (dilation of the pupils in the dark)—remain. Disappearance of unneeded reflexes on schedule is a sign that motor pathways in the cortex have been partially myelinated, enabling a shift to voluntary behavior. Thus we can evaluate a baby's neurological development by seeing whether certain reflexes are present or absent.

What is normal, however, varies somewhat from culture to culture (D. G. Freedman, 1979). For example, differences show up in the Moro reflex. To elicit this reflex, the baby's body is lifted, supporting the head. Then the head support is released, and the head is allowed to drop slightly. Caucasian newborns reflexively extend both arms and legs, cry persistently, and move about agitatedly. Navajo babies do not extend their limbs in the same way, rarely cry, and almost immediately stop any agitated motion. Since these reflexive differences are displayed soon after birth, they may reflect innate variability among ethnic groups.

CHECKPOINT

Can you . . .

- ✔ Describe the most important features of brain development before and after birth?
- ✔ Explain the functions of inborn reflex behaviors and why some of these reflexes drop out during the early months of life while others remain?

Molding the Brain

The brain growth spurt that begins at about the third trimester of gestation and continues until at least the fourth year of life is important to the development of neurological functioning (Gabbard, 1996). Smiling, babbling, crawling, walking, and talking—all the major sensory, motor, and cognitive milestones of infancy and toddlerhood—are made possible by the rapid development of the brain, particularly the cerebral cortex.

Until the middle of the twentieth century, scientists believed that the brain grew in an unchangeable, genetically determined pattern. This does seem to be largely true before birth. But it is now widely believed, largely on the basis of animal studies, that the postnatal brain is "molded" by experience. This is so especially during the early months of life, when the cortex is still growing rapidly and organizing itself (Black, 1998). The technical term for this malleability, or modifiability, of the brain is **plasticity.** Early synaptic connections, some of which depend on sensory stimulation, refine and stabilize the brain's genetically designed "wiring." Thus, early experience can have lasting effects on the capacity of the central nervous system to learn and store information (Black, 1998; Chugani, 1998; Greenough, Black, & Wallace, 1987; Pally, 1997; Wittrock, 1980).

plasticity
Modifiability, or "molding," of the brain through experience.

In one series of experiments, rats were raised in cages with wheels to run on, rocks to climb on, levers to manipulate, or other animals to interact with. These animals were then compared with littermates raised in standard cages or in isolation. The "enriched" animals had heavier brains with thicker cortical layers, more cells in the visual cortex, more complex cells, and higher levels of neurochemical activity, making it easier to form synaptic connections (Rosenzweig, 1984; Rosenzweig & Bennett, 1976).

By the same token, early abuse or sensory impoverishment may leave an imprint on the brain (Black, 1998). In one experiment, kittens fitted with goggles that allowed them to see only vertical lines grew up unable to see horizontal lines and bumped into horizontal boards in front of them. Other kittens, whose goggles allowed them to see only horizontal lines, grew up blind to vertical columns (H. V. Hirsch & Spinelli, 1970). This did not happen when the same procedure was carried out with adult cats. Apparently, neurons in the visual cortex became programmed to respond only to lines running in the direction the kittens were permitted to see. Thus, if certain cortical connections are not made early in life, these circuits may "shut down" forever.

Early emotional development, too, may depend on experience. Infants whose mothers are severely depressed show less activity in the left frontal lobe, the part of the brain that is involved in positive emotions such as happiness and joy, and more activity in the right frontal lobe, which is associated with negative emotions (Dawson, Klinger, Panagiotides, Hill, & Spieker, 1992; Dawson, Frey, Panagiotides, Osterling, & Hessl, 1997).

Sometimes corrective experience can make up for past deprivation (Black, 1998). Plasticity continues throughout life as neurons change in size and shape in response to environmental experience (Diamond, 1988; Pally, 1997). Brain-damaged rats, when raised in an enriched setting, grow more dendritic connections (Diamond, 1988). Such findings have sparked successful efforts to stimulate the physical and mental development of children with Down syndrome and to help victims of brain damage recover function.

Consider this . . .

- In view of what is now known about the plasticity of the infant brain, should society make sure that every baby has access to an appropriately stimulating environment? If so, how can and should this be done?

Ethical constraints prevent controlled experiments on the effects of environmental deprivation on human infants; but the discovery of thousands of infants and young children who had spent virtually their entire lives in overcrowded Romanian orphanages offered an opportunity for a natural experiment (Ames, 1997). Discovered after the fall of the dictator Nicolae Ceausescu in December 1989, these abandoned children appeared to be starving, passive, and emotionless. They had spent much of their time lying quietly in their cribs or beds, with nothing to look at. They had had little contact with one another or with their caregivers and had heard little conversation or even noise. Most of the 2- and 3-year-olds did not walk or talk, and the older children played aimlessly. PET scans of their brains showed extreme inactivity in the temporal lobes, which regulate emotion and receive sensory input.

Many of these children were adopted by foreign families. Researchers at Simon Fraser University in British Columbia studied 46 children, ages 8 months to 5 1/2 years, who had been adopted by Canadian parents (Ames, 1997; Morison, Ames, & Chisholm, 1995). At the time of adoption, all the children showed delayed motor, language, or psychosocial development, and nearly 8 out of 10 were behind in all these areas. Three years later, when compared with children left behind in the Romanian institutions, they showed remarkable progress. Even when compared with Canadian children reared in their own homes from birth, about one-third had no serious problems and were doing well—in a few cases, better than the average home-raised child. Another one-third—generally those who had been in institutions the longest—still had serious developmental problems. The rest were moving toward average performance and behavior.

However, another study suggests that age of adoption makes a difference. Among 111 Romanian children adopted in England before age 2, those adopted *before* age 6 months had largely caught up physically and had made a complete cognitive recovery by age 4, as compared with a control group of English adopted children. However, 85 percent of the English adoptees were more cognitively advanced than the average Romanian child adopted *after* 6 months of age (Rutter & the English and Romanian Adoptees [ERA] Study Team, 1998). Apparently, then, it may take very early environmental stimulation to fully overcome the effects of extreme deprivation.

CHECKPOINT

Can you . . .

✔ Discuss the role of early experience in brain growth and development?

Early Sensory Capacities

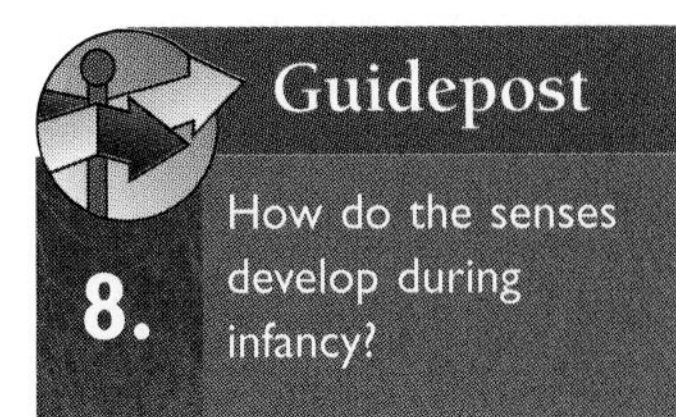

Guidepost
8.
How do the senses develop during infancy?

"The baby, assailed by eyes, ears, nose, skin, and entrails at once, feels that all is one great blooming, buzzing confusion," wrote the psychologist William James in 1890. We now know that this is far from true. The developing brain enables newborn infants to make fairly good sense of what they touch, see, smell, taste, and hear; and their senses develop rapidly in the early months of life.

Touch and Pain

Touch seems to be the first sense to develop, and for the first several months it is the most mature sensory system. When a hungry newborn's cheek is stroked near the mouth, the baby responds by trying to find a nipple. Early signs of this rooting reflex (refer back to Table 4-4) show up in the womb, 2 months after conception. By 32 weeks of gestation, all body parts are sensitive to touch, and this sensitivity increases during the first 5 days of life (Haith, 1986).

Often physicians performing surgery on newborn babies have omitted anesthesia because of a mistaken belief that neonates cannot feel pain, or feel it only briefly. Actually, even on the first day of life, babies can and do feel pain; and they become more sensitive to it during the next few days. Furthermore, pain experienced during the neonatal period may sensitize an infant to later pain, perhaps by affecting the neural pathways that process painful stimuli. In one study, circumcised 4- and 6-month-olds had stronger reactions to the pain of vaccination than uncircumcised infants; the reaction was muted among infants who had been treated with a painkilling cream before being circumcised (Taddio, Katz, Ilersich, & Koren, 1997). The American Academy of Pediatrics (1999) now maintains that pain relief is essential during circumcision.

Smell and Taste

The senses of smell and taste also begin to develop in the womb (refer back to Chapter 3). The flavors and odors of foods an expectant mother consumes may be transmitted to the fetus through the amniotic fluid. After birth, a similar transmission occurs through breast milk (Mennella & Beauchamp, 1996b).

Newborns seem to show by their expression that they like the way vanilla and strawberries smell but do not like the smell of rotten eggs or fish (Steiner, 1979). A preference for pleasant odors seems to be learned in utero and during the first few days after birth, and the odors transmitted through the mother's breast milk may contribute to this learning (Bartoshuk & Beauchamp, 1994).

Six-day-old breast-fed infants prefer the odor of their mother's breast pad over that of another nursing mother, but 2-day-olds do not, suggesting that babies need a few days' experience to learn how their mothers smell (Macfarlane, 1975). Bottle-fed babies do not make such a distinction (Cernoch & Porter, 1985). This preference for the fragrance of the mother's breast may well be a survival mechanism.

Certain taste preferences seem to be largely innate (Bartoshuk & Beauchamp, 1994). Newborns prefer sweet tastes to sour or bitter ones. The sweeter the fluid, the harder they suck and the more they drink (Haith, 1986). Sweetened water calms crying newborns, whether full-term or two to three weeks premature—evidence that not only the taste buds themselves (which seem to be fairly well developed by 20 weeks of gestation), but the mechanisms that produce this calming effect are functional before normal term (B. A. Smith & Blass, 1996). An inborn "sweet tooth" may help a baby adapt to life outside the womb, since breast milk is quite sweet. Newborns' rejection of bitter tastes is probably a survival mechanism, since many bitter substances are toxic (Bartoshuk & Beauchamp, 1994).

Hearing

Hearing, too, is functional before birth; fetuses respond to sounds and seem to learn to recognize them. As we reported in Chapter 3, babies less than 3 days old respond differently to a story heard while in the womb than to other stories, by sucking more on a nipple that activates a recording of the story heard prenatally (DeCasper & Spence, 1986). They also can tell their mother's voice from a stranger's, and they prefer their native language to a foreign language (DeCasper & Fifer, 1980; C. Moon, Cooper, & Fifer, 1993). Early recognition of voices and language heard in the womb may lay a foundation for the relationship between parents and child.

Auditory discrimination develops rapidly after birth. Three-day-old infants can tell new speech sounds from those they have heard before (L. R. Brody, Zelazo, & Chaika, 1984). At 1 month, babies can distinguish sounds as close as "ba" and "pa" (Eimas, Siqueland, Jusczyk, & Vigorito, 1971).

CHECKPOINT

Can you . . .

- ✔ Give evidence for the early development of the sense of touch?
- ✔ Give evidence of newborns' senses of smell and taste and tell how breast-feeding plays a part in their development?
- ✔ Tell how auditory discrimination in newborns is related to fetal hearing?
- ✔ List at least three ways in which newborns' vision is underdeveloped?

Sight

Vision is the least developed sense at birth. The eyes of newborns are smaller than those of adults, the retinal structures are incomplete, and the optic nerve is underdeveloped. Newborns blink at bright lights. Their peripheral vision is very narrow; it more than doubles between 2 and 10 weeks of age (E. Tronick, 1972). The ability to follow a moving target also develops rapidly in the first months, as does color perception. By about 2 months, babies can tell red from green; by about 3 months, they can distinguish blue (Haith, 1986). Four-month-old babies can discriminate among red, green, blue, and yellow. Like most adults, they prefer red and blue (M. Bornstein, Kessen, & Weiskopf, 1976; Teller & Bornstein, 1987).

Vision becomes more acute during the first year, reaching the 20/20 level by about the sixth month (Aslin, 1987). (This measure of vision means that a person can read letters on a specified line on a standard eye chart from 20 feet away.) *Binocular vision*—the use of both eyes to focus, allowing perception of depth and distance—usually does not develop until 4 or 5 months (Bushnell & Boudreau, 1993).

Motor Development

Guidepost

9. What are some early milestones in motor development, and what are some influences on it?

Babies do not have to be taught such basic motor skills as grasping, crawling, and walking. They just need room to move and freedom to see what they can do. When the central nervous system, muscles, and bones are ready and the environment offers the right opportunities for exploration and practice, babies keep surprising the adults around them with their new abilities.

Milestones of Motor Development

Motor development is marked by a series of "milestones": achievements a child masters before going on to more difficult ones. These milestones are not isolated achievements; they develop systematically, each newly mastered ability preparing a baby to tackle the next. Babies first learn simple skills and then combine them into increasingly complex **systems of action,** which permit a wider or more precise range of movement and more effective control of the environment. In developing the precision grip, for example, an infant first tries to pick things up with the whole hand, fingers closing against the palm (the *ulnar grasp*). Later the baby masters the *pincer grasp,* in which thumb and index finger meet at the tips to form a circle, making it possible to pick up tiny objects. In learning to walk, an infant first gains control of separate movements of the arms, legs, and feet before putting these movements together to take that momentous first step.

systems of action Increasingly complex combinations of simpler, previously acquired skills, which permit a wider or more precise range of movement and more control of the environment.

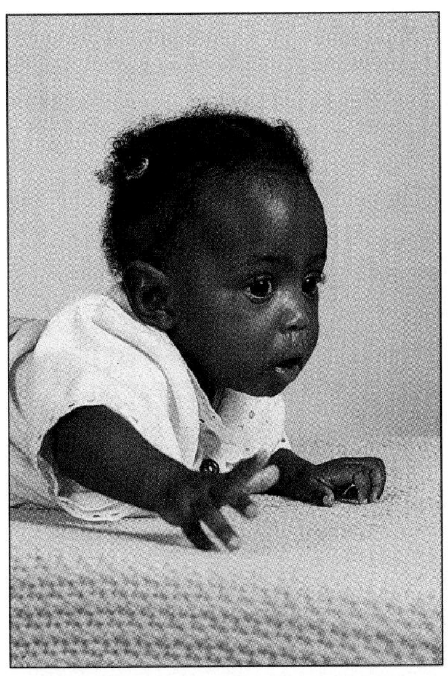

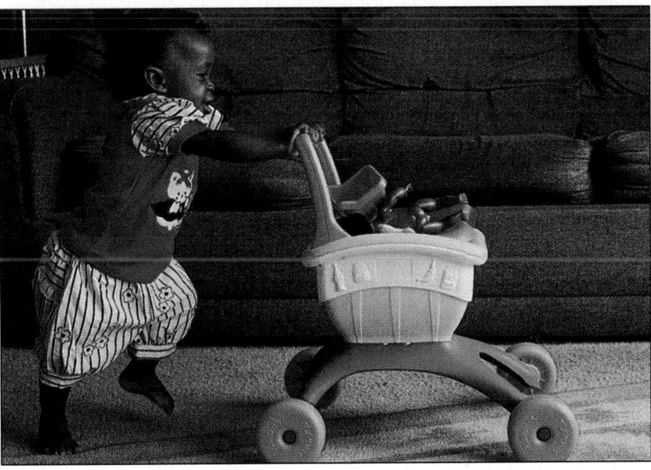
Lifting and holding up the head from a prone position, crawling along the floor to reach something enticing, such as a furry cat's tail, and walking well enough to push a doll's carriage are important early milestones of motor development.

The **Denver Developmental Screening Test** (Frankenburg, Dodds, Fandal, Kazuk, & Cohrs, 1975) is used to chart normal progress between the ages of 1 month and 6 years and to identify children who are not developing normally. The test measures **gross motor skills** (those using large muscles), such as rolling over and catching a ball, and **fine motor skills** (using small muscles), such as grasping a rattle and copying a circle. It also assesses language development (for example, knowing the definitions of words) and personality and social development (such as smiling spontaneously and dressing without help).

The newest edition, the Denver II Scale (Frankenburg et al., 1992), includes revised norms (see Table 4-5 for examples). A child who cannot yet do something that 90 percent of children the same age can already do is considered developmentally delayed.

When we talk about what the "average" baby can do, we refer to the 50 percent Denver norms. Actually, normality covers a wide range; about half of all babies master these skills before the ages given, and about half afterward. Also, the Denver norms were developed with reference to a western population and are not necessarily valid in assessing children from other cultures. For example, southeast Asian children who were given the Denver test did not play pat-a-cake, did not pick up raisins, and did not dress themselves at the expected ages (V. Miller, Onotera, & Deinard, 1984). Yet that did not indicate slow development. In their culture, children do not play pat-a-cake; raisins look like a medicine they

Denver Developmental Screening Test
Screening test given to children 1 month to 6 years old to determine whether they are developing normally; it assesses gross motor skills, fine motor skills, language development, and personality and social development.

gross motor skills
Physical skills such as jumping and running, which involve the large muscles.

fine motor skills
Abilities such as buttoning and copying figures, which involve the small muscles and eye-hand coordination.

Table 4-5 Milestones of Motor Development

Skill	50 Percent	90 Percent
Rolling over	3.2 months	5.4 months
Grasping rattle	3.3 months	3.9 months
Sitting without support	5.9 months	6.8 months
Standing while holding on	7.2 months	8.5 months
Grasping with thumb and finger	8.2 months	10.2 months
Standing alone well	11.5 months	13.7 months
Walking well	12.3 months	14.9 months
Building tower of two cubes	14.8 months	20.6 months
Walking up steps	16.6 months	21.6 months
Jumping in place	23.8 months	2.4 years
Copying circle	3.4 years	4.0 years

Note: This table shows the approximate ages when 50 percent and 90 percent of children can perform each skill, according to the Denver Training Manual II.

Source: Adapted from Frankenburg et al., 1992.

are taught to avoid; and their parents continue to help them dress much longer than western parents do.

As we trace typical progress in head control, hand control, and locomotion, notice how these developments follow the *cephalocaudal* (head to tail) and *proximodistal* (inner to outer) principles outlined earlier.

Head Control At birth, most infants can turn their heads from side to side while lying on their backs. While lying chest down, many can lift their heads enough to turn them. Within the first 2 to 3 months, they lift their heads higher and higher—sometimes to the point where they lose their balance and roll over on their backs. By 4 months of age, almost all infants can keep their heads erect while being held or supported in a sitting position.

Hand Control Babies are born with a grasping reflex. If the palm of an infant's hand is stroked, the hand closes tightly. At about $3\frac{1}{2}$ months, most infants can grasp an object of moderate size, such as a rattle, but have trouble holding a small object. Next they begin to grasp objects with one hand and transfer them to the other, and then to hold (but not pick up) small objects. Some time between 7 and 11 months, their hands become coordinated enough to pick up a tiny object, such as a pea, using the pincer grasp. After that, hand control becomes increasingly precise. By 15 months, the average baby can build a tower of two cubes. A few months after the third birthday, the average toddler can copy a circle fairly well.

Locomotion After 3 months, the average infant begins to roll over deliberately (rather than accidentally, as before)—first from front to back and then from back to front. The average baby can sit without support by 6 months and can assume a sitting position without help about $2\frac{1}{2}$ months later.

Between 6 and 10 months, most babies begin to get around under their own power by means of various forms of creeping or crawling. This new achievement of self-locomotion has striking cognitive and psychosocial ramifications (see Box 4-2).

By holding onto a helping hand or a piece of furniture, the average baby can stand at a little past 7 months of age. A little more than 4 months later, after dogged practice in pulling themselves to an upright posture, most babies let go and stand alone. The average baby can stand well about 2 weeks or so before the first birthday.

Box 4-2

The Far-Reaching Implications of Crawling

Between 7 and 9 months, babies change greatly in many ways. They show an understanding of such concepts as "near" and "far." They imitate more complex behaviors, and they show new fears; but they also show a new sense of security around their parents and other caregivers. Since these changes involve so many different psychological functions and processes and occur during such a short time span, some observers tie them all in with a reorganization of brain function. This neurological development may be set in motion by a skill that emerges at this time: the ability to crawl, which makes it possible to get around independently. Crawling has been called a "setting event" because it sets the stage for other changes in the infant and his or her relationships with the environment and the people in it (Bertenthal & Campos, 1987; Bertenthal, Campos, & Barrett, 1984; Bertenthal, Campos, & Kermoian, 1994).

Crawling exerts a powerful influence on babies' cognitive development by giving them a new view of the world. Infants become more sensitive to where objects are, how big they are, whether they can be moved, and how they look. Crawling helps babies learn to judge distances and perceive depth. As they move about, they see that people and objects look different close up than far away. Crawling babies can differentiate similar forms that are unlike in color, size, or location (J. Campos, Bertenthal, & Benson, 1980). Babies are more successful in finding a toy hidden in a box when they crawl around the box than when they are carried around it (Benson & Uzgiris, 1985).

The ability to crawl gets babies into new situations. As they become more mobile, they begin to hear such warnings as "Come back!" and "Don't touch!" They receive loving help as adult hands pick them up and turn them in a safer direction. They learn to look to caregivers for clues as to whether a situation is secure or frightening—a skill known as social referencing (see Chapter 6). Crawling babies do more social referencing than babies who have not yet begun to crawl (J. B. Garland, 1982). Crawling babies also may develop fear of heights; they learn to be afraid of places from which they might fall.

The ability to move from one place to another has other emotional and social implications. Crawling babies are no longer "prisoners" of place. If Ashley wants to be close to her mother and far away from a strange dog, she can move toward the one and away from the other. This is an important step in developing a sense of mastery, enhancing self-confidence and self-esteem.

Thus the physical milestone of crawling has far-reaching effects in helping babies see and respond to their world in new ways.

All these developments are milestones along the way to the major motor achievement of infancy: walking. Humans begin to walk later than other species, possibly because babies' heavy heads and short legs make balance difficult. For some months before they can stand without support, babies practice "cruising" while holding onto furniture. Soon after they can stand alone well, at about $11^1/_2$ months, most infants take their first unaided steps. Within a few weeks, soon after the first birthday, the child is walking well and thus achieves the status of toddler.

During the second year, children begin to climb stairs one at a time, putting one foot after another on each step; later they will alternate feet. Walking down stairs comes later. In their second year, toddlers run and jump. By age $3^1/_2$, most children can balance briefly on one foot and begin to hop.

How Motor Development Occurs: Maturation in Context

The sequence we have just described was traditionally thought to be genetically programmed—a largely automatic, preordained series of steps directed by the maturing brain. Today, many developmentalists consider this view too simplistic. Instead, according to Esther Thelen (1995), motor development is a continuous process of interaction between baby and environment.

As evidence of the shortcomings of maturational theory, Thelen points to the *walking reflex:* stepping movements a neonate makes when held upright with the feet touching a surface. This behavior usually disappears by the fourth month. Not until the latter part of the first year, when a baby is getting ready to walk, do such movements appear again. The usual explanation is a shift to cortical control:

an older baby's deliberate walking is seen as a new skill masterminded by the developing brain. But, Thelen observes, a newborn's stepping involves the same kinds of movements neonates make while lying down and kicking. Why would stepping stop, only to reappear months later, whereas kicking continues? The answer, she suggests, may be that babies' legs become thicker and heavier during the early months, but not yet strong enough to carry the increased weight (Thelen & Fisher, 1982, 1983). In fact, when young infants are held in warm water, which helps support the legs, stepping reappears. The ability to produce the movement has not changed—only the physical and environmental conditions that inhibit or promote it.

Maturation alone cannot adequately explain such observations, says Thelen. Infant and environment form an interconnected system, and development has interacting causes. One is the infant's motivation to do something (say, pick up a toy or get to the other side of the room). The infant's physical characteristics and his or her position in a particular setting (for example, lying in a crib or being held upright in a pool) offer opportunities and constraints that affect whether and how the goal can be achieved. Ultimately, a solution emerges as a result of trying out behaviors and retaining those that most efficiently reach the goal. Rather than being solely in charge of this process, says Thelen, the maturing brain is only one part of it.

According to Thelen, normal babies develop the same skills in the same order because they are built approximately the same way and have similar physical challenges and needs. Thus they eventually discover that walking is more efficient than crawling in most situations. The idea that this discovery arises from each particular baby's experience in a particular context may help explain why some babies learn to walk earlier than others.

Motor Development and Perception

Thelen's work builds in part on earlier studies by Eleanor and James Gibson, which point to a bidirectional connection between perception and motion. Sensory perceptions help infants learn about their environment so they can navigate in it. Motor experience sharpens and modifies infants' perceptions of what will happen if they move in a certain way.

How do crawling babies decide whether to attempt to cross a muddy patch or climb a hill? Crawling and, later, walking require infants to continually per-

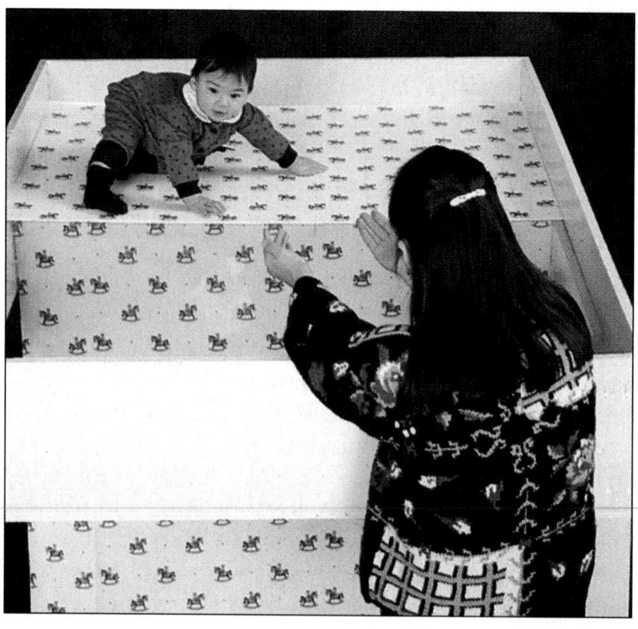

No matter how enticing a mother's arm are, this baby is staying away from them. As young as she is, she can perceive depth and wants to avoid falling off what looks like a cliff.

ceive the "fit," or *affordance,* between their own changing physical abilities and the characteristics of a variety of terrains—smooth or rough, flat or sloping (J. J. Gibson, 1979).

When and how do infants become aware of affordances? In a classic experiment (Walk & Gibson, 1961), researchers put babies on a plexiglass tabletop over a checkerboard pattern that created the illusion of a vertical drop in the center of the table—a **visual cliff.** Would infants perceive the illusion of depth and sense danger?

visual cliff
Apparatus designed to give an illusion of depth and used to assess depth perception in infants.

Six-month-old babies did see a difference between the "ledge," which seemed to afford them safe passage, and the "drop," which did not. They crawled freely on the "ledge" but avoided the "drop," even when they saw their mothers beckoning on the far side of the table. When even younger infants, ages 2 and 3 months, were placed face down over the visual cliff, their hearts slowed down, suggesting that **depth perception,** the ability to perceive objects and surfaces three-dimensionally, is either innate or learned very early (Campos, Langer, & Krowitz, 1970).

depth perception
Ability to perceive objects and surfaces three-dimensionally.

However, a slowed heart rate, which indicates interest, does not mean that the younger infants were afraid of falling; fear would be indicated by a *faster* heart rate. Not until babies can get around by themselves do they learn from experience, or from a caregiver's warnings, that a steep dropoff can be dangerous (Bertenthal et al., 1994).

Later studies explored how motor experience sensitizes infants and toddlers to the affordances of slopes of varying steepness. When crawling and walking babies (average ages 8½ and 14 months) were placed on a walkway with an adjustable slope, neither the crawlers nor the walkers hesitated to climb uphill, a task that posed little danger. Going downhill was a different story. The inexperienced crawlers plunged down even the steepest slopes. The older and more experienced walkers walked down a shallow slope but slid down a steep one or avoided it altogether (Eppler, Adolph, & Weiner, 1996).

In a companion longitudinal study, infants were tested on various surfaces every three weeks from the time they began to crawl until a few weeks after they began to walk. The goal was to get a microgenetic picture of how the infants adapted their perceptions of affordance to their changing motor abilities. As crawling infants became more experienced, their judgments seemed to become more accurate and their explorations more efficient. However, this learning did not generalize to a new type of movement: when they began to walk, they had to learn to cope with slopes all over again (Adolph, 1997).

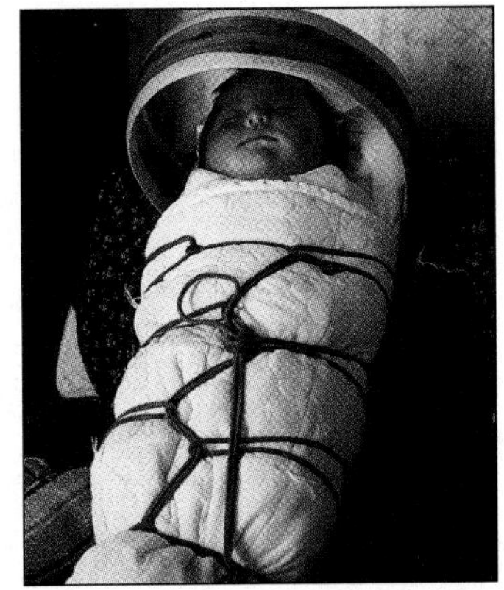

Some observers have suggested that babies from the Yucatan develop motor skills later than American babies because they are swaddled. However, Navajo babies like this one also are swaddled for most of the day, and they begin to walk at about the same time as other American babies, suggesting a hereditary explanation.

Cultural Influences on Motor Development

Although motor development follows a virtually universal sequence, its pace does seem to respond to certain contextual factors. When children are well fed and well cared for and have physical freedom and the chance to explore their surroundings, their motor development is likely to be normal. However, what is normal in one culture may not be in another.

African babies tend to be more advanced than U.S. and European infants in sitting, walking, and running. In Uganda, for example, babies typically walk at 10 months, as compared with 12 months in the United States and 15 months in France (Gardiner et al., 1998). Asian babies tend to develop these skills more slowly. Such differences may in part be related to ethnic differences in temperament (H. Kaplan & Dove, 1987; see Chapter 6) or may reflect a culture's child-rearing practices (Gardiner et al., 1998).

Some cultures actively encourage early development of motor skills. A Somali infant is placed face down while her older sister shows her how to crawl to a nearby object. A Japanese father folds his baby's legs into a sitting position (Broude, 1995). In many African and West Indian cultures with advanced infant motor development, adults use special "handling routines," such as bouncing and stepping exercises, to strengthen babies' muscles (Hopkins & Westra, 1988).

In one study, Jamaican infants, whose mothers used such handling routines daily, sat, crawled, and walked at about the ages the mothers had predicted when the infants were 1 month old. English infants, whose mothers gave them no such special handling, sat and walked later (Hopkins & Westra, 1990).

On the other hand, some cultures discourage early motor development. Children of the Ache in eastern Paraguay do not begin to walk until 18 to 20 months of age—about 9 months later than U.S. babies (H. Kaplan & Dove, 1987). Ache mothers pull their babies back to their laps when the infants begin to crawl away. The Ache mothers closely supervise their babies to protect them from the hazards of nomadic life, and also because the women's primary responsibility is child raising rather than subsistence labor. Yet, as 8- to 10-year-olds, Ache children climb tall trees, chop branches, and play in ways that enhance their motor skills (H. Kaplan & Dove, 1987). Normal development, then, need not follow the same timetable to reach the same destination.

Training Motor Skills Experimentally

Can systematic training speed up motor development? For many years, developmental scientists thought the answer was no. In a famous experiment, Arnold Gesell (1929) trained one monozygotic twin, but not the other, in stair-climbing, block-building, and hand coordination. As the children got older, the untrained twin became just as expert as the trained one, showing, said Gesell, "the powerful influence of maturation." According to Gesell, children perform certain activities when they are ready, and training gives no advantage.

Yet culturally induced differences in rates of motor development (discussed in the preceding section) seem to challenge Gesell's view; and more recent experimental findings indicate that early training *can* influence walking. In one study, infants trained in stepping at 8 weeks walked at an average of 10 months, while those in an untrained control group did not begin walking until an average of $12\frac{1}{3}$ months (P. R. Zelazo, Zelazo, & Kolb, 1972). Why did this happen? Perhaps there is a critical period during which the newborn's repetitive walking response can be translated into a specific later voluntary action. Then again, practice in one such behavior pattern might promote maturation of the brain's ability to control related activities. Another possibility, in line with Thelen's view, is that training strengthened the infants' legs, allowing them to resume stepping at an earlier-than-usual age.

Can training in one skill facilitate the learning of another? A randomized follow-up experiment suggests that the answer is no. Six-week-old healthy baby boys who were trained for 7 weeks, either in stepping alone or in stepping and sitting, stepped more than those untrained in stepping movements; and infants trained either in sitting alone or in stepping and sitting sat more than infants untrained in sitting. Infants trained in sitting alone did not step more, and infants trained in stepping alone did not sit more (N. A. Zelazo, Zelazo, Cohen, & Zelazo, 1993). Apparently early training can accelerate a *specific* behavior, but the training does not carry over to other abilities.

These studies do not indicate whether changes in the brain or in muscle strength, or both, are involved; but they do seem to rule out a view of early motor development as purely biologically determined and suggest that learning plays a greater role than has generally been believed.

In recent years, many U.S. parents have put their babies in mobile walkers, in the belief that walkers help babies learn to walk earlier. Actually, this belief is mistaken; by restricting babies' motor exploration, and sometimes their view of their own movements, walkers may *delay* motor skill development. In one study, infants who used walkers sat, crawled, and walked later than babies who did not use walkers, and they also scored lower on tests of cognitive development (Siegel & Burton, 1999). Furthermore, walkers are dangerous. They were responsible for an estimated 25,000 injuries in the United States in 1993 and 11 deaths in the previ-

CHECKPOINT

Can you . . .

- ✔ Trace a typical infant's progress in head control, hand control, and locomotion, according to the Denver norms?
- ✔ Discuss how maturation, perception, environmental influence, and training relate to early motor development?

ous five years. The American Academy of Pediatrics has called for a ban on their manufacture and sale (AAP Committee on Injury and Poison Prevention, 1995).

By the time small children can run, jump, and play with toys requiring fairly sophisticated coordination, they are very different from the neonates described at the beginning of this chapter. The cognitive changes that have taken place are equally dramatic, as we discuss in Chapter 5.

Consider this . . .

- Is it advisable to try to teach babies skills such as walking before they develop them on their own?

Summary

The Birth Process

Guidepost 1. What happens during each of the four stages of childbirth?

- Birth normally occurs after a preparatory period of **parturition** and consists of four stages: (1) dilation of the cervix; (2) descent and emergence of the baby; (3) expulsion of the umbilical cord and the placenta; (4) contraction of the uterus and recovery of the mother.
- **Electronic fetal monitoring** is widely used (and may be overused) during labor and delivery. It is intended to detect signs of fetal distress, especially in high-risk births.

Guidepost 2. What alternative methods and settings of delivery are available today?

- Almost 21 percent of births in the United States are by **cesarean delivery.** Critics claim that many cesareans, which carry special risks to mother and baby, are unnecessary.
- There is disagreement over the effects on a newborn of anesthesia given to a laboring mother. **Natural childbirth** or **prepared childbirth** can minimize the need for pain-killing drugs and maximize parents' active involvement. Modern epidurals can give effective pain relief with smaller doses of medication than in the past.
- Delivery at home or in birth centers, and attendance by midwives, are alternatives to physician-attended hospital delivery for women with normal, low-risk pregnancies who want to involve family members and make the experience more intimate and personal. The presence of a doula can provide physical benefits as well as emotional support.

The Newborn Baby

Guidepost 3. How do newborn infants adjust to life outside the womb?

- The **neonatal period** is a time of transition from intrauterine to extrauterine life. During the first few days, the **neonate** loses weight and then regains it; the **lanugo** (prenatal hair) falls off and the protective coating of **vernix caseosa** dries up. The **fontanels** (soft spots) in the skull close within the first 18 months.
- At birth, the circulatory, respiratory, gastrointestinal, and temperature regulation systems become independent of the mother's. If a newborn cannot start breathing within about 5 minutes, brain injury due to **anoxia** may occur.
- Newborns have a strong sucking reflex and secrete **meconium** from the intestinal tract. They are commonly subject to **neonatal jaundice,** due to immaturity of the liver.
- A newborn's **state of arousal** is governed by periodic cycles of wakefulness, sleep, and activity, which seem to be inborn. Sleep takes up the major amount of a neonate's time. Newborns' activity levels may be early indicators of temperament.

Survival and Health

Guidepost 4. How can we tell whether a new baby is healthy and is developing normally?

- At 1 minute and 5 minutes after birth, the neonate is assessed by the **Apgar scale** to determine how well he or she is adjusting to extrauterine life. The neonate also may be screened for one or more medical conditions. The **Brazelton Neonatal Behavioral Assessment Scale** may be given to assess responses to the environment and to predict future development.

Guidepost 5. What complications of childbirth can endanger newborn babies' adjustment or even their lives?

- A small minority of infants suffer lasting effects of **birth trauma.** Other complications include **low birthweight** and **postmature** birth.
- Low-birthweight babies may be either **preterm (premature) infants** or **small-for-date (small-for-gestational age) infants.** Low birthweight is a major factor in infant mortality and can cause long-term physical and cognitive problems.

Guidepost 6. How can we enhance babies' chances of survival and health?

- A supportive postnatal environment and other **protective factors** often can improve the outcome for babies suffering from birth complications. However, very-low-birthweight babies (those weighing $3\frac{1}{2}$ pounds or less) have a less promising prognosis than those who weigh more.
- Although the **infant mortality rate** in the United States has improved, it is still disturbingly high, especially for African American babies. Birth defects are the leading

cause of death in the first year; for black infants, low birthweight is the leading cause.

- **Sudden infant death syndrome (SIDS)** is the third leading cause of death in infants in the United States. Exposure to smoke and sleeping in the prone position are major risk factors.
- Rates of immunization have improved worldwide and have reached record highs in the United States, but many preschoolers are not fully protected.

Early Physical Development

Guidepost 7. What influences the growth of body and brain?

- Normal physical growth and motor development proceed according to the cephalocaudal and proximodistal principles.
- A child's body grows most dramatically during the first year of life; growth proceeds at a rapid but diminishing rate throughout the child's first 3 years.
- Breast-feeding offers many benefits. However, the quality of the relationship between parents and infant may be more important than the feeding method in promoting healthy development. Babies should not get cow's milk until 1 year of age and should not start solid foods and fruit juices until 6 months of age.
- Sleep patterns change dramatically; by the second half of the first year, babies do most of their sleeping at night.
- The **central nervous system** controls sensorimotor functioning. **Brain growth spurts** coincide with changes in cognitive behavior. **Lateralization** enables each hemisphere of the brain to specialize in different functions.
- The brain grows most rapidly during the months before and immediately after birth as **neurons** migrate to their assigned locations, form synaptic connections, and undergo the processes of **integration** and **differentiation. Cell death** and **myelination** improve the efficiency of the nervous system.
- **Reflex behaviors**—primitive, locomotor, and postural—are indications of neurological status. Most early reflexes drop out during the first year as voluntary, cortical control develops.
- Due to the brain's **plasticity,** especially during the early period of rapid growth, environmental experience can influence brain development positively or negatively.

Guidepost 8. How do the senses develop during infancy?

- Sensory capacities, present from birth and even in the womb, develop rapidly in the first months of life. Very young infants show pronounced abilities to discriminate between stimuli.
- Touch seems to be the first sense to develop and mature. Newborns are sensitive to pain. Smell, taste, and hearing also begin to develop in the womb.
- Vision is the least well developed sense at birth. Peripheral vision, color perception, acuteness of focus, binocular vision, and the ability to follow a moving object with the eyes all develop within the first few months.

Guidepost 9. What are some early milestones in motor development, and what are some influences on it?

- Motor skills develop in a certain sequence, which may depend largely on maturation but also on context, experience, and motivation. Simple skills are combined into increasingly complex **systems of action.**
- The **Denver Developmental Screening Test** is widely used to assess **gross motor skills** and **fine motor skills,** as well as linguistic and personality and social development.
- Self-locomotion seems to be a "setting event," bringing about changes in all domains of development.
- Studies with the **visual cliff** suggest that **depth perception** is present at a very early age and is related to motor development.
- Environmental factors, including cultural practices, may affect the pace of early motor development.
- Training or practice can accelerate infants' acquisition of specific motor skills.

Key Terms

parturition (110)
electronic fetal monitoring (110)
cesarean delivery (111)
natural childbirth (112)
prepared childbirth (112)
neonatal period (page 114)
neonate (114)
fontanels (115)
lanugo (115)
vernix caseosa (115)
anoxia (115)
meconium (115)
neonatal jaundice (115)
state of arousal (116)
Apgar scale (117)
Brazelton Neonatal Behavioral Assessment Scale (NBAS) (117)
birth trauma (118)
low birthweight (118)
preterm (premature) infants (118)
small-for-date (small-for-gestational age) infants (118)
postmature (121)
protective factors (123)
infant mortality rate (123)
sudden infant death syndrome (SIDS) (125)
central nervous system (130)
brain growth spurts (131)
lateralization (131)
neurons (132)
integration (133)
differentiation (133)
cell death (133)
myelination (134)
reflex behaviors (134)
plasticity (137)
systems of action (140)
Denver Developmental Screening Test (141)
gross motor skills (141)
fine motor skills (141)
visual cliff (145)
depth perception (145)

Chapter 5

Cognitive Development During the First Three Years

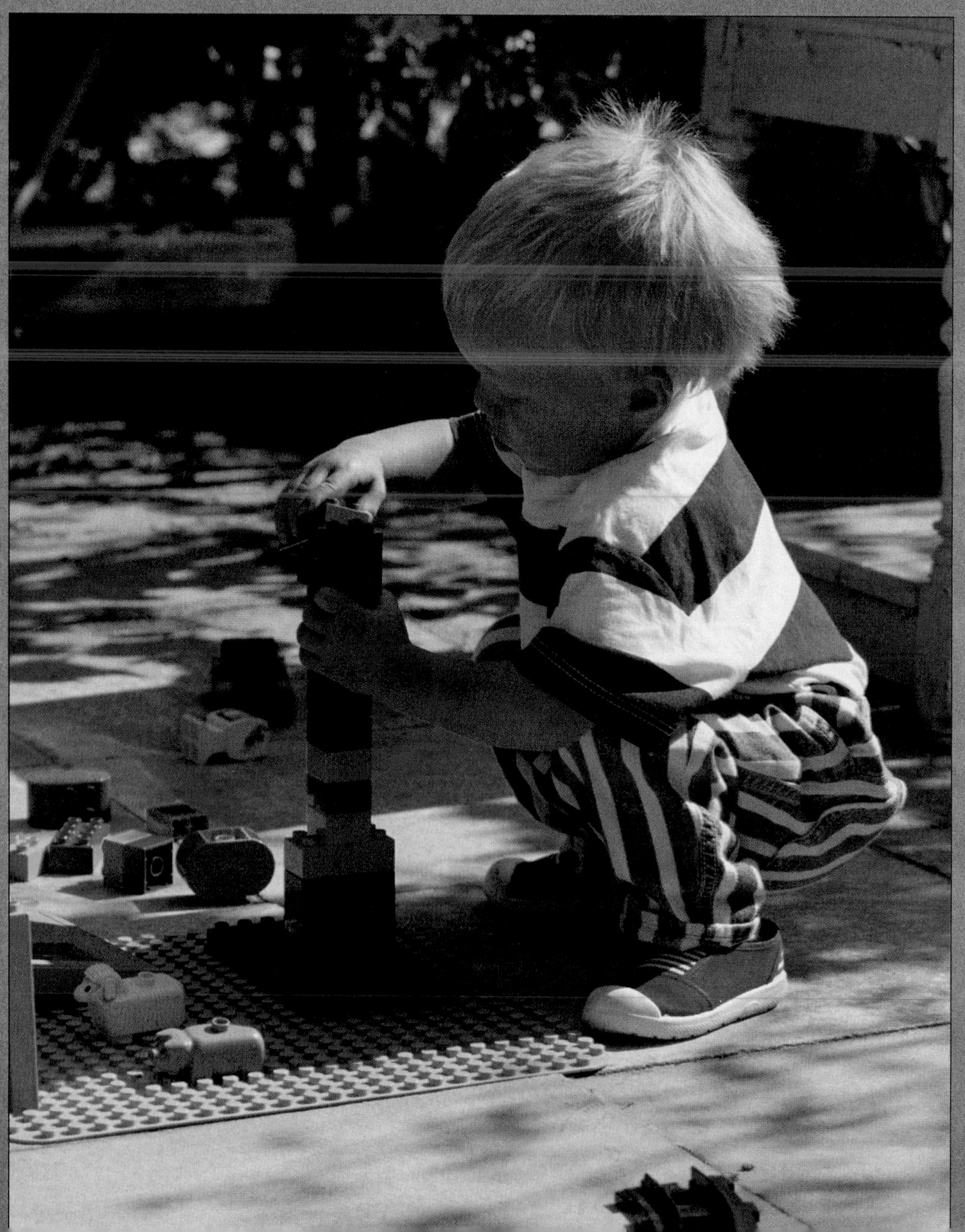

So runs my dream; but what am I? An infant crying in the night; An infant crying for the light, And with no language but a cry.

Alfred, Lord Tennyson, *In Memoriam*, Canto 54

OUTLINE

Charles and "Doddy" Darwin

Focus: William Erasmus (Doddy) Darwin, Naturalist's Son

On December 27, 1839, when the naturalist Charles Darwin was 30 years old, his wife, Emma, gave birth to their first baby, William Erasmus Darwin, affectionately known as Doddy. That day—twenty years before the publication of Charles Darwin's *Origin of Species,* which outlined his theory of evolution based on natural selection—the proud father began keeping a diary of observations of his newborn son. It was these notes, published in 1877,* that first called scientific attention to the developmental nature of infant behavior.

What abilities are babies born with? How do they learn about their world? How do they communicate, first nonverbally and then through language? These were among the questions Darwin set out to answer—questions still central to the study of cognitive development.

Darwin's keen eye illuminates how coordination of physical and mental activity helps an infant adapt to the world—as in this entry written when Doddy was 4 months old:

> Took my finger to his mouth & as usual could not get it in, on account of his own hand being in the way; then he slipped his own back & so got my finger in.—This was not chance & therefore a kind of reasoning. (Diary, p. 12; quoted in Keegan & Gruber, 1985, p. 135)

*The source for analysis of Darwin's diary was Keegan and Gruber (1985).

In Darwin's notes, we can see Doddy developing new cognitive skills through interaction not only with his father's finger, but with other objects as well. The diary depicts a series of recurring encounters with reflected images. In these episodes we see Doddy gaining knowledge, not in sudden bursts or jumps, but through gradual integration of new experience with existing patterns of mental and physical behavior. In Darwin's view—as, later, in Piaget's—this was not merely a matter of piling new knowledge upon old; it involved an actual transformation of the way the mind is organized.

When Doddy, at 4½ months, saw his likeness and his father's in a mirror, Darwin noted that the baby "seemed surprised at my voice coming from behind him, my image being in front" (Diary, p. 18; quoted in Keegan & Gruber, 1985, p. 135). Two months later, Doddy apparently had solved the mystery: now, when his father, standing behind him, made a funny face in the mirror, the infant "was aware that the image . . . was not real & therefore . . . turned round to look" (Diary, pp. 21–22; quoted in Keegan & Gruber, pp. 135–136).

At first, this newfound understanding did not generalize to other reflective materials. Two weeks later, Doddy seemed puzzled to see his father's reflection in a window. By 9 months, however, the boy realized that "the shadow of a hand, made by a candle, was to be looked for behind, in [the] same manner as in [a] looking glass" (Diary, p. 23; quoted in Keegan & Gruber, 1985, p. 136). His recognition that reflections could emanate from objects behind him now extended to shadows, another kind of two-dimensional image.

Darwin was particularly interested in documenting his son's progress in communication. He believed that language acquisition is a natural process, akin to earlier physical expressions of feelings. Through smiling, crying, laughing, facial expressions, and sounds of pleasure or pain, Doddy managed to communicate quite well with his parents even before uttering his first word. One of his first meaningful verbal expressions was "Ah!"—uttered when he recognized an image in a glass.

Darwin made these observations more than 160 years ago, at a time when infants' cognitive abilities were widely underestimated. We now know — as Darwin inferred from his observations of Doddy — that normal, healthy infants are born with the ability to learn and remember and with a capacity for acquiring and using speech. They use their growing sensory and cognitive capacities to exert control over their behavior and their world.

In this chapter we look at infants' and toddlers' cognitive abilities from three classic perspectives — behaviorist, psychometric, and Piagetian — and then from three newer perspectives: information processing, cognitive neuroscientific, and social-contextual. We trace the early development of language and discuss how it comes about. Finally, we see how adults help infants and toddlers become more competent with language.

After you have read and studied this chapter, you should be able to answer the following questions:

CH 5

Guideposts for Study

1. How do infants learn, and how long can they remember?
2. Can infants' and toddlers' intelligence be measured, and how can it be improved?
3. How did Piaget describe infants' and toddlers' cognitive development, and how have his claims stood up under later scrutiny?
4. How can we measure infants' ability to process information, and how does this ability relate to future intelligence?
5. When do babies begin to think about characteristics of the physical world?
6. What can brain research reveal about the development of cognitive skills?
7. How does social interaction with adults advance cognitive competence?
8. How do babies develop language?
9. What influences contribute to linguistic progress?

Studying Cognitive Development: Classic Approaches

When Doddy Darwin, at 4 months, figured out how to get his father's finger into his mouth by moving his own hand out of the way, he showed **intelligent behavior.** Intelligent behavior has two key aspects. First, it is goal-oriented: conscious and deliberate. Second, it is adaptive: directed at adjusting to the circumstances and conditions of life. Intelligence—the array of mental abilities underlying intelligent behavior—is influenced by both inheritance and experience. Intelligence enables people to acquire, remember, and use knowledge; to understand concepts and relationships; and to solve everyday problems.

How and when do babies learn to solve problems? How and when does memory develop? What accounts for individual differences in cognitive abilities? Can we measure a baby's intelligence? Can we predict how smart that baby will be in the future? Many investigators have taken one of three classic approaches to the study of such questions:

- The **behaviorist approach** studies the basic *mechanics* of learning. It is concerned with how behavior changes in response to experience.
- The **psychometric approach** seeks to measure individual differences in *quantity* of intelligence by using intelligence tests. The higher a person scores, the more intelligent she or he is presumed to be.
- The **Piagetian approach** looks at changes, or stages, in the *quality* of cognitive functioning. It is concerned with how the mind structures its activities and adapts to the environment.

All three approaches, as well as the three newer ones we discuss in the following section—the information-processing, cognitive neuroscience, and social-contextual approaches—help us understand intelligent behavior. Let's see what each of the three classic approaches can tell us about the cognitive development of infants and toddlers.

intelligent behavior
Behavior that is goal-oriented (conscious and deliberate) and adaptive to circumstances and conditions of life.

behaviorist approach
Approach to the study of cognitive development based on learning theory, which is concerned with the basic mechanics of learning.

psychometric approach
Approach to the study of cognitive development that seeks to measure the quantity of intelligence a person possesses.

Piagetian approach
Approach to the study of cognitive development based on Piaget's theory, which describes qualitative stages, or typical changes, in children's and adolescents' cognitive functioning.

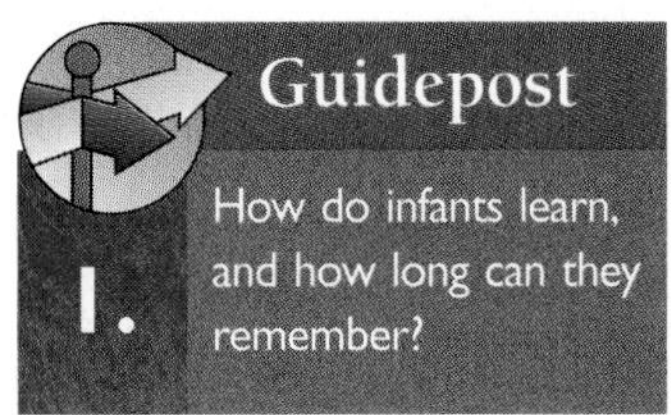

Behaviorist Approach: Basic Mechanics of Learning

Babies are born with the ability to learn from what they see, hear, smell, taste, and touch, and they have at least some ability to remember what they learn. Of course, maturation is essential to this process. But while learning theorists recognize maturation as a limiting factor, they do not focus on it. Their main interest is in mechanisms of learning.

Let's look first at two simple learning processes that behaviorists study: *classical conditioning* and *operant conditioning*. Later we will consider *habituation*, another simple form of learning, which information-processing researchers study.

Classical Conditioning

classical conditioning Kind of learning in which a previously neutral stimulus (one that does not originally elicit a particular response) acquires the power to elicit the response after the stimulus is repeatedly associated with another stimulus that ordinarily does elicit the response.

In Chapter 2, we described how 11-month-old Anna, after her father had taken many pictures of her, eventually blinked *before* the flashbulb on his camera went off. This is an example of **classical conditioning,** in which a person or animal learns to make a reflex response (in this case, blinking) to a stimulus (the camera) that originally did not provoke the response. As Figure 5-1 shows, the camera initially was a neutral stimulus; it did not make Anna blink. The flash was an unconditioned stimulus (UCS); Anna's blinking when she saw it go off was an unconditioned response (UCR). After Anna learned to connect the camera with the flash, the camera became a conditioned stimulus (CS); Anna's blinking before the flash was a conditioned response (CR).

Classical conditioning enables infants to anticipate an event before it happens by forming associations between stimuli (such as the camera and the flash) that regularly occur together. Classically conditioned learning will fade, or become *extinct,* if it is not reinforced. Thus, if Anna frequently saw the camera without the flash, she eventually would stop blinking.

Newborns can be classically conditioned most readily when the association between stimuli has survival value. For example, babies only 2 hours old will turn their heads and suck when their foreheads are stroked at the same time that they are given a bottle of sweetened water. After classical conditioning, they will turn and suck in response to forehead-stroking alone (Blass et al., 1984, in Rovee-Collier, 1987).

Operant Conditioning and Infant Memory

operant conditioning Form of learning in which a person tends to repeat a behavior that has been reinforced or to cease a behavior that has been punished.

In classical conditioning, the learner is passive, absorbing and automatically reacting to stimuli. By contrast, in **operant conditioning**—as when a baby learns that smiling brings loving attention—the learner acts, or operates, on the envi-

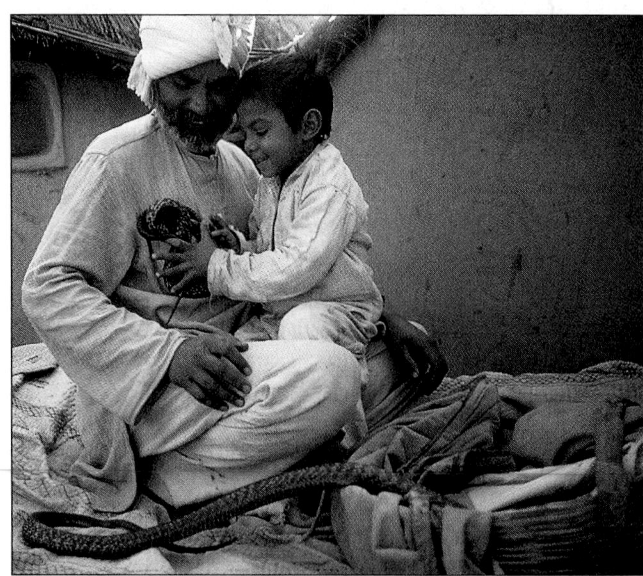

An Indian snake charmer's son eagerly plays with a snake the father has trained, showing that fear of snakes is a learned response. Children can be conditioned to fear animals that are associated with unpleasant or frightening experiences, as "Little Albert" was in a classic study by John B. Watson and Rosalie Rayner.

Stage 1: Before conditioning
Camera
Child does not blink
Neutral stimulus
Interest—no blinking
Neutral stimulus does not produce blinking.

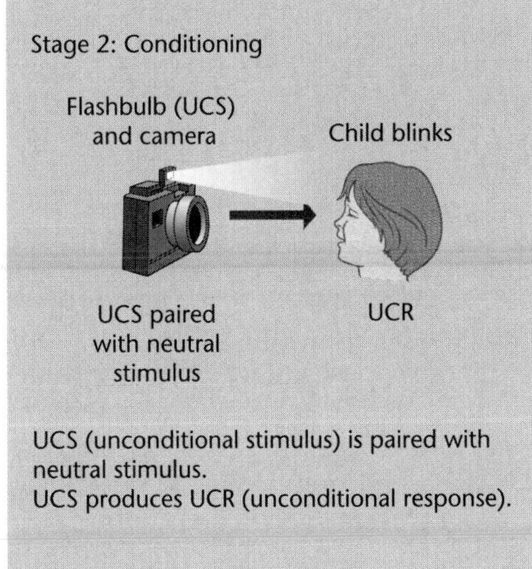
Stage 2: Conditioning
Flashbulb (UCS) and camera
Child blinks
UCS paired with neutral stimulus
UCR
UCS (unconditional stimulus) is paired with neutral stimulus.
UCS produces UCR (unconditional response).

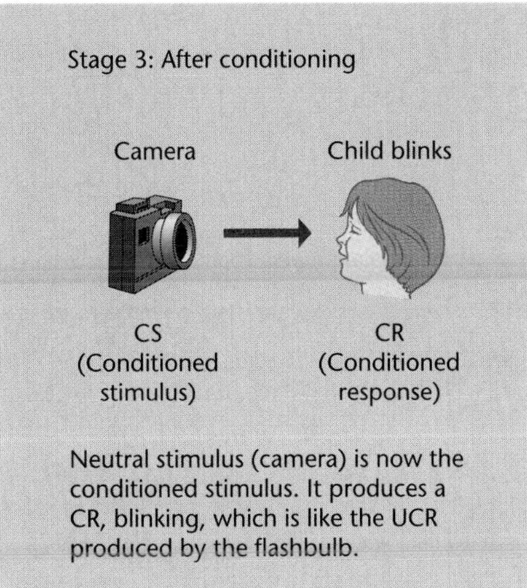
Stage 3: After conditioning
Camera
Child blinks
CS (Conditioned stimulus)
CR (Conditioned response)
Neutral stimulus (camera) is now the conditioned stimulus. It produces a CR, blinking, which is like the UCR produced by the flashbulb.

Figure 5-1
Three steps in classical conditioning.

ronment. The infant learns to make a certain response to an environmental stimulus (smiling at sight of the parents) in order to produce a particular effect (parental attention).

Studies using operant conditioning have been used to test infants' memory. These studies have found that babies will repeat an action days or weeks later—*if* they are tested in a situation very similar to the one in which they were originally trained.

In a series of experiments by Carolyn Rovee-Collier and her associates, infants have been operantly conditioned to kick to activate a mobile attached to one ankle by a ribbon. Babies 2 to 6 months old, when again shown the mobiles days or weeks later, repeat the kicking, even though their legs are no longer attached to the mobiles. When the infants see the mobiles, the babies kick more than before the conditioning, showing that recognition of the mobiles triggers a memory of their initial experience with them (Rovee-Collier, 1996). In a similar task designed for older infants and toddlers, the child is conditioned to press a lever to make a miniature train go around a track (Hartshorn et al., 1998).

The length of time a conditioned response can be retained increases with age, from 2 days for 2-month-olds to 13 weeks for 18-month-olds (see Figure 5-2). The retention time of very young infants can be increased by dividing the training into more sessions (Hartshorn et al., 1998; Rovee-Collier, 1996). A flagging memory can be reactivated by a reminder—a brief periodic exposure to the original stimulus or the context in which the baby first encountered it. Older infants are quicker than younger ones to retrieve a memory after such a reminder—evidence that the speed of information processing, like the duration of memories, increases with age (Rovee-Collier & Boller, 1995).

CHECKPOINT

Can you . . .

- ✔ Distinguish the goals of the behaviorist, psychometric, and Piagetian approaches to the study of cognitive development?
- ✔ Identify conditions under which newborns can be classically or operantly conditioned?

Figure 5-2
Maximum number of weeks that infants of varying ages show retention of how to operate either a mobile or a miniature train.
(Source: Rovee-Collier & Boller, 1995, p. 7.)

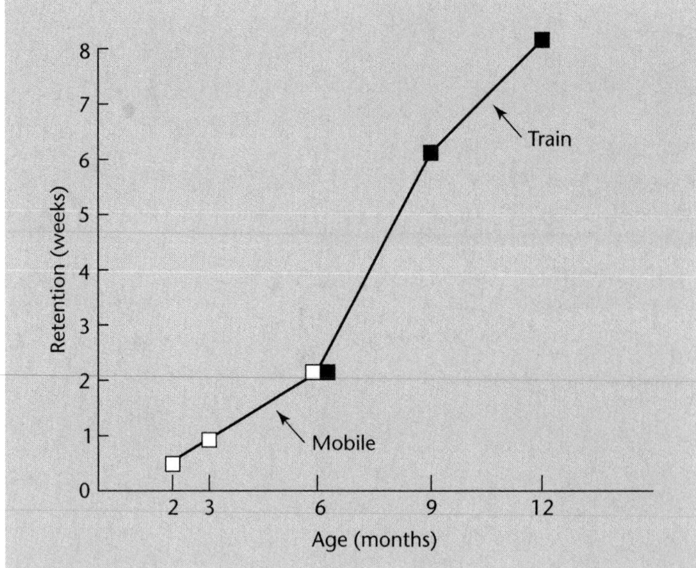

time window
Limited period of time following an event, during which an infant can integrate new information with the memory of it.

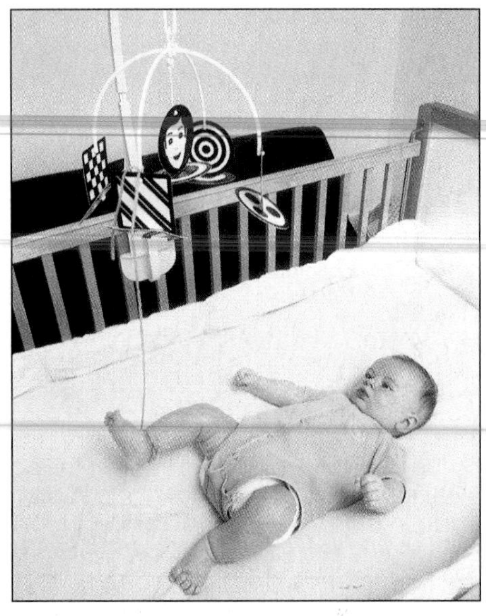
Babies 2 to 6 months old can remember, after a hiatus of 2 days to 2 weeks, that they were able to activate a mobile by kicking; they show this by kicking as soon as they see the mobile.

Young infants' memory of a behavior seems to be specifically linked to the original context. Babies who are given the mobile training in playpens hung with patterns of stripes, squares, dots, or triangles remember to kick if retested in a playpen with the same pattern. If retested in a different context, such as a differently patterned playpen, or with the same pattern but in a different room, they do not kick. However, infants do respond more flexibly when trained with a variety of cues or in more than one context, or if the cue or the context is changed shortly after the original training. Babies trained with different mobiles on different days learn to expect a different one each time, and act accordingly (Rovee-Collier, 1996; Rovee-Collier & Boller, 1995).

There seems to be a **time window:** a limited period of time following an event, during which an infant can integrate new information with the memory of the original event. The time window closes when the infant has forgotten the original event; after that, the infant perceives a modified experience as a new, unique event. For example, 3-month-olds retain the mobile response for as long as 8 days if the training occurs in two sessions no more than 3 days apart, but not if the second session is 4 days after the first. However, the time window widens each time the original memory is retrieved within that window, making it possible to add new information after longer and longer intervals (Rovee-Collier, 1995; Rovee-Collier & Boller, 1995).

Psychometric Approach: Developmental and Intelligence Testing

The precise nature of the ability or abilities that make up intelligence has been debated for many years, as has the best way to measure it (or them). Sir Francis Galton (1822–1911), a cousin of Charles Darwin, proposed that intelligence could be measured by such characteristics as head size and reaction time. The American psychologist James McKeen Cattell (1860–1944) developed mental tests that scored strength of hand squeeze, pain sensitivity, weight discrimination, judgment of time, and rote recall. However, these tests had little predictive value.

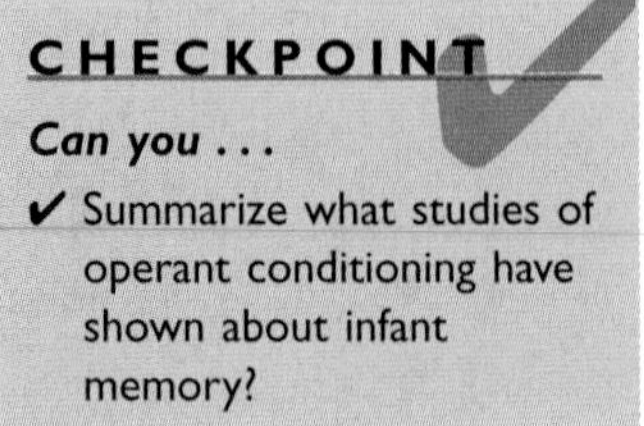
CHECKPOINT

Can you . . .

✔ Summarize what studies of operant conditioning have shown about infant memory?

Then, at the beginning of the twentieth century, school administrators in Paris asked the psychologist Alfred Binet to devise a way to identify children who could not handle academic work and who should be removed from regular classes and given special training. The test that Binet and his colleague Theodore Simon developed was the forerunner of psychometric tests, used for children of all levels of ability, which score intelligence by numbers. One is the Stanford-Binet Intelligence Scale, an American version of the traditional Binet-Simon tests (see Chapter 7).

Guidepost
2.
Can infants' and toddlers' intelligence be measured, and how can it be improved?

The goals of psychometric testing are to measure quantitatively the factors that are thought to make up intelligence (such as comprehension and reasoning), and, from the results of that measurement, to predict future performance (such as school achievement). **IQ (intelligence quotient) tests** consist of questions or tasks that are supposed to show how much of the measured abilities a person has, by comparing her or his performance with that of other test-takers. A child's score is compared with **standardized norms:** standards obtained from the scores of a large, representative sample of children the same age who were given the test while it was being developed.

IQ (intelligence quotient) tests
Psychometric tests that seek to measure how much intelligence a person has by comparing her or his performance with standardized norms.

standardized norms
Standards for evaluating performance of persons who take an intelligence test, obtained from scores of a large, representative sample who took the test while it was in preparation.

Test developers devise techniques to try to ensure that tests have high **validity** (the tests measure the abilities they claim to measure) and **reliability** (the test results are reasonably consistent from one time to another). Tests can be meaningful and useful only if they are both valid and reliable. For school-age children, intelligence test scores can predict school performance fairly accurately and reliably. Testing infants' and toddlers' intelligence is another matter.

validity
Capacity of a test to measure what it is intended to measure.

reliability
Consistency of a test in measuring performance.

Testing Infants' and Toddlers' Intelligence

Infants are intelligent from birth, but measuring their intelligence is not easy. Since babies cannot tell us what they know and how they think, the most obvious way to gauge their intelligence is by assessing what they can do. But if they do not grasp a rattle, it is hard to tell whether they do not know how, do not feel like doing it, do not realize what is expected of them, or have simply lost interest.

Still, sometimes there are reasons to test an infant's intelligence. If parents are worried because a baby is not doing the same things as other babies the same age, developmental testing may reassure them that development is normal—or may alert them to a problem. Developmental tests compare a baby's performance on a series of tasks with norms established by observing what large numbers of infants and toddlers can do at particular ages.

The **Bayley Scales of Infant Development** (Bayley, 1969, 1993; see Table 5-1) are widely used for these purposes. The Bayley-II, revised in 1993, is designed to assess the developmental status of children from 1 month to $3\frac{1}{2}$ years. It is used primarily with children suspected of being at risk for abnormal development (B. Thompson et al., 1994). The Bayley-II has three sections: a *mental scale,* which measures such abilities as perception, memory, learning, and vocalization; a *motor scale,* which measures gross (large-muscle) and fine (manipulative) motor skills, including sensorimotor coordination; and a *behavior rating scale* to be completed by the examiner. Separate scores, called *developmental quotients (DQs),* are calculated for each scale. DQs are most useful for early detection of emotional disturbances, learning problems, and sensory, neurological, and environmental deficits.

Bayley Scales of Infant Development
Standardized test of infants' mental and motor development.

Although these scores give a reasonably accurate picture of a child's current developmental status, they have little value in predicting future functioning (Anastasi & Urbina, 1997). One reason, as we'll see, is that environmental influences affect cognitive development, especially as children approach age 3 (Klebanov, Brooks-Gunn, McCarton, & McCormick, 1998). Another reason is that the developmental tests traditionally used for babies measure mostly sensory and motor abilities, whereas intelligence tests for older children place more emphasis on verbal abilities (Bornstein & Sigman, 1986; Colombo, 1993; McCall & Carriger, 1993). Not until at least the third year of life, when children may be tested with

Table 5-1 Sample Tasks in the Bayley Scales of Infant Development

Age (in months)	Mental Scale*	Motor Scale*
1	Eyes follow moving person	Lifts head when held at shoulder
3	Reaches for suspended ring	Turns from back to side
6	Manipulates bell, showing interest in detail	Turns from back to stomach
9	Jabbers expressively	Raises self to standing position
12	Pats toy in imitation	Walks alone
14–16	Uses two different words appropriately	Walks up stairs with help
20–22	Names three objects	Jumps off floor with both feet
26–28	Matches four colors	Imitates hand movements
32–34	Uses past tense	Walks up stairs, alternating feet
38–42	Counts	Walks down stairs, alternating feet

*Task most children this age can do

Source: Bayley, 1993.

the Stanford-Binet, do a child's IQ scores, along with such factors as the parents' IQ and educational level, usually help to predict later test scores (Kopp & Kaler, 1989; Kopp & McCall, 1982; McCall & Carriger, 1993). As children approach their fifth birthday, the relationship between current scores and those in later childhood becomes stronger (Bornstein & Sigman, 1986), and IQ tests given near the end of kindergarten are among the best predictors of future school success (Tramontana, Hooper, & Selzer, 1988).

Developmental tests are most accurate in predicting the future IQ of infants with disabilities or prenatal problems, especially if they are raised in impoverished, unstimulating environments (McCall & Carriger, 1993). However, human beings have a strong *self-righting tendency;* given a favorable environment, infants will follow normal developmental patterns unless they have suffered severe damage. Thus even some children born with mental or motor problems make impressive strides in tested intelligence as they grow older (Kopp & Kaler, 1989; Kopp & McCall, 1982).

Socioeconomic Status, Parenting Practices, and IQ

The correlation between socioeconomic status and IQ is well documented (Neisser et al., 1996). Poor children tend to have lower IQs than more well-to-do children, especially if the family has been poor for a long time. This seems to be true regardless of such factors as the composition of the household and the mother's educational level (Duncan, Brooks-Gunn, & Klebanov, 1994).

As an ecological analysis suggests, poverty can affect children by limiting parents' ability to provide educational resources and by exerting a negative psychological effect on the parents and their parenting practices (McLoyd, 1990, 1998; see Chapter 10). Even in well-functioning families, specific aspects of parenting associated with socioeconomic status can influence cognitive development. An observational study suggests how (B. Hart & Risley, 1992, 1996).

Once a month for more than two years, until the participating children turned 3, researchers visited the homes of 40 families with diverse marital, racial, and socioeconomic characteristics and observed parent-child interactions. Parents in higher-income families spent more time with their children, gave them more attention, talked more with them, and showed more interest in what they had to say. Children whose parents did these things tended to do well on IQ tests at age

3 and again at age 9. They also did better in school and on language and achievement tests. Much more of the talk of the lower-income parents included such negative words as "stop," "quit," and "don't"; and the children of parents who talked that way had lower IQs and achievement. This study pinpoints differences in early parenting practices that may help account for typical differences in future IQ and school performance of children from higher- and lower-income families. It shows what specific practices may help children do better in school (B. Hart & Risley, 1989, 1992, 1996; D. Walker, Greenwood, Hart, & Carta, 1994).

In another longitudinal study covering the first 3 years of life, characteristics of the home environment largely accounted for the influences of socioeconomic status, neighborhood income, and family risk factors on developmental and IQ scores at ages 1 to 3 (Klebanov et al., 1998).

Assessing the Impact of the Home Environment

How do researchers measure the characteristics of the early home environment that influence intelligence? Using the **Home Observation for Measurement of the Environment (HOME)** (R. H. Bradley, 1989; Caldwell & Bradley, 1984) trained observers rate the resources and atmosphere in a child's home and interview the parents. Versions of HOME are available for infants, preschoolers, and school-age children.

Home Observation for Measurement of the Environment (HOME) Instrument to measure the influence of the home environment on children's cognitive growth.

One important factor is parental responsiveness. HOME gives credit to the parent of an infant or toddler for caressing or kissing the child during an examiner's visit; to the parent of a preschooler for spontaneously praising the child at least twice during the visit; and to the parent of an older child for answering the child's questions. Examiners evaluate how parent and child talk to each other, and they give high ratings for a parent's friendly, nonpunitive attitude. A longitudinal study found positive correlations between parents' responsiveness to their 6-month-old babies, as measured by HOME, and the children's IQ and achievement test scores at age 10, as well as between the 6-month parental responsiveness scores and teachers' ratings of classroom behavior at age 10 (R. Bradley & Caldwell, 1982; R. Bradley, Caldwell, & Rock, 1988).

HOME also assesses the number of books in the home, the presence of playthings that encourage the development of concepts, and parents' involvement in children's play. High scores on all these factors are fairly reliable in predicting children's IQ. In one study, researchers compared HOME scores for low-income 2-year-olds with the children's Stanford-Binet intelligence test scores two years later. The single most important factor in predicting high intelligence was the mother's ability to create and structure an environment that fostered learning (Stevens & Bakeman, 1985).

Among 931 African American, Mexican American, and white children up to age 3, socioeconomic status and other aspects of their inner-city environment were less closely related to cognitive development than were such day-to-day aspects of the home environment as parental responsiveness and access to stimulating play materials (R. H. Bradley et al., 1989). In all three ethnic groups, a responsive and stimulating home environment could offset problems in infancy; but when both early development *and* early home environment were poor, the chances for a good outcome were much smaller. In a subsample of 347 low-birthweight babies from the control groups of the Infant Health and Development Study (introduced in Chapter 4), the association between family and neighborhood income and cognitive test scores at ages 2 and 3 was attributable to the home environment as measured by HOME (Klebanov et al., 1998).

Of course, we cannot be sure on the basis of correlational findings that parental responsiveness or an enriched home environment actually increases a child's intelligence. All we can say is that these factors are associated with high intelligence. Intelligent, well-educated parents may be more likely to provide a positive, stimulating home environment; and since they also pass their genes on

CHECKPOINT

Can you . . .

- ✔ Tell why developmental tests are sometimes given to infants and toddlers and describe one such widely used test?
- ✔ Explain why tests of infants and toddlers are unreliable in predicting later IQ?
- ✔ Discuss the relationship between socioeconomic status, parenting practices, and cognitive development?
- ✔ Identify specific aspects of the home environment that seem to influence measured intelligence?

Consider this . . .

- The HOME scale assesses the relationship between the home environment and a child's later cognitive functioning. If you were designing such a measure, what aspects of the home situation, if any, would you add to those mentioned in the text?

to their children, there may be a genetic influence as well. (This is an example of a *passive genotype-environment correlation,* described in Chapter 3.)

Adoption studies support a genetic influence. In one statistical analysis, the correlation between HOME scores of 12- and 24-month-olds and their performance on the Bayley Mental Development Scale was greater for biological siblings than for adoptive siblings (Braungart, Fulker, & Plomin, 1992). And, in a longitudinal study of adoptive and nonadoptive children, most apparent correlations between the home environment during infancy and IQ at age 7 turned out to be indirectly attributable to a genetic factor: the parents' IQs (Coon, Fulker, DeFries, & Plomin, 1990).

Early Intervention

developmental priming mechanisms
Preparatory aspects of the home environment that seem to be necessary for normal cognitive and psychosocial development to occur.

In other research, six **developmental priming mechanisms**—aspects of the home environment that pave the way for normal cognitive and psychosocial development and help make children ready for school—have repeatedly been associated with positive outcomes. The six mechanisms are: (1) encouragement to explore; (2) mentoring in basic cognitive and social skills, such as labeling, sequencing, sorting, and comparing; (3) celebration and reinforcement of new accomplishments; (4) guidance in practicing and expanding new skills; (5) protection from inappropriate punishment, teasing, or disapproval for mistakes or unintended consequences of exploring and trying out new skills; and (6) stimulation of language and other symbolic communication. The consistent presence of all six of these conditions early in life may be essential to normal brain development (C. T. Ramey & S. L. Ramey, 1998a, 1998b; S. L. Ramey & C. T. Ramey, 1992).

early intervention
Systematic process of planning and providing therapeutic and educational services to families that need help in meeting infants', toddlers', and preschool children's developmental needs.

What can be done to help children who do not get such developmental support? **Early intervention** is a systematic process of providing therapeutic and educational services to families that need help in meeting young children's developmental needs.

How effective is early intervention? Results from randomly assigned, controlled studies have found positive effects, especially among the most at-risk children—those whose parents are very poor, have little education, and in many cases are unmarried (C. T. Ramey & S. L. Ramey, 1998b). Project CARE (Wasik, Ramey, Bryant, & Sparling, 1990) and the Abecedarian project (C. T. Ramey & Campbell, 1991) involved a total of 174 North Carolina babies from at-risk homes. In each project, from 6 weeks of age until kindergarten, an experimental group was enrolled in a full-day, year-round early childhood education program, Partners for Learning, at a university child development center. The program had a low child-teacher ratio and used learning games to foster specific cognitive, linguistic, perceptual-motor, and social skills. Control groups were not enrolled in Partners for Learning but (like the experimental groups) did receive pediatric and social work services, formula, and home visits.

CHECKPOINT

Can you . . .

✔ Identify six developmental priming mechanisms that help make children ready for formal learning?

In both projects, the children who received the early educational intervention demonstrated a widening advantage over the control groups in developmental test scores during the first 18 months. By age 3, the average IQ of the Abecedarian children was 101, and of CARE children, 105—equal to or better than average for the general population—as compared with only 84 and 93 for the control groups (C. T. Ramey & S. L. Ramey, 1998b).

Consider this . . .

- On the basis of the six developmental priming mechanisms listed in the text, can you suggest specific ways to help infants and toddlers get ready for schooling?

As often happens with early intervention programs, these early gains were not fully maintained. IQs dropped between ages 3 and 8, especially among children from the most disadvantaged homes. However, scores tended to be higher and more stable among children who had been in Partners for Learning than in the control groups, suggesting that early educational intervention can moderate the negative effects of low socioeconomic status (Burchinal, Campbell, Bryant, Wasik, & Ramey, 1997). At age 15, the children in the Abecedarian Project who had been enrolled in Partners for Learning continued to outdo the control group, with an average IQ of 97.7 as compared with 92.6. They also did better on reading and math achievement tests and were less likely to have repeated a grade in school (C. T. Ramey et al., 2000).

These findings show that early educational intervention can boost cognitive development. The most effective early interventions are those that (1) start early and continue throughout the preschool years; (2) are highly time-intensive; (3) provide direct educational experiences, not just parental training; (4) take a comprehensive approach, including health, family counseling, and social services; and (5) are tailored to individual differences and needs. As in the two North Carolina projects, initial gains tend to diminish unless there is adequate, ongoing environmental support for further progress (C. T. Ramey & S. L. Ramey, 1996, 1998a).

CHECKPOINT

Can you . . .

✔ Summarize findings about the value of early intervention in improving disadvantaged children's IQs?

Piagetian Approach: The Sensorimotor Stage

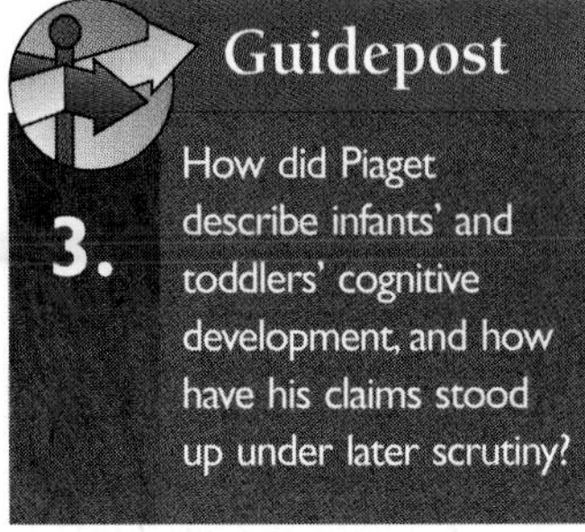

Guidepost
3.
How did Piaget describe infants' and toddlers' cognitive development, and how have his claims stood up under later scrutiny?

As a young man studying in Paris, Piaget set out to standardize the tests Binet and Simon had developed to assess the intelligence of French schoolchildren. Piaget became intrigued by the children's wrong answers, seeing them as clues to what is special and important about children's thought processes. To examine these processes, Piaget observed his own and other children from infancy on. Children's thinking, he concluded, is qualitatively different (different in kind) from adult thought. Whereas psychometricians measure individual differences in how much intelligence children (or adults) have, Piaget looked at the way children's thinking developed throughout infancy, childhood, and adolescence and proposed universal sequences of cognitive growth.

The first of Piaget's four stages of cognitive development (refer back to Table 2-2 in Chapter 2) is the **sensorimotor stage.** During this stage (birth to approximately age 2), said Piaget, infants learn about themselves and their world—as Doddy Darwin seemed to do—through their developing sensory and motor activity. Babies change from creatures who respond primarily through reflexes and random behavior into goal-oriented toddlers.

sensorimotor stage
In Piaget's theory, the first stage in cognitive development, during which infants (from birth to approximately 2 years) learn through their developing senses and motor activity.

Piaget's theory has inspired much research on cognition in infancy and early childhood. Some of this research, as we will see, has shown that—as important as Piaget's contributions were—he underestimated young children's abilities.

Substages of the Sensorimotor Stage

According to Piaget, the sensorimotor stage consists of six substages (see Table 5-2), which flow from one to another as a baby's **schemes,** organized patterns of behavior, become more elaborate. During the first five substages, babies learn to coordinate input from their senses and organize their activities in relation to their environment. During the sixth and last substage, they progress from trial-and-error learning to the use of symbols and concepts to solve simple problems.

schemes
In Piaget's terminology, basic cognitive structures consisting of organized patterns of behavior used in different kinds of situations.

Much of this early cognitive growth comes about through **circular reactions,** in which an infant learns to reproduce pleasurable or interesting events originally discovered by chance. The process is based on operant conditioning. Initially, an activity produces a sensation so enjoyable that the baby wants to repeat it. The repetition then feeds on itself in a continuous cycle in which cause and effect keep reversing (see Figure 5-3). The originally chance behavior has been consolidated into a new scheme.

circular reactions
In Piaget's terminology, processes by which an infant learns to reproduce desired occurrences originally discovered by chance.

In the *first substage* (birth to about 1 month), as neonates exercise their inborn reflexes, they gain some control over them. They begin to engage in a behavior even when the stimulus that normally elicits it is not present. For example, newborns suck reflexively when their lips are touched. They soon learn to find the nipple even when they are not touched, and they suck at times when they are not

Table 5-2 Six Substages of Piaget's Sensorimotor Stage of Cognitive Development

Substage	Description
Substage 1 (birth to 1 month) *Use of reflexes*	Infants exercise their inborn reflexes and gain some control over them. They do not coordinate information from their senses. They do not grasp an object they are looking at.
Substage 2 (1 to 4 months) *Primary circular reactions*	Infants repeat pleasurable behaviors that first occur by chance (such as thumb sucking). Activities focus on infant's body rather than the effects of the behavior on the environment. Infants make first acquired adaptations; that is, they suck different objects differently. They begin to coordinate sensory information and grasp objects.
Substage 3 (4 to 8 months) *Secondary circular reactions*	Infants become more interested in the environment; they repeat actions that bring interesting results (such as shaking a rattle) and prolong interesting experiences. Actions are intentional but not initially goal-directed.
Substage 4 (8 to 12 months) *Coordination of secondary schemes*	Behavior is more deliberate and purposeful (intentional) as infants coordinate previously learned schemes (such as looking at and grasping a rattle) and use previously learned behaviors to attain their goals (such as crawling across the room to get a desired toy). They can anticipate events.
Substage 5 (12 to 18 months) *Tertiary circular reactions*	Toddlers show curiosity and experimentation; they purposefully vary their actions to see results (for example, by shaking different rattles to hear their sounds). They actively explore their world to determine what is novel about an object, event, or situation. They try out new activities and use trial and error in solving problems.
Substage 6 (18 to 24 months) *Mental combinations*	Since toddlers can mentally represent events, they are no longer confined to trial and error to solve problems. Symbolic thought allows toddlers to begin to think about events and anticipate their consequences without always resorting to action. Toddlers begin to demonstrate insight. They can use symbols, such as gestures and words, and can pretend.

Note: Infants show enormous cognitive growth during Piaget's sensorimotor stage, as they learn about the world through their senses and their motor activities. Note their progress in problem solving and the coordination of sensory information. All ages are approximate.

hungry. Thus infants modify and extend the scheme for sucking as they begin to initiate activity.

In the *second substage* (about 1 to 4 months), babies learn to repeat a pleasant bodily sensation first achieved by chance (say, sucking their thumbs, as in the first part of Figure 5-3). Piaget called this a *primary circular reaction.* They begin to turn toward sounds, showing the ability to coordinate different kinds of sensory information (vision and hearing).

The *third substage* (about 4 to 8 months) coincides with a new interest in manipulating objects and learning about their properties. Babies engage in *secondary circular reactions:* intentional actions repeated not merely for their own sake, as in the second substage, but to get results *beyond the infant's own body.* For example, a baby this age will repeatedly shake a rattle to hear its noise, or (as in the second part of Figure 5-3) coo when a friendly face appears, so as to make the face stay longer.

By the time infants reach the *fourth substage, coordination of secondary schemes* (about 8 to 12 months), they have built on the few schemes they were born with. They have learned to generalize from past experience to solve new problems and to distinguish means from ends. They will crawl to get something they want, grab it, or push away a barrier to it (such as someone else's hand). They try out, modify, and coordinate previous schemes, to find one that works. Thus this substage marks the beginning of *intentional* behavior.

In the *fifth substage* (about 12 to 18 months), babies begin to experiment with new behavior to see what will happen. Once they begin to walk, they can more easily explore their environment. They now engage in *tertiary circular reactions, varying* an action to get a similar result, rather than merely *repeating* pleasing behavior they have accidentally discovered. For example, a toddler may squeeze a rubber duck that squeaked when stepped on, to see whether it will squeak again (as in the third part of Figure 5-3). For the first time, children show originality in problem solving. By trial and error, they try out behaviors until they find the best way to attain a goal.

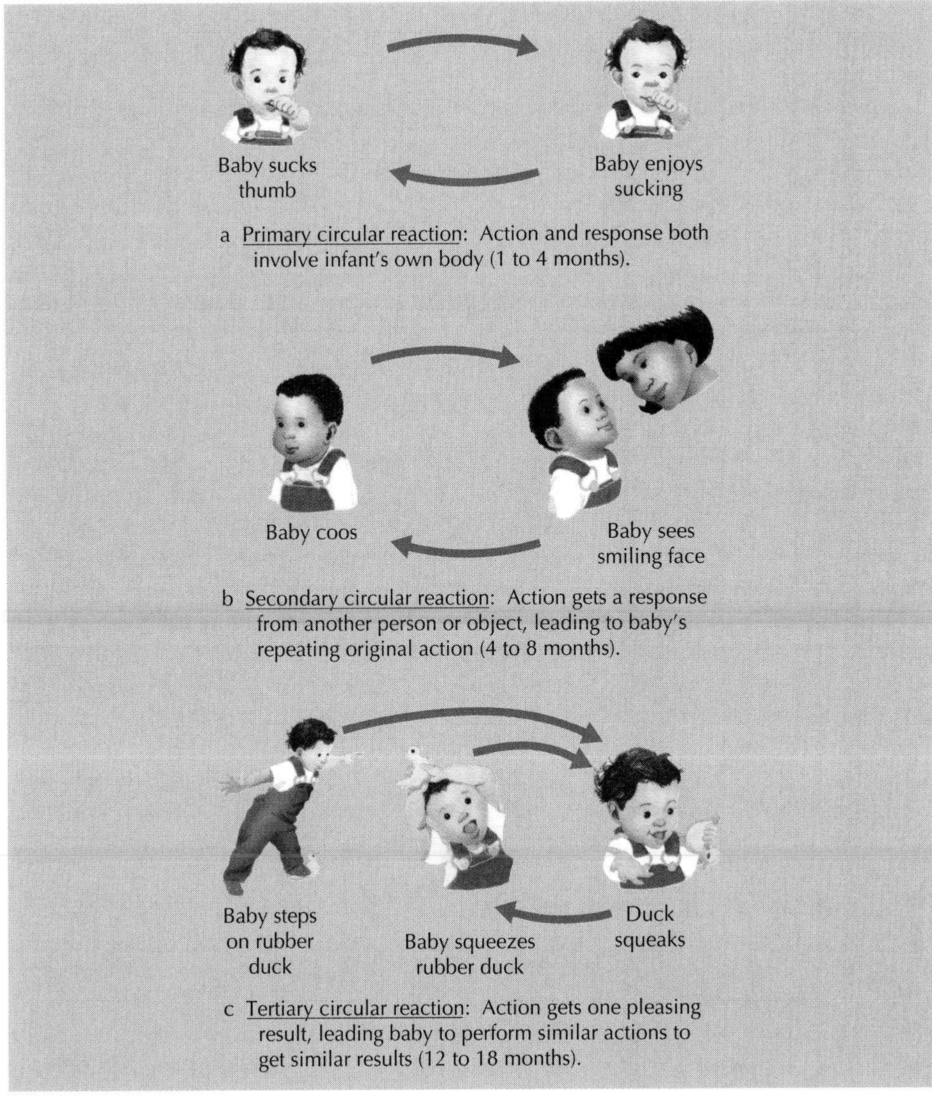
Baby sucks thumb
Baby enjoys sucking
a Primary circular reaction: Action and response both involve infant's own body (1 to 4 months).
Baby coos
Baby sees smiling face
b Secondary circular reaction: Action gets a response from another person or object, leading to baby's repeating original action (4 to 8 months).
Baby steps on rubber duck
Baby squeezes rubber duck
Duck squeaks
c Tertiary circular reaction: Action gets one pleasing result, leading baby to perform similar actions to get similar results (12 to 18 months).

Figure 5-3
Primary, secondary, and tertiary circular reactions. According to Piaget, infants learn to reproduce pleasurable events they discover accidentally. *(a)* Primary circular reaction: A baby happens to suck a thumb, enjoys sucking, and puts the thumb back into the mouth or keeps it there. The stimulus (thumb) elicits the sucking reflex; pleasure then stimulates the baby to keep on sucking. *(b)* Secondary circular reaction: This involves something outside the baby's body. The baby coos; the mother smiles; and because the baby likes to see the mother smile, the baby coos again. *(c)* Tertiary circular reaction: The baby tries different ways to reproduce an accidentally discovered response. When the baby steps on a rubber duck, the duck squeaks. The baby then tries to produce the squeak in other ways, perhaps by squeezing it or sitting on it.

The *sixth substage, mental combinations* (about 18 months to 2 years) is a transition into the preoperational stage of early childhood. **Representational ability**—the ability to mentally represent objects and actions in memory, largely through symbols such as words, numbers, and mental pictures—blossoms. The ability to manipulate symbols frees children from immediate experience. They can now engage in **deferred imitation,** imitating actions they no longer see in front of them. They can pretend, as Anna did at 20 months when she was given a tea set and immediately "served tea" to her parents. They can use symbols to *think* about actions before taking them. Since they now have some understanding of cause and effect, they no longer have to go through laborious trial and error to solve problems. Piaget's daughter Lucienne seemed to show representational ability when, in figuring out how to pry open a partially closed matchbox to remove a watch chain, she opened her mouth wider to represent her idea of widening the slit in the box (Piaget, 1936/1952).

representational ability
In Piaget's terminology, capacity to mentally represent objects and experiences, largely through the use of symbols.

deferred imitation
In Piaget's terminology, reproduction of an observed behavior after the passage of time by calling up a stored symbol of it.

Development of Knowledge about Objects and Space

The *object concept*—the idea that objects have their own independent existence, characteristics, and location in space—is fundamental to an orderly view of physical reality. The object concept is the basis for children's awareness that they themselves exist apart from objects and other people. It is essential to understanding a world full of objects and events. Doddy Darwin's struggle to understand the existence and location of reflective images was part of his development of an object concept.

Piaget believed that infants develop knowledge about objects and space by seeing the results of their own actions: in other words, by coordinating visual and motor information. Before they can get around on their own, infants' knowledge about sizes and shapes of objects, how close or far away they are, and their relative positions in space does not extend much farther than the infant's grasp. With the coming of self-locomotion—first crawling, then walking—babies can get close to an object, size it up, and compare its location with that of other objects (refer back to Box 4-2 in Chapter 4).

Research supports this shift. Infants can follow their mother's gaze or her pointing finger to a nearby object at an earlier age than to a distant object. The latter ability seems to develop between 12 and 15 months, when most infants begin to walk (Butterworth & Jarrett, 1991; Morissette, Ricard, & Decarie, 1995). During approximately the same period, infants become better able to judge the location of an object or event in relation to themselves (Newcombe, Huttenlocher, Drummey, & Wiley, 1998). However, it is not clear whether self-locomotion helps bring about these changes or merely accompanies them (Haith & Benson, 1998).

object permanence
In Piaget's terminology, the understanding that a person or object still exists when out of sight.

A, not-B, error
Tendency, noted by Piaget, for 8- to 12-month-old infants to search for a hidden object in a place where they previously found it, rather than in the place where they most recently saw it being hidden.

One aspect of the object concept is **object permanence,** the realization that an object or person continues to exist when out of sight. It is object permanance that allows a child whose parent has left the room to feel secure in the knowledge that the parent still exists and will return. The development of this concept in many cultures can be seen in the game of peekaboo (see Box 5-1).

According to Piaget, object permanence develops gradually during the sensorimotor stage (refer back to Table 5-3). At first, infants have no such concept. By the third substage, from about 4 to 8 months, they will look for something they have dropped, but if they cannot see it, they act as if it no longer exists. In the fourth substage, about 8 to 12 months, they will look for an object in a place where they first found it after seeing it hidden, even if they later saw it being moved to another place. (Piaget called this the **A, not-B error.**) In the fifth substage, 12 to 18 months, they no longer make this error; they will search for an object in the *last* place they saw it hidden. However, they will *not* search for it in a place where they did *not* see it hidden. By the sixth substage, 18 to 24 months, object permanence is fully achieved; toddlers will look for an object even if they did not see it hidden.

CHECKPOINT

Can you . . .

- ✔ Summarize major developments during the six substages of Piaget's sensorimotor stage?
- ✔ Explain how circular reactions work, and distinguish between primary, secondary, and tertiary circular reactions?
- ✔ Tell why the development of representational ability is important?
- ✔ Summarize Piaget's views on the development of object permanence and spatial knowledge?

An analysis of 30 studies verified the prevalence of the A, not-B error (Wellman, Cross, & Bartsch, 1986). Say a 9-month-old finds a doll hidden behind a pillow (location A). Then he watches closely as the doll is hidden again, this time under a table (location B). But instead of looking under the table (B), where the infant just saw the doll hidden, he again looks behind the pillow (A).

Piaget saw this A, not-B error as a sign of incomplete understanding of the object concept, together with an egocentric (self-centered) view of spatial relations. He reasoned that the infant must believe that the doll's existence is linked to a particular location (the one where it was first found) and to the infant's own action in retrieving it from that location. More recent research suggests that infants—and even toddlers and preschoolers—may simply find it hard to restrain the impulse to repeat a previous behavior that was previously reinforced by success (Diamond, Cruttenden, & Neiderman, 1994; Zelazo, Reznick, & Spinazzola, 1998).

What Abilities May Develop Earlier Than Piaget Thought?

Piaget has made monumental contributions to our understanding of cognitive development; but while research has supported some of his claims, it has challenged others. According to Piaget, the journey from reflex behavior to the beginnings of thought is a long, slow one. For a year and a half or so, babies learn only from their senses and movements. Not until the last half of the second year do they make the breakthrough to conceptual thought. Today there is growing

Box 5-1
Playing Peekaboo

In a mud hut in rural South Africa, a mother smiles at her 9-month-old son, covers her eyes with her hands, and asks, "Uphi?" (Where?) After 3 seconds, the mother says, "Here!" and uncovers her eyes to the baby's delight. In a Tokyo apartment a Japanese mother, using different language and covering her eyes with a cloth, plays the same game with her 12-month-old daughter, who shows the same joyous response.

Peekaboo is played across diverse cultures, using similar routines (Fernald & O'Neill, 1993). In all cultures in which the game is played,* the moment when the mother or other caregiver reappears is exhilarating. It is marked by exaggerated gestures and voice tones. Infants' pleasure from the immediate sensory stimulation of the game is heightened by their fascination with faces and voices, especially the high-pitched tones the adult usually uses.

The game is not only fun; it serves several important purposes. Psychoanalysts maintain that it helps babies master anxiety when their mother disappears. Cognitive psychologists see it as a way babies play with developing ideas about the existence, disappearance, and reappearance of objects—the concept of object permanence. It may also be a social routine that helps babies learn the kinds of rules that govern conversation, such as taking turns. It may provide practice in paying attention, a prerequisite for learning.

As babies develop the cognitive competency to predict future events, the game takes on new dimensions. Between 3 and 5 months, the baby's smiles and laughter as the adult's face moves in and out of view signal the infant's developing expectation of what will happen next. At 5 to 8 months, the baby shows anticipation by looking and smiling as the adult's voice alerts the infant to the adult's imminent reappearance. By 1 year, babies are no longer merely observers but usually initiate the game, actively engaging adults in play. Now it is the adult who generally responds to the baby's physical or vocal cues, which can become quite insistent if the adult doesn't feel like playing.

To help infants who are in the process of learning peekaboo or other games, parents often use *scaffolding* (see Chapter 2). They encourage babies to move to a higher level of mastery by prompting them to perform at their highest current level of competence.

In an 18-month longitudinal study at the University of Montreal, 25 mothers were videotaped playing peekaboo with their babies, using a doll as a prop (Rome-Flanders, Cronk, & Gourde, 1995). The amount of scaffolding on the mother's part, and the particular type of scaffolding behavior, varied with the infant's age and skill. Mothers frequently tried to attract a 6-month-old's attention to begin the game; this became less and less necessary as time went on. Modeling (performing the peekaboo sequence to encourage a baby to imitate it) also was most frequent at 6 months and decreased significantly by 12 months, when there was an increase in direct verbal instruction ("Cover the doll") as babies became more able to understand spoken language. Indirect verbal instruction ("Where is the doll?"), used to focus attention on the next step in the game, remained constant throughout the entire age range. Reinforcement (showing satisfaction with the infant's performance, for example, by saying "Peekaboo!" when the infant uncovered the doll) was fairly constant from 9 months on. The overall amount of scaffolding dropped substantially at 24 months, by which time most babies have fully mastered the game.

*The cultures included in this report are found in Malaysia, Greece, India, Iran, Russia, Brazil, Indonesia, Korea, and South Africa.

evidence that some of the limitations Piaget saw in infants' cognitive abilities may instead have reflected their immature linguistic and motor skills. Researchers using simplified tasks and modern research tools have built an impressive case for babies' cognitive strengths.

For example, Piaget may have underestimated young infants' grasp of object permanence because of his testing methods. Babies may fail to search for hidden objects because they cannot yet carry out a two-step sequence of actions, such as moving a cushion or lifting the cover of a box before grasping the object. When object permanence is tested with a more age-appropriate procedure, in which the object is hidden only by darkness and thus can be retrieved in one motion, infants in the third substage (4 to 8 months) perform surprisingly well. In one study of object permanence, $6\frac{1}{2}$-month-olds saw a ball drop down a chute and land in one of two spots, each identifiable by a distinctive sound. When the light was turned off, and the procedure was repeated, the babies reached for the ball in the appropriate location, guided only by the sound (Goubet & Clifton, 1998). This showed that they knew the ball continued to exist and could tell where it had gone.

Methods based only on what infants look at, and for how long, eliminate the need for *any* motor activity and thus can be used with even younger infants. As we report later in this chapter, studies since the late 1970s, using information-processing methodology, suggest that very young infants may form mental representations—images or memories of objects not physically present—an ability Piaget said does not emerge before 18 months. According to this research, the interpretation of which is in dispute, infants as young as 3 or 4 months old seem to have a sense of object permanence, know certain principles about the physical world, understand categorization and causality, and have a rudimentary concept of number. Other research deals with infants' and toddlers' ability to remember and imitate what they see. (Table 5-3 compares these findings with Piaget's views.)

invisible imitation
Imitation with parts of one's body that one cannot see; e.g., the mouth.

visible imitation
Imitation with parts of one's body that one can see, such as the hands and the feet.

Piaget maintained that **invisible imitation**—imitation using parts of the body that a baby cannot see, such as the mouth—develops at about 9 months, after **visible imitation**—the use of hands or feet, for example, which babies can see. Yet in a series of studies by Andrew Meltzoff and M. Keith Moore (1983, 1989), babies less than 72 hours old appeared to imitate adults by opening their mouths and sticking out their tongues, as well as by duplicating adults' head movements.

Table 5-3 Key Developments of the Sensorimotor Stage

Concept or Skill	Piaget's View	More Recent Findings
Object permanence	Develops gradually between third and sixth substage. Infants in fourth substage (8–12 months) make A, not-B error.	Infants as young as $3\,^1/_2$ months (second substage) seem to show object knowledge, though interpretation of findings is in dispute. A, not-B error may persist into second year or longer.
Spatial knowledge	Development of object concept and spatial knowledge is linked to self-locomotion and coordination of visual and motor information.	Research supports Piaget's timetable and relationship of spatial judgments to decline of egocentrism. Link to motor development is less clear.
Causality	Develops slowly between 4–6 months and 1 year, based on infant's discovery, first of effects of own actions and then of effects of outside forces.	Some evidence suggests early awareness of specific causal events in the physical world, but general understanding of causality may be slower to develop.
Number	Depends on use of symbols, which begins in sixth substage (18–24 months).	Infants as young as 5 months may recognize and mentally manipulate small numbers, but interpretation of findings is in dispute.
Categorization	Depends on representational thinking, which develops during sixth substage (18–24 months).	Infants as young as 3 months seem to recognize perceptual categories.
Imitation	Invisible imitation develops around 9 months, deferred imitation after development of mental representations in sixth substage (18–24 months).	Controversial studies have found invisible imitation of facial expressions in newborns and deferred imitation as early as 6 weeks. Deferred imitation of complex activities seems to exist as early as 6 months.

However, a review of Meltzoff and Moore's work on invisible imitation, and of attempts to replicate it, found clear, consistent evidence only with regard to one movement—sticking out the tongue (Anisfeld, 1996)—and that response disappears by about 2 months of age. Since it seems unlikely that an early and short-lived imitative capacity would be limited to one gesture, some researchers have instead suggested that the tongue thrust may serve other purposes—perhaps as an early attempt to interact with the mother, or simply as exploratory behavior aroused by the intriguing sight of an adult tongue (Bjorklund, 1997; S. S. Jones, 1996). Pending further research, the age when invisible imitation begins will remain in doubt.

Piaget also held that children under 18 months cannot engage in *deferred imitation* of an act they saw some time before. Yet babies as young as 6 *weeks* have imitated an adult's facial movements after a 24-hour delay, in the presence of the same adult, who this time was expressionless. This suggests that very young babies can retain a mental representation of an event (Meltzoff & Moore, 1994, 1998).

Six- to 9-month-olds have shown deferred imitation of a complex sequence of actions they observed but did not immediately have an opportunity to try (Meltzoff & Moore, 1998). In one experiment in New Zealand, infants of various ages watched a researcher pull a mitten off a puppet, jingle a bell inside the mitten three times, and then put the mitten back on the puppet. Infants as young as 9 months mimicked these actions 24 hours later, if they were in the same place and with the same people. Even 6-month-olds, if given extra time for demonstration sessions, were able to repeat the first part of the sequence after a day; but older infants imitated more accurately (Barr, Dowden, & Hayne, 1996).

During a child's second year, specific contextual links between the training and test situations become less critical. After 24 hours, 12-month-olds will show deferred imitation only if the puppet's color and shape are virtually identical to the original ones. Eighteen-month-olds will respond if differences in color and form are minor (as in a rabbit and a mouse); 21-month-olds will respond to a substantially different puppet (a cow as compared with a duck). The time between training and testing also is a factor. If the delay is only 10 minutes, 12-month-olds will imitate a stimulus of a different color from the original one, and 14-month-olds will imitate a stimulus of a different shape (Barnat, Klein, & Meltzoff, 1996; Hayne, MacDonald, & Barr, 1997). In other research, 14- to 18-month-olds who watched other children play with objects (for example, putting beads in a cup or sounding a buzzer), either in a laboratory or in a day care center, repeated the behavior when given the same objects at home 2 days later—evidence that toddlers are capable of deferred imitation in a totally different context (Hanna & Meltzoff, 1993).

Can imitation occur after a much longer delay? In one study, 16- to 20-month-olds reproduced such activities as illuminating an orange panel by touching their foreheads to it—a procedure they had been shown 2 to 4 months earlier (Meltzoff, 1995).

Overall, then, infants and toddlers seem to be far more cognitively competent than Piaget imagined and show earlier signs of conceptual thought (Flavell, Miller, & Miller, 1993). This does not mean that infants come into the world with minds fully formed. Piaget seems to have been right in his view that immature forms of cognition give way to more mature forms. We can see this, for example, in the errors young infants make in searching for hidden objects. But Piaget may have been wrong in his emphasis on motor experience as the primary "engine" of cognitive growth. Infants' perceptions are far ahead of their motor abilities, and today's methods allow researchers to make observations and inferences about those perceptions. Just how perception relates to cognition is a major area of investigation, as we will see in the next section (Flavell et al., 1993).

Consider this . . .

- What comments might Piaget have made about Darwin's diary entries on his son's early cognitive development?
- On the basis of observations by Piaget and the research they inspired, what factors would you consider in designing or purchasing a toy or book for an infant or toddler?

CHECKPOINT

Can you . . .

✔ Explain why Piaget may have underestimated some of infants' cognitive abilities, and discuss the implications of research on imitation in infants and toddlers?

Studying Cognitive Development: Newer Approaches

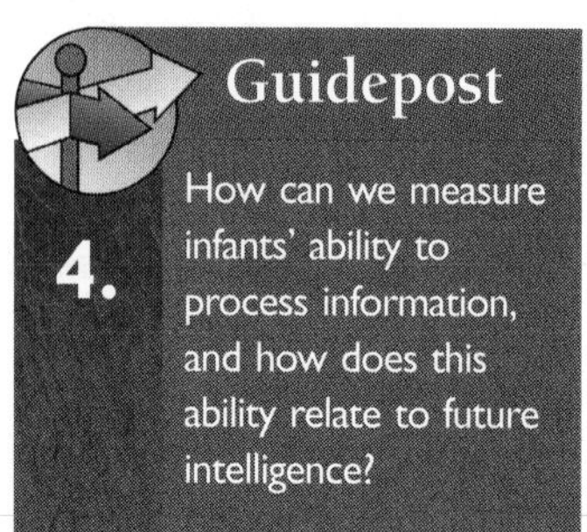
Guidepost
4.
How can we measure infants' ability to process information, and how does this ability relate to future intelligence?

information-processing approach
Approach to the study of cognitive development by observing and analyzing the mental processes involved in perceiving and handling information.

cognitive neuroscience approach
Approach to the study of cognitive development by examining brain structures and measuring neurological activity.

social-contextual approach
Approach to the study of cognitive development by focusing on the influence of environmental aspects of the learning process, particularly parents and other caregivers.

During the past few decades, researchers have turned to three new approaches to add to our knowledge about infants' and toddlers' cognitive development:

- The **information-processing approach** focuses on the processes involved in perception, learning, memory, and problem solving. It seeks to discover what people do with information from the time they encounter it until they use it.
- The **cognitive neuroscience approach** examines the "hardware" of the central nervous system. It attempts to identify what brain structures are involved in specific aspects of cognition.
- The **social-contextual approach** examines environmental aspects of the learning process, particularly the role of parents and other caregivers.

Information-Processing Approach: Perceptions and Representations

Like the psychometric approach, information-processing theory is concerned with individual differences in intelligent behavior. Unlike the psychometric approach, it attempts to describe the mental processes involved in acquiring and remembering information or solving problems, rather than merely inferring differences in mental functioning from answers given or problems solved. Information-processing research uses new methods to test ideas about children's cognitive development that sprang from the psychometric and Piagetian approaches. For example, information-processing researchers analyze the separate parts of a complex task, such as Piaget's object search tasks, to figure out what abilities are necessary for each part of the task and at what age these abilities develop. Information-processing research also seeks to measure what infants pay attention to, and for how long.

Habituation

habituation
Simple type of learning in which familiarity with a stimulus reduces, slows, or stops a response. Compare *dishabituation*.

dishabituation
Increase in responsiveness after presentation of a new stimulus. Compare *habituation*.

At about 6 weeks, André lies peacefully in his crib near a window, sucking a pacifier. It is a cloudy day, but suddenly the sun breaks through, and an angular shaft of light appears on the end of the crib. André stops sucking for a few moments, staring at the pattern of light and shade. Then he looks away and starts sucking again.

We don't know what was going on in André's mind when he saw the shaft of light, but we can tell by his sucking and looking behavior at what point he began paying attention and when he stopped. These simple behaviors can be indicators of sensory perception and discrimination and even of future intelligence.

Much information-processing research with infants is based on **habituation,** a type of learning in which repeated or continuous exposure to a stimulus (such as the shaft of light) reduces attention to that stimulus. In other words, familiarity breeds loss of interest. As infants habituate, they transform the novel into the familiar, the unknown into the known (Rheingold, 1985).

Researchers study habituation in newborns by repeatedly presenting a stimulus (usually a sound or visual pattern) and then monitoring such responses as heart rate, sucking, eye movements, and brain activity. A baby who has been sucking typically stops when the stimulus is first presented and does not start again until after it has ended. After the same sound or sight has been presented again and again, it loses its novelty and no longer causes the baby to stop sucking. Uninterrupted sucking shows that the infant has habituated to the stimulus. A new sight or sound, however, will capture the baby's attention and the baby will again stop sucking. This increased response to a new stimulus is called **dishabituation.**

Can this baby tell the difference between Raggedy Ann and Raggedy Andy? This researcher may find out by seeing whether the baby has habituated—gotten used to one face—and then stops sucking on the nipple when a new face appears, showing recognition of the difference.

Researchers gauge the efficiency of infants' information processing by measuring how quickly babies habituate to familiar stimuli, how fast their attention recovers when they are exposed to new stimuli, and how much time they spend looking at the new and the old. Efficiency of habituation correlates with later signs of cognitive development, such as a preference for complexity, rapid exploration of the environment, sophisticated play, quick problem solving, and the ability to match pictures. In fact, as we will see, speed of habituation and other information-processing abilities show promise as predictors of intelligence (Bornstein & Sigman, 1986; Colombo, 1993; McCall & Carriger, 1993).

Habituation has been used to study topics ranging from infants' ability to detect differences between visual patterns to the ability to categorize people, objects, and events—abilities that would seem to require mental representations. For example, 3-month-olds who have been looking at a picture of a dog will look longer at a picture of a cat than at another picture of a dog, showing that they know the difference between cats and dogs (Quinn, Eimas, & Rosenkrantz, 1993). However, it is important not to overstate the results of such research. The fact that an infant pays closer attention to a new shape or pattern than to a familiar one shows that the infant can see a difference between the two but does not reveal what *cognitive* meaning, if any, the infant attaches to that difference (Haith & Benson, 1998).

Early Perceptual and Processing Abilities

The amount of time a baby spends looking at different sights is a measure of **visual preference,** which is based on the ability to make visual distinctions. Classic research by Robert Fantz and his colleagues revealed that babies less than 2 days old prefer curved lines to straight lines, complex patterns to simple patterns, three-dimensional objects to two-dimensional objects, pictures of faces to pictures of other things, and new sights to familiar ones (Fantz, 1963, 1964, 1965; Fantz, Fagen, & Miranda, 1975; Fantz & Nevis, 1967).

visual preference
Tendency of infants to spend more time looking at one sight than another.

If infants pay more attention to new stimuli than to familiar ones—a phenomenon called *novelty preference*—they can tell the new from the old. Therefore, say information-processing theorists, they must be able to remember the old. Their ability to compare new information with information they already have suggests that they can form mental representations (P. R. Zelazo, Kearsley, & Stack, 1995). The efficiency of information processing depends on the speed with which they form and refer to such images.

Contrary to Piaget's view, habituation and novelty preference studies suggest that this ability exists at birth or very soon after, and it quickly becomes more efficient. Newborns can tell sounds they have already heard from those they have not. In one study, infants who heard a certain speech sound 1 day after birth appeared to remember that sound 24 hours later, as shown by a reduced tendency to turn their heads toward the sound and even a tendency to turn away (Swain, Zelazo, & Clifton, 1993). Indeed, as we reported in Chapter 4, newborns seem to remember sounds they heard in the womb.

Piaget believed that the senses are unconnected at birth and are only gradually integrated through experience. If so, this integration begins very early. The fact that newborns will look at a source of sound shows that they associate hearing and sight. A more sophisticated ability is **cross-modal transfer,** the ability to use information gained from one sense to guide another—as when a person negotiates a dark room by feeling for the location of familiar objects, or identifies objects by sight after feeling them with eyes closed. In one study, 1-month-old infants showed that they could transfer information gained from sucking (touch) to vision. When the infants saw a rigid object (a hard plastic cylinder) and a flexible one (a wet sponge) being manipulated by a pair of hands, the infants looked longer at the object they had just sucked (Gibson & Walker, 1984). The use of cross-modal transfer to judge some other properties of objects, such as shape, does not seem to develop until a few months later (Maurer, Stager, & Mondloch, 1999).

cross-modal transfer
Ability to use information gained by one sense to guide another.

Speed of processing increases rapidly during the first year of life. It continues to increase during the second and third years, when interference from previously processed information comes under better control (P. R. Zelazo et al., 1995).

Information Processing as a Predictor of Intelligence

Because of the weak correlation between infants' scores on developmental tests and their later IQ, many psychologists believed that the cognitive functioning of infants had little in common with that of older children and adults—in other words, that there was a discontinuity in cognitive development (Kopp & McCall, 1982). Piaget believed this too. However, when researchers assess how infants and toddlers process information, some aspects of mental development seem to be fairly continuous from birth (Bornstein & Sigman, 1986; Colombo, 1993; Colombo & Janowsky, 1998; Dougherty & Haith, 1997; McCall & Carriger, 1993; L. A. Thompson, Fagan, & Fulker, 1991). Children who, from the start, were efficient at taking in and interpreting sensory information score well on intelligence tests.

In many longitudinal studies, habituation and attention-recovery abilities during the first 6 months to 1 year of life were moderately useful in predicting scores on IQ tests between ages 1 and 8. So was **visual recognition memory**—the ability to distinguish familiar sights from unfamiliar ones when shown both at the same time, as measured by the tendency to look longer at the new (Bornstein & Sigman, 1986; Colombo, 1993; McCall & Carriger, 1993). In one study, babies who, at 5 and 7 months, preferred looking at new pictures rather than ones they had seen before tended to score higher on the Bayley scales at 2 years and the Stanford-Binet at 3 years. They also showed stronger language skills and memory ability at age 3 (L. A. Thompson et al., 1991). In another study, a combination of visual recognition memory at 7 months and cross-modal transfer at 1 year predicted IQ at age 11 and also showed a modest (but nonetheless remarkable after 10 years!) relationship to processing speed and memory at that age (Rose & Feldman, 1995, 1997).

visual-recognition memory
Ability to distinguish a familiar visual stimulus from an unfamiliar one when shown both at the same time.

An infant's *visual reaction time* and *visual anticipation* can be measured by the *visual expectation paradigm.* A series of computer-generated pictures briefly appears, some on the right and some on the left sides of an infant's peripheral visual field. The same sequence of pictures is repeated several times. The infant's eye movements are measured to see how quickly his or her gaze shifts to a picture that has just appeared (reaction time) or to the place where the infant expects the next picture to appear (anticipation). These measurements may indicate attentiveness and processing speed, as well as the tendency to form expectations on the basis of experience. In a longitudinal study, visual reaction time and visual anticipation at 3 1/2 months correlated with IQ at age 4 (Dougherty & Haith, 1997).

Sensitivity to auditory distinctions may be another early indicator of cognitive ability. Research has found significant correlations between the ability to discriminate sounds at 4 months of age and IQ scores at 5 years (O'Connor, Cohen, & Parmelee, 1984).

All in all, there is much evidence that the abilities infants use to process sensory information are related to the cognitive abilities intelligence tests measure. Still, we need to be cautious in interpreting these findings. Most of the studies used small samples. Also, the predictability of childhood IQ from measures of habituation and recognition memory is only modest. It is no higher than the predictability from parental education and socioeconomic status, and not as high as the predictability from some other infant behaviors, such as early vocalization. Predictions based on information-processing measures alone do not take into account the influence of environmental factors (Colombo & Janowsky, 1998; Laucht, Esser, & Schmidt, 1994; McCall & Carriger, 1993). For example, maternal responsiveness in early infancy seems to play a part in the link between early attentional abilities and cognitive abilities later in childhood (Bornstein & Tamis-LeMonda, 1994) and even at age 18 (Sigman, Cohen, & Beckwith, 1997).

Violation of Expectations and the Development of Thought

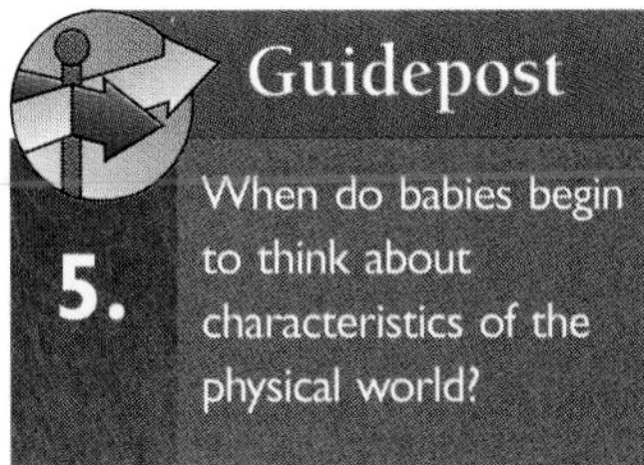

Guidepost
5.
When do babies begin to think about characteristics of the physical world?

According to **violation-of-expectations** research, infants begin to think and reason about the physical world much earlier than Piaget believed. In the violation-of-expectations method, infants are first habituated to seeing an event happen as it normally would. Then the event is changed in a way that conflicts with (violates) normal expectations. An infant's tendency to look longer at the changed event (dishabituation) is interpreted as evidence that the infant recognizes it as surprising.

violation-of-expectations Research method in which dishabituation to a stimulus that conflicts with previous experience is taken as evidence that an infant recognizes the new stimulus as surprising.

Researchers using this method claim that some of the concepts Piaget described as developing toward the end of the sensorimotor stage, such as object permanence, number, and causality, all of which depend on formation of mental representations, actually arise much earlier (refer back to Table 5-4). It has been proposed that infants may be born with reasoning abilities—*innate learning mechanisms* that help them make sense of the information they encounter—or may acquire these abilities very early (Baillargeon, 1994). Some investigators go further, suggesting that infants at birth may already have intuitive *knowledge* about basic physical principles—knowledge that then develops further with experience (Spelke, 1994, 1998). As we will see, these interpretations and conclusions are highly controversial.

Object Permanence Using the violation-of-expectations method, Renée Baillargeon and her colleagues claim to have found evidence of object permanence in infants as young as 3 1/2 months. The babies appeared surprised by the failure of a tall carrot that slid behind a screen of the same height to

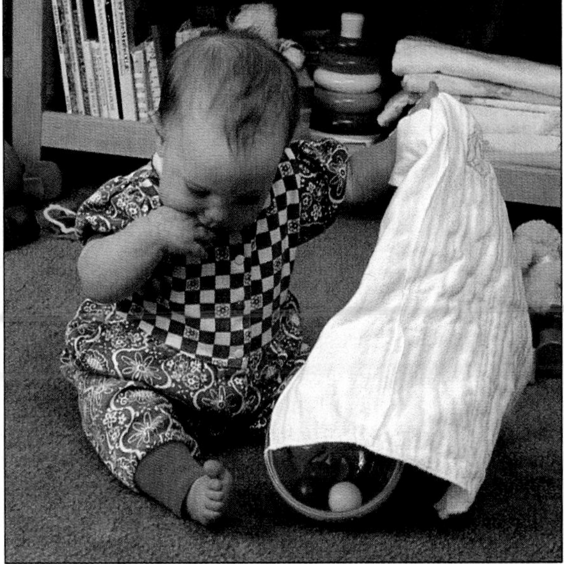

This baby seems to be showing at least the beginning of the concept of object permanence by searching for an object that is partially hidden. She will probably have the complete concept by 18 months of age, when she will look for objects or people even when she has not seen where they were hidden.

show up in a large notch in the upper part of the screen before appearing again on the other side (Baillargeon & DeVos, 1991; see Figure 5-4). Of course, since this task is so different from Piaget's, it may not assess precisely the same ability. Recognition that an object that disappeared on one side of a screen is the same as the object that reappears on the other side need not imply knowledge that the object should have continued to exist behind the screen (Meltzoff & Moore, 1998). Still, this experiment suggests that at least a rudimentary form of object permanence may be present in the early months of life.

Critics point to two practical challenges to the early emergence of object permanence (Haith & Benson, 1998). If infants as young as $3^1/_2$ months have such a concept, then why is it not until several months after they can grasp objects that they begin to search for something they saw hidden? And why, as we have seen, do they make errors in their searches? One answer is that a rudimentary form of object knowledge may exist in early infancy and may become more sophisticated as infants gain experience in reaching for and handling objects (Spelke, 1998).

Number Violation-of-expectations research also suggests that an understanding of number may begin long before Piaget's sixth substage, when he claimed children first begin to use symbols. In a series of experiments, Karen Wynn (1992) tested whether 5-month-old babies can add and subtract small numbers of objects (see Figure 5-5). The infants watched as Mickey Mouse dolls were placed behind a screen, and a doll was either added or taken away. The screen then was lifted to reveal either the expected number or a different number of dolls. In all the experiments, the babies looked longer at surprising "wrong" answers than at expected "right" ones, suggesting (according to Wynn) that they had mentally "computed" the right answers. Other researchers who replicated these experiments got similar results, even when one of the dolls was replaced with a different doll, indicating that it was the *number* of dolls, and not their physical appearance or identity, to which the infants were responding (Simon, Hespos, & Rochat, 1995).

According to Wynn, this research raises the possibility that numerical concepts are inborn—that when parents teach their babies numbers, they may only be teaching them the names ("one, two, three") for concepts the babies already know. However, the idea of an innate ability is only speculation, since the infants in these studies were already 5 and 6 months old. Furthermore, simple sensory memory

Habituation Events

Short carrot event

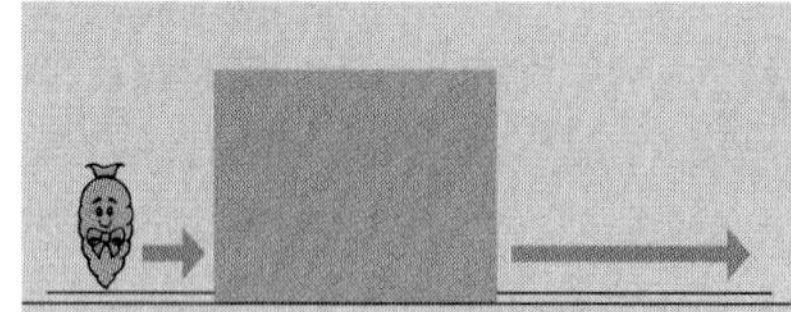

Tall carrot event

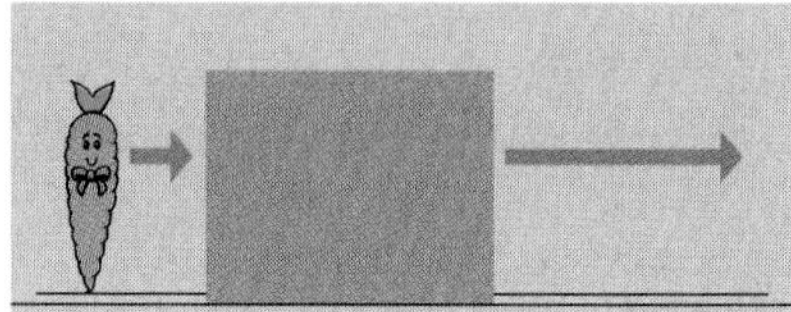

Test Events

Possible event

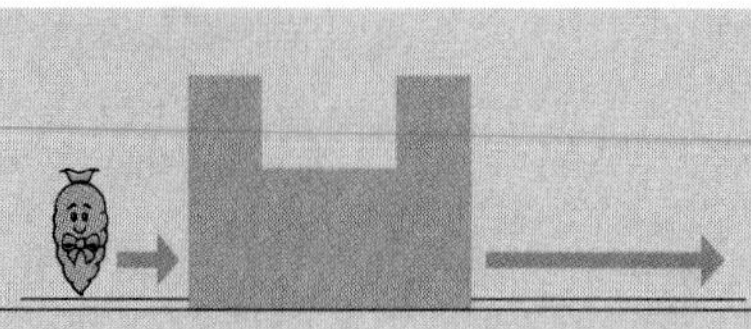

Impossible event

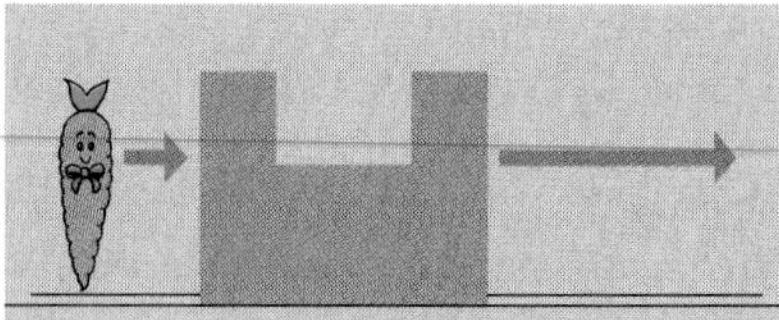

Figure 5-4
Object permanence in infants. In this experiment, $3^1/_2$-month-old infants watched a short and then a tall carrot slide along a track, disappear behind a screen, and then reappear. After they became accustomed to seeing these events, the opaque screen was replaced by a screen with a large notch at the top. The short carrot did not appear in the notch when passing behind the screen; the tall carrot, which should have appeared in the notch, also did not. The babies looked longer at the tall than at the short carrot event, suggesting that they were surprised that the tall carrot did not reappear.
(Source: Baillargeon & DeVos, 1991.)

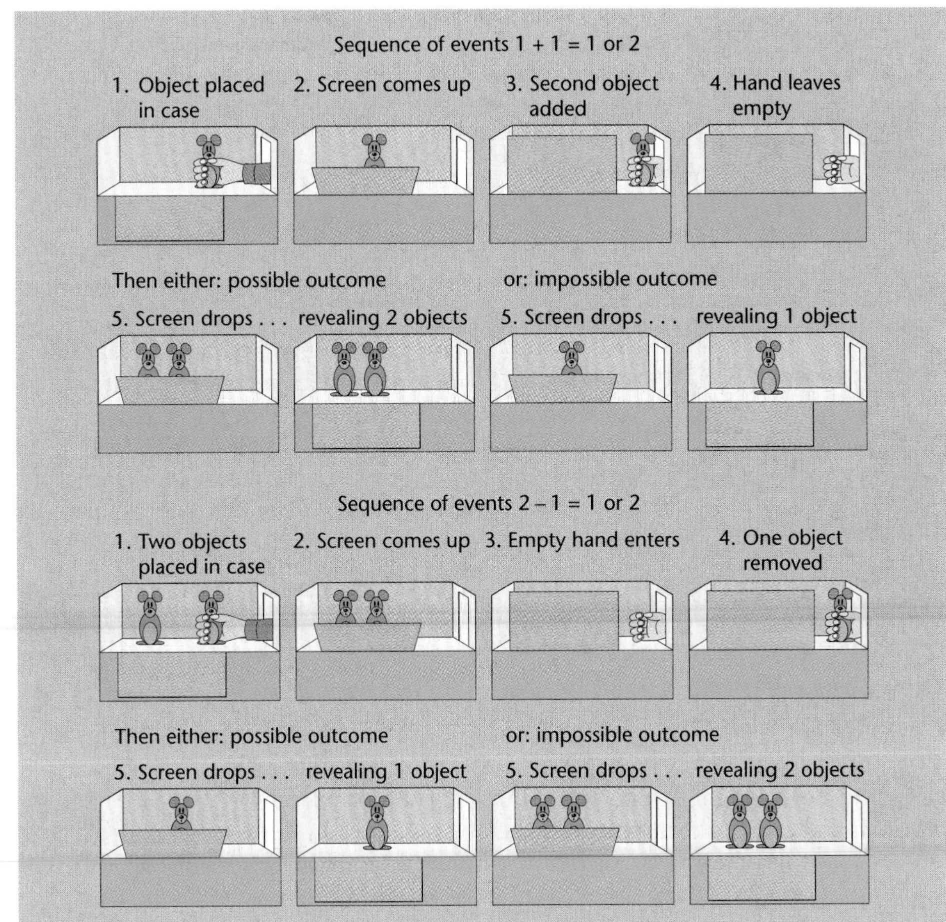
Sequence of events 1 + 1 = 1 or 2
1. Object placed in case
2. Screen comes up
3. Second object added
4. Hand leaves empty
Then either: possible outcome
5. Screen drops . . . revealing 2 objects
or: impossible outcome
5. Screen drops . . . revealing 1 object
Sequence of events 2 – 1 = 1 or 2
1. Two objects placed in case
2. Screen comes up
3. Empty hand enters
4. One object removed
Then either: possible outcome
5. Screen drops . . . revealing 1 object
or: impossible outcome
5. Screen drops . . . revealing 2 objects

Figure 5-5

Can 5-month-old infants count? For the problem "1 plus 1," a researcher showed a baby one doll, then hid it behind a screen. The baby saw a hand place another doll behind the screen; then the screen was pulled away, revealing two dolls. Sometimes there was a false answer; the baby saw only one doll or three dolls. In the "2 minus 1" trials the researcher showed two dolls, then took one away, and the baby saw either one or two dolls. Babies consistently looked longer at the surprising "wrong" answers than at the expected right ones, which suggests that they had "computed" the right answers in their minds.

(Source: Wynn, 1992).

may explain the findings. Infants may simply be responding to the puzzling presence of a doll they saw removed from behind the screen, or the absence of a doll they saw placed there (Haith, 1998; Haith & Benson, 1998).

Causality Piaget believed that an understanding of *causality,* the principle that one event causes another, develops slowly during the first year of life. At about 4 to 6 months, as infants become able to grasp objects, they begin to recognize that they can act on their environment. Thus the concept of causality is rooted in a dawning awareness of the power of their own intentions. However, according to Piaget, infants do not yet know that causes must come before effects; and not until close to 1 year do they realize that forces outside of themselves can make things happen.

Some research suggests that a mechanism for recognizing causality exists much earlier (Mandler, 1998). In habituation-dishabituation experiments, infants $6\frac{1}{2}$ months old have seen a difference between events that flow into other events (such as a brick striking a second brick, which is then pushed out of position) and events that occur with no apparent cause (such as a brick moving away from another brick without having been struck by it). Thus, at an early age, infants seem aware of the continuity of relationships in time and space—a first step toward understanding causality (Leslie, 1982). Follow-up studies suggest that infants see something special about causal events as compared with other sequences of events (Leslie & Keeble, 1987). One hypothesis is that infants have a special brain "module" that acts as a causal-motion detector, directing attention to causally linked events(Leslie, 1988, 1994).

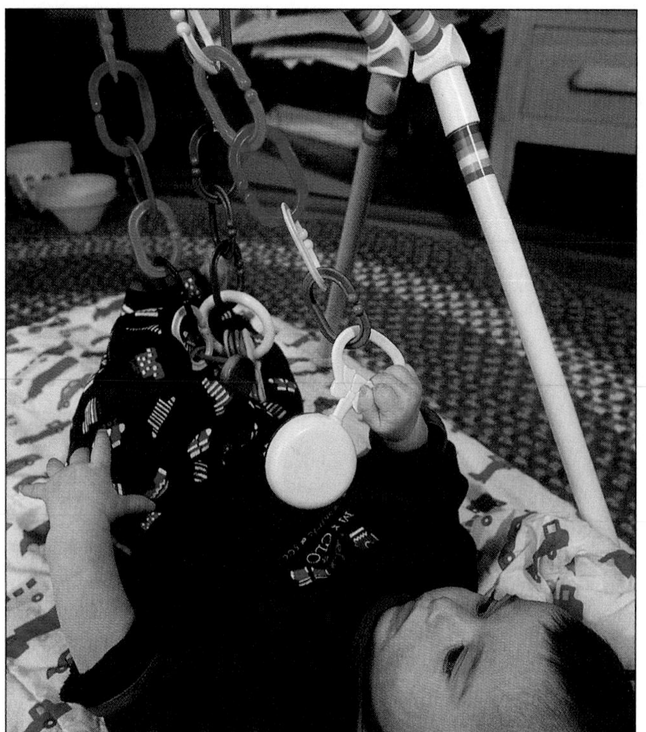

This 5-month-old baby is discovering that he can make a dangling chain rattle and swing by pulling it. As infants this age become able to grasp objects, said Piaget, they become aware of the power of their own intentions—a first step toward understanding causality.

Investigators who support Piaget's slower timetable for the development of causal understanding attribute this understanding to a gradual improvement in information-processing skills (Cohen & Oakes, 1993; Oakes, 1994). Younger infants may make causal interpretations about a particular set of objects and circumstances, but they do not yet apply a general concept of causality to all objects in all circumstances. As infants accumulate more information about how objects behave, they are better able to see causality in a variety of situations.

Evaluating Violation-of-Expectations Reasearch There is some skepticism about what violation-of-expectations studies show. Does the infant's reaction reveal a conceptual understanding of the way things work, or merely a perceptual awareness that something novel or unusual has happened? The fact that an infant looks longer at one scene than at another may show only that the infant can see a difference between the two. It does not show what the infant knows about the difference, or that the infant is actually surprised. The "mental representation" the infant refers to may be no more than a brief sensory memory of something just seen. It's also possible that an infant, in becoming accustomed to the habituation event, develops the expectations that are then violated by the "surprising" event, and did not have such knowledge or expectations before (Goubet & Clifton, 1998; Haith, 1998; Haith & Benson, 1998; Mandler, 1998; Munakata, in press; Munakata, McClelland, Johnson, & Siegler, in press).

Defenders of the new research insist that a conceptual interpretation best accounts for the evidence (Baillargeon, in press; Spelke, 1998), but a recent variation on one of Baillargeon's experiments suggests otherwise. In her original research Baillargeon (1994) showed infants of various ages a "drawbridge" rotating 180 degrees. When the infants became habituated to the rotation, a barrier was introduced in the form of a box. At $4^1/_2$ months, infants seemed to show (by longer looking) that they realized the drawbridge could not move through the entire box (see Figure 5-6). Later investigators replicated the experiment but eliminated the box. Five-month-olds still looked longer at the 180-degree rotation than at a lesser degree of rotation, even though no barrier was present—suggesting that the explanation might simply be a preference for greater movement (Rivera, Wakeley, & Langer, 1999).

Further research may clarify these issues. In the meantime, developmental scientists need to be cautious about inferring the existence of adultlike cognitive abilities that are not conclusively established, when the data may have simpler explanations or may represent only partial achievement of mature abilities (Haith, 1998).

CHECKPOINT

Can you . . .

- ✔ Describe the violation-of-expectations method, tell how and why it is used, and list some criticisms of it?
- ✔ Discuss three areas in which violation-of-expectations research seems to contradict Piaget's account of development?

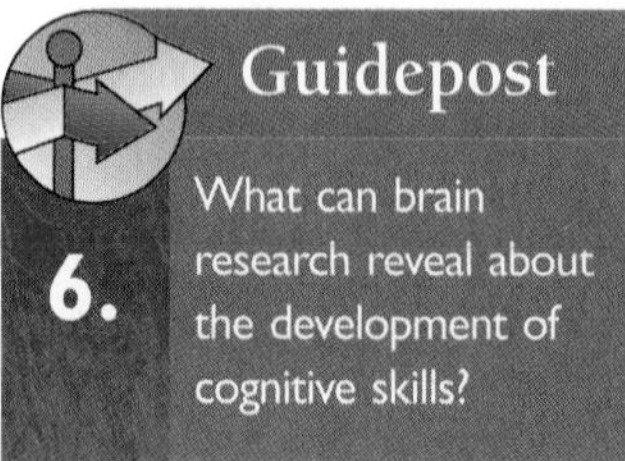

Guidepost
6.
What can brain research reveal about the development of cognitive skills?

Cognitive Neuroscience Approach: The Brain's Cognitive Structures

Piaget's belief that neurological maturation is a major factor in cognitive development was merely a supposition. Today research in cognitive neuroscience, the study of the brain structures that govern thinking and memory, bears him out.

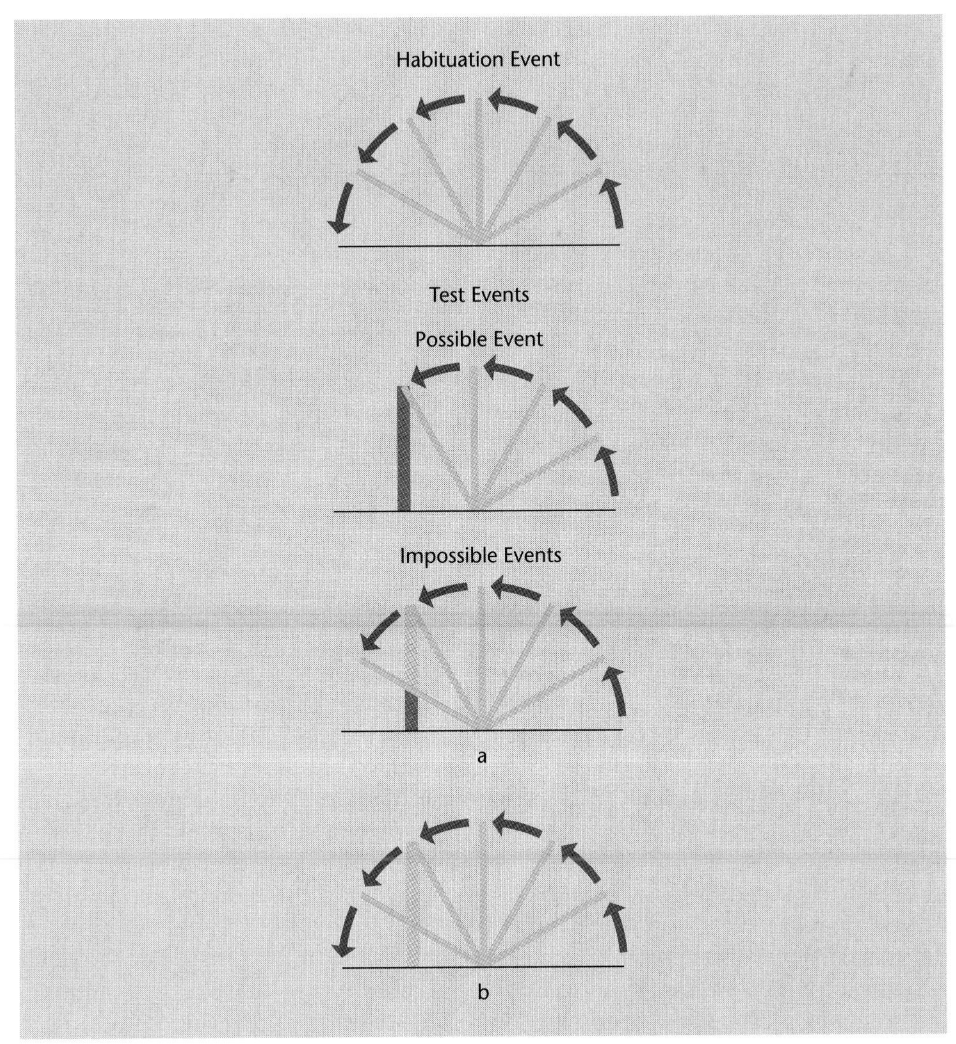

Figure 5-6
Test for infants' understanding of how a barrier works. Infants first become accustomed to seeing a "drawbridge" rotate 180 degrees on one edge. Then a box is placed beside the drawbridge. In the possible event, the drawbridge stops when it reaches the edge of the box. In the impossible events, the drawbridge rotates through part or all of the space occupied by the box. On the basis of how long they stare at each event, $4^1/_2$-month-old infants seem to know that the drawbridge cannot pass through the entire box *(b)*; but not until $6^1/_2$ months do infants recognize that the drawbridge cannot pass through 80 percent of the box *(a)*.
(Source: Adapted from Baillargeon, 1994)

We are learning about infant neurological development both indirectly, from studies of monkeys, rabbits, and other animals, and directly, from instruments that measure human brain activity. Studies of infant brain functioning have made use of behaviorist principles (classical and operant conditioning) and Piagetian tasks (such as deferred imitation and object permanence). Other studies have looked at the physical side of information processing. Measurements taken on an infant's scalp have recorded brain wave changes associated with visual recognition memory (Nelson & Collins, 1991, 1992), auditory recognition memory (Thomas & Lykins, 1995), and cross-modal transfer (Nelson, Henschel, & Collins, 1993), as well as physical responses involved in habituation, visual anticipation, and reaction time.

Scientists are getting an increasingly clear picture of which brain structures affect which aspects of memory (refer back to Figure 4-6 and the discussion of brain development in Chapter 4). Studies of normal and brain-damaged adults point to two separate long-term memory systems—*explicit* and *implicit*—which acquire and store different kinds of information for long periods of time. **Explicit memory** is conscious or intentional recollection, usually of facts, names, events, or other things that people can state, or declare. **Implicit memory** refers to remembering that occurs without effort or even conscious awareness; it generally pertains to habits and skills, such as knowing how to throw a ball or ride a bicycle. Brain scans have provided direct physical evidence of the existence and location of these distinct memory systems (Squire, 1992; Vargha-Khadem, et al., 1997).

explicit memory
Memory, generally of facts, names, and events, which is intentional and conscious. Compare *implicit memory.*

implicit memory
Memory, generally of habits and skills, which does not require conscious recall; sometimes called *procedural memory.* Compare *explicit memory.*

Implicit memory seems to develop earlier and mature faster than explicit memory. Two kinds of implicit memory develop during the first few months of life: memory for procedures (such as anticipating the next light in a sequence), which seems to be centered in the *striatum;* and conditioning, which appears to depend on the *cerebellum* and cell nucleii deep in the *brain stem.* At the same time, a reflexlike precursor to explicit memory apparently develops; it is chiefly dependent on the *hippocampus,* a seahorse-shaped structure deep in the central portion of the brain, the *medial temporal lobe.* This preexplicit memory system permits infants to remember specific sights or sounds for a few seconds—long enough to show simple novelty preferences (Nelson, 1995).

Sometime between 6 and 12 months, a more sophisticated form of explicit memory modifies or replaces the preexplicit form. It draws upon cortical structures, which are the primary site of general knowledge *(semantic memory),* as well as structures associated with the hippocampus, which govern memory of specific experiences *(episodic memory)* (Nelson, 1995; Vargha-Khadem et al., 1997). This advance is responsible for the emergence of complex forms of cross-modal transfer.

The large area of the frontal lobe called the *prefrontal cortex* (the portion of the frontal lobe directly behind the forehead) is believed to control many aspects of cognition. This part of the brain develops more slowly than any other (Johnson, 1998). During the second half of the first year, the prefrontal cortex and associated circuitry develop the capacity for **working memory,** short-term storage of information the brain is actively processing, or working on. It is in working memory that mental representations are prepared for, or recalled from, storage.

working memory
Short-term storage of information being actively processed.

The relatively late appearance of working memory may be largely responsible for the slow development of object permanence, which seems to be seated in the *dorsolateral* (rear and side) area of the prefrontal cortex (Nelson, 1995). Electroencephalogram (EEG) studies support a link between prefrontal cortex functioning and success in a delayed search (Bell & Fox, 1992). By 12 months, the dorsolateral prefrontal cortex—though not yet fully mature—may be developed enough to permit an infant, not only to remember where an object was hidden, but to avoid the A, not-B, error by controlling the impulse to search in a place where the object was previously found (Diamond, 1991).

CHECKPOINT

Can you . . .

- ✔ Name the brain structures apparently involved in implicit, preexplicit, explicit, and working memory and mention at least one task made possible by each?
- ✔ Tell how brain research helps explain Piagetian developments and information-processing skills, and give examples?

Brain development also may explain the abrupt transition at 21 to 22 months to the use of landmarks to aid in remembering where an object was hidden (Newcombe et al., 1998). This change may be related to maturation of the hippocampus (Mangan, Franklin, Tignor, Bolling, & Nadel, 1994; Newcombe et al., 1998).

Although explicit memory and working memory continue to develop beyond infancy, the early emergence of the brain's memory structures underlines the importance of environmental stimulation during the first months of life (refer back to Chapter 4). Social-contextual theorists and researchers pay particular attention to the impact of environmental influences.

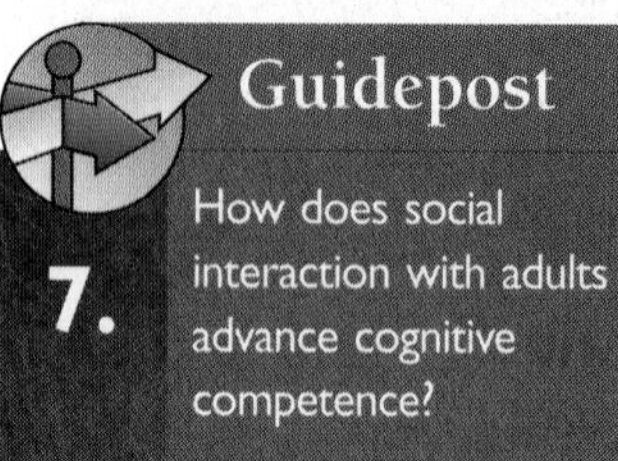

Guidepost
7.
How does social interaction with adults advance cognitive competence?

Social-Contextual Approach: Learning from Interactions with Caregivers

As we have seen, parents' responsiveness and ability to create a stimulating home environment are positively related to infants' information-processing abilities and future IQ. Researchers influenced by Vygotsky's sociocultural theory study how the cultural context affects early social interactions that may promote cognitive competence.

guided participation
Participation of an adult in a child's activity in a manner that helps to structure the activity and to bring the child's understanding of it closer to that of the adult.

The concept of **guided participation** (Rogoff, 1990, 1998; Rogoff, Mistry, Göncü, & Mosier, 1993) was inspired by Vygotsky's zone of proximal development (refer back to Chapter 2) and his view of learning as a collaborative process. Guided participation refers to mutual interactions with adults that help structure children's activities and bridge the gap between the child's understanding and the adult's. Guided participation often occurs in shared play and in ordinary, everyday activities in which children learn informally the skills, knowledge, and values important in their culture.

In one cross-cultural study (Rogoff et al., 1993), researchers visited the homes of 14 one- to two-year-olds in each of four communities: a Mayan town in Guatemala, a tribal village in India, and middle-class urban neighborhoods in Salt Lake City and Turkey. The investigators interviewed caregivers about their childrearing practices and watched them help the toddlers learn to dress themselves and to play with objects the children had not seen before, such as a set of nesting dolls.

In the Guatemalan town, toddlers normally saw their mothers sewing and weaving at home to help support the family; in the Indian village, they accompanied their mothers at work in the fields. Toddlers in these communities were expected to play alone or with older siblings while the mother worked nearby. The Turkish and U.S. toddlers had full-time homemaker mothers or, in Salt Lake City, were in day care. These middle-class children interacted with their parents in play—in the context of their own childhood milieu—rather than in the parents' work or social worlds.

These cultural differences were reflected in the types of guided participation the researchers observed the parents using. After initial demonstration and instruction by a caregiver (the mother, the father, or another adult), the Guatemalan and Indian children took the lead in their own learning, while the caregiver remained available to respond to requests for help. Communication was mostly nonverbal. The U.S. caregivers, by contrast, emphasized verbal instruction; they spoke with the children as peers and managed their learning, using praise, mock excitement, and other motivators. The Turkish families, who were in transition from a rural to an urban way of life, showed a pattern somewhere between these two.

The cultural context, then, influences the way caregivers contribute to cognitive development. These researchers suggest that direct adult involvement in children's play and learning may be less adaptive in a rural village or small town in a developing country, in which children frequently observe and participate in adult activities, than in a middle-class urban community, in which homemaker mothers have more time, greater verbal skills, and possibly more interest in children's play and learning.

We will look again at interaction with caregivers in relation to language learning.

CHECKPOINT

Can you . . .

✔ Compare two cultural patterns of guided participation in toddlers' learning?

Language Development

Guidepost 8. How do babies develop language?

The ability to use **language,** a communication system based on words and grammar, is a crucial element of cognitive development. Children can use words to represent objects and actions, to reflect on observations and experiences, and to communicate their needs, feelings, and ideas in order to exert control over their lives.

The growth of language illustrates the interaction of all aspects of development. As the physical structures needed to produce sounds mature, and the neuronal connections necessary to associate sound and meaning become activated, social interaction with adults introduces babies to the communicative nature of speech. Let's look at the typical sequence of language development (see Table 5-4), at some characteristics of early speech, at how babies acquire language and make progress in using it, and at how parents and other caregivers help toddlers prepare for **literacy,** the ability to read and write.

language
Communication system based on words and grammar.

literacy
Ability to read and write.

Sequence of Early Language Development

The word *infant* is based on the Latin for "without speech," but this is actually a misnomer. Before babies can use words, they make their needs and feelings known—as Doddy Darwin did—through sounds that progress from crying to

prelinguistic speech Forerunner of linguistic speech; utterance of sounds that are not words. Includes crying, cooing, babbling, and accidental and deliberate imitation of sounds without understanding their meaning.

cooing and babbling, then to accidental imitation, and then deliberate imitation. These sounds are known as **prelinguistic speech.** Infants also grow in the ability to recognize and understand speech sounds and to use meaningful gestures. Around the end of the first year, babies typically say their first word, and about eight months to a year later, toddlers begin speaking in sentences.

Early Vocalization

Crying is a newborn's only means of communication. Different pitches, patterns, and intensities signal hunger, sleepiness, or anger (Lester & Boukydis, 1985).

Between 6 weeks and 3 months, babies start *cooing* when they are happy—squealing, gurgling, and making vowel sounds like "ahhh." At about 3 to 6 months, babies begin to play with speech sounds, matching the sounds they hear from people around them.

Babbling—repeating consonant-vowel strings, such as "ma-ma-ma-ma"—occurs between 6 and 10 months of age and is often mistaken for a baby's first word. Babbling is not real language, since it does not hold meaning for the baby, but it becomes more wordlike.

Language development continues with accidental *imitation of language sounds* babies hear and then imitation of themselves making these sounds. At about 9 to 10 months, infants deliberately imitate sounds without understanding them. Once they have a repertoire of sounds, they string them together in patterns that sound like language but seem to have no meaning.

Table 5-4 Language Milestones from Birth to 3 Years

Age in Months	Development
Birth	Can perceive speech, cry, make some response to sound.
$1\frac{1}{2}$ to 3	Coos and laughs.
3	Plays with speech sounds.
$4\frac{1}{2}$ to 6	Begins to store sound patterns in memory and to link sounds with meaning, especially own and parents' names.
6 to 10	Babbles in strings of consonants and vowels.
6 to 12	Recognizes basic sounds of own language and begins to become aware of its rules.
9 to 10	Imitates sounds.
9 to 12	Begins to use gestures to communicate; uses conventional social gestures.
10 to 12	No longer can discriminate sounds not in own language.
10 to 14	Says first word (usually a label for something).
10 to 18	Says single words.
13	Understands symbolic function of naming.
13	Uses representational gestures.
14	Uses symbolic gestures.
16 to 24	Learns many new words, expanding vocabulary rapidly from about 50 words to as many as 400; uses verbs and adjectives.
18 to 24	Says first sentence (2 words).
20	Uses fewer gestures; names more things.
20 to 22	Has comprehension spurt.
24	Uses many two-word phrases; no longer babbles; wants to talk.
30	Learns new words almost every day; speaks in combinations of three or more words; understands very well; makes grammatical mistakes.
36	Says up to 1,000 words, 80 percent intelligible; makes some mistakes in syntax.

Note: These ages are averages.

Sources: Bates, O'Connell, & Shore, 1987; Capute, Shapiro, & Palmer, 1987; Kuhl, Williams, Lacerda, Stevens, & Lindblom, 1992; Lalonde & Werker, 1995; Lenneberg, 1969; Lock, Young, Service, & Chandler, 1990; Mandel, Jusczyk, & Pisoni, 1995; Marcus, Vijayan, Rao, & Vishton, 1999; Owens, 1996; Tincoff & Jusczyk, 1999.

Recognizing Language Sounds

The ability to perceive differences between sounds is essential to language development. As we have seen, this ability is present from or even before birth, and it becomes more refined during the first year of life. In getting ready to understand and use speech, infants first become familiar with the sounds of words and phrases and later attach meanings to them (Jusczyk & Hohne, 1997).

The process apparently begins in the womb. In one experiment, two groups of Parisian women in their thirty-fifth week of pregnancy each recited a different nursery rhyme, saying it three times a day for 4 weeks. At the end of that time, researchers played recordings of both rhymes close to the women's abdomens. The fetuses' heart rates slowed when the rhyme the mother had spoken was played, but not for the other rhyme. Since the voice on the tape was not that of the mother, the fetuses apparently were responding to the linguistic sounds they had heard the mother use. This suggests that hearing the "mother tongue" before birth may "pretune" an infant's ears to pick up its sounds (DeCasper, Lecanuet, Busnel, Granier-Deferre, & Maugeais, 1994).

By 6 months of age, babies have learned to recognize the basic sounds, or *phonemes,* of their native language, and to adjust to slight differences in the way different speakers form those sounds. In one study, 6-month-old Swedish and U.S. babies routinely ignored variations in sounds common in their own language but noticed variations in an unfamiliar language (Kuhl, Williams, Lacerda, Stevens, & Lindblom, 1992).

Before infants can connect sounds to meanings, they seem to recognize sound patterns they hear frequently, such as their own names. Four-and-a-half-month-olds listen longer to their own names than to other names, even names with stress patterns similar to theirs (Mandel, Jusczyk, & Pisoni, 1995). Six-month-olds look longer at a video of their mothers when they hear the word *mommy* and of their fathers when they hear *daddy,* suggesting that they are beginning to associate sound with meaning—at least with regard to special people (Tincoff & Jusczyk, 1999). By 8 months, infants store other sound patterns in memory; they listen longer to a list of words from stories they heard 2 weeks earlier than to an unrelated list of words (Jusczyk & Hohne, 1997).

By about 10 months, babies lose their earlier sensitivity to sounds that are not part of the language they hear spoken. For example, Japanese infants no longer make a distinction between "ra" and "la," a distinction that does not exist in the Japanese language. Although the ability to perceive nonnative sounds is not entirely lost—it can be revived, with effort, in adulthood—the brain no longer routinely discriminates them (Bates, O'Connell, & Shore, 1987; Lalonde & Werker, 1995; Werker, 1989).

Meanwhile, during the second half of the first year, as babies become increasingly familiar with the sounds of their language, they begin to become aware of its phonological rules—how sounds are arranged in speech. In one series of experiments (Marcus, Vijayan, Rao, & Vishton, 1999), 7-month-olds listened longer to "sentences" containing a different order of nonsense sounds (such as "wo fe wo," or ABA) from the order to which the infants had been habituated (such as "ga ti ti," or ABB). The sounds used in the test were different from those used in the habituation phase, so the infants' discrimination must have been based on the patterns of repetition alone. This finding suggests that infants may have a mechanism for discerning abstract rules of sentence structure, lending support to the *nativist* theory of language acquisition discussed later in this chapter.

Gestures

At 9 months Antonio *pointed* to an object, sometimes making a noise to show that he wanted it. Between 9 and 12 months, he learned some *conventional social gestures:* waving bye-bye, nodding his head to mean *yes,* and shaking his head to signify *no.* By about 13 months, he used more elaborate *representational gestures;* for

This toddler is communicating with his father by pointing at something that catches his eye. Gesturing seems to come naturally to young children and may be an important part of language learning.

example, he would hold an empty cup to his mouth or hold up his arms to show that he wanted to be picked up.

Symbolic gestures, such as blowing to mean *hot,* or sniffing to mean *flower,* often emerge around the same time as babies say their first words, and they function much like words. By using them, children show an understanding that symbols can refer to specific objects, events, desires, and conditions. Gestures usually appear before children have a vocabulary of 25 words and drop out when children learn the word for the idea they were gesturing and can say it instead (Lock, Young, Service, & Chandler, 1990).

Some parents fear that encouraging the use of gestures will deter a baby from learning words. Apparently, the opposite is true: learning gestures seems to confer a linguistic advantage. In one experiment (Goodwyn & Acredolo, 1998), 11-month-olds learned eight gestures by watching their parents perform the gestures and say the corresponding words. Between 15 and 36 months, when tested on vocal language development, these children outperformed two other groups—one whose parents had only said words and another that had received neither vocal nor gestural training. Gestures, then, can be a valuable alternative or supplement to words, especially during the period of early vocabulary formation.

Gesturing seems to come naturally. In an observational study, blind children and adolescents used gestures while speaking, as much as sighted children did, and even while speaking to a blind listener. Thus the use of gestures does not depend on having either a model or an observer, but seems to be an inherent part of the speaking process (Iverson & Goldin-Meadow, 1998).

First Words

linguistic speech
Verbal expression designed to convey meaning.

holophrase
Single word that conveys a complete thought.

Doddy Darwin, at 11 months, said his first word—"ouchy"—which he attached to a number of objects. Doddy's development was typical in this respect. The average baby says a first word sometime between 10 and 14 months, initiating **linguistic speech**—verbal expression that conveys meaning. Before long, the baby will use many words and will show some understanding of grammar, pronunciation, intonation, and rhythm. For now, an infant's total verbal repertoire is likely to be "mama" or "dada." Or it may be a simple syllable that has more than one meaning depending on the context in which the child utters it. "Da" may mean "I want that," "I want to go out," or "Where's Daddy?" A word like this, which expresses a complete thought, is called a **holophrase.**

Babies understand many words before they can use them; that is, their *passive vocabulary* develops faster and is larger than their *active vocabulary.* The first words most babies understand are the ones they are likely to hear most often: their own names and the word *no,* as well as words with special meaning for them.

By 13 months, most children understand that a word stands for a specific thing or event, and they can quickly learn the meaning of a new word (Woodward, Markman, & Fitzsimmons, 1994). Addition of new words to their *expressive* (spoken) vocabulary is slower at first. As children come to rely more on words than on gestures to express themselves, the sounds and rhythms of speech grow more elaborate.

As babies work on attaching meaning to sounds, they may temporarily pay less attention to fine auditory discrimination. In one cross-sectional study (Stager & Werker, 1997), when spoken nonsense words were paired with pictures of objects, 14-month-olds failed to notice the difference between "bih" and "dih," a distinction they easily detected when viewing a meaningless pattern. Eight-month-olds, who were not yet focused on learning word meanings, distinguished the sounds equally well in both kinds of tasks. Apparently inattention to phonetic detail is adaptive during the period when babies are concentrating on understanding the sounds they hear and do not yet have to deal with many similar-sounding words.

Vocabulary continues to grow throughout the single-word stage, which generally lasts until about 18 months of age. Sometime between 16 and 24 months a "naming explosion" occurs. Within a few weeks, a toddler may go from saying about 50 words to saying about 400 (Bates, Bretherton, & Snyder, 1988). These rapid gains in spoken vocabulary reflect a steady increase in the speed and accuracy of word recognition during the second year of life (Fernald, Pinto, Swingley, Weinberg, & McRoberts, 1998).

The most common early spoken words in English are *names* of things (nouns), either general ("bow-wow" for *dog*) or specific ("Unga" for one particular dog). Others are *action* words ("bye-bye"), *modifiers* ("hot"), words that arise out of *personal feelings or social relationships* (the ever-popular "no"), and a few *functional* words ("for") (Nelson, 1973, 1981). After the first 100 words, this pattern shifts, and the proportion of verbs to nouns begins to increase (Owens, 1996).

The kinds of words children initially use may depend on the patterns of their native language. In one small observational study, 9 out of 10 Mandarin-speaking toddlers in Beijing, China, used more verbs than nouns—hardly surprising, since verbs are especially prominent in the Mandarin language (Tardif, 1996).

First Sentences

The next important linguistic breakthrough comes when a toddler puts two words together to express one idea ("Dolly fall"). Generally, children do this between 18 and 24 months, about 8 to 12 months after they say their first word. However, this age range varies greatly. Although prelinguistic speech is fairly closely tied to chronological age, linguistic speech is not. Most children who begin talking fairly late catch up eventually—and many make up for lost time by talking nonstop to anyone who will listen!

A child's first sentence typically deals with everyday events, things, people, or activities (Braine, 1976; Rice, 1989; Slobin, 1973). Children at first use **telegraphic speech,** which, like most telegrams, includes only a few essential words. When Rita says, "Damma deep," she seems to mean "Grandma is sweeping the floor." Telegraphic speech was once thought to be universal, but we now know that children's use of it varies (Braine, 1976). Its form varies, too, depending on the language being learned (Slobin, 1983). Word order tends to conform to what a child hears; Rita does not say "Deep Damma" when she sees her grandmother pushing a broom.

telegraphic speech
Early form of sentence consisting of only a few essential words.

Does the omission of functional words such as *is* and *the* mean that a child does not know these words? Not necessarily; the child may merely find them hard to reproduce. Even during the first year, infants are sensitive to the presence of functional words; at $10^1/_2$ months, they can tell a normal passage from one in which the functional words have been replaced by similar-sounding nonsense words. Between 14 and 16 months, they show that they know where functional words typically appear in a sentence (Jusczyk, in press).

Sometime between 20 and 30 months, children show increasing competence in **syntax,** the rules for putting sentences together in their language. They become somewhat more comfortable with articles *(a, the)*, prepositions *(in, on)*, conjunctions *(and, but)*, plurals, verb endings, past tense, and forms of the verb *to be (am, are, is)*. They also become increasingly aware of the communicative purpose of speech and of whether their words are being understood—a sign of growing sensitivity to the mental lives of others (see Box 5-2). In one experiment, $2^1/_2$-year-olds who had been prompted to ask for a toy persisted more in clarifying the request when the listener's verbal reply indicated misunderstanding of what the child had asked for than when the listener appeared to understand, regardless of whether the listener gave the child the toy (Shwe & Markman, 1997). By age 3, speech is fluent, longer, and more complex; although children often omit parts of speech, they get their meaning across well.

syntax
Rules for forming sentences in a particular language.

Box 5-2

Can Toddlers "Read" Others' Wishes?

At what age can babies begin to "read" what is on other people's minds? In Chapter 7, we discuss the development of *empathy,* the ability to feel what another person is feeling, and its relationship to understanding of mental states. How far back do the beginnings of this understanding go?

Twelve-month-olds will give an object to a person who points to it and asks for it. But does the baby realize that the request reflects an inner desire, or is the child merely responding to observable behavior (pointing)? Eighteen-month-olds will offer a toy to a crying child. But do they realize that their comforting may change the other child's mental state, or are they merely trying to change an overt behavior (crying)? And, since they usually offer a toy they themselves would find comforting, are they capable of distinguishing another person's state of mind from their own?

It's hard to answer such questions, since most toddlers can't talk well enough to tell us what they are thinking. So one research team (Repacholi & Gopnik, 1997) designed a nonverbal experiment to test toddlers' ability to discern another person's food preferences.

The researchers recruited 159 children, about half of them 14 months old and the other half 18 months old. Each child was invited to participate in an individual free play session in a human development laboratory at the University of California, Berkeley. In the course of the session, the child and an experimenter were offered two bowls of snacks: one that young children typically like (goldfish crackers) and one that they typically do not like (raw broccoli flowerets). The child was first given a chance to taste the snacks, and then the experimenter did. As expected, more than 9 out of 10 children (93 percent) preferred the crackers.

Equal numbers of boys and girls of each age were randomly assigned to two testing conditions: one in which the experimenter's apparent food preference matched the child's expected preference and one in which it did not. In the "matched" condition, the experimenter showed pleasure after tasting the cracker ("Mmm!") and disgust after tasting the broccoli ("Eww"). In the "mismatched" condition, the experimenter acted as if she preferred the broccoli.

Next, the experimenter placed one hand, palm up, halfway between the two bowls, and asked the child to give her some food, without indicating whether she wanted the broccoli or the crackers. The child was also given another opportunity to taste the snacks. This was done to see whether the children's food preferences had been influenced by the experimenter's expressed preferences. Only 6 children (4 percent) changed their apparent preference.

What did the children do when the experimenter asked for some food? Nearly 7 out of 10 of the 14-month-olds did not respond, even when the request was repeated. About 1 in 3 "teased" the experimenter by offering the crackers and then pulling back. Most of the 14-month-olds who did respond (including the teasers) offered crackers, regardless of which food the experimenter seemed to prefer. By contrast, only 3 out of 10 of the 18-month-olds failed to respond to the request; and, of those who did, 3 out of 4 gave the experimenter the food she had shown a liking for, whether or not it was the one they themselves liked.

Thus 18-month-olds, but not 14-month-olds, seem able to use another person's emotional cues to figure out what that person likes and wants, even when that person's desire is different from their own, and then to apply the information in a different situation in which there are no visible cues to the other person's preference. This suggests a rather sophisticated understanding of mental states: an awareness that two people can have opposite feelings about the same thing.

An interesting finding is that 14-month-olds were much less likely to respond to the experimenter's request for food when she had seemed to like broccoli than when she had seemed to like crackers. Perhaps those who did not respond in the "mismatched" situation found it hard to believe that someone might like and want broccoli; but unlike the children who instead gave the experimenter crackers, they may have been in a transitional stage, in which they noticed that another person's desires were different from their own and did not know what to do with this surprising information.

Young children who can interpret another person's desire are on their way to developing a *theory of mind,* a topic we discuss in Chapter 7.

Characteristics of Early Speech

Early speech is not just an immature version of adult speech. It has a character all its own—no matter what language a child is speaking (Slobin, 1971).

As we have seen, children *simplify.* They use telegraphic speech to say just enough to get their meaning across ("No drink milk!"). Early speech also has several other distinct characteristics.

Children *understand grammatical relationships they cannot yet express.* At first, Erica may understand that a dog is chasing a cat, but she cannot string together enough words to express the complete action. Her sentence comes out as "Puppy chase" rather than "Puppy chase kitty."

Children *underextend word meanings.* Lisa's uncle gave her a toy car, which the 13-month-old called her "koo-ka." Then her father came home with a gift, saying, "Look, Lisa, here's a little car for you." Lisa shook her head. "Koo-ka," she said, and ran and got the one from her uncle. To her, *that* car—and *only* that car—was a little car, and it took some time before she called any other toy cars by the same name. Miranda was underextending the word *car* by restricting it to a single object.

Children also *overextend word meanings.* At 14 months, Eddie jumped in excitement at the sight of a gray-haired man on the television screen and shouted, "Gampa!" Eddie was overgeneralizing, or *overextending,* a word; he thought that because his grandfather had gray hair, all gray-haired men could be called "Grandpa." As children develop a larger vocabulary and get feedback from adults on the appropriateness of what they say, they overextend less. ("No, honey, that man looks a little like Grandpa, but he's somebody else's grandpa, not yours.")

Children *overregularize rules*: they apply them rigidly, not knowing that some rules have exceptions. When John says "mouses" instead of "mice" or Megan says "I thinked" rather than "I thought," this represents progress. Both children initially used the correct forms of these irregular words, but merely in imitation of what they heard. Once children learn the rules for plurals and past tense (a crucial step in learning language), they apply them universally. The next step is to learn the exceptions to the rules, which they generally do by early school age.

CHECKPOINT

Can you . . .

- ✔ Trace the typical sequence of milestones in early language development, pointing out the influence of the language babies hear around them?
- ✔ Describe five ways in which early speech differs from adult speech?

Classic Theories of Language Acquisition: The Nature-Nurture Debate

The sequence of children's language development, especially during the early years, has been exhaustively documented. Less clear is just how—by what processes—children gain access to the secrets of verbal communication. Is linguistic ability learned or inborn? In the 1950s, a debate raged between two schools of thought: one led by B. F. Skinner, the foremost proponent of learning theory, the other by the linguist Noam Chomsky.

Skinner (1957) maintained that language learning, like other learning, is based on experience. According to classic learning theory, children learn language through operant conditioning. At first, babies utter sounds at random. Caregivers reinforce the sounds that happen to resemble adult speech with smiles, attention, and praise. Infants then repeat these reinforced sounds. Sounds that are not part of the native language are not reinforced, and the child gradually stops making them. According to social-learning theory, babies imitate the sounds they hear adults make and, again, are reinforced for doing so. Word learning depends on selective reinforcement; the word *kitty* is reinforced only when the family cat appears. As this process continues, children are reinforced for speech that is more and more adultlike. Sentence formation is a more complex process: the child learns a basic word order (subject-verb-object—"I want ice cream"), and then learns that other words can be substituted in each category ("Daddy eats meat").

Observation, imitation, and reinforcement probably do contribute to language development, but, as Chomsky (1957) persuasively argued, they cannot fully explain it (Flavell, Miller, & Miller, 1993; Owens, 1996). For one thing, word combinations and nuances are so many and so complex that they cannot all be acquired by specific imitation and reinforcement. Then, caregivers often reinforce utterances that are not strictly grammatical, as long as they make sense. ("Gampa go bye-bye.") Adult speech itself is an unreliable model to imitate, as it is often ungrammatical, containing false starts, unfinished sentences, and slips of the tongue. Also, learning theory does not account for children's imaginative ways of saying things they have never heard—as when 2-year-old Anna described a sprained ankle as a "sprangle" and said she didn't want to go to sleep yet because she wasn't "yawny."

nativism
Theory that human beings have an inborn capacity for language acquisition.

language acquisition device (LAD)
In Chomsky's terminology, an inborn mechanism that enables children to infer linguistic rules from the language they hear.

Chomsky's own view is called **nativism.** Unlike Skinner's learning theory, nativism emphasizes the active role of the learner. Since language is universal among human beings, Chomsky (1957, 1972) proposed that the human brain has an innate capacity for acquiring language; babies learn to talk as naturally as they learn to walk. He suggested that an inborn **language acquisition device (LAD)** programs children's brains to analyze the language they hear and figure out its rules. More recently, Chomsky (1995) has sought to identify a simple set of universal principles and parameters that underlie all languages, and a single multipurpose mechanism for connecting sound to meaning.

Support for the nativist position comes from newborns' ability to differentiate similar sounds (Eimas et al., 1971). One researcher suggests that neonates can put sounds into categories because all human beings are "born with perceptual mechanisms that are tuned to the properties of speech" (Eimas, 1985, p. 49). Nativists point out that almost all children master their native language in the same age-related sequence without formal teaching. Furthermore, the brains of human beings, the only animals with fully developed language, contain a structure that is larger on one side than on the other, suggesting that an inborn mechanism for language may be localized in the larger hemisphere—the left for most people. A similar imbalance in the size of this brain structure, the *planum temporale,* has now been discovered in chimpanzees, which also show some ability to learn language (Gannon, Holloway, Broadfield, & Braun, 1998). Still, the nativist approach does not explain precisely how such a mechanism operates. It does not tell us why some children acquire language more rapidly and efficiently than others, why children differ in linguistic skill and fluency, or why (as we'll see) speech development appears to depend on having someone to talk with, not merely on hearing spoken language.

Aspects of both learning theory and nativism have been used to explain how deaf babies learn sign language, which is structured much like spoken language and is acquired in the same sequence. Deaf babies of deaf parents seem to copy the sign language they see their parents using, just as hearing babies copy vocal utterances. Using hand motions more systematic and deliberate than those of

Almost all children, like this Japanese baby, learn their native language, mastering the basics in the same age-related sequence without formal teaching. Nativists say this shows that all human beings are born with the capacity to acquire language.

hearing babies, deaf babies first string together meaningless motions and repeat them over and over in what has been called *hand-babbling* (Petitto & Marentette, 1991). As parents reinforce these gestures, the babies attach meaning to them.

However, some deaf children make up their own sign language when they do not have models to follow—evidence that environmental influences alone cannot explain the emergence of linguistic expression (Goldin-Meadow & Mylander, 1998). Furthermore, learning theory does not explain the correspondence between the ages at which linguistic advances in hearing and nonhearing babies typically occur (Padden, 1996). Deaf babies begin hand-babbling before 10 months of age, about the same period when hearing infants begin voice-babbling (Petitto & Marentette, 1991). Deaf babies also begin to use sentences in sign language at about the same time that hearing babies begin to speak in sentences (Meier, 1991; Newport & Meier, 1985). This suggests that an inborn language capacity may underlie the acquisition of both spoken and signed language and that advances in both kinds of language are tied to brain maturation.

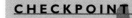

CHECKPOINT

Can you . . .

✔ Summarize how learning theory and nativism seek to explain language acquisition, and point out strengths and weaknesses of each?

Most developmentalists today believe that language acquisition, like most other aspects of development, depends on an intertwining of nature and nurture. Children, whether hearing or deaf, probably have an inborn capacity to acquire language, which may be activated or constrained by experience.

Influences on Language Development

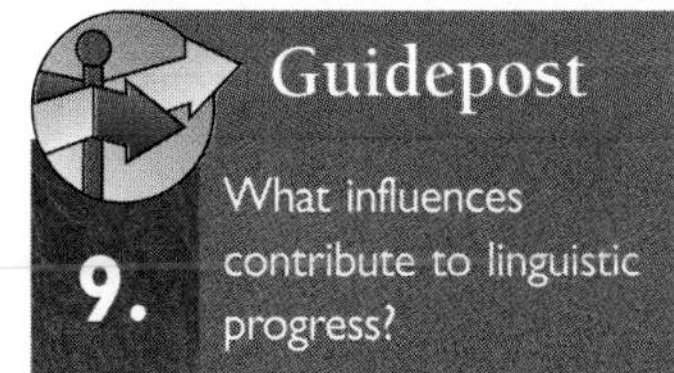

Guidepost

9. What influences contribute to linguistic progress?

What determines how quickly and how well children learn to understand and use language? Research during the past two or three decades has focused on specific influences, both within and outside the child.

Maturation of the Brain

During the early months and years of life, the brain undergoes tremendous growth and reorganization. Some of these changes are closely linked with the development of language.

Which brain structures control which language functions, and when do these structures develop and mature? Scientists have two basic methods of seeking answers to that question. The first is to study specific language deficiencies in people who have suffered damage to particular regions of the brain. The second is to observe brain activity in normal people as they engage in particular language functions. Both approaches have been greatly aided by the development of modern techniques that produce images of what is going on in the brain.

The results of such research suggest that linguistic processes are extremely complex and may involve different components in different people (Caplan, 1992). These processes seem to flow, not from the operation of separate, isolated brain structures, but from the coordination of a variety of structures (Owens, 1996), including those involved in such related cognitive activities as visual perception. For example, the structures involved in recognizing faces and those involved in recognizing words seem to be located near each other and to be organized similarly (Nobre & Plunkett, 1997).

Do certain neurological events underlie key linguistic developments, such as the first word or the first sentence? Here our knowledge is limited. We do not know, for example, whether the naming explosion in the second half of the second year reflects actual physical changes in the brain, or merely a fine-tuning of preexisting structures and representations (Nobre & Plunkett, 1997).

We do know that the cortical regions associated with language do not fully mature until at least the late preschool years or beyond—some, not even until adulthood. A newborn's cries are controlled by the *brain stem* and *pons,* the most primitive parts of the brain and the earliest to develop (refer back to Figure 4-6). Repetitive babbling may emerge with the maturation of parts of the *motor cortex,* which control movements of the face and larynx. Not until early in the second year, when most children begin to talk, do the pathways that link auditory and motor activity mature (Owens, 1996).

How linguistic processes come to be organized in the brain may depend heavily on experience during maturation (Nobre & Plunkett, 1997). Language (unlike some sensory and motor capacities) is highly lateralized (see Chapter 4). In about 98 percent of people, the left hemisphere is dominant for language, though the right hemisphere participates as well. It has been widely believed that this lateralization may be genetically determined. However, studies of brain-damaged children suggest that a sensitive period exists before lateralization of language is firmly fixed. Whereas an adult whose left hemisphere is removed will be severely language-impaired, a young child who undergoes this procedure may eventually have nearly normal speech and comprehension. The plasticity of the infant brain seems to allow functions to be transferred from damaged areas to other regions (Nobre & Plunkett, 1997; Owens, 1996).

Do brains of normal children show similar plasticity? Recent research says yes. The investigators measured brain activity at various places on the scalp as babies listened to a series of words, some of which they did not understand. Between ages 13 and 20 months, a period of marked vocabulary growth, the infants showed increasing lateralization and localization of comprehension (Mills, Cofley-Corina, & Neville, 1997). Other evidence of neural plasticity comes from findings that the upper regions of the temporal lobe, which are involved in hearing and understanding speech, can be activated by a congenitally deaf person's use of sign language (Nishimura et al., 1999). Such findings suggest that the assignment of language functions to brain structures may be a gradual process linked to verbal experience and cognitive development (Nobre & Plunkett, 1997).

CHECKPOINT

Can you . . .

- ✔ Name two important areas of the brain involved in use of language, and tell the function of each?
- ✔ Give evidence for plasticity in the brain's linguistic areas?

Social Interaction: The Role of Parents and Caregivers

Language is a social act. Parents and other caregivers play an important role at each stage of an infant's language development.

At the babbling stage, adults help an infant advance toward true speech by repeating the sounds the baby makes; the baby soon joins in the game and repeats the sounds back. Parents' imitation of babies' sounds affects the pace of language learning (Hardy-Brown & Plomin, 1985; Hardy-Brown, Plomin, & DeFries, 1981). It also helps babies experience the social aspect of speech, the sense that a conversation consists of taking turns, an idea most babies seem to grasp at about $7\frac{1}{2}$ to 8 months of age.

A baby's comprehension grows by discovering through language what another person is thinking. Caregivers may help babies understand spoken words by, for example, pointing to a doll and saying, "Please give me Kermit." If the baby doesn't respond, the adult may pick up the doll and say, "Kermit." In one naturalistic observational study, researchers videotaped 40 mothers playing with their 9-month-old infants at home and rated the mothers' verbal sensitivity. Did a mother respond to her baby's interest in a toy by naming that toy? Did she continue to talk about the toy as long as the baby was paying attention to it and pick up on the baby's signal when the baby's attention shifted? The mother's verbal sensitivity turned out to be an important predictor of the baby's language comprehension (as reported by the mother) 4 months later (Baumwell, Tamis-LeMonda, & Bornstein, 1997).

When babies begin to talk, parents or caregivers often help them by repeating their first words and pronouncing them correctly. Again, sensitivity counts. Vocabulary gets a boost when an adult seizes an appropriate opportunity to teach a child a new word. If Jordan's mother says, "This is a ball" when Jordan is looking at the ball, he is more likely to remember the word than if he were playing with something else and she tried to divert his attention to the ball (Dunham,

Dunham & Curwin, 1993). Adults help a toddler who has begun to put words together by expanding on what the child says. If Christina says "Mommy sock," her mother may reply, "Yes, that is Mommy's sock."

Babies learn by listening to what adults say. A strong relationship has appeared between the frequency of various words in mothers' speech and the order in which children learn these words (Huttenlocher, Haight, Bryk, Seltzer, & Lyons, 1991), as well as between mothers' talkativeness and the size of toddlers' vocabularies (Huttenlocher, 1998).

In households where two languages are spoken, babies often use elements of both languages at first, sometimes in the same utterance—a phenomenon called **code mixing.** Still, as we have seen, even young infants do learn to discriminate between languages. A naturalistic observation of five 2-year-olds in Montreal (Genesee, Nicoladis, & Paradis, 1995) suggests that children in dual-language households differentiate between the two languages, using French, for example, with a predominantly French-speaking father and English with a predominantly English-speaking mother. This ability to shift from one language to another is called **code switching.**

code mixing
Use of elements of two languages, sometimes in the same utterance, by young children in households where both languages are spoken.

code switching
Process of changing one's speech to match the situation, as in people who are bilingual.

From early in their second year, children talk to their parents about what they see on television. They label objects, repeat slogans and jingles, and ask questions. Parents who build on the children's interest and lead them into exchanges of thoughts enhance language development (Lemish & Rice, 1986). Such exchanges are crucial; hearing speech on television is not enough.

The *kinds* of things adults say to children may be almost as important as *how much* they speak. One factor in the delayed speech that is typical of twins, whose mothers must divide their attention between them, is that when their mothers speak to them, much of what the mothers say consists of telling them what to do (Tomasello, Mannle, & Kruger, 1986). Among 2-year-olds in day care centers in Bermuda, children whose caregivers spoke to them often to give or ask for information rather than to control behavior had better language skills than children who did not have such conversations (McCartney, 1984).

Socioeconomic status seems to affect the amount and quality of verbal interaction between parents and children, and also the children's long-range language and cognitive development. In a longitudinal study of 40 midwestern families (described earlier in this chapter) that began when their babies were 7 months old, parents with lower incomes and lower educational and occupational levels tended to spend less time talking with their children in positive ways. These children were exposed to less varied language and were given less opportunity to talk, and their spoken vocabulary was more limited (Hart & Risley, 1989, 1992, 1996)—disadvantages later reflected in linguistic and academic performance between ages 5 and 10 (Walker, Greenwood, Hart, & Carta, 1994).

CHECKPOINT

Can you . . .

- ✔ Explain the importance of social interaction and give at least three examples of how parents or caregivers help babies learn to talk?
- ✔ Tell how socioeconomic status and other family characteristics may influence language development?

Child-Directed Speech

You do not have to be a parent to speak "parentese." If, when you talk to an infant or toddler, you speak slowly in a high-pitched voice with exaggerated ups and downs, simplify your speech, exaggerate vowel sounds, and use short words and sentences and much repetition, you are using **child-directed speech (CDS).** Most adults, and even children, do it naturally. Such "baby talk" may well be universal; it has been documented in many languages and cultures (Kuhl et al., 1997).

child-directed speech (CDS)
Form of speech often used in talking to babies or toddlers; includes slow, simplified speech, a high-pitched tone, exaggerated vowel sounds, short words and sentences, and much repetition. Also called *parentese.*

Many researchers believe that CDS helps children to learn their native language, or at least to pick it up faster. In one cross-cultural observational study, mothers in the United States, Russia, and Sweden were audiotaped speaking to their 2- to 5-month-old infants. Whether the mothers were speaking English, Russian, or Swedish, they produced more exaggerated vowel sounds when talking to the infants than when talking to other adults. Apparently this kind of linguistic input helps infants hear the distinguishing features of speech

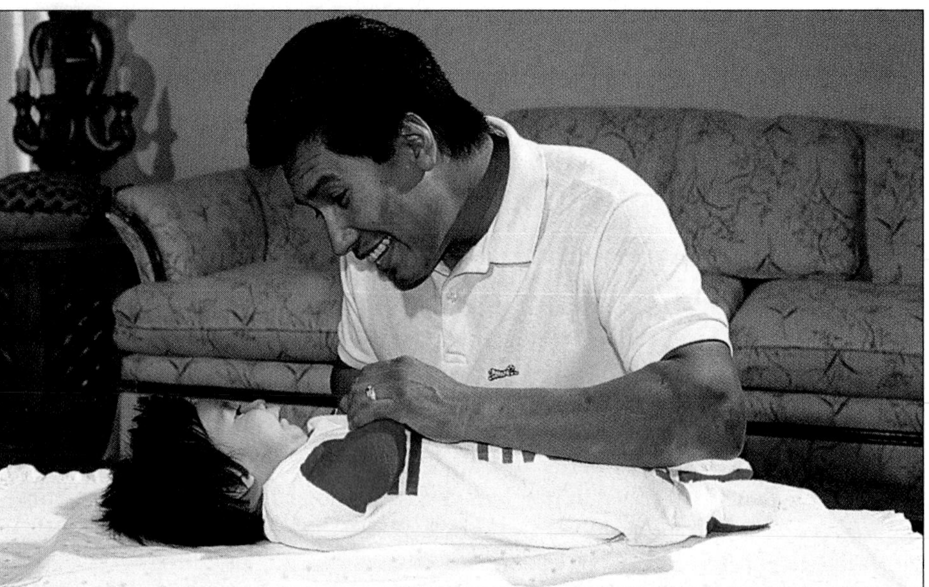

"Parentese," or child-directed speech, is a simplified form of language used for speaking to babies and toddlers. It seems to come naturally, not only to parents, but also to other adults and slightly older children.

sounds. At 20 weeks, the babies' babbling contained distinct vowels that reflected the phonetic differences to which their mothers' speech had alerted them (Kuhl et al., 1997).

CDS also seems to serve other cognitive, social, and emotional functions (Fernald, 1984; Fernald & Simon, 1984). It teaches babies how to carry on a conversation: how to introduce a topic, comment on and add to it, and take turns talking. It teaches them how to use new words, structure phrases, and put ideas into language. Because CDS is confined to simple, down-to-earth topics, infants and toddlers can use their own knowledge of familiar things to help them work out the meanings of the words they hear. CDS also helps babies develop a relationship with adults and enables them to respond to emotional cues.

Adults' use of CDS teaches children the norms of their culture along with the rules of their language. In a cross-sectional study of 30 Japanese and 30 U.S. mothers with 6-, 12-, and 19-month-old babies (Fernald & Morikawa, 1993), both the Japanese and American mothers simplified their language, repeated often, and spoke differently to babies of different ages, but the mothers' ways of interacting with the babies reflected cultural values about child rearing. American mothers labeled objects more, to expand the babies' vocabulary ("That's a car. See the car? You like it? It's got nice wheels"). Japanese mothers encouraged politeness by give-and-take routines ("Here! It's a vroom vroom. I give it to you. Now give this to me. Yes! Thank you"). Japanese mothers use CDS longer and more extensively than U.S. mothers, whose culture places a higher value on fostering independence in children.

Some investigators challenge the value of CDS. They contend that babies speak sooner and better if they hear and can respond to more complex adult speech. In fact, some researchers say, children discover the rules of language faster when they hear complex sentences that use these rules more often and in more ways (Gleitman, Newport, & Gleitman, 1984). Normal adult conversations among older family members may be a useful model. In a Canadian observational study, English-speaking secondborn 21-month olds were directly spoken to less often than firstborn children but overheard more complex conversations between caregivers and older siblings. These secondborns were more advanced in the use of personal pronouns at age 2 than firstborns the same age, even though the general language development of the two groups was about equal (Oshima-Takane, Goodz, & Derevensky, 1996).

Nonetheless, infants themselves prefer simplified speech. This preference is clear before 1 month of age, and it does not seem to depend on any specific experience (Cooper & Aslin, 1990; Kuhl et al., 1997).

Infants' preference for CDS crosses language barriers. In one experiment, $4^{1}/_{2}$- and 9-month-old babies of immigrants to Canada from Hong Kong, whose native tongue was Cantonese, were more attentive, happy, and excited when shown a videotape of a Cantonese-speaking woman using CDS than when the woman used normal adult speech—and so were the babies of English-speaking parents (Werker, Pegg, & McLeod, 1994). The preference for CDS is not limited to spoken language. In an observational study in Japan, deaf mothers were videotaped reciting everyday sentences in sign language, first to their deaf 6-month-old infants and then to deaf adult friends. The mothers signed more slowly and with more repetition and exaggerated movements when directing the sentences to the infants, and other infants the same age paid more attention and appeared more responsive when shown these tapes (Masataka, 1996). What's more, 6-month-old *hearing* infants who had never been exposed to sign language also showed a preference for infant-directed sign. This is powerful evidence that infants, whether hearing or deaf, are universally attracted to CDS (Masataka, 1998).

Preparing for Literacy: The Benefits of Reading Aloud

Most babies love to be read to, and the frequency with which parents or caregivers read to them, as well as the way they do it, can influence how well children speak and eventually how well and how soon they read. Children who learn to read early are generally those whose parents read to them very frequently when they were very young.

Reading to an infant or toddler offers opportunities for emotional intimacy and fosters parent-child communication. Adults help a child's language development when they paraphrase what the child says, expand on it, talk about what interests the child, remain quiet long enough to give the child a chance to respond, and ask specific questions (Rice, 1989). Read-aloud sessions offer a perfect opportunity for this kind of interaction.

A child will get more out of such sessions if adults ask challenging, open-ended questions rather than those calling for a simple yes or no ("What is the cat doing?" instead of "Is the cat asleep?"). In one study, 21- to 35-month-olds whose parents did this—and who added to the child's answers, corrected wrong ones, gave alternative possibilities, encouraged the child to tell the story, and bestowed

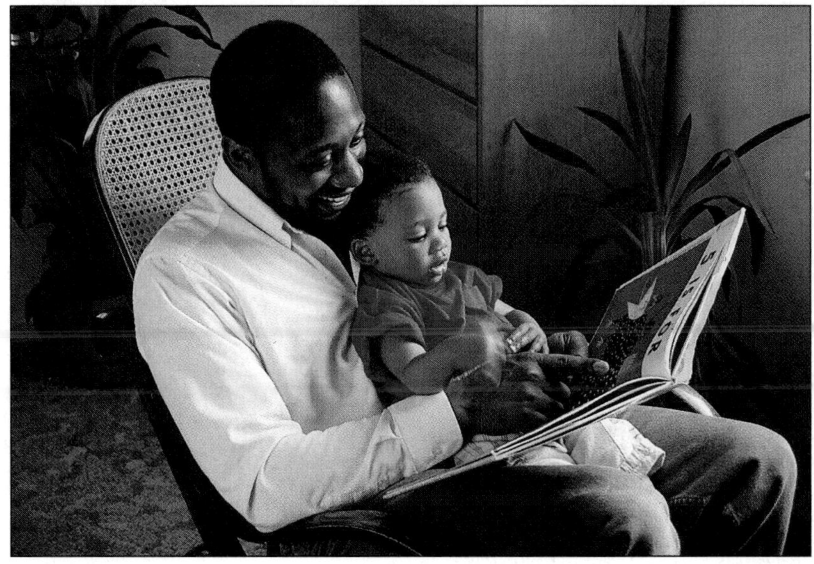

By reading aloud to his 2-year-old son and asking questions about the pictures in the book, this father is helping the boy build language skills and prepare to become a good reader.

CHECKPOINT

Can you . . .

✔ Assess the arguments for and against the value of child-directed speech (CDS)?

✔ Tell why reading aloud to children at an early age is beneficial?

✔ Describe an effective way of reading aloud to infants and toddlers?

praise—scored 6 months higher in vocabulary and expressive language skills than did a control group whose parents did not use these practices in reading to the children. The experimental group also got a boost in *preliteracy skills,* the competencies helpful in learning to read, such as learning how letters look and sound (Arnold & Whitehurst, 1994; Whitehurst et al., 1988). Children who are read to often, especially in this way, when they are 1 to 3 years old show better language skills at ages $2^1/_2$, $4^1/_2$, and 5 and better reading comprehension at age 7 (Crain-Thoreson & Dale, 1992; Wells, 1985).

Social interaction in reading aloud, play, and other daily activities is a key to much of childhood development. Children call forth responses from the people around them and, in turn, react to those responses. In Chapter 6, we will look more closely at these bidirectional influences as we explore early psychosocial development.

Summary

Studying Cognitive Development: Classic Approaches

Guidepost 1. How do infants learn, and how long can they remember?

- The **behaviorist approach** to the study of **intelligent behavior** is concerned with the mechanics of learning. Two simple types of learning that behaviorists study are **classical conditioning** and **operant conditioning.**
- Research using operant conditioning has found that infants' memory span increases with age. Infants' memory of an action is closely linked to contextual cues. New contextual information can be added during a limited **time window.**

Guidepost 2. Can infants' and toddlers' intelligence be measured, and how can it be improved?

- The **psychometric approach** seeks to determine and measure quantitatively the factors that make up intelligence, usually through **IQ (intelligence quotient) tests** based on **standardized norms.** To be useful, psychometric tests must have **validity** and **reliability.**
- A widely used developmental test for infants and toddlers is the **Bayley Scales of Infant Development.** In normal infants, psychometric tests can indicate current functioning but are generally poor predictors of later intelligence.
- Socioeconomic status, parenting practices, and the home environment can affect measured intelligence. According to research using the **Home Observation for Measurement of the Environment (HOME),** parental responsiveness and the ability to create a stimulating home environment are important factors in cognitive development.
- If the **developmental priming mechanisms** necessary for normal development are not present, **early intervention** may be needed.

Guidepost 3. How did Piaget describe infants' and toddlers' cognitive development, and how have his claims stood up under later scrutiny?

- The **Piagetian approach** is concerned with qualitative stages of cognitive development. During the **sensorimotor stage,** from about birth to 2 years, infants' cognitive and behavioral **schemes** become more elaborate. They progress from primary to secondary to tertiary **circular reactions** and finally to the development of **representational ability,** which makes possible **deferred imitation,** pretending, and problem solving.
- According to Piaget, self-locomotion promotes development of the object concept. **Object permanence** develops gradually throughout the sensorimotor stage. Piaget saw the **A, not-B, error** as a sign of incomplete object knowledge and the persistence of egocentric thought.
- Research suggests that a number of abilities develop earlier than Piaget described. For example, he may have underestimated young infants' grasp of object permanence because his testing methods required complex motor coordination. **Invisible imitation**—which, according to Piaget, develops at about 9 months, after **visible imitation**—has been reported in newborns, though this finding is in dispute. Deferred imitation, which Piaget placed in the last half of the second year, has been reported as early as 6 weeks.

Studying Cognitive Development: Newer Approaches

Guidepost 4. How can we measure infants' ability to process information, and how does this ability relate to future intelligence?

- The **information-processing approach** is concerned with mental processes—what people do with the information they perceive. Contrary to Piaget, information-processing research suggests that the ability to form and remember mental representations is present virtually from birth.

- Indicators of the efficiency of infants' information processing include speed of **habituation** and **dishabituation, visual preference,** and **cross-modal transfer.** These and other processing abilities, such as **visual recognition memory,** tend to predict later intelligence.

Guidepost 5. When do babies begin to think about characteristics of the physical world?

- **Violation-of-expectations** research suggests that infants as young as $3^1/_2$ to 5 months may have a rudimentary grasp of object permanence, a sense of number, the beginning of an understanding of **causality,** and an ability to reason about other characteristics of the physical world. Some researchers suggest that infants may have innate learning mechanisms for acquiring such knowledge. However, the meaning of these research findings is in dispute.

Guidepost 6. What can brain research reveal about the development of cognitive skills?

- The **cognitive neuroscience approach** is the study of brain structures that govern thought and memory. Such studies have found that some forms of **implicit memory** develop during the first few months of life. **Explicit memory** and **working memory** emerge between 6 and 12 months of age. Neurological developments help explain the emergence of Piagetian skills and information-processing abilities.

Guidepost 7. How does social interaction with adults advance cognitive competence?

- The **social-contextual approach** looks at social interactions with adults and how they contribute to cognitive competence. Through **guided participation** in play and other shared everyday activities, parents or caregivers help children learn the skills, knowledge, and values important in their culture.

Language Development

Guidepost 8. How do babies develop language?

- The acquisition of **language** is an important aspect of cognitive development.
- **Prelinguistic speech** includes crying, cooing, babbling, and imitating language sounds. Neonates can distinguish speech sounds; by 6 months, babies have learned the basic sounds of their language and begin to become aware of its phonological rules and to link sound with meaning.
- Before they say their first word, babies use gestures, including pointing, conventional social gestures, representational gestures, and symbolic gestures.
- The first word typically comes sometime between 10 and 14 months, initiating **linguistic speech;** often it is a **holophrase.** Passive vocabulary grows faster than active vocabulary. A "naming explosion" typically occurs sometime between 16 and 24 months of age.
- The first brief sentences, or **telegraphic speech,** generally come between 18 and 24 months. By age 3, **syntax** and communicative abilities are fairly well developed.
- Early speech is characterized by simplification, underextending and overextending word meanings, and overregularizing rules.
- Historically, two opposing views about how children acquire language were learning theory, which emphasizes the roles of reinforcement and imitation, and Chomsky's **nativism,** which maintains that children have an inborn **language acquisition device (LAD).** Today, most developmentalists hold that an inborn capacity to learn language may be activated or constrained by experience.

Guidepost 9. What influences contribute to linguistic progress?

- Influences on language development include brain maturation and social interaction. Communication with parents or caregivers plays a vital role at each stage of language development.
- Family characteristics, such as socioeconomic status, affect verbal interaction and language learning. Children in households where two languages are spoken tend to do **code mixing** and **code switching.**
- **Child-directed speech (CDS)** seems to have cognitive, emotional, and social benefits, and infants show a preference for it. However, some researchers dispute its value.
- Reading aloud to a child from an early age helps pave the way for **literacy.**

Key Terms

intelligent behavior (153)
behaviorist approach (153)
psychometric approach (153)
Piagetian approach (153)
classical conditioning (154)
operant conditioning (154)
time window (156)
IQ (intelligence quotient) tests (157)
standardized norms (157)
validity (157)
reliability (157)
Bayley Scales of Infant Development (157)
Home Observation for Measurement of the Environment (HOME) (159)
developmental priming mechanisms (160)
early intervention (160)
sensorimotor stage (161)
schemes (161)
circular reactions (161)
representational ability (163)
deferred imitation (163)
object permanence (164)
A, not-B, error (164)
invisible imitation (166)
visible imitation (166)
information-processing approach (168)
cognitive neuroscience approach (168)
social-contextual approach (168)
habituation (168)
dishabituation (168)
visual preference (169)
cross-modal transfer (170)
visual recognition memory (170)
violation-of-expectations (171)
explicit memory (175)
implicit memory (175)
working memory (176)
guided participation (176)
language (177)
literacy (177)
prelinguistic speech (178)
linguistic speech (180)
holophrase (180)
telegraphic speech (181)
syntax (181)
nativism (184)
language acquisition device (LAD) (184)
code mixing (187)
code switching (187)
child-directed speech (CDS) (187)

Chapter 6

Psychosocial Development During the First Three Years

I'm like a child trying to do everything say everything and be everything all at once

John Hartford, "Life Prayer," 1971

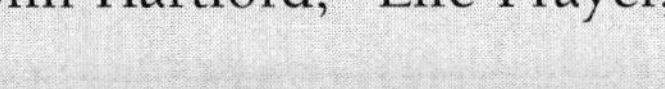

OUTLINE

Helen Keller

Focus: Helen Keller and the World of the Senses*

"What we have once enjoyed we can never lose," the author Helen Keller (1880–1968) once wrote. "A sunset, a mountain bathed in moonlight, the ocean in calm and in storm—we see these, love their beauty, hold the vision to our hearts. All that we love deeply becomes a part of us" (Keller, 1929, p.2).

This quotation is especially remarkable—and especially poignant—in view of the fact that Helen Keller never saw a sunset, or a mountain, or moonlight, or an ocean, or anything else after the age of 19 months. It was then that she contracted a mysterious fever, which left her deaf and with inexorably ebbing sight.

Helen, before her illness, had been a normal, healthy baby—lively, friendly, and affectionate. Now she became expressionless and unresponsive. At 1 year, she had begun to walk; now she clung to her mother's skirts or sat in her lap. She had also begun to talk; one of her first words was *water*. After her illness, she continued to say "wah-wah," but not much else.

Her distraught parents first took her to a mineral spa and then to medical specialists, but there was no hope for a cure. The sensory gateways to the exploration of Helen's world had slammed shut—but not entirely. Deprived of two senses, she leaned more heavily on the other three, especially smell and touch. Memories of the daylight world she had once inhabited helped her make sense of the unrelieved night in which she now found herself.

Helen realized that she was not like other people, but at first she had no clear sense of who or what she was. "I lived in a world that was a no-world. . . . I did not know

*Sources of information about Helen Keller included Keller (1905, 1920) and Lash (1980).

that I knew [anything], or that I lived or acted or desired" (1920, p. 113). Sometimes, when family members were talking to each other, she would stand between them and touch their lips, and then frantically move her own—but nothing happened. Her frustration found its outlet in violent, inconsolable tantrums; she would kick and scream until she was exhausted.

Her parents, out of pity, indulged her whims. Finally, more in desperation than in hope, they engaged a teacher for her: a young woman named Anne Sullivan, who herself had limited vision and who had been trained in a school for the blind. Arriving at the Keller home, Sullivan found 6-year-old Helen to be "wild, wilful, and destructive" (Lash, 1980, p. 348). Once, after figuring out how to use a key, she locked her mother in the pantry. Another time, frustrated by her teacher's attempts to spell the word *doll* into her palm, Helen hurled her new doll to the floor, smashing it to bits.

Yet, that same day, the little girl made her first linguistic breakthrough. As she and her teacher walked in the garden, they stopped to get a drink at the pump. Sullivan placed Helen's hand under the spout, at the same time spelling "w-a-t-e-r" over and over into her other hand. "I stood still," Keller later wrote, "my whole attention fixed upon the motions of her fingers. Suddenly I felt a misty consciousness as of something forgotten—a thrill of returning thought; and somehow the mystery of language was revealed to me. I knew then that 'w-a-t-e-r' meant the wonderful cool something that was flowing over my hand. That living word awakened my soul, gave it light, hope, joy, set it free!" (Keller, 1905, p. 35).

The story of how Anne Sullivan tamed this unruly child and brought her into the light of language and social communion is a familiar and inspiring one. For our present purposes, the lesson to be drawn from Helen Keller's early life is the extent to which psychosocial development rests on physical and cognitive footings. Deprived of vision and hearing, Helen reverted to an infantile emotional state, afraid to leave her mother's side yet unable to trust or to develop positive attachments. Once this "difficult" child began to master language, her window to the world of social experience opened, enabling her to control and express her feelings (which she later did in more than half a dozen published books), become more independent, and interact with others in a wholesome way — tasks she normally would have begun to master in toddlerhood. Her relationship with her teacher, Anne Sullivan, remained a special one throughout her life.

In this chapter we first examine foundations of psychosocial development: emotions, temperament, and early experiences with parents. We consider Erik Erikson's theories about the formation of trust and the growth of autonomy. We look at patterns of attachment and their long-term effects, at how the sense of self develops, and at how toddlers begin to regulate their own behavior according to socially accepted standards. We explore relationships with siblings and other children. Finally, we consider the increasingly widespread impact of parental employment and early child care.

After you have read and studied this chapter, you should be able to answer the following questions:

CH. 6

Guideposts *for* **Study**

1. When and how do emotions develop, and how do babies show them?

2. How do infants show temperamental differences, and how enduring are those differences?

3. What roles do mothers and fathers play in early personality development?

4. How do infants gain trust in their world and form attachments?

5. How do infants and caregivers "read" each other's nonverbal signals?

6. When does the sense of self arise?

7. How do toddlers develop autonomy and standards for socially acceptable behavior?

8. How do infants and toddlers interact with siblings and other children?

9. How do parental employment and early child care affect infants' and toddlers' development?

Foundations of Psychosocial Development

While babies share common patterns of development, they also—from the start—show distinct personalities, which reflect both inborn and environmental influences. From infancy on, personality development is intertwined with social relationships (see Table 6-1).

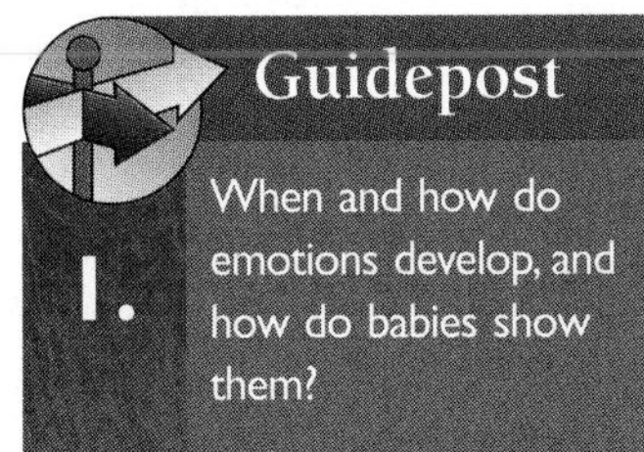

Guidepost

1. When and how do emotions develop, and how do babies show them?

emotions
Subjective reactions to experience that are associated with physiological and behavioral changes.

Emotions

Emotions, such as sadness, joy, and fear, are subjective reactions to experience that are associated with physiological and behavioral changes. All normal human beings have the same range of emotions, but people differ in how often they feel a particular emotion, in the kinds of events that may produce it, in the physical manifestations they show (such as heart rate changes), and in how they act as a result. A person's characteristic pattern of emotional reactions begins to develop during infancy and is a basic element of personality.

From an ethological perspective, emotions serve several functions important to human survival and well-being. One is to communicate a person's inner condition to others and elicit a response. This communicative function is crucial for infants, who must depend on caring adults to meet their basic needs. A second function is to guide and regulate behavior—a function that begins to shift during toddlerhood from the caregiver to the child. Such emotions as fear and surprise mobilize action in emergencies. Other emotions, such as interest and excitement, promote exploration of the environment, which can lead to learning that is useful in protecting or sustaining life.

Human emotions are flexible and modifiable. Cognitive development plays an important role in emotion as infants learn to appraise the meaning of a situation or event in its context and to gauge what is happening against expectations based on past experience. Eight-month-old Melissa's fear of a stranger who tries to pick her up involves memory for faces, the ability to compare the stranger's appearance with her mother's, and perhaps the recollection of situations in which she has been left with a stranger. If Melissa is allowed to get used to the stranger

Table 6-1 Highlights of Infants' and Toddlers' Psychosocial Development, Birth to 36 Months

Approximate Age, Months	Characteristics
0–3	Infants are open to stimulation. They begin to show interest and curiosity, and they smile readily at people.
3–6	Infants can anticipate what is about to happen and experience disappointment when it does not. They show this by becoming angry or acting warily. They smile, coo, and laugh often. This is a time of social awakening and early reciprocal exchanges between the baby and the caregiver.
6–9	Infants play "social games" and try to get responses from people. They "talk" to, touch, and cajole other babies to get them to respond. They express more differentiated emotions, showing joy, fear, anger, and surprise.
9–12	Infants are intensely preoccupied with their principal caregiver, may become afraid of strangers, and act subdued in new situations. By 1 year, they communicate emotions more clearly, showing moods, ambivalence, and gradations of feeling.
12–18	Toddlers explore their environment, using the people they are most attached to as a secure base. As they master the environment, they become more confident and more eager to assert themselves.
18–36	Toddlers sometimes become anxious because they now realize how much they are separating from their caregiver. They work out their awareness of their limitations in fantasy and in play and by identifying with adults.

Source: Adapted from Sroufe, 1979.

gradually in a familiar setting, she may not show a negative reaction (Lewis, 1997; Sroufe, 1997).

Early Signs of Emotion

Newborns plainly show when they are unhappy. They let out piercing cries, flail their arms and legs, and stiffen their bodies. It is harder to tell when they are happy. During the first month, they become quiet at the sound of a human voice or when they are picked up, and they may smile when their hands are moved together to play pat-a-cake. As time goes by, infants respond more to people by smiling, cooing, reaching out, and eventually going to them.

These early signals or clues to babies' feelings are important steps in development. When babies want or need something, they cry; when they feel sociable, they smile or laugh. When their messages bring a response, their sense of connection with other people grows. Their sense of control over their world grows, too, as they see that their cries bring help and comfort and that their smiles and laughter elicit smiles and laughter in return. They become more able to actively participate in regulating their states of arousal and their emotional life.

As time goes by, the meaning of babies' emotional signals changes. At first, crying signifies physical discomfort; later, it more often expresses psychological distress. An early smile comes spontaneously as an expression of well-being; around 3 to 6 weeks, a smile may show pleasure in social contact. As babies get older, smiles and laughter at novel or incongruous situations reflect increasing cognitive awareness and growing ability to handle excitation (Sroufe, 1997).

Crying Crying is the most powerful way—and sometimes the only way—that infants can communicate their needs. Almost all adults around the world respond quickly to a crying infant (Broude, 1995).

Some research has distinguished four patterns of crying (Wolff, 1969): the basic *hunger cry* (a rhythmic cry, which is not always associated with hunger); the *angry cry* (a variation of the rhythmic cry, in which excess air is forced through the vocal cords); the *pain cry* (a sudden onset of loud crying without preliminary moaning, sometimes followed by holding the breath); and the *frustration cry* (two or three drawn-out cries, with no prolonged breath-holding).

Some parents worry that they will spoil a child by responding too much to crying. Early research concluded that this is not so. By the end of the first year, babies whose mothers had regularly responded to their crying cried less, suggesting that the mothers' responsiveness gave the babies confidence in their power to affect their condition (Ainsworth & Bell, 1977; Bell & Ainsworth, 1972). By 1 year, these babies were communicating more in other ways—through babbling, gestures, and facial expressions—while babies whose mothers punished or ignored them continued to cry more. However, more recent observational research found that infants whose mothers were slow in responding to their crying cried *less* often by 6 months. The reason may lie in the distinction between two kinds of crying: cries of extreme distress, which require a prompt response, and mild fussing. Delays in responding to fussing may help babies learn to deal with minor irritations on their own (Hubbard & van IJzendoorn, 1991). On the other hand, if parents wait until cries of distress escalate to shrieks of rage, it may become more difficult to soothe the baby; and such a pattern, if experienced repeatedly, may interfere with infants' developing the ability to regulate, or manage, their own emotional state (R. A. Thompson, 1991).

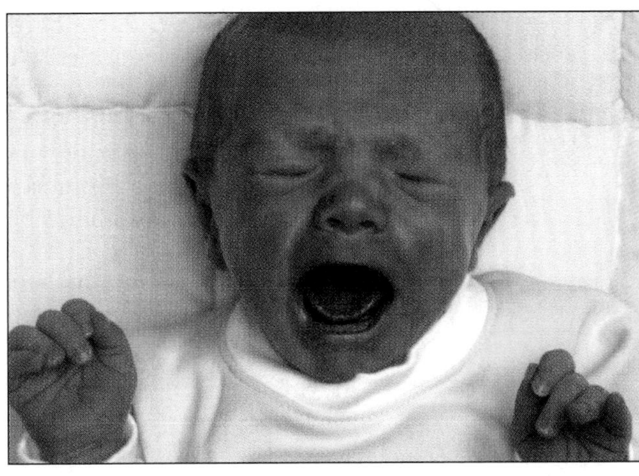

Crying is the most powerful way, and sometimes the only way, that babies can communicate their needs. Parents may soon learn to recognize whether their baby is crying because of hunger, anger, frustration, or pain.

Smiling and Laughing The earliest faint smiles occur spontaneously soon after birth, apparently as a result of alternating cycles of excitation and relaxation in subcortical nervous system activity. These involuntary smiles frequently appear during periods of REM sleep (refer back to Chapter 4). They become less frequent during the first 3 months as the cortex matures (Sroufe, 1997).

The earliest *waking* smiles may be elicited by mild sensations, such as gentle jiggling or blowing on the infant's skin. In the second week, a baby may smile drowsily after a feeding. By the third week, most infants begin to smile when they are alert and paying attention to a caregiver's nodding head and voice. At about 1 month, smiles generally become more frequent and more social. During the second month, as visual recognition develops, babies smile more at visual stimuli, such as faces they know (Sroufe, 1997; Wolff, 1963).

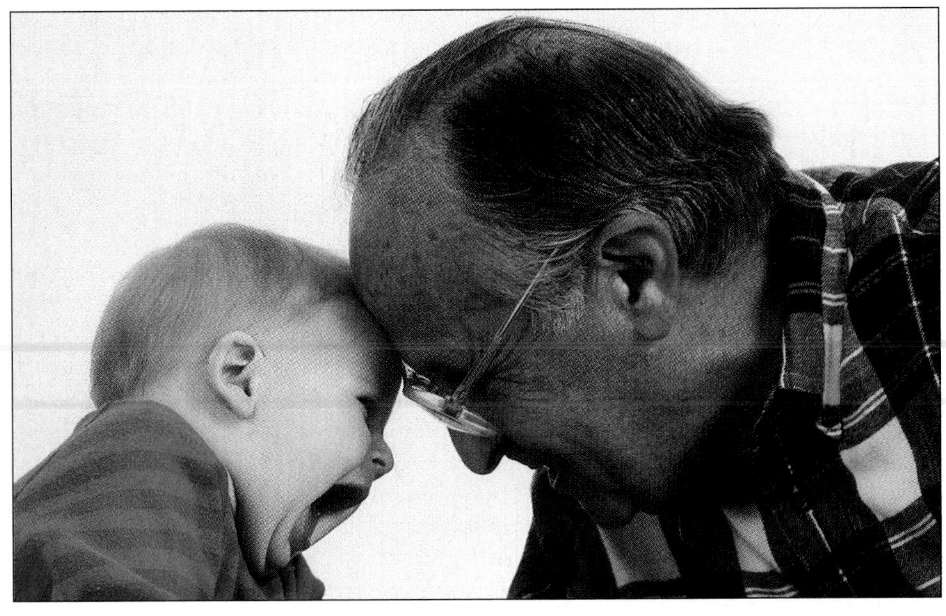

At 6 months, butting heads with his grandfather makes Jackson laugh. Laughter at unusual or unexpected occurrences reflects growing cognitive understanding.

At about the fourth month, infants start to laugh out loud when kissed on the stomach or tickled ("I'm going to get you!") As babies grow older, they laugh more often and at more things. A 6-month-old may giggle in response to unusual sounds or seeing the mother with a towel over her face; an 8-month-old may laugh in a game of peekaboo. This change reflects cognitive development: by laughing at the unexpected, older babies show that they know what to expect. Laughter also helps babies discharge tension, such as fear of a threatening object (Sroufe, 1997).

A longitudinal study of children with Down syndrome underscores the connection between emotional development and cognition. As infants, these mildly to severely retarded children went through the normal sequence of emotional development, but at a slower-than-usual pace. They showed marked delays in the emergence of smiling and laughing and also of fear (Cicchetti & Beeghly, 1990; Cicchetti & Sroufe, 1976, 1978).

When Do Various Emotions Develop?

At what age do sadness, joy, fear, and other emotions develop? To answer that question, we need to determine that an infant of a certain age is showing a particular emotion. Identifying infants' emotions is a challenge because babies cannot tell us what they feel. Still, parents, caregivers, and researchers learn to recognize clues. For example, Carroll Izard and his colleagues have videotaped infants' facial expressions and have interpreted them as showing joy, sadness, interest, and fear, and to a lesser degree anger, surprise, and disgust (Izard, Huebner, Resser, McGinness, & Dougherty, 1980). Of course, we do not know that these babies actually had the feelings they were credited with, but their facial expressions were remarkably similar to adults' expressions when experiencing these emotions.

Facial expressions are not the only, or necessarily the best, index of infants' emotions; motor activity, body language, and physiological changes also are important indicators. An infant can be fearful without showing a "fear face"; the baby may show fear by turning away or averting the gaze, or by a faster heartbeat, and these signs do not necessarily accompany each other. Different criteria may point to different conclusions about the timing of emergence of specific emotions. In addition, this timetable shows a good deal of individual variation (Sroufe, 1997).

Nevertheless, theory and research suggest that the process of emotional development is an orderly one. Emotions do not arise full-blown. Just as the spontaneous neonatal smile is a forerunner of smiles of pleasure in response to people or events, complex emotions seem to build on earlier, simpler ones (Sroufe, 1997). According to one model (Lewis, 1997; see Figure 6-1), soon after birth babies show signs of contentment, interest, and distress. These are diffuse, reflexive, mostly physiological responses to sensory stimulation or internal processes. During the next six months or so, these early emotional states differentiate into true emotions: joy, surprise, sadness, disgust, and last, anger and fear—reactions to events that have meaning for the infant. As we'll discuss in the next section, the emergence of these basic, or primary, emotions seems to be related to the biological "clock" of neurological maturation.

Although the repertoire of basic emotions seems to be universal, there are cultural variations in their expression. A number of cultures discourage children from showing anger and fear (Broude, 1995). In laboratory observations, videotaped faces of 11-month-old Chinese infants whose arms were briefly restrained, or who were approached by a growling gorilla head, were less expressive of emotion than those of American and Japanese infants who underwent the same treatments (Camras et al., 1998). It is unclear whether these findings reflect cultural attitudes or innate differences in emotional reactivity.

Self-conscious emotions, such as embarrassment, empathy, and envy, arise only after children have developed **self-awareness:** the cognitive understanding that they are functioning beings, separate from the rest of their world.

self-awareness
Realization that one's existence and functioning are separate from those of other people and things.

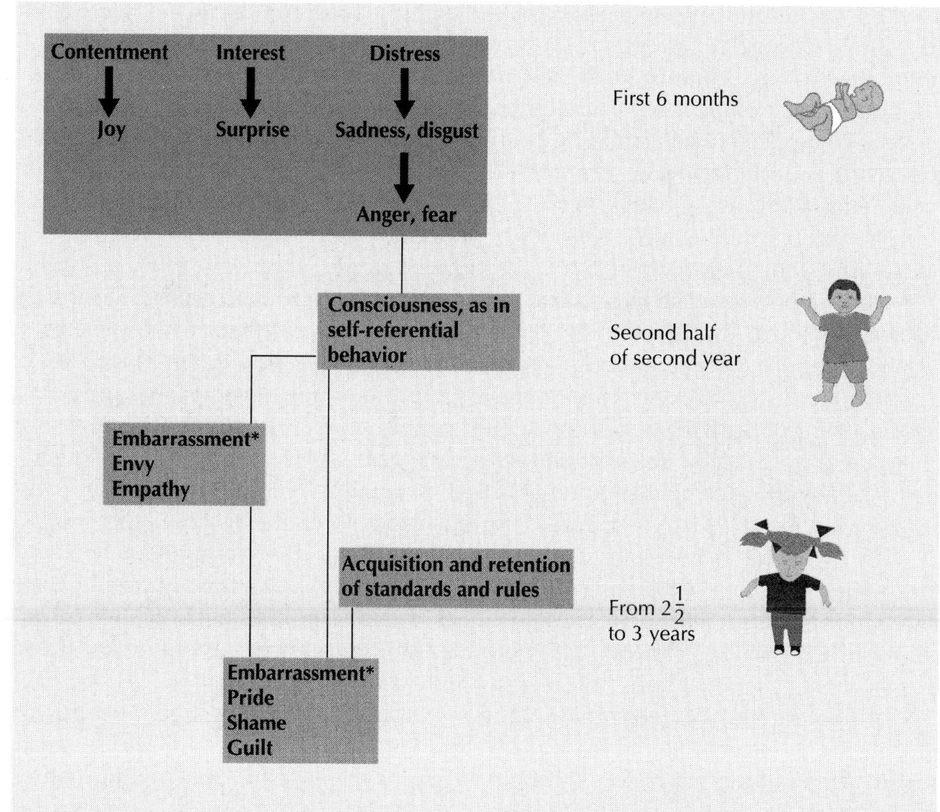

Figure 6-1
Differentiation of emotions during the first three years. The primary, or basic emotions emerge during the first 6 months or so; the self-conscious emotions develop beginning in the second half of the second year, as a result of the emergence of self-awareness (consciousness of self) together with accumulation of knowledge about societal standards and rules.
**Note:* There are two kinds of embarrassment. The earlier form does not involve evaluation of behavior and may simply be a response to being singled out as the object of attention. The second kind, evaluative embarrassment, which emerges during the third year, is a mild form of shame.
(Source: Adapted from Lewis, 1997, Figure 1, p. 120.)

Consciousness of self seems to emerge between 15 and 24 months, when (according to Piaget) infants become able to make mental representations—of themselves as well as other people and things. Self-awareness is necessary before children can be aware of being the focus of attention, identify with what other "selves" are feeling, or wish they had what someone else has. During the third year, having acquired a good deal of knowledge about their society's accepted standards, rules, and goals—largely from parental attitudes and reactions to their behavior—children develop *self-evaluative* emotions, such as pride, shame, and guilt. They now can evaluate their own thoughts, plans, desires, and behavior against what is considered socially appropriate (Lewis, 1995, 1997, 1998). (We'll return to the topic of the sense of self later in this chapter.)

Brain Growth and Emotional Development

The growth of the brain after birth, including the proliferation of neural pathways (described in Chapters 4 and 5), is closely connected with changes in emotional life. This is a bidirectional process: social and emotional experience not only are affected by brain development but can have long-lasting effects on the structure of the brain (Mlot, 1998; Sroufe, 1997).

Some research suggests that separate but interacting regions of the brain (refer back to Figure 4-6 in Chapter 4) may be responsible for various emotional states. For example, fear seems to be seated in the *amygdala,* an almond-shaped structure in the center of the brain, but the left side of the prefrontal cortex can modulate its activity (LeDoux, 1989; Mlot, 1998).

Several kinds of evidence support the role of neurological maturation in emotional development. Developmental changes in electroencephalograph (EEG) recordings, sleep patterns, the *autonomic nervous system* (which controls involuntary activity of the glands and internal organs), and the brain's anatomy (as revealed by animal studies and autopsies of human infants) point to four major shifts in brain organization, which roughly correspond to changes in emotional processes (Schore, 1994; Sroufe, 1997).

During the first 3 months, differentiation of basic emotions begins as the *cerebral cortex* becomes functional, bringing cognitive perceptions into play. REM sleep and reflexive behavior, including the spontaneous neonatal smile, diminish. The social smile reflects a growing desire to seek and maintain contact with outside stimuli.

The second shift occurs around 9 or 10 months, when the *frontal lobes* mature and limbic structures such as the *hippocampus* become larger and more adultlike. Connections between the *hypothalamus* and limbic system, which process sensory information, and the frontal cortex may facilitate the relationship between the emotional and cognitive spheres. As these connections become denser and more elaborate, an infant can experience and interpret emotions at the same time. The development of recognition and recall, object permanence, and other cognitive advances make it possible to coordinate past and present events and future expectations. A baby this age may become upset when a ball rolls under a couch and may smile or laugh when it is retrieved. Fear of strangers often develops at this time.

The third shift takes place during the second year, when infants develop self-awareness, self-conscious emotions, and a greater capacity for regulating their own emotions and activities. These changes, which coincide with greater physical mobility and exploratory behavior, may be related to myelination of the frontal lobes.

The emergence of evaluative emotions around age 3 may both reflect and produce hormonal changes in the developing brain. A shift away from dominance of the autonomic nervous system by the *sympathetic system,* which prepares the body for action, and the maturation of the *parasympathetic system,* which is involved in excretion and sexual excitation, may underlie the development of such emotions as shame. The experience of shame may in turn activate the inhibitory circuits of the limbic system and deactivate the excitatory circuits, eventually bringing the two circuits into balance. Also, an increase in left-hemisphere activity supports the emergence of language, which advances social interaction and awareness of parental and societal standards.

Neurological factors also may play a part in temperamental differences (Mlot, 1998), the topic we turn to next.

CHECKPOINT

Can you . . .

- ✔ Cite two important functions of emotions?
- ✔ Explain the significance of patterns of crying, smiling, and laughing?
- ✔ Trace a typical sequence of emergence of the basic, self-conscious, and evaluative emotions, and explain its connection with cognitive and neurological development?

Temperament

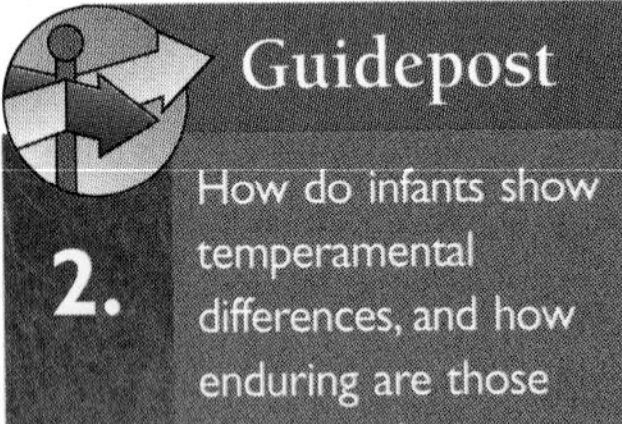

Guidepost
2.
How do infants show temperamental differences, and how enduring are those differences?

Temperament, sometimes defined as a person's characteristic way of approaching and reacting to people and situations, is the *how* of behavior: not *what* people do, but how they go about doing it. Two toddlers, for example, may be equally able to dress themselves and may be equally motivated, but one may do it more quickly than the other, be more willing to put on a new outfit, and be less distracted if the cat jumps on the bed.

temperament Person's characteristic disposition, or style of approaching and reacting to people and situations.

What does temperament consist of? How and when does it develop? How does it affect social adjustment? Is it subject to change?

Aspects and Patterns of Temperament: The New York Longitudinal Study

The New York Longitudinal Study (NYLS), begun in 1956 by Alexander T. Thomas, Stella C. Chess, and Herbert B. Birch, is considered the pioneering study on temperament. These researchers followed 133 infants into adulthood, interviewing, testing, and observing them and interviewing their parents and teachers.

The researchers looked at how active the children were; how regular they were in hunger, sleep, and bowel habits; how readily they accepted new people and situations; how they adapted to changes in routine; how sensitive they were

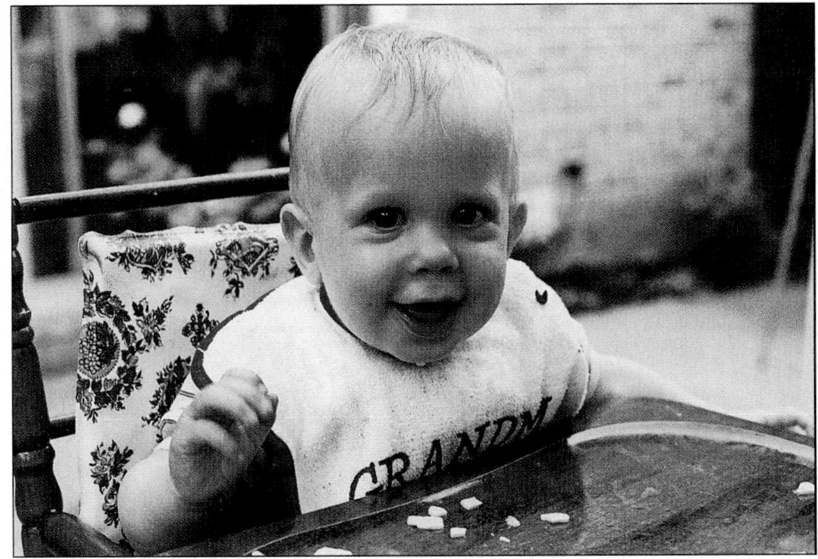

Seven-month-old Daniel's ready smile and willingness to try a new food are signs of an easy temperament.

to noise, bright lights, and other sensory stimuli; how intensely they responded; whether their mood tended to be pleasant, joyful, and friendly or unpleasant, unhappy, and unfriendly; and whether they persisted at tasks or were easily distracted (A. Thomas, Chess, & Birch, 1968). The children differed in all these characteristics, almost from birth, and the differences tended to continue. However, many children, like Helen Keller after her illness, changed their behavioral style, apparently reacting to special experiences or parental handling (Lerner & Galambos, 1985; A. Thomas & Chess, 1984).

To better appreciate how temperament can affect behavior, let's look at three sisters. Amy, the eldest, was a cheerful, calm baby who ate, slept, and eliminated at regular times. She greeted each day and most people with a smile, and the only sign that she was awake during the night was the tinkle of the musical toy in her crib. When Brooke, the second sister, woke up, she would open her mouth to cry before she even opened her eyes. She slept and ate little and irregularly; she laughed and cried loudly, often bursting into tantrums; and she had to be convinced that new people and new experiences were not threatening before she would have anything to do with them. The youngest sister, Christina, was mild in her responses, both positive and negative. She did not like most new situations, but if allowed to proceed at her own slow pace, she would eventually become interested and involved.

Almost two-thirds of the children in the NYLS fell into one of three categories exemplified by these three sisters (see Table 6-2). Forty percent were **easy children** like Amy: generally happy, rhythmic in biological functioning, and accepting of new experiences. Ten percent were what the researchers called **difficult children** like Brooke: more irritable and harder to please, irregular in biological rhythms, and more intense in expressing emotion. Fifteen percent were **slow-to-warm-up children** like Christina: mild but slow to adapt to new people and situations (A. Thomas & Chess, 1977, 1984).

Many children (including 35 percent of the NYLS sample) do not fit neatly into any of these three groups. A baby may eat and sleep regularly but be afraid of strangers. A child may be easy most of the time, but not always. Another child may warm up slowly to new foods but adapt quickly to new baby-sitters. All these variations are normal (A. Thomas & Chess, 1984).

According to the NYLS, the key to healthy adjustment is **goodness of fit**—the match between a child's temperament and the environmental demands and constraints the child must deal with. If a very active child is expected to sit still

easy children
Children with a generally happy temperament, regular biological rhythms, and a readiness to accept new experiences.

difficult children
Children with irritable temperament, irregular biological rhythms, and intense emotional responses.

slow-to-warm-up children
Children whose temperament is generally mild but who are hesitant about accepting new experiences.

goodness of fit
Appropriateness of environmental demands and constraints to a child's temperament.

Table 6-2 Three Temperamental Patterns

Easy Child	Difficult Child	Slow-to-Warm-Up Child
Has moods of mild to moderate intensity, usually positive	Displays intense and frequently negative moods; cries often and loudly; also laughs loudly	Has mildly intense reactions, both positive and negative
Responds well to novelty and change	Responds poorly to novelty and change	Responds slowly to novelty and change
Quickly develops regular sleep and feeding schedules	Sleeps and eats irregularly	Sleeps and eats more regularly than difficult child, less regularly than easy child
Takes to new foods easily	Accepts new foods slowly	Shows mildly negative initial response to new stimuli (a first encounter with a new person, place, or situation)
Smiles at strangers	Is suspicious of strangers	
Adapts easily to new situations	Adapts slowly to new situations	
Accepts most frustrations with little fuss	Reacts to frustration with tantrums	
Adapts quickly to new routines and rules of new games	Adjusts slowly to new routines	Gradually develops liking for new stimuli after repeated, unpressured exposures

Source: Adapted from A. Thomas & Chess, 1984.

for long periods, if a slow-to-warm-up child is constantly pushed into new situations, or if a persistent child is constantly taken away from absorbing projects, trouble may occur.

When parents recognize that a child acts in a certain way, not out of willfulness, laziness, or stupidity, but largely because of inborn temperament, they are less likely to feel guilty, anxious, or hostile or to be rigid or impatient. Rather than seeing a child's temperament as an impediment, they can anticipate the child's reactions and help the child adapt. For example, a "difficult" child may need extra warning time before being expected to put toys away, or may require especially careful preparation before a family move. Sometimes all that is required is a simple adjustment in parents' demands (Chess, 1997).

How Stable Is Temperament?

Even in the womb, fetuses show distinct personalities. They have different activity levels and heart rates, which seem to forecast differences in disposition after birth (DiPietro, Hodgson, Costigan, & Johnson, 1996; see Chapter 3). This and other evidence suggests that temperament is inborn and largely hereditary (Braungart, Plomin, DeFries, & Fulker, 1992; Emde et al., 1992; Schmitz, Saudino, Plomin, Fulker, & DeFries, 1996; A. Thomas & Chess, 1977, 1984). It also tends to be fairly stable. Newborn babies show different patterns of sleeping, fussing, and activity, and these differences tend to persist to some degree (Korner et al., 1985; Korner, 1996).

Early temperament can foreshadow adult personality. In one longitudinal study, temperamental differences among 900 three-year-olds predicted social adjustment 18 years later. Children rated by examiners as well-adjusted, confident, or reserved at age 3 showed normal social functioning at age 21, whereas those who had been rated as inhibited tended to be less sociable. Children rated as undercontrolled (irritable, impulsive, overactive, inattentive, emotionally unstable, and lacking in persistence) grew up to have a broad array of social problems (Newman, Caspi, Moffitt, & Silva, 1997). Undercontrolled 3-year-olds tended, at age 18, to be aggressive or alienated and low in constraint (a combination of harm avoidance, control, and high moral standards). These personality traits, in turn, predicted a greater likelihood of risky behavior at 21: alcohol dependence, violent crime, unsafe sex, and dangerous driving (Caspi et al., 1997).

Some research (introduced in Chapter 3) has focused on an aspect of temperament called *inhibition to the unfamiliar*, which has to do with how sociable a child is with strange children and how boldly or cautiously the child approaches unfamiliar objects and situations. This characteristic seems to have a genetic basis and is associated with differences in physical features and brain functioning. Four-month-olds who are highly reactive—that is, who show much motor activity and distress, or who fret or cry readily in response to new stimuli—are more likely to show the inhibited pattern at 14 and 21 months. Babies who are highly inhibited or uninhibited seem to maintain these patterns to some degree during childhood and adolescence (Kagan, 1997; Kagan & Snidman, 1991a, 1991b).

However, experience can moderate these early tendencies. In a longitudinal study of 193 white, middle-class infants, only about 25 percent of those judged high-reactive were markedly withdrawn and shy at age $4^1/_2$, and a similar proportion of low-reactive infants were spontaneous and outgoing at $4\,^1/_2$. Nearly 70 percent of the sample were neither extremely inhibited nor extremely uninhibited. Still, fewer than 5 percent switched from one temperamental type to the other (Kagan, Snidman, & Arcus, 1998).

In another longitudinal study, firstborn male toddlers who were inclined to be fearful and shy were more likely to remain so at age 3 if their parents were highly accepting of the child's reactions. If parents encouraged their sons to venture into new situations, the boys tended to become less inhibited. This research suggests that parents need not just passively accept a child's temperament; sometimes, by being less "sensitive" and more "intrusive," they may help the child overcome tendencies that will make it harder to get along in the world (Park, Belsky, Putnam, & Crnic, 1997).

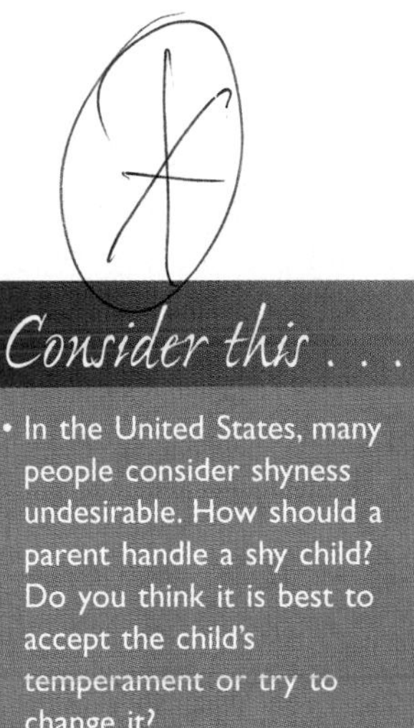

Consider this . . .

- In the United States, many people consider shyness undesirable. How should a parent handle a shy child? Do you think it is best to accept the child's temperament or try to change it?

Cross-Cultural Differences

Studies have found ethnic differences in temperament. If a Caucasian American newborn's nose is briefly pressed with a cloth, the baby will normally turn away or swipe at the cloth. Chinese American babies are more likely to open their mouths immediately to restore breathing, without a fight (Freedman & Freedman, 1969).

Inhibited behavior also varies across cultures. Four-month-old U.S. babies react more strongly than Irish babies the same age to stimulating sights, loud sounds, and strong smells—by crying, fussing, kicking, arching their backs, and otherwise showing irritability—and Irish babies react more strongly than Chinese babies (Kagan et al., 1994). Such temperamental differences tend to predict how fearful or outgoing the infants will be as toddlers (Kagan & Snidman, 1991a, 1991b).

Do these findings reflect genetic variations across cultures? We don't know. Temperament may be affected by prenatal experience or, in older babies, by culturally influenced childraising practices. For example, infants in Malaysia, an island group in Southeast Asia, tend to be less adaptable, more wary of new experiences, and more readily responsive to stimuli than U.S. babies. This may be because Malay parents do not often expose young children to situations that require adaptability, and they encourage children to be acutely aware of sensations, especially uncomfortable ones such as the need for a diaper change (Banks, 1989).

In a cross-cultural study of Chinese and Canadian 2-year-olds, Canadian mothers of inhibited children tended to be punitive or overprotective, whereas Chinese mothers of such children were warm and accepting and encouraged them to achieve. The Chinese toddlers were significantly more inhibited than the Canadian ones; but because this was a correlational study, we don't know whether

CHECKPOINT

Can you . . .

✔ List and describe nine aspects and three patterns of temperament identified by the New York Longitudinal Study?

✔ Discuss evidence for the stability of temperament, and explain the importance of "goodness of fit"?

CHECKPOINT

Can you . . .

✔ Give evidence of cultural differences in temperament, and discuss ways of interpreting it?

the children's temperament was a consequence or a cause of their mothers' treatment, or perhaps a bidirectional effect. In Western countries such as Canada, shy, inhibited children tend to be seen as incompetent, immature, and unlikely to accomplish much. Their mothers may show disappointment by emotionally rejecting them or may think they need special guidance and protection. In China, shyness and inhibition are socially approved. The Confucian principle of filial piety emphasizes obedience to parents; a shy child is considered well behaved and is likely to get adult approval. Thus a naturally inhibited Chinese child may be less motivated to come out of his or her shell than a Canadian one (Chen et al., 1998).

Earliest Social Experiences: The Infant in the Family

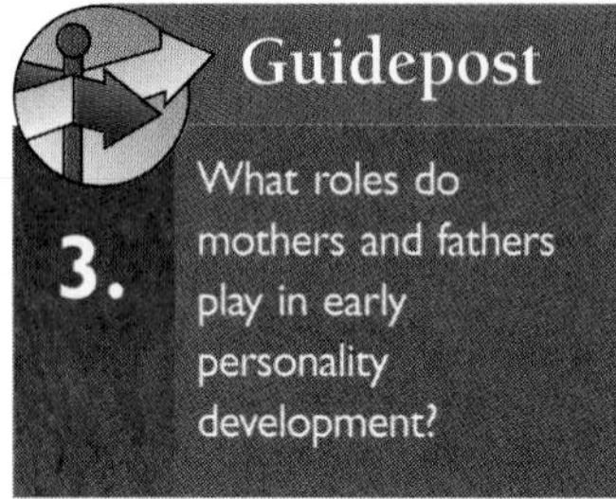

Guidepost
3.
What roles do mothers and fathers play in early personality development?

In the past, research on infant psychosocial development focused almost exclusively on mothers and babies, but now researchers are studying relationships between infants and their fathers, siblings, and other caregivers, as well as characteristics of the family as a whole. How old are the parents? Are they healthy? What is their financial status? How many people live at home? Do the parents act differently when either one is alone with a baby than when all three are together? How does the quality of the marital relationship affect the relationship each spouse has with the baby? How does living in a single-parent household, in a stepfamily, or with grandparents or other relatives affect an infant's development? Are there older siblings, and how do they respond to the newcomer? By looking at the family as a functioning unit, we get a fuller picture of the network of relationships among all its members.

Childraising practices and patterns of social interaction vary greatly around the world. For example, infants among the Efe people of the African country of Zaire typically receive care from five or more people in a given hour and are routinely breast-fed by other women as well as by their mothers, even though the mother is the major caregiver. At age 3, they spend about 70 percent of their time with people other than their mothers (Tronick, Morelli, & Ivey, 1992). Unlike U.S. babies, who spend more time alone or with just one or two family members and may learn to amuse themselves earlier than Efe babies, the Efe may learn to be more sociable at an earlier age.

The fathering role is recognized in all cultures, but it may be taken or shared by someone other than the biological father: the mother's brother, as in Botswana (where young mothers remain with their own childhood family until their partners are in their forties), or a grandfather, as in Vietnam (Engle & Breaux, 1998; Richardson, 1995; Townsend, in press). Sometimes the father is not even present; 32 percent of families in the United States are headed by women (mostly single mothers), and even higher rates are reported in Norway and in some African and Caribbean countries. This is a growing trend in developing countries, reflecting urbanization, employment of women, and a decline in male employment (Engle & Breaux, 1998).

Classic ethnographic research by Robert LeVine (1974, 1989, 1994) among the Gusii people in western Kenya highlighted differences in childraising behaviors in preindustrial and industrial societies. Because infant mortality in preindustrial societies is high, parents tend to keep their infants close to them, respond quickly when they cry, and feed them on demand. Urban-industrial parents—to help their children acquire cognitive skills that will equip them for success in a competitive marketplace—stress sensory stimulation, social interaction, and vocal exchanges with their babies.

Now a naturalistic observation of Aka foragers (hunter-gatherers) and Ngandu farmers in central Africa has found distinctive child-raising styles in these two kinds of small, preindustrial societies (Hewlett, Lamb, Shannon, Leyendecker, & Schölmerich, 1998). The Aka move around frequently in small, tightly knit groups marked by extensive sharing, cooperation, and concern about danger. Aka parents hold their babies almost all the time, nurse them frequently, and respond promptly to signs of distress. The Ngandu, who tend to live farther apart and to stay in one place for long periods of time, are more likely to leave their infants alone and to let them fuss or cry, smile, vocalize, or play.

We need to remember, then, that patterns of psychological development we take for granted may be culture-based. With that caution in mind, let's look first at the roles of the mother and father: how they care for and play with their babies, and how their influence begins to shape personality differences between boys and girls. Later in this chapter, we look more deeply at relationships with parents and at the influence of siblings. In Chapter 16, we examine the influence of grandparents.

The Mother's Role

In a series of pioneering experiments by Harry Harlow and his colleagues, rhesus monkeys were separated from their mothers 6 to 12 hours after birth and raised in a laboratory. The infant monkeys were put into cages with one of two kinds of surrogate "mothers": a plain cylindrical wire-mesh form or a form covered with terry cloth. Some monkeys were fed from bottles connected to the wire "mothers"; others were "nursed" by the warm, cuddly cloth ones. When the monkeys were allowed to spend time with either kind of "mother," they all spent more time clinging to the cloth surrogates, even if they were being fed only by the wire ones. In an unfamiliar room, the babies "raised" by cloth surrogates showed more natural interest in exploring than those "raised" by wire surrogates, even when the appropriate "mothers" were there.

Apparently, the monkeys also remembered the cloth surrogates better. After a year's separation, the "cloth-raised" monkeys eagerly ran to embrace the terry-cloth forms, whereas the "wire-raised" monkeys showed no interest in the wire forms (Harlow & Zimmerman, 1959). None of the monkeys in either group grew up normally, however (Harlow & Harlow, 1962), and none were able to nurture their own offspring (Suomi & Harlow, 1972).

It is hardly surprising that a dummy mother would not provide the same kinds of stimulation and opportunities for development as a live mother. These experiments show that feeding is not the most important thing babies get from their mothers. Mothering includes the comfort of close bodily contact and, in monkeys, the satisfaction of an innate need to cling. Human infants also have needs that must be satisfied if they are to grow up normally, as the research on children raised in Romanian orphanages (discussed in Chapter 4) shows. A major task of developmental research is to find out what those needs are.

In a series of classic experiments, Harry Harlow and Margaret Harlow showed that food is not the most important way to a baby's heart. When infant rhesus monkeys could choose whether to go to a wire surrogate "mother" or a warm, soft terry-cloth "mother," they spent more time clinging to the cloth mother, even if they were being fed by bottles connected to the wire mother.

How and when does the special intimacy between mothers and their babies form? In another classic study, Konrad Lorenz (1957) waddled, honked, and flapped his arms—and got newborn ducklings to follow him as they would the mother duck. Lorenz showed that newly hatched ducklings will follow the

imprinting
Instinctive form of learning in which, during a critical period in early development, a young animal forms an attachment to the first moving object it sees, usually the mother.

mother-infant bond
Close, caring connection between mother and newborn.

first moving object they see, whether or not it is a member of their own species. This phenomenon is called **imprinting**, and Lorenz believed that it is automatic and irreversible. Usually, this first attachment is to the mother; but if the natural course of events is disturbed, other attachments (like the one to Lorenz)—or none at all—can form. Imprinting, said Lorenz, is the result of a *predisposition toward learning*: the readiness of an organism's nervous system to acquire certain information during a brief critical period in early life.

Does something similar to imprinting happen between human newborns and their mothers? Is there a critical period for bonding?

In 1976, two researchers proposed that if mother and baby are separated during the first hours after birth, the **mother-infant bond**—the close, caring connection between mother and newborn—may not develop normally (Klaus & Kennell, 1976). However, follow-up research has not confirmed a critical time for bonding (Chess & Thomas, 1982; Lamb, 1982a, 1982b). The original advocates of this idea later changed their position, saying that contact immediately after birth is *not* essential for strong mother-child bonding (Klaus & Kennell, 1982). This finding has relieved the worry and guilt sometimes felt by adoptive parents and parents who had to be separated from their infants after birth. (Later in this chapter we discuss *attachment*, a linkage that develops later in infancy and has greater emotional meaning for the infant.)

Newly hatched chicks will follow and become attached to the first moving object they see. The ethologist Konrad Lorenz, who got newborn ducklings to "love him like a mother," called this behavior *imprinting*.

The Father's Role

The father's role, like the mother's, entails emotional commitments, and often direct involvement in the care and upbringing of children (Engle & Breaux, 1998). Many fathers form close bonds with their babies soon after birth. Fathers who are present at the birth of a child often see the event as a "peak emotional experience" (May & Perrin, 1985), but a man can become emotionally committed to his newborn whether or not he attended the birth (Palkovitz, 1985).

Still, in most cultures women are children's primary caregivers (Harkness & Super, 1995). While fathers' roles vary greatly (see Box 6-1), most fathers are not nearly as involved in their children's day-to-day lives as mothers are (Engle & Breaux, 1998). Among white and African American middle-class families and in Jamaica, fathers spend as much time playing with their babies as mothers do, but less time feeding or bathing them (Bailey, 1994; Broude, 1995; Hossain & Roopnarine, 1994; Roopnarine, Brown, Snell-White, & Riegraft, 1995). Even mothers who work full time spend more time taking care of their infants than fathers do (Bailey, 1994).

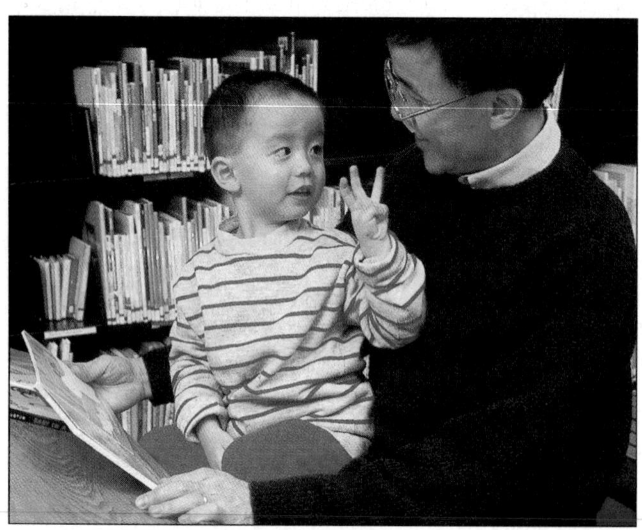

By taking his 2-year-old to the library and reading to him frequently and lovingly, this father encourages his son's cognitive development.

In the United States, fathers tend to "play rough": they toss infants up in the air and wrestle or "box" with toddler sons, whereas mothers typically play gentler games and sing and read to babies (Kelley, Smith, Green, Berndt, & Rogers, 1998; Parke & Tinsley, 1981; Yogman, 1984). However, a highly physical style of play is not typical of fathers in all cultures. Swedish and German fathers usually do not play with their babies this way (Lamb, Frodi, Frodi, & Hwang, 1982; Parke, Grossman, & Tinsley, 1981). African Aka fathers (Hewlett, 1987) and those in New Delhi, India, also tend to play gently with small children (Roopnarine, Hooper, Ahmeduzzaman, & Pollack, 1993; Roopnarine, Talokder, Jain, Josh, & Srivastav, 1992). Such cross-cultural variations suggest that rough play is *not* a function of male biology, but instead is culturally influenced.

Research has found a relationship between a father's close involvement with his baby and the baby's

Box 6-1
Fatherhood in Three Cultures

Fatherhood has different meanings in different cultures. In some cultures, fathers are more involved in their young children's lives—economically, emotionally, and in time spent—than in other cultures. In many parts of the world, what it means to be a father has changed—and is changing (Engle & Breaux, 1998*).

Urbanization in West Africa and Inner Mongolia

In Cameroon and other rural areas of West Africa (Nsamenang, 1987, 1992a, 1992b), men have more than one wife, and children grow up in large extended families linked to kinship-based clans. Although children guarantee the perpetuation of a man's family line, they belong to the kinship group, not just to the parents. After weaning, they may have multiple caregivers or may even be given to other members of the group to raise.

The father has the dominant position in the family and gives his children their connection with the clan. The mother is literally the breadwinner, responsible for providing her children's food, but the father controls his wives and their earnings; and wives compete for their husbands' favor. Fathers are primarily disciplinarians and advisers. They have little contact with infants but serve as guides, companions, and models for older children.

With the coming of urbanization and western values, these traditional patterns are breaking up. Many men are pursuing financial goals and are spending almost no time with their children. With the vanishing of traditional folkways, men no longer know how to be fathers. They can no longer tell folktales to young children around the fire or teach their sons how to do a man's work.

Among the Huhot of Inner Mongolia, too, fathers traditionally are responsible for discipline and mothers for nurturing; but fathers also provide economic support (Jankowiak, 1992). Children have strong bonds with mothers, who live in the homes of their mothers-in-law and have no economic power. Fathers are stern and aloof, and their children respect and fear them. Men almost never hold infants; they are believed to be incapable of it. Fathers interact more with toddlers but perform child care duties reluctantly, and only if the mother is absent.

Here, as in Cameroon, urbanization is changing these attitudes—but in the opposite direction. Families now live in very small quarters, and women work outside the home. Fathers—especially college-educated ones—now seek more intimate relationships with children, especially sons. China's official one-child policy has accentuated this change, leading both parents to be more deeply involved with their only child (Engle & Breaux, 1998).

Aka Pygmies

The Aka are hunter-gatherers in the tropical forests of central Africa who move frequently from camp to camp in small, tightly knit groups and are highly protective of young children. In contrast with fathers in the other two cultures just described, Aka fathers are just as nurturant and emotionally supportive as Aka mothers. In fact, "Aka fathers provide more direct infant care than fathers in any other known society" (Hewlett, 1992, p. 169). They hold their babies frequently and hug, kiss, clean, and play gently with them (Hewlett, 1987).

This behavior is in line with *family systems theory*, which predicts that fathers will be more involved in the care of young children in cultures in which husbands and wives frequently cooperate in subsistence tasks and other activities (Hewlett, 1992). Among the Aka and other societies with high paternal involvement in infant care, the key is not just that both parents participate in such activities, but that they do it together. The father's role in child care is part and parcel of his role in the family.

*Unless otherwise referenced, this box is based on Engle & Breaux, 1998.

cognitive development (Easterbrooks & Goldberg, 1984; Nugent, 1991). In an observational study of 54 African American 1- to 3-year-olds, those whose fathers showed sensitivity during free play (for example, by letting the child set the pace and control the choice of activities) tended to have better self-help and motor skills than the other children. Toddlers whose fathers valued strictness and obedience tended to have less advanced cognitive and social development. Of course, here again, children influence the adults around them; toddlers with more advanced skills may elicit more sensitivity from their fathers (Kelley et al., 1998).

Consider this . . .

- "Despite the increasingly active role today's fathers play in child raising, a mother will always be more important to babies and young children than a father." Do you agree or disagree?
- Should parents try to treat male and female infants and toddlers alike?

How Parents Shape Gender Differences

Being male or female affects how people look, how they move their bodies, and how they work, play, and dress. It influences what they think about themselves and what others think of them. All those characteristics—and more—are included in the word **gender:** what it means to be male or female.

gender Significance of being male or female.

Measurable differences between baby boys and girls are few. Males are physically more vulnerable than females from conception on. On the other hand, baby boys are a bit longer and heavier than baby girls and may be slightly stronger. Newborn boys and girls react differently to stress, possibly suggesting genetic, hormonal, or temperamental differences (Davis & Emory, 1995). An analysis of a large number of studies found baby boys more active than baby girls, though this difference is not consistently documented (Eaton & Enns, 1986). The two sexes are equally sensitive to touch and tend to teethe, sit up, and walk at about the same ages (Maccoby, 1980).

gender-typing Socialization process by which children, at an early age, learn appropriate gender roles.

Parental shaping of boys' and girls' personalities appears to begin very early. Fathers, especially, promote **gender-typing,** the process by which children learn behavior that their culture considers appropriate for each sex (Bronstein, 1988). Fathers treat boys and girls more differently than mothers do, even during the first year (M. E. Snow, Jacklin, & Maccoby, 1983). During the second year, fathers talk more and spend more time with sons than with daughters (Lamb, 1981). Mothers talk more, and more supportively, to daughters than to sons. Overall, fathers are less talkative and supportive—but also less negative—in their speech than mothers are. These differences are especially pronounced with toddlers, whose mothers typically spend much more time with them than fathers do (Leaper, Anderson, & Sanders, 1998). Fathers of toddlers play more roughly with sons and show more sensitivity to daughters (Kelley et al., 1998).

CHECKPOINT

Can you . . .

- ✔ Discuss the implications of research on infant monkeys "raised" by inanimate "mothers"?
- ✔ Compare the roles of fathers and mothers, and describe cultural differences in the ways fathers play with their babies?
- ✔ Describe the influences of mothers and fathers on gender-typing, especially during toddlerhood?

Home observations of 12-month-old, 18-month-old, and 5-year-old children found the biggest gender differences at 18 months, when both mothers and fathers fostered gender-typed play. Parents encouraged girls to communicate but discouraged boys' efforts to do so. Boys received more positive reactions to aggressive behavior and to play with "boys'" toys and fewer positive responses from their fathers (but not their mothers) when they played with "girls'" toys. By the time children were 5 years old, parents treated both sexes about the same—possibly because the children had already become gender-typed and "needed" no more influence in that direction (Fagot & Hagan, 1991).

We discuss gender-typing and gender differences in more depth in Chapter 8.

Developmental Issues in Infancy

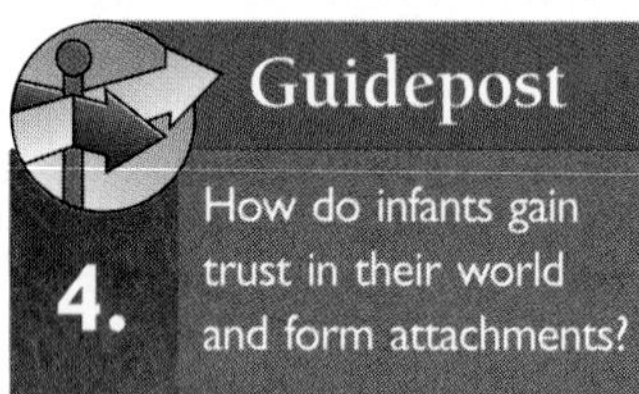

Guidepost
4.
How do infants gain trust in their world and form attachments?

How does a dependent newborn, with a limited emotional repertoire and pressing physical needs, become a 3-year-old with complex feelings, a strong will, and the beginnings of a conscience? Much of this development revolves around issues regarding the self in relation to others. In this section, we look at the development of trust and attachment in infancy and at emotional communication between infants and caregivers—developments that pave the way for the very different issues of toddlerhood. We also look at three phenomena widely believed to be common during late infancy: stranger anxiety, separation anxiety, and social referencing.

Developing Trust

basic trust versus basic mistrust In Erikson's theory, the first crisis in psychosocial development, occurring between birth and about 18 months, in which infants develop a sense of the reliability of people and objects in their world.

For a far longer period than the young of other mammals, human babies are dependent on other people for food, for protection, and for their very lives. How do they come to trust that their needs will be met? According to Erikson (1950), early experiences are the key.

The first of the eight crises, or critical developmental stages, Erikson identified (refer back to Table 2-2 in Chapter 2) is **basic trust versus basic mistrust.** This stage begins in infancy and continues until about 18 months. In these early

According to Erikson, this newborn infant will develop trust in the world through reliance on the mother's sensitive, responsive, consistent caregiving.

months, babies develop a sense of how reliable the people and objects in their world are. They need to develop a balance between trust (which lets them form intimate relationships) and mistrust (which enables them to protect themselves). If trust predominates, as it should, children develop the "virtue" of *hope:* the belief that they can fulfill their needs and obtain their desires (Erikson, 1982). If mistrust predominates, children will view the world as unfriendly and unpredictable and will have trouble forming relationships.

The critical element in developing trust is sensitive, responsive, consistent caregiving. Erikson saw the feeding situation as the setting for establishing the right mix of trust and mistrust. Can the baby count on being fed when hungry, and can the baby therefore trust the mother as a representative of the world? Trust enables an infant to let the mother out of sight "because she has become an inner certainty as well as an outer predictability" (Erikson, 1950, p. 247).

CHECKPOINT

Can you . . .

✔ Explain the importance of Erikson's crisis of basic trust versus basic mistrust and identify what he saw as the critical element in its resolution?

Developing Attachments

Attachment is a reciprocal, enduring emotional tie between an infant and a caregiver, each of whom contributes to the quality of the relationship. Attachments have adaptive value for babies, ensuring that their psychosocial as well as physical needs will be met. According to ethological theory (see Chapter 2), infants and parents are biologically predisposed to become attached to each other. As Mary Ainsworth (1979), a pioneering researcher on attachment, has said, it may be "an essential part of the ground plan of the human species for an infant to become attached to a mother figure" (p. 932).

attachment
Reciprocal, enduring tie between infant and caregiver, each of whom contributes to the quality of the relationship.

Virtually any activity on a baby's part that leads to a response from an adult can be an attachment-seeking behavior: sucking, crying, smiling, clinging, or looking into the caregiver's eyes. As early as the eighth week of life, babies direct some of these behaviors more to their mothers than to anyone else. These overtures are successful when the mother responds warmly, expresses delight, and gives the baby frequent physical contact and freedom to explore (Ainsworth, 1969). Attachment behaviors vary across cultures. Among the Gusii, for example, infants are greeted with handshakes, and Gusii infants reach out for a parent's hand much as western infants cuddle up for a hug (van IJzendoorn & Sagi, 1999).

Ainsworth (1964) described four overlapping stages of attachment behavior during the first year:

1. Before about 2 months, infants respond indiscriminately to anyone.
2. At about 8 to 12 weeks, babies cry, smile, and babble more to the mother than to anyone else but continue to respond to others.

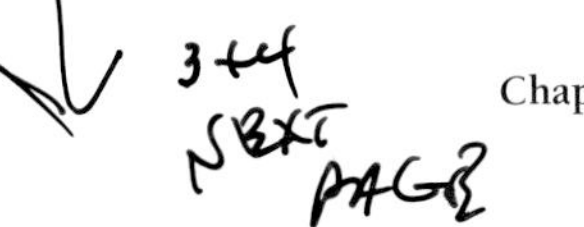

3. At 6 or 7 months, babies show a sharply defined attachment to the mother. Fear of strangers may appear between 6 and 8 months.
4. Meanwhile, babies develop an attachment to one or more other familiar figures, such as the father and siblings.

This sequence may vary in cultures in which infants have multiple caregivers from birth on.

Studying Patterns of Attachment

Ainsworth first studied attachment in the early 1950s with John Bowlby (1951). Then, after studying attachment in African babies in Uganda through naturalistic observation in their homes (Ainsworth, 1967), Ainsworth changed her approach and devised the laboratory-based **Strange Situation,** a now-classic technique designed to assess attachment patterns between an infant and an adult. Typically, the adult is the mother (though other adults have taken part as well), and the infant is 10 to 24 months old.

Strange Situation
Laboratory technique used to study attachment.

The Strange Situation consists of a sequence of eight episodes, which take less than half an hour. During that time, the mother twice leaves the baby in an unfamiliar room, the first time with a stranger. The second time she leaves the baby alone, and the stranger comes back before the mother does. The mother then encourages the baby to explore and play again and gives comfort if the baby seems to need it (Ainsworth, Blehar, Waters, & Wall, 1978). Of particular concern is the baby's response each time the mother returns.

When Ainsworth and her colleagues observed 1-year-olds in the Strange Situation and at home, they found three main patterns of attachment: **secure attachment** (the most common category, into which 66 percent of U.S. babies fell) and two forms of anxious, or insecure, attachment: **avoidant attachment** (20 percent of U.S. babies) and **ambivalent, or resistant, attachment** (12 percent).

secure attachment
Attachment pattern in which an infant cries or protests when the primary caregiver leaves and actively seeks out the caregiver upon the caregiver's return.

avoidant attachment
Attachment pattern in which an infant rarely cries when separated from the primary caregiver and avoids contact upon his or her return.

ambivalent (resistant) attachment
Attachment pattern in which an infant becomes anxious before the primary caregiver leaves, is extremely upset during his or her absence, and both seeks and resists contact on his or her return.

disorganized-disoriented attachment
Attachment pattern in which an infant, after being separated from the primary caregiver, shows contradictory behaviors upon his or her return.

Babies with *secure* attachment cry or protest when the mother leaves and greet her happily when she returns. They use her as secure base, leaving her to go off and explore but returning occasionally for reassurance. They are usually cooperative and relatively free of anger. Babies with *avoidant* attachment rarely cry when the mother leaves, and they avoid her on her return. They tend to be angry and do not reach out in time of need. They dislike being held but dislike being put down even more. Babies with *ambivalent (resistant)* attachment become anxious even before the mother leaves and are very upset when she goes out. When she returns, they show their ambivalence by seeking contact with her while at the same time resisting it by kicking or squirming. Resistant babies do little exploration and are hard to comfort. These three attachment patterns are universal in all cultures in which they have been studied—cultures as different as those in Africa, China and Israel—though the percentage of infants in each category varies (van IJzendoorn & Kroonenberg, 1988; van IJzendoorn & Sagi, 1999).

Later research (Main & Solomon, 1986) has identified a fourth pattern, **disorganized-disoriented attachment**. Babies with the disorganized pattern often show inconsistent, contradictory behaviors. They greet the mother brightly when she returns but then turn away or approach without looking at her. They seem confused and afraid. This may be the least secure pattern. It is most likely to occur in babies whose mothers are single or are insensitive, intrusive, or abusive (Carlson, 1998).

Much research on attachment has been based on the Strange Situation, but some investigators have questioned its validity. The Strange Situation *is* strange; it is also artificial. It sets up a series of eight brief, controlled episodes. It asks mothers not to initiate interaction, exposes babies to repeated comings and goings of adults, and expects the infants to pay attention to them. Since attachment influences a wider range of behaviors than are seen in the Strange Situation, some researchers have called for a more comprehensive, sensitive method to measure it, one that would show how mother and infant interact during natural, nonstressful situations (T. M. Field, 1987).

It has been suggested that the Strange Situation may be especially inappropriate for studying attachment in children of employed mothers, since these children are used to routine separations from their mothers and the presence of other caregivers (K. A. Clarke-Stewart, 1989; L. W. Hoffman, 1989). However, a comparison of 1,153 randomly sampled 15-month-olds born in 10 U.S. cities, who had received varying amounts, types, and quality of day care starting at various ages, found "no evidence . . . that the Strange Situation was less valid for children with extensive child-care experience than for those without" (NICHD Early Child Care Research Network, 1997a, p. 867).

The Strange Situation may be less valid in some nonwestern cultures, which have different expectations for babies' interaction with their mothers and in which mothers may encourage different kinds of attachment-related behavior. Research on Japanese infants, who are less commonly separated from their mothers than U.S. babies, showed high rates of resistant attachment, which may reflect the extreme stressfulness of the Strange Situation for these babies (Miyake, Chen, & Campos, 1985).

Some researchers have begun to supplement the Strange Situation with methods that allow children to be studied in their natural settings. Using a Q-sort technique, observers sort a set of descriptive words or phrases ("cries a lot"; "tends to cling") into categories ranging from most to least characteristic of the child. The Waters and Deane (1985) Attachment Q-set (AQS) has raters (either mothers or other observers) compare descriptions of children's everyday behavior with expert descriptions of the "hypothetical most secure child."

In a cross-cultural study using the AQS, mothers in China, Colombia, Germany, Israel, Japan, Norway, and the United States decribed their children as behaving more like than unlike the "most secure child." Furthermore, the mothers' descriptions of "secure-base" behavior were about as similar across cultures as within a culture. These findings suggest that the tendency to use the mother as a secure base is universal, though it may take somewhat varied forms (Posada et al., 1995).

The Preschool Assessment of Attachment (PAA) (Crittenden, 1993), an instrument for measuring attachment after 20 months of age, takes into account older preschoolers' more complex relationships and language abilities. We will undoubtedly learn more about attachment as researchers develop and use more diversified ways to measure it.

How Attachment Is Established

Both mothers and babies contribute to security of attachment by their personalities and behavior and the way they respond to each other. On the basis of a baby's interactions with the mother, said Ainsworth, the baby builds a "working model" of what can be expected from her. The various patterns of emotional attachment represent different cognitive representations that result in different expectations. As long as the mother continues to act the same way, the model holds up. If her behavior changes—not just once or twice but consistently—the baby may revise the model, and security of attachment may change.

A baby's working model of attachment is related to Erikson's concept of basic trust. Secure attachment evolves from trust; insecure attachment reflects mistrust. Securely attached babies have learned to trust not only their caregivers but their own ability to get what they need.

Many studies show that mothers of securely attached infants and toddlers tend to be sensitive and responsive (Ainsworth et al., 1978; De Wolff & van IJzendoorn, 1997; Isabella, 1993; NICHD Early Child Care Research Network, 1997a). Equally important are other aspects of mothering, such as mutual

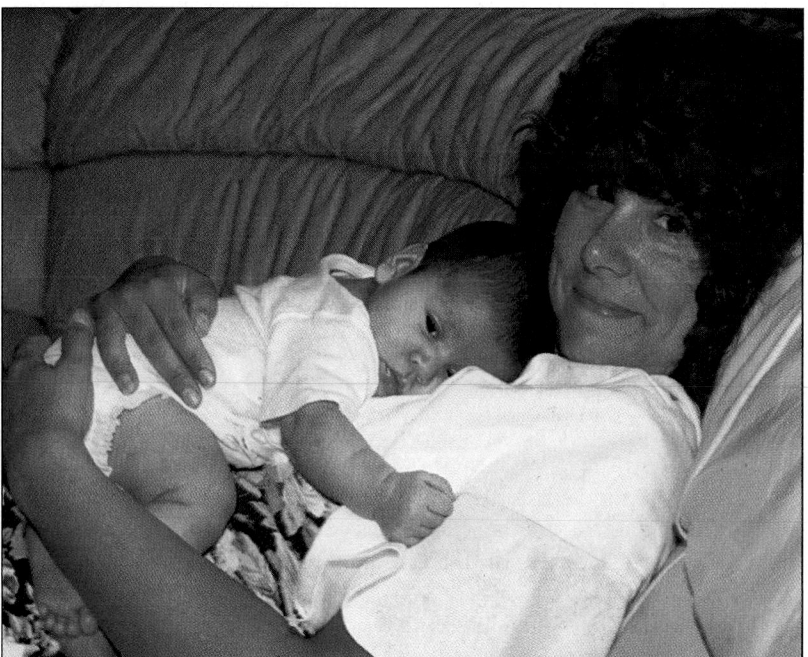

Both Anna and Diane contribute to the attachment between them by the way they act toward each other. The way the baby molds herself to her mother's body shows her trust and reinforces Diane's feelings for her child, which she displays through sensitivity to Anna's needs.

interaction, stimulation, a positive attitude, warmth and acceptance, and emotional support (De Wolff & van IJzendoorn, 1997).

Contextual factors may influence attachment (De Wolff & van IJzendoorn, 1997). One such factor is a mother's employment and her attitude toward the separation it causes. Babies of employed mothers who are highly anxious about being away from home tend to develop avoidant attachments, as measured at 18 months by the Strange Situation (Stifter, Coulehan, & Fish, 1993).

Contrary to Ainsworth's original findings, babies seem to develop attachments to both parents at about the same time, and security of attachment to father and mother is usually quite similar (Fox, Kimmerly, & Schafer, 1991). However, a secure attachment to the father can sometimes offset an insecure attachment to the mother (Engle & Breaux, 1998). Fathers who show delight in their 3-month-olds, who see themselves as important in their babies' development, who are sensitive to their needs, and who place a high priority on spending time with them are likely to have infants who are securely attached at 1 year (Cox, Owen, Henderson, & Margand, 1992).

The usual similarity of type of attachment to the two parents suggests that the baby's temperament may be an important factor (Fox et al., 1991). However, researchers disagree about how much influence temperament exerts and in what ways (Susman-Stillman, Kalkoske, Egeland, & Waldman, 1996; Vaughn et al., 1992). Some studies have identified frustration levels, amounts of crying, and irritability as predictors of attachment (Calkins & Fox, 1992; Izard, Porges, Simons, Haynes, & Cohen, 1991). Neurological or physiological conditions may underlie temperamental differences in attachment. For example, variability in heart rate is associated with irritability, and heart rate seems to vary more in insecurely attached infants (Izard, Porges, et al., 1991). A study of infants from 6 to 12 months and their families (which used frequent home observations, maternal reports, and Q-sorts in addition to the Strange Situation) suggests that both a mother's sensitivity and her baby's temperament are important in establishing attachment patterns (Seifer, Schiller, Sameroff, Resnick, & Riordan, 1996).

Consider this . . .

- Ainsworth's (1964) finding that attachment to the mother develops well before attachment to the father appears to be contradicted by more recent research. Can you suggest possible reasons for the difference in the later findings?

A baby's temperament may have not only a direct impact on attachment but also an indirect impact through its effect on the parents. In one longitudinal study of 114 white middle-class mothers and their babies, infants who were fussy, demanding, and easily frustrated at $2^1/_2$ months tended to be insecurely attached at 13 months (as measured by the Strange Situation). Also, their mothers were more insecure and less emotionally responsive than the mothers of the securely attached infants. The mothers' and babies' emotional states probably fed on each other. The insecure babies' behavior may have made their mothers feel sad, angry, and helpless, though they tended not to show their emotions; and the mothers' emotional inaccessibility may have led the babies to seek attention by crying frequently (Izard, Haynes, Chisholm, & Baak, 1991). As with other issues concerning temperament, "goodness of fit" between parent and child may well be a key to understanding security of attachment.

Intergenerational Transmission of Attachment Patterns

The way a mother remembers her attachment to her parents seems to predict the way her children will be attached to *her.* Parents who can clearly, coherently, and consistently describe their own early experiences with attachment figures—whether those experiences were favorable or unfavorable, secure or insecure—tend to have babies who become securely attached to them (Main, 1995; Main, Kaplan, & Cassidy, 1985).

The **Adult Attachment Interview (AAI)** (George, Kaplan, & Main, 1985) is a semistructured interview that asks adults to recall and interpret feelings and experiences related to their childhood attachments. An analysis of eighteen studies using the AAI found that the clarity, coherence, and consistency of responses reliably predicts the security with which the respondent's own child will be attached to him or her (van IJzendoorn, 1995).

Adult Attachment Interview (AAI)
Instrument for measuring the clarity, coherence, and consistency of an adult's memories of attachment to her or his parents.

Apparently, the way adults recall early experiences with parents or caregivers affects the way they treat their own children. Let's say that Katya, an insecurely attached baby with a rejecting mother, grows up with a mental working model of herself as unlovable. Unless this distorted self-image is later revised, Katya's memory of her relationship with her mother may lead her to misinterpret her baby's attachment behaviors and respond inappropriately. ("How can this child want to love me? How could anybody?") In turn, Katya's insensitivity to the baby's signals misleads the baby, making it difficult for the infant to form a working model of a loving, accepting mother and a lovable self. On the other hand, a mother who was securely attached to *her* mother, or who understands why she was insecurely attached, can accurately recognize the baby's attachment behaviors, respond encouragingly, and help the baby form a secure attachment to her (Bretherton, 1990).

The working model a mother retains from her childhood can affect her relationship with her own child well beyond infancy. Mothers with secure working models (as measured by the AAI) tend to have securely attached toddlers and preschoolers (as measured by the Attachment Q-set) and to show more sensitivity in interacting with them than insecure mothers do (Eiden, Teti, & Corns, 1995). This line of research shows promise for identifying prospective parents at risk of developing unhealthy attachment patterns with their children.

Stranger Anxiety and Separation Anxiety

Sophie used to be a friendly baby, smiling at strangers and going to them, continuing to coo happily as long as someone—anyone—was around. Now, at 8 months, she turns away when a new person approaches and howls when her parents try to leave her with a baby-sitter. Sophie is experiencing both **stranger anxiety,** wariness of a person she does not know, and **separation anxiety,** distress when a familiar caregiver leaves her.

stranger anxiety
Wariness of strange people and places, shown by some infants during the second half of the first year.

separation anxiety
Distress shown by an infant when a familiar caregiver leaves.

Separation anxiety and stranger anxiety used to be considered emotional and cognitive milestones of the second half of infancy, reflecting attachment to the mother. However, newer research suggests that although stranger anxiety and separation anxiety are fairly typical, they are not universal. Whether a baby cries

Sitting on Santa's lap is not a very merry experience for this baby, who may be showing stranger anxiety. Wariness of unfamiliar people and places commonly occurs during the second half of the first year.

when a parent leaves or when someone new approaches may say more about the baby's temperament or life circumstances than about security of attachment (R. J. Davidson & Fox, 1989).

Babies rarely react negatively to strangers before 6 months of age, commonly do so by 8 or 9 months, and do so more and more throughout the rest of the first year (Sroufe, 1997). Even then, however, a baby may react positively to a new person, especially if the mother speaks positively about the stranger (Feinman & Lewis, 1983) or if the person waits a little while and then approaches the baby gradually, gently, and playfully (Sroufe, 1997).

Babies of different ages handle their anxiety differently. In one laboratory experiment (Mangelsdorf, Shapiro, & Marzolf, 1995), 6-month-olds tended to fuss and look away from a stranger, 12-month-olds to soothe themselves by sucking their thumbs, and 18-month-olds to turn their attention elsewhere or try to direct the interaction with the stranger. There are individual and cultural differences, too. Navajo infants show less fear of strangers during the first year of life than Anglo infants do; and Navajo babies who have many opportunities to interact with other people—who have frequent contact with relatives or live close to a trading post—are even less wary of new people than other Navajo infants (Chisholm, 1983).

Separation anxiety may be due, not so much to the separation itself, as to the quality of substitute care. When substitute caregivers are warm and responsive and play with 9-month-olds *before* they cry, the babies cry less than when they are with less responsive caregivers (Gunnar, Larson, Hertsgaard, Harris, & Brodersen, 1992).

Stability of substitute care also is important. The pioneering work by René Spitz (1945, 1946) on institutionalized children emphasizes the need for care as close as possible to good mothering. Research has underlined the value of continuity and consistency in caregiving, so children can form early emotional bonds with their caregivers.

Today, neither intense fear of strangers nor intense protest when the mother leaves is considered to be a sign of secure attachment. Researchers measure attachment more by what happens when the mother returns than by how many tears the baby sheds at her departure.

Long-Term Effects of Attachment

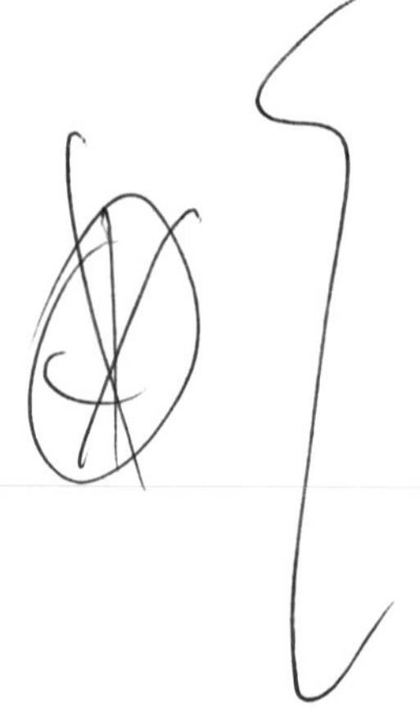

Attachment theory proposes that security of attachment affects children's emotional, social, and cognitive competence (van IJzendoorn & Sagi, 1997). Research tends to bear this out. The more secure a child's attachment to a nurturing adult, the easier it seems to be for the child eventually to become independent of that adult and to develop good relationships with others. The relationship between attachment in infancy and characteristics observed years later underscores the continuity of development and the interrelationship of various aspects of development.

Securely attached toddlers are more sociable with peers and unfamiliar adults than those who are insecurely attached (Elicker, Englund, & Sroufe, 1992; Main, 1983). At 18 to 24 months, they have more positive interactions with peers, and their friendly overtures are more likely to be accepted (Fagot, 1997). From ages 3 to 5, securely attached children are more curious, competent, empathic, resilient, and self-confident, get along better with other children, and are more likely to form close friendships (Arend, Gove, & Sroufe, 1979; Elicker et al., 1992; J. L. Jacobson & Wille, 1986; Waters, Wippman, & Sroufe, 1979; Youngblade & Belsky, 1992). They interact more positively with parents, preschool teachers, and peers and are better able to resolve conflicts (Elicker et al., 1992). They are also more independent, seeking help from teachers only when they need it (Sroufe, Fox, & Pancake, 1983). As preschoolers and kindergartners, they tend to have a more positive self-image (Elicker et al., 1992; Verschueren, Marcoen, & Schoefs, 1996).

Their advantages continue into middle childhood and adolescence (Sroufe, Carlson, & Shulman, 1993). When 10- and 11-year-olds were observed in summer day camp, those with histories of secure attachment were better at making and keeping friends and functioning in a group than children who had been classified as avoidant or resistant. They were also more self-reliant, self-assured, and adaptable and better physically coordinated. In a reunion of 15-year-olds who had gone to camp together, the adolescents who had been securely attached in infancy were rated higher on emotional health, self-esteem, ego resiliency, and peer competence by their counselors and peers and by the researchers who observed them.

If children, on the basis of early experience, have positive expectations about their ability to get along with others and engage in social give and take, and if they think well of themselves, they may set up social situations that tend to reinforce these beliefs and the gratifying interactions that result from them (Elicker et al., 1992; Sroufe et al., 1993). And if children, as infants, had a secure base and could count on parents' or caregivers' responsiveness, they are likely to feel confident enough to be actively engaged in their world. In one study, children with secure working models of attachment at age 7 were rated by teachers at ages 9, 12, and 15 as more attentive and participatory, as having better grades, and as seeming to feel more secure about themselves than children who had had insecure working models of attachment (Jacobsen & Hofmann, 1997).

Conversely, insecurely attached children often have later problems: inhibitions at age 2, hostility toward other children at age 5, and dependency during the school years (Calkins & Fox, 1992; Lyons-Ruth, Alpern, & Repacholi, 1993; Sroufe et al., 1993). Those with disorganized attachment tend to have behavior problems at all levels of schooling and psychiatric disorders at age 17 (Carlson, 1998). However, it may be that the correlations between attachment in infancy and later development stem, not from attachment itself, but from personality characteristics that affect both attachment and parent-child interactions *after* infancy (Lamb, 1987).

CHECKPOINT

Can you . . .

- ✔ Describe four patterns of attachment?
- ✔ Discuss how attachment is established, including the roles of mothers and fathers and of the baby's temperament?
- ✔ Discuss factors affecting stranger anxiety and separation anxiety?
- ✔ Describe long-term behavioral differences influenced by attachment patterns?

Emotional Communication with Caregivers: Mutual Regulation

The interaction between infant and caregiver that influences the quality of attachment depends on the ability of both to respond appropriately to signals about each other's emotional states. This process is called **mutual regulation.** Infants take an active part in this regulatory process. They are not just passive receivers of caregivers' actions; they actively influence how caregivers act toward them.

Guidepost

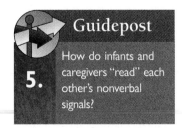

5. How do infants and caregivers "read" each other's nonverbal signals?

Healthy interaction occurs when a caregiver "reads" a baby's signals accurately and responds appropriately. When a baby's goals are met, the baby is joyful, or at least interested (E. Z. Tronick, 1989). If a caregiver ignores an invitation to play or insists on playing when the baby has signaled "I don't feel like it," the baby may feel frustrated or sad. When babies do not achieve the desired results, they keep on sending signals to repair the interaction. Normally, interaction moves back and forth between well-regulated and poorly regulated states, and babies learn from these shifts how to send signals and what to do when their initial signals do not result in a comfortable emotional balance.

mutual regulation
Process by which infant and caregiver communicate emotional states to each other and respond appropriately.

Relationships with parents and other caregivers help babies learn to "read" others' behavior and to develop expectations about it. Even very young infants can perceive emotions expressed by others and can adjust their own behavior accordingly (Lelwica & Haviland, 1983; Termine & Izard, 1988).

"still-face" paradigm Research method used to measure mutual regulation in infants 2 to 9 months old.

The **"still-face" paradigm** is a research method used to measure mutual regulation in infants from 2 to 9 months old. In the *still-face* episode, which follows a normal face-to-face interaction, the mother suddenly becomes stony-faced, silent, and unresponsive. Then, a few minutes later, she resumes normal interaction (the *reunion* episode). During the still-face episode, infants tend to stop smiling and looking at the mother. They may make faces, sounds, or gestures or may touch themselves, their clothing, or a chair, apparently to comfort themselves or to relieve the emotional stress created by the mother's unexpected behavior (Cohn & Tronick, 1983; E. Z. Tronick, 1980; 1989; Weinberg & Tronick, 1996).

How do infants react during the reunion episode? One study combined a microanalysis of 6-month-olds' facial expressions during this episode with measures of heart rate and nervous system reactivity. The infants' reactions were mixed. On the one hand, they showed even more positive behavior—joyous expressions and utterances, and gazes and gestures directed toward the mother—than before the still-face episode. On the other hand, the persistence of sad or angry facial expressions, "pick-me-up" gestures, distancing, and indications of stress, as well as an increased tendency to fuss and cry, suggested that while infants welcome the resumption of interaction with the mother, the negative feelings stirred by the still-face episode are not readily eased. These complex reactions indicate how difficult it must be for babies to cope with repairing a mismatched interaction, such as with a depressed mother (Weinberg & Tronick, 1996; see Box 6-2).

Consider this . . .

- In view of the discussion of ethics of research in Chapter 2, do you see any ethical problems with the still-face paradigm? Are there comparable problems with the Strange Situation? Do you think the benefits of these kinds of research are worth the risks?

Gender differences in mutual regulation have been found as early as 6 months of age. In a laboratory observation using the still-face paradigm, 6-month-old boys seemed to have a harder time than girls in regulating their own emotions. They made their needs known to their mothers through a wider variety of expressive behavior—both positive and negative—than girls did. In normal face-to-face interaction, mothers and sons maintained better coordination of emotional signals than mothers and daughters, but also took longer to repair mismatches (Weinberg, Tronick, Cohn, & Olson, 1999).

According to the mutual regulation model, this baby's playful attempt to "feed" his mother is more than just a game; it is a way of initiating interaction between them. When the mother "reads" her baby's behaviors accurately and responds appropriately, she helps him learn how to send and receive signals.

Box 6-2
How Does a Mother's Depression Affect Her Baby?

Reading emotional signals lets mothers assess and meet babies' needs; and it lets babies influence or respond to the mother's behavior toward them. What happens, then, if that communication system seriously breaks down, and what can be done about it?

Temporary postpartum depression, which affects 10 to 40 percent of new mothers (Kendall-Tackett, 1997), may have little or no impact on the way a mother interacts with her baby, but severe or chronic depression lasting six months or more (which is far less common) can have serious effects (Campbell, Cohn, & Meyers, 1995; Teti, Gelfand, Messinger, & Isabella, 1995). Babies of depressed mothers may give up on sending emotional signals and try to comfort themselves by sucking or rocking. If this defensive reaction becomes habitual, babies learn that they have no power to draw responses from other people, that their mothers are unreliable, and that the world is untrustworthy. They also tend to become depressed themselves (Gelfand & Teti, 1995; Teti et al., 1995).

Do infants become depressed through a failure of mutual regulation with a depressed, unresponsive mother? Or do they inherit a predisposition to depression, or acquire it prenatally through exposure to hormonal or other physiological influences? Evidence is inconclusive (T. Field, 1995). Newborns of mothers with depressive symptoms are less expressive, less active and robust, more excitable, and less oriented to sensory stimuli than other newborns. This would seem to indicate an inborn tendency; but it is possible that, even shortly after birth, negative interactions with a depressed mother have taken a toll (Lundy, Field, & Pickens, 1996). It may well be that a combination of genetic, prenatal, and environmental factors—such as malnutrition, prenatal exposure to cocaine, preterm birth, and the absence of a father or grandmother who could assume some of a depressed mother's caregiving responsibilities—puts infants of depressed mothers at risk of becoming depressed (T. Field, 1995).

We do know that babies of depressed mothers tend to show unusual patterns of brain activity, similar to the mothers' own patterns, though a link between those brain patterns and infants' behavior has not been established. The left frontal region of the human brain seems to be specialized for "approach" emotions such as joy and anger, whereas the right frontal region controls "withdrawal" emotions such as distress and disgust. In one pair of studies, toddlers with depressed mothers showed relatively less activity in the left frontal region than children of nondepressed mothers, both when playing with their mothers and with another familiar adult. This was true of infants both of teenaged, unmarried, low-income mothers, many of whom had substance abuse and other psychological problems, and of infants of adult, married, middle-class mothers without known pathology (G. Dawson, Klinger, Panagiotides, Hill, & Spieker, 1992; G. Dawson et al., 1999). Infants of depressed mothers have shown reduced activity in the left frontal region as early as 3 months and 1 month of age (T. Field, Fox, Pickens, Nawrocki, & Soutollo, 1995; N. A. Jones, Field, Fox, Lundy, & Davalos, 1997) and even within 24 hours after birth. Newborns of depressed mothers also have lower scores on the Brazelton Neonatal Behavior Assessment Scale and lower vagal tone, which is associated with attention and learning. These findings suggest that mothers' depressive symptoms during pregnancy may contribute to newborns' neurological and behavioral functioning (N. A. Jones et al., 1998).

Both as infants and as preschoolers, children with severely or chronically depressed mothers tend to be insecurely attached to them (Gelfand & Teti, 1995; Teti et al., 1995) and seem less upset than other infants when separated from their mothers (Dawson et al., 1992). As infants, they are more likely than other babies to be drowsy or tense, to cry frequently, to look sad or angry more often, and to show interest less often (T. Field, Morrow, & Adelstein, 1993; Pickens & Field, 1993). They are less motivated to explore or to examine and manipulate toys and more apt to prefer relatively unchallenging tasks (Hart, Field, del Valle, & Pelaez-Nogueras, 1998; Redding, Harmon, & Morgan, 1990).

As toddlers these children tend to have trouble suppressing frustration and tension (Cole, Barrett, & Zahn-Waxler, 1992). Toddlers 18 months to 3 years old may respond to signs of a mother's emotional withdrawal by first attempting to reengage the mother's attention and then, when those attempts fail, by moving away from her, making negative bids for attention (such as hitting the mother

Apparently the still-face reaction is universal and is not limited to interactions with mothers. A laboratory observation of 94 four-month-olds found that fathers are equally sensitive to their infants' signals, and infants react similarly to fathers and mothers (Braungart-Rieker, Garwood, Powers, & Notaro, 1998). In a cross-cultural experiment, Chinese 3- to 6-month-olds responded similarly to mothers and fathers—and also to strangers—in comparison with control groups that did

—*Continued*

or a toy, or throwing something at her), staring vacantly, wandering around the room, or simply doing nothing (Seiner & Gelfand, 1995). These children engage in less symbolic play than children of nondepressed mothers. Later they are likely to grow poorly and to perform poorly on cognitive measures, to have accidents, and to have behavior problems (T. M. Field et al., 1985; Gelfand & Teti, 1995; B. S. Zuckerman & Beardslee, 1987).

Professional or paraprofessional home visitors have helped depressed mothers by putting them in touch with community resources, such as parenting groups, and by modeling and reinforcing positive interactions. Interactions with a nondepressed adult—the father or a day care teacher—can help infants compensate for the effects of depressed mothering (T. Field, 1995).

Techniques that may help improve a depressed mother's mood include listening to music, visual imagery, aerobics, yoga, relaxation, and massage therapy (T. Field, 1995). Massage also can help depressed babies. One- to 3-month-old infants of depressed teenage single mothers, when given 6 weeks of biweekly 15-minute massage treatments, were more alert, slept better, cried less, showed less stress, gained more weight, and were more soothable and more sociable than a control group who were rocked instead (T. Field et al., 1996). Massage may have effects on neurological activity. In one study, 10 minutes of massage therapy reduced the asymmetrical pattern of left-right frontal lobe activity typical in infants of depressed mothers (N. A. Jones et al., 1998).

not experience the still-face episode. When the data on responses to the mothers were compared with results of similar studies of Canadian infants, no significant differences emerged, even though Canadian mothers' play with their babies involved more body contact (Kisilevsky et al., 1998).

Social Referencing

If, at a formal dinner party, you have ever cast a sidelong glance to see which fork the person next to you was using, you have read another person's nonverbal signals to get information on how to act. Through **social referencing,** one person forms an understanding of how to act in an ambiguous, confusing, or unfamiliar situation by seeking out and interpreting another person's perception of it. Babies seem to use social referencing when they look at their caregivers upon encountering a new person or toy. This pattern of behavior may begin some time after 6 months of age, when infants begin to judge the possible consequences of events, imitate complex behaviors, and distinguish among and react to various emotional expressions.

social referencing
Understanding an ambiguous situation by seeking out another person's perception of it.

In a study using the visual cliff (a measure of depth perception described in Chapter 4), when the drop looked very shallow or very deep, 1-year-olds did not look to their mothers; they were able to judge for themselves whether to cross over or not. When they were uncertain about the depth of the "cliff," however, they paused at the "edge," looked down, and then looked up at their mothers. Most of the babies whose mothers showed joy or interest crossed the "drop," but very few whose mothers looked angry or afraid crossed it (Sorce, Emde, Campos, & Klinnert, 1985).

However, the idea that infants engage in social referencing has been challenged. Are babies less than 1 year old aware of their own need for knowledge and someone else's ability to furnish it? Although infants as young as 8 or 9 months old do spontaneously look at caregivers in ambiguous situations, it is not clear that they are looking for information; they may be seeking comfort, attention, sharing of feelings, or simply reassurance of the caregiver's presence—typical attachment behaviors (Baldwin & Moses, 1996).

CHECKPOINT

Can you . . .

- ✔ Describe how mutual regulation works?
- ✔ Discuss how a mother's depression can affect her baby?
- ✔ Tell what social referencing is, and give arguments for and against infants' use of it?

About halfway between their first and second birthdays, babies become toddlers. This transformation can be seen not only in such physical and cognitive skills as walking and talking, but in how children express their personalities and interact with others. Let's look at three psychological issues that toddlers—and their caregivers—have to deal with: the emerging *sense of self;* the growth of *autonomy,* or self-determination; and the *internalization of behavioral standards.*

Guidepost

6. When does the sense of self arise?

The Emerging Sense of Self

Before children can take responsibility for their own activities, they must have a cognitive sense of themselves as physically distinct persons separate from the rest of the world, whose characteristics and behavior can be described and evaluated. Self-awareness is the first step toward developing standards of behavior; it lets children understand that a parent's response to something they have done is directed at *them* and not just at the act itself.

How does the **self-concept,** or sense of self, begin to develop? After interviewing the mothers of 123 children 14 to 40 months old, a team of researchers (Stipek, Gralinski, & Kopp, 1990) identified this sequence:

self-concept
Sense of self; descriptive and evaluative mental picture of one's abilities and traits.

1. *Physical self-recognition and self-awareness:* Toddlers recognize themselves in mirrors or pictures by 18 to 24 months, showing awareness of themselves as physically distinct beings. In a classic line of research, investigators dabbed rouge on the noses of 6- to 24-month-olds and sat them in front of a mirror. Three-fourths of 18-month-olds and all 24-month-olds touched their red noses more often than before, whereas babies younger than 15 months never did. This behavior suggests that the older babies knew they didn't normally have red noses and that they recognized the image in the mirror as their own (Lewis, 1997; Lewis & Brooks, 1974). By 20 to 24 months, toddlers begin to use first-person pronouns, another sign of self-awareness (Lewis, 1997).
2. *Self-description and self-evaluation:* Once they have a concept of themselves as distinct beings, children begin to apply descriptive terms ("big" or "little"; "straight hair" or "curly hair") and evaluative ones ("good," "pretty," or "mean") to themselves. This normally occurs sometime between 19 and 30 months, as representational ability and vocabulary expand.
3. *Emotional response to wrongdoing:* The third stage has arrived when children show that they are upset by a parent's disapproval and will stop doing something they are not supposed to do—at least while they are being watched. This stage, which lays the foundation for moral understanding and the development of conscience, comes about more gradually than the second stage, and there is some overlap.

This toddler's attempt to dress himself—clumsy as it may be at first—expresses his strong urge for autonomy.

According to the mothers in this study, children as young as 14 months showed an urge for *autonomy,* or self-determination—refusing help, acting contrary, and resisting attempts to dress or diaper them or pick them up (Stipek et al., 1990). Erikson's theory focuses on autonomy as the main development of toddlerhood.

Guidepost

7. How do toddlers develop autonomy and standards for socially acceptable behavior?

Developing Autonomy

As children mature—physically, cognitively, and emotionally—they are driven to seek independence from the very adults to whom they are attached. Erikson (1950) identified the period from about 18 months to 3 years as the second

autonomy versus shame and doubt
In Erikson's theory, the second crisis in psychosocial development, occurring between about 18 months and 3 years, in which children achieve a balance between self-determination and control by others.

negativism
Behavior characteristic of toddlers, in which they express their desire for independence by resisting authority.

CHECKPOINT

Can you ...

- ✔ Trace three stages in the development of the sense of self during toddlerhood?
- ✔ Describe Erikson's crisis of autonomy versus shame and doubt?
- ✔ Explain why the "terrible twos" are a normal phenomenon?

stage, or crisis, in personality development, **autonomy versus shame and doubt**, which is marked by a shift from external control to self-control. Having come through infancy with a sense of basic trust in the world and an awakening self-awareness, toddlers begin to substitute their own judgment for their caregivers'. The "virtue" that emerges during this stage is *will*. Toilet training is an important step toward autonomy and self-control. So is language; as children are better able to make their wishes understood, they become more powerful and independent.

Since unlimited freedom is neither safe nor healthy, said Erikson, shame and doubt have a necessary place. As in all of Erikson's stages, an appropriate balance is crucial. Self-doubt helps children recognize what they are not yet ready to do, and shame helps them learn to live by reasonable rules. Toddlers need adults to set appropriate limits, and shame and doubt help them recognize the need for those limits.

The "terrible twos" are a normal manifestation of the drive for autonomy. Toddlers have to test the new notion that they are individuals, that they have some control over their world, and that they have new, exciting powers. They are driven to try out their own ideas, exercise their own preferences, and make their own decisions. This drive typically shows itself in the form of **negativism,** the tendency to shout "No!" just for the sake of resisting authority. Almost all children show negativism to some degree; it usually begins before 2 years of age, tends to peak at about $3^1/_2$ to 4, and declines by age 6. Parents and other caregivers who view children's expressions of self-will as a normal, healthy striving for independence, not as stubbornness, can help them learn self-control, contribute to their sense of competence, and avoid excessive conflict. (Box 6-3 gives specific, research-based suggestions for dealing with the "terrible twos.")

Socialization and Internalization: Developing a Conscience

socialization
Process of developing the habits, skills, values, and motives shared by responsible, productive members of a particular society.

internalization
Process by which children accept societal standards of conduct as their own; fundamental to socialization.

Socialization is the process by which children develop habits, skills, values, and motives that make them responsible, productive members of society. Some investigators argue that compliance with parental expectations is a first step toward compliance with societal standards. Socialization rests on **internalization** of these standards. Children who are successfully socialized no longer merely obey rules or commands to get rewards or avoid punishment; they have made society's standards their own (Grusec & Goodnow, 1994; Kochanska & Aksan, 1995; Kochanska, Tjebkes, & Forman, 1998).

Developing Self-Regulation

self-regulation
Child's independent control of behavior to conform to understood social expectations.

Katy, age 2, is about to poke her finger into an electric outlet. In her "child-proofed" apartment, the sockets are covered, but not here in her grandmother's home. When Katy hears her father shout "No!" the toddler pulls her arm back. The next time she goes near an outlet, she starts to point her finger, hesitates, and then says "No." She has stopped herself from doing something she remembers she is not supposed to do. She is beginning to show **self-regulation:** control of her own behavior to conform to a caregiver's demands or expectations, even when the caregiver is not present.

Self-regulation is the foundation of socialization, and it links all domains of development—physical, cognitive, social, and emotional. Until Katy was physically able to get around on her own, electric outlets posed no hazard. To stop herself from poking her finger into an outlet requires that she consciously understand and remember what her father told her. Cognitive awareness, however, is not enough; restraining herself also requires emotional control.

By "reading" their parents' emotional responses to their behavior, children continually absorb information about what conduct their parents approve of. As children process, store, and act upon this information, their strong desire to

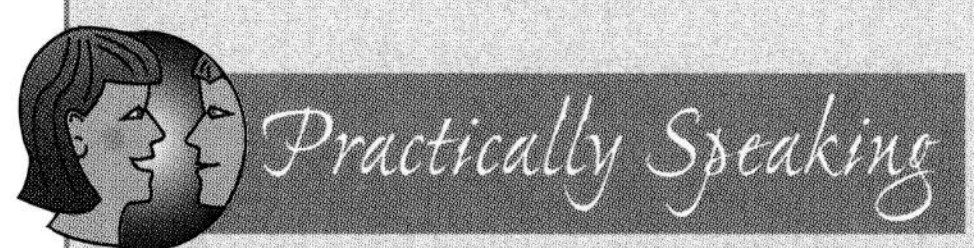

Box 6-3

Dealing with the "Terrible Twos"

The following research-based guidelines can help parents and toddlers get through the "terrible twos" by discouraging negativism and encouraging socially acceptable behavior (Haswell, Hock, & Wenar, 1981; Kochanska & Aksan, 1995; Kopp, 1982; Kuczynski & Kochanska, 1995; Power & Chapieski, 1986):

- *Be flexible.* Learn the child's natural rhythms and special likes and dislikes. The most flexible parents tend to have the least resistant children.
- *Think of yourself as a safe harbor,* with safe limits, from which a child can set out and discover the world—and keep coming back for support.
- *Make your home "child-friendly."* Fill it with unbreakable objects that are safe to explore.
- *Avoid physical punishment.* It is often ineffective and may even lead a toddler to do more damage.
- *Offer a choice*—even a limited one—to give the child some control. For example, "Would you like to have your bath now, or after we read a book?"
- *Be consistent* in enforcing necessary requests. Many children refuse to obey to show their control—but do not really mean what they say and will eventually comply.
- *Don't interrupt an activity unless absolutely necessary.* Try to wait until the child's attention has shifted to something else.
- *If you must interrupt, give warning:* "We have to leave the playground soon." This gives the child time to prepare and either finish an activity or think about resuming it another time.
- *Suggest alternative activities.* When Ashley is throwing sand in Keiko's face, say, "Oh, look! Nobody's on the swings now. Let's go over and I'll give you a good push!"
- *Suggest; don't command.* Accompany requests with smiles or hugs, not criticism, threats, or physical restraint.
- *Link requests with pleasurable activities:* "It's time to stop playing, so that you can go to the store with me."
- *Remind the child of what you expect:* "When we go to this playground, we *never* go outside the gate."
- *Wait a few moments before repeating a request* when a child doesn't comply immediately.
- *Use "time out"* to end conflicts. In a nonpunitive way, remove either yourself or the child from a situation. Very often this results in the resistance diminishing or even disappearing.
- *Expect less self-control during times of stress* (illness, divorce, the birth of a sibling, or a move to a new home).
- *Expect it to be harder for toddlers to comply with "do's" than with "don'ts."* "Clean up your room" takes more effort than "Don't write on the furniture."
- Above all, *keep the atmosphere as positive as possible.* Maintaining a warm, enjoyable relationship is the key to making children *want* to cooperate.

please their parents leads them to do as they know their parents want them to, whether or not the parents are there to see. Mutual regulation of emotional states during infancy contributes to the development of self-control, especially in temperamentally "difficult" children, who may need extra help in achieving it (R. Feldman, Greenbaum, & Yirmiya, 1999).

The growth of self-regulation parallels the development of the self-conscious and evaluative emotions, such as empathy, shame, and guilt (Lewis, 1995, 1997, 1998). It requires flexibility and the ability to wait for gratification. When young children want very badly to do something, however, they easily forget the rules; they may run into the street after a ball or take a forbidden cookie. In most children, then, the full development of self-regulation takes at least three years (Kopp, 1982).

CHECKPOINT

Can you . . .

✔ Tell when and how self-regulation develops and how it contributes to socialization?

Origins of Conscience: Committed Compliance

Internalization of societal standards is essential to the development of **conscience,** which includes both emotional discomfort about doing something wrong and the ability to refrain from doing it (Kochanska, 1993). Conscience depends on the

conscience
Internal standards of behavior, which usually control one's conduct and produce emotional discomfort when violated.

willingness to do the right thing because a child believes it is right, not (as in self-regulation) just because someone else has said so. *Inhibitory control*—conscious, or effortful, control of behavior, a mechanism of self-regulation that emerges during toddlerhood and may be linked to temperament—may contribute to the underpinnings of conscience by first enabling the child to comply with parental do's and don'ts (Kochanska, Murray, & Coy, 1997).

Grazyna Kochanska (1993, 1995, 1997a, 1997b) and her colleagues have sought the origins of conscience in a longitudinal study of a socioeconomically and ethnically mixed group of toddlers and mothers in urban and rural areas of Iowa. Researchers videotaped 103 children ages 26 to 41 months and their mothers playing together for 2 to 3 hours, both at home and in a homelike laboratory setting (Kochanska & Aksan, 1995). After a free-play period, the mother gave the child 15 minutes to put the toys away. The laboratory also had a special shelf with unusually attractive toys, such as a bubble gum machine, a walkie-talkie, a music box, a fishing set, and a beautiful doll. The child was told not to touch anything on the shelf during the entire session. After about an hour, the experimenter asked the mother to go into an adjoining room, leaving the child with the toys. A few minutes later, a strange woman entered, played with several of the toys on the forbidden shelf, and then left the child alone for 8 minutes.

committed compliance
In Kochanska's terminology, a toddler's wholehearted obedience of a parent's orders without reminders or lapses.

situational compliance
In Kochanska's terminology, a toddler's obedience of a parent's orders only in the presence of prompting or other signs of ongoing parental control.

Children were judged to show **committed compliance**, which seems to be an early form of conscience, if they willingly followed the orders to clean up and not to touch the toys, without reminders or lapses. Children showed **situational compliance** if they needed prompting to obey; their compliance depended on ongoing parental control.

Committed compliance is strongly related to internalization of parental values and rules. Children whose mothers rated them as having internalized household rules refrained from touching the forbidden toys even when left alone with them, whereas children whose compliance was only situational tended to yield to temptation when their mothers were out of sight. In a follow-up observation when the children were $3\frac{1}{2}$ to $4\frac{1}{2}$ years old, those who, as toddlers, had shown committed compliance were more likely to show it as they got older, and they also were more likely to have internalized adult rules (Kochanska, Aksan, & Koenig, 1995).

Committed compliance and situational compliance seem to be distinct patterns of behavior, and their roots go back to infancy. The two kinds of compliance can be distinguished in children as young as 13 months. Toddlers who show committed compliance tend to be receptive to maternal teaching. They also tend to be those who, at 8 to 10 months, could focus attention on a set of blocks and could refrain from reaching for an attractive plant when told "No!" Committed compliance increases with age, while situational compliance decreases. Girls are more likely than boys to show committed compliance (Kochanska et al., 1998).

Consider this . . .

- How would you expect each of the three early stages in self-concept development to affect the parent-child relationship?
- In line with stage theorists' belief that each developmental stage lays the groundwork for the next, what difference might security of attachment make in the way a child experiences the next developmental task, development of autonomy?
- In view of Kochanska's research on the roots of conscience, what questions would you ask about the early socialization of antisocial adolescents and adults, whose conscience

Factors in the Success of Socialization

Some children internalize societal standards more readily than others. The way parents go about their job, together with a child's temperament and the quality of the parent-child relationship, may help predict how hard or easy it will be to socialize a child (Kochanska, 1993, 1995, 1997a, 1997b).

A warm, mutually responsive parent-child relationship during the infant and toddler years seems to foster committed compliance and promote smoother, more successful socialization. (Kochanska et al., 1998). This early socialization can have profound long-range echoes: lack of maternal responsiveness in infancy has been linked with the risk of disruptive behavior problems during middle childhood (Wakschlag & Hans, 1999). Children may more readily comply with parental demands when the parent has repeatedly affirmed the child's autonomy—for example, by following the child's lead during play (Kochanska, 1997b).

Mothers of committed compliers are more likely than mothers of situational compliers to rely on gentle guidance rather than force, threats, or other forms of negative control (Kochanska & Aksan, 1995). Gentle guidance seems particularly suited to temperamentally fearful or anxious children, who tend to become upset when they misbehave. Such a child will readily internalize parental messages with a minimum of prodding; displays of power would merely make the child more anxious. Something more is needed with bolder children, but they too are likely to respond better to appeals to cooperate than to threats, and they are more likely to comply if they are securely attached (Kochanska, 1995, 1997a).

CHECKPOINT

Can you . . .

- ✔ Distinguish between committed and situational compliance in relation to conscience?
- ✔ Discuss how temperament and parenting practices affect socialization?

Contact with Other Children

Although parents exert a major influence on children's lives, relationships with other children—both in the home and out of it—are important too, from infancy on.

Guidepost

8. How do infants and toddlers interact with siblings and other children?

Siblings

If you have brothers or sisters, your relationships with them are likely to be the longest-lasting you'll ever have. You and your siblings may have fought continually as children, or you may have been each other's best friends. Either way, they share your roots; they "knew you when," they accepted or rejected the same parental values, and they probably deal with you more candidly than almost anyone else you know.

The Arrival of a New Baby

Children react in various ways to the arrival of a sibling. To bid for the mother's attention, some suck their thumbs, wet their pants, ask to suck from breast or bottle, or use baby talk. Others withdraw, refusing to talk or play. Some suggest taking the baby back to the hospital, giving it away, or flushing it down the toilet. Some take pride in being the "big ones," who can dress themselves, use the potty, eat with the grown-ups, and help care for the baby.

Much of the variation in children's adjustment to a new baby may have to do with such factors as the older child's age, the quality of his or her relationship with the mother, and the family atmosphere. Not surprisingly, attachment to the mother often becomes less secure. According to one longitudinal study, this is most likely to happen to firstborns who are more than 24 months old when the new baby arrives or whose mothers show signs of depression, anxiety, or hostility. Between the third trimester of the pregnancy and one or two months after the birth, security decreased more for 2- to 5-year-olds than for younger children, perhaps because children under 2 are not yet mature enough to see the newcomer as an intruder or a threat. Firstborns younger than 24 months may have a delayed reaction to a new baby as their social and cognitive awareness sharpens. In any event, a lapse in security of attachment is likely to be only temporary unless the birth brings a serious disruption in the caregiving environment (Teti, Sakin, Kucera, Corns, & Eiden, 1996).

The birth of a younger sibling may change the way a mother acts toward an older child. The mother is likely to play less with the older child, to be less sensitive to her or his interests, to give more orders, to have more confrontations, to use physical punishment, and to initiate fewer conversations and games that help develop skills. An older boy, especially, may show temporary behavior problems. This decline in positive interaction with the mother tends to be temporary unless the siblings are less than $2^1/_2$ years apart (Baydar, Greek, & Brooks-Gunn, 1997; Baydar, Hyle, & Brooks-Gunn, 1997; Dunn, 1985; Dunn & Kendrick, 1982). The child's personality makes a difference. Children who take the initiative to start a conversation or play with the mother show less sibling rivalry than those who withdraw. Also, older siblings generally adjust better if their fathers give them extra time and attention to make up for the mother's involvement with the infant (Lamb, 1978).

If the mother has been working outside the home and does not return to work, the arrival of a new baby may mean that the mother can spend more, rather than less, time with the older child. However, with less family income and another mouth to feed, fewer resources for learning (such as play materials and outings) may be available to the older child. Also, financial worries may affect the mother's emotional well-being, contributing to negative maternal interactions with the older sibling. On the positive side, the arrival of a baby tends to enhance the older child's language development, perhaps because the child talks more than before with the father and other family members. In economically disadvantaged families, however, detrimental effects on academic skill development appear by the time the younger sibling is 4 years old and the older one is in school (Baydar, Greek, & Brooks-Gunn, 1997; Baydar, Hyle, & Brooks-Gunn, 1997).

How Siblings Interact

Young children usually become attached to their older brothers and sisters. Babies become upset when their siblings go away, greet them when they come back, prefer them as playmates, and go to them for security when a stranger enters the room. Although rivalry is often present, so is affection. The more securely attached siblings are to their parents, the better they get along with each other (Teti & Ablard, 1989).

Nevertheless, as babies begin to move around and become more assertive, they inevitably come into conflict with older siblings over toys and territory and begin to interfere with their freedom to play. Sibling conflict increases dramatically during the second half of the younger child's second year (Vandell & Bailey, 1992). During this time, younger siblings begin to participate more fully in family interactions and become more involved in family disputes. As they do, they become more aware of others' intentions and feelings. Their actions and expressions suggest that they are beginning to recognize what kind of behavior will upset or annoy an older brother or sister and what behavior is considered "naughty" or "good." They can anticipate what will happen when rules are broken; they show a great deal of interest in older siblings' transgressions and may attempt to support or comfort a sister or brother in trouble (Dunn & Munn, 1985).

This growing cognitive and social understanding accompanies changes in the quality of sibling conflict. Conflict tends to become more constructive and less coercive, with the younger sibling participating in attempts to reconcile. Constructive conflict is limited to the issue at hand, is not highly emotional, and usually leads to a negotiated settlement. It helps children recognize each other's needs, wishes, and point of view, and it helps them learn how to fight, disagree, and compromise within the context of a safe, stable relationship (Vandell & Bailey, 1992).

Infants and toddlers become closely attached to their older brothers and sisters, especially when, as with these Chinese children, the older siblings assume a large measure of care for the younger ones.

Squabbling arises in part from what parents do—or fail to do. When parents show favoritism, are cold, are hostile or punitive, are depressed or unhappy, do not give their children enough attention, fight with each other, or deal inconsistently with sibling conflicts, such conflicts are more likely to occur. Conflicts are less frequent and more constructive when parents reason with children, recognize their feelings and needs, explain a younger child's behavior to the older one, refer to rules, and suggest solutions (Vandell & Bailey, 1992).

Sociability with Nonsiblings

Although the family is the center of a baby's social world, infants and—even more so—toddlers show interest in people outside the home, particularly people their own size. During the first few months, they show interest in other babies in about the same way they respond to their mothers: by looking, smiling, and cooing (T. M. Field, 1978). During the last half of the first year, they increasingly smile at, touch, and babble to another baby, especially when they are not distracted by the presence of adults or toys (Hay, Pedersen, & Nash, 1982).

At about 1 year, when the biggest items on their agenda are learning to walk and to manipulate objects, babies pay more attention to toys and less to other people (T. M. Field & Roopnarine, 1982). This stage does not last long, though; from about $1^1/_2$ years of age to almost 3, they show more interest in what other children do and increasing understanding of how to deal with them. This insight seems to accompany awareness of themselves as separate individuals. A 10-month-old who holds out a toy to another baby pays no attention to whether the other's back is turned, but an 18-month-old toddler knows when the offer has the best chance of being accepted and how to respond to another child's overtures (Eckerman, Davis, & Didow, 1989; Eckerman & Stein, 1982).

Toddlers learn by imitating one another. Imitative games such as follow-the-leader help toddlers connect with other children and pave the way for more complex games during the preschool years (Eckerman et al., 1989). As with siblings, conflict, too, can have a purpose: helping children learn how to negotiate and resolve disputes. In one study, groups of three toddlers who had not known one another before were observed playing with toys. Overall, the children got along well—sharing, showing, and demonstrating toys to one another, even just before and after squabbling over them. Two-year-olds got into more conflicts than 1-year-olds but also resolved them more often—for example, by sharing toys when there were not enough to go around (Caplan, Vespo, Pedersen, & Hay, 1991).

Some children, of course, are more sociable than others, reflecting such temperamental traits as their usual mood, readiness to accept new people, and ability to adapt to change. Sociability is also influenced by experience; babies who spend time with other babies become sociable earlier than those who spend all their time at home alone. As children grow older and enter more and more into the world beyond the home, social skills become increasingly important. For many children the first step into that wider world is entrance into organized child care.

CHECKPOINT

Can you . . .

- ✔ Discuss factors affecting adjustment to a new baby?
- ✔ Describe changes in sibling interaction and sibling conflict during toddlerhood?
- ✔ Trace changes in sociability during the first 3 years?

Children of Working Parents

In 1998, almost 58 percent of women with children under the age of 3, and nearly 54 percent of mothers of infants in their first year of life, were in the labor force (Bureau of Labor Statistics, 1999a). Early nonparental child care is now a way of life for most U.S. families, and its impact is the subject of much debate.

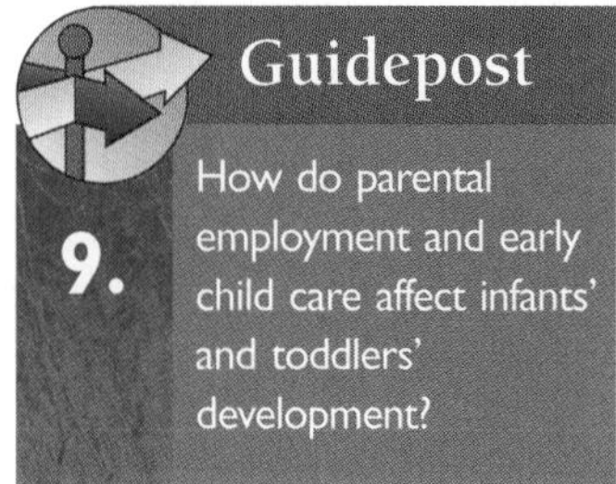

Guidepost
9.
How do parental employment and early child care affect infants' and toddlers' development?

Effects of Parental Employment

What are the short-term and long-term consequences of a mother's going to work during the first 3 years of her child's life? Hardly any, according to a recent study based on the National Longitudinal Survey of Youth (NLSY).

The NLSY is an annual survey of some 12,600 women, accompanied by assessments of their children. Earlier studies of effects of maternal employment based on NLSY data yielded conflicting results, probably because of methodological inconsistencies. Also, the original sample contained unrepresentatively large proportions of low-income and minority women.

Now, a reanalysis of 1994 NLSY data, based on a larger and more representative sample (Harvey, 1999), has found little or no effect of early maternal employment on children's compliance, behavior problems, self-esteem, cognitive development, or academic achievement. Three- and 4-year-olds whose mothers had returned to work later were slightly more compliant than children the same age whose mothers had returned to work sooner, and children whose mothers had worked long hours during the first 3 years scored slightly lower on tests of vocabulary and achievement during the early school years; but these differences were small and faded over time. As in a number of other studies, early maternal employment seemed to benefit children in low-income families by increasing the family's resources. The study found no significant effects of fathers' working hours.

In Chapter 10, we'll discuss effects of parents' work on older children.

The Impact of Early Child Care

One way parents' working affects children is through substitute child care. When we think about effects of early child care, we need to consider variations in type, quality, amount, and stability of care, as well as the age at which children start receiving it.

In 1995, of the nearly 21 million children under the age of 5 who were not yet in school, about 60 percent received nonparental child care—21 percent from other relatives, 31 percent in child care centers, 14 percent in family child care homes, and 4 percent from sitters in the child's home (Hofferth, 1996). (Some children received more than one type of care.) In home settings, where most U.S. babies stay during the first year of life, quality of care is related to income. In child care centers, which are more popular for older children, poor and affluent children receive better quality care than those in the middle, who usually do not benefit from federal subsidies (NICHD Early Child Care Research Network, 1997b). Most child care centers do not meet all recommended guidelines for child-staff ratios, group sizes, teacher training, and teacher education (NICHD Early Child Care Research Network, 1998b). Table 6-3 lists guidelines for judging quality of care.

The most important element in the quality of care is the caregiver; stimulating interactions with responsive adults are crucial to early cognitive and linguistic as well as emotional and social development (Burchinal, Roberts, Nabors, & Bryant, 1996). Low staff turnover is critical; infants need consistent caregiving in order to develop trust and secure attachments. In one longitudinal study, 4-year-olds who had formed secure attachments to child care providers tended to be more sociable, sensitive, em-

These children in a high-quality group day care program are likely to do at least as well cognitively and socially as children cared for full time at home. The most important element of infant day care is the caregiver or teacher, who exerts a strong influence on the children in her care.

Table 6-3 Checklist for Choosing a Good Child Care Facility

- Is the facility licensed? Does it meet minimum state standards for health, fire, and safety? (Many centers and home care facilities are not licensed or regulated.)
- Is the facility clean and safe? Does it have adequate indoor and outdoor space?
- Does the facility have small groups, a high adult-to-child ratio, and a stable, competent, highly involved staff?
- Are caregivers trained in child development?
- Are caregivers warm, affectionate, accepting, responsive, and sensitive? Are they authoritative but not too restrictive, and neither too controlling nor merely custodial?
- Does the program promote good health habits?
- Does it provide a balance between structured activities and free play? Are activities age-appropriate?
- Do the children have access to educational toys and materials, which stimulate mastery of cognitive and communicative skills at a child's own pace?
- Does the program nurture self-confidence, curiosity, creativity, and self-discipline?
- Does it encourage children to ask questions, solve problems, express feelings and opinions, and make decisions?
- Does it foster self-esteem, respect for others, and social skills?
- Does it help parents improve their child-rearing skills?
- Does it promote cooperation with public and private schools and the community?

Sources: AAP, 1986; Belsky, 1984; Clarke-Stewart, 1987; NICHD Early Child Care Research Network, 1996; S. W. Olds, 1989; Scarr, 1998.

pathic, and better liked than those who were insecurely attached (Howes, Matheson, & Hamilton, 1994).

The most comprehensive research on early child care to date is sponsored by the National Institute of Child Health and Human Development (NICHD). This ongoing longitudinal study of 1,364 children and their families began in 1991 in ten university centers across the United States, shortly after the children's birth. The sample was diverse socioeconomically, educationally, and ethnically; nearly 35 percent of the families were poor or near-poor. Most infants entered nonmaternal care before 4 months of age and received, on average, 33 hours of care each week. Child care arrangements varied widely in type and quality (Peth-Pierce, 1998).

The study was designed to measure the contribution child care makes to developmental outcomes, apart from the influences of family characteristics, the child's characteristics, and the care the child receives at home. Through observation, interviews, questionnaires, and tests, researchers measured the children's social, emotional, cognitive, and physical development at frequent intervals from 1 month of age through the first 7 years of life. So far, results have been published for the first 3 years (Peth-Pierce, 1998). What do they show?

The quantity and quality of care children receive, as well as the type and stability of care, influence several aspects of development—emotional, social, and cognitive (Peth-Pierce, 1998; see Table 6-4). However, factors related to child care seem to be less influential than family characteristics, such as income and the mother's educational level. These characteristics strongly predict developmental outcomes, regardless of whether children are in child care more than 30 hours a week or less than 10 hours (NICHD Early Child Care Research Network, in press).

Children who spend longer hours in outside care do tend to receive less sensitive mothering and to be less engaged with their mothers, suggesting that the amount of time mother and child spend together may influence their ease and comfort with each other. Also, children in high-quality care tend to receive more sensitive mothering than children in lower-quality care; perhaps sensitive, involved caregivers provide mothers with positive role models or emotional support. However, these correlations are modest, particularly in comparison with family characteristics. The mother's education, for example, is a stronger

Table 6-4 Aspects of Development Affected by Characteristics of Early Child Care*

	Attachment	Parent-Child Relationships	Cooperation	Problem Behaviors	Cognitive Development and School Readiness	Language Development
Quality	•	•		+	+	+
Amount	•	•		•		
Type			•	•	+	+
Stability	•		•			

+Consistent effects; • Effects under some conditions.
*Results after taking into account all family and child variables.

Source: Peth-Pierce, 1998, summary table of findings, p. 15.

predictor of the mother's sensitivity than either quantity or quality of care (NICHD Early Child Care Research Network, 1999a). Similarly, caregivers' sensitivity and responsiveness influence toddlers' self-control and compliance and the likelihood of problem behavior, but the mother's sensitivity has a greater influence (NICHD Early Child Care Research Network, 1998a).

Sometimes family and child care characteristics work together. For example, child care itself has no direct effect on attachment (as measured at 15 months by the Strange Situation), no matter how early infants enter care or how many hours they spend in it. Nor do the stability or quality of care matter, in and of themselves. However, when unstable, poor quality, or more-than-minimal amounts of child care (10 or more hours a week) are added to the impact of insensitive, unresponsive mothering, insecure attachment is more likely. On the other hand, high-quality care may help to offset insensitive mothering (NICHD Early Child Care Research Network, 1997a).

Quality of care contributes to cognitive and psychosocial development. Children in child care centers with low child-staff ratios, small group sizes, and trained caregivers who provide positive interaction and language stimulation score higher on tests of language comprehension and readiness for school. Their mothers report fewer behavior problems (NICHD Early Child Care Research Network, 1997c; NICHD Early Child Care Research Network, 1999b). Cognitive benefits are independent of income level or ethnic background, and children in full-time mother-care show no advantage. Once again, though, family income, the mother's vocabulary, the home environment, and the amount of mental stimulation the mother provides are even more influential (NICHD Early Child Care Research Network, 1997c).

It should not be surprising that what look on the surface like effects of child care may often be effects of family characteristics. After all, stable families with high incomes and educational backgrounds and favorable home environments are more likely to place their children in high-quality care. It will be illuminating to follow the long-term progress of the NICHD sample; in some earlier longitudinal studies, apparent early effects of child care faded out during the school years, while family characteristics continued to be important (Scarr, 1997b).

CHECKPOINT

Can you . . .

- ✔ List at least five criteria for good child care?
- ✔ Compare the impact of child care and of family characteristics on emotional, social, and cognitive development?

Even if child care may have little long-term effect on most children, those from low-income families or stressful homes do seem to benefit from care that supplies emotional support and cognitive stimulation, which may otherwise be lacking in their lives (Scarr, 1997b). Disadvantaged children in good child care programs tend not to show the declines in IQ often seen when such children reach school age, and they may be more motivated to learn (AAP, 1986; Belsky, 1984; Bronfenbrenner, Belsky, & Steinberg, 1977). Even modest improvements in care may make a difference. Among 79 African American 1-year-olds who had been in poor to mediocre urban community-based day care centers full time for two months or more, those getting mediocre care scored higher on the Bayley scales, as well as on measures of language and communicative skills, even after adjusting for such factors as gender, poverty, and characteristics of the home environment (Burchinal et al., 1996).

However infants and toddlers are cared for, the experiences of the first 3 years lay the foundation for future development. In Part Three, we'll see how young children build on that foundation.

Consider this . . .

- In the light of findings about effects of early child care, what advice would you give a new mother about the timing of her return to work and the selection of child care?

Summary

Foundations of Psychosocial Development

Guidepost 1. When and how do emotions develop, and how do babies show them?

- The development and expression of various **emotions** seem to be tied to brain maturation and cognitive development.
- Crying, smiling, and laughing are early signs of emotion. Other indices of emotion include facial expressions, motor activity, body language, and physiological changes.
- The repertoire of basic emotions seems to be universal, but there are cultural variations in their expression.
- Complex emotions seem to develop from earlier, simpler ones. Self-conscious and evaluative emotions arise after the development of **self-awareness.**
- Separate but interacting regions of the brain may be responsible for various emotional states.

Guidepost 2. How do infants show temperamental differences, and how enduring are those differences?

- Children seem to fall into three categories of **temperament: easy children, difficult children,** and **slow-to-warm-up children.** These temperamental patterns, as well as an aspect of temperament called *inhibition to the unfamiliar,* appear to be largely inborn and are generally stable but can be modified by experience.
- **Goodness of fit** between a child's temperament and environmental demands aids adjustment.
- Cross-cultural differences in temperament may reflect genetic variations, prenatal experience, or culturally influenced childraising practices.

Guidepost 3. What roles do mothers and fathers play in early personality development?

- Childraising practices and caregiving roles vary around the world.
- Unlike the phenomenon of **imprinting** in animals, there does not seem to be a critical period for forming the **mother-infant bond.** However, infants do have strong needs for maternal closeness and warmth as well as physical care.
- In most cultures, mothers, even when employed outside the home, do more infant care than fathers. Mothers and fathers in some cultures have different styles of play with babies.
- Significant **gender** differences typically do not appear until after infancy. However, parents begin **gender-typing** boys and girls almost from birth.

Developmental Issues in Infancy

Guidepost 4. How do infants gain trust in their world and form attachments?

- According to Erikson, infants in the first 18 months of life experience the first crisis in personality development, **basic trust versus basic mistrust.** Sensitive, responsive, consistent caregiving is the key to successful resolution of this crisis.
- Most research on **attachment** is based on the **Strange Situation.** Three main patterns have been found: **secure attachment** and two types of insecure attachment, **avoidant attachment** and **ambivalent (resistant) attachment.** A fourth pattern, **disorganized-disoriented attachment,** may be the least secure.
- Newer instruments have been developed for measuring attachment in natural settings and in cross-cultural research. The **Adult Attachment Interview (AII)** can predict the security of attachment on the basis of a parent's memories of her or his own childhood attachment.
- Attachment patterns may depend on a baby's temperament, as well as on the quality of parenting, and may have long-term implications for development.
- **Separation anxiety** and **stranger anxiety** may arise during the second half of the first year. Although once thought to be signs of attachment, they appear to be related to temperament and circumstances.

Guidepost 5. How do infants and caregivers "read" each other's nonverbal signals?

- **Mutual regulation** enables babies to play an active part in regulating their emotional states by sending and receiving emotional signals. Researchers gauge mutual regulation by the **"still-face" paradigm.**
- A mother's depression, especially if severe or chronic, can have serious consequences for her infant's development.
- The belief that babies, after about 6 months of age, display **social referencing** is in dispute.

Developmental Issues in Toddlerhood

Guidepost 6. When does the sense of self arise?

- The **self-concept** begins to emerge in the following sequence, beginning at about 18 months: (1) physical self-recognition and self-awareness, (2) self-description and self-evaluation, and (3) emotional response to wrongdoing.

Guidepost 7. How do toddlers develop autonomy and standards for socially acceptable behavior?

- Erikson's second crisis (about 18 months to 3 years) concerns **autonomy versus shame and doubt. Negativism** is a normal manifestation of the shift from external control to self-control.
- **Socialization,** which rests on **internalization** of societally approved standards, begins with the development of **self-regulation.** A precursor of **conscience** is **committed compliance** to a caregiver's demands; toddlers who show committed compliance tend to internalize adult rules more readily than those who show merely **situational compliance.**
- Parenting practices, a child's temperament, and the quality of the parent-child relationship may be factors in the ease and success of socialization.

Contact with Other Children

Guidepost 8. How do infants and toddlers interact with siblings and other children?

- Siblings influence each other both positively and negatively from an early age. Parents' actions and attitudes affect sibling relationships.
- Contact with other children, especially during toddlerhood, affects cognitive and psychosocial development.

Children of Working Parents

Guidepost 9. How do parental employment and early child care affect infants' and toddlers' development?

- Mothers' workforce participation during a child's first three years seems to have little or no impact on the child's development.
- Substitute child care varies widely in type and quality. The most important element in quality of care is the caregiver.
- Although quality, quantity, stability, and type of care have some influence on psychosocial and cognitive development, the influence of family characteristics seems greater.
- Low-income children, especially, benefit from good child care.

Key Terms

emotions (197)
self-awareness (200)
temperament (202)
easy children (203)
difficult children (203)
slow-to-warm-up children (203)
goodness of fit (203)
imprinting (208)
mother-infant bond (208)
gender (210)
gender-typing (210)
basic trust versus basic mistrust (210)
attachment (211)
Strange Situation (212)
secure attachment (212)
avoidant attachment (212)
ambivalent (resistant) attachment (212)
disorganized-disoriented attachment (212)
Adult Attachment Interview (AAI) (215)
stranger anxiety (215)
separation anxiety (215)
mutual regulation (217)
"still-face" paradigm (218)
social referencing (220)
self-concept (221)
autonomy versus shame and doubt (222)
negativism (222)
socialization (222)
internalization (222)
self-regulation (222)
conscience (223)
committed compliance (224)
situational compliance (224)

Part Three

Early Childhood

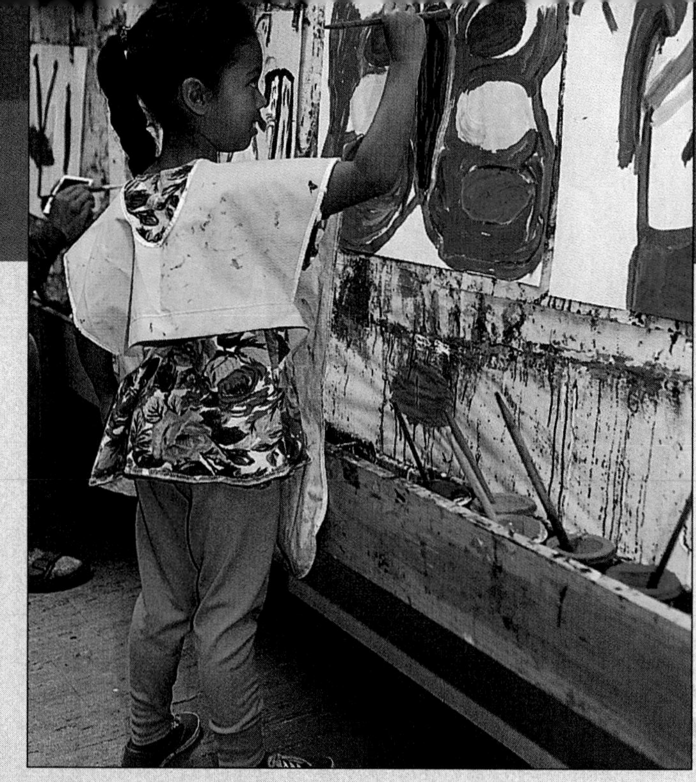

During the years from 3 to 6, often called the preschool years, *children make the transition from toddlerhood to childhood. Their bodies become slimmer, their motor and mental abilities sharper, and their personalities and relationships more complex.*

The 3-year-old is no longer a baby, but a sturdy adventurer, at home in the world and eager to explore its possibilities as well as the developing capabilities of his or her own body and mind. A child of this age has come through a relatively dangerous time of life—the years of infancy and toddlerhood—to enter a healthier, less threatening phase.

Growth and change are less rapid in early childhood than in infancy and toddlerhood, but, as we see in Chapters 7 and 8, all aspects of development—physical, cognitive, emotional, and social—continue to intertwine.

Linkups to Look For

- As muscles come under more conscious control, children can tend to more of their own personal needs, such as dressing and toileting, and thus gain a greater sense of competence and independence.
- Eating and sleep patterns are influenced by cultural attitudes.
- Even the common cold can have emotional and cognitive implications. Occasional minor illnesses not only build immunity; they help children learn to cope with physical distress and understand its causes.
- Social interaction plays a major role in the development of preliteracy skills, memory, and measured intelligence.
- Cognitive awareness of gender has far-reaching psychosocial implications, affecting children's sense of self and their attitudes toward the roles the two sexes play in their society.
- Environmental influences, including the parents' life circumstances, affect health and safety. The link between developmental realms is especially evident in the tragic results of child abuse and neglect; although the most obvious effects may be physical, these conditions can stunt cognitive growth and can leave lasting emotional scars.

Early Childhood: *A Preview*

Chapter 7

Physical and Cognitive Development in Early Childhood

Growth is steady; appearance becomes more slender and proportions more adultlike.
Appetite diminishes, and sleep problems are common.
Handedness appears; fine and gross motor skills and strength improve.
Thinking is somewhat egocentric, but understanding of other people's perspectives grows.
Cognitive immaturity leads to some illogical ideas about the world.
Memory and language improve.
Intelligence becomes more predictable.
Preschool experience is common, and kindergarten more so.

Chapter 8

Psychosocial Development in Early Childhood

Self-concept and understanding of emotions become more complex; self-esteem is global.
Independence, initiative, and self-control increase.
Gender identity develops.
Play becomes more imaginative, more elaborate, and usually more social.
Altruism, aggression, and fearfulness are common.
Family is still the focus of social life, but other children become more important.

Chapter 7

Physical and Cognitive Development in Early Childhood

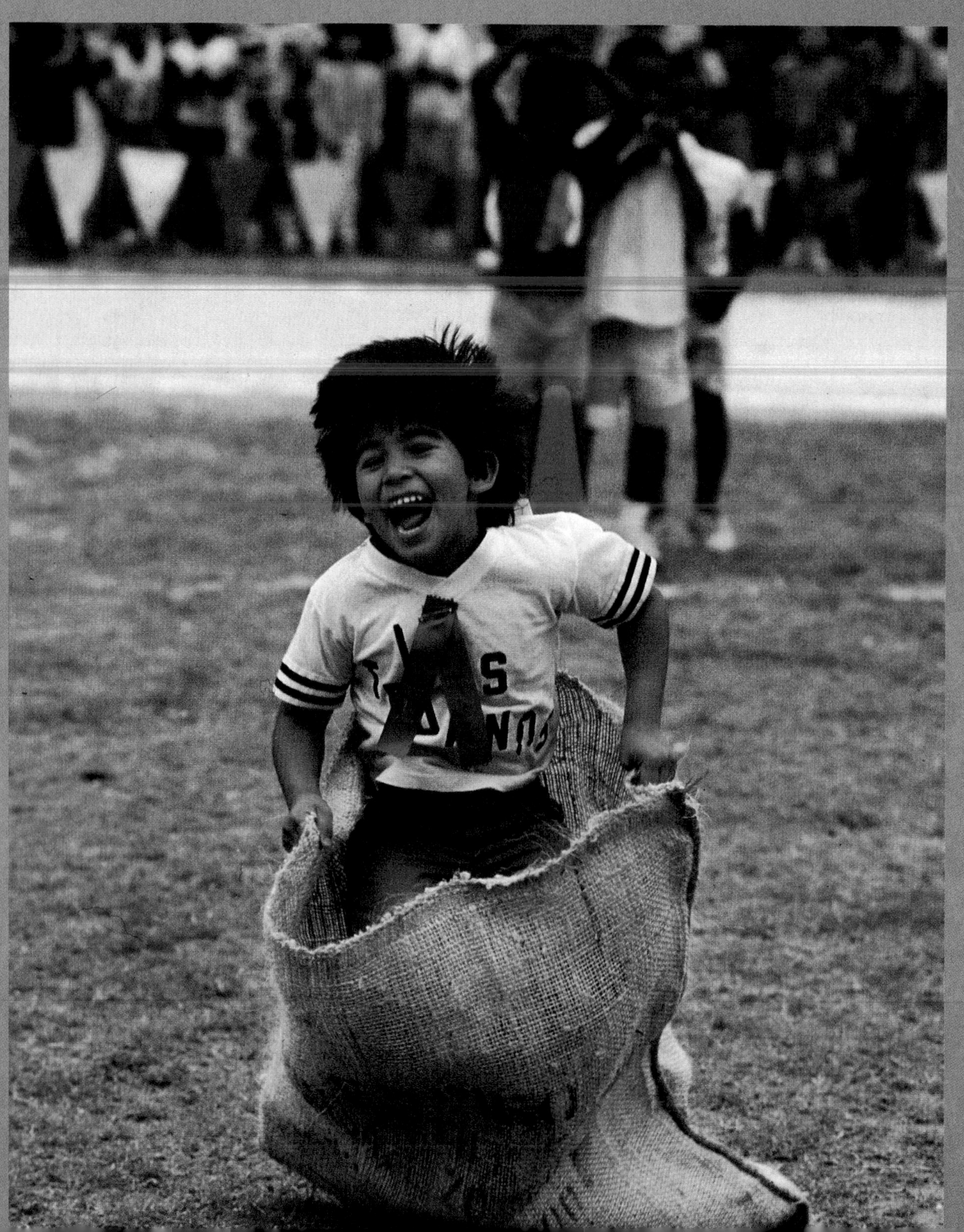

Children live in a world of imagination and feeling. . . . They invest the most insignificant object with any form they please, and see in it whatever they wish to see.

Adam G. Oehlenschlager

OUTLINE

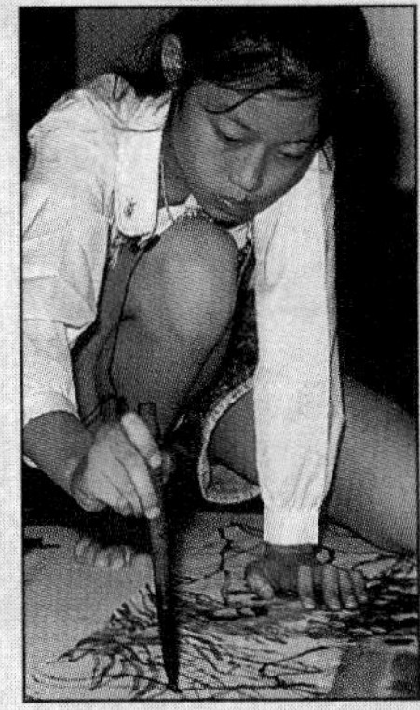

Wang Yani

Focus: Wang Yani, Self-Taught Artist*

Wang Yani (b. 1975) is a gifted young Chinese artist. Now in her twenties, she had her first exhibit in Shanghai at the age of 4 and produced 4,000 paintings by the time she turned 6. Since she was 10, her work has been shown throughout Asia and in Europe and the United States. Yet, as a child, she never took art lessons.

Yani (her given name)** began painting at 2½. Her father, Wang Shiqiang, was a professional artist and educator. One day she picked up a piece of charcoal and began drawing on the wall, imitating her father as she stood back, head tilted, arm on hip, to examine her creation. Her father gave her big brushes and large sheets of paper to permit bold strokes. Rather than teach her, he let her learn by doing, in her own way, and always praised her work. In contrast with traditional Chinese art education, which emphasizes conformity and imitation, he allowed his daughter's imagination free rein.

Yani went through the usual stages in preschoolers' drawing, from scribbling to pictorial, but far more quickly than usual. Her early paintings after the scribble stage were made up of dots, circles, and apparently meaningless lines, which stood for people, birds, or fruit. By the age of 3, she painted recognizable but highly original forms.

*Sources of biographical information about Wang Yani were Bond (1989), Costello (1990), Ho (1989), Stuart (1991), and Zhensun & Low (1991).

**In Chinese custom, the given name follows the family name.

Yani's father encouraged her to paint what she saw outdoors near their home in the scenic riverside town of Gongcheng. Like traditional Chinese artists, she did not paint from life but constructed her brightly colored compositions from mental images—vivid memories of what she had seen. Her visual memory has been called astounding. When she was only 4, her father taught her Chinese characters (letters) of as many as 25 strokes by "writing" them in the air with his finger. Yani immediately put them down on paper.

Her father helped develop her powers of observation and imagery by carrying her on his shoulders as he hiked in the fields and mountains or lying with her in the grass and telling stories about the passing clouds. The pebbles along the riverbank reminded her of the monkeys at the zoo, which she painted over and over between the ages of 3 and 6. Yani made up stories about the monkeys she created. They often represented Yani herself—eating a snack, refereeing an argument among friends, or trying to conquer her fear of her first shot at the doctor's office. Painting, to Yani, was not an objective representation of reality; it was a mirror of her mind, a way to transform her sensory impressions into simple but powerful semiabstract images onto which she projected her thoughts, feelings, and dreams.

Because of her short arms, Yani's brush strokes at first were short. Her father trained her to hold her brush tightly, by trying to grab it from behind when she was not looking. She learned to paint with her whole arm, twisting her wrist to produce the effect she wanted. As her physical dexterity and experience grew, her strokes became more forceful, varied, and precise: broad, wet strokes to define an animal's shape; fuzzy, nearly dry ones to suggest feathers, fur, or tree bark.

As she grew older, Yani's subjects expanded to include landscapes, pine trees, and lotus flowers. The materials she used—bamboo brushes, ink sticks, and rice paper—were traditional, but her style—popularly called *xieyi,* "idea writing"—was not. It was, and remains, playful, free, and spontaneous.

With quick reflexes, a fertile imagination, remarkable visual abilities, strong motivation, and her father's sensitive guidance, Yani's artistic progress has been swift. As a young adult, she is considered an artist of great promise. Yet she herself finds painting very simple: "You just paint what you think about. You don't have to follow any instruction. Everybody can paint" (Zhensun & Low, 1991, p. 9).

Although Wang Yani's artistic growth has been unusual, it rested on typical developments of early childhood: rapid improvement in muscular control and eye-hand coordination, accompanied by a growing understanding of the world around her—an understanding guided by her powers of observation and memory and her verbal interactions with her father. Together these physical, cognitive, and social influences helped her express her thoughts and emotions through art.

In this chapter, we look at physical and cognitive development during the years from 3 to 6. Youngsters in this age group grow more slowly than before, but still at a fast pace; and they make so much progress in muscle development and coordination that they can do much more. Children also make enormous advances in the abilities to think, speak, and remember. In this chapter, we trace all these developing capabilities and consider several important concerns. We also assess the increasingly common experience of early childhood education.

After you have read and studied this chapter, you should be able to answer the following questions:

cH. 7

Guideposts *for* Study

1. How do children's bodies change between ages 3 and 6, and what are their nutritional needs?

2. What sleep patterns and problems tend to develop during early childhood?

3. What are the main motor achievements of early childhood?

4. What are the major health and safety risks for children?

5. What are some typical cognitive advances and some immature aspects of young children's thinking?

6. How does language improve, and what happens when its development is delayed?

7. What memory abilities expand in early childhood?

8. How is preschoolers' intelligence measured, and what are some influences on it?

9. What purposes does early childhood education serve, and how do children make the transition to kindergarten?

Physical Development

Aspects of Physiological Development

In early childhood, children slim down and shoot up. They need less sleep than before and are more likely to develop sleep problems. They improve in running, hopping, skipping, jumping, and throwing balls. They also become better at tying shoelaces (in bows instead of knots), drawing with crayons (on paper rather than on walls), and pouring cereal (into the bowl, not onto the floor); and they begin to show a preference for either the right or left hand.

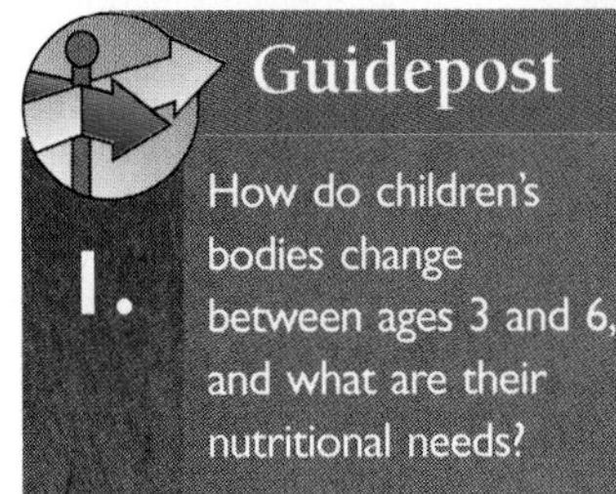

Guidepost

1. How do children's bodies change between ages 3 and 6, and what are their nutritional needs?

Bodily Growth and Change

At about age 3, children begin to take on the slender, athletic appearance of childhood. As abdominal muscles develop, the toddler potbelly tightens. The trunk, arms, and legs grow longer. The head is still relatively large, but the other parts of the body continue to catch up as body proportions steadily become more adultlike.

The pencil mark on the wall that shows Eve's height at 3 years is a little more than 37 inches from the floor, and she now weighs more than 31 pounds. Her twin brother, Isaac, like most boys this age, is slightly taller and heavier and has more muscle per pound of body weight, whereas Eve, like most girls, has more fatty tissue. Both boys and girls typically grow 2 to 3 inches a year during early childhood and gain 4 to 6 pounds annually. Boys' slight edge in height and weight continues until the growth spurt of puberty.

These changes in appearance reflect developments inside the body. Muscular and skeletal growth progresses, making children stronger. Cartilage turns to bone at a faster rate than before, and bones become harder, giving the child a firmer shape and protecting the internal organs. These changes, coordinated by the maturing brain and nervous system, promote the development of a wide range of motor skills. The increased capacities of the respiratory and circulatory systems build physical stamina and, along with the developing immune system, keep children healthier.

Nutrition and Dentition

Preschoolers eat less in proportion to their size than infants do; as growth slows, they need fewer calories per pound of body weight. Preschoolers who are allowed to eat when they are hungry and are not pressured to eat everything given to them are more likely to regulate their own caloric intake than are children fed on schedule (S. L. Johnson & Birch, 1994). In one study of self-regulated feeding, 15 children ages 2 to 5 took in roughly the same number of calories every day for six days, even though they often ate very little at one meal and a great deal at another (Birch, Johnson, Andersen, Peters, & Schulte, 1991).

Children over age 2 should get only about 30 percent of their total calories from fat, and less than 10 percent of the total from saturated fat. Lean meat and dairy foods should remain in the diet to provide protein, iron, and calcium. Milk and other dairy products can now be skim or low-fat (AAP Committee on Nutrition, 1992a). A study that followed a predominantly Hispanic group of 215 healthy 3- to 4-year-olds for one to two years found no negative effects on height, weight, or body mass from a moderately low-fat diet (Shea et al., 1993).

Obesity today is more common among preschoolers (especially girls, who tend to be less active than boys) than twenty-five years ago. Between the early 1970s and 1994, the proportion of 4- and 5-year-old girls who were above the 95th percentile in standard growth curves of weight for height increased from 5.8 percent to 10.8 percent; for boys, the increase was from 4.4 to 5 percent (Ogden et al., 1997).

Consider this . . .

- Much television advertising aimed at young children fosters poor nutrition by promoting fats and sugars rather than proteins and vitamins. How might parents counteract these pressures?

Although a fat baby is usually no cause for concern, a fat child may be. Overweight children, especially those who have overweight parents, tend to become overweight adults (Whitaker, Wright, Pepe, Seidel, & Dietz, 1997), and excess body mass can be a threat to health. A tendency to obesity is partly hereditary, but it also depends on fat intake and exercise (Jackson et al., 1997; Klesges, Klesges, Eck, & Shelton, 1995; Leibel, 1997; Ogden et al., 1997). Early to middle childhood is a good time to treat obesity, when a child's diet is still subject to parental influence or control (Whitaker et al., 1997). Obesity is discussed further in Chapters 9 and 11.

CHECKPOINT

Can you . . .

✔ Describe typical physiological changes around the age of 3?

✔ Summarize preschoolers' dietary needs and explain why obesity and tooth decay can become concerns at this age?

By age 3, all the primary, or deciduous, teeth are in place. The permanent teeth, which will begin to appear at about age 6, are developing. Tooth decay is a major problem among poor children; more than 90 percent of 3- to 5-year-olds in Head Start programs have cavities. Tooth decay in early childhood often stems from overconsumption of sweetened milk and juices in infancy, together with lack of regular dental care, and the pain resulting from infection may contribute to slowed growth by interfering with normal eating and sleep. In one study of 300 three-year-olds, nearly 14 percent of those with serious tooth decay weighed less than 80 percent of their ideal weight. After a year and a half of dental rehabilitation, these children caught up in weight with a comparison group who had had relatively healthy teeth and normal weight (Acs, Shulman, Ng, & Chussid, 1999).

Sleep Patterns and Problems

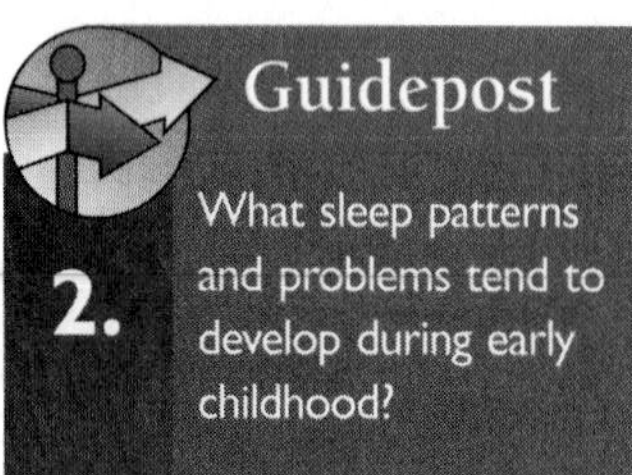
Guidepost
2.
What sleep patterns and problems tend to develop during early childhood?

Sleep patterns change throughout life, and early childhood has its own distinct rhythms. Young children usually sleep more deeply at night than they will later in life, but most still need a daytime nap or quiet rest until about age 5.

Cultural expectations affect these patterns. Children in different cultures may get the same amount of sleep each day, but its timing may vary. In many traditional cultures, such as the Gusii of Kenya, the Javanese in Indonesia, and the Zuni in New Mexico, young children have no regular bedtime and are allowed to stay up watching adult activities until they are sleepy. Among the Canadian Hare, 3-year-olds do not take naps but are put to sleep right after dinner and are allowed to sleep as long as they wish in the morning (Broude, 1995).

Young children who do have specified bedtimes, as is common in the United States, may develop elaborate routines to put off retiring, and it may take them longer than before to fall asleep. About 20 to 30 percent of children in their first 4 years engage in *bedtime struggles* lasting more than an hour and wake their parents frequently at night (Lozoff, Wolf, & Davis, 1985).

Children are likely to want a light left on and to sleep with a favorite toy or blanket (Beltramini & Hertzig, 1983). Such **transitional objects,** used repeatedly as bedtime companions, help a child shift from the dependence of infancy to the independence of later childhood. Parents sometimes worry if their child cannot fall asleep without a tattered blanket or stuffed animal, but such worry seems unfounded. In one longitudinal study, 11-year-olds who at age 4 had insisted on taking cuddly objects to bed were now outgoing, sociable with adults, and self-confident; they enjoyed playing by themselves and tended not to be worriers. At age 16, they were just as well adjusted as children who had not used transitional objects (Newson, Newson, & Mahalski, 1982).

transitional objects
Objects used repeatedly by a child as bedtime companions.

Walking and talking during sleep are fairly common in early childhood and are usually harmless. However, persistent sleep disturbances may indicate an emotional problem that needs to be examined.

Sleep Disturbances

About 25 percent of children ages 3 to 8, mostly boys, have night terrors or nightmares (Hartmann, 1981). A child who experiences a *night terror* awakens abruptly from a deep sleep in a state of panic. The child may scream and sit up in bed, breathing rapidly and staring. Yet he is not really awake, quiets down quickly, and the next morning remembers nothing about the episode. Night terrors alarm parents more than children and may simply be an effect of very deep sleep; they rarely signify a serious emotional problem and usually go away by age 6. If they are severe and long-lasting and occur once a week or more, some physicians prescribe a short course of therapy with an antihistamine or antidepressant drug (McDaniel, 1986).

A *nightmare* is a frightening dream, often brought on by staying up too late, eating a heavy meal close to bedtime, or overexcitement—for example, from watching an overstimulating television program. Unlike night terrors, which usually occur within an hour after falling asleep, nightmares come toward morning and are often vividly recalled. An occasional bad dream is no cause for alarm, but frequent or persistent nightmares, especially those that make a child fearful or anxious during waking hours, may signal excessive stress. A repeated theme may point to a specific problem the child cannot solve while awake.

Bed-Wetting

Most children stay dry, day and night, by 3 to 5 years of age; but **enuresis,** repeated urination in clothing or in bed, is common, especially at night. A child may be diagnosed as having primary, or persistent, enuresis if wetting occurs at least twice a week for at least three months after age 5, or if the condition is causing significant stress or impairment at school or in other everyday activities. About 7 percent of 5-year-old boys and 3 percent of girls wet the bed regularly, but most outgrow the condition without special help (American Psychiatric Association [APA], 1994). Fewer than 1 percent of bed-wetters have a physical disorder. Nor is persistent enuresis primarily an emotional problem.

enuresis
Repeated urination in clothing or in bed.

Enuresis runs in families. About 75 percent of bed-wetters have a close relative who also wets the bed, and identical twins are more concordant for the condition than fraternal twins (APA, 1994; Fergusson, Horwood, & Shannon, 1986).

The discovery of the approximate site of a gene linked to enuresis (Eiberg, Berendt, & Mohr, 1995) points to heredity as a major factor, possibly in combination with such other factors as slow motor maturation, allergies, and poor behavioral control (Goleman, 1995). The gene does not appear to account for occasional bed-wetting.

Children and their parents need to be reassured that enuresis is common and not serious. The child is not to blame and should not be punished. Generally parents need not do anything unless children themselves see bed-wetting as a problem. The most effective treatments include rewarding children for staying dry; waking them when they begin to urinate by using devices that ring bells or buzzers; and teaching children to practice controlling the sphincter muscles and to stretch the bladder (Rappaport, 1993). As a last resort, hormones or antidepressant drugs may be given for a short time (Goleman, 1995b; McDaniel, 1986).

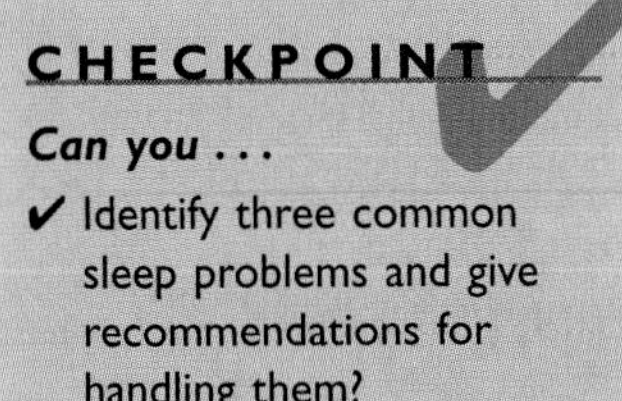

Can you . . .

✔ Identify three common sleep problems and give recommendations for handling them?

Motor Skills

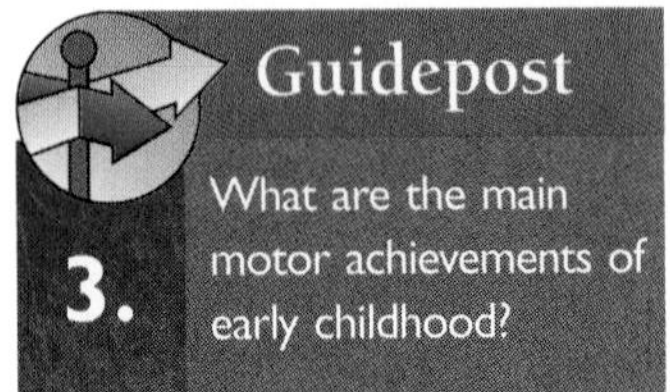

Guidepost
3.
What are the main motor achievements of early childhood?

Children between ages 3 and 6 make great advances in **gross motor skills,** such as running and jumping, which involve the large muscles (see Table 7-1). Development of the sensory and motor areas of the cortex permits better coordination between what children want to do and what they can do. Their bones and muscles are stronger, and their lung capacity is greater, making it possible to run, jump, and climb farther, faster, and better.

Children vary in adeptness, depending on their genetic endowment and their opportunities to learn and practice motor skills. Those under age 6 are rarely ready to take part in any organized sport. Only 20 percent of 4-year-olds can throw a ball well, and only 30 percent can catch well (AAP Committee on Sports Medicine and Fitness, 1992). Physical development blossoms best in active, unstructured free-play.

gross motor skills
Physical skills that involve the large muscles.

fine motor skills
Physical skills that involve the small muscles and eye-hand coordination.

Fine motor skills, such as buttoning shirts and drawing pictures, involve eye-hand and small-muscle coordination. Gains in these skills allow young children to take more responsibility for their personal care. At 3, Winnie can pour milk into her cereal bowl, eat with silverware, and use the toilet alone. She can also draw a circle and a rudimentary person—without arms. At 4, Michael can dress himself with help. He can cut along a line, draw a fairly complete person, make designs and crude letters, and fold paper into a double triangle. At 5, Juan can dress himself without much help, copy a square or triangle, and draw a more elaborate person than before.

As they develop both types of motor skills, preschoolers continually merge abilities they already have with those they are acquiring, to produce more complex capabilities. Such combinations of skills are known as **systems of action.**

systems of action
Combinations of motor skills that permit increasingly complex activities.

Table 7-1 Gross Motor Skills in Early Childhood

3-Year-Olds	4-Year-Olds	5-Year-Olds
Cannot turn or stop suddenly or quickly	Have more effective control of stopping, starting, and turning	Can start, turn, and stop effectively in games
Can jump a distance of 15 to 24 inches	Can jump a distance of 24 to 33 inches	Can make a running jump of 28 to 36 inches
Can ascend a stairway unaided, alternating feet	Can descend a long stairway alternating feet, if supported	Can descend a long stairway unaided, alternating feet
Can hop, using largely an irregular series of jumps with some variations added	Can hop four to six steps on one foot	Can easily hop a distance of 16 feet

Source: Corbin, 1973.

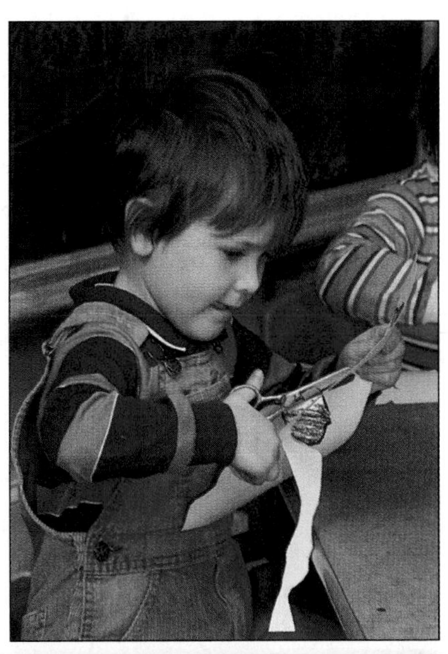

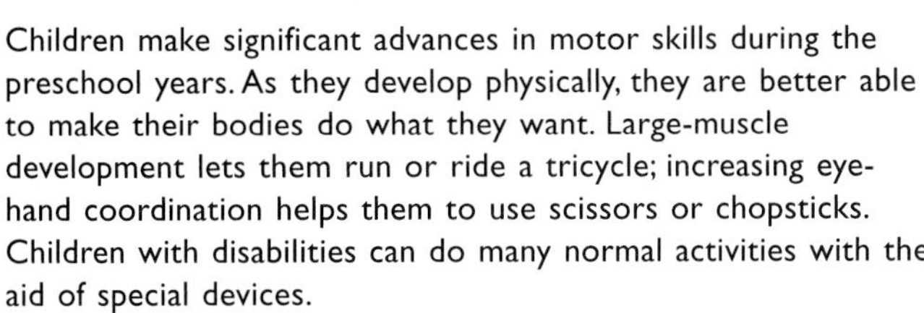

Children make significant advances in motor skills during the preschool years. As they develop physically, they are better able to make their bodies do what they want. Large-muscle development lets them run or ride a tricycle; increasing eye-hand coordination helps them to use scissors or chopsticks. Children with disabilities can do many normal activities with the aid of special devices.

Handedness

Handedness, the preference for using one hand over the other, is usually evident by 3 years of age. Since the left hemisphere of the brain, which controls the right side of the body, is usually dominant, most people favor their right side. In people whose brains are more symmetrical, the right hemisphere tends to dominate, making them left-handed. Handedness is not always clear-cut; not everybody prefers one hand for every task. Boys are more likely to be left-handed than girls.

handedness
Preference for using a particular hand.

Is handedness genetic or learned? That question has been controversial. A new theory proposes the existence of a single gene for right-handedness. According to this theory, people who inherit this gene from either or both parents—about 82 percent of the population—are right-handed. Those who do not inherit the gene still have a 50–50 chance of being right-handed; otherwise they will be left-handed or ambidextrous. Random determination of handedness among those who do not receive the gene could explain why some monozygotic twins have differing hand preferences, as well as why 8 percent of the offspring of two right-handed parents are left-handed. The theory closely predicted the proportion of left-handed offspring in a three-generational sample of families recruited through advertisements (Klar, 1996).

CHECKPOINT

Can you . . .

- ✔ List at least three gross motor skills and three fine motor skills, and tell when they typically develop?
- ✔ Tell how brain functioning is related to physical skills and handedness?

Figure 7-1
Artistic development in early childhood. There is a great difference between the very simple shapes shown in (a) and the detailed pictorial drawings in (e). The challenge for adults is to encourage children's creativity while acknowledging their growing facility in drawing.
Source: Kellogg, 1970.

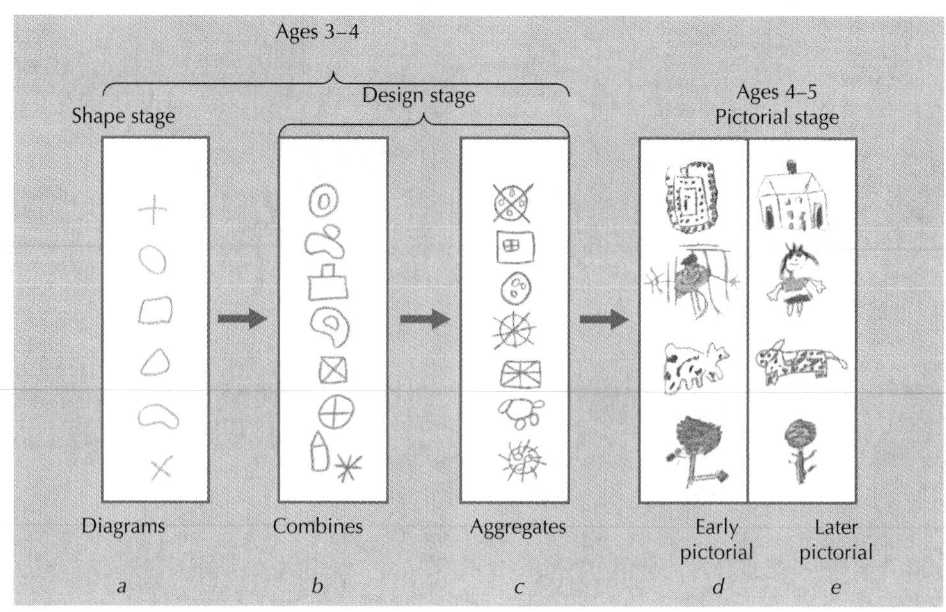

> ***Consider this . . .***
>
> - Drawings from children's early pictorial stage show energy and freedom; those from the later pictorial stage show care and accuracy. Why do you think these changes occur? How would you evaluate them?

> **CHECKPOINT**
>
> ***Can you . . .***
>
> ✔ Identify four stages of early artistic development?

Artistic Development

Changes in young children's drawings seem to reflect maturation of the brain as well as of the muscles (Kellogg, 1970; see Figure 7-1). Two-year-olds *scribble*—not randomly but in patterns, such as vertical and zigzag lines. By age 3, children draw *shapes*—circles, squares, rectangles, triangles, crosses, and Xs—and then begin combining the shapes into more complex *designs*. The *pictorial* stage typically begins between ages 4 and 5; Wang Yani reached this stage at age 3.

The switch from abstract form and design to depicting real objects marks a fundamental change in the purpose of children's drawing, reflecting cognitive development of representational ability. However, greater pictorial accuracy—often encouraged by adults—may come at the cost of the energy and freedom shown in children's early efforts. This was not so in Yani's case. While her father refrained from influencing her artistic style, he gave her big sheets of paper and trained her to paint with her whole arm, using large muscles as well as small ones. Her pictorial forms retained a free-flowing, semiabstract quality that gave them the stamp of originality.

Health and Safety

Guidepost
4.
What are the major health and safety risks for children?

What used to be a very vulnerable time of life is much safer now. Because of widespread immunization, many of the major diseases of childhood are now fairly rare in western industrialized countries. In the developing world, however, such vaccine-preventable diseases as measles, pertussis (whooping cough), and tuberculosis still take a large toll. Diarrheal infections account for nearly one-fifth of the 11.2 million deaths of children under age 5 in these regions each year (Wegman, 1999; see Figure 7-2).

In the United States, children's death rates from all kinds of illness have come down in recent years (National Center for Health Statistics [NCHS], 1998a). Deaths in childhood are relatively few compared with deaths in adulthood, and most are caused by injury rather than illness (NCHS, 1998a). Still, environmental influences make this a less healthy time for some children than for others.

Minor Illnesses

Coughs, sniffles, stomachaches, and runny noses are a part of early childhood. These minor illnesses typically last a few days and are seldom serious enough to need a doctor's attention. Because the lungs are not fully developed, respiratory problems are common, though less so than in infancy. Three- to 5-year-olds catch an average of seven to eight colds and other respiratory illnesses a year. It's a good thing they do, since these illnesses help build natural immunity (resistance to disease). During middle childhood, when the respiratory system is more fully developed, children average fewer than six such illnesses a year (Denny & Clyde, 1983). Minor illnesses may have emotional and cognitive benefits as well. Repeated experience with illness helps children learn to cope with physical distress and understand its causes, increasing their sense of competence (Parmelee, 1986).

Accidental Injuries

Because young children are naturally venturesome and often unaware of danger, it is hard for caregivers to protect them from harm without *over*protecting them. Although most cuts, bumps, and scrapes are "kissed away" and quickly forgotten, some accidental injuries result in lasting damage or death. Indeed, accidents are the leading cause of death throughout childhood and adolescence in the United States. Most of these deaths are from motor vehicle injuries (Rivara, 1999; NCHS, 1998a). Deaths from pedestrian injuries have fallen by 65 percent since the late 1970s, but the risk of serious brain damage and lifelong disability from head injuries remains high (Rivara, 1999).

Many deaths in automobile collisions are preventable. All fifty states and the District of Columbia have laws requiring young children to be restrained in cars, either in specially designed seats or by standard seat belts. Four-year-olds who "graduate" from car seats to lap and shoulder belts may need booster seats until they grow bigger. Airbags designed to inflate rapidly so as to protect adults riding in the front seat of a car in high-impact collisions *increase* the risk of fatal injury to children under age 13 by as much as 34 percent (Rivara, 1999). It is safer, therefore, for young children always to ride in the back seat.

Laws requiring "childproof" caps on medicine bottles, mandatory helmets for bicycle riders, and safe storage of firearms have improved child safety. In

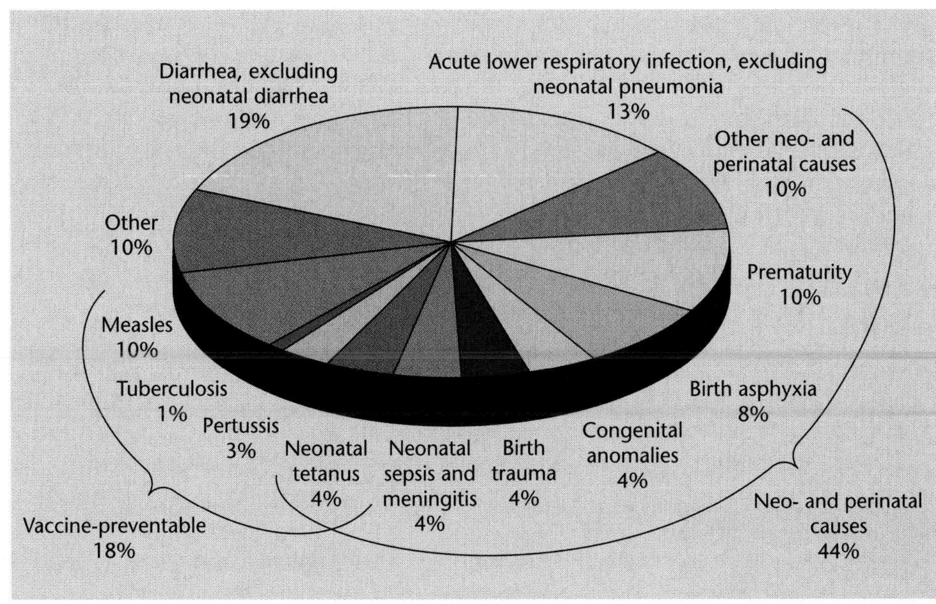

Figure 7-2
Leading causes of death for children under age 5 in the developing world, 1995. Total deaths: 11.2 million.
Source: Adapted from Wegman, 1999, p. 651; data from World Health Organization.

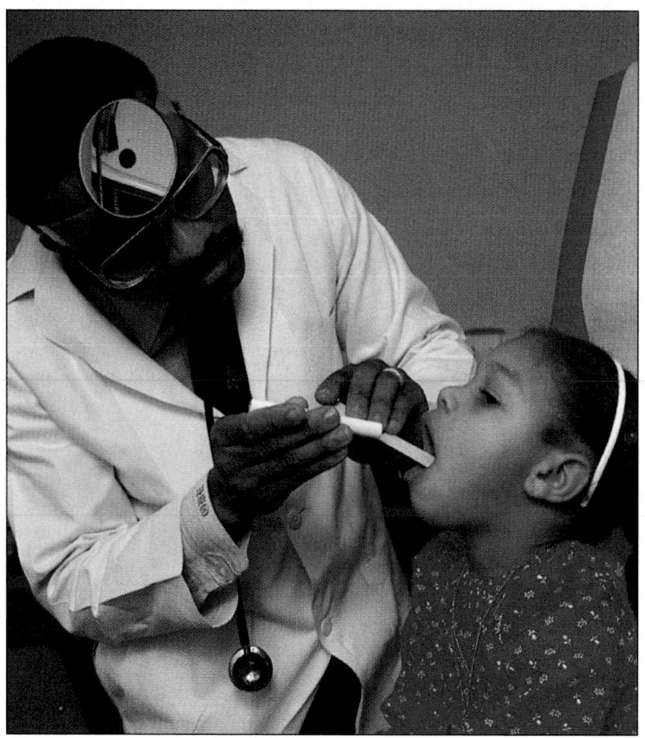

Although sore throats and other minor illnesses are common among 3- to 6-year-olds, they are usually not serious enough to require visits to the doctor. This 5-year-old will probably have fewer colds and sore throats in the next few years, as her respiratory and immune systems mature.

twelve states that passed laws requiring that guns be inaccessible to children, unintentional shooting deaths of children younger than 15 fell by 23 percent (Cummings, Grossman, Rivara, & Koepsell, 1997). Still, the United States has by far the highest rates of childhood deaths due to homicide, suicide, and unintentional firearm-related injuries among twenty-six industrialized countries. Of all firearm-related deaths of children under age 15 in the most recently reported year in each of these countries, 86 percent occurred in the United States ("Rates of Homicide," 1997).

Making playgrounds safer would be another valuable measure. An estimated 3 percent of children in day care are hurt badly enough each year to need medical attention, and about half of accidents at child care centers occur on playgrounds. Nearly 1 in 5 are from falls, often resulting in skull injury and brain damage (Briss, Sacks, Addiss, Kresnow, & O'Neil, 1994).

CHECKPOINT

Can you . . .

- ✔ Identify two benefits of minor illnesses?
- ✔ Tell where and how young children are most likely to be injured, and list ways in which injuries can be avoided?

Children are less likely to be injured in day care, however, than in and around the home (Thacker, Addiss, Goodman, Holloway, & Spencer, 1992), where most fatal nonvehicular accidents occur. Children drown in bathtubs, pools, and buckets containing liquids (as well as in lakes, rivers, and oceans); are burned by scalding or in fires or explosions; fall from heights; drink or eat poisonous substances; get caught in mechanical contrivances; and suffocate in traps, such as abandoned refrigerators. Another dangerous place is the supermarket shopping cart (U.S. Consumer Product Safety Commission, 1991).

Health in Context: Environmental Influences

Why do some children have more illnesses or injuries than others? The genetic heritage contributes: some children seem predisposed toward some medical conditions. In addition, as Bronfenbrenner's bioecological theory would predict, the home, the child care facility, the neighborhood, and the larger society play major roles.

Exposure to Stress

stress
Response to physical or psychological demands.

Stress is a response to physical or psychological demands. Family situations involving stress increase vulnerability to illness and accidents. In a study of all children born in Tennessee between 1985 and 1994, children born to mothers under 20 years old, with less than a high school education and three or more other children to deal with, were 15 times as likely to die of injuries before the age of 5 as children whose mothers were college educated, more than 30 years old, and had fewer than three other children. If the mortality rate for all children could be reduced to that of this lowest-risk group, injury-related deaths might be reduced by more than 75 percent (Scholer, Mitchel, & Ray, 1997). Home visitation programs to teach parents to use car restraints and smoke detectors, lower water heater thermostats to avoid scalding, and undertake other safety measures can substantially reduce injuries (Roberts, Kramer, & Suissa, 1996).

Stressful events in the family, such as moves, job changes, divorce, and death, are related to increased frequency of minor illnesses and home accidents. In one study, children whose families had experienced 12 or more such stressful events were more than twice as likely to have to go into the hospital as children from families that had experienced fewer than 4 traumatic events (Beautrais, Fergusson, & Shannon, 1982). Entry into child care is stressful for many children. Children also can be affected by adults' stress. A distraught adult may forget to make sure that a child washes before eating, or to fasten a gate or put a cup of hot coffee, a kitchen knife, or a noningestible cleaning fluid out of a child's reach (Craft, Montgomery, & Peters, 1992).

Exposure to Smoking

Parental smoking is an important preventable cause of childhood illness and death. In the United States, 43 percent of children 2 months to 11 years old live with smokers and are exposed daily to secondhand smoke (Pirkle et al., 1996). This passive exposure increases the risk of contracting a number of medical problems, including pneumonia, bronchitis, serious infectious illnesses, otitis media (middle ear infection), burns, and asthma. It also may lead to cancer in adulthood (Aligne & Stoddard, 1997; AAP Committee on Environmental Health, 1997; U.S. Environmental Protection Agency, 1994). The (AAP) Committee on Environmental Health (1997) recommends that children be raised in a smoke-free environment.

Poverty

Poverty is stressful, unhealthy, and dangerous. Low income is the *chief* factor associated with poor health of children and adolescents, over and above race and family structure (Montgomery, Kiely, & Pappas, 1996; see Table 7-2).

A growing proportion of children in the United States are poor: nearly 1 in 5 in 1997, as compared with about 1 in 7 in 1973. Young families have been particularly hard hit. Although poverty strikes all parts of the population, it besets

Table 7-2 Poor Health Outcomes for Poor Children

Outcome	Poor Children's Higher Risk Relative to Nonpoor Children
Death in childhood	1.5 to 3 times more likely
Stunted growth	2.7 times more likely
Iron deficiency in preschool years	3 to 4 times more likely
Partial or complete deafness	1.5 to 2 times more likely
Partial or complete blindness	1.2 to 1.8 times more likely
Serious physical or mental disabilities	About 2 times more likely
Fatal accidental injuries	2 to 3 times more likely
Pneumonia	1.6 times more likely

Source: Adapted from Children's Defense Fund, 1998, p. xiv; from Sherman, 1997.

minorities disproportionately. About 37 percent of black children and 36 percent of Hispanic children are poor, as compared with 11 percent of white children. Still, 3 out of 5 poor children are white, 1 in 3 lives in a suburb, 1 in 3 lives with married parents, and 2 out of 3 have working parents (Children's Defense Fund, 1998; Federal Interagency Forum on Child and Family Statistics, 1999). Child poverty rates in the United States are $1^1/_2$ to 8 times as high as in other major industrialized countries (Children's Defense Fund, 1996, 1997a; see Figure 7-3).

The health problems of poor children often begin before birth. Many poor mothers do not eat well and do not receive adequate prenatal care; their babies are more likely than babies of nonpoor mothers to be of low birthweight or to die in infancy (NCHS, 1998a). Poor children who do not eat properly do not grow properly, and thus are weak and susceptible to disease. Many poor families live in crowded, unsanitary housing, and the children may lack adequate supervision, especially when the parents are at work. They are more likely than other children to suffer lead poisoning, hearing and vision loss, and iron-deficiency anemia, as well as such stress-related conditions as asthma, headaches, insomnia, and irritable bowel. They also tend to have more behavior problems, psychological disturbances, and learning disabilities (J. L. Brown, 1987; Egbuono & Starfield, 1982; Santer & Stocking, 1991; Starfield, 1991).

About 12 percent of poor children have elevated blood lead levels, as compared with only 2 percent of high-income children (Lanphear, Weitzman, & Eberly, 1996; McLoyd, 1998; NCHS, 1998a). Lead poisoning can seriously interfere with cognitive development and can lead to a variety of neurological and behavioral problems (Needleman, Riess, Tobin, Biesecker, & Greenhouse, 1996;

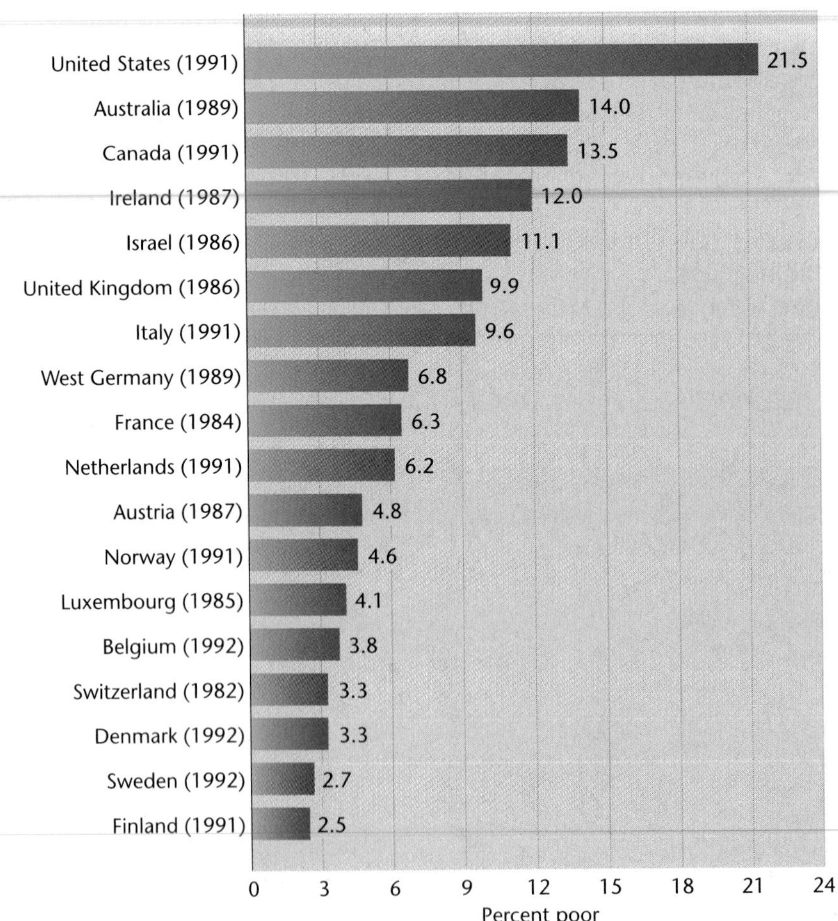

Figure 7-3

Child poverty rates in 18 industrialized countries. The poverty rate for children in the United States is higher than that in 17 other industrialized countries; yet upper- and middle-class children in the United States are much better off than in those countries.

(Source: Luxembourg Income Study; reprinted in Children's Defense Fund, 1996, p. 6.)

Tesman & Hills, 1994) or to seizures, mental retardation, or death (AAP Committee on Environmental Health, 1993). Yet it is totally preventable by removing sources of lead, such as lead paint, from children's environment (Tesman & Hills, 1994). Regular, thorough home cleaning to remove lead dust can be somewhat effective (Rhoads et al., 1999). Some of the effects of severe lead poisoning may be irreversible (AAP Committee on Environmental Health, 1993). Moderate lead poisoning can be treated (Ruff, Bijur, Markowitz, Ma, & Rosen, 1993), but reduced exposure may only partially reverse the cognitive effects (Tong, Baghurst, Sawyer, Burns, & McMichael, 1998).

Many poor children do not get the medical care they need, often because they are uninsured (NCHS, 1998a). Black and Hispanic children are more likely to lack regular care and insurance than white children (Federal Interagency Forum on Child and Family Statistics, 1999; Simpson, Bloom, Cohen, & Parsons, 1997). Between 1977 and 1996, the proportion of uninsured children grew 14 percent, largely due to loss of employer-provided coverage (Children's Defense Fund, 1998). By 1997, an estimated 10 million children—1 out of 7—were uninsured (Health Care Financing Administration, 1997).

Important "safety nets" for poor children in the United States have been federally funded Aid to Families with Dependent Children (AFDC) and Medicaid. AFDC has been eliminated, responsibility for welfare has been shifted to the states, and Medicaid has not grown fast enough to offset losses in private insurance coverage (Children's Defense Fund, 1998). In 1997, the federal government authorized $24 billion in matching funds over a 5-year period to help states expand health care coverage to uninsured children (Health Care Financing Administration, 1997).

Homelessness

An estimated 43 percent of the $2\frac{1}{2}$ to 3 million homeless in the United States are families with children, the fastest-growing segment of this population (AAP Committee on Community Health Services, 1996). Typically these families are headed by single mothers in their twenties (Buckner, Bassuk, Weinreb, & Brooks, 1999). As low-cost housing has become scarce in a booming economy, homelessness has become more widespread (Children's Defense Fund, 1998).

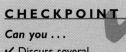

CHECKPOINT

Can you . . .

✔ Discuss several environmental influences that endanger children's health and development?

Many homeless children spend their crucial early years in unstable, insecure, and often unsanitary environments. They and their parents are cut off from a supportive community, family ties, and institutional resources and from ready access to medical care and schooling (AAP Committee on Community Health Services,

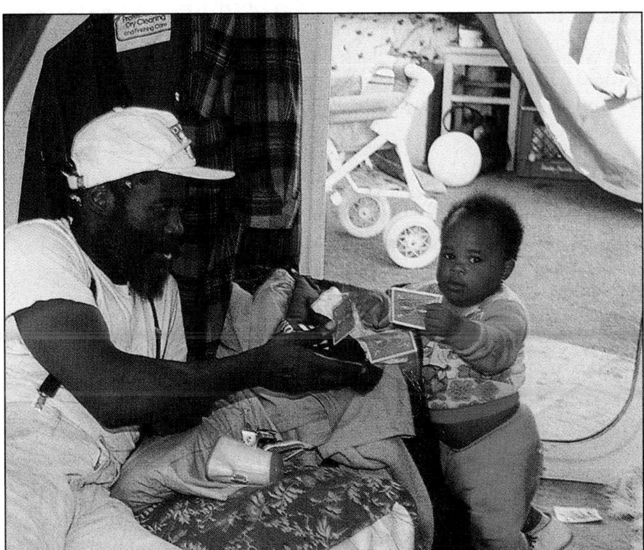

Homeless children who spend their early years in crowded, unsanitary environments tend to have more health problems than children with homes.

1996; J. L. Bass, Brennan, Mehta, & Kodzis, 1990; Bassuk, 1991; Bassuk & Rosenberg, 1990; Rafferty & Shinn, 1991).

From birth, these children suffer more health problems than poor children who have homes, and they are more likely to die in infancy. They are three times more likely than other children to lack immunizations, and two to three times more likely to have iron deficiency anemia. They experience high rates of diarrhea; hunger and malnourishment; obesity (from eating excessive carbohydrates and fats); tooth decay; asthma and other chronic diseases; respiratory, skin, and eye and ear infections; scabies and lice; trauma-related injuries; and elevated levels of lead. Homeless children also tend to suffer severe depression and anxiety and to have neurological and visual deficits, developmental delays, behavior problems, and learning difficulties (AAP Committee on Community Health Services, 1996; Bassuk, 1991; Buckner et al., 1999; Rafferty & Shinn, 1991; Rubin et al., 1996).

Consider this . . .

- Who should be responsible for children's well-being when parents cannot provide adequate food, clothing, shelter, and health care: government, religious and community institutions, the private sector, or a combination of these?

To combat homelessness, a number of communities and community development groups are building low-income housing units and reclaiming neighborhoods with the help of federal, state, local, foundation, and private financing (Children's Defense Fund, 1998).

COGNITIVE DEVELOPMENT

Piagetian Approach: The Preoperational Child

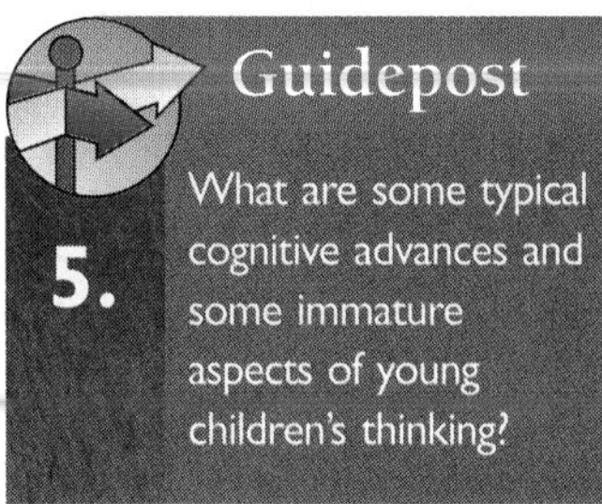

Guidepost
5.
What are some typical cognitive advances and some immature aspects of young children's thinking?

Jean Piaget named early childhood the **preoperational stage.** In this second major stage of cognitive development, which lasts from approximately ages 2 to 7, children gradually become more sophisticated in their use of symbolic thought, which emerges at the end of the sensorimotor stage (see Chapter 5). However, according to Piaget, they cannot think logically until the stage of concrete operations in middle childhood (Chapter 9).

Let's look at some advances and immature aspects of preoperational thought (see Tables 7-3 and 7-4), including recent research findings, some of which challenge Piaget's conclusions.

preoperational stage
In Piaget's theory, the second major stage of cognitive development (approximately from age 2 to age 7), in which children become more sophisticated in their use of symbolic thought but are not yet able to use logic.

Advances of Preoperational Thought

Advances in symbolic thought are accompanied by a growing understanding of identities, space, causality, categorization, and number. Some of these understandings have roots in infancy and toddlerhood; others begin to develop in early childhood but are not fully achieved until middle childhood.

The Symbolic Function

"I want ice cream!" announces Kerstin, age 4, trudging indoors from the hot, dusty backyard. She has not seen anything that triggered this desire—no open freezer door, no television commercial. She no longer needs this kind of sensory cue to think about something. She remembers ice cream, its coldness and taste, and she purposefully seeks it out. This absence of sensory or motor cues characterizes the **symbolic function:** the ability to use symbols, or mental representations—words, numbers, or images to which a person has attached meaning. Having symbols for things helps children to remember and think about them without having them physically present, as Wang Yani did when she drew or painted from memory.

symbolic function
In Piaget's terminology, ability to use mental representations (words, numbers, or images) to which a child has attached meaning.

Children show the symbolic function through deferred imitation, pretend play, and language. *Deferred imitation,* which appears to begin in infancy (refer

Table 7-3 Cognitive Advances During Early Childhood

Advance	Significance	Example
Use of symbols	Children do not need to be in sensorimotor contact with an object, person, or event in order to think about it.	Simon asks his mother about the elephants they saw on their trip to the circus several months earlier.
	Children can imagine that objects or people have properties other than those they actually have.	Rolf pretends that a slice of apple is a vacuum cleaner "vrooming" across the kitchen table.
Understanding of identities	Children are aware that superficial alterations do not change the nature of things.	Jeffrey knows that his teacher is dressed up as a pirate but that he is still his teacher underneath the costume.
Understanding of cause and effect	Children realize that events have causes.	Seeing a ball roll from behind a wall, Marie looks behind the wall for the person who kicked the ball.
Ability to classify	Children organize objects, people, and events into meaningful categories.	Emily sorts the pine cones she collected on a nature walk into two piles according to their size: "big" and "little."
Understanding of number	Children can count and deal with quantities.	Lindsay shares some candy with her friends, counting to make sure that each girl gets the same amount.
Empathy	Children become more able to imagine how others might feel.	James tries to comfort his friend when he sees that his friend is upset.
Theory of mind	Children become more aware of mental activity and the functioning of the mind.	Jennifer wants to save some cookies for herself, so she hides them from her brother in a pasta box. She knows her cookies will be safe there because her brother will not look in a place where he doesn't expect to find cookies.

back to Chapter 5), is based on retention of a mental representation of an observed action (like Yani's early imitation of her father drawing with charcoal). In *pretend play* (also called *symbolic play, fantasy play, dramatic play*, or *imaginative play*), which we discuss in Chapter 8, children make a [illegible] ize) something else; for example, a doll may repres[illegible] cussed later in this chapter, involves the use of a c[illegible] (words) to communicate.

Understanding of Identities

The world becomes more orderly and predictable as c[illegible] derstanding of *identities:* the concept that people an[illegible] the same even if they change in form, size, or appe[illegible] underlies the emerging self-concept (see Chapters 6 a[illegible]

Spatial Thinking

The growth of representational thinking enables chil[illegible] judgments about spatial relationships. By 19 months [illegible] picture is a representation of something else (DeLo[illegible] Rosengren, & Gottlieb, 1998), but until age 3 they hav[illegible] tionships between pictures, maps, or scale models an[illegible] represent (DeLoache, Miller, & Pierroutsakos, 1998). In one experiment, $2\frac{1}{2}$-year-olds who were told that a "shrinking machine" had shrunk a room to

Table 7-4 Limitations of Preoperational Thought (according to Piaget)

Limitation	Description	Example
Centration: inability to decenter	Children focus on one aspect of a situation and neglect others.	Timothy teases his younger sister that he has more juice than she does because his juice box has been poured into a tall, skinny glass, but hers has been poured into a short, wide glass.
Irreversibility	Children fail to understand that some operations or actions can be reversed, restoring the original situation.	Timothy does not realize that the juice in each glass can be poured back into the juice box from which it came, contradicting his claim that he has more than his sister.
Focus on states rather than transformations	Children fail to understand the significance of the transformation between states.	In the conservation task, Timothy does not understand that transforming the shape of a liquid (pouring it from one container into another) does not change the amount.
Transductive reasoning	Children do not use deductive or inductive reasoning; instead they jump from one particular to another and see cause where none exists.	Sarah was mean to her brother. Then her brother got sick. Sarah concludes that she made her brother sick.
Egocentrism	Children assume everyone else thinks, perceives, and feels as they do.	Kara doesn't realize that she needs to turn a book around so that her father can see the picture she is asking him to explain to her. Instead, she holds the book directly in front of her, where only she can see it.
Animism	Children attribute life to objects not alive.	Amanda says that spring is trying to come but winter is saying, "I won't go! I won't go!"
Inability to distinguish appearance from reality	Children confuse what is real with outward appearance.	Courtney is confused by a sponge made to look like a rock. She states that it looks like a rock and it really is a rock.

the size of a miniature model were more successful in finding a toy hidden in the room on the basis of its position in the model (and vice versa) than were children the same age who were told that the "little room" was just like the "big room" (DeLoache, Miller, & Rosengren, 1997). According to the **dual representation hypothesis,** what makes the second task harder is that it requires a child to mentally represent both the symbol (the "little room") and its relationship to the thing it stands for (the "big room") at the same time. With the "shrinking machine," children do not have to perform this dual operation, because they are told that the room and the model are one and the same. Three-year-olds do not seem to have this problem with models.

dual representation hypothesis
Proposal that children under the age of 3 have difficulty grasping spatial relationships because of the need to keep more than one mental representation in mind at the same time.

Preschoolers can use simple maps, and they can transfer the spatial understanding gained from working with models to maps and vice versa (DeLoache, Miller, & Pierroutsakos, 1998). In one experiment, 4- to 7-year-olds who had been shown a simple map of a playhouse learned a specific route through the playhouse more easily than children who had not seen the map before entering the playhouse (Uttal & Wellman, 1989).

Causality

Although Piaget recognized that toddlers have some understanding of a connection between actions and reactions, he maintained that preoperational children cannot yet reason logically about cause and effect. Instead, he maintained, they reason by **transduction.** They view one situation as the basis for another situation, often one occurring at about the same time, whether or not there is logically a causal relationship. For example, they may think that their "bad" thoughts or behavior caused their own or another child's illness or their parents' divorce. Yet when tested on situations they can understand, young children do accurately link cause and effect.

In one study, preschoolers were shown a row of blocks touching each other. When a rod was pushed against the first block, the entire row tumbled like dominos. Even 3-year-olds could predict that removing some of the center blocks would prevent the ones on the far end from falling. They also knew that using a glass rod instead of a wooden one would make no difference (Bullock, Gelman, & Baillargeon, 1982). Apparently, then, young children's understanding of familiar events in the physical world enables them to think logically about causation, even though they cannot yet do so in some other areas (Wellman & Gelman, 1998).

Some research even suggests that preschoolers can see analogies involving familiar items—an ability that, according to Piaget, does not develop until the stage of formal operations in adolescence. When shown a picture of a chocolate bar paired with a picture of melted chocolate, even some 3-year-olds realize that the analogous pair for a picture of a snowman is a melted snowman, and not a melted crayon, a dirty snowman, a scarecrow, or a sled (Goswami & Brown, 1989).

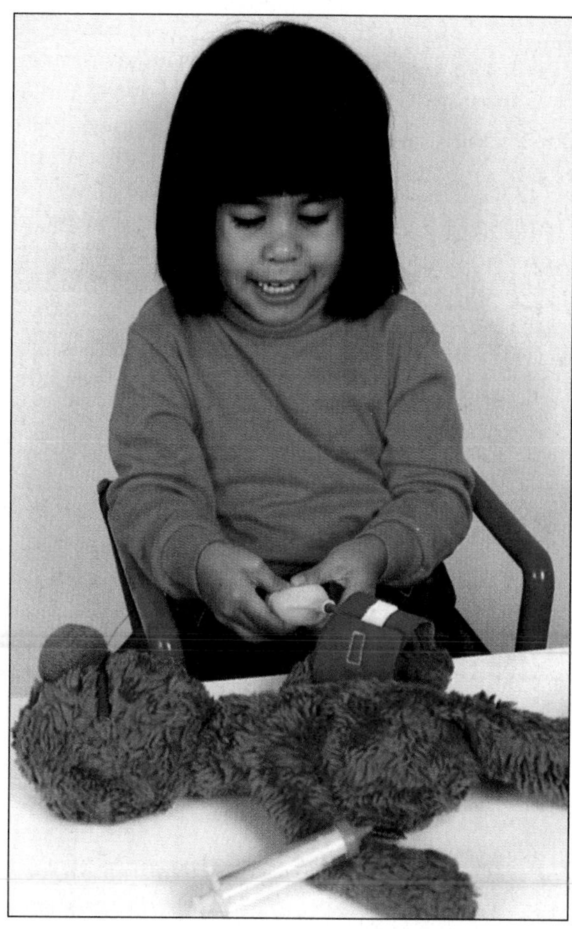

As Anna pretends to take Grover's blood pressure, she is showing a major cognitive achievement: deferred imitation, the ability to act out an action she observed some time before.

Preschoolers' unrealistic views about causes of illness may reflect a belief that all causal relationships are equally and absolutely predictable. In one series of experiments, 3- to 5-year-olds predicted, for example, that all children in a classroom who played with a sick visitor would get sick; a control group of adults saw the outcome as less certain. Preschoolers, unlike adults, were just as sure that a person who does not wash hands before eating will get sick as they were that a person who jumps up will come down (Kalish, 1998).

transduction
In Piaget's terminology, a preoperational child's tendency to mentally link particular experiences, whether or not there is logically a causal relationship.

Categorization and Biological Understanding

Categorization, or classification, requires identification of similarities and differences. By age 4, many children can classify by two criteria, such as color and shape. Children use this ability to order many aspects of their lives, categorizing people as "good," "bad," "friend," "nonfriend," and so forth. Thus categorization is a cognitive ability with emotional and social implications.

What characteristics distinguish living from nonliving things? When Piaget asked young children whether the wind and the clouds were alive, their answers led him to think they were confused about what is alive and what is not. (The tendency to attribute life to objects that are not alive is called **animism.**) But when later researchers questioned 3- and 4-year-olds about something more familiar to them—differences between a rock, a person, and a doll—the children showed they understood that people are alive and rocks and dolls are not (Gelman, Spelke, & Meck, 1983). They did not attribute thoughts or emotions to rocks, and they cited the fact that dolls cannot move on their own as evidence that dolls are not alive.

animism
Tendency to attribute life to objects that are not alive.

Of course, plants do not move on their own either, nor do they utter sounds, as most animals do. Yet preschoolers know that both plants and animals can grow and decay and, when injured, can heal themselves (Rosengren et al., 1991; Wellman & Gelman, 1998).

Culture can affect such beliefs. Five- to 9-year-olds in Israel, Japan, and the United States were questioned about characteristics of people, other animals, plants, and inanimate objects (Hatano et al., 1993). Israeli children, whose tradition views plants primarily in terms of their usefulness as food, were less likely than children from the other two countries to attribute to plants the qualities shared by all living things, such as respiration, growth, and death. On the other hand, Japanese children were more likely to attribute such qualities to inanimate objects, which, in their culture, are sometimes viewed as if they were alive and had feelings.

Number

By age 3 or 4, children have words for comparing quantities. They can say one tree is *bigger* than another, or one cup holds *more* juice than another. They know that if they have one cookie and then get another cookie, they have more cookies than they had before, and that if they give one cookie to another child, they have fewer cookies. Such quantitative knowledge appears to be universal, though it develops at different rates, depending on how important counting is in a particular family or culture (Resnick, 1989; Saxe, Guberman, & Gearhart, 1987).

By age 5, most children can count to 20 or more and know the relative sizes of the numbers 1 through 10. Some can do simple, single-digit addition and subtraction (Siegler, 1998). Children intuitively devise strategies for adding, by counting on their fingers or by using other objects.

Sometime in early childhood, children come to recognize five principles of counting (Gelman & Gallistel, 1978; Sophian, 1988):

1. The *1-to-1 principle:* Say only one number-name for each item being counted ("One . . . two . . . three . . . ").
2. The *stable-order principle:* Say number-names in a set order ("One, two, three . . . " rather than "Three, one, two . . . ").
3. The *order-irrelevance principle:* Start counting with any item, and the total count will be the same.
4. The *cardinality principle:* The last number-name used is the total number of items being counted. (If there are five items, the last number-name will be "5.")
5. The *abstraction principle:* The principles above apply to any kind of object. (Seven buttons are equal in number to seven birds.)

CHECKPOINT

Can you . . .

✔ Summarize findings about preschool children's understanding of symbols, identities, space, causality, biological categories, and number?

There is debate about whether children need to understand these principles before they can learn to count (Gelman & Gallistel, 1978) or whether they deduce the principles from experience with counting (Ho & Fuson, 1998; Siegler, 1998).

How quickly children learn to count depends in part on the number system of their culture. At age 3, when most number learning is focused on counting from 1 through 10, U.S. and Chinese children perform about equally well. At ages 4 and 5, when U.S. youngsters are still counting by ones between 11 and 20, Chinese youngsters learn their culture's more efficient system based on tens and ones (10 + 1, 10 + 2, and so forth). It's not surprising, then, that U.S. children's performance begins to lag (Miller, Smith, Zhu, & Zhang, 1995).

Immature Aspects of Preoperational Thought

centration
In Piaget's theory, a limitation of preoperational thought that leads the child to focus on one aspect of a situation and neglect others, often leading to illogical conclusions.

According to Piaget, one of the main characteristics of preoperational thought is **centration:** the tendency to focus on one aspect of a situation and neglect others. He said preschoolers come to illogical conclusions because they cannot

decenter—think about several aspects of a situation at one time. Centration can limit young children's thinking about both physical and social relationships.

decenter
In Piaget's terminology, to think simultaneously about several aspects of a situation; characteristic of operational thought.

Conservation

A classic example is the failure to understand **conservation,** the fact that two things that are equal remain so if their appearance is altered, so long as nothing is added or taken away. Piaget found that children do not fully grasp this principle until the stage of concrete operations and that they develop different kinds of conservation at different ages. Table 7-5 shows how various dimensions of conservation have been tested.

conservation
In Piaget's terminology, awareness that two objects that are equal according to a certain measure (such as length, weight, or quantity) remain equal in the face of perceptual alteration (for example, a change in shape) so long as nothing has been added to or taken away from either object.

In one type of conservation task, conservation of liquid, a 5-year-old we'll call Jeffrey is shown two identical clear glasses, each one short and wide and each holding the same amount of water. Jeffrey is asked whether the amount of water in the two glasses is equal. When he agrees, the water in one glass is poured into a third glass, a tall, thin one. Jeffrey is now asked whether both contain the same amount of water or whether one contains more, and why. In early childhood—even after watching the water poured out of one of the short, fat glasses into a tall, thin glass or even after pouring it himself—Jeffrey will say that either the taller glass or the wider one contains more water. When asked why, he says, "This one is bigger this way," stretching his arms to show the height or width. Preoperational children cannot consider height *and* width at the same time. Since they center on one aspect, they cannot think logically, said Piaget.

The ability to conserve is also limited by **irreversibility:** failure to understand that an operation or action can go two or more ways. Once Jeffrey can imagine restoring the original state of the water by pouring it back into the other glass, he will realize that the amount of water in both glasses is the same.

irreversibility
In Piaget's terminology, a limitation on preoperational thinking consisting of failure to understand that an operation can go in two or more directions.

Preoperational children commonly think as if they were watching a filmstrip with a series of static frames: they *focus on successive states,* said Piaget, and do

Table 7-5 Tests of Various Kinds of Conservation

Conservation Task	Show Child (and Have Child Acknowledge) That Both Items Are Equal	Perform Transformation	Ask Child	Preoperational Child Usually Answers
Number	Two equal, parallel rows of candies	Space the candies in one row farther apart.	"Are there the same number of candies in each row or does one row have more?"	"The longer one has more."
Length	Two parallel sticks of the same length	Move one stick to the right.	"Are both sticks the same size or is one longer?"	"The one on the right (or left) is longer."
Liquid	Two identical glasses holding equal amounts of liquid	Pour liquid from one glass into a taller, narrower glass.	"Do both glasses have the same amount of liquid or does one have more?"	"The taller one has more."
Matter (mass)	Two balls of clay of the same size	Roll one ball into a sausage shape.	"Do both pieces have the same amount of clay or does one have more?"	"The sausage has more."
Weight	Two balls of clay of the same weight	Roll one ball into a sausage shape.	"Do both weigh the same or does one weigh more?"	"The sausage weighs more."
Area	Two toy rabbits, two pieces of cardboard (representing grassy fields), with blocks or toys (representing barns on the fields); same number of "barns" on each board	Rearrange the blocks on one piece of board.	"Does each rabbit have the same amount of grass to eat or does one have more?"	"The one with the blocks close together has more to eat."
Volume	Two glasses of water with two equal-sized balls of clay in them	Roll one ball into a sausage shape.	"If we put the sausage back in the glass, will the water be the the same height in each glass, or will one be higher?"	"The water in the glass with the sausage will be higher."

not recognize the transformation from one state to another. In the conservation experiment, they focus on the water as it stands in each glass rather than on the water being poured from one glass to another, and so they fail to realize that the amount of water is the same.

Egocentrism

egocentrism
In Piaget's terminology, inability to consider another person's point of view; a characteristic of preoperational thought.

Egocentrism is a form of centration. According to Piaget, young children center so much on their own point of view that they cannot take in another's. Three-year-olds are not as egocentric as newborn babies; but, said Piaget, they still think the universe centers on them. Egocentrism may help explain why young children (as we will see) sometimes have trouble separating reality from what goes on inside their own heads and why they may show confusion about what causes what. When Jeffrey believes that his "bad thoughts" have made his sister sick, or that he caused his parents' marital troubles, he is thinking egocentrically.

To study egocentrism, Piaget designed the *three-mountain task* (see Figure 7-4). A child sits facing a table that holds three large mounds. A doll is placed on a chair at the opposite side of the table. The investigator asks the child how the "mountains" would look to the doll. Piaget found that young children usually could not answer the question correctly; instead, they described the "mountains" from their own perspective. Piaget saw this as evidence that preoperational children cannot imagine a different point of view (Piaget & Inhelder, 1967).

However, another experimenter who posed a similar problem in a different way got different results (Hughes, 1975). In the *doll and police officer task,* the child sits in front of a square board with dividers that separate it into four sections. A toy police officer is put at the edge of the board; a doll is set in one section and then moved from one section to another. After each move the child is asked, "Can the police officer see the doll?" Then another toy police officer is brought into the action, and the child is told to hide the doll from both officers. In this study, 30 children between the ages of $3^1/_2$ and 5 were correct 9 out of 10 times.

CHECKPOINT

Can you . . .

- ✔ Tell how centration limits preoperational thought?
- ✔ Give several reasons why preoperational children have difficulty with conservation?
- ✔ Discuss research that challenges Piaget's views on egocentrism in early childhood?

Why were these children able to take another person's point of view (the police officer's) when those doing the mountain task were not? It may be because the "police officer" task calls for thinking in more familiar, less abstract ways. Most children do not look at mountains and do not think about what other people might see when looking at one, but most 3-year-olds know about dolls and police officers and hiding. Thus young children may show egocentrism primarily in situations beyond their immediate experience.

empathy
Ability to put oneself in another person's place and feel what that person feels.

Research also challenges Piaget's belief that egocentrism delays the development of **empathy,** the ability to understand what another person is feeling. Even 10- to 12-month-old babies cry when they see another child crying; by 13 or 14 months, they pat or hug a crying child; by 18 months they may hold out a new

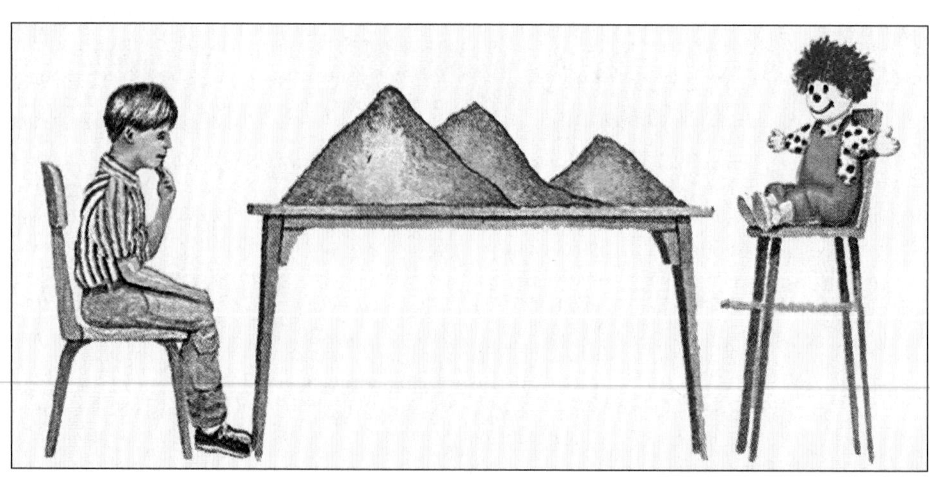

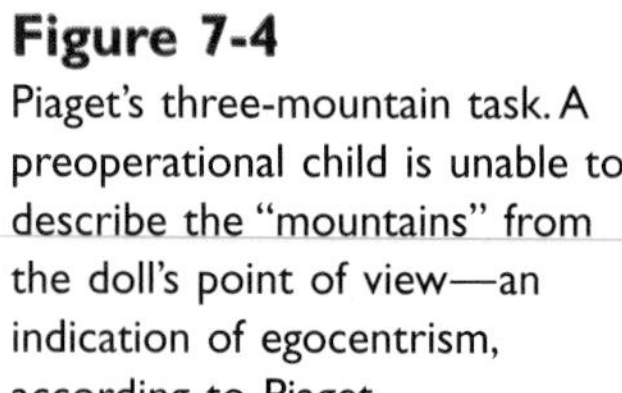

Figure 7-4
Piaget's three-mountain task. A preoperational child is unable to describe the "mountains" from the doll's point of view—an indication of egocentrism, according to Piaget.

toy to replace a broken one or give a bandage to someone with a cut finger (Yarrow, 1978). In early childhood, empathy shows itself more and more. This kind of understanding usually comes earlier to children in families that talk a lot about feelings and causality (Dunn, Brown, Slomkowski, Tesla, & Youngblade, 1991; Dunn, 1991).

Do Young Children Have Theories of Mind?

theory of mind Awareness and understanding of mental processes.

Piaget (1929) was the first scholar to investigate children's **theory of mind,** their emerging awareness of their own mental processes and those of other people. He asked children such questions as "Where do dreams come from?" and "What do you think with?" On the basis of the answers, he concluded that children younger than 6 cannot distinguish between thoughts or dreams and real physical entities and have no theory of mind. However, more recent research indicates that between ages 2 and 5, children's knowledge about mental processes—their own and others'—grows dramatically (Astington, 1993; Bower, 1993; Flavell, Green, & Flavell, 1995).

Again, methodology seems to have made the difference. Piaget's questions were abstract, and he expected children to be able to put their understanding into words. Contemporary researchers use vocabulary and objects children are familiar with. Instead of talking in generalities, they observe children in everyday activities or give them concrete examples. In this way, we have learned, for example, that 3-year-olds can tell the difference between a boy who has a cookie and a boy who is thinking about a cookie; they know which boy can touch, share, and eat it (Astington, 1993). They know that people who get what they want are likely to feel happy, and people who don't get what they want are likely to feel sad (Flavell et al., 1995).

Young children's theory of mind continues to develop throughout early childhood. Let's look at several aspects of it.

Knowledge about Thinking

Young children know something about what thinking is, but they are less aware of when it occurs and what people are thinking about. Between ages 3 and 5, children come to understand that thinking goes on inside the mind; that it can deal with either real or imaginary things; that someone can be thinking of one thing while doing or looking at something else; that a person whose eyes and ears are covered can think about objects; that someone who looks pensive is probably thinking; and that thinking is different from seeing, talking, touching, and knowing (Flavell et al., 1995).

However, preschoolers generally believe that mental activity starts and stops. They seem unaware that the mind is constantly engaged in thought. Not until middle childhood do children know that the mind is continuously active (Flavell, 1993; Flavell et al., 1995). Preschoolers also have little or no awareness that they or other people think in words, or "talk to themselves in their heads," or that they think while they are looking, listening, reading, or talking (Flavell, Green, Flavell, & Grossman, 1997).

Distinguishing between Fantasy and Reality

Sometime between 18 months and 3 years, children learn to distinguish between real and imagined events. Three-year-olds know the difference between a real dog and a dog in a dream, and between something invisible (such as air) and something imaginary. They can pretend and can tell when someone else is pretending (Flavell et al., 1995).

Still, the line between fantasy and reality may seem to blur at times, as with Wang Yani and the monkeys in her paintings, who seemed more real to her than the live monkey her father once gave her. In one study (Harris, Brown, Marriott,

Whittall, & Harmer, 1991), 40 four- to six-year-olds were shown two cardboard boxes. They were asked to pretend that there was a monster in one box and a bunny in the other. Each box had a small hole in it, and the children were asked whether they wanted to put a finger or a stick in the holes. The experimenter then left the room "to fetch something," and some of the children did touch the boxes. Even though most of the children claimed they were just pretending about both the bunny and the monster, most preferred to touch the box holding the imaginary bunny, and more put their fingers in that box and put the stick in the monster box.

This research suggests that even though young children understand the distinction between fantasy and reality, they sometimes act as if the creatures of their imagination could exist. On the other hand, the children may simply have been carrying on the unfinished pretend game in the experimenter's absence. That was the conclusion of a partial replication of the study, in which the experimenter remained in the room and clearly ended the pretense. Only about 10 percent of the children touched or looked in the boxes, and when questioned, almost all showed a clear understanding that the creatures were imaginary (Golomb & Galasso, 1995). It's possible, though, that if the experimenter had left the room, as in the previous study, the children might have felt more free to act on their fantasies, since the presence of adults has been found to inhibit children's magical thinking (Woolley, 1997).

A review of the literature suggests that magical or wishful thinking in children age 3 and older does not stem from a basic confusion between fantasy and reality. Nor, it is claimed, is children's magical thinking fundamentally different from that of many adults who believe in astrology or who avoid walking under ladders. However, the fantasy-reality distinction may be less firmly established in children than in adults. Often magical thinking is a way to explain events that do not seem to have obvious realistic explanations (usually because children lack knowledge about them), or simply to indulge in the pleasures of pretending—as with the belief in the tooth fairy or Santa Claus or in imaginary playmates (see Box 7-1). Children, like adults, generally are aware of the magical nature of such fantasy figures but are more willing to entertain the possibility that they may be real. Furthermore, adults tend to encourage children's fascination with the imaginary by immersing them in a culture of fairy tales and dragons (Woolley, 1997). It is difficult to know, when questioning children about "pretend" objects, whether children are giving "serious" answers or are still keeping up the pretense (M. Taylor, 1997).

False Beliefs and Deception

Five-year-old Mariella is shown a candy box and is asked what is in it. "Candy," she says. But when she opens the box, she finds crayons, not candy. "What will a child who hasn't opened the box think is in it?" the researcher asks. "Candy!" shouts Mariella, grinning at the joke. When the researcher repeats the same procedure with 3-year-old Bobby, he too answers the first question with "Candy." But after seeing the crayons in the box, when asked what another child would think was in the box, he says "Crayons." And then he says that he himself originally thought crayons would be in the box (Flavell, 1993; Flavell et al., 1995).

Not until children are 4 or 5 years old, according to this and some other research, do they understand that they or other people can have false beliefs (Moses & Flavell, 1990). This understanding flows from the realization that people hold mental representations of reality, which can sometimes be wrong; and 3-year-olds, at least in some studies, appear to lack such an understanding (Flavell et al., 1995). Other researchers claim that 3-year-olds have at least a rudimentary understanding of false beliefs but may not show it when presented with complicated situations (Hala & Chandler, 1996).

Three-year-olds' failure to recognize false beliefs may stem more from egocentric thinking than from lack of awareness of mental representations. Children that age do see a relationship between belief and surprise: they know, for exam-

Box 7-1

Imaginary Playmates

At $3^1/_2$, Anna had 23 "sisters" with such names as Och, Elmo, Zeni, Aggie, and Ankie. She often talked to them on the telephone, since they lived about 100 miles away, in the town where her family used to live. During the next year, most of the sisters disappeared, but Och continued to visit, especially for birthday parties. Och had a cat and a dog (which Anna had begged for in vain), and whenever Anna was denied something she saw advertised on television, she announced that she already had one at her sister's house. But when a live friend came over and Anna's mother happened to mention one of her imaginary companions, Anna quickly changed the subject.

All 23 sisters—and some "boys" and "girls" who have followed them—lived only in Anna's imagination, as she well knew. Like an estimated 25 to 65 percent of children between ages 3 and 10 (Woolley, 1997), she created imaginary companions, with whom she talked and played. This normal phenomenon of childhood is seen most often in bright, creative firstborn and only children (Manosevitz, Prentice, & Wilson, 1973). Girls are more likely than boys to have imaginary playmates (or at least to acknowledge them); girls' imaginary playmates are usually human, whereas boys' are more often animals (D. G. Singer & Singer, 1990). However, this was not true of Wang Yani; the monkeys she painted often served as imaginary companions with whom she acted out everyday problems or experiences.

Children who have imaginary companions can distinguish fantasy from reality, but in free-play sessions they are more likely to engage in pretend play than are children without imaginary companions (M. Taylor, Cartwright, & Carlson, 1993). They play more happily and more imaginatively than other children and are more cooperative with other children and adults (D. G. Singer & Singer, 1990; J. L. Singer & Singer, 1981). They are more fluent with language, watch less television, and show more curiosity, excitement, and persistence during play. In one study, 4-year-olds—regardless of verbal intelligence—who reported having imaginary companions did better on theory of mind tasks (such as differentiating appearance and reality and recognizing false beliefs) than children who did not create such companions (M. Taylor & Carlson, 1997).

Children use imaginary companions to help them get along better in the real world. Imaginary playmates are good company for an only child (like Anna and Wang Yani). They provide wish-fulfillment mechanisms ("There was a monster in my room, but Elmo scared it off with magic dust"), scapegoats ("I didn't eat those cookies—Och must have done it!"), displacement agents for the child's own fears ("Aggie is afraid she's going to be washed down the drain"), and support in difficult situations. (One 6-year-old "took" her imaginary companion with her to see a scary movie.)

ple, that a child who believes she is getting hot oatmeal for breakfast will be surprised if she gets cold spaghetti instead (Wellman & Banerjee, 1991). But they have difficulty recognizing that another person's belief or desire may be different from a very strong belief or desire that they themselves hold (Moore et al., 1995).

Older preschoolers' more advanced understanding of mental representations seems to be related to a decline in egocentrism. Four-year-olds understand that people who see or hear different versions of the same event may come away with different beliefs. Not until about age 6, however, do children realize that two people who see or hear the *same* thing may interpret it differently (Pillow & Henrichon, 1996).

Children whose teachers rate them high in social skills are better able to recognize false beliefs. This may be a bidirectional relationship. Frequent, successful social interactions may help children learn about connections between thoughts and behavior. Conversely, children who understand such connections may have an advantage in social situations (Watson, Nixon, Wilson, & Capage, 1999).

Deception is an effort to plant a false belief in someone else's mind, and it requires a child to suppress the impulse to be truthful. Some studies have found that children become capable of deception as early as age 2 or 3, others, at 4 or 5. The difference may have to do with the means of deception children are expected to use. In a series of experiments, 3-year-olds were asked whether they would like to play a trick on an experimenter by giving a false clue about which of

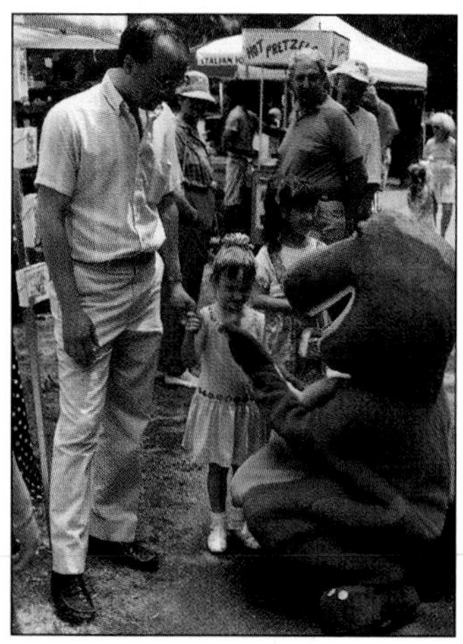

Is it really Barney? This young girl doesn't seem quite sure. The ability to distinguish appearance from reality develops between ages 3 and 6.

two boxes a ball was hidden in. The children were better able to carry out the deception when asked to put a picture of the ball on the wrong box, or to point to that box with an arrow, than when they pointed with their fingers, which children this age are accustomed to do nondeceptively (Carlson, Moses, & Hix, 1998).

According to Piaget, young children do not understand the difference between a deception and a mistake; they regard all falsehoods—intentional or not—as lies. However, when 3- to 6-year-olds were told a story about a subject close to their experience—the danger of food contamination—and were given a choice between interpreting a character's action as a lie or a mistake, about three-fourths of the children in all age groups characterized it accurately (Siegal & Peterson, 1998). Apparently, then, even 3-year-olds have some understanding of the role of intent in deception.

Distinguishing Between Appearance and Reality

Related to awareness of false beliefs is the ability to distinguish between appearance and reality: both require a child to refer to two conflicting mental representations at the same time. According to Piaget, not until about age 5 or 6 do children understand the distinction between what *seems* to be and what *is*. Much research bears him out, though some studies have found this ability beginning to emerge between ages 3 and 4 (Friend & Davis, 1993; C. Rice, Koinis, Sullivan, Tager-Flusberg, & Winner, 1997).

In one series of experiments (Flavell, Green, & Flavell, 1986), 3-year-olds confused appearance and reality in a variety of tests. For example, the experimenters showed preschoolers a red car and then covered it with a filter that made it look black. When the children were asked what color the car really was, they said "Black." When the children put on special sunglasses that made milk look green, they said the milk *was* green, even though they had just seen white milk. When an experimenter put on a Halloween mask in front of the children, they thought the experimenter was someone else. In another study, which dealt not only with physical appearances (the colors of animal cutouts, which were altered by transparent plastic filters) but also with recognition of a story character's real versus feigned emotional state (looking happy while actually feeling sad), 5- and 6-year-olds did much better than 4-year-olds (Friend & Davis, 1993).

CHECKPOINT

Can you . . .

- ✔ Give examples of research that challenges Piaget's views on young children's cognitive limitations?
- ✔ Describe changes between the ages of 3 and 6 in children's knowledge about the way their minds work?

Other Aspects of Cognitive Development

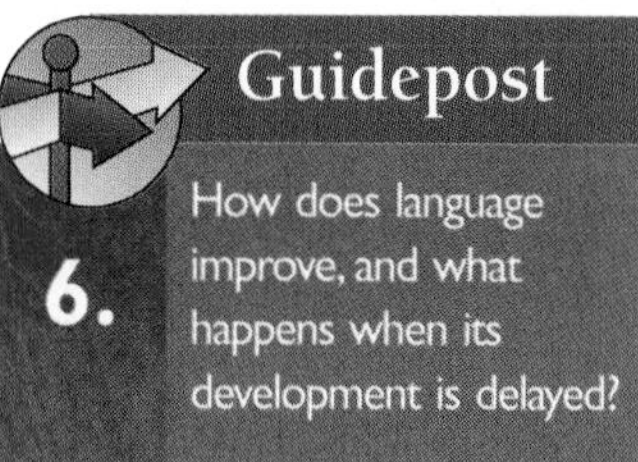

Guidepost
6.
How does language improve, and what happens when its development is delayed?

During early childhood Anna was full of questions: "How many sleeps until tomorrow?" "Who filled the river with water?" "Do babies have muscles?" "Do smells come from inside my nose?" Young children's growing facility with language helps them express their own unique view of the world. As they become more competent in memory and other information-processing abilities, they form and use concepts they can share with others. And, as children apply their intelligence to solving puzzling problems, individual differences become more apparent and more measurable.

Language

Preschoolers make rapid advances in vocabulary, grammar, and syntax. The child who, at 3, describes how Daddy "hatches" wood (chops with a hatchet), or asks Mommy to "piece" her food (cut it into little pieces) may, by the age of 5, tell her mother, "Don't be ridiculous!" or proudly point to her toys and say, "See how I organized everything?"

Vocabulary

At 3, the average child can use 900 to 1,000 different words and uses about 12,000 each day. By the age of 6, a child typically has a spoken vocabulary of 2,600 words and understands more than 20,000 (Owens, 1996), having learned an average of 9 new words a day since about $1\frac{1}{2}$ years of age (M. L. Rice, 1982). With the help of formal schooling, a youngster's passive, or receptive, vocabulary (words she can understand) will grow four times as large—to 80,000 words—by the time of entry into high school (Owens, 1996).

How do children expand their vocabularies so quickly? Apparently they do it by **fast mapping,** which allows them to absorb the meaning of a new word after hearing it only once or twice in conversation. On the basis of the context, children seem to form a quick hypothesis about the meaning of the word and store it in memory. Linguists are not sure how fast mapping works, but it seems likely that children draw on what they know about the rules for forming words, about similar words, about the immediate context, and about the subject under discussion.

fast mapping
Process by which a child absorbs the meaning of a new word after hearing it once or twice in conversation.

Names of objects (nouns) seem to be easier to fast map than names of actions (verbs), which are less concrete. Yet one experimental study showed that children just under 3 years old can fast map a new verb and apply it to another situation in which the same action is being performed (Golinkoff, Jacquet, Hirsh-Pasek, & Nandakumar, 1996). Many 3- and 4-year-olds seem able to tell when two words refer to the same object or action—an impressive feat (Savage & Au, 1996).

Grammar and Syntax

The ways in which children combine syllables into words and words into sentences grow increasingly sophisticated during early childhood (Owens, 1996). At 3, children typically begin to use plurals, possessives, and past tense and know the difference between *I, you,* and *we.* However, they still make errors of overregularization because they have not yet learned exceptions to rules (refer back to Chapter 5). Their sentences are generally short and simple, often leaving out small words such as *a* and *the,* but including some pronouns, adjectives, and prepositions. Most of their sentences are declarative ("Kitty wants milk"), but they can ask—and answer—*what* and *where* questions. (*Why* and *how* are harder to grasp.)

Between ages 4 and 5, sentences average four to five words and may be declarative, negative ("I'm not hungry"), interrogative ("Why can't I go outside?"), or imperative ("Catch the ball!"). Four-year-olds use complex, multiclause sentences ("I'm eating because I'm hungry") more frequently if their parents often use such sentences (Huttenlocher, Boyle, Cymerman, & Vasilyeva, in preparation). Children this age tend to string sentences together in long run-on stories (" . . . And then . . . And then . . . "). In some respects, comprehension may be immature. For example, 4-year-old Noah can carry out a command that includes more than one step ("Pick up your toys and put them in the cupboard"). However, if his mother tells him "You may watch TV after you pick up your toys," he may process the words in the order in which he hears them and think he can first watch television and then pick up his toys.

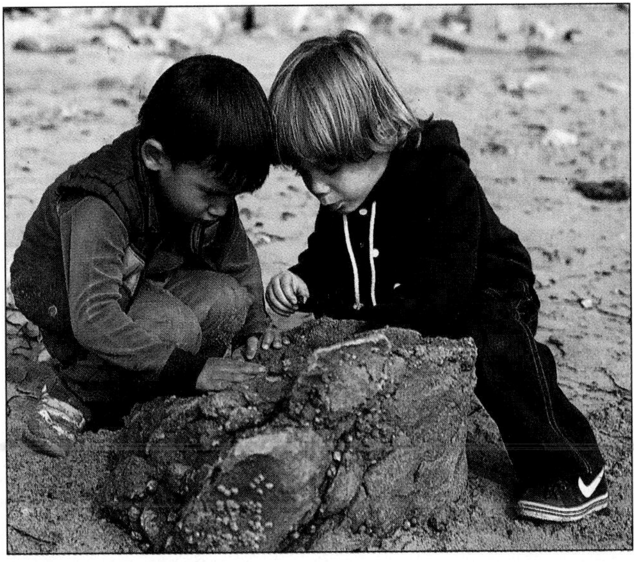

Although Piaget believed that most of young children's speech is egocentric, research shows that children like these boys playing on the beach communicate, both verbally and through gestures, from an early age.

By ages 5 to 7, children's speech has become quite adultlike. They speak in longer and more complicated sentences. They use more conjunctions, prepositions, and articles. They use compound and complex sentences and can handle all parts of speech. Still, while children this age speak fluently, comprehensibly, and fairly grammatically, they have yet to master many fine points of language.

Pragmatics and Social Speech

pragmatics
The practical knowledge needed to use language for communicative purposes.

social speech
Speech intended to be understood by a listener.

As children learn vocabulary, grammar, and syntax, they become more competent in **pragmatics**—the practical knowledge of how to use language to communicate. This includes knowing how to ask for things, how to tell a story or joke, how to begin and continue a conversation, and how to adjust comments to the listener's perspective (M. L. Rice, 1982). These are all aspects of **social speech:** speech intended to be understood by a listener.

As we'll see, Piaget characterized much of young children's speech as egocentric. But, as we reported in Chapter 5, research shows that children use both gestures and speech communicatively from an early age. By age 2, they engage in conversation, trying to make their own speech relevant to what someone else has said. However, children this age have trouble keeping a conversation going without changing the subject (Owens, 1996).

With improved pronunciation and grammar, it becomes easier for others to understand what children say. Most 3-year-olds are quite talkative, and they pay attention to the effect of their speech on others. If people cannot understand them, they try to explain themselves more clearly. Four-year-olds, especially girls, use "parentese" when speaking to 2-year-olds (Owens, 1996; Shatz & Gelman, 1973; see Chapter 5). Three- to 5-year-olds communicate very differently with a person who can see than with one who cannot; they will point to a toy for a sighted listener but describe it to a blindfolded one (Maratsos, 1973).

Most 5-year-olds can adapt what they say to what the listener knows. They can now use words to resolve disputes, and they use more polite language and fewer direct commands in talking to adults than to other children. Almost half of all 5-year-olds can stick to a conversational topic for about a dozen turns—if they are comfortable with their partner and if the topic is one they know and care about (Owens, 1996).

Private Speech

private speech
Talking aloud to oneself with no intent to communicate.

Anna, age 4, was alone in her room painting. When she finished, she was overheard saying aloud, "Now I have to put the pictures somewhere to dry. I'll put them by the window. They need to get dry now. I'll paint some more dinosaurs."

Private speech—talking aloud to oneself with no intent to communicate with others—is normal and common in childhood, accounting for 20 to 50 percent of what 4- to 10-year-old children say (Berk, 1986a). Two to 3-year-olds playfully repeat rhythmic sounds; older children "think out loud" or mutter in barely audible tones.

Piaget (1923/1962) saw private speech as egocentric, a sign of cognitive immaturity. Unable to communicate meaningfully or to recognize others' viewpoints, young children simply vocalize whatever is on their own minds. Another reason young children talk while they do things, said Piaget, is that the symbolic function is not fully developed: they do not yet distinguish between words and the actions the words stand for. With cognitive maturation and social experience, children by the end of the preoperational stage become less egocentric and more capable of symbolic thought, and so discard private speech.

Like Piaget, Vygotsky (1934/1962) believed that private speech helps young children to integrate language with thought. However, Vygotsky did not look upon private speech as egocentric. He saw it as a special form of communication: conversation with the self. As such, he said, it serves a very important function in the transition between early social speech (often experienced in the form of adult commands) and inner speech (thinking in words)—a transition toward the internalization of socially derived control of behavior ("Now I have to put the pictures somewhere to dry"). Vygotsky suggested that private speech follows an inverted U-shaped curve, increasing during the preschool years as children use it for self-regulation and then fading away during the early elementary school years as they become more able to guide and master their actions.

Research generally supports Vygotsky. In an observational study of 93 low- to middle-income 3- to 5-year-olds, 86 percent of the children's remarks were *not* egocentric (Berk, 1986a). The most sociable children, and those who engage in the most social speech, tend to use the most private speech as well, apparently supporting Vygotsky's view that private speech is stimulated by social experience (Berk, 1986a, 1986b, 1992; Berk & Garvin, 1984; Kohlberg, Yaeger, & Hjertholm, 1968).

There also is evidence for the role of private speech in self-regulation (Berk & Garvin, 1984; Furrow, 1984). Private speech tends to increase when children are trying to do difficult tasks, especially without adult supervision (Berk, 1992; Berk & Garvin, 1984). Private speech serves other functions for younger children. Two-year-olds often engage in "crib talk," playing with sounds and words. For 4- and 5-year-olds, private speech may be a way to express fantasies and emotions (Berk, 1992; Small, 1990).

According to one ranking (Bivens & Berk, 1988), children progress through at least three levels of private speech: (1) speech that is purely self-expressive (word play, repetition of syllables, expression of feelings, or talking to dolls or imaginary playmates); (2) vocal statements relevant to a task at hand (commenting on what one is doing or needs to do or has done, asking and then answering one's own questions, or sounding out words); and (3) external signs of task-directed inner speech (inaudible muttering or lip and tongue movements). Preschool girls, who tend to be more verbally advanced than preschool boys, use more mature forms of private speech; and middle-income children use more mature forms than low-income children (Berk, 1986a).

How much do children engage in private speech? Research initially supported Vygotsky's U-shaped curve (Berk, 1986a, 1986c; Kohlberg et al., 1968), but the pattern now appears more complex. Some studies have reported no age changes in overall use of private speech; others have found variations in the timing of its decline. The brightest children tend to use it earliest. Whereas Vygotsky considered the need for private speech a universal stage of cognitive development, studies have found a wide range of individual differences, with some children using it very little or not at all (Berk, 1992).

Understanding the significance of private speech has practical implications, especially in school (Berk, 1986b). Talking to oneself or muttering should not be considered misbehavior; a child may be struggling with a problem and may need to think out loud.

CHECKPOINT

Can you . . .

- ✔ Trace normal progress in 3- to 6-year-olds' vocabulary, grammar, syntax, and conversational abilities?
- ✔ Give reasons why children of various ages use private speech?

Delayed Language Development

About 3 percent of preschool-age children show language delays, though their intelligence is usually average or better (M. L. Rice, 1989). Boys are more likely than girls to be late talkers (Plomin et al., 1998).

It is unclear why some children speak late. They do not necessarily lack linguistic input at home. These children may have a cognitive limitation that makes it hard for them to learn the rules of language (Scarborough, 1990). Some late speakers have a history of otitis media (an inflammation of the middle ear) between 12 and 18 months of age; these children improve in language ability when the infection, with its related hearing loss, clears up (Lonigan, Fischel, Whitehurst, Arnold, & Valdez-Menchaca, 1992).

Some current investigations focus on problems in fast mapping. Children with delayed language skills may need to hear a new word more often than other children do before they can incorporate it into their vocabularies (M. L. Rice, 1989; M. L. Rice, Oetting, Marquis, Bode, & Pae, 1994). Heredity seems to play a role in the most severe cases of language delay. Among 3,039 pairs of 2-year-old twins, if one monozygotic twin fell in the bottom 5 percent in vocabulary knowledge, the other twin had an 80 percent chance of being equally delayed. With dizygotic twins, the chances of equivalent delays were only 42 percent (Plomin et al., 1998).

Many children who speak late—especially those whose comprehension is normal—eventually catch up (Thal, Tobias, & Morrison, 1991). Still, delayed language development can have far-reaching cognitive, social, and emotional consequences. Children who show an unusual tendency to mispronounce words at age 2, who have poor vocabulary at age 3, or who have trouble naming objects at age 5 are apt to have reading disabilities later on (M. Rice et al., 1994; Scarborough, 1990). Children who do not speak or understand as well as their peers tend to be judged negatively by adults and other children (M. L. Rice, Hadley, & Alexander, 1993) and to have trouble finding playmates or friends (Gertner, Rice, & Hadley, 1994). Children viewed as unintelligent or immature may "live down" to these expectations, and their self-image may suffer.

Speech and language therapy for children with delayed language development should begin with professional assessment of both child and family. It may include therapeutic strategies focusing on specific language forms, a specialized preschool program targeting language skills, and follow-up programs either in or out of school during the elementary school years (M. L. Rice, 1989).

A promising technique, both for normal children and for those who show language delays or are at risk of developing reading problems, is called *dialogic reading*. In this method, reading picture books becomes a vehicle for parent-child dialogue. Parents are taught to ask "what" questions, to follow up the child's answers with more questions, to repeat and expand on what the child says, to correct wrong answers and give alternative possibilities, to help the child as needed, and to give praise and encouragement. With older preschoolers, they encourage the child to relate a story to the child's own experience ("Have you ever seen a duck swimming? What did it look like?"). In one experiment, 3- to 6-year-olds with mild-to-moderate language delays whose mothers were trained in dialogic reading tended to give more verbal responses to questions than before and to use a greater variety of words and longer utterances. These children improved more than a comparison group whose mothers had been trained to use similar principles in talking with their children, but not about books (Dale, Crain-Thoreson, Notari-Syverson, & Cole, 1996).

Why is shared reading more effective than just talking with a child? Shared reading affords a natural opportunity for giving information and increasing vocabulary. It provides a focus for attention and for asking and responding to questions. In addition, it is enjoyable for both children and adults; it fosters emotional bonding while enhancing cognitive development.

Social Interaction and Preparation for Literacy

emergent literacy Preschoolers' development of skills, knowledge, and attitudes that underlie reading and writing.

Emergent literacy is the development of skills, knowledge, and attitudes that underlie reading and writing. Besides general linguistic skills, such as vocabulary, syntax, and the understanding that language is used to communicate, these include such specific preliteracy skills as the realization that words are composed of distinct sounds, or *phonemes*, and the ability to link phonemes with the corresponding alphabetic letters or combinations of letters (Whitehurst & Lonigan, 1998).

As children learn the skills they will need to translate the written word into speech, they also learn that writing can express ideas, thoughts, and feelings. Preschool children pretend to write by scribbling, lining up their marks from left to right (Brenneman, Massey, Machado, & Gelman, 1996). Later they begin using letters, numbers, and letterlike shapes to represent words, syllables, or phonemes.

Often their spelling is so inventive that they may not be able to read it themselves (Whitehust & Lonigan, 1998)!

Social interaction can promote emergent literacy. Children are more likely to become good readers and writers if, during the preschool years, parents provide conversational challenges the children are ready for—if they use a rich vocabulary and center dinner-table talk on the day's activities or on questions about why people do things and how things work. Such conversations help young children learn to choose words and put sentences together coherently (Snow, 1990, 1993).

In a longitudinal study of 24 white, middle-class two-parent families (Reese, 1995), the quality of mother-child conversation at ages 3 and 4—particularly about past events—was a strong predictor of literacy skills prior to entering first grade. Most influential was mothers' use of questions and comments that helped children elaborate on events or link them with other incidents. Children who took the lead in these conversations were more likely to be competent storytellers as kindergartners.

As we discussed in Chapter 5, reading to children is one of the most effective paths to literacy. Children who are read to from an early age learn that reading and writing move from left to right and from top to bottom and that words are separated by spaces (Siegler, 1998; Whitehurst & Lonigan, 1998). They also are motivated to learn to read.

Adults tend to use one of three styles of reading to children: the *describer style, comprehender style,* and *performance-oriented style.* A *describer* focuses on describing what is going on in the pictures ("What are the Mom and Dad having for breakfast?"). A *comprehender* encourages the child to make inferences and predictions ("What do you think the lion will do now?"). A *performance-oriented* reader reads the story straight through, introducing the main themes beforehand and asking questions afterward. Among 50 four-year-olds in Dunedin, New Zealand, the describer style (similar to dialogic reading) produced the greatest overall benefits for vocabulary and print skills, but the performance-oriented style was more beneficial for children who started out with large vocabularies (Reese & Cox, 1999).

Too much time spent watching television can rob children of such interactive language opportunities, but moderate exposure to educational television can help prepare children for literacy, especially if parents talk with children about what they see. In one study, the more time 3- to 5-year-olds spent watching *Sesame Street,* the more their vocabulary improved (M. L. Rice, Huston, Truglio, & Wright, 1990).

CHECKPOINT

Can you . . .

✔ Discuss possible causes, consequences, and treatment of delayed language development?

✔ Identify factors in preparation for literacy?

Memory and Other Information-Processing Skills

During early childhood, children show significant improvement in attention and in the speed and efficiency with which they process information; and they begin to form long-lasting memories.

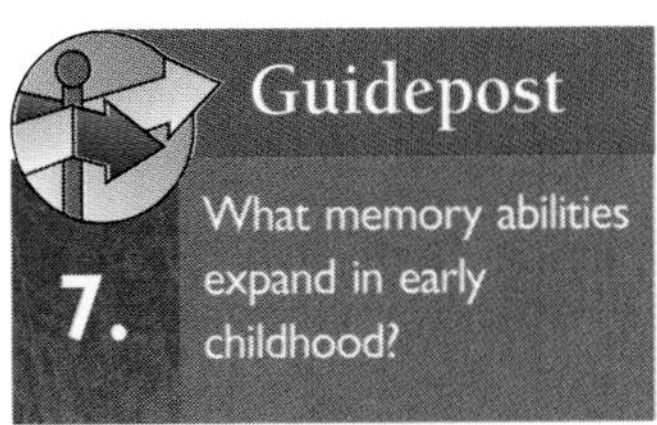

Guidepost
7.
What memory abilities expand in early childhood?

Recognition and Recall

Recognition is the ability to identify something encountered before (for example, to pick out a missing mitten from a lost-and-found box). **Recall** is the ability to reproduce knowledge from memory (for example, to describe the mitten to someone). Preschool children, like all age groups, do better on recognition than on recall, but both abilities improve with age (Lange, MacKinnon, & Nida, 1989; Myers & Perlmutter, 1978). The more familiar children are with an item, the better they can recall it.

Recall depends both on motivation to master skills and on the way a child approaches a task. In one observational study (Lange, MacKinnon, & Nida, 1989),

recognition
Ability to identify a previously encountered stimulus. Compare *recall.*

recall
Ability to reproduce material from memory. Compare *recognition.*

CHECKPOINT

Can you . . .

✔ Compare preschoolers' recognition and recall ability?

3- and 4-year-olds handled two assortments of toys in succession and then tried to name them from memory. The best predictor of success was *mastery motivation*: the tendency to be independent, self-directed, and generally resourceful, as rated by the child's teacher. The only other relevant factor was what the child did while studying the toys. The more children named or grouped the toys, or spent time thinking about or repeating their names (in other words, used strategies to help them remember), the better their recall.

Forming Childhood Memories

Can you remember anything that happened to you before you were 3 years old? The chances are you can't. This inability to remember early events is called *infantile amnesia.* One explanation, held by Piaget (1969) and others, is that early events are not stored in memory at all. Freud believed that early memories are repressed because they are emotionally troubling. Some information-processing theorists suggested that early memories become inaccessible because they are not *encoded* (prepared for storage), as later memories are. None of these explanations is supported by more recent research (Nelson, 1992, 1993b). Very young children do seem to remember things that happened to them. Even children younger than 2 can talk about events that occurred a month before, and 4-year-olds recall trips they took at age 2 (Nelson, 1992). Why, then, don't these early memories last? And how do children begin to form permanent memories? To answer that question, one investigator has distinguished between three types of childhood memory: *generic, episodic,* and *autobiographical* (Nelson, 1993b).

generic memory
Memory that produces a script of familiar routines to guide behavior.

script
General remembered outline of a familiar, repeated event, used to guide behavior.

episodic memory
Long-term memory of specific experiences or events, linked to time and place.

Generic memory, which begins at about age 2, produces a **script,** or general outline of a familiar, repeated event without details of time or place. The script contains routines for situations that come up again and again; it helps a child know what to expect and how to act. For example, a child may have scripts for riding the bus to preschool or having lunch at Grandma's house.

Episodic memory is the awareness of having experienced a particular incident that occurred at a specific time and place. It depends on the emerging recognition that general knowledge is based on specific experiences (Welch-Ross, 1997). Young children remember more clearly events that are unique or new. Three-year-olds may recall details about a trip to the circus for a year or longer (Fivush, Hudson, & Nelson, 1983), whereas generic memories of frequent events (such as going to the park) tend to blur together. However, given a young child's limited memory capacity, episodic memories are temporary. Unless they recur several

"Remember when we went on the airplane to visit Grandma and Grandpa?" Young children better remember events that are unique and new, and they may recall many details from a special trip for a year or longer.

times (in which case they are transferred to generic memory), they last for a few weeks or months and then fade. One reason young children do not remember events well is that they pay attention to exact details of an event, which are easily forgotten, whereas older children and adults focus on the gist of what happened. Also, young children, because of their lesser knowledge of the world, may fail to notice important aspects of a situation. The reliability of children's episodic memory has become an important issue in lawsuits involving charges of child abuse (see Box 7-2).

Autobiographical memory refers to memories that form a person's life history. These memories are specific and long-lasting. Although autobiographical memory is a type of episodic memory, not everything in episodic memory becomes part of it—only those memories that have special meaning to the child.

autobiographical memory Memory of specific events in one's own life.

Autobiographical memory begins for most people around age 4, and rarely before age 3. It increases slowly between ages 5 and 8; memories from then on may be recalled for twenty, forty, or more years. Individuals differ in the onset of autobiographical memory; some people have vivid memories from the age of 3, while others do not remember much before age 8 (Nelson, 1992).

This timetable suggests that autobiographical memory (and the decline of infantile or childhood amnesia) is linked with the development of language. The

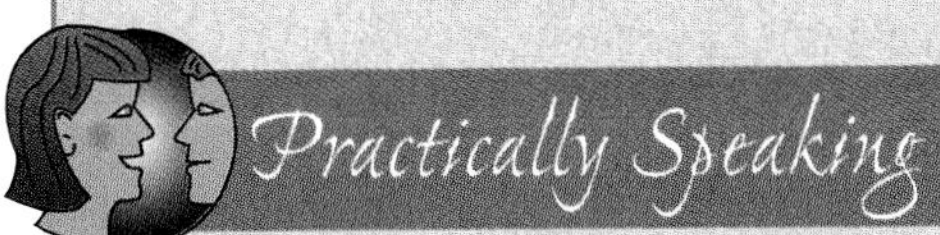

Box 7-2
How Reliable Is Children's Eyewitness Testimony?

Child abuse is a crime that often can be proved only by the testimony of preschool children. If a child's testimony is inaccurate, an innocent adult may be unfairly punished.

Children responding to adults' suggestions have been known to "remember" events that never occurred. For eleven consecutive weeks, an interviewer told a 4-year-old, "You went to the hospital because your finger got caught in a mousetrap. Did this ever happen to you?" At first the boy said, "No, I've never been to the hospital." In the second interview he said, "Yes, I cried." By the eleventh interview, he gave a detailed recital of the event and the trip to the hospital, which he now said had happened the day before (Ceci, in Goleman, 1993).

It is very difficult to detect a false story if a child has come to believe it and has been supplied with details by a biased interviewer (Bruck & Ceci, 1997; Bruck, Ceci, & Hembrooke, 1998). This can happen through the use of guided imagery. Children who have been asked to imagine or pretend that an event occurred may begin to think it *did* occur (Bruck & Ceci, 1997).

Preschoolers tend to be more suggestible than older children. This difference may be due to younger children's weaker episodic memory and their greater vulnerability to bribes, threats, and adult expectations (Bruck, Ceci, & Hembrooke, 1998; Ceci & Bruck, 1993; Leichtman & Ceci, 1995). Young children also tend to have difficulty in *source monitoring* (identifying how memories originated); they may not know whether they "remember" something from experience or from imagining or being told or asked about it (Woolley & Bruell, 1996).

In one experiment, researchers had a man called "Sam Stone" drop in at a child care center for a few minutes (Leichtman & Ceci, 1995). The visitor commented on a story that was being read, strolled around the room, and then waved good-bye and left. Some of the children who witnessed the event were repeatedly told stories about "Sam Stone" before his visit, depicting him as a well-meaning bumbler. Others, when interviewed after the visit, were given false suggestions that he had ripped a book and soiled a teddy bear. A third group received both the stereotyped advance preparation and the misleading questioning.

After four weekly interviews, nearly half of the 3- and 4-year-olds and 30 percent of 5- and 6-year-olds in the third group spontaneously reported the book-ripping and teddy-bear-soiling to a new interviewer; and when asked probing questions, nearly 3 out of 4 of the younger children said the visitor had done one or both. Lesser proportions of the groups that had received *only* advance preparation or suggestive questioning gave false reports, generally in response to probing. By contrast, none of the children in a control group, which had received neither advance preparation nor suggestive questioning, freely made false reports; and very few did so even when probed, showing that young children's testimony *can* be accurate when elicited neutrally.

Reports are likely to be more reliable if children are interviewed only once, soon after the event, by people who do not have an opinion about what took place, who do not ask leading questions, who ask open-ended rather than yes/no questions, who do not repeatedly ask the same questions,

Practically Speaking —Continued

who are patient and nonjudgmental, and who do not selectively reward or reinforce responses or convey veiled threats or accusations. The likelihood of a false report increases if an interviewer uses more than one suggestive technique (Bruck & Ceci, 1997; Bruck, Ceci, & Hembrooke, 1998; Leichtman & Ceci, 1995; Steward & Steward, 1996).

Most 4- to 6-year-olds—4 out of 5 in one study—are unlikely to accept false suggestions concerning an event in which they were personally involved (being touched on the leg rather than the arm), but they are more suggestible when asked leading questions. Suggestibility seems to diminish after age $4^1/_2$ (Portwood & Repucci, 1996). However, some children, regardless of age, are more suggestible than others (Bruck & Ceci, 1997).

According to some research, many children, given anatomically correct dolls, will insert fingers or sticks into a doll's vagina or anus, reporting that someone did that to them, even when it did not happen (Bruck & Ceci, 1997; Ceci & Bruck, 1993). In other studies, use of dolls did *not* increase false reports but rather produced more complete reports. Young children may need such external cues as prods to memory (Steward & Steward, 1996).

Shame may inhibit some children from reporting sexual abuse. When questioned about doctors' examinations, 5- and 7-year-old girls, even when using dolls, gave almost no false reports of genital contact. They were far more likely to *fail* to report contact that *did* occur (Saywitz, Goodman, Nicholas, & Moan, 1991). The relative privacy and impersonality of a computer-assisted interview may encourage disclosure (Steward & Steward, 1996).

Young children are apt to err in recalling precise details of an event that varies with repetition (Powell & Thomson, 1996). They tend to confuse what happened during the episode in question with what happened during other, similar episodes; all may blur together in memory into a generic "script." Thus a child may have trouble answering questions about a *specific instance* of abuse, even though the child accurately remembers a *pattern* of abuse.

Often young children's testimony is excluded because they cannot demonstrate a clear understanding of the difference between truth and falsehood and of the morality and consequences of telling a lie. Often they do not understand such questions the way they are asked or cannot explain the concepts involved. Furthermore, abused children often have seriously delayed language skills. The Lyon-Saywitz Oath-Taking Competency Picture Task avoids these problems by simply asking a prospective young witness whether a child in a story is telling the truth about a pictured event and what would happen if the child told a lie. Among 192 maltreated 4- to 7-year-olds awaiting court appearances, a majority of 5-year-olds successfully performed this task, and even 4-year-olds did better than chance would predict (Lyon & Saywitz, 1999).

Issues concerning the reliability of young children's testimony are still being sorted out, but it appears that children *can* give reliable testimony if care is taken to avoid biased interviewing techniques. Researchers are trying to develop and validate "model" interview techniques that will expose adults who harm children while protecting those who may be falsely accused (Bruck, Ceci, & Hembrooke, 1998).

ability to talk about an event may not be necessary for a young child to remember it, but verbal skills may affect whether and how memories can be carried forward into later life (Fivush & Schwarzmueller, in press). Not until children can put memories into words can they hold them in their minds, reflect on them, and compare them with the memories of others.

Consider this . . .

- What information would you seek and what factors would you consider in deciding whether to believe a preschooler's testimony in a child abuse case?

According to the **social interaction model,** based on Vygotsky's sociocultural theory, children collaboratively construct autobiographical memories as they talk with parents or other significant adults about shared past events, as Wang Yani continually did with her father (Nelson, 1993a). Parents initiate and guide these conversations, which enable children to learn how memories are organized in narrative form in their culture (Welch-Ross, 1997). When parents prompt 2- and 3-year-olds with frequent questions about context ("When did you find the pine cone?" "Where did you find it?" "Who was with you?"), children soon learn to include this information (Peterson & McCabe, 1994). When parents of 3-year-olds comment on subjective reactions ("You *wanted* to go on the slide," "It was a *huge* bowl," "Mommy was *wrong*"), the children at $5^1/_2$ are more likely to weave such comments into their reminiscences (Haden, Haine, & Fivush, 1997).

social interaction model Model, based on Vygotsky's sociocultural theory, which proposes that children construct autobiographical memories through conversation with adults about shared events.

It is important to keep in mind that most research on memory has focused on middle-class U.S. or western European children, most of whom have been talking since at least age 2. We are only beginning to learn about the relationship between memory and language among children who begin to speak later because of different social and cultural practices, or among deaf children of hearing parents who cannot as easily converse with them (Nelson, 1993b).

Influences on Autobiographical Memory

Why do some early memories last longer than others? One factor, as we've seen, is the uniqueness of the event. A second factor is children's active participation, either in the event itself or in its retelling or reenactment. A third factor is parents' way of talking with children about past events. Finally, the child's theory of mind may play a role.

Preschoolers tend to remember things they *did* better than things they merely *saw*. A study in New Zealand (Murachver, Pipe, Gordon, Owens, & Firush, 1996) measured 5- and 6-year-olds' recall of a novel event (visiting a "pirate") that they either observed, were told a story about, or experienced directly. A few days later, the children recalled details (such as trying on pirate clothes, steering the ship, making a treasure map, and finding the treasure) more completely, more accurately, and in a more organized way when they themselves had participated, and they required less prompting or reminding. The effect of direct experience was qualified by how often the event was repeated and with what variations, how logically the event was structured, and whether the children were asked to reenact the event or just describe it (Murachver et al., 1996).

The way adults talk with a child about a shared experience can influence how well the child will remember it (Haden & Fivush, 1996; Reese & Fivush, 1993). When a child gets stuck, adults with a *repetitive* conversational style tend to repeat their own previous statements or questions. Adults with an *elaborative* style are more likely to move on to a new aspect of the event or add more information. A repetitive-style parent might ask, "Do you remember how we traveled to Florida?" and then, receiving no answer, ask, "How did we get there? We went in the ______." An elaborative-style parent might instead follow up the first question by saying, "Did we go by car or by plane?" Elaborative parents seem more focused on having a mutually rewarding conversation and affirming the child's responses, whereas repetitive parents are more focused on checking the child's memory performance. Three-year-olds of elaborative-style parents take part in longer conversations about events and remember more details, and they tend to remember the events better at ages 5 and 6 (Reese, Haden, & Fivush, 1993).

CHECKPOINT

Can you . . .

- ✔ Explain how language development may contribute to the onset of autobiographical memory?
- ✔ Identify factors that affect how well a preschool child will remember an event?

Implicit Memory

Some memories—the kinds we have been discussing—are conscious (explicit); others, as we mentioned in Chapter 5, are preserved in unconscious (implicit) form (Lie & Newcombe, 1999; Newcombe & Fox, 1994). In one study, 9- and 10-year-olds were shown photos of preschool classmates they had not seen for five years, along with photos of children they had never known. Only 1 out of 5 children recognized their former classmates. Researchers measured the children's *skin conductance* (movement of electrical impulses through the skin) as they viewed the pictures. In a small but significant number of cases, positive responses appeared when the children saw pictures of their former classmates, even when they did not consciously recognize the faces (Newcombe & Fox, 1994). Similarly, when 8-year-olds were tested on implicit memory by asking them to match front views of children's faces with side views showing only partial features, the children made fewer errors with faces of former classmates than with faces of unknown children (Lie & Newcombe, 1999). These findings suggest that people may retain early memories of which they are not aware, and which may affect behavior.

Consider this . . .

- Since an elaborative conversational style seems most effective in developing young children's autobiographical memory, would you favor training parents to use it? Why or why not? What difficulties would you anticipate?

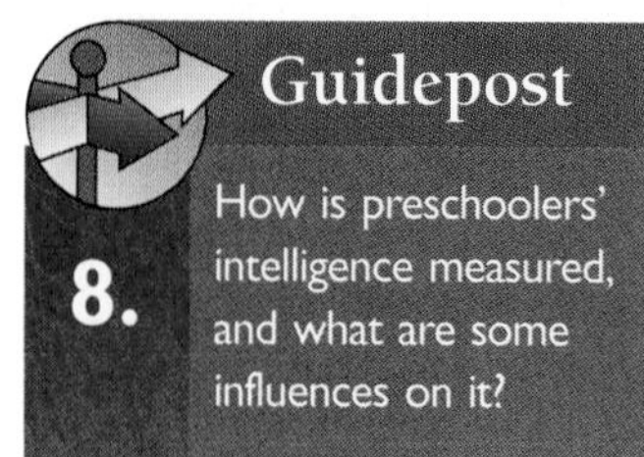

Guidepost
8.
How is preschoolers' intelligence measured, and what are some influences on it?

Intelligence: Psychometric and Vygotskian Approaches

One factor that may affect how early children develop both language and memory is intelligence. Let's look at two ways intelligence is measured—through traditional psychometric tests and through newer tests of cognitive potential—and at influences on children's performance.

Traditional Psychometric Measures

Because children of 3, 4, and 5 are more proficient with language than younger children, intelligence tests can now include more verbal items; and these tests produce more reliable results than the largely nonverbal tests used in infancy. As children approach age 5, there is a higher correlation between their scores on intelligence tests and the scores they will achieve later (Bornstein & Sigman, 1986). IQ tests given near the end of kindergarten are among the best predictors of future school success (Tramontana, Hooper, & Selzer, 1988).

Although preschool children are easier to test than infants and toddlers, they still need to be tested individually. The two most commonly used individual tests for preschoolers are the Stanford-Binet Intelligence Scale and the Wechsler Preschool and Primary Scale of Intelligence. The **Stanford-Binet Intelligence Scale,** the first individual childhood intelligence test to be developed, takes 30 to 40 minutes. The child is asked to define words, string beads, build with blocks, identify the missing parts of a picture, trace mazes, and show an understanding of numbers. The child's score is supposed to measure memory, spatial orientation, and practical judgment in real-life situations.

Stanford-Binet Intelligence Scale
Individual intelligence test used to measure memory, spatial orientation, and practical judgment.

Wechsler Preschool and Primary Scale of Intelligence, Revised (WPPSI-R)
Individual intelligence test for children ages 3 to 7, which yields verbal and performance scores as well as a combined score.

The fourth edition of the Stanford-Binet, revised in 1985, includes an equal balance of verbal and nonverbal, quantitative, and memory items. Instead of providing the IQ as a single overall measure of intelligence, the revised version assesses patterns and levels of cognitive development. The updated standardization sample is well balanced geographically, ethnically, socioeconomically, and by gender, and it includes children with disabilities.

The **Wechsler Preschool and Primary Scale of Intelligence, Revised (WPPSI-R),** an hour-long individual test used with children ages 3 to 7, yields separate verbal and performance scores as well as a combined score. Its separate scales are similar to those in the Wechsler Intelligence Scale for Children (WISC-III), discussed in Chapter 9. The 1989 revision includes new subtests and new picture items. It too has been restandardized on a sample of children representing the population of preschool-age children in the United States. Because children of this age tire quickly and are easily distracted, the test may be given in two separate sessions.

Parents of children with high IQs tend to be warm, loving, and sensitive and to encourage independence and creativity. Giving suggestions and strategies for solving a puzzle or problem—without showing strong approval or disapproval—can foster cognitive growth.

Influences on Measured Intelligence: The Family

Many people believe that IQ scores represent a fixed quantity of intelligence a person is born with. That is not so: the score is simply a measure of how well a child can do certain tasks in comparison with others of the same age. Test scores of children in industrialized countries have risen steadily since testing began, forcing test developers to raise standardized norms. This is called the *Flynn effect* (Flynn, 1984, 1987). The reasons for this upward trend are in dispute; it may in part reflect exposure to educational television, preschools, better-educated parents, and a wider variety of experiences, as well as changes in the tests themselves.

How well a particular child does on intelligence tests is influenced by many factors. These include temperament, the match between cognitive style and the tasks posed, social and emotional maturity, ease in the testing situation, preliteracy or literacy skills, socioeconomic status, and ethnic background. (We will examine several of these factors in Chapter 9.)

At one time it was believed that the family environment played a major role in cognitive development. Now the extent of that influence is in question. We don't know how much of parents' influence on intelligence comes from their genetic contribution, and how much from the fact that they provide a child's earliest environment for learning.

Twin and adoption studies suggest that family life has its strongest influence in early childhood, and this influence diminishes greatly by adolescence (McGue, 1997; Neisser et al., 1996). However, these studies have been done largely with white, middle-class samples; their results may not apply to low-income and nonwhite families (Neisser et al., 1996). In two recent longitudinal studies of low-income African American children, although the influence of the home environment did diminish between infancy and middle childhood, it remained substantial—at least as strong as the influence of the mother's IQ (Burchinal, Campbell, Bryant, Wasik, & Ramey, 1997).

As we discussed in Chapter 5, family economic circumstances can exert a powerful influence, not so much in themselves but in the way they affect parenting practices and the atmosphere in the home. But socioeconomic status is only one of several social and family risk factors. Assessments of 152 children at ages 4 and 13 revealed no single pattern of risk. Instead, a child's IQ was related to *the total number* of such risk factors as the mother's behavior, mental health, anxiety level, education, and beliefs about children's development; family size and social support; stressful life events; parental occupations; and disadvantaged status. The more risk factors there were, the lower the child's IQ score (Sameroff, Seifer, Baldwin, & Baldwin, 1993).

Testing and Teaching Based on Vygotsky's Theory

A form of testing developed in Russia and now becoming influential in the United States is based on Vygotsky's (1978) sociocultural theory, introduced in Chapter 2. According to Vygotsky, children learn by internalizing the results of their interactions with adults. Adults direct children's learning most effectively in the *zone of proximal development (ZPD),* that is, with regard to tasks children are almost ready to accomplish on their own.

Tests based on Vygotsky's approach emphasize potential rather than present achievement. These tests contain items up to two years above a child's current level of competence. The items a child can answer with help determine the ZPD, or potential level of development. Vygotsky (1956) gives an example of two children, each with a mental age of 7 years (based on ability to do various cognitive tasks). With the help of leading questions, examples, and demonstrations, Natasha can easily solve problems geared to a mental age of 9, two years beyond her mental age; but Ivan, with the same kind of help, can do tasks at only a $7^1/_2$-year-old level. If we measure these children by what they can do on their own (as traditional IQ tests do), their intelligence seems about the same; but if we measure them by their immediate potential development (their ZPD), they are quite different.

The ZPD, in combination with the related concept of *scaffolding* (refer back to Chapter 2), can help parents and teachers efficiently guide children's cognitive progress. The less able a child is to do a task, the more direction an adult must give. As the child can do more and more, the adult helps less and less. When the child can do the job alone, the adult takes away the "scaffold" that is no longer needed.

In one study, 3- and 4-year-olds were asked to give their parents directions for finding a hidden mouse in a dollhouse. The parents gave the children feedback when their directions needed clarifying. The parents proved to be highly sensitive to the children's scaffolding needs; they gave more directive prompts to 3-year-olds, whose directions tended to be less clear than those of 4-year-olds. The parents used fewer directive prompts as the children gained experience in giving clear directions (Plumert & Nichols-Whitehead, 1996).

CHECKPOINT

Can you . . .

✔ Describe two commonly used individual intelligence tests for preschoolers?

✔ Discuss several influences on measured intelligence?

✔ Explain why an intelligence test score using the ZPD might be significantly different from a traditional psychometric test score?

Consider this . . .

- How meaningful is intelligence testing of young children? If you were a preschool or kindergarten teacher, how helpful do you think it would be to know a child's IQ? The child's ZPD?
- Can you think of an effective way in which you have used scaffolding, or seen it used?

Ryan, 1997). Since the 1960s, large-scale programs have been developed to help such children compensate for what they have missed and to prepare them for school.

The best-known compensatory preschool program for children of low-income families in the United States is Project Head Start, launched in 1965. Head Start's administrators adopted a "whole child" approach. Their goals were to improve physical health, enhance cognitive skills, and foster self-confidence, relationships with others, social responsibility, and a sense of dignity and self-worth for the child and the family. The program provides medical, dental, and mental health care, social services, and at least one hot meal a day. Due to inadequate funding, Head Start serves only about one-third of eligible 3- and 4-year-olds (Children's Defense Fund, 1998).

Has Head Start lived up to its name? By and large, yes. The program has probably had its strongest impact on physical health and well-being (Zigler & Styfco, 1994). Head Start children also have shown substantial cognitive and language gains, with the neediest children benefiting most. Being healthier, Head Start children are absent less. They also do better on tests of motor control and physical development (Collins & Deloria, 1983). Head Start has had a positive impact on self-esteem, socialization, and social maturity (McKey et al., 1985). The most successful Head Start programs have been those with the most parental participation, the best teachers, the smallest groups, and the most extensive services.

A major concern has been that gains in IQ do not last. Although Head Start children do better on intelligence tests than other children from comparable backgrounds, this advantage disappears after the children start school. Nor have Head Start children equaled the average middle-class child in school achievement or on standardized tests (Collins & Deloria, 1983; Zigler & Styfco, 1993, 1994). Still, children from Head Start and other such programs are less likely to be placed in special education or to repeat a grade and are more likely to finish high school than low-income children who did not attend compensatory preschool programs (Neisser et al., 1996).

Advocates of compensatory programs say the results point to a need for earlier and longer-lasting intervention (Zigler & Styfco, 1993, 1994). In another large-scale federally funded compensatory program, the Chicago Child Parent Centers, which extends from preschool through third grade, the added years of academic enrichment signicantly increased achievement (Reynolds, 1994). And, on the basis of experience with Head Start and other compensatory preschool programs, educational researchers in recent years have focused attention on earlier interventions for infants and toddlers.

Some positive effects of Head Start and other compensatory preschool programs have persisted through elementary or high school or even beyond. A number of studies have found long-term benefits for children enrolled in high-quality compensatory preschool programs (Darlington, 1991; Haskins, 1989). A major benefit is a lesser likelihood of juvenile delinquency (see Chapter 12). Poor African American children who participated in the Perry Preschool Program of the High/Scope Educational Research Foundation (which predated Head Start) have been followed to age 27. They were much more likely than a comparison group who lacked preschool experience to finish high school, to enroll in college or vocational training, and to be employed. They also did better on tests of competence and were less likely to be on welfare or to have been arrested, and the women were less likely to have become pregnant in their teens (Berrueta-Clement, Schweinhart, Barnett, Epstein, & Weikart, 1985; Schweinhart, Barnes, & Weikart, 1993). It seems, then, that early childhood education can help compensate for deprivation and that well-planned programs produce long-term benefits that far exceed the original cost (Haskins, 1989; Schweinhart et al., 1993).

CHECKPOINT

Can you . . .

✔ Assess the benefits of compensatory preschool education?

Consider this . . .

- Is publicly funded compensatory education the best way to help poor children catch up?

The Transition to Kindergarten

For most U.S. children today, kindergarten is the beginning of formal schooling. The bell that marks the beginning of the first day of kindergarten represents an abrupt change in a child's life (Ladd, 1996).

Historically a year of transition between the relative freedom of home or preschool and the structure of "real school," kindergarten now has become more like first grade. Children spend less time on self-chosen activities and more time on worksheets and preparing to read. Possibly for the first time, they may receive critical evaluation of their abilities. In many districts, kindergartners go to school all day. There also are proposals to lengthen the school year, not only for kindergarten but for all grades. When an elementary school in a midsize, southeastern city added 30 days to its school year, kindergartners who went through the resulting 210-day program outperformed students in a traditional 180-day program on tests of math, reading, general knowledge, and cognitive competence at the beginning of first grade (Frazier & Morrison, 1998).

Although age 5 is the traditional time for kindergarten entrance, more and more children are starting at, or close to, age 6. As the academic and emotional pressures of kindergarten mount, many parents hold children back a year. Some schools offer a preliminary year of developmental kindergarten designed to provide a more gradual transition to "regular" kindergarten.

How do children adjust to kindergarten? The answer may depend on both the child's characteristics—age, gender, cognitive and social competencies, and coping skills—and the support or stress generated by the home, school, and neighborhood environments. Children with extensive preschool experience tend to be less anxious and to adjust more easily than those who spent little or no time in preschool. Children who played cooperatively in preschool tend to be well liked in kindergarten, but those who were aggressive or antisocial in preschool tend to be hostile, disruptive, and unpopular in kindergarten. Girls are more likely than boys to underrate their abilities, while boys are more likely to behave inappropriately in class. Children who start kindergarten with peers they know and like, or who have a "secure base" of ongoing neighborhood friendships, generally do better (Ladd, 1996; see Chapter 8).

The relationship with the kindergarten teacher greatly affects a child's success. Children who are close to their teachers tend to do well academically and to be highly involved in classroom activities. Children who are either overdependent on, or antagonistic toward, the teacher tend to do poorly, to dislike school, and to be less involved (Birch & Ladd, 1997).

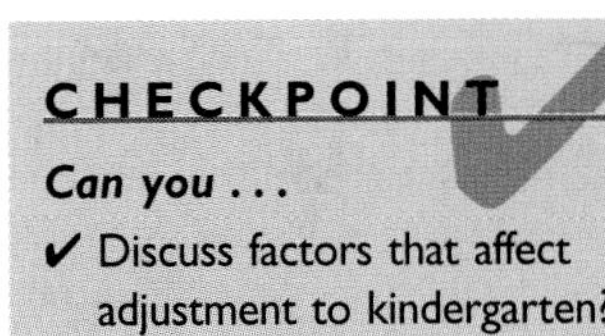

CHECKPOINT
Can you . . .
✔ Discuss factors that affect adjustment to kindergarten?

The burgeoning physical and cognitive skills of early childhood have psychosocial implications, as we'll see in Chapter 8.

Summary

PHYSICAL DEVELOPMENT

Aspects of Physiological Development

Guidepost 1. How do children's bodies change between ages 3 and 6, and what are their nutritional needs?

- Physical growth increases during the years from 3 to 6, but more slowly than during infancy and toddlerhood. Boys are on average slightly taller, heavier, and more muscular than girls. Internal body systems are maturing, and all primary teeth are present.
- Preschool children generally eat less for their weight than before, but the prevalence of obesity has increased.

Guidepost 2. What sleep patterns and problems tend to develop during early childhood?

- Sleep patterns change during early childhood, as they do throughout life, and are affected by cultural expectations.

- It is normal for preschool children to develop bedtime rituals that delay going to sleep and to rely on **transitional objects.** Prolonged bedtime struggles or persistent night terrors or nightmares may indicate emotional disturbances that need attention.
- **Enuresis** is common and is usually outgrown without special help.

Guidepost 3. What are the main motor achievements of early childhood?

- Children progress rapidly in **gross motor skills, fine motor skills,** and eye-hand coordination, developing more complex **systems of action.**
- **Handedness** is usually evident by age 3, reflecting dominance by one hemisphere of the brain.
- Stages of art production, which appear to reflect brain development, are the scribbling stage, shape stage, design stage, and pictorial stage.

Health and Safety

Guidepost 4. What are the major health and safety risks for children?

- Many major contagious illnesses are rare today in industrialized countries due to widespread immunization, and death rates have declined. Preventable disease continues to be a major problem in the developing world.
- Minor illnesses, such as colds and other respiratory illnesses, are common during early childhood and help build immunity to disease.
- Accidents, most commonly motor vehicle injuries, are the leading cause of death in childhood in the United States but have declined. Most fatal nonvehicular accidents occur at home.
- Environmental factors such as exposure to **stress,** smoking, poverty, and homelessness increase the risks of illness or injury. Lead poisoning can have serious physical, cognitive, and behavioral effects.

COGNITIVE DEVELOPMENT

Piagetian Approach: The Preoperational Child

Guidepost 5. What are some typical cognitive advances and some immature aspects of young children's thinking?

- Children in the **preoperational stage** of cognitive development, from approximately 2 years to 7 years of age, show several important advances, as well as some immature aspects of thought.
- The **symbolic function** enables children to reflect upon people, objects, and events that are not physically present. It is shown in deferred imitation, pretend play, and language.
- Preoperational children can understand the concept of identity. No longer limited by the **dual representation hypothesis,** they can make more accurate judgments about spatial relationships. They are becoming proficient at classification and can understand principles of counting and quantity.
- Although Piaget maintained that preoperational children reason by **transduction,** more recent research suggests that they can think logically about causation of familiar physical events. Their ability to categorize living and nonliving things challenges Piaget's attribution of **animism** to children this age.
- **Centration,** or inability to **decenter,** keeps preoperational children from understanding principles of **conservation.** Their logic is also limited by **irreversibility** and a focus on states rather than transformations.
- Although preoperational children show **egocentrism,** they appear to be less egocentric than Piaget thought; for example, they (and even younger children) are capable of **empathy.**
- The **theory of mind,** which seems to develop markedly between the ages of 3 and 5, includes awareness of a child's own thought processes, ability to distinguish fantasy from reality, understanding that people can hold false beliefs, ability to deceive, and ability to distinguish appearance from reality.

Other Aspects of Cognitive Development

Guidepost 6. How does language improve, and what happens when its development is delayed?

- During early childhood, vocabulary increases greatly, apparently through **fast mapping,** and grammar and syntax become fairly sophisticated. Children become more competent in **pragmatics** as they engage in **social speech.**
- **Private speech** is normal and common; it may aid in the shift to self-regulation and usually disappears by age 10.
- Causes of delayed language development are unclear. If untreated, it may have serious cognitive, social, and emotional consequences.
- Interaction with adults can promote **emergent literacy.**

Guidepost 7. What memory abilities expand in early childhood?

- At all ages, **recognition** is better than **recall,** but both increase during early childhood.
- Early **episodic memory** is only temporary; it fades or is transferred to **generic memory,** which produces a **script** of familiar routines to guide behavior. **Autobiographical memory** begins at about age 4 and may be related to language development. According to the **social interaction model,** children and adults co-construct autobiographical memories by talking about shared experiences.
- Children are more likely to remember unusual activities that they actively participate in. The way adults talk with children about events influences memory formation, as does a child's theory of mind.
- Implicit memories may unconsciously affect behavior.

Guidepost 8. How is preschoolers' intelligence measured, and what are some influences on it?

- The two most commonly used psychometric intelligence tests for young children are the **Stanford-Binet Intelligence Scale** and the **Wechsler Preschool and Primary Scale of Intelligence, Revised (WPPSI-R).**

- Intelligence test scores may be influenced by social and emotional functioning, as well as by parent-child interaction and socioeconomic factors. The family environment seems to have its greatest impact in early childhood.
- Newer tests based on Vygotsky's concept of the zone of proximal development (ZPD) are an indication of immediate potential for achievement. Such tests, when combined with scaffolding, can help parents and teachers guide children's progress.

Early Childhood Education

Guidepost 9. What purposes does early childhood education serve, and how do children make the transition to kindergarten?

- Goals of preschool education vary in different cultures. Since the 1970s, the academic content of early childhood education programs in the United States has increased, causing concern about the effects of academic pressure on young children. A similar trend has occurred in some Japanese preschools. For low-income children in the United States, academically oriented programs seem to be less effective than child-centered ones.
- Compensatory preschool programs, such as Project Head Start, have had positive outcomes, but participants generally have not equalled the performance of middle-class children.
- Adjustment to kindergarten may depend on interaction among the child's characteristics and those of the home, school, and neighborhood environments.

Key Terms

transitional objects (241)
enuresis (241)
gross motor skills (242)
fine motor skills (242)
systems of action (242)
handedness (243)
stress (246)
preoperational stage (250)
symbolic function (250)
dual representation hypothesis (252)
transduction (253)
animism (253)
centration (254)
decenter (255)
conservation (255)
irreversibility (255)
egocentrism (256)
empathy (256)
theory of mind (257)
fast mapping (261)
pragmatics (262)
social speech (262)
private speech (262)
emergent literacy (264)
recognition (265)
recall (265)
generic memory (266)
script (266)
episodic memory (266)
autobiographical memory (267)
social interaction model (268)
Stanford-Binet Intelligence Scale (270)
Wechsler Preschool and Primary Scale of Intelligence, Revised (WPPSI-R) (270)

Chapter 8

Psychosocial Development in Early Childhood

Children's playings are not sports and should be deemed as their most serious actions.

Montaigne, *Essays*

OUTLINE

Eva Perón

Focus: Eva Perón, "Woman of the People"*

Eva Perón (1919–1952) was an enigma, a woman of myth and mystery who (as dramatized in Andrew Lloyd Webber's musical *Evita*) rose from tawdry origins to become first lady of Argentina, transforming herself from a bastard waif to one of the most powerful women of all time. Her followers depicted her as a selfless friend of downtrodden workers and a champion of women's rights. Her enemies denounced her as power-hungry, manipulative, and ruthless. Even the basic facts of her life are in question, for she destroyed records and intimidated interviewers, and her biographies are full of contradictions. One point, however, is clear: the origins of her resolute drive for advancement went back to early childhood.

Eva (affectionately known as Evita) began life on May 7, 1919, in the small, isolated, dusty village of Los Toldos, on the *pampas* (agricultural plains) about 200 miles west of Buenos Aires. She was the fifth and youngest illegitimate child of Juana Ibarguren, an uneducated peasant woman, and Juan Duarte, a small rancher and magistrate who had left a wife and three daughters in the nearby town of Chivilcoy. When Eva was nearly a year old, her father returned to his first family.

While Duarte was living with Doña Juana and her children, they had enjoyed a comfortable lifestyle. Now they were reduced to poverty. They moved to a tiny house by the railroad tracks, and Doña Juana took in sewing, often working into the night. She saw to it that her children were well dressed and did not go hungry, but their few toys were damaged or secondhand.

*Sources of biographical information on Eva Perón were Barager (1968), Barnes (1978), Blanksten (1953), Flores (1952), Fraser & Navarro (1996), Guillermoprieto (1996), Ortiz (1996), Perón (1951), and J. M. Taylor (1979).

The children were stung not only by abandonment and deprivation but by the stigma of illegitimacy and the whispers of villagers. Even after Duarte left, Doña Juana was regarded as a kept woman. Although it was not unusual for an Argentinian man to have a mistress, Eva and her older brother and sisters were shunned by respectable people, and "nice" children were forbidden to play with them. These early years of poverty, shame, and insecurity awakened Eva's strong sense of injustice and led her to identify with the common people who accepted her and her family and to hate the "upstanding" people who would have nothing to do with them.

Eva was 6 years old when her father died. His funeral was a formative event, bringing home the humiliation of her dubious identity. There is disagreement as to whether her mother attempted to attend or only sent the children. Whatever the case, the dead man's legitimate daughters barred the interlopers' way, and a violent argument erupted. According to one version of the story, Eva's godfather, a friend of her father's, got the children admitted to the wake and carried little Eva in on his arm, a perch from which she "stare[d] down at her half-sisters with . . . implacable animosity" (Flores, 1952, p. 18). In another version, it was the mayor of the town, the dead man's brother-in-law, who interceded and obtained permission for the outcasts to pay quick final respects and then trail behind the other mourners following the coffin to the cemetery. "Eva, the youngest, was last in line. . . . [She] swore to herself that, one day, she would be first" (Ortiz, 1996, p. 13).

An intense, frail girl given to tantrums and driven by dreams of glory, Eva at age 15 made her way to Buenos Aires and began her meteoric rise to become the consort and ultimately the wife of the military dictator Juan Perón. At the height of her power, Eva Perón, bedecked in diamonds, met the crowned heads of Europe, owned three newspapers, and established a multimillion-dollar foundation, which built hospitals, clinics, and schools with funds her opponents charged were extorted from workers. Still, she was beloved by the masses, and until her death from cancer at age 33, she never forgot her humble origins. She knew from firsthand observation that hundreds of thousands of Argentine children lacked food, homes, education, and basic hygiene. It was these early lessons that Eva had in mind when she called herself a "woman of the people."

Eva Perón's experiences in early childhood fueled her hatred of the establishment, her will to power, and her hunger for love and esteem—themes that defined her personality. As a young child she learned what it meant in her society to be poor, illegitimate, and female. She saw that the path to security for a woman of her class was through a man—an insight she brilliantly turned to advantage.

The years from ages 3 to 6 are pivotal ones in children's psychosocial development, as they were for Eva Perón. As children's self-concept grows stronger, they learn what sex they are and begin to act accordingly. Their behavior also becomes more socially directed.

In this chapter we discuss preschool children's understanding of themselves and their feelings. We see how their identification of themselves as male or female arises and how it affects their behavior. We describe the activity on which children typically spend most of their time: play. We consider the influence, for good or ill, of what parents do. Finally, we discuss relationships with siblings and other children.

After you have read and studied this chapter, you should be able to answer the following questions:

Guideposts
for Study

1. How does the self-concept develop during early childhood, and how do children advance in understanding their emotions?
2. How do young children develop initiative and self-esteem?
3. How do boys and girls become aware of the meaning of gender, and what explains differences in behavior between the sexes?
4. How do preschoolers play, and how does play contribute to and reflect development?
5. What forms of discipline do parents use, and how do parenting styles and practices influence development?
6. Why do young children help or hurt others, and why do they develop fears?
7. Why are some children abused or neglected, and what are the effects of maltreatment?
8. How do young children get along with (or without) siblings?
9. How do young children choose playmates and friends, and why are some children more popular than others?

The Developing Self

"Who in the world am I? Ah, *that's* the great puzzle," said Alice in Wonderland, after her size had abruptly changed—again. Solving Alice's "puzzle" is a lifelong process of getting to know one's self.

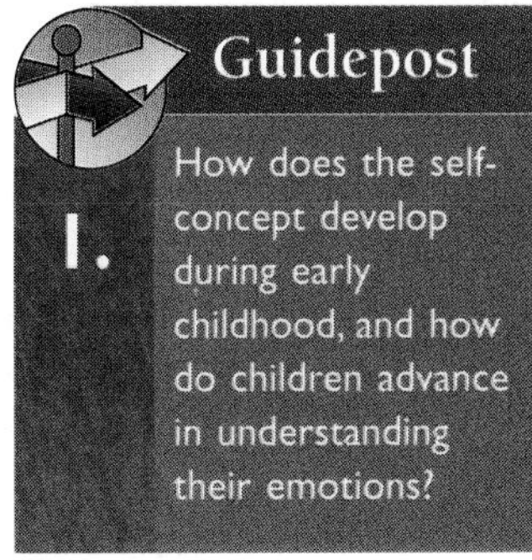
Guidepost
1.
How does the self-concept develop during early childhood, and how do children advance in understanding their emotions?

The Self-Concept and Cognitive Development

The **self-concept** is our image of ourselves. It is what we believe about who we are—our total picture of our abilities and traits. It is "a *cognitive construction, . . .* a system of descriptive and evaluative representations about the self," which determines how we feel about ourselves and guides our actions (Harter, 1996, p. 207). The sense of self also has a social aspect: like Evita Duarte, branded with the stigma of illegitimacy, children incorporate into their self-image their growing understanding of how others see them.

self-concept
Sense of self; descriptive and evaluative mental picture of one's abilities and traits.

The picture of the self comes into focus in toddlerhood, as infants gradually learn that they are separate from other people and things (refer back to Chapter 6). The self-concept becomes clearer and more compelling as a person gains in cognitive abilities and deals with the developmental tasks of childhood, of adolescence, and then of adulthood.

How does the self-concept change in early childhood? By age 4, Jason's attempts at **self-definition** are becoming more comprehensive as he begins to identify a cluster of characteristics to describe himself:

self-definition
Cluster of characteristics used to describe oneself.

> My name is Jason and I live in a big house with my mother and father and sister, Lisa. I have a kitty that's orange and a television set in my own room. . . . I like pizza and I have a nice teacher. I can count up to 100, want to hear me? I love my dog, Skipper. I can climb to the top of the jungle gym, I'm not scared! Just happy. You can't be happy *and* scared, no way!

A young child's self-concept is based mainly on external characteristics, such as physical features.

I have brown hair, and I go to preschool. I'm really strong. I can lift this chair, watch me! (Harter, 1996, p. 208)

The way Jason describes himself is typical of children his age. He talks mostly about concrete, observable behaviors; external characteristics, such as physical features; preferences; possessions; and members of his household. He mentions particular skills (running and climbing) rather than general abilities (being athletic). His self-descriptions are unrealistically positive, and they frequently spill over into demonstrations; what he *thinks* about himself is almost inseparable from what he *does.* Not until middle childhood (around age 7) will he describe himself in terms of generalized traits, such as *popular, smart,* or *dumb*; recognize that he can have conflicting emotions; and be self-critical while holding a positive overall self-concept.

single representations
In neo-Piagetian terminology, first stage in development of self-definition, in which children describe themselves in terms of individual, unconnected characteristics and in all-or-nothing terms.

real self
The self one actually is. Compare *ideal self.*

ideal self
The self one would like to be. Compare *real self.*

representational mappings
In neo-Piagetian terminology, the second stage in development of self-definition, in which a child makes logical connections between aspects of the self but still sees these characteristics in all-or-nothing terms.

During the past twenty-five years, researchers have become interested in pinpointing the intermediate changes that make up this "age 5 to 7 shift." An analysis based on neo-Piagetian theory (Case, 1985, 1992; Fischer, 1980) describes the 5 to 7 shift as occurring in three steps, which actually form a continuous progression.* At 4, Jason is at the first step: his statements about himself are **single representations**—isolated, one-dimensional items. His thinking jumps from particular to particular, without logical connections. At this stage he cannot imagine having two emotions at once ("You can't be happy *and* scared"). He cannot decenter, in part because of his limited working memory capacity, and so he cannot consider different aspects of himself at the same time. His thinking is all-or-nothing. He cannot acknowledge that his **real self,** the person he actually is, is not the same as his **ideal self,** the person he would like to be. So he describes himself as a paragon of virtue and ability.

At about age 5 or 6, Jason moves up to the second step, as he begins to link one aspect of himself to another: "I can run fast, and I can climb high. I'm also strong. I can throw a ball real far, I'm going to be on a team some day!" (Harter, 1996, p. 215) However, these **representational mappings**—logical connections between parts of his image of himself—are still expressed in completely positive, all-or-nothing terms. Since good and bad are opposites, he cannot see how he might be good at some things and not at others.

The third step, *representational systems,* takes place in middle childhood (see Chapter 10), when children begin to integrate specific features of the self into a general, multidimensional concept. As all-or-nothing thinking declines, Jason's self-descriptions will become more balanced ("I'm good at hockey but bad at arithmetic").

Understanding Emotions

Understanding their own emotions helps children to control the way they show their feelings and to be sensitive to how others feel (Garner & Power, 1996). A progression similar to the shift in self-concept seems to characterize children's understanding of emotions.

Preschoolers know something about their emotions, but they still have much to learn. They can talk about their feelings and often can discern the feelings of others, and they understand that emotions are connected with experiences and

*This discussion of children's developing understanding of themselves from age 4 on, including their understanding of their emotions, is indebted to Susan Harter (1990, 1993, 1996, 1998).

desires (Saarni, Mumme, & Campos, 1998). However, they still lack a full understanding of such self-directed emotions as shame and pride, and they have trouble reconciling apparently conflicting emotions.

Emotions Directed Toward the Self

As we discussed in Chapter 6, emotions directed toward the self, such as shame and pride, develop during the third year, after children gain self-awareness. These emotions are "socially derived" (Harter, 1996, p. 225); they depend on internalization of parental standards of behavior. But even children a few years older often lack the cognitive sophistication to recognize such emotions and what brings them on.

In one study (Harter, 1993), 4- to 8-year-olds were told two stories. In the first story, a child takes a few coins from a jar after being told not to do so; in the second story, a child performs a difficult gymnastic feat—a flip on the bars. Each story was presented in two versions: one in which a parent sees the child doing the act, and another in which the child is not observed. The children were asked how they and the parent would feel in each circumstance.

The answers revealed a gradual progression in understanding of feelings about the self (Harter, 1996). At ages 4 to 5, children did not say that either they or their parents would feel pride or shame. Instead they used such terms as "worried" or "scared" (for the money jar incident) and "excited" or "happy" (about the gymnastic accomplishment). At 5 to 6, children said their parents would be ashamed or proud of them but did not acknowledge feeling these emotions themselves. At 6 to 7, children said they would feel proud or ashamed, but only if they were observed. At 7 to 8, children acknowledged that even if no one saw them, they would feel ashamed or proud of themselves. By this age, the standards that produce pride and shame appear to be fully internalized. Until that happens, children need the prod of parental observation—a sort of emotional "scaffolding."

Simultaneous Emotions

Part of the confusion in young children's understanding of their feelings is inability to recognize that they can experience different emotional reactions at the same time ("You can't be happy *and* scared"). The problem has two dimensions: the quality of the emotion (positive or negative) and the target toward which it is directed. One study (Harter & Buddin, 1987) suggests that children gradually acquire an understanding of simultaneous emotions between ages 4 and 12 (Harter, 1996) as they move through five levels of development (a more detailed breakdown related to the stages of self-concept development already described):

- *Level 0:* At first children do not understand that *any* two feelings can coexist. A child at the stage of single representations may say, "You can't have two feelings at the same time because you only have one mind!" The child cannot even acknowledge feeling two *similar* emotions at once (such as happy and glad).
- *Level 1:* Children are developing separate categories—one for positive emotions and one for negative emotions—and can differentiate emotions within each category, such as "happy" and "glad," or "mad" and "sad." They can now be aware of two emotions at the same time, but only if both are either positive or negative and are directed toward the same target ("If my brother hit me, I would be mad and sad"). A child at this level cannot understand the possibility of feeling simultaneous emotions toward two different people or feeling contradictory emotions toward the same person.
- *Level 2:* Children capable of representational mappings can recognize having two feelings of the same kind directed toward different targets ("I was excited about going to Mexico and glad to see my grandparents").

However, they cannot acknowledge holding contradictory feelings ("I couldn't feel happy and scared at the same time; I would have to be two people at once!").

- *Level 3:* Children who have developed representational systems can integrate their sets of positive and negative emotions. They can understand having contrary feelings at the same time, but only if they are directed toward different targets. Ashley can express a negative feeling toward her baby brother ("I was mad at Tony, so I pinched him") and a positive feeling toward her father ("I was happy my father didn't spank me"), but she cannot recognize that she has positive and negative feelings (anger and love) toward both.
- *Level 4:* Older children can describe conflicting feelings toward the same target ("I'm excited about going to my new school, but I'm a little scared too").

CHECKPOINT

Can you . . .

✔ Trace self-concept development between ages 3 and 6?

✔ Describe a typical progression in understanding of (1) emotions directed toward the self and (2) simultaneous emotions?

✔ Identify factors that may influence emotional regulation and behavior problems?

In this study, not until children were 10 or 11 did they seem to understand conflicting emotions (Level 4). However, that does not necessarily mean they did not *feel* conflicting emotions—only that they could not find a way to cognitively reconcile them. In later research, children completing kindergarten, especially girls, showed such an understanding (J. R. Brown & Dunn, 1996). The difference may be one of methodology. In the earlier study, the children were asked to tell their own stories involving mixed feelings; thus, narrative skills as well as understanding of emotions were involved. In the later study only 1 in 4 kindergartners was able to recount such a story from his or her own experience. However, when *told* a story about, for example, a child receiving a present but not being allowed to open it, or riding a two-wheeled bicycle for the first time, 1 in 3 could identify conflicting emotions, and most of the children were able to explain the emotions when told what they were.

Individual differences in emotional understanding seem to go back at least to age 3. Children who, at that age, could identify whether a face looked happy or sad and could tell how a puppet felt when enacting a situation involving happiness, sadness, anger, or fear were better able at the end of kindergarten to explain a story character's conflicting emotions. These children tended to come from families in which there was much discussion of why people behave as they do (J. R. Brown & Dunn, 1996).

Erikson: Initiative versus Guilt

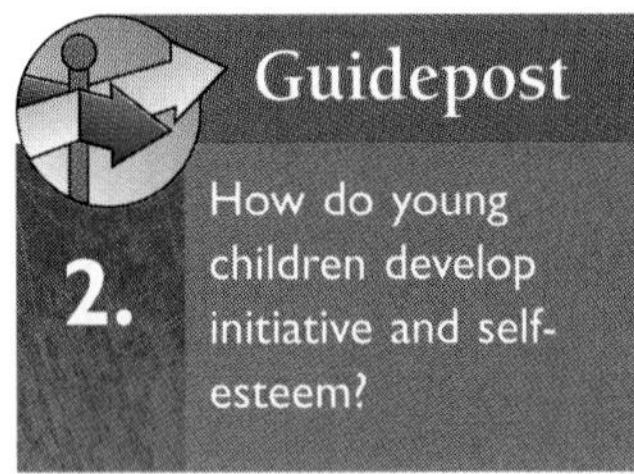

Guidepost
2.
How do young children develop initiative and self-esteem?

The need to deal with conflicting feelings about the self is at the heart of the third crisis of personality development identified by Erik Erikson (1950): **initiative versus guilt.** The conflict arises from the growing sense of purpose, which lets a child plan and carry out activities, and the growing pangs of conscience the child may have about such plans.

Preschool children can do—and want to do—more and more. At the same time, they are learning that some of the things they want to do meet social approval, while others do not. How do they reconcile their desire to *do* with their desire for approval?

This conflict marks a split between two parts of the personality: the part that remains a child, full of exuberance and a desire to try new things and test new powers, and the part that is becoming an adult, constantly examining the propriety of motives and actions. Children who learn how to regulate these opposing drives develop the "virtue" of *purpose,* the courage to envision and pursue goals without being unduly inhibited by guilt or fear of punishment (Erikson, 1982).

initiative versus guilt
In Erikson's theory, the third crisis in psychosocial development, occurring between the ages of 3 and 6, in which children must balance the urge to pursue goals with the moral reservations that may prevent carrying them out.

If this crisis is not resolved adequately, said Erikson, a child may turn into an adult who is constantly striving for success or showing off, or who is inhibited and unspontaneous or self-righteous and intolerant, or who suffers from impotence or psychosomatic illness. With ample opportunities to do things on their own—but under guidance and consistent limits—children can attain a healthy balance between the tendency to overdo competition and achievement and the tendency to be repressed and guilt-ridden.

Self-Esteem

Children cannot articulate a concept of self-worth until about age 8, but they show by their behavior that they have one (Harter, 1990, 1993, 1996). Young children's **self-esteem**—the judgment they make about their worth—is not based on a realistic appraisal of abilities or personality traits. In fact, young children usually overrate their abilities. Although they can make judgments about their competence at various activities, they are not yet able to rank them in importance; and they tend to accept the judgments of adults, who often give positive, uncritical feedback (Harter, 1990, 1996, 1998).

self-esteem
The judgment a person makes about his or her self-worth.

Self-esteem in early childhood tends to be global—"I am good" or "I am bad" (Harter, 1996, 1998). Parents' supportive behaviors—listening to a child, reading stories, making snacks, kissing away tears—are major contributors to self-esteem (Haltiwanger & Harter, 1988). Not until middle childhood do personal evaluations of competence and adequacy (based on internalization of parental and societal standards) normally become critical in shaping and maintaining a sense of self-worth (Harter, 1990, 1996, 1998).

Consider this . . .

- Looking back, can you think of ways in which your parents or other adults helped you develop self-esteem?

When self-esteem is high, a child is motivated to achieve. However, if self-esteem is *contingent* on success, children may view failure or criticism as an indictment of their worth and may feel helpless to do better. About one-third to one-half of preschoolers, kindergartners, and first-graders show elements of this "helpless" pattern: self-denigration or self-blame, negative emotion, lack of persistence, and lowered expectations for themselves (Burhans & Dweck, 1995; Ruble & Dweck, 1995).

CHECKPOINT

Can you . . .

✔ Explain the significance of Erikson's third crisis of personality development?

✔ Tell how young children's self-esteem differs from that of school-age children?

Instead of trying a different way to complete a puzzle, as a child with unconditional self-esteem might do, "helpless" children feel ashamed and give up, or go back to an easier puzzle they have already done. They do not expect to succeed, and so they do not try. Whereas older children who fail may conclude that they are dumb, preschoolers interpet poor performance as a sign of being "bad." Furthermore, they believe that "badness" is permanent. This sense of being a bad person may persist into adulthood. To avoid fostering the "helpless"

This mother's approval of her 3-year-old son's artwork is an important contributor to his self-esteem. Not until middle childhood do children develop strong internal standards of self-worth.

pattern, parents and teachers can give children specific, focused feedback rather than criticizing the child as a person ("Look, the tag on your shirt is showing in front," not "Can't you see your shirt is on backwards? When are you going to learn to dress yourself?").

Gender

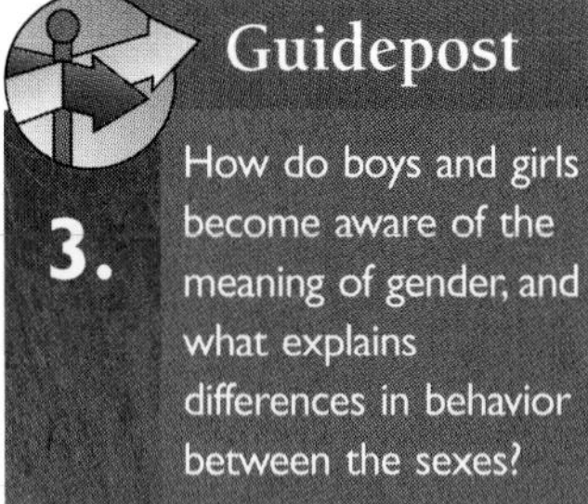

Guidepost

3. How do boys and girls become aware of the meaning of gender, and what explains differences in behavior between the sexes?

gender identity Awareness, developed in early childhood, that one is male or female.

Gender identity, awareness of one's gender and all it implies, is an important aspect of the developing self-concept. How different are young boys and girls? What causes those differences? How do children develop gender identity, and how does it affect their attitudes and behavior?

Gender Differences

Gender differences are psychological or behavioral differences between the sexes. Although some gender differences become more pronounced after age 3, boys and girls on average remain more alike than different. A landmark review of more than 2,000 studies found few significant gender differences (Maccoby & Jacklin, 1974). The clearest difference is that boys, from preschool age on, act more aggressively than girls, both physically and verbally (Coie & Dodge, 1998; Turner & Gervai, 1995). Some studies suggest that girls are more empathic, compliant, and cooperative with parents and seek adult approval more than boys do (N. Eisenberg, Fabes, Schaller, & Miller, 1989; M. L. Hoffman, 1977; Maccoby, 1980; Turner & Gervai, 1995). Also, as we'll discuss later in this chapter, boys and girls play differently. One of the earliest differences, appearing as early as age 2 and more consistently from age 3 on, is in the choice of toys and play activities and of playmates of the same sex (Turner & Gervai, 1995).

Is one sex smarter than the other? Overall, intelligence test scores show no gender differences. This is not surprising, since the most widely used tests are designed to eliminate gender bias (Neisser et al., 1996). Females tend to do better at verbal tasks (but not analogies), at mathematical computation, and at tasks requiring fine motor and perceptual skills, while males excel in most spatial abilities and in abstract mathematical and scientific reasoning (Halpern, 1997).

Some of these differences, which seem to exist across cultures, begin quite early in life. Girls' superiority in perceptual speed and verbal fluency appears during infancy and toddlerhood, and boys' greater ability to mentally manipu-

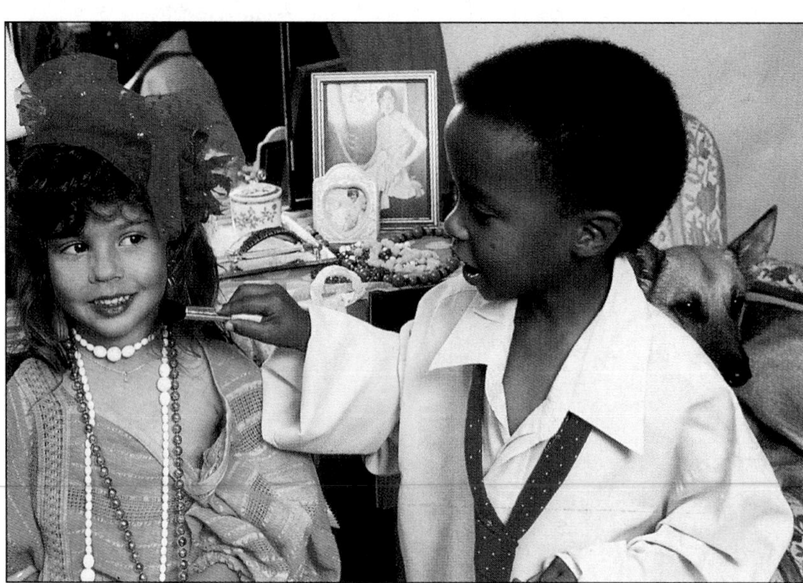

These preschoolers playing dress-up already show a strong awareness of gender identity and gender roles.

late figures and shapes can be observed as soon as it can be tested, at about age 3. Other differences do not become apparent in children of average ability until preadolescence or beyond (Halpern, 1997). In a statistical analysis of 286 studies of spatial abilities, few significant differences appeared before adolescence (Voyer, Voyer, & Bryden, 1995).

We need to remember, of course, that gender differences are valid for large groups of boys and girls but not necessarily for individuals (Turner & Gervai, 1995). By knowing a child's sex, we cannot predict whether that *particular* boy or girl will be faster, stronger, smarter, more obedient, or more assertive than another child.

CHECKPOINT

Can you . . .

✔ Summarize the main behavioral and cognitive differences between boys and girls?

Perspectives on Gender Development: Nature and Nurture

What accounts for gender differences, and why do some of them emerge with age? The most influential explanations, until recently, centered on the differing experiences and social expectations that boys and girls meet almost from birth (Halpern, 1997; Neisser et al., 1996). These experiences and expectations concern three related aspects of gender identity: *gender roles, gender-typing,* and *gender stereotypes.*

Gender roles are the behaviors, interests, attitudes, skills, and personality traits considered appropriate for males or females. All societies have gender roles. Historically, in most cultures, women have been expected to devote most of their time to caring for the household and children, while men were providers and protectors. Women were expected to be compliant and nurturant; men, to be active, aggressive, and competitive. In Eva Péron's Argentina, an ambitious woman with leadership qualities could rise to the highest echelons—but only on the arm of a man. Today, gender roles in western cultures have become more diverse and more flexible. **Gender-typing** (refer back to Chapter 6), the acquisition of a gender role, takes place early in childhood; but children vary in the degree to which they take on gender roles.

gender roles
Behaviors, interests, attitudes, skills, and traits that a culture considers appropriate for males or for females.

gender-typing
Socialization process whereby children, at an early age, learn appropriate gender roles.

Gender stereotypes are preconceived generalizations about male or female behavior ("All females are passive and dependent; all males are aggressive and independent"). Gender stereotypes pervade many cultures. They are seen to some degree in children as young as $2^1/_2$ or 3, increase during the preschool years, and reach a peak at age 5 (Haugh, Hoffman, & Cowan, 1980; Ruble & Martin, 1998; J. E. Williams & Best, 1982). As we might expect from our discussion of self-concept, younger preschoolers often attribute positive qualities to their own sex and negative qualities to the other sex. Still, even at this early age they call boys strong, fast, and cruel, and girls fearful and helpless (Ruble & Martin, 1998).

gender stereotypes
Preconceived generalizations about male or female role behavior.

How do young children acquire gender roles, and why do they adopt gender stereotypes? Are these purely social constructs, or do they reflect underlying biological differences between males and females? Do social and cultural influences create gender differences, or merely accentuate them?

Today investigators are uncovering evidence of biological explanations for gender differences: genetic, hormonal, and neurological. These explanations are not either-or. Both nature and nurture probably play important parts in what it means to be male or female. Biological influences are not necessarily universal, inevitable, or unchangeable; nor are social and cultural influences easily overcome.

Let's look, then, at four perspectives on gender development (summarized in Table 8-1): *biological, psychoanalytic, cognitive,* and *socialization-based* approaches. Each of these perspectives can contribute to our understanding; none fully explains why boys and girls turn out differently in some respects and not in others.

Biological Approach

The existence of similar gender roles in many cultures suggests that some gender differences, at least, may be biologically based. On the other hand, psychological and behavioral similarities among people of the same sex are much larger than the differences between the sexes, suggesting that the role of biology is limited.

Table 8-1 Four Perspectives on Gender Development

Theories	Major Theorists	Key Processes	Basic Beliefs
Biological Approach		Genetic, neurological, and hormonal activity	Many or most behavioral differences between the sexes can be traced to biological differences.
Psychoanalytic Approach			
Psychosexual theory	Sigmund Freud	Resolution of unconscious emotional conflict	Gender identity occurs when child identifies with same-sex parent.
Cognitive Approach			
Cognitive-developmental theory	Lawrence Kohlberg	Self-categorization	Once child learns she is a girl or he is a boy, child sorts information about behavior by gender and acts accordingly.
Gender-schema theory	Sandra Bem, Carol Lynn Martin, & Charles F. Halverson	Self-categorization based on processing of cultural information	Child organizes information about what is considered appropriate for a boy or a girl on the basis of what a particular culture dictates, and behaves accordingly. Child sorts by gender because the culture dictates that gender is an important schema.
Socialization Approach			
Social cognitive theory	Albert Bandura	Modeling, reinforcement, and teaching	Gender-typing is a result of interpretation, evaluation, and internalization of socially transmitted standards.

By age 5, when the brain reaches approximate adult size, boys' brains are about 10 percent larger than girls' brains, mostly because boys have more gray matter in the cerebral cortex. This difference in volume may be related to girls' greater neuronal density in the cerebral cortex. In most other respects, brain development is similar in the two sexes. What these findings may tell us about early similarities and differences in brain organization and functioning is a topic for future study (Reiss, Abrams, Singer, Ross, & Denckla, 1996).

We do have evidence that size differences in the *corpus callosum*, the band of tissue joining the right and left hemispheres, are correlated with verbal fluency (Hines, Chiu, McAdams, Bentler, & Lipcamon, 1992). Since girls have a larger, more bulbous corpus callosum, better coordination between the two hemispheres may help explain girls' superior verbal abilities (Halpern, 1997).

Hormones circulating in the bloodstream before or about the time of birth may affect the developing brain and influence gender differences. The male hormone testosterone, along with low levels of the neurotransmitter serotonin, seems related to aggressiveness, competitiveness, and dominance, perhaps through action on certain brain structures, such as the hypothalamus and amygdala (Bernhardt, 1997). Attempts also have been made to link prenatal hormonal activity with other aspects of brain functioning, such as those involved in gender differences in spatial and verbal skills (Neisser et al., 1996), but this research is quite controversial (Ruble & Martin, 1998).

Other research focuses on children with unusual hormonal histories. Girls with a disorder called congenital adrenal hyperplasia (CAH) have high prenatal levels of *androgens* (male sex hormones). Although raised as girls, they tend to develop into "tomboys," showing preferences for "boys' toys," rough play, and male playmates, as well as strong spatial skills. *Estrogens* (female hormones), on the other hand, seem to have less influence on boys' gender-typed behavior. Since these studies are natural experiments, they cannot establish cause and effect; other factors besides hormonal differences, such as early interactions with parents, may play a role. Also, hormonal differences may themselves be affected by environmental or other factors. In any case, such atypical patterns of behavior have not been found in children with normal hormonal variations (Ruble & Martin, 1998).

Perhaps the most dramatic examples of biologically based research have to do with infants born with ambiguous sexual structures (part male and part female). John Money and his colleagues (Money, Hampson, & Hampson, 1955) developed guidelines for such cases, recommending that the child be assigned as early as possible to the gender that holds the potential for the most nearly normal functioning and for stable gender identity.

In the case of a 7-month-old boy whose penis was accidentally cut off during circumcision, the decision was made at 17 months to rear the child as a girl, and four months later doctors performed surgical reconstruction (Money & Ehrhardt, 1972). Although initially described as developing into a normal female, the child later rejected female identity and, at puberty, switched to living as a male. After a second surgical reconstruction, he married a woman and adopted her children. This case seems to suggest that gender identity may be rooted in chromosomal structure or prenatal development and cannot easily be changed (Diamond & Sigmundson, 1997).

However, the only other documented case of this kind had a different outcome. This time, the accident occurred at 2 months, and penile removal and sexual reassignment took place by 7 months. When interviewed at ages 16 and 26, the patient identified as a female, was living as a woman, and had had sexual relationships with both men and women (Bradley, Oliver, Chernick, & Zucker, 1998). Thus assignment of gender—at least during early infancy—may have some flexibility after all.

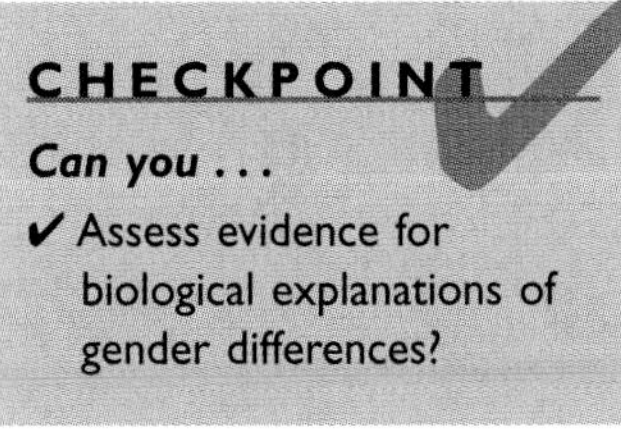

CHECKPOINT
Can you . . .
✔ Assess evidence for biological explanations of gender differences?

Psychoanalytic Approach

"Dad, where will you live when I grow up and marry Mommy?" asks Timmy, age 4. From the psychoanalytic perspective, Timmy's question is part of his acquisition of gender identity. That process, according to Freud, is one of **identification,** the adoption of characteristics, beliefs, attitudes, values, and behaviors of the parent of the same sex. Freud and other classical psychoanalytic theorists considered identification an important personality development of early childhood; some social-learning theorists also have used the term.

identification
In Freudian theory, the process by which a young child adopts characteristics, beliefs, attitudes, values, and behaviors of the parent of the same sex.

According to Freud, identification will occur for Timmy when he represses or gives up the wish to possess the parent of the other sex (his mother) and identifies with the parent of the same sex (his father). Although this explanation for gender development has been influential, it has been difficult to test. Despite some evidence that preschoolers tend to act more affectionately toward the opposite-sex parent and more aggressively toward the same-sex parent (Westen, 1998), the theory has little research support. Studies have found that children's gender-typed behavior is not much like that of their parents and that identification seems to be a result, not a cause, of gender-typing (Maccoby, 1992). Most developmental psychologists today therefore favor other explanations.

Cognitive Approach

Sarah finds out she is a girl because people call her a girl. She figures out what things girls are supposed to do and does them. She comes to understand gender the same way she comes to understand everything else: by thinking about her experience. This is the heart of Lawrence Kohlberg's (1966) cognitive-developmental theory.

According to Kohlberg, children do their own gender-typing. They classify themselves and others as male or female and then organize their behavior around

In one study, children saw three photos of this little boy: nude, dressed in boys' clothes, and dressed in girls' clothes. Preschoolers who identified the child's sex by genitals rather than by dress were more likely to show gender constancy—to know that they themselves would remain the sex they were.

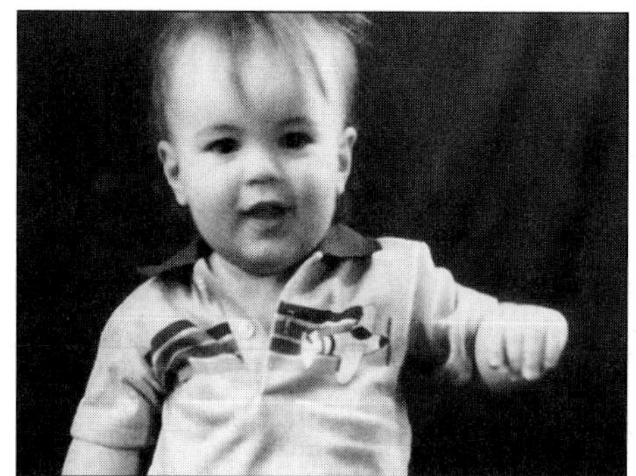

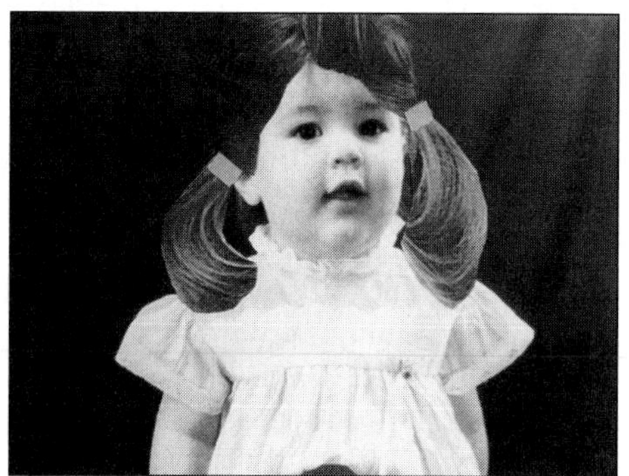

that classification. They do this by adopting behaviors they perceive as consistent with their gender. Thus, Sarah prefers dolls to trucks because she views playing with dolls as consistent with her idea of herself as a girl. According to Kohlberg, **gender constancy,** more recently called *sex-category constancy*—a child's realization that his or her sex will always be the same—leads to the acquisition of gender roles. Once children realize they are permanently male or female, they adopt what they see as gender-appropriate behaviors.

gender constancy
Awareness that one will always be male or female. Also called *sex-category constancy.*

When does gender constancy emerge? Answers vary from ages 3 to 7. This wide range in findings may be due to the kinds of questions asked, to differing criteria for gender constancy, to differences in the kinds of reasoning children use at different ages, or to methodological differences (Ruble & Martin, 1998; Szkrybalo & Ruble, in press).

One reason for the variability of findings may be that gender constancy does not appear all at once. Instead, it seems to occur in three stages: *gender identity, gender stability,* and *gender consistency* (Ruble & Martin, 1998; Szkrybalo & Ruble, in press). *Gender identity* (awareness of one's own gender and that of others) typically arrives between ages 2 and 3. *Gender stability* comes when a girl realizes that she will grow up to be a woman, and a boy that he will grow up to be a man—in other words, that gender remains the same across time. However, children at this stage may base judgments about gender on superficial external appearances and stereotyped behaviors. The final stage, *gender consistency,* is the realization that a girl remains a girl even if she has a short haircut and wears pants, and a boy remains a boy even if he has long hair and earrings.

There is little evidence for Kohlberg's view that gender constancy is the key to gender-typing. Long before children attain the final stage of gender constancy, they show gender-typed preferences (Bussey & Bandura, 1992; Ruble & Martin, 1998). They categorize activities and objects by gender, know a lot about what males and females do, and often acquire gender-appropriate behaviors (G. D. Levy & Carter, 1989; Luecke-Aleksa, Anderson, Collins, & Schmitt, 1995). Even at $2^1/_2$, girls show more interest in dolls and boys in cars, and both begin to prefer being with children of their own sex (Ruble & Martin, 1998).

It is possible that gender constancy, once achieved, may further sensitize children to gender-related information (Ruble & Martin, 1998). Five-year-old boys who have reached or are on the brink of gender constancy pay more attention to male characters on television and watch more sports and action programs than other boys their age (Luecke-Aleksa et al., 1995). Later, children tend to develop more complex beliefs about gender and to become more flexible in their views about gender roles (Ruble & Martin, 1998; M. G. Taylor, 1996; see Box 8-1).

gender-schema theory
Theory, proposed by Bem, that children socialize themselves in their gender roles by developing a mentally organized network of information about what it means to be male or female in a particular culture.

A second cognitive approach, which incorporates information-processing concepts and stresses societal influences, is **gender-schema theory.** Among its leading proponents is Sandra Bem (1983, 1985, 1993); others are Carol Lynn Martin and Charles F. Halverson (1981). A *schema* (somewhat like the schemes in

Box 8-1

Children's Beliefs about Gender

If you had been raised on an island with only members of the other sex, what kinds of interests, abilities, and personal characteristics would you be likely to have? In what ways, if any, would you be different from what you are today? Your answers most likely depend on your beliefs about the relative contributions of nature and nurture to gender-related behavior.

To find out what children in early and middle childhood think about such questions, one researcher (M. G. Taylor, 1996) presented 80 mostly white, middle-class 4-, 5-, 8-, 9-, and 10-year-old boys and girls and 16 college students with an imaginary situation similar to the one just described. There were eight male and eight female participants in each age group. The children were tested individually; the college students filled out a questionnaire.

The experimenter showed each child a picture of a baby with very little hair, wearing gender-neutral pajamas, and told the following story:

> Once there was a baby girl named Chris. When Chris was a tiny baby, she went to live with her uncle on a beautiful island. On this island there were only boys and men; Chris was the only girl. Chris lived a very happy life on the island, but she never saw another girl or woman.

The experimenter described the same situation involving a male baby named Pat, also with little hair and wearing gender-neutral pajamas, who lived on an all-female island. After hearing each story, the children were asked a series of questions about what Chris (or Pat) would be like at age 10. Would Chris (or Pat) like to play with dolls? Like to play football? Wear dresses? Have short hair? Cry a lot? Get into fights a lot? Want to be a nurse? Want to be a soldier? Be good at taking care of babies? Be good at playing baseball? Have a body like a girl's or boy's? Grow up to be a mommy or daddy?

A randomly assigned control group of 80 children of the same ages and 16 college students instead heard a story in which a baby grew up on an island with only people of the baby's own sex. This was done to make sure that the stereotyped items asked about Chris (or Pat) were ones that children of these ages would consider typically masculine or feminine.

What were the results? The 5- to 8-year-olds recognized *no* environmental influence on gender roles: they seemed to believe that a boy will develop stereotypically male characteristics (and a girl, female ones) regardless of upbringing. Interestingly, 4-year-olds, though they responded similarly, did recognize some environmental influence. Nine- and 10-year-olds and college students distinguished between such characteristics as hair style, dress, play activities, skills, and ambitions, which probably would be affected by the social environment, and biological characteristics, which would not.

Apparently, young children who have come to a firm understanding of gender categories at first develop a rigid idea of gender; they seem to view gender differences as immutable and to believe that boys and girls are essentially different in nature, much as cats and dogs are, and will grow up in a certain way regardless of their surroundings. By age 9 or 10, as children gain more life experience and information, they develop more flexible ideas about what the categories of gender imply.

Piaget's theory) is a mentally organized network of gender-related information that influences behavior. According to gender-schema theory, once children know what sex they are, they begin to take on gender roles by developing a concept of what it means to be male or female in their culture. They do this by organizing their observations around the schema of gender. They organize information on this basis because they see that their society classifies people that way: males and females wear different clothes, play with different toys, and use separate bathrooms. Children then match their own behavior to their culture's gender schema—what boys and girls are "supposed" to be and do.

According to this theory, gender schemas promote gender stereotypes by influencing judgments about behavior. When a new boy his age moves in next door, 4-year-old Brandon knocks on his door, carrying a toy truck. He assumes that the new boy will like the same toys he likes: "boys' toys." Children are quick to accept gender labels; when told that an unfamiliar toy is for the other sex, they will drop it like a hot potato (even if it is very attractive), and they expect others to do the same (C. L. Martin, Eisenbud, & Rose, 1995; Ruble & Martin, 1998). However, it is not clear that gender schemas are at the root of this behavior. Nor does gender-schema theory explain why some children show less stereotyped behavior than others (Bussey & Bandura, 1992, 1999; Ruble & Martin, 1998).

Another problem with gender-schema theory (as with Kohlberg's theory) is that gender-typing does not necessarily become stronger with increased gender knowledge; in fact, the opposite is often true (Bussey & Bandura, 1999). A proposed explanation, which has some research support, is that while children are constructing and then consolidating their gender schemas (around ages 4 to 6), they notice and remember only information consistent with them. Later, around age 8, schemas become more complex as children begin to take in and integrate contradictory information (Ruble & Martin, 1998; Welch-Ross & Schmidt, 1996).

Cognitive approaches to gender development have made an important contribution by exploring how children think about gender and what they know about it at various ages. However, these approaches do not fully explain the link between knowledge and conduct. What prompts children to act out gender roles, and why do some children become more strongly gender-typed than others? The answers, according to some investigators, lie in socialization (Bussey & Bandura, 1992).

Socialization-Based Approach

Anna, at age 5, insisted on dressing in a new way. She wanted to wear leggings with a skirt over them, and boots—indoors and out. When Diane asked her why, Anna replied, "Because Katie dresses like this—and Katie's the king of the girls!"

According to Albert Bandura's (1986; Bussey & Bandura, 1999) *social cognitive theory,* an expanded version of social-learning theory, children learn gender roles through socialization. Bandura sees gender development as the outcome of a complex array of interacting influences, personal and social. The way a child interprets experiences with parents, teachers, peers, and cultural institutions plays a central part.

As in traditional social-learning theory (refer back to Chapter 2), children initially acquire gender roles as they learn other kinds of behavior: by observing models. Children generally pick models they see as powerful or nurturing. Typically, one model is a parent, often of the same sex, but children also pattern their behavior after other adults or (as Anna did) after peers. Behavioral feedback, together with direct teaching by parents and other adults, reinforces gender-typing. A boy who models his behavior after his father or male peers is commended for acting "like a boy." A girl gets compliments on a pretty dress or hairstyle.

The socialization process begins in infancy (refer back to Chapter 6), long before a conscious understanding of gender begins to form. Gradually, as children begin to regulate their own activities, standards of gender-related behavior become internalized. A child no longer needs praise, rebukes, or a model's presence to act in socially appropriate ways. Biological makeup, emotional reactions, and cognitive judgments enter into the creation of these internalized standards, which vary with the individual. Children feel good about themselves when they live up to their internal standards and feel bad if they don't. A substantial part of this shift from socially guided control to self-regulation of gender preferences may take place between ages 3 and 4 (Bussey & Bandura, 1992).

Early childhood is a prime period for socialization. Let's look more closely at how parents, peers, and the media influence gender development.

Parental Influences It makes sense that if parents steer children toward gender-appropriate activities, express gender stereotypes, and model traditional gender roles, the children will become highly gender-typed. However, it is not clear how much effect such parental influences actually have (Ruble & Martin, 1998). Some studies have found that parental treatment affects children's gender *knowledge* more than their *behavior* (Fagot & Leinbach, 1995; Turner & Gervai, 1995). A girl may know that baseball bats are "supposed" to be for boys but may want to use one anyway.

One reason for discrepancies in findings may be that researchers study different kinds of gender-related behavior and use different measuring instruments (Turner & Gervai, 1995). Gender-typing has many facets, and the particular combination of "masculine" and "feminine" traits and behaviors that a child acquires is an individual matter. Also, today many parents' own gender roles are less sterotyped than they once were.

In general, boys are more strongly gender-socialized with regard to play preferences than girls. Parents, especially fathers, tend to show more discomfort if a boy plays with a doll than if a girl plays with a truck (Lytton & Romney, 1991). Girls have more freedom than boys in the clothes they wear, the games they play, and their choice of playmates (Miedzian, 1991).

In egalitarian households, the father's role in gender-socialization seems especially important (Fagot & Leinbach, 1995). In an observational study of 4-year-olds in Cambridge, England, and Budapest, Hungary, boys and girls whose fathers did more housework and child care were less aware of gender stereotypes and engaged in less gender-typed play (Turner & Gervai, 1995). Gender-role socialization also tends to be untraditional in single-parent families headed by mothers or fathers who must play both the customary masculine and feminine roles (Leve & Fagot, 1997).

A father who encourages his son to engage in traditionally masculine activities, such as adjusting a bicycle seat, delivers a powerful message about what kinds of interests are appropriate for a boy.

Peer Influences Even in early childhood, the peer group is a major influence on gender-typing (Turner & Gervai, 1995). Peers begin to reinforce gender-typed behavior by age 3, and their influence increases with age. Children show more disapproval of boys who act "like girls" than of girls who are tomboys (Ruble & Martin, 1998). As we have seen, both 3- and 4-year-olds are aware of what kinds of behavior peers consider gender-appropriate, but 4-year-olds are more consistent in applying these judgments to themselves (Bussey & Bandura, 1992).

In the observational study described in the last section, British and Hungarian 4-year-olds' play preferences seemed less affected by the parents' gender-typing than were other aspects of their behavior; at this age, such choices may be more strongly influenced by peers and the media than by the models children see at home (Turner & Gervai, 1995). Generally, however, peer and parental attitudes reinforce each other. Social cognitive theory sees peers, not as an independent influence for socialization but as part of a complex cultural system that encompasses parents and other socializing agents as well (Bussey & Bandura, 1999).

Consider this . . .

- "Males are innately more aggressive, and females more nurturing. Although these traits can be altered to some degree, the basic tendencies will remain." To what extent does research support these statements? Whether true or not, what implications do these widely held beliefs have for personality development?
- Where would you place your own views on the continuum between the following extremes? Explain.
    1. Family A thinks girls should wear only ruffly dresses and boys should never wash dishes or cry.
    2. Family Z treats sons and daughters exactly alike, without making any references to the children's sex.

Cultural Influences: The Media A major channel for the transmission of cultural attitudes toward gender is television. Although women in television programs and advertisements are now more likely to be working outside the home and men are sometimes shown caring for children or doing the marketing, for the most part life as portrayed on television continues to be more stereotyped than life in the real world (Coltrane & Adams, 1997; Ruble & Martin, 1998).

Social cognitive theory predicts that children who watch a lot of television will become more gender-typed by imitating the models they see on the screen. Dramatic supporting evidence emerged from a natural experiment in several Canadian towns that obtained access to television transmission for the first time. Children who had had relatively unstereotyped attitudes showed marked increases in traditional views two years later (Kimball, 1986). In another study, children who watched a series of nontraditional episodes, such as a father and son cooking together, had less stereotyped views than children who had not seen the series (J. Johnston & Ettema, 1982).

Children's books have long been a source of gender stereotypes. Today, friendship between boys and girls is portrayed more often, and girls are braver and more resourceful. Still, male characters predominate, females are more likely to need help, and males are more likely to give it (Beal, 1994; Evans, 1998). So pervasive is the influence of these stereotypes that when children are exposed to an

CHECKPOINT

Can you . . .

✔ Distinguish among four basic approaches to the study of gender development?

✔ Compare how various theories explain the acquisition of gender roles, and assess the support for each theory?

alternative, nonsexist version of a fairy tale, they expect it to follow the usual stereotyped patterns and may even be indignant when it does not (Evans, 1998).

Major strengths of the socialization approach include the breadth and multiplicity of processes it examines and the scope for individual differences it reveals. But this very complexity makes it difficult to establish clear causal connections between the way children are raised and the way they think and act. Just what aspects of the home environment and the peer culture promote gender-typing? Underlying this question is a chicken-and-egg problem: Do parents and peers treat boys and girls differently because they *are* different, or because the culture says they *should be* different? Does differential treatment *produce* or *reflect* gender differences? Perhaps, as social cognitive theory suggests, there is a bidirectional relationship. Further research may help to show how socializing agents mesh with children's own tendencies with regard to gender-related attitudes and behavior.

Play: The Business of Early Childhood

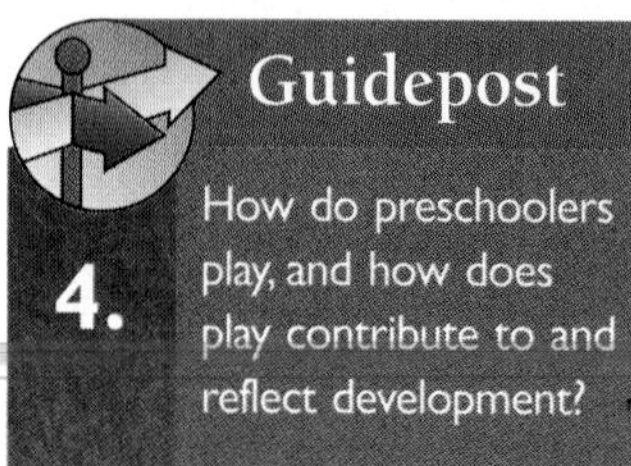
Guidepost

4. How do preschoolers play, and how does play contribute to and reflect development?

Play is the work of the young, and it contributes to all domains of development. Through play, children stimulate the senses, learn how to use their muscles, coordinate sight with movement, gain mastery over their bodies, and acquire new skills. Through pretending, they try out roles, cope with uncomfortable emotions, gain understanding of other people's viewpoints, and construct an image of the social world. They develop problem-solving skills, experience the joy of creativity, and become more proficient with language (Bodrova & Leong, 1998; J. I. F. Davidson, 1998; Furth & Kane, 1992; J. E. Johnson, 1998; Nourot, 1998; Singer & Singer, 1990). By making "tickets" for an imaginary train trip or "reading" eye charts in a "doctor's office," they build emergent literacy (Christie, 1991, 1998). As they sort blocks of different shapes, count how many they can pile on each other, or announce that "my tower is bigger than yours," they lay the foundation for mathematical concepts (Jarrell, 1998). As they play with computers, they learn new ways of thinking (Silvern, 1998).

Preschoolers engage in different types of play at different ages. Particular children have different styles of play, and they play at different things. Researchers categorize children's play by its *content* (what children do when they play) and its *social dimension* (whether they play alone or with others). What can we learn about children by seeing how they play?

Types of Play

Carol, at $2^1/_2$, "talked for" a doll, using a deeper voice than her own. Michael, at 3, wore a kitchen towel as a cape and "flew" around as Batman. These children were engaged in pretend play involving make-believe people or situations.

Pretend play is one of four categories of play identified by Piaget and others as showing increasing levels of cognitive complexity (Piaget, 1951; Smilansky, 1968). The simplest form, which begins during infancy, is active **functional play** involving repetitive muscular movements (such as rolling or bouncing a ball). As gross motor skills improve, preschoolers run, jump, skip, hop, throw and aim (see Chapter 7). Toward the end of this period and into middle childhood (see Chapter 9), *rough-and-tumble play* involving wrestling, kicking, and sometimes chasing, becomes more common; this kind of play is sometimes mistaken for aggressive behavior, which we discuss later in this chapter (Pellegrini, 1998).

functional play In Piaget's and Smilansky's terminology, the lowest cognitive level of play, involving repetitive muscular movements.

constructive play In Piaget's and Smilansky's terminology, the second cognitive level of play, involving use of objects or materials to make something.

The second level of cognitive complexity is seen in toddlers' and preschoolers' **constructive play** (using objects or materials to make something, such as a house of blocks or a crayon drawing). Four-year-olds in preschools or day care centers may spend more than half their time in this kind of play, which becomes more elaborate by ages 5 and 6 (J. E. Johnson, 1998).

Pretend play, also called *fantasy play, dramatic play,* or *imaginative play,* rests on the symbolic function, which emerges near the end of the sensorimotor stage (Piaget, 1962). Three-year-olds show that they understand the concept of pretense when they excuse an action by saying "I was only pretending" (Lloyd & Goodwin, 1995). Pretend play typically begins during the last part of the second year, increases during the preschool years, and then declines as school-age children become more involved in the fourth cognitive level of play, *formal games with rules,* such as hopscotch and marbles.

This young "veterinarian" examining his toy dog is showing an important cognitive development of early childhood, which underlies imaginative play: the ability to use symbols to stand for people or things in the real world.

An estimated 10 to 17 percent of preschoolers' play and 33 percent of kindergartners' is pretend play, often using dolls and real or imaginary props, such as a block for a telephone (Bretherton, 1984; Garner, 1998; J. E. Johnson, 1998; K. H. Rubin, Fein, & Vandenberg, 1983). Children who often play imaginatively tend to cooperate more with other children and to be more popular and more joyful than those who don't (Singer & Singer, 1990). Children who watch a great deal of television play less imaginatively, perhaps because they are accustomed to passively absorbing images rather than generating their own (Howes & Matheson, 1992). Television also seems to have influenced the kinds of roles preschoolers choose to play. Instead of modeling their dramatic play after real people in the community, such as teachers, shopkeepers, doctors, and nurses, they more often pretend to be television adventure heroes (French & Pena, 1991).

pretend play
In Piaget's and Smilansky's terminology, the third cognitive level of play, involving imaginary people or situations; also called *fantasy play, dramatic play,* or *imaginative play.*

The Social Dimension of Play

In the 1920s, Mildred B. Parten (1932) observed 2- to 5-year-olds during free-play periods at nursery school. She identified six types of play, ranging from the least to the most social (see Table 8-2). She found that as children get older, their play tends to become more interactive and more cooperative. At first they play alone, then alongside other children, and finally, together.

Is solitary play less mature than social play? Parten thought so. She and some other observers suggest that young children who play alone may be at risk

Table 8-2 Parten's Categories of Social and Nonsocial Play

Category	Description
Unoccupied behavior	The child does not seem to be playing, but watches anything of momentary interest.
Onlooker behavior	The child spends most of the time watching other children play. The onlooker talks to them, asking questions or making suggestions, but does not enter into the play. The onlooker is definitely observing particular groups of children rather than just anything that happens to be exciting.
Solitary independent play	The child plays alone with toys that are different from those used by nearby children and makes no effort to get close to them.
Parallel play	The child plays independently but among other children, playing with toys like those used by the other children, but not necessarily playing with them in the same way. Playing *beside* rather than *with* the others, the parallel player does not try to influence the other children's play.
Associative play	The child plays with other children. They talk about their play, borrow and lend toys, follow one another, and try to control who may play in the group. All the children play similarly if not identically; there is no division of labor and no organization around any goal. Each child acts as she or he wishes and is interested more in being with the other children than in the activity itself.
Cooperative or organized supplementary play	The child plays in a group organized for some goal—to make something, play a formal game, or dramatize a situation. One or two children control who belongs to the group and direct activities. By a division of labor, children take on different roles and supplement each other's efforts.

Source: Adapted from Parten, 1932, pp. 249–251.

of developing social, psychological, and educational problems. However, most researchers now view Parten's characterization of children's play development as too simplistic. Nonsocial play does not necessarily diminish through the years, to be replaced by social play; instead, children of all ages engage in all of Parten's categories of play. Although solitary active play becomes less common between ages 3 and 6, solitary constructive play does not. Furthermore, playing near other children and watching what they do is often a prelude to joining in their play (K. H. Rubin, Bukowski, & Parker, 1998).

Much nonsocial play consists of activities that foster cognitive, physical, and social development. In one study of 4-year-olds, some kinds of nonsocial play, such as *parallel constructive play* (for example, working on puzzles near another child) were most common among children who were good problem solvers, were popular with other children, and were seen by teachers as socially skilled (K. Rubin, 1982). Such play may reflect independence and maturity, not poor social adjustment. Children need some time alone to concentrate on tasks and problems, and some simply enjoy individual activities more than group activities. We need to look, then, at what children *do* when they play, not just at whether they play alone or with someone else (K. H. Rubin et al., 1998). Some investigators have modified Parten's system to more realistically gauge developmental and individual differences in play by assessing both its cognitive and social dimensions (Coplan & Rubin, 1998).

Consider this . . .

- How do you think play with computers might affect children's cognitive and social development? What skills might they learn that they otherwise would not? What disadvantages, if any, do you see in preschoolers' use of computers?

CHECKPOINT

Can you . . .

✔ Describe four cognitive levels of play, according to Piaget and others, and six categories of social and nonsocial play, according to Parten?

✔ Explain the connection between the cognitive and social dimensions of play?

One kind of play that does become more social during the preschool years is imaginative play, which shifts from solitary pretending to dramatic play involving other children (K. H. Rubin et al., 1998; Singer & Singer, 1990). Young children follow unspoken rules in organizing dramatic play, staking out territory ("I'm the daddy; you're the mommy"), negotiating ("Okay, I'll be the daddy tomorrow"), or setting the scene ("Watch out—there's a train coming!"). As imaginative play becomes increasingly collaborative, story lines become more complex, and themes become more innovative. Dramatic play offers rich opportunities to practice interpersonal and language skills and to explore social roles and conventions (Bodrova & Leong, 1998; Christie, 1991; J. E. Johnson, 1998; Nourot, 1998). It is easy to envision how little Eva Duarte might have acted out her dreams of power and glory in early childhood.

How Gender Influences Play

A tendency toward sex segregation in play seems to be universal across cultures. It is common among preschoolers as young as 3 and becomes even more common in middle childhood (Maccoby, 1988, 1990, 1994; Ramsey & Lasquade, 1996; Snyder, West, Stockemer, Gibbons, & Almquist-Parks, 1996).

Boys and girls typically play differently, and neither sex seems to like the other's style (Serbin, Moller, Gulko, Powlishta, & Colburne, 1994). Most boys like rough-and-tumble play in fairly large groups; girls are inclined to quieter play with one playmate (Benenson, 1993). The difference is not just based on liking different kinds of activities. Even when boys and girls play with the same toys, they play more socially with others of the same sex (Neppl & Murray, 1997). At age 4, when playing in a large school-based group, boys pair off more frequently, though for a shorter time. At 6, boys engage in more coordinated group activity (Benenson, Apostoleris, & Parnass, 1997). Boys play more boisterously; girls play more cooperatively, taking turns to avoid clashes (Maccoby, 1980).

Children's developing gender concepts seem to influence dramatic play. Whereas boys' stories often involve danger and discord (such as mock battles), girls' plots generally focus on maintaining or restoring orderly social relationships (playing house) (Fagot & Leve, 1998; Nourot, 1998).

From an evolutionary viewpoint, gender differences in children's play, found in all cultures, provide practice for adult behaviors important for reproduction and survival. Boys' rough-and-tumble play mirrors adult males' competition for dominance and status, and for fertile mates. Girls' play parenting prepares them to care for the young (Geary, 1999).

How Culture Influences Play

Both the social and cognitive dimensions of play can be seen in cultures around the world. However, the frequency of specific forms of play differs across cultures and is influenced by the play environments adults set up for children, which in turn reflect cultural values (Bodrova & Leong, 1998).

One observational study compared 48 middle-class Korean American and 48 middle-class Anglo American children in separate full-day, year-round preschools (Farver, Kim, & Lee, 1995). The Anglo American preschools, in keeping with typical American values, encouraged independent thinking, problem solving, and active involvement in learning by letting children select from a wide range of activities. The Korean American preschool, in keeping with traditional Korean values, emphasized developing academic skills and completing tasks. The Anglo American preschools encouraged social interchange among children and collaborative activities with teachers. In the Korean American preschool, with its structured schedule, children were allowed to talk and play only during outdoor recess.

Not surprisingly, the Anglo American children engaged in more social play, whereas the Korean Americans engaged in more unoccupied or parallel play. The Korean Americans also showed less imaginative play—again, not surprising, since their classroom offered few materials that would stimulate pretending, such as "dress-up" clothes or dolls. In addition, the greater amount of pretend play among the Anglo American children may have been influenced by the greater value American culture places on individuality and self-expression. Korean American children played more cooperatively, often offering toys to other children—very likely a reflection of their culture's emphasis on group harmony. Anglo American children were more aggressive and often responded negatively to other children's suggestions, reflecting the competitiveness of American culture.

CHECKPOINT

Can you . . .

✔ Tell how gender and culture influence the way children play, and give examples?

Parenting

As children gradually become their own persons, their upbringing can be a complex challenge. Parents must deal with small people who have minds and wills of their own, but who still have a lot to learn about what kinds of behavior work well in a civilized society. How do parents discipline children and teach them self-discipline? Are some ways of parenting more effective than others?

Guidepost 5. What forms of discipline do parents use, and how do parenting styles and practices influence development?

Forms of Discipline

Discipline refers to methods of teaching children character, self-control, and acceptable behavior. It can be a powerful tool for socialization.

What forms of discipline work best? Research inspired by learning theory has compared reinforcement and punishment. Other researchers have looked at a wider range of disciplinary techniques.

discipline
Tool of socialization, which includes methods of molding children's character and of teaching them to exercise self-control and engage in acceptable behavior.

Reinforcement and Punishment

"What are we going to do with that child?" Noel's mother says. "The more we punish him, the more he misbehaves!"

Parents sometimes punish children to stop undesirable behavior, but children usually learn more from being reinforced for good behavior. *External* reinforcements may be tangible (candy, money, toys, or gold stars) or intangible (a smile, a word of praise, a hug, extra attention, or a special privilege). Whatever the reinforcement, the child must see it as rewarding and must receive it fairly consistently after showing the desired behavior. Eventually, the behavior should provide its own *internal* reward: a sense of pleasure or accomplishment. In Noel's case, his parents ignore him most of the time when he behaves well but scold or spank him when he acts up. In other words, they unwittingly reinforce his *mis*-behavior by giving him attention when he does what they do *not* want him to do.

Still, at times some kind of punishment does seem necessary. Children may have to be immediately and forcefully prevented from running out into traffic or bashing another child over the head with a wooden hammer. Sometimes a child is willfully defiant. In such situations, punishment, if administered prudently, may be effective. Prudent punishment is consistent, immediate, and clearly tied to the offense. It is administered calmly, in private. It is aimed at eliciting compliance, not guilt. It is most effective when accompanied by a short, simple explanation to make sure the child understands why she or he is being punished (AAP Committee on Psychosocial Aspects of Child and Family Health, 1998; Baumrind, 1996a, 1996b).

Imprudent punishment can be counterproductive. Children who are punished harshly and frequently may have trouble interpreting other people's actions and words; they may attribute hostile intentions where none exist (B. Weiss, Dodge, Bates, & Pettit, 1992). On the other hand, such children may become passive because they feel helpless. Children may become frightened if parents lose control and yell, scream, chase, or hit the child. A child may eventually try to avoid a punitive parent, undermining the parent's ability to influence behavior (Grusec & Goodnow, 1994).

Spanking, which is very common in early childhood, can have negative consequences. Aside from the risk of injury to the child, some research suggests that physical punishment may stimulate aggressive behavior by leading children to imitate the punisher and to consider infliction of pain an acceptable response to problems. As with any punishment, the effectiveness of spanking diminishes with repeated use; children may feel free to misbehave if they are willing to take the consequences. Reliance on physical punishment may weaken parents' authority when children become teenagers and spanking becomes inappropriate—if not impractical (AAP Committee on Psychosocial Aspects of Child and Family Health, 1998; McCord, 1996). In the long run, spanking can have more serious effects. In a survey of 4,888 residents of Ontario, Canada, ages 15 to 64, those who recalled being spanked or slapped sometimes or often during childhood were more likely to report having had anxiety disorders, alcohol problems, or antisocial behavior than those who never had been spanked (MacMillan et al., 1999).

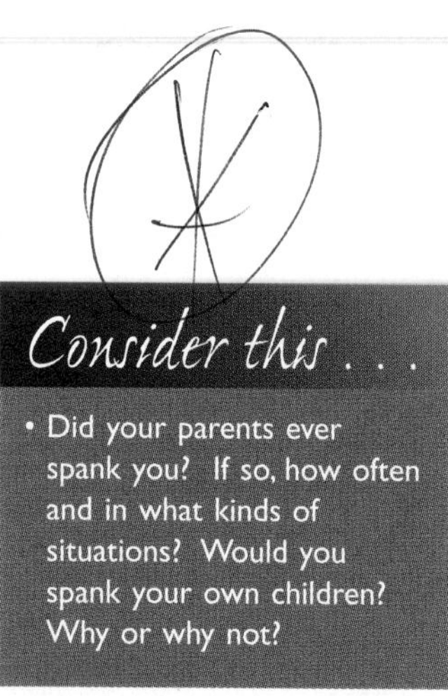

Consider this . . .

- Did your parents ever spank you? If so, how often and in what kinds of situations? Would you spank your own children? Why or why not?

As alternatives to spanking, the American Academy of Pediatrics Committee on Psychosocial Aspects of Child and Family Health (1998) suggests such inductive methods as helping children learn to use words to express feelings, giving children choices and helping them evaluate the consequences, and modeling orderly behavior and collaborative conflict resolution. The committee recommends positive reinforcement to encourage desired behaviors, and verbal reprimands, "time-outs," or removal of privileges to discourage undesired behaviors—all within the context of a positive, supportive, loving parent-child relationship.

power assertion
Disciplinary strategy designed to discourage undesirable behavior through physical or verbal enforcement of parental control. Compare *inductive techniques* and *withdrawal of love*.

inductive techniques
Disciplinary techniques designed to induce desirable behavior by appealing to a child's sense of reason and fairness. Compare *power assertion* and *withdrawal of love*.

Power Assertion, Induction, and Withdrawal of Love

Reinforcement and punishment are not the only ways to influence behavior. Contemporary research has focused on three broader categories of discipline: *power assertion, induction,* and *temporary withdrawal of love.*

Power assertion is intended to stop or discourage undesirable behavior through physical or verbal enforcement of parental control; it includes demands, threats, withdrawal of privileges, spanking, and other punishments. **Inductive**

techniques are designed to induce desirable behavior (or discourage undesirable behavior) by appealing to a child's sense of reason and fairness; they include setting limits, demonstrating logical consequences of an action, explaining, discussing, and getting ideas from the child. **Withdrawal of love** may take the form of ignoring, isolating, or showing dislike for a child. The choice and effectiveness of a disciplinary strategy may depend on the personality of the parent, the personality and age of the child, and the quality of their relationship, as well as on culturally based customs and expectations (Grusec & Goodnow, 1994).

Most parents call upon more than one strategy, depending on the situation. Parents tend to use reasoning to get a child to show concern for others or to teach table manners. They use power assertion to stop play that gets too rough, and they use both power assertion and reasoning to deal with lying and stealing (Grusec & Goodnow, 1994).

The strategy parents choose may depend not only on their belief in its effectiveness but on their confidence that they can carry it out, and mothers and fathers may differ on these points. In one observational study of how parents of preschoolers handle sibling conflicts, mothers were more likely to use inductive techniques, which they believed to be more effective than asserting parental control. Fathers were more likely to use power-assertive strategies, which they had more confidence they could perform. Still, beliefs and behavior frequently did not match; despite their expressed preference for either inductive or power-assertive techniques, what both mothers and fathers did most often was not to intervene at all (Perozynski & Kramer, 1999).

An important goal of socialization is to help a child internalize parental teachings in the form of self-discipline. Analysis of data from a number of studies suggests that induction is usually the most effective method, and power assertion the least effective, of getting children to accept parental standards (M. L. Hoffman, 1970a, 1970b). Among 54 poor, inner-city African American kindergartners, children whose mothers reported using reasoning were more likely to see the moral wrongness of behavior that hurts other people (as opposed to merely breaking rules) than children whose mothers took away privileges (Jagers, Bingham, & Hans, 1996). This may be because punishment encourages children to focus on themselves and their own feelings rather than on the way their behavior affects others (McCord, 1996).

The effectiveness of parental discipline may hinge on how well the child understands and accepts the parent's message, both cognitively and emotionally (Grusec & Goodnow, 1994). For the child to accept the message, the child has to recognize it as appropriate; so parents need to be fair and accurate, and clear and consistent about their expectations. They need to fit their actions to the misdeed and to the child's temperament and cognitive and emotional level. A child may be more motivated to accept the message if the parents are normally warm and responsive, if they arouse the child's empathy for the victim of the misdeed, and if they make the child feel less secure in their affections as a result of the misbehavior (Grusec & Goodnow, 1994).

One point on which experts agree is that a child interprets and responds to discipline in the context of an ongoing relationship with a parent. Some researchers therefore have looked beyond specific parental practices to overall styles, or patterns, of parenting.

"Young lady, don't get gutsy with me."

Power assertion, consisting of threats, demands, or physical punishment, is usually less effective than other types of discipline. However, the choice and effectiveness of a disciplinary strategy may depend on the personalities of parent and child, the child's age, the quality of their relationship, and the culture.

withdrawal of love Disciplinary strategy that may involve ignoring, isolating, or showing dislike for a child. Compare *power assertion* and *inductive techniques*.

CHECKPOINT

Can you . . .

✔ Compare various forms of discipline, and identify factors that influence their effectiveness?

Consider this . . .

- As a parent, what forms of discipline would you favor in what situations? Give specific examples, and tell why.

Parenting Styles

Why does Stacy hit and bite the nearest person when she cannot finish a jigsaw puzzle? What makes David sit and sulk when he cannot finish the puzzle, even though his teacher offers to help him? Why does Consuelo work on the puzzle for 20 minutes and then shrug and try another? Why are children so different in their responses to the same situation? Temperament is a major factor, of course; but some research suggests that styles of parenting may affect children's competence in dealing with their world.

Baumrind's Model

In her pioneering research, Diana Baumrind (1971, 1996b; Baumrind & Black, 1967) studied 103 preschool children from 95 families. Through interviews, testing, and home studies, she measured how children were functioning, identified three parenting styles, and described typical behavior patterns of children raised according to each.

authoritarian
In Baumrind's terminology, parenting style emphasizing control and obedience. Compare *authoritative* and *permissive*.

permissive
In Baumrind's terminology, parenting style emphasizing self-expression and self-regulation. Compare *authoritarian* and *authoritative*.

authoritative
In Baumrind's terminology, parenting style blending respect for a child's individuality with an effort to instill social values. Compare *authoritarian* and *permissive*.

Authoritarian parents value control and unquestioning obedience. They try to make children conform to a set standard of conduct and punish them arbitrarily and forcefully for violating it. They are more detached and less warm than other parents. Their children tend to be more discontented, withdrawn, and distrustful.

Permissive parents value self-expression and self-regulation. They consider themselves resources, not models. They make few demands and allow children to monitor their own activities as much as possible. When they do have to make rules, they explain the reasons for them. They consult with children about policy decisions and rarely punish. They are warm, noncontrolling, and undemanding. Their preschool children tend to be immature—the least self-controlled and the least exploratory.

Authoritative parents value a child's individuality but also stress social constraints. They have confidence in their ability to guide children, but they also respect children's independent decisions, interests, opinions, and personalities. They are loving and accepting, but also demand good behavior, are firm in maintaining standards, and are willing to impose limited, judicious punishment—even occasional, mild spanking—when necessary, within the context of a warm, supportive relationship. They explain the reasoning behind their stands and encourage verbal give-and-take. Their children apparently feel secure in knowing both that they are loved and what is expected of them. These preschoolers tend to be the most self-reliant, self-controlled, self-assertive, exploratory, and content.

Eleanor Maccoby and John Martin (1983) added a fourth parenting style—*neglectful,* or *uninvolved*—to describe parents who, sometimes because of stress or depression, focus on their own needs rather than on those of the child. Neglectful parenting, discussed later in this chapter, has been linked with a variety of behavioral disorders in childhood and adolescence (Baumrind, 1991; Parke & Buriel, 1998; R. A. Thompson, 1998).

Why does authoritative parenting seem to enhance children's competence? It may be because authoritative parents set sensible expectations and realistic standards. By making clear, consistent rules, they let children know what is expected of them. In authoritarian homes, children are so strictly controlled that often they cannot make independent choices about their own behavior. In permissive homes, children receive so little guidance that they may become uncertain and anxious about whether they are doing the right thing. In authoritative homes, children know when they are meeting expectations and can decide whether it is worth risking parental displeasure or other unpleasant consequences to pursue a goal. These children are expected to perform well, fulfill commitments, and participate actively in family duties as well as family fun. They know the satisfaction of meeting responsibilities and achieving success. Parents who make reasonable demands show that they believe their children can meet them—and that the parents care enough to insist that they do.

Support and Criticisms of Baumrind's Model

Baumrind's work has inspired much research, and the superiority of authoritative parenting (or similar conceptions of parenting style) has repeatedly been supported (Baumrind, 1989; Darling & Steinberg, 1993). A longitudinal study of 585 ethnically and socioeconomically diverse families in Tennessee and Indiana from prekindergarten through grade 6 found that four aspects of early "supportive" parenting—warmth, use of inductive discipline, interest and involvement in children's contacts with peers, and proactive teaching of social skills—predicted children's later behavioral, social, and academic outcomes (Pettit, Bates, & Dodge, 1997).

However, because Baumrind's model seems to suggest that there is one "right" way to raise children well, it has provoked some controversy. Since Baumrind's findings were correlational, they merely establish associations between each parenting style and a particular set of child behaviors. They do not show that different styles of child rearing *cause* children to be more or less competent. Sandra Scarr (1992, 1993), for example, argues that heredity normally exerts a much greater influence than parenting practices.

It is also impossible to know whether the children Baumrind studied were, in fact, raised in a particular style. It may be that some of the better-adjusted children were raised inconsistently, but by the time of the study their parents had adopted the authoritative pattern. Furthermore, parents often behave inconsistently in differing situations (Holden & Miller, 1999).

In addition, Baumrind did not consider innate factors, such as temperament, that might have affected children's competence and exerted an influence on the parents. Parents of "easy" children may be more likely to respond to the child in a permissive or authoritative manner, while parents of "difficult" children may become more authoritarian.

Cultural Differences in Parenting Styles

Baumrind's categories reflect the dominant North American view of child development and may be misleading when applied to some cultures or socioeconomic groups. Among Asian Americans, obedience and strictness—rather than being associated with harshness and domination—have more to do with caring, concern, and involvement and with maintaining family harmony. Traditional Chinese culture, with its emphasis on respect for elders, stresses adults' responsibility to maintain the social order by teaching children socially proper behavior. This obligation is carried out through firm and just control and governance of the child. Although Asian American parenting is frequently described as authoritarian, the warmth and supportiveness that characterize Chinese American family relationships more closely resemble Baumrind's authoritative parenting—but without the emphasis on the American values of individuality, choice, and freedom (Chao, 1994).

The question of *how much* freedom children should be allowed is a major source of conflict between parents and children in mainstream American culture. Most U.S. parents believe that even preschoolers are entitled to their own opinions and should have control over some aspects of their lives so as to promote competence and self-esteem. However, the precise boundaries where a child's area of autonomy ends and the area of parental control begins are matters of negotiation and may vary among ethnic and socioeconomic groups (Nucci & Smetana, 1996).

From the perspective of authoritative parenting, the processes by which parents and children resolve "boundary disputes" may be more important than the specific outcomes. Through participation in family conflict, children can learn about rules and standards of behavior. They also can learn what kinds of issues

Consider this . . .

- To what extent would you like your children to adopt your values and behavioral standards? Can you give examples?

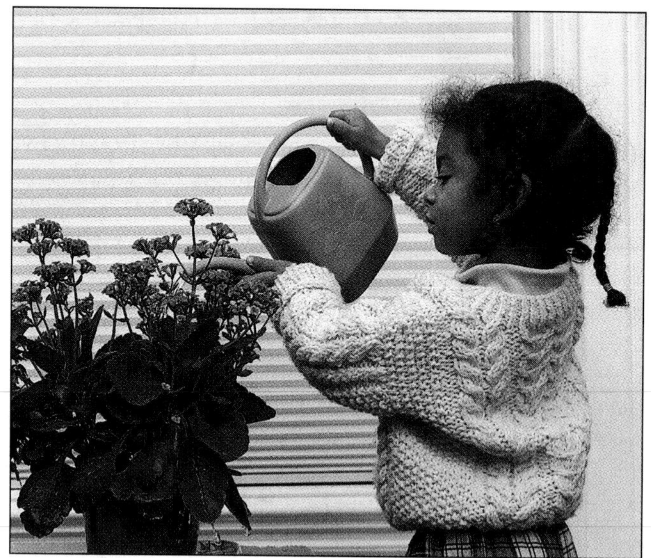

Children given responsibilities at home tend to develop prosocial qualities, such as cooperation and helpfulness. This 3-year-old girl, who is learning to care for plants, is likely to have caring relationships with people as well.

are worth arguing about and what strategies are effective (Eisenberg, 1996). When a conflict arises, an authoritative parent may take the opportunity to teach the child positive ways to communicate his or her own point of view and negotiate acceptable alternatives. ("If you don't want to throw away those smelly clam shells you found, where do you think we should keep them?") Internalization of this broader set of skills, not just of specific behavioral demands, may well be a key to the success of authoritative parenting (Grusec & Goodnow, 1994).

CHECKPOINT

Can you . . .

- ✔ Describe and evaluate Baumrind's model of parenting styles?
- ✔ Discuss how parents' way of resolving conflicts with young children over issues involving autonomy and control can contribute to the success of authoritative child rearing?

Some researchers have identified a parenting style in African American families that falls somewhere between Baumrind's authoritarian and authoritative styles. This style, called "no nonsense parenting," combines warmth and affection with firm parental control. "No nonsense" parents regard stringent control and insistence on obedience to rules as necessary safeguards for children growing up in dangerous neighborhoods, and such children see this kind of parenting as evidence of concern about their well-being (Brody & Flor, 1998). It may be misleading, then, to consider parenting styles without looking at the goals parents are trying to achieve and the constraints their life circumstances present.

Promoting Altruism and Dealing with Aggression and Fearfulness

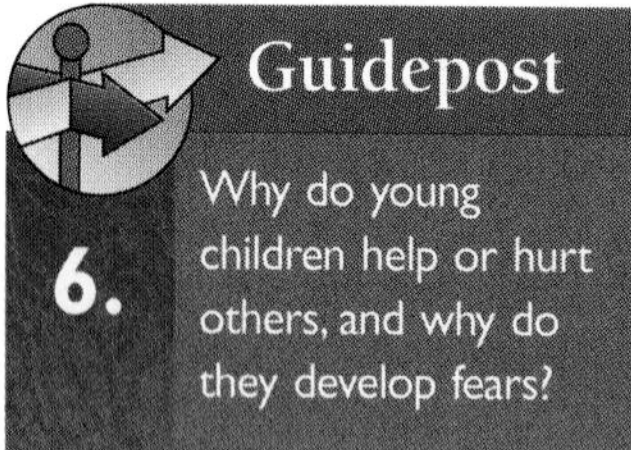

Guidepost
6.
Why do young children help or hurt others, and why do they develop fears?

Three specific issues of especial concern to parents, caregivers, and teachers of preschool children are how to promote altruism, curb aggression, and deal with fears that often arise at this age.

Altruism, or Prosocial Behavior

altruism, or prosocial behavior
Behavior intended to help others without external reward.

Anna, at $3^1/_2$, responded to two fellow preschoolers' complaints that they did not have enough modeling clay, her favorite plaything, by giving them half of hers. Anna was showing **altruism,** or **prosocial behavior**—acting out of concern for another person with no expectation of reward. Prosocial acts like Anna's often entail cost, self-sacrifice, or risk.

Even before the second birthday, children often help others, share belongings and food, and offer comfort (refer back to Chapter 7). Such behaviors may reflect a growing ability to imagine how another person might feel (Zahn-Waxler, Radke-Yarrow, Wagner, & Chapman, 1992). An analysis of 179 studies found increasing evidence of concern for others from infancy throughout childhood and adolescence (Fabes & Eisenberg, 1996). Although girls are generally thought to be more prosocial than boys, actual gender differences in altruistic behavior are small (Eisenberg & Fabes, 1998).

The family is important as a model and as a source of explicit standards of behavior (Eisenberg & Fabes, 1998). Parents of prosocial children typically are altruistic themselves. They point out models of prosocial behavior and steer children toward stories, films, and television programs, such as *Barney and Friends,* which depict cooperation, sharing, and empathy and encourage sympathy, generosity, and helpfulness (Singer & Singer, 1998). Relationships with siblings (discussed later in this chapter) provide an important "laboratory" for trying out caring behavior and learning to see another person's point of view. Peers and teachers also can be models and reinforcers of prosocial behavior (Eisenberg, 1992; Eisenberg & Fabes, 1998).

Parents encourage prosocial behavior when they use inductive disciplinary methods instead of power-assertive techniques (Eisenberg & Fabes, 1998). When Sara took candy from a store, her father did not lecture her on honesty, spank her, or tell her what a bad girl she had been. Instead, he explained how the owner of the store would be harmed by her failure to pay for the candy, and he took her back to the store to return it. When such incidents occur, Sara's parents ask "How do you think Mr. Jones feels?" or "How would you feel if you were Mr. Jones?" In one study of 106 three- to six-year-olds, the most prosocial children were disciplined by such inductive techniques (C. H. Hart, DeWolf, Wozniak, & Burts, 1992).

Motives for altruistic behavior may change as children grow older and develop more mature moral reasoning (see Chapters 9 and 11). Preschoolers tend to show egocentric motives, such as the desire to earn praise and avoid disapproval. They weigh the costs and benefits to themselves and consider how they would like others to act toward them. As children grow older, their motives become less self-centered. They adopt societal standards of "being good," which eventually become internalized in the form of principles and values (Eisenberg & Fabes, 1998).

Cultures vary in the degree to which they foster prosocial behavior. Traditional cultures in which people live in extended family groups and work is shared seem to inculcate prosocial values more than cultures that emphasize individual achievement (Eisenberg & Fabes, 1998).

Consider this . . .

- In a society in which "good Samaritans" are sometimes reviled for "butting into other people's business" and sometimes attacked by the very persons they try to help, is it wise to encourage children to offer help to strangers?

instrumental aggression Aggressive behavior used as a means of achieving a goal.

Aggression

A young child who roughly snatches a toy away from another child is usually interested only in getting the toy, not in hurting or dominating the other child. This is **instrumental aggression,** or aggression used as an instrument to reach a goal—the most common type of aggression in early childhood. Between ages $2\frac{1}{2}$ and 5, children commonly struggle over toys and the control of space. Aggression surfaces mostly during social play; the children who fight the most also tend to be the most sociable and competent. In fact, the ability to show some instrumental aggression may be a necessary step in social development.

Between ages 2 and 4, as children develop more self-control and become better able to express themselves verbally and to wait for what they want, they typically shift from showing aggression with blows to doing it with words (Coie & Dodge, 1998). However, individual differences remain; children who more frequently hit or grab toys from other children at age 2 are likely to be more physically aggressive at age 5 (Cummings, Iannotti, & Zahn-Waxler, 1989). After age 6 or 7, most children become less aggressive as they become more cooperative, less egocentric, and more empathic and can communicate better. They

The kind of aggression involved in fighting over a toy, without intention to hurt or dominate the other child, is known as *instrumental aggression.* It surfaces mostly during social play and normally declines as children learn to ask for what they want.

hostile aggression Aggressive behavior intended to hurt another person.

overt aggression Aggression that is openly directed at its target.

relational aggression Aggression aimed at damaging or interfering with another person's relationships, reputation, or psychological well-being; also called *covert, indirect,* or *psychological aggression.*

can now put themselves in someone else's place, can understand why the other person may be acting in a certain way, and can develop more positive ways of dealing with that person. As aggression declines overall, **hostile aggression**—action intended to hurt another person—proportionately increases (see Chapter 10). Some children do not learn to control aggression; they continue to be destructive and antisocial throughout life (Coie & Dodge, 1998).

Are boys more aggressive than girls? As we mentioned earlier, many studies say yes. Indeed, it has been suggested that the male hormone testosterone may underlie aggressive behavior. From infancy, boys are more likely to grab things from others. As children learn to talk, girls are more likely to rely on words to protest and to work out conflicts (Coie & Dodge, 1998).

However, girls may be more aggressive than they seem; they just show aggressiveness differently (McNeilly-Choque, Hart, Robinson, Nelson, & Olsen, 1996). Boys engage in more **overt aggression,** either instrumental or hostile. Overt aggression, either physical or verbal, is openly directed against its target. Girls tend to practice **relational aggression** (also called *covert, indirect,* or *psychological aggression*). This more subtle kind of aggression consists of damaging or interfering with relationships, reputation, or psychological well-being. It may involve spreading rumors, name-calling, withholding friendship, or excluding someone from a group.

Sources and Triggers of Aggression What are the sources of aggression, and what sets it off? Why are some children more aggressive than others?

As we've mentioned, biology may play a part. So may temperament: children who are intensely emotional and low in self-control tend to express anger aggressively (Eisenberg, Fabes, Nyman, Bernzweig, & Pinuelas, 1994). Evidence suggests that exposure to real or televised violence can trigger aggression (see Chapter 10).

A negative early relationship with the mother is an important factor, which may interact with other risk factors, such as low socioeconomic status and single parenthood. In longitudinal studies, insecure attachment and lack of maternal warmth and affection in infancy have been predictors of aggressiveness in early childhood (Coie & Dodge, 1998).

Parents of children who become antisocial often fail to reinforce good behavior and are harsh or inconsistent, or both, in stopping or punishing misbehavior (Coie & Dodge, 1998). Parents who back down when confronted with a preschooler's coercive demands (such as whining or yelling when scolded for not going to bed) may reinforce repetition of the undesirable behavior (G. R. Patterson, 1995). On the other hand, as we've mentioned, harsh punishment, especially spanking, can backfire; children who are spanked not only suffer frustration, pain, and humiliation (which can be spurs to aggression) but also see aggressive behavior in an adult model.

In a classic social-learning experiment (Bandura, Ross, & Ross, 1961), 3- to 6-year-olds individually watched adult models play with toys. One experimental group saw the adult play quietly. The model for a second experimental group began to assemble Tinker Toys, but then spent the rest of the 10-minute session punching, throwing, and kicking a life-size inflated doll. A control group did not see any model. After the sessions, the children, who were mildly frustrated by seeing toys they were not allowed to play with, went into another playroom. The children who had seen the aggressive model acted much more aggressively than those in the other groups, imitating many of the same things they had seen the model say and do. Both boys and girls were more strongly influenced by an aggressive male model than an aggressive female. The children who had been with the quiet model were less aggressive than the control group. This finding suggests that parents may be able to moderate the effects of frustration by showing nonaggressive behavior to their children.

Influence of Culture How much influence does culture have on aggressive behavior? One research team asked closely matched samples of 30 Japanese and 30 U.S. middle- to upper-middle-class preschoolers to choose pictured solutions to hypothetical conflicts or stressful situations (such as having one's block tower knocked down, having to stop playing and go to bed, being hit, hearing parents argue, or fighting on a jungle gym). The children also were asked to act out and complete such situations using dolls and props. The U.S. children showed more anger, more aggressive behavior and language, and less control of emotions than the Japanese children (Zahn-Waxler, Friedman, Cole, Mizuta, & Hiruma, 1996).

These results are consistent with childrearing values in the two cultures. In Japanese culture, anger and aggression are seen as clashing with the emphasis on harmonious relationships. Japanese mothers are more likely than U.S. mothers to discipline by reasoning and inducing guilt, pointing out how aggressive behavior hurts others. Japanese mothers also strongly show their disappointment when children do not meet their behavioral standards. However, the cross-cultural difference in children's anger and aggressiveness was significant even apart from mothers' behavior, suggesting that temperamental differences may also be at work (Zahn-Waxler et al., 1996).

On the other hand, a correlational study of 207 Russian 3- to 6-year-olds, based on parental questionnaires and nursery school teachers' ratings of children's behavior, identified much the same family influences on aggression as have studies in western cultures: parental coercion and lack of responsiveness. Coercive (power-assertive) discipline by either parent was linked with overt aggression in both boys and girls (C. H. Hart, Nelson, Robinson, Olsen, & McNeilly-Choque, 1998).

Consider this . . .

- Are there situations in which a child should be encouraged to be aggressive?

Fearfulness

Passing fears are common in early childhood. Many 2- to 4-year-olds are afraid of animals, especially dogs. By 6 years, children are more likely to be afraid of the dark. Other common fears are of thunderstorms, doctors, and imaginary creatures (DuPont, 1983; Stevenson-Hinde & Shouldice, 1996). Most of these disappear as children grow older and lose their sense of powerlessness.

Young children's fears stem largely from their intense fantasy life and their tendency to confuse appearance with reality. Sometimes their imaginations get carried away, making them worry about being attacked by a lion or being abandoned. Young children are more likely to be frightened by something that looks scary, such as a cartoon monster, than by something capable of doing great harm, such as a nuclear explosion (Cantor, 1994). For the most part, older children's fears are more realistic and self-evaluative (for example, fear of failing a test), since they know they are being evaluated by others (Stevenson-Hinde & Shouldice, 1996; see Table 8-3).

Fears may come from personal experience (conditioning) or from hearing about experiences of others (Muris, Merckelbach, & Collaris, 1997). A preschooler whose mother is sick in bed may become upset by a story about a mother's death, even if it is an animal mother. Often fears come from appraisals of danger, such as the likelihood of being bitten by a dog, or are triggered by events, as when a child who was hit by a car becomes afraid to cross the street. Children who have lived through an earthquake, a kidnapping, or some other frightening event may fear that it will happen again (Kolbert, 1994).

Parents can help prevent children's fears by instilling a sense of trust and normal caution without being too protective, and also by overcoming their own unrealistic fears. They can help a fearful child by reassurance and by encouraging open expression of feelings. Ridicule ("Don't be such a baby!"), coercion ("Pat the nice doggie—it won't hurt you"), and logical persuasion ("The closest bear is 20 miles away, locked in a zoo!") are not helpful. Not until elementary school can children tell themselves that what they fear is not real (Cantor, 1994).

CHECKPOINT

Can you . . .

✔ Discuss how parental and other influences contribute to altruism, aggression, and fearfulness?

Age	Fears
0–6 months	Loss of support, loud noises
7–12 months	Strangers; heights, sudden, unexpected, and looming objects
1 year	Separation from parent, toilet, injury, strangers
2 years	A multitude of stimuli, including loud noises (vacuum cleaners, sirens and alarms, trucks, and thunder), animals, dark rooms, separation from parent, large objects or machines, changes in personal environment, unfamiliar peers
3 years	Masks, dark, animals, separation from parent
4 years	Separation from parent, animals, dark, noises (including noises at night)
5 years	Animals, "bad" people, dark, separation from parent, bodily harm
6 years	Supernatural beings (e.g., ghosts, witches), bodily injury, thunder and lightning, dark, sleeping or staying alone, separation from parent
7–8 years	Supernatural beings, dark, media events (e.g., news reports on the threat of nuclear war or child kidnapping), staying alone, bodily injury
9–12 years	Tests and examinations in school, school performances, bodily injury, physical appearance, thunder and lightning, death, dark

Table 8-3 Childhood Fears

Source: Adapted from Morris & Kratochwill, 1983; Stevenson-Hinde & Shouldice, 1996.

Children also can be helped to overcome fears by *systematic desensitization,* a therapeutic technique involving gradual exposure to a feared object or situation. This technique has been used successfully to help children overcome fears ranging from snakes to elevators (Murphy & Bootzin, 1973; Sturges & Sturges, 1998).

Maltreatment: Abuse and Neglect

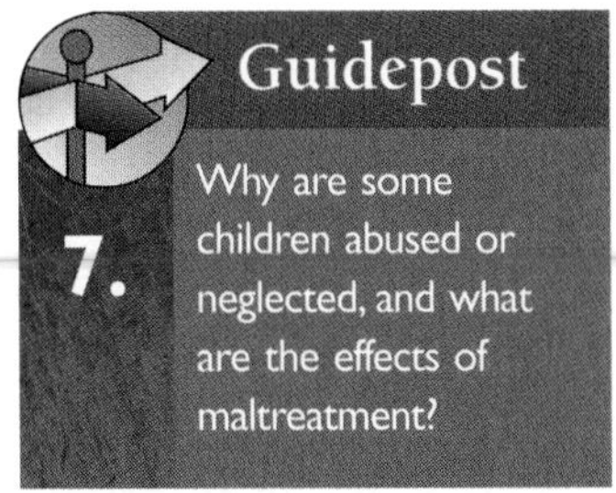
Guidepost
7.
Why are some children abused or neglected, and what are the effects of maltreatment?

physical abuse
Action taken to endanger a child involving potential bodily injury.

neglect
Failure to meet a child's basic needs.

sexual abuse
Sexual activity involving a child and an older person responsible for the child's care.

emotional maltreatment
Action or inaction that may cause behavioral, cognitive, emotional, or mental disorders.

Although most parents are loving and nurturing, some cannot or will not take proper care of their children, and some deliberately hurt or kill them. *Maltreatment,* whether perpetrated by parents or others, is deliberate or avoidable endangerment of a child; it takes several specific forms. In general, *abuse* refers to action that inflicts harm; *neglect* refers to inaction that leads to harm. **Physical abuse** involves injury to the body through punching, beating, kicking, or burning. **Neglect** is failure to meet a child's basic needs, such as food, clothing, medical care, protection, and supervision. **Sexual abuse** is sexual activity involving a child and an older person. **Emotional maltreatment** includes acts of abuse or neglect that may cause behavioral, cognitive, emotional, or mental disorders (U.S. Department of Health and Human Services [USDHHS], 1999a). It may include rejection, terrorization, isolation, exploitation, degradation, ridicule, or failure to provide emotional support, love, and affection. Any one form of maltreatment is likely to be accompanied by one or more of the others (Belsky, 1993).

Maltreatment: Facts and Figures

Maltreatment is more widely recognized than in the past, but its incidence remains hard to determine. The steep rise in reported cases and serious injuries since 1976, when the first national statistics were compiled, may reflect an increase in maltreatment, better recognition and reporting of abuse and neglect, or (more likely) both.

The reported number of abused and neglected children in the United States has declined slightly since its peak in 1993. Still, the number of cases investigated and confirmed by state child protective services agencies in 1997 was close to 1 million, and the actual number may well have been considerably higher (USDHHS, 1999c). Many, if not most, cases are never reported to protective agencies, and many of those reported are not investigated (USDHHS, 1999a). Children and families are often caught between conflicting values: protecting children's safety versus preserving families and respecting privacy. Many allegations of maltreatment are never confirmed, and adults who are unjustly accused suffer grievously and unfairly. On the other hand, many children whose precarious situation is known to authorities or neighbors are left in the hands of abusive or neglectful parents, often with fatal results.

In 1996, 6 out of 10 reported cases of maltreatment involved neglect or emotional maltreatment, and nearly 1 out of 4 involved physical abuse. Most neglect cases occur in very poor families; yet most low-income parents, like Eva Duarte's mother, do not neglect their children. Emotional maltreatment is hard to identify; its effects may not surface immediately and may be difficult to distinguish from signs of emotional disturbance and other developmental problems (USDHHS, 1999a).

Abused and neglected children are of all ages, but more than half of reported victims are 7 or younger, and about one-fourth are below age 4 (National Clearinghouse on Child Abuse and Neglect Information, 1997). Girls are three times as likely as boys to be sexually abused, whereas boys are more likely to be emotionally neglected or seriously injured (Sedlak & Broadhurst, 1996). The people most likely to abuse or neglect a child are the child's parents (USDHHS, 1999a, 1999b).

Maltreatment has become a major cause of death among young children, and, again, the full incidence of such deaths is unknown. According to one estimate, fatal maltreatment claimed more than 1,000 lives in 1996, half through abuse and half through neglect. Three out of four of the victims were less than 4 years old (USDHHS, 1999a). On the basis of a review of all deaths of children under 11 years old in North Carolina between 1985 and 1994, it has been estimated that more than 3 times as many child deaths nationally are due to abuse as are officially reported (9,467 as opposed to 2,973). In 63 percent of the North Carolina cases, biological parents were the perpetrators (Herman-Giddens et al., 1999).

Contributing Factors: An Ecological View

Why do adults hurt or neglect children? Which children, in what kinds of families, are most likely to be mistreated? What are the characteristics of the perpetrators? What other influences are at work? The answers are not clear-cut (USDHHS, 1999a).

Maltreatment by parents is a symptom of extreme disturbance in child rearing, usually aggravated by other family problems, such as poverty, alcoholism, or antisocial behavior. A disproportionate number of abused and neglected children are in large, poor, or single-parent families, which tend to be under stress and to have trouble meeting children's needs (Sedlak & Broadhurst, 1996). Yet, what pushes one parent over the edge, another may take in stride. By looking at maltreatment through Bronfenbrenner's ecological perspective, we can see that abuse and neglect reflect the interplay of many contributing factors involving the child, the family, the community, and the larger society (USDHHS, 1999a).

The Child in the Family Many abusers are lonely, unhappy, anxious, depressed, angry, or aggressive. They tend to have low self-esteem and poor impulse control and coping skills. About one-third of abusing parents were abused themselves as children (National Research Council [NRC], 1993b; Schmitt & Kempe, 1983; USDHHS, 1999a; Wolfe, 1985). Substance abuse is a factor in at least one-third of substantiated cases of abuse and neglect (USDHHS, 1999a).

Unlike neglectful parents, who tend to be apathetic, incompetent, irresponsible, or emotionally withdrawn (Wolfe, 1985), abusive parents are overly involved with the child. Often deprived of good parenting themselves, they are greatly upset by behavior that most parents accept as normal (J. R. Reid, Patterson, & Loeber, 1982; Wolfe, 1985). Abuse may begin when a parent who is already anxious, depressed, or hostile tries to control a child physically, but loses self-control and ends up shaking or beating the child (USDHHS, 1999a). When parents who had troubled childhoods, think poorly of themselves, and find negative emotions hard to handle have children who are particularly needy or demanding, who cry a lot, or who are unresponsive, the likelihood of maltreatment increases (NRC, 1993b; J. R. Reid et al., 1982; USDHHS, 1999a).

Abusive parents tend to have marital problems and to fight physically. Their households tend to be disorganized, and they experience more stressful events than other families (J. R. Reid et al., 1982; Sedlak & Broadhurst, 1996). Many abusive parents cut themselves off from others, leaving them with no one to turn to in times of stress and no one to see what is happening.

Neighborhood and Social Support The outside world can create a climate for family violence. Poverty, unemployment, job dissatisfaction, social isolation, and lack of assistance for the primary caregiver are closely correlated with child and spouse abuse. None of these, however, are determining factors.

What makes one low-income neighborhood a place where children are highly likely to be maltreated, while another, matched for ethnic population and income levels, is safer? In one inner-city Chicago neighborhood, the proportion of children who died from maltreatment (1 death for every 2,541 children) was about twice the proportion in another inner-city neighborhood. Researchers who interviewed community leaders found a depressed atmosphere in the high-abuse community. Criminal activity was rampant, and facilities for community programs were dark and dreary. This was an environment with "an ecological conspiracy against children" (Garbarino & Kostelny, 1993, p. 213). In the low-abuse neighborhood, people described their community as a poor but decent place to live. They painted a picture of a neighborhood with robust social support networks, well-known community services, and strong political leadership. In a community like this, maltreatment is less likely to occur.

Cultural Values and Patterns Two cultural factors associated with child abuse are societal violence and physical punishment of children. In countries where violent crime is infrequent and children are rarely spanked, such as Japan, China, and Tahiti, child abuse is rare (Celis, 1990).

By comparison, the United States is a violent place. Homicide, wife battering, and rape are common. A 1977 Supreme Court ruling that school personnel may strike disobedient children is still in effect, with some qualifications. Many states still permit corporal punishment in schools. According to a 1995 Gallup poll, more than 5 percent of parents admit to punishing their children so brutally that it amounts to abuse.

Effects of Maltreatment

Maltreatment can produce grave consequences—not only physical, but emotional, cognitive, and social. Maltreated children often speak late (Coster, Gersten, Beeghly, & Cicchetti, 1989). They are more likely to repeat a grade, to do poorly on cognitive tests, and to have discipline problems in school (Eckenrode, Laird, & Doris, 1993). They often have disorganized-disoriented attachments to their parents (refer back to Chapter 5) and negative, distorted self-concepts. Deprived of early positive social interactions, they do not develop social skills and have difficulty making friends (Price, 1996). Chronic neglect during early childhood has especially negative effects on later school performance, social relationships, adaptability, and problem solving (NRC, 1993b).

Maltreated children may become either overly aggressive or withdrawn (USDHHS, 1999a). Physically abused youngsters tend to be fearful, uncooperative, less able to respond appropriately to friendly overtures, and, consequently, less well liked than other children (Coie & Dodge, 1998; Haskett & Kistner, 1991; Salzinger, Feldman, Hammer, & Rosario, 1993).

Although most abused children do not become delinquent, criminal, or mentally ill, abuse makes it likelier that they will (Dodge, Bates, & Pettit, 1990; NRC,

Table 8-4 Developmentally Related Reactions to Sexual Abuse

Age	Most Common Symptoms
Preschoolers	Anxiety Nightmares Inappropriate sexual behavior
School-age children	Fear Mental illness Aggression Nightmares School problems Hyperactivity Regressive behavior
Adolescents	Depression Withdrawn, suicidal, or self-injurious behaviors Physical complaints Illegal acts Running away Substance abuse

Source: Adapted from Kendall-Tackett, Williams, & Finkelhor, 1993.

1993b; Widom, 1989). Teenagers who were abused when they were younger may react by running away, which may be self-protective, or may abuse drugs, which is not (NRC, 1993b).

Consequences of sexual abuse vary with age (see Table 8-4), but fearfulness and low self-esteem often continue into adulthood. Adults who were sexually abused as children tend to be anxious, depressed, angry, or hostile; not to trust people; to feel isolated and stigmatized; to be sexually maladjusted (Browne & Finkelhor, 1986); and to abuse alcohol or drugs (NRC, 1993b; USDHHS, 1999a).

Emotional maltreatment is more subtle than physical maltreatment, and its effects may be harder to pin down. It has been linked to lying, stealing, low self-esteem, emotional maladjustment, dependency, underachievement, depression, aggression, learning disorders, homicide, and suicide, as well as to psychological distress later in life (S. N. Hart & Brassard, 1987).

Still, many maltreated children show remarkable resilience, especially if they have been able to form an attachment to a supportive person (Egeland & Sroufe, 1981). Above average intelligence, advanced cognitive abilities, and high self-esteem seem to help. Also important is the child's interpretation of the abuse or neglect. Children who see it as coming from a parent's weaknesses or frustrations seem to cope better than those who take it as parental rejection (Garmezy, Masten, & Tellegen, 1984; Zimrin, 1986).

Growing up to be an abuser is far from an inevitable result of being abused as a child (Kaufman & Zigler, 1987; USDHHS, 1999a). Abused children who grow up to be *non*abusing parents are likely to have had someone to whom they could turn for help, to have received therapy, and to have good marital or love relationships. They are likely to have been abused by only one parent and to have had a loving, supportive relationship with the other (Egeland, Jacobvitz, & Sroufe, 1988; Kaufman & Zigler, 1987; NRC, 1993b).

Helping Families in Trouble or at Risk

Since maltreatment is a multifactorial problem, it needs many-pronged solutions. Effective community prevention and intervention strategies should be comprehensive, neighborhood-based, centered on protecting children, and aimed at strengthening families if possible and removing children if necessary (USDHHS, 1999a).

Some abuse-prevention programs teach basic parenting skills (USDHHS, 1999a; Wolfe, Edwards, Manion, & Koverola, 1988). Other programs offer subsidized

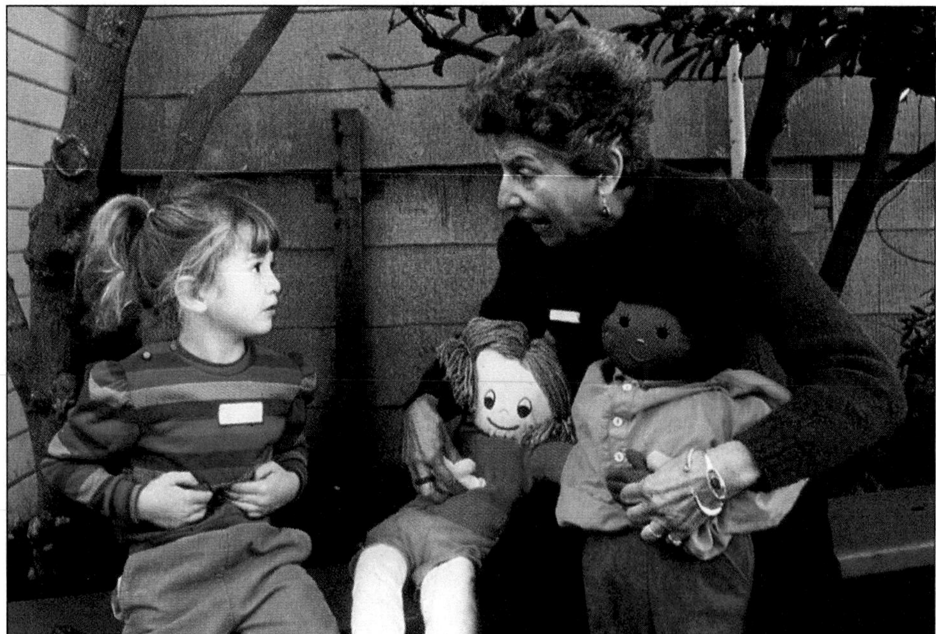

This adult volunteer uses dolls to help young children realize that they have control over their bodies and need not let anyone—even friends or family members—touch them. Such programs for preventing sexual abuse need to walk a fine line between alerting children to danger and frightening them or discouraging appropriate affection.

day care, volunteer homemakers, home visitors, and temporary "respite homes" or "relief parents" to take over occasionally.

One way to stop maltreatment that is already occurring is to treat abusers as criminal offenders; people arrested for family violence are less likely to repeat the offense (Bouza, 1990; Sherman & Berk, 1984). Services for abused children and adults include shelters, education in parenting skills, and therapy. Parents Anonymous and other organizations offer free, confidential support groups. Abused children may receive play or art therapy and day care in a therapeutic environment. In communities where abuse or neglect is widespread, school-based programs can be effective.

When authorities remove children from their homes, the usual alternative is foster care, which has increased markedly since the 1980s. Foster care removes a child from immediate danger, but it is often unstable, may also turn out to be an abusive situation, and further alienates the child from the family. It is intended as a temporary, emergency measure; but in some cities the average stay is five years, often with a series of placements in different homes (NRC, 1993b).

The plight of abused and neglected children is one for which society needs to find more effective remedies. Without help, maltreated children often grow up with serious problems, at great cost to themselves and to society, and may continue the cycle of maltreatment when they have children of their own.

CHECKPOINT

Can you . . .

- ✔ Define four types of child abuse and neglect?
- ✔ Discuss the incidence of maltreatment and explain why it is hard to measure?
- ✔ Identify contributing factors having to do with the child, the family, the neighborhood, and the wider society?
- ✔ Give examples of effects of child abuse and neglect?
- ✔ Describe ways to prevent or stop maltreatment and help its victims?

Relationships with Other Children

Although the most important people in young children's world are the adults who take care of them, relationships with siblings and playmates become more important in early childhood. Virtually every characteristic activity and personality issue of this age, from gender development to prosocial or aggressive behavior, involves other children. Sibling and peer relationships provide a measuring stick for **self-efficacy,** children's growing sense of capability to master challenges and achieve their goals. By competing with and comparing themselves with other children, they can gauge their physical, social, cognitive, and linguistic competencies and gain a more realistic sense of self (Bandura, 1994).

self-efficacy
Sense of capability to master challenges and achieve goals.

Siblings—or Their Absence

Ties between brothers and sisters often set the stage for later relationships. Let's look at sibling relationships, and then at children who grow up with no siblings.

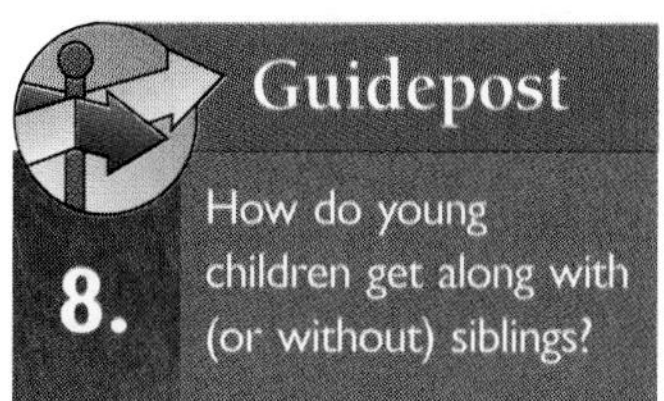

8. How do young children get along with (or without) siblings?

Brothers and Sisters

"It's mine!"
"No, it's mine!"
"Well, I was playing with it first!"

The earliest, most frequent, and most intense disputes among siblings are over property rights—who owns a toy or who is entitled to play with it—and some of these quarrels become so serious that parents or caregivers step in. Although exasperated adults may not always see it that way, sibling disputes and their settlement can be viewed as socialization opportunities, in which children learn to stand up for moral principles—even though those principles may not be the ones adults go by.

Among 40 pairs of 2- and 4-year-old siblings, property disputes arose, on average, about every 15 minutes during a 9-hour observation period. Even children as young as $2\frac{1}{2}$ argued on the basis of clear principles: the owner's right to a toy should take precedence over who was currently using it, but when property was commonly owned (as was true in about half the disputes), the possessor should have exclusive rights. Parents, on the other hand, did not clearly favor claims based on either ownership or possession but were more inclined to stress sharing and avoidance of damage or to suggest alternate playthings (Ross, 1996).

Despite the frequency of conflict, sibling rivalry is *not* the main pattern between brothers and sisters early in life. While some rivalry exists, so do affection, interest, companionship, and influence. Observations spanning three and a half years, which began when younger siblings were about $1\frac{1}{2}$ years old and the older ones ranged from 3 to $4\frac{1}{2}$, found prosocial and play-oriented behaviors to be more common than rivalry, hostility, and competition (Abramovitch, Corter, & Lando, 1979; Abramovitch, Corter, Pepler, & Stanhope, 1986; Abramovitch, Pepler, & Corter, 1982). Older siblings initiated more behavior, both friendly and unfriendly; younger siblings tended to imitate the older ones. Siblings got along better when their mother was not with them. (Squabbling can be a bid for parental attention.) As the younger children reached their fifth birthday, the siblings became less physical and more verbal, both in showing aggression (through commands, insults, threats, tattling, put-downs, bribes, and teasing) and in showing care and affection (by compliments and comforting rather than hugs and kisses).

At least one finding of this research has been replicated in many studies: same-sex siblings, particularly girls, are closer and play together more peaceably than boy-girl pairs (Kier & Lewis, 1998). The quality of relationships with brothers and sisters often carries over to relationships with other children; a child who is aggressive with siblings is likely to be aggressive with friends as well. However, a child who is dominated by an older sibling may be able to take a dominant role with a playmate. Usually children are more prosocial and playful with playmates than with siblings (Abramovitch et al., 1986).

CHECKPOINT

Can you . . .

- ✔ Explain how the resolution of sibling disputes contributes to socialization?
- ✔ Tell how birth order and gender affect typical patterns of sibling interaction?

The Only Child

People often think of only children as spoiled, selfish, lonely, or maladjusted, but research does not bear out this stereotype. According to an analysis of 115 studies of children of various ages and backgrounds, "onlies" do comparatively well (Falbo & Polit, 1986; Polit & Falbo, 1987). In occupational and educational achievement and intelligence, they surpass children with siblings. Only children also

CHECKPOINT

Can you . . .

✔ Compare development of only children with that of children with siblings?

tend to be more mature and motivated to achieve and to have higher self-esteem. They do not differ, however, in overall adjustment or sociability. Perhaps these children do better because their parents spend more time and focus more attention on them, talk to them more, do more with them, and expect more of them.

Research in China, which mandates one-child families, has produced encouraging findings about only children (see Box 8-2).

Box 8-2
A Nation of Only Children

In 1979, to control its exploding population, the People's Republic of China established an official policy of limiting families to one child each. In addition to propaganda campaigns and incentives (housing, money, child care, health care, and preference in school placement) to induce voluntary compliance, there have been millions of involuntary abortions and sterilizations. People who have had children without first getting a permit faced fines and loss of jobs. By 1985, at least 8 out of 10 young urban couples and half of those in rural areas had only one child (Yang, Ollendick, Dong, Xia, & Lin, 1995), and by 1997, the country's estimated population growth was holding steady at a little more than 1 percent—well within the planners' target.

Today the one-child policy is unevenly enforced. Economic growth is exerting a natural check on family size and also making it easier for families who want a second child to pay the fine (Faison, 1997). The State Family Planning Commission has now prohibited forced sterilizations and abortions and has begun to switch to a kinder, gentler system stressing education, contraceptive choice, and heavy taxation for families with more than one child. In a small but growing number of counties, fixed quotas and permit requirements have been eliminated (Rosenthal, 1998).

Still, in many Chinese cities, kindergartens and primary classrooms are almost completely filled with children who have no brothers or sisters. This situation marks a great change in Chinese society, in which newlyweds were traditionally congratulated with the wish, "May you have a hundred sons and a thousand grandsons." What kind of future population are the Chinese raising?

Early research suggested that only children were more egocentric, less persistent, less cooperative, and less well liked than children with siblings (Jiao, Ji, & Jing, 1986). However, more recent research contradicts these findings. Among 4,000 third- and sixth-graders from urban and rural districts, personality differences between only children and those with siblings—as rated by parents, teachers, peers, and the children themselves—were few. In academic achievement and physical growth, only children did about the same as, or better than, those with siblings (Falbo & Poston, 1993). A review of the literature found no significant differences in behavior problems; the small number of severe problems that did appear in only children were attributed to parental overindulgence and overprotection (Tao, 1998).

Indeed, only children now seem to be at a distinct psychological advantage in China. When questionnaires were administered to 731 urban children and adolescents, children with siblings reported higher levels of fear, anxiety, and depression than only children, regardless of sex or age. Apparently children with siblings are less well adjusted in a society that favors and rewards the only child (Yang et al., 1995).

Only children seem to do better cognitively, too. A randomized study in Beijing schools (Jiao, Ji, & Jing, 1996) found that only children outperformed first-grade classmates with siblings in memory, language, and mathematics skills. This finding may reflect the greater attention, stimulation, hopes, and expectations that parents shower on a baby they know will be their first and last. Fifth-grade only children, who were born before the one-child policy was strongly enforced—and whose parents may have originally planned on a larger family—did not show a pronounced cognitive edge.

Both of these studies used urban samples. Further research may reveal whether the findings hold up in rural areas and small towns, where children with siblings are more numerous, and whether only children maintain their cognitive superiority as they move through school.

China's population policy has wider implications. If it succeeds, most Chinese will eventually lack aunts, uncles, nephews, nieces, and cousins, as well as siblings. How this will affect individuals, families, and the social fabric is incalculable.

A more sinister question is this: what happened to the girls? A 1990 census suggests that 5 percent of all infant girls born in China (some half a million infants born alive each year) are unaccounted for. Suspicions are that many parents, being permitted only one child, had their baby girls killed or let them die of neglect to allow the parents the chance to bear and raise more highly valued sons. A more benign explanation is that these girls were hidden and raised secretly to evade the one-child policy (Kristof, 1991, 1993). In either case, China's one-child policy appears to be having ramifications its developers may not have considered, and concern about these unforeseen effects may be one factor in the current relaxation of enforcement.

Playmates and Friends

Toddlers play alongside or near each other, but not until about age 3 do children begin to have friends. Through friendships and interactions with more casual playmates, young children learn how to get along with others. They learn that being a friend is the way to have a friend. They learn how to solve problems in relationships, they learn how to put themselves in another person's place, and they see models of various kinds of behavior. They learn moral values and gender-role norms, and they practice adult roles.

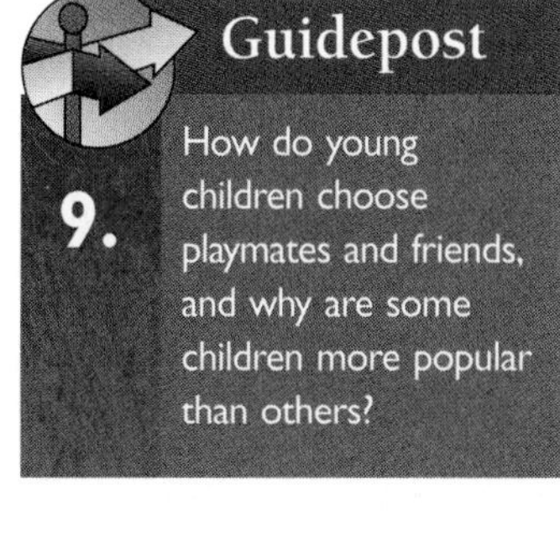

Guidepost
9.
How do young children choose playmates and friends, and why are some children more popular than others?

Choosing Playmates and Friends

Preschoolers are choosy about playmates. Not only do they usually like to play with children of their own age and sex, but they are quite selective about *which* children they play with. In preschool classrooms, they tend to spend most of their time with a few other children—usually those with whom they have previously had positive experiences and whose behavior is similar to their own. Children who have frequent positive experiences with each other are most likely to become friends (Rubin et al., 1998; Snyder et al., 1996). About 3 out of 4 preschoolers have such mutual friendships (Hartup & Stevens, 1999).

The traits that young children look for in a playmate are similar to the traits they look for in a friend (C. H. Hart et al., 1992). In one study, 4- to 7-year-olds rated the most important features of friendships as doing things together, liking and caring for each other, sharing and helping one another, and to a lesser degree, living nearby or going to the same school. Younger children rated physical traits, such as appearance and size, higher than did older ones and rated affection and support lower (Furman & Bierman, 1983). Preschool children prefer prosocial playmates (C. H. Hart et al., 1992). They reject disruptive, demanding, intrusive, or aggressive children and ignore those who are shy, withdrawn, or tentative (Ramsey & Lasquade, 1996; Roopnarine & Honig, 1985).

Well-liked preschoolers and kindergartners, and those who are rated by parents and teachers as socially competent, generally cope well with anger. They respond directly, in ways that minimize further conflict and keep relationships going. They avoid insults and threats. Unpopular children tend to hit back or tattle (Fabes & Eisenberg, 1992).

Not all children without playmates have poor social adjustment, however. Among 567 kindergartners, almost 2 out of 3 socially withdrawn children were rated (through direct observation, teacher questionnaires, and interviews with classmates) as socially and cognitively competent; they simply preferred to play alone (Harrist, Zain, Bates, Dodge, & Pettit, 1997).

Characteristics and Effects of Friendships

Preschoolers act differently with their friends than with other children. They have more positive, prosocial interactions, but also more quarrels and fights (Rubin et al., 1998). Children may get just as angry with a friend as with someone they dislike, but they are more likely to control their anger and express it constructively (Fabes, Eisenberg, Smith, & Murphy, 1996).

Friendships are more satisfying—and more likely to last—when children see them as relatively harmonious and as validating their self-worth. Being able to confide in

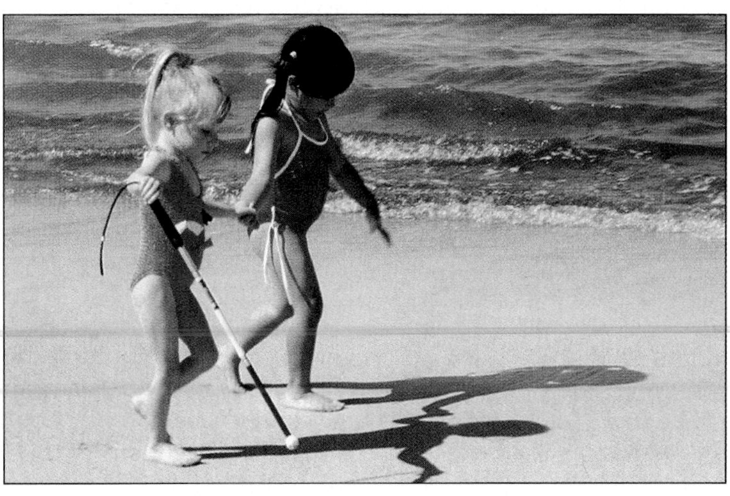

Young children learn the importance of *being* a friend in order to *have* a friend. One way of being a friend can involve a sighted child's helping a blind playmate to enjoy the feel of the sand and the sound of the surf.

friends and get help from them is less important at this age than when children get older (Ladd, Kochenderfer, & Coleman, 1996).

Children with friends enjoy school more (Ladd & Hart, 1992). Among 125 kindergartners, those who had friends in their class when they entered in August liked school better two months later, and those who kept up these friendships continued to like school better the following May. Children whose friendships are a source of help and self-validation are happier, have more positive attitudes toward school, and feel they can look to classmates for support (Ladd et al., 1996).

Parenting and Popularity

Parenting styles and practices can influence peer relationships. Popular children generally have warm, positive relationships with both mother and father. The parents are likely to be authoritative, and the children to be both assertive and cooperative (Isley, O'Neil, & Parke, 1996; Kochanska, 1992; Roopnarine & Honig, 1985). Children who are insecurely attached or whose parents are harsh, neglectful, or depressed or have troubled marriages are at risk of developing unattractive social and emotional patterns and of being rejected by peers (Rubin et al., 1998). Negative mother-daughter or father-son relationships can be especially harmful, since they serve as models for interactions with same-sex peers (Isley et al., 1996).

Children whose parents rely on power-assertive discipline tend to use coercive tactics in peer relations; children whose parents engage in give-and-take reasoning are more likely to resolve conflicts with peers that way (Crockenberg & Lourie, 1996). Children whose parents clearly communicate disapproval rather than anger, as well as strong positive feelings, are more prosocial, less aggressive, and better liked (Boyum & Parke, 1995). Children whose physical play with their fathers is characterized—on both sides—by pouting, whining, anger, teasing, mocking, or boredom tend to share less than other children, to be more verbally and physically aggressive, and to avoid social contact (Carson & Parke, 1996).

Helping Children with Peer Relations

Adults can help young children's relationships with peers by getting them together with other children, monitoring their play, and suggesting strategies to use in approaching other children.

Children whose parents arrange play dates for them have more playmates, see them more often, and initiate more get-togethers themselves (Ladd & Colter, 1988; Ladd & Hart, 1992). They also tend to be more outgoing and cooperative in kindergarten. In arranging and supervising play dates, parents promote prosocial behavior as well as sociability by prompting children to think about the needs and wishes of their guests. Since children who behave prosocially tend to be more popular, such guidance can have long-lasting consequences (Ladd & Hart, 1992).

Other helpful strategies include making a special effort to find a play group for young children who do not often have the opportunity to be with other youngsters; encouraging "loners" to play with another lone child or a small group of two or three children, or just to play side by side with other children at first; praising signs of empathy and responsiveness; and teaching friendship skills indirectly through puppetry, role-playing, and books about animals and children who learn to make friends (Ramsey & Lasquade, 1996; Roopnarine & Honig, 1985).

Since preschoolers respond to peers on the basis of past experience, it is important to help children learn effective strategies before they become tagged as outsiders (Ramsey & Lasquade, 1996). If that has already happened, a change in the child's behavior may not help unless something is done to change the other children's perceptions of that child—or to find a new group of children for the child to associate with (Snyder et al., 1996).

CHECKPOINT

Can you . . .

- ✔ Explain how preschoolers choose playmates and friends, how they behave with friends, and how they benefit from friendships?
- ✔ Discuss how relationships at home can influence relationships with peers?

Peer relationships become even more important during middle childhood, which we examine in Chapters 9 and 10.

Summary

The Developing Self

Guidepost 1. How does the self-concept develop during early childhood, and how do children advance in understanding their emotions?

- The **self-concept** undergoes major change in early childhood. According to neo-Piagetians, **self-definition** shifts from **single representations** to **representational mappings.** Young children cannot acknowledge the difference between the **real self** and the **ideal self.**
- Understanding of emotions directed toward the self and of simultaneous emotions develops gradually during early childhood.

Guidepost 2. How do young children develop initiative and self-esteem?

- According to Erikson, the chief developmental crisis of early childhood is **initiative versus guilt.** Successful resolution of this conflict results in the "virtue" of *purpose.*
- **Self-esteem** in early childhood tends to be global and unrealistic, reflecting adult approval. If self-esteem is contingent on success, children may develop a "helpless" pattern of thought and behavior.

Gender

Guidepost 3. How do boys and girls become aware of the meaning of gender, and what explains differences in behavior between the sexes?

- **Gender identity** is an important aspect of the developing self-concept.
- The main gender difference in early childhood is boys' greater aggressiveness. Some cognitive differences appear early; others not until preadolescence or later.
- Children learn **gender roles** at an early age through **gender-typing. Gender stereotypes** peak during the preschool years.
- Four major perspectives on gender development are the biological, psychoanalytic, cognitive, and socialization approaches.
- Evidence of differences in brain size and prenatal hormonal activity suggests that some gender differences may be biologically based.
- In Freudian theory, a child develops gender identity through **identification** with the same-sex parent after giving up the wish to possess the other parent.
- Cognitive-developmental theory maintains that gender identity develops from thinking about experience. According to Kohlberg, **gender constancy** leads to acquisition of gender roles.
- **Gender-schema theory** holds that children organize their concept of gender and their gender-related behavior around information about what males and females are and do in their culture.
- According to social cognitive theory, children learn gender roles through socialization, which includes observation of models, reinforcement of gender-appropriate behavior, and internalization of standards. Parents, peers, and the media influence gender-typing.

Play

Guidepost 4. How do preschoolers play, and how does play contribute to and reflect development?

- Play has many physical, cognitive, and psychosocial benefits. Changes in the types of play children engage in reflect cognitive and social development.
- According to Piaget and Smilansky, children progress cognitively from **functional play** to **constructive play, pretend play,** and then formal games with rules. Pretend play becomes increasingly common during early childhood and helps children develop social and cognitive skills. Rough-and-tumble play also begins during early childhood.
- According to Parten, play becomes more social during early childhood. However, later research has found that nonsocial play is not necessarily immature, depending on what children do when they play.
- Children prefer to play with (and play more socially with) others of their sex.
- Both the cognitive and social aspects of play are influenced by the culturally approved environments adults create for children.

Parenting

Guidepost 5. What forms of discipline do parents use, and how do parenting styles and practices influence development?

- **Discipline** can be a powerful tool for socialization.
- Both positive reinforcement and prudently administered punishment can be appropriate tools of discipline within the context of a positive parent-child relationship.
- **Power assertion, inductive techniques,** and **withdrawal of love** each can be effective in certain situations. Discipline based on induction is generally the most effective and power assertion the least effective in promoting internalization of parental standards. Spanking can have negative consequences.
- Baumrind identified three childrearing styles: **authoritarian, permissive,** and **authoritative.** According to much research, authoritative parents tend to raise more competent children. These categories and results may be misleading when applied to some cultures or socioeconomic groups.
- Family conflict can be used to help children learn rules and standards of behavior and negotiating skills.

Guidepost 6. Why do young children help or hurt others, and why do they develop fears?

- The roots of **altruism, or prosocial behavior,** appear early and can be cultivated by parental modeling and encouragement.
- **Instrumental aggression**—first physical, then verbal—is the most common type of aggression in early

childhood. Most children become less aggressive after age 6 or 7. However, the proportion of **hostile aggression** increases. Boys tend to practice **overt aggression,** whereas girls engage in **relational aggression.** Aggression may be influenced by the home and culture.
- Preschool children show temporary fears of real and imaginary objects and events; older children's fears tend to be more realistic. Some fears can be overcome by systematic desensitization.

Guidepost 7. Why are some children abused or neglected, and what are the effects of maltreatment?

- The incidence of reported maltreatment of children has increased greatly since the 1970s, and the actual number of cases may be far higher than reported.
- Maltreatment includes **physical abuse, neglect, sexual abuse,** and **emotional maltreatment**. It can have grave long-term effects.
- Characteristics of the abuser, the victim, the family, the community, and the larger culture all contribute to child abuse and neglect.
- Maltreatment can interfere with physical, cognitive, emotional, and social development, and its effects can continue into adulthood. Still, many maltreated children show remarkable resilience.

Relationships with Other Children

Guidepost 8. How do young children get along with (or without) siblings?

- Sibling and peer relationships contribute to **self-efficacy.**
- Most sibling interactions are positive. Older siblings tend to initiate activities, and younger ones to imitate. Same-sex siblings, especially girls, get along best. Siblings tend to resolve disputes on the basis of moral principles, though not necessarily the same ones parents use.
- The kind of relationship children have with siblings often carries over into other peer relationships.
- Only children seem to develop at least as well as children with siblings.

Guidepost 9. How do young children choose playmates and friends, and why are some children more popular than others?

- Preschoolers choose playmates and friends who are like them. Aggressive children are less popular than prosocial children.
- Friends have more positive and negative interactions than other playmates.
- Parenting can affect children's social competence with peers.

Key Terms

self-concept (281)
self-definition (281)
single representations (282)
real self (282)
ideal self (282)
representational mappings (282)
initiative versus guilt (284)
self-esteem (285)
gender identity (286)
gender roles (287)
gender-typing (287)
gender stereotypes (287)
identification (289)
gender constancy (290)
gender-schema theory (290)
functional play (294)
constructive play (294)
pretend play (295)
discipline (297)
power assertion (298)
inductive techniques (298)
withdrawal of love (299)
authoritarian (300)
permissive (300)
authoritative (300)
altruism, or prosocial behavior (302)
instrumental aggression (303)
hostile aggression (304)
overt aggression (304)
relational aggression (304)
physical abuse (306)
neglect (306)
sexual abuse (306)
emotional maltreatment (306)
self-efficacy (310)

Part Four

Middle Childhood

The middle years of childhood, from about age 6 to about age 11, are often called the school years. School is the central experience during this time—a focal point for physical, cognitive, and psychosocial development. As we see in Chapter 9, children grow taller, heavier, and stronger and acquire the motor skills needed to participate in organized games and sports. They also make major advances in thinking, in moral judgment, in memory, and in literacy. Individual differences become more evident and special needs more important, as competencies affect success in school.

Competencies also affect self-esteem and popularity, as we see in Chapter 10. Although parents continue to be important, the peer group is more influential than before. Children develop physically, cognitively, and emotionally, as well as socially, through contacts with other youngsters.

Linkups to Look For

- Obese children often suffer social rejection.
- Moral development may be linked to cognitive growth.
- IQ can be affected by nutrition, socioeconomic status, culture, rapport with the examiner, and familiarity with the surroundings.
- Parenting styles can affect school achievement.
- Physical appearance plays a large part in self-esteem.
- A decline in egocentric thinking permits deeper, more intimate friendships.
- Children who are good learners and problem solvers tend to be resilient in coping with stress.

Middle Childhood: *A Preview*

Chapter 9

Physical and Cognitive Development in Middle Childhood

Growth slows.

Strength and athletic skills improve.

Respiratory illnesses are common, but health is generally better than at any other time in the life span.

Egocentrism diminishes. Children begin to think logically but concretely.

Memory and language skills increase.

Cognitive gains permit children to benefit from formal schooling.

Some children show special educational needs and strengths.

Chapter 10

Psychosocial Development in Middle Childhood

Self-concept becomes more complex, affecting self-esteem.

Coregulation reflects a gradual shift in control from parents to child.

Peers assume central importance.

Chapter 9

Physical and Cognitive Development in Middle Childhood

*W*hat we must remember above all in the education of our children is that their love of life should never weaken.

Natalia Ginzburg, *The Little Virtues*, 1985

Theodore Roosevelt

Focus: Theodore Roosevelt, Rough Rider*

Theodore Roosevelt (1858–1919), the twenty-sixth president of the United States, was a vigorous man who enjoyed the outdoor life. As a young boy, he showed an intense interest in nature and wanted to be a zoologist. He filled notebooks with his observations and, on a family trip to Europe at age 10, visited every museum of natural history he could find. Earlier, he had started his own natural history museum, keeping his specimens in his room until a chambermaid found a collection of dead mice in his dresser drawer.

An avid reader, he loved adventure stories. As an adult, he had adventures of his own. Before becoming president, he lived for two years on a ranch in North Dakota and organized and led a volunteer cavalry regiment, Roosevelt's Rough Riders. After leaving the White House, he conducted a big-game hunting expedition in East Africa, which captured 296 animals, and an exploratory expedition to South America, which resulted in the discovery of a tributary of the Madeira River. He wrote several books on these experiences, one of which was called *The Strenuous Life* (1900).

Yet, as a child in Manhattan, "Teedie," as he was then called, was weak and sickly, subject to asthma. He and his two sisters and brother spent summers in the country, running barefoot, swimming, rowing, hiking, picking apples, hunting frogs, and riding a Shetland pony. Still, despite all this healthful exercise, he "continued to have his gasping nights, his days of exhausted reaction, his pipestem legs, his pale face, and his

*Sources of biographical information about Theodore Roosevelt were Pringle (1931), Putnam (1958), and Roosevelt (1929).

digestive upsets" (Putnam, 1958, p. 33). Too ill most of the time to go to school, he was tutored at home.

When Teedie was 10 or 11, his father—a big, powerful man, who came from sturdy Dutch stock—told him he must build up his physical condition. "You have the mind but not the body," the elder Roosevelt told him, "and without the help of the body the mind cannot go as far as it should" (Pringle, 1931, p. 17).

A large second-floor room in the family's brownstone house at 28 East Twentieth Street near Union Square was converted into a gymnasium. There the boy dutifully worked out with punching bag and dumbbells and on the horizontal bars. Later an asthma attack caused his family to send him to Moosehead Lake. On the way there, a couple of boys on the stagecoach teased him unmercifully, and he found himself too weak to fight them off. Humiliated, he resolved to improve his health and strength and immediately began boxing lessons. As he grew in stature and breadth of chest, he gained in self-confidence.

Asthma had not been his only problem. At 13, when he began learning to shoot, he discovered that he was nearsighted. At first he noticed his companions aiming at targets he could not see. One day they read aloud to him a distant billboard advertisement. Although it was printed in huge letters, he could not make them out. Now he understood why, throughout his childhood, he had been at a disadvantage in studying nature: "the only things I could study were those I ran against or stumbled over" (Roosevelt, 1929, p. 17).

Putting on his first pair of glasses changed Roosevelt's outlook on life and "opened an entirely new world" to him. "I had been a clumsy and awkward little boy," he wrote in his autobiography, "and . . . a good deal of it was due to the fact that I could not see and yet was wholly ignorant that I was not seeing." The memory of his undiagnosed childhood disability gave him "a keen sympathy" with efforts to "remove the physical causes of deficiency in children, who are often unjustly blamed for being obstinate or unambitious, or mentally stupid" (Roosevelt, 1929, p. 18).

As Theodore Roosevelt's father recognized, a sound body and mind are keys to positive development. And, as Roosevelt himself discovered, physical competence has cognitive and psychosocial ramifications.

Despite frequent colds and sore throats, middle childhood is a healthy time for most children; but many, like Theodore Roosevelt, are not as healthy or as physically fit as they should be. Although motor abilities improve less dramatically in middle childhood than before, these years are an important time for the development of the strength, stamina, endurance, and motor proficiency needed for active sports.

In this chapter we look at these physical developments, beginning with normal growth, which depends on proper nutrition and good health. Cognitively, we see how entrance into Piaget's stage of concrete operations enables children to think logically and to make more mature moral judgments. As children improve in memory and problem solving, intelligence tests become more accurate in predicting school performance. The abilities to read and write open the door to participation in a wider world. We look at factors affecting the transition to grade school and school achievement. We examine the controversies over IQ testing, methods of teaching reading, and second-language education. Finally, we see how schools educate children with exceptional needs.

After you have read and studied this chapter, you should be able to answer the following questions:

CH. 9

Guideposts *for* Study

1. What gains in growth and motor development occur during middle childhood, and what nutritional hazards do children face?
2. What are the principal health, fitness, and safety concerns about school-age children?
3. How is school-age children's thinking and moral reasoning different from that of younger children?
4. What advances in memory and other information-processing skills occur during middle childhood?
5. How accurately can schoolchildren's intelligence be measured?
6. How do communicative abilities and literacy expand during middle childhood?
7. What influences school achievement?
8. How do schools meet the needs of foreign-speaking children and those with learning problems?
9. How is giftedness assessed and nurtured?

Physical Development

Aspects of Physical Development

Guidepost

1. What gains in growth and motor development occur during middle childhood, and what nutritional hazards do children face?

If we were to walk by a typical elementary school just after the closing bell, we would see a virtual explosion of children of all shapes and sizes. Tall ones, short ones, husky ones, and skinny ones would be bursting out of the school doors into the open air. Some of these children, who have spent much of the day sitting in school, will go home, get a snack, and dash outside to jump rope, play ball, skate, cycle, or throw snowballs. Some, especially those with working parents, may stay at school for organized after-school programs. Many children, however, go inside after school, not to emerge for the rest of the day. Instead of practicing skills that stretch their bodies, they do homework or sit in front of the television set. When we talk about physical development in middle childhood, then, we need to look closely at individual children.

Growth

Compared with its rapid pace in early childhood, growth in height and weight during middle childhood slows considerably. Still, although day-by-day changes may not be obvious, they add up to a startling difference between 6-year-olds, who are still small children, and 11-year-olds, many of whom are now beginning to resemble adults.

On average, school-age children in the United States grow about 1 to 3 inches each year and gain about 5 to 8 pounds or more, doubling their body weight. Late in this stage, girls begin a growth spurt, gaining about 10 pounds a year. Suddenly they are taller and heavier than the boys in their class, and they remain so until about age 12 or 13, when the boys begin their spurt and overtake the girls (see Chapter 11). Girls retain somewhat more fatty tissue than boys, a characteristic that will persist through adulthood.

African American boys and girls tend to grow faster than white children and thus to be a bit taller and heavier at the same age. By about age 6, African American girls have more muscle and bone mass than white or Mexican American girls. Mexican American girls have a higher percentage of body fat than white girls the same size (Ellis, Abrams, & Wong, 1997).

Nutrition and Dentition

Most schoolchildren have good appetites and eat far more than younger children. To support their steady growth and constant exertion, children need, on average, 2,400 calories every day—more for older children and less for younger ones. Breakfast should supply about one-fourth of total calories. Daily food intake should include high levels of complex carbohydrates, found in such foods as potatoes, pasta, bread, and cereals. Simple carbohydrates, found in sweets, should be kept to a minimum. Although protein is necessary to build and repair muscles, most people in the United States eat more protein than they need. The government-recommended daily allowance (RDA) for 7- to 10-year-olds is 28 grams, but the average intake for both boys and girls is 71 grams (Bittman, 1993).

Nutritionists recommend a varied diet including plenty of grains, fruits, and vegetables, which are high in natural nutrients. Studies find that U.S. children of all ages eat too much fat and sugar and artificially fortified or low-nutrient food (Muñoz, Krebs-Smith, Ballard-Barbash, & Cleveland, 1997; Subar, Krebs-Smith, Cook, & Kahle, 1998).

Tooth Development and Dental Care

Most of the adult teeth arrive early in middle childhood. The primary teeth begin to fall out at about age 6 and are replaced by permanent teeth at a rate of about four teeth per year for the next five years.

A major health concern in the United States until recently was the high rate of dental problems among children. Now the picture is brighter, thanks to better dental care and widespread use of fluoride in toothpaste, mouthwash, and water used for drinking and food preparation. More than half (55 percent) of U.S. children ages 5 to 17 have cavity-free permanent teeth, compared with only about one-fourth (26 percent) of 6- to 17-year-olds in 1971–1974. Much of the improvement in children's dental health is attributed to use of adhesive sealants on the rough, chewing surfaces, which more than doubled between 1986–1987 and 1988–1991 (L. J. Brown, Kaste, Selwitz, & Furman, 1996).

CHECKPOINT

Can you . . .

- ✔ Summarize typical growth patterns of boys and girls in middle childhood?
- ✔ Discuss nutritional needs of school-age children?
- ✔ Tell why dental health has improved in recent years?

Obesity, Cardiac Risk, and Body Image

Obesity in children has become a major health issue in the United States. The proportion of children ages 6 to 17 who are obese more than doubled between 1981 and 1991—from 5 percent to nearly 11 percent (Centers for Disease Control and Prevention [CDC], 1994). A child whose *body mass index* (weight in comparison with height) was in the 95th percentile (that is, higher than that of 95 percent of children of the same age and sex in a standardized sample) was considered obese. Furthermore, standards have become more lenient, obscuring the full extent of the problem. About one-third of 5- to 14-year-olds in cross-sectional studies in Bogalusa, Louisiana, in 1992 to 1994 would have been considered obese by the standard used in 1973, which was based on the 85th percentile rather than the 95th (Freedman, Srinivasan, Valdez, Williamson, & Berenson, 1997).

Overweight often results from an inherited tendency, aggravated by too little exercise and too much, or the wrong kinds of, food. Researchers have identified at least three genes that seem to be involved in obesity (Clément et al., 1998; Jackson et al.,

1997; Montague et al., 1997; Ristow, Muller-Wieland, Pfeiffer, Kroner, & Kahn, 1998). One of these genes governs production of a brain protein called *leptin,* which seems to help regulate body fat through appetite control (Campfield, Smith, Guisez, Devos, & Burn, 1995; Friedman & Halaas, 1998; Halaas et al., 1995; Kristensen et al., 1998; Montague et al., 1997; Pelleymounter et al., 1995; Zhang et al., 1994).

Inactivity may be a major factor in the sharp rise in obesity (Freedman et al., 1997; Harrell, Gansky, Bradley, & McMurray, 1997). Although a causal connection has not been established, children who watch four or more hours of television each day (as more than one-fourth of U.S. children do) have more body fat and a higher body mass index than those who watch less than two hours a day (Andersen, Crespo, Bartlett, Cheskin, & Pratt, 1998). After a 6-month school-sponsored program to monitor and reduce third- and fourth-graders' television, videotape, and video game use, participants showed decreases in body mass index, triceps skinfold thickness, waist circumference, and waist-to-hips ratio, as compared with children who did not participate (Robinson, 1999).

Obese children often suffer emotionally because of rejection by peers. They also tend to become overweight adults, at risk of high blood pressure, heart disease, orthopedic problems, and diabetes. Childhood overweight may be a stronger predictor of some diseases than adult overweight (Must, Jacques, Dallal, Bajerna, & Dietz, 1992). Body mass index and blood pressure, both cardiac risk factors, tend to be higher in African American and Mexican American children than in white children (Winkleby, Robinson, Sundquist, & Kraemer, 1999).

Another cardiac risk factor is *cholesterol,* a waxy substance found in human and animal tissue. High levels of one type of cholesterol (LDL, or "bad" cholesterol) can dangerously narrow blood vessels, leading to heart disease. This condition is called *atherosclerosis.* Since atherosclerosis begins in childhood, so should heart disease prevention.

Even brief interventions can have excellent results. An 8-week program of health and diet education for third- and fourth-graders in North Carolina schools, combined with aerobic activity in place of regular physical education classes, reduced cardiovascular risks—cholesterol levels, body mass index, and body fat—in comparison with a control group who did not participate (Harrell et al., 1998).

Weight management programs should begin early and should consist of gradual, targeted increases in activity and reductions in high-fat, high-calorie foods (Barlow & Dietz, 1998). Unfortunately, children who try to lose weight are not always the ones who need to do so. Concern with **body image**—how one believes one looks—begins to be important toward the end of middle childhood, especially to girls, and may develop into eating disorders that become more common in adolescence (see Chapter 12). As preadolescent girls begin to fill out and add body fat, some—perhaps influenced by the ultrathin models in the media—see this normal development as undesirable. According to one study, about 40 percent of 9- and 10-year-old girls, especially those whose mothers have told them they are too fat, work at trying to lose weight (Schreiber et al., 1996).

body image
Descriptive and evaluative beliefs about one's appearance.

Malnutrition

More than half of the young children in south Asia, 30 percent of those in sub-Saharan Africa, and 10 percent in the western hemisphere are believed to suffer from malnutrition (World Health Organization [WHO], 1996). In the United States in the early 1990s, 2 to 4 million children under 12 years old sometimes or often did not get enough to eat (Lewit & Kerrebrock, 1997a).

Because undernourished children usually live in poverty and suffer other kinds of environmental deprivation, the specific effects of malnutrition may be hard to isolate. However, taken together, these deprivations may negatively affect not only growth and physical well-being but cognitive and psychosocial development as well (Espinosa, Sigman, Neumann, Bwibo, & McDonald, 1992; Lewit & Kerrebrock, 1997b; McDonald, Sigman, Espinosa, & Neumann, 1994; Ricciuti, 1993; WHO, 1996).

Schooling can make a difference. One longitudinal study followed approximately 1,400 Guatemalan children in impoverished rural villages, many of whom had stunted growth due to malnutrition and who lived in unsanitary, infection-causing conditions. Those who completed at least four years of school did better on tests of cognition during adolescence than those who dropped out earlier (Gorman & Pollitt, 1996).

Effects of malnutrition early in life can be largely reversed with improvements in diet (Lewit & Kerrebrock, 1997b). In Massachusetts, when low-income third- to sixth-graders took part in a school breakfast program, their scores on achievement tests rose (Meyers, Sampson, Weitzman, Rogers, & Kayne, 1989).

Since malnutrition affects all aspects of development, its treatment may need to go beyond physical care. One longitudinal study (Grantham-McGregor, Powell, Walker, Chang, & Fletcher, 1994) followed two groups of Jamaican children with low developmental levels who were hospitalized for severe malnourishment in infancy or toddlerhood. The children came from extremely poor and often unstable homes. Health care paraprofessionals played with an experimental group in the hospital and, after discharge, visited them at home every week for three years, showing the mothers how to use homemade toys and encouraging them to interact with their children. A control group received only standard medical care.

Three years after the program stopped, the experimental group's IQs were well above those of the control group (though not as high as those of a third, well-nourished group); and their IQs remained significantly higher 7, 8, 9, and 14 years after leaving the hospital. Apparently the continuity of the program was important; not only did it last 3 years, but the mothers in the experimental group enrolled their children in preschools at an earlier age than children in the control group.

CHECKPOINT

Can you . . .

✔ Discuss possible causes of the increase in childhood obesity, and tell how it can affect health in adulthood?

✔ Describe effects of malnutrition and identify factors that may influence the long-term outcome?

Motor Development

During the middle years, children's motor abilities continue to improve (see Table 9-1). Children keep getting stronger, faster, and better coordinated—and they derive great pleasure from testing their bodies and learning new skills.

Children's lives today are more tightly organized than they were a generation ago. They spend less time in free, unstructured play and more time in organized sports (Hofferth & Sandberg, 1998).

Consider this . . .

- If obesity "runs in families," either because of heredity or lifestyle, how can parents who have not been able to control their own weight help their children?
- In view of childhood malnutrition's long-term effects on physical, social, and cognitive development, what can and should various sectors of society—government agencies, community groups, and private organizations—do to combat it?

Table 9-1 Motor Development in Middle Childhood

Age	Selected Behaviors
6	Girls are superior in movement accuracy; boys are superior in forceful, less complex acts. Skipping is possible. Can throw with proper weight shift and step.
7	One-footed balancing without looking becomes possible. Can walk 2-inch-wide balance beams. Can hop and jump accurately into small squares. Can execute accurate jumping-jack exercise.
8	Have 12-pound pressure on grip strength. Number of games participated in by both sexes is greatest at this age. Can engage in alternate rhythmic hopping in a 2-2, 2-3, or 3-3 pattern. Girls can throw a small ball 40 feet.
9	Boys can run 16½ feet per second. Boys can throw a small ball 70 feet.
10	Can judge and intercept pathways of small balls throw from a distance. Girls can run 17 feet per second.
11	Standing broad jump of 5 feet is possible for boys; 6 inches less for girls.

Source: Adapted from Cratty, 1986.

Rough-and-Tumble Play

Should you come across a couple of schoolboys tumbling over each other, you may hardly be able to tell whether they are fighting or playing except by the expressions on their faces. About 10 percent of schoolchildren's free-play at recess in the early grades consists of **rough-and-tumble play,** vigorous play that involves wrestling, kicking, tumbling, grappling, and sometimes chasing, often accompanied by laughing and screaming. This kind of play peaks in middle childhood; the proportion typically drops to about 5 percent at age 11, about the same as in early childhood (refer back to Chapter 7).

rough-and-tumble play Vigorous play involving wrestling, tumbling, kicking, grappling, and sometimes chasing, often accompanied by laughing and screaming.

Rough-and-tumble play may look like fighting, but it generally is not. Unpopular children tend to be aggressive; popular children typically engage in rough-and-tumble play (Pellegrini, 1998; Pellegrini & Smith, 1998). Rough-and-tumble play allows children to jockey for dominance in the peer group by assessing their own and each other's strength. Children usually choose others of approximately their own status to tussle with (Pellegrini & Smith, 1998). Boys around the world engage in rough-and-tumble play more than girls do, a fact generally attributed to a combination of hormonal differences and socialization (Pellegrini, 1998; Pellegrini & Smith, 1998).

Gender Differences in Motor Skills

Although there is little difference in the motor skills of young boys and girls, differences become greater as children approach puberty. Part of this gender difference is due to boys' growing size and strength and girls' greater fleshiness, but much of it may be due to differing cultural expectations and experiences, differing levels of coaching, and differing rates of participation.

The type of skill also makes a difference. Tasks that require extensive movement or support of body weight, such as the standing long jump, are more affected by body fat (Smoll & Schutz, 1990). Among 2,309 five- to nine-year-olds, boys did better in the 50-meter dash, standing broad jump, 600-meter run, and shuttle run, and in strength of grip. Girls did better in the lateral jump, backward balancing, flexibility, and manual dexterity. However, no more than 10 percent of the variance in performance was attributable to gender. Since these prepubertal differences were small, they may reflect the kinds of activities that boys and girls like or are encouraged to do (Krombholz, 1997).

Participation in organized sports has risen among both sexes—a 50 percent increase since 1981—but boys still spend twice as much time on team sports as girls do (Hofferth & Sandberg, 1998). Even though athletic programs are more open to girls than in the past, opportunities and standards may not be the same as for boys (Butterfield & Loovis, 1993), and many girls may lack the confidence or motivation to participate (Trost et al., 1996). The disparity in time boys and girls spend in sports increases as children grow older (Hofferth & Sandberg, 1998).

CHECKPOINT

Can you . . .

- ✔ Explain the significance of rough-and-tumble play?
- ✔ Discuss how gender differences in motor skills are related to age and the influences of physical and environmental factors?

Health and Safety

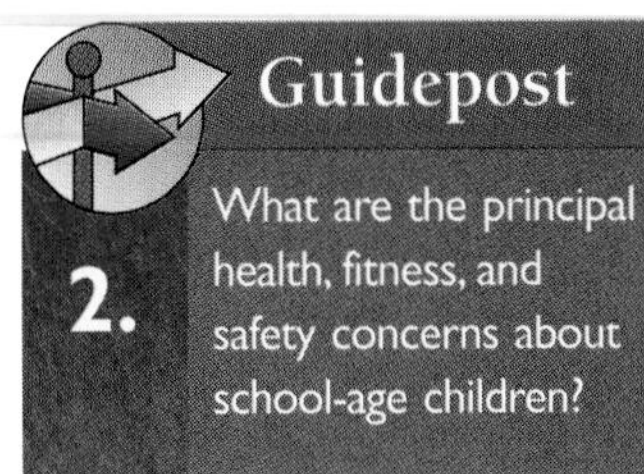

Guidepost

2. What are the principal health, fitness, and safety concerns about school-age children?

The development of vaccines for major childhood illnesses has made middle childhood a relatively safe time of life. Since immunizations are required for school admission, children this age are likely to be protected. The death rate in these years is the lowest in the life span. Still, many children get too little exercise to maintain physical fitness; some suffer from acute or chronic medical conditions; and some are injured in accidents. As children's experience with illness increases, so does their cognitive understanding of the causes of health and illness and of the steps people can take to promote their own health (see Box 9-1).

Box 9-1

Children's Understanding of Health and Illness

When Angela was sick, she overheard her doctor refer to *edema* (an accumulation of fluid, which causes swelling), and she thought her problem was "a demon." Being sick is frightening at any age. For young children, who do not understand what is happening, it can be especially distressing and confusing.

From a Piagetian perspective, children's understanding of health and illness is tied to cognitive development. As they mature, their explanations for disease change. Before middle childhood, children are egocentric; they tend to believe that illness is magically produced by human actions, often their own ("I was a bad boy, so now I feel bad"). Later they explain all diseases—only a little less magically—as the doing of all-powerful germs; the only "protection" is a variety of superstitious behaviors to ward them off. "Watch out for germs," a child may say. As children approach adolescence, they see that there can be multiple causes of disease, that contact with germs does not automatically lead to illness, and that people can do much to keep healthy.

Children's understanding of AIDS seems to follow the same developmental sequence as their understanding of colds and of cancer, but they understand the cause of colds earlier than they do the causes of the other two illnesses, probably because they are more familiar with colds. Interviews with 361 children in kindergarten through sixth grade (Schonfeld, Johnson, Perrin, O'Hare, & Cicchetti, 1993) found that children often give superficially correct explanations but lack real understanding of the processes involved. For example, although 96 children mentioned drug use as a cause of AIDS, most did not seem to realize that the disease is spread through blood adhering to a needle shared by drug users. One second-grader gave this version of how someone gets AIDS: "Well, by doing drugs and something like that . . . by going by a drug dealer who has AIDS. . . . Well, you go by a person who's a drug dealer and you might catch the AIDS from 'em by standing near 'em" (Schonfeld et al., 1993, p. 393).

From a young child's point of view, such a statement may be a logical extension of the belief that germs cause disease. The child may wrongly assume that AIDS can be caught, as colds are, from sharing cups and utensils, from being near someone who is coughing or sneezing, or from hugging and kissing. One AIDS education program (Sigelman et al., 1996) sought to replace such intuitive "theories" with scientifically grounded ones and to test Piaget's idea that if children have not mastered a concept, they are probably not yet ready to do so. The developers of the program hypothesized that what young children lack is knowledge about disease, not the ability to think about it.

A carefully scripted program was tried on 306 third-, fifth-, and seventh-graders—mostly low-income Mexican Americans—in Catholic schools in Tucson. Trained health instructors conducted two 50-minute sessions consisting of lectures, video clips, drawings, and discussion, and using vocabulary appropriate for third-graders. Content included an introduction to contagious and noncontagious diseases; specific information about the AIDS virus; an overview of the immune system; the meaning of the letters in "AIDS"; differences between transmission of colds and of AIDS; misconceptions about how the AIDS virus is transmitted; risk factors for AIDS; how the disease develops; and how it can be prevented. The curriculum emphasized that there are only a few ways to get AIDS and that normal contact with people infected with the virus is not one of them. Flip charts summarized key points.

Experimental and control groups were tested before the program began and again about two weeks afterward. Students who had received instruction knew more about AIDS and its causes than those who had not, were no more (and no less) worried about it than before, and were more willing to be with people with AIDS. Another test almost a year later found that gains generally were retained. Third-graders gained about as much from the program as seventh-graders. It was somewhat less effective with fifth-graders, perhaps because children that age already know more about AIDS than younger children and find it less relevant to their own lives than older ones do. The success of this program shows that, contrary to Piaget, even relatively young children can grasp complex scientific concepts about disease if teaching is geared to their level of understanding.

Maintaining Health and Fitness

As Theodore Roosevelt's father knew, exercise is important because it promotes health and fitness. Most U.S. schoolchildren get enough exercise to meet national goals, but many children are not as active as they should be—and could be. Among a nationally representative sample of 8- through 16-year-olds examined between 1988 and 1994, 80 percent said they play or exercise vigorously—enough to work up a sweat or breathe hard—at least three times a week outside of physical education classes. However, 15 percent of boys and 26 percent of girls did not meet that standard (Andersen et al., 1998).

Unfortunately, most physical activities, in and out of school, are team and competitive sports and games. These activities usually will be dropped after leaving school and typically are aimed at the fittest and most athletic youngsters. In a multiethnic sample of 2,410 third-graders in four states, the most active children were those who were good at sports and were encouraged to participate. Again, boys were more active than girls—a finding echoed in a number of studies—and white children were more active than black or Hispanic children (Simons-Morton et al., 1997).

A sound physical education program for *all* children should emphasize skill mastery based on realistic goals, rather than winning or losing. It should include a variety of sports that can be part of a lifetime fitness regimen, such as tennis, bowling, running, swimming, golf, and skating (American Academy of Pediatrics [AAP] Committee on Sports Medicine and Committee on School Health, 1989).

CHECKPOINT

Can you . . .

✔ Explain the importance of maintaining physical fitness, and give some recommendations for doing so?

Medical Problems

Illness in middle childhood tends to be brief and transient. **Acute medical conditions**—occasional, short-term conditions, such as infections, allergies, and warts are common. Six or seven bouts a year with colds, flu, or viruses are typical at this age, as germs pass freely among youngsters at school or at play (Behrman, 1992). Upper-respiratory illnesses, sore throats, strep throats, and ear infections decrease with age; but acne, headaches, and transitory emotional disturbances increase as youngsters approach puberty (Starfield et al., 1984).

acute medical conditions Occasional illnesses that last a short time.

chronic medical conditions Physical, developmental, behavioral, and/or emotional disorders or impairments requiring special health services.

According to a nationwide survey of 30,032 families, an estimated 18 percent of children under age 18 in 1994 had **chronic medical conditions:** physical, developmental, behavioral, and/or emotional conditions requiring special health services beyond those that children normally need. Children with special health needs spend three times as many days sick in bed and miss school three times as often as other children (Newacheck et al., 1998).

Socioeconomic status and ethnicity play an important part in children's health (refer back to Chapter 7). Poor children (who are disproportionately minority children) and those living with a single parent are more likely than other children to have chronic conditions and to face barriers to health care (Newacheck et al., 1998). These disadvantaged children tend to be in fair or poor health, to have been hospitalized, and to have health-related limitations on activities. Why is this so? Parents with higher socioeconomic status tend to know more about good health habits and have better access to preventive health care; and two-parent families tend to have higher incomes and more wholesome diets than single-parent families (Collins & LeClere, 1997).

Children with chronic conditions tend to be remarkably resilient. Most do not exhibit problems in mental health, behavior, or schooling (AAP Committee on Children with Disabilities and Committee on Psychosocial Aspects of Child and Family Health, 1993). Still, certain specific conditions—such as vision and hearing problems, asthma, and AIDS—can greatly affect everyday living.

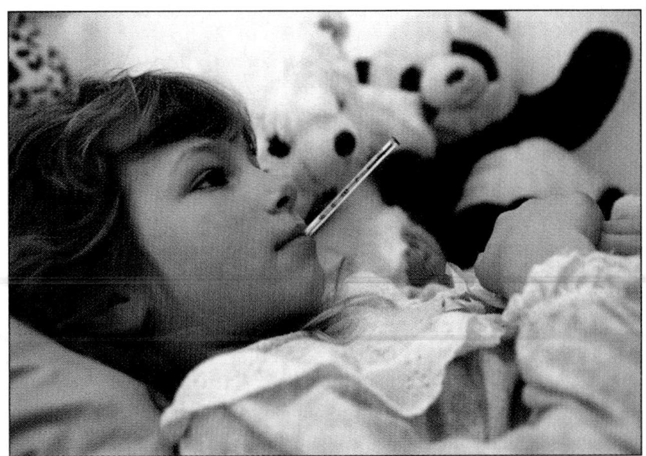

Colds, flu, and viruses are common in middle childhood. Illnesses at this age tend to be brief and transient.

Vision and Hearing Problems

Most youngsters in middle childhood have keener vision than when they were younger. Children under 6 years old tend to be farsighted. By age 6, vision is more acute; and because the two eyes are better coordinated, they can focus better.

Still, almost 13 percent of children under 18 are estimated to be blind or to have visual impairments, as Theodore Roosevelt did. Vision problems are reported more often for white and Latino children than for African Americans (Newacheck, Stoddard, & McManus, 1993). About 15 percent of 6- to 19-year-olds, preponderantly boys, have some degree of hearing loss. Current screening guidelines may miss many children with very high frequency impairments. This may be of concern, since even slight hearing loss can affect communication, behavior, and social relationships (Niskar et al., 1998).

Asthma

Asthma, a chronic respiratory disease from which Roosevelt also suffered, seems to have an allergic basis. It is characterized by sudden attacks of coughing, wheezing, and difficulty in breathing; and it can be fatal. It is now the most prevalent chronic illness in childhood, affecting 5.6 million children under age 18, an 80 percent increase since 1984. Death rates tripled during the same period, despite improved diagnosis and treatment. The cause of the asthma explosion is unknown, but some experts point to more tightly insulated houses that permit less air circulation and early exposure to environmental toxins and allergens (Nugent, 1999; Stapleton, 1998).

Poor and minority children are most severely affected (Stapleton, 1998), perhaps because of inadequate access to health care. Poor children with asthma miss more days of school, must limit their activities more, and spend more days in bed at home or in the hospital than do children from better-off families (Halfon & Newacheck, 1993).

Consider this . . .

- Which of the following measures do you think would be most helpful to poor children with asthma? How could these suggestions be implemented and funded? What other solutions might work?
  1. Evening and weekend hours for community health centers
  2. Education in detecting symptoms and avoiding triggers of attacks (such as smoking and allergy-causing substances)
  3. Classes in self-management of the disease

HIV and AIDS

Children infected with the human immunodeficiency virus (HIV) are at a high risk to develop AIDS (acquired immune deficiency syndrome). Ninety percent of these children acquired the AIDS virus from their mothers, almost all of them in the womb (AAP Committee on Pediatric AIDS and Committee on Infectious Diseases, 1999; refer back to Chapter 3).

In addition to the devastating physical effects of this usually fatal disease, the child's entire family may be stigmatized, and the child may be shunned or kept out of school even though there is virtually no risk of infecting classmates (refer back to Box 9-1). Children who carry the AIDS virus do not need to be isolated, either for their own health or for that of other children. They should be encouraged to participate in all school activities to the extent they are able (AAP Committee on Pediatric AIDS and Committee on Infectious Diseases, 1999).

Children with AIDS may develop central nervous system dysfunction that can interfere with their ability to learn and also can cause behavior problems (AAP Task Force on Pediatric AIDS, 1991). In one study at a developmental diagnostic and treatment center, most of the children in a sample of 5- to 14-year-olds who had been diagnosed with HIV infection had cognitive, linguistic, or emotional problems, although the children were living longer and doing better than predicted (Papola, Alvarez, & Cohen, 1994).

CHECKPOINT

Can you . . .

✔ Distinguish between acute and chronic medical conditions, and discuss how chronic conditions can affect everyday life?

Accidental Injuries

Injuries increase between ages 5 and 14, as children become involved in more physical activities and are supervised less. As in early childhood, accidental injuries are the leading cause of death (National Center for Health Statistics [NCHS], 1998a).

Children may get hurt because they overestimate their physical abilities. In one study, 6-year-olds' whose estimation of their abilities was the most inaccurate were the most accident prone (Plumert, 1995).

Parents tend to overestimate the safety skills of young children. Many kindergartners and first-graders walk alone to school, often crossing busy streets without traffic lights, although they do not have the skills to do this safely. Many such accidents could be prevented by providing school-operated transportation or more crossing guards (Dunne, Asher, & Rivara, 1992; Rivara, Bergman, & Drake, 1989).

Each year about 140,000 head injuries and 400 deaths of children and adolescents, as well as about 450,000 visits to emergency rooms for treatment of nonfatal injuries, are attributed to bicycle accidents (Sosin, Sacks, & Webb, 1996). The dangers of riding a bicycle can be reduced dramatically by using safety-approved helmets (D. C. Thompson, Rivara, & Thompson, 1996). Protective headgear also is vital for football, roller skating, roller blading, skateboarding, horseback riding, hockey, speed sledding, and tobogganing (Weiss, 1992).

In 1996, an estimated 83,400 trampoline-related injuries were treated in U.S. hospital emergency rooms—a 140 percent increase since 1990—and more than two-thirds of the victims were 5 to 14 years old (AAP Committee on Injury and Poison Prevention and Committee on Sports Medicine and Fitness, 1999). Because of the need for stringent safety precautions and constant supervision, the American Academy of Pediatrics (AAP Committee on Injury and Poison Prevention, 1999) recommends that parents never buy trampolines, nor should children use them on playgrounds or at school.

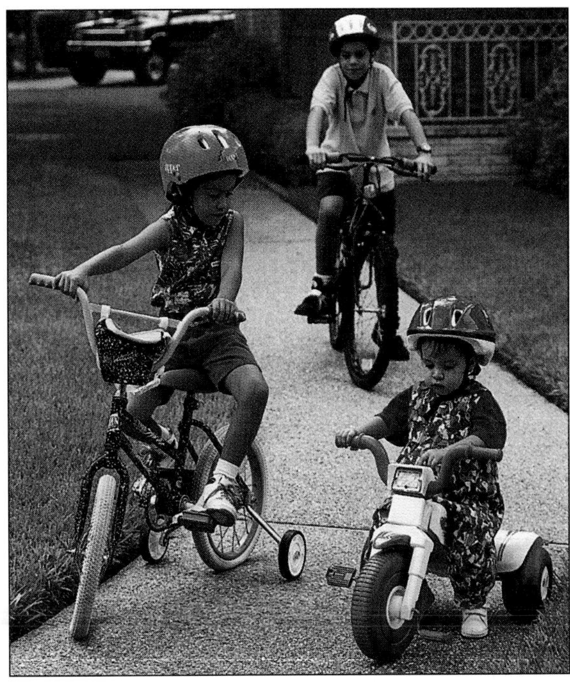

Safety-approved helmets protect children of all ages from disabling or fatal head injuries.

CHECKPOINT

Can you . . .

✔ Identify factors that increase risks of injury?

Cognitive Development

Piagetian Approach: The Concrete Operational Child

At about age 7, according to Piaget, children enter the stage of **concrete operations,** when they can use mental operations to solve concrete (actual) problems. Children now can think logically because they can take multiple aspects of a situation into account. However, children are still limited to thinking about real situations in the here and now.

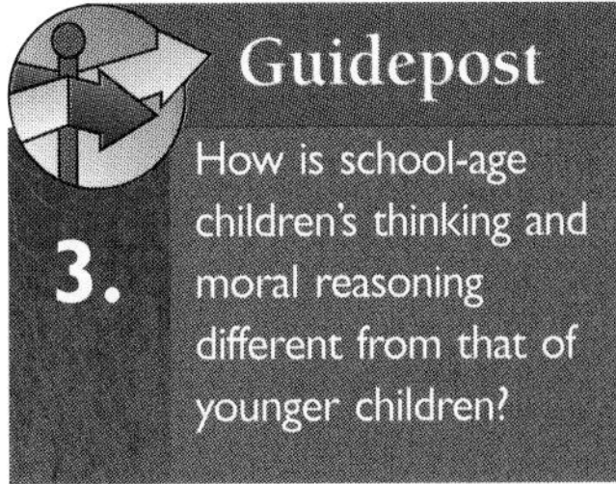

Guidepost

3. How is school-age children's thinking and moral reasoning different from that of younger children?

concrete operations Third stage of Piagetian cognitive development (approximately from ages 7 to 12), during which children develop logical but not abstract thinking.

Cognitive Advances

Children in the stage of concrete operations can perform many tasks at a much higher level than they could in the preoperational stage (see Table 9-2). They have a better understanding of spatial concepts, of causality, of categorization, of conservation, and of number.

Space

Why can 6- or 7-year-olds be trusted to find their way to and from school, whereas most younger children cannot? One reason is that children in the stage of concrete operations can better understand spatial relationships. They have a clearer idea of how far it is from one place to another and how long it will take to get there, and they can more easily remember the route and the landmarks along the way. Experience plays a role in this development. Much as a baby who begins to crawl gains a better understanding of the immediate spatial environment by

Table 9-2 Advances in Selected Cognitive Abilities During Middle Childhood

Ability	Example
Spatial thinking	Danielle can use a map or model to help her search for a hidden object and can give someone else directions for finding the object. She can find her way to and from school, can estimate distances, and can judge how long it will take her to go from one place to another.
Cause and effect	Douglas knows which physical attributes of objects on each side of a balance scale will affect the result (i.e., number of objects matters but color does not). He does not yet know which spatial factors, such as position and placement of the objects, make a difference.
Classification	Elena can sort objects into categories, such as shape, color or both. She knows that a subclass (roses) has fewer members than the class of which it is a part (flowers).
Seriation and transitive inference	Catherine can arrange a group of sticks in order, from the shortest to the longest, and can insert an intermediate-size stick into the proper place. She knows that if one stick is longer than a second stick, and the second stick is longer than a third, then the first stick is longer than the third.
Inductive and deductive reasoning	Dara can solve both inductive and deductive problems and knows that inductive conclusions (based on particular premises) are less certain than deductive ones (based on general premises).
Conservation	Stacy, at age 7, knows that if a clay ball is rolled into a sausage, it still contains the same amount of clay (conservation of substance). At age 9, she knows that the ball and the sausage weigh the same. Not until early adolescence will she understand that they displace the same amount of liquid if dropped in a glass of water.
Number and mathematics	Kevin can count in his head, can add by counting up from the smaller number, and can do simple story problems.

exploring it from a variety of positions and vantage points, a child who goes to school becomes more familiar with the neighborhood outside the home.

Both the ability to use maps and models and the ability to communicate spatial information improve with age (Gauvain, 1993). Although 6-year-olds can search for and find hidden objects, they usually do not give well-organized directions for finding the same objects—perhaps because they lack the appropriate vocabulary or do not realize what information the other person needs (Plumert, Pick, Marks, Kintsch, & Wegesin, 1994). In one study (Gauvain & Rogoff, 1989), 9-year-olds were better able than 6-year-olds to give "mental tours" of a funhouse. The 9-year-olds described the layout, as well as the route through the funhouse; but the younger children merely listed places in no particular order.

Causality

Judgments about cause and effect improve during middle childhood. When 5- to 12-year-olds were asked to predict how levers and balance scales would perform under varying conditions, the older children gave more correct answers than the younger children. Children understood the influence of physical attributes (the number of objects on each side of a scale) earlier than they recognized the influence of spatial factors (the distance of objects from the center of the scale). Awareness of which variables *do* have an effect seems unrelated to awareness of which *do not* (for example, the color of the objects). Apparently, these two mental processes develop separately as experience helps children revise their intuitive theories about how things work (Amsel, Goodman, Savoie, & Clark, 1996).

Categorization

Categorization now includes such sophisticated abilities as *seriation, transitive inference,* and *class inclusion.* Children show that they understand **seriation** when they can arrange objects in a series according to one or more dimensions, such as weight (lightest to heaviest) or color (lightest to darkest). Piaget (1952) tested this ability by asking children to put sticks in order from shortest to longest. By age 4 or 5, children can pick out the smallest and the largest sticks. By 5 or 6, they can arrange the rest of the sticks by trial and error. Finally, at 7 or 8, they can grasp the relationships among the sticks on sight, picking out the shortest, then the next shortest, and so on to the longest.

seriation
Ability to order items along a dimension.

Transitive inference is the ability to recognize a relationship between two objects by knowing the relationship between each of them and a third object. Catherine is shown three sticks: a yellow one, a green one, and a blue one. She is shown that the yellow stick is longer than the green one, and the green one is longer than the blue. Without physically comparing the yellow and blue sticks, she knows that the yellow one is longer than the blue one. She bases her answer on how the length of each of these sticks compares with the length of the green stick (Chapman & Lindenberger, 1988; Piaget & Inhelder, 1967).

transitive inference
Understanding of the relationship between two objects by knowing the relationship of each to a third object.

Class inclusion is the ability to see the relationship between a whole and its parts. If preoperational children are shown a bunch of 10 flowers—7 roses and 3 carnations—and are asked whether there are more roses or more flowers, they are likely to say there are more roses, because they are comparing the roses with the carnations rather than with the whole bunch. Not until the stage of concrete operations do children come to realize that roses are a subclass of flowers and that, therefore, there cannot be more roses than flowers (Flavell, 1963).

class inclusion
Understanding of the relationship between a whole and its parts.

The ability to categorize helps children think logically. According to Piaget, children in the stage of concrete operations use **inductive reasoning.** Starting with observations about particular members of a class of people, animals, objects, or events, they then draw general conclusions about the class as a whole. ("My dog barks. So does Terry's dog and Melissa's dog. So it looks as if all dogs bark.") **Deductive reasoning,** which Piaget believed does not develop until adolescence, is central to formal logic. Deductive reasoning starts with a general statement (premise) about a class and applies it to particular members of the class. If the premise is true of the whole class, and the reasoning is sound, then the conclusion must be true: "All dogs bark. Spot is a dog. Spot barks." Inductive conclusions are less certain than deductive ones because it is always possible to come across new information that does not support the conclusion.

inductive reasoning
Type of logical reasoning that moves from particular observations about members of a class to a general conclusion about that class.

deductive reasoning
Type of logical reasoning that moves from a general premise about a class to a conclusion about a particular member or members of the class.

Researchers gave 16 inductive and deductive problems to 16 kindergartners, 17 second-graders, 16 fourth-graders, and 17 sixth-graders. The problems were designed so as *not* to call upon knowledge of the real world. For example, one deductive problem was: "All poggops wear blue boots. Tombor is a poggop. Does Tombor wear blue boots?" The corresponding inductive problem was: "Tombor is a poggop. Tombor wears blue boots. Do all poggops wear blue boots?" Contrary to Piagetian theory, second-graders (but not kindergartners) were able to correctly answer both kinds of problems, to see the difference between them, and to explain their responses, and they (appropriately) expressed more confidence in their deductive answers than in their inductive ones (Galotti, Komatsu, & Voelz, 1997).

Consider this . . .

- How can parents and teachers help children improve their reasoning ability?

Conservation

In solving various types of conservation problems, children in the stage of concrete operations can work out the answers in their heads; they do not have to measure or weigh the objects.

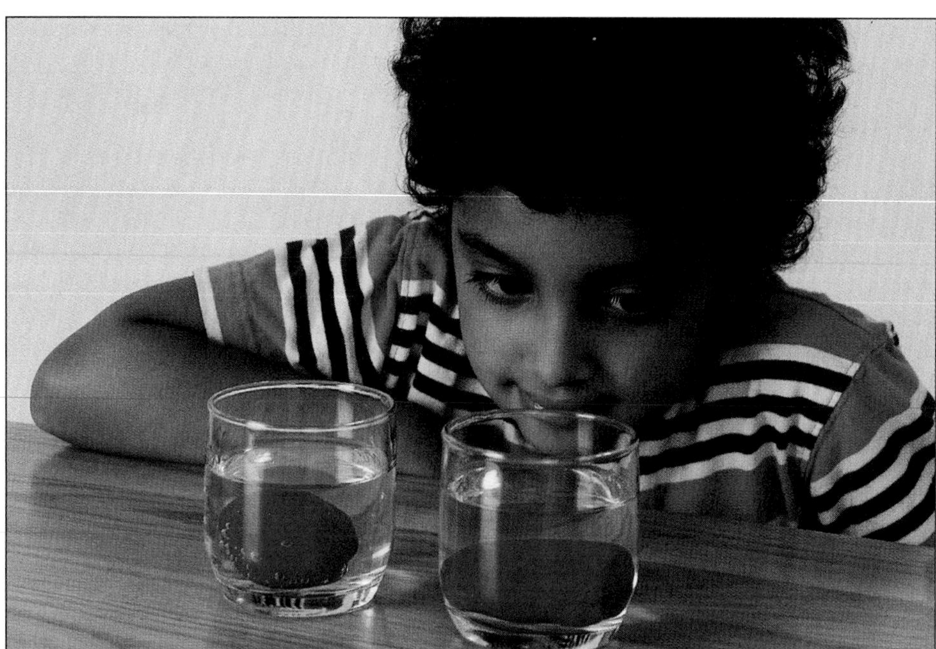

Does one ball of clay displace more water than the other? A child who has achieved conservation of volume knows that the answer does not depend on the ball's shape.

If one of two identical clay balls is rolled or kneaded into a different shape, say, a long, thin "sausage," Felipe, who is in the stage of concrete operations will say that the ball and the "sausage" still contain the same amount of clay. Stacy, who is in the preoperational stage, is deceived by appearances. She says the long, thin roll contains more clay because it looks longer.

Felipe, unlike Stacy, understands the principle of *identity:* he knows the clay is still the same clay, even though it has a different shape. He also understands the principle of *reversibility:* he knows he can change the sausage back into a ball. And he can *decenter:* he can focus on both length and width. He recognizes that although the ball is shorter than the "sausage," it is also thicker. Stacy centers on one dimension (length) while excluding the other (thickness).

Typically, children can solve problems involving conservation of substance, like this one, by about age 7 or 8. However, in tasks involving conservation of weight—in which they are asked, for example, whether the ball and the "sausage" weigh the same—children typically do not give correct answers until about age 9 or 10. In tasks involving conservation of volume—in which children must judge whether the "sausage" and the ball displace an equal amount of liquid when placed in a glass of water—correct answers are rare before age 12.

horizontal décalage
In Piaget's terminology, a child's inability to transfer learning about one type of conservation to other types, because of which the child masters different types of conservation tasks at different ages.

Piaget's term for this inconsistency in the development of different types of conservation is **horizontal décalage.** Children's thinking at this stage is so concrete, so closely tied to a particular situation, that they cannot readily transfer what they have learned about one type of conservation to another type, even though the underlying principles are the same.

Number and Mathematics

Children intuitively devise strategies for adding, by counting on their fingers or by using other objects. By age 6 or 7, many children can count in their heads. They also learn to *count on:* to add 5 and 3, they start counting at 5 and then go on to 6, 7, and 8 to add the 3. They can reverse the numbers as well, starting with 3 and adding 5 to it. It may take two or three more years for them to perform a comparable operation for subtraction, but by age 9 most children can either count up from the smaller number or down from the larger number to get the answer (Resnick, 1989).

Children also become more adept at solving simple story problems, such as: "Pedro went to the store with $5 and spent $2 on candy. How much did he have left?" When the original amount is unknown ("Pedro went to the store, spent $2 and had $3 left. How much did he start out with?"), the problem is harder because the operation needed to solve it (addition) is not as clearly indicated. Few children can solve this kind of problem before age 8 or 9 (Resnick, 1989).

Research with minimally schooled people in developing countries suggests that the ability to add develops nearly universally and often intuitively, through concrete experience in a cultural context (Guberman, 1996; Resnick, 1989). In a study of Brazilian street vendors ages 9 to 15, a researcher acting as a customer says, "I'll take two coconuts." Each one costs 40 cruzeiros; she pays with a 500-cruzeiros bill and asks, "What do I get back?" The child counts up from 80: "Eighty, 90, 100 . . ." to arrive at the correct answer, 420 cruzeiros. However, when this same child is given a similar problem in the classroom ("What is 420 + 80?"), he arrives at the wrong answer by incorrectly using a series of steps learned in school (Carraher, Schliemann, & Carraher, 1988).

Some intuitive understanding of fractions seems to exist by age 4 (Mix, Levine, & Huttenlocher, 1999), as children show when they deal a deck of cards or distribute portions of pizza (Frydman & Bryant, 1988; Sophian, Garyantes, & Chang, 1997). However, calculating with fractions is hard because they cannot be counted (Gelman & Meck, 1992). Children tend not to think about the quantity a fraction represents; instead, they focus on the numerals that make it up. Thus they may say that $^1/_2$ plus $^1/_3$ equals $^2/_5$. Also difficult for many children to grasp at first is the fact that $^1/_2$ is bigger than $^1/_4$—that the smaller fraction ($^1/_4$) has the larger denominator (Siegler, 1998; Sophian & Wood, 1997).

Influences of Neurological Development and Culture

Cross-cultural studies support a progression from the rigid, illogical thinking of younger children to the flexible, logical thinking of older ones (Broude, 1995; Gardiner, Mutter, & Kosmitzki, 1998). Piaget maintained that this shift depends on neurological maturation and adaptation to the environment and is not tied to cultural experience.

Support for a neurological basis of conservation of volume comes from scalp measurements of brain activity during a conservation task. Children who had achieved conservation of volume showed different brain wave patterns from those who had not yet achieved it, suggesting that they were using different brain regions for the task (Stauder, Molenaar, & Van der Molen, 1993). Contrary to Piaget, however, certain types of training seem to affect the brain's efficiency. In one study, piano instruction and solving computer math puzzles boosted second-graders' scores on tests of fractions and proportions. The musical and computer training may have enhanced the brain's "wiring" for spatial-temporal reasoning (the ability to mentally manipulate objects in space and time). The training also seemed to improve the ability to think ahead in going through the steps of a problem (Graziano, Peterson, & Shaw, 1999).

While the characteristics of concrete operational thinking and the sequence of progression in cognitive abilities appear to be universal, the *rate* of development in certain domains may depend on cultural factors (Dasen, 1994). In a number of studies, children in nonwestern cultures took as much as seven years longer than western children to achieve conservation and other advances of the stage of concrete operations (Broude, 1995; Gardiner et al., 1998). However, most of these studies had methodological problems. When 48 Micmac Indian 10- and 11-year-olds on Cape Breton Island, Canada, were tested in English by European examiners on conservation of substance, weight, and volume, the Indian children lagged behind a comparison group of white

CHECKPOINT

Can you . . .

- ✔ Identify cognitive abilities that emerge or strengthen during middle childhood?
- ✔ Name three principles that help school-aged children understand conservation, and explain why children master different kinds of conservation at different ages?
- ✔ Weigh the evidence for influences of neurological development and cultural experience on Piagetian tasks?

English-speaking Canadian children. Yet when interviewed by examiners from their own culture, who spoke their native language, the Indian children did about as well as the English-speaking group (Nyiti, 1982). It may well be, then, that findings of cultural differences in acquisition of conservation reflect the methods of the researchers rather than the abilities of the children (Gardiner et al., 1998).

Abilities such as conservation may depend in part on familiarity with the materials being manipulated. Children can think more logically about things they know something about. Mexican children who make pottery understand that a clay ball is still made of clay when its shape is changed sooner than they understand other types of conservation (Broude, 1995); and these children show signs of conservation of substance earlier than children who do not make pottery (Price-Williams, Gordon, & Ramirez, 1969). Thus, understanding of conservation may come not only from new patterns of mental organization, but also from culturally defined experience with the physical world.

Moral Reasoning

To draw out children's moral thinking, Piaget (1932) would tell them a story about two little boys: "One day Augustus noticed that his father's inkpot was empty and decided to help his father by filling it. While he was opening the bottle, he spilled a lot of ink on the tablecloth. The other boy, Julian, played with his father's inkpot and spilled a little ink on the cloth." Then Piaget would ask, "Which boy was naughtier, and why?"

Children younger than 7 usually considered Augustus naughtier, since he made the bigger stain. Older children recognized that Augustus meant well and made the large stain by accident, whereas Julian made a small strain while doing something he should not have been doing. Immature moral judgments, Piaget concluded, center only on the degree of offense; more mature judgments consider intent.

According to Piaget, moral development is linked to cognitive growth. Piaget maintained that children make sounder moral judgments when they can look at things from more than one perspective. He proposed that moral reasoning develops in two stages (summarized in Table 9-3). Children may go through these stages at varying ages, but the sequence is the same.

morality of constraint First of Piaget's two stages of moral development, characterized by rigid, egocentric judgments.

morality of cooperation Second of Piaget's two stages of moral development, characterized by flexible, subtle judgments and formulation of one's own moral code.

In the first stage, **morality of constraint** (up to about age 7, corresponding with the preoperational stage), the young child thinks rigidly about moral concepts. In this stage children are quite egocentric; they cannot imagine more than one way of looking at a moral issue. They believe that rules cannot be bent or changed, that behavior is right or wrong, and that any offense (like Augustus's) deserves punishment, regardless of intent (unless they themselves are the offenders!).

The second stage, **morality of cooperation** (ages 7 up, corresponding with the stages of concrete operations and formal operations) is characterized by flexibility. As children mature, they interact with more people and come into contact with a wider range of viewpoints. They discard the idea that there is a single, absolute standard of right and wrong, and they begin to formulate their own moral code. Because they can consider more than one aspect of a situation, they can make more subtle moral judgments, such as taking into consideration the intent behind Augustus's and Julian's behavior.

Consider this . . .

- Do you agree with Piaget's view that intent is an important factor in morality? In what ways does the criminal justice system reflect this view?

The increasing popularity of games with rules in middle childhood is related to the development of moral reasoning, according to Piaget (1932). Not until children enter the stage of morality of cooperation (usually beginning at age 7 or 8), he observed, do they see the need for mutual agreement on rules and on the consequences of breaking them. Beginning at ages 11 or 12, children codify their own

Table 9-3 Piaget's Two Stages of Moral Development

	Stage I: Morality of Constraint	Stage II: Morality of Cooperation
Point of view	Children cannot put themselves in place of others. They view an act as either totally right or totally wrong and think everyone sees it the same way.	Children put themselves in place of others. They are not absolutist in judgments but see that more than one point of view is possible.
Intention	Child judges acts in terms of actual physical consequences, not the motivation behind them.	Child judges acts by intentions, not consequences.
Rules	Child obeys rules because they are sacred and unalterable.	Child recognizes that rules are made by people and can be changed by people. Children consider themselves just as capable of changing rules as anyone else.
Respect for authority	Unilateral respect leads to feeling of obligation to conform to adult standards and obey adult rules.	Mutual respect for authority and peers allows children to value their own opinions and abilities and to judge other people realistically.
Punishment	Child favors severe punishment. Child feels that punishment itself defines the wrongness of an act; an act is bad if it will elicit punishment.	Child favors milder punishment that compensates the victim and helps the culprit recognize why an act is wrong, thus leading to reform.
Concept of justice	Child confuses moral law with physical law and believes that any physical accident or misfortune that occurs after a misdeed is a punishment willed by God or some other supernatural force.	Child does not confuse natural misfortune with punishment.

Source: Adapted partly from M. L. Hoffman, 1970b; Kohlberg, in M. L. Hoffman & Hoffman, 1964.

complex sets of rules to cover all contingencies. If disagreements arise, the participants find ways to work them out. Rules are no longer externally imposed, but a result of mutual self-regulation (DeVries, 1998).

Lawrence Kohlberg's influential theory of moral development, which builds on Piaget's, is discussed in Chapter 11.

CHECKPOINT

Can you . . .

✔ Describe Piaget's two stages of moral development and explain their link to cognitive maturation?

Other Approaches to Cognitive Development

Unlike Piaget, who described broad changes in the way school-age children's minds operate, information-processing researchers focus on improvements in the *efficiency* of mental operations: how much information children can handle at a given time and how quickly and accurately they can process it. More efficient processing makes it easier for children to learn and remember. Differences in efficiency of processing may help account for scores on psychometric intelligence tests, which now become more reliable predictors of school performance.

Information-Processing Approach: Memory and Other Processing Skills

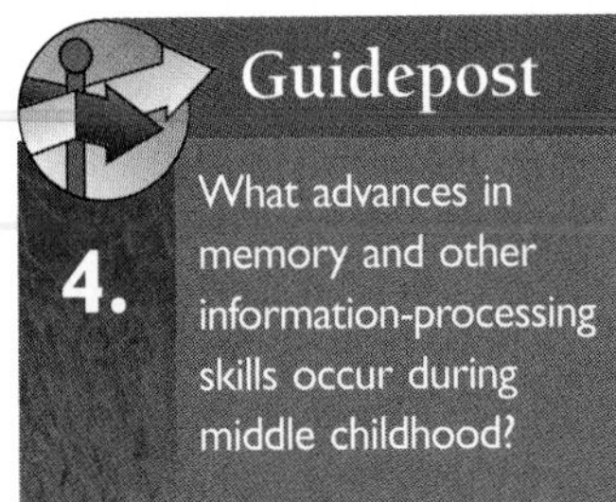

Guidepost
4.
What advances in memory and other information-processing skills occur during middle childhood?

As children move through the school years, they make steady progress in their abilities to process and retain information. They understand more about how memory works, and this knowledge enables them to use strategies, or deliberate plans, to help them remember. In addition, as their knowledge expands, they become more aware of what kinds of information are important to pay attention to and commit to memory.

Basic Processes and Capacities

Information-processing theorists think of memory as a filing system that has three steps, or processes: *encoding, storage,* and *retrieval.* **Encoding** is like putting information in a folder to be filed in memory; it attaches a "code" or "label" to the information to prepare it for storage, so that it will be easier to find when needed. Events are encoded along with information about the context in which they were encountered. Children between ages 5 and 7 become increasingly able to recall such details as when and where an event occurred (Janowsky & Carper, 1996). **Storage** is putting the folder away in the filing cabinet. The last step, **retrieval,** occurs when the information is needed; the child then searches for the file and takes it out. Retrieval may involve either recognition or recall. Difficulties in any of these processes can interfere with efficiency.

Information-processing models depict the mind as containing three "storehouses": *sensory memory, working memory,* and *long-term memory.* **Sensory memory** is the system's initial entry point; a temporary "holding tank" for incoming sensory information. Without processing (encoding), sensory memories fade quickly. Sensory memory shows little change with age; a 5-year-old's immediate recall is about as good as that of an adult (Siegler, 1998).

Information that is being encoded or retrieved is kept in **working memory,** a short-term "storehouse" for information a person is actively working on (trying to understand or remember). Researchers may assess the capacity of working memory by asking children to recall a series of spoken digits in reverse order (for example, "2–8–3–7–5–1" if they heard "1–5–7–3–8–2"). The capacity of working memory increases rapidly in middle childhood (Cowan, Nugent, Elliott, Ponomarev, & Saults, 1999). At ages 5 to 6, children usually remember only two digits; the typical adolescent remembers six.

According to a widely used model, a **central executive** controls the processing of information in working memory (Baddeley, 1981, 1986). The central executive orders information encoded for transfer to **long-term memory,** a "storehouse" of virtually unlimited capacity that holds information for long periods of time. The central executive also retrieves information from long-term memory for processing in working memory. The central executive can temporarily expand the capacity of working memory by moving information into two separate subsidiary systems. One of these keeps verbal information, and the other, visual and spatial images, "on hold" while the central executive is occupied with other tasks.

The central executive seems to mature sometime between ages 8 and 10. Ten-year-olds are less likely than younger children to become confused when given a visual task (identifying the colors of numbers flashed on a computer screen) while trying to do a verbal task (committing the numbers to memory). This suggests that the visual and verbal components of working memory have become independent of each other (Hale, Bronik, & Fry, 1997). Similarly, when children were asked to recall lists of numbers they heard while paying attention to a computer game in which they had to match up pictures with rhyming names, first-graders recalled fewer numbers than adults did under the same conditions, but fourth-graders recalled just as many as the adults (Cowan et al., 1999).

During middle childhood, reaction time improves, and processing speed for such tasks as matching pictures, adding numbers in one's head, and recalling spatial information increases rapidly as unneeded synapses, or neural connections in the brain, are pruned away (Hale et al., 1997; Janowsky & Carper, 1996; Kail, 1991, 1997; Kail & Park, 1994). Faster, more efficient processing increases the amount of information a child can keep in working memory, making possible better recall and more complex, higher-level thinking (Flavell, Miller, & Miller, 1993).

encoding
Process by which information is prepared for long-term storage and later retrieval.

storage
Retention of memories for future use.

retrieval
Process by which information is accessed or recalled from memory storage.

sensory memory
Initial, brief, temporary storage of sensory information.

working memory
Short-term storage of information being actively processed.

central executive
In Baddeley's model, element of working memory that controls the processing of information.

long-term memory
Storage of virtually unlimited capacity, which holds information for very long periods.

CHECKPOINT

Can you . . .

- ✔ Identify several ways in which information processing improves during middle childhood?
- ✔ Describe the three steps in memory?

Metamemory: Understanding Memory

Metamemory, knowledge about one's own memory, improves with age. Between ages 5 and 7, the brain's frontal lobes may undergo significant development and reorganization, making metamemory—and improved recall—possible (Janowsky & Carper, 1996). From kindergarten through fifth grade, children advance steadily in understanding of memory (Flavell et al., 1993; Kreutzer, Leonard, & Flavell, 1975). Kindergartners and first-graders know that people remember better if they study longer, that people forget things with time, and that relearning something is easier than learning it for the first time. By third grade, children know that some people remember better than others and that some things are easier to remember than others.

metamemory
Understanding of processes of memory.

One pair of experiments looked at preschoolers', first-graders', and third-graders' beliefs about what influences remembering and forgetting. Most children in all three age groups believed that important events in a story about a birthday party (such as a guest falling into the cake) were more likely to be retained than minor details (such as a guest bringing a ball as a present). Most first- and third-graders, but not most preschoolers, believed that a later experience (playing with a friend who was not at the party) might color a child's recollection of who was at the party. Not until third grade did most children recognize that memory can be distorted by suggestions from others—say, a parent who suggests that the friend was at the party (O'Sullivan, Howe, & Marche, 1996).

Mnemonics: Strategies for Remembering

Devices to aid memory are called **mnemonic strategies.** The most common mnemonic strategy among both children and adults is use of *external memory aids.* Other common mnemonic strategies include *rehearsal, organization,* and *elaboration.*

mnemonic strategies
Techniques to aid memory.

external memory aids
Mnemonic strategies using something outside the person.

rehearsal
Mnemonic strategy to keep an item in working memory through conscious repetition.

Writing down a telephone number, making a list, setting a timer, and putting a library book by the front door are examples of **external memory aids:** prompting by something outside the person. Saying a telephone number over and over after looking it up, so as not to forget it before dialing, is a form of **rehearsal,** or

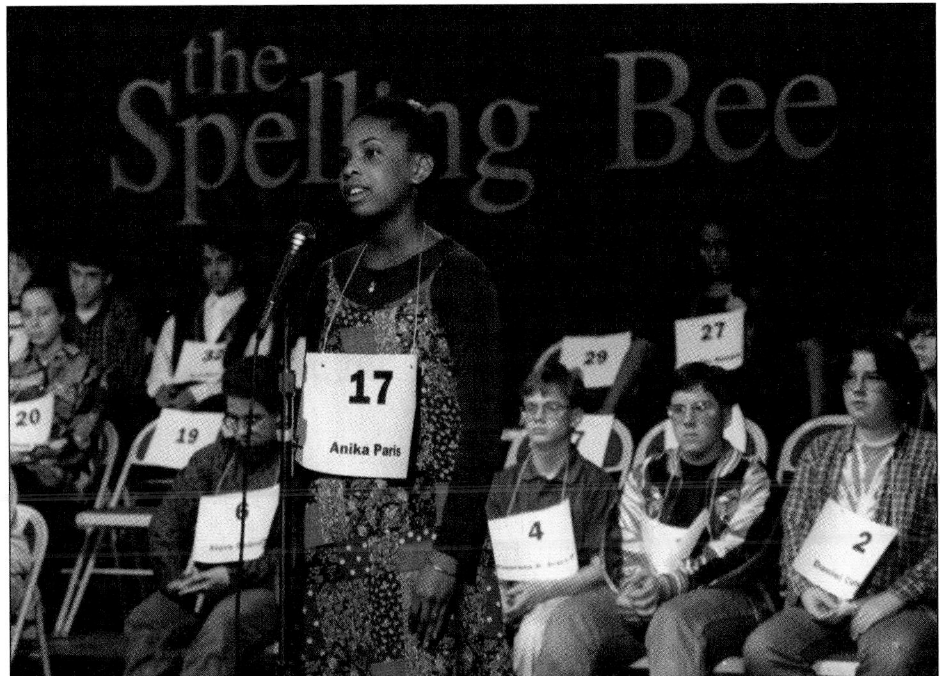

Contestants in a spelling bee can make good use of mnemonic strategies—devices to aid memory—such as rehearsal (repetition), organization, and elaboration.

organization Mnemonic strategy of categorizing material to be remembered.

elaboration Mnemonic strategy of making mental associations involving items to be remembered.

conscious repetition. **Organization** is mentally placing information into categories (such as animals, furniture, vehicles, and clothing) to make it easier to recall. In **elaboration,** children associate items with something else, such as an imagined scene or story. To remember to buy lemons, ketchup, and napkins, for example, a child might imagine a ketchup bottle balanced on a lemon, with a pile of napkins handy to wipe up spilled ketchup.

As children get older, they develop better strategies, use them more effectively, and tailor them to meet specific needs (Bjorklund, 1997). Even kindergartners recognize the value of *external aids,* and as children mature, they use them more (Kreutzer et al., 1975). Children usually do not use *rehearsal* spontaneously until after first grade; and if taught to do so in one situation, they usually do not apply it to another (Flavell, Beach, & Chinsky, 1966; Flavell et al., 1993; Keeney, Canizzo, & Flavell, 1967). The picture is similar for the other two types of mnemonic strategies, though there is some evidence that even preschoolers, when taught to use *organization,* can generalize this learning to other situations. Again, older children are more likely than younger ones to use *elaboration* spontaneously and to transfer it to other tasks (Flavell et al., 1993), and they remember better when they think up the elaborations themselves. Younger children remember better when someone else makes up the elaboration (Paris & Lindauer, 1976; H. W. Reese, 1977).

Children often use more than one strategy for a task and choose different kinds of strategies for different problems. In one study, second-, third-, and fourth-graders were given 2 minutes to memorize 18 words and then were asked to recall them in any order. The same procedure was repeated four more times with different sets of words. Older children used more strategies, more effectively, than younger children, but even second-graders tended to use more than one strategy for each set of words; and children of all ages who used more strategies recalled more words (Coyle & Bjorklund, 1997).

Selective Attention

School-age children can concentrate longer than younger children and can focus on the information they need and want while screening out irrelevant information. For example, they can summon up the appropriate meaning of a word they read and suppress other meanings that do not fit the context (Simpson & Foster, 1986; Simpson & Lorsbach, 1983). Fifth-graders are better able than first-graders to keep discarded information from reentering working memory and vying with other material for attention (Harnishfeger & Pope, 1996). This growing ability to control the intrusion of older thoughts and associations and redirect attention to current, relevant ones is believed to be due to neurological maturation. It is one of the reasons memory functioning improves during middle childhood (Bjorklund & Harnishfeger, 1990; Harnishfeger & Bjorklund, 1993).

The ability to consciously direct attention may help explain why older children make fewer mistakes in recall than younger ones. It may enable them to select what they want to remember and what they want to forget (Lorsbach & Reimer, 1997).

CHECKPOINT

Can you . . .

- ✔ Name four of the most common mnemonic aids and discuss developmental differences in their use?
- ✔ Explain the importance of metamemory and selective attention?

Information Processing and Piagetian Tasks

Improvements in information processing may help explain the advances Piaget described. For example, 9-year-olds may be better able than 5-year-olds to find their way to and from school because they can scan a scene, take in its important features, and remember objects in context, in the order in which they were encountered (Allen & Ondracek, 1995).

Improvements in memory may contribute to the mastery of conservation tasks. Young children's working memory is so limited that, even if they are able to master the concept of conservation, they may not be able to remember all the relevant information (Siegler & Richards, 1982). They may forget that two differently shaped pieces of clay were originally identical. Gains in short-term memory may contribute to the ability to solve problems like this in middle childhood.

Robbie Case (1985, 1992), a neo-Piagetian theorist (refer back to Chapter 2), suggests that as a child's application of a concept or scheme becomes more automatic, it frees space in working memory to deal with new information. This may help explain horizontal décalage: children may need to become comfortable enough with one kind of conservation to use it without conscious thought before they can extend and adapt that scheme to other kinds of conservation.

CHECKPOINT

Can you . . .

✔ Give examples of how improved information processing may help explain cognitive advances Piaget described?

Psychometric Approach: Assessment of Intelligence

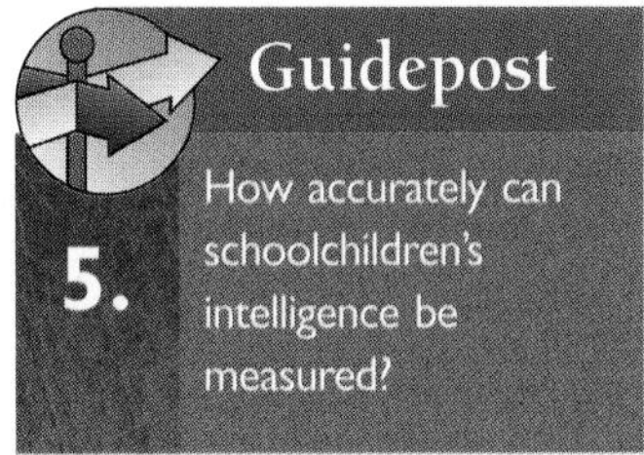

Guidepost
5.
How accurately can schoolchildren's intelligence be measured?

Intelligence tests (or IQ tests) are called **aptitude tests:** they claim to measure the capacity to learn, as contrasted with **achievement tests,** which assess how much children have already learned in various subject areas. However, as we'll see, it is virtually impossible to design a test that requires no prior knowledge. In addition, intelligence tests are validated against measures of achievement, such as school performance, and such measures are affected by factors beyond innate intelligence. For this and other reasons, there is strong disagreement over how accurately IQ tests assess differences among children.

Traditional Group and Individual Tests

aptitude tests
Tests that measure children's general intelligence, or capacity to learn.

achievement tests
Tests that assess how much children know in various subject areas.

Otis-Lennon School Ability Test
Group intelligence test for kindergarten through twelfth grade.

Wechsler Intelligence Scale for Children (WISC-III)
Individual intelligence test for schoolchildren, which yields verbal and performance scores as well as a combined score.

The original IQ tests, such as those of Alfred Binet and Lewis M. Terman (see Chapter 5), were designed to be given to individuals, and their modern versions still are used that way. The first group tests, developed during World War I to screen army recruits for appropriate assignments, became models for the group tests now given in schools. As both individual and group tests have been refined, their developers have turned from the original emphasis on general intelligence to more sophisticated distinctions among various kinds of abilities and have sought to adapt the tests to special needs (Anastasi & Urbina, 1997; Daniel, 1997).

One popular group test, the **Otis-Lennon School Ability Test,** has levels for kindergarten through twelfth grade. Children are asked to classify items, to show an understanding of verbal and numerical concepts, to display general information, and to follow directions. Separate scores for verbal comprehension, verbal reasoning, pictorial reasoning, figural reasoning, and quantitative reasoning can identify strengths and weaknesses.

The most widely used individual test is the **Wechsler Intelligence Scale for Children (WISC-III).** This test for ages 6 through 16 measures verbal and performance abilities, yielding separate scores for each, as well as a total score. Separate subtest scores makes it easier to pinpoint a child's strengths and to diagnose specific problems. For example, if a child does well on verbal tests (such as understanding a written passage and knowing vocabulary words) but poorly on performance tests (such as figuring out mazes and copying a block design), the child may be slow in perceptual or motor development. A child who does well on performance tests but poorly on verbal tests may have a language problem. Another commonly used individual test is the Stanford-Binet Intelligence Scale (see Chapter 7).

Pros and Cons of Intelligence Testing

The use of psychometric intelligence tests is controversial. On the positive side, because IQ tests have been standardized and widely used, there is extensive information about their norms, validity, and reliability (see Chapter 5). IQ scores during middle childhood are fairly good predictors of school achievement, especially for highly verbal children, and scores are more reliable than during the preschool year. IQ scores account for about one-quarter of the variance among children's grades and are the single best predictor of how long a child will stay in school (Neisser et al., 1996). They can help in selecting students for advanced or slow-paced classes and can aid in decision making about college applications and admissions.

Nevertheless, critics claim that IQ tests are unfair to many children. For one thing, they may underestimate the intelligence of children who, for one reason or another, do not do well on tests (Anastasi, 1988; Ceci, 1991). Because the tests are timed, they equate intelligence with speed and penalize a child who works slowly and deliberately.

A more fundamental criticism, as we've already mentioned, is that IQ tests infer intelligence from what children already know; and much of this knowledge is culturally derived. Consider the following item: "Hat is to head as shoe is to ______." This problem would mean nothing to a child from a culture in which nobody wears hats and shoes. Critics claim that IQ tests are unfair to minorities because they are subject to **cultural bias:** a tendency to include questions that use vocabulary or call for information or skills more familiar or meaningful to some cultural groups than to others (Sternberg, 1985a, 1987).

cultural bias
Tendency of intelligence tests to include items calling for knowledge or skills more familiar or meaningful to some cultural groups than to others, thus placing some test-takers at an advantage or disadvantage due to their cultural background.

Test developers have tried to design **culture-free** tests—tests with no culture-linked content—by posing tasks that do not require language, such as tracing mazes, putting the right shapes in the right holes, and completing pictures. But they have been unable to eliminate all cultural influences. For example, an Asian child, when asked what was missing in a picture of a face with no mouth, said the body was missing, since, in his culture, faces are not drawn without bodies (Anastasi, 1988). Test designers also have found it virtually impossible to produce **culture-fair** tests consisting only of experiences common to people in various cultures. On a simple sorting task, for example, a child in a western culture will categorize things by what they *are* (say, putting *bird* and *fish* in the category *animal*). Kpelle tribespeople in Nigeria consider it more intelligent to sort things by what they *do* (say, grouping *fish* with *swim*) (Sternberg, in Quinby, 1985; Sternberg, 1985a, 1986).

culture-free
Describing an intelligence test that, if it were possible to design, would have no culturally linked content. Compare *culture-fair.*

culture-fair
Describing an intelligence test that deals with experiences common to various cultures, in an attempt to avoid cultural bias. Compare *culture-free.*

Another serious criticism is that IQ tests focus almost entirely on abilities that are useful in school. They do *not* cover other important aspects of intelligent behavior, such as common sense, social skills, creative insight, and self-knowledge. Yet these abilities, in which some children with modest academic skills excel, may become equally or more important in later life (Gardner, 1993; Sternberg, 1985a, 1987). Two of the chief advocates of this position are Howard Gardner and Robert Sternberg.

theory of multiple intelligences
Gardner's theory that distinct, multiple forms of intelligence exist in each person.

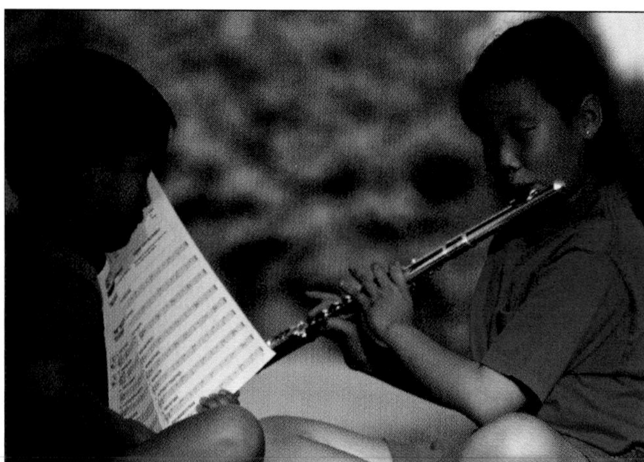

According to Howard Gardner, musical ability—which includes the ability to perceive and create patterns of pitch and rhythm—is one of several separate kinds of intelligence.

Gardner and Sternberg: Is There More Than One Intelligence?

In his **theory of multiple intelligences,** Howard Gardner (1993) defines *intelligence* as the ability to solve problems or create culturally valued products. He maintains that people have at least seven separate kinds of intelligence. Conventional intelligence tests tap only three of these "intelligences": *linguistic, logical-mathematical,* and, to some extent, *spatial.* The other four, which are not reflected in IQ scores, are *musical, bodily-kinesthetic, interpersonal,* and *intrapersonal.* Gardner (1998) recently added an eighth intelligence, *naturalist intelligence* (perhaps as exemplified by Theodore Roosevelt), to his original list. (See Table 9-4 for definitions and examples of fields in which each "intelligence" is useful.)

High intelligence in one area is not necessarily accompanied by high intelligence in any of the others.

Table 9-4 Eight Intelligences, According to Gardner

Intelligence	Definition	Fields or Occupations Where Used
Linguistic	Ability to use and understand words and nuances of meaning	Writing, editing, translating
Logical-mathematical	Ability to manipulate numbers and solve logical problems	Science, business, medicine
Musical	Ability to perceive and create patterns of pitch and rhythm	Musical composition, conducting
Spatial	Ability to find one's way around in an environment and judge relationships between objects in space	Architecture, carpentry, city planning
Bodily-kinesthetic	Ability to move with precision	Dancing, athletics, surgery
Interpersonal	Ability to understand and communicate with others	Teaching, acting, politics
Intrapersonal	Ability to understand the self	Counseling, psychiatry, spiritual leadership
Naturalist	Ability to distinguish species	Hunting, fishing, farming, gardening, cooking

Source: Based on Gardner, 1993, 1998.

A person may be extremely gifted in art (a spatial ability), precision of movement (bodily-kinesthetic), social relations (interpersonal), or self-understanding (intrapersonal), but not have a high IQ. The various intelligences also develop at different rates. For example, logical-mathematical ability tends to develop earlier and to decline more quickly in late life than interpersonal ability.

Gardner would assess each intelligence directly by observing its products—how well a child can tell a story, remember a melody, or get around in a strange area. Extended observation could reveal strengths and weaknesses so as to help children realize their potential, rather than to compare individuals (Gardner, 1995; Scherer, 1985). Of course, such assessments would be far more time-consuming and more open to observer bias than paper-and-pencil tests.

Robert Sternberg (1997) defines *intelligence* as a group of mental abilities necessary for children or adults to adapt to any environmental context, and also to select and shape the contexts in which they live and act. Intelligent behavior may differ from one culture to another—in England it is intelligent to drive on the left side of the road, in the United States on the right—but the mental processes that produce such behavior are the same.

Sternberg's (1985a) **triarchic theory of intelligence** embraces three elements, or aspects, of intelligence: *componential, experiential,* and *contextual.* A person may be strong in one, two, or all three.

- The **componential element** is the *analytic* aspect of intelligence; it determines how efficiently people process information. It tells people how to solve problems, how to monitor solutions, and how to evaluate the results.
- The **experiential element** is *insightful;* it determines how people approach novel or familiar tasks. It allows people to compare new information with what they already know and to come up with new ways of putting facts together—in other words, to think originally.
- The **contextual element** is *practical;* it determines how people deal with their environment. It is the ability to size up a situation and decide what to do: adapt to it, change it, or get out of it.

triarchic theory of intelligence
Sternberg's theory describing three types of intelligence: componential (analytical ability), experiential (insight and originality), and contextual (practical thinking).

componential element
In Sternberg's triarchic theory, term for the analytic aspect of intelligence, which determines how efficiently people process information and solve problems.

experiential element
In Sternberg's triarchic theory, term for the insightful aspect of intelligence, which determines how effectively people approach both novel and familiar tasks.

contextual element
In Sternberg's triarchic theory, term for the practical aspect of intelligence, which determines how effectively people deal with their environment.

Consider this . . .

- Which of Gardner's or Sternberg's types of intelligence are you strongest in? Did your education include a focus on any of these aspects? How might such teaching be integrated into a school curriculum?

Kaufman Assessment Battery for Children (K-ABC)
Nontraditional individual intelligence test for children ages $2\frac{1}{2}$ to $12\frac{1}{2}$, which seeks to provide fair assessments of minority children and children with disabilities.

Sternberg Triarchic Abilities Test (STAT)
Test that seeks to measure componential, experiential, and contextual intelligence in verbal, quantitative, and figural (spatial) domains.

CHECKPOINT

Can you . . .

- ✔ Name and describe two traditional intelligence tests for schoolchildren?
- ✔ Give arguments for and against IQ tests?
- ✔ Compare Gardner's and Sternberg's theories, and name and describe the specific abilities proposed by each?
- ✔ Describe several new types of intelligence tests?

Conventional IQ tests measure mainly componential ability; and since this ability is the kind most school tasks require, it's not surprising that the tests are fairly good predictors of school performance. Their failure to measure experiential (insightful) or contextual (practical) intelligence, says Sternberg, may explain why they are less useful in predicting success in the outside world.

Alternative Directions in Intelligence Testing

Ever since intelligence tests were born, researchers have been trying to improve them. One relatively new diagnostic and predictive tool, based on neurological research and information processing theory, is the **Kaufman Assessment Battery for Children (K-ABC)** (A. S. Kaufman & Kaufman, 1983). This individual test for children $2\frac{1}{2}$ to $12\frac{1}{2}$ years old has separate scales for aptitude (processing abilities) and achievement. So as to fairly assess children from cultural minorities and children with disabilities, members of these groups were included in the standardization sample. There is also a nonverbal scale for children with hearing impairments or speech or language disorders and for those whose primary language is not English. The K-ABC incorporates the concept of scaffolding (see Chapters 2 and 7): if a child fails any of the first three items on a subtest, the examiner can clarify what kind of response is expected by using different words or gestures or a different language. Other new tests are based on Vygotsky's zone of proximal development (ZPD) (see Chapter 7). These tests, which seek to capture the dynamic nature of intelligence formation, offer an alternative to traditional "static" tests that measure a child's abilities at a given moment.

Sternberg has developed tests consistent with his theory of intelligence. The **Sternberg Triarchic Abilities Test (STAT)** (Sternberg, 1993) seeks to measure each of the three components of intelligence—*analytic, creative,* and *practical*—through multiple-choice and essay questions in three domains: *verbal, quantitative,* and *figural* (or spatial). For example, a test of practical-quantitative intelligence might be to solve an everyday math problem having to do with buying tickets to a ball game. A creative-verbal item might ask children to solve deductive reasoning problems that start with factually false premises (such as, "Money falls off trees"). An analytical-figural item might ask children to identify the missing piece of a figure. The test has levels for elementary, high school, and college students. Preliminary validation has found correlations with several other tests of critical thinking, creativity, and practical problem solving (Sternberg, 1997; Sternberg & Clinkenbeard, 1995).

Despite such innovations, it seems likely that conventional psychometric intelligence tests will continue to dominate the field for some time to come (Daniel, 1997). They are widely entrenched, heavily researched, and readily available, and their developers continue to respond to criticisms with each new revision. With or without intelligence tests, decisions will be made about children's abilities and educational placement. Without the tests, such judgments might be made on a less justifiable basis, such as the opinion of a biased teacher. Even though current tests are far from perfect, if they are well designed, carefully administered, and wisely interpreted in the light of other relevant information, they can benefit both children and society.

Influences on Measured Intelligence: Ethnicity and Schooling

When we talk about interpreting test results wisely, we are talking, among other things, about the need to be aware of the many influences that can affect a child's performance. These include genetic endowment, temperament, social and emotional maturity, ease in the testing situation, and verbal and numerical skills. They also include such environmental factors as the family setting, socioeconomic status, ethnic background, and schooling. We have discussed some of these factors in earlier chapters. Let's look now at ethnicity and schooling.

Although there is considerable overlap in IQ among ethnic groups, some intergroup differences exist. Although some African Americans score higher than most whites, on average African Americans score about 15 points lower than white Americans and show a comparable lag on school achievement tests. Average IQ scores of Hispanic children fall between those of black and white children, and their scores, too, tend to predict school achievement. Yet Asian Americans, whose scholastic achievements consistently outstrip those of other ethnic groups, do not seem to have a significant edge in IQ—a reminder of the limited predictive power of intelligence testing (Neisser et al., 1996). Instead, as we'll show later in this chapter, Asian American children's strong scholastic achievement seems to be best explained by cultural factors.

What accounts for ethnic differences in IQ? Some writers have argued that part of the cause is genetic (Herrnstein & Murray, 1994; Jensen, 1969). However, while there is strong evidence of a genetic influence on individual differences in intelligence, there is *no* direct evidence that differences among ethnic, cultural, or racial groups are hereditary (Neisser et al., 1996).

Many scholars attribute such differences to inequalities in environment—in income, in nutrition, in living conditions, in intellectual stimulation, in schooling, in culture, or in other circumstances such as the effects of oppression and discrimination, which can affect self-esteem, motivation, and academic performance (Kamin, 1974, 1981; Kottak, 1994; Miller-Jones, 1989) and even the very structure of the brain. The IQ and achievement test gaps between white and black Americans appear to be narrowing (Neisser et al., 1996) as the life circumstances and educational opportunities of many African American children improve.

In one study of 5-year-olds who had been low-birthweight babies, when analysts adjusted for socioeconomic differences between black and white children (including differences in home environment), they virtually eliminated the difference in average IQ (Brooks-Gunn, Klebanov, & Duncan, 1996). Generally, however, while socioeconomic status and IQ are strongly correlated, SES does not seem to explain the entire intergroup variance in IQ (Neisser et al., 1996; Suzuki & Valencia, 1997).

Some critics attribute ethnic differences in IQ to cultural bias. They argue that intelligence tests are built around the dominant thinking style and language of white people of European ancestry, putting minority children at a disadvantage (Heath, 1989; Helms, 1992). Language difficulties may well explain the lower IQs of Latino children, who tend to do better on performance tasks than on verbal tasks; the same is generally true of American Indians (Neisser et al., 1996). Language may play a part in the black-white differential as well; some test items may be confusing to children who hear black English rather than standard English at home.

Cultural bias also may affect the testing situation. A child from a culture that stresses sociability and cooperation may be handicapped taking a test alone (Kottak, 1994). Rapport with the examiner and familiarity with the surroundings make a difference. African American and Latino children, disabled children, and children from low socioeconomic levels often make higher scores when tested in their own classrooms by their own teachers, rather than in unfamiliar rooms by examiners they do not know (D. Fuchs & Fuchs, 1986; L. S. Fuchs & Fuchs, 1986).

Still, while cultural bias may play a part in some children's performance, controlled studies have failed to show that it contributes substantially to overall group differences in IQ. Although many answers have been suggested, and some seem more plausible than others, the mystery of ethnic differences in IQ remains just that—a mystery that needs much more investigation (Neisser et al., 1996).

There is evidence that schooling increases tested intelligence (Ceci & Williams, 1997; Neisser et al., 1996). This is not surprising, since children learn information

Consider this . . .

- Since intelligence tests are only moderately good predictors of school achievement, and less useful in predicting eventual job performance, is there a value in giving them? Or do they do more harm than good?
- Is the impossibility of eliminating cultural bias from IQ tests sufficient reason to abandon them? If so, what evaluation system, if any, should take their place?
- Is intelligence related to how well a person adapts to the dominant culture, or should intelligence tests be designed to take a minority culture into account?

CHECKPOINT

Can you . . .

✔ Assess various explanations that have been advanced for differences in the performance of children of various ethnic groups on psychometric intelligence tests?

and skills in school that help them on tests of "aptitude" as well as of achievement. In a comparison of identical twins raised in different homes, differences in IQ were directly related to the number of years of education each twin had had (Bronfenbrenner, 1979). IQ scores drop during summer vacation (Ceci & Williams, 1997). Among a national sample of 1,500 children, language, spatial, and conceptual scores improved much more between October and April, the bulk of the school year, than between April and October, which includes summer vacation and the beginning and end of the school year (Huttenlocher, Levine, & Vevea, 1998). Of course, the quality of schooling makes a difference. In very poor quality schools, children may fall further behind national IQ norms each year, with older siblings scoring lower than younger ones (Neisser et al., 1996).

Language and Literacy

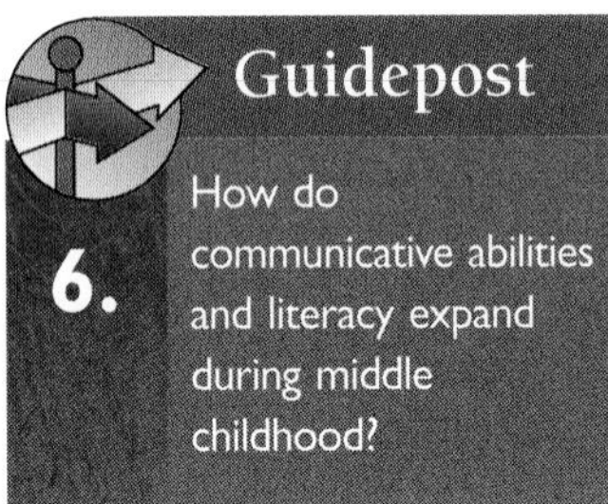

Guidepost
6.
How do communicative abilities and literacy expand during middle childhood?

Language abilities continue to grow during middle childhood. Children are now better able to understand and interpret oral and written communication and to make themselves understood.

Vocabulary, Grammar, and Syntax

As vocabulary grows during the school years, children use increasingly precise verbs to describe an action (*hitting, slapping, striking, pounding*). They learn that a word like *run* can have more than one meaning, and they can tell from the context which meaning is intended. They learn, not only to use many more words, but to select the right word for a particular use. *Simile* and *metaphor,* figures of speech in which a word or phrase that usually designates one thing is compared or applied to another, become increasingly common (Owens, 1996; Vosniadou, 1987). Although grammar is quite complex by age 6, children during the early school years rarely use the passive voice (as in "The sidewalk is being shoveled"), verb tenses that include the auxiliary *have* ("I have already shoveled the sidewalk"), and conditional sentences ("If Barbara were home, she would help shovel the sidewalk") (C. S. Chomsky, 1969).

Up to and possibly after age 9, children's understanding of rules of *syntax* (how words are organized into phrases and sentences) becomes more sophisticated. Carol S. Chomsky (1969) found considerable variation in the ages at which children grasp certain syntactic structures. For example, most children under 5 or 6 years old think the sentences "John promised Bill to go shopping" and "John told Bill to go shopping" both mean that Bill is the one to go to the store. Their confusion is understandable, since almost all English verbs other than *promised* that might be used in such a sentence (such as *ordered, wanted,* and *expected*) would have that meaning. Many 6-year-olds have not yet learned how to deal with constructions such as the one in the first sentence, even though they know what a promise is and can use and understand the word correctly in other sentences. By age 8, most children can interpret the first sentence correctly, and by age 9 virtually all children can.

Sentence structure continues to become more elaborate. Older children use more subordinate clauses ("The boy *who delivers the newspapers* rang the doorbell"), and they now look at the semantic effect of a sentence as a whole, rather than focusing on word order as a signal of meaning. Still, some constructions, such as clauses beginning with *however* and *although,* do not become common until early adolescence (Owens, 1996).

Pragmatics

By the school years, most children have mastered the basic rules of form and meaning. They are better able to take the viewpoint of another person and to engage in social give-and-take. Their major area of linguistic growth is in

pragmatics: the practical use of language to communicate.* This includes both conversational and narrative skills.

pragmatics
Set of linguistic rules that govern the use of language for communication.

Good conversationalists probe by asking questions before introducing a topic with which the other person may not be familiar. They quickly recognize a breakdown in communication and do something to repair it. There are wide individual differences in such conversational skills; some 7-year-olds are better conversationalists than some adults (Anderson, Clark, & Mullin, 1994).

Schoolchildren are highly conscious of adults' power and authority. First-graders respond to adults' questions with simpler, shorter answers than they give their peers. They tend to speak differently to parents than to other adults, issuing more demands and engaging in less extended conversation.

When children this age tell stories, they usually do not make them up; they are more likely to relate a personal experience. Most 6-year-olds can retell the plot of a short book, movie, or television show. They are beginning to describe motives and causal links.

By second grade, children's stories become longer and more complex. Fictional tales often have conventional beginnings and endings ("Once upon a time . . ." and "They lived happily ever after," or simply "The end"). Word use is more varied than before, but characters do not show growth or change, and plots are not fully developed.

Older children usually "set the stage" with introductory information about the setting and characters, and they clearly indicate changes of time and place during the story. They construct more complex episodes than younger children do, but with less unnecessary detail. They focus more on the characters' motives and thoughts, and they think through how to resolve problems in the plot.

Literacy

Learning to read and write frees children from the constraints of face-to-face communication. Now they have access to the ideas and imagination of people in faraway lands and long-ago times.

Reading

The developmental processes that improve reading comprehension during the school years are similar to those that improve memory. As word recognition becomes faster and more automatic (see Box 9-2), children can focus on the meaning of what they read and look for inferences and connections.

Metacognition—awareness of what is going on in their own minds—helps children monitor their understanding of what they read and develop strategies to clear up any problems (such as rereading difficult passages, reading more slowly, trying to visualize what is being described, and thinking of examples). Children also learn to adjust their reading speed and attentional resources to the importance and difficulty of the material. As their store of knowledge increases, they can more readily check new information against what they already know (Siegler, 1998).

metacognition
Awareness of a person's own mental processes.

Some school-based programs help children develop interpretive strategies through literary discussion. Teachers model effective strategies (such as making associations with prior knowledge, summarizing, visualizing relationships, and making predictions) and coach students on how to select and use them. After a year in one such program, low-achieving second-graders did significantly better on standardized measures of comprehension than a control group (R. Brown & Pressley, 1994; R. Brown, Pressley, Schuder, & Van Meter, 1994).

*This section is largely indebted to Owens (1996).

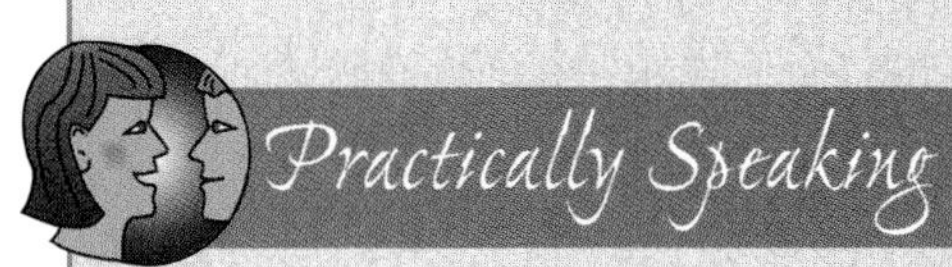

Box 9-2

Teaching Reading: Phonics versus Whole Language

Traditionally, most children learned to read by mastering a phonetic code that matches the printed alphabet to spoken sounds. A child who knows this code can "sound out," and thus "decode," unfamiliar words. Teaching methods that stress phonics take a *code emphasis* approach.

The *whole-language* approach (sometimes called *literature-based* or *process-oriented*), which is in widespread use today, is based on very different principles. Whole-language advocates believe that children can learn to read and write naturally, through discovery, much as they learn to understand and use speech. They claim that phonetic instruction hampers this natural process by obscuring the purpose of written language—to communicate meaning—and produces readers who can decode but cannot comprehend.

The whole-language method emphasizes *visually based retrieval:* the child looks at a whole word and then retrieves it from memory, with the help of contextual cues if necessary. Whole-language programs are built around real literature and open-ended, student-initiated activities, in contrast with the more rigorous, teacher-directed tasks involved in phonics instruction. Proponents argue that children learn to read better—and enjoy it more—if they see written language as a way to gain information and express ideas and feelings, not as a system of isolated sounds and syllables that must be learned by memorization and drill.

Despite the popularity of the whole-language approach, reviews of the literature have found little support for its claims (Stahl, McKenna, & Pagnucco, 1994; Stahl & Miller, 1989). Critics hold it largely responsible for the failure of an estimated 20 to 25 percent of schoolchildren to learn to read (Stedman & Kaestle, 1987). Due to difficulty in word identification, most children up to seventh or eighth grade do not understand what they read as well as what they hear (Sticht & James, 1984). Furthermore, attitudes toward reading—both recreational and academic—worsen from first grade on, especially among boys. Motivation for recreational reading declines fastest in the worst readers, and this trend grows stronger throughout elementary school (McKenna, Kear, & Ellsworth, 1995).

Critics claim that whole-language teaching encourages children to skim through a text, guessing at words and their meaning, and not to try to correct reading or spelling errors as long as the results "make sense." They say that reading, unlike talking, is a skill that must be taught; the brain is not programmed to acquire it. A long line of research supports the view that phonemic awareness and early phonics training are keys to reading proficiency (Hatcher, Hulme, & Ellis, 1994; Liberman & Liberman, 1990).

One phonological ability that has been shown to predict later reading scores is recognition of words that have the same beginning sounds (alliteration) or ending sounds (rhyme). In a well-known experiment in England (Bradley & Bryant, 1983, 1985), 4- and 5-year-olds who had tested poorly on alliteration and rhyme were trained not only in these skills but also in how letters "spell out" sounds (phonics). After two years of training, these children were eight to ten months ahead of a group that had been trained to categorize pictures and words by meaning, and they were also several months ahead of a third group trained only in alliteration and rhyme.

Some experts seek to combine the best of both the phonetic and whole-language approaches by teaching children phonetic skills along with strategies to help them understand what they read. Children who can select either visually based or phonetic strategies—using visual retrieval for familiar words and phonetic decoding as a backup for unfamiliar words—tend to develop stronger mental associations and can perform visual retrieval faster and more efficiently (Siegler, 1998).

Recently, efforts to improve the teaching of reading seem to be paying off. The 1998 National Assessment of Educational Progress showed significant increases in average reading scores in grades 4, 8, and 12 since 1994—the first time all three grades' averages have risen since the nationwide testing program began in 1971.

Writing

The acquisition of writing skill goes hand in hand with the development of reading. As children learn to translate the written word into speech, they also learn that they can reverse the process—that they can use written words to express spoken or unspoken ideas, thoughts, and feelings.

Writing is difficult for younger children, and early compositions are usually quite short. Often school writing assignments involve unfamiliar topics; children must organize diverse information from long-term memory and other sources. Unlike conversation, which offers constant feedback, writing provides no immediate sign of how well the child's communicative goals have been met. The child also must keep in mind a variety of rules regarding spelling, punctuation, grammar, and capitalization, as well as the basic physical task of forming letters (Siegler, 1998).

Young children, whose thinking is still somewhat egocentric, have difficulty separating what they know about a topic from what they can expect their readers to know, and they have more trouble finding errors in their own work than in the work of others. As children get older and can take more than one perspective, they spend more time planning their writing so as to present it in a way that their audience will understand. This forces them to notice any gaps, blind alleys, or contradictions in their own thinking. They begin to see weaknesses in their work and can revise it accordingly.

In the typical classroom children are discouraged from discussing their work with other children. This practice is based on the belief that children, especially friends, will distract one another, turn learning time into playtime, and prevent one another from doing their best work. Research based on Vygotsky's social interaction model of language development suggests that this is not so.

In one study, fourth-graders progressed more when they wrote with other children, especially friends. Children working in pairs wrote stories with more solutions to problems, more explanations and goals, and fewer errors in syntax and word use than did children working alone. Friends concentrated better than acquaintances and collaborated in complex ways, elaborating on each other's ideas, working as a team, and posing alternative ideas (Daiute, Hartup, Sholl, & Zajac, 1993).

CHECKPOINT

Can you . . .

- ✔ Summarize improvements in language skills during middle childhood?
- ✔ Compare the whole-language and code-emphasis methods of teaching reading and present arguments for each?
- ✔ Tell how and why reading comprehension improves?
- ✔ Explain why writing is harder for younger children than for older ones and why social interaction may improve children's writing?

The Child in School

"What will the teacher be like?" 6-year-old Julia wonders as she walks up the steps to the big red-brick schoolhouse, wearing her new backpack. "Will the work be too hard? Will the kids like me? What games will we play at recess?"

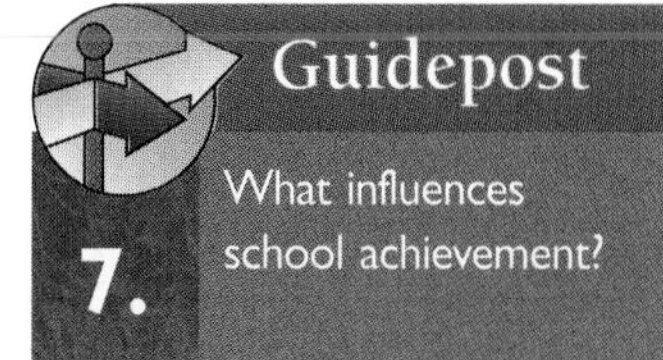
Guidepost
7.
What influences school achievement?

Even today, when many children go to preschool and most go to kindergarten, the start of first grade is often approached with a mixture of eagerness and anxiety. The first day of "regular" school is a milestone—a sign of the internal advances that make this new status possible.

Entering First Grade

The first-grade experience lays the foundation for a child's entire school career. Schooling is cumulative: the curriculum in each grade builds on what went before. So does the file that follows the child from year to year. This "paper trail" helps shape each new teacher's perceptions and expectations—expectations that can affect a student's achievement in the middle grades and even in high school. The first-grade report card is a forecast of what is to come—a more accurate predictor than initial test scores (Entwisle & Alexander, 1998).

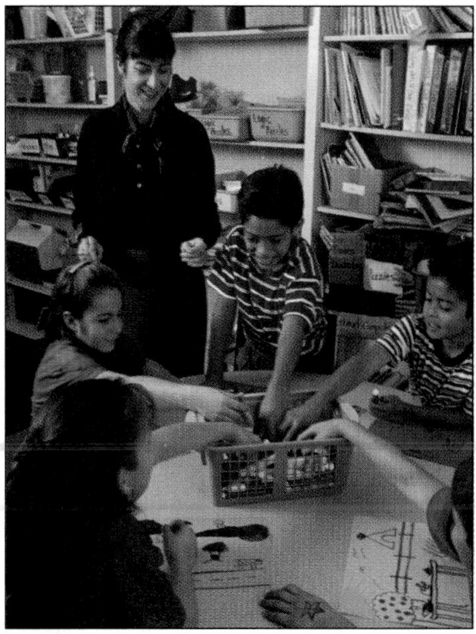

Children who participate actively tend to do well in school.

The Beginning School Study (BSS) has followed 790 randomly selected African American and white children in Baltimore since 1982, when they entered first grade (Entwisle & Alexander, 1998), and has identified factors that can ease the first-grade transition. One is the amount of kindergarten experience a child has had. Children who had attended full-day kindergarten did better on achievement tests and got higher marks in reading and math early in first grade than those who had attended kindergarten half days or not at all. Although the difference in test scores petered out by spring, the early advantage enjoyed by children with more kindergarten experience may have helped them get off to a better start.

Like many other studies, the BSS found that children in two-parent families did better than children in single-parent families, apparently because of economic disparities. However, children who lived with a mother and grandmother gained more in reading skills during first grade than other children of single parents, even though their economic situation was similar. Children whose grandmothers lived with them had better work habits, which translated into better marks. These findings are important because small differences in first-grade performance tend to enlarge later on. In the BSS, a 20-point gap on a standardized test of reading between first-graders from high-income and low-income families widened to more than 60 points five years later (Entwisle, Alexander, & Olson, 1997).

Interest, attention, and active participation (but not cooperativeness and compliance) were associated with achievement test scores and, even more so, with teachers' marks from first grade through at least fourth grade (K. L. Alexander, Entwisle, & Dauber, 1993). Apparently, to make the most academic progress, a child need not be polite and helpful but does need to be involved in what is going on in class. Since patterns of classroom behavior seem to be established in first grade, this crucial year offers a "window of opportunity" for parents and teachers to help a child form good learning habits.

CHECKPOINT

Can you . . .

✔ Explain the impact of the first-grade experience on a child's school career, and identify factors that affect success in first grade?

Environmental Influences on School Achievement

In addition to children's own characteristics, each level of the context of their lives, from the immediate family to what goes on in the classroom to the messages they receive from the larger culture (such as "It's not cool to be smart"), influences how well they do in school. Let's look at this "nest" of environmental influences.

The Family

Parents of achieving children provide a place to study and to keep books and supplies; they set times for meals, sleep, and homework; they monitor how much television their children watch and what their children do after school; and they show interest in their children's lives by talking with them about school and being involved in school activities. Parents' attitudes about homework directly affect their children's willingness to do it. As children get older, the responsibility for seeing that schoolwork gets done shifts from parent to child (Cooper, Lindsay, Nye, & Greathouse, 1998).

How do parents motivate children to do well? Some use *extrinsic* (external) means—giving children money or treats for good grades or punishing them for bad ones. Others encourage children to develop *intrinsic* (internal) motivation by praising them for ability and hard work. Intrinsic motivation seems more effective. In fact, some educators claim that even praise should be used sparingly, as it shifts the focus from the child's own motivation to the need to please others (Aldort, 1994). In a study of 77 third- and fourth-graders, those who were interested in the work itself did better in school than those who mainly sought grades or parents' approval (Miserandino, 1996).

Parenting styles may affect motivation. In one study, the highest achieving fifth-graders had *authoritative* parents (refer back to Chapter 8). These children were curious and interested in learning; they liked challenging tasks and enjoyed solving problems by themselves. *Authoritarian* parents, who kept after children to do their homework, supervised closely, and relied on extrinsic motivation, tended to have lower-achieving children. Perhaps such external control undermines children's ability to trust their own judgment about what they need to do to achieve success. Children of *permissive* parents, who were uninvolved and did not seem to care how the children did in school, also tended to be low achievers. Of course, since this was a correlational study, we cannot draw firm conclusions about the direction of causation. Parents of poor achievers may resort to bribes and threats and

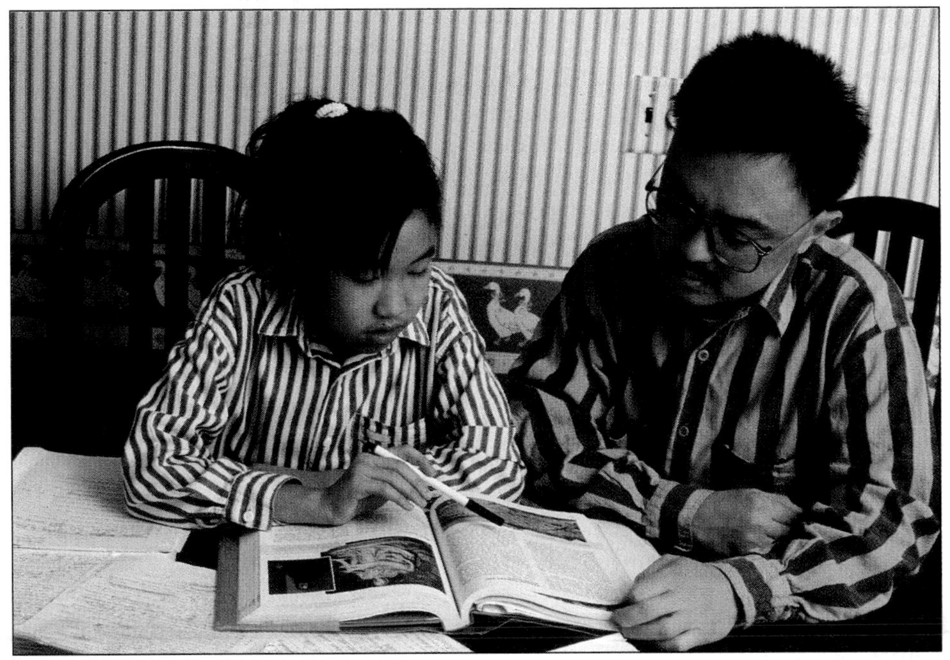

A parent's attitude about the importance of homework tends to "rub off" on a child. A parent whose child is motivated to achieve does not need to bribe or threaten to make sure that homework gets done.

may feel obliged to make sure homework gets done, while parents of children who are motivated and successful may not feel the need to offer rewards or punishments or to take such an active supervisory role (G. S. Ginsburg & Bronstein, 1993).

Socioeconomic status can have long-lasting effects on school achievement. When researchers followed 1,253 second- through fourth-graders for two to four years, those from low-income families tended to have lower reading and math achievement test scores, and the income gap in math achievement widened as time went on (Pungello, Kupersmidt, Burchinal, & Patterson, 1996). Apparently, socioeconomic status itself does not determine school achievement; the difference comes from its effects on family life. In a study of 90 rural African American families with firstborn children ages 9 to 12, parents with more education were likely to have higher incomes and to be more involved in the child's schooling. Higher-income families also tended to be more supportive and harmonious. Children growing up in a positive family atmosphere, whose mothers were involved in their schooling, tended to develop better self-regulation and to do better in school (G. H. Brody, Stoneman, & Flor, 1995).

In one longitudinal study, 8-year-olds whose home environment was cognitively stimulating had higher intrinsic motivation for academic learning at ages 9, 10, and 13 than children who lived in less stimulating homes. This was true over and above effects of SES (Gottfried, Fleming, & Gottfried, 1998).

Of the low-income African American children who attended the Perry Preschool (see Chapters 7 and 12), some did much better in school—and in adult life—than others. An important factor in the success of the higher-achieving children was the positive influence of parents who placed a high value on education and helped them overcome obstacles to obtaining it. Parents' expectations for their children also seemed to play a role, though it is hard to know whether children did well because their parents expected them to achieve or whether parents expected more of children who showed the potential to succeed (Luster & McAdoo, 1996).

Teacher Expectations

According to the principle of the **self-fulfilling prophecy,** children live up to—or down to—other people's expectations for them. In the "Oak School" experiment, teachers were falsely told at the beginning of the term that some students

self-fulfilling prophecy
False expectation or prediction of behavior that tends to come true because it leads people to act as if it already were true.

had shown unusual potential for cognitive growth, when these children actually had been chosen at random. Yet several months later, many of them showed unusual gains in IQ (R. Rosenthal & Jacobson, 1968).

Later analyses cast doubt on the power of the self-fulfilling prophecy, showing that its effects, on average, are small. Still, under certain conditions teachers' expectations can and do function as self-fulfilling prophecies (Jussim, Eccles, & Madon, 1996). This is why the early entries in a student's cumulative file can be so important. Performance can become self-perpetuating by fueling teacher expectations, which, in turn, influence student achievement as a child passes from class to class (Entwisle & Alexander, 1998).

Low achievers, especially, seem sensitive to the influence of teachers' positive perceptions. In a study of 1,539 sixth-grade math students in southeastern Michigan, previous low achievers whose teachers overestimated their ability in relation to their records made considerable gains on seventh-grade fall achievement tests (Madon, Jussim, & Eccles, 1997).

The Educational System

How can school best enhance children's development? Conflicting views, along with historical events, have brought great swings in educational theory and practice during the twentieth century. The traditional curriculum, centered on the "three R's" (reading, 'riting, and 'rithmetic), gave way first to "child-centered" methods that focused on children's interests and then, during the late 1950s, to an emphasis on science and mathematics to overcome the Soviet Union's lead in the space race. During the turbulent 1960s and early 1970s, rigorous studies were replaced by student-directed learning, electives, and "open classrooms," in which children chose their own activities. Then, a decline in high school students' scores on the Scholastic Aptitude Test (SAT) in the mid-1970s sent schools back to the "basics." In the 1980s, a series of governmental and educational commissions proposed plans for improvement, ranging from more homework to a longer school day and school year to a total reorganization of schools and curricula.

Today, many educators recommend teaching children in the primary grades in a way that integrates subject matter fields and builds on children's natural interests and talents: teaching reading and writing, for example, in the context of a social studies project or teaching math concepts through the study of music. They favor cooperative projects, hands-on problem solving, and close parent-teacher cooperation (Rescorla, 1991).

Consider this . . .

- Which approach to education do you favor for children in the primary grades: instruction in the "basics," or a more flexible, child-centered curriculum, or a combination of the two?

Many contemporary educators also emphasize a "fourth R": reasoning. Children who are taught thinking skills in the context of academic subject matter perform better on intelligence tests and in school (R. D. Feldman, 1986; Sternberg, 1984, 1985a, 1985c). Research on Sternberg's triarchic theory suggests that students learn better when taught in a variety of ways, emphasizing creative and practical skills as well as memorization and critical thinking (Sternberg, Torff, & Grigorenko, 1997, cited in Sternberg, 1997).

Opinions on homework have undergone swings reflecting the broad shifts in educational philosophy just outlined. Advocates of homework view it as an important way to discipline children's minds and develop good work habits, as well as to cover more ground than can be accomplished in the classroom alone. Champions of child-centered education claim that too much homework puts unnecessary pressure on children and keeps them from self-initiated activities.

In a survey of 709 second- through twelfth-graders and their parents and teachers, there was a strong relationship between upper-grade students' achievement and the amount of homework they completed (but not the amount the teacher assigned). The relationship between completed homework and achievement was weaker for children in the lower grades. The more homework younger children were given, the more negative their attitudes toward it; in fact, about one-third of the lower-grade students said they typically did not finish their homework. In the upper grades, too, students who received lengthy assignments tended not to complete them. These findings suggest that homework has value in moderation, but that teachers should consider students' developmental level. Sixth-graders are better able to take responsibility for doing their own homework than are second-graders (Cooper et al., 1998).

When the Chicago public schools in 1996 ended **social promotion,** the practice of promoting children who do not meet academic standards, many observers hailed the change, part of a multipronged effort to improve achievement in the city's schools. However, some educators maintain that forcing failing students to go to summer school or repeat a grade—a policy that could affect up to 15 percent of students in some inner-city schools—is a poor solution (Bronner, 1999). Although retention in some cases can be a "wake-up call," more often it is the first step on a remedial track that leads to lowered expectations, poor performance, and ultimately dropping out of school (J. M. Fields & Smith, 1998; McLeskey, Lancaster, & Grizzle, 1995). A number of countries with well-regarded educational systems, such as Denmark, Sweden, Norway, Japan, and South Korea have automatic promotion policies. Many educators say the only real solution to a high failure rate is to identify at-risk students early and intervene *before* they fail (Bronner, 1999).

social promotion
Policy in which children are automatically promoted from one grade to another even if they do not meet academic standards for the grade they are completing.

Computer literacy and the ability to navigate the World Wide Web are becoming classroom "musts," opening new possibilities for individualized instruction, global communication, and early training in independent research skills. Under the Telecommunications Act of 1997, the U.S. Federal Communications Commission has allotted $2.25 billion to help schools acquire the equipment necessary to make universal classroom Internet service a reality. However, this new tool poses dangers. Beyond the risk of exposure to harmful or inappropriate material, which involves issues of censorship, there is a need to teach students to critically evaluate information they find in cyberspace (some of which is inaccurate) and to separate facts from opinion and advertising (J. Lee, 1998). A focus on "visual literacy" may divert financial resources from other areas of the curriculum. Nor does use of computers necessarily improve basic skills. In a major international math and science examination, fourth-graders from 7 other countries out of 26 significantly outperformed U.S. fourth-graders on the math section, and teachers in 5 of these countries reported that students never or almost never used computers in class (Mullis et al., 1997).

CHECKPOINT

Can you . . .

✔ Tell how parental beliefs and practices can influence school success?

✔ Discuss the impact of socioeconomic status on school achievement?

✔ Evaluate the effects of teachers' perceptions and expectations?

✔ Trace major changes in educational philosophy and practice during the twentieth century?

The Culture

Why do so many students of East Asian extraction make such a strong showing in school? Cultural influences in these children's countries of origin, which carry over to children of the immigrant generation, may hold the key.

Educational practices in East Asian societies differ markedly from those in the United States (Song & Ginsburg, 1987; H. W. Stevenson, 1995; Stigler, Lee, & Stevenson, 1987). The school day and year are longer, and the curriculum is set centrally. Classes are larger (about 40 to 50), and teachers spend more time teaching the whole class, whereas U.S. children spend more time working alone or in small groups and thus receive more individual attention but less total instruction.

Although Asian cultures vary greatly, East Asian cultures share certain values that foster educational success, such as obedience, responsibility, and respect for elders (Chao, 1994). In Japan, a child's entrance into school is a major occasion for celebration. Japanese and Korean parents spend a great deal of time helping children with schoolwork. Japanese children who fall behind are tutored or go to *jukus,* private remedial and enrichment schools (McKinney, 1987; Song & Ginsburg, 1987).

Chinese and Japanese mothers view academic achievement as a child's most important pursuit (H. W. Stevenson, 1995; H. W. Stevenson, Chen, & Lee, 1993; H. W. Stevenson, Lee, Chen, & Lummis, 1990; H. W. Stevenson, Lee, Chen, Stigler,

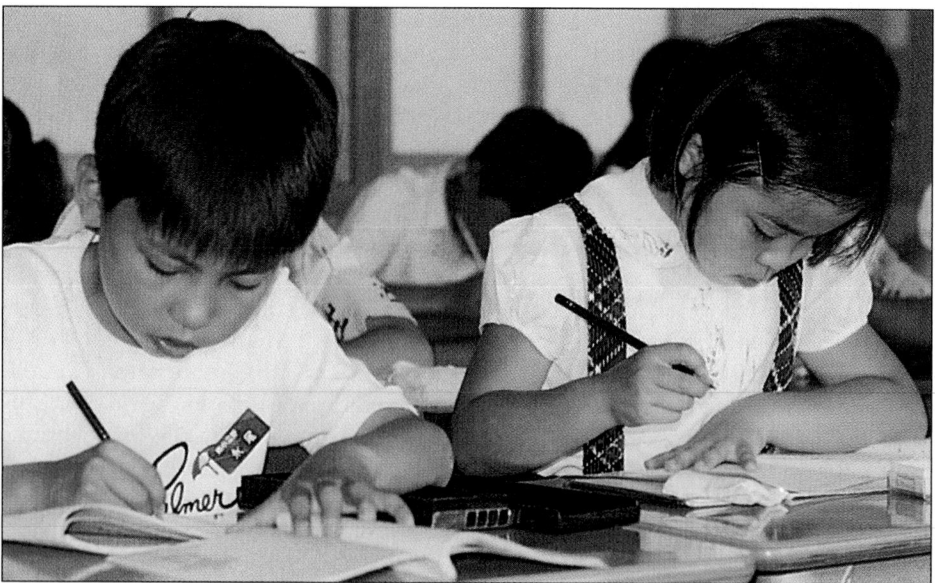

Children of East Asian extraction often do better in school than other U. S. youngsters. The reasons seem to be cultural, not genetic.

et al., 1990). Their children spend more time on homework, like it better, and get more parental help than U.S. children (C. Chen & Stevenson, 1989). Whereas U.S. students socialize after school and engage in sports and other activities, Asian students devote themselves almost entirely to study (Fuligni & Stevenson, 1995; H. W. Stevenson, 1995; H. W. Stevenson et al., 1993). Asian parents communicate an attitude that learning is valuable, mastery is satisfying, and effort is more important than ability; and their children are highly motivated to achieve (H. W. Stevenson, 1995).

Many Asian American families see education as the best route to upward mobility (Chao, 1996; Sue & Okazaki, 1990). Chinese American parents are strongly motivated to see that their children succeed in school. This means training them early in the values of hard work and discipline, teaching them specific skills, supervising homework, and, if necessary, driving them to excel. The child's school success is seen as a prime goal of parenting (Chao, 1994, 1996; Huntsinger & Jose, 1995).

Of course, as Asian American children grow up in U.S. culture and absorb its values, their attitudes toward learning may change (C. Chen & Stevenson, 1995). The influence of Asian culture may become weaker from one generation to the next. Research on second-, third-, and fourth-generation Asian Americans may help sort out the cultural influences on educational achievement.

Contrary to the experience of Asian Americans, some minority children whose cultures value different kinds of behavior than the dominant culture does are at a disadvantage in school (Helms, 1992; Tharp, 1989). The Kamehameha Early Education Program (KEEP) has produced dramatic improvements in primary-grade Hawaiian children's cognitive performance by designing educational programs to fit cultural patterns. Whereas children in non-KEEP classes score very low on standard achievement tests, children in KEEP classes approach national norms. A KEEP program also was established on the Navajo reservation in northern Arizona. Among the issues KEEP addresses are the following (Tharp, 1989):

- *Organization of the classroom:* Since Hawaiian culture values collaboration, cooperation, and assisted performance, children are placed in small groups of four to five students, who continually teach and learn from one another. For Navajo children, who are trained in self-sufficiency and are separated by sex from about age 8, groupings are most effectively limited to two or three children of the same sex.

- *Accommodation for language styles:* Hawaiians typically overlap one another's speech, a style of social involvement often interpreted by non-Hawaiian teachers as rude. By contrast, Navajos speak slowly, with frequent silent pauses. Non-Navajo teachers often interrupt, misinterpreting such pauses as signaling the end of a response. When teachers adjust their styles of speaking to their students', children participate more freely.
- *Adjustment for learning styles:* Whereas most western teaching stresses verbal and analytic thought, American Indians tend to think in visual, holistic patterns and learn by imitation, with little verbal instruction. Contrary to typical American classroom practice, Native American parents expect children to listen to an entire story without interruption before discussing it. Teachers can help children by acknowledging culturally different learning styles and helping children adjust to an unfamiliar style.

CHECKPOINT

Can you . . .

✔ Give reasons for the superior achievement of children of East Asian extraction, and identify some ways of addressing cultural differences in the classroom?

Second-Language Education

Guidepost

8. How do schools meet the needs of foreign-speaking children and those with learning problems?

Between 1979 and 1995, with rising immigration, the number of U.S. schoolchildren who have difficulty speaking English nearly doubled, from 1.25 million to 2.44 million (National Center for Education Statistics [NCES], 1997). A goal of the federal Equal Education Opportunity Act is for foreign-speaking students to learn English well enough to compete academically with native English speakers. How can this best be done?

Some schools use an **English-immersion** approach (sometimes called ESL, or English as a Second Language), in which minority children are immersed in English from the beginning, in special all-day or part-time classes. Other schools have adopted programs of **bilingual education,** in which children are taught in two languages, first learning academic subjects in their native language and then switching to English when they become more proficient in it. These programs can encourage children to become **bilingual** (fluent in two languages) and to feel pride in their cultural identity.

English-immersion
Approach to teaching English as a second language in which instruction is presented only in English from the outset of formal education.

bilingual education
A system of teaching foreign-speaking children in two languages—their native language and English—and later switching to all-English instruction after the children develop enough fluency in English.

bilingual
Fluent in two languages.

Advocates of early English-immersion claim that the sooner children are exposed to English and the more time they spend speaking it, the better they learn it (Rossel & Ross, 1986). Support for this view would seem to come from findings that the effectiveness of second-language learning declines from early childhood through late adolescence (Newport, 1991). On the other hand, proponents of bilingual programs claim that children progress faster academically in their

Advocates of bilingual instruction claim that children who learn in their native language as well as in English, like these fourth-graders, make faster academic progress than in English alone.

native language and later make a smoother transition to all-English classrooms (Padilla et al., 1991). Some educators maintain that the English-only approach stunts children's cognitive growth; because foreign-speaking children can understand only simple English at first, the curriculum must be watered down, and children are less prepared to handle complex material later (Collier, 1995).

Findings on the relative success of these approaches have been mixed. Furthermore, until recently most studies have focused only on how well children learn English, not on how well they do in school and society (Hakuta & Garcia, 1989). Now, large-scale research on the long-term academic achievement of children in high-quality second-language programs offers strong support for a bilingual approach (Collier, 1995; W. P. Thomas & Collier, 1995).

Researchers examined the elementary and high school records of 42,000 foreign-speaking students in five districts across the United States and compared their standardized achievement test scores and grade-point averages with those of native English speakers. In the primary grades, the type of language teaching made little difference; but from seventh grade on, differences were dramatic. Children who had remained in bilingual programs at least through sixth grade caught up with or even surpassed their native English-speaking peers, while the relative performance of those who had been in traditional immersion programs began to decline. By the end of high school, those in part-time ESL (immersion) programs—the least successful type—trailed 80 percent of native English speakers their age.

two-way (dual-language) learning
Approach to second-language education in which English speakers and foreign speakers learn together in their own and each other's languages.

Most successful was a third, less common approach: **two-way (dual-language) learning**, in which English-speaking and foreign-speaking children learn together in their own and each other's languages. This approach avoids any need to place minority children in separate classes. By valuing both languages equally, it helps build self-esteem and thus improve school performance. An added advantage is that English speakers learn a foreign language at an early age, when they can acquire it most easily (Collier, 1995; W. P. Thomas & Collier, 1995).

These findings echo earlier ones: the more bilingually proficient children are, the higher their cognitive achievement—as long as school personnel value bilingualism and the second language is added at no sacrifice to the first (Diaz, 1983; Padilla et al., 1991). Knowing one language does not interfere with learning a second, and learning the second does not rob a child of fluency in the first (Hakuta, Ferdman, & Diaz, 1987; Hakuta & Garcia, 1989). As we mentioned in Chapter 5, code switching seems to come naturally to children; they learn very early, for example, to talk differently to parents than to friends. When bilingualism rises to the level of *biliteracy* (proficiency in reading and writing two languages), which makes possible full participation in both cultures, we see the most positive effects (Huang, 1995).

CHECKPOINT

Can you . . .

✔ Describe and evaluate various types of second-language education?

Consider this . . .

- On the basis of the descriptions given, which approach to second-language education do you favor?

Children with Learning Problems

Just as educators have become more sensitive to teaching children from varied cultural backgrounds, they have also sought to meet the needs of children with special educational needs. Three of the most frequent sources of learning problems are mental retardation, attention deficit disorders, and learning disabilities.

Mental Retardation

mental retardation
Significantly subnormal cognitive functioning.

Mental retardation is significantly subnormal cognitive functioning. It is indicated by an IQ of about 70 or less, coupled with a deficiency in age-appropriate adaptive behavior (such as communication, social skills, and self-care), appearing before age 18. IQ alone is not enough for a diagnosis; the behavioral component is also important. About 1 percent of the U.S. population are mentally retarded; about 3 boys are affected for every 2 girls (APA, 1994).

Mildly retarded persons and those considered "borderline" (with IQs ranging from 70 up to about 85) can hold jobs and function fairly well in society. The profoundly retarded need constant care and supervision, usually in institutions.

In about 30 to 40 percent of cases, the cause of mental retardation is unknown. Known causes include problems in embryonic development, such as those caused by a mother's alcohol or drug use (30 percent); mental disorders, such as autism, and environmental influences, such as lack of nurturance (15 to 20 percent); problems in pregnancy and childbirth, such as fetal malnutrition or birth trauma (10 percent); hereditary conditions, such as Tay-Sachs disease (5 percent); and medical problems in childhood, such as trauma or lead poisoning (5 percent) (APA, 1994). Many cases of retardation may be preventable through such measures as genetic counseling, prenatal care, amniocentesis, routine screening and health care for newborns, and nutritional services for pregnant women and infants.

With a supportive and stimulating early environment and continued help and guidance, many mentally retarded children can expect a reasonably good outcome. Intervention programs have helped people who are mildly or moderately retarded to be more independent and to live in the community. Day care centers, hostels for retarded adults, and homemaking services for families caring for retarded children are less costly and more humane alternatives to institutional care. Most retarded children can benefit from schooling to enable them to become contributing members of society to the best of their ability.

Learning Disabilities

Nelson Rockefeller, former vice president of the United States, had so much trouble reading that he ad-libbed speeches instead of using a script. Rockefeller is one of many eminent persons, such as the World War II hero General George Patton, the inventor Thomas Edison, and the actress Whoopi Goldberg, who apparently have suffered from **dyslexia,** a developmental reading disorder in which reading achievement is substantially below the level predicted by IQ or age.

dyslexia
Developmental disorder in which reading achievement is substantially lower than predicted by IQ or age.

Dyslexia is the most commonly diagnosed of a large number of **learning disabilities (LDs),** disorders that interfere with specific aspects of school achievement, resulting in performance substantially lower than would be expected given a child's age, intelligence, and amount of schooling (APA, 1994). A growing number of children are classified as learning disabled—2.6 million in the 1995–1996 school year (T. D. Snyder, Hoffman, & Geddes, 1997). Learning-disabled (LD)

learning disabilities (LDs)
Disorders that interfere with specific aspects of learning and school achievement.

Children with dyslexia have trouble reading and writing, and often doing arithmetic, because they may confuse up and down and left and right. Dyslexia may be part of a more general language impairment.

children often have near-average to higher-than-average intelligence and normal vision and hearing, but they seem to have trouble processing sensory information. They tend to be less task oriented and more easily distracted than other children; they are less well organized as learners and less likely to use memory strategies (Feagans, 1983). Learning disabilities can have devastating effects on self-esteem as well as on the report card.

Four out of five learning-disabled children have dyslexia. Estimates of its prevalence range from 5 to 17.5 percent of the school population; it seems to affect boys and girls equally. Although some observers claim that what looks like dyslexia is often the result of poor teaching, it is now generally considered to be a chronic, persistent medical condition. It is heritable and runs in families (S. E. Shaywitz, 1998).

Most cases of dyslexia are believed to result from a neurological defect in processing speech sounds: an inability to recognize that words consist of smaller units of sound, which are represented by printed letters. This defect in phonological processing makes it hard to decode words but generally does not affect comprehension. Dyslexic children also may be weak in short-term verbal memory and other linguistic and cognitive skills (Morris et al., 1998; S. E. Shaywitz, 1998).

Brain imaging has revealed differences in the regions of the brain activated during phonological tasks in dyslexic as compared with normal readers (Horwitz, Rumsey, & Donohue, 1998; Shaywitz et al., 1998). In one such study, dyslexic boys used five times as much brain area to do oral language tasks as nondyslexic boys. The researchers also found chemical differences in brain functioning (T. L. Richards et al., 1999).

Dyslexia does not go away. Although dyslexic children can be taught to read through systematic phonological training, the process never becomes automatic, as it does with most readers (S. E. Shaywitz, 1998).

Mathematical disabilities involve difficulty in counting, comparing numbers, calculating, and remembering basic arithmetic facts. Each of these may involve distinct disabilities. One cause may be a neurological deficit. Of course, not all children who have trouble with arithmetic are learning disabled. Some haven't been taught properly, are anxious or have trouble reading or hearing directions, lack motivation to learn math, or have a developmental delay, which eventually disappears (Geary, 1993; Ginsburg, 1997; Roush, 1995).

Hyperactivity and Attention Deficits

attention-deficit/hyperactivity disorder (ADHD) Syndrome characterized by persistent inattention and distractibility, impulsivity, low tolerance for frustration, and inappropriate overactivity.

Attention-deficit/hyperactivity disorder (ADHD) is the behavioral disorder most commonly diagnosed in children (National Institutes of Health [NIH], 1998), affecting an estimated 2 to 11 percent or more of school-age children worldwide (Zametkin & Ernst, 1999) and 3 to 5 percent in the United States (NIH, 1998). It is marked by persistent inattention, distractibility, impulsivity, low tolerance for frustration, and a great deal of activity at the wrong time and the wrong place, such as the classroom (APA, 1994).

The disorder consists of a combination of two different sets of symptoms. Some children are inattentive but not hyperactive; others show the reverse pattern. However, in 85 percent of cases, the two kinds of behavior go together (Barkley, 1998a). These characteristics appear to some degree in most children; there is cause for concern when they are unusually frequent and so severe as to interfere with the child's functioning in school and in daily life (AAP Committee on Children with Disabilities and Committee on Drugs, 1996; Barkley, 1998b). Boys are at least three times as likely to be diagnosed as girls, perhaps because boys' behavior may be more disruptive (Barkley, 1998b; Zametkin & Ernst, 1999). More than 1 in 4 children with learning disabilities also has ADHD (Roush, 1995; Zametkin, 1995).

ADHD has a substantial genetic basis, with heritability approaching 80 percent (APA, 1994; Barkley, 1998b; Elia, Ambrosini, & Rapoport, 1999; Zametkin,

1995; Zametkin & Ernst, 1999). Other factors that may play a part in ADHD include premature birth, a mother's alcohol or tobacco use, exposure to high levels of lead, and brain injuries (Barkley, 1998b). Research has failed to substantiate any link between ADHD and food additives, such as artificial colorings and flavorings and the sugar substitute aspartame—or, for that matter, sugar itself (Barkley, 1998b; B. A. Shaywitz et al., 1994; Zametkin, 1995).

Brain imaging studies suggest that children with ADHD have unusually small brain structures in the prefrontal cortex and basal ganglia, the regions that inhibit impulses and regulate attention and self-control (refer back to Figure 4–6). Genetic alteration in these structures may diminish or delay the achievement of four essential cognitive functions: holding information in working memory; internalizing self-directed speech; controlling emotions and motivation; and analyzing and synthesizing behaviors in new ways so as to pursue goals. Children with ADHD tend to forget responsibilities, to speak aloud rather than giving themselves silent directions, to be easily frustrated or angered, and to give up when they don't see how to solve a problem. Parents and teachers may be able to help children with ADHD by giving them a structured environment: breaking down tasks into small "chunks," providing frequent prompts about rules and time, and giving frequent, immediate rewards for small accomplishments (Barkley, 1998b).

Although symptoms tend to decline with age, ADHD often persists into adolescence and adulthood and, if untreated, can lead to excessive injuries, academic problems, antisocial behavior, risky driving, and substance abuse (Barkley, 1998b; Barkley, Murphy, & Kwasnik, 1996; Elia et al., 1999; McGee, Partridge, Williams, & Silva, 1991; NIH, 1998; Wender, 1995; Zametkin, 1995). ADHD is generally treated with drugs, sometimes combined with behavioral therapy (see Chapter 2), counseling, training in social skills, and special classroom placement. Stimulants such as Ritalin, used in proper doses, appear to be safe and effective in the short run, but their long-run effects have not yet been shown (NIH, 1998; Rodrigues, 1999). They can dramatically improve concentration and behavior (AAP Committee on Children with Disabilities and Committee on Drugs, 1996; Elia et al., 1999; NIH, 1998; Zametkin, 1995; Zametkin & Ernst, 1999).

A 14-month randomized study of 579 children with ADHD, conducted by researchers at six universities assembled by the National Institutes of Health, found a carefully monitored program of Ritalin treatment, alone or in combination with behavior modification, more effective than the behavioral therapy alone or standard community care. In some children with related problems, such as depression, anxiety, and disruptive behavior, the combined treatment was more beneficial and sometimes led to better school achievement, relationships with parents, and social skills (MTA Cooperative Group, 1999).

Educating Children with Disabilities

The Individuals with Disabilities Education Act (IDEA) ensures a free, appropriate public education for all children with disabilities in the United States. More than half (51 percent) of covered children are learning disabled, 22 percent are speech-impaired, 11 percent are mentally retarded, and 9 percent have serious emotional disturbances (Terman, Larner, Stevenson, & Behrman, 1996).

Under the law, an individualized program must be designed for each child, with parental involvement. Children must be educated in the "least restrictive environment" appropriate to their needs: that means, whenever possible, the regular classroom. Many of these students can be served by "inclusion" programs, in which they are integrated with nondisabled youngsters for all or part of the day. Inclusion can help children with disabilities learn to get along in society and can let nondisabled children know and understand people with disabilities.

CHECKPOINT

Can you . . .

- ✔ Describe the causes and prognoses for three common types of conditions that interfere with learning?
- ✔ Discuss the impact of federal requirements for the education of children with disabilities?

One potential problem with inclusion is that children with learning disabilities may be evaluated by unrealistic standards, resulting in their being held back and made to repeat grades. This has already happened on a large scale in some schools, despite evidence that retention is ineffective even with children of normal abilities (McLeskey et al., 1995).

Gifted Children

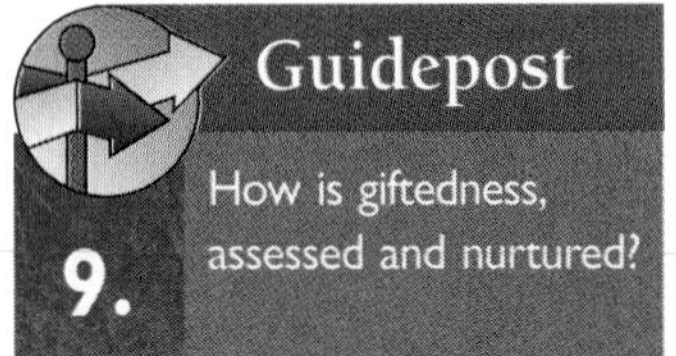

Giftedness, like intelligence, is hard to define and measure. Educators disagree on who qualifies as gifted and on what basis, and what kinds of educational programs these children need. Another source of confusion is that creativity and artistic talent are sometimes viewed as aspects or types of giftedness and sometimes as independent of it (Hunsaker & Callahan, 1995).

Identifying Gifted Children

The traditional criterion of giftedness is high general intelligence, as shown by an IQ score of 130 or higher. This definition tends to exclude highly creative children (whose unusual answers often lower their test scores), children from minority groups (whose abilities may not be well developed, though the potential is there), and children with specific aptitudes (who may be only average or even show learning problems in other areas). Most states and school districts have therefore adopted a broader definition, which includes children who have shown high *potential* or *achievement* in one or more of the following: general intellect, specific aptitude (such as in mathematics or science), creative or productive thinking, leadership, talent in the arts (such as painting, writing, music, or acting), and psychomotor ability (Cassidy & Hossler, 1992). Many school districts now use multiple criteria for admission to programs for the gifted, including achievement test scores, grades, classroom performance, creative production, parent and teacher nominations, and student interviews; but IQ remains an important, and sometimes the determining, factor (Reis, 1989).

CHECKPOINT

Can you . . .

✔ Tell how gifted children are identified?

The Lives of Gifted Children

A classic longitudinal study of gifted children began in 1921, when Lewis M. Terman (who brought the Binet intelligence test to the United States) identified more than 1,500 California children with IQs of 135 or higher. The study de-

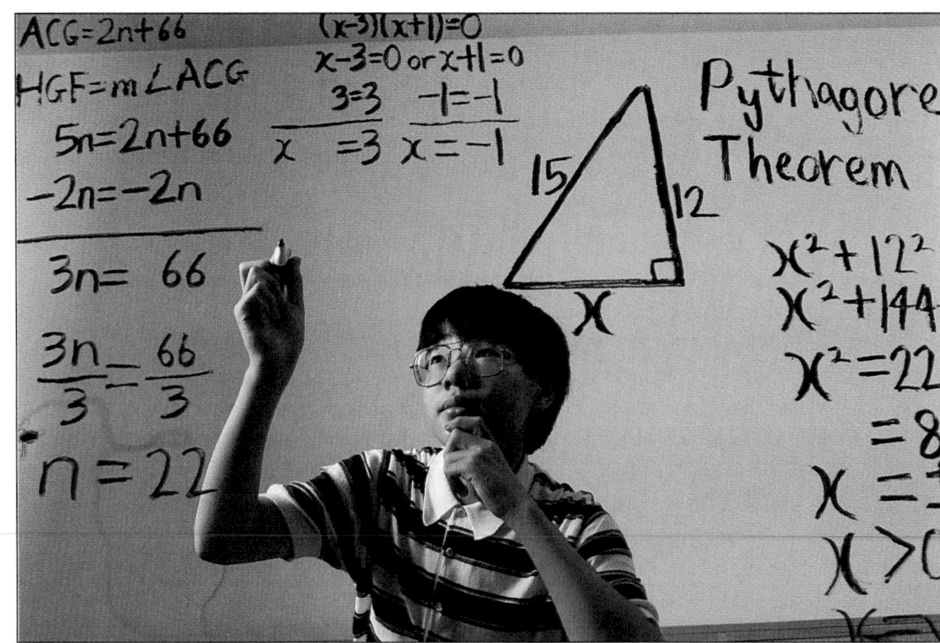

Mahito Takahashi of New Jersey made a perfect score in a worldwide mathematics Olympiad and has won close to 200 other awards. A well-rounded youngster, he signs in a chamber choir and acted in a school production of Shakespeare's *Romeo and Juliet.* The key to helping such children achieve lies in recognizing and nurturing their natural gifts.

molished the widespread stereotype of the bright child as a puny, pasty-faced bookworm. These children were taller, healthier, better coordinated, better adjusted, and more popular than the average child (Wallach & Kogan, 1965), and their cognitive, scholastic, and vocational superiority has held up for nearly eighty years. They were ten times more likely than a comparison group to graduate from college and three times more likely to be elected to honorary societies such as Phi Beta Kappa. By midlife, they were highly represented in such listings as *Who's Who in America*. Almost 90 percent of the men were in the professions or in higher echelons of business, and the women also made a good showing, at a time when there was far less emphasis on careers for women than there is today (Terman & Oden, 1959). (In Chapter 17, we discuss findings on the Terman group in late life.)

On the other hand, none of Terman's sample grew up to be Einsteins, and those with the highest IQs became no more illustrious than those who were only moderately gifted. This lack of a close correlation between childhood giftedness and adult eminence has been supported by later research (Winner, 1997). Although most gifted children are highly motivated, they may lack the insatiable drive and "furious impulse to understand" (Michelmore, 1962, p. 24) that characterize an Einstein.

Defining and Measuring Creativity

One definition of *creativity* is the ability to see things in a new light—to produce something never seen before or to discern problems others fail to recognize and find new and unusual solutions. High creativity and high academic intelligence do not necessarily go hand in hand. The Terman sample did not produce a great musician, an exceptional painter, or a Nobel Prize winner. Other classic research found only modest correlations between creativity and IQ (Anastasi & Schaefer, 1971; Getzels, 1964, 1984; Getzels & Jackson, 1962, 1963). Creative thinking seems to require different abilities from those needed to do exceptionally well in school.

J. P. Guilford (1956, 1959, 1960, 1967, 1986) distinguished between two kinds of thinking: *convergent* and *divergent*. **Convergent thinking**—the kind IQ tests measure—seeks a single correct answer; **divergent thinking** comes up with a wide array of fresh possibilities. Tests of creativity call for divergent thinking. The Torrance Tests of Creative Thinking (Torrance, 1966, 1974; Torrance & Ball, 1984), among the most widely known tests of creativity, include such tasks as listing unusual uses for a paper clip, completing a figure, and writing down what a sound brings to mind.

One problem with many of these tests is that the score depends partly on speed, which is not a hallmark of creativity. Moreover, although the tests yield fairly reliable results, there is dispute over whether they are valid—whether they identify children who are creative in everyday life (Anastasi, 1988; Mansfield & Busse, 1981; Simonton, 1990). As Guilford recognized, divergent thinking may not be the only, or even the most important, factor in creative performance.

convergent thinking
Thinking aimed at finding the one "right" answer to a problem. Compare *divergent thinking*.

divergent thinking
Thinking that produces a variety of fresh, diverse possibilities. Compare *convergent thinking*.

enrichment
Approach to educating the gifted, which broadens and deepens knowledge and skills through extra activities, projects, field trips, or mentoring.

acceleration
Approach to educating the gifted, which moves them through the curriculum, or part of it, at an unusually rapid pace.

Educating Gifted, Creative, and Talented Children

Most states have special programs for the gifted; about 6 percent of public school children participate (U.S. Department of Education, 1996). These programs either supplement or substitute for the usual curriculum. They generally follow one of two approaches: *enrichment* or *acceleration*. **Enrichment** broadens and deepens knowledge and skills through extra classroom activities, research projects, field trips, or coaching by mentors (experts in a child's field of talent or interest). **Acceleration,** often recommended for highly gifted children, speeds up their education by early school entrance, by grade skipping, by placement in fast-paced classes, or by advanced courses in specific subjects, offered through university-based programs. Moderate acceleration does not seem to harm social adjustment, at least in the long run (Winner, 1997).

CHECKPOINT

Can you . . .

- ✔ Discuss the relationships between giftedness and life achievements and between IQ and creativity?
- ✔ Describe two approaches to education of gifted children?

> ## Consider this . . .
>
> - On the basis of the information in this section, would you favor strengthening, cutting back, or eliminating special educational programs for gifted students? Should IQ carry more or less weight than other factors in admitting students to such programs?

Children in gifted programs not only make academic gains but also tend to improve in self-concept and social adjustment (Ford & Harris, 1996). However, competition for funding and opposition to "elitism" threatens the continuation of these programs (Purcell, 1995; Winner, 1997). Some educators advocate moving away from an all-or-nothing definition of giftedness and including a wider range of students in more flexible programs (J. Cox, Daniel, & Boston, 1985; Feldhusen, 1992; R. D. Feldman, 1985). Some say that if the level of education were significantly improved for all children, only the most exceptional would need special classes (Winner, 1997). In the coming years, the nation will continue to grapple with how best to educate its most promising children while not shortchanging other children.

There is no firm dividing line between being gifted and not being gifted, creative and not creative. All children benefit from being encouraged in their areas of interest and ability. What we learn about fostering intelligence, creativity, and talent in the most able youngsters may help all children make the most of their potential. The degree to which they do this will affect their self-concept and other aspects of personality, as we discuss in Chapter 10.

Summary

PHYSICAL DEVELOPMENT

Aspects of Physical Development

Guidepost 1. What gains in growth and motor development occur during middle childhood, and what nutritional hazards do children face?

- Physical development is less rapid in middle childhood than in earlier years. Boys are slightly larger than girls at the beginning of this period, but girls undergo the growth spurt of adolescence earlier and thus tend to be larger than boys at the end of middle childhood.
- On average, children need 2,400 calories a day for normal growth and health.
- The permanent teeth arrive in middle childhood. Dental health has improved, mainly because of use of fluoride and better dental care.
- Obesity is increasingly common among U.S. children. It is influenced by genetic and environmental factors. Concern with **body image,** especially among girls, may lead to eating disorders.
- Malnutrition can affect all aspects of development.
- Because of improved motor development, boys and girls in middle childhood can engage in a wider range of motor activities than preschoolers.
- About 10 percent of schoolchildren's free-play is **rough-and-tumble play.** It is more common among boys than among girls.
- Differences in boys' and girls' motor abilities increase as puberty approaches, in part due to boys' growing size and strength and in part due to cultural expectations and experience.

Health and Safety

Guidepost 2. What are the principal health, fitness, and safety concerns about school-age children?

- Middle childhood is a relatively healthy period; most children are immunized against major illnesses, and the death rate is the lowest in the life span. However, many children, especially girls, do not meet fitness standards.
- Respiratory infections and other **acute medical conditions** are common at this age. **Chronic medical conditions,** such as asthma, are most prevalent among poor and minority children. Children's understanding of health and illness is related to their cognitive level.
- Vision becomes keener during middle childhood, but a minority of children have defective vision or hearing.
- Children who are HIV-positive or have AIDS may suffer from social stigma and from cognitive, linguistic, or emotional problems.
- Accidents are the leading cause of death in middle childhood. Use of bicycle helmets and avoidance of trampolines can greatly reduce injuries.

COGNITIVE DEVELOPMENT

Piagetian Approach: The Concrete Operational Child

Guidepost 3. How is school-age children's thinking and moral reasoning different from that of younger children?

- A child from about age 7 to age 12 is in Piaget's stage of **concrete operations.** Children are less egocentric than before and are more proficient at tasks requiring logical reasoning, such as spatial thinking, understanding of causality, categorization (including **seriation, transitive inference,** and **class inclusion**), **inductive reasoning, deductive reasoning,** conservation, and working with numbers. However, their reasoning is largely limited to the here and now. This concreteness of thought results in **horizontal décalage.**

- Cultural experience seems to contribute to the rate of development of Piagetian skills.
- According to Piaget, moral development is linked with cognitive maturation and occurs in two stages: **morality of constraint,** which corresponds roughly to the preoperational stage, and **morality of cooperation,** which corresponds to the stages of concrete operations and formal operations.

Other Approaches to Cognitive Development

Guidepost 4. What advances in memory and other information-processing skills occur during middle childhood?

- Information-processing models describe three steps in memory: **encoding, storage,** and **retrieval.**
- Although **sensory memory** shows little change with age, the capacity of **working memory** increases greatly during middle childhood. The **central executive,** which controls the flow of information to and from **long-term memory,** seems to mature between ages 8 and 10. Reaction time, processing speed, selective attention, and concentration also increase. These gains in information-processing abilities may help explain the advances Piaget described.
- **Metamemory** and selective attention improve during these years, and children become more adept at using **mnemonic strategies,** such as **external memory aids, rehearsal, organization,** and **elaboration.**

Guidepost 5. How accurately can schoolchildren's intelligence be measured?

- The intelligence of school-age children may be assessed by group tests such as the **Otis-Lennon School Ability Test** or individual tests such as the **Wechsler Intelligence Scale for Children (WISC-III)** and Stanford-Binet. Although these are intended as **aptitude tests,** not **achievement tests,** they are validated against measures of achievement.
- IQ tests are good predictors of school success but may be unfair to some children. Attempts to devise **culture-free** or **culture-fair** tests, so as to avoid **cultural bias,** have not been successful.
- Conventional IQ tests may miss important aspects of intelligent behavior. IQ tests tap only three of the "intelligences" in Howard Gardner's **theory of multiple intelligences.** According to Robert Sternberg's **triarchic theory of intelligence,** IQ tests measure mainly the **componential element** of intelligence, not the **experiential** and **contextual elements.**
- New directions in intelligence testing include such tools as the **Kaufman Assessment Battery for Children (K-ABC)** and the **Sternberg Triarchic Abilities Tests (STAT).**
- Differences in IQ among ethnic groups appear to result at least in part from socioeconomic and other environmental differences. Schooling seems to increase measured intelligence.

Language and Literacy

Guidepost 6. How do communicative abilities and literacy expand during middle childhood?

- Use of vocabulary, grammar, and syntax become increasingly sophisticated, but the major area of linguistic growth is in **pragmatics.**
- **Metacognition** contributes to progress in reading. Early phonics training is a key to proficiency in decoding words.
- Interaction with peers aids in the development of writing skills.

The Child in School

Guidepost 7. What influences school achievement?

- Because schooling is cumulative, the foundation laid in first grade is very important.
- Parents influence children's learning by becoming involved in their schooling, motivating them to achieve, and transmitting attitudes about learning. Socioeconomic status can influence parental behavior and attitudes.
- Although the power of the **self-fulfilling prophecy** may not be as great as was once thought, teachers' perceptions and expectations can have a strong influence, especially on low achievers.
- Shifts in educational philosophy affect such issues as amount of homework assigned and **social promotion.** Computer literacy is becoming a universal requirement.
- The superior achievement of children of East Asian extraction seems to stem from cultural factors. Some minority children can benefit from educational programs adapted to their cultural styles.

Guidepost 8. How do schools meet the needs of foreign-speaking children and those with learning problems?

- Many school districts have implemented programs of second-language education. Some programs take an **English-immersion** approach, but high-quality programs of **bilingual education,** which enable children to become **bilingual** and feel pride in their cultural identity, appear to be more effective. Most effective of all is a less widely used approach: **two-way (dual-language) learning.**
- Three frequent sources of learning problems are **mental retardation, learning disabilities (LDs),** and **attention-deficit/hyperactivity disorder (ADHD). Dyslexia,** the most common learning disability, is believed to stem from a defect in phonological processing.
- In the United States, all children with disabilities are entitled to a free, appropriate education. Children must be educated in the least restrictive environment possible, often in the regular classroom.

Guidepost 9. How is giftedness assessed and nurtured?

- An IQ of 130 or higher is a common standard for identifying gifted children for special programs. Broader definitions of giftedness include **creativity,** artistic talent, and other attributes and rely on multiple criteria for identification. Minorities are underrepresented in programs for the gifted.

- In Terman's classic longitudinal study of gifted children, most turned out to be well adjusted and successful, but not outstandingly so.
- Creativity and IQ are not closely linked. Tests of creativity attempt to measure **divergent thinking** rather than **convergent thinking,** but their validity has been questioned.
- Special educational programs for gifted, creative, and talented children stress **enrichment** or **acceleration.** Critics consider such programs elitist, but they do benefit the children involved.

Key Terms

body image (325)
rough-and-tumble play (327)
acute medical conditions (329)
chronic medical conditions (329)
concrete operations (331)
seriation (333)
transitive inference (333)
class inclusion (333)
inductive reasoning (333)
deductive reasoning (333)
horizontal décalage (334)
morality of constraint (336)
morality of cooperation (336)
encoding (338)
storage (338)
retrieval (338)
sensory memory (338)
working memory (338)
central executive (338)
long-term memory (338)
metamemory (339)
mnemonic strategies (339)
external memory aids (339)
rehearsal (339)
organization (340)
elaboration (340)
aptitude tests (341)
achievement tests (341)
Otis-Lennon School Ability Test (341)
Wechsler Intelligence Scale for Children (WISC-III) (341)
cultural bias (342)
culture-free (342)
culture-fair (342)
theory of multiple intelligences (342)
triarchic theory of intelligence (343)
componential element (343)
experiential element (343)
contextual element (343)
Kaufman Assessment Battery for Children (K-ABC) (344)
Sternberg Triarchic Abilities Test (STAT) (344)
pragmatics (347)
metacognition (347)
self-fulfilling prophecy (351)
social promotion (353)
English-immersion (355)
bilingual education (355)
bilingual (355)
two-way (dual-language) learning (356)
mental retardation (356)
dyslexia (357)
learning disabilities (LDs) (357)
attention-deficit/hyperactivity disorder (ADHD) (358)
convergent thinking (361)
divergent thinking (361)
enrichment (361)
acceleration (361)

Chapter 10

Psychosocial Development in Middle Childhood

OUTLINE

Have you ever felt like nobody? Just a tiny speck of air. When everyone's around you, And you are just not there.

Karen Crawford, age 9

Marian Anderson

Focus: Marian Anderson, Operatic Trailblazer*

The African American contralto Marian Anderson (1902–1993) had—in the words of the great Italian conductor Arturo Toscanini—a voice heard "once in a hundred years." She was also a pioneer in breaking racial barriers. Turned away by a music school in her home town of Philadelphia, she studied voice privately and in 1925 won a national competition to sing with the New York Philharmonic. She performed in European capitals throughout the 1930s but was often forced to put up with second-class treatment at home. When she was refused the use of a concert hall in Washington, D.C., First Lady Eleanor Roosevelt arranged for her to sing on the steps of the Lincoln Memorial. The unprecedented performance on Easter Sunday, 1939, drew 75,000 people and was broadcast to millions. Several weeks later, Marian Anderson was the first black singer to perform at the White House. But not until 1955, a year after the Supreme Court outlawed segregated public schools, did Anderson, at age 57, become the first person of her race to sing with New York's Metropolitan Opera.

A remarkable story lies behind this woman's "journey from a single rented room in South Philadelphia" (McKay, 1992, p. xxx). It is a story of nurturing family ties—bonds of mutual support, care, and concern that extended from generation to generation.

Marian Anderson was the eldest child of John and Annie Anderson. Two years after her birth, the family left their one-room apartment to move in with her father's parents and then, after two more baby girls came along, into a small rented house nearby. John Anderson supported his family by peddling coal and ice, among other jobs.

Marian's parents encouraged her love of singing. At the age of 6, she joined the junior choir at church. There she made a friend, Viola Johnson, who lived across the street from the Andersons. Within a year or two, they sang a duet together—Marian's first public performance. Two years later, Marian began singing with the senior choir, doing duets with her aunt, who also arranged for her to perform in a benefit concert.

When Marian was 10, her beloved father died, and the family again moved in with his parents, his sister, and her two daughters. Marian's grandfather had a steady job. Her grandmother took care of all the children, her aunt ran the house, and her mother contributed by cooking dinners, working as a cleaning woman, and taking in laundry, which Marian and her sister Alyce delivered.

Years later, the singer had vivid memories of her grandmother: "What she said was law. . . . Grandmother loved children and always had scads of them living in her house. . . . [She] saw to it that we each had our little jobs to do. . . . And there were useful things for us to learn, . . . how to share a home with others, how to understand their ways and respect their rights and privileges" (Anderson, 1992, pp. 17–18).

But the most important influence in Marian Anderson's life was the counsel, example, and spiritual guidance of her hardworking, unfailingly supportive mother. Annie Anderson, who had been a teacher in her home state of Virginia, placed great importance on her children's schooling and saw to it that they didn't skimp on homework. Even when she was working full time, she cooked their dinner every night, and she taught Marian to sew her own clothes. "Not once can I recall . . . hearing Mother lift her voice to us in anger," Marian wrote. "When she corrected us she used a conversational tone. She could be firm, and we learned to respect her wishes" (Anderson, 1992, p. 92).

When Marian Anderson became a world-renowned concert artist, she often returned to her old neighborhood in Philadelphia. Her mother and sister Alyce shared a modest house, and the other sister, Ethel, lived next door with her son.

"It is the pleasantest thing in the world to go into that home and feel its happiness, . . ." the singer wrote. "They are all comfortable, and they cherish and protect one another. . . . I know that it warms [Mother] to have her grandson near her as he grows up, just as I think that when he gets to be a man, making his own life, he will have pleasant memories of his home and family" (1992, p. 93). In 1992, Marian Anderson—widowed, childless, and frail at age 95—went to live with that nephew, James DePriest, then music director of the Oregon Symphony. She died of a stroke at his home the following year.

*The chief source of biographical material about Marian Anderson and her family was Anderson (1992). Some details come from Kernan (1993) and from obituaries published in *Time* (April 19, 1993), *People Weekly, The New Yorker,* and *Jet* (April 26, 1993).

Marian Anderson "lived through momentous changes in America and the world" and in African American life (McKay, 1992, p. xxiv), but one thing that never changed was the strong, supportive network of relationships that sustained her and her family. The kind of household a child lives in, and the relationships within the household, can have profound effects on psychosocial development in middle childhood, when children are developing a stronger sense of what it means to be responsible, contributing members, first of a family, and then of society. The family is part of a web of contextual influences, including the peer group, the school, and the neighborhood in which the family lives. Marian

Anderson's first friend, her church choir, and the neighbors for whom she did odd jobs to earn the price of a violin all played parts in her development. Above and beyond these influences were the overarching cultural patterns of time and place, which presented special challenges to African American families and communities and called forth mutually supportive responses.

In this chapter, we trace the rich and varied emotional and social lives of school-age children. We see how youngsters develop a more realistic concept of themselves and how they become more independent, self-reliant, and in control of their emotions. Through being with peers (like Marian Anderson's friend Viola Johnson) they make discoveries about their own attitudes, values, and skills. Still, as Anderson's story shows, the family remains a vital influence. Children's lives are affected, not only by the way parents approach the task of child raising, but by whether and how they are employed, by the family's economic circumstances, and by its structure, or composition — whether the child lives with one parent or two; whether or not the child has siblings, and how many; and whether or not the household includes other relatives, such as Anderson's grandparents, aunt, and cousins. Although most children are emotionally healthy, some have mental health problems; we look at several of these. We also describe resilient children, who emerge from the stresses of childhood healthier and stronger.

After you have read and studied this chapter, you should be able to answer the following questions:

Guideposts *for* Study

1. How do school-age children develop a realistic self-concept, and what contributes to self-esteem?
2. How do school-age children show emotional growth?
3. How do parent-child relationships change in middle childhood?
4. What are the effects of parents' work and of poverty on family atmosphere?
5. What impact does family structure have on children's development?
6. How are relationships with grandparents affected by divorce, mothers' employment, and other family situations?
7. How do siblings influence and get along with one another?
8. How do relationships with peers change in middle childhood, and what influences popularity and choice of friends?
9. What are the most common forms of aggressive behavior in middle childhood, and what influences contribute to it?
10. What are some common emotional disturbances, and how are they treated?
11. How do the stresses of modern life affect children, and what enables "resilient" children to withstand them?

The Developing Self

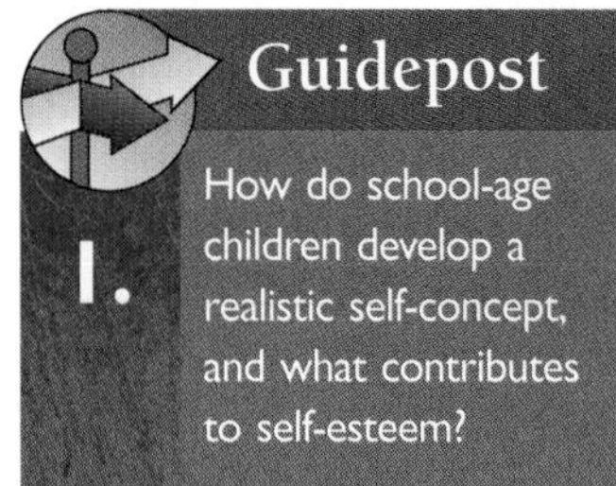
Guidepost
1.
How do school-age children develop a realistic self-concept, and what contributes to self-esteem?

The cognitive growth that takes place during middle childhood enables youngsters to develop more complex concepts of themselves and to grow in emotional understanding and control.

Representational Systems: A Neo-Piagetian View

Children as young as 4 show by their behavior that they have a sense of self-worth, but judgments about the self become more realistic, more balanced, more comprehensive, and more consciously expressed in middle childhood (Harter, 1996, 1998).

"At school I'm feeling pretty smart in certain subjects, Language Arts and Social Studies," says 8-year-old Lisa. "I got A's in these subjects on my last report card and was really proud of myself. But I'm feeling really dumb in Arithmetic and Science, particularly when I see how well the other kids are doing. . . . I still like myself as a person, because Arithmetic and Science just aren't that important to me. How I look and how popular I am are more important" (Harter, 1996, p. 208).

representational systems In neo-Piagetian terminology, third stage in development of self-definition, characterized by breadth, balance, and the integration and assessment of various aspects of the self.

Around age 7 or 8, children reach the third of the neo-Piagetian stages of self-concept development described in Chapter 8. Children now have the cognitive ability to form **representational systems:** broad, inclusive self-concepts that integrate different aspects of the self (Harter, 1993, 1996, 1998). Lisa can focus on more than one dimension of herself. She has outgrown an all-or-nothing, black-or-white self-definition; she recognizes that she can be "smart" in certain subjects and "dumb" in others. Her self-descriptions are more balanced; she can verbalize her self-concept better, and she can weigh different aspects of it ("How I look and how popular I am are more important . . . "). She can compare her *real self* with her *ideal self* and can judge how well she measures up to social standards in comparison with others. All of these changes contribute to the development of self-esteem, her assessment of her *global self-worth* ("I like myself as a person").

Self-Esteem

Kendall has high self-esteem. He is confident, curious, and independent. He trusts his own ideas, approaches challenges and initiates new activities with confidence, describes himself positively, and takes pride in his work. He adjusts fairly easily to change, tolerates frustration, perseveres in pursuing a goal, and can handle criticism. Kerry, by contrast, has low self-esteem. He describes himself negatively, does not trust his own ideas, lacks confidence and pride in his work, seems depressed, sits apart from other children, and hangs back and watches instead of exploring on his own. He gives up easily when frustrated and reacts immaturely to stress.

What accounts for the striking difference between these two boys? Why does one have such positive feelings about himself, while the other has such negative ones?

industry versus inferiority In Erikson's theory, the fourth critical alternative of psychosocial development, occurring during middle childhood, in which children must learn the productive skills their culture requires or else face feelings of inferiority.

According to Erikson (1982), a major determinant of self-esteem is children's view of their capacity for productive work. The issue to be resolved in the crisis of middle childhood is **industry versus inferiority.** The "virtue" that develops with successful resolution of this crisis is *competence,* a view of the self as able to master skills and complete tasks.

Children have to learn skills valued in their society. Arapesh boys in New Guinea learn to make bows and arrows and to lay traps for rats; Arapesh girls learn to plant, weed, and harvest. Inuit children of Alaska learn to hunt and fish. Children in industrialized countries learn to read, write, count, and use computers. Like Marian Anderson, many children learn household skills and help out with odd jobs. Children compare their abilities with those of their peers; if they feel inadequate, they may retreat to the protective embrace of the family. If, on

Middle childhood, according to Erikson, is a time for learning the skills one's culture considers important. In driving geese to market, this Vietnamese girl is developing a sense of competence and gaining self-esteem. In addition, by taking on responsibilities to match her growing capabilities, she learns about how her society works, her role in it, and what it means to do a job well.

the other hand, they become too industrious, they may neglect social relationships and turn into "workaholics."

A different view of the sources of self-worth comes from research by Susan Harter (1985, 1990, 1993). Harter (1985) asked 8- to 12-year olds to rate their appearance, behavior, school performance, athletic ability, and acceptance by other children and to assess how much each of these areas affected their opinion of themselves. The children rated physical appearance most important. Social acceptance came next. Less critical were schoolwork, conduct, and athletics. In contrast, then, to the high value Erikson placed on mastery of skills, Harter suggests that today's school-age children, at least in North America, judge themselves more by good looks and popularity.

A major contributor to self-esteem is social support—first, from parents and classmates, then from friends and teachers. Do they like and care about the child? Do they treat the child as a person who matters and has valuable things to say? Even if Mike thinks it's important to be handsome and smart and considers himself both, his self-esteem will suffer if he does not feel valued by the important people in his life. Still, social support generally will not compensate for a low self-evaluation. If Juanita thinks sports are important but that she is not athletic, she will lose self-esteem no matter how much praise she gets from others.

Children who are socially withdrawn or isolated (like Kerry in our opening example) may be overly concerned about their performance in social situations. They may attribute rejection to their own personality deficiencies, which they believe they are helpless to change. Rather than trying new ways to gain approval, they repeat unsuccessful strategies or just give up. (This is similar to the "helpless pattern" in younger children, described in Chapter 8.) Children like Kendall, on the other hand, tend to attribute failure to factors outside themselves or to the need to try harder. If initially unsuccessful, they persevere, trying new strategies until they find one that works (Erdley, Cain, Loomis, Dumas-Hines, & Dweck, 1997).

CHECKPOINT

Can you . . .

✔ From a neo-Piagetian perspective, tell how the self-concept develops in middle childhood as compared with early childhood?

✔ Compare Erikson's and Harter's views about sources of self-esteem?

✔ Describe how the "helpless pattern" can affect children's reactions to social rejection?

Emotional Growth

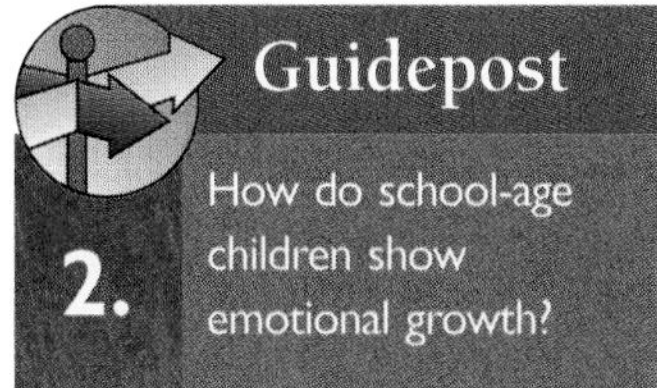
Guidepost
2.
How do school-age children show emotional growth?

By age 7 or 8, children typically have internalized shame and pride (refer back to Chapter 8). These emotions, which depend on awareness of the implications of their actions and on what kind of socialization children have received, affect their opinion of themselves (Harter, 1993, 1996). Children also become able to verbalize conflicting emotions. As Lisa says, "Most of the boys at school are pretty yukky. I don't feel that way about my little brother Jason, although he does get on my nerves. I love him but at the same time, he also does things that make me mad. But I control my temper, I'd be ashamed of myself if I didn't" (Harter, 1996, p. 208).

As children grow older, they are more aware of their own and other people's feelings. They can better regulate their emotional expression in social situations, and they can respond to others' emotional distress (Saarni, Mumme, & Campos, 1998).

One aspect of emotional growth is control of negative emotions. Children learn what makes them angry, fearful, or sad and how other people react to a display of these emotions, and they learn to adapt their behavior accordingly. They also learn the difference between having an emotion and expressing it. Kindergartners believe that a parent can make a child less sad by telling the child to stop crying, or can make a child less afraid of a dog by telling the child there is nothing to be afraid of. Sixth-graders know that a suppressed emotion still exists (Rotenberg & Eisenberg, 1997).

Why do children suppress emotion? The most common reason is self-protection—to avoid ridicule or rejection. Another reason is so as not to upset another person. Fifth-graders are more aware of social "rules" about showing emotion than first-graders. Girls are more willing than boys to show sadness or pain and are more likely to expect emotional support (Zeman & Garber, 1996). Children whose mothers encourage them to express feelings constructively and help them focus on solving the root problem tend to cope more effectively and have better social skills than children whose mothers devalue their feelings by minimizing the seriousness of the situation (Eisenberg, Fabes, & Murphy, 1996).

Even very young children show *empathy,* or understanding of what another person is feeling (refer back to Chapter 8), but children become more empathic and more inclined to prosocial behavior in middle childhood. Prosocial behavior is a sign of positive adjustment. Prosocial children tend to act appropriately in social situations, to be relatively free from negative emotion, and to cope with problems constructively (Eisenberg et al., 1996).

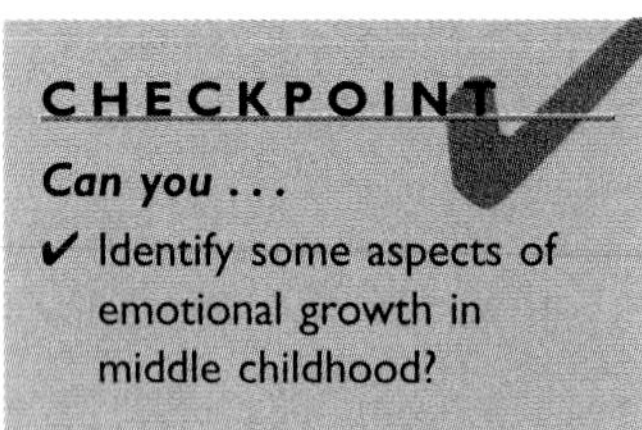

CHECKPOINT
Can you ...
✔ Identify some aspects of emotional growth in middle childhood?

The Child in the Family

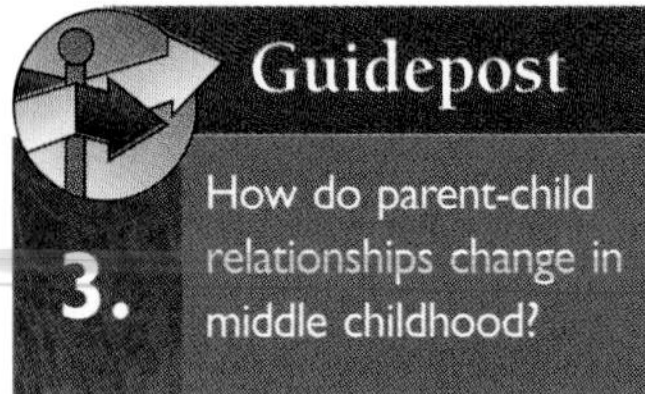

Guidepost
3.
How do parent-child relationships change in middle childhood?

School-age children spend more time away from home than when they were younger and become less close to their parents (Hofferth, 1998). With the upsurge in dual-earner and single-parent families, greater emphasis on education, and the tighter pace of family life, children spend more time at school or in child care and in organized activities than a generation ago. They have less free time for unstructured play, outdoor activities, and leisurely family dinners. Much of the time parents and children spend together is task-centered: shopping, preparing meals, cleaning house, and doing homework (Hofferth & Sandberg, 1998). Still, home and the people who live there remain an important part of a child's life.

To understand the child in the family we need to look at the family environment—its atmosphere and structure. These in turn are affected by what goes on beyond the walls of the home. As Bronfenbrenner's theory describes, additional layers of influence—including parents' work and socioeconomic status and societal trends such as urbanization, changes in family size, divorce, and remarriage—help shape the family environment and, thus, children's development.

Beyond these influences are cultural experiences and values that define rhythms of family life and roles of family members. Children generally are socialized differently in ethnic minority families than in white families. For example, African American families like Marian Anderson's have carried on African extended-family traditions, which have helped them adapt to life in the United States. These traditions include living near or with kin, frequent contacts with relatives, a strong sense of family obligation, willingness to take additional relatives into the household, and a system of mutual aid. Important goals of parenting include teaching children how to deal with racial discrimination (such as Anderson's rejection by the music school) and instilling ethnic pride (Parke & Buriel, 1998).

As we look at the child in the family, then, we need to be aware of outside influences that impinge upon it.

Family Atmosphere

The most important influences of the family environment on children's development come from the atmosphere within the home. Is it supportive and loving, or conflict-ridden? Does the family have enough money to provide for basic needs? Often these two facets of family atmosphere are interrelated.

Parenting Issues: Coregulation and Discipline

As children's lives change, so do the issues between them and their parents, and the ways in which issues are resolved. During the course of childhood, control of behavior gradually shifts from parents to child. A preschooler's acquisition of self-regulation (refer back to Chapter 6) reduces the need for constant supervision, since the child can (usually!) be relied upon to follow parental rules when the parent is not present. However, power resides wholly in the parents. Not until adolescence or even later are many young people permitted to decide how late to stay out and how to spend their money.

Middle childhood is the transitional stage of **coregulation,** in which parent and child share power: parents oversee, but children exercise moment-to-moment self-regulation (Maccoby, 1984). With regard to problems with peers, for example, parents now rely less on direct management or supervision and more on consultation and discussion with their own child (Parke & Buriel, 1998). Children are more apt to follow their parents' wishes or advice when they recognize that the parents are fair and are concerned about the child's welfare and that they may "know better" because of experience. It also helps if parents try to defer to children's maturing judgment and take strong stands only on important issues (Maccoby, 1984).

coregulation
Transitional stage in the control of behavior in which parents exercise general supervision and children exercise moment-to-moment self-regulation.

The processes by which parents and children resolve conflicts may be more important than the specific outcomes. Through family conflict, children learn about rules and standards of behavior. They also learn what kinds of issues are worth arguing about and what strategies can be effective (A. R. Eisenberg, 1996).

As children become preadolescents, and their striving for autonomy becomes more insistent, the quality of family problem solving and negotiation often deteriorates. In one study, 63 two-parent families with fourth-grade children videotaped home discussions of two problems (for example, over allowance, bedtime, or chores) that had come up within the past month—one topic of the child's choosing and one of the parents' choosing. The families repeated the procedure two years later. Between the ages of 9 and 11, the children's participation became more negative, especially when discussing topics the parents had chosen. It made no difference what the topic was; the basic issue, apparently, was "who is in charge" (Vuchinich, Angelelli, & Gatherum, 1996).

Although school-age children spend less time at home than before, parents continue to be very important in children's lives. Parents who enjoy being with their children tend to raise children who feel good about themselves—and about their parents.

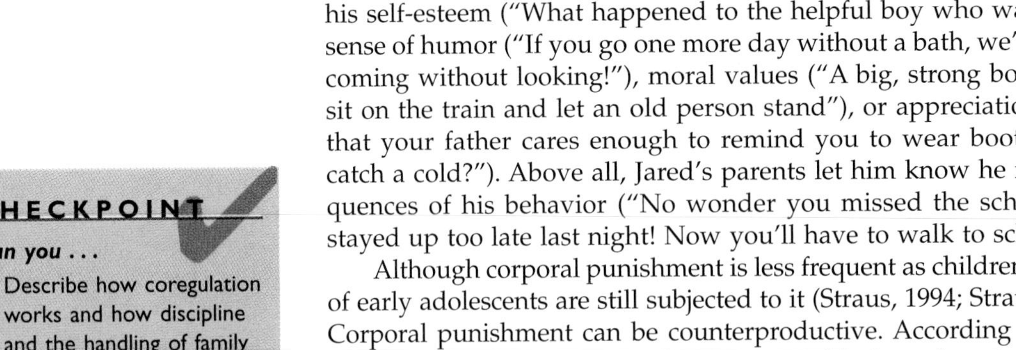

The shift to coregulation affects how parents handle discipline (Maccoby, 1984; Roberts, Block, & Block, 1984). Parents of school-age children are more likely to use inductive techniques that include reasoning. For example, 8-year-old Jared's father points out how his actions affect others: "Hitting Jermaine hurts him and makes him feel bad." In other situations, Jared's parents may appeal to his self-esteem ("What happened to the helpful boy who was here yesterday?"), sense of humor ("If you go one more day without a bath, we'll know when you're coming without looking!"), moral values ("A big, strong boy like you shouldn't sit on the train and let an old person stand"), or appreciation ("Aren't you glad that your father cares enough to remind you to wear boots so that you won't catch a cold?"). Above all, Jared's parents let him know he must bear the consequences of his behavior ("No wonder you missed the school bus today—you stayed up too late last night! Now you'll have to walk to school").

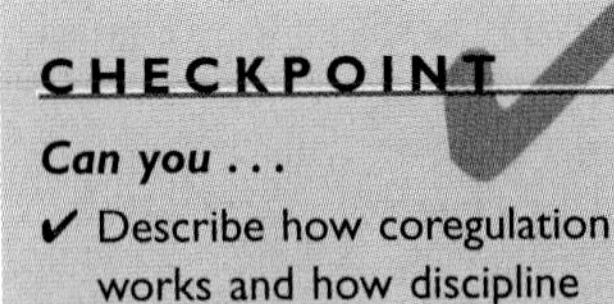

CHECKPOINT

Can you . . .

✔ Describe how coregulation works and how discipline and the handling of family conflict change during middle childhood?

Although corporal punishment is less frequent as children get older, about half of early adolescents are still subjected to it (Straus, 1994; Straus & Donnelly, 1993). Corporal punishment can be counterproductive. According to interviews with a national sample of mothers of 6- to 9-year-olds, it tends to increase rather than reduce antisocial behavior; the more frequent the spankings and the longer they continue, the greater the chance of problems (Straus, Sugarman, & Giles-Sims, 1997).

Effects of Parents' Work

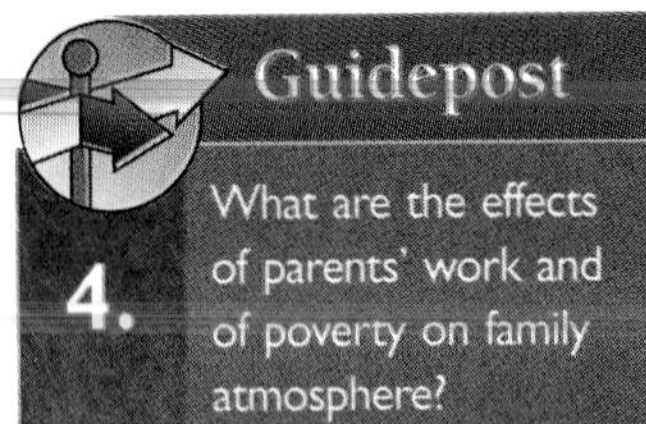

Guidepost

4. What are the effects of parents' work and of poverty on family atmosphere?

Today, about 3 out of 4 mothers of school-age children are in the U.S. workforce (Children's Defense Fund, 1998). In Canada, almost three-fourths of women in the prime childbearing and childraising years (ages 25 to 34) are gainfully employed (Sorrentino, 1990). With more than half of all new mothers in the United States going to work within a year after giving birth (Bureau of Labor Statistics, 1999a), many children have never known a time when their mothers were *not* working for pay. The impact of a mother's work depends on many factors, including the child's age, sex, temperament, and personality; whether the mother works full or part time; why she is working, and how she feels about her work; whether she has a supportive or unsupportive mate, or none; the family's socioeconomic status; and the kind of care the child receives before and/or after school.

When good child care is available and affordable, children are likely to do well (Parke & Buriel, 1998). Some children whose parents work outside the home are supervised after school by baby-sitters or relatives; others go to structured after-school programs. Like good child care for preschoolers, good after-school programs have relatively low enrollment, low child-staff ratios, and well-educated staff (Rosenthal & Vandell, 1996). An estimated 10 percent of 8- to 10-year-olds and 32 percent of 11- to 12-year-olds regularly care for themselves at home without adult supervision (Hofferth, Brayfield, Deich, & Holcomb, 1991). This arrangement can work if a child is mature, responsible, and resourceful and knows how to get help in an emergency, and if a parent stays in touch by telephone.

Often a single mother like Marian Anderson's must work to stave off economic disaster. How her working affects her children may hinge on how much time and energy she has left over to spend with them and what sort of role model she provides (B. L. Barber & Eccles, 1992)—clearly, a positive one in Annie Anderson's case.

The more satisfied a mother is with her employment status, the more effective she is likely to be as a parent (Parke & Buriel, 1998). Many employed mothers feel more competent, more economically secure, and more in charge of their lives than mothers who do not work for pay (Demo, 1992).

School-age children of employed mothers tend to live in more structured homes than children of full-time homemakers, with clear-cut rules giving them more household responsibilities. They are also encouraged to be more independent (Bronfenbrenner & Crouter, 1982), and they have more egalitarian attitudes about gender roles (Parke & Buriel, 1998).

How does maternal employment affect school achievement? Both boys and girls in low-income families seem to benefit academically from the more favorable environment a working mother's income can provide (Goldberg, Greenberger, & Nagel, 1996; Vandell & Ramanan, 1992). In middle-class families, however, sons of working mothers tend to do less well in school than sons of homemakers, whereas daughters usually do as well or better when mothers work (Goldberg et al., 1996; Heyns & Catsambis, 1986). These gender differences in middle-class families may have to do with boys' greater need for supervision and guidance (Goldberg et al., 1996). Independence seems to help girls to become more competent, to achieve more in school, and to have higher self-esteem (Bronfenbrenner & Crouter, 1982).

As children approach adolescence, how well parents keep track of them may be more important than whether the mother works for pay. In one study, 9- to 12-year-old boys whose parents did not closely monitor their activities earned poorer grades than more closely monitored children (Crouter, MacDermid, McHale, & Perry-Jenkins, 1990).

Poverty and Parenting

Poverty can inspire people like Marian Anderson's mother to work hard and make a better life for their children—or it can crush their spirits. Poverty can harm children's development through its impact on parents' emotional state and parenting practices and on the home environment they create (Brooks-Gunn & Duncan, 1997; Brooks-Gunn et al., in press).

Vonnie McLoyd's (1990, 1998) ecological analysis of the effects of poverty traces a route that leads to adult psychological distress, to effects on child rearing, and finally to emotional, behavioral, and academic problems in children. Parents who live in poor housing (or have none), who have lost their jobs, who are worried about their next meal, and who feel a lack of control over their lives are likely to become anxious, depressed, or irritable. They may become less affectionate with, and less responsive to, their children. They may discipline inconsistently, harshly, and arbitrarily. They may ignore good behavior and pay attention only to misbehavior. The children, in turn, tend to become depressed themselves, to have trouble getting along with peers, to lack self-confidence, and to engage in antisocial acts (Brooks-Gunn et al., in press; McLoyd, 1990, 1998).

Families under economic stress are less likely to monitor their children's activities, and lack of monitoring is associated with poorer school performance and social adjustment (Bolger, Patterson, Thompson, & Kupersmidt, 1995). In a nationally representative study of 11,760 children ages 6 to 17, one-third of those with family incomes below poverty level were behind the normal grade level for their age (J. M. Fields & Smith, 1998).

Lack of financial resources can make it harder for mothers and fathers to support each other in parenting. One study looked at 9- to 12-year-olds and their married parents with incomes ranging from $2,500 to $57,500. In many of the poor families, parents worked several fatiguing jobs to make ends meet. These parents were less optimistic and more depressed than parents in better-off families. They found it harder to communicate and cooperate with each other and often fought over child raising. These contradictory parental messages led to behavioral and scholastic problems in the children (Brody et al., 1994).

Persistent poverty can be particularly damaging. Among 534 schoolchildren in Charlottesville, Virginia, those from persistently deprived families had lower self-esteem, got along less well with peers, and were more likely to have behavior problems than children whose families experienced intermittent hardship or none at all (Bolger et al., 1995).

Antisocial behavior tends to be bred from early childhood by a combination of a stressful and unstimulating home atmosphere; harsh discipline; lack of

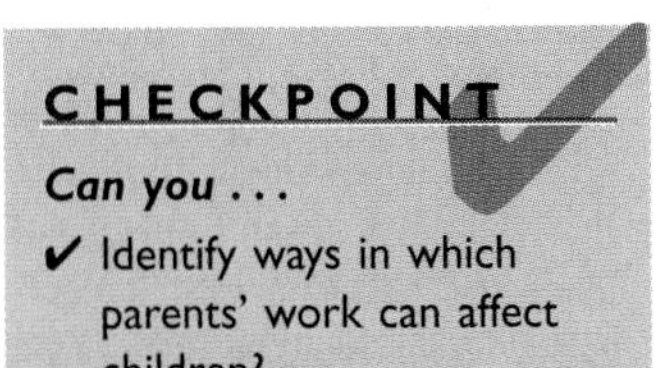

maternal warmth and social support; exposure to aggressive adults and neighborhood violence; and transient peer groups, which prevent stable friendships. Through such negative socializing experiences, children growing up in poor, high-risk surroundings may absorb antisocial attitudes, sometimes despite their parents' best efforts (Dodge, Pettit, & Bates, 1994).

However, this bleak picture is not etched in stone. Parents who can turn to relatives (as Annie Anderson did) or to community representatives for emotional support, help with child care, and childrearing information often can parent their children more effectively.

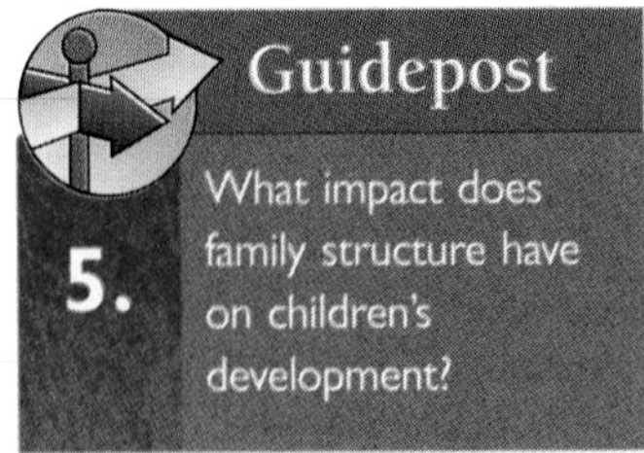

Family Structure

Families in the United States have changed dramatically in recent decades. Although most children under 18 live with two parents, the proportion has decreased drastically since 1970 (see Figure 10-1). Many two-parent families are stepfamilies, resulting from divorce and remarriage. There also are a growing number of other nontraditional families, including single-parent families, gay and lesbian families, and grandparent-headed families.

Traditional and Nontraditional Families: An Overview

traditional (intact) families Families that include a married couple and their biological children, or children adopted in infancy.

Much research has found that children tend to do better in **traditional (intact) families**—those that include two biological parents or two parents who adopted the child in infancy (Bray & Hetherington, 1993; Bronstein, Clauson, Stoll, & Abrams, 1993; D. A. Dawson, 1991; Hetherington, Bridges, & Insabella, 1998). In a nationwide study of 17,110 children under 18, those living with single or remarried mothers were more likely than those living with both biological parents to have repeated a grade of school, to have been expelled, to have health problems, or to have been treated for emotional or behavioral troubles in the previous year (D. A. Dawson, 1991). Children from divorced and remarried families are also likely to be less socially responsible and competent, to think less of themselves, and to have trouble relating to parents, siblings, and peers (Hetherington et al., 1998).

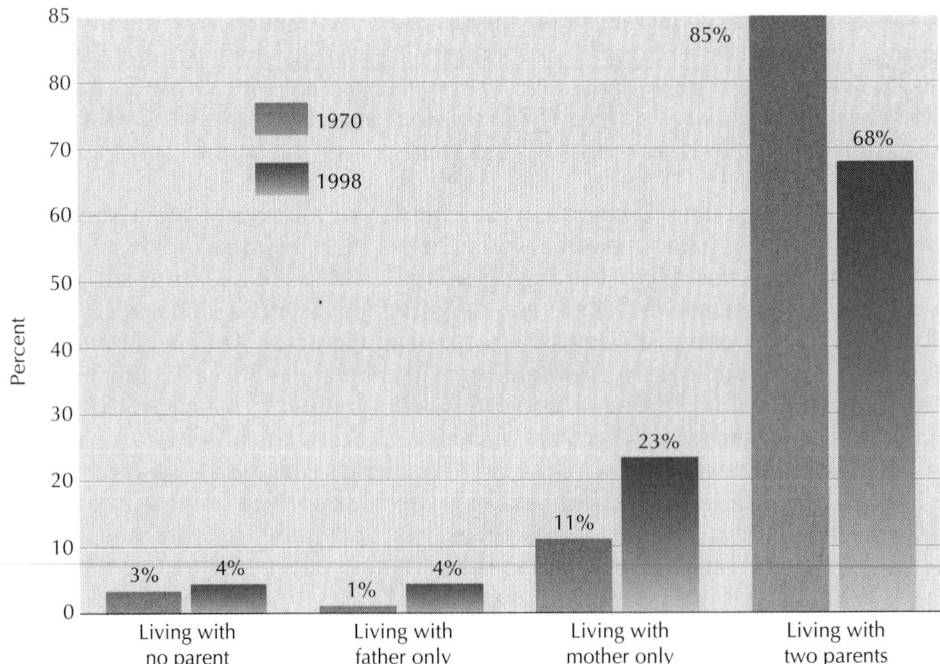

Figure 10-1
Living arrangements of children younger than 18, 1970–1995. Most children under 18 in the United States live with two parents, but this proportion dropped during the past quarter-century. Many of these two-parent families are stepfamilies. Note: Percentages do not add up to 100 percent because fractional amounts have been dropped.
Source: U.S. Department of Commerce, 1996; Lugaila, 1998, Table A.)

The structure of the family in itself is less important than its effect on family atmosphere. Traditional families have not had to deal with the stress and disruption caused by divorce or the death of a parent; with the financial, psychological, and time pressures on single parents; or with the possible need to adjust to a new household or to remarriage. Not only objective changes in family life, but parents' emotional responses to those changes, can be stressful for children. What may affect children most is how these stresses influence the way the family functions day by day, bringing about changes in roles, relationships, and parenting practices (Hetherington et al., 1998).

Among 136 fifth-graders, those in traditional families were better adjusted than children in nontraditional families. Traditional parents did more with their children, talked with them more, disciplined them more appropriately, and were likely to share parenting responsibilities more cooperatively than nontraditional parents. Not surprisingly, the children in the traditional families were better adjusted. Deficiencies in family relationships in single-mother households were almost entirely linked to socioeconomic status (Bronstein et al., 1993). In other studies, however, even when income was controlled, children in divorced families had more problems than those in intact families (Hetherington et al., 1998).

In a traditional family, a father's involvement is usually deeper when there is at least one son. Fathers are more likely to play with, supervise, and discipline sons than daughters. A father's involvement with his children may be a gauge of whether the parents will stay together. When a father is heavily involved, the mother is likely to be more satisfied and to expect the marriage to last (Katzev, Warner, & Acock, 1994).

Adoptive Families

Anna Victoria Finlay, who was born in Santiago, Chile, is the adoptive daughter of Diane E. Papalia, one of the authors of this book. Anna is among the approximately 2 percent of people in the United States who are children adopted by nonrelatives (Brodzinsky, 1993). Married couples, single people, older people, and homosexual couples have become adoptive parents. Overall, about 60 percent of legal adoptions are by relatives, usually stepparents or grandparents (Goodman, Emery, & Haugaard, 1998; Haugaard, 1998).

Advances in contraception and legalization of abortion have reduced the number of adoptable healthy white U.S. babies. The percentage of babies, born to never-married white women, who were given up for adoption dropped from 19.3 percent in the early 1970s to only 1.7 percent in the early 1990s (Chandra, Abma, Maza, & Bachrach, 1999). Black women have consistently been far less likely to put their babies up for adoption. Thus a greater percentage of the children available for adoption today are disabled, are beyond infancy, or are of foreign birth. Adoptions take place through public or private agencies or through independent agreements between birth parents and adoptive parents. Independent adoptions have become increasingly common (Brodzinsky, 1997; Goodman et al., 1998).

Adopting a child carries special challenges. Besides the usual issues of parenthood, adoptive parents need to deal with integrating the adopted child into the family, explaining the adoption to the child, helping the child develop a healthy sense of self, and perhaps eventually helping the child to contact the biological parents.

A common belief is that adopted children are bound to have problems because they have been deprived of their biological parents. A review of the literature found few significant differences in adjustment between adopted and nonadopted children; any problems seemed to occur mainly around the time of sexual maturation (Goodman et al., 1998). Children adopted as infants are least likely to have adjustment problems (Sharma, McGue, & Benson, 1996b).

Does adopting a foreign-born child make a difference? A number of studies have found no detrimental effects (Sharma, McGue, & Benson, 1996a). One study

Because of a decrease in the number of adoptable American babies, many children adopted today are of foreign birth. Adoptive parents face special challenges, such as the need to explain the adoption to the child. But most adoptive children view their adoption positively and see it as playing only a minor role in their identity.

looked at 100 Israeli families, half of whom had adopted South American children and half Israeli children. The two groups of 7- to 13-year-olds, all of whom had been adopted soon after birth, showed no significant differences in psychological adjustment, in school adjustment and performance, in observed behavior at home, or in the way they coped with being adopted (Levy-Shiff, Zoran, & Shulman, 1997).

open adoption
Adoption in which the birth parents and adoptive parents know each other's identities and share information or have direct contact.

Traditionally, adoptions were confidential, with no contact between the birth mother and the adoptive parents, and the identity of the birth mother was kept secret. In recent years, **open adoption,** in which the parties share information or have direct contact, has become more common. Contrary to what are sometimes considered the risks of open adoption, one study found that with direct contact the adoptive parents tend to feel more confident that the arrangement is permanent and that the birth mother will not try to reclaim the child. At the same time, they are more likely to recognize the child's interest in knowing about her or his origins (Grotevant, McRoy, Elde, & Fravel, 1994). In one survey of 1,059 California families who had adopted children three years earlier, whether or not an adoption was open seemed to bear no relation to the children's adjustment or to the parents' satisfaction with the adoption, both of which were very high (Berry, Dylla, Barth, & Needell, 1998).

When Parents Divorce

The annual number of divorces has tripled since 1960; more than 1 million children are involved in divorces each year (Harvey & Pauwels, 1999). No matter how unhappy a marriage has been, its breakup usually comes as a shock to a child. Children may feel afraid of the future, guilty about their own (usually imaginary) role in causing the divorce, hurt by the parent who moves out, and angry at both parents.

Adjusting to Divorce Most children of divorce do gradually readjust (Masten, Best, & Garmezy, 1990). Although different children react differently, readjustment generally involves six "tasks" (Wallerstein, 1983; Wallerstein & Kelly, 1980): (1) acknowledging the reality of the marital rupture; (2) disengaging from parental conflict and distress and resuming customary pursuits; (3) resolving loss—of the parent they are not living with, of security in feeling loved and cared for by both parents, of familiar daily routines and family traditions; (4) resolving anger and self-blame; (5) accepting the permanence of the divorce; and (6) achieving realistic hope for their own intimate relationships.

What influences a child's adjustment to divorce? The child's age or maturity, gender, temperament, and psychological and social adjustment are important factors. So is the way parents handle such issues as custody and visitation arrangements, finances, reorganization of household duties, contact with the noncustodial parent, remarriage, and the child's relationship with a stepparent.

Younger children are more anxious about divorce, have less realistic perceptions of what caused it, and are more likely to blame themselves; but they may adapt more quickly than older children, who better understand what is going on. School-age children are sensitive to parental pressures and loyalty conflicts; like younger children, they may fear abandonment and rejection. Boys generally find it harder to adjust than girls do. However, this difference may be less significant than was once thought and may depend largely on how involved the father remains (Bray, 1991; Hetherington, Stanley-Hagan, & Anderson, 1989; Hetherington et al., 1998; Hines, 1997; Masten et al., 1990; Parke & Buriel, 1998).

In most divorce cases the mother gets custody, but paternal custody is a growing trend (Meyer & Garasky, 1993). Children do better when the custodial parent creates a stable, structured, and nurturing environment and does not expect the children to take on more responsibility than they are ready for (Hetherington et al., 1989).

Boys, especially, benefit from reliable, frequent contact with a noncustodial father (J. B. Kelly, 1987). The more recent the separation, the closer the father lives to his children, and the higher his socioeconomic status, the more involved he is likely to be (Amato & Keith, 1991a; Parke & Buriel, 1998). Noncustodial fathers are more likely to lose contact if they have biological children from a new marriage (Cooksey & Craig, 1998). Noncustodial mothers keep up twice as much contact with their children as noncustodial fathers and are less likely to break contact after remarriage (Hetherington et al., 1998). After a divorce or separation, children living with their mothers do better in school if they have warm, responsive relationships with their fathers (Coley, 1998). Children also perform better academically if their nonresident fathers are involved in their schools (National Center for Education Statistics [NCES], 1998b).

Most research has found few advantages of *joint custody,* custody shared by both parents (Hetherington et al., 1998). When parents have joint *legal* custody, they share the right and responsibility to make decisions regarding the child's welfare. When parents have joint *physical* custody (which is less common), the child is supposed to live part time with each of them. The main determinant of the success of joint custody is the amount of conflict between the parents (Parke & Buriel, 1998). In a three-year study of 1,100 families with both types of joint custody, only about one-fourth of the parents managed to cooperate, more than one-fourth were hostile, and the rest avoided contact (Maccoby & Mnookin, 1992).

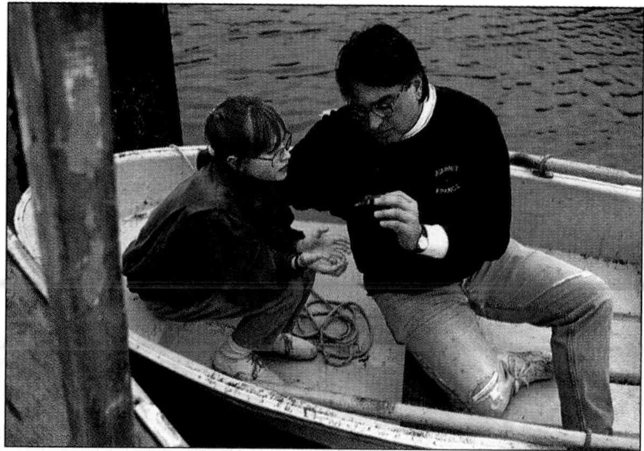

Children of divorce tend to be better adjusted if they have reliable, frequent contact with the noncustodial parent, usually the father.

Children's emotional or behavioral problems may stem from parental conflict, both before and after divorce,

Box 10-1

Should Parents Stay Together for the Sake of the Children?

A generation ago, when divorce was far less common than it is today, it was widely believed that parents in troubled marriages should stay together for the sake of the children. More recent research has found that marital strife harms children more than divorce does—that children are better adjusted if they grow up in a harmonious single-parent household than in a two-parent home marked by discord and discontent (Hetherington et al., 1998; Hetherington & Stanley-Hagan, 1999). However, that finding may need some qualifying.

Clearly, watching parents' spats can be hard on children. Aside from the distress, worry, or fear children may feel, marital dissension may affect the way parents treat children and may diminish parents' responsiveness to children's needs. Young boys growing up in an atmosphere of parental anger and discord tend to become aggressive; girls, to become withdrawn and anxious. Children do not get used to marital conflict; the more they are exposed to it, the more sensitive they become (E. M. Cummings, 1994). Children see destructive parental quarrels as threatening their own security and that of the family (Davies & Cummings, 1998).

In one study, 5-year-olds whose fathers expressed anger by withdrawing emotionally during conflicts with the mother tended to be seen by teachers three years later as self-blaming, distressed, and ashamed. Five-year-olds whose parents insulted, mocked, and disparaged each other were likely at age 8 to be disobedient, unwilling to obey rules, and unable to wait their turn. These patterns held true whether or not the parents had separated by then (Katz & Gottman, 1993).

Still, not all conflict is destructive. When children see that parents can resolve their disputes—especially if the parents make clear that the child was not to blame—children learn that conflict is normal and can be handled constructively (E. M. Cummings, 1994). Exposure to parental disagreements may help children learn to control their own emotions and work out their own interpersonal conflicts. Violent clashes, conflicts about a child to which the child is directly exposed, and those in which a child feels caught in the middle are the most damaging (Hetherington & Stanley-Hagan, 1999).

The *amount* of conflict in a marriage may make a difference. A 15-year longitudinal study, which followed a nationwide sample originally consisting of 2,033 married people (Amato & Booth, 1997), suggests that in only about 30 percent of divorces involving children is there so much discord that the children are better off if the marriage ends. About 70 percent of cases, according to this research, involve low-conflict marriages, in which children would benefit "if parents remained together until children are grown" (p. 238).

In many divorced families—as many as 1 in 5—conflict continues or escalates. Two years after a divorce, children suffer more from dissension in a divorced family than do children in a nondivorced family. Thus, if conflict is going to *continue,* children may be better off in an acrimonious two-parent household than if the parents divorce. On the other hand, if conflict *lessens* after a divorce, the children may be better off than they were before. Unfortunately, the amount of bickering after a divorce is not always easy to anticipate (Hetherington & Stanley-Hagan, 1999).

In evaluating the effects of divorce, then, we need to look at particular circumstances. Sometimes divorce may improve a child's situation by reducing the amount of conflict within the family, and sometimes not. Children's personal characteristics make a difference; intelligent, socially competent children without serious behavior problems, who have a sense of control over their own lives, can cope better with both parental conflict and divorce (Hetherington & Stanley-Hagan, 1999). And, while the immediate effects of a marital breakup may be traumatic, in the long run some youngsters may benefit from having learned new coping skills that make them more competent and independent (B. L. Barber & Eccles, 1992).

as well as from the separation itself (Amato, Kurdek, Demo, & Allen, 1993; E. M. Cummings, 1994; Parke & Buriel, 1998; see Box 10-1). If parents can control their anger, cooperate in parenting, and avoid exposing the children to quarreling, the children are less likely to have problems (Bray & Hetherington, 1993; Hetherington et al., 1989). Unfortunately, the strains of divorce make it harder for a couple to be effective parents (Hines, 1997).

Although most children of divorce eventually adjust reasonably well, some remain troubled. They are more than twice as likely to drop out of high school as children in intact families (McLanahan & Sandefur, 1994). Family ties may be weakened, sometimes leading to antisocial behavior (Parke & Buriel, 1998). However, since all research on effects of divorce is correlational, we cannot be sure that the divorce caused children's later problems. Children may still be reacting to conflict preceding or surrounding the dissolution of the marriage.

An analysis of 37 studies involving more than 81,000 people found that adult children of divorced parents tend to be slightly more depressed, to have more marital problems, to be in poorer health, and to have lower socioeconomic status than adults who grew up in intact families (Amato & Keith, 1991b). These differences were small and were most pronounced among people who had sought counseling or therapy. The association between parental divorce and problems in adulthood was weaker than in earlier studies, perhaps because divorce is a more normative event than it used to be. In a nationally representative British study based on data gathered on children from birth on, the vast majority of those whose parents divorced came through well by their early twenties (Chase-Lansdale, Cherlin, & Kiernan, 1995). In the United States, between 1973 and 1996, the chances of children of divorce ending their own marriages declined by almost 50 percent, from 2.5 to 1.4 times as likely as for children of intact families (Wolfinger, 1999).

Living in a One-Parent Family

One-parent families result from divorce or separation, unwed parenthood, or death. The number of single-parent families in the United States has more than quadrupled since 1960 (Harvey & Pauwels, 1999). Today a child has at least a 50 percent chance of living with only one parent at some point, usually the mother (Bianchi, 1995; Hines, 1997; NCES, 1998b). Children in divorced families typically spend five years in a single-parent home, usually the mother's, before she remarries (Bray & Hetherington, 1993).

Although the growth of one-parent families is slowing, in 1998 they comprised about 32 percent of U.S. families with children under 18—62 percent of African American families, 36 percent of Hispanic families, and 27 percent of white families—as compared with only 13 percent of all families in 1970 (Bryson, 1996; U.S. Bureau of the Census, 1998). The United States has the highest percentage of single-parent families among eight industrialized countries: Australia, France, Japan, Sweden, United Kingdom, United States, Soviet Union, and West Germany (A. Burns, 1992). In Canada the proportion of such families in 1996 was 15 percent, less than half the U.S. rate (Statistics Canada, 1996).

In 1998, about 84 percent of U.S. children who lived with a single parent lived with their mothers (Lugaila, 1998). The number of father-only families has more than quadrupled since 1974, apparently due largely to an increase in the number of fathers having custody after divorce (Garasky & Meyer, 1996; U.S. Bureau of the Census, 1998). In 1998, about one-sixth of all single-parent families were headed by fathers (U.S. Bureau of the Census, 1998).

Since the 1970s delayed marriage and unwed motherhood have created more single-mother families than has divorce (Bianchi, 1995). By 1994 nearly 1 in 3 births—up from fewer than 1 in 25 in 1940—was to an unwed mother (National Center for Health Statistics [NCHS], 1993, 1994b; Rosenberg, Ventura, Maurer, Heuser, & Freedman, 1996). The trend has been especially marked among white and college-educated women (Bachu, 1993; U.S. Bureau of the Census, 1993c). In 1998, about 4 out of 10 children who lived with a single mother lived with a mother who had never been married (Lugaila, 1998). Out-of-wedlock births have increased dramatically in many other developed countries as well (Bruce, Lloyd, & Leonard, 1995; WuDunn, 1996).

Compared with children in intact families, children in one-parent families have more behavioral and academic problems, especially when the absence of a parent is due to divorce (Hetherington et al., 1998; Walker & Hennig, 1997). Children in one-parent families are more on their own. They have more household responsibility, more conflict with siblings, less family cohesion, and less support, control, or discipline from fathers, if it is the father who is absent from the household (Amato, 1987; Coley, 1998; Walker & Hennig, 1997). Single fathers tend to be more satisfied with parenting and to report fewer behavior problems with their children than single mothers do (Walker & Hennig, 1997).

Children in single-parent families are disproportionately likely to be poor, and financial hardship can have negative effects on children's health, well-being, and school achievement. Nearly three times as many mother-only families as father-only families are poor—35 percent as compared with 13 percent (U.S. Bureau of the Census, 1996a).

It is widely believed that most mother-only families suffer from the mother's greatly reduced income after divorce and the father's failure to pay child support. However, a study of a random sample of 378 couples who divorced in Maricopa County, Arizona, in 1986 suggests that the data supporting this belief may be methodologically flawed (Braver & O'Connell, 1998).

For one thing, the Census Bureau's statistics on child support are based on mothers' reports. Not surprisingly, the researchers in Maricopa County found a wide disparity between what fathers say they have paid and what custodial mothers say the fathers have paid. The findings suggest that fathers (as long as they are employed) pay more than is generally assumed. As for the much-deplored "feminization of poverty," the researchers found that, on average, men and women tend to fare about the same economically after divorce. The investigators reached this conclusion by taking into consideration such factors as tax advantages to the custodial mother, costs of establishing a new household, other "hidden" costs to the noncustodial father, and the difficulty of establishing equivalent poverty levels for households of different sizes. The analysis showed that families of *never-married* single mothers—many of whom are teenagers from low socioeconomic backgrounds—but *not* divorced mothers tend to be below the poverty level (Braver & O'Connell, 1998).

Consider this . . .

- If finances permit, should either the mother or the father stay home to take care of the children?
- Would you advise parents who want a divorce to stay married until their children have grown up? Why or why not?

Living in a Blended Family

Since about 75 percent of divorced mothers and 80 percent of divorced fathers remarry, families made up of "yours, mine, and ours" are common. Eighty-six percent of children in remarriages live with their biological mother and a stepfather (Bray & Hetherington, 1993).

The stepfamily—also called the *blended,* or *reconstituted,* family—is different from the "natural" family. It has a larger cast, which may include the relatives of up to four adults (the remarried pair, plus one or two former spouses); and it has many stressors. Because of losses from death or divorce, children and adults may be afraid to trust or to love. A child's loyalties to an absent or dead parent may interfere with forming ties to a stepparent. Past emotional and behavior problems often resurface. Adjustment is harder when there are many children, including those from both the man's and the woman's previous marriages, or when a new child is born (Hetherington et al., 1989). Furthermore, because the increase in blended families is fairly recent, social expectations for such families have not caught up. In combining two family units, each with its own web of customs and relationships, remarried families must invent their own ways of doing things (Hines, 1997). For these reasons, among others, remarriages are more likely to fail than first marriages, especially during the first 5 years (Parke & Buriel, 1998).

Findings on the impact of remarriage on children are mixed (Parke & Buriel, 1998). Some studies have found that boys, who often have more trouble than girls in adjusting to divorce and single-parent living (usually with the mother), benefit from a stepfather. A girl, on the other hand, may find the new man in the house a threat to her independence and to her close relationship with her mother and may be less likely to accept him (Bray & Hetherington, 1993; Hetherington, 1987; Hetherington et al., 1989; Hetherington et al., 1998; Hines, 1997).

Stepparents often assume a "hands-off" attitude toward children of the custodial parent, though stepmothers may take—or be expected to take—a more active role than stepfathers (Hetherington et al., 1989; Hetherington et al., 1998;

Parke & Buriel, 1998; Santrock, Sitterle, & Warshak, 1988). Still, a stepchild's most enduring ties are with the custodial parent. Life generally goes more smoothly when stepparents support the natural parent and do not try to step in themselves (Hetherington et al., 1998).

Living with Gay or Lesbian Parents

The number of children of gay and lesbian parents is unknown; conservative estimates range from 6 to 14 million (C. J. Patterson, 1992; C. J. Patterson & Redding, 1996). There are an estimated 1 to 5 million lesbian mothers and 1 to 3 million gay fathers (Gottman, 1990). These numbers are probably low because many gay and lesbian parents do not openly acknowledge their sexual orientation. Some are raising children born of previous heterosexual relationships. Others conceive by artificial means (see Chapter 13), become foster parents, or adopt children (C. J. Patterson, 1997).

Several studies have focused on the personal development of children of gays and lesbians, including sense of self, moral judgment, and intelligence, and on their social relationships. Although research is still sparse and studies vary in adequacy of methodology, none has indicated psychological concerns (C. J. Patterson, 1992, 1995a, 1995b, 1997). Contrary to popular belief, openly gay or lesbian parents usually have positive relationships with their children (P. H. Turner et al., 1985), and the children are no more likely than children raised by heterosexual parents to have social or psychological problems (Chan, Raboy, & Patterson, 1998; C. J. Patterson, 1992, 1995a, 1997). Abuse by gay or lesbian parents is rare (R. L. Barrett & Robinson, 1990; Cramer, 1986).

Children of gays and lesbians are no more likely to be homosexual themselves, or to be confused about their gender, than are children of heterosexuals (B. M. King, 1996; C. J. Patterson, 1997). In one study, the vast majority of adult sons of gay fathers were heterosexual (Bailey, Bobrow, Wolfe, & Mikach, 1995). Likewise, in a longitudinal study of adult children of lesbians, a large majority identified themselves as heterosexual (Golombok & Tasker, 1996).

Such findings can have social policy implications for legal decisions on custody and visitation disputes, foster care, and adoptions.

CHECKPOINT

Can you . . .

- ✔ Differentiate between traditional (intact) and nontraditional family structures?
- ✔ List the psychological "tasks" children face in adjusting to divorce, and identify factors that affect adjustment?
- ✔ Assess the impact of parental divorce on children?
- ✔ Tell three ways in which a one-parent family can be formed, and how living in such a household can affect children's well-being?
- ✔ Discuss how parents and stepparents handle the issues and challenges of a blended family?
- ✔ Discuss the outcomes of child raising by gay and lesbian parents?

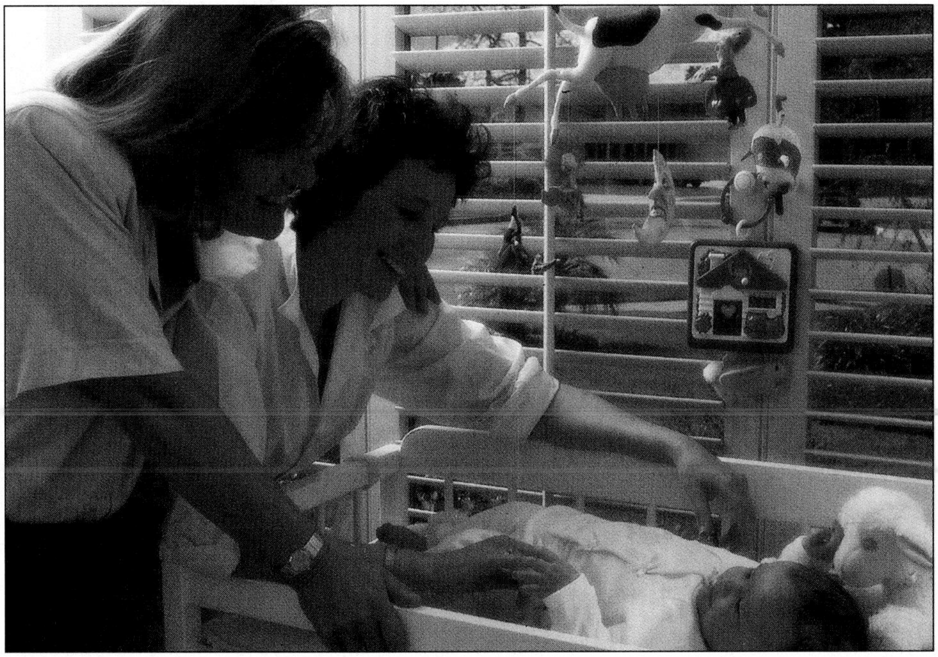

This baby has two mothers—and both obviously dote on the child. Contrary to popular stereotypes, children living with homosexual parents are no more likely than other children to have social or psychological problems or to turn out to be homosexual themselves.

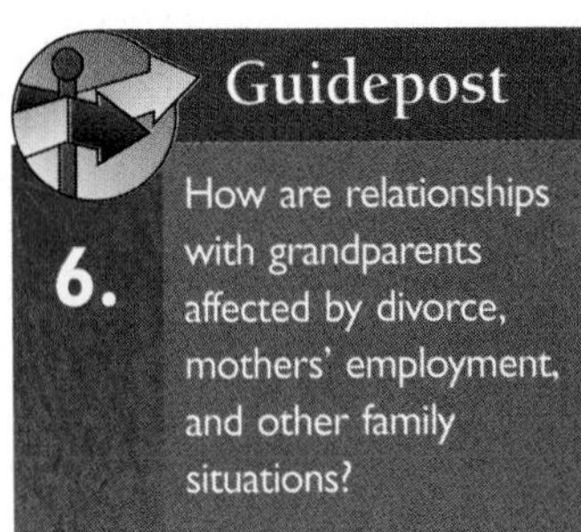

Guidepost
6.
How are relationships with grandparents affected by divorce, mothers' employment, and other family situations?

Relationships with Grandparents

During the school years, children may spend less time with grandparents than before, but the bond remains a special one. A grandparent can serve as caregiver, teacher, role model, confidant, and sometimes negotiator between child and parent. Grandparents' warmth, indulgence, and acceptance can be a "release valve" from the pressure of parental expectations. Grandparents can be sources of guidance and symbols of family continuity (Weissbourd, 1996).

One unfortunate byproduct of divorce and remarriage may be the weakening or severing of grandparent-grandchild relations. Because the mother usually has custody, her parents tend to have more contact and stronger relationships with their grandchildren than the father's parents (Cherlin & Furstenberg, 1986b; Myers & Perrin, 1993). The mother's remarriage increases the likelihood that the paternal grandparents will be displaced or that the family will move away, making contact more difficult (Cherlin & Furstenberg, 1986b). Since 1965 every state in the Union has given grandparents (and in some states, great-grandparents, siblings, and others) the right to visitation after a divorce or the death of a parent, but only if a judge finds it in the best interest of the child.

Many grandparents provide child care for working parents. In one survey, 32 percent of grandparents had provided child care or supervision for at least 1 hour during the previous week, and 9 percent had done it for 20 or more hours (Bass & Caro, 1996). In 1997, nearly 4 million grandchildren, especially in the south and in central cities, lived in grandparents' homes, as Marian Anderson did—in most cases, along with a young, poor single parent (Casper & Bryson, 1998; see Figure 10-2). But an increasing number of grandparents and even great-grandparents are serving as "parents by default" for children whose parents are addicted to drugs or alcohol, divorced, dead, physically or mentally ill, unwed, underage, unemployed, abusive, neglectful, or in jail, or who have simply abandoned them (Casper & Bryson, 1998; Chalfie, 1994; Minkler & Roe, 1996).

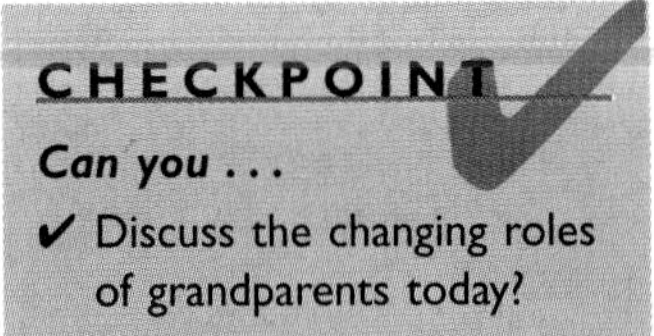

CHECKPOINT
Can you . . .
✔ Discuss the changing roles of grandparents today?

Most grandparents who take on this responsibility do it because they do not want their grandchildren placed in a stranger's foster home. However, the age

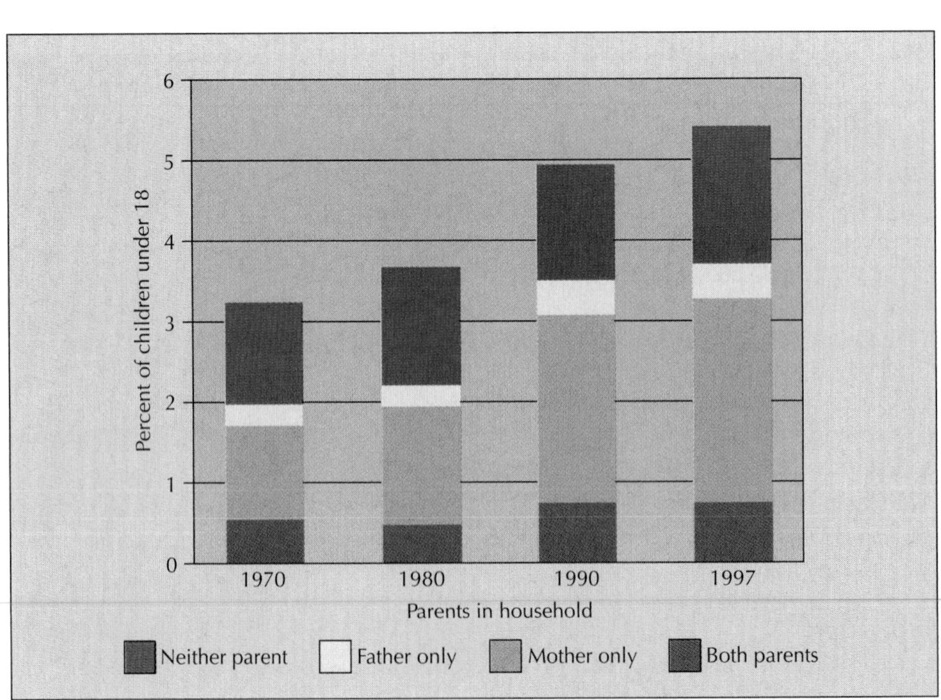

Figure 10-2
Granchildren living in grandparents' homes, with and without parents, 1970–1997. A growing proportion of children under 18 live with their grandparents, most of them along with a single mother. In many grandparent-headed households, neither parent is present.
(Source: Casper & Bryson, 1998, Figure 1. Data from U.S. Bureau of the Census.)

difference can be a barrier, and both generations may feel cheated out of their traditional roles (Crowley, 1993; Larsen, 1990–1991). Also, there are practical problems. Working grandparents raising grandchildren need good, affordable child care and family-friendly workplace policies, such as health insurance coverage for grandchildren and time off to care for a sick child (Chalfie, 1994; Simon-Rusinowitz, Krach, Marks, Piktialis, & Wilson, 1996).

Consider this . . .

- How can or should society help grandparents who are raising grandchildren?

Sibling Relationships

Guidepost
7.
How do siblings influence and get along with one another?

In nonindustrialized societies, such as those in remote rural areas or villages of Asia, Africa, Oceania, and Central and South America, it is common to see older girls caring for three or four younger siblings: feeding, comforting, and toilet-training them; disciplining them; assigning chores; and generally keeping an eye on them. In a poor agricultural or pastoral community, older siblings have an important, culturally defined role. Parents train children early to teach younger sisters and brothers how to gather firewood, carry water, tend animals, and grow food. Younger siblings absorb intangible values, such as respecting elders and placing the welfare of the group above that of the individual. Siblings may fight and compete, but they do so within the bounds of societal rules and roles (Cicirelli, 1994).

In industrialized societies, parents generally try not to "burden" older children with the care of younger ones (Weisner, 1993). Some caretaking does take place, but it is typically sporadic. Older siblings do teach younger ones, but this usually happens informally, by chance, and not as an established part of the social system (Cicirelli, 1994). However, sibling relationships among some American working families and ethnic minority groups are closer to the pattern of nonindustrialized cultures than to that of the majority culture in the United States (C. L. Johnson, 1985).

Consider this . . .

- Should older siblings in industrialized societies have regular formal duties in taking care of younger ones, as is true in nonindustrialized societies?

The number of siblings in a family and their spacing, birth order, and gender determine roles and relationships in nonindustrialized societies. The larger number of siblings in these societies helps the family carry on its work and provide for aging members. The definition of *siblings* may even include cousins, aunts, uncles, grandparents, or same-age peers, who are expected to fulfill the obligations of brothers and sisters. In industrialized societies, the number and spacing of siblings vary from family to family; siblings tend to be fewer and farther apart in age, making it easier for parents to pursue careers or other interests and to focus more resources and attention on each child (Cicirelli, 1994).

Two longitudinal studies, one in England and one in Pennsylvania, based on naturalistic observation of siblings and mothers and interviews with the mothers, found no clear pattern of change in sibling relationships during the transition to middle childhood. Negative changes were most often described as happening when one sibling was between ages 7 and 9 and completing the primary grades. Often both mothers and children attributed these changes to outside friendships, which led to jealousy and competitiveness or loss of interest in, and intimacy with, the sibling. Sometimes the younger sibling's growing assertiveness played a part (Dunn, 1996).

Sibling relations are a laboratory for conflict resolution. Siblings are impelled to make up after quarrels, since they

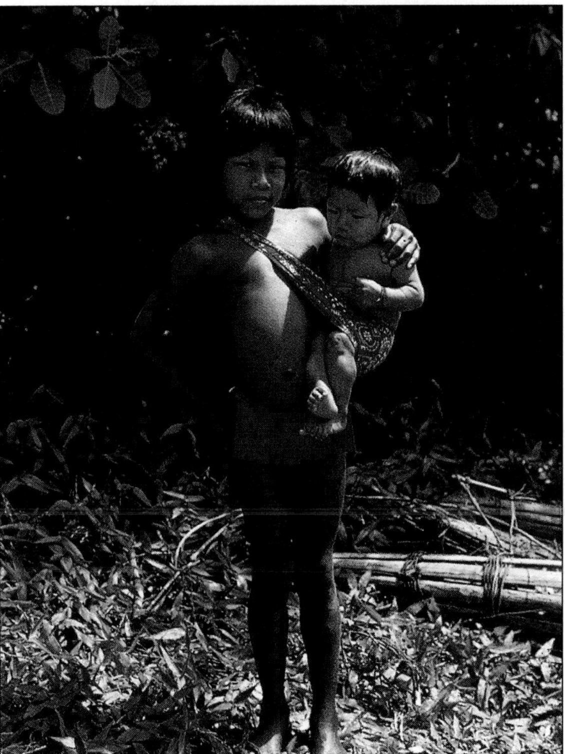

This boy in Surinam has an important responsibility: taking care of his younger brother. Siblings in nonindustrialized societies have clear, culturally defined roles throughout life.

CHECKPOINT

Can you . . .

✔ Compare the roles and responsibilities of siblings in industrialized and nonindustrialized countries?

✔ Discuss how siblings affect each other's development during middle childhood?

know they will see each other every day. They learn that expressing anger does not end a relationship. Firstborns tend to be bossy and are more likely to attack, interfere with, ignore, or bribe their siblings. Younger siblings plead, reason, and cajole; they often become quite skillful at sensing other people's needs, negotiating, and compromising. Children are more apt to squabble with same-sex siblings; two brothers quarrel more than any other combination (Cicirelli, 1976, 1995).

Siblings influence each other, not only *directly,* through their own interactions, but *indirectly* through their impact on each other's relationship with the parents. Conversely, behavior patterns established with parents tend to "spill over" into behavior with siblings. An older child's positive relationship with the mother or father can mitigate the effects of that child's "difficult" temperament on sibling interactions. Also, a father's positive relationship with an "easy" younger sibling can bolster that child in dealing with a "difficult" older sibling (Brody, Stoneman, & Gauger, 1996).

The Child in the Peer Group

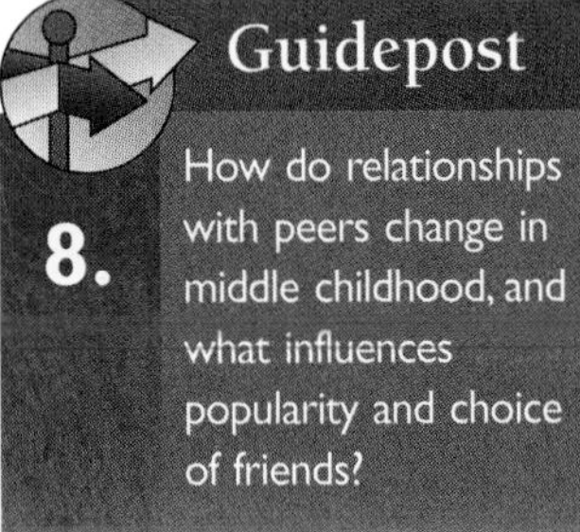

Guidepost

8. How do relationships with peers change in middle childhood, and what influences popularity and choice of friends?

It is in middle childhood that the peer group comes into its own. Groups form naturally among children who live near one another or go to school together; thus peer groups often consist of children of the same racial or ethnic origin and similar socioeconomic status. Children who play together are usually close in age, though a neighborhood play group may include mixed ages. Too wide an age range brings differences, not only in size, but in interests and ability levels. Groups are usually all girls or all boys (Hartup, 1992). Children of the same sex have common interests; girls are generally more mature than boys, and girls and boys play and talk to one another differently. Same-sex groups help children to learn gender-appropriate behaviors and to incorporate gender roles into their self-concept (Hibbard & Buhrmester, 1998).

Today we are seeing new social patterns as technology changes the tools and habits of leisure. Television and videocassettes turn some children into "couch potatoes." Computer games demand few social skills. Organized sports have adult rules and adult referees to settle disputes so that children do not need to find ways to resolve matters among themselves. Still, children spend more time with others their own age than they did in early childhood.

How does the peer group influence children? What determines their acceptance by peers and their ability to make friends? Why do some children become bullies and others, victims?

Positive and Negative Effects of Peer Relations

Children benefit from doing things with peers. They develop skills needed for sociability and intimacy, they enhance relationships, and they gain a sense of belonging. They are motivated to achieve, and they attain a sense of identity. They learn leadership and communication skills, cooperation, roles, and rules (Zarbatany, Hartmann, & Rankin, 1990).

As children begin to move away from parental influence, the peer group opens new perspectives and frees them to make independent judgments. Testing values they previously accepted unquestioningly against those of their peers helps them decide which to keep and which to discard. In comparing themselves with others their age, children obtain a more realistic gauge of their abilities and a clearer sense of self-efficacy (Bandura, 1994). The peer group helps children learn how to get along in society—how to adjust their needs and desires to those of others, when to yield, and when to stand firm. The peer group also offers emotional security. It is reassuring for children to find out that they are not alone in harboring thoughts that might offend an adult.

Among their peers, children get a sense of how smart, how athletic, and how likable they are. Both competition and shared confidences build the self-concept, helping children develop social skills and a sense of belonging. Peer groups tend to be of the same sex, enabling boys and girls to learn gender-appropriate behaviors.

The peer group also can have negative effects. To be part of a peer group, a child is expected to accept its values and behavioral norms; even though these may be undesirable, children may not have the strength to resist. It is usually in the company of peers that children shoplift, begin to use drugs, and act in other antisocial ways. Preadolescent children are especially susceptible to pressure to conform, and this pressure may change a troublesome child into a delinquent one. Children who already have antisocial leanings are the ones most likely to gravitate toward other antisocial youngsters and to be further influenced by them (Hartup, 1992). Peer group influence is especially strong when issues are unclear. Of course, some degree of conformity to group standards is healthy. It is unhealthy when it becomes destructive or prompts people to act against their own better judgment.

Another negative influence of the peer group may be a tendency to reinforce **prejudice:** unfavorable attitudes toward "outsiders," especially members of certain racial or ethnic groups. A study done in Montreal, Canada, where tensions exist between French-speaking and English-speaking citizens, found signs of prejudice in a sample of 254 English-speaking boys and girls in kindergarten through sixth grade (Powlishta, Serbin, Doyle, & White, 1994). The children were given brief descriptions of positive and negative traits (such as *helpful, smart, mean,* and *naughty*) and were asked whether one or both of two cartoon children—one English-speaking and the other French-speaking—would be likely to possess each trait. A similar procedure was followed with regard to male and female figures (using gender stereotypes such as *ambitious* and *gentle*) and figures of overweight and normal-weight children. The researchers also asked the children which of two pictured children they would like to play with.

prejudice
Unfavorable attitude toward members of certain groups outside one's own, especially racial or ethnic groups.

CHECKPOINT

Can you . . .

- ✔ Tell some ways in which members of a peer group tend to be alike?
- ✔ Identify positive and negative effects of the peer group?

In general, children showed biases in favor of children like themselves, but these biases (except for a preference for children of the same sex) diminished with age and cognitive development. Girls were more biased with regard to gender, and boys with regard to ethnicity. However, individual differences were significant, and a child who was highly prejudiced in one respect was not necessarily prejudiced in another.

Prejudice may be lessened or eliminated by broadening children's experience. The most effective programs get children from different groups to work together toward a common goal, as on athletic teams (Gaertner, Mann, Murrell, & Dovidio, 1989).

Consider this . . .

- How can parents and schools reduce racial, religious, and ethnic prejudice?

Popularity

Popularity gains importance in middle childhood. Youngsters spend more time with other children, and their self-esteem is greatly affected by opinions of peers. Peer relationships in middle childhood are strong predictors of later adjustment (Masten & Coatsworth, 1998). Schoolchildren whose peers like them are likely to be well adjusted as adolescents. Those who have trouble getting along with peers are more likely to develop psychological problems, drop out of school, or become delinquent (Hartup, 1992; Kupersmidt & Coie, 1990; Morison & Masten, 1991; Newcomb, Bukowski, & Pattee, 1993; Parker & Asher, 1987).

Popular children typically have good cognitive abilities, are high achievers, are good at solving social problems, help other children, and are assertive without being disruptive or aggressive. They are trustworthy, loyal, and self-disclosing and provide emotional support. Their superior social skills make others enjoy being with them (Masten & Coatsworth, 1998; Newcomb et al., 1993).

Children can be unpopular for many reasons, some of which may not be fully within their control. Some unpopular youngsters are aggressive, some are hyperactive and inattentive, and some are withdrawn (Dodge, Coie, Pettit, & Price, 1990; Masten & Coatsworth, 1998; Newcomb et al., 1993; A. W. Pope, Bierman, & Mumma, 1991). Others act silly and immature or anxious and uncertain. They are often insensitive to other children's feelings and do not adapt well to new situations (Bierman, Smoot, & Aumiller, 1993). Some show undue interest in being with groups of the other sex (Sroufe, Bennett, Englund, Urban, & Shulman, 1993). Some unpopular children *expect* not to be liked, and this becomes a self-fulfilling prophecy (Rabiner & Coie, 1989).

It is often in the family that children acquire behaviors that affect popularity (Masten & Coatsworth, 1998). Authoritative parents tend to have more popular children than authoritarian parents (Dekovic & Janssens, 1992). Children of parents who punish and threaten are likely to threaten or act mean with other children; they are less popular than children whose parents reason with them and try to help them understand how another person might feel (C. H. Hart, Ladd, & Burleson, 1990).

In both western and Chinese cultures, there is a bidirectional link between academic achievement and social competence. High achievers tend to be popular and socially skilled; and well-adjusted, well-liked children tend to do well in school (X. Chen, Rubin, & Li, 1997). One difference is that shyness and sensitivity are valued in China, but not in western cultures. Thus, children who show these traits are more likely to be popular in China—at least in middle childhood (see Box 10-2).

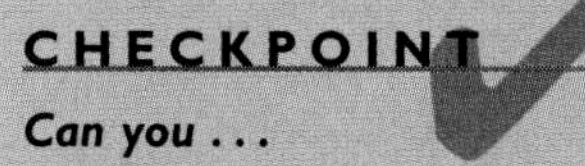

CHECKPOINT

Can you . . .

- ✔ Describe characteristics of popular and unpopular children?
- ✔ Identify family and cultural influences on popularity?

Children can be trained in social skills. In one experiment, fifth- and sixth-graders learned how to carry on a conversation: how to share information about themselves, how to show interest in others by asking questions, and how to give help, suggestions, invitations, and advice. When they had a chance to practice their new conversational skills in a group project with other children, they became better liked by the others and interacted more with them (Bierman & Furman, 1984).

Friendship

Children may spend much of their free time in groups, but only as individuals do they form friendships. Popularity is the peer group's opinion of a child, but friendship is a two-way street. The strongest friendships involve equal commitment and mutual give-and-take (George & Hartmann, 1996; Hartup, 1992; Newcomb & Bagwell, 1995).

A friend is someone a child feels affection for, is comfortable with, likes to do things with, and can share feelings and secrets with. Children look for friends who are like them: of the same age, sex, and ethnic group and with common interests (Hartup, 1992).

Box 10-2

Popularity: A Cross-cultural View

How does culture affect popularity? Would a child who has what it takes to be popular in one culture be equally popular in another? Researchers compared 480 second- and fourth-graders in Shanghai, China, with 296 children the same ages in Ontario, Canada (X. Chen, Rubin, & Sun, 1992). Although the two samples were quite different—for example, none of the Canadian children came from peasant families, but many of the Chinese children did—both samples were representative of school-age children in the two countries.

The researchers assessed the children's popularity by means of two kinds of peer perceptions. The children filled out a sociometric rating telling which three classmates they most and least liked to be with and which three classmates were their best friends. The results showed that certain traits are valued similarly in both cultures. A sociable, cooperative child is likely to be popular in both China and Canada, and an aggressive child is likely to be rejected in both countries. However, one important difference emerged: shy, sensitive children are well liked in China, but not in Canada. This is not surprising. Chinese children are encouraged to be cautious, to restrain themselves, and to inhibit their urges; thus a quiet, shy youngster is considered well behaved. In a western culture such as Canada's, by contrast, such a child is likely to be seen as socially immature, fearful, and lacking in self-confidence.

A follow-up study at ages 8 and 10 (X. Chen, Rubin, & Li, 1995) again found that shy, sensitive Chinese children were popular with peers. They also were rated by teachers as socially competent, as leaders, and as academic achievers. However, by age 12, an interesting twist had occurred: shy, sensitive Chinese children were no longer popular. In fact, they tended to be rejected by their peers, just as in western cultures.

It may be, then, that shyness and sensitivity take on different social meanings in China as children enter adolescence, when peer relationships become more important and adult approval becomes less so. As in the west, a shy early adolescent may lack the assertiveness and communication skills needed to establish and maintain strong peer relationships.

This research suggests that the influence of culture may be tempered by developmental processes that are more or less universal. Even in China, with its strong tradition of obedience to authority, the influence of adult social standards may wane as children's urge to make their own independent judgments of their peers asserts itself.

Children's concepts of friendship, and the ways they act with their friends, change with age, reflecting cognitive and emotional growth. Preschool friends play together, but friendship among school-age children is deeper and more stable. Children cannot be or have true friends until they achieve the cognitive

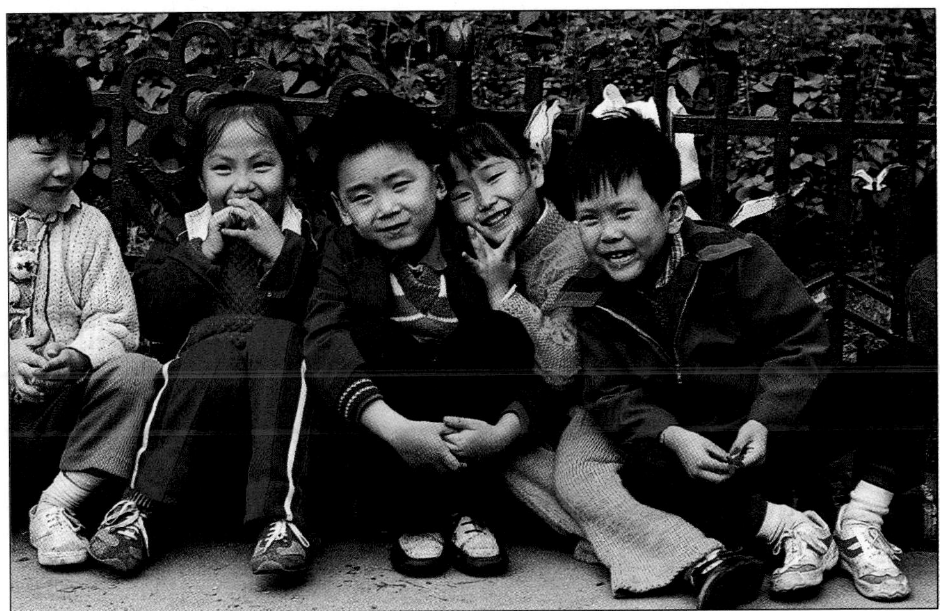

During middle childhood, shy, sensitive children are better liked in China than in western cultures, because they are considered well-behaved. Children this age tend to accept adult standards of behavior.

School-age friends often share secrets—and laughs—as Anna and her friend Christina are doing. Friendship becomes deeper and more stable in middle childhood, reflecting cognitive and emotional growth. Girls tend to have fewer friends, but more intimate ones, than boys do.

maturity to consider other people's views and needs as well as their own (Hartup, 1992; Hartup & Stevens, 1999; Newcomb & Bagwell, 1995).

On the basis of interviews with more than 250 people between ages 3 and 45, Robert Selman (1980; Selman & Selman, 1979) traced changing conceptions of friendship through five overlapping stages (see Table 10-1). He found that most school-age children are in stage 2 (reciprocal friendship based on self-interest). Older children, from about age 9 up, may be in stage 3 (intimate, mutually shared relationships).

School-age children distinguish "best friends," "good friends," and "casual friends" on the basis of how intimate they are and how much time they spend together (Hartup & Stevens, 1999). Children this age typically have three to five "best" friends with whom they spend most of their free time, but they usually play with only one or two at a time (Hartup, 1992; Hartup & Stevens, 1999). Twelve percent of children this age have only one friend or none (Hofferth, 1998).

School-age girls care less about having many friends than about having a few close friends they can rely on; boys have more friendships, but they tend to be less intimate and affectionate (Furman, 1982; Furman & Buhrmester, 1985; Hartup & Stevens, 1999). In one study, 56 same-sex threesomes of third-, fourth-, and fifth-graders were observed discussing personal issues, doing a puzzle together, playing a competitive game, and engaging in free-play. Although intimate sharing was more common among girls and aggressive behavior among boys, there were no differences in responsiveness, dominance, exuberance, or ability to cooperate (Lansford & Parker, 1999).

Friendship seems to help children to feel good about themselves, though it's also likely that children who feel good about themselves have an easier time making friends. Friends know each other well, trust each other, feel a sense of commitment to each other, and treat each other as equals. They can help each other get through stressful transitions, such as starting a new school or adjusting to parents' divorce. Of course, the bond needs to be sturdy enough to withstand the inevitable quarrels. Learning to resolve conflict is an important function of friendship (Furman, 1982; Hartup, 1992, 1996a, 1996b; Hartup & Stevens, 1999; Newcomb & Bagwell, 1995).

Friendship can have cognitive benefits. As we reported in Chapter 9, friends who do written assignments together tend to produce better writing. Friends

Table 10-1 Selman's Stages of Friendship

Stage	Description	Example
Stage 0: Momentary playmateship (ages 3 to 7)	On this *undifferentiated* level of friendship, children are egocentric and have trouble considering another person's point of view; they tend to think only about what they want from a relationship. Most very young children define their friends in terms of physical closeness and value them for material or physical attributes.	"She lives on my street" or "He has the Power Rangers."
Stage 1: One-way assistance (ages 4 to 9)	On this *unilateral* level, a "good friend" does what the child wants the friend to do.	"She's not my friend anymore, because she wouldn't go with me when I wanted her to" or "He's my friend because he always says yes when I want to borrow his eraser."
Stage 2: Two-way fair-weather cooperation (ages 6 to 12)	This *reciprocal* level overlaps stage 1. It involves give-and-take but still serves many separate self-interests, rather than the common interests of the two friends.	"We are friends; we do things for each other" or "A friend is someone who plays with you when you don't have anybody else to play with."
Stage 3: Intimate, mutually shared relationships (ages 9 to 15)	On this *mutual* level, children view a friendship as having a life of its own. It is an ongoing, systematic, committed relationship that incorporates more than doing things for each other. Friends become possessive and demand exclusivity.	"It takes a long time to make a close friend, so you really feel bad if you find out that your friend is trying to make other friends too."
Stage 4: Autonomous interdependence (beginning at age 12)	In this *interdependent* stage, children respect friends' needs for both dependency and autonomy.	"A good friendship is a real commitment, a risk you have to take; you have to support and trust and give, but you have to be able to let go too."

Source: Selman, 1980; Selman & Selman, 1979.

usually cooperate more effectively than mere acquaintances. Friendships among antisocial children are more conflictual, and behavior problems increase when children have antisocial friends (Hartup, 1996a, 1996b; Hartup & Stevens, 1999).

Even unpopular children can make friends. However, they have fewer friends than popular children and tend to find them among younger children, other unpopular children, or children in a different class or a different school (George & Hartmann, 1996). Peer rejection and friendlessness in middle childhood may influence long-term adjustment. In one longitudinal study, fifth-graders who had no friends were more likely than their classmates to show symptoms of depression in young adulthood. Young adults who had had friends in childhood had higher self-esteem (Bagwell, Newcomb, & Bukowski, 1998).

CHECKPOINT

Can you . . .

- ✔ Distinguish between popularity and friendship?
- ✔ List characteristics children look for in friends?
- ✔ Summarize how friendships change with age?
- ✔ Compare boys' and girls' friendships?

Aggression and Bullying

During the school years, aggression declines and changes in form (Coie & Dodge, 1998). *Hostile* aggression (aggression aimed at hurting its target) becomes more common than *instrumental aggression* (aggression aimed at achieving an objective), the hallmark of the preschool period (Coie & Dodge, 1998). *Overt* aggression (physical force or verbal threats) gives way to *relational*, or social, aggression ("putting down" or spreading rumors about another person, teasing, manipulation, and bids for control; see Chapter 8). Relational aggression becomes especially prevalent among girls. Nine-year-olds and older children recognize such behavior as aggressive; they realize that it stems from anger and is aimed at hurting others (Crick, Bigbee, & Howes, 1996; Galen & Underwood, 1997).

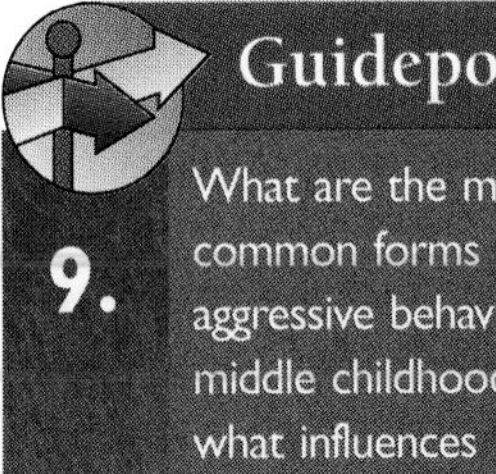

Guidepost
9.
What are the most common forms of aggressive behavior in middle childhood, and what influences contribute to it?

Aggressors tend to be unpopular and to have social and psychological problems, but it is not clear whether aggression causes these problems or is a reaction to them (Crick & Grotpeter, 1995). Highly aggressive children tend to seek out friends like themselves and to egg each other on to antisocial acts (Hartup, 1989, 1992, 1996a; Hartup & Stevens, 1999; Masten & Coatsworth, 1998).

Aggression and Social Information Processing

What makes children act aggressively? One answer may lie in the way they process social information: what features of the social environment they pay attention to, and how they interpret what they perceive (Crick & Dodge, 1994, 1996).

Hostile (also called *reactive*) aggressors tend to have a *hostile bias;* they see other children as trying to hurt them, and they strike out angrily in retaliation or self-defense (Crick & Dodge, 1996; Waldman, 1996). Children who seek dominance and control may be especially sensitive to slights, provocations, or other threats to their status. They may attribute such behavior to hostility and react aggressively (Erdley et al., 1997). Rejected children also tend to have a hostile bias (Coie & Dodge, 1998; Masten & Coatsworth, 1998). Since people often *do* become hostile toward someone who acts aggressively toward them, a hostile bias may become a self-fulfilling prophecy, setting in motion a cycle of aggression.

Instrumental (or *proactive*) aggressors view force and coercion as effective ways to get what they want. They act deliberately, not out of anger. In social-learning terms, they are aggressive because they expect to be rewarded for it; and when they *are* rewarded, their belief in the effectiveness of aggression is reinforced (Crick & Dodge, 1996).

Adults can help children curb *hostile* aggression by teaching them how to recognize when they are getting angry and how to control their anger. *Instrumental* aggression tends to stop if it is not rewarded. Above all, aggressive children need help in altering the way they process social information, so that they do not interpret aggression as either justified or useful (Crick & Dodge, 1996).

Does Televised Violence Lead to Aggression?

Reports of the amount of time U.S. and Canadian children spend watching television range from 12 to 25 hours a week (Hofferth, 1998; Sege & Dietz, 1994; Statistics Canada, 1997). In the United States, 58 percent of all programs in 1994–1995 and 61 percent in 1995–1996 contained some violence, according to a three-year National Television Violence Study (Aidman, 1997). According to one estimate, acts intended to injure or harm others appear about 8 to 12 times an hour on prime-time programs and about 20 times an hour on children's programs, including cartoons (Sege & Dietz, 1994). Thirty-nine percent of children's programs on British television contain violence, mostly shootings or other physical assaults (Gunter & Harrison, 1997).

Research shows that children who see televised violence tend to act aggressively. The long-term influence is particularly great in middle childhood.

Research since the 1960s shows that children who see televised violence behave more aggressively (Coie & Dodge, 1998; National Institute of Mental Health [NIMH], 1982; Strasburger & Donnerstein, 1999). This is true across geographic locations and socioeconomic levels, for both boys and girls, and for normal children as well as for those with emotional problems. These correlations do not, of course, prove that viewing televised violence *causes* aggression, though the findings strongly suggest it. It is possible that children already prone to aggression may watch more violent television and may become more aggressive than other children do after seeing violence on-screen. Still, evidence from a wide range of other research, including experimental and longitudinal studies, supports a causal relationship between watching televised violence and acting aggressively (Coie & Dodge, 1998; Green, 1994; Huston et al., 1992; Strasburger & Donnerstein, 1999).

Children, especially those whose parents use harsh discipline, are more vulnerable than adults to the influence of televised violence (Coie & Dodge, 1998). Classic social-learning research suggests that children imitate filmed models even more than live ones (Bandura, Ross, & Ross, 1963). The influence is stronger if the child believes the violence on the screen is real, identifies with the violent character, and watches without parental supervision (Coie & Dodge, 1998; Huesmann & Eron, 1986).

When children see televised violence, they may absorb the values depicted and come to view aggression as acceptable behavior. Most violent programs do not show victims suffering or perpetrators being punished. On the contrary, they glorify and glamorize violence. Violent acts are usually rewarded and often are depicted as humorous. Children who see both heroes and villains on television getting what they want through violence may conclude that violence is an effective way to resolve conflicts and may become less sensitive to the pain it causes. They may learn to take violence for granted and may be less likely to intervene when they see it (Gunter & Harrison, 1997; National Television Violence Study, 1996; NIMH, 1982; Sege & Dietz, 1994; M. E. Smith, 1993). Of course, some children are more impressionable, more impulsive, and more easily influenced than others (M. O. Johnson, 1996).

The long-term influence of televised violence is greater in middle childhood than at earlier ages; 8- to 12-year-olds seem particulary susceptible (Eron & Huesmann, 1986). Among 427 young adults whose viewing habits had been studied at age 8, the best predictor of aggressiveness in 19-year-old men and women was the degree of violence in the shows they had watched as children (Eron, 1980, 1982). In a follow-up study, the amount of television viewed at age 8, and the preference among boys for violent shows, predicted the severity of criminal offenses at age 30 (Huesmann, 1986; Huesmann & Eron, 1984).

The American Psychological Association (1993) has called for a major effort to reduce violence on television, including limits on violence shown between 6 A.M. and 10 P.M. and warning labels on videotapes containing violent material. In 1996, Congress enacted a law requiring all new television sets to be equipped with an electronic blocking device that parents can use to screen out objectionable programs. The law also prods the networks to devise a violence rating system (Mifflin, 1996).

CHECKPOINT

Can you . . .

✔ Tell how aggression changes in form during middle childhood and how social information processing and televised violence can contribute to it?

Consider this . . .

- What can and should be done about children's exposure to violent television programs?

Bullies and Victims

Aggression becomes **bullying** when it is deliberately, persistently directed against a particular target: a victim who, typically, is weak, vulnerable, and defenseless. Male bullies tend to use physical force (overt aggression) and to select either boys or girls as victims. Female bullies use verbal or psychological means (relational aggression) and are more likely to victimize other girls (Boulton, 1995).

bullying
Aggression deliberately and persistently directed against a particular target, or victim, typically one who is weak, vulnerable, and defenseless.

Patterns of bullying and victimization may become established as early as kindergarten. As tentative peer groups form, aggression is directed at various targets. Aggressors get to know which children make the easiest "marks" and focus their aggression on them.

Victims tend to be anxious and submissive and cry easily, or to be argumentative and provocative (Hodges, Boivin, Vitaro, & Bukowski, 1999; Olweus, 1995). They are apt to have low self-esteem—though it is not clear whether low self-esteem leads to or follows from victimization. Male victims tend to be physically weak (Boulton & Smith, 1994; Olweus, 1995). Children who are bullied may develop such behavior problems as hyperactivity and overdependence, and they may become more aggressive themselves (Schwartz, McFadyen-Ketchum, Dodge,

Pettit, & Bates, 1998). Having a best friend seems to provide some protection against victimization (Hodges et al., 1999).

Middle childhood is a prime time for bullying in many industrialized countries. In one British study, about 1 in 3 eight- and nine-year-olds was identified by peers as a bully or victim. All of the bullies were boys; victims were evenly divided between boys and girls. These identifications persisted through the beginning of the next school year, even when classes and classmates changed (Boulton & Smith, 1994).

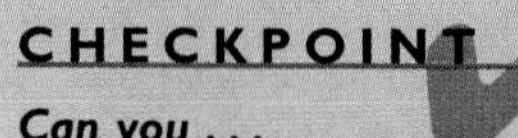

Can you . . .

✔ Describe how patterns of bullying and victimization become established and change?

The likelihood of being bullied, but not of being a bully, seems to decrease steadily throughout middle childhood and adolescence. As children get older, most of them may learn how to discourage bullying, leaving a smaller "pool" of available victims for bullies to pick on (P. K. Smith & Levan, 1995).

Bullying can be stopped or prevented. One intervention program in grades 4 through 7 in Norwegian schools cut bullying in half and also reduced other antisocial behavior. This was accomplished through creation of an authoritative atmosphere marked by warmth, interest, and involvement combined with firm limits and consistent, nonphysical punishment. Better supervision and monitoring at recess and lunch time, class rules against bullying, and serious talks with bullies, victims, and parents were part of the program (Olweus, 1995).

Consider this . . .

- What can and should adults do to help unpopular children, bullies, and victims?

Mental Health

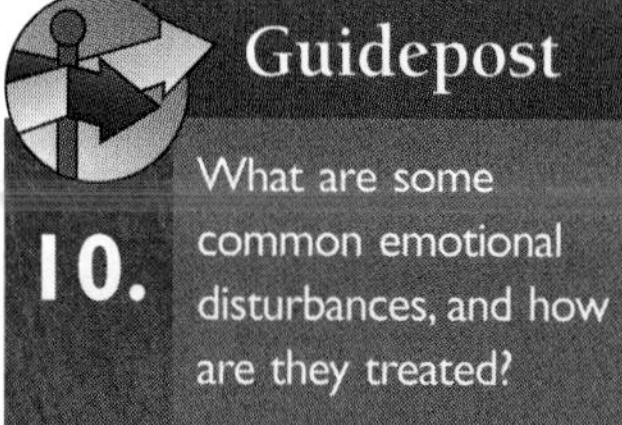

10. What are some common emotional disturbances, and how are they treated?

Among 2,466 children ages 7 to 16 in 1989, more than 8 percent had had mental health services during the previous year and more than 18 percent of the remainder were judged by parents or teachers to have problems that might need clinical treatment. Among these were *withdrawal or social problems* (wanting to be alone or to play with younger children or being secretive, sulky, overly dependent, or lethargic); *attention or thinking problems* (impulsiveness, hyperactivity, or difficulty in concentrating and doing schoolwork); *anxiety or depression* (feeling sad, unloved, nervous, fearful, or lonely); and *aggression or delinquency* (being mean, stubborn, hot-tempered, disobedient, destructive, or antisocial). Some problems seem to be associated with a particular phase of a child's life and will go away on their own, but others need to be treated to prevent future trouble (Achenbach & Howell, 1993). A study of parent-reported mental health problems of more than 13,000 children in Australia, Belgium, China, Germany, Greece, Israel, Jamaica, the Netherlands, Puerto Rico, Sweden, Thailand, and the United States found remarkably similar complaints across cultures (Crijnen, Achenbach, & Verhulst, 1999).

Not all types of social withdrawal point to mental health problems, nor are they equally problematic. Researchers have identified four categories: *passive-anxious, unsociable, active-isolates*, and *sad/depressed. Passive-anxious* children are temperamentally shy; they want to play with others but are too inhibited. *Unsociable* children are socially competent; they simply prefer playing with things to playing with people, and in turn tend to be ignored by peers. In a longitudinal study that followed 567 kindergartners of mixed ethnic and socioeconomic backgrounds for four years, passive-anxious and unsociable children suffered fewer social problems than the other two types. The most socially dysfunctional were *active-isolates*: immature or aggressive children who were social rejects. *Sad/depressed* children tended to be timid, immature, and unpopular and to be rejected or neglected by peers (Harrist, Zaia, Bates, Dodge, & Pettit, 1997).

Common Emotional Disturbances

It is during elementary school that children increasingly are referred for mental health treatment. Let's look at three common types of disturbances: disruptive behavior disorders, anxiety disorders, and depression.

Disruptive Behavior Disorders

Temper tantrums and defiant, argumentative, hostile, deliberately annoying behavior—common among 4- and 5-year-olds—typically are outgrown by middle childhood. When such a pattern of behavior persists until age 8, children (usually boys) may be diagnosed with **oppositional defiant disorder (ODD).** Some children with ODD move on to a repetitive, persistent pattern of aggressive, antisocial acts, such as truancy, setting fires, habitual lying, fighting, vandalism, and use of guns. This is called **conduct disorder (CD).** In the United States, about 9 percent of boys and 2 percent of girls have conduct disorder (APA, 1994); in Canada, it affects about 7 percent of boys and 3 percent of girls (Offord, Boyle, & Racine, 1989). Many youngsters with conduct disorder also have attention-deficit hyperactivity disorder (refer back to Chapter 9). Some 11- to 13-year-olds progress from conduct disorder to criminal violence—mugging, rape, and break-ins—and by age 17 may be frequent, serious offenders (Coie & Dodge, 1998; see the discussion of juvenile delinquency in Chapter 12).

oppositional defiant disorder (ODD)
Pattern of behavior, persisting into middle childhood, marked by negativity, hostility, and defiance.

conduct disorder (CD)
Repetitive, persistent pattern of aggressive, antisocial behavior violating societal norms or the rights of others.

School Phobia and Other Anxiety Disorders

Nicole wakes up on a school morning complaining of nausea, stomachache, or headache. Soon after she receives permission to stay home, the symptom clears up. This goes on day after day, and the longer she is out of school, the harder it is to get her back.

Nicole's behavior is typical of children with **school phobia,** an unrealistic fear of going to school. Some children have realistic reasons to avoid going to school: a sarcastic teacher, overly demanding work, or a bully in the schoolyard (Kochenderfer & Ladd, 1996). In such instances, the environment may need changing, not the child.

school phobia
Unrealistic fear of going to school; may be a form of *separation anxiety disorder* or *social phobia.*

True school phobia may be a type of **separation anxiety disorder,** a condition involving excessive anxiety for at least four weeks concerning separation from home or from people to whom the child is attached. Separation anxiety disorder affects some 4 percent of children and young adolescents and may persist through the college years. These children often come from close-knit, caring families. They may develop the disorder after the death of a pet, an illness, or a move to a new school (APA, 1994).

separation anxiety disorder
Condition involving excessive, prolonged anxiety concerning separation from home or from people to whom a child is attached.

School phobia also may be a form of **social phobia:** extreme fear and/or avoidance of social situations. Social phobia is much more common than was once believed, affecting about 5 percent of children and 8 percent of adults. Social phobias run in families, so there may be a genetic component. Often these phobias are triggered by traumatic experiences, such as a child's mind going blank when the child is called on in class. Children also can develop social phobias by observing how their parents respond to social situations (Beidel & Turner, 1998).

social phobia
Extreme fear and/or avoidance of social situations.

School-phobic children tend to be average or good students. They tend to be timid and inhibited away from home, but willful, stubborn, and demanding with their parents (G. A. Bernstein & Garfinkel, 1988). The most important element in treatment is an early, gradual return to school. Usually children go back without too much trouble once treatment is begun.

Anxiety disorders such as separation anxiety and social phobia are among the most prevalent mental health problems in the United States for children and adults; they are twice as common among girls and women as among boys and men. The heightened female vulnerability to anxiety begins as early as age 6. Females also are more susceptible to depression, which is similar to anxiety in some ways and often goes hand-in-hand with it (Lewinsohn, Gotlib, Lewinsohn, Seeley, & Allen, 1998). Both anxiety and depression may involve a neurologically based *behavior inhibition system:* apprehensiveness, diminished motor activity, and watchful waiting for anticipated danger. A tendency to anxiety and depression may stem from early experiences that make children feel a lack of control over what happens around them (Chorpita & Barlow, 1998).

Childhood Depression

childhood depression Affective disorder characterized by such symptoms as a prolonged sense of friendlessness, inability to have fun or concentrate, fatigue, extreme activity or apathy, feelings of worthlessness, weight change, physical complaints, and thoughts of death or suicide.

"Nobody likes me" is a common complaint among school-age children, who tend to be popularity-conscious; but a prolonged sense of friendlessness may be one sign of **childhood depression:** a disorder of mood that goes beyond normal, temporary sadness. Other symptoms may include inability to have fun or concentrate, fatigue, extreme activity or apathy, crying, sleep problems, feelings of worthlessness, weight change, physical complaints, or frequent thoughts about death or suicide. Any five of these symptoms, lasting at least two weeks, may point to depression (APA, 1994). If symptoms persist, the child should be given psychological help. Depression may lead to an attempted suicide and often signals the beginning of a recurrent problem that, if present during adolescence, is likely to persist into adulthood (Birmaher, 1998; Birmaher et al., 1996; Cicchetti & Toth, 1998; Kye & Ryan, 1995; Weissman et al., 1999).

Twin studies have found the heritability of childhood depression to be only modest. Depressed children tend to come from dysfunctional families, with high levels of parental depression, anxiety, substance abuse, or antisocial behavior. Early interactions with caregivers may lay the groundwork for the emergence of childhood depression. Infants of depressed mothers may fail to develop normal systems for regulating attention, arousal, and emotional states (refer back to Box 6-2). These infants tend to develop insecure attachments and, as toddlers, to lack a healthy sense of self (Cicchetti & Toth, 1998).

Depression often emerges during the transition to middle school and may be related to academic pressures (Cicchetti & Toth, 1998). The prevalence of depression increases during adolescence. As many as 2.5 percent of children and 8.3 percent of adolescents have major depression at a given time, and 15 to 20 percent may experience an episode sometime during adolescence. Between 10 and 35 percent of boys and 15 to 40 percent of girls who have not sought psychotherapy experience depressed moods (Petersen et al., 1993).

Beginning in adolescence, girls are more subject to depression than boys (Birmaher et al., 1996; Cicchetti & Toth, 1998). The reasons for the difference are unclear; it has been attributed to genetic factors, to biological changes connected with puberty, to cognitive predispositions, to the greater female tendency to anxiety disorders, and to the way girls are socialized (Birmaher et al., 1996).

individual psychotherapy Psychological treatment in which a therapist sees a troubled person one-on-one, to help the patient gain insight into his or her personality, relationships, feelings, and behavior.

Girls may be more vulnerable to depression because gender-typing leads them to be less self-confident than boys, to have lower self-esteem, and to be more pessimistic about their capabilities. They are more likely to attribute their successes to outside, undependable forces (such as luck) and their failures to their own faults (Ruble, Greulich, Pomerantz, & Gochberg, 1993). Adolescent girls also tend to be unhappier about their looks than adolescent boys (Tobin-Richards, Boxer, & Petersen, 1983; see Chapter 12). Males may have more effective ways of coping with a depressed mood: they typically distract themselves until the mood lifts, whereas females tend to look for reasons for their depression (Petersen, Kennedy, & Sullivan, 1991).

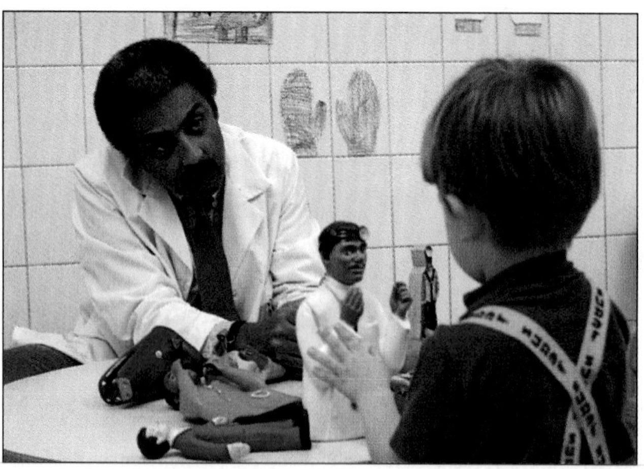

Therapists who work with troubled children often encourage them to express themselves through play, which helps bring out their emotions.

Treatment Techniques

Psychological treatment for emotional disturbances can take several forms. In **individual psychotherapy,** a therapist sees a child one-on-one, to help the child gain insights into his or her personality and relationships and to interpret feelings and behavior. Such treatment may be helpful at a time of stress, such as the death of a parent or parental divorce, even when a child has not shown signs of disturbance. Child psychotherapy is usually more effective when combined with counseling for the parents.

In **family therapy,** the therapist sees the family together, observes how members interact, and points out both growth-producing and growth-inhibiting or destructive patterns of family functioning. Sometimes the child whose problem brings the family into therapy is, ironically, the healthiest member, responding openly to a troubled family situation. Therapy can help parents confront their own conflicts and begin to resolve them. This is often the first step toward resolving the child's problems as well.

family therapy
Psychological treatment in which a therapist sees the whole family together to analyze patterns of family functioning.

Behavior therapy, or *behavior modification* (refer back to Chapter 2), is a form of psychotherapy that uses principles of learning theory to eliminate undesirable behaviors (such as temper tantrums) or to develop desirable ones (such as putting away toys after play). In the latter example, every time the child puts toys away, she or he gets a reward, such as praise, a treat, or a token to be exchanged for a new toy.

behavior therapy
Therapeutic approach using principles of learning theory to encourage desired behaviors or eliminate undesired ones; also called *behavior modification.*

A statistical analysis of many studies found that, in general, psychotherapy is effective with children and adolescents, especially with adolescent girls. Behavior therapy was more effective than nonbehavioral methods. Results were best when treatment was targeted to specific problems and desired outcomes (Weisz, Weiss, Han, Granger, & Morton, 1995).

During the 1980s, the use of **drug therapy** to treat childhood emotional disorders increased (Tuma, 1989). In Chapter 9, we mentioned the use of Ritalin to treat hyperactivity. Antidepressants are commonly prescribed for depression, and antipsychotics for severe psychological problems. Yet many studies have found antidepressants no more effective than *placebos* (substances with no active ingredients) in treating depression in children and adolescents (Fisher & Fisher, 1996; Sommers-Flanagan & Sommers-Flanagan, 1996).

drug therapy
Administration of drugs to treat emotional disorders.

A randomly controlled trial did find fluoxetine (Prozac), the most popular of a new and widely used class of drugs called *serotonin selective reuptake inhibitors (SSRIs),* superior to placebos. It is safer and has more tolerable side effects than other classes of drugs (Birmaher, 1998). A team from the National Institutes of Mental Health found strong support for the safety and short-term efficacy of SSRIs (Rodrigues, 1999). However, Prozac can produce sleep disturbances and behavioral changes, and its long-term effects are unknown. There also is concern that SSRIs may be used instead of psychological therapies, rather than along with them (Rushton, Clark, & Freed, 1999).

CHECKPOINT

Can you . . .

✔ Identify causes and symptoms of aggressive conduct disorders, social phobias, and childhood depression?

✔ Describe and evaluate four common types of therapy for emotional disorders?

Stress and Resilience

Stressful events are part of childhood, and most children learn to cope. Stress that becomes overwhelming, however, can lead to psychological problems. Illness, the birth of a sibling, day-to-day frustration, and parents' temporary absence are common sources of stress for almost every child. Divorce or death of parents, hospitalization, parental substance abuse, and the day-in, day-out grind of homelessness and poverty affect many children. Some children undergo the trauma of war, earthquakes, kidnapping, or child abuse. Such severe stressors may have long-term effects on physical and psychological well-being. Yet some children show remarkable resilience in surviving such ordeals.

Guidepost

11. How do the stresses of modern life affect children, and what enables "resilient" children to withstand them?

Stresses of Modern Life

The child psychologist David Elkind (1981, 1984, 1986, 1997) has called today's child the "hurried child." He warns that the pressures of modern life are forcing children to grow up too soon and are making their childhood too stressful. Today's children are expected to succeed in school, to compete in sports, and to meet parents' emotional needs. Children are exposed to many adult problems on television and in real life before they have mastered the problems of childhood.

They know about sex and violence, and if they live in single-parent homes or dual-earner families, they often must shoulder adult responsibilities. Many children move frequently and have to change schools and leave old friends (Fowler, Simpson, & Schoendorf, 1993; G. A. Simpson & Fowler, 1994). The tightly scheduled pace of life also can be stressful (Hofferth & Sandberg, 1998). Yet children are not small adults. They feel and think like children, and they need the years of childhood for healthy development.

Given how much stress children are exposed to, it should not be surprising that they worry a lot. In a survey and interviews of 272 ethnically diverse second- through sixth-graders in a large metropolitan area (Silverman, La Greca, & Wasserstein, 1995), school emerged as one of the children's chief concerns. So did health—their own or someone else's. However, the worry reported by the largest number of children (56 percent of the sample) was personal harm from others: being robbed, stabbed, or shot.

These children were not in a high-crime area, nor had they personally experienced many attacks. Their intense anxiety about their safety seemed to reflect the high rates of crime and violence in the larger society, as reported in the media. How much more stressful life must be, then, for children who are in real, constant danger—such as a 6-year-old in Washington, D.C., who saw her mother punched in the face by a drug addict, or a 10-year-old who ran away in terror after seeing a man shot in the back on the street! These inner-city children are typical of many who live in the midst of violence and are fearful, anxious, distressed, or depressed (Garbarino, Dubrow, Kostelny, & Pardo, 1992, 1998).

Children who grow up surrounded by violence often have trouble concentrating because fears keep them from getting enough sleep. They may be afraid that their mothers will abandon them. Some become aggressive in order to hide their fear or protect themselves, or simply in imitation of what they have seen. Some become desensitized to brutality and come to take it for granted. Many do not allow themselves to become attached to other people, for fear of more hurt and loss (Garbarino et al., 1992, 1998). Children who first see or experience violence before age 11 are three times more likely to develop psychiatric symptoms than if first exposed to it as teenagers (Davidson & Smith, 1990). (Table 10-2 gives typical reactions to violence at different ages.) Children with multiple risks—those who live in violent communities, who are poor, and who receive inadequate parenting, education, and health care—are the most likely to suffer permanent developmental damage (Rutter, 1987).

Table 10-2 Typical Reactions to Violence at Different Ages

Age	Reaction
Early childhood	Passive reactions and regression (such as bed-wetting, clinging, speaking less); fear of leaving the mother or of sleeping alone; aggressive play; sleep problems
School age	Aggressiveness, inhibition, somatic complaints (headaches, stomachaches, etc.); learning difficulties (forgetfulness, trouble concentrating); psychological difficulties (anxiety, phobias, withdrawal, denial); grief and loss reactions (hopelessness, despair, depression, inability to play, suicidal thoughts, uncaring behavior, destructiveness); acting tough to hide fears; constricted activities
Adolescence	Some of the same reactions as school-age children, plus acting-out and self-destructive behavior (drug abuse, delinquency, promiscuity, life-threatening reenactments of the trauma); identification with the aggressor (becoming violent, joining a gang)

Source: Garbarino et al., 1992.

Children who live in high-crime areas are not the only ones directly exposed to violence. In a government survey of 1,234 public schools throughout the United States, 57 percent of principals had reported incidents of crime or violence to law enforcement officials during the 1996–1997 school year, and 10 percent of the schools had been scenes of serious violent crime (murder, rape, suicide, robbery, or attacks or fights involving weapons). Most such incidents occurred in middle schools and high schools, but 45 percent of elementary schools reported violent incidents, and 4 percent, violent crimes. Most schools (84 percent) had no guards or metal detectors (NCES, 1998a).

To reduce violence, the American Academy of Pediatrics (1992) recommends regulating and restricting ownership of handguns and ammunition; stopping the romanticizing of gun use in television and movies; and targeting adolescents at high risk for becoming violent (chiefly teenage boys and drug and alcohol abusers) for community service. The American Psychological Association's Commission on Violence and Youth recommends community recreational and vocational training programs (Youngstrom, 1992).

Coping with Stress: The Resilient Child

Two children of the same age and sex are exposed to the same stressful experience. One crumbles while the other remains emotionally healthy. Why?

Resilient children are those who weather circumstances that would blight most others, who maintain their composure and competence under challenge or threat, or who bounce back from traumatic events. These children do not possess mysterious qualities. They simply have managed, despite adverse circumstances, to hold onto the basic systems and resources that promote positive development in normal children (see Table 10-3). The two most important **protective factors,** which seem to help children overcome stress and contribute to resilience, are good *family relationships* and *cognitive functioning* (Masten & Coatsworth, 1998).

resilient children
Children who weather adverse circumstances, function well despite challenges or threats, or bounce back from traumatic events that would have a highly negative impact on the emotional development of most children.

protective factors
Influences that reduce the impact of early stress and tend to predict positive outcomes.

Resilient children are likely to have good relationships and strong bonds with at least one supportive parent (Pettit, Bates, & Dodge, 1997) or caregiver. If not, the child may be close to at least one other caring, competent adult (Masten & Coatsworth, 1998).

Resilient children tend to have high IQs and to be good problem solvers. Their superior information-processing skills may help them cope with adversity, protect themselves, regulate their behavior, and learn from experience. They may attract the interest of teachers, who can act as guides, confidants, or mentors (Masten & Coatsworth, 1998).

Table 10-3 Characteristics of Resilient Children and Adolescents

Source	Characteristic
Individual	Good intellectual functioning Appealing, sociable, easygoing disposition Self-efficacy, self-confidence, high self-esteem Talents Faith
Family	Close relationship to caring parent figure Authoritative parenting, warmth, structure, high expectations Socioeconomic advantages Connections to extended supportive family networks
Extrafamilial context	Bonds to prosocial adults outside the family Connections to prosocial organizations Attending effective schools

Source: Masten & Coatsworth, 1998, p. 212.

Other frequently cited protective factors (Eisenberg et al., 1997; Masten et al., 1990; Masten & Coatsworth, 1998; E. E. Werner, 1993) include:

- *The child's personality:* Resilient children are adaptable. They are friendly, well liked, independent, and sensitive to others. They feel and are competent and have high self-esteem. They are creative, resourceful, independent, and pleasant to be with.
- *Reduced risk:* Children who have been exposed to only one of a number of factors strongly related to psychiatric disorder (such as parental discord, low social status, a disturbed mother, a criminal father, and experience in foster care or an institution) are often better able to overcome stress than children who have been exposed to more than one risk factor.
- *Compensating experiences:* A supportive school environment or successful experiences in studies, in sports, in music, or with other children or adults can help make up for a destructive home life. In adulthood, a good marriage can compensate for poor relationships earlier in life.

CHECKPOINT

Can you . . .

✔ Explain Elkind's concept of the "hurried child"?

✔ Name the most common source of fear and anxiety in urban children and tell how fears change with age?

✔ Identify protective factors that contribute to resilience?

All this does not mean that bad things which happen in a child's life do not matter. In general, children with unfavorable backgrounds have more problems in adjustment than children with more favorable backgrounds. Some outwardly resilient children may suffer internal distress that may have long-term consequences (Masten & Coatsworth, 1998). Still, what is heartening about these findings is that negative childhood experiences do not necessarily determine the outcome of a person's life and that many children have the strength to rise above the most difficult circumstances.

The findings on resilience also point to potential pathways to promote more positive development. This might be done by eliminating or reducing the impact of risk factors such as low birthweight and homelessness, adding compensating resources, or bolstering adaptational processes by improving parent-child relationships and designing experiences that build self-efficacy (Masten & Coatsworth, 1998).

Consider this . . .

- How can adults contribute to children's resilience? Give examples.

Adolescence, too, is a stressful, risk-filled time—more so than middle childhood. Yet most adolescents develop the skills and competence to deal with the challenges they face, as we'll see in Chapters 11 and 12.

Summary

The Developing Self

Guidepost 1. How do school-age children develop a realistic self-concept, and what contributes to self-esteem?

- The self-concept becomes more realistic during middle childhood. According to neo-Piagetian theory, cognitive development allows children around age 7 or 8 to form **representational systems**—pictures of the self that are broader and more balanced than before.
- According to Erikson, the chief source of self-esteem is children's view of their productive competence. This is the "virtue" that develops through resolution of the crisis of middle childhood, **industry versus inferiority.** According to Susan Harter's research, self-esteem, or global self-worth, arises primarily from social support as well as from a child's self-evaluation.

Guidepost 2. How do school-age children show emotional growth?

- School-age children have internalized shame and pride and can better understand and control negative emotions.
- Empathy and prosocial behavior increase.

The Child in the Family

Guidepost 3. How do parent-child relationships change in middle childhood?

- School-age children spend less time with, and are less close to, parents than before; but relationships with parents continue to be important. Culture influences family relationships and roles.
- **Coregulation** is an intermediate stage in the transfer of behavioral control from parent to child. It may affect how families handle conflicts and how parents handle discipline.

Guidepost 4. What are the effects of parents' work and of poverty on family atmosphere?

- The family environment has two major components: family structure and family atmosphere. Family atmosphere includes both emotional tone and economic well-being.
- The impact of mothers' employment depends on such factors as the child's age, sex, temperament, and personality; whether the mother works full time or part time; how she feels about her work; whether she has a supportive mate; the family's socioeconomic status; and the kind of care the child receives. Homes with employed mothers tend to be more structured and more egalitarian than homes with at-home mothers. Maternal employment has a positive influence on school achievement in low-income families, but boys in middle-class families tend to do less well.
- Parents living in persistent poverty may have trouble providing effective discipline and monitoring and emotional support.

Guidepost 5. What impact does family structure have on children's development?

- Many children today grow up in nontraditional family structures: one-parent families, stepfamilies, gay and lesbian families, and families headed by grandparents or other relatives. Children tend to do better in **traditional (intact) families.** The structure of the family is less important in itself than in its effects on family atmosphere.
- Although adopted children face special challenges, they are generally well adjusted. **Open adoption** does not seem to affect children's adjustment or parents' satisfaction.
- Children's adjustment to divorce depends on such factors as age, gender, temperament, and social adjustment; the way the parents handle the situation; custody and visitation arrangements; financial circumstances; contact with the noncustodial parent (usually the father); and circumstances surrounding a parent's remarriage. The amount of conflict in a marriage and the likelihood of its continuing after divorce may influence whether or not children are better off if the parents stay together.
- Unwed motherhood creates more single-parent families than does divorce. Children living with only one parent are at heightened risk of behavioral and academic problems.
- Remarriages are more likely to fail than first marriages. Boys tend to have more trouble than girls in adjusting to divorce and single-parent living but tend to adjust better to the mother's remarriage.
- Despite public concern about children living with homosexual parents, studies have found no ill effects.

Guidepost 6. How are relationships with grandparents affected by divorce, mothers' employment, and other family situations?

- Divorce can weaken ties between grandparents (usually the paternal grandparents) and grandchildren. Many grandparents provide child care for working parents or take a single parent and children into their homes. An increasing number of children are being raised by grandparents or other relatives.

Guidepost 7. How do siblings influence and get along with one another?

- The roles and responsibilities of siblings in nonindustrialized societies are more structured than in industrialized societies.
- Siblings learn about conflict resolution from their relationships with each other. Relationships with parents affect sibling relationships.

The Child in the Peer Group

Guidepost 8. How do relationships with peers change in middle childhood, and what influences popularity and choice of friends?

- The peer group becomes more important in middle childhood. Peer groups generally consist of children who are similar in age, sex, ethnicity, and socioeconomic status, and who live near one another or go to school together.
- The peer group helps children develop social skills, allows them to test and adopt values independent of parents, gives them a sense of belonging, and helps develop the self-concept. One negative effect is encouragement of conformity; another is reinforcement of **prejudice** toward outsiders.
- Popularity influences self-esteem and future adjustment. Popular children tend to have good cognitive abilities and social skills. Behaviors that affect popularity may be derived from family relationships and cultural values.
- Intimacy and stability of relationships increase during middle childhood. Boys tend to have more friends, whereas girls have closer friends.

Guidepost 9. What are the most common forms of aggressive behavior in middle childhood, and what influences contribute to it?

- During middle childhood, aggression typically declines. Relational aggression becomes more common than overt aggression, especially among girls. Also, instrumental aggression gives way to hostile aggression. Highly aggressive children tend to be unpopular and maladjusted.
- Aggression may be provoked by faulty social information processing (a hostile bias). Aggressiveness promoted by exposure to televised violence in middle childhood can extend into adult life.
- Middle childhood is a prime time for **bullying;** patterns may be established as early as kindergarten. Victims tend to be weak and submissive, or argumentative and provocative. They generally have poor athletic skills and low self-esteem. The likelihood of being bullied decreases during middle childhood and adolescence.

Mental Health

Guidepost 10. What are some common emotional disturbances, and how are they treated?

- Common emotional and behavioral disorders among school-age children include **oppositional defiant**

disorder (ODD), conduct disorder (CD), school phobia (a form of **separation anxiety disorder**), and **childhood depression.**

- Treatment techniques include **individual psychotherapy, family therapy, behavior therapy,** and **drug therapy.**

Guidepost 11. How do the stresses of modern life affect children, and what enables "resilient" children to withstand them?

- As a result of the pressures of modern life, many children are experiencing a shortened and stressful childhood. Children tend to worry about school, health, and personal safety.
- **Resilient children** are better able than others to withstand stress. **Protective factors** related to cognitive ability, family relationships, personality, degree of risk, and compensating experiences are associated with resilience.

Key Terms

representational systems (370)
industry versus inferiority (370)
coregulation (373)
traditional (intact) families (376)
open adoption (378)
prejudice (387)
bullying (393)
oppositional defiant disorder (ODD) (395)
conduct disorder (CD) (395)
school phobia (395)
separation anxiety disorder (395)
social phobia (395)
childhood depression (396)
individual psychotherapy (396)
family therapy (397)
behavior therapy (397)
drug therapy (397)
resilient children (399)
protective factors (399)

Adolescence

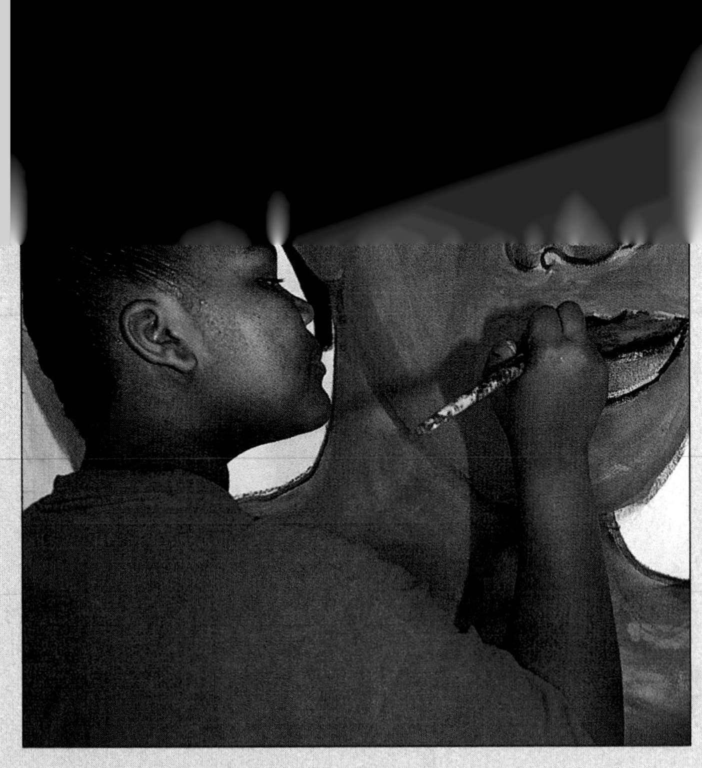

In adolescence, young people's appearance changes; as a result of the hormonal events of puberty, they take on the bodies of adults. Their thinking changes, too; they are better able to think abstractly and hypothetically. Their feelings change about almost everything. All areas of development converge as adolescents confront their major task: establishing an identity—including a sexual identity—that will carry over to adulthood.

In Chapters 11 and 12, we see how adolescents incorporate their drastically changed appearance, their puzzling physical yearnings, and their new cognitive abilities into their sense of self. We see how the peer group serves as the testing ground for teenagers' ideas about life and about themselves. We look at risks and problems that arise during the teenage years, as well as at characteristic strengths of adolescents.

Linkups to **Look For**

- Both hormonal and social influences may contribute to heightened emotion and moodiness in adolescence.
- Early or late physical maturation can affect emotional and social adjustment.
- Conflict between adolescents and their parents may sometimes stem from immature aspects of adolescent thinking.
- Parental involvement and parenting styles influence academic achievement.
- The ability of low-income youngsters to do well in school may depend on the availability of family and community resources.
- Physical characteristics play an important part in molding adolescents' self-concept.
- Girls who are knowledgeable about sex are most likely to postpone sexual activity.
- The intensity and intimacy of adolescent friendships is in part due to cognitive development.

Adolescence: *A Preview*

Chapter 11

Physical and Cognitive Development in Adolescence

Physical growth and other changes are rapid and profound.
Reproductive maturity occurs.
Major health risks arise from behavioral issues, such as eating disorders and drug abuse.
Ability to think abstractly and use scientific reasoning develops.
Immature thinking persists in some attitudes and behaviors.
Education focuses on preparation for college or vocations.

Chapter 12

Psychosocial Development in Adolescence

Search for identity, including sexual identity, becomes central.
Peer groups help develop and test self-concept but also may exert an antisocial influence.
Relationships with parents are generally good.

Chapter 11

Physical and Cognitive Development in Adolescence

What I like in my adolescents is that they have not yet hardened. We all confuse hardening and strength. Strength we must achieve, but not callousness.

Anaïs Nin, *The Diaries of Anaïs Nin,* Vol. IV

OUTLINE

Anne Frank

Focus: Anne Frank, Diarist of the Holocaust*

For her thirteenth birthday on June 12, 1942, Anne Frank's parents gave her a diary. This small, cloth-covered volume was the first of several notebooks in which Anne recorded her experiences and reflections during the next two years. Little did she dream that her jottings would become one of the most famous published accounts of victims of the Holocaust during World War II.

Anne Frank (1929–1945), her parents, Otto and Edith Frank, and her older sister, Margot, were German Jews who fled to Amsterdam after Hitler came to power in 1933, only to see the Netherlands fall to Nazi conquest seven years later. In the summer of 1942, when the Nazis began rounding up Dutch Jews for deportation to concentration camps, the family went into hiding on the upper floors of the building occupied by Otto Frank's pharmaceutical firm. Behind a door concealed by a movable cupboard, a steep stairway led to the four rooms Anne called the "Secret Annexe." For two years, they stayed in those confined quarters with a couple named "Van Daan," their 15-year-old son, "Peter," and a middle-aged dentist, "Albert Dussel,"** who shared Anne's room. Then,

*Sources of biographical information about Anne Frank were Bloom (1999); Frank (1958, 1995), Lindwer (1991), Müller (1998), and Netherlands State Institute for War Documentation (1989). Page references are to the 1958 paperback version of the diary.

**Fictional names Anne invented for use in her diary.

on August 4, 1944, German and Dutch security police raided the "Secret Annexe" and sent its occupants to concentration camps, where all but Anne's father died.

Anne's writings, published by Otto Frank after the war, describe the life the fugitives led. During the day they had to be completely quiet so as not to alert people in the offices below. They saw no one except a few trusted Christian helpers who risked their lives to bring food, books, newspapers, and essential supplies. To venture outside—which would have been necessary to replace Anne's quickly outgrown clothes or to correct her worsening nearsightedness—was unthinkable.

The diary reveals the thoughts, feelings, daydreams, and mood swings of a high-spirited, introspective adolescent coming to maturity under traumatic conditions. Anne wrote of her concern about her "ugly" appearance, of her wish for "a real mother who understands me," and of her adoration for her father (Frank, 1958, pp. 36, 110). She expressed despair at the adults' constant criticism of her failings and at her parents' apparent favoritism toward her sister. She wrote about her fears, her urge for independence, and her aspirations for a writing career.

As tensions rose in the "Secret Annexe," Anne lost her appetite and began taking antidepressant medication. But as time went on, she became less self-pitying and more serious-minded. When she thought back to her previous carefree existence, she felt like a different person from the Anne who had "grown wise within these walls" (p. 149).

She was deeply conscious of her sexual awakening: "I think what is happening to me is so wonderful, and not only what can be seen on my body, but all that is taking place inside. . . . Each time I have a period . . . I have the feeling that . . . I have a sweet secret, and . . . I always long for the time that I shall feel that secret within me again" (pp. 115–116).

Anne originally had regarded Peter as shy and gawky—a not-very-promising companion; but eventually she began visiting his attic room for long, intimate talks and finally, her first kiss. Her diary records the conflict between her stirring sexual passion and her strict moral upbringing.

One of the last diary entries is dated July 15, 1944, less than three weeks before the raid and eight months before Anne's death: " . . . in spite of everything, I still believe that people are really good at heart. . . . I hear the ever approaching thunder, which will destroy us too, I can feel the suffering of millions and yet, if I look up into the heavens, I think that it will all come right, that this cruelty too will end, and that peace and tranquillity will return again" (p. 233).

The moving story of Anne Frank's tragically abbreviated adolescence points up the insistent role of biology and its interrelationships with inner and outer experience. Anne's "coming of age" occurred under highly unusual conditions. Yet her normal physical maturation went on, along with a host of cognitive and psychosocial changes heightened by her stressful circumstances.

In this chapter, we describe the physical transformations of adolescence and how they affect young people's feelings. We consider the impact of early and late maturation, and we discuss health issues associated with this time of life. Turning to cognitive development, we examine the Piagetian stage of formal operations, which makes it possible for a young person like Anne to visualize an ideal world. We also look at some immature aspects of adolescents' thought and at their moral development. Finally, we explore issues of education and vocational choice, which continued to concern Anne even in her constricted situation.

After you have read and studied this chapter, you should be able to answer the following questions:

CH. 11

Guideposts *for* Study

1. What is adolescence, when does it begin and end, and what opportunities and risks does it entail?
2. What physical changes do adolescents experience, and how do these changes affect them psychologically?
3. What are some common health problems and risks of adolescence?
4. How does adolescents' thinking differ from that of younger children?
5. On what basis do adolescents make moral judgments?
6. What influences affect success in secondary school, and why do some students drop out?
7. What are some factors in educational and vocational planning?

Adolescence: A Developmental Transition

Rituals to mark a child's "coming of age" are common in many societies. Rites of passage may include religious blessings, separation from the family, severe tests of strength and endurance, marking the body in some way (see Box 11-1), or acts of magic. The ritual may be held at a certain age; for example, bar mitzvah and bat mitzvah ceremonies mark a 13-year-old Jewish boy's or girl's assumption of responsibility for following traditional religious observance. Or a ritual may be tied to a specific event, such as a girl's first menstruation, which Apache tribes celebrate with a four-day ritual of sunrise-to-sunset chanting.

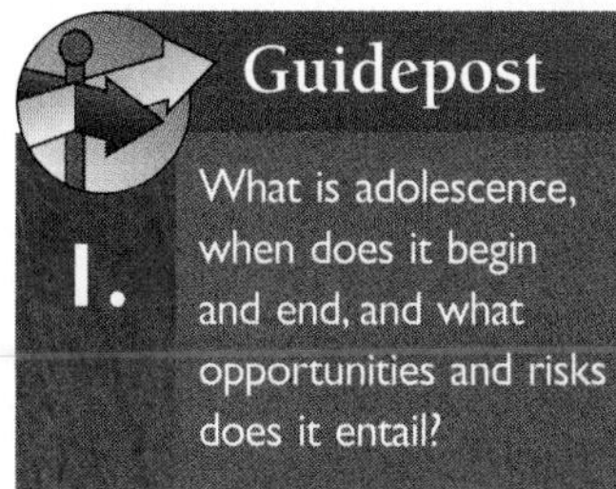

Guidepost

1. What is adolescence, when does it begin and end, and what opportunities and risks does it entail?

In modern industrial societies, the passage to adulthood is generally less abrupt and less clearly marked. Instead, these societies recognize a long transitional

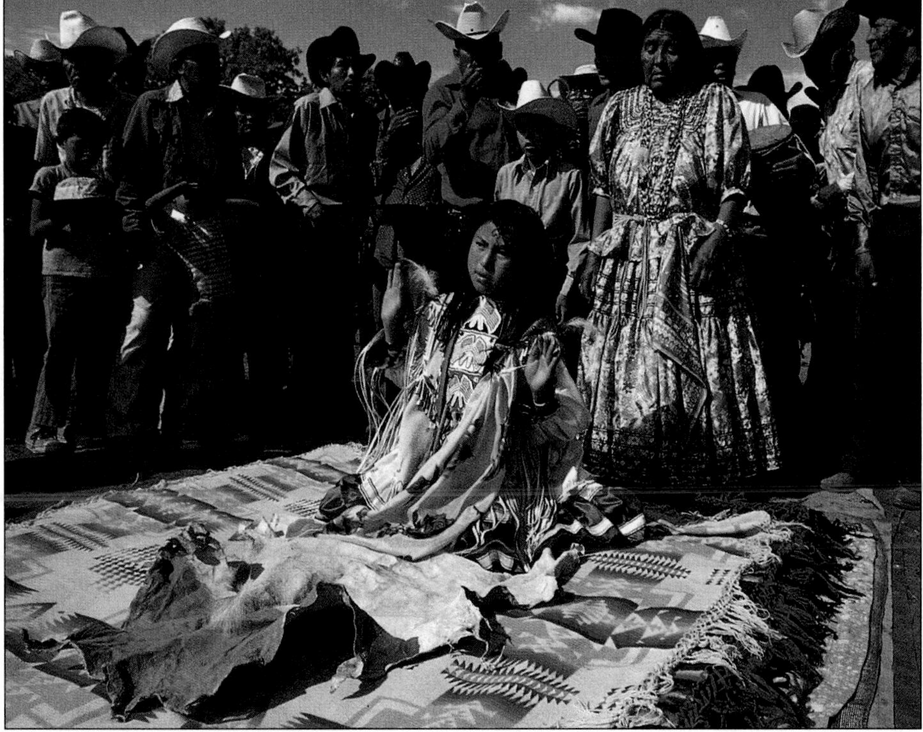

The Apache Indians of the southwestern United States celebrate a girl's entrance into puberty with a four-day ritual that includes special clothing, a symbolic blanket, and singing from sunrise to sunset.

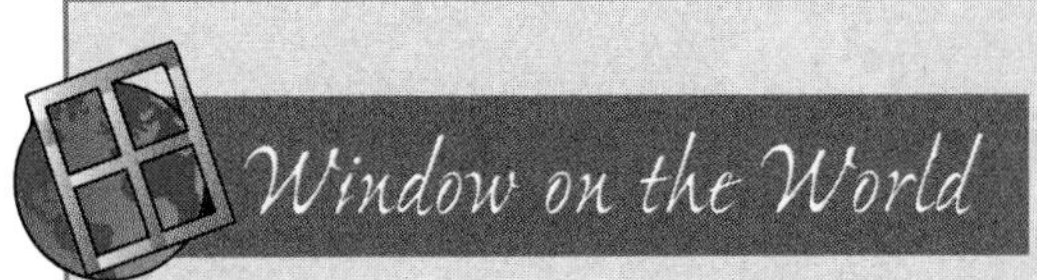

Box 11-1
Female Genital Mutilation

Many traditional societies have coming-of-age rituals that signal membership in the adult community. One custom widely practiced in some parts of Africa, the Middle East, southeastern Asia, and Central and South America is surgery to alter the female genitals (Samad, 1996).

This 4,000-year-old practice, euphemistically called *female circumcision,* is termed *female genital mutilation (FGM)* by the World Health Organization. The operation—which is performed, usually without anesthesia, on girls of varying ages from infancy to puberty—entails *clitoridectomy,* the removal of part or all of the clitoris. Its most extreme form, *infibulation,* includes total clitoridectomy plus removal of parts of the labia (the lips of the vulva), the raw edges of which are then sewn together with catgut or held by thorns, leaving only a tiny opening for menstrual blood and urine. When a woman marries, the scar may be cut open and then enlarged for childbirth (Council on Scientific Affairs, 1995; Samad, 1996). An estimated 100 million women worldwide have had such surgery, and 4 million to 5 million girls undergo it each year (American Academy of Pediatrics [AAP], 1998).

The purposes of these procedures include preserving (and proving) virginity before marriage, reducing sexual appetite, maintaining cleanliness, increasing fertility, enhancing beauty, and affirming femininity through removal of the "malelike" clitoris. In some cultures, an uncircumcised girl is not considered marriageable (Council on Scientific Affairs, 1995; Lightfoot-Klein, 1989; Samad, 1996).

Besides loss of sexual fulfillment, the consequences of FGM can include psychological dysfunction and various immediate or long-term medical problems, such as shock, infection, hemorrhaging, damage to the urethra or anus, tetanus, inability to urinate normally, painful intercourse, complications of childbirth, sterility, or even death (Council on Scientific Affairs, 1995; Lightfoot-Klein, 1989; Samad, 1996).

In more than twenty countries where these operations are practiced, government officials, physicians, and women's groups have tried to end them. However, because many women believe in FGM and because it is sanctioned by some religious leaders, the practice continues (MacFarquhar, 1996; Samad, 1996). In a survey of 5,868 Sudanese women, close to 90 percent had had or planned to have their daughters "circumcised," and about half favored the most severe form of the procedure (Williams & Sobieszczyk, 1997). FGM has been practiced among African refugees in Europe and North America—an estimated 40,000 procedures each year in the United States alone (MacFarquhar, 1996).

The U.S. Congress outlawed the practice in 1996, and a number of countries, including Britain, France, Sweden, and Switzerland, also have banned it. In 1999, a Paris court sentenced an African woman to eight years in prison for cutting the genitals of 48 girls (Simons, 1999). A ban by the Egyptian Health Ministry in 1996 met widespread local defiance but in late 1997 was upheld by Egypt's Supreme Administrative Court.

The World Health Organization, the World Medical Association, the American Medical Association Council on Scientific Affairs, and the American Academy of Pediatrics condemn FGM as harmful and abusive. A British organization, the Foundation for Women's Health Research and Development (FORWARD), formed to raise awareness of FGM, views it as a violation of human rights. Despite some resistance to interfering with a practice that reflects cultural beliefs (Samad, 1996), these organizations have urged physicians not to participate in such surgery and to educate patients and their families to its dangers.

adolescence
Developmental transition between childhood and adulthood entailing major physical, cognitive, and psychosocial changes.

puberty
Process by which a person attains sexual maturity and the ability to reproduce.

period known as **adolescence,** a developmental transition between childhood and adulthood that entails major, interrelated physical, cognitive, and psychosocial changes.

Adolescence lasts about a decade, from about age 11 or 12 until the late teens or early twenties. Neither its beginning nor its end point is clearly marked. Adolescence is generally considered to begin with **puberty,** the process that leads to sexual maturity, or fertility—the ability to reproduce.* Before the twentieth century, children in western cultures entered the adult world when they matured physically or when they began a vocational apprenticeship. Today entry into adulthood takes longer and is less clear-cut. Puberty begins earlier than it used to; and entrance into a vocation tends to occur later, since complex societies re-

*Some people use the term *puberty* to mean the end point of sexual maturation and refer to the process as *pubescence,* but our usage conforms to that of most psychologists today.

quire longer periods of education or vocational training before a young person can take on adult responsibilities.

Contemporary American society has a variety of markers of entrance into adulthood. There are *legal* definitions: at 17, young people may enlist in the armed forces; at age 18, in most states, they may marry without their parents' permission; at 18 to 21 (depending on the state), they may enter into binding contracts. Using *sociological* definitions, people may call themselves adults when they are self-supporting or have chosen a career, have married or formed a significant relationship, or have started a family. There also are *psychological* definitions. Cognitive maturity is often considered to coincide with the capacity for abstract thought. Emotional maturity may depend on such achievements as discovering one's identity, becoming independent of parents, developing a system of values, and forming relationships. Some people never leave adolescence, no matter what their chronological age.

Early adolescence (approximately ages 11 or 12 to 14), the transition out of childhood, offers opportunities for growth—not only in physical dimensions, but also in cognitive and social competence, autonomy, self-esteem, and intimacy. This period also carries great risks. Some young people have trouble handling so many changes at once and may need help in overcoming dangers along the way. Adolescence is a time of increasing divergence between the majority of young people, who are headed for a fulfilling and productive adulthood, and a sizable minority (about 1 out of 5) who will be dealing with major problems (Offer, 1987; Offer & Schonert-Reichl, 1992).

U.S. adolescents today face greater hazards to their physical and mental well-being than did their counterparts in earlier years (Petersen, 1993; Takanishi, 1993). Among these hazards are early pregnancy and childbearing (see Chapter 12) and high death rates from accidents, homicide, and suicide (National Center for Health Statistics [NCHS], 1998a). These problems are not typical in other developed countries (Petersen, 1991). Behavior patterns that contribute to these risks, such as heavy drinking, drug abuse, sexual and gang activity, motorcycling without helmets, and use of firearms, are established early in adolescence (Petersen, 1993; Rivara & Grossman, 1996). Yet, despite the risks of this period, most young people come through the teenage years in good physical and mental health.

Consider this . . .

- What are some implications of attaining sexual maturity years before the customary age of marriage and attaining physical maturity years before attaining independence from parents?
- Some people argue that banning female genital mutilation is imposing western cultural values on nonwestern cultures. How would you respond?

CHECKPOINT

Can you . . .

✔ Distinguish among three ways of defining entrance into adulthood?

✔ Identify some risky behavior patterns common during adolescence?

Physical Development

Puberty: The End of Childhood

The biological changes of puberty, which signal the end of childhood, result in rapid growth in height and weight, changes in body proportions and form, and attainment of sexual maturity. These dramatic physical changes are part of a long, complex process of maturation that begins even before birth, and their psychological ramifications continue into adulthood.

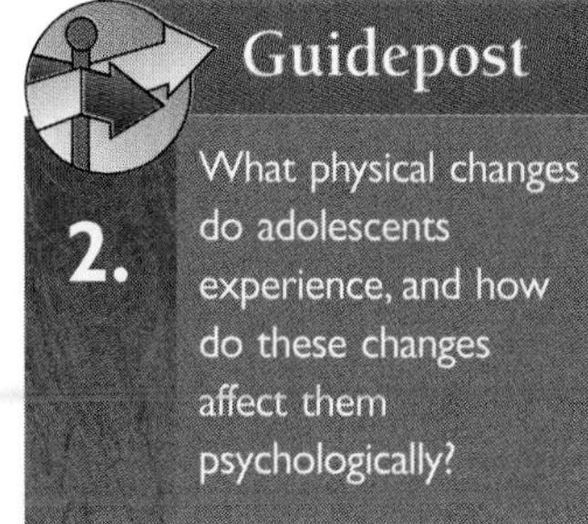

Guidepost
2.
What physical changes do adolescents experience, and how do these changes affect them psychologically?

How Puberty Begins

Puberty begins with a sharp increase in production of sex hormones. First, sometime between ages 5 and 9, the adrenal glands begin secreting larger amounts of androgens, which will play a part in the growth of pubic, axillary (armpit), and facial hair. A few years later, in girls, the ovaries step up their output of estrogen, which stimulates growth of female genitals and development of breasts. In boys, the testes increase the manufacture of androgens, particularly testosterone, which stimulate growth of male genitals, muscle mass, and body hair. Boys and girls have both types of hormones, but girls have higher levels of estrogen and boys have higher levels of androgens; in girls, testosterone influences growth of the clitoris, as well as of the bones and of pubic and axillary hair.

The precise time when this burst of hormonal activity begins seems to depend on reaching a critical weight level. Studies of mice and humans show that leptin, a protein hormone secreted by fatty tissue and identified as having a role in obesity (refer back to Chapter 9), is needed to trigger the onset of puberty (Chehab, Mounzih, Lu, & Lim, 1997; Clément et al., 1998; O'Rahilly, 1998; Strobel, Camoin, Ozata, & Strosberg, 1998). An accumulation of leptin in the bloodstream may stimulate the hypothalamus, a structure at the base of the brain, to send pulsating signals to the nearby pituitary gland, which in turn, may signal the sex glands to increase their secretion of hormones. This may explain why overweight girls tend to enter puberty earlier than thin girls.

Some research attributes the heightened emotionality and moodiness of early adolescence—so apparent in Anne Frank's diary—to hormonal changes. Hormones are associated with aggression in boys and with both aggression and depression in girls (Brooks-Gunn, 1988; Buchanan, Eccles, & Becker, 1992). However, other influences, such as sex, age, temperament, and the timing of puberty, may moderate or even override hormonal ones. Hormones seem more strongly related to moods in boys than in girls, and especially in early adolescents, who are still adjusting to pubertal changes. Environmental factors also make a difference (Buchanan et al., 1992). Although there is a relationship between hormone production and sexuality, adolescents tend to begin sexual activity more in accord with what their friends do than with what their glands secrete (Brooks-Gunn & Reiter, 1990).

Timing, Sequence, and Signs of Maturation

There is about a seven-year range for the onset of puberty in both boys and girls. The process typically takes about four years for both sexes and begins about two or three years earlier in girls than in boys.

Physical changes in both boys and girls during puberty include the adolescent growth spurt, the development of pubic hair, a deeper voice, and muscular growth. The maturation of reproductive organs brings the beginning of menstruation in girls and the production of sperm in boys. These changes unfold in a sequence that is much more consistent than their timing (see Table 11-1), though it does vary somewhat. One girl, for example, may be developing breasts and body hair at about the same rate; in another, body hair may grow so fast that it shows an adult pattern a year or so before her breasts develop. Similar variations occur among boys.

secular trend
Trend that can be seen only by observing several generations, such as the trend toward earlier attainment of adult height and sexual maturity, which began a century ago.

On the basis of historical sources, developmentalists have found a **secular trend** (a trend that spans several generations) in the onset of puberty: a lowering of the age when puberty begins and when young people reach adult height and sexual maturity. The trend, which also involves increases in adult height and weight, began about 100 years ago and has occurred in the United States, western Europe, and Japan. The most likely explanation seems to be a higher standard of living. Children who are healthier, better nourished, and better cared for mature earlier and grow bigger. Thus, the average age of sexual maturity is later in less developed countries than in more industrialized ones. Although the secular trend was believed to have ended in the United States, it now appears that girls—but not boys—are maturing one to two years earlier than previous studies showed (Herman-Giddens et al., 1997; Kaplowitz et al., 1999).

The average age for boys' entry into puberty is 12, but boys may begin to show changes any time between 9 and 16. Girls, on average, begin to show pubertal changes at 8 to 10 years of age. However, it is normal for girls to show breast budding and pubic hair as early as age 6 (for African American girls) or 7

Table 11-1 Usual Sequence of Physiological Changes in Adolescence

Female Characteristics	Age of First Appearance
Growth of breasts	6–13
Growth of pubic hair	6–14
Body growth	9.5–14.5
Menarche	10–16.5
Underarm hair	About 2 years after appearance of pubic hair
Increased output of oil- and sweat-producing glands (which may lead to acne)	About the same time as appearance of underarm hair
Male Characteristics	**Age of First Appearance**
Growth of testes, scrotal sac	10–13.5
Growth of pubic hair	12–16
Body growth	10.5–16
Growth of penis, prostate gland, seminal vesicles	11–14.5
Change in voice	About the same time as growth of penis
First ejaculation of semen	About 1 year after beginning of growth of penis
Facial and underarm hair	About 2 years after appearance of pubic hair
Increased output of oil- and sweat-producing glands (which may lead to acne)	About the same time as appearance of underarm hair

(for white girls) and as late as 14. African American girls, who tend to be heavier than white girls, enter puberty about a year earlier (Chumlea, 1982; Ellis, Abrams, & Wong, 1997; Herman-Giddens et al., 1997; Kaplowitz et al., 1999).

The Adolescent Growth Spurt

In Anne Frank's diary, she made rueful references to her physical growth—to shoes she could no longer get into and vests "so small that they don't even reach my tummy" (p. 71). Anne apparently was in the **adolescent growth spurt**—a rapid increase in height and weight, which generally begins in girls between ages $9^1/_2$ and $14^1/_2$ (usually at about 10) and in boys, between $10^1/_2$ and 16 (usually at 12 or 13). The growth spurt typically lasts about two years; soon after it ends, the young person reaches sexual maturity. Since girls' growth spurt usually occurs earlier than that of boys, girls between ages 11 and 13 are taller, heavier, and stronger than boys the same age. After their growth spurt, boys are again larger, as before. Both boys and girls reach virtually their full height by age 18 (Behrman, 1992).

adolescent growth spurt Sharp increase in height and weight that precedes sexual maturity.

Boys and girls grow differently, of course. A boy becomes larger overall: his shoulders wider, his legs longer relative to his trunk, and his forearms longer relative to his upper arms and his height. A girl's pelvis widens to make childbearing easier, and layers of fat are laid down just under the skin, giving her a more rounded appearance.

The adolescent growth spurt affects practically all skeletal and muscular dimensions; muscular growth peaks at age $12^1/_2$ for girls and $14^1/_2$ for boys. Even the eye grows faster, causing (as in Anne Frank's case) an increase in nearsightedness, a problem that affects about one-fourth of 12- to 17-year-olds (Gans, 1990). The lower jaw becomes longer and thicker, the jaw and nose project more, and the incisor teeth become more upright. Because each of these changes follows its own timetable, parts of the body may be out of proportion for a while. The result is the familiar teenage gawkiness Anne noticed in Peter Van Daan, which accompanies unbalanced, accelerated growth.

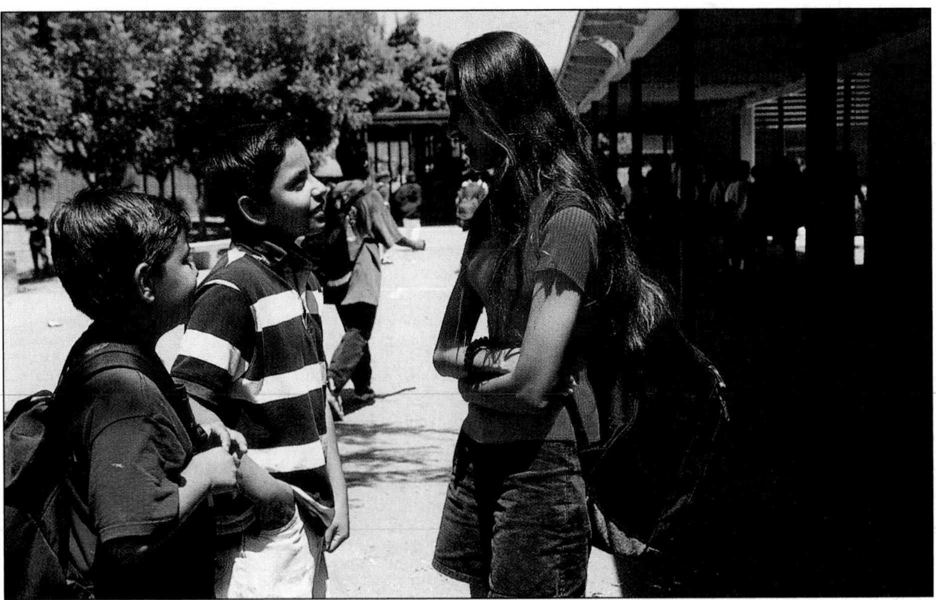

During the years from ages 11 to 13, girls are, on the average, taller, heavier, and stronger than boys, who reach their adolescent growth spurt later than girls do.

These dramatic physical changes have psychological ramifications. Most young teenagers are more concerned about their looks than about any other aspect of themselves, and many do not like what they see in the mirror. Girls tend to be unhappier about their looks than boys, reflecting the greater cultural emphasis on women's physical attributes (Rosenblum & Lewis, 1999). Girls, especially those who are advanced in pubertal development, tend to think they are too fat (Richards, Boxer, Petersen, & Albrecht, 1990; Swarr & Richards, 1996), and this negative body image can lead to eating problems (discussed later in this chapter).

Primary and Secondary Sex Characteristics

primary sex characteristics Organs directly related to reproduction, which enlarge and mature during adolescence. Compare *secondary sex characteristics*.

secondary sex characteristics Physiological signs of sexual maturation (such as breast development and growth of body hair) that do not involve the sex organs. Compare *primary sex characteristics*.

The **primary sex characteristics** are the organs necessary for reproduction. In the female, the sex organs are the ovaries, fallopian tubes, uterus, and vagina; in the male, the testes, penis, scrotum, seminal vesicles, and prostate gland. During puberty, these organs enlarge and mature. In boys, the first sign of puberty is the growth of the testes and scrotum. In girls, the growth of the primary sex characteristics is not readily apparent because these organs are internal.

The **secondary sex characteristics** are physiological signs of sexual maturation that do not directly involve the sex organs: for example, the breasts of females and the broad shoulders of males. Other secondary sex characteristics are changes in the voice and skin texture, muscular development, and the growth of pubic, facial, axillary, and body hair.

The first reliable sign of puberty in girls is the growth of the breasts. The nipples enlarge and protrude, the *areolae* (the pigmented areas surrounding the nipples) enlarge, and the breasts assume first a conical and then a rounded shape. Some adolescent boys, much to their distress, experience temporary breast enlargement; this is normal and may last up to 18 months.

The voice deepens, partly in response to the growth of the larynx and partly, especially in boys, in response to the production of male hormones. The skin becomes coarser and oilier. Increased activity of the sebaceous glands (which secrete a fatty substance) may give rise to pimples and blackheads. Acne is more common in boys and seems related to increased amounts of testosterone.

Pubic hair, which at first is straight and silky and eventually becomes coarse, dark, and curly, appears in different patterns in males and females. Adolescent boys are usually happy to see hair on the face and chest; but girls are usually dismayed at the appearance of even a slight amount of hair on the face or around the nipples, though this is normal.

Signs of Sexual Maturity: Sperm Production and Menstruation

In males, the principal sign of sexual maturity is the production of sperm. A boy may wake up to find a wet spot or a hardened, dried spot on the sheets—the result of a *nocturnal emission,* an involuntary ejaculation of semen (commonly referred to as a *wet dream*). Most adolescent boys have these emissions, sometimes in connection with an erotic dream. There is little research on boys' feelings about the first ejaculation (**spermarche**), which occurs at an average age of 13; most boys in one study reported positive reactions, though about two-thirds were somewhat frightened (Gaddis & Brooks-Gunn, 1985).

spermarche
Boy's first ejaculation.

The principal sign of sexual maturity in girls is *menstruation,* a monthly shedding of tissue from the lining of the womb—what Anne Frank called her "sweet secret." The first menstruation, called **menarche,** occurs fairly late in the sequence of female development (refer back to Table 11–1). On average, a white girl in the United States first menstruates shortly before her thirteenth birthday, and a black girl shortly after her twelfth (Kaplowitz et al., 1999). Menarche typically occurs about two years after breasts have begun to develop and the uterus has begun to grow, and shortly after the growth spurt has slowed down. However, the normal timing of menarche can vary from ages 10 to $16^1/_2$.

menarche
Girl's first menstruation.

A combination of genetic, physical, emotional, and environmental influences may affect the timing of menarche. Strenuous exercise, as in competitive athletics, can delay it. Nutrition also is a factor. In one study (Graber, Brooks-Gunn, & Warren, 1995), 75 girls were examined at ages 10 to 14, before starting to menstruate, and again after menarche. Their age of first menstruation turned out to be similar to that of their mothers. Bigger girls and those whose breasts were more developed tended to menstruate earlier. Even when these factors were controlled, girls with early menarche tended to show aggression or depression or reported poor family relationships (conflict with parents, lack of parental approval and warmth, or negative feelings about the home environment). This last finding supports previous suggestions of a link between family conflict and early menarche (Moffitt, Caspi, Belsky, & Silva, 1992; Steinberg, 1988).

Another longitudinal study suggests that the relationship with the father may be the key to pubertal timing. Among 173 randomly selected girls in Tennessee and Indiana, those who, as preschoolers, had close, supportive relationships with their parents—especially with an affectionate, involved father—showed later pubertal development than girls whose parental relationships had been cold or distant. Also, girls raised by single mothers tended to reach puberty earlier than girls from two-parent homes (Ellis, McFadyen-Ketchum, Dodge, Pettit, & Bates, 1999).

The mechanism by which family relationships may affect pubertal development is not clear. One suggestion is that human males, like some animals, may give off *pheromones,* odorous chemicals that attract mates. As a natural incest-prevention mechanism, sexual development may be inhibited in girls who are heavily exposed to their fathers' pheromones, as would happen in a close father-daughter relationship. On the other hand, frequent exposure to the pheromones of unrelated adult males, such as stepfathers or a single mother's boyfriends, may speed up pubertal development (Ellis & Garber, in press). Since both the father's absence and early pubertal timing have been identified as risk factors for sexual promiscuity and teenage pregnancy, these findings suggest that the father's early presence and active involvement may be important to girls' healthy sexual development (Ellis et al., 1999).

Psychological Effects of Early and Late Maturation

The effects of early and late maturing are not clear-cut and differ in boys and girls.

Some research done during the past several decades has found early-maturing boys to be more poised, relaxed, good-natured, popular with peers, likely to be leaders, and less impulsive than late maturers. Other studies have found them to be more worried about being liked, more cautious, more reliant on others, and more bound by rules and routines. Some studies suggest that early maturers retain a head start in cognitive performance into late adolescence and adulthood (Graber, Lewinsohn, Seeley, & Brooks-Gunn, 1997; R. T. Gross & Duke, 1980; M. C. Jones, 1957; Tanner, 1978). Late maturers have been found to feel more inadequate, self-conscious, rejected, and dominated; to be more dependent, aggressive, insecure, or depressed; to have more conflict with parents and more trouble in school; to have poorer social and coping skills; and to think less of themselves (Graber et al., 1997; Mussen & Jones, 1957; Peskin, 1967, 1973; Siegel, 1982).

Apparently there are pluses and minuses in both situations. Boys like to mature early, and those who do so seem to gain in self-esteem (Alsaker, 1992; Clausen, 1975). Being more muscular than late maturers, they are stronger and better in sports and have a more favorable body image. They also have an edge in dating (Blyth et al., 1981). However, an early maturer sometimes has trouble living up to expectations that he should act as mature as he looks.

Unlike most boys, girls tend *not* to like maturing early; they are generally happier if their timing is about the same as that of their peers. Early-maturing girls tend to be less sociable, less expressive, and less poised; more introverted and shy; and more negative about menarche (M. C. Jones, 1958; Livson & Peskin, 1980; Ruble & Brooks-Gunn, 1982; Stubbs, Rierdan, & Koff, 1989). Perhaps because they feel rushed into confronting the pressures of adolescence before they are ready, they are more vulnerable to psychological distress and remain so at least through the midteens (ages 15 to 16). They are more likely to associate with antisocial peers (Ge, Conger, & Elder, 1996). They may have a poor body image and lower self-esteem than later-maturing girls (Alsaker, 1992; Graber et al., 1997; Simmons, Blyth, Van Cleave, & Bush, 1979). However, some research has found that maturational status in itself does not affect self-esteem, which depends more on the overall social context (Brooks-Gunn, 1988). Early-maturing girls are at in-

Consider this . . .

- Did you mature early, late, or "on time"? How did the timing of your maturation affect you psychologically?

The wide range of sizes and body shapes that can be seen among a group of early adolescents results from the six- to seven-year variation in the onset of puberty. Boys tend to like maturing early, but girls do not.

creased risk of mental health problems, including depression, disruptive behavior, eating disorders, substance abuse, and attempted suicide (Graber et al., 1997).

It is hard to generalize about the psychological effects of timing of puberty because they depend on how the adolescent and other people in his or her world interpret the accompanying changes. Effects of early or late maturation are most likely to be negative when adolescents are much more or less developed than their peers; when they do not see the changes as advantageous; and when several stressful events occur at about the same time (Petersen, 1993; Simmons, Blyth, & McKinney, 1983). As we will see, early maturation is associated with a tendency toward risky behavior in both girls and boys (D. P. Orr & Ingersoll, 1995). Adults need to be sensitive to the potential impact of pubertal changes so as to help young people experience these changes as positively as possible.

CHECKPOINT

Can you . . .

✔ Tell how puberty begins and how its timing and length vary?

✔ Describe typical pubertal changes in boys and girls, and identify factors that affect psychological reactions to these changes?

Physical and Mental Health

Most adolescents have low rates of disability and chronic disease, and dental health has improved among both children and adolescents. Still, about one-fifth of 10- to 18-year-olds in the United States have at least one serious physical or mental health problem, and many more need counseling or other health services (Dougherty, 1993). Among 3,818 students who visited school health facilities at three Denver high schools during a four-year period, 29 percent had emotional problems. Other major reasons for seeking care included respiratory problems (11 percent), reproductive health problems (11 percent), and substance abuse problems (8 percent) (Anglin, Naylor, & Kaplan, 1996).

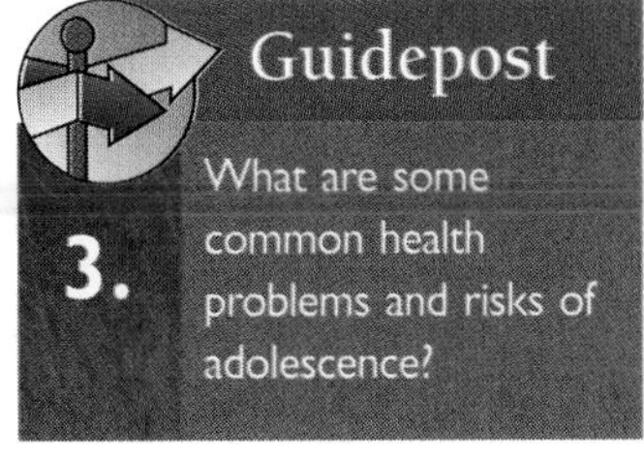

Guidepost
3.
What are some common health problems and risks of adolescence?

Health problems frequently stem from lifestyle or poverty. Across ethnic and social-class lines, many early adolescents use drugs, drive while intoxicated, and become sexually active, and these behaviors increase throughout the teenage years (see Figure 11-1). Adolescents whose families have been disrupted by parental separation or death are more likely to start these activities early and to engage in them more frequently during the next few years (Millstein et al., 1992).

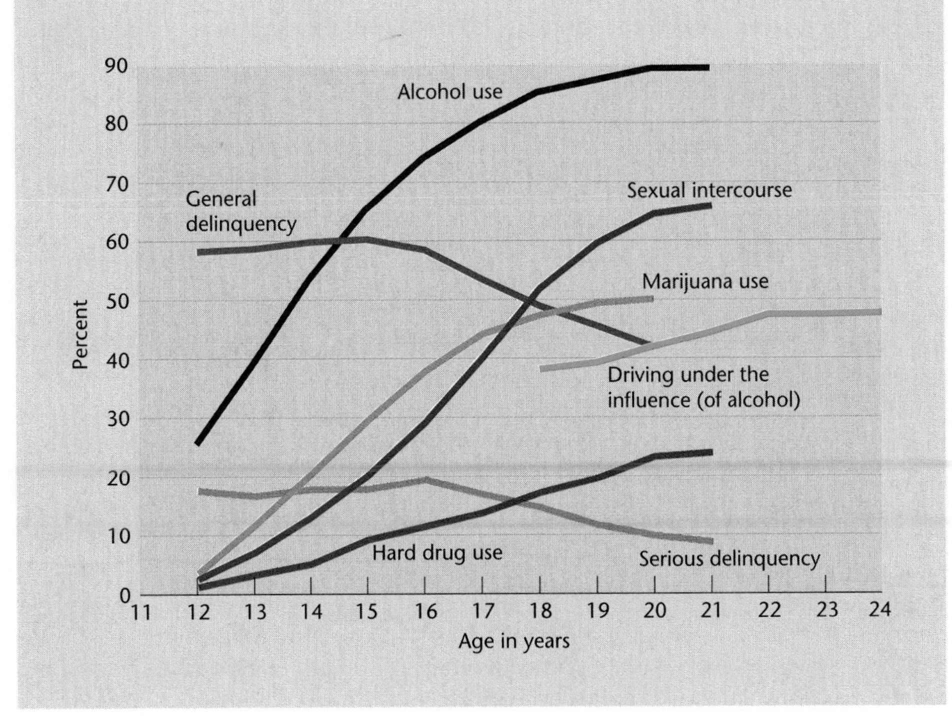

Figure 11-1
Age-specific rates for prevalence of some high-risk behaviors, averaged out over three years.
(Source: Adapted from Elliott, 1993.)

Boys and girls who enter puberty early or whose cognitive maturation is delayed are especially prone to risky behavior (D. P. Orr & Ingersoll, 1995). So are gay, lesbian, and bisexual young people (Garofalo, Wolf, Kessel, Palfrey, & DuRant, 1998).

Adolescents are less likely than younger children to see a physician regularly. An estimated 14 percent of young people under age 18, especially African Americans and Hispanic Americans, do not receive the medical care they need (Gans, 1990; Lieu, Newacheck, & McManus, 1993). Adolescents with mental health problems are more likely to turn to family or friends (if anyone) than to professionals (Offer & Schonert-Reichl, 1992).

Let's look at several specific health concerns: physical fitness, sleep needs, eating disorders, drug abuse, and causes of death in adolescence. (Anxiety and depression were discussed in Chapter 10.)

Physical Fitness

Many boys and girls become less active during adolescence (NIH Consensus Development Panel on Physical Activity and Cardiovascular Health, 1996). Only 50 percent of high school boys and 25 percent of girls report participating in vigorous physical activity at least three days a week (Heath, Pratt, Warren, & Kann, 1994).

Exercise—or lack of it—affects both mental and physical health. Even moderate physical activity, such as brisk walking, bicycling, swimming, or yard work, has health benefits if done regularly for at least 30 minutes on most, and preferably all, days of the week. A sedentary lifestyle that carries over into adulthood may result in increased risk of obesity, diabetes, heart disease, and cancer (NIH Consensus Development Panel, 1996). In a British study, 16-year-olds who participated in team or individual sports had fewer physical or emotional problems and felt better about themselves than less active classmates (Steptoe & Butler, 1996).

Sleep Needs

Many adolescents do not get enough sleep. They go to bed later than younger children and, on school days, get up as early or earlier. Yet adolescents need just as much sleep as before—about 9 hours per night. Nor does "sleeping in" on weekends make up for the loss. Adolescents who are sleep-deprived or who have irregular sleep schedules tend to be chronically sleepy in the daytime, show symptoms of depression, have sleep problems, and do poorly in school. In a survey of 3,120 Rhode Island high school students, total sleep time (on school nights and weekends) diminished by 40 to 50 minutes between ages 13 and 19, and students who got the least sleep got the worst grades (Wolfson & Carskadon, 1998).

Why do teenagers stay up late? Many people assume that it's because they need to study, enjoy talking on the phone with friends, or want to act "grown up." Actually, adolescents undergo a shift in the brain's natural sleep cycle, or *circadian timing system.* The timing of secretion of *melatonin,* a hormone detectable in saliva, is a gauge of when the brain is ready for sleep. After puberty, this secretion takes place later at night than before (Carskadon, Acebo, Richardson, Tate, & Seifer, 1997). Thus adolescents need to go to bed later and get up later than younger children. Yet most secondary schools start earlier than elementary schools. Their schedules are out of sync with students' biological rhythms.

These findings fit in with adolescents' daily mood cycles, which also may be hormonally related. Teenagers tend to be least alert and most stressed early in the morning. Starting school later, or at least offering difficult courses later in the day, would maximize students' ability to concentrate (Crouter & Larson, 1998).

CHECKPOINT

Can you . . .

- ✔ Summarize the status of adolescents' health and health care?
- ✔ Explain why physical activity is important in adolescence, and assess risks and benefits of athletic activity for adolescent girls?
- ✔ Explain why adolescents often get too little sleep and how sleep deprivation can affect them?

Nutrition and Eating Disorders

Nutrition continues to be important in adolescence. Teenagers (like everyone else) should avoid "junk foods" such as french fries, soft drinks, ice cream, and snack chips and dips, which are high in cholesterol, fat, and calories, and low in nutrients.

Adolescents' most common mineral deficiencies are of calcium, zinc, and iron. The need for calcium, which supports bone growth, is best met by drinking enough milk; young people who are lactose intolerant (unable to digest milk) may obtain calcium from other foods, such as calcium-fortified orange juice. Girls who avoid milk for fear of gaining weight should try skim milk, which has a higher calcium content than whole milk. Calcium supplements can increase bone density and—together with regular weight-bearing exercise, such as walking or running—may protect against osteoporosis (Lloyd et al., 1993).

Foods containing zinc—meats, eggs, seafood, and whole-grain cereal products—belong in the diet; even a mild zinc deficiency can delay sexual maturity. Iron-deficiency anemia is common among U.S. adolescents. Teenagers need a steady source of iron-fortified breads, dried fruits, and green leafy vegetables. Iron has cognitive benefits; giving iron supplements to adolescent girls who were not anemic but did have iron deficiency improved their verbal learning and memory (Bruner, Joffe, Duggan, Casella, & Brandt, 1996).

Obesity

The average teenage girl needs about 2,200 calories per day; the average teenage boy needs about 2,800. Many adolescents eat more calories than they expend and thus accumulate excess body fat. Obesity is the most common eating disorder in the United States; 11.5 percent of 12-to 17-year-olds are in the 95th percentile of body mass (weight for height) for their age and sex (NCHS, 1997).

Some causes of obesity—too little physical activity and poor eating habits—are within a person's control. Weight-loss programs that use behavioral modification to help adolescents make changes in diet and exercise have had some success. However, genetic and other factors having nothing to do with willpower or lifestyle choices seem to make some people susceptible to obesity (see Chapters 9 and 13). Among these factors are faulty regulation of metabolism, inability to recognize body cues about hunger and satiation, and development of an abnormally large number of fat cells.

Obese teenagers tend to become obese adults, subject to physical, social, and psychological risks (Gortmaker, Must, Perrin, Sobol, & Dietz, 1993). According to a 60-year longitudinal study, overweight in adolescence can lead to life-threatening chronic conditions in adulthood, even if the excess weight is lost (Must, Jacques, Dallal, Bajema, & Dietz, 1992).

Anorexia Nervosa and Bulimia Nervosa

Sometimes a determination *not* to become obese can result in graver problems than obesity itself. Eating disorders such as anorexia nervosa and bulimia nervosa involve abnormal patterns of food intake, together with excessive concern with body image (refer back to Chapter 9) and weight control. Such chronic disorders affect an estimated 5 million Americans each year (Becker, Grinspoon, Klibanski, & Herzog, 1999), typically adolescent girls and young women, but about 5 to 15 percent of sufferers are male (Andersen, 1995). These disorders are especially common among girls driven to excel in ballet, competitive swimming, long-distance running, figure skating, and gymnastics ("Eating Disorders—Part II," 1997; Skolnick, 1993).

Eating disorders occur in all major ethnic groups and social classes (Becker et al., 1999; "Eating Disorders—Part II," 1997). They tend to run in families, suggesting a possible genetic basis (Becker et al., 1999; "Eating Disorders—Part I,"

Gymnast Christy Henrich died of multiple organ failure at age 22, after having suffered from anorexia and bulimia as a teenager. These eating disorders are especially common among female gymnasts, figure skaters, ballet dancers, and competitive swimmers.

1997; Kendler et al., 1991). Other apparent causes are neurochemical, developmental, and social-cultural (Becker et al., 1999).

Eating disorders are most prevalent in industrialized societies, where food is abundant and attractiveness is equated with slimness (APA, 1994; Becker et al., 1999). Girls' normal increase in body fat at puberty may lead to a negative body image (Swarr & Richards, 1996). Girls tend to become more critical of their bodies over the course of adolescence, while boys became more satisfied with theirs (Rosenblum & Lewis, 1999). Fashion magazines, which promote unrealistic ideals of thinness, influence girls' displeasure with their bodies (A. E. Field, Cheung, Wolf, Herzog, Gortmaker, & Colditz, 1999). In one survey of fifth- through eighth-grade girls, 31 percent said they were dieting, 9 percent sometimes fasted, and 5 percent had induced vomiting ("Eating Disorders—Part II," 1997).

Relationships with parents may be a factor. In a study of 240 suburban white girls in grades 5 through 9, girls who had positive relationships with their parents had fewer weight and eating concerns, both at the time of the original testing and two years later (Swarr & Richards, 1996).

Let's look more closely at anorexia and bulimia.

Anorexia Susanna, 14, diets obsessively. She is preoccupied with food—cooking it, talking about it, and urging others to eat—but she eats very little herself. Yet she has a distorted body image: she thinks she is too fat. Her weight becomes less than 85 percent of what is considered normal for her height and age (APA, 1994). Meanwhile, she stops menstruating, and thick soft hair spreads over her body. To hide what she is doing to herself, she may wear baggy clothes or quietly pocket food and later throw it away; yet she denies that her behavior is abnormal or dangerous. She is a good student, described by her parents as a "model" child, is compulsive about exercising, and participates in gymnastics. She is also withdrawn and depressed and engages in repetitive, perfectionist behavior ("Eating Disorders—Part I," 1997; Garner, 1993).

anorexia nervosa
Eating disorder characterized by self-starvation.

This is a typical scenario for **anorexia nervosa,** or self-starvation. This potentially life-threatening eating disorder occurs mostly in young women, typically beginning during adolescence. An estimated 0.5 to 1 percent of late adolescent girls and a smaller but growing percentage of boys are affected (APA, 1994; "Eating Disorders—Part I," 1997; Garner, 1993).

Anorexia may be due to a combination of genetic and environmental factors. Some authorities point to a deficiency of a crucial chemical in the brain, a disturbance of the hypothalamus, or high levels of opiate-like substances in the spinal fluid ("Eating Disorders–Part I," 1997). Researchers in London, Sweden, and Germany have found reduced blood flow to certain parts of the brain, including an area thought to control visual self-perception and appetite (Gordon, Lask, Bryantwaugh, Christie, & Timini, 1997). Others see anorexia as a psychological disturbance related to fear of growing up or fear of sexuality or to a malfunctioning family that seems harmonious while members are actually overdependent, overly involved in each other's lives, and unable to deal with conflict ("Eating Disorders—Part I," 1997; Garner, 1993). As discussed earlier, anorexia may in part be a reaction to societal pressure to be slender.

Early warning signs include determined, secret dieting; dissatisfaction after losing weight; setting new, lower weight goals after reaching an initial desired weight; excessive exercising; and interruption of regular menstruation.

bulimia nervosa
Eating disorder in which a person regularly eats huge quantities of food and then purges the body by laxatives, induced vomiting, fasting, or excessive exercise.

Bulimia In **bulimia nervosa**, a person—usually an adolescent girl or a young woman—regularly goes on huge eating binges within a short time, usually two hours or less, and then tries to undo the high caloric intake by self-induced vomiting, strict dieting or fasting, engaging in excessively vigorous exercise, or taking laxatives, enemas, or diuretics to purge the body. These episodes occur at least twice a week for at least three months (APA, 1994). (Binge eating without purging is a separate disorder associated with obesity.)

Bulimia is at least two or three times as common as anorexia, and, as with anorexia, most sufferers are females. An estimated 1 to 3 percent of adolescent girls and young women have the disorder, about ten times the number of males. Between 4 and 10 percent of women may become bulimic at some time in their lives (APA, 1994; "Eating Disorders—Part I," 1997; Kendler et al., 1991).

People with bulimia are obsessed with their weight and shape. They do not become abnormally thin, but they become overwhelmed with shame, self-contempt, and depression over their eating habits. They also experience extensive tooth decay (caused by repeated vomiting of stomach acid), gastric irritation, skin lesions, and loss of hair. There is some overlap between anorexia and bulimia; some victims of anorexia have bulimic episodes, and some people with bulimia lose weight ("Eating Disorders—Part I," 1997; Edwards, 1993; Kendler et al., 1991). However, the two are separate disorders.

Bulimia may have a biological basis; it seems to be related to low levels of the brain chemical serotonin ("Eating Disorders—Part I," 1997; K. A. Smith, & Cowen, 1999). However, this association does not necessarily mean that low serotonin levels *cause* bulimia. Then there is a psychoanalytic explanation: people with bulimia use food to satisfy their hunger for love and attention. This interpretation rests on reports by some bulimic patients that they felt abused, neglected, and deprived of parental nurturing ("Eating Disorders—Part I," 1997; Humphrey, 1986). Women likely to become bulimic are age 30 or under. They have low self-esteem, a slim ideal body image, and a history of wide weight fluctuation, dieting, or frequent exercise (Kendler et al. 1991). Many people with bulimia also are alcoholics or substance abusers or have other mental health problems, which may arise from the physical effects of the disorder ("Eating Disorders—Part I," 1997; Edwards, 1993; Kendler et al. 1991).

Consider this . . .

- Can you suggest ways to reduce the prevalence of eating disorders?

Treatment and Outcomes for Anorexia and Bulimia The outlook for people with bulimia is better than for those with anorexia. In a seven-and-a-half-year longitudinal study of 225 Boston girls and women with eating disorders who sought treatment during a three-year period, 74 percent of those with bulimia eventually stopped binging and purging, and 99 percent improved. By contrast, only one-third of those with anorexia recovered, though 83 percent began eating enough to gain some weight (Herzog et al., 1999). Treatment for bulimia tends to be more successful because the patients generally want treatment. But while treatment may speed recovery at first, it does not seem to affect the long-term outcome; symptoms often disappear by the age of 40, even without treatment. ("Eating Disorders—Part II," 1997; Keel & Mitchell, 1997).

Anorexia can be treated, but the relapse rate is high. Up to 25 percent of patients with anorexia progress to chronic invalidism, and between 2 and 10 percent die prematurely (APA, 1994; Beumont, Russell, & Touyz, 1993; "Eating Disorders—Part I," 1997; Herzog, Keller, & Lavori, 1988).

The immediate goal of treatment for anorexia is to get patients to eat and gain weight. They are likely to be admitted to a hospital, where they may be given 24-hour nursing, drugs to encourage eating and inhibit vomiting, and behavior therapy, which rewards eating with such privileges as being allowed to get out of bed and leave the room (Beumont et al., 1993). Bulimia also may be treated with behavior therapy. Patients keep daily diaries of their eating patterns and are taught ways to avoid the temptation to binge. Individual, group, or family psychotherapy can help both anorexics and bulimics, usually after initial behavior therapy has brought symptoms under control. Since these patients are at risk for depression and suicide, antidepressant drugs can be helpful in treating bulimia and in stabilizing recovery from anorexia (Becker et al., 1999; Edwards, 1993; Fluoxetine-

CHECKPOINT

Can you . . .

- ✔ Summarize the normal nutritional needs of adolescent boys and girls?
- ✔ Discuss risk factors, effects, treatment, and prognosis for obesity, anorexia nervosa, and bulimia nervosa?

Bulimia Collaborative Study Group, 1992; Hudson & Pope, 1990; Kaye, Weltzin, Hsu, & Bulik, 1991).

People with anorexia often have long-term psychological problems even after they have stopped starving themselves and have gained some weight. As much as twelve years after recovery, many continue to have an unrealistic body image, to be unusually thin, and to remain preoccupied with weight and eating. They tend to show perfectionist tendencies and to suffer from depression, anxiety disorders, or alcohol dependence (Sullivan, Bulix, Fear, & Pickering, 1998).

Use and Abuse of Drugs

substance abuse
Repeated, harmful use of a substance, usually alcohol or other drugs.

substance dependence
Addiction (physical or psychological, or both) to a harmful substance.

Substance abuse means harmful use of alcohol or other drugs. It is a poorly adaptive behavior pattern, lasting more than one month, in which a person continues to use a substance after knowingly being harmed by it or uses it repeatedly in a hazardous situation, such as driving while intoxicated (APA, 1994). Abuse can lead to **substance dependence** (addiction), which may be physiological or psychological, or both, and is likely to continue into adulthood (Kandel, Davies, Karus, & Yamaguchi, 1986).

Trends and Factors in Drug Use

Use of illicit drugs among U.S. adolescents leveled off in 1997 and dropped slightly in 1998 after increasing throughout most of the 1990s. (The decline for eighth-graders began in 1997.) However, use of crack cocaine continued to increase. The rise in drug use had accompanied a decline in perception of its dangers and a softening of peer disapproval. That trend has now begun to reverse itself, especially among eighth-graders. Throughout the decade, drug use remained less prevalent than during the late 1970s and early 1980s (Mathias, 1999; University of Michigan News and Information Services, 1998a; Zickler, 1999; see Figure 11-2).

These findings come from the latest in a series of annual government surveys of a nationally representative sample of nearly 50,000 eighth-, tenth-, and twelfth-graders in 422 public and private schools across the United States. These surveys

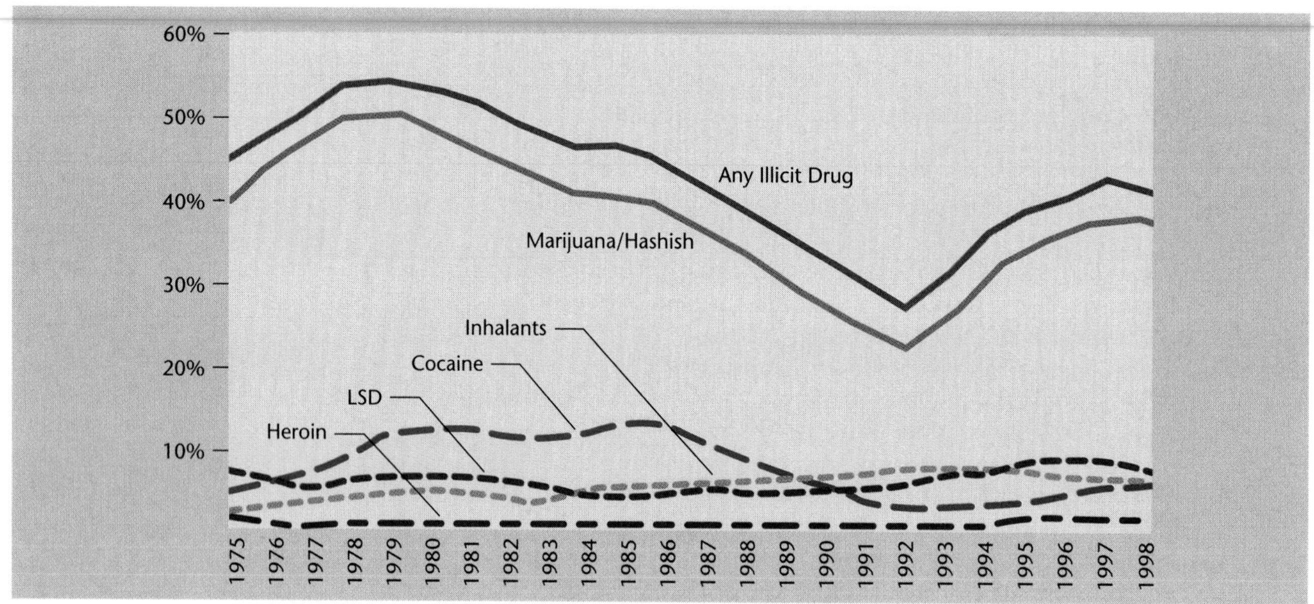

Figure 11-2

Trends in past-year use of drugs by high school seniors. A sharp increase in marijuana use during the 1990s accounts for most of the increase in use of illicit drugs. The rise in use of marijuana accompanied an increase in ease of availability and a decrease in young people's perception of risk of harm from using the drug. Marijuana can be a "gateway" to use of harder drugs.

(Source: Mathias, 1999, p. 58.)

probably underestimate adolescent drug use since they do not reach high school dropouts, who are likely to have higher rates.

What makes it likely that a particular young person will abuse drugs? Research has pinpointed a number of risk factors: (1) poor impulse control and a tendency to seek out sensation rather than avoid harm (which may have a biochemical basis and may appear as early as kindergarten), (2) family influences (such as a genetic predisposition to alcoholism, parental use or acceptance of drugs, poor or inconsistent parenting practices, family conflict, troubled or distant family relationships, and not living with two biological or adoptive parents), (3) "difficult" temperament, (4) early and persistent behavior problems, particularly aggression, (5) academic failure and lack of commitment to education, (6) peer rejection, (7) associating with drug users, (8) alienation and rebelliousness, (9) favorable attitudes toward drug use, and (10) early initiation into drug use. The earlier young people start using a drug, the more frequently they are likely to use it and the greater the tendency to abuse it. Contrary to popular belief, poverty is not linked with drug abuse unless deprivation is extreme (Hawkins, Catalano, & Miller, 1992; Johnson, Hoffmann, & Gerstein, 1996; Masse & Tremblay, 1997; USDHHS, 1996b). The more risk factors that are present, the greater the chance that an adolescent or young adult will abuse drugs.

Drug use often begins as children move from elementary school to middle school, where they meet new friends and become more vulnerable to peer pressure. Cigarettes, beer, and inhalants are more frequently used by fourth- to sixth-graders than marijuana or harder drugs (National Parents' Resource Institute for Drug Education, 1999).

An important early influence may be the omnipresence of substance use in the media. According to one study, alcohol, tobacco, or illicit drugs are shown in 70 percent of prime time network television dramas, 38 out of 40 top-grossing movies, and half of all music videos (Gerbner & Ozyegin, 1997). Among 50 children's animated feature films available on videotape from five major Hollywood studios, more than two-thirds show characters smoking or drinking, with no indication or warning of negative health effects (Goldstein, Sobel, & Newman, 1999).

Gateway Drugs: Alcohol, Marijuana, and Tobacco

Alcohol, marijuana, and tobacco, the three drugs most popular with adolescents, are sometimes called **gateway drugs,** because their use often leads to use of more addictive substances, such as cocaine and heroin (Gerstein & Green, 1993). Young people who smoke or drink often associate with peers who introduce them to harder drugs as they grow older.

gateway drugs
Drugs such as alcohol, tobacco, and marijuana, the use of which tends to lead to use of more addictive drugs.

Alcohol Alcohol is a potent, mind-altering drug and is a very serious problem nationwide. Alcohol use among teenagers, which had drifted upward during most of the 1990s, has begun to decline along with illicit drug use. Still, one-third of high school seniors admit to having been drunk during the past month (University of Michigan News and Information Services, 1998a). This is worrisome because young people who begin drinking before age 15 are four times as likely to become alcohol-dependent as those who do not start drinking until age 20 or later (Grant & Dawson, 1998).

Marijuana Despite a decline in marijuana use since 1979, it is still by far the most widely used illicit drug in the United States. Marijuana accounted for most of the rise and much of the more recent fall in illicit drug use during the 1990s. Still, in 1998 nearly one-quarter of eighth-graders and about one-half of high school seniors admitted to having tried marijuana (Mathias, 1999; University of Michigan News and Information Services, 1998a).

Adolescents try marijuana for many of the same reasons they try alcohol: they are curious, they want to do what their friends do, and they want to be like

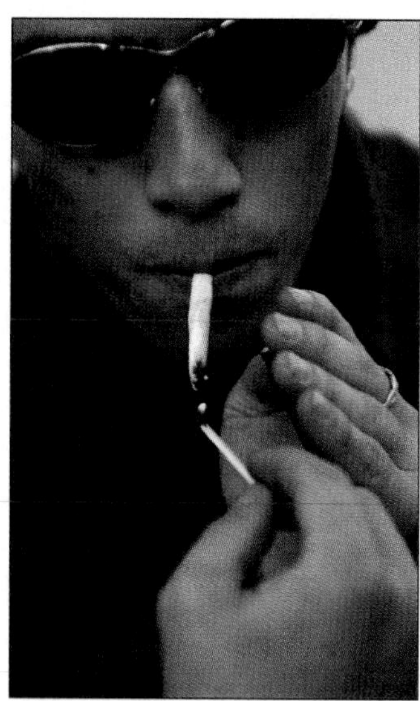

Marijuana is the most widely used illicit drug in the United States; about half of high school seniors say they have tried it. Aside from its own ill effects, marijuana use may lead to addiction to hard drugs.

adults. Marijuana also can be a symbol of rebellion against parental values, but this attraction may be waning, since today's teenagers are much more likely to have parents who have smoked (or now smoke) it themselves.

Heavy use of marijuana can damage the brain, heart, lungs, and immune system; its smoke typically contains more than 400 carcinogens. Using marijuana can impede memory, learning, perception, judgment, and the motor skills needed to drive a vehicle. It can contribute to traffic accidents, nutritional deficiencies, respiratory infections, and other physical problems. It may also lessen motivation, interfere with schoolwork and other activities, cut down on alertness and attention span, and cause family problems (AAP Committee on Drugs, 1980; Farrow, Rees, & Worthington-Roberts, 1987; National Institute on Drug Abuse [NIDA], 1996).

Contrary to a common belief, marijuana may be addictive. Injecting rats with marijuana initially produces a "high" by increasing levels of a brain chemical called *dopamine*. As with heroin, cocaine, and other addictive drugs, the brain's ability to produce dopamine gradually diminishes, creating a greater craving for the drug (Tanda, Pontieri, & DiChiara, 1997).

Tobacco After the release of a U.S. Surgeon General's report in 1964, which linked cigarette smoking to lung cancer, heart disease, emphysema, and several other illnesses, smoking among high school seniors dropped sharply. As with other drugs, an upturn in usage during the 1990s began to reverse itself in 1997–1998, along with a rise in the proportion of young people who see smoking as dangerous. Still, cigarette use remains very high. Nearly 1 in 5 eighth-graders, more than 1 in 4 tenth-graders, and more than 1 in 3 high school seniors reports smoking within the past month (University of Michigan News and Information Services, 1998b).

The prevalence of early smoking is especially serious in light of recent findings that smoking during childhood or adolescence may damage the DNA in the lungs; this increases the danger of lung cancer even in people who later stop smoking (Wiencke et al., 1999). Furthermore, youngsters who begin smoking by age 11 are twice as likely as other young people to engage in risky behaviors, such as riding in a car with a drinking driver; carrying knives or guns to school; using inhalants, marijuana, or cocaine; and making suicide plans. Early use of alcohol and marijuana also are associated with multiple risk behaviors, according to a survey of 2,000 students in North Carolina middle schools (DuRant, Smith, Kreiter, & Krowchuk, 1999).

Consider this . . .

- Should marijuana be legal, like alcohol? Why or why not?
- Should there be tighter restrictions on cigarette advertising? If so, what kinds of restrictions would you favor?
- How can adolescents be helped to avoid or change risky behaviors, such as the use of drugs?

Peer influence on smoking has been documented extensively (Center on Addiction and Substance Abuse at Columbia University [CASA], 1996). Other research points to the family. One 6-year longitudinal study followed 312 adolescents—most of them from white, college-educated, two-parent families—who were *not* smoking at ages 11 and 13. Those whose families were not close and whose parents smoked were more than twice as likely as others in the sample to smoke by ages 17 to 19 (Doherty & Allen, 1994).

Tobacco advertising may be an even stronger factor (N. Evans, Farkas, Gilpin, Berry, & Pierce, 1995). National Health Interview Surveys found a sudden, marked increase in cigarette smoking by girls under 18 after the launching in 1967 of advertising campaigns specifically targeted to women (Pierce, Lee, & Gilpin, 1994). Although the tobacco industry claims that it does not target adolescents, an analysis of advertisements in 39 popular magazines found that cigarette brands popular with 10- to 15-year-olds are more likely than adult brands to be advertised in magazines with young readers (King, Siegel, Celebucki, & Connolly, 1998).

Death in Adolescence

Not every death in adolescence is as poignant as Anne Frank's, but death at this time of life is always tragic. When adolescents die, it is usually from violence. The leading causes of death among 15- to 24-year-olds in the United States—accidents, homicide, and suicide—reflect cultural pressures and adolescents' inexperience and immaturity, which often lead to risk taking and carelessness. The death rate is nearly three times as high for 15- to 24-year-old males as for females and almost twice as high for black as for white young people. Automobile accidents are the leading cause for young whites. For African Americans, homicide is the number one killer–among black males, at a rate almost nine times greater than among white males (Hoyert, Kochanek, & Murphy, 1999). Still, death rates for this age group have dropped 26 percent in the past twenty years, largely because of decreases in alcohol-related motor vehicle accidents and suicide (USDHHS, 1999b). (We discuss teenage suicide in Chapter 19.)

Many teenagers grow up with handgun violence as a fact of daily life. In 1997, more than 8,000 15- to 24-year-olds died from firearm injuries, either deliberate or accidental (Hoyert et al., 1999). However, youth homicide rates have declined since their peak in 1993, partly due to police confiscation of guns on the streets (T. B. Cole, 1999) and to the fact that fewer young people carry weapons (USDHHS, 1999b). Still, about one-third of U.S. homes contain firearms. In more than one-fifth of these households, many of which include children and adolescents, guns are loaded and unlocked (Stennies, Ikeda, Leadbetter, Houston, & Sacks, 1999). Guns in the home increase the risk of teenage homicide more than threefold and of suicide more than tenfold (Rivara & Grossman, 1996).

CHECKPOINT

Can you . . .

- ✔ Summarize recent trends in drug use among adolescents?
- ✔ Discuss factors and risks connected with use of drugs, specifically alcohol, marijuana, and tobacco?
- ✔ Name the three leading causes of death among adolescents, and discuss the dangers of firearm injury?

Cognitive Development

Aspects of Cognitive Maturation

Despite the perils of adolescence, most young people emerge from the teenage years with mature, healthy bodies and a zest for life. Their cognitive development has continued, too. Adolescents not only look different from younger children; they also think differently. Although their thinking may remain immature in some ways, they are capable of abstract reasoning and sophisticated moral judgments, and they can plan more realistically for the future.

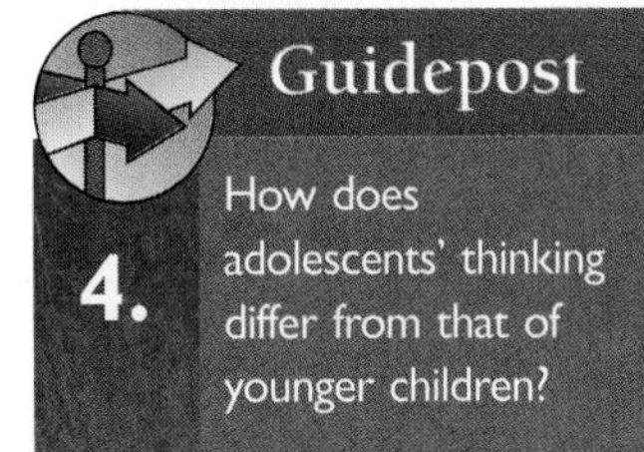

Guidepost
4.
How does adolescents' thinking differ from that of younger children?

Piaget's Stage of Formal Operations

According to Piaget, adolescents enter the highest level of cognitive development—**formal operations**—when they develop the capacity for abstract thought. This development, usually around age 11, gives them a new, more flexible way to manipulate information. No longer limited to the here and now, they can understand historical time and extraterrestrial space. They can use symbols for symbols (for example, letting the letter X stand for a numeral, such as 15) and thus can learn algebra and calculus. They can better appreciate metaphor and allegory and thus can find richer meanings in literature. They can think in terms of what *might* be, not just what *is*. They can imagine possibilities and can form and test hypotheses.

formal operations In Piaget's theory, the final stage of cognitive development, characterized by the ability to think abstractly.

The ability to think abstractly has emotional implications. Earlier, a child could love a parent or hate a classmate. Now "the adolescent can love freedom or hate exploitation. . . . The possible and the ideal captivate both mind and feeling" (H. Ginsburg & Opper, 1979, p. 201). Thus could Anne Frank, in her attic hideout, express her ideals and her hopes for the future.

What determines how fast the pendulum swings: the length of the string? the weight of the object suspended from it? the height from which the object is released? the amount of force used to push the object? According to Piaget, an adolescent who has achieved the stage of formal operations can form a hypothesis and figure out a logical way to test it. However, many people never figure out how to solve this problem.

Hypothetical-Deductive Reasoning

To appreciate the difference formal reasoning makes, let's follow the progress of a typical child in dealing with a classic Piagetian problem, the pendulum problem.* The child, Adam, is shown the pendulum—an object hanging from a string. He is then shown how he can change any of four factors: the length of the string, the weight of the object, the height from which the object is released, and the amount of force he may use to push the object. He is asked to figure out which factor or combination of factors determines how fast the pendulum swings. (This and other Piagetian tasks for assessing the achievement of formal operations are pictured in Figure 11-3.)

When Adam first sees the pendulum, he is not yet 7 years old and is in the preoperational stage. Unable to formulate a plan for attacking the problem, he tries one thing after another in a hit-or-miss manner. First he puts a light weight on a long string and pushes it; then he tries swinging a heavy weight on a short string; then he removes the weight entirely. Not only is his method random; he also cannot understand or report what has happened.

Adam next encounters the pendulum at age 10, when he is in the stage of concrete operations. This time, he discovers that varying the length of the string and the weight of the object affects the speed of the swing. However, because he varies both factors at the same time, he cannot tell which is critical or whether both are.

Adam is confronted with the pendulum for a third time at age 15, and this time he goes at the problem systematically. He designs an experiment to test all the possible hypotheses, varying one factor at a time—first, the length of the string; next, the weight of the object; then the height from which it is released; and finally, the amount of force used—each time holding the other three factors constant. In this way, he is able to determine that only one factor—the length of the string—determines how fast the pendulum swings.

Adam's solution of the pendulum problem shows that he has arrived at the stage of formal operations. He is now capable of **hypothetical-deductive reasoning.** He can develop a hypothesis and can design an experiment to test it. He considers all the relationships he can imagine and goes through them systematically, one by one, to eliminate the false and arrive at the true. Hypothetical-deductive reasoning gives him a tool to solve problems, from fixing the family car to constructing a political theory.

hypothetical-deductive reasoning
Ability, believed by Piaget to accompany the state of formal operations, to develop, consider, and test hypotheses.

Microgenetic studies of problem-solving behavior support Piaget's analysis of how concrete operations differ from formal operations. In one such study, fifth- and sxith-graders and noncollege-educated adults were asked to design experiments to understand physical phenomena (Schauble, 1996). For example, they were to vary the depth of water in a model canal and the size, shape, and weight of boats traveling through it, so as to maximize the speed of the vessels. Preadolescents were less systematic than adults in exploring such problems, typically varying more than one factor at the same time, as Adam did with the pendulum at that age.

To solve such problems, people need to think like scientists. They need theories and hypotheses to guide their problem-solving strategies, and they need to modify or abandon a hypothesis when the evidence does not fit. On the other hand, they should not rule out a hypothesis before testing it, just because it seems unlikely to be true—a common mistake among children (DeLoache, Miller, & Pierroutsakos, 1998). Above all, they need to know what theories and strategies they are following. Many preadolescents do not have coherent theories and

*This description of age-related differences in the approach to the pendulum problem is adapted from H. Ginsburg & Opper, 1979.

Figure 11-3

Piagetian tasks for measuring attainment of formal operations. (a) Pendulum. The pendulum's string can be shortened or lengthened, and weights of varying sizes can be attached to it. The student must determine what variables affect the speed of the pendulum's swing. (b) Motion in a horizontal plane. A spring device launches balls of varying sizes, which roll in a horizontal plane. The student must predict their stopping points. (c) Balance beam. A balance scale comes with weights of varying sizes, which can be hung at different points along the crossbar. The student must determine what factors affect whether or not the scale will balance. (d) Shadows. A board containing a row of peg holes is laid perpendicular to a screen at its base. A light source and rings of varying diameters can be placed in the holes, at varying distances from the screen. The student must produce two shadows of the same size, using different-sized rings.

(Source: Adapted from Small, 1990, Fig. 8-12.)

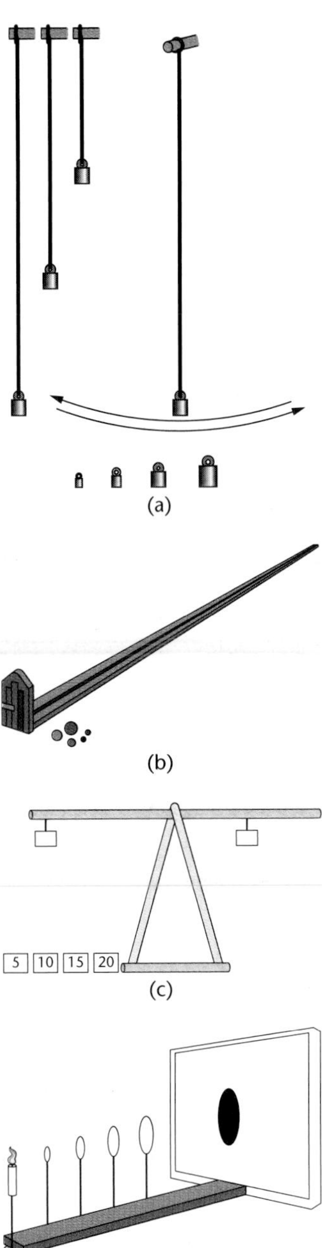

strategies or do not consciously think about them (Kuhn, Garcia-Mila, Zohar, & Anderson, 1995).

What brings about the shift to formal reasoning? Piaget attributed it to a combination of brain maturation and expanding environmental opportunities. Both are essential: even if young people's neurological development has advanced enough to permit formal reasoning, they can attain it only with appropriate environmental stimulation. One way this happens is through cooperative effort. When college students (average age, $18^1/_2$) were given a chemistry problem and told to set up their own experiments to solve it, students randomly assigned to work in pairs solved more problems than those who worked alone. The more the partners challenged each other's reasoning, the greater were the advances in thinking (Dimant & Bearison, 1991).

As with the development of concrete operations, schooling and culture seem to play a role—as Piaget (1972) ultimately recognized. French 10- to 15-year-olds in the 1990s did better on Piagetian tests of formal operations than their counterparts two to three decades earlier, at a time when fewer French adolescents (or their parents) had secondary school educations (Flieller, 1999). (This apparent speedup in cognitive development may help explain the *Flynn effect,* a steady rise in IQ scores over time, which has occurred in France and many other countries during the twentieth century.) When adolescents in New Guinea and Rwanda were tested on the pendulum problem, none were able to solve it. On the other hand, Chinese children in Hong Kong, who had been to British schools, did at least as well as U.S. or European children. Schoolchildren in Central Java and New South Wales also showed some formal operational abilities (Gardiner et al., 1998). Apparently, this kind of thinking is a learned ability that is not equally necessary or equally valued in all cultures.

Evaluating Piaget's Theory

Piaget's analysis of the development of formal reasoning seems fairly accurate, as far as it goes. However, there are several advances, both in middle childhood and in adolescence, that it does not adequately take into account. Among them are the gradual accumulation of knowledge and expertise in specific fields; the gain in information-processing capacity; and growth in *metacognition,* awareness and monitoring of one's own mental processes and strategies (Flavell et al., 1993).

While research has not seriously challenged the overall *sequence* of development Piaget described (Lourenco & Machado, 1996), it has questioned his assertion of definite stages of development. For example, the distinction between the stages of concrete and formal operations may be less clear-cut than Piaget's theory suggests. His own writings provide many examples of children displaying aspects of scientific thinking well before adolescence. At the same time, Piaget seems to have *over*estimated older children's abilities. Many late adolescents and adults—perhaps one-third to one-half—seem incapable of abstract thought as

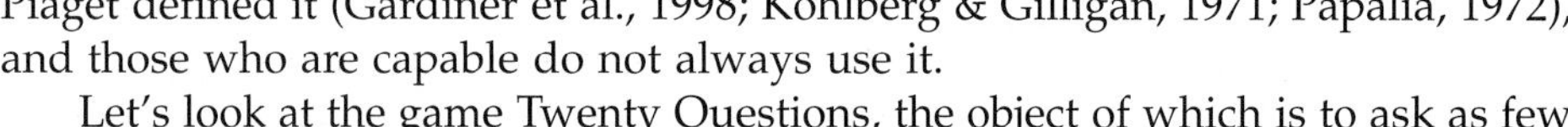

Piaget defined it (Gardiner et al., 1998; Kohlberg & Gilligan, 1971; Papalia, 1972), and those who are capable do not always use it.

Let's look at the game Twenty Questions, the object of which is to ask as few yes-or-no questions as necessary to discover the identity of a person, place, or thing. The efficiency with which young people can do this, by systematically narrowing down the categories within which the answer might fall, generally improves between middle childhood and late adolescence. However, in one study (Drumm & Jackson, 1996), high school students, especially boys, showed a greater tendency than either early adolescents or college students to jump to guessing the answer. This pattern of guesswork may reflect a penchant for impulsive, risky behavior—whether it be in driving, drug use, or sexual activity—at a time when young people have more autonomy than before and more choices to make.

CHECKPOINT

Can you . . .

- ✔ Explain the difference between formal operational and concrete operational thinking, as exemplified by the pendulum problem?
- ✔ Cite factors influencing adolescents' development of formal reasoning?
- ✔ Evaluate strengths and weaknesses of Piaget's theory?

Brain research suggests a possible reason for adolescents' rash judgments. In one study, 16 adolescents (ages 10 to 18) and 18 young adults were asked to look at pictures of people with fearful expressions, while researchers used magnetic resonance imaging (MRI) to examine their brains. Adults tended to process the pictures with the frontal lobes, which are involved in rational thinking. In adolescents, whose frontal lobes are not yet fully developed, the pictures aroused more activity in the amygdala, a small, almond-shaped structure deep in the temporal lobe that is heavily involved in emotional and instinctual reactions (refer back to Figure 4-6 in Chapter 4). This was especially true of the younger adolescents, suggesting that immature brain development may permit feelings to override reason (Baird et al., 1999).

Consider this . . .

- How can parents and teachers help adolescents improve their reasoning ability?

The familiarity of a situation and how much a child knows about it can greatly influence the sophistication of the child's reasoning. Yet Piaget, in most of his writings, paid little attention to individual differences, to variations in a child's performance of different kinds of tasks, or to social and cultural influences (Flavell et al., 1993). In his later years, Piaget himself "came to view his earlier model of the development of children's thinking, particularly formal operations, as flawed because it failed to capture the essential *role of the situation* in influencing and constraining . . . children's thinking" (Brown, Metz, & Campione, 1996, pp. 152–153).

Elkind: Immature Characteristics of Adolescent Thought

On the basis of clinical work with adolescents, the psychologist David Elkind (1984, 1998) has described immature behaviors and attitudes that may stem from young people's inexperienced ventures into abstract thought:

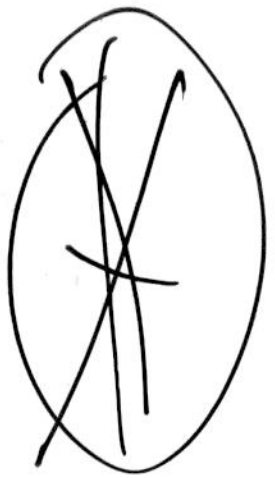

- *Argumentativeness:* Adolescents are constantly looking for opportunities to try out—and show off—their newfound reasoning abilities. They often become argumentative as they explore the nuances of a problem or build a case for staying out later than their parents think they should.
- *Indecisiveness:* Because they are now more aware of how many choices life offers, many teenagers have trouble making up their minds even about such simple things as whether to go to the mall with a friend or to the computer to work on a school assignment.
- *Finding fault with authority figures:* Adolescents now realize that the adults they once worshiped and the world for which they hold adults responsible fall far short of their ideals; and they feel compelled to say so, as Anne Frank did when writing about her mother ("I face life with more courage than Mummy; my feeling for justice is immovable, and truer than hers. . . . I shall not remain insignificant, I shall work in the world and for mankind!" [Frank, 1958, pp. 184–185]).
- *Apparent hypocrisy:* Young adolescents often do not recognize the difference between expressing an ideal and making the sacrifices necessary to live up

to it. In one example Elkind (1998) gives, teenagers concerned about animal welfare demonstrated in front of a furrier's shop but waited until a warm spring day to do it—thus avoiding having to stand outside in cloth coats in wintry weather.

- *Self-consciousness:* In their preoccupation with their own mental state, adolescents often assume that everyone else is thinking about the same thing they are thinking about: themselves. Elkind refers to this self-consciousness as the **imaginary audience,** a conceptualized "observer" who is as concerned with a young person's thoughts and behavior as he or she is. The imaginary audience fantasy is especially strong in the early teens; the early entries in Anne Frank's diary contain many references to what she thinks the others in the "Secret Annexe" think of her.
- *Assumption of invulnerability:* Elkind uses the term **personal fable** to denote a belief by adolescents that they are special, that their experience is unique, and that they are not subject to the rules that govern the rest of the world ("Other people get hooked from taking drugs, not me," or, "No one has ever been in love as I am"). According to Elkind, this special form of egocentrism underlies much risky, self-destructive behavior.

imaginary audience
In Elkind's terminology, an observer who exists only in an adolescent's mind and is as concerned with the adolescent's thoughts and actions as the adolescent is.

personal fable
In Elkind's terminology, conviction that one is special, unique, and not subject to the rules that govern the rest of the world.

The imaginary audience and the personal fable, says Elkind (1998), persist to a lesser degree in adult life. The imaginary audience may surface when, for example, a person drops a fork on the tile floor of a noisy restaurant and imagines that everyone in the room is watching. The personal fable is what enables people to take necessary risks, such as driving a car despite statistics on highway deaths. Perhaps it was what led Anne Frank's parents to believe that by hiding in a building on a city street they would be safe from the fate of the Jewish families around them.

The concepts of the imaginary audience and the personal fable have been widely accepted, but their validity as especially strong earmarks of adolescence has little independent research support. One study of the personal fable compared 86 mostly white, middle-class teenagers; their parents; and 95 mostly male, nonwhite teenagers in homes for adolescents with legal and substance abuse problems. Participants were asked to estimate their risk of being in a car accident, having an unwanted pregnancy, becoming alcoholic, being mugged, or becoming sick from air pollution. All three groups saw themselves as facing less risk than others they knew; this attitude was no more pronounced in teenagers than in adults. In fact, for some risks adolescents considered themselves in *more* danger than their parents considered themselves (Quadrel, Fischoff, & Davis, 1993). Similarly, in another study, adolescents were more likely than college students or adults to see themselves as vulnerable to alcohol and other drug problems (Millstein, in press).

Rather than universal features of adolescents' cognitive development, the imaginary audience and personal fable may be related to specific social experiences, such as the transition to middle school. And, since these concepts grew out of Elkind's clinical observations, they may be more characteristic of youngsters who are experiencing difficulties in adjustment (Vartanian & Powlishta, 1996).

CHECKPOINT

Can you . . .

✔ Describe Elkind's seven proposed aspects of immature adolescent thought, and give examples of each?

Consider this . . .

- In your experience, are the attitudes Elkind called the *imaginary audience* and *personal fable* more characteristic of adolescents than of adults?

Moral Reasoning: Kohlberg's Theory

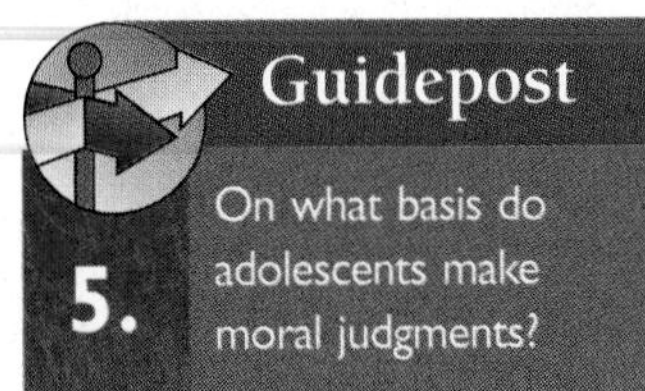

Guidepost
5.
On what basis do adolescents make moral judgments?

A woman is near death from cancer. A druggist has discovered a drug that doctors believe might save her. The druggist is charging $2,000 for a small dose—ten times what the drug costs him to make. The sick woman's husband, Heinz, borrows from everyone he knows but can scrape together only $1,000. He begs the druggist to sell him the drug for $1,000 or let him pay the rest later. The druggist refuses, saying "I discovered the drug and I'm going to make money from it." Heinz, desperate, breaks into the man's store and steals the drug. Should Heinz have done that? Why or why not? (Kohlberg, 1969).

Heinz's problem is the most famous example of Lawrence Kohlberg's approach to studying moral development. Starting in the 1950s, Kohlberg and his colleagues posed hypothetical dilemmas like this one to 75 boys ages 10, 13, and 16, and continued to question them periodically for more than thirty years. At the heart of each dilemma was the concept of justice. By asking respondents how they arrived at their answers, Kohlberg concluded that how people think about moral issues reflects cognitive development and that people arrive at moral judgments on their own, rather than merely internalizing standards of parents, teachers, or peers.

Kohlberg's Levels and Stages

preconventional morality First level of Kohlberg's theory of moral reasoning, in which control is external and rules are obeyed in order to gain rewards, or avoid punishment, or out of self-interest.

Moral development in Kohlberg's theory bears some similarity to Piaget's (refer back to Chapter 9), but his model is more complex. On the basis of thought processes shown by responses to his dilemmas, Kohlberg (1969) described three levels of moral reasoning, each divided into two stages (see Table 11-2):

- *Level I:* **Preconventional morality.** People act under external controls. They obey rules to avoid punishment or reap rewards, or act out of self-interest. This level is typical of children ages 4 to 10.

Table 11-2 Kohlberg's Six Stages of Moral Reasoning

Levels	Stages of Reasoning	Typical Answers to Heinz's Dilemma
Level I: Preconventional morality (ages 4 to 10) Emphasis in this level is on external control. The standards are those of others, and they are observed either to avoid punishment or to reap rewards, or out of self-interest.	*Stage 1: Orientation toward punishment and obedience.* "What will happen to me?" Children obey the rules of others to avoid punishment. They ignore the motives of an act and focus on its physical form (such as the size of a lie) or its consequences (for example, the amount of physical damage).	*Pro:* "He should steal the drug. It isn't really bad to take it. It isn't as if he hadn't asked to pay for it first. The drug he'd take is worth only $200; he's not really taking a $2,000 drug." *Con:* "He shouldn't steal the drug. It's a big crime. He didn't get permission; he used force and broke and entered. He did a lot of damage, stealing a very expensive drug and breaking up the store, too."
	Stage 2: Instrumental purpose and exchange. "You scratch my back, I'll scratch yours." Children conform to rules out of self-interest and consideration for what others can do for then in return. They look at an act in terms of the human needs it meets and differentiate this value from the act's physical form and consequences,	*Pro:* "It's all right to steal the drug, because his wife needs it and he wants her to live. It isn't that he wants to steal, but that's what he has to do to get the drug to save her." *Con:* "He shouldn't steal it. The druggist isn't wrong or bad; he just wants to make a profit. That's what you're in business for—to make money."
Level II: Conventional mortality (ages 10 to 13 or beyond) Children now want to please other people. They still observe the standard of others, but they have internalized these standards to some extent. Now they want to be considered "good" by those persons whose opinions are important to them. They are now able to take the roles of authority figures well enough to decide whether an action is good by their standards.	*Stage 3: Maintaining mutual relations, approval of others, the golden rule.* "Am I a good boy or girl?" Children want to please and help others, can judge the intentions of others, and develop their own ideas of what a good person is. They evaluate an act according to the motive behind it or the person performing it, and they take circumstances into account.	*Pro:* "He should steal the drug. He is only doing something that is natural for a good husband to do. You can't blame him for doing something out of love for his wife. You'd blame him if he didn't love his wife enough to save her." *Con:* "He shouldn't steal. If his wife dies, he can't be blamed. It isn't because he's heartless or that he doesn't love her enough to do everything that he legally can. The druggist is the selfish or heartless one."

(Continued)

- *Level II:* **Conventional morality (or morality of conventional role conformity).** People have internalized the standards of authority figures. They are concerned about being "good," pleasing others, and maintaining the social order. This level is typically reached after age 10; many people never move beyond it, even in adulthood.
- *Level III:* **Postconventional morality (or morality of autonomous moral principles.** People now recognize conflicts between moral standards and make their own judgments on the basis of principles of right, fairness, and justice. People generally do not reach this level of moral reasoning until at least early adolescence, or more commonly in young adulthood, if ever.

Kohlberg later added a transitional level between levels II and III, when people no longer feel bound by society's moral standards but have not yet developed rationally derived principles of justice. Instead, they base their moral decisions on personal feelings.

In Kohlberg's theory, it is the reasoning underlying a person's response to a moral dilemma, not the answer itself, which indicates the stage of moral development. As illustrated in Table 11-2, two people who give opposite answers may be at the same stage if their reasoning is based on similar factors.

conventional morality (or morality of conventional role conformity)
Second level in Kohlberg's theory of moral reasoning, in which the standards of authority figures are internalized.

postconventional morality (or morality of autonomous moral principles)
Third level in Kohlberg's theory of moral reasoning, in which people follow internally held moral principles of right, fairness, and justice, and can decide among conflicting moral standards.

	Stage 4: Social concern and conscience. "What if everybody did it?" People are concerned with doing their duty, showing respect for higher authority, and maintaining the social order. They consider an act always wrong, regardless of motive or circumstances, if it violates a rule and harms others.	*Pro:* "You should steal it. If you did nothing, you'd be letting your wife die. It's your responsibility if she dies. You have to take it with the idea of paying the druggist." *Con:* "It is a natural thing for Heinz to want to save his wife, but it's still always wrong to steal. He still knows that he's stealing and taking a valuable drug from the man who made it."
Level III: Postconventional mortality (early adolescence, or not until young adulthood, or never) This level marks the attainment of true morality. For the first time, the person acknowledges the possibility of conflict between two socially accepted standards and tries to decide between them. The control of conduct is now internal, both in the standards observed and in the reasoning about right and wrong. Stages 5 and 6 may be alternative expressions of the highest level of moral reasoning.	*Stage 5: Morality of contract, of individual rights, and of democratically accepted law.* People think in rational terms, valuing the will of the majority and the welfare of society. They generally see these values as best supported by adherence to the law. While they recognize that there are times when human need and the law conflict, they believe that it is better for society in the long run if they obey the law.	*Pro:* "The law wasn't set up for these circumstances. Taking the drug in this situation isn't really right, but it's justified." *Con:* "You can't completely blame someone for stealing, but extreme circumstances don't really justify taking the law into your own hands. You can't have people stealing whenever they are desperate. The end may be good, but the ends don't justify the means."
	Stage 6: Morality of universal ethical principles. People do what they as individuals think is right, regardless of legal restrictions or the opinions of others. They act in accordance with internalized standards, knowing that they would condemn themselves if they did not.	*Pro:* "This is a situation that forces him to choose between stealing and letting his wife die. In a situation where the choice must be made, it is morally right to steal. He has to act in terms of the principle of preserving and respecting life." *Con:* "Heinz is faced with the decision of whether to consider the other people who need the drug just as badly as his wife. Heinz ought to act not according to his particular feelings toward his wife, but considering the value of all the lives involved."

Source: Adapted from Kohlberg, 1969; Lickona, 1976.

Kohlberg's early stages correspond roughly to Piaget's stages of moral development in childhood, but his advanced stages go into adulthood. Some adolescents, and even some adults, remain at Kohlberg's level I. Like young children, they seek to avoid punishment or satisfy their own needs. Most adolescents, and most adults, seem to be at level II. They conform to social conventions, support the status quo, and do the "right" thing to please others or to obey the law. (Toward the end of Anne Frank's diary, we can see her begin to emerge from this stage as she argues with her father and herself about the morality of a more physically intimate relationship with Peter.)

Very few people reach level III, when they can choose between two socially accepted standards. In fact, at one point Kohlberg questioned the validity of stage 6, since so few people seem to attain it. Later, however, he proposed a seventh, "cosmic" stage (see Chapter 13), in which people consider the effect of their actions not only on other people but on the universe as a whole (Kohlberg, 1981; Kohlberg & Ryncarz, 1990).

One reason the ages attached to Kohlberg's levels are so variable is that factors besides cognition, such as emotional development and life experience, affect moral judgments. People who have achieved a high level of cognitive development do not always reach a comparably high level of moral development. Thus a certain level of cognitive development is *necessary* but not *sufficient* for a comparable level of moral development.

Evaluating Kohlberg's Theory

Kohlberg and Piaget brought about a profound shift in the way we look at moral development. Instead of viewing morality solely as the attainment of control over self-gratifying impulses, investigators now look at how children make moral judgments based on their growing understanding of the social world. However, in analyzing early moral development, both Kohlberg and Piaget may have overemphasized external factors, such as obedience to rules and fear of punishment, and overlooked young children's ability to recognize the impact of their actions on others (Turiel, 1998).

Research has supported some aspects of Kohlberg's theory but has left others in question. The American boys that Kohlberg and his colleagues followed through adulthood progressed through Kohlberg's stages in sequence, and none skipped a stage. Their moral judgments correlated positively with age, education, IQ, and socioeconomic status (Colby, Kohlberg, Gibbs, & Lieberman, 1983).

However, research has noted a lack of a clear relationship between moral reasoning and moral behavior. People at postconventional levels of reasoning do not necessarily act more morally than those at lower levels (Colby & Damon, 1992; Kupfersmid & Wonderly, 1980). Perhaps one problem is the remoteness from young people's experience of such dilemmas as the "Heinz" situation. On the other hand, juvenile delinquents (particularly boys) consistently show developmental delays in Kohlbergian tests of moral reasoning (Gregg, Gibbs, & Basinger, 1994).

A practical problem in using Kohlberg's system is its time-consuming testing procedures. The standard dilemmas need to be presented to each person individually and then scored by trained judges. One alternative is the Defining Issues Test (DIT), which can be given quickly to a group and scored objectively (Rest, 1975). Its results correlate moderately well with scores on Kohlberg's traditional tasks. When the DIT was administered to large samples of people of varying ages, from early adolescent to adult, participants relied most consistently on Kohlbergian principles when they were clearly in one stage or another. When they were in transition, more conflict and confusion appeared (Thoma & Rest, 1999).

Consider this . . .

- Kohlberg's method of assessing moral development by evaluating participants' reactions to moral dilemmas is widely used. Does this seem like the most appropriate method? Why or why not? Can you suggest an alternative measure?

Family Influences Neither Piaget nor Kohlberg considered parents important to children's moral development. More recent research, however, emphasizes parents' contribution in both the cognitive and the emotional realms.

In one study, parents of 63 students in grades 1, 4, 7, and 10 were asked to talk with their children about two dilemmas: a hypothetical one and an actual one that the child described (L. J. Walker & Taylor, 1991). The children and adolescents who, during the next two years, showed the greatest progress through Kohlberg's stages were those whose parents had used humor and praise, listened to them, and asked their opinions. These parents had asked clarifying questions, reworded answers, and checked to be sure the children understood the issues. They reasoned with their children at a slightly higher level than the children were currently at, much as in the method of scaffolding. The children who advanced the least were those whose parents had lectured them or challenged or contradicted their opinions.

Validity for Women and Girls Carol Gilligan (1982), on the basis of research on women, argued that Kohlberg's theory is oriented toward values more important to men than to women. According to Gilligan, women see morality not so much in terms of justice and fairness as of responsibility to show care and avoid harm.

Research has not supported Gilligan's claim of a male bias in Kohlberg's stages, and she has since modified her position (see Chapter 13). However, some research has found gender differences in moral judgments in early adolescence, with girls scoring *higher* than boys (Garmon, Basinger, Gregg, & Gibbs, 1996; Skoe & Gooden, 1993). This may be because girls generally mature earlier and have more intimate social relationships (Garmon et al., 1996; Skoe & Diessner, 1994). Early adolescent girls do tend to emphasize care-related concerns more than boys do, especially when tested with open-ended questions ("How important is it to keep promises to a friend?") or self-chosen moral dilemmas related to their own experience (Garmon et al., 1996).

Cross-cultural Validity Cross-cultural studies support Kohlberg's sequence of stages—up to a point. Older people from countries other than the United States do tend to score at higher stages than younger people. However, people in nonwestern cultures rarely score above stage 4 (Edwards, 1981; Nisan & Kohlberg, 1982; Snarey, 1985). It is possible that these cultures do not foster higher moral development, but it seems more likely that some aspects of Kohlberg's definition of morality may not fit the cultural values of some societies (see Chapter 13).

Kohlberg himself observed that before people can develop a fully principled morality, they must recognize the relativity of moral standards. Adolescents begin to understand that every society evolves its own definitions of right and wrong; in some cases, the values of one culture may even seem shocking to members of another (refer back to Box 11-1). Many young people question their earlier views about morality when they enter high school or college and encounter people whose values, culture, and ethnic background are different from their own.

CHECKPOINT

Can you . . .

- ✔ List Kohlberg's levels and stages, and discuss factors that influence how rapidly children and adolescents progress through them?
- ✔ Evaluate Kohlberg's theory, especially with regard to family influences, gender, and cultural validity?

Educational and Vocational Issues

School is a central organizing experience in most adolescents' lives. It offers opportunities to learn information, master new skills, and sharpen old ones; to participate in sports, the arts, and other activities; to explore vocational choices; and to be with friends. It widens intellectual and social horizons. Some adolescents, however, experience school not as an opportunity but as one more hindrance on the road to adulthood.

Let's examine influences on school achievement. Then we'll look at why some young people drop out of school, and what penalties they pay. Finally, we'll consider planning for higher education and vocations.

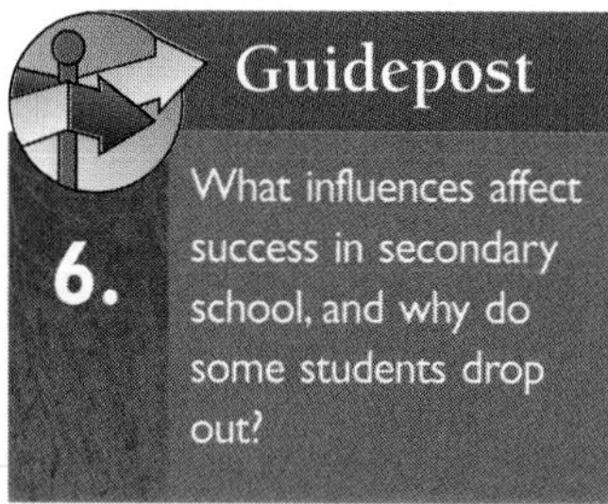

Guidepost
6.
What influences affect success in secondary school, and why do some students drop out?

Influences on School Achievement

Today, nearly 83 percent of Americans age 25 or older—more than ever before—have completed high school. Furthermore, the proportion is growing in younger cohorts: Among 25- to 29-year-olds, it is about 88 percent (Day & Curry, 1998).

Historically in the United States, education has been the ticket to economic and social advancement and to a successful adult life. However, for some students, school does not serve this vital purpose.

Self-Efficacy Beliefs and Academic Motivation

self-efficacy
Sense of capability to master challenges and achieve goals.

What makes one student strive for good grades while another fails? According to Albert Bandura (Bandura, Barbaranelli, Caprara, & Pastorelli, 1996; Zimmerman, Bandura, & Martinez-Pons, 1992), whose social-cognitive theory we discussed in Chapters 2 and 8, an important factor is **self-efficacy.** Students who believe that they can master academic material and regulate their own learning are more likely to try to achieve and more likely to succeed than students who do not believe in their own abilities.

Self-regulated learners are interested in learning. They set challenging goals and use appropriate strategies to achieve them. They try hard, persist in the face of difficulties, and seek help when necessary. Students who do not believe in their ability to succeed tend to become frustrated and depressed—feelings that make success harder to attain.

In one study that found a link between self-efficacy beliefs and academic achievement, 116 ninth- and tenth-graders of various ethnic backgrounds in two eastern high schools answered a questionnaire about their ability to learn and to regulate their own learning (Zimmerman et al., 1992; see Table 11-3). The students' perceived self-efficacy predicted the social studies grades they hoped for, expected, and achieved. Students' goals were influenced by their parents' goals for them, but that influence was tempered by the students' beliefs about their own abilities. The message is clear: if parents want their children to do well in school, they must do more than set high expectations. They also must see that children have learning experiences that build a belief in their ability to succeed.

Several factors, including parental beliefs and practices, socioeconomic status, and peer influence, affect parents' power to shape children's achievement. As with other aspects of development, parents' own perceived self-efficacy—their belief in their ability to promote their children's academic growth—affects their success in doing so. Parents who are economically secure and who have high aspirations for their children and a strong sense of parental efficacy tend to have children with high academic goals and achievement, who can resist negative peer pressures (Bandura et al., 1996).

Parental Involvement and Parenting Styles

Parents also can affect their children's educational achievement by becoming involved in their children's schooling: acting as advocates for their children and impressing teachers with the seriousness of the family's educational goals (Bandura et al., 1996). Students whose parents are closely involved in their school lives and monitor their progress fare best in high school. This is particularly true of fathers, whose involvement varies more than that of mothers (NCES, 1985).

Parents' involvement may be related to their style of child rearing (refer back to Chapter 8). *Authoritative parents* urge adolescents to look at both sides of issues, admit that children sometimes know more than parents, and welcome their par-

Table 11-3 Self-Efficacy Questionnaire for High School Students

Self-efficacy for Self-regulated Learning
How well can you:
1. finish homework assignments by deadlines?
2. study when there are other interesting things to do?
3. concentrate on school subjects?
4. take notes on class instruction?
5. use the library to get information for class assignments?
6. plan your schoolwork?
7. organize your schoolwork?
8. remember information presented in class and textbooks?
9. arrange a place to study without distractions?
10. motivate yourself to do schoolwork?
11. participate in class discussions?
Self-efficacy for Academic Achievement
How well can you:
1. learn general mathematics?
2. learn algebra?
3. learn science?
4. learn biology?
5. learn reading and writing language skills?
6. learn to use computers?
7. learn foreign languages?
8. learn social studies?
9. learn English grammar?

Source: Adapted from Zimmerman et al., 1992, Table 1, p. 668.

Even though adolescents are more independent than younger children, the home atmosphere continues to influence school achievement. Parents help not only by monitoring homework but by taking an active interest in other aspects of teenagers' lives. Children of authoritative parents, who discuss issues openly and offer praise and encouragement, tend to do best in school.

ticipation in family decisions. These parents strike a balance between making demands and being responsive. Their children receive praise and privileges for good grades; poor grades bring encouragement to try harder and offers of help. *Authoritarian parents* tell adolescents not to argue with or question adults and tell them they will "know better when they are grown up." Good grades bring admonitions to do even better; poor grades upset the parents, who may punish by reducing allowances or "grounding." *Permissive parents* seem not to care about grades, make no rules about watching television, do not attend school functions, and neither help with nor check their children's homework. These parents may not be neglectful or uncaring, but simply convinced that teenagers should be responsible for their own lives.

Research has consistently found that the positive effects of authoritative parenting continue during adolescence. Among about 6,400 California high school students, children of authoritative parents tended to do better in school than children of authoritarian and permissive parents (Dornbusch, Ritter, Leiderman, Roberts, & Fraleigh, 1987; Steinberg & Darling, 1994; Steinberg, Lamborn, Dornbusch, & Darling, 1992). Adolescents raised authoritatively not only achieve better academically but are more socially competent, are more emotionally healthy, and show fewer behavior problems than children raised in an authoritarian or permissive manner (Glasgow, Dornbusch, Troyer, Steinberg, & Ritter, 1997).

What accounts for the academic success of authoritatively raised adolescents? Authoritative parents' greater involvement in schooling may be a factor, as well as their encouragement of positive attitudes toward work. A more subtle mechanism, consistent with Bandura's findings, may be parents' influence on how children explain success or failure. In a study of 2,353 students at six high schools in California and three high schools in Wisconsin, youngsters who saw their parents as nonauthoritative were more likely than their peers to attribute poor grades to external causes or to low ability—forces beyond their control—rather than to their own efforts. A year later, such students tended to pay less attention in class and to spend less time on homework (Glasgow et al., 1997). Thus a sense of helplessness associated with nonauthoritative parenting may become a self-fulfilling prophecy, discouraging students from trying to succeed.

Ethnicity and Peer Influence

The findings about the value of authoritative parenting do *not* seem to hold true among some ethnic and cultural groups. In one study, Latino and African American students—even those with authoritative parents—did not do as well as white students, apparently because of lack of peer support for academic achievement (Steinberg, Dornbusch, & Brown, 1992). On the other hand, Asian American students, whose parents are sometimes described as authoritarian, get high grades and score higher than white students on math achievement tests, apparently because both parents *and* peers prize achievement (C. Chen & Stevenson, 1995). In addition to having parents and peers with high academic standards, who value hard work, Asian American students tend to go to good schools, to take challenging courses, and to like math. They also spend more time studying than white students and less time socializing with friends, and they are less likely to hold outside jobs (see Box 11–2).

Among some ethnic groups, then, parenting styles may be less important than other factors that affect motivation. Young people who are interested in what they are learning and whose parents and peers value education are more motivated to succeed. The strong school achievement of many first- and second-generation youngsters from immigrant backgrounds—not only East Asian, but also Filipino, Mexican, and European—reflects their families' and friends' strong emphasis on and support of educational success (Fuligni, 1997).

Practically Speaking

Box 11-2
Should Teenagers Work Part Time?

Many teenagers today hold part-time jobs. This trend fits in with a long-standing American belief in the moral benefits of work. However, some research challenges the value of part-time employment for high school students. Let's look at both sides of the issue.

On the positive side, paid work is generally believed to teach young people to handle money and to help them develop good work habits. A good part-time job requires a teenager to assume responsibility and to get along with people of different ages and backgrounds. It enables an adolescent to learn workplace skills, such as how to find a job and how to get along with employers, coworkers, and sometimes the public. It may improve the self-concept by giving young people a greater sense of competence, independence from parents, and status with peers. By helping them learn more about particular fields of work, it may guide them in choosing careers and may lead to higher attainment in those fields (Elder & Caspi, 1990; Mortimer & Shanahan, 1991; National Commission on Youth, 1980; Phillips & Sandstrom, 1990; Steel, 1991). Also, by showing adolescents how demanding and difficult the world of work is and how unprepared they are for it, part-time jobs sometimes motivate young people to continue their education.

On the negative side, most high school students who work part time have low-level, repetitive jobs in which they do not learn skills useful later in life. According to some research, teenagers who work are no more independent in making financial decisions and are unlikely to earn any more money as adults than those who do not hold jobs during high school. By assuming adult burdens they are not yet ready to deal with, young people may miss out on the opportunity to explore their identity and develop close relationships. Outside work may require a stressful juggling of other commitments and cut down on active involvement in school (Greenberger & Steinberg, 1986). There is some evidence that long hours of work may undermine school performance and increase the likelihood of dropping out, especially when teenagers work more than 15 to 20 hours per week (NCES, 1987). However, findings about the influence of employment on grades are mixed (Mortimer, Finch, Ryu, Shanahan, & Call, 1996).

Paid work can have other hidden costs. Young people who work long hours are less likely to eat breakfast, exercise, get enough sleep, or have enough leisure time (Bachman & Schulenberg, 1993). They spend less time with their families and may feel less close to them. They usually have little contact with adults on the job, and their jobs usually reinforce gender stereotypes. Some teenagers spend their earnings on alcohol or drugs, develop cynical attitudes toward work, and cheat or steal from their employers (Greenberger & Steinberg, 1986; Steinberg, Fegley, & Dornbusch, 1993). Such conduct may be tied in with a premature assumption of adult roles—an effort to grow up too soon (Bachman & Schulenberg, 1993). Some of the undesirable effects that have been attributed to part-time work may result, not from working itself, but from the factors that motivate some teenagers to take jobs. Some may want to work because they are already uninterested in school or feel alienated from their families or because they want money to buy drugs or liquor.

A longitudinal study that followed 1,000 randomly selected ninth-graders in St. Paul, Minnesota, through four years of high school suggests that some of the harmful effects of work may have been overstated (Mortimer et al., 1996). Each year, the students filled out questionnaires designed to measure their mental health and behavioral adjustment. They were asked about their grade point average, how much time they spent doing homework, and how much they drank and smoked. They also reported on whether they worked for pay and, if so, for how many hours a week.

According to these questionnaire reports, the number of hours an adolescent worked did not seem to reduce self-esteem or mastery motivation. Nor were employed students unusually likely to be depressed. During the first 3 years, working had no effect on homework time or grades. Only during senior year did students who worked more than 20 hours a week tend to do less homework than other students, and even so, their grades and motivation to do well in school did not suffer in comparison with nonworking peers. Furthermore, students who worked 20 or fewer hours during their senior year had *higher* grades than either those who worked longer hours or those who did not work at all. Working was not related to smoking or behavioral problems at school. However, working more than 20 hours a week was associated with increased alcohol use.

This research does not give a definitive answer to the question of whether outside work is good or bad for adolescents. For one thing, the data come entirely from self-reports. Furthermore, they do not deal with the influence of working on illegal drug use, cheating in school, delinquency, sexual behavior, or a number of other possible concerns. Finally, the study addressed only how *much* young people work, and not the quality of their work experience. Another study of more than 12,000 randomly selected seventh- through twelfth-graders nationwide (also based largely on self-reports) found that teenagers who work 20 or more hours a week are more likely to feel stress, to smoke, drink, or use marijuana, and to begin sexual activity early (Resnick et al., 1997). Still other studies suggest that such factors as advancement opportunity, the chance to learn useful skills, and the kinds of responsibilities adolescents have at work may determine whether the experience is a positive or negative one (Call, Mortimer, & Shanahan, 1995; Finch, Shanahan, Mortimer, & Ryu, 1991; Shanahan, Finch, Mortimer, & Ryu, 1991).

Socioeconomic Status and the Family Environment

Socioeconomic status can be a powerful factor in educational achievement—not in and of itself, but through its influence on family atmosphere, on choice of neighborhood, and on parents' way of rearing children (NRC, 1993a). Children of poor, uneducated parents are more likely to experience negative family and school atmospheres and stressful events (Felner et al., 1995). The neighborhood a family can afford generally determines the quality of schooling available, as well as opportunities for higher education; and the availability of such opportunities, together with attitudes in the neighborhood peer group, affects motivation.

When a school has a predominance of low-income children, negative effects of low socioeconomic status spread through the school population as a whole. This may help explain why schools in which a majority of students come from single-parent homes (many of which are low-income) tend to have lower eighth-grade math and reading achievement scores (Pong, 1997).

social capital
Family and community resources upon which a person can draw.

Still, many young people from nontraditional families and disadvantaged neighborhoods do well in school and improve their condition in life. What may make the difference is **social capital:** the family and community resources children can draw upon. Parents who invest time and effort in their children and who have a strong network of community support build the family's social capital (J. S. Coleman, 1988). Single parents and stepparents who establish relationships with other parents may become better aware of school programs and operations and thus foster their children's achievement (Pong, 1997).

In a 20-year study of 252 children born to mostly poor and African American teenage mothers in Baltimore, those who—regardless of parents' income, education, and employment—had more social capital (according to such measures as those listed in Table 11-4) were more likely by the end of adolescence to have completed high school and in some cases to have gone to college, or to have entered the labor force and to be enjoying stable incomes (Furstenberg & Hughes, 1995).

Table 11-4 Factors Contributing to Social Capital

Within Family
Family cohesion
Mother's support to and from own mother.
Parents see siblings or grandparents weekly?
Father in home:
Biological father or long-term stepfather?
Parent help with homework
Child's activities with parents
Parents' expectations for school performance
Parents' educational aspirations for child
Mother's encouragement of child
Mother's attendance at school meetings
Number of child's friends mother knows
Family Links to Community
Religious involvement
Strong help network
Mother sees close friend weekly?
Child ever changed schools due to move?
Child's friends' educational expectations
School quality
Neighborhood as a place to grow up

Source: Adapted from Furstenberg & Hughes, 1995.

Quality of Schooling

An important factor in students' achievement is the quality of the schools they attend. A good high school has an orderly, unoppressive atmosphere; an active, energetic principal; and teachers who take part in making decisions. Principal and teachers have high expectations for students, place greater emphasis on academics than on extracurricular activities, and closely monitor student performance (Linney & Seidman, 1989).

The educational practice known as *tracking*, or grouping students by abilities, may contribute to failure. Students placed in low-track classes lack the stimulation of higher-ability peers and often get poorer teaching. They rarely move up to higher tracks, and many lose interest in trying to do better (NRC, 1993a). Furthermore, since school failure and contact with antisocial peers are often related to antisocial behavior, grouping poor achievers together may solidify problem behaviors (Dishion, Patterson, Stoolmiller, & Skinner, 1991). Some research suggests that mixed-ability classes have cognitive, social, and psychological benefits for these young people while not holding back more competent students (Oakes, Gamoran, & Page, 1992; Rutter, 1983). However, other research has found that gifted students achieve better and are more motivated when grouped with their intellectual peers (Feldhusen & Moon, 1992).

Schools that tailor teaching to students' abilities get better results than schools that try to teach all students in the same way. Research on Sternberg's triarchic theory of intelligence (refer back to Chapter 9) has found that students high in practical or creative intelligence do better when taught in a way that allows them to capitalize on those strengths and compensate for their weaknesses (Sternberg, 1997).

Some big-city school systems, such as New York's, Philadelphia's, and Chicago's, are experimenting with small schools, either freestanding or within larger schools—small enough for students, teachers, and parents to form a learning community united by a common vision of good education. The curriculum may have a special focus, such as ethnic studies. Teaching is flexible, innovative, and personalized; teachers work together closely and get to know students well (Meier, 1995; Rossi, 1996). In Central Park East, a complex of four small, ethnically diverse elementary and secondary schools in New York's East Harlem, 90 percent of the students finish high school and 9 out of 10 of those go on to college, as compared with an average citywide graduation rate of 50 percent (Meier, 1995).

Dropping out of High School

Society suffers when young people do not finish school. Dropouts are more likely to be unemployed or to have low incomes, to end up on welfare, and to become involved with drugs, crime, and delinquency. In addition, the loss of taxable income burdens the public treasury (NCES, 1987, 1999).

Fewer students are dropping out these days, and some eventually go back to school to earn a high school equivalency certificate. In 1997, only 4.6 percent of students dropped out of high school. Hispanic students were almost twice as likely to drop out as African Americans (9.5 percent as compared with 5 percent), and nearly three times as likely to drop out as non-Hispanic whites (3.6 percent). Among all 16- to 24-year-olds, 11 percent are high school dropouts: 7.6 percent of whites, 13.4 percent of blacks, and 25.3 percent of Hispanics. The higher dropout rates among Hispanics may be due at least in part to recent immigration (NCES, 1999).

Low-income students are much more likely to drop out than middle- or high-income students (NCES, 1999). The higher dropout rates among minority groups living in poverty may stem in part from the poor quality of their schools as compared with those attended by more advantaged children. Among other possible reasons for the high Latino dropout rates are language difficulties, financial pressures, and a culture that puts family first, since these students often leave school to help support their families (U.S. Department of Education, 1992).

Students in single-parent and remarried households—even relatively affluent ones—are more likely to drop out than students living with both parents (Finn & Rock, 1997; Zimiles & Lee, 1991). Frequent moves may contribute to the effects of family instability. Changing schools may reduce a family's social capital. Families that move a lot generally have weaker social connections, know less about the children's school, and are less able to make wise decisions about schooling (Teachman, Paasch, & Carver, 1996).

Perhaps the most important factor in whether or not a student will finish school is *active engagement:* the extent to which the student is actively involved in schooling. On the most basic level, active engagement means coming to class on time, being prepared, listening and responding to the teacher, and obeying school rules. A second level of engagement consists of getting involved with the coursework—asking questions, taking the initiative to seek help when needed, or doing extra projects. Both levels of active engagement tend to pay off in positive school performance by at-risk students. In a nationwide sample of 1,803 low-income African American and Hispanic students, active engagement was the chief distinction between those who graduated from high school on time, got reasonably good grades, and did fairly well on achievement tests and those who did not (Finn & Rock, 1997).

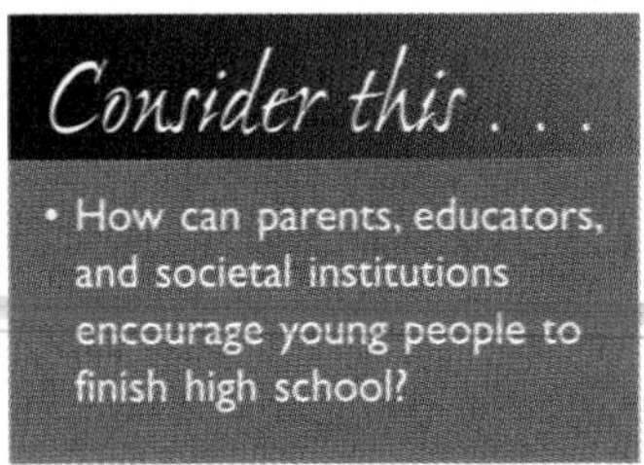

Consider this . . .
• How can parents, educators, and societal institutions encourage young people to finish high school?

What factors promote active engagement? Family encouragement is undoubtedly one. Others may be small class size and a warm, supportive school environment. Since engaged or alienated behavior patterns tend to be set early in a child's school career, dropout prevention should start early, too (Finn & Rock, 1997).

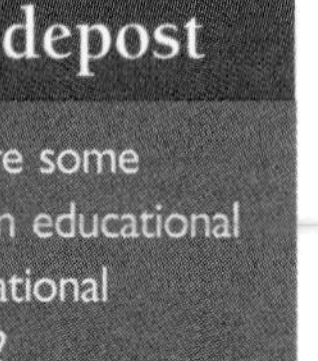

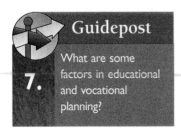

Guidepost

7. What are some factors in educational and vocational planning?

Educational and Vocational Planning

How do young people develop career goals? How do they decide whether or not to go to college and, if not, how to enter the world of work? Many factors enter in, including individual ability and personality, education, socioeconomic and ethnic background, the advice of school counselors, life experiences, and societal values. Let's look at some influences on educational and vocational aspirations. Then we'll examine what happens to young people who do not go to college.

Influences on Students' Aspirations

Students' self-efficacy beliefs—their confidence in their educational and vocational prospects—shape the occupational options they consider and the way they prepare for careers (Bandura et al., 1996). Parental aspirations and financial support often influence youngsters' plans. In fact, parental encouragement predicts high ambition better than social class (T. E. Smith, 1981).

Despite the greater flexibility in career goals today, gender—and gender-stereotyping—often influence vocational choice. Interviews with students ages 3 to 18 in a coeducational urban private school in Australia found that, except among the youngest children, boys had more restrictive ideas than girls about proper occupations for each sex. Boys knew more about the requirements for traditionally male occupations and girls about traditionally female ones. Older adolescent boys generally found school career programs helpful, while girls did not (McMahon & Patton, 1997).

A 1992 report by the American Association of University Women (AAUW) Educational Foundation claimed that schools shortchange girls by steering them away from science and math and into gender-typed pursuits. Even girls who did well in science and math were less likely than boys to choose careers in those fields. Six years later, a follow-up study (AAUW Educational Foundation, 1998a,

1998b) reported that girls were taking more science and math than before and doing better in those subjects. According to the National Center for Education Statistics (1997), male and female high school seniors are equally likely to plan careers in math or science, but boys are much more likely to expect to go into engineering. Fewer girls than boys take physics and computer science, but more girls take chemistry. In vocational education and career exploration programs, girls cluster in traditionally female occupations. On the other hand, boys take fewer English classes and lag in communications skills (AAUW Educational Foundation, 1998b; NCES, 1998a; Weinman, 1998).

The educational system itself may act as a subtle brake on some students' vocational aspirations. The relatively narrow range of abilities valued and cultivated in many schools gives certain students the inside track. Students who can memorize and analyze tend to do well on intelligence tests that hinge on those abilities and in classrooms where teaching is geared to those abilities. Thus, as predicted by the tests, these students are achievers in a system that stresses the abilities in which they happen to excel. Meanwhile, students whose strength is in creative or practical thinking—areas critical to success in certain fields—never get a chance to show what they can do. These young people may be frozen out of career paths or forced into less challenging and rewarding ones because of test scores and grades too low to put them on track to success (Sternberg, 1997). Recognition of a broader range of "intelligences" (see Chapter 9), combined with more flexible teaching and career counseling at all levels, could allow more students to get the education and enter the occupations they desire and to make the contributions of which they are capable.

Guiding Students Not Bound for College

About 33 percent of high school graduates in the United States do not immediately go on to college, and about 23 percent enroll in two-year community colleges (NCES, 1999). Yet most vocational counseling in high schools is oriented toward college-bound youth.

Most other industrialized countries offer some kind of structured guidance to non-college-bound students. Germany, for example, has an apprenticeship system, in which high school students go to school part time and spend the rest of the week in paid on-the-job training supervised by an employer-mentor. About 60 percent of German high school students take advantage of this program each year, and 85 percent of those who complete it find jobs (Hopfensperger, 1996).

In the United States, whatever vocational training programs do exist are less comprehensive and less closely tied to the needs of businesses and industries. Most young people get necessary training on the job or in community college courses. Many, ignorant about the job market, do not obtain the skills they need. Others take jobs beneath their abilities. Some do not find work at all (NRC, 1993a).

In some communities, demonstration programs help in the school-to-work transition. The most successful ones offer instruction in basic skills, counseling, peer support, mentoring, apprenticeship, and job placement (NRC, 1993a). In 1994, Congress passed the School to Work Opportunities Act, which allocated $1.1 billion to help states and local governments develop vocational training programs.

Consider this . . .

- Would you favor an apprenticeship program like Germany's in the United States? How successful do you think it would be in helping young people make realistic career plans? What negative effects, if any, might it have?

CHECKPOINT

Can you . . .

✔ Assess factors in adolescents' academic achievement?

✔ Discuss influences on educational and vocational planning?

Vocational planning is one aspect of an adolescent's search for identity. The question "What shall I do?" is very close to "Who shall I be?" People who feel they are doing something worthwhile, and doing it well, feel good about themselves. Those who feel that their work does not matter—or that they are not good at it—may wonder about the meaning of their lives. A prime personality issue in adolescence, which we discuss in Chapter 12, is the effort to define the self.

Summary

Adolescence: A Developmental Transition

Guidepost 1. What is adolescence, when does it begin and end, and what opportunities and risks does it entail?

- **Adolescence** is the transition from childhood to adulthood. Neither its beginning nor its end is clearly marked in western societies; it lasts about a decade, between ages 11 or 12 and the late teens or early twenties. Legal, sociological, and psychological definitions of entrance into adulthood vary. In some nonwestern cultures, "coming of age" is signified by special rites.
- Adolescence is fraught with risks to healthy development, as well as with opportunities for physical, cognitive, and psychosocial growth. Risky behavior patterns, such as drinking alcohol, drug abuse, sexual and gang activity, and use of firearms tend to be established early in adolescence. However, about 4 out of 5 young people do not experience major problems.

PHYSICAL DEVELOPMENT

Puberty: The End of Childhood

Guidepost 2. What physical changes do adolescents experience, and how do these changes affect them psychologically?

- **Puberty** is triggered by hormonal changes, which may affect moods and behavior. Puberty takes about four years, typically begins earlier in girls than in boys, and ends when a person can reproduce.
- During puberty, both boys and girls undergo an **adolescent growth spurt.** A **secular trend** toward earlier attainment of adult height and sexual maturity began about 100 years ago, probably because of improvements in living standards.
- **Primary sex characteristics** (the reproductive organs) enlarge and mature during puberty. **Secondary sex characteristics** also appear.
- The principal signs of sexual maturity are production of sperm (for males) and menstruation (for females). **Spermarche,** a boy's first ejaculation, typically occurs at age 13. **Menarche,** the first menstruation, occurs, on average, between the ages of 12 and 13 in the United States.
- Teenagers, especially girls, tend to be sensitive about their physical appearance. Girls who mature early tend to adjust less easily than early maturing boys.

Physical and Mental Health

Guidepost 3. What are some common health problems and risks of adolescence?

- For the most part, the adolescent years are relatively healthy. Health problems often result from poverty or a risk-taking lifestyle. Adolescents are less likely than younger children to get regular medical care.
- Most high school students, especially girls, do not engage in regular vigorous physical activity.
- Many adolescents do not get enough sleep because the high school schedule is out of sync with their circadian timing system.
- Three common eating disorders in adolescence are obesity, **anorexia nervosa,** and **bulimia nervosa.** All can have serious long-term effects. Anorexia and bulimia affect mostly girls. Outcomes for bulimia tend to be better than for anorexia.
- **Substance abuse,** which can lead to **substance dependence,** is less common among adolescents today than during recent decades, despite a rise in drug use during most of the 1990s. Drug use often begins as children move into middle school. Marijuana, alcohol, and tobacco, which are called **gateway drugs,** are most popular with adolescents. All involve serious risks.
- The three leading causes of death among adolescents are accidents, homicide, and suicide. Access to firearms is a major factor in homicide and suicide.

COGNITIVE DEVELOPMENT

Aspects of Cognitive Maturation

Guidepost 4. How does adolescents' thinking differ from that of younger children?

- People in Piaget's stage of **formal operations** can engage in **hypothetical-deductive reasoning.** They can think in terms of possibilities, deal flexibly with problems, and test hypotheses. Since experience plays an important part in attaining this stage, not all people become capable of formal operations. Adolescents' immature brain development may permit emotions to interfere with rational thinking.
- Piaget's stage of formal operations does not take into account such developments as accumulation of domain-specific knowledge and expertise, gains in information-processing capacity, and the growth of metacognition. Piaget also paid little attention to individual differences, between-task variations, and the role of the situation in influencing thinking.
- According to Elkind, immature thought patterns characteristic of adolescence include finding fault with authority figures, argumentativeness, indecisiveness, apparent hypocrisy, self-consciousness (which he calls the **imaginary audience**), and an assumption of uniqueness and invulnerability (which he calls the **personal fable**). However, research has cast doubt on the special prevalence of the latter two patterns during adolescence.

Guidepost 5. On what basis do adolescents make moral judgments?

- According to Kohlberg, moral reasoning is rooted in the development of a sense of justice and occurs on three main levels: **preconventional morality, conventional morality (or morality of conventional role**

conformity), and **postconventional morality (or morality of autonomous moral principles).**

- Kohlberg's theory has been criticized on several grounds, including failure to credit parents' influence. The applicability of Kohlberg's system to women and girls and to people in nonwestern cultures has been questioned.

Educational and Vocational Issues

Guidepost 6. What influences affect success in secondary school, and why do some students drop out?

- Academic motivation, parenting styles, ethnicity, socioeconomic status, and quality of schooling influence educational achievement. **Self-efficacy** beliefs and parental and peer attitudes can influence motivation to achieve. Poor families whose children do well in school tend to have more **social capital** than poor families whose children do not do so well.
- Although most Americans graduate from high school, the dropout rate is higher among poor, Hispanic, and African American students and among those not living with both parents. Active engagement in studies is an important factor in keeping adolescents in school.

Guidepost 7. What are some factors in educational and vocational planning?

- Educational and vocational aspirations are influenced by several factors, including parental encouragement and gender stereotypes. About 33 percent of high school graduates do not immediately go on to college.
- Outside work seems to have both positive and negative effects on educational, social, and occupational development.

Key Terms

adolescence (410)
puberty (410)
secular trend (412)
adolescent growth spurt (413)
primary sex characteristics (414)
secondary sex characteristics (414)
spermarche (415)
menarche (415)
anorexia nervosa (420)
bulimia nervosa (420)
substance abuse (422)
substance dependence (422)
gateway drugs (423)
formal operations (425)
hypothetical-deductive reasoning (426)
imaginary audience (429)
personal fable (429)
preconventional morality (430)
conventional morality (or morality of conventional role conformity) (431)
postconventional morality (or morality of autonomous moral principles) (431)
self-efficacy (434)
social capital (438)

Chapter 12

Psychosocial Development in Adolescence

This face in the mirror stares at me demanding Who are you? What will you become? *And taunting,* You don't even know. *Chastened, I cringe and agree and then because I'm still young, I stick out my tongue.*

—Eve Merriam, "Conversation with Myself," 1964

Jackie Robinson

Focus: Jackie Robinson, Baseball Legend*

On April 15, 1947, when 28-year-old Jack Roosevelt ("Jackie") Robinson (1919–1972) put on a Brooklyn Dodgers uniform and strode onto Ebbets Field, he became the first African American in the twentieth century to play major league baseball. By the end of a spectacular first season in which he was named Rookie of the Year, Robinson's name had become a household word. Two years later, he was voted baseball's Most Valuable Player. During his ten years with the Dodgers, the team won six pennants, and Robinson played in six consecutive All-Star games. After his retirement, he won first-ballot election to the Hall of Fame.

His triumph did not come easily. When the Dodgers' manager, Branch Rickey, decided to bring Robinson up from the Negro Leagues, several players petitioned to keep him off the team. But Robinson's athletic prowess and dignified demeanor in the face of racist jibes, threats, hate mail, and attempts at bodily harm won the respect of the baseball world. Within the next decade, most major league teams signed African American players. Baseball had become "one of the first institutions in modern society to accept blacks on a relatively equal basis" (Tygiel, 1983).

*Sources of biographical information about Jackie Robinson were Falkner (1995), Rampersad (1997), J. Robinson (1995), S. Robinson (1996), and Tygiel (1983, 1997). Page references from Robinson's autobiography are to the 1995 edition.

Behind the Jackie Robinson legend is the story of a prodigiously talented boy growing up in a nation in which opportunities for black youth were extremely limited. His grandfather had been a slave. Jackie's father, a Georgia sharecropper, abandoned his wife and five children when the boy was 6 months old. His mother, Mallie Robinson, was a determined, deeply religious woman, who imbued her children with moral strength and pride. Intent on providing them with a good education, she moved her family to Pasadena, California. But Pasadena turned out to be almost as rigidly segregated as the Deep South.

Jackie Robinson lived for sports. He idolized his older brother Mack, who won a silver medal in the 1936 Olympics. By the time Jackie was in junior high school, he was a star in his own right. He also did odd jobs after school.

Still, he had time on his hands. He joined a street gang of poor black, Mexican, and Japanese boys who seethed with "a growing resentment at being deprived of some of the advantages the white kids had" (J. Robinson, 1995, p. 6). The gang's activities were serious enough to get them in trouble—throwing rocks at cars and street lamps, smashing windows, and swiping apples from fruitstands. But once they were taken to jail at gunpoint merely for swimming in the reservoir when they were not allowed entrance to the whites-only municipal pool.

Robinson later reflected that he "might have become a full-fledged juvenile delinquent" had it not been for the influence of two men. One was an auto mechanic, Carl Anderson, who pointed out that "it didn't take guts to follow the crowd, that courage and intelligence lay in being willing to be different" (J. Robinson, 1995, pp. 6–7). The other was a young African American minister, Karl Downs, who lured Robinson and his friends into church-sponsored athletics, listened to their worries, helped them find jobs, and got them to help build a youth center—"an alternative to hanging out on street corners" (J. Robinson, 1995, p. 8). Later, while at UCLA, Robinson served as a volunteer Sunday school teacher at the church.

Adolescence is a time of opportunities and risks. Teenagers are on the threshold of love, of life's work, and of participation in adult society. Yet adolescence is also a time when some young people engage in behavior that closes off their options and limits their possibilities. Today, research is increasingly focusing on how to help young people whose environments are not optimal to avoid hazards that can keep them from fulfilling their potential. What saved Jackie Robinson—in addition to the influence of his indomitable, hardworking mother, his older brothers, and his adult mentors—were his talent and his passion for athletics, which ultimately enabled him to channel his drive, energy, audacity, and rebellion against racism in a positive direction.

In Chapter 11 we looked at some physical and cognitive factors, such as appearance and school achievement, that contribute to an adolescent's sense of self. In this chapter, we turn to psychosocial aspects of the quest for identity. We discuss how adolescents come to terms with their sexuality. We consider how teenagers' burgeoning individuality expresses itself in relationships with parents, siblings, and peers. We examine sources of antisocial behavior and ways of reducing the risks of adolescence. Finally, we compare adolescents' views of themselves and their lives around the world.

After you have read and studied this chapter, you should be able to answer the following questions:

Guideposts *for* **Study**

1. How do adolescents form an identity?

2. What determines sexual orientation?

3. What sexual attitudes and practices are common among adolescents, and what leads some teenagers to engage in high-risk sexual behavior?

4. How common are sexually transmitted diseases and teenage pregnancy, and what are the usual outcomes?

5. How typical is "adolescent rebellion"?

6. How do adolescents relate to parents, siblings, and peers?

7. What are the root causes of antisocial behavior and juvenile delinquency, and what can be done to reduce these and other risks of adolescence?

8. How does adolescence vary across cultures, and what are some common features?

The Search for Identity

The search for identity, which Erikson defined as confidence in one's inner continuity amid change, comes into focus during the teenage years. Adolescents' cognitive development now enables them to construct a "theory of the self" (Elkind, 1998). As Erikson (1950) emphasized, a teenager's effort to make sense of the self is not "a kind of maturational malaise." It is part of a healthy, vital process that builds on the achievements of earlier stages—on trust, autonomy, initiative, and industry—and lays the groundwork for coping with the crises of adult life.

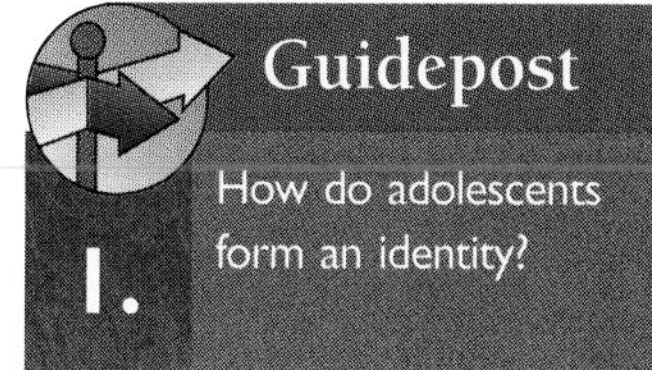

Guidepost

1. How do adolescents form an identity?

Erikson: Identity versus Identity Confusion

The chief task of adolescence, said Erikson (1968), is to confront the crisis of **identity versus identity confusion** (or *role confusion*), so as to become a unique adult with a coherent sense of self and a valued role in society. The identity crisis is unlikely to be fully resolved in adolescence; issues concerning identity crop up again and again throughout adult life.

identity versus identity confusion
In Erikson's theory, the fifth crisis of psychosocial development, in which an adolescent seeks to develop a coherent sense of self, including the role she or he is to play in society. Also called *identity versus role confusion.*

Erikson's concept of the identity crisis was based on his own life and his research on adolescents in various societies. Growing up in Germany as the son of a Danish mother and a Jewish adoptive father, Erikson had felt confusion about his identity. He never knew his biological father; he floundered before settling on a vocation; and when he came to the United States, he needed to redefine his identity as an immigrant. All these issues found echoes in the "identity crises" he observed among disturbed adolescents, soldiers in combat, and members of minority groups (Erikson, 1968, 1973; L. J. Friedman, 1999).

According to Erikson, adolescents form their identity not by modeling themselves after other people, as younger children do, but by modifying and synthesizing earlier identifications into "a new psychological structure, greater than the sum of its parts" (Kroger, 1993, p. 3). To form an identity, adolescents must ascertain and organize their abilities, needs, interests, and desires so they can be expressed in a social context.

Erikson saw the prime danger of this stage as identity (or role) confusion, which can greatly delay reaching psychological adulthood. (He himself did not

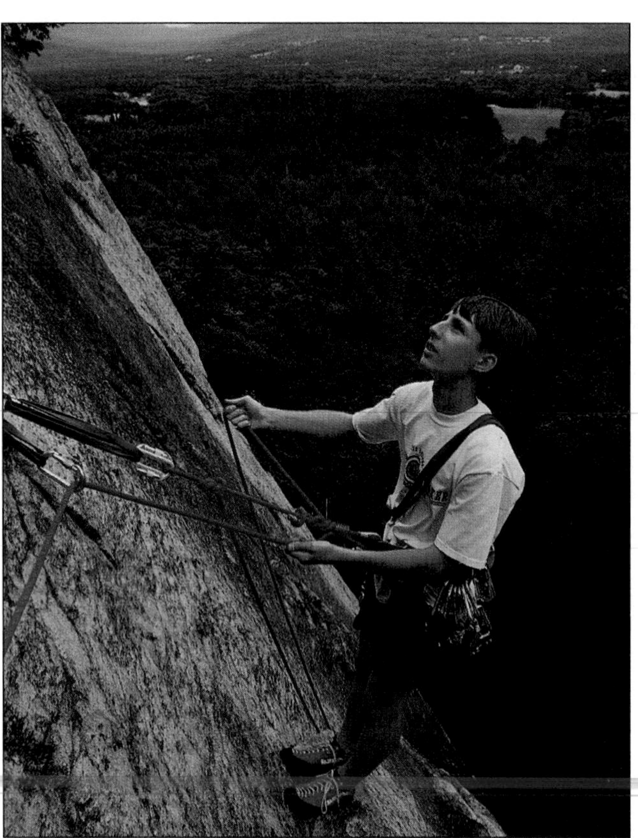

Mastering the challenge of rock climbing may help this adolescent boy assess his abilities, interests, and desires. According to Erikson, this process of self-assessment helps adolescents resolve the crisis of *identity versus identity confusion.*

resolve his own identity crisis until his midtwenties.) Some degree of identity confusion is normal. It accounts for both the seemingly chaotic nature of much adolescent behavior and teenagers' painful self-consciousness. Cliquishness and intolerance of differences—both hallmarks of the adolescent social scene—are defenses against identity confusion. Adolescents also may show confusion by regressing into childishness to avoid resolving conflicts or by committing themselves impulsively to poorly thought-out courses of action.

Identity forms as young people resolve three major issues: the choice of an occupation, the adoption of values to believe in and live by, and the development of a satisfying sexual identity. During the crisis of middle childhood, that of *industry versus inferiority,* children acquire skills needed for success in their culture. Now, as adolescents, they need to find ways to use these skills. When young people have trouble settling on an occupational identity—or when their opportunities are artificially limited, as they were for Jackie Robinson and his friends—they are at risk of behavior with serious negative consequences, such as criminal activity or early pregnancy.

During the *psychosocial moratorium*—the "time out" period that adolescence provides—many young people search for commitments to which they can be faithful. These youthful commitments, both ideological and personal, may shape a person's life for years to come. Jackie Robinson's commitments, which remained lifelong ones, were to develop his athletic potential and to help improve the position of African Americans in society. The extent to which young people remain faithful to commitments influences their ability to resolve the identity crisis. Adolescents who satisfactorily resolve that crisis develop the "virtue" of *fidelity:* sustained loyalty, faith, or a sense of belonging to a loved one or to friends and companions. Fidelity also can mean identification with a set of values, an ideology, a religion, a political movement, a creative pursuit, or an ethnic group (Erikson, 1982). Self-identification emerges when young people choose values and people to be loyal to, rather than simply accepting their parents' choices.

Fidelity is an extension of trust. In infancy, it is important for trust of parents to outweigh mistrust; in adolescence, it becomes important to be trustworthy oneself. In addition, adolescents now extend their trust to mentors or loved ones. In sharing thoughts and feelings, an adolescent clarifies a tentative identity by seeing it reflected in the eyes of the beloved. However, these adolescent "intimacies" differ from mature intimacy, which involves greater commitment, sacrifice, and compromise.

Erikson's theory describes male identity development as the norm. According to Erikson, a man is not capable of real intimacy until after he has achieved a stable identity, whereas women define themselves through marriage and motherhood (something that may have been truer when Erikson developed his theory than it is today). Thus, said Erikson, women (unlike men) develop identity *through* intimacy, not before it. As we'll see, this male orientation of Erikson's theory has prompted criticism. Still, Erikson's concept of the identity crisis has inspired much valuable research.

Marcia: Identity Status—Crisis and Commitment

Kate, Andrea, Nick, and Mark are all about to graduate from high school. Kate has considered her interests and her talents and plans to become an engineer. She has narrowed her college choices to three schools that offer good programs in this field. She knows that college will either confirm her interest in engineering or lead her in another direction. She is open to both possibilities.

Andrea knows exactly what she is going to do with her life. Her mother, a union leader at a plastics factory, has arranged for Andrea to enter an apprenticeship program there. Andrea has never considered doing anything else.

Nick, on the other hand, is agonizing over his future. Should he attend a community college or join the army? He cannot decide what to do now or what he wants to do eventually.

Mark still has no idea of what he wants to do, but he is not worried. He figures he can get some sort of a job—maybe at a supermarket or fast-food restaurant—and make up his mind about the future when he is ready.

These four young people are involved in identity formation. What accounts for the differences in the way they go about it, and how will these differences affect the outcome? According to research by the psychologist James E. Marcia (1966, 1980), these students are in four different states of ego (self) development, or **identity statuses,** which seem to be related to certain aspects of personality.

Through 30-minute, semistructured *identity-status interviews* (see Table 12-1), Marcia found four types of identity status: *identity achievement, foreclosure, moratorium,* and *identity diffusion.* The four categories differ according to the presence or absence of **crisis** and **commitment,** the two elements Erikson saw as crucial to forming identity (see Table 12-2). Marcia defines *crisis* as a period of conscious decision making, and *commitment* as a personal investment in an occupation or system of beliefs (ideology). He found relationships between identity status and such characteristics as anxiety, self-esteem, moral reasoning, and patterns of behavior. Building on Marcia's theory, other researchers have identified other

identity statuses
In Marcia's terminology, states of ego development that depend on the presence or absence of crisis and commitment.

crisis
In Marcia's terminology, period of conscious decision making related to identity formation.

commitment
In Marcia's terminology, personal investment in an occupation or system of beliefs.

Table 12-1 Identity-Status Interview

Sample Questions	Typical Answers for the Four Statuses
About occupational commitment: "How willing do you think you'd be to give up going into ____ if something better came along?"	*Identity achievement.* "Well, I might, but I doubt it. I can't see what 'something better' would be for me."
	Foreclosure. "Not very willing. It's what I've always wanted to do. The folks are happy with it and so am I."
	Moratorium. "I guess that if I knew for sure, I could answer that better. It would have to be something in the general area—something related . . ."
	Identity diffusion. "Oh, sure. If something better came along, I'd change just like that."
About ideological commitment: "Have you ever had any doubts about your religious beliefs?"	*Identity achievement.* "Yes, I even started wondering whether there is a God. I've pretty much resolved that now, though. The way it seems to me is . . ."
	Foreclosure. "No, not really; our family is pretty much in agreement on these things."
	Moratorium: "Yes, I guess I'm going through that now. I just don't see how there can be a God and still so much evil in the world . . ."
	Identity diffusion. "Oh, I don't know. I guess so. Everyone goes through some sort of stage like that. But it really doesn't bother me much. I figure that one religion is about as good as another!"

Source: Adapted from Marcia, 1966.

Identity Status	Crisis (Period of Considering Alternatives)	Commitment (Adherence to a Path of Action)
Identity achievement	Resolved	Present
Foreclosure	Absent	Present
Moratorium	In crisis	Absent
Identity diffusion	Absent	Absent

Table 12-2 Criteria for Identity Statuses

Source: Adapted from Marcia, 1980.

personality and family variables related to identity status (see Table 12-3). Here is a thumbnail sketch of people in each of the four identity statuses:

identity achievement
Identity status, described by Marcia, that is characterized by commitment to choices made following a crisis, a period spent in exploring alternatives.

1. **Identity achievement** (*crisis leading to commitment*). Kate has resolved her identity crisis. During the crisis period, she devoted much thought and some emotional struggle to major issues in her life. She has made choices and expresses strong commitment to them. Her parents have encouraged her to make her own decisions; they have listened to her ideas and given their opinions without pressuring her to adopt them. Kate is thoughtful but not so introspective as to be unable to act. She has a sense of humor, functions well under stress, is capable of intimate relationships, and holds to her standards while being open to new ideas. Research in a number of cultures has found people in this category to be more mature and more competent in relationships than people in the other three (Marcia, 1993).

foreclosure
Identity status, described by Marcia, in which a person who has not spent time considering alternatives (that is, has not been in crisis) is committed to other people's plans for his or her life.

2. **Foreclosure** (*commitment without crisis*). Andrea has made commitments, not as a result of a crisis, which would involve questioning and exploring possible choices, but by accepting someone else's plans for her life. She is happy and self-assured, perhaps even smug and self-satisfied, and she becomes dogmatic when her opinions are questioned. She has close family ties, is obedient, and tends to follow a powerful leader (like her mother), who accepts no disagreement.

Table 12-3 Family and Personality Factors Associated with Adolescents in Four Identity Statuses*

Factor	Identity Achievement	Foreclosure	Moratorium	Identity Diffusion
Family	Parents encourage autonomy and connection with teachers; differences are explored within a context of mutuality.	Parents are overly involved with their children; families avoid expressing differences.	Adolescents are often involved in an ambivalent struggle with parental authority	Parents are laissez-faire in childrearing attitudes; are rejecting or not available to children.
Personality	High levels of ego development, moral reasoning, internal locus of control, self-certainty, self-esteem, performance under stress, and intimacy.	Highest levels of authoritarianism and stereotypical thinking, obedience to authority, external locus of control, dependent relationships, low levels of anxiety.	Most anxious and fearful of success; high levels of ego development, moral reasoning, and self-esteem.	Mixed results, with low levels of ego development, moral reasoning, cognitive complexity, and self-certainty; poor cooperative abilities.

*These associations have emerged from a number of separate studies. Since the studies have all been correlational, and not longitudinal, it is impossible to say that any factor caused placement in any identity status.

Source: Kroger, 1993.

3. **Moratorium** (*crisis with no commitment yet*). Nick is in crisis, struggling with decisions. He is lively, talkative, self-confident, and scrupulous, but also anxious and fearful. He is close to his mother but also resists her authority. He wants to have a girlfriend but has not yet developed a close relationship. He will probably come out of his crisis eventually with the ability to make commitments and achieve identity.
4. **Identity diffusion** (*no commitment, no crisis*). Mark has not seriously considered options and has avoided commitments. He is unsure of himself and tends to be uncooperative. His parents do not discuss his future with him; they say it's up to him. Some people in this category become aimless drifters without goals. They tend to be unhappy, and they are often lonely because they have only superficial relationships.

moratorium
Identity status, described by Marcia, in which a person is currently considering alternatives (in crisis) and seems headed for commitment.

identity diffusion
Identity status, described by Marcia, which is characterized by absence of commitment and lack of serious consideration of alternatives.

These categories are not permanent, of course; they may change as people continue to develop (Marcia, 1979). From late adolescence on, more and more people are in moratorium or achievement: seeking or finding their own identity. Still, many people, even as young adults, remain in foreclosure or diffusion (Kroger, 1993). Although people in foreclosure seem to have made final decisions, that is often not so; when adults in midlife look back on their lives, they most commonly trace a path from foreclosure to moratorium to achievement (Kroger & Haslett, 1991).

Consider this . . .

- On the basis of the criteria presented in the text, which of Marcia's identity statuses do you think you fit into as an adolescent? Has your identity status changed since then? If so, how?

Gender Differences in Identity Formation

Much research supports Erikson's view that, for women, identity and intimacy develop together. Indeed, intimacy matters more to girls than to boys even in grade school friendships (Blyth & Foster-Clark, 1987). Rather than view this pattern as a departure from a male norm, however, some researchers see it as pointing to a weakness in Erikson's theory, which, they claim, is based on male-centered western concepts of individuality, autonomy, and competitiveness. According to Carol Gilligan (1982, 1987a, 1987b; L. M. Brown & Gilligan, 1990), the female sense of self develops not so much through achieving a separate identity as through establishing relationships. Girls and women, says Gilligan, judge themselves on their handling of their responsibilities and on their ability to care for others as well as for themselves. Even high-achieving women attain identity more through cooperation than through competition.

Some developmental scientists, however, have begun to question how different the male and female paths to identity really are—especially today—and to suggest that individual differences may be more important than gender differences (Archer, 1993; Marcia, 1993). Indeed, Marcia (1993) argues that relationships and an ongoing tension between independence and connectedness are at the heart of all of Erikson's psychosocial stages for *both* men and women.

Self-esteem, during adolescence, develops largely in the context of relationships with peers, particularly those of the same sex. In line with Gilligan's view, male self-esteem seems to be linked with striving for individual achievement, whereas female self-esteem depends more on connections with others. In one longitudinal study, 84 mostly white, socioeconomically diverse young adults, whose self-esteem had been measured at ages 14 and 18, described memories about important experiences with others. Men who had had high self-esteem during adolescence tended to recall wanting to assert themselves with male friends, whereas women who had had high self-esteem recalled efforts to help female friends—efforts that involved asserting themselves in a collaborative rather than a competitive way (Thorne & Michaelieu, 1996).

Some research suggests that adolescent girls have lower self-esteem than adolescent boys (Chubb, Fertman, & Ross, 1997). Highly publicized studies during the early 1990s found that girls' self-confidence and self-esteem stay fairly high until age 11 or 12 and then tend to falter (American Association of University

Consider this . . .

- Do findings that adolescent girls lose self-esteem ring true, in your experience? What do you think might explain the conflicting findings on this question?

Women [AAUW] Educational Foundation, 1992; L. M. Brown & Gilligan, 1990)—news that, other researchers suggest, may have served as a self-fulfilling prophecy (refer back to Chapter 9). A recent analysis of hundreds of studies involving nearly 150,000 respondents concluded that boys and men do have higher self-esteem than girls and women, especially in late adolescence, but the difference is small. Contrary to the earlier finding, both males and females seem to gain self-esteem with age (Kling, Hyde, Showers, & Buswell, 1999).

Ethnic Factors in Identity Formation

What happens to young people's identity when the values of their own ethnic community conflict with those of the larger society—for example, when American Indians are expected to participate in a tribal ceremony on a day when they are also supposed to be in school? Or when young people face and perhaps internalize (take into their own value system) prejudice against their ethnic group? Or when discrimination limits their occupational choice, as it did for Jackie Robinson's brother Mack, who, after his Olympic glory, came home to a succession of menial jobs? All these situations can lead to identity confusion.

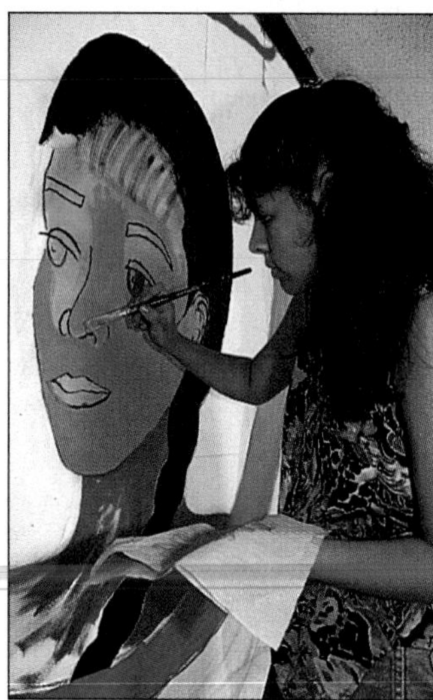

Identity development can be especially complicated for young people from minority groups. Ethnicity—and the conflicts with the dominant culture it entails—may play a central part in their self-concept.

Identity formation is especially complicated for young people in minority groups. In fact, for some adolescents ethnicity may be central to identity formation (Phinney, 1993). Skin color and other physical features, language differences, and stereotyped social standing can be extremely influential in molding minority adolescents' self-concept (Spencer & Markstrom-Adams, 1990). At a time when adolescents want to fit in—when they are painfully self-conscious about physical differences—minority adolescents cannot help but stand out (Spencer & Dornbusch, 1998).

Teenagers have wider social networks and more mobility than younger children, and greater cognitive awareness of cultural attitudes and distinctions. Caught between two cultures, many minority youth are keenly conscious of conflicts between the values stressed at home and those dominant in the wider society. Despite positive appraisals by parents, teachers, community, and peers, minority adolescents' self-perceptions may reflect negative views of their group by the majority culture. Faced with a dearth of successful black role models, African American young people in inner cities who "act white" may be rejected by both white and black peers. Many Asian American adolescents find it easier to assimilate, but this means subscribing to values such as autonomy, which may conflict with their parents' desire to maintain traditions of family cohesion and obedience to authority (Spencer & Dornbusch, 1998).

Research using Marcia's identity-status measures has shown a disproportionately large number of minority teenagers in foreclosure (Spencer & Markstrom-Adams, 1990). However, for them, this status may be adaptive. For example, Latino adolescents living in predominantly Latino communities may find social recognition, strength, and a robust sense of identity through following the customs and values of their culture.

CHECKPOINT

Can you . . .

- ✔ List the three major issues involved in identity formation, according to Erikson?
- ✔ Describe four types of identity status found by Marcia?
- ✔ Discuss how gender and ethnicity can affect identity formation?

Elkind: The Patchwork Self

As Erikson and Marcia observed, not everyone achieves a strong sense of identity, during or after adolescence. Why is this so?

According to Elkind (1998), there are two paths to identity. The first, and healthiest, is a process of *differentiation* and *integration:* becoming aware of the many ways in which one differs from others, and then integrating these distinctive parts of oneself into a unified, unique whole. This inner-directed process requires much time and reflection; but when a person has achieved a sense of identity in this way, it is almost impossible to break down.

The second, initially easier, path is that of *substitution:* replacing one, childlike, set of ideas and feelings about the self with another by simply adopting other people's attitudes, beliefs, and commitments as one's own. A sense of self built mainly by substitution is what Elkind calls a **patchwork self**—a self put together from borrowed, often conflicting, bits and pieces. Young people with patchwork selves tend to have low self-esteem. They find it hard to handle freedom, loss, or failure. They may be anxious, conforming, angry, frightened, or self-punishing. They are highly susceptible to outside influence and highly vulnerable to stress because they have no inner compass, no distinctive sense of direction to guide them.

Elkind attributes increases in drug abuse, gun violence, risky sexual behavior, and teenage suicide (discussed in Chapter 19) to the growing number of young people who have elements of the patchwork self. Today, says Elkind, with both parents working (or only one parent, or none, in the home), the consumer culture beckoning, and the sexual sophistication that is widely taken for granted, many adolescents "have a premature adulthood thrust upon them" (1998, p. 7). They lack the time or opportunity for the psychosocial moratorium Erikson described—the protected "time out" period necessary to build a stable, inner-directed self.

Authoritative parenting (discussed later in this chapter) can help. If young people see their parents acting according to firm, deeply held principles, they are more likely to develop firm, deeply held principles of their own. If parents show adolescents effective ways of dealing with stress, youngsters will be less likely to succumb to the pressures that threaten the patchwork self.

patchwork self
In Elkind's terminology, a sense of identity constructed by substituting other people's attitudes, beliefs, and commitments for one's own.

CHECKPOINT

Can you . . .

✔ Distinguish the two paths of identity development described by Elkind, and explain how he links risky behavior with the patchwork self?

Consider this . . .

- What similarities and differences do you see between Elkind's description of identity development and those of Erikson and Marcia?

Sexuality

Seeing oneself as a sexual being, recognizing one's sexual orientation, coming to terms with sexual stirrings, and forming romantic or sexual attachments all are parts of achieving sexual identity. This urgent awareness of sexuality is an important aspect of identity formation, profoundly affecting self-image and relationships. Although this process is biologically driven, its expression is in part culturally defined.

Guidepost

2. What determines sexual orientation?

Sexual Orientation

Although present in younger children, it is in adolescence that a person's **sexual orientation** generally becomes a pressing issue: whether that person will consistently be sexually, romantically, and affectionately attracted to persons of the other sex **(heterosexual)** or of the same sex **(homosexual)** or of both sexes (**bisexual**).

The incidence of homosexuality among adolescents is hard to pinpoint. In one study of 38,000 American students in grades 7 through 12, about 88 percent described themselves as predominantly heterosexual and only 1 percent as predominantly homosexual or bisexual. About 11 percent, mostly younger students, were unsure of their sexual orientation (Remafedi, Resnick, Blum, & Harris, 1992).

Although homosexuality once was considered a mental illness, several decades of research have found no association between sexual orientation and emotional or social problems (American Psychological Association, undated; C. J. Patterson, 1992, 1995a, 1995b). These findings eventually led the psychiatric profession to stop classifying homosexuality as a mental disorder. The 1994 edition of the American Psychiatric Association's *Diagnostic and Statistical Manual of Mental Disorders* contains no references to it at all.

sexual orientation
Focus of consistent sexual, romantic, and affectionate interest, either heterosexual, homosexual, or bisexual.

heterosexual
Describing a person whose sexual orientation is toward the other sex.

homosexual
Describing a person whose sexual orientation is toward the same sex.

bisexual
Describing a person whose sexual orientation is toward both the same sex and the other sex.

Other common explanations for homosexuality—all of which lack convincing scientific support—point to disturbed relationships with parents; parental encouragement of unconventional, cross-gender behavior; imitation of homosexual parents; or chance learning through seduction by a homosexual. Many young people have one or more homosexual experiences as they are growing up, usually before age 15. However, isolated experiences, or even homosexual attractions or fantasies, do not determine sexual orientation.

According to one theory, sexual orientation may be influenced by a complex prenatal process involving both hormonal and neurological factors (Ellis & Ames, 1987). If the levels of sex hormones in a fetus of either sex between the second and fifth months of gestation are in the typical female range, the person is likely to be attracted to males after puberty. If the hormone levels are in the male range, the person is likely to be attracted to females. Whether and how hormonal activity may affect brain development, and whether and how differences in brain structure may affect sexual orientation have not been established (Golombok & Tasker, 1996), but an anatomical difference between homosexual and heterosexual men in an area of the brain that governs sexual behavior has been reported (LeVay, 1991).

There also is evidence that sexual orientation may be at least partly genetic. An identical twin of a homosexual has about a 50 percent probability of being homosexual himself or herself, while a fraternal twin has only about a 20 percent likelihood and an adopted sibling 10 percent or less (Gladue, 1994). One series of studies linked male homosexuality to a small region of the X chromosome inherited from the mother (Hamer, Hu, Magnuson, Hu, & Pattatucci, 1993, Hu et al., 1995). However, later research failed to replicate this finding (G. Rice, Anderson, Risch, & Ebers, 1999).

Controversy remains as to whether or not sexual orientation is decisively shaped either before birth or at an early age. There also is dispute as to the relative contributions of biological, psychological, and social influences (Baumrind, 1995; C. J. Patterson, 1995b). These influences may well be "impossible to untangle," and their relative strength may differ among individuals (Baumrind, 1995, p. 132).

Sexual Attitudes and Behavior

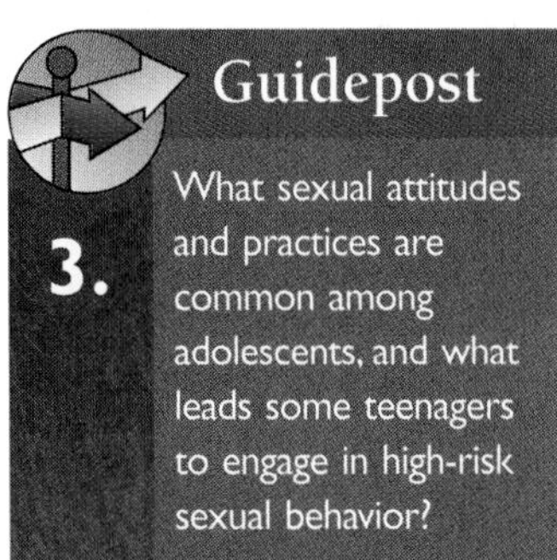

Guidepost
3.
What sexual attitudes and practices are common among adolescents, and what leads some teenagers to engage in high-risk sexual behavior?

It is difficult to do research on sexual expression. People willing to answer questions about sex tend to be sexually active and liberal in their attitudes toward sex and thus are not representative of the population. Also, there is often a discrepancy between what people say about sex and what they do, and there is no way to corroborate what people say. Some may conceal sexual activity; others may exaggerate. Problems multiply in surveying young people. For one thing, parental consent is often required, and parents who grant permission may not be typical. Methodology can make a difference: adolescent boys are more open in reporting certain types of sexual activity when surveys are self-administered by computer (C. F. Turner et al., 1998). Still, even if we cannot generalize findings to the population as a whole, within the groups that take part in surveys we can see trends that reveal changes in sexual mores.

How have sexual attitudes and behavior changed in recent decades?

The early 1920s through the late 1970s witnessed an evolution in sexual attitudes and behavior. This sexual evolution has brought greater acceptance of and indulgence in premarital sex, especially in a committed relationship, together with a decline in the *double standard:* the code that gives males more sexual freedom than females. One reason for this change is the secular trend toward earlier sexual maturity (see Chapter 11), coupled with a societal trend toward later marriage (see Chapter 14).

In 1965, at a large southern university, 33 percent of male students and 70 percent of female students called premarital sexual intercourse immoral. By

1985, only about 16 percent of the men and 17 percent of the women thought so (I. Robinson, Ziss, Ganza, Katz, & Robinson, 1991). Rates of premarital sexual activity have risen accordingly, especially among girls. In the mid-1950s, 1 out of 4 girls had sexual experience by age 18. Today more than 1 out of 2 girls and nearly 3 out of 4 boys have had intercourse by that age. The average girl now has her sexual initiation at 17, only one year later than the average boy (Alan Guttmacher Institute [AGI], 1994; American Academy of Pediatrics [AAP] Committee on Adolescence, 1999; Children's Defense Fund, 1997a, 1998; see Figure 12-1).

The double standard is not dead, however. In a telephone survey of 500 high school students, more boys said that sex was pleasurable and that they felt good about their sexual experiences, whereas more girls said that they were in love with their last sexual partner and that they should have waited until they were older before having sex (Lewin, 1994).

The wave of sexual liberation may be ebbing. After a steady rise since the 1970s, two government surveys found a decline between 1990 and 1995 in the proportion of 15- to 19-year-olds who report being sexually active. Among girls, the percentage who have had intercourse dropped from 55 to 50 percent (Abma, Chandra, Mosher, Peterson, & Piccinino, 1997), and among never-married boys, from 60 to 55 percent ("Teen sex down," 1997). A 1995 survey of more than 240,000 entering freshman at colleges and universities found 43 percent approving of casual sex, down from 52 percent in 1987 (Sax et al., 1996).

The sexual evolution has brought more acceptance of homosexuality. In 1995, 31 percent of 240,082 college freshmen in a major survey said homosexual relations should be prohibited, down from 53 percent in 1987 (Sax et al., 1996). Still, teenagers who openly identify as gay or lesbian often feel isolated in a hostile environment and may be subject to prejudice and even violence (C. J. Patterson, 1995b).

Attitudes toward sexuality have liberalized during the past fifty years. This "sexual evolution" includes more open acceptance of sexual activity and a decline in the double standard by which males are freer sexually than females.

CHECKPOINT

Can you . . .

- ✔ Discuss theories and research regarding origins of sexual orientation?
- ✔ Describe trends in sexual attitudes and activity among adolescents?

Sexual Risk Taking

Two major concerns about teenage sexual activity are the risks of contracting **sexually transmitted diseases (STDs)**—diseases spread by sexual contact—and of pregnancy. (Both of these topics are discussed in subsequent sections.) Most in

sexually transmitted diseases (STDs) Diseases spread by sexual contact.

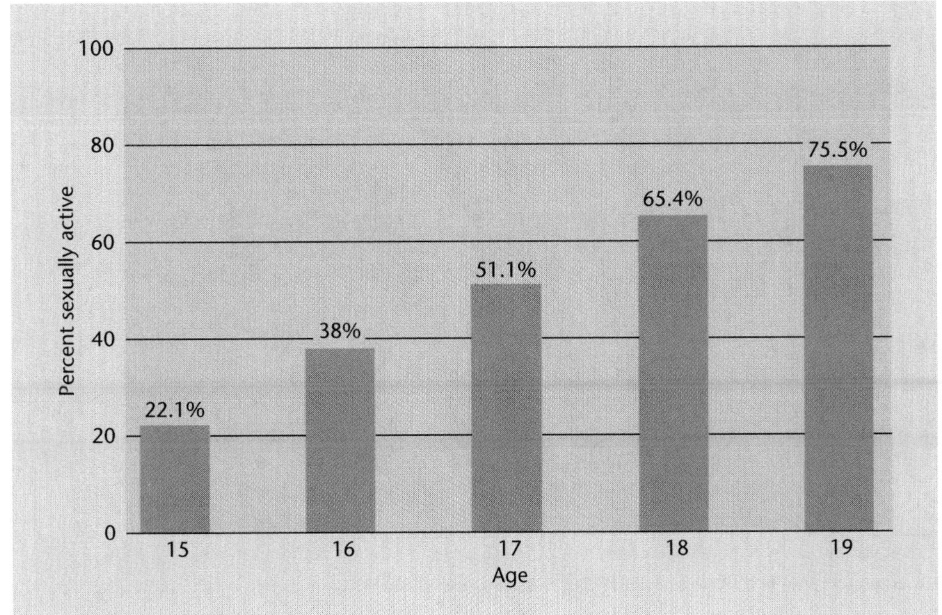

Figure 12-1
Percentage of teenage girls who have had intercourse after menarche, by age, 1995. More than half of teenage girls become sexually active by age 17.
(Source: Based on data from Abma et al., 1997.)

danger are teenagers who start sexual activity early, who have multiple partners, who do not use contraceptives, and who have inadequate information—or misinformation—about sex.

Early Sexual Activity

Various factors—including early entrance into puberty, poverty, poor school performance, lack of academic and career goals, a history of sexual abuse or parental neglect, and cultural or family patterns of early sexual experience—influence the likelihood of early sexual activity (AAP Committee on Adolescence, 1999; Kroger, 1993; see Table 12-4).

One of the most powerful influences is young adolescents' perception of peer group norms. Among 1389 sixth-graders in Philadelphia public schools, the strongest predictor of which youngsters would begin sexual activity by the end of the school year was the intention to do so, and that intention was most strongly influenced by the belief that most of their friends had already had intercourse (Kinsman, Romer, Furstenberg, & Schwarz, 1998).

Teenage girls (and, to a lesser extent, boys) often feel under pressure to engage in activities they do not feel ready for. Social pressure was the chief reason given by 73 percent of the girls and 50 percent of the boys in a Harris poll when asked why many teenagers do not wait to engage in sex until they are older (Louis Harris & Associates, 1986). Some girls who begin having sexual relations early are coerced into it by older men (AGI, 1994; Children's Defense Fund, 1998). Sixteen percent of women whose first intercourse took place before age 16, and 22 percent of those whose first experience was before age 15, report that it was not voluntary (Abma et al., 1997).

Use of Contraceptives

The best safeguard for sexually active teens is regular use of condoms, which gives some protection against STDs as well as against pregnancy. Condom use has increased dramatically in recent years, probably due to educational campaigns aimed at preventing AIDS. About three-fourths of girls and women who began premarital sexual activity voluntarily between 1990 and 1995 say they used some kind of protection the first time they engaged in sex. More than half (54 percent) report that their partners used condoms, as compared with only 18 percent of women whose first sexual experience was before 1980 (Abma et al., 1997).

Table 12-4 Some Factors Associated with Timing of First Intercourse

	Factors Associated with Early Age	Factors Associated with Later Age
Timing of puberty	Early	Late
Personality style and behavior	Risk taking, impulsive	Traditional values, religious orientation
	Depressive symptoms Antisocial or delinquent	Prosocial or conventional behavior
Substance use	Use of drugs, alcohol, tobacco	Nonuse
Education	Fewer years of schooling	More years of schoolig; valuing academic achievement
Family structure	Single-parent family	Two-parent family
Socioeconomic status	Disadvantaged	Advantaged
Ethnicity	African American	White, Latino

Source: Adapted from B. C. Miller & Moore, 1990; Sonenstein, Pleck, & Ku, 1991.

The younger a girl is when becoming sexually active, the less likely she is to use contraception at first intercourse (Abma et al., 1997). Adolescents who do not use contraceptives, or who use them irregularly or ineffectively, tend to be in their early teens. They are relatively inexperienced with sex, ignorant about it, and ashamed of engaging in it, and typically they are not in committed relationships. They tend to have low educational and career aspirations, to be uninvolved in sports or other activities, and to use alcohol or drugs (AGI, 1994; Louis Harris & Associates, 1986; Luster & Small, 1994; B. C. Miller & Moore, 1990).

Many teenagers with multiple sex partners do not use reliable protection. Almost one-fifth of sexually active high school students report having had four or more sex partners (AAP Committee on Adolescence, 1999). Teenagers in this high-risk group tend to have low grades, to be frequent drinkers, to have little parental supervision or support; and to have been abused by parents (Luster & Small, 1994).

Where Do Teenagers Get Information about Sex?

The more teenagers know about sex, the more responsible thay are likely to be about it, and today's teenagers tend to know more about sex than their predecessors did. In 1995, about 96 percent of 18- to 19-year-olds (as compared with only 80 percent of 25- to 29-year-olds and 65 percent of 35- to 39-year-olds) reported having had formal sex instruction. This instruction typically covered birth control methods, sexually transmitted diseases, safe sex to prevent HIV infection, and how to say no to sex (Abma et al., 1997). This is important because teenagers who are knowledgeable about sex are more likely to use contraceptives and to use them consistently (Ku, Sonenstein, & Pleck, 1992; Louis Harris & Associates, 1986; Luster & Small, 1994). They are also more likely to postpone sexual intimacy—the most effective means of birth control (Conger, 1988; Jaslow, 1982). Teenagers who can go to their parents or other adults with questions about sex and those who get sex education from school or community programs have a better chance of avoiding pregnancy and other risks connected with sexual activity (see Box 12-1).

Unfortunately, nearly 4 out of 10 teenagers get their sex education from the media (Princeton Survey Research Associates, 1996), which present a distorted view of sexual activity, associating it with fun, excitement, competition, danger, or violence, and rarely showing the risks of unprotected sexual relations (AAP Committee on Communications, 1995b).

Not surprisingly, then, adolescents who get their information about sex from television and who lack well-formed value systems, critical viewing skills, and strong family influence may accept the idea of premarital and extramarital intercourse with multiple partners and without protection against pregnancy and disease. Furthermore, television tends to reinforce a stereotypical double standard, in which women, but not men, consider marriage important. Also, movies and rock music lyrics have become more and more sexually explicit; music videos are full of sexual images and violence against women (AAP Committee on Communications, 1995b).

Several studies suggest a link between media influence and early sexual activity (Strasburger & Donnerstein, 1999). For example, the National Surveys of Children found that boys who watched more television (especially those who watched television without their families) were more likely to have early sexual relations (Peterson, Moore, & Furstenberg, 1991). But the amount of time young people spend watching television may be less important an influence than their involvement with what they see. Among a multiethnic sample of 314 college undergraduates, students who said they identified strongly with the characters in

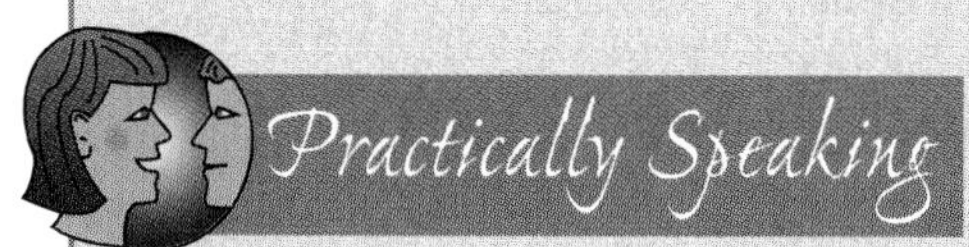

Box 12-1

Preventing Teenage Pregnancy

Teenage pregnancy rates in the United States are many times higher than in other industrialized countries, where adolescents begin sexual activity just as early or earlier than in the United States (AAP Committee on Adolescence, 1999; Children's Defense Fund, 1998).

Experts disagree about the causes of teenage pregnancy. Some observers point to such factors as the reduced stigma on unwed motherhood, media glorification of sex, the lack of a clear message that sex and parenthood are for adults, the influence of childhood sexual abuse, and failure of parents to communicate with children. The European experience suggests the importance of two other factors: sex education and access to contraception (AAP Committee on Adolescence, 1999).

Europe's industrialized countries have long provided universal, comprehensive sex education—a more recent development in the United States. Comprehensive programs encourage young teenagers to delay intercourse but also aim to improve contraceptive use among adolescents who are sexually active. Such programs include education about sexuality and acquisition of skills for responsible sexual decision making and communication with partners. They provide information about risks and consequences of teenage pregnancy, about birth control methods, and about where to get medical and contraceptive help (AGI, 1994; Kirby, 1997; I. C. Stewart, 1994). Programs aimed at male adolescents emphasize the wisdom of delaying fatherhood and the need to take responsibility when it occurs (Children's Defense Fund, 1998).

Contrary to some critics, community- and school-based sex education does not lead to more sexual activity (Children's Defense Fund, 1998; Eisen & Zellman, 1987). However, the content of sex education programs has become a political issue. The 1996 federal welfare reform law funded a massive, state-administered sex education program, to begin in 1998, stressing abstinence only, with

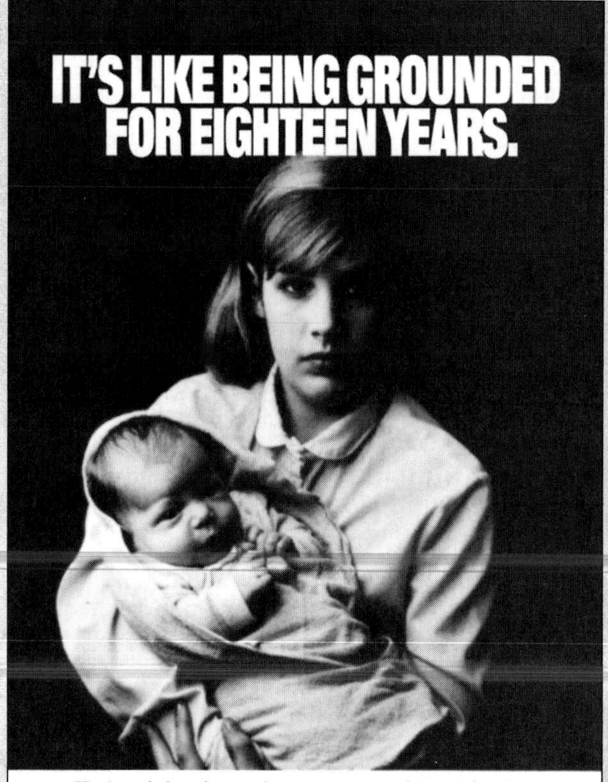

IT'S LIKE BEING GROUNDED FOR EIGHTEEN YEARS.
Having a baby when you're a teenager can do more than just take away your freedom, it can take away your dreams.
THE CHILDREN'S DEFENSE FUND

To many teenagers, one of the most persuasive arguments against sexual risk taking is the danger that pregnancy will ruin their lives. Teenage girls respond better when the advice comes from other girls close to their own age.

situation comedies dealing with sexual issues, or who judged the portrayals as very realistic, tended to endorse recreational attitudes toward sex. They also tended to be more sexually experienced and to expect more sexual activity among peers than students who were less involved with what they saw on screen (Ward & Rivadeneyra, 1999). Thus television seems to help shape young people's views of what is normative and expected.

In ironic contrast to the blatantly irresponsible portrayals of sexuality in television programming, network executives have almost universally refused to show contraceptive advertisements, claiming that they would be controversial and offensive and might encourage sexual activity. However, there is no evidence for the latter claim, and trial advertisements in limited markets have brought mostly commendations instead of complaints (AAP Committee on Communications, 1995b).

CHECKPOINT

Can you . . .

- ✔ Identify and discuss factors that increase the risks of sexual activity?

—*Continued*

no authorization for teaching about contraception. Some experts fear that this program may actually increase teenage pregnancy by failing to teach sexually active young people how to prevent it (Children's Defense Fund, 1997b). Although abstinence programs may be appropriate for some youngsters, especially for younger adolescents, there is inadequate evidence as to their effectiveness (Kirby, 1997).

Of course, parents are young people's first and often best teachers. Teenagers whose parents have talked with them about sex from an early age, have communicated healthy attitudes, and have been available to answer questions tend to wait longer for sexual activity (J. J. Conger, 1988; Jaslow, 1982). However, many adolescents are uncomfortable talking about sex with parents. Programs that include peer counseling can be effective; teenagers often heed peers when they might not pay attention to the same advice from an older person (Jay, DuRant, Shoffitt, Linder, & Litt, 1984).

Another factor in preventing pregnancy is access to reproductive services. Contraceptives are provided free to adolescents in Britain, France, Sweden, and, in many cases, the Netherlands. Sweden showed a fivefold reduction in the teenage birth rate following introduction of contraceptive education, free access to contraceptives for young people, and free abortion on demand (Bracher & Santow, 1999). Swedish parents cannot be told that their children have sought contraceptives if the teenagers request privacy.

When similar programs are proposed in the United States, they generally are not adopted for fear that they might seem to endorse sexual activity among teenagers. Yet U.S. teenagers say that making birth control services free, readily accessible (close to schools), and confidential are the three most effective ways to encourage contraception (Louis Harris & Associates, 1986; Zabin & Clark, 1983). Many adolescents do not go to public health clinics because they fear being judged by adults (Children's Defense Fund, 1998).

Providing contraceptives is not enough. In the long run, preventing teenage pregnancy requires attention to underlying factors that put teenagers and families at risk: reducing poverty, school failure, behavioral, and family problems, and expanding employment, skills training, and family life education (AGI, 1994; Children's Defense Fund, 1998; Kirby, 1997). The Perry Preschool Project and an intervention program for elementary school students in Seattle (both discussed later in this chapter) have shown that comprehensive early intervention can reduce teenage pregnancy (Hawkins, Catalano, Kosterman, Abbott, & Hill, 1999; Schweinhart, Barnes, & Weikart, 1993).

Since adolescents who have high aspirations are less likely to become pregnant, programs that focus on motivating young people to achieve and raising their self-esteem—not merely on the mechanics of contraception—have achieved some success (Carrera, 1986). One promising program, Teen Outreach, has grown dramatically; by 1998, it was offered to girls and boys in 107 schools in 16 states (Children's Defense Fund, 1998). At 25 randomly assigned sites where the program was given between 1991 and 1995, rates of teenage pregnancy, school failure, and suspension were less than half the rates in a control group (Allen, Philliber, Herrling, & Kuperminc, 1997). Teen Outreach does not explicitly focus on these problems; instead, it seeks to help teenagers make decisions, handle emotions, and deal with peers and adults. The program includes volunteer community service linked to classroom discussions of future life decisions. By allowing students to select their volunteer activity, the program helps them see themselves as autonomous and competent. This is evidence that teenage pregnancy and school failure are not isolated problems but are part of a larger developmental picture.

Sexually Transmitted Diseases (STDs)

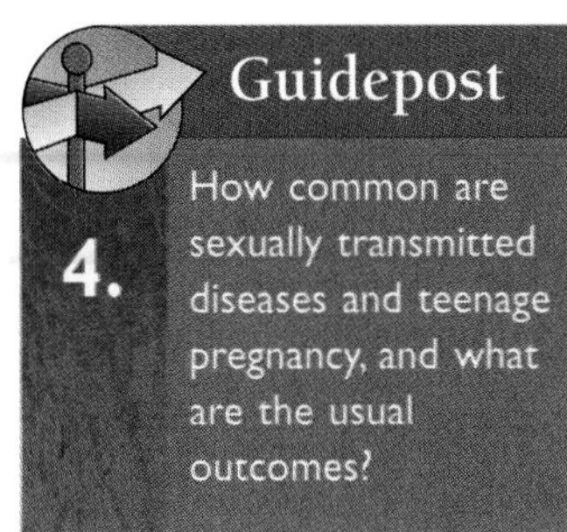

Guidepost
4.
How common are sexually transmitted diseases and teenage pregnancy, and what are the usual outcomes?

Sexually transmitted diseases (STDs) are diseases spread by sexual contact. Rates in the United States are among the highest in the industrialized world; 1 out of 4 Americans is likely to contract an STD (AGI, 1994).

One in three cases of STDs occurs among adolescents; the younger the teenager, the greater the chance of infection. The chief reasons for the spread of STDs among adolescents are early sexual activity, which increases the likelihood of having multiple high-risk partners, and failure to use condoms or to use them regularly and correctly. An estimated 25 percent of young people may develop an STD before high school graduation (AAP Committee on Adolescence, 1994).

The most prevalent STD, according to some estimates, is human papilloma virus (HPV), which sometimes produces warts on the genitals (AAP Committee on Adolescence, 1994). Next is genital herpes simplex, a chronic, recurring, often painful, and highly contagious disease caused by a virus (AGI, 1994). The condition can be fatal to a person with a deficiency of the immune system or to the newborn infant of a mother who has an outbreak at the time of delivery. There is no cure, but the antiviral drug acyclovir can prevent active outbreaks. Both diseases have been associated, in women, with increased incidence of cervical cancer. The most common *curable* STD is chlamydia, which causes infections of the urinary tract, rectum, and cervix and can lead, in women, to pelvic inflammatory disease (PID), a serious abdominal infection. Table 12-5 summarizes some common STDs: their causes, most frequent symptoms, treatment, and consequences.

STDs are more likely to develop undetected in women than in men, and in adolescents as compared with adults. Symptoms may not appear until the disease has progressed to the point of causing serious long-term complications. Programs that promote abstention from or postponement of sexual activity, responsible decision making, and ready availability of condoms for those who are sexually active may have some effect in controlling the spread of STDs (AAP Committee on Adolescence, 1994; AGI, 1994; Ku et al., 1992).

Although AIDS is not as prevalent as some other STDs, it is the seventh leading cause of death among 15- to 24-year-olds in the United States (Hoyert et al., 1999). AIDS results from the human immunodeficiency virus (HIV), which attacks the body's immune system, leaving affected persons vulnerable to a variety of fatal diseases. HIV is transmitted through bodily fluids (mainly blood and semen) and is believed to stay in the body for life, even though the person carrying it may show no signs of illness. Symptoms of AIDS—which include extreme fatigue, fever, swollen lymph nodes, weight loss, diarrhea, and night sweats—may not appear until 6 months to 10 or more years after initial infection. As of now, AIDS is incurable, but increasingly, the related infections that kill people are being stopped with antiviral therapy, including protease inhibitors (Palella et al., 1998). Many HIV-infected people lead active lives for years.

CHECKPOINT

Can you . . .

- ✔ Identify and describe the most common sexually transmitted diseases?
- ✔ List risk factors for developing an STD during adolescence, and state effective prevention methods?

Teenage Pregnancy and Childbearing

In the United States, about 1 in 10 girls ages 15 to 19—an estimated 1 million girls—become pregnant each year, and 85 percent of these pregnancies are unplanned. Who are these girls? They are inexperienced: 50 percent had their first intercourse within the past six months (AGI, 1994; Children's Defense Fund, 1998; Ventura, Mathews, & Curtin, 1999). Some were coerced or sexually abused: nearly two-thirds had partners who were 21 or older (AAP Committee on Adolescence, 1999). Low-income girls, those who come from dysfunctional families, those who show early behavioral problems or fail in school, and those who already have given birth are most likely to become pregnant (Children's Defense Fund, 1998).

More than half of pregnant teenagers have their babies and plan to raise them themselves. About one-third have abortions, and one-seventh miscarry. Very few place their infants for adoption (AAP Committee on Adolescence, 1999; AGI, 1994; Children's Defense Fund, 1998). More than 8 out of 10 adolescent mothers are from poor families (AGI, 1994); pregnant girls from advantaged families are more likely to choose abortion.

Teenage pregnancy and birthrates have fallen during the 1990s, reflecting the trends toward delay in sexual activity and increased use of contraceptives. The

Table 12-5 Common Sexually Transmitted Diseases

Disease	Cause	Symptoms: Male	Symptoms: Female	Treatment	Consequences if Untreated
Chlamydia	Bacterial infection	Pain during urination, discharge from penis	Vaginal discharge, abdominal discomfort†	Tetracycline or erythromycin	Can cause pelvic inflammatory disease or eventual sterility
Trichomoniasis	Parasitic infection, sometimes passed on in moist objects such as towels and bathing suits	Often absent	May be absent, or may include vaginal discharge, discomfort during intercourse, odor, painful urination	Oral antibiotic	May lead to abnormal growth of cervical cells
Gonorrhea	Bacterial infection	Discharge from penis, pain during urination*	Discomfort when urinating, vaginal discharge, abnormal menses†	Penicillin or other antibiotics	Can cause pelvic inflammatory disease or eventual sterility; also can cause arthritis, dermatitis, and meningitis
HPV (genital warts)	Human papiloma virus	Painless growths that usually appear on penis, but also may appear on urethra or in rectal area*	Small, painless growths on genitals and anus; also may occur inside the vagina without external symptoms*	Removal of warts; but infection often reappears	May be associated with cervical cancer. In pregnancy, warts enlarge and may obstruct birth canal.
Herpes	Herpes simplex virus	Painful blisters anywhere on the genitalia, usually on the penis*	Painful blisters on the genitalia, sometimes with fever and aching muscles; women with sores on cervix may be unaware of outbreaks*	No known cure, but controlled with antiviral drug acyclovir	Possible increased risk of cervical cancer
Hepatitis B	Hepatitis B virus	Skin and eyes become yellow	Skin and eyes become yellow	No specific treatment; no alcohol	Can cause liver damage, chronic hepatitis
Syphillis	Bacterial infection	In first stage, reddish-brown sores on the mouth or genitalia, or both which may disappear, through the bacteria remain; in the second more infectious stage, a widespread skin rash*	Same as in men	Penicillin or other antibiotics	Paralysis, convulsions, brain damage, and sometimes death
AIDS (acquired immune deficiency syndrome)	Human immunodeficiency virus (HIV)	Extreme fatigue, fever, swollen lymph nodes, weight loss, diarrhea, night sweats, susceptibility to other diseases*	Same as in men	No known cure; protease inhibitors and other drugs appear to extend life	Death, usually due to other diseases, such as cancer

*May be asymptomatic.
†Often asymptomatic.

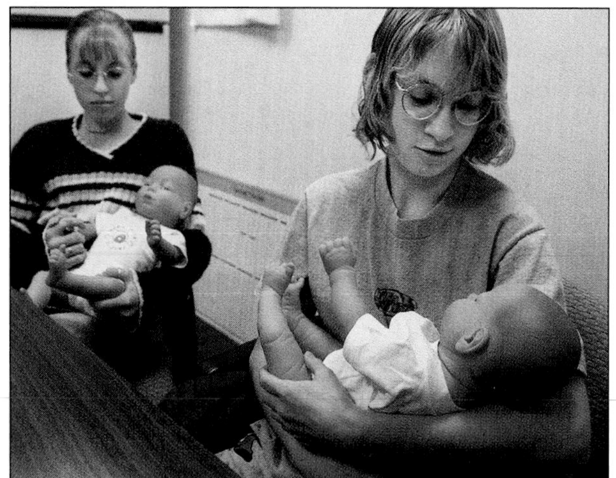

At the Child Support Agency in Appleton, Wisconsin, teenage girls try to comfort computerized dolls that cry and fuss like real babies. The program is designed to dramatize what it means to become mothers at an early age.

birthrate for 15- to 19-year-old girls dropped 18 percent from its high point in 1991, from about 62 births per 1,000 to about 51 in 1998, partly reversing a 24 percent increase from 1986 to 1991. The birthrate has fallen more sharply among black than among white teenagers, but black girls are still nearly twice as likely to have babies as white girls; and birthrates for Hispanic teenagers now are highest of all. Nearly 79 percent of teenage births are to unmarried girls (Ventura et al., 1999). The birthrate for unwed teens is almost three times as high as in the early 1960s, when girls married younger (Children's Defense Fund, 1997b, 1998).

CHECKPOINT

Can you . . .

✔ Summarize trends in teenage pregnancy and birthrates?

✔ Discuss problems and outcomes of teenage pregnancy?

✔ Identify ways to prevent teenage pregnancy?

Teenage pregnancies often have poor outcomes. Many of the mothers are impoverished and poorly educated, and some are drug users. Many do not eat properly, do not gain enough weight, and get inadequate prenatal care or none at all. Their babies are likely to be premature or dangerously small and are at heightened risk of neonatal death, disability, or health problems (AAP Committee on Adolescence, 1999; Children's Defense Fund, 1998). Babies of more affluent teenage mothers also are at risk. Among more than 134,000 white, largely middle-class girls and women in Utah who had their first babies between 1970 and 1990, 13- to 19-year-olds were more likely than 20- to 24-year-olds to have low-birthweight babies, even when the mothers were married and well educated and had adequate prenatal care. Good prenatal care apparently cannot always overcome the biological disadvantage inherent in being born to a still-growing girl whose own body may be competing for vital nutrients with the developing fetus (Fraser, Brockert, & Ward, 1995).

Consider this . . .

- Since girls generally bear the burdens of adolescent pregnancy, should teenage girls be urged to follow a stricter standard of sexual behavior than teenage boys? Should more emphasis be placed on encouraging teenage boys to be more responsible sexually? Or both?
- Under what circumstances do you think each of the following choices might be best for a teenage girl who discovers that she is pregnant: marry the father and raise the child, stay single and raise the child, give the baby to adoptive parents, or have an abortion?

Teenage unwed mothers and their families are likely to suffer financial hardship. Although paternity now can be clearly established through DNA testing, child support laws are spottily enforced, and court-ordered payments are often inadequate. If the fathers are also adolescents, they often have poor school records, high dropout rates, and limited financial resources and income potential. Even if they want to be involved in their children's lives, they may not know how (AAP Committee on Adolescence, 1999). In the past, many teenage mothers went on public assistance, but under the 1996 federal welfare reform law such assistance is severely limited. Unmarried parents under age 18 are now eligible only if they live with their parents and go to school.

Many teenage mothers eventually finish high school and obtain employment, but their immaturity and lack of parenting skills can take a toll on their children. During the preschool years, children born to teenage mothers are more likely than children born to older mothers to show cognitive delays, high levels of aggression, and impulsive behavior. As adolescents, they are more likely to fail in school, to be delinquent, to be incarcerated, to abuse drugs, and to become pregnant (AAP Committee on Adolescence, 1999; Children's Defense Fund, 1998). However, these outcomes are far from universal. A 20-year study of more than 400 teenage mothers in Baltimore found that two-thirds of their daughters did not become teenage mothers themselves, and most graduated from high school (Furstenberg, Levine, & Brooks-Gunn, 1990).

Age becomes a powerful bonding agent in adolescence. Adolescents spend more time with peers and less with family. However, most teenagers' fundamental values (like Jackie Robinson's) remain closer to their parents' than is generally realized (Offer & Church, 1991). Even as adolescents turn to peers for companionship and intimacy, they look to parents for a "secure base" from which they can try their wings (Laursen, 1996).

Is Adolescent Rebellion a Myth?

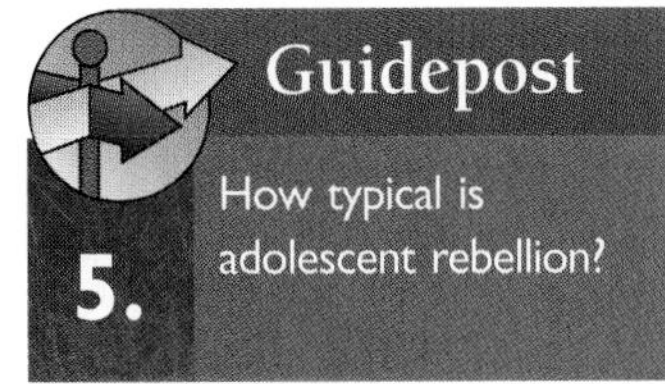

Guidepost

5. How typical is adolescent rebellion?

The teenage years have been called a time of **adolescent rebellion,** involving emotional turmoil, conflict within the family, alienation from adult society, reckless behavior, and rejection of adults' values. Yet research on adolescents in the United States and other countries the world over suggests that fewer than 1 in 5 teenagers—at least among those who remain in school—fits this pattern (Brooks-Gunn, 1988; Offer, 1987; Offer, Ostrov, & Howard, 1989; Offer, Ostrov, Howard, & Atkinson, 1988; Offer & Schonert-Reichl, 1992).

adolescent rebellion Pattern of emotional turmoil, characteristic of a minority of adolescents, which may involve conflict with family, alienation from adult society, reckless behavior, and rejection of adults' values.

The idea of adolescent rebellion may have been born in the first formal theory of adolescence, that of the psychologist G. Stanley Hall. Hall (1904/1916) believed that young people's efforts to adjust to their changing bodies and to the imminent demands of adulthood usher in a period of "storm and stress," which produces conflict between the generations. Sigmund Freud (1935/1953) and his daughter, Anna Freud (1946), described "storm and stress" as universal and inevitable, growing out of a resurgence of early sexual drives toward the parents. However, the anthropologist Margaret Mead (1928, 1935), who studied adolescence on South Pacific islands, concluded that when a culture provides a gradual, serene transition from childhood to adulthood, "storm and stress" is not typical—an observation later supported by research in 186 preindustrial societies (Schlegel & Barry, 1991).

Full-fledged rebellion now appears to be uncommon even in western societies, at least among middle-class youngsters who are in school. In classic studies, Daniel Offer (1969) found a high level of bickering over minor issues between 12- and 14-year-old boys and their parents, but little turmoil. Less than one-fifth of these boys experienced a tumultuous adolescence (Offer & Offer, 1974). Similarly, in more recent research, only 15 to 25 percent of families with adolescents reported significant conflict, and many of those families had had problems before the children reached their teens (W. A. Collins, 1990; J. P. Hill, 1987; Offer et al., 1989). Although adolescents may defy parental authority with some regularity, the emotions attending this transition do not normally lead to family conflict of major proportions or to a sharp break with parental or societal standards (Arnett, 1999; Offer & Church, 1991; Offer et al., 1989). Most young people feel close to and positive about their parents, share similar opinions on major issues, and value their parents' approval (J. P. Hill, 1987; Offer et al., 1989; Offer et al., 1988). "Adolescent rebellion" frequently amounts to little more than a series of minor skirmishes.

Nonetheless, adolescence—at least in middle-class western families—can be a difficult time. Family conflict, mood swings, and risky behavior are more common than during other parts of the life span (Arnett, 1999). Despite wide individual differences, negative moods and depression tend to increase during these years (Larson & Lampman-Petraitis, 1989; Petersen et al., 1993; see Chapter 10). Many adolescents feel self-conscious, embarrassed, awkward, lonely, nervous, or ignored (Larson & Richards, 1994). And, while not all engage in fast driving, drug use, or unprotected sex, most do take occasional risks (Arnett, 1999).

Consider this . . .

- Can you think of values you hold that are different from those of your parents? How did you come to develop these values?
- When teenagers complain that their parents "don't understand" them, what do you think they mean?

To what extent is such behavior rooted in the biological changes of puberty? Hormonal changes probably contribute to emotional volatility, especially during early adolescence, but their effect seems to be small and to depend on interaction with other factors. Some investigators point to genes that may be "turned on" at this time; developmental changes in emotional regulation, aggressiveness, and sensation-seeking; and sleep-deprivation, which often results from the discrepancy between adolescents' changing sleep needs and their school schedules (Arnett, 1999; see Chapter 11).

The fact that "storm and stress" is not universal or inevitable suggests that its main sources are not biological. Adolescence is most difficult in cultures such as the dominant one in the United States, which emphasize individuality and the need to achieve independence. The relative tranquillity of adolescence in many traditional societies (and in some minority U.S. subcultures) may change with their growing adoption of western values.

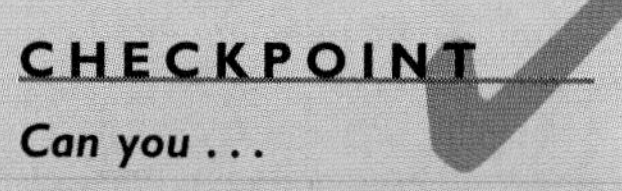

Can you . . .

✔ Assess the extent of adolescent rebellion and of storm and stress during the teenage years?

Recognizing that adolescence tends to be a difficult time can help parents and teachers put troubling behavior in perspective. On the other hand, adults who assume that adolescent turmoil is normal and necessary may erroneously believe that teenagers will outgrow problems and may fail to recognize when a young person needs help.

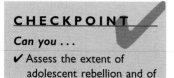

How Adolescents Spend Their Time—and with Whom

Guidepost
6.
How do adolescents relate to parents, siblings, and peers?

What do teenagers do on a typical day? With whom do they do it, and how do they feel about what they are doing?

According to sequential research with 220 white middle- and working-class suburban youngsters who carried beepers and reported what they were doing each time the beepers sounded, the amount of time spent with families declines dramatically between ages 10 and 18, from 35 percent to 14 percent of waking hours (Larson, Richards, Moneta, Holmbeck, & Duckett, 1996). This disengagement is not a rejection of the family, but a response to developmental needs. Early adolescents often retreat to their rooms; they seem to need time alone to step back from the demands of social relationships, regain emotional stability, and reflect on identity issues (Larson, 1997). High schoolers spend more of their free time with peers, with whom they identify and feel comfortable (Larson & Richards, 1991).

Adolescents' social and emotional life follows a weekly cycle. The weekend assumes special importance in high school, when youngsters have more freedom, become more mobile, and spend more time with friends, away from home (Larson & Richards, 1998). School days become less enjoyable, and weekend evenings become "the emotional high point of the week" (p. 43). Friday and Saturday nights typically are a time for being with a romantic partner or "cruising" with a group. Sometimes these parties become occasions for risky behavior, such as daredevil driving and using alcohol or drugs.

The character of family interactions changes during these years. Adolescents and their parents may spend less time than before watching television together, but just as much—and among girls, more—in one-on-one conversations. As adolescents grow older, they increasingly see themselves as taking the lead in these discussions, and their feelings about contact with parents become more positive (Larson et al., 1996). In one study of 121 rural New England high school students (average age, 17), adolescents were as close to mothers as to friends. Parents' influence remained high even as contact diminished (Laursen, 1996).

African American teenagers, who may look upon their families as havens in a hostile world, maintain more intimate family relationships and less intense peer relations than white teenagers, according to interviews with a representative cross section of 942 adolescents in Toledo, Ohio. Black teenagers also tend to be more flexible in their choice of friends and less dependent on peer approval (Giordano, Cernkovich, & DeMaris, 1993).

Mexican American boys tend to become closer to their parents during puberty. This may reflect the unusually close-knit nature of Mexican American families and their greater adaptability to change. Or—since this pattern does not appear among girls—it may reflect the importance Hispanic families place on the traditional male role (Molina & Chassin, 1996).

With such ethnic variations in mind, let's look more closely at relationships with parents, and then with siblings and peers.

CHECKPOINT

Can you . . .

✔ Identify age and cultural differences in how young people spend their time?

Adolescents and Parents

Just as adolescents feel tension between dependency on their parents and the need to break away, parents often have mixed feelings, too. They want their children to be independent, yet they find it hard to let go. Parents have to walk a fine line between giving adolescents enough independence and protecting them from immature lapses in judgment. These tensions often lead to family conflict, and parenting styles can influence its shape and outcome. Also, as with younger children, parents' life situation—their work and marital and socioeconomic status—impinges on their relationships with teenage children.

Family Conflict

Much family conflict is over the pace of adolescents' growth toward independence (Arnett, 1999). Arguments between teenagers and their parents often focus on "how much" or "how soon": how much freedom teenagers should have to plan their own activities or how soon they can take the family car. Most arguments concern day-to-day matters—chores, schoolwork, dress, money, curfews, dating, and friends—rather than fundamental values (B. K. Barber, 1994). However, some of these "minor" issues are "proxies" for more serious ones, such as substance use, safe driving, and sex. Furthermore, an accumulation of frequent "hassles" can add up to a stressful family atmosphere (Arnett, 1999).

Subjects of conflict are similar in married and divorced families (Smetana, Yau, Restrepo, & Braeges, 1991) and across ethnic lines. However, white parents report more frequent clashes with teenagers than black or Hispanic parents, who tend to enforce higher behavioral expectations as a means of survival in the majority culture (B. K. Barber, 1994). Working-class Chinese adolescents in Hong Kong, whose culture stresses family obligations and harmony, report fewer conflicts with parents than European American adolescents (Yau & Smetana, 1996).

Family conflict is most frequent during early adolescence but most intense in midadolescence (Laursen, Coy, & Collins, 1998). The frequency of strife in early adolescence may be related to the strains of puberty and the need to assert autonomy. The more highly charged arguments in midadolescence and, to a lesser extent, in late adolescence may reflect the emotional strains that occur as adolescents try their wings. The reduced frequency of conflict in late adolescence may signify adjustment to the momentous changes of the teenage years and a renegotiation of the balance of power between parent and child. Or older adolescents may argue less with parents simply because they spend less time with them (Fuligni & Eccles, 1993; Laursen et al., 1998; Molina & Chassin, 1996; Steinberg, 1988).

These patterns, too, have ethnic variations. In African American families in the rural South, religiosity influences the levels of family cohesion and conflict during preadolescence and early adolescence. Highly religious parents tend to get along better with each other and with their children (Brody, Stoneman, & Flor, 1996).

Asian American youngsters experience more family conflict during late adolescence than during early adolescence, and their perceptions of their parents' warmth and understanding do not seem to improve as much as in European American families. This may be because Asian cultures stress control of emotions and expectations for respect and obedience. By college age, when many European American young people have already renegotiated their relationships with parents, Asian American parents and adolescents are struggling over control of the young person's friends, activities, and private life (Greenberger & Chen, 1996). Conflict in both cultures is more likely with mothers than with fathers (Greenberger & Chen, 1996; Laursen et al., 1998; Steinberg, 1981, 1987), perhaps because most mothers have been more closely involved with their children and may have mixed feelings about giving up that involvement.

Consider this . . .

- What kinds of issues do you recall as causing the most conflict in your family when you were a teenager, and how were they resolved? If you lived with both parents, did your mother and father handle such issues similarly or differently?

Regardless of ethnicity, the level of family discord seems to hinge primarily on teenagers' personalities and on their parents' treatment of them. These factors may explain why disagreements in some families tend to blow over, whereas in other families they escalate into major confrontations. Dissension is most likely when parents see a teenager as having negative personality characteristics (such as a hot temper, meanness, or anxiety) and a history of problem behavior, and when parents use coercive discipline (B. K. Barber, 1994). In a study of 335 two-parent rural midwestern families with teenagers, conflict declined in warm, supportive families during early to middle adolescence but worsened in a hostile, coercive, or critical family atmosphere (Rueter & Conger, 1995).

Parenting Styles

Although adolescents are different from younger children, authoritative parenting still seems to work best (Baumrind, 1991). Authoritative parents insist on important rules, norms, and values but are willing to listen, explain, and negotiate. They encourage teenagers to form their own opinions (Lamborn, Mounts, Steinberg, & Dornbusch, 1991). They exercise appropriate control over the child's conduct but not the child's sense of self (Steinberg & Darling, 1994).

Overly strict, authoritarian parenting may be especially counterproductive as children enter adolescence and feel a need to be treated more as adults. When parents do not adjust to this need, their children may reject parental influence and seek peer support and approval at all costs. Among 1,771 predominantly white, middle-class sixth- and seventh-graders, those who saw their parents as giving them little opportunity to be involved in decisions affecting them were apt to do virtually anything to gain popularity with peers, even if it meant breaking family rules and neglecting schoolwork and their own talents. This was not true of

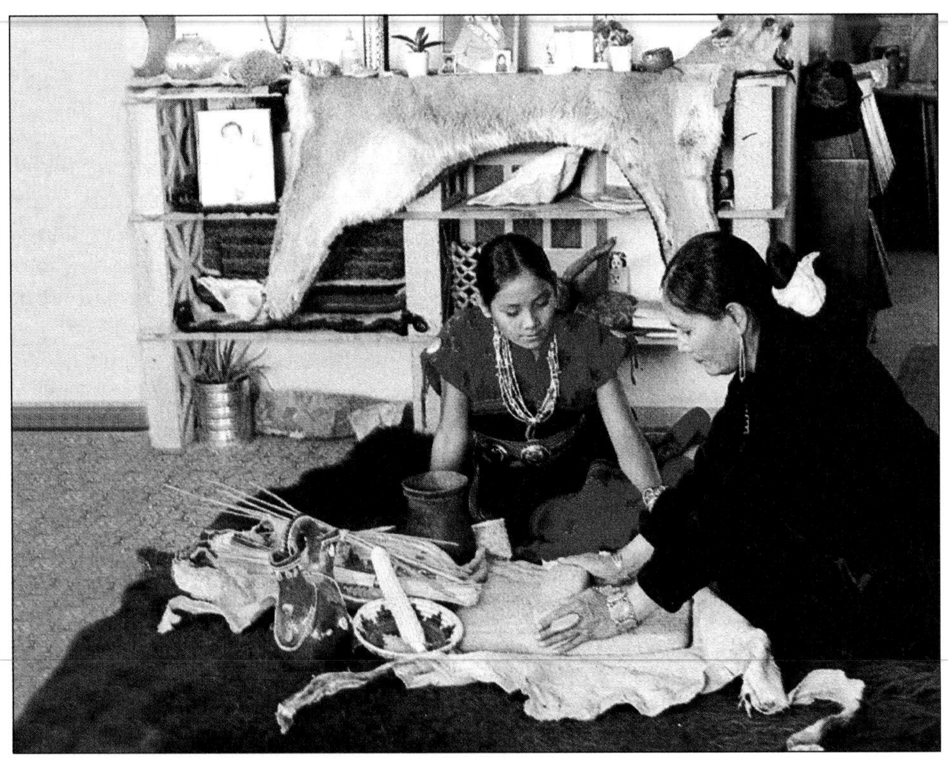

Communication between parents and adolescents may flow more naturally when they are engaged in a shared pursuit. Grinding corn in the traditional manner strengthens the bond between this Navajo mother and daughter. Most adolescents feel close to and positive about their parents, appreciate their approval, and have similar values on major issues.

students whose parents simply monitored their activities. Apparently it is power assertion, not appropriate supervision, that evokes negative reactions (Fuligni & Eccles, 1993). Parents who show disappointment in their teenagers' misbehavior are more effective in motivating them to behave responsibly than are parents who punish them harshly (Krevans & Gibbs, 1996).

Authoritative parenting can help young people internalize standards that insulate them against negative peer influences and open them to positive ones. In a study of 500 ninth- through eleventh-graders, students whose close friends were drug users tended to increase their own self-reported drug use, but that was less true of those who saw their parents as highly authoritative. Adolescents whose close friends were academic achievers tended to improve their grades, but that was less true of students whose parents were *not* authoritative (Mounts & Steinberg, 1995).

Effects of Parents' Life Situation

Many adolescents today live in families that are very different from families a few decades ago. Most mothers, like Jackie Robinson's, work outside the home, and teenagers often care for themselves after school. Many youngsters, like Robinson, live with single parents; others live with stepparents. Many families, like Robinson's, must cope with severe economic stress.

How do these family situations affect adolescents? A combination of factors may be involved. The impact of a mother's employment, for example, may depend on whether there are two parents or only one in the home. Often a single mother must work to stave off economic disaster; how her working affects her teenage children may hinge on how much time and energy she has left over to spend with them and what sort of role model she provides. These factors, in turn, may be influenced by others: what kind of work she does, how many hours she works, how much she earns, and how much she likes her work (B. L. Barber & Eccles, 1992).

Parents' Employment Most research about how parents' work affects adolescents deals with mothers' employment. Some research has found that adolescent children of working mothers tend to be better adjusted socially than other teenagers; they feel better about themselves, have more of a sense of belonging, and get along better with families and friends. On the negative side, they tend to spend less time on homework and leisure reading and more time watching television (Gold & Andres, 1978; Milne, Myers, Rosenthal, & Ginsburg, 1986).

Teenagers may like being freer to direct their own activities when their mothers are out of the house. However, with less supervision adolescents are more susceptible to peer pressure. A survey of 3,993 ninth-graders in six school districts in southern California, who came from a wide range of ethnic and socioeconomic backgrounds, found that students who are unsupervised after school tend to smoke, drink, use marijuana, or engage in other risky behavior; to be depressed; and to have low grades. As long as parents know where their son or daughter is, a lack of supervision in itself does not significantly increase the risk of problems; but the less consistently parents monitor their child's activities and the more hours the young person is unsupervised, the greater the risk. Lack of supervision seems to have the most detrimental effect on girls, who otherwise are less prone to problems than boys (Richardson, Radziszewska, Dent, & Flay, 1993).

When parents feel overworked, parent-child conflict tends to rise. Mothers who feel overloaded tend to become less caring and accepting, and their children often show behavior problems (Galambos, Sears, Almeida, & Kolaric, 1995). When mothers are stressed, tensions between adolescents and fathers increase as well (Almeida & McDonald, 1998).

In the 1950s, 1960s, and 1970s, when most mothers who could afford to stay home did so, adolescent sons of working women held less stereotyped attitudes about female roles than did sons of at-home mothers. Daughters of employed women had higher and less gender-stereotyped career aspirations, were more outgoing, scored higher on several academic measures, and seemed better adjusted on social and personality measures (L. W. Hoffman, 1979). Today, a mother's work status seems to be just one of many factors that shape adolescents' attitudes toward women's roles (Galambos, Petersen, & Lenerz, 1988). In fact, maternal employment in itself does not seem to affect teenagers much; whatever effect it has is filtered through other factors, such as the warmth in a relationship (Galambos et al., 1995) and a woman's satisfaction with her dual roles. Teenage sons of working mothers tend to have more flexible attitudes toward gender roles when they have warm relationships with their mothers, and teenage daughters show unstereotyped attitudes when their mothers are happy with their roles (Galambos et al., 1988).

Surprisingly, some of the strongest gender-typing occurs in families with full-time employed mothers. Gender divisions may be more egalitarian during the week, when everyone is occupied with work or school. On weekends, however, girls—like their mothers—do a larger share of the housework and of care of younger siblings (Crouter & Maguire, 1998).

Family Structure Growing up in a household with two parents is an advantage during childhood (refer back to Chapter 10), and it continues to be an advantage during adolescence, at least in terms of avoiding risky behaviors. An analysis of data on approximately 22,000 young people ages 12 to 17 from the 1991, 1992, and 1993 National Household Survey of Drug Abuse found that adolescents living with two biological or adoptive parents are less likely than adolescents living in other family structures to use alcohol, cigarettes, or illegal drugs, or to report problems associated with their use (R. A. Johnson, Hoffmann, & Gerstein, 1996).

Still, divorce and single parenting do not necessarily produce problem adolescents. Indeed, a review of the literature suggests that some of the detrimental effects of living in a "broken home" may have been overstated (B. L. Barber & Eccles, 1992). For example, a number of studies have found that children of divorce do worse in school than those in two-parent families. By adolescence, however, the differences are usually minor and may be nonexistent when other factors, such as socioeconomic status and parental conflict, are held constant. Similarly, findings of lower self-esteem and differences in attitudes toward gender roles are small, inconsistent, or inconclusive. Furthermore, most of these studies are cross-sectional and thus do not show changes in the same young person before and after a divorce.

In evaluating the effects of divorce and single parenting, then, we need to look at particular circumstances. Sometimes divorce can improve the situation by reducing the amount of conflict within the home (refer back to Box 10-1). And, while the immediate effects of a marital breakup may be traumatic, in the long run some adolescents may benefit from having learned new coping skills that make them more competent and independent (B. L. Barber & Eccles, 1992).

Parental support may be more important than family structure. In one study of 254 urban African American adolescent boys, those living with a single mother were no more likely than those in two-parent, stepparent, or extended family households to use alcohol or drugs, to become delinquent, to drop out of school, or to have psychological problems. The only difference was a positive one: sons in single-mother households experienced more parental support than other youths. It may be that the mothers (like Jackie Robinson's) provided extra support to compensate for the fathers' absence. However, many fathers also continued to be involved in their sons' lives, and this involvement was related to positive outcomes (M. A. Zimmerman, Salem, & Maton, 1995).

Adolescents find it especially difficult to adjust to a parent's remarriage. In one study, 9- to 13-year-olds in remarried families were less socially and scholastically competent than children from nondivorced families and tended to be disruptive or depressed and withdrawn. Two years later, they showed little improvement (Hetherington & Clingempeel, 1992).

Economic Stress A major problem in many single-parent families is economic stress. Poverty can complicate family relationships and harm children's development through its impact on parents' emotional state (refer back to Chapter 10). Adolescents may experience such indirect effects of economic hardship, too. One study looked at single African American mothers of seventh- and eighth-graders in a midwestern city that was experiencing widespread manufacturing layoffs. Unemployed mothers, especially those without outside help and support, tended to become depressed; and depressed mothers tended to be negative in their perception of their maternal role and punitive toward their children. Young people who saw their relationships with their mothers deteriorate tended to become depressed themselves and to have trouble in school (McLoyd, Jayaratne, Ceballo, & Borquez, 1994).

Of course, economic stress can strike two-parent families as well. Among 378 intact white families in an economically declining area of rural Iowa, financial conflicts between parents and adolescents were worsened by parental depression and marital conflict. Parents who fought with each other and with their children over money tended to be hostile and coercive, increasing the risk of teenage behavior problems (R. C. Conger, Ge, Elder, Lorenz, & Simons, 1994).

On the other hand, many adolescents in economically distressed families like Jackie Robinson's benefit from accumulated social capital (refer back to Chapter 11)—the support of kin and community. In 51 poor, urban African American families in which teenagers were living with their mothers, grandmothers, or aunts, the women who had strong kinship networks tended to be psychologically healthy, and so were the youngsters. The more social support the women received, the greater their self-esteem and acceptance of their children. The women with stronger support exercised firmer control and closer monitoring while granting appropriate autonomy, and their teenage charges were more self-reliant and had fewer behavior problems (R. D. Taylor & Roberts, 1995).

CHECKPOINT

Can you . . .

- ✔ Identify factors that affect conflict with parents?
- ✔ Discuss the impact on adolescents of parenting styles and of parents' employment, marital status, and socioeconomic status?

Adolescents and Siblings

As teenagers begin to separate from their families and spend more time with peers, they have less time and less need for the emotional gratification they used to get from the sibling bond. Adolescents are less close to siblings than to either parents or friends, are less influenced by them, and become even more distant as they move through adolescence (Laursen, 1996).

Changes in sibling relationships may well precede similar changes in the relationship between adolescents and parents: more independence on the part of the younger person and less authority exerted by the older person. As children reach high school, their relationships with their siblings become progressively more equal. Older siblings exercise less power over younger ones and fight with them less (Buhrmester & Furman, 1990). Adolescents still show intimacy, affection, and admiration for their brothers and sisters (Raffaelli & Larson, 1987), but their relationships are less intense (Buhrmester & Furman, 1990).

These changes seem to be fairly complete by the time the younger sibling is about 12 years old (Buhrmester & Furman, 1990). By this time, the younger child no longer needs as much supervision, and differences in competence and independence between older and younger siblings are shrinking. (A 6-year-old is vastly more competent than a 3-year-old, but a 15-year-old and a 12-year-old are more nearly equal.)

Consider this . . .

- If you have one or more brothers or sisters, did your relationships with them change during adolescence? If so, how? What factors do you think influenced any such changes?

Older and younger siblings tend to have different feelings about their changing relationship. As the younger sibling grows up, the older one has to give up some of his or her accustomed power and status and may look on a newly assertive younger brother or sister as a pesky annoyance. On the other hand, younger siblings still tend to look up to older ones—as Jackie Robinson did to his brother Mack—and try to feel more "grown up" by identifying with and emulating them (Buhrmester & Furman, 1990). Even by age 17, younger siblings are more likely to get advice about plans and problems from older siblings, to be influenced by them, and to be satisfied with the support they receive from them than the other way around (Tucker, Barber, & Eccles, 1997).

CHECKPOINT

Can you . . .

✔ Describe typical changes in sibling relationships during adolescence?

Siblings born farther apart tend to be more affectionate toward each other and to get along better than those who are closer in age. The quarreling and antagonism between closely spaced brothers and sisters may reflect more intense rivalry, since their capabilities are similar enough to be frequently compared—by themselves and others. Same-sex siblings are usually closer than a brother and sister (Buhrmester & Furman, 1990).

Adolescents and Peers

As Jackie Robinson found, an important source of emotional support during the complex transition of adolescence, as well as a source of pressure for behavior that parents may deplore, is a young person's growing involvement with peers.

Adolescents going through rapid physical changes take comfort from being with others going through like changes. Teenagers challenging adult standards and parental authority find it reassuring to turn for advice to friends who are in the same position themselves. Adolescents questioning their parents' adequacy as models of behavior, but not yet sure enough of themselves to stand alone, look to peers to show them what's "in" and what's "out." The peer group is a source of affection, sympathy, understanding, and moral guidance; a place for experimentation; and a setting for achieving autonomy and independence from parents. It is a place to form intimate relationships that serve as "rehearsals" for adult intimacy (Buhrmester, 1996; Coleman, 1980; Gecas & Seff, 1990; Laursen, 1996; P. R. Newman, 1982).

The peer group is an important source of emotional support during adolescence. Young people going through rapid physical changes feel more comfortable with peers who are experiencing similar changes.

Peer Group Status

In sociometric studies, children are generally asked to name the classmates they like most and those they like least. Such studies have identified five *peer status groups: popular* (youngsters who receive many positive nominations), *rejected* (those who receive many negative nominations), *neglected* (those who receive few nominations of either kind), *controversial* (those who receive many positive and many negative nominations), and *average* (those who do not receive an unusual number of nominations of either kind).

A study of 1,041 preteens (ages 10 to 12) and 862 teenagers (ages 13 to 16) in northern Greece used this technique along with teacher ratings and self-ratings (Hatzichristou & Hopf, 1996). The young people also were asked to name two classmates who best fit certain behavioral descriptions (for example, "quarrels often with other students," "liked by everybody and helps everybody," or "gets into trouble with the teacher"). By combining and comparing the various evaluations, the researchers were able to fill out a portrait of rejected, neglected, and controversial adolescents.

As in U.S. studies, *rejected* youngsters had the greatest adjustment problems. They also had academic difficulties and low achievement test scores. Rejected boys, particularly younger ones, tended to be aggressive and antisocial; rejected girls were more likely to be shy, isolated, and unhappy, and to have a negative self-image. The latter characteristics also were typical of rejected boys in junior high and high school, apparently because shyness and sensitivity become more of a social liability as young people move into their teens (refer back to Box 10-2).

The *neglected* group—which, by high school age, included more boys than girls—were not much different from the average, except that they were less prosocial and had some learning difficulties, which contributed to a poor self-image. The transitions from elementary to junior high school and from junior high to high school seem to be particularly hard for rejected and neglected youngsters.

Controversial youngsters often were viewed differently by teachers and peers. Since the controversial group tended to do well in school, teachers did not see them as having behavioral problems. Peers, particularly in elementary school, often rated the girls in this category as well-behaved but snobbish and arrogant—perhaps reflecting girls' tendency to form cliques at this age. The boys were seen as aggressive and antisocial—but also as leaders, perhaps because peers expect and accept aggressiveness in young boys. By high school, the girls in the controversial category were better liked than before and were also seen as leaders.

Consider this . . .

- On the basis of the specific characteristics of rejected and neglected children described in this section, what do you think can be done to help such children?

Friendships

Friendships are fundamentally different from family relationships. They are more egalitarian than relationships with parents, who hold greater power, or with siblings, who are usually older or younger. Friendships are based on choice and commitment. By the same token, they are more unstable than family relationships. Awareness of the distinctive character of friendships, and of what it takes to maintain them, emerges in adolescence. Adolescents quarrel less angrily and resolve conflicts more equitably with friends than with family members, perhaps because they realize that too much conflict could cost them a friendship (Laursen, 1996).

Adolescents, like younger children, tend to choose friends who are like them, and friends influence each other to become even more alike (Berndt, 1982; Berndt & Perry, 1990). Friends usually are of the same race (Giordano et al., 1993) and have similar status within the peer group (Berndt & Perry, 1990).

Parents have considerable indirect influence on teenagers' choice of friends. In a study of 3,781 high school students (B. B. Brown, Mounts, Lamborn, & Steinberg, 1993), the extent to which parents monitored adolescents' behavior and schoolwork, encouraged achievement, and allowed joint decision making were related to academic achievement, drug use, and self-reliance. These behaviors, in turn, were linked with membership in such peer groups as "populars, jocks, brains, normals, druggies, and outcasts" (p. 471).

The intensity and importance of friendships, as well as time spent with friends, are probably greater in adolescence than at any other time in the life span. Friendships become more reciprocal in adolescence. Early adolescents begin to rely more on friends than on parents for intimacy and support. Friends now regard loyalty as more critical, and they share confidences more than younger friends. Intimacy, loyalty, and sharing are features of adult friendship; their appearance in adolescence marks a transition to adultlike relationships (Berndt & Perry, 1990; Buhrmester, 1990, 1996; Hartup & Stevens, 1999; Laursen, 1996). Intimacy with same-sex friends increases during early to midadolescence, after which it typically declines as intimacy with the other sex grows (Laursen, 1996).

The increased intimacy of adolescent friendship reflects cognitive development. Adolescents are now better able to express their private thoughts and feelings. They also can more readily consider another person's point of view, and so it is easier for them to understand a friend's thoughts and feelings. Increased intimacy also reflects early adolescents' concern with getting to know themselves. Confiding in a friend helps young people explore their own feelings, define their identity, and validate their self-worth. Friendship provides a safe place to venture opinions, admit weaknesses, and get help in coping with problems (Buhrmester, 1996).

The capacity for intimacy is related to psychological adjustment and social competence. Adolescents who have close, stable, supportive friendships generally have a high opinion of themselves, do well in school, are sociable, and are unlikely to be hostile, anxious, or depressed (Berndt & Perry, 1990; Buhrmester, 1990; Hartup & Stevens, 1999). A bidirectional process seems to be at work: good friendships foster adjustment, which in turn fosters good friendships.

Friendship in adolescence requires more advanced social skills than friendship in childhood. Because friendships become more talk-oriented, teenagers need to be able to start and sustain conversations. They need to know how to seek out friends, call them up, and make plans. They need to know how to handle conflicts and disagreements. They need to know how and when to share confidences and how and when to offer emotional support. Friendships help adolescents develop these skills by offering opportunities to use them and feedback on their effectiveness (Buhrmester, 1996).

Sharing of confidences and emotional support seem to be more vital to female friendships than to male friendships during adolescence and throughout life. Boys' friendships focus less on conversation than on shared activity, usually sports and competitive games (Blyth & Foster-Clark, 1987; Buhrmester, 1996; Bukowski & Kramer, 1986). Girls feel better after telling a friend about an upsetting experience than boys do; boys may express support by just spending time doing things together (Denton & Zarbatany, 1996). As we have seen, boys tend to gain self-esteem from competition with friends, girls from helping them.

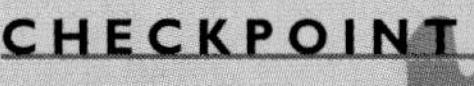

Can you . . .

✔ Describe characteristics that affect adolescents' popularity?

✔ Discuss important features of adolescent friendships?

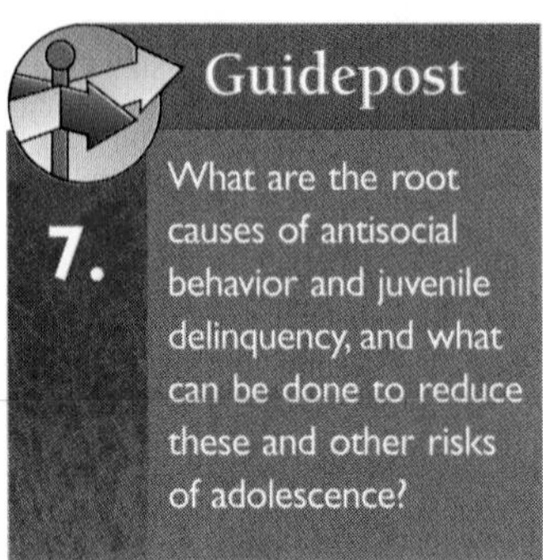

Guidepost
7.
What are the root causes of antisocial behavior and juvenile delinquency, and what can be done to reduce these and other risks of adolescence?

Adolescents in Trouble: Antisocial Behavior and Juvenile Delinquency

What influences young people to engage in—or refrain from—violence (see Box 12-2) or other antisocial acts? What determines whether or not a juvenile delinquent will grow up to be a hardened criminal?

As we examine the roots of delinquency, we need to keep in mind an important distinction. Some adolescents occasionally commit an antisocial act. A smaller group of chronic (repeat) offenders habitually commit a variety of serious antisocial acts, such as stealing, setting fires, breaking into houses or cars, destroying property, physical cruelty, frequent fighting, and rape. Chronic offend-

Box 12-2
The Youth Violence Epidemic

On April 20, 1999, 18-year-old Eric Harris and 17-year-old Dylan Klebold entered Columbine High School in Littleton, Colorado, wearing black trench coats and carrying a rifle, a semiautomatic pistol, two sawed-off shotguns, and more than 30 homemade bombs. Laughing and taunting, they began spraying bullets at fellow students, killing twelve classmates and one teacher before fatally shooting themselves.

The massacre in Littleton was one of a string of incidents that add up to what has been called an epidemic of youth violence. Between 1985 and 1995, the number of gun-related murders committed by juveniles in the United States rose by 249 percent (Federal Bureau of Investigation, 1995).

The contemporary prevalence of youth violence has been attributed to social trends that affect the atmosphere in which young people grow up (Staub, 1996): the rise in divorce and single parenthood, changing gender roles, drug use, unemployment and poverty due to economic shifts, and ethnic prejudice and discrimination. Some scholars point to a lack of structure in the home; a weakening of guiding values and standards; harsh discipline; abuse and neglect; and family conflict, which mirrors the violence in adult society.

Parents and teachers in Littleton seem to have been unaware that Harris and Klebold presented a serious threat, but psychologists point to potential warning signs that might avert future tragedies. Adolescents who are likely to commit violence often refuse to listen to authority figures, such as parents and teachers; ignore the feelings and rights of others; mistreat people; rely on violence or threatened violence to solve problems; and believe that life has treated them unfairly. They tend to do poorly in school; cut classes or play truant; be suspended or drop out; use alcohol, inhalants, and/or drugs; join gangs; and fight, steal, or destroy property (American Psychological Association and American Academy of Pediatrics [AAP], 1996).

In 3 out of 4 assaults or murders by young people, the perpetrators are members of gangs (American Psychological Association, undated). For many adolescents, gangs satisfy unfulfilled needs for identity, connection, and a sense of power and control. For youngsters who lack positive family relationships, a gang can become a substitute family. Gangs promote a sense of "us-versus-them"; violence against outsiders is accompanied by bonds of loyalty and support within the gang (Staub, 1996).

Violence and antisocial behavior have roots in childhood. Eight-year-olds who are unusually aggressive in school are likely to be antisocial in adolescence and adulthood (American Psychological Association Commission on Violence and Youth, 1994). Children who are raised in a rejecting or coercive atmosphere, or in an overly permissive or chaotic one, tend to show aggressive behavior; and the hostility they evoke in others increases their own

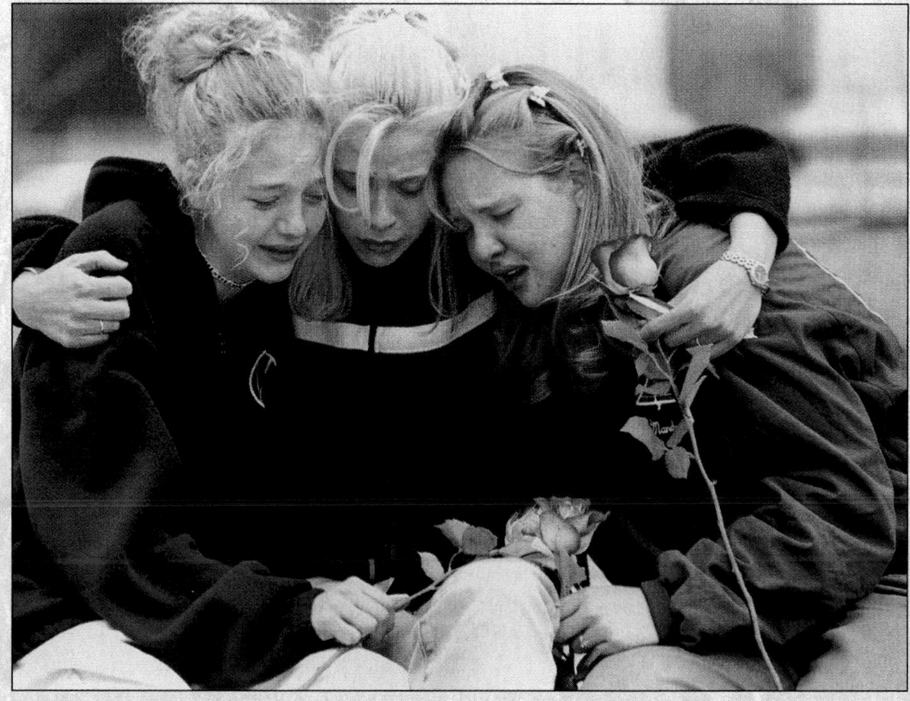

These sixteen-year-old girls console each other at a vigil service for victims of a shooting spree by teenage gunmen at Columbine High School in Littleton, Colorado, on April 20, 1999. This and other school shootings are part of what has been called an epidemic of youth violence.

Digging Deeper —Continued

aggression. Their negative self-image prevents them from succeeding at school or developing other constructive interests, and they generally associate with peers who reinforce their antisocial attitudes and behavior (Staub, 1996). Young people who are impulsive or fearless, or who have low IQs or learning difficulties, also may be violence-prone. Boys in poor, unstable neighborhoods are most likely to become involved in violence—one reason that the incident at Columbine, a middle-class suburban school, was so shocking (American Psychological Association, undated).

Of course, not all youngsters who grow up in difficult circumstances become violent. Factors that contribute to resilience (refer back to Chapter 10) include positive role models; a close, trusting bond with a parent or other adult; supportive relationships with teachers and peers; development of self-esteem and self-efficacy; strong social skills; ability to take refuge in hobbies, work, or creative pursuits; and a sense of control over one's life (American Psychological Association, undated).

Adolescents are more likely to turn violent if they have witnessed or have been victims of violence, such as physical abuse or neighborhood fights. Heavy exposure to media violence has a significant impact by desensitizing viewers to violence and depicting situations in which aggression is rewarded or justified (American Psychological Association, undated; Strasburger & Donnerstein, 1999; see Chapter 10). One in 5 rock music videos portrays overt violence, and 1 in 4 shows weapon carrying (DuRant et al., 1997). The media's contribution to real-life violence has been estimated at 5 to 15 percent (Strasburger & Donnerstein, 1999).

Fortunately, despite occasional well-publicized tragedies such as the one in Littleton, there are signs that the epidemic of youth violence is abating. Between 1991 and 1997, the percentage of high school students nationwide who reported carrying a weapon dropped by 30 percent, from about 26 percent to about 18 percent. There also were reductions in self-reported physical fighting and injury (Brener, Simon, Krug, & Lowry, 1999).

Successful preventive programs have given parents help in reducing the stress of child raising (American Psychological Association, undated) and training in socialization skills. Cooperative learning practices in schools and multicultural education can create a sense of community and reduce the us-versus-them mentality. Giving young people serious responsibilities and the opportunity to participate in making rules can help them understand how the individual's behavior affects the group (Staub, 1996). Some specific, practical suggestions for parents of older children and adolescents are to limit and monitor television viewing; encourage participation in sports and other supervised after-school activities; use nonphysical methods of discipline, such as grounding; store firearms unloaded and locked; and teach young people to stand up against violence when they see it (American Psychological Association and AAP, 1996).

ers are responsible for most juvenile crime and are most likely to continue their criminal activity in adulthood (Yoshikawa, 1994). Adolescents who were aggressive or got in trouble when they were younger—lying, being truant, stealing, or doing poorly in school—are more likely than other youngsters to become chronic delinquents (Loeber & Dishion, 1983; Yoshikawa, 1994).

How do "problem behaviors" escalate into chronic delinquency—an outcome Jackie Robinson managed to avoid? Research points to early patterns of parent-child interaction that pave the way for negative peer influence, which reinforces and promotes antisocial behavior. Neighborhood characteristics play a part as well.

Parental Influences

Parenting practices help shape prosocial or antisocial behavior by meeting or failing to meet children's basic emotional needs (Krevans & Gibbs, 1996; Staub, 1996). Parents of chronic delinquents often failed to reinforce good behavior in early childhood and were harsh or inconsistent, or both, in punishing misbehavior. Through the years these parents have not been closely and positively involved in their children's lives (G. R. Patterson, DeBaryshe, & Ramsey, 1989). The children may get payoffs for antisocial behavior: when they act up, they may gain attention or get their own way.

Ineffective parenting tends to continue in adolescence. Antisocial behavior at this age is closely related to parents' leniency and inability to keep track of their children's activities (G. R. Patterson & Stouthamer-Loeber, 1984). A longitudinal study of 132 white families found that the way mothers communicate with early adolescents about such issues as the young person's keeping his or her room clean can predict whether he or she will engage in severely delinquent behavior at age 19. The highest rates of criminal arrests and convictions occurred in families in which poor maternal communication and problem-solving skills were combined with parental conflict, divorce, or a mother's depression (Klein, Forehand, Armistead, & Long, 1997).

Teenagers' behavior also can be indirectly influenced by the way their friends are brought up. Among 4,431 high school students of varied ethnic backgrounds, those whose friends described their parents as authoritative were more likely to do well in school and less likely to use drugs or get in trouble with the law. This was true over and above the effect of a young person's own parenting (Fletcher, Darling, Steinberg, & Dornbusch, 1995). Apparently, authoritative parents tend to raise well-adjusted teenagers, who seek out other well-adjusted teenagers as friends. Thus the peer group reinforces the beneficial results of effective parenting.

Peer Influences

How much does the peer group contribute to delinquency? Parents often worry about a child's "falling in with the wrong crowd." Young people who take drugs, drop out of school, and commit delinquent acts usually do all these in the company of friends. However, children do not usually "fall in" with a group; they tend to seek out friends like themselves. Antisocial youngsters tend to have antisocial friends, and their antisocial behavior increases when they associate with each other (Dishion, McCord, & Poulin, 1999; Hartup & Stevens, 1999).

In the early grades, children with behavior problems tend to do poorly in school and do not get along with well-behaved classmates. Unpopular and low-achieving youngsters gravitate toward each other and influence one another toward further misconduct (G. R. Patterson, Reid, & Dishion, 1992). Grouping students with similar academic skills in the same classroom ("tracking") may make the problem worse by keeping low-achieving, antisocial youngsters together (Dishion, Patterson, Stoolmiller, & Skinner, 1991).

A young person with moderately deviant tendencies can be pushed further in that direction by associating with deviant peers. In one study of 868 low-income boys in Montreal, those who had been identified by teachers at ages 11 and 12 as moderately disruptive in class were more likely to be delinquent at age 13 if they had friends who were rated by peers as highly aggressive and disturbing (Vitaro, Tremblay, Kerr, Pagani, & Bukowski, 1997).

The way antisocial teenagers talk among themselves constitutes a sort of "deviancy training." By laughing, nodding, or showing other positive reactions to talk about rule breaking, they reinforce each other in antisocial behavior; youngsters who do not show antisocial tendencies ignore such talk. When researchers videotaped problem 25-minute discussions among 206 thirteen- and fourteen-year-old Oregon boys and their friends, conversations characterized by deviancy training predicted an increased probability of delinquency, drug use, and violent behavior at 15 and 16. What's more, deviancy training accounted for 35 percent of the variation in adult maladjustment five years later (Dishion et al., 1999).

Neighborhood Influences

Delinquency, like adult crime, tends to be concentrated in poor, overcrowded urban neighborhoods with dilapidated housing, high unemployment rates, and predominantly minority or recent immigrant populations (NRC, 1993a; Yoshikawa, 1994). However, neighbors who join together to exercise informal social control—keeping an eye on each other's children, confronting teenagers who hang out on street corners and harass passersby, and demanding basic community services, such as police protection and housing code enforcement—can help deter delinquency (Sampson, 1997; Sampson, Raudenbush, & Earls, 1997).

Long-Term Prospects

Most juvenile delinquents do not become adult criminals; many who are not hard-core offenders simply outgrow their "wild oats" (L. W. Shannon, 1982). Delinquency peaks at about age 15 and then declines, unlike alcohol use and sexual activity, which become more prevalent with age (refer back to Figure 11-1). Since alcohol and sexual activity are accepted parts of adult life, it is not surprising that as teenagers grow older they increasingly want to engage in them (Petersen, 1993). Antisocial behavior that is not accepted in adulthood may diminish as most adolescents and their families come to terms with young people's need to assert independence.

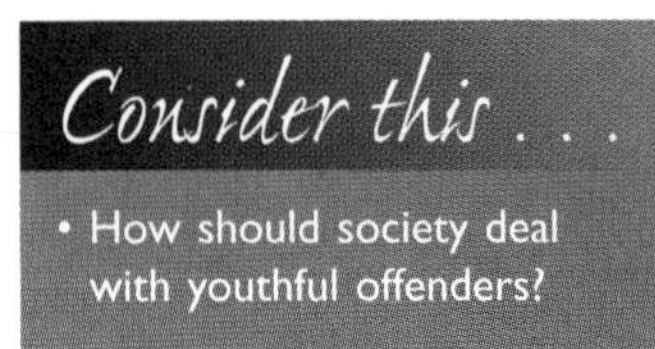

Consider this . . .
• How should society deal with youthful offenders?

Middle- and high-income adolescents may experiment with problem behaviors and then drop them, but low-income teenagers who do not see positive alternatives are more likely to adopt a permanently antisocial lifestyle (Elliott, 1993). A youth who sees that the only rich people in the neighborhood are drug dealers may be seduced into a life of crime.

Preventing Delinquency

Since juvenile delinquency seems to have roots early in childhood, so must preventive efforts. Young people who suffer from poor parenting are at less risk if their parents get effective community support. Effective programs attack the multiple risk factors that can lead to delinquency (Yoshikawa, 1994; Zigler, Taussig, & Black, 1992).

Research has found that adolescents who had taken part in certain early childhood intervention programs were less likely to get in trouble with the law (Yoshikawa, 1994; Zigler et al., 1992). For example, the Perry Preschool Project (refer back to Chapters 7 and 9), which focused on preparing children for school, had a "snowball effect." The children's teachers had a more positive attitude toward better-prepared kindergartners, the children liked school better, and they achieved more in later grades. The children developed higher self-esteem and aspirations for the future, both of which tend to deter antisocial behavior. Even though the early benefits to school performance did not always hold up, Perry "graduates" showed less antisocial behavior in adolescence and young adulthood than equally disadvantaged peers (Berrueta-Clement et al., 1985; Berrueta-Clement, Schweinhart, Barnett, & Weikart, 1987; Schweinhart et al., 1993).

Other early childhood interventions that have achieved impressive long-term results in preventing antisocial behavior and delinquency include the Syracuse Family Development Research Project, the Yale Child Welfare Project, and the Houston Parent Child Development Center. Each of these programs targeted high-risk urban children and lasted at least 2 years during the child's first 5 years of life. All influenced children directly, through high-quality day care or education, and at the same time indirectly, by offering families assistance and support geared to their needs (Yoshikawa, 1994; Zigler et al., 1992). Some programs taught parents how to discipline and motivate their children and how to build relationships with the children's teachers (Seitz, 1990).

In terms of Bronfenbrenner's bioecological theory (refer back to Chapter 2), these programs operated on the mesosystem by affecting interactions between two or more settings (the home and the educational or child care center) of which a child was a part. The programs also went one step further to the exosystem, by creating supportive parent networks and linking parents with community providers of prenatal and postnatal health care, educational and vocational counseling, and other services (Yoshikawa, 1994; Zigler et al., 1992). Through their multipronged approach, these interventions made an impact on several early risk factors for delinquency.

A preventive program for first- through sixth-graders in multiethnic high-crime areas of Seattle significantly reduced adolescent criminal behavior, as well as heavy drinking and sexual activity. Rather than attacking those issues directly, the program gave teachers, parents, and students training in skills designed to increase youngsters' academic and social competencies and attachment to school. Teachers learned instructional methods and classroom management skills to foster cooperative learning. Parents learned how to manage children's behavior and help them succeed in school. Children learned how to solve problems with peers without resorting to aggression and how to resist negative peer pressure—to stay out of trouble without losing friends. Six years later, at age 18, youngsters who had been in the program were 19 percent less likely than a control group to have committed violent acts. They also were 38 percent less likely to drink heavily, 13 percent less likely to have had sexual intercourse, 19 percent less likely to have had multiple sex partners, and 35 percent less likely to have become pregnant or caused a pregnancy (Hawkins et al., 1999).

Interventions need to target older youngsters as well. In addition to spotting characteristics of troubled adolescents, it is important to find ways of reducing young people's exposure to high-risk settings that encourage antisocial behavior. One way to do this is to monitor adolescents' activities, especially after school, on weekend evenings, and in summer, when they are most likely to be idle and get into trouble. As Jackie Robinson's experience shows, getting teenagers involved in constructive activities during their free time can pay long-range dividends (Larson, 1998). Training parents may help (Dishion et al., 1999), especially in families undergoing parental conflict, divorce, or depression (Klein et al., 1997). Some programs have helped by teaching delinquents social and vocational skills (NRC, 1993a).

However, interventions that focus on promoting prosocial attitudes within the peer group can boomerang by inadvertently offering enhanced opportunities for deviancy training. In one experiment, high-risk teenagers randomly assigned to a peer-focused intervention showed greater subsequent increases in smoking, aggressive classroom behavior, and delinquency as compared with groups assigned to parent-focused training or no special training. The results were no better for teenagers who had the parent-focused as well as the peer-focused intervention (Dishion et al., 1999).

Fortunately, the great majority of adolescents do not get into serious trouble. Those who do show disturbed behavior can—and should—be helped. With love, guidance, and support, adolescents can avoid risks, build on their strengths, and explore their possibilities as they approach adult life.

CHECKPOINT

Can you . . .

- ✔ Explain how parental, peer, and neighborhood influences can promote or prevent antisocial behavior and juvenile delinquency?
- ✔ Give examples of programs that have been successful in preventing delinquency and other risky behavior?

Is There a "Universal Adolescent"?

How much does the psychosocial world of adolescence vary in cultures as diverse as those of Australia and Bangladesh? Is the communication revolution making the world a "global village" and breaking down cultural differences among the young people who inhabit it?

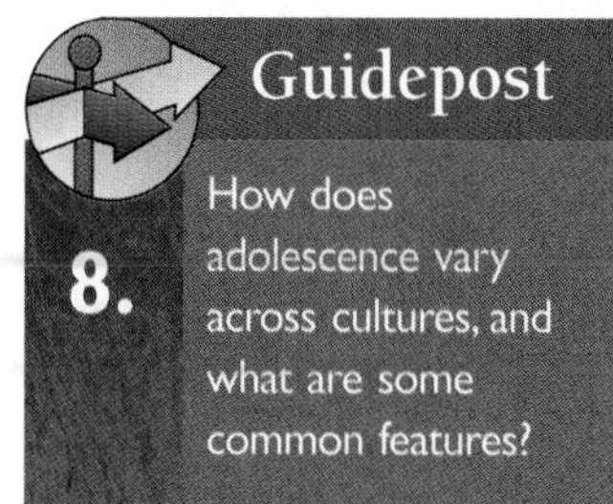

Guidepost
8.
How does adolescence vary across cultures, and what are some common features?

To answer questions like these, Daniel Offer and his colleagues (Offer et al., 1988) administered the Offer Self-Image Questionnaire to 5,938 adolescents in ten countries: Australia, Bangladesh, Hungary, Israel, Italy, Japan, Taiwan, Turkey, the United States, and West Germany. The young people answered questions about five aspects of themselves: (1) the *psychological self:* impulse control, fluctuations in mood and emotions, and feelings about their bodies, (2) the *social self:* peer relations, moral attitudes, and educational and vocational goals, (3) the *sexual self:* attitudes toward sexuality and sexual behavior, (4) the *familial self:*

These Israeli adolescents, growing up in a small nation wracked by internal tensions and surrounded by hostile neighbors, have had very different experiences from those of teenagers in the United States. Yet Daniel Offer and his colleagues found underlying similarities in self-image between adolescents in these and other countries the world over.

feelings about parents and the atmosphere in the home, and (5) the *coping self:* ability to deal with the world.

The researchers found cross-cultural commonalities in each of the five "selves," particularly familial, social, and coping. About 9 out of 10 adolescents in each country had positive feelings toward their parents, valued work and friendship, and tried to learn from failure. There was less consistency in the psychological and sexual areas; here socioeconomic circumstances and local customs were more crucial. In general, however, these "universal adolescents" described themselves as happy; felt able to cope with life, make decisions, and use self-control; cared about others and liked being with and learning from them; enjoyed a job well done; were confident about their sexuality; did not harbor grudges against their parents; saw their mothers and fathers as getting along well most of the time; and expected to be able to take responsibility for themselves as they grew older. All in all, the researchers judged at least 73 percent of the total sample to have "a healthy adolescent self-image" (p. 124).

In each country, teenagers showed characteristic strengths and weaknesses; in no country were adolescents better or worse adjusted in all respects. In Bangladesh, one of the world's poorest countries, even middle-class teenagers were low in impulse control; felt lonely, sad, and vulnerable; and had a poor body image. They also reported the most problems with peers and the highest rate of depression (48 percent). In Taiwan, where traditional sexual taboos still operate, large numbers of young people seemed to be afraid of sex or inhibited about it. On the other hand, Bengali and Taiwanese youths seemed superior in their enjoyment of solving difficult problems and in their willingness to find out how to deal with new situations. The lower a country's economic output and the higher the proportion of adolescents who had to compete for places in school and for jobs, the less positive were the teenagers' emotional tone and peer relationships.

Some consistent age and gender differences emerged across cultures. Older adolescents were less self-conscious than younger ones, more willing to learn from others, and better able to take criticism without resentment. Older adolescents also were more comfortable with their sexuality and more realistic in their view of family relationships.

Boys felt surer of themselves than girls, less afraid of competition, more in control of their emotions, prouder of their bodies, and more interested in sex. Girls were more empathic, caring, and socially responsible, and more committed to work and study. Similarly, in questionnaires completed by 154 high school boys and 119 high school girls in Turkey, the boys tended to evaluate themselves in terms of physical attributes and cognitive abilities, whereas girls stressed altruism and social and communication skills (Yildirim, 1997).

Offer and his colleagues attributed the "surprising unity of adolescent experience" across cultures largely to the media, which give young people a "collective consciousness" of what is going on in one another's lives all over the world (Offer et al., 1988, p. 114). Through the eye of television, adolescents see themselves as part of a world culture.

We need to be careful about drawing overly broad generalizations from these findings. The samples included only young people in school, mostly urban or suburban and middle class. Also, some of the questionnaire items may have taken on different meanings in translation. Nevertheless, this research draws a fascinating picture of the universal and not-so-universal aspects of adolescence.

CHECKPOINT

Can you . . .

✔ Identify cross-cultural commonalities and differences in adolescents' self-image, attitudes, and personalities?

The normal developmental changes in the early years of life are obvious and dramatic signs of growth. The infant lying in the crib becomes an active, exploring toddler. The young child enters and embraces the worlds of school and society.

The adolescent, with a new body and new awareness, prepares to step into adulthood.

Growth and development do not screech to a stop after adolescence. People change in many ways throughout early, middle, and late adulthood, as we will see in the remainder of this book.

Summary

The Search for Identity

Guidepost 1. How do adolescents form an identity?

- A central concern during adolescence is the search for identity, which has occupational, sexual, and values components. Erik Erikson described the psychosocial crisis of adolescence as the conflict of **identity versus identity confusion.** The "virtue" that should arise from this crisis is *fidelity*.
- James Marcia, in research based on Erikson's theory, described four **identity statuses** with differing combinations of **crisis** and **commitment: identity achievement** (crisis leading to commitment), **foreclosure** (commitment without crisis), **moratorium** (crisis with no commitment yet), and **identity diffusion** (no commitment, no crisis).
- Researchers differ on whether girls and boys take different paths to identity formation. Some research suggests that girls' self-esteem tends to fall at adolescence, but later research does not support that finding.
- Ethnicity is an important part of identity, especially among minority adolescents.
- According to David Elkind, healthy, stable identity development is achieved by a slow process of differentiation and integration. Today many young people instead develop a **patchwork self** that is highly vulnerable to stress and outside influence.

Sexuality

Guidepost 2. What determines sexual orientation?

- **Sexual orientation—heterosexual, homosexual,** or **bisexual**—appears to be influenced by an interaction of biological and environmental factors and may be at least partly genetic.

Guidepost 3. What sexual attitudes and practices are common among adolescents, and what leads some teenagers to engage in high-risk sexual behavior?

- Sexual attitudes and behaviors are more liberal than in the past. There is more acceptance of premarital sexual activity and homosexuality, and there has been a decline in the double standard.
- Teenage sexual activity involves risks of pregnancy and sexually transmitted disease. Adolescents at greatest risk are those who begin sexual activity early, have multiple partners, do not use contraceptives, and are ill-informed about sex.

Guidepost 4. How common are sexually transmitted diseases and teenage pregnancy, and what are the usual outcomes?

- **Sexually transmitted diseases (STDs)** have become far more prevalent since the 1960s; rates in the United States are highest in the industrialized world. One out of three cases occurs among adolescents. STDs are more likely to develop undetected in women than in men, and in adolescents as compared with adults.
- Teenage pregnancy and birthrates in the United States have declined during the 1990s. Most of these births are to unmarried mothers. Teenage pregnancy and childbearing often have negative health outcomes. Teenage mothers and their families tend to suffer financial hardship, and the children often suffer from ineffective parenting.

Relationships with Family, Peers, and Adult Society

Guidepost 5. How typical is "adolescent rebellion"?

- Although relationships between adolescents and their parents are not always smooth, full-scale **adolescent rebellion** does not seem usual, and parents and their teenage children often hold similar values.

Guidepost 6. How do adolescents relate to parents, siblings, and peers?

- Adolescents spend an increasing amount of time with peers, but relationships with parents continue to be close and influential.
- Conflict with parents tends to be most frequent during early adolescence and most intense during middle adolescence. Authoritative parenting is associated with the most positive outcomes.
- The effect of maternal employment on adolescents' development depends on such factors as mothers' warmth and role satisfaction, stress at home and at work, and whether the mother works full or part time. The effects of divorce and single parenting may be less severe than has been believed and may depend on individual circumstances. Economic stress affects relationships in both single-parent and two-parent families.
- Relationships with siblings tend to become more equal and more distant during adolescence.
- The peer group can have both positive and negative influences. Youngsters who are rejected by peers tend to have the greatest adjustment problems.

- Friendships, especially among girls, become more intimate and supportive in adolescence.

Guidepost 7. What are the root causes of antisocial behavior and juvenile delinquency, and what can be done to reduce these and other risks of adolescence?

- Most juvenile delinquents grow up to be law-abiding. Chronic delinquency is associated with multiple interacting risk factors, including ineffective parenting, school failure, peer influence, and low socioeconomic status. Programs that attack such risk factors at an early age have had success.

Is There a Universal Adolescent?

Guidepost 8. How does adolescence vary across cultures, and what are some common features?

- Cross-cultural research has found striking commonalities in adolescents' self-image, attitudes, and coping ability. There is less consistency in the psychological and sexual areas. Age and gender differences exist across cultures.

Key Terms

identity versus identity confusion (447)
identity statuses (449)
crisis (449)
commitment (449)
identity achievement (450)
foreclosure (450)
moratorium (451)
identity diffusion (451)
patchwork self (453)
sexual orientation (453)
heterosexual (453)
homosexual (453)
bisexual (453)
sexually transmitted diseases (STDs) (455)
adolescent rebellion (463)

Part Six

Young Adulthood

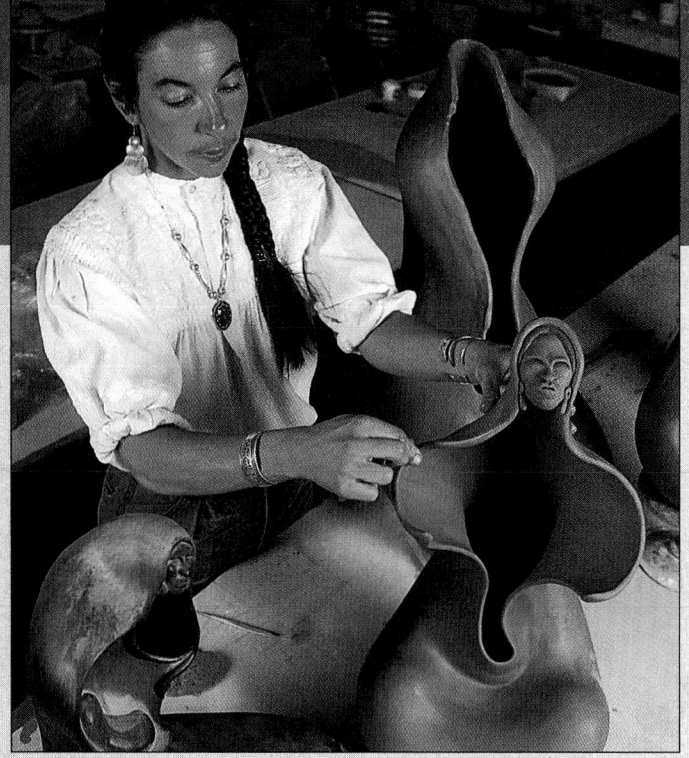

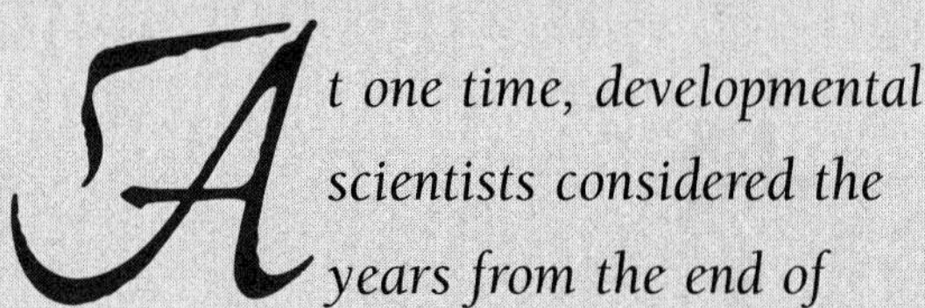

At one time, developmental scientists considered the years from the end of adolescence to the onset of old age a relatively uneventful plateau, but research tells us that this is not so. Growth and decline go on throughout life, in a balance that differs for each individual. Choices and events during young adulthood (which we define approximately as the span between ages 20 and 40) have much to do with how that balance is struck.

During these two decades, human beings build a foundation for much of their later development. This is when people typically leave their parents' homes, start jobs or careers, get married or establish other intimate relationships, have and raise children, and begin to contribute significantly to their communities. They make decisions that will affect the rest of their lives—their health, their happiness, and their success.

During young adulthood, as throughout life, all aspects of development—physical, cognitive, and psychosocial—intertwine. In Chapters 13 and 14 we see, for example, how income, education, and lifestyle—even marital status—influence health; how emotions may play a part in intelligence; and how pressures in the workplace can affect family life.

Linkups to Look For

- Knowledge about health affects adults' physical condition.
- Cognitive and moral development reflect life experience.
- Gender-typing may affect women's choice of careers and use of their talents.
- The gender revolution has diminished differences in men's and women's life course and health patterns.
- Infertility can lead to marital problems.
- People without friends or family are more likely to become ill and die.

Young Adulthood: *A Preview*

Chapter 13

Physical and Cognitive Development in Young Adulthood

Physical condition peaks, then declines slightly.

Lifestyle choices influence health.

Cognitive abilities and moral judgments assume more complexity.

Educational and career choices are made.

Chapter 14

Psychosocial Development in Young Adulthood

Personality traits and styles become relatively stable, but changes in personality may be influenced by life stages and events.

Decisions are made about intimate relationships and personal lifestyles.

Most people marry, and most become parents.

Chapter 13

Physical and Cognitive Development in Young Adulthood

OUTLINE

If . . . happiness is the absence of fever then I will never know happiness. For I am possessed by a fever for knowledge, experience, and creation.

Diary of Anaïs Nin (1931–1934),
written when she was between 28 and 31

Arthur Ashe

Focus: Arthur Ashe, Tennis Champion*

The tennis champion Arthur Ashe (1943–1993) was one of the most respected athletes of all time. "Slim, bookish and bespectacled" (Finn, 1993, p. B1), he was known for his quiet, dignified manner on and off the court; he did not dispute calls, indulge in temper tantrums, or disparage opponents.

The only African American to win the Wimbledon tournament and the United States and Australian Opens, Ashe grew up in Richmond, Virginia, where he began playing on segregated public courts. In 1955, the boy was barred from a city tennis tournament because of his race. As the only black star in a white-dominated game, Ashe was a target for bigotry; but his father, a park policeman, had taught him to maintain his composure and to channel his aggressive impulses into the game.

Ashe felt a responsibility to use his natural physical gifts and stellar reputation to combat racism and increase opportunity for disadvantaged youth. He conducted tennis clinics and helped establish tennis programs for inner-city youngsters. Twice refused a visa to play in the South African Open, he was finally allowed to compete in 1973 and again in 1974 and 1975. Despite South Africa's rigid apartheid system of racial separation, he insisted on unsegregated seating at his matches.

Ashe continued to work against apartheid, for the most part quietly, behind the scenes. Accused of being an "Uncle Tom" by angry militants who shouted him down while

*Sources of biographical information about Arthur Ashe were Ashe and Rampersad (1993), Finn (1993), and Witteman (1993).

he was giving a speech, he politely rebuked them: "What do you expect to achieve when you give in to passion and invective and surrender the high moral ground that alone can bring you to victory?" (Ashe & Rampersad, 1993, pp. 117, 118). Several years later, he was arrested in a protest outside the South African embassy in Washington, D.C. He felt tremendous pride when he saw Nelson Mandela, the symbol of opposition to apartheid, released from prison in 1990, riding in a ticker-tape parade in New York City. But Ashe would not live to see Mandela become president of South Africa.

In 1979, at age 36, at the height of a brilliant career, Ashe had suffered the first of several heart attacks and had undergone quadruple bypass surgery. Forced to retire from competitive play, he served for five years as captain of the U.S. Davis Cup team. In 1985, barely past young adulthood, he was inducted into the Tennis Hall of Fame.

One summer morning in 1988, Ashe woke up and could not move his right arm. He was given two options: immediate brain surgery, or wait and see. He opted for action. Preparatory blood tests showed that he was HIV-positive, probably from a blood transfusion during his heart surgery five years earlier. The surgery revealed a parasitic infection linked to AIDS, and the virus had progressed to AIDS itself. Like an athlete who is outscored but still in the game, Ashe refused to panic or to give up. Relying on the best medical knowledge, he chose to do all he could to fight his illness. He also chose to keep quiet about it—in part to protect his family's privacy and in part because, as he insisted, "I am not sick." He played golf, appeared on the lecture circuit, wrote columns for the *Washington Post,* was a television commentator for HBO and ABC Sports, and composed a three-volume history of African American athletes.

In 1992, warned that *USA Today* planned to reveal his secret, Ashe called a press conference and announced that he had AIDS. He became a tireless leader in the movement for AIDS research, establishing a foundation and launching a $5 million fund-raising campaign.

Ashe died of AIDS-related pneumonia in 1993, at age 49. Shortly before, he had summed up his situation in his usual style: "I am a fortunate, blessed man. Aside from AIDS and heart disease, I have no problems" (Ashe & Rampersad, 1993, p. 328).

Arthur Ashe's characteristic way of coping with trouble or bigotry was to meet it as he did an opponent on the tennis court: with grace, determination, moral conviction, and coolness under fire. Again and again, he turned adversity into opportunity. Arthur Ashe was a "can-do" person.

Even for people who lack Ashe's outstanding athletic skills, young adulthood typically is a "can-do" period. Most people at this age are on their own for the first time, setting up and running households and proving themselves in their chosen pursuits. Every day, they test and expand their physical and cognitive abilities. They encounter the "real world" and find their way through or around problems of everyday living. They make decisions that help determine their health, their careers, and the kinds of people they wish to be. For some, though, especially those who do not continue their education or acquire marketable skills, this can be a period of floundering.

In this chapter, we look at young adults' physical functioning, which is usually at its height; and we note factors that can affect health in young adulthood and in later life. We then discuss aspects of intelligence that come to the fore in adulthood, and how education can stimulate cognitive growth. We examine routes to moral maturity. Finally, we discuss one of the most important tasks during this period: entering the world of work.

After you have read and studied this chapter, you should be able to answer the following questions:

Guideposts *for* **Study**

1. In what physical condition is the typical young adult, and how do lifestyle, behavior, and other factors affect present and future health and well-being?
2. What are some sexual and reproductive issues at this time of life?
3. What is distinctive about adult thought and intelligence?
4. How do moral reasoning and faith develop?
5. How do higher education and work affect cognitive development?
6. How does age influence work performance and attitudes toward work?
7. How can continuing education help adults meet workplace demands?
8. How do ethnicity and gender affect educational and occupational attainment?

Physical Development

Aspects of Physical Development and Health

Young adults generally take their physical capabilities and good health for granted. Yet it is in young adulthood that the foundation for physical functioning throughout the rest of the life span is laid. What young adults eat, how physically active they are, whether they smoke, drink, or use drugs—all these factors contribute greatly to present and future health and well-being.

Your favorite spectator sport may be tennis, basketball, figure skating, or football. Whatever it is, most of the athletes you root for (like Arthur Ashe in his time) are young adults, people in prime physical condition. Young adults typically are at the peak of strength, energy, and endurance. They also are at a peak of sensory and motor functioning. By the middle twenties, most body functions are fully developed. Visual acuity is keenest from about age 20 to age 40; and taste, smell, and sensitivity to pain and temperature generally remain undiminished until at least 45. However, a gradual hearing loss, which typically begins during adolescence, becomes more apparent after 25, especially for higher-pitched sounds.

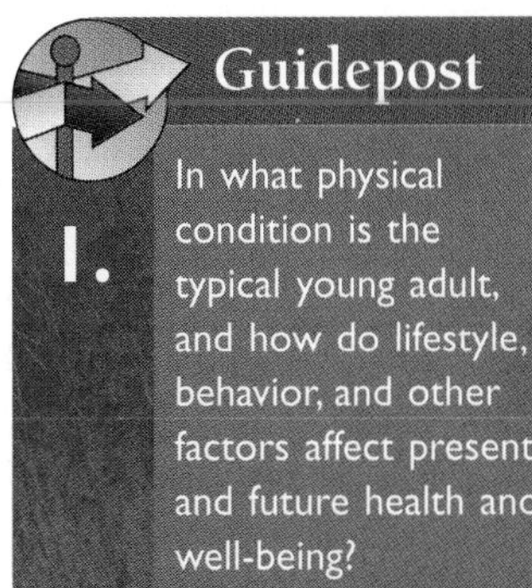

Guidepost

1. In what physical condition is the typical young adult, and how do lifestyle, behavior, and other factors affect present and future health and well-being?

Health Status

Most young adults in the United States are in good health. Many are never seriously ill or incapacitated, and the vast majority have no chronic conditions or impairments. When young adults do get sick, it is usually from a cold or other respiratory illness, which they easily shake off.

Since most young adults are healthy, it is not surprising that accidents are the leading cause of death for Americans ages 25 to 44. Next comes cancer, then heart disease, followed by suicide, AIDS, and homicide (Hoyert, Kochanek, & Murphy, 1999). Death rates for young adults have dropped, as have mortality rates for all other age groups except the oldest old, those above 85 (Hoyert et al., 1999). Cancer, heart disease, and strokes are down (Hoyert et al., 1999; USDHHS, 1999b; Wingo et al., 1999). On the other hand, too many adults—even young ones—are overweight and not active enough and engage in health-threatening behaviors.

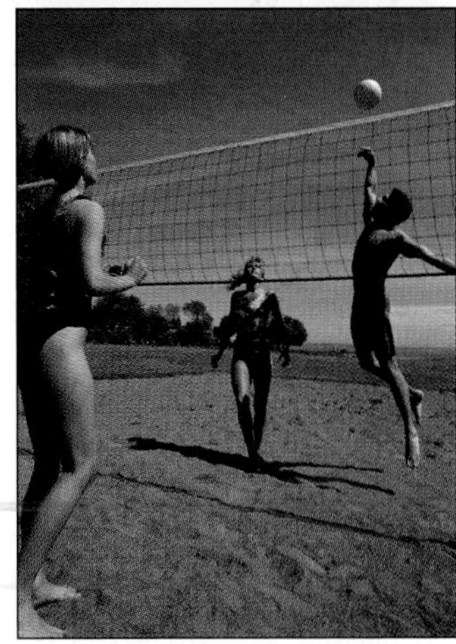

Playing volleyball takes strength, energy, endurance, and muscular coordination, and young adults like these typically are in prime physical condition.

Behavioral Influences on Health and Fitness

Good health is not just a matter of luck. People can seek health by pursuing some activities and refraining from others.

In a study of 7,000 adults ages 20 to 70, health was directly related to several common habits: eating regular meals, including breakfast, and not snacking; eating and exercising moderately; sleeping regularly 7 to 8 hours each night; not smoking; and drinking in moderation. Ten or more years later, people who did not follow these health habits were twice as likely to be disabled as people who followed most or all of them (Breslow & Breslow, 1993).

Medical care that focuses on preventing health problems can pay big dividends. Regular immunizations and screening tests, such as mammograms, can prevent diseases or catch them in early, treatable stages.

The link between behavior and health points up the interrelationship among physical, cognitive, and emotional aspects of development. What people know about health affects what they do, and what they do affects how they feel. Knowing about good health habits is not enough, however. Personality, emotions, and social surroundings often outweigh what people know they should do and lead them into unhealthful behavior.

Let's look at several lifestyle factors that are strongly and directly linked with health and fitness: nutrition and obesity, physical activity, and substance use and abuse. (In Chapter 15 we'll discuss the influence of stress.) In the next section of this chapter we'll consider indirect influences: socioeconomic status, ethnicity, gender, and relationships.

Nutrition

The saying "You are what you eat" sums up the importance of nutrition for physical and mental health. What people eat affects how they look, how they feel, and how likely they are to get sick.

People who eat plenty of fruits and vegetables, which increase the antioxidant capacity of the blood (Cao, Booth, Sadowski, & Prior, 1998), lessen their chance of heart disease (Rimm et al., 1996), stroke (Gillman et al., 1995), and cancer. Indeed, following a mostly plant-based diet—together with staying active, maintaining a healthy weight, and refraining from tobacco use—can cut cancer risk by as much as 70 percent. Just eating five servings of fruits and vegetables daily could lower the risk by 20 percent (World Cancer Research Fund and American Institute for Cancer Research, 1997).

A diet high in animal fat has been linked with colon cancer (Willett, Stampfer, Colditz, Rosner, & Speizer, 1990). However, some studies point only to the fat in red meat—or to other components of red meat, such as protein, iron, or substances that become cancer-producing when cooked—as likely culprits (Willett, 1994). Fat consumption does not seem to be related to breast cancer (Holmes et al., 1999) but does seem to be implicated in prostate cancer (Giovannucci et al., 1993; Hebert et al., 1998; Willett, 1994; Willett et al., 1992). A six-year study of nearly 48,000 men found that eating tomato-based sauces reduces the risk of prostate cancer by as much as 45 percent. Tomatoes are rich in lycopene, an antioxidant that may protect against the disease (Giovannucci et al., 1995).

Eating habits also play an important part in heart disease—which, as Arthur Ashe's story shows, is not necessarily limited to later life. Fat consumption increases cardiovascular risks, particularly cholesterol levels (Brunner et al. 1997; Matthews et al., 1997). Excess cholesterol deposited in blood vessels can narrow them so much as to cut off the blood supply to the heart, causing a heart attack. In a 25-year study of more than 12,000 men in five European countries, the United States, and Japan, cholesterol levels were directly related to the risk of death from coronary heart disease (Verschuren et al., 1995). Controlling cholesterol through diet and medication can significantly lower this risk (Lipid Research Clinics

Program, 1984a, 1984b; Scandinavian Simvastatin Survival Study Group, 1994; Shepherd et al., 1995).

Cholesterol—in combination with proteins and triglycerides (fatty acids)—circulates through the bloodstream, carried by low-density lipoprotein (LDL), commonly called "bad" cholesterol. More than 1 in 2 American men age 35 and older and women 45 and older have undesirably high LDL levels (Liebman, 1995b). High-density lipoprotein (HDL)—commonly called "good" cholesterol—flushes cholesterol out of the system. Since HDL is protective, a key to preventing heart disease is the ratio between total cholesterol and HDL. Current guidelines recommend total cholesterol of 200 milligrams per deciliter or less and HDL of 35 or more. A more healthful goal, according to some cardiologists, is an HDL of at least 45 for men and 50 for women, with a 4 to 1 ratio of total cholesterol to HDL ("What Is a Healthy Cholesterol Level?" 1998).

One way to lower LDL and total cholesterol is to replace saturated fats (as in meat, cheese, butter, and whole milk) and trans-fats (in margarine, cakes, pies, frostings, and processed foods made with partially hydrogenated oil) with polyunsaturated fats (soybean, corn, or safflower oil). Monounsaturated fats (olive oil and canola oil), which lower LDL but have no effect on HDL, are an even better choice (Blackburn, 1999). It is also helpful to eat more soluble fiber (in oats, beans, fruits, and vegetables); lose excess weight; exercise; drink alcohol only in moderation; and stop smoking ("Cholesterol: New Advice," 1993; Liebman, 1995b). An analysis of 17 randomized controlled studies found that behavioral interventions can achieve modest reductions in cardiovascular risk that are maintained for at least 9 to 18 months (Brunner et al., 1997). Drug treatment may be advisable for people whose LDL remains very high even after adjusting the diet (Adult Treatment Panel II, 1994).

Obesity

The World Health Organization (WHO) has called obesity a worldwide epidemic (WHO, 1998). Obesity more than doubled in the United Kingdom between 1980 and 1994, and similar increases have been reported in Brazil, Canada, and several countries in Europe, the Western Pacific, Southeast Asia, and Africa (Taubes, 1998). In the United States, nearly 18 percent of adults were obese in 1998, as compared with 12 percent in 1991, according to a randomized survey by the Centers for Disease Control and Prevention (CDC)* (Mokdad et al., 1999). Obesity is increasing in both sexes and all segments of the population, but especially among 18- to 29-year-olds and people with some college education (Mokdad et al., 1999).

What explains the obesity epidemic? Some experts point to availability of inexpensive "fast foods" in "supersized" portions; high-fat diets; labor-saving technologies; and sedentary recreational pursuits, such as television and computers (Brownell, 1998; Hill & Peters, 1998; Taubes, 1998).

In a society that values slenderness, being overweight can lead to emotional problems; it also carries risks of high blood pressure, heart disease, stroke, diabetes, gallstones, and some cancers (National Task Force on the Prevention and Treatment of Obesity, 1993; Wickelgren, 1998). In a 14-year longitudinal study of more than 1 million U.S. men and women, the risk of death from all causes, especially cardiovascular disease, increased with the degree of overweight (Calle, Thun, Petrelli, Rodriguez, & Heath, 1999). An estimated 300,000 deaths a year have been attributed to overweight, second only to the 400,000 deaths a year believed to be caused by cigarette smoking. A 16-year study of 115,195 female nurses found that even a moderate gain of 22 pounds after age 18 increases the risk of death in middle age (Manson et al., 1995).

*Obesity in adults is measured by *body mass index,* the number of kilograms of weight per square meter of height. According to the WHO's classifications, an adult with a BMI of 25 or more is overweight, and one with a BMI of 30 or more is obese. The CDC survey used the latter definition.

However, it is not clear whether these increased risks come from overweight itself or from inactivity and lack of cardiovascular fitness, which often accompany overweight. And, while weight loss can reduce blood pressure and blood sugar and increase HDL (good cholesterol) levels, it has not yet been shown that these effects are lasting, or that losing weight results in longer life (Wickelgren, 1998). Instead of focusing on weight loss, therefore, some scientists and physicians advocate treatments aimed at improving metabolic fitness (Campfield, Smith, & Burn, 1998). Since overweight becomes more prevalent with age, prevention of weight gain during young adulthood through healthy diet and regular physical activity may be the most practical approach (Wickelgren, 1998).

As we discussed in Chapters 3 and 9, a tendency toward obesity can be inherited, and this genetic tendency may interact with environmental and behavioral factors (Comuzzie & Allison, 1998). Researchers have identified a genetic mutation in mice that may disrupt the appetite control center in the brain by inhibiting production of the protein *leptin,* which tells the brain when the body has consumed enough (Campfield, Smith, Guisez, Devos, & Burns, 1995; Halaas et al., 1995, Pelleymounter et al., 1995; Zhang et al., 1994; refer back to Chapter 9). In humans, overeating may result from the brain's failure to respond to this protein's signals (Campfield et al., 1998; Travis, 1996). Eventually this research may lead to identification and treatment of people predisposed to obesity.

Anti-obesity drugs generally work by suppressing appetite. Orlistat, a promising new drug now under review, works by inhibiting fat absorption (Campfield et al., 1998). In a large-scale, randomized 2-year trial, orlistat, together with a controlled diet, was modestly effective in taking off weight and keeping it off (Davidson et al., 1999). However, there is no evidence that drugs can meaningfully reduce health risks without changes in diet and lifestyle; and the long-term effects of these drugs are unknown (Williamson, 1999).

The healthiest course for overweight people—which is, of course, usually difficult—is to lose weight slowly and then maintain the loss. The most effective ways to lose weight are to eat less, decrease the amount of fat in the diet, use behavior modification techniques to change eating patterns, and exercise more (National Task Force, 1993).

Regular physical activity brings many benefits. It helps people feel and look good, builds muscles, strengthens heart and lungs, keeps weight down, and protects against various disorders.

Physical Activity

Adults who are physically active reap many benefits. Aside from helping to maintain desirable body weight, physical activity builds muscles; strengthens heart and lungs; lowers blood pressure; protects against heart disease, stroke, diabetes, cancer, and osteoporosis (a thinning of the bones that is most prevalent in middle-aged and older women, causing fractures); relieves anxiety and depression; and lengthens life (American Heart Association [AHA], 1995; I.-M. Lee & Paffenbarger, 1992; P. R. Lee, Franks, Thomas, & Paffenbarger, 1981; McCann & Holmes, 1984; Notelovitz & Ware, 1983; Pratt, 1999).

Even moderate exercise has health benefits (I.-M. Lee, Hsieh, & Paffenbarger, 1995; NIH Consensus Development Panel on Physical Activity and Cardiovascular Health, 1996). Incorporating more physical activity into daily life—for example, by walking instead of driving short distances, and climbing stairs instead of taking elevators—can be as effective as structured exercise (Andersen et al., 1999; Dunn et al., 1999; Pratt, 1999).

Keeping physically active may prevent early death. In a longitudinal study of 15,902 healthy Finnish men and women ages 25 to 64, those who got even occasional exercise were less likely to die within the next 19 years, regardless of genetic or familial factors (Kujala, Kaprio, Sarna, & Koskenvuo, 1998). A 5-year follow-up of nearly 10,000 men found a 44 percent reduction in mortality risk among those who had been sedentary and became moderately fit (Blair et al., 1995).

If adults—and children as well—engaged in 30 minutes of moderate physical activity daily, an estimated 250,000 deaths a year could be avoided, most of them from cardiovascular disease (NIH Consensus Development Panel, 1996; Pate, Pratt, Blair, Haskell, & Macera, 1995). The total time spent exercising is more important than the type, intensity, or continuity of activity. Even brief periods of exercise throughout the day can add up to lifesaving protection.

Smoking

Smoking is the leading preventable cause of death in the United States (AHA, 1995). It kills about 400,000 people yearly and disables millions. When victims of passive smoking—inhaling other people's smoke—are added, the death toll may reach more than 450,000 (Bartecchi, MacKenzie, & Schrier, 1995).

The link between smoking and lung cancer is well established. Smoking and exposure to environmental smoke are estimated to be responsible for about 90 percent of lung cancer in the United States (Wingo et al., 1999). Lung cancer is now the leading cause of cancer deaths in women as well as in men (Hoyert et al., 1999). Smoking is also linked to cancer of the larynx, mouth, esophagus, bladder, kidney, pancreas, and cervix; to gastrointestinal problems, such as ulcers; to respiratory illnesses, such as bronchitis and emphysema; to osteoporosis; and to heart disease (He, Vupputuri, Prerost, Hughes, & Whelton, 1999; Hopper & Seeman, 1994; National Institute on Aging [NIA], 1993; Slemenda, 1994; USDHHS, 1987). Smoking strains the heart. By constricting the blood vessels, it makes the heart beat faster, raises blood pressure, and reduces the oxygen supply (AHA, 1995). Smokers are five times as likely as nonsmokers to have heart attacks in their thirties or forties (Parish et al., 1995).

As the risks have become known, smoking in the United States has declined more than 37 percent since 1965 (AHA, 1995). However, the trend among 18- to 25-year-olds has begun to reverse (Substance Abuse and Mental Health Services Administration [SAMHSA], 1998b) as smoking among high school and college students has increased (Wechsler, Rigotti, Gledhill-Hoyt, & Lee, 1998; Wingo et al., 1999; refer back to Chapter 11). Currently about 1 in 4 Americans age 18 and over is a smoker (NCHS, 1998a), as is about 1 in 3 people over age 15 worldwide (Pianezza, Sellers, & Tyndale, 1998).

In view of the known risks of smoking, why do so many people do it? One reason is that smoking is addictive. A tendency to addiction may be genetic, and recently identified genes may affect the ability to quit (Lerman et al., 1999; Pianezza et al., 1998; Sabol et al., 1999). Although African Americans smoke less than white Americans, they metabolize more nicotine in the blood, are more subject to lung cancer, and have more trouble breaking the habit. Possible reasons may be genetic, biological, or behavioral (Caraballo et al., 1998; Pérez-Stable, Herrera, Jacob III, & Benowitz, 1998; Sellers, 1998).

Giving up smoking reduces the risks of heart disease and stroke (Kawachi et al., 1993; NIA, 1993; Wannamethee, Shaper, Whincup, & Walker, 1995). Men and women who stop smoking have virtually no greater risk of heart attack, or of dying from heart disease within 3 to 20 years, than those who never have smoked (Rosenberg, Palmer, & Shapiro, 1990; Stamler, Dyer, Shekelle, Neaton, & Stamler, 1993; see Figure 13-1).

Nicotine chewing gum, nicotine patches, and nicotine nasal sprays and inhalers, especially when combined with counseling, can help addicted persons taper off gradually and safely (Cromwell, Bartosch, Fiore, Hasselblad, & Baker, 1997; Hughes, Goldstein, Hurt, & Shiffman, 1999; NIA, 1993). Bupropion, an antidepressant medication, can increase the effectiveness of treatment with nicotine patches (Ferry & Burchette, 1994; Heishman et al., 1998). However, nicotine replacement should not be continued indefinitely, as it may have long-term toxic effects (Macklin, Maus, Pereira, Albuquerque, & Conti-Fine, 1998; Maus et al., 1998). In one study, coupling vigorous exercise with a cognitive-behavioral smoking cessation program that did not include nicotine replacement doubled the program's success rate (Marcus et al., 1999).

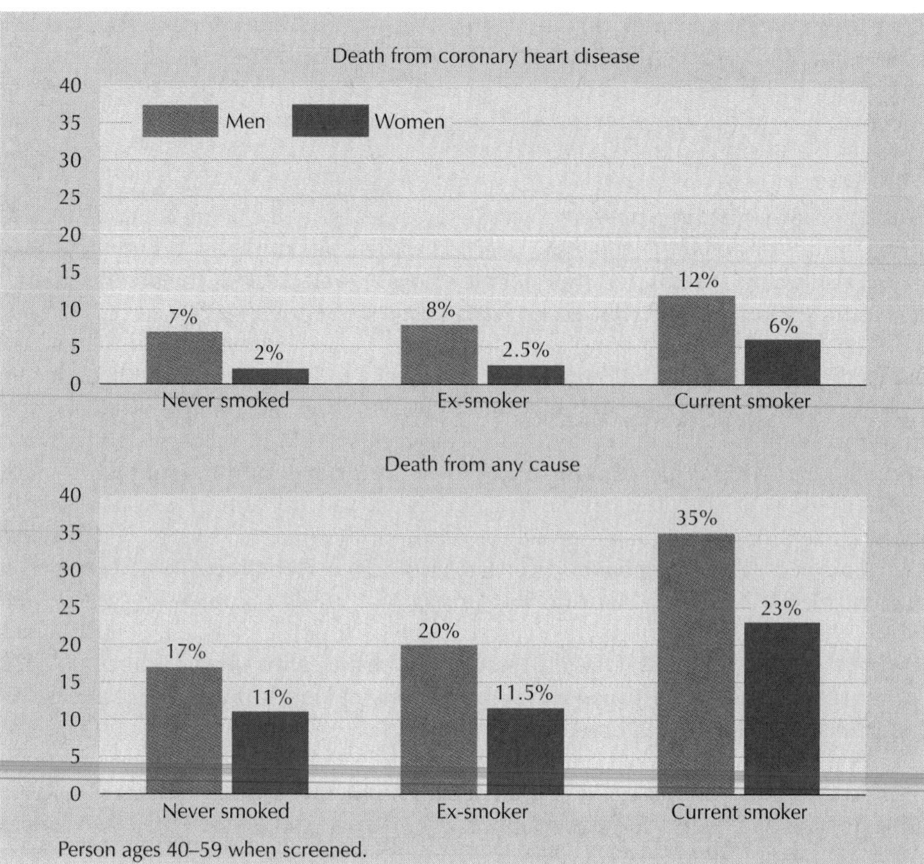

Figure 13-1
Death rates in 20 years for smokers, ex-smokers, and those who never smoked. Among 40,000 adults ages 18 to 74 screened during the years 1968–1973 to identify high risk factors for coronary heart disease, those who had quit smoking were only slightly more likely to die within the next 20 years than those who had never smoked. Smokers had much higher death rates from heart disease and all other causes than the other two groups.
(Source: Adapted from Stamler, Stamler, & Garside, undated.)

Substance Use and Abuse

The United States is a drinking society. Advertising equates liquor, beer, and wine with the good life and with being "grown up." About 60 percent of 21- to 39-year-olds report using alcohol, and the youngest adults tend to be the heaviest drinkers. Nearly half (46 percent) of 18- to 25-year-olds, predominantly young men, are binge drinkers, downing five or more drinks at a session (SAMHSA, 1998b).

Alcohol use is risky and is associated with other risks characteristic of young adulthood, such as traffic accidents, crime, and HIV infection (Leigh, 1999). Driving under the influence of alcohol or other drugs can be deadly. A nationally representative survey estimates that nearly 1 in 4 drivers—most commonly a young adult—gets behind the wheel within 2 hours after drinking, and 1 in 20 drives after using other drugs, resulting in more than 16,000 deaths and 1 million injuries each year (SAMHSA, 1998a). Alcohol is also implicated in deaths from drowning, suicide, fire, and falls; and it is often a factor in family violence (National Institute on Alcohol Abuse and Alcoholism [NIAAA], 1981). It is estimated that a majority of homicides involve alcohol (APA, 1994).

Although moderate alcohol consumption seems to reduce the risk of fatal heart disease, the definition of *moderate* has become more restricted. Men who take more than one drink a day have much higher death rates from cancer, which outweigh any benefits to the heart (Camargo, Gaziano, Hennekens, Manson, & Stampfer, 1994). Women can safely drink only about half as much as men (Fuchs et al., 1995; Urbano-Marquez et al., 1995).

College is a prime time and place for drinking and drugs. The overwhelming majority of college students use alcohol, and as many as 40 percent binge drink at least once in 2 weeks (Johnston, O'Malley, & Bachman, 1999). Students who binge drink tend to miss classes, get in trouble with authorities, cause property damage, drive after drinking, and engage in unplanned, unsafe sexual activity or sexual aggression (NIAAA, 1995). Collegiate marijuana use rose by 21 percent between 1993 and 1997 (Wechsler et al., 1998) and now involves 1 out of 4 students. Marijuana users, like binge drinkers, tend to get lower grades, to spend less time studying and more time socializing, and to participate in other high-risk behaviors (Bell, Wechsler, & Johnston, 1997; Wechsler, Dowdall, Davenport, & Castillo, 1995).

As young adults mature, settle down, and take more responsibility for their future, they tend to cut down on alcohol and drug use, especially if their friends also are doing so (Labouvie, 1996). Although about half of all young adults have tried illicit drugs, most commonly marijuana, only 7.4 percent of 26- to 34-year-olds are current users (SAMHSA, 1998b).

Substance abuse can carry short-term and long-term health risks. Chronic, heavy cocaine use can impair cognitive functioning (Bolla, Cadet, & London, 1998; Bolla, Rothman, & Cadet, 1999). Many "baby boomers" who began using drugs in their teens or early twenties, and continued to do so, now have severe drug-related medical problems (SAMHSA, 1998b). Over the years, heavy drinking may lead to cirrhosis of the liver, other gastrointestinal disorders (including ulcers), pancreatic disease, certain cancers, heart failure, stroke, damage to the nervous system, psychoses, and other medical problems (AHA, 1995; Fuchs et al., 1995; NIAAA, 1981). The risks of cancer of the mouth, throat, and esophagus are greater for excessive drinkers who smoke (NIAAA, 1998a). Regular, long-term drinking increases the risk of breast cancer (Smith-Warner et al., 1998).

alcoholism
Chronic disease involving dependence on use of alcohol, causing interference with normal functioning and fulfillment of obligations.

Alcoholism has been called the nation's major mental health problem (Horton & Fogelman, 1991). It is a chronic disease involving pathological dependence on alcohol, causing interference with normal functioning and fulfillment of obligations. It may include periods of remission and relapse. Alcoholism runs in families; close relatives of people who are addicted to alcohol are three to four times as likely to become dependent on it as people whose relatives are not addicted (APA, 1994; McGue, 1993). Although men are more likely than women to be problem drinkers, this gap appears to be closing (Prescott, Neale, Corey, & Kendler, 1997).

Alcoholism, like other addictions, seems to result from long-lasting changes in patterns of neural signal transmission in the brain. Exposure to a substance that creates a euphoric mental state brings about neurological adaptations that produce feelings of discomfort and craving when it is no longer present. Six to 48 hours after the last drink, alcoholics experience strong physical withdrawal symptoms (anxiety, agitation, tremors, elevated blood pressure, and sometimes seizures). Alcoholics, like drug addicts, develop a tolerance for the substance and need more and more to get the desired high. As researchers come to understand precisely how these neurological processes work, they can devise treatments to alter them (NIAAA, 1996b).

Depending on the severity of the condition, current treatment for alcoholism may include detoxification (removing all alcohol from the body), hospitalization, medication, individual and group psychotherapy, involvement of the family, and referral to a support organization, such as Alcoholics Anonymous. While not a cure, treatment can give alcoholics new tools for coping with their addiction and leading a productive life. Prevention of relapse is a key goal; no more than half of patients recovering from alcoholism and other substance use disorders remain abstinent for as long as a year (Friedmann, Saitz, & Samet, 1998).

CHECKPOINT

Can you . . .

- ✔ Summarize the typical health status of young adults in the United States?
- ✔ List the leading causes of death in young adulthood?
- ✔ Tell how diet can affect the likelihood of cancer and heart disease?
- ✔ Give reasons for the "obesity epidemic"?
- ✔ Cite benefits of exercise?
- ✔ Discuss the risks involved in smoking and substance use and abuse?

Consider this . . .

- What specific things could you do to have a healthier lifestyle?

Indirect Influences on Health and Fitness

Apart from the things people do, or refrain from doing, which affect their health directly, there are indirect influences on health. Among the most important are income, education, and ethnicity. Gender also makes a difference, as do relationships.

Income is a major influence on health. This homeless family may not be getting the nutrition and medical care needed for good health.

Socioeconomic Status and Ethnicity

The connection between socioeconomic status and health has been widely documented. Although death rates have declined overall in the United States since 1960, the disparity between the high death rates of poor and poorly educated people and the lower death rates of more affluent, better-educated people has increased (Pappas, Queen, Hadden, & Fisher, 1993). Higher-income and white people rate their health better and live longer than lower-income and black people, a disproportionate number of whom are poor. (In 1996, 28.4 percent of African Americans were below the poverty line, as compared with 11.2 percent of white people.) Education is important, too. The less schooling people have had, the greater the chance that they will develop and die from communicable diseases, injuries, or chronic ailments (such as heart disease), or that they will become victims of homicide or suicide (NCHS, 1998a).

This does not mean, of course, that income and education *cause* good health; instead, they are related to lifestyle factors that are likely to be causative. Poverty often results in poor nutrition, substandard housing, and (in the United States) limited access to health care (Otten, Teutsch, Williamson, & Marks, 1990; NCHS, 1998a). Better-educated and more affluent people have healthier diets and better preventive health care and medical treatment. They exercise more, are less likely to be overweight, and smoke less. They are more likely to use alcohol, but to use it in moderation (NCHS, 1998a; SAMHSA, 1998b).

The associations between income, education, living conditions, and health help explain the deplorable state of health in some minority populations. Young black adults are 20 times more likely to have high blood pressure than young white adults (Agoda, 1995). And African Americans are more than twice as likely as white people to die in young adulthood, in part because young black men are about 7 times as likely to be victims of homicide (Hoyert et al., 1999). Ethnic differences in health are not wholly attributable to socioeconomic factors; for example, we have already mentioned the greater physiological impact of smoking on black people. (We will further discuss the relationship between ethnicity and health in Chapter 15.)

Gender

Which sex is healthier: women or men? One reason this question is hard to answer is that until recently women have been excluded from many important studies of health problems that affect both sexes (Healy, 1991; Rodin & Ickovics, 1990). As a result, much of what we know applies only to men. Of course, certain health problems—those affecting the female reproductive system—are limited to women; others, such as prostate and testicular cancer, affect only men. Some diseases, such as lung cancer, are more common among men, though this difference has decreased (NCHS, 1998a; Wingo et al., 1999). Others, such as heart disease, tend to strike men (like Arthur Ashe) earlier in life than women. Still others, such as eating disorders (refer back to Chapter 11), rheumatoid arthritis, and osteoporosis (see Chapter 17), are more common among women.

We do know that women have a higher life expectancy than men and lower death rates throughout life (Hoyert et al., 1999; see Figure 13-2 and Chapter 17). Women's greater longevity has been attributed to genetic protection given by the

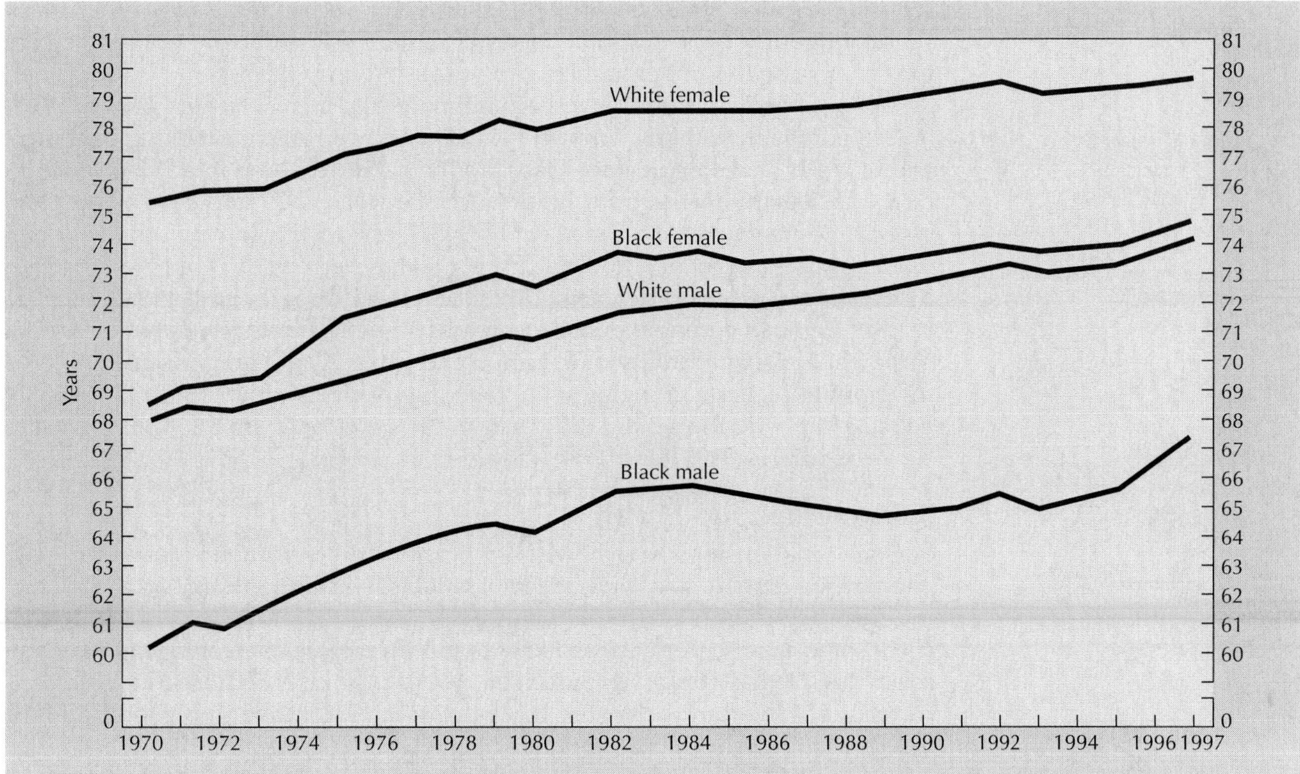

Figure 13-2

Life expectancy by sex, 1970–1997.

(Source: Hoyert et al., 1999, Fig. 3, p. 7.)

second X chromosome (which men do not have) and, before menopause, to beneficial effects of the female hormone estrogen, particularly on cardiovascular health (Rodin & Ickovics, 1990; USDHHS, 1992). However, psychosocial and cultural factors, such as men's greater propensity for risk taking and their preference for meat and potatoes rather than fruits and vegetables, also may play a part (Liebman, 1995a; Schardt, 1995).

Despite their longer life, women report being ill more often than men, are more likely to seek treatment for minor illnesses, and report more unexplained symptoms. Men, by contrast, have longer hospital stays, and their health problems are more likely to be chronic and life-threatening (Kroenke & Spitzer, 1998; NCHS, 1998a; Rodin & Ickovics, 1990). This is probably because men wait longer before seeking medical help.

Women's greater tendency to seek medical care does not necessarily mean that women are in worse health than men, nor that they are imagining ailments or are preoccupied with illness (Kroenke & Spitzer, 1998). They may simply be more health-conscious. Menstruation and childbearing make women aware of the body and its functioning, and cultural standards encourage medical management of those processes. Many women see doctors on a regular basis, not only during pregnancy, but for routine gynecological tests (Schardt, 1995). Women generally know more than men about health, think and do more about preventing illness, are more aware of symptoms and susceptibility, and are more likely to talk about their medical worries. Men may feel that illness is not "masculine" and thus may be less likely to admit that they do not feel well. It may be that the better care women take of themselves helps them live longer than men.

For example, testicular cancer, the most common cancer among young men, is a highly curable disease if detected early, with cure rates of well over 90 percent (Bosl & Motzer, 1997; Young, 1998). It can be detected by monthly self-examinations, followed up by a visit to a physician, who may order ultrasound and other tests. Yet some men put off going to a doctor because they are too embarrassed to undergo these procedures (Young, 1998).

As women's lifestyles have become more like men's, so—in some ways—have their health patterns. Women have been slower to stop smoking than men, and in recent years many have taken up the habit, resulting in a 182 percent increase in female deaths from lung cancer between 1970 and 1993, more than seven times the increase for men (USDHHS, 1996a). The gap between men's and women's use of alcohol and illicit drugs also has narrowed. Women become addicted more easily and develop substance-related diseases earlier than men do (CASA, 1996). In addition, public awareness of men's health issues has increased. Meanwhile, the availability of the impotence drug Viagra and of screening tests for prostate cancer is bringing more men into doctor's offices. Such trends may help explain why the gender difference in life expectancy shrank from 7 years to 5.8 years between 1991 and 1997 (Hoyert et al., 1999).

Relationships and Health

Personal relationships may be vital to health. Adults without friends or loved ones are susceptible to a wide range of troubles, including traffic accidents, eating disorders, and suicide (Baumeister & Leary, 1995). People isolated from friends and family are twice as likely to fall ill and die as people who maintain social ties (House, Landis, & Umberson, 1988). Of course, because this research is correlational, we cannot be sure that relationships contribute to good health. It may be that healthy people are more likely to maintain relationships.

What is it about relationships that might promote good health—or about their absence that might undermine it? Social ties may foster a sense of meaning or coherence in life. Emotional support may help minimize stress. People who are in touch with others may be more likely to eat and sleep sensibly, get enough exercise, avoid substance abuse, and get necessary medical care (House et al., 1988).

Married people, especially men, tend to be healthier physically and, in some research, psychologically than those who are never-married, widowed, separated, or divorced (Horwitz, White, & Howell-White, 1996; Ross, Mirowsky, & Goldsteen, 1990). Married people have fewer disabilities or chronic conditions that limit their activities; and when they go to the hospital, their stays are generally short. Married people live longer, too, according to a study in 16 industrial countries (Hu & Goldman, 1990). Married people, especially men, seem to lead healthier, safer lives. They take fewer risks and encourage their spouses to pay more attention to their health (Rogers, 1995).

Married people also tend to be better off financially, a factor associated with physical and mental health (Ross et al., 1990). In a study of more than 36,000 men and women ages 25 to 64, married people were less likely to die than unmarrieds. However, people with high incomes, married or single, were more likely to survive than were married people with low incomes; the highest mortality was among low-income singles (Rogers, 1995).

Marriage is related differently to mental and physical health in husbands than in wives, according to two studies with mostly white, middle-class samples. In a seven-year longitudinal survey of 1,201 young adults, men who got married and stayed married were less likely to become depressed, and the women who did so were less likely to develop alcohol problems, than those who remained single (Horwitz et al., 1996). In an observational study, 90 newlywed couples, ages 20 to 37, were videotaped trying to resolve points of disagreement in their marriage. Blood samples taken beforehand and afterward showed larger endocrine and blood pressure changes in women than in men. Apparently marital conflict and the stresses of daily home life have greater physiological and emotional effects on wives than on husbands (Kiecolt-Glaser et al., 1996).

CHECKPOINT

Can you . . .

- ✔ Point out some differences in health and mortality that reflect income, education, ethnicity, and gender?
- ✔ Discuss how relationships, particularly marriage, may affect physical and mental health?

Sexual and Reproductive Issues

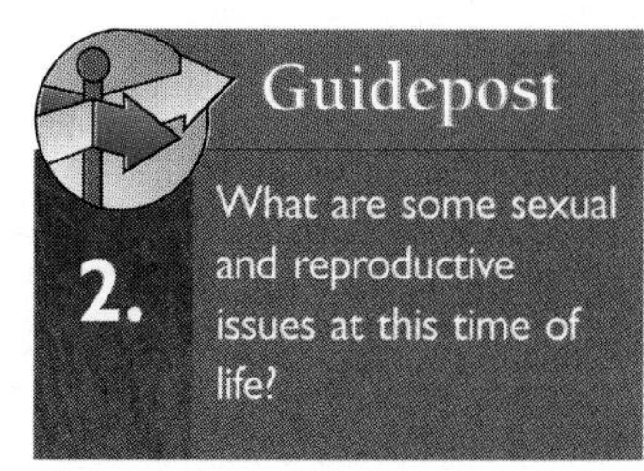

Sexual and reproductive activity can bring pleasure and sometimes parenthood. These natural and important functions also may involve physical concerns. Four such concerns are sexual dysfunction, sexually transmitted disease, menstrual problems, and infertility.

Sexual Dysfunction

sexual dysfunction
Persistent disturbance in sexual desire or sexual response.

For a surprising proportion of adults, sex is not easy or enjoyable. **Sexual dysfunction** is a persistent disturbance in sexual desire or sexual response. It can include a variety of problems, such as lack of interest in or pleasure from sex, painful intercourse, difficulty in arousal, premature orgasm or ejaculation, inability to reach climax, and anxiety about sexual performance. Sexual dysfunction is most common in young women and in middle-aged and older men, among whom it often takes the form of *erectile dysfunction,* or impotence (Laumann, Paik, & Rosen, 1999; see Chapter 15).

In in-depth interviews with a nationally representative sample of 1,749 women and 1,410 men ages 18 to 59, 43 percent of the women and 31 percent of the men reported some form of sexual dysfunction (Laumann et al., 1999). The most common problem for young women was lack of interest in sex; 27 percent of 18- to 29-year-old women reported finding sex nonpleasurable, 21 percent reported physical pain, and 16 percent reported anxiety about sex. Young men were about as likely as older men to experience premature ejaculation, anxiety about performance, and nonpleasurable sex.

Although sexual dysfunction can have physical causes, some risk factors are connected with general health, lifestyle, and emotional well-being. Married and college-educated men and women have fewer sexual problems than unmarried or less educated ones. Stress caused by a sudden drop in income tends to increase sexual dysfunction. Men and women who were victims of childhood sexual abuse tend to have poor sexual adjustment (Laumann et al., 1999).

These findings suggest that sexual dysfunction is a widespread, and largely unsuspected, public health problem. Unfortunately, according to this study, only 10 percent of men and 20 percent of women who have the problem seek medical treatment (Laumann et al., 1999).

Sexually Transmitted Diseases (STDs)

The risks of unprotected sexual activity with multiple partners are no different in young adulthood than in adolescence (refer back to Chapter 12). Sexually transmitted diseases (STDs)—some of which also can be acquired through other means, such as, in Arthur Ashe's case, blood transfusions—are a major public health problem among young adults.

Worldwide, some 33.4 million people are estimated to have HIV, the virus that causes AIDS. People of working age are at highest risk (Satcher, 1999). In many South African countries, 20 to 26 percent of 15- to 49-year-olds are infected. Life expectancy there is predicted to fall from 64 to 47 years by 2015, reversing decades of progress through disease control (Satcher, 1999).

In the United States, where about 665,000 people are infected (Satcher, 1999), the AIDS epidemic has begun to come under control. In 1995 AIDS became the leading cause of death for 25- to 44-year-olds. By 1997 it had dropped to fifth, though it remained the leading cause of death for African American young adults. In that year, for the population as a whole, deaths from HIV infection fell 47.7 percent, toppling it from the eighth to the fourteenth leading cause of death (Hoyert et al., 1999).

Globally, most HIV-infected adults are heterosexual (Altman, 1992). In the United States, HIV has been most prevalent among drug abusers who share contaminated hypodermic needles, homosexual and bisexual men, people who (like

Arthur Ashe) have received transfusions of infected blood or blood products, people who have had sexual contact with someone in one of these high-risk groups, and infants who have been infected in the womb or during birth (Edlin et al., 1994). The incidence of HIV among homosexual men and injection drug users in their early twenties has slowed, but heterosexual transmission has increased, particularly among minorities. The result is a growing incidence of infection in young minority women alongside a dramatic reduction in incidence in young white men (Rosenberg & Biggar, 1998).

Voluntary testing is a critical element of STD control. Unfortunately, it is not easy to motivate people to have it done. In one study, college psychology students viewed a film on unsafe sexual behavior and vulnerability to HIV infection. The students filled out questionnaires before and after seeing the film, and again four weeks later. Although the film heightened sexually active students' perceptions of personal risk, only 17 percent subsequently got tested, asked their partners to be tested, or initiated inquiries about testing (Rothman, Kelly, Weinstein, & O'Leary, 1999).

Educating people to use condoms, the most effective means of preventing STDs, is not always easy either. Among 822 inner-city women (average age, about 26), only 7 percent reported consistent condom use by their main partners, and 12 percent by other partners, even though most of the women were knowledgeable and concerned about AIDS. Women who reported consistent condom use, and those who were seriously considering it, tended to have a stronger sense of self-efficacy, or confidence in their ability to achieve their goals, than those who were not yet contemplating it. Self-efficacy may help women to be more assertive with partners who resist using condoms (Stark et al., 1998).

CHECKPOINT

Can you . . .

- ✔ Identify several types and causes of sexual dysfunction?
- ✔ Discuss ways to control the spread of STDs?

Counseling can help. In a controlled, randomized study of 617 African American and Hispanic women with gonorrhea and chlamydia (average age, about 21), female facilitators from the participants' own ethnic group conducted three sessions of culturally sensitive small-group counseling (Shain et al., 1999). Participants had significantly lower reinfection rates during the following year than a control group who had undergone standard counseling (16.8 versus 26.9 percent).

Problems Related to Menstruation

Although women enjoy valuable protection due to hormonal activity during the reproductive years, the menstrual cycle can produce health problems. **Premenstrual syndrome (PMS)** is a disorder involving physical discomfort and emotional tension during the one to two weeks before a menstrual period. Symptoms may include fatigue, food cravings, headaches, swelling and tenderness of the breasts, swollen hands or feet, abdominal bloating, nausea, constipation, weight gain, anxiety, depression, irritability, mood swings, tearfulness, and difficulty concentrating or remembering ("PMS: It's Real," 1994; Reid & Yen, 1981). These symptoms are not distinctive in themselves; it is their timing that identifies PMS.

premenstrual syndrome (PMS)
Disorder producing symptoms of physical discomfort and emotional tension during the one to two weeks before a menstrual period.

Unlike *dysmenorrhea*, or menstrual cramps, which tend to afflict adolescents and younger women, PMS typically affects women in their thirties or older. Up to 70 percent of menstruating women may have some symptoms, but in fewer than 10 percent do they create significant health problems (Freeman, Rickels, Sondheimer, & Polansky, 1995; "PMS: It's Real," 1994).

Although some people believe PMS has emotional origins, a double-blind study established that it is an abnormal response to normal monthly surges of the female hormones estrogen and progesterone, possibly due to differences in the brain receptors for those hormones. By artificially administering the hormones, researchers induced PMS symptoms in women who had the syndrome but not in women who did not have it or in women who received a placebo, which has no active ingredients (Schmidt, Nieman, Danaceau, Adams, & Rubinow, 1998).

How to treat PMS is controversial. One widely used treatment—administration of progesterone in the form of a pill or suppository—proved in a large, randomized, controlled study to be no more beneficial than a placebo (Freeman, Rickels, Sondheimer, & Polansky, 1990). In a follow-up study, anti-anxiety pills proved more effective (Freeman et al., 1995). For milder symptoms, some doctors recommend exercise and dietary changes, such as avoiding fat, sodium, caffeine, and alcohol ("PMS: It's Real," 1994).

Infertility

An estimated 8 to 17 percent of U.S. couples experience **infertility:** inability to conceive a baby after 12 to 18 months of trying (ISLAT Working Group, 1998; Mosher & Pratt, 1991).

infertility
Inability to conceive after 12 to 18 months of trying.

The most common cause of infertility in men is production of too few sperm. Although only one sperm is needed to fertilize an ovum, a sperm count lower than 60 to 200 million per ejaculation makes conception unlikely. Sometimes an ejaculatory duct is blocked, preventing the exit of sperm; or sperm may be unable to "swim" well enough to reach the cervix. Some cases of male infertility seem to have a genetic basis (King, 1996; Phillips, 1998; Reijo, Alagappan, Patrizio, & Page, 1996).

If the problem is with the woman, she may not be producing ova; the ova may be abnormal; mucus in the cervix may prevent sperm from penetrating it; or a disease of the uterine lining may prevent implantation of the fertilized ovum. A major cause of declining fertility in women after age 30 is deterioration in the quality of their ova (van Noord-Zaadstra et al., 1991). However, the most common female cause is blockage of the fallopian tubes, preventing ova from reaching the uterus. In about half of these cases, the tubes are blocked by scar tissue from sexually transmitted diseases (King, 1996).

Infertility burdens a marriage emotionally. Women, especially, often have trouble accepting the fact that they cannot do what comes so naturally and easily to others. Partners may become frustrated and angry with themselves and each other and may feel empty, worthless, and depressed (Abbey, Andrews, & Halman, 1992; H. W. Jones & Toner, 1993). Their sexual relationship may suffer as sex becomes a matter of "making babies, not love." Such couples may benefit from professional counseling or support from other infertile couples.

About 50 percent of infertile couples eventually conceive, with or without artificial help (see Box 13-1), and some adopt children (refer back to Chapter 10). An increasing proportion get medical treatment (H. W. Jones & Toner, 1993). Hormone treatment may raise a man's sperm count or increase a woman's ovulation. Sometimes drug therapy or surgery can correct the problem. However, fertility drugs increase the likelihood of multiple, and often premature, births (King, 1996). Also, men undergoing fertility treatment are at increased risk of producing sperm with chromosomal abnormalities (Levron et al., 1998).

CHECKPOINT

Can you . . .

- ✔ Describe symptoms and treatments of premenstrual syndrome (PMS)?
- ✔ Identify several causes of male and female infertility?

Consider this . . .

- If you or your partner were infertile, would you seriously consider or undertake one of the methods of assisted reproduction described in Box 13-1? Why or why not?

Practically Speaking

Box 13-1
Assisted Reproduction

Since human beings seldom abandon their desires simply because they run into obstacles, it is no surprise that many infertile adults who want children embrace techniques that bypass ordinary biological processes. Technology now enables many people to have children who are genetically at least half their own.

Artificial insemination—injection of sperm into a woman's cervix—can be done when a man has a low sperm count. Sperm from several ejaculations can be combined for one injection. If the woman has no explainable cause of infertility, the chances of success can be greatly

(Continued)

Practically Speaking —*Continued*

In *in vitro fertilization,* a microscopically tiny needle (right) injects a single male sperm cell into a ripe egg (center), which has been surgically removed from a woman's body. A flat-nosed pipette (left) is used to hold the egg steady during the insertion. The fertilized egg is then implanted in the womb. This technique is one of several forms of assisted reproduction that are helping some infertile couples to reproduce.

increased by stimulating her ovaries to produce excess ova and injecting semen directly in the uterus (Guzick et al., 1999). If the man is infertile, a couple may choose *artificial insemination by a donor (AID).* The donor may be matched with the prospective father for physical characteristics, and the two men's sperm may be mixed so that no one knows which one is the biological father.

An increasing number of couples are attempting *in vitro fertilization (IVF),* fertilization outside the mother's body. First, fertility drugs are given to increase production of ova. Then a mature ovum is surgically removed, fertilized in a laboratory dish, and implanted in the mother's uterus. This method also can address male infertility, since a single sperm can be injected into the ovum. Many couples conceive only after several tries, if at all; estimates of success rates range from 12 to 20 percent. Usually several ova are fertilized and implanted, to increase the chances of success (de Lafuente, 1994; Gabriel, 1996), and the procedure often results in multiple births (P. Brown, 1993; Templeton & Morris, 1998). Although children conceived through IVF tend to be small, their head circumference and mental development are normal (Brandes et al., 1992). Two newer techniques with higher success rates are *gamete intrafallopian transfer (GIFT)* and *zygote intrafallopian transfer (ZIFT),* in which the egg and sperm or the fertilized egg are inserted in the fallopian tube (Society for Assisted Reproductive Technology, 1993).

A woman who is producing poor-quality ova or who has had her ovaries removed may try *ovum transfer.* In this procedure (the female counterpart of AID), an ovum, or *donor egg*—provided, usually anonymously, by a fertile young woman—is fertilized in the laboratory and implanted in the prospective mother's uterus (Lutjen et al., 1984). Alternatively, the ovum can be fertilized in the donor's body by artificial insemination. The donor's uterus is flushed out a few days later, and the embryo is retrieved and inserted into the recipient's uterus. Ovum transfer has been used by women past menopause (Sauer, Paulson, & Lobo, 1990, 1993).

In *surrogate motherhood,* a fertile woman is impregnated by the prospective father, usually by artificial insemination. She carries the baby to term and gives the child to the father and his mate. Surrogate motherhood is in legal limbo; courts in most states view surrogacy contracts as unenforceable (A. Toback, personal communication, January 23, 1997), and some states have either banned the practice or placed strict conditions on it. The American Academy of Pediatrics Committee on Bioethics (1992) recommends that surrogacy be considered a tentative, preconception adoption agreement in which the surrogate is the sole decision maker before the birth. The AAP committee also recommends a prebirth agreement on the period of time in which the surrogate may assert her parental rights.

Perhaps the most objectionable aspect of surrogacy, aside from the possibility of forcing the surrogate to relinquish the baby, is the payment of money. The creation of a "breeder class" of poor and disadvantaged women who carry the babies of the well-to-do strikes many people as wrong. Similar concerns have been raised about payment for donor eggs. Exploitation of the would-be parents is an issue, too. Some observers worry about the rapid growth of fertility clinics driven by the profit motive that may prey on desperate couples through misleading claims (Gabriel, 1996).

New and unorthodox means of conception raise serious questions, and only a few states have adopted regulations to address them (ISLAT Working Group, 1998). Must people who use fertility clinics be infertile, or should people be free to make such arrangements simply for conven-

Practically Speaking —Continued

ience? Should single people and cohabiting and homosexual couples have access to these methods? What about older people, who may become frail or die before the child grows up? Should the children know about their parentage? Should genetic tests be performed on prospective donors and surrogates, to identify potential abnormalities or susceptibility to certain diseases or disorders? What about routine screening for existing disease? Should there be legal limits on the number of embryos implanted? Should fertility clinics be required to disclose risks, options, and success rates? What happens if a couple who contracted with a surrogate divorce before the birth? When a couple chooses in vitro fertilization, what should be done with any unused embryos? (In more than one court case, a couple who had arranged for the freezing of excess embryos later divorced. The woman then wanted to be able to use the embryos to conceive; the man wanted them destroyed.)

Another concern is the psychological risk to children conceived with donated eggs or sperm. Will the lack of a genetic bond with one or both parents, together with strains created by the usual secrecy of such procedures and lingering disappointment about infertility, color the family atmosphere? One study suggests that the answer is no—that a strong desire for parenthood is more important than genetic ties. The quality of parenting was *better* when a child was conceived by in vitro fertilization or donor insemination than in the usual way; and no overall differences appeared in the children's feelings, behavior, or relationships with their parents (Golombok, Cook, Bish, & Murray, 1995).

One thing seems certain: as long as there are people who want children but are unable to conceive or bear them, human ingenuity and technology will come up with new ways to satisfy their need.

Cognitive Development

Perspectives on Adult Cognition

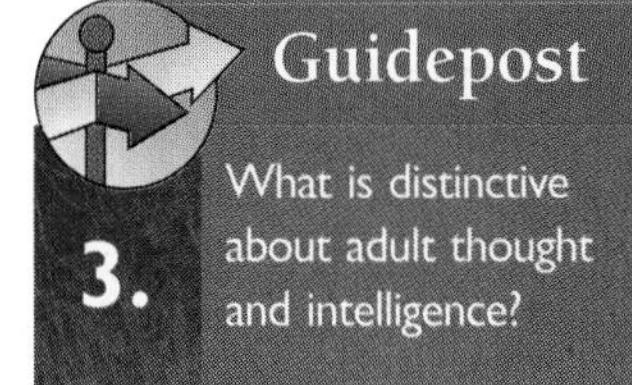

Guidepost
3.
What is distinctive about adult thought and intelligence?

Common sense tells us that adults think differently from children or adolescents. They hold different kinds of conversations, understand more complicated material, and use their broader experience to solve practical problems. Is common sense correct? Developmental theorists and researchers have studied adult cognition from a variety of perspectives. Some investigators such as Jan Sinnott and K. Warner Schaie, take a stage approach, seeking to identify what is distinctive about the way adults think, as Piaget did for children's thinking. Other investigators, such as Robert Sternberg, focus on types or aspects of intelligence, overlooked by psychometric tests, that tend to come to the fore in adulthood. One current theory highlights the role of emotion in intelligent behavior.

Beyond Piaget: The Shift to Postformal Thought

Although Piaget described the stage of formal operations as the pinnacle of cognitive achievement, some developmental scientists maintain that changes in cognition extend beyond that stage. According to Piaget's critics, formal reasoning is not the only, and perhaps not even the most important, capability of mature thought (Moshman, 1998).

Research and theoretical work since the 1970s suggest that mature thinking may be far richer and more complex than the abstract intellectual manipulations Piaget described (Arlin, 1984; Labouvie-Vief, 1985, 1990a; Labouvie-Vief & Hakim-Larson, 1989; Sinnott, 1984, 1989a, 1989b, 1991, 1998). Thought in adulthood often appears to be flexible, open, adaptive, and individualistic. It draws on intuition and emotion as well as on logic to help people cope with a seemingly chaotic world. It applies the fruits of experience to ambiguous situations. It is characterized by the ability to deal with uncertainty, inconsistency, contradiction, imperfection, and compromise (as Arthur Ashe did when faced with physical limitations on his ability to continue his tennis career). This higher stage of adult cognition is sometimes called **postformal thought.**

postformal thought
Mature type of thinking, which relies on subjective experience and intuition as well as logic and is useful in dealing with ambiguity, uncertainty, inconsistency, contradiction, imperfection, and compromise.

Postformal thought is relativistic. Immature thinking sees black and white (right versus wrong, intellect versus feelings, mind versus body); postformal thinking sees shades of gray. It often develops in response to events and interactions that open up unaccustomed ways of looking at things and challenge a simple, polarized view of the world. It enables adults to transcend a single logical system (such as a particular theory of human development, or an established political system) and reconcile or choose among conflicting ideas or demands, each of which, from its own perspective, may have a valid claim to truth (Labouvie-Vief, 1990a, 1990b; Sinnott, 1996, 1998).

One prominent researcher, Jan Sinnott (1984, 1998), has proposed several criteria of postformal thought. Among them are:

- *Shifting gears.* Ability to shift back and forth between abstract reasoning and practical, real-world considerations. ("This might work on paper but not in real life.")
- *Multiple causality, multiple solutions.* Awareness that most problems have more than one cause and more than one solution, and that some solutions are more likely to work than others. ("Let's try it your way; if that doesn't work, we can try my way.")
- *Pragmatism.* Ability to choose the best of several possible solutions and to recognize criteria for choosing. ("If you want the most practical solution, do this; if you want the quickest solution, do that.")
- *Awareness of paradox.* Recognition that a problem or solution involves inherent conflict. ("Doing this will give him what he wants, but it will only make him unhappy in the end.")

Postformal thinking deals with information in a social context. Unlike the problems Piaget studied, which involve physical phenomena and require dispassionate, objective observation and analysis, social dilemmas are less clearly structured and often fraught with emotion. It is in these kinds of situations that mature adults tend to call on postformal thought (Berg & Klaczynski, 1996; Sinnott, 1996, 1998).

One study (Labouvie-Vief, Adams, Hakim-Larson, Hayden, & DeVoe, 1987) asked people from preadolescence through middle age to consider the following problem:

> John is a heavy drinker, especially at parties. His wife, Mary, warns him that if he gets drunk once more, she will take the children and leave him. John does come home drunk after an office party. Does Mary leave John?

Preadolescents and most early adolescents answered "yes": Mary would leave John because she had said she would. More mature adolescents and adults took into account the problem's human dimensions; they realized that Mary might not go through with her threat. The *most* mature thinkers recognized that there are a number of ways to interpret the same problem, and that the way people look at such questions often depends on their life experience. The ability to envision multiple outcomes was only partly age-related; although it did not appear until late adolescence or early adulthood, adults in their forties did not necessarily think more maturely than adults in their twenties.

Other research, however, has found a general, age-related progression toward postformal thought throughout young and middle adulthood, especially when emotions are involved (Blanchard-Fields, 1986). In one study, participants were asked to judge what caused the outcomes of a series of hypothetical situations, such as a marital conflict. Adolescents and young adults tended to blame individuals, whereas middle-aged people were more likely to attribute behavior to the interplay among persons and environment. The more ambiguous the situation, the greater were the age differences in interpretation (Blanchard-Fields & Norris, 1994). Later in this chapter we discuss teaching methods designed to help adults develop postformal thought.

Although a number of studies support the existence of postformal thought (Berg & Klaczynski, 1996; Sinnott, 1996, 1998), critics say the concept has a thin research base. Much of the supporting research has taken the form of extensive, time-consuming interviews that probe participants' views of hypothetical situations and then compare their responses to subjective criteria. Such studies are not easy to replicate, so the validity of their conclusions cannot easily be tested. Future research may determine whether reliable, objective measures of postformal thinking can be developed. (We'll further discuss postformal thought in Chapter 15.)

CHECKPOINT

Can you . . .

✔ Explain why postformal thought may be especially suited to solving social problems?

Schaie: A Life-Span Model of Cognitive Development

One of the few investigators to propose a full life-span model of stages of cognitive development from childhood through late adulthood is K. Warner Schaie (1977–1978; Schaie & Willis, 2000). Schaie's model looks at the developing *uses* of intellect within a social context. His seven stages (see Figure 13-3) revolve around objectives that come to the fore at various stages of life. These objectives shift from acquisition of information and skills *(what I need to know)* to practical integration of knowledge and skills *(how to use what I know)* to a search for meaning and purpose *(why I should know).* The seven stages are as follows:

acquisitive stage
First of Schaie's seven cognitive stages, in which children and adolescents learn information and skills largely for their own sake or as preparation for participation in society.

achieving stage
Second of Schaie's seven cognitive stages, in which young adults use knowledge to gain competence and independence.

responsible stage
Third of Schaie's seven cognitive stages, in which middle-aged people are concerned with long-range goals and practical problems related to their responsibility for others.

executive stage
Fourth of Schaie's seven cognitive stages, in which middle-aged people responsible for societal systems deal with complex relationships on several levels.

1. **Acquisitive stage** (childhood and adolescence). Children and adolescents acquire information and skills mainly for their own sake or as preparation for participation in society.
2. **Achieving stage** (late teens or early twenties to early thirties). Young adults no longer acquire knowledge merely for its own sake; they use what they know to pursue goals, such as career and family.
3. **Responsible stage** (late thirties to early sixties). Middle-aged people use their minds to solve practical problems associated with responsibilities to others, such as family members or employees.
4. **Executive stage** (thirties or forties through middle age). People in the executive stage, which may overlap with the achieving and responsible stages, are responsible for societal systems (such as governmental or business organizations) or social movements. They deal with complex relationships on multiple levels.

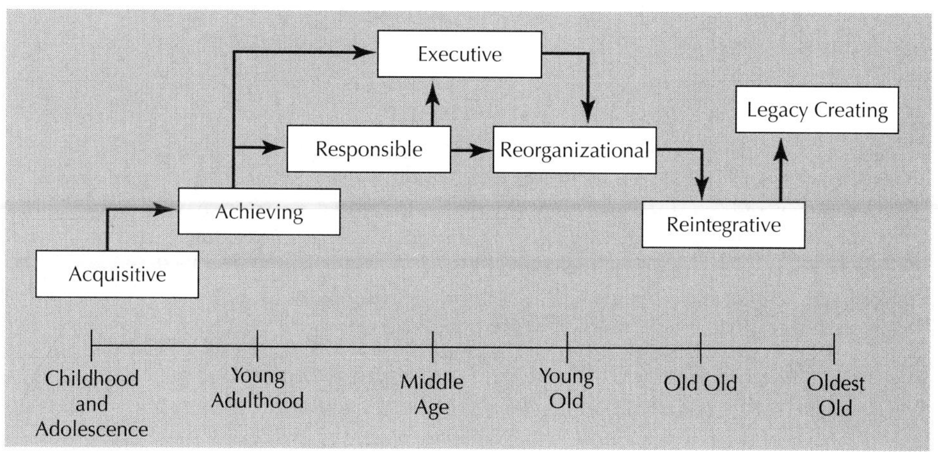

Figure 13-3
Stages of cognitive development in adults.
(Source: Based on Schaie & Willis, 2000.)

reorganizational stage
Fifth of Schaie's seven cognitive stages, in which adults entering retirement reorganize their lives around nonwork-related activities.

reintegrative stage
Sixth of Schaie's seven cognitive stages, in which older adults choose to focus limited energy on tasks that have meaning to them.

legacy creating stage
Seventh of Schaie's seven cognitive stages, in which very old people prepare for death by recording their life stories, distributing possessions, and the like.

5. **Reorganizational stage** (end of middle age, beginning of late adulthood). People who enter retirement reorganize their lives and intellectual energies around meaningful pursuits that take the place of paid work.
6. **Reintegrative stage** (late adulthood). Older adults, who may have let go of some social involvement and whose cognitive functioning may be limited by biological changes, are often more selective about what tasks they expend effort on. They focus on the purpose of what they do and concentrate on tasks that have the most meaning for them.
7. **Legacy creating stage** (advanced old age). Near the end of life, once reintegration has been completed (or along with it), older people may create instructions for the disposition of prized possessions, make funeral arrangements, provide oral histories, or write their life stories as a legacy for their loved ones. All of these tasks involve the exercise of cognitive competencies within a social and emotional context.

Not everyone goes through all the stages within the suggested time frames. Arthur Ashe as a boy in the *acquistitive stage* gained the knowledge and skills needed to become a top tennis player. While still in high school and college, he was already entering the *achieving stage,* refining his knowledge and skills as he used them to win amateur tournaments and lay the groundwork for a professional tennis career. In his thirties he moved into the *responsible stage,* helping to found a tennis players' union, serving as its president, and then becoming captain of the U.S. Davis Cup team. He also became more keenly aware of his responsibility to use his position to promote racial justice and equal opportunity. Shifting into the *executive stage,* he served as chairman of the National Heart Association and on the boards of directors of corporations, and established tennis programs for inner-city youth in several cities. Meanwhile, his early retirement from tennis and then his struggle with AIDS led him into the *reorganizational stage,* lecturing, writing, playing golf, and acting as a television sports commentator. His ultimate decision to "go public" with the news of his illness pushed him into the *reintegrative* and *legacy creating stages:* spearheading a nationwide movement for AIDS research and education and writing books on African American history—projects that would have a lasting impact.

If adults do go through stages such as these, then traditional psychometric tests, which use the same kinds of tasks to measure intelligence at all periods of life, may be inappropriate for them. Tests developed to measure knowledge and skills in children may not be suitable for measuring cognitive competence in adults, who use knowledge and skills to solve practical problems and achieve self-chosen goals. If conventional tests fail to tap abilities central to adult intelligence, we may need measures that have what Schaie (1978) calls **ecological validity**—tests that show competence in dealing with real-life challenges, such as balancing a checkbook, reading a railroad timetable, and making informed decisions about medical problems. Robert Sternberg has taken a step in this direction.

ecological validity
Characteristic of adult intelligence tests that indicate competence in dealing with real problems or challenges faced by adults.

CHECKPOINT

Can you . . .

✔ Describe Schaie's seven stages of cognitive development and give reasons why intelligence tests devised for children may not be valid for adults?

Sternberg: Insight and Know-How

> Each of us knows individuals who succeed in school but fail in their careers, or conversely, who fail in school but succeed in their careers. We have watched as graduate students, at the top of their class in the initial years of structured coursework, fall by the wayside when they must work independently on research and a dissertation. Most of us know of colleagues whose brilliance in their academic fields is matched only by their incompetence in social interactions. (Sternberg, Wagner, Williams, & Horvath, 1995, p. 912)

Alix, Barbara, and Courtney applied to graduate programs at Yale University. Alix had earned almost straight A's in college, scored high on the Graduate Record Examination (GRE), and had excellent recommendations. Barbara's grades were only fair, and her GRE scores were low by Yale's standards, but her letters of recommendation enthusiastically praised her exceptional research and creative ideas. Courtney's grades, GRE scores, and recommendations were good but not among the best.

Alix and Courtney were admitted to the graduate program. Barbara was not admitted but was hired as a research associate and took graduate classes on the side. Alix did very well for the first year or so, but less well after that. Barbara confounded the admissions committee by doing outstanding work. Courtney's performance in graduate school was only fair, but she had the easiest time getting a good job afterward (Trotter, 1986).

According to Sternberg's (1985a, 1987) triarchic theory of intelligence (introduced in Chapter 9), Barbara and Courtney were strong in two aspects of intelligence that psychometric tests miss: creative insight (what Sternberg calls the *experiential element)* and practical intelligence (the *contextual element).* Since insight and practical intelligence are very important in adult life, psychometric tests are much less useful in gauging adults' intelligence and predicting their life success than in measuring children's intelligence and predicting their school success. As an undergraduate, Alix's *componential* (analytical) ability helped her sail through examinations. However, in graduate school, where original thinking is expected, Barbara's superior *experiential* intelligence—her fresh insights and innovative ideas—began to shine. So did Courtney's practical, *contextual* intelligence—her "street smarts." She knew her way around. She chose "hot" research topics, submitted papers to the "right" journals, and knew where and how to apply for jobs.

Studies suggest that creative production and the ability to solve practical problems grow at least until midlife (see Chapter 15), while the ability to solve academic problems generally declines (Sternberg, Wagner, Williams, & Horvath, 1995). Practical problems emerge from personal experience, as does the information needed to solve them. Being more relevant to the solver, they evoke more careful thinking and provide a better gauge of cognitive ability than academic problems, which are made up by someone else, provide all necessary information, and are disconnected from everyday life. Academic problems generally have a definite answer and one right way to find it; practical problems are often ill-defined and have a variety of possible solutions and ways of reaching them, each with its advantages and disadvantages (Neisser, 1976; Sternberg & Wagner, 1989; Wagner & Sternberg, 1985). Life experience helps adults solve such problems.

An important aspect of practical intelligence is **tacit knowledge:** "inside information," "know-how," or "savvy" that is not formally taught or openly expressed (Sternberg & Wagner, 1993; Sternberg et al., 1995; Wagner & Sternberg, 1986). Tacit knowledge, acquired largely on one's own, is useful knowledge of how to act to achieve personal goals. It is "commonsense" knowledge of how to get ahead—how to win a promotion or cut through red tape. Tacit knowledge may include *self-management* (knowing how to motivate oneself and organize time and energy), *management of tasks* (knowing, for example, how to write a term paper or grant proposal), and *management of others* (knowing when to reward or criticize subordinates).

tacit knowledge
In Sternberg's terminology, information that is not formally taught or openly expressed but is necessary to get ahead.

Sternberg's method of testing tacit knowledge is to compare a test-taker's chosen course of action in hypothetical, work-related situations (such as how best to angle for a promotion) with the choices of experts in the field and with accepted "rules of thumb." Tacit

These colleagues conferring informally about their work will be helped to achieve professional success by their tacit knowledge—practical, "inside" information about how things are done, which is not formally taught but must be gained from experience.

knowledge, measured in this way, seems to be unrelated to IQ and predicts job performance better than do psychometric tests, which by themselves account for only 4 to 25 percent of the variation in how well people do in real-life situations (Sternberg et al., 1995).

Of course, tacit knowledge is not all that is needed to succeed; other aspects of intelligence count, too. In studies of business managers, tests of tacit knowledge together with IQ and personality tests predicted virtually *all* of the variance in performance, as measured by such criteria as salary, years of management experience, and the company's success (Sternberg et al., 1995). In a more recent study, tacit knowledge was related to the salaries managers earned at a given age and to how high their positions were, independent of family background and education. Interestingly, the most knowledgeable managers were not those who had spent many years with a company or many years as managers, but those who had worked for the most companies, perhaps gaining a greater breadth of experience (W. M. Williams & Sternberg, in press).

Further research is needed to determine how and when tacit knowledge is acquired, why some people acquire it more efficiently than others, and how it can best be measured. In the meantime, tests of practical intelligence, such as these, can be a valuable supplement to the aptitude tests now widely used in hiring and promotion.

Emotional Intelligence

In the mid-1980s, half of Metropolitan Life Insurance Company's sales force—unable to take the constant frustration of being turned down during cold calls—quit during their first year on the job, and 4 out of 5 stayed less than four years. The company asked the psychologist Martin Seligman to design a test to predict which prospective salespeople would stick it out. Job applicants were asked to choose between two responses to a series of hypothetical problems, such as this one (Park, 1995, p. 65):

> You fall down a great deal while skiing.
>
> A. Skiing is difficult.
>
> B. The trails were icy.

The answer Seligman was looking for was *B*. Success, he reasoned, is related to self-esteem. He expected optimistic people, who view failure as a setback due to temporary conditions and not as a reflection of their own inadequacy, to be better able to handle rejection. Sure enough, on the job, "superoptimists"—who had done exceptionally well on Seligman's test but had failed the company's usual screening test—outperformed those who had done well on the regular test by 21 percent in the first year and 57 percent in the second (Gibbs, 1995).

The observation that emotional qualities such as optimism influence success is not new, of course, nor does it apply only to adults. However, it is in adult life, with its "make-or-break" challenges, that we can perhaps see most clearly the role of the emotions in influencing how effectively people use their minds—as Arthur Ashe demonstrated again and again.

In 1990, two psychologists, Peter Salovey and John Mayer, coined the term **emotional intelligence** (sometimes called *EQ*). It refers to the ability to understand and regulate emotions—to recognize and deal with one's own feelings and the feelings of others. In other words, emotional intelligence is the ability to process emotional information. Daniel Goleman (1995a), the psychologist and science writer who popularized the concept, expanded it to include such qualities as optimism, conscientiousness, motivation, empathy, and social competence.

emotional intelligence
In Salovey's and Mayer's terminology, ability to understand and regulate emotions; an important component of effective, intelligent behavior.

According to Goleman, these abilities may be more important to success, on the job and elsewhere, than is IQ. As some corporate personnel executives have noted, "IQ gets you hired, but EQ gets you promoted" (Gibbs, 1995, p. 66).

Goleman cites studies of nearly 500 corporations in which people who scored highest on EQ rose to the top. Emotional intelligence may play a part in the ability to acquire tacit knowledge. It also may affect how well people navigate intimate relationships.

Emotional intelligence is not the opposite of cognitive intelligence, says Goleman; some people are high in both, while others have little of either. He speculates that emotional intelligence may be largely set by midadolescence, when the parts of the brain that control how people act on their emotions mature. Men and women seem to have differing emotional strengths. On an EQ test given to 4,500 men and 3,200 women, the women scored higher on empathy and social responsibility, the men on stress tolerance and self-confidence (Murray, 1998). Different kinds of tasks call for different kinds of emotional intelligence.

Emotional intelligence echoes some other developmental theories and concepts. It is reminiscent of Gardner's proposed intrapersonal and interpersonal intelligences (refer back to Chapter 9). It also resembles postformal thought in its connection between emotion and cognition.

Although research supports the role of emotions in intelligent behavior, the concept of emotional intelligence is controversial. Hard as it is to assess cognitive intelligence, emotional intelligence may be even harder to measure. For one thing, lumping the emotions together can be misleading. How do we assess someone who can handle fear but not guilt, or who can face stress better than boredom? Then too, the usefulness of a certain emotion may depend on the circumstances. Anger, for example, can lead to either destructive or constructive behavior. Anxiety may alert a person to danger but also may block effective action (Goleman, 1995a). Furthermore, most of the alleged components of emotional intelligence are usually considered personality traits. One investigation found that objective measures of EQ, as presently defined, are unreliable, and those that depend on self-ratings are almost indistinguishable from personality tests (Davies, Stankov, & Roberts, 1998).

Ultimately, acting on emotions often comes down to a value judgment. Is it smarter to obey or disobey authority? To inspire others or exploit them? "Emotional skills, like intellectual ones, are morally neutral. . . . Without a moral compass to guide people in how to employ their gifts, emotional intelligence can be used for good or evil" (Gibbs, 1995, p. 68). Let's look next at the development of that "moral compass" in adulthood.

Consider this . . .

- In what kinds of situations would postformal thought be most useful? Give specific examples. Do the same for tacit knowledge and emotional intelligence.
- Who is the most intelligent person you know? Why do you consider this person exceptionally intelligent? Would you ask this person for advice about a personal problem? Why or why not?

CHECKPOINT

Can you . . .

✔ Compare several theoretical views of adult cognition?

✔ Cite criticisms of the concepts of postformal thought and emotional intelligence?

Moral Development

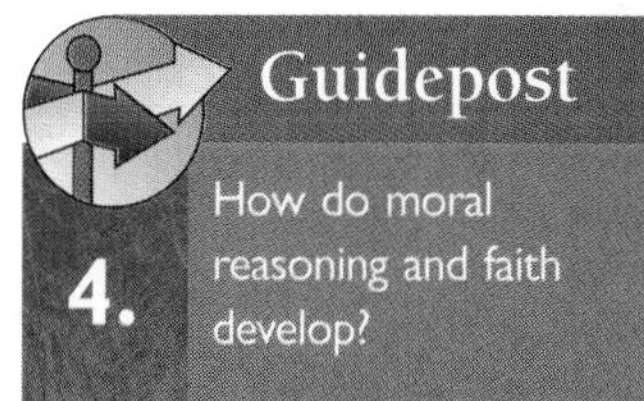

Guidepost
4.
How do moral reasoning and faith develop?

In Lawrence Kohlberg's influential theory, moral development of children and adolescents is a rational process accompanying cognitive maturation. Youngsters advance in moral judgment as they shed egocentric thought and become capable of abstract thought. In adulthood, however, moral judgments often seem more complex; experience and emotion play an increasingly important role. Let's look at how Kohlberg dealt with these issues, and then at the work of Carol Gilligan, who investigated moral development in women and challenged the values at the heart of Kohlberg's theory.

Live and Learn: The Role of Experience in Kohlberg's Theory

According to Kohlberg, advancement to the third level of moral reasoning—fully principled, postconventional morality—is chiefly a function of experience (refer back to Chapter 11). Most people do not reach this level until their twenties, if ever. Although cognitive awareness of higher moral principles often develops in adolescence, people typically do not commit themselves to such principles until adulthood (Kohlberg, 1973). Two experiences that spur moral development in young adults are encountering conflicting values away from home (as happens in college or the armed services or sometimes in foreign travel) and being responsible for the welfare of others (as in parenthood).

Experience leads adults to reevaluate their criteria for what is right and fair. Some adults spontaneously offer personal experiences as reasons for their answers to moral dilemmas. For example, people who have had cancer, or whose relatives or friends have had cancer, are more likely to condone a man's stealing an expensive drug to save his dying wife, and to explain this view in terms of their own experience (Bielby & Papalia, 1975). Arthur Ashe's experiences in a highly competitive environment, captaining the U.S. Davis Cup team, led him to be more activist and outspoken in his advocacy of an end to apartheid in South Africa. Such experiences, strongly colored by emotion, trigger rethinking in a way that hypothetical, impersonal discussions cannot and are more likely to help people see other points of view.

CHECKPOINT

Can you . . .

✔ Give examples of the role of experience in adult moral development?

With regard to moral judgments, then, cognitive stages do not tell the whole story. Of course, someone whose thinking is still egocentric is unlikely to make moral decisions at a postconventional level; but even someone who can think abstractly may not reach the highest level of moral development unless experience catches up with cognition. Many adults who are capable of thinking for themselves do not break out of a conventional mold unless their experiences have prepared them for the shift. Furthermore, experience is interpreted within a cultural context.

Cultural Differences

People born and raised on a kibbutz (collective farming or industrial settlement) in Israel are imbued with a socialist perspective. How do such people score on a problem such as Heinz's dilemma, which weighs the value of human life against a druggist's right to charge what the traffic will bear? Interviewers using Kohlberg's standardized scoring manual ran into trouble in trying to classify the following response:

> The medicine should be made available to all in need; the druggist should not have the right to decide on his own. . . . The whole community or society should have control of the drug.

Responses such as this one were coupled with statements about the importance of obeying the law and thus were confusing to the interviewers, who estimated them as fitting in with conventional stage 4 reasoning or as being in transition between stages 4 and 5. However, from the perspective of an Israeli kibbutz dweller, such a response may represent a postconventional moral principle missing from Kohlberg's description of stage 5. If membership in a kibbutz is viewed as a commitment to certain social values, including cooperation and equality for all, then concern about upholding the system may be not merely for its own sake, but aimed at protecting those principles (Snarey, 1985).

When Kohlberg's dilemmas were tested in India, Buddhist monks from Ladakh, a Tibetan enclave, scored lower than laypeople. Apparently Kohlberg's model, while capturing the preconventional and conventional elements of Buddhist thinking, was inadequate for understanding postconventional Buddhist principles of cooperation and nonviolence (Gielen & Kelly, 1983). Also, in Indian culture, people tend not to be held responsible for transgressions provoked by outside forces. When told a story about a man who hit two strangers with a rolled-up magazine after they made fun of his facial deformities, Indian participants were more likely than Americans to excuse the deformed man's behavior as due to emotional duress (Bersoff & Miller, 1993).

Heinz's dilemma was revised for use in Taiwan. In the revision, a shopkeeper will not give a man *food* for his sick wife. This version would seem unbelievable to Chinese villagers, who are more accustomed to hearing a shopkeeper in such a situation say, "You have to let people have things whether they have money or not" (Wolf, 1968, p. 21).

Whereas Kohlberg's system is based on justice, the Chinese ethos leans toward conciliation and harmony. In Kohlberg's format, respondents make an either-or decision based on their own value systems. In Chinese society, people faced with a moral dilemma discuss it openly, are guided by community standards, and try to find a way of resolving the problem to please as many parties as possible. In the west, even good people may be harshly punished if, under the force of circumstances, they break a law. The Chinese are unaccustomed to universally applied laws; they prefer to abide by the decisions of a wise judge (Dien, 1982).

Consider this . . .

- Have you ever had an experience with a person from another culture involving differences in moral principles?

The Seventh Stage

Kohlberg, shortly before his death in 1987, proposed a seventh stage of moral reasoning, which moves beyond considerations of justice and has much in common with the concept of self-transcendence in eastern traditions. In the seventh stage, adults reflect on the question, "*Why* be moral?" (Kohlberg & Ryncarz, 1990, p. 192; emphasis added). The answer, said Kohlberg, lies in achieving a cosmic perspective: "a sense of unity with the cosmos, nature, or God," which enables a person to see moral issues "from the standpoint of the universe as a whole" (Kohlberg & Ryncarz, 1990, pp. 191, 207). In experiencing oneness with the universe, people come to see that everything is connected; each person's actions affect everything and everyone else, and the consequences rebound on the doer.

This idea was eloquently expressed in a letter written in the mid–nineteenth century by the American Indian Chief Seattle, leader of the Suquamish and Duwamish tribes, when the U.S. government sought to buy tribal land:

> We are part of the earth and it is part of us. . . . Man did not weave the web of life, he is merely a strand in it. Whatever he does to the web, he does to himself. . . . So, if we sell you our land, love it as we have loved it. Care for it as we have cared for it. . . . As we are part of the land, you too are part of the land. We are brothers after all. (Chief Seattle, quoted in Campbell & Moyers, 1988, pp. 34–35)

The achievement of such a perspective is so rare that Kohlberg himself had questions about calling it a stage of development, and it has had little research exploration. Kohlberg did note that it parallels the most mature stage of faith that the theologian James Fowler (1981) identified (see Box 13-2), in which "one experiences a oneness with the ultimate conditions of one's life and being" (Kohlberg & Ryncarz, 1990, p. 202).

Box 13-2

The Development of Faith Across the Life Span

Can faith be studied from a developmental perspective? Yes, according to James Fowler (1981, 1989). Fowler defined faith as a way of seeing or knowing the world. To find out how people arrive at this knowledge, Fowler and his students at Harvard Divinity School interviewed more than 400 people of all ages with various ethnic, educational, and socioeconomic backgrounds and various religious or secular identifications and affiliations.

Fowler's theory focuses on the *form* of faith, not its content or object; it is not limited to any particular belief system. Faith can be religious or nonreligious: people may have faith in a god, in science, in humanity, or in a cause to which they attach ultimate worth and which gives meaning to their lives.

According to Fowler, faith develops—as do other aspects of cognition—through interaction between the maturing person and the environment. As in other stage theories, Fowler's stages of faith progress in an unvarying sequence, each building on those that went before. New experiences—crises, problems, or revelations—that challenge or upset a person's equilibrium may prompt a leap from one stage to the next. The ages at which these transitions occur are variable, and some people never leave a particular stage.

Fowler's stages correspond roughly to those described by Piaget, Kohlberg, and Erikson and to the "eras" of adult psychosocial development described by Daniel

(Continued)

—*Continued*

Levinson (see Chapter 14). The beginnings of faith, says Fowler, come at about 18 to 24 months of age, after children become self-aware, begin to use language and symbolic thought, and have developed what Erikson called *basic trust:* the sense that their needs will be met by powerful others.

- *Stage 1: Intuitive-projective faith* (ages 18–24 months to 7 years). As young children struggle to understand the forces that control their world, they form powerful, imaginative, often terrifying, and sometimes lasting images of God, heaven, and hell, drawn from the stories adults read to them. These images are often irrational, since preoperational children tend to be confused about cause and effect and may have trouble distinguishing between reality and fantasy. Still egocentric, they have difficulty distinguishing God's point of view from their own or their parents'. They think of God mainly in terms of obedience and punishment.
- *Stage 2: Mythic-literal faith* (ages 7 to 12 years). Children are now more logical and begin to develop a more coherent view of the universe. Not yet capable of abstract thought, they tend to take religious stories and symbols literally, as they adopt their family's and community's beliefs and observances. They can now see God as having a perspective beyond their own, which takes into account people's effort and intent. They believe that God is fair and that people get what they deserve.
- *Stage 3: Synthetic-conventional faith* (adolescence or beyond). Adolescents, now capable of abstract thought, begin to form ideologies (belief systems) and commitments to ideals. As they search for identity, they seek a more personal relationship with God. However, their identity is not on firm ground; they look to others (usually peers) for moral authority. Their faith is unquestioning and conforms to community standards. This stage is typical of followers of organized religion; about 50 percent of adults may never move beyond it.
- *Stage 4: Individuative-reflective faith* (early to middle twenties or beyond). Adults who reach this postconventional stage examine their faith critically and think out their own beliefs, independent of external authority and group norms. Since young adults are deeply concerned with intimacy, movement into this stage is often triggered by divorce, the death of a friend, or some other stressful event.
- *Stage 5: Conjunctive faith* (midlife or beyond). Middle-aged people become more aware of the limits of reason. They recognize life's paradoxes and contradictions, and they often struggle with conflicts between fulfilling their own needs and sacrificing for others. As they begin to anticipate death, they may achieve a deeper understanding and acceptance by integrating into their faith aspects of their earlier beliefs.
- *Stage 6: Universalizing faith* (late life). In this rare, ultimate category Fowler placed such moral and spiritual leaders as Mahatma Gandhi, Martin Luther King, and Mother Teresa, whose breadth of vision and commitment to the well-being of all humanity profoundly inspire others. Consumed with a sense of "participation in a power that unifies and transforms the world," they seem "more lucid, more simple, and yet somehow more fully human than the rest of us" (Fowler, 1981, p. 201). Because they threaten the established order, they often become martyrs; and though they love life, they do not cling to it. This stage parallels Kohlberg's proposed seventh stage of moral development.

As one of the first researchers to systematically study how faith develops, Fowler has had great impact; his work has become required reading in many divinity schools. It also has been criticized on several counts (Koenig, 1994). Critics say Fowler's concept of faith is at odds with conventional definitions, which involve acceptance, not introspection. They challenge his emphasis on cognitive knowledge and claim that he underestimates the maturity of a simple, solid, unquestioning faith (Koenig, 1994). Critics also question whether faith develops in universal stages—at least in those Fowler identified. Fowler himself has cautioned that his advanced stages should not be seen as better or truer than others, though he does portray people at his highest stage as moral and spiritual exemplars.

Fowler's sample was not randomly selected; it consisted of paid volunteers who lived in or near North American cities with major colleges or universities. Thus the findings may be more representative of people with above average intelligence and education (Koenig, 1994). Nor are the findings representative of nonwestern cultures. Also, the initial sample included few people over age 60. To remedy this weakness, Richard N. Shulik (1988) interviewed 40 older adults and found a strong relationship between their stages of faith and their Kohlbergian levels of moral development. However, he also found that older people at intermediate levels of faith development were less likely to be depressed than older people at higher or lower stages; perhaps those with more advanced cognition were more aware of changes associated with aging. Thus Fowler's theory may overlook the adaptive value of conventional religious belief for many older adults (Koenig, 1994; see Box 18-1 in Chapter 18).

Some of these criticisms resemble those made against other models of life-span development. Piaget's, Kohlberg's, and Erikson's initial samples were not randomly selected either. More research is needed to confirm, modify, or extend Fowler's theory, especially in nonwestern cultures.

Gilligan's Theory: Women's Moral Development

Carol Gilligan (center) studied moral development in women and, later, in men and concluded that concern for others is at the highest level of moral thought.

Because Kohlberg's original studies were done on boys and men, Carol Gilligan (1982, 1987a, 1987b) has argued that his system gives a higher place to "masculine" values (justice and fairness) than to "feminine" values (compassion, responsibility, and caring). According to Gilligan, a woman's central moral dilemma is the conflict between her own needs and those of others. While most societies typically expect assertiveness and independent judgment from men, they expect from women self-sacrifice and concern for others.

To find out how women make moral choices, Gilligan (1982) interviewed 29 pregnant women about their decisions to continue or end their pregnancies. These women saw morality in terms of selfishness versus responsibility, defined as an obligation to exercise care and to avoid hurting others. Gilligan concluded that women think less about abstract justice and fairness than men do and more about their responsibilities to specific people. (Table 13-1 lists Gilligan's proposed levels of moral development in women.)

Does other research bear out gender differences in moral reasoning? Some studies based on Kohlberg's dilemmas have shown differences in the levels achieved by men and women—differences that consistently favored men. However, a large-scale analysis comparing results from many studies found no significant differences in men's and women's responses to Kohlberg's dilemmas across the life span (L. J. Walker, 1984). In the few studies in which men scored

Table 13-1 Gilligan's Levels of Moral Development in Women

Stage	Description
Level 1: Orientation of individual survival	The woman concentrates on herself—on what is practical and what is best for her.
Transition 1: From selfishness to responsibility	The woman realizes her connection to others and thinks about what the responsible choice would be in terms of other people (including her unborn baby), as well as herself.
Level 2: Goodness as self-sacrifice	This conventional feminine wisdom dictates sacrificing the woman's own wishes to what other people want—and will think of her. She considers herself responsible for the actions of others, while holding others responsible for her own choices. She is in a dependent position, one in which her indirect efforts to exert control often turn into manipulation, sometimes through the use of guilt.
Transition 2: From goodness to truth	The woman assesses her decisions not on the basis of how others will react to them but on her intentions and the consequences of her actions. She develops a new judgment that takes into account her own needs, along with those of others. She wants to be "good" by being responsible to others, but also wants to be "honest" by being responsible to herself. Survival returns as a major concern.
Level 3: Morality of nonviolence	By elevating the injunction against hurting anyone (including herself) to a principle that governs all moral judgment and action, the woman establishes a "moral equality" between herself and others and is then able to assume the responsibility for choice in moral dilemmas.

Source: Based on Gilligan, 1982.

Consider this . . .

- Which (if either) do you consider to be higher moral priorities: justice and rights, or compassion and care?
- In your opinion, is faith in a divine being required in order to live a moral life?

CHECKPOINT

Can you . . .

✔ Compare Kohlberg's proposed seventh stage with Fowler's highest stage of faith development?

✔ State Gilligan's original position on gender differences in moral development, and summarize research findings on the subject?

slightly higher, the findings were not clearly gender-related, since the men generally were better educated and had better jobs than the women. A more recent study of male and female college and university students found no evidence that men's thinking is more principled and women's more relationship-oriented (Orr & Luszcz, 1994). Thus the weight of evidence does not appear to back up either of Gilligan's original contentions: a male bias in Kohlberg's theory or a distinct female perspective on morality (L. Walker, 1995). In one study, researchers asked college students about the morality of sexual behavior that could lead to the transmission of STDs. The researchers scored the responses according to both Kohlberg's stages and Gilligan's concept of moral orientation (justice and rights versus care and responsibility). There were no significant gender differences (Jadack, Hyde, Moore, & Keller, 1995).

In her own later research, Gilligan has described moral development in *both* men and women as evolving beyond abstract reasoning. In studies using real-life moral dilemmas (such as whether a woman's lover should confess their affair to her husband), rather than hypothetical dilemmas like the ones Kohlberg used, Gilligan and her colleagues found that many people in their twenties become dissatisfied with a narrow moral logic and become more able to live with moral contradictions (Gilligan, Murphy, & Tappan, 1990). It seems, then, that if the "different voice" in Gilligan's earlier research reflected an alternative value system, it was not gender-based. At the same time, with the inclusion of his seventh stage, Kohlberg's thinking evolved to a point of greater agreement with Gilligan's. Both theories now place responsibility to others at the highest level of moral thought. Both recognize the importance for both sexes of connections with other people and of compassion and care.

Education and Work

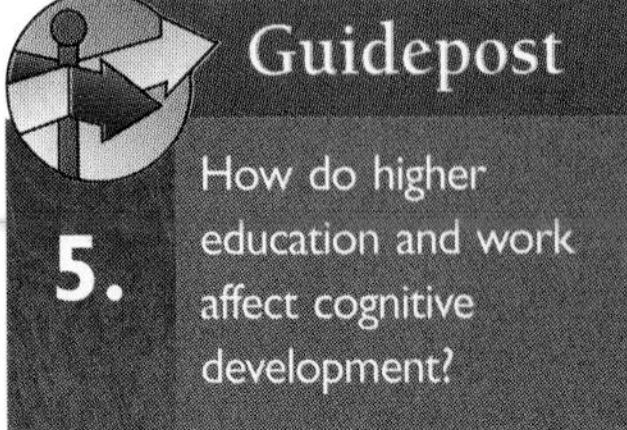

Guidepost

5. How do higher education and work affect cognitive development?

Educational and vocational choices after high school flow from the cognitive developments of earlier years and often present opportunities for further cognitive growth. Today about 2 out of 3 high school graduates go directly to college, about two-thirds of them to four-year institutions and one-third to two-year community colleges, and most of those who complete their first year go on to earn degrees. In 1998, 31 percent of 25- to 29-year-old high school graduates had completed at least four years of college (NCES, 1999). Most young adults who do not enroll in college, or do not finish, enter the job market, but many return later to finish their schooling. In 1997, about 36 percent of college undergraduates were age 25 and over (U.S. Department of Education, Office of Educational Research and Improvement, 1999).

For young people in transition from adolescence to adulthood, exposure to a new educational or work environment, sometimes far away from the childhood home, offers a chance to hone abilities, question long-held assumptions, and try out new ways of looking at the world. For the increasing number of students of nontraditional age, college or workplace education can rekindle intellectual curiosity, improve employment opportunities, and enhance work skills.

Cognitive Growth in College

College can be a time of intellectual discovery and personal growth. Students change in response to the curriculum, which offers new insights and new ways of thinking; to other students who challenge long-held views and values; to the student culture, which is different from the culture of society at large; and to faculty members, who provide new role models.

The choice of a college major can represent the pursuit of a passionate interest or a prelude to a future career. It also tends to affect thinking patterns. In a longitudinal study of 165 undergraduates, freshmen majoring in the natural sciences, humanities, and social sciences showed improvement in everyday reasoning by their senior year, but different courses of study promoted different *kinds* of reasoning. Training in the social sciences led to gains in *statistical and methodological* reasoning—the ability to generalize patterns. Students majoring in the humanities and natural sciences had better *conditional* reasoning—formal deductive logic, like that used in computer programming and mathematics. These two groups also improved in *verbal* reasoning—the ability to recognize arguments, evaluate evidence, and detect analogies (Lehman & Nisbett, 1990).

Beyond improvement in reasoning abilities, the college experience may lead to a fundamental change in the way students think. In a classic study that foreshadowed current research on the shift to postformal thought, William Perry (1970) interviewed 67 Harvard and Radcliffe students throughout their undergraduate years and found that their thinking progressed from *rigidity* to *flexibility* and ultimately to *freely chosen commitments*. Many students come to college with rigid ideas about truth; they cannot conceive of any answer but the "right" one. As students begin to encounter a wide range of ideas and viewpoints, said Perry, they are assailed by uncertainty. They consider this stage temporary, however, and expect to learn the "one right answer" eventually. Next, they come to see all knowledge and values as relative. They recognize that different societies and different individuals have their own value systems. They now realize that their opinions on many issues are as valid as anyone else's, even those of a parent or teacher; but they cannot find meaning or value in this maze of systems and beliefs. Chaos has replaced order. Finally, they achieve *commitment within relativism*: they make their own judgments and choose their own beliefs and values despite uncertainty and the recognition of other valid possibilities.

Can college students be taught to use postformal thought? Sinnott (1998) has developed specific methods for doing so. Jointly creating a grading system, brainstorming ways to design a research project, debating fundamental questions about the meaning of life, presenting arguments in a mock courtroom trial, and trying to find several explanations for an event are a few of many ways instructors can help students to recognize that there is more than one way to examine and solve a problem, to appreciate the logic of competing systems, and to see the ultimate need to commit to one.

Consider this . . .

- From your observation, does college students' thinking typically seem to follow the stages Perry outlined?

An estimated one-third of full-time and two-thirds of part-time college students work to help pay their bills. How does juggling work and study affect cognitive development? One longitudinal study followed a random sample of

College students majoring in anatomy are likely to improve in deductive reasoning and ability to weigh evidence.

incoming freshmen at 23 two- and four-year colleges and universities in 16 states through their first 3 years of college. Each year the students took tests in reading comprehension skills, mathematical reasoning, and critical thinking. During the first 2 years, on- or off-campus work had little or no effect on the test results. By the third year, part-time work had a positive effect, perhaps because employment forces students to organize their time efficiently and learn better work habits. However, working on campus more than 15 hours a week or off campus more than 20 hours a week tended to have a negative impact (Pascarella, Edison, Nora, Hagedorn, & Terenzini, 1998).

Cognitive Complexity of Work

The nature of work is changing. During the 1980s, for the first time there were more Americans in executive, professional, and technical jobs (nearly 1 in 3 workers) than in manufacture or transport of goods (1 in 5 workers) (U.S. Bureau of the Census, 1990). Work arrangements are becoming more varied and less stable. More and more adults are self-employed, working at home, telecommuting, or acting as independent contractors (Clay, 1998; McGuire, 1998). In May 1997, nearly 27 percent of U.S. employees were on flexible work schedules (Bureau of Labor Statistics, 1998).

Do people change as a result of the kind of work they do? Some research says yes: people seem to grow in challenging jobs, the kind that are becoming increasingly prevalent today.

A combination of cross-sectional and longitudinal studies (Kohn, 1980) revealed a reciprocal relationship between the **substantive complexity** of work—the degree of thought and independent judgment it requires—and a person's flexibility in coping with cognitive demands. People doing more complex work tend to become more flexible thinkers; and flexible thinkers are likely to do more complex work.

substantive complexity
Degree to which a person's work requires thought and independent judgment.

This circular relationship may begin early. "Children from culturally advantaged families develop skills and other qualities that result in their being placed in classroom situations and tracks that are relatively complex and demanding, which in turn contribute to further development of intellectual flexibility" (Smelser, 1980, p. 16). In adulthood the gap between flexible and inflexible thinkers widens. Flexible thinkers go into increasingly complex work, while people who show less flexibility do less complex work, and their cognitive abilities grow more slowly or not at all (Kohn, 1980).

CHECKPOINT

Can you . . .

- ✔ Tell how college, and working while in college, can affect cognitive development?
- ✔ Summarize current changes in the workplace?
- ✔ Explain the relationship between substantive complexity of work and cognitive development?

Why is the complexity of work linked with cognitive growth? In a society in which work plays a central role in people's lives, mastery of complex tasks may give workers confidence in their ability to handle problems. It also may open their minds to new experience and stimulate them to become more self-directed.

Brain research casts light on how people deal with complex work. Full development of the frontal lobes during young adulthood may equip people to handle several tasks at the same time. Magnetic resonance imaging reveals that the most frontward part of the frontal lobes, the *fronto-polar prefrontal cortex (FPPC),* which is much more highly developed in human beings than in other primates, has a special function in problem solving and planning. The FPPC springs into action when a person needs to put an unfinished task "on hold" and shift attention to another—a process called *branching.* The FPPC permits a worker to keep the first task in working memory while attending to the second—for example, to resume reading a report after being interrupted by the telephone (Koechlin, Basso, Pietrini, Panzer, & Grafman, 1999).

Cognitive growth need not stop at the end of the work day. According to the **spillover hypothesis,** cognitive gains from work carry over to nonworking hours. Studies support this hypothesis: substantive complexity of work strongly influences the intellectual level of leisure activities (Kohn, 1980; K. Miller & Kohn, 1983).

spillover hypothesis
Hypothesis that there is a positive correlation between intellectuality of work and of leisure activities because of a carryover of learning from work to leisure.

Work and Age

Guidepost

6. How does age influence work performance and attitudes toward work?

How well do young adults do their work as compared with older ones? Does age affect adults' ability to handle certain kinds of jobs?

In general, performance improves with age, at least until midlife; and some workers continue to increase their productivity late in life (see Chapter 18). Age differences may depend on how performance is measured and on the demands of a specific kind of work. A job requiring quick responses is likely to be done better by a young person; a job that depends on precision, a steady pace, and mature judgment may be better handled by an older person (Forteza & Prieto, 1994; Warr, 1994). A key factor may be experience rather than age: when older people perform better, it may be because they have been on a job, or have done similar work, longer (Warr, 1994).

Attitudes toward work can affect performance. Young adults tend to be less satisfied with their work than older ones (Salthouse & Maurer, 1996). They are less involved with their work, less committed to their employers, less well paid, and more likely to change jobs. Young adults may have higher goals and expectations and may look at their jobs more critically, since they are still establishing careers, are generally more attractive to employers, and can change companies or career directions more easily than can older workers (Forteza & Prieto, 1994; Rhodes, 1983; Warr, 1994).

Again, we have to be careful about drawing conclusions from cross-sectional studies. For example, older people's commitment to the "work ethic"—the idea that hard work develops character—may reflect a difference between cohorts, not how long a person has lived (Warr, 1994). Also, there may be a developmental difference in the relative importance of certain *aspects* of work. Younger workers tend to be more satisfied if they receive recognition and get along well with supervisors and colleagues, whereas older workers are more concerned about pay and the type of work they do (Forteza & Prieto, 1994). A 4-year longitudinal study in the Netherlands focused on the changing value young adults attach to their work. As the 18- to 26-year-old participants grew older, the intrinsic motivation they found in their work grew more important to them, while the value of status, money, and social contacts diminished (van der Velde, Feij, & van Emmerik, 1998).

Consider this . . .

- If you were competing for a job, would you rather compete against someone your own age or someone younger or older than you? Would the type of job affect your answer?

Workplace Education and Adult Literacy

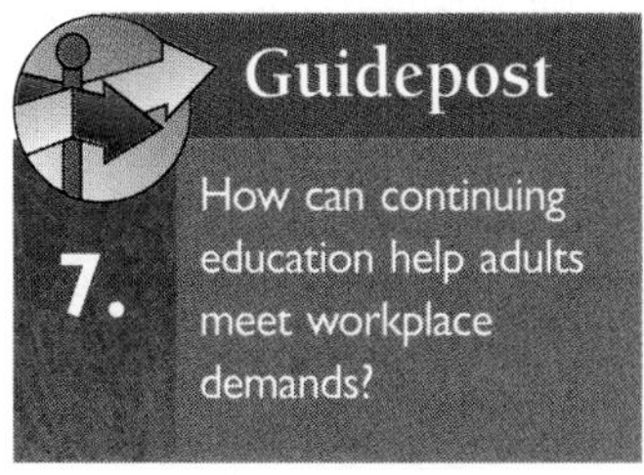

Guidepost
7.
How can continuing education help adults meet workplace demands?

About 38 percent of adults in the United States participate in part-time educational activities. Three out of 4 participants are between 25 and 54 years old, and nearly 3 out of 5 take courses to improve or advance in their work. Much of this work-related education is employer-supported (Kopka, Schantz, & Korb, 1998)—and for good reason. More than 40 percent of the workforce and more than 50 percent of high school graduates lack basic skills needed in their jobs, according to a government-assisted survey of more than 40 public and private employers in a variety of fields. Employers see benefits of workplace education in improved morale, increased quality of work, better teamwork and problem solving, and greater ability to cope with new technology and other changes in the workplace. Employees also gain in such basic skills as reading, math, and critical thinking (Conference Board, 1999).

Literacy is a fundamental requisite for participation not only in the workplace but in all facets of a modern, information-driven society. Literate adults are those who can use printed and written information to function in society, achieve their goals, and develop their knowledge and potential. At the turn of the century, a person with a fourth-grade education was considered literate; today, a high school diploma is barely adequate.

literacy
In an adult, ability to use printed and written information to function in society, achieve goals, and develop knowledge and potential.

At least 40 million U.S. adults—1 in 5—cannot read, write, or do arithmetic well enough to handle many everyday tasks, such as finding information in a newspaper article and filling out a bank deposit slip; and another 50 million are only marginally literate, according to the National Adult Literacy Survey (Kirsch, Jenkins, Jungeblut, & Kolstad, 1993).

In an International Adult Literacy Survey in 12 industrialized countries,* literacy was directly related to occupational status and earnings; less literate workers tended to be in blue-collar jobs, while those at the highest literacy level held professional or managerial positions. People at the lowest literacy levels were more likely to be unemployed or out of the labor force than those with better literacy skills (Binkley, Matheson, & Williams, 1997). For U.S. test-takers, the single most important factor in literacy in the international study was the level of educational attainment, and the disparity based on education was greater than in any other country. U.S. college graduates did better on the literacy test than college graduates in every other country except Belgium; but U.S. high school dropouts did more poorly than in any other country but Poland (NCES, 1999).

CHECKPOINT

Can you . . .

- ✔ Discuss the relationship between age and job performance?
- ✔ Explain the need for workplace education?
- ✔ State the relationship between literacy and occupational status?

Globally, almost 1 billion adults are illiterate. Illiteracy rates in sub-Saharan Africa, the Arab states, and southern Asia range from 43 to nearly 50 percent (UNESCO, 1998). Illiteracy is especially common among women in developing countries, where education typically is considered unimportant for females. In 1990, the United Nations launched literacy programs in developing countries such as Bangladesh, Nepal, and Somalia (Linder, 1990). In the United States, the National Literacy Act requires the states to establish literacy training centers with federal funding assistance.

Equal Opportunity Issues

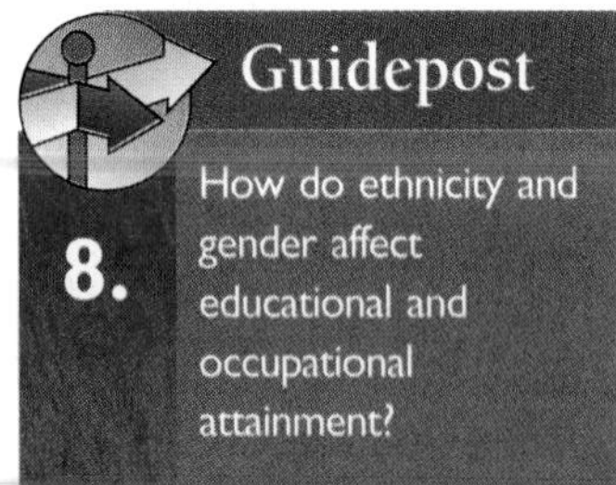

Guidepost
8.
How do ethnicity and gender affect educational and occupational attainment?

The links between cognitive ability, educational attainment, and occupational opportunity are complex ones, and are complicated further by such factors as ethnicity and gender. Despite laws mandating equal opportunity in employment, minorities and women are more likely to be unemployed and tend to earn less than white males. (In subsequent chapters we'll discuss other work-related issues, such as work-family conflict, occupational stress, unemployment, and career changes.)

Ethnicity

Despite great strides in educational attainment of African Americans and steady strides for Hispanic Americans since the early 1970s, their schooling, employment, and earnings have not kept pace with those of white Americans. The reasons are complex.

African Americans are now nearly as likely to finish high school as white Americans; 88.2 percent of black 25- to 29-year-olds have diplomas or equivalency certificates as compared with 93.6 percent of whites and 62.8 percent of Hispanics. However, black and Hispanic high school seniors, many of whom come from underprivileged backgrounds and attend low-quality schools, continue to lag (though less than in the 1970s) on national reading, math, and science assessments. This indicates that, on average, they are not as prepared for college as their white classmates.

Students from different ethnic and income backgrounds who are academically well prepared for college and who take the necessary steps to apply are equally likely to be accepted and to enroll; but black and Hispanic students are less likely to stay in college and earn a degree. White 25- to 29-year-olds who have completed high school are approximately twice as likely as blacks or Hispanics to have earned bachelor's degrees or higher—34.5 percent versus 17.9 percent and 16.5 percent, respectively (NCES, 1999).

*The countries were Canada, Germany, the Netherlands, Poland, Sweden, Switzerland, Australia, Flemish-speaking Belgium, Ireland, New Zealand, the United Kingdom, and the United States.

These statistics have practical effects. Along with promoting cognitive development, education expands employment opportunities and earning power. Even in a booming economy, in mid-1999, the unemployment rate for adults age 25 and over with no more than a high school diploma was twice as high—and for high school dropouts more than three times as high—as for college graduates (Bureau of Labor Statistics, 1999d). And median earnings of college graduates were nearly twice the earnings of high school graduates—$842 a week as compared with $481 (Bureau of Labor Statistics, 1999b). At the same time, unemployment rates for African Americans (7.3 percent) and Hispanic Americans (6. 8 percent) were nearly twice as high as for whites (3.8 percent); and the unemployment rate for black males ages 16 to 19, many of whom were high school dropouts, was nearly 27 percent (Bureau of Labor Statistics, 1999d).

The loss of well-paid manufacturing jobs and the shift to lower-paid service positions has been financially disastrous for young African American men who lack college education (Bernstein, 1995). Overall, black men working full time earn only 76.8 percent as much as white men, and black women make 85.5 percent as much as white women. Median earnings of Hispanics ($387 a week) are lower than those of either black ($443) or white ($560) workers (Bureau of Labor Statistics, 1999c). Even at the highest professional levels, income disparities are great. Black professional men earn only 79 percent, and black professional women only 60 percent, of what white men in similar positions earn (Federal Glass Ceiling Commission, 1995).

Gender

In the 1970s, women were less likely than men to go to college and less likely to finish. Today, women have more than caught up. In 1998, 29 percent of 25- to 29-year-old women had college degrees as compared with 25.6 percent of men their age (Day & Curry, 1998). During the 1990s, the number of men enrolled in college and graduate school has declined steadily in relation to the rising number of women (Lewin, 1998; U.S. Department of Education, Office of Educational Research & Improvement, 1999). However, women still tend to major in traditionally "feminine" fields, such as education, nursing, and psychology. The great majority of engineering, computer science, and mathematics degrees go to men, though the gender gap in the life sciences has reversed in the past twenty years (NCES, 1999).

According to the U.S. Department of Labor, Women's Bureau (1994), 99 percent of women in the United States will work for pay sometime during their lives. The increase in women's employment is an international phenomenon. Trends toward later marriage, later childbearing, and smaller families, as well as flexible schedules and job sharing, have made it easier for women in developed countries to pursue occupational goals, even though most mothers continue to be primary caregivers for their children. However, especially during the childrearing years, women the world over tend to work in part-time or low-status clerical and service jobs, where they earn less than men (Bruce, Lloyd, & Leonard, 1995; O'Grady-LeShane, 1993; United Nations, 1991). In some Latin American and Caribbean countries, the disparity in income is as much as 50 percent (Lim, 1996).

In the United States, women's occupational choices are far more varied than in the past, and their relative earnings have improved, as more women have moved into traditionally male fields. Women now hold about half of all executive, managerial, administrative, and

Justice Leah J. Sears was appointed to the Georgia Supreme Court in 1992, the first African American woman to serve on the court. Vocational opportunities for women and minorities have greatly expanded but, overall, are not yet equal to opportunities for white men.

professional positions (Bureau of Labor Statistics, 1999b), though the top echelons of business, government, and the professions are still largely male-dominated (Daily, Certo, & Dalton, 1999; Federal Glass Ceiling Commission, 1995).

On average, for every dollar men earn, women who work full time earn only 76.5 cents (Bureau of Labor Statistics, 1999c), and the picture is no brighter for women in managerial and professional positions. Still college-educated women's earnings (adjusted for inflation) have risen nearly 22 percent since 1979, while college-educated men's real earnings increased less than 8 percent. Young women under age 25 earn nearly as much as their male counterparts (91 percent), suggesting that the income gap may be on the way to closing as this cohort moves up in the working world (Bureau of Labor Statistics, 1999b).

CHECKPOINT

Can you . . .

✔ Discuss differences in educational attainment and employment opportunities and rewards for minorities and women?

Work affects day-to-day life, not only on the job but at home, and it brings both satisfaction and stress. In Chapter 14, we'll explore the effects of work on relationships as we look at psychosocial development in young adulthood.

Summary

PHYSICAL DEVELOPMENT

Aspects of Physical Development and Health

Guidepost 1. In what physical condition is the typical young adult, and how do lifestyle, behavior, and other factors affect present and future health and well-being?

- The typical young adult is in good condition; physical and sensory abilities are usually excellent.
- Accidents are the leading cause of death for 25- to 44-year-olds, followed by cancer, heart disease, suicide, AIDS, and homicide.
- Lifestyle factors such as diet, obesity, exercise, smoking, and substance use or abuse can affect health. **Alcoholism** is a major health problem.
- Good health is related to higher income and education.
- Women tend to live longer than men, in part for biological reasons, but perhaps also because they are more health-conscious.
- Social relationships, especially marriage, tend to be associated with physical and mental health.

Guidepost 2. What are some sexual and reproductive issues at this time of life?

- Sexual dysfunction, sexually transmitted disease, menstrual problems, and infertility can be concerns during young adulthood.
- **Sexual dysfunction** is especially common among young women.
- The AIDS epidemic is coming under control in the United States, but heterosexual transmission has increased, particularly among minority women. Voluntary testing is an important element of STD control.
- Hormones of the menstrual cycle have protective effects but also can cause health problems, notably **premenstrual syndrome (PMS).**
- The most common cause of **infertility** in men is a low sperm count; the most common cause in women is blockage of the fallopian tubes. Infertile couples now have several options for assisted reproduction, but these techniques may involve thorny ethical and practical issues.

COGNITIVE DEVELOPMENT

Perspectives on Adult Congnition

Guidepost 3. What is distinctive about adult thought and intelligence?

- Some investigators propose a distinctively adult stage of cognition beyond formal operations, called **postformal thought.** It is generally applied in social situations and involves the ability to shift between abstract reasoning and practical considerations; awareness that problems can have multiple causes and solutions; pragmatism in choosing solutions; and awareness of inherent conflict.
- Schaie has proposed seven stages of age-related cognitive development based on social roles and objectives of learning: **acquisitive stage** (childhood and adolescence), **achieving stage** (young adulthood), **responsible stage** and **executive stage** (middle adulthood), and **reorganizational, reintegrative,** and **legacy creating stages** (late adulthood). This model suggests a need to develop new kinds of intelligence tests that have **ecological validity** for adults.
- According to Sternberg's triarchic theory of intelligence, the experiential (creative, insightful) and contextual (practical) elements become particularly important during adulthood. Tests that measure **tacit knowledge,** an aspect of practical intelligence, are useful complements to traditional intelligence tests.
- **Emotional intelligence** may play an important part in intelligent behavior and life success. However, emotional intelligence as a distinct construct is controversial and hard to measure.

Moral Development

Guidepost 4. How do moral reasoning and faith develop?

- According to Lawrence Kohlberg, moral development in adulthood depends primarily on experience, though it cannot exceed the limits set by cognitive development. Experience may be interpreted differently in various cultural contexts.
- Kohlberg, shortly before his death, proposed a seventh stage of moral development, which involves seeing moral issues from a cosmic perspective. This is similar to the highest stage of faith proposed by James Fowler.
- Carol Gilligan initially proposed that women have moral concerns and perspectives that are not tapped in Kohlberg's theory and research. However, later research (including her own) has not supported a distinction between men's and women's moral outlook.

Education and Work

Guidepost 5. How do higher education and work affect cognitive development?

- Depending on their major field, college students often show specific kinds of improvements in reasoning abilities.
- According to Perry, college students' thinking tends to progress from rigidity to flexibility to freely chosen commitments.
- Research has found a relationship between **substantive complexity** of work and cognitive growth. According to the **spillover hypothesis,** people who do more complex work tend to engage in more intellectually demanding leisure activities.

Guidepost 6. How does age influence work performance and attitudes toward work?

- In general, job performance improves with age and experience; however, younger workers may do better in work requiring quick responses. Younger workers tend to be less committed to their present jobs than older workers.

Guidepost 7. How can continuing education help adults meet workplace demands?

- Workplace education can help adults develop basic job skills, which many lack.
- Adults with low **literacy** skills are at a severe disadvantage in a modern economy. In developed countries, literacy is directly linked to occupational status and income. In developing countries, illiteracy is more common among women than among men.

Guidepost 8. How do ethnicity and gender affect educational and occupational attainment?

- Despite equal opportunity laws and progress in educational attainment of African Americans and Hispanic Americans, they still are more likely to be unemployed and tend to earn less than white Americans. The changing workplace poses special challenges for adults who lack college education.
- Although more women than men now are going to college, the fields that men and women choose to study differ markedly. Still, an increasing number of women are pursuing careers in traditionally male-dominated fields and are moving into managerial and professional positions.
- Worldwide, women tend to earn less than men and to do lower-paid, lower-status work.

Key Terms

alcoholism (493)
sexual dysfunction (497)
premenstrual syndrome (PMS) (498)
infertility (499)
postformal thought (502)
acquisitive stage (503)
achieving stage (503)
responsible stage (503)
executive stage (503)
reorganizational stage (504)
reintegrative stage (504)
legacy creating stage (504)
ecological validity (504)
tacit knowledge (505)
emotional intelligence (506)
substantive complexity (514)
spillover hypothesis (514)
literacy (515)

Chapter 14

Psychosocial Development in Young Adulthood

OUTLINE

Every adult is in need of help, of warmth, of protection . . . in many ways differing (from) and yet in many ways similar to the needs of the child.

Erich Fromm, *The Sane Society*, 1955

Focus: Ingrid Bergman, "Notorious" Actress*

Ingrid Bergman

Ingrid Bergman (1915–1982) was one of the world's most distinguished stage and screen actresses. Perhaps best remembered for her starring role in *Casablanca*, she won Academy Awards for *Gaslight, Anastasia,* and *Murder on the Orient Express;* the New York Film Critics' Award for *Autumn Sonata;* and an Emmy for *The Turn of the Screw.* In 1981, a year before her death, she came out of retirement to play the Israeli prime minister Golda Meir in the Emmy-winning *A Woman Called Golda.*

Bergman's personal life was as dramatic as any movie plot. One of her film titles, *Notorious,* sums up the abrupt change in her public image in 1949, when Bergman—known as a paragon of wholesomeness and purity—shocked the world by leaving her husband and 10-year-old daughter for the Italian film director Roberto Rossellini. Compounding the scandal was the news that Bergman was pregnant by Rossellini, a married man.

Bergman had been obsessed with acting since she had seen her first play at the age of 11 in her native Sweden. Tall, awkward, and shy, she came alive onstage. Plucked out of Stockholm's Royal Dramatic School at 18 to make her first film, she braved the wrath of the school's director, who warned that movies would destroy her talent.

At 22, she married Dr. Petter Lindstrom, a handsome, successful dentist eight years her senior, who later became a prominent brain surgeon. It was he who urged her to accept the producer David Selznick's invitation to go to Hollywood to make *Intermezzo.* At 23, she arrived, to be joined later by her husband and infant daughter, Pia.

*Sources of biographical information about Ingrid Bergman were Bergman & Burgess (1980) and Spoto (1997).

Her filmmaking was punctuated by periodic spells of domesticity. "I have plenty to do as usual, and having a home, husband and child ought to be enough for any woman's life," she wrote during one such interlude. "But still I think every day is a lost day. As if only half of me is alive." (Bergman & Burgess, 1980, p. 110).

Bergman began to see her husband—whom she had always leaned on for help and decision making—as overprotective, controlling, jealous, and critical. The couple spent long hours, days, and weeks apart—she at the studio or on tour, he at the hospital.

Meanwhile, Bergman was becoming dissatisfied with filming on studio lots. When she saw Rossellini's award-winning *Open City,* she was stunned by its power and realism and by Rossellini's artistic freedom and courage. She wrote to him, offering to come to Italy and work with him. The result was *Stromboli*—and the end of what she now saw as a constrictive, unfulfilling marriage. "It was not my intention to fall in love and go to Italy forever," she wrote to Lindstrom apologetically. "But how can I help it or change it?"

At 33, Bergman, who had been number one at the box office, became a Hollywood outcast. Her affair made headlines worldwide. So did the illegitimate birth of Robertino in 1950, Bergman's hurried Mexican divorce and proxy marriage there to Rossellini (who had had his own marriage annulled), the birth of twin daughters in 1952, and the struggle over visitation rights with Pia, who took her father's side and did not see her guilt-ridden mother for six years.

The tempestuous Bergman-Rossellini love match did not last. Every picture they made together failed, and finally, so did the marriage. But their mutual bond with their children, to whom Bergman gave Rossellini custody to avoid another bitter battle, made these ex-spouses a continuing part of each other's lives. In 1958, at the age of 43, Ingrid Bergman—her career, by this time, rehabilitated and peace made with her eldest daughter—began her third marriage, to Lars Schmidt, a Swedish-born theatrical producer. It lasted sixteen years, despite constant work-related separations, and ended in an amicable divorce. Schmidt and Bergman remained close friends for the rest of her life.

Ingrid Bergman's story is a dramatic reminder of the impact of cultural change on personal attitudes and behavior. The furor over her affair with Rossellini may seem strange today, when cohabitation, extramarital sex, divorce, and out-of-wedlock birth, all of which were shocking fifty years ago, have become more common. Still, now as then, personal choices made in young adulthood establish a framework for the rest of life. Bergman's marriages and divorces, the children she bore and loved, her passionate pursuit of her vocation, and her agonizing over her unwillingness to put family before work were much like the life events and issues that confront many young women today.

Did Bergman change with maturity and experience? On the surface, she seemed to keep repeating the same cycle again and again. Yet, in her handling of her second and third divorces, she seemed calmer, more pragmatic, and more in command. Still, her basic approach to life remained the same: she did what she felt she must, come what may.

Does personality stop growing when the body does? Or does it keep developing throughout life? In this chapter, we look at theories and research on adult psychosocial development and at effects of cultural attitudes and social change. We examine the choices that frame personal and social life: adopting a sexual lifestyle; marrying, cohabiting, or remaining single; having children or not; and establishing and maintaining friendships.

After you have read and studied this chapter, you should be able to answer the following questions:

Guideposts *for* **Study**

1. Does personality change during adulthood, and if so, how?
2. What is intimacy, and how is it expressed in friendship, sexuality, and love?
3. Why do some people remain single?
4. How do homosexuals deal with "coming out," and what is the nature of gay and lesbian relationships?
5. What are the pros and cons of cohabitation?
6. What do adults gain from marriage, what cultural patterns surround entrance into marriage, and why do some marriages succeed while others fail?
7. When do most adults become parents, and how does parenthood affect a marriage?
8. Why do some couples choose to remain childless?
9. How do dual-earner couples divide responsibilities and deal with role conflicts?
10. Why have divorce rates risen, and how do adults adjust to divorce, remarriage, and stepparenthood?

Psychosocial Development: Four Approaches

Whether personality primarily shows stability or change depends in part on how we study and measure personality (Caspi, 1998). Four major approaches to adult psychosocial development are represented by *trait models, typological models, normative-crisis models,* and the *timing-of-events model.*

Trait models focus on mental, emotional, temperamental, and behavioral traits, or attributes, such as cheerfulness and irritability. Trait-based studies find that adult personality changes very little. **Typological models** identify broader personality types, or styles; they represent how personality traits are organized within the individual. These models, too, tend to find considerable stability in personality.

On the other hand, models that focus on the life course find considerable evidence of change. **Normative-crisis models** portray a typical sequence of age-related development that continues throughout the adult life span, much as in childhood and adolescence. Normative-crisis research has found major, predictable changes in adult personality. The **timing-of-events model** holds that change is related not so much to age as to the expected or unexpected occurrence and timing of important life events. This model emphasizes individual and contextual differences.

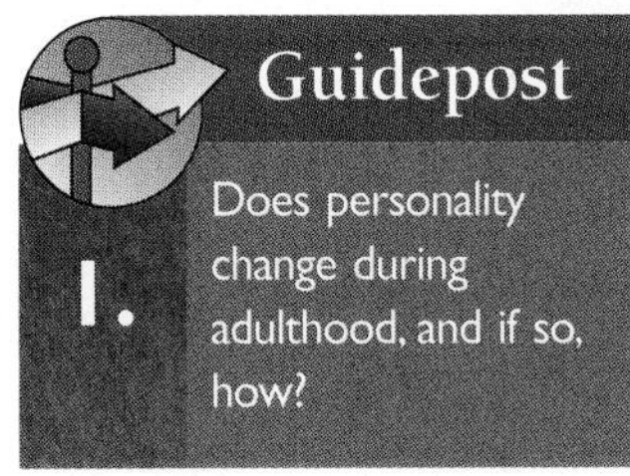

Guidepost

1. Does personality change during adulthood, and if so, how?

trait models
Theoretical models that focus on mental, emotional, temperamental, and behavioral traits, or attributes.

typological models
Theoretical models that identify broad personality types, or styles.

normative-crisis models
Theoretical models that describe psychosocial development in terms of a definite sequence of age-related changes.

timing-of-events model
Theoretical model that describes adult psychosocial development as a response to the expected or unexpected occurrence and timing of important life events.

Trait Models: Costa and McCrae's Five Factors

Rather than measure each of hundreds of distinct personality traits, Paul T. Costa and Robert R. McCrae, researchers with the National Institute on Aging, have developed and tested a **five-factor model** consisting of factors that seem to underlie five groups of associated traits (the "Big Five"). They are: (1) *neuroticism,* (2) *extraversion,* (3) *openness to experience,* (4) *conscientiousness,* and (5) *agreeableness* (see Figure 14-1).

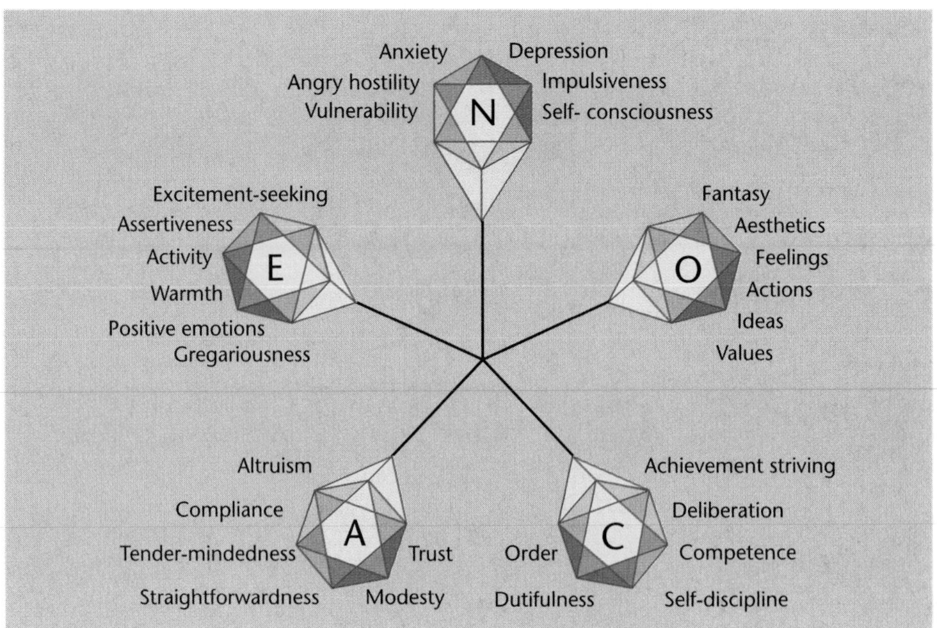

Figure 14-1
Costa and McCrae's five-factor model. Each factor, or domain of personality, represents a cluster of related traits or facets. N = neuroticism, E = extraversion, O = openness to experience, A = agreeableness, C = conscientiousness.
(Source: Adapted from Costa & McCrae, 1980.)

five-factor model Theoretical model, developed and tested by Costa and McCrae, based on the "Big Five" factors underlying clusters of related personality traits: neuroticism, extraversion, openness to experience, conscientiousness, and agreeableness.

Neuroticism is a cluster of six negative traits indicating emotional instability: anxiety, hostility, depression, self-consciousness, impulsiveness, and vulnerability. Highly neurotic people are nervous, fearful, irritable, easily angered, and sensitive to criticism. They may feel sad, hopeless, lonely, guilty, and worthless. *Extraversion* also has six facets: warmth, gregariousness, assertiveness, activity, excitement-seeking, and positive emotions. Extraverts are sociable and like attention. They keep busy and active; they are constantly looking for excitement, and they enjoy life. We can speculate that Ingrid Bergman would have had fairly high scores on some facets of neuroticism and extraversion and low scores on others.

People who are *open to experience* are willing to try new things and embrace new ideas. They have vivid imagination and strong feelings. They appreciate beauty and the arts and question traditional values. Ingrid Bergman probably would have scored high in these areas.

Conscientious people are achievers: they are competent, orderly, dutiful, deliberate, and disciplined. *Agreeable* people are trusting, straightforward, altruistic, compliant, modest, and easily swayed. Some of these characteristics could be identified with Ingrid Bergman in her youth but seem less descriptive of her as she got older.

By analyzing cross-sectional, longitudinal, and sequential data from several large samples of men and women of all ages, Costa and McCrae (1980, 1988, 1994a, 1994b; Costa et al., 1986; McCrae & Costa, 1984; McCrae, Costa, & Busch, 1986) found remarkable stability in all five domains. However, they did find age-related differences between college students and young and middle-aged adults (Costa & McCrae, 1994b). "Somewhere between age 21 and age 30 personality appears to take its final, fully developed form," these researchers conclude (Costa & McCrae, 1994a, p. 34). Adaptations may occur in response to new responsibilities and demands, traumatic events, or major cultural transformations (such as the feminist movement), but basic tendencies remain unchanged and influence the way a person adapts to these new circumstances (Caspi, 1998; Clausen, 1993; Costa & McCrae, 1994a). This underlines the importance of "goodness of fit" between person and environment (refer back to Chapter 6) and helps explain why people tend to find "niches" compatible with their nature (refer back to Chapter 3).

This body of work has made a powerful case for continuity of personality. Other researchers using somewhat different systems of trait classification have had similar results (Costa & McCrae, 1995). Comparable systems have emerged when personality was rated in languages other than English (Saucier & Ostendorf, 1999). In a study of representative samples of adults ages 25 to 65 in the United States and Germany, the "Big Five" (especially neuroticism) and other personality dimensions largely accounted for variations in subjective feelings of health and well-being (Staudinger, Fleeson, & Baltes, 1999).

Still, the five-factor model has critics. Jack Block (1995a, 1995b) argues that analysis of factors in personality (like analysis of factors in intelligence, which forms the basis of psychometric IQ tests) presents statistical and methodological problems. Because the five-factor model is based largely on self-ratings and ratings by spouses and peers, it may lack validity unless supplemented by other measures. The selection of factors and their associated facets is arbitrary and perhaps not all-inclusive; other researchers have chosen different factors and have divided up the associated traits differently. (Is warmth a facet of extraversion or agreeableness?) Finally, personality is more than a collection of traits. A model limited to studying individual differences in trait groupings offers no theoretical framework for understanding how personality works within the person.

Typological Models

Block (1971) was a pioneer in the *typological approach.* This approach looks at personality as a functioning whole that affects and reflects attitudes, values, behavior, and social interactions. Typological research is not necessarily in conflict with trait research, but seeks to complement and expand it (Caspi, 1998).

Using a variety of techniques, including interviews, clinical judgments, Q-sorts (refer back to Chapter 6), behavior ratings, and self-reports, a number of researchers, working independently, have identified several basic personality types. Most of this research is quite new; classifications may be further refined or expanded as additional studies are done (Caspi, 1998).

Three types that have emerged in a number of studies are *ego-resilient, overcontrolled,* and *undercontrolled.* People of these three types differ in **ego-resiliency,** or adaptability under stress, and **ego-control,** or self-control. *Ego-resilient* people are well adjusted: self-confident, independent, articulate, attentive, helpful, cooperative, and task-focused. *Overcontrolled* people are shy, quiet, anxious, and dependable; they tend to keep their thoughts to themselves and to withdraw from conflict, and they are the most subject to depression. *Undercontrolled* people are active, energetic, impulsive, stubborn, and easily distracted. These or similar personality types seem to exist in both sexes, across cultures and ethnic groups, and in children, adolescents, and adults (Caspi, 1998; Hart, Hofmann, Edelstein, & Keller, 1997; Pulkkinen, 1996; Robins, John, Caspi, Moffitt, & Stouthamer-Loeber, 1996; van Lieshout, Haselager, Riksen-Walraven, & van Aken, 1995).

ego-resiliency
Adaptability under potential sources of stress.

ego-control
Self-control.

In a longitudinal study in New Zealand, observer-rated personality types of 1,024 boys and girls at age 3 (similar to the three categories just described) showed predictable relationships to self-reported personality characteristics at age 19 (Caspi & Silva, 1995). In a Finnish study, "adjusted" or "conflicted" personality styles at age 27 had roots in emotional regulation and self-control during the early school years. Adjusted or conflicted styles also tended to predict "Big Five" personality traits at age 33. Some gender differences appeared. For example, women who were judged conflicted at 27 tended to have been more anxious and passive at age 8 than adjusted women, whereas conflicted men had been more aggressive and less prosocial than adjusted men. However, at age 33, both conflicted men and conflicted women tended to be more neurotic and less agreeable than adjusted men and women (Pulkkinen, 1996).

Of course, the finding of a tendency toward continuity of attitudes and behavior does not mean that personalities never change, or that certain people are condemned to a life of maladjustment. Undercontrolled children may get along better in early adulthood if they find niches in which their energy and spontaneity are considered a plus rather than a minus. Overcontrolled youngsters, like Ingrid Bergman in her youth, may come out of their shell if they find that their quiet dependability is valued.

Although personality traits or types established in childhood may predict *trajectories,* or long-term patterns of behavior, certain events may change the life course (Caspi, 1998). For some young adults, military service offers a "time-out" period and an opportunity to redirect their lives. For young people with adjustment problems, marriage to a supportive spouse can be a turning point, leading to more positive outcomes.

Some theorists who look at the life course focus, not on individual trajectories and transitions, but on age-related changes connected with events or developments that occur in most people's lives. Let's look now at these.

Normative-Crisis Models

Erik Erikson broke with Freud in part because of his conviction that personality is not frozen at puberty—that it changes throughout adult life. Variations on Erikson's theory grew out of pioneering studies by George Vaillant and Daniel Levinson. These *normative-crisis models,* all of which originally were based on research with men, hold that everyone follows the same basic sequence of age-related social and emotional changes. The changes are *normative* in that they seem to be common to most members of a population; and they emerge in successive periods, often marked by emotional *crises* that pave the way for further development.

Erikson: Intimacy versus Isolation

intimacy versus isolation
According to Erikson, the sixth critical alternative of psychosocial development, in which young adults either make commitments to others or face a possible sense of isolation and consequent self-absorption.

Erikson's sixth crisis of psychosocial development, **intimacy versus isolation,** is the major issue of young adulthood. If young adults cannot make deep personal commitments to others, said Erikson, they may become isolated and self-absorbed. However, they do need a certain amount of isolation to think about their lives. As they work to resolve conflicting demands of intimacy, competitiveness, and distance, they develop an ethical sense, which Erikson considered the mark of the adult.

Intimate relationships demand sacrifice and compromise. Young adults who have developed a strong sense of self—the chief task of adolescence, according to Erikson—are ready to fuse their identity with that of another person. They are willing to risk temporary loss of self in coitus and orgasm, as well as in very close friendships.

Erikson distinguished sexual *intimacies,* which may take place in casual encounters, from mature *intimacy with a capital "I,"* which goes beyond mere sexuality (E. Hall, 1983). Not until a person is ready for this kind of intimacy, said Erikson, can "true genitality" occur—what he defined as mutual orgasm in a loving heterosexual relationship.

Intimacy, the major achievement of young adulthood in Erikson's theory of personality development, comes about through commitment to a relationship that may demand sacrifice and compromise. According to Erikson, intimacy is possible for a man only after he has achieved his own identity, but women achieve identity *through* intimacy. Gilligan and other researchers propose a different sequence for women, who, they say, often achieve intimacy first and then go on to find identity later, sometimes years later.

Resolution of this crisis results in the "virtue" of *love:* mutual devotion between partners who have chosen to share their lives, have children, and help those children achieve their own healthy development. A decision not to fulfill the natural procreative urge has serious consequences for development, according to Erikson. His model has been criticized for excluding single, celibate, homosexual, and childless lifestyles from his blueprint for healthy development, as well as for taking male development of intimacy after identity as the norm (refer back to Chapter 12). However, we need to remember that Erikson developed his theory in a different societal context from the one in which we now live.

Erikson's Heirs: Vaillant and Levinson

In 1938, 268 eighteen-year-old Harvard undergraduates—self-reliant and emotionally and physically healthy—were selected for the Grant Study. By the time they reached midlife, Vaillant (1977) saw a typical pattern. At age 20, many of the men were still dominated by their parents. During their twenties, and sometimes their thirties, they established themselves: achieved autonomy, married, had children, and deepened friendships. Somewhere between the twenties and the forties, these men entered a stage of *career consolidation.* They worked hard at strengthening their careers and devoted themselves to their families. They followed the rules, strove for promotions, and accepted "the system," rarely questioning whether they had chosen the right woman or the right occupation. The excitement, charm, and promise they had radiated as students disappeared; now they were described as "colorless, hardworking, bland young men in gray flannel suits" (Vaillant, 1977, p. 217).

In comparing how the young men in the Grant Study adapted to the circumstances of their lives, Vaillant identified four characteristic patterns, or **adaptive mechanisms:** (1) *mature* (such as using humor or helping others), (2) *immature* (such as developing aches and pains with no physical basis), (3) *psychotic* (distorting or denying reality), and (4) *neurotic* (repressing anxiety or developing irrational fears). Men who used mature mechanisms were mentally and physically healthier, as well as happier, than others; they got more satisfaction from work, enjoyed richer friendships, made more money, and seemed better adjusted.

adaptive mechanisms
Vaillant's term to describe four characteristic ways people adapt to life circumstances: mature, immature, psychotic, and neurotic.

Levinson (1978, 1980, 1986) and his colleagues at Yale University conducted in-depth interviews and personality tests with 40 men ages 35 to 45—industrial workers, business executives, biologists, and novelists. From this study, as well as from biographical sources and other research, Levinson formed a theory of personality development in adulthood. Shortly before his death, Levinson (1996) completed a companion study of 45 women.

At the heart of Levinson's theory is an evolving **life structure:** "the underlying pattern or design of a person's life at a given time" (1986, p. 6). This structure is built around whatever a person finds most important, usually work and family.

life structure
In Levinson's theory, the underlying pattern of a person's life at a given time, built on whatever aspects of life the person finds most important.

People shape their life structures during overlapping eras of about twenty to twenty-five years each. The eras are divided into entry and culminating phases. Each phase has its own tasks, whose accomplishment becomes the foundation for the next life structure. The eras and phases are linked by transitional periods, when people reappraise, and think about restructuring, their lives. Indeed, according to Levinson, people spend nearly half their adult lives in transitions, which may involve crises.

In the entry phase of young adulthood (ages 17 to 33), a man builds his first provisional life structure. He leaves his parents' home, perhaps to go to college or into the armed services, and becomes financially and emotionally independent. He chooses an occupation and forms important relationships, usually leading to marriage and parenthood.

Two important tasks of this phase are forming a dream and finding a mentor. A *dream* of the future usually has to do with a career: a vision of, say, winning a Nobel Prize. The realization, generally in midlife, that a cherished dream will not come true may trigger an emotional crisis; and the ability to substitute more attainable goals determines how well a man will cope with life. Success during these years is influenced by a *mentor*—a slightly older man who offers guidance and inspiration and passes on wisdom, moral support, and practical help in both career and personal matters.

In the age-30 transition, a man reevaluates his entry life structure and seeks to improve it. Then, in the culminating phase of early adulthood, he settles down. He sets goals (a professorship, for instance, or a certain level of income) and a time for achieving them (say, by age 40). He anchors his life in family, occupation, and community. At the same time, he chafes under authority; he wants to become his own man. He may discard his mentor and be at odds with his wife, children, lover, boss, friends, or coworkers. How he deals with the issues of this phase will affect the midlife transition (see Chapter 16).

Women go through similar eras, phases, and transitions, according to Levinson (1996); but because of traditional cultural divisions between masculine and feminine roles, women may face different psychological and environmental constraints in forming their life structures, and their transitions tend to take longer.

Evaluating Normative-Crisis Models

The idea of a predictable sequence of age-related changes throughout adult life has been influential. Normative-crisis studies have identified developmental threads that run through the lives of many people. However, the validity of these studies is questionable. It is risky to generalize from studies with such limited samples. Both the Grant Study and Levinson's early work were based on small groups of all or mostly white middle-class to upper-middle-class men born in the 1920s or 1930s. Likewise, Levinson's small sample of women born between about 1935 and 1945 was not representative.

These men's and women's development was most likely influenced by societal events that did not affect earlier or later cohorts, as well as by their socioeconomic status, ethnicity, and gender. Many of the men in Vaillant's and Levinson's studies grew up during the economic depression of the 1930s. They benefited from an expanding economy after World War II and may have succeeded at work far beyond their early expectations, and then burned out early (see Chapter 16). Levinson's women lived through a time of great change in women's roles brought about by the women's movement, economic trends, and changing patterns in family life and in the workplace. As gender roles continue to change, both women's and men's personality development will be affected. In addition, the findings of normative crisis research do not apply to other cultures, some of which have very different patterns of life course development (see Box 16-1 in Chapter 16).

Cohort differences challenge the very heart of normative-crisis theory: the idea that development follows a predictable, age-linked sequence. Although age can be fairly indicative of children's development, it may be less so for adults. In childhood and adolescence, internal maturational events signal the transition from one developmental stage to another. A baby says the first word, takes the first step, loses the first tooth; a child's body changes at the onset of puberty. As young people enter the adult world, choose diverse lifestyles, and have varying experiences, environmental circumstances and life events become more significant, and these are not the same for everyone.

The most important message of normative-crisis models is that adults continue to change, develop, and grow. Whether or not people grow in the particular ways suggested by these models, they have challenged the notion that hardly anything important happens to personality after adolescence.

Timing-of-Events Model

Instead of looking at adult personality development as a function of age, the *timing-of-events model,* supported by Bernice Neugarten and others (Neugarten, Moore, & Lowe, 1965; Neugarten & Neugarten, 1987), holds that the course of development depends on when certain events occur in people's lives.

As we discussed in Chapter 1, **normative life events** (also called *normative age-graded events)* are those that happen to most adults at certain times of life—such events as marriage, parenthood, grandparenthood, and retirement. Events that occur when expected, such as graduating from high school at age 18, are *on time;* events that occur earlier or later than usual, such as becoming a widow at age 25 or a mother at 50, are *off time.* Events that are normative when they are "on time" become nonnormative when they are "off time." Marrying at age 14 or, for the first time, at 41 would be a nonnormative event.

normative life events
In the timing-of-events model, commonly expected life experiences that occur at customary times.

Crises result, not from reaching a certain age (as in normative-crisis models), but from the unexpected occurrence and timing of life events. If events occur as expected, development proceeds smoothly. If not, stress can result. Stress may come from an unexpected event (such as losing a job), an event that happens earlier or later than expected (being widowed at age 35, having a first child at 45, being forced to retire at 55), or the failure of an expected event to occur at all (never being married, or being unable to have a child). Personality differences influence the way people respond to life events and (as typological theorists would suggest) may even influence their timing. For example, a resilient person is likely to experience an easier transition to adulthood and the tasks that lie ahead than an overcontrolled person, who may be paralyzed by anxiety and may put off marriage or career decisions.

People usually are keenly aware of their own timing and describe themselves as "early," "late," or "on time" in marrying, having children, settling on careers, or retiring. They gauge themselves by a **social clock,** their society's norms or expectations for the appropriate timing of life events.

social clock
Set of cultural norms or expectations for the times of life when certain important events, such as marriage, parenthood, entry into work, and retirement, should occur.

The typical timing of events varies from culture to culture and from generation to generation. One illustration is the rise in the average age when adults first marry in the United States (U.S. Bureau of the Census, 1996b); another is the trend toward delayed first childbirth (see Figure 14-2). A timetable that seems right to people in one cohort may not seem so to the next.

Since the mid–twentieth century, western societies have become less age-conscious; the feeling that there is a "right time" to do certain things is less rigid, and the acceptable range of age norms is wider (C. C. Peterson, 1996). Today people

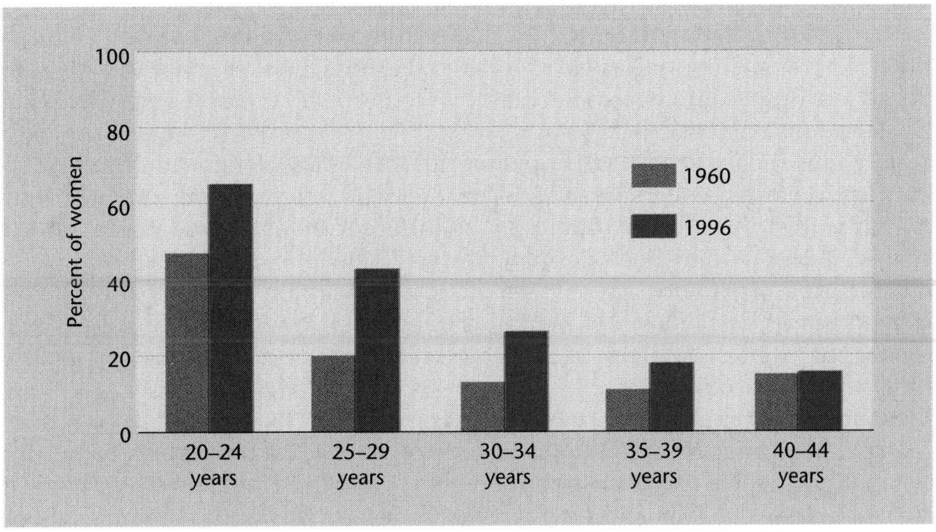

Figure 14-2
Proportion of women ages 20 to 44 who had not yet given birth, 1960 and 1996. Today, women tend to have children later in life than their mothers did. More women now have a first child after age 30.
(Source: Data from NCHS, 1998, Table 4.)

Consider this . . .

- Is there a best age to leave one's parents' home? Get married? Have a child? Start a new career? Take time off to travel? Become a grandparent? Retire? If so, what are those ages?

are more accepting of 40-year-old first-time parents and 40-year-old grandparents, 50-year-old retirees and 75-year-old workers, 60-year-olds in jeans and 30-year-old college presidents. Such rapid social change undermines the predictability on which the timing-of-events model is based.

The timing-of-events model has made an important contribution to our understanding of adult personality by emphasizing the individual life course and challenging the idea of universal, age-related change. However, its usefulness may well be limited to cultures and historical periods in which norms of behavior are stable and widespread.

Integrating Approaches to Psychosocial Development

The four approaches to psychosocial development described in the preceding sections ask different questions about adult development, look at different aspects of development, and use different methods. For example, trait researchers rely heavily on personality inventories and questionnaires, whereas normative-crisis models were built on in-depth interviews and biographical materials. It is not surprising, then, that researchers within each of these traditions often come out with results that are difficult to reconcile or even to compare.

Advocates of personality stability and advocates of change often defend their positions zealously, but it seems plain that personality development entails some of both. In the 1970s, theories of normative change took center stage, only to yield to the timing-of-events model. Since then, trait and typological researchers have redirected attention to the essential stability of personality.

Recently, there have been efforts to pull these diverse approaches together. One leading team of trait researchers (Costa & McCrae, 1994a) has mapped six interrelated elements that "make up the raw material of most personality theories" (p. 23). These elements are *basic tendencies, external influences, characteristic adaptations, self-concept, objective biography,* and *dynamic processes.*

Basic tendencies include not only personality traits, but physical health, appearance, gender, sexual orientation, intelligence, and artistic abilities. These tendencies, which may be either inherited or acquired, interact with *external* (environmental) *influences* to produce certain *characteristic adaptations:* social roles, attitudes, interests, skills, activities, habits, and beliefs. For example, it takes a combination of musical inclination (a basic tendency) and exposure to an instrument (an external influence) to produce musical skill (a characteristic adaptation). Basic tendencies and characteristic adaptations, in turn, help shape the *self-concept,* which bears only a partial resemblance to the *objective biography,* the actual events of a person's life. Thus a woman may think of herself as having more musical ability than she has objectively demonstrated, and her behavior may be influenced by that self-image. *Dynamic processes* link the other five elements; one such process is learning, which enables people to adapt to external influences (for example, to become accomplished in playing a musical instrument).

Various theorists emphasize one or another of these elements. Trait models focus on basic tendencies, which are the least likely to change, though they may manifest themselves differently at different times. For example, an extraverted 25-year-old shoe salesman may, at 70, be lobbying against cuts in social security. Typological models seek to identify certain characteristic adaptations, such as resiliency. Normative-crisis models and the timing-of-events model highlight dynamic processes that reflect universal or particular aspects of the objective biography.

Another attempt to integrate various approaches to psychosocial development is that of Ravenna Helson, whose work we discuss further in Chapter 16. For more than three decades Helson and her associates have followed 140 women from the classes of 1958 and 1960 at Mills College in Oakland, California. Using

Figure 14-3

Changes in femininity with age. In a sample fo 79 Mills College women who took the California Psychological Inventory (CPI) at ages 21, 27, 43, and 52, traits associated with femininity became stronger between ages 21 and 27, then weaker at midlife and into the early fifties.

(Source: Adapted from Helson, 1993, p. 101.)

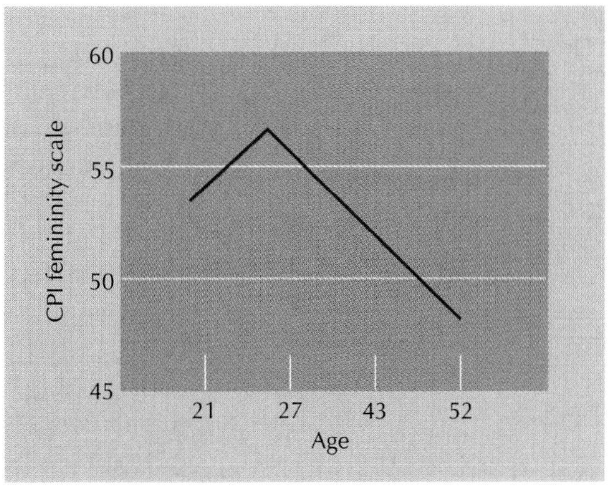

a combination of techniques, such as personality ratings, Q-sorts, and self-reports in response to open-ended questions, these researchers found evidence of systematic personality change.

One normative change in young adulthood was an increase and then a decline in traits associated with femininity (sympathy and compassion combined with a sense of vulnerability, self-criticism, and lack of confidence and initiative). Between ages 27 and 43, the women developed more self-discipline and commitment, independence, confidence, and coping skills (Helson & Moane, 1987; see Figure 14-3). The Mills researchers also found certain changes related to specific personality patterns. For example, women identified as willful, or excessively self-absorbed, at age 21 became more effective, happier, more sociable, and more confident by age 27 but by midlife tended to have problems with drugs, relationships, and careers (Wink, 1991, 1992).

The Mills studies found that "personality does change from youth to middle age in consistent and often predictable ways" (Helson & Moane, 1987, p. 185); but there were important areas of stability as well. For example, certain persistent traits, such as optimism, affected quality of life at various ages (Mitchell & Helson, 1990).

Of course, the experience of these Mills graduates has to be considered in terms of their socioeconomic status, cohort, and culture. They are a group of educated, predominantly white, upper-middle-class women who lived through a time of great change in women's roles. Thus the normative changes found in the Mills research are not necessarily the same as maturational changes. Today's young women, in turn, may be developing differently from the women in the Mills sample.

CHECKPOINT

Can you . . .

✔ Summarize and compare four major theoretical approaches to adult psychosocial development?

Consider this . . .

- Which of the models presented seems to you to most accurately describe psychosocial development in adulthood? Which model seems to have the most solid research support?

Foundations of Intimate Relationships

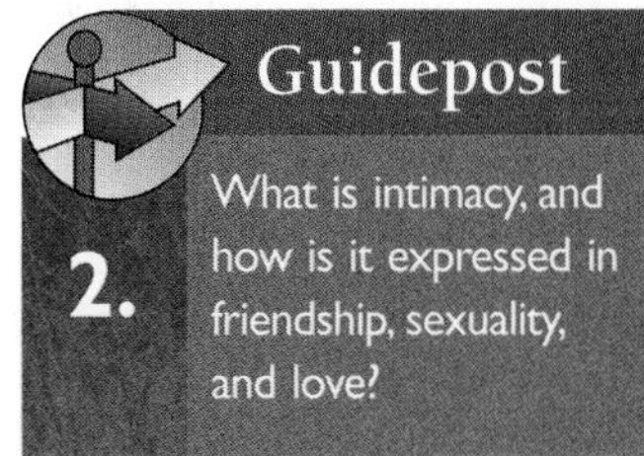

Guidepost

2. What is intimacy, and how is it expressed in friendship, sexuality, and love?

Young adulthood typically is a time of dramatic change in personal relationships as people establish, renegotiate, or cement bonds based on friendship, sexuality, and love. As young adults take responsibility for themselves and exercise the right to make their own decisions, they must redefine their relationships with their parents (Mitchell, Wister, & Burch, 1989). Adolescent friendships or "crushes" may become lifelong attachments or may fade away, to be replaced by new relationships, often with people met at college or at work.

According to Erikson, developing intimate relationships is the crucial task of this period. In today's highly mobile, open society, friendships may come and go, and so may lovers and sexual partners. Still, relationships remain pivotal as young adults decide to marry, form unwed or homosexual partnerships, or live alone, and to have or not to have children.

Intimacy is a "close, warm, communicative experience" (Rosenbluth & Steil, 1995), which may or may not include sexual contact. An important element of intimacy is *self-disclosure*: "revealing important information about oneself to another" (Collins & Miller, 1994, p. 457). People become intimate—and remain intimate—through shared disclosures, responsiveness to one another's needs, and mutual acceptance and respect (Harvey & Omarzu, 1997; Reis & Patrick, 1996).

Intimacy includes a sense of belonging. The need to belong to someone—to form strong, stable, close, caring relationships—is a powerful motivator of human behavior. The strongest emotions—both positive and negative—are evoked by intimate attachments. And, as we mentioned in Chapter 13, people tend to be healthier, physically and mentally, and to live longer, if they have satisfying close relationships (Baumeister & Leary, 1995; Myers & Diener, 1995).

Friendship

Friendships during young and middle adulthood tend to center on work and parenting activities and the sharing of confidences and advice (Hartup & Stevens, 1999). Friendships usually are based on mutual interests and values and develop among people of the same generation or at the same stage of family life, who validate each other's beliefs and behavior (Dykstra, 1995).

Of course, friendships vary in character and quality. Some are extremely intimate and supportive; others are marked by frequent conflict. Some friends have many interests in common; others are based on a single shared activity, such as bowling or bridge. Some friendships are lifelong; others are fleeting (Hartup & Stevens, 1999). Some "best friendships" are more stable than ties to a lover or spouse (K. E. Davis, 1985).

Young singles rely more on friendships to fulfill their social needs than young marrieds or young parents do (Carbery & Buhrmester, 1998); but newlyweds have the greatest *number* of friends. The number of friends and the amount of time spent with them generally decreases by middle age. Young adults who are building careers and perhaps caring for babies have limited time to spend with friends. Still, friendships are important to them. People with friends tend to have a sense of well-being; either having friends makes people feel good about themselves, or people who feel good about themselves have an easier time making friends (Hartup & Stevens, 1999).

CHECKPOINT

Can you . . .

- ✔ Identify factors that promote and maintain intimacy?
- ✔ Describe characteristic features of friendship in young adulthood?

Young women—whether single or married, and whether or not they have children—tend to have more of their social needs met by friends than young men do (Carbery & Buhrmester, 1998). Women typically have more intimate friendships than men and find friendships with other women more satisfying than those with men. Men are more likely to share information and activities, not confidences, with friends (Rosenbluth & Steil, 1995). Among 150 adults, two-thirds of whom were college students and one-third no longer in school, most people's close and best friends were of the same sex, though 27 percent had best friends of the other sex (K. E. Davis, 1985).

Love

Most people like love stories, including their own. In a sense, says Robert J. Sternberg (1995), love *is* a story. The lovers are its authors, and the kind of story they make up reflects their personalities and their feelings about the relationship. Love "stories" also differ historically and across cultures (see Box 14-1).

The idea of love as a story suggests that people do not fall in love; they create it. A couple's love story may be based on a familiar "script," which they modify to fit their situation. Love, to some people, is an ad-

Couples in love tend to have similar interests and temperament. These roller-bladers may have been drawn together by their sense of adventure and enjoyment of risk-taking.

diction—a strong, anxious, clinging attachment. Others think of it as a fantasy, in which one party (usually the woman) expects to be saved by a "knight in shining armor" (usually the man). Still others think of love as a game, a war, or a power relationship, with a winner and loser or governor and governed. Love can be a horror story, with abuser and victim, a mystery, or a detective story, in which one partner constantly tries to keep tabs on the other. Or it can be the story of a garden that needs to be tended and nurtured.

Stories, once begun, are hard to change because that would involve reinterpreting and reorganizing everything the couple have understood about the relationship. When something occurs that conflicts with that understanding (such as Ingrid Berman's affair with Rossellini), people resist changing their story. Instead they try to interpret the new information to fit it ("Something must be wrong with Ingrid; this is not the wife I know"). In Piaget's terms (refer back to Chapter 2), people prefer to *assimilate* the new information into the existing story line rather than *accommodate* the story to it.

Box 14-1

Cultural Conceptions of Love

In William Shakespeare's *A Midsummer Night's Dream,* a fairy king who wants to play a trick on his queen squeezes the juice of a magic flower into her sleeping eyes so that she will fall in love with the first person she sees upon awakening—who turns out to be an actor wearing a donkey's head. That tale is one source of the old saying, "Love is blind."

Actually, students of love find that chance plays a much smaller role than the cultural context. Although love seems to be virtually universal (Goleman, 1992), its meaning and expression vary across time and space.

According to Anne E. Beall and Robert Sternberg (1995),* people in different cultures define love differently, and the way they think about love affects what they feel. Love, say these investigators, is a *social construction* (refer back to Chapter 1)—a concept people create out of their culturally influenced perceptions of reality. This concept influences what is considered normal, acceptable, or ideal. Culture influences not only the definition of love, but the features considered desirable in choosing a beloved, the feelings and thoughts expected to accompany love, and how lovers act toward each other. Social approval and support from family and friends reinforce satisfaction with and commitment to a relationship.

In many cultures, love has been considered a dangerous distraction, disruptive of a social order based on arranged marriages. During the past two centuries, in western societies and in some nonwestern ones as well (Goleman, 1992), marriage has come to be built on love—a trend accelerated by women's increasing economic self-sufficiency. Romantic love is more commonly accepted in individualistic societies than in collectivist ones. In Communist China, for example, such love is frowned upon. Chinese see themselves in terms of social roles and relationships, and self-indulgent emotional displays as weakening the social fabric.

Within western civilization, ideas about love have changed radically. In ancient Greece, homosexual love was prized above heterosexual relationships. In some cultures, love has been separated from sexuality. In King Arthur's court, love involved a nonsexual chivalry rather than intimacy; knights undertook feats of bravery to impress fair ladies but didn't seek to marry them. In the Roman Catholic Church, love of God is considered superior to love of a human being, and priests and nuns remain celibate so as to devote themselves completely to their calling. In Victorian England, love was viewed as a noble emotion, but sex was considered a necessary evil, required only for producing children. The Victorian poets placed the beloved on a pedestal. A more modern view is that of loving a person for who he or she is, warts and all.

Ideas about love are influenced by how a culture looks at human nature. For example, during the eighteenth-century European Enlightenment, love—like other aspects of human experience—was thought to be subject to scientific understanding and rational control, and people were expected to hold their passions in check. By the nineteenth century, disillusionment with the power of science and reason had set in. People were seen as creatures of sensation, prejudice, and irrational emotion, and love was described as an uncontrollable passion. Today, the popularity of marriage counseling suggests a reassertion of the possibility of consciously affecting the course of love.

*Unless otherwise noted, this discussion is indebted to Beall & Sternberg, 1995.

triangular theory of love Sternberg's theory that patterns of love hinge on the balance among three elements: intimacy, passion, and commitment.

Thinking of love as a story may help us see how people select and mix the elements of the "plot." According to Sternberg's **triangular theory of love** (1985b; Sternberg & Barnes, 1985; Sternberg & Grajek, 1984), the three elements of love are intimacy, passion, and commitment. *Intimacy,* the emotional element, involves self-disclosure, which leads to connection, warmth, and trust. *Passion,* the motivational element, is based on inner drives that translate physiological arousal into sexual desire. *Commitment,* the cognitive element, is the decision to love and to stay with the beloved. The degree to which each of the three elements is present determines what kind of love people have (see Table 14-1). Mismatches can lead to problems.

Do opposites attract? Not as a rule. Just as people choose friends with whom they have something in common, they tend to choose life partners much like themselves (E. Epstein & Gutmann, 1984). According to the *matching hypothesis,* dating partners who are about equally attractive are most likely to develop close relationships (Harvey & Pauwels, 1999). Lovers often resemble each other in physical appearance, mental and physical health, intelligence, popularity, and warmth. They are likely to be similar in the degree to which their parents are happy as individuals and as couples, and in such factors as socioeconomic status, race, religion, education, and income (Murstein, 1980). Couples often have similar temperaments, too; risk takers tend to marry other risk takers—though they may be risking early divorce! (Zuckerman, 1994)

Consider this . . .

- Other than sexual attraction, what difference, if any, do you see between a friend and a lover?
- If you have ever been in love, do any of the theories and hypotheses presented in this section ring true, in your experience?

Evolutionary psychologists hold that men, by nature, are motivated to produce multiple offspring so as to increase the chances of perpetuating their genetic legacy; thus they look for women who are young, attractive, and healthy. Women are biologically motivated to protect their young; they seek older mates who will be good providers (Buss, 1994a, 1994b; Harvey & Pauwels, 1999). Thus the traits that make women attractive are less controllable than those that make men attractive. This analysis may help explain why women are more subject than men to negative moods, depression, low self-esteem, and dissatisfaction with body image (Ben Hamida, Mineka, & Bailey, 1998).

Table 14-1 Patterns of Loving

Type	Description
Nonlove	All three components of love—intimacy, passion, and commitment—are absent. This describes most personal relationships, which are simply casual interactions.
Liking	Intimacy is the only component present. There is closeness, understanding, emotional support, affection, bondedness, and warmth. Neither passion nor commitment is present.
Infatuation	Passion is the only component present. This is "love at first sight," a strong physical attraction and sexual arousal, without intimacy or commitment. This can flare up suddenly and die just as fast—or, given certain circumstances, can sometimes last for a long time.
Empty love	Commitment is the only component present. This is often found in long-term relationships that have lost both intimacy and passion, or in arranged marriages.
Romantic love	Intimacy and passion are both present. Romantic lovers are drawn to each other physically and bonded emotionally. They are not, however, committed to each other.
Companionate love	Intimacy and commitment are both present. This is a long-term, committed friendship, often occurring in marriages in which physical attraction has died down but in which the partners feel close to each other and have made the decision to stay together.
Fatuous love	Passion and commitment are present, without intimacy. This is the kind of love that leads to a whirlwind courtship, in which a couple make a commitment on the basis of passion without allowing themselves the time to develop intimacy. This kind of love usually does not last, despite the initial intent to commit.
Consummate love	All three components are present in this "complete" love, which many people strive for, especially in romantic relationships. It is easier to reach it than to hold onto it. Either partner may change what he or she wants from the relationship. If the other partner changes, too, the relationship may endure in a different form. If the other partner does not change, the relationship may dissolve.

Source: Sternberg, 1985b.

Sexuality: Issues and Attitudes

The change in attitudes toward premarital sex among young adults in the United States since the 1960s is striking. Between 1965 and 1994, disapproval of sex before marriage fell from 63 percent to 30 percent among men and from 80 percent to 44 percent among women (Scott, 1998).

In some other respects, however, the change in sexual attitudes and behavior is not so dramatic. Neither men nor women appear to be as promiscuous as is sometimes thought. In a nationally representative survey of 3,432 randomly selected 18- to 59-year-olds, half the respondents said they had had fewer than four sex partners during their lifetime. Many adults, because of the threat of AIDS, say they have modified their sexual behavior by having fewer partners, choosing them more carefully, using condoms, or abstaining from sex (Laumann, Gagnon, Michael, & Michaels, 1994; Michael, Gagnon, Laumann, & Kolata, 1994).

Negative attitudes toward homosexuality are slowly diminishing in the United States, but nearly 3 out of 4 men and more than 2 out of 3 women still disapprove. Disapproval of extramarital sex is even greater—94 percent—though perhaps not as intense or as publicly expressed as in Ingrid Bergman's time. The pattern of strong disapproval of homosexuality, even stronger disapproval of extramarital sex, and far weaker disapproval of premarital sex also holds true in Britain, Ireland, Germany, Sweden, and Poland, though degrees of disapproval differ from one country to another. The United States has more restrictive attitudes than any of these countries except Ireland, where the influence of the Catholic Church is strong. For example, in Germany and Sweden only 3 to 7 percent of adults disapprove of premarital sex (Scott, 1998). In China, sexual attitudes and premarital and extramarital sexual activity have liberalized dramatically despite official prohibition of sex outside marriage (Gardiner et al., 1998).

Between adolescence and young adulthood, gender differences in frequency of intercourse and incidence of masturbation increase. American men are much more likely than American women to masturbate and to approve of casual premarital sex. However, an overview of 177 studies done from 1966 through 1990, which included nearly 59,000 males and 70,000 females (largely young adults), found *no* gender differences in sexual satisfaction or participation in oral sex. Also, the sexes were quite similar in *attitudes* about such issues as masturbation, homosexuality, and civil liberties for gays and lesbians (Oliver & Hyde, 1993).

Acquaintance rape is a problem on many college campuses. College women are approximately three times more likely to become rape victims than women in the population as a whole (Gidycz, Hanson, & Layman, 1995). Rape-prevention programs have had some success. In one study, college men who participated in an hour-long session designed to provide accurate information about rape and debunk myths about it became more empathic toward rape victims than a control group and also became more aware of what constitutes rape (Pinzone-Glover, Gidycz, & Jacobs, 1998).

CHECKPOINT

Can you . . .

- ✔ Discuss theories and research about the nature of love and how men and women choose mates?
- ✔ Summarize recent trends and gender differences in sexual attitudes and behavior?

Nonmarital and Marital Lifestyles

Today's rules for acceptable behavior are more elastic than they were during the first half of the twentieth century. Current norms no longer dictate that people must get married, stay married, or have children, and at what ages. Lifestyle options include staying single, living with a partner of either sex, divorce, remarriage, and childlessness; and people's choices may change.

Marriage is no longer the central organizing institution of U.S. society, and that is even more true in many other industrialized countries. According to randomized nationwide surveys, the proportion of U.S. households consisting of married couples with children dropped from 45 percent in 1972 to 26 percent in 1998. Meanwhile, the proportion of households consisting of unmarried people with no children doubled, from 16 percent to 32 percent, becoming the most common living arrangement in the country. People marry later nowadays, if at all; more have children outside of marriage, if at all; and more break up their marriages. Economics may be part of the picture; the decline in marriage is mainly among working-class families (T. Smith, 1999).

In this section, we look at marriage and its alternatives. In the next section we examine family life.

Single Life

Guidepost
3.
Why do some people remain single?

The number of young adults who have not yet married has increased dramatically. In 1998, nearly 35 percent of 25- to 34-year-olds, including more than 53 percent of African Americans that age, had never married (U.S. Bureau of the Census, 1993b, 1996a, 1998).

Some people remain single because they have not found the right mate. In a study of 300 black, white, and Latina single women in the Los Angeles area (Tucker & Mitchell-Kernan, 1998), members of all three groups had difficulty finding eligible men with similar educational and social backgrounds; but unlike the other two groups, African American women, whose average age was 40, seemed relatively untroubled by the situation. Perhaps, as the timing-of-events model might predict, this is because they saw singlehood as normative in their ethnic group—a condition due largely to widespread unemployment and high death rates among young African American men (Manning & Landale, 1996; Tucker & Mitchell-Kernan, 1998; Tucker, Taylor, & Mitchell-Kernan, 1993).

Some young adults stay single by choice. More women today are self-supporting, and there is less social pressure to marry. Some people want to be free to take risks, experiment, and make changes—move across the country or across the world, shift careers, further their education, or do creative work without worrying about how their quest for self-fulfillment affects another person. Some enjoy sexual freedom. Some find the lifestyle exciting. Some just like being alone. And some postpone or avoid marriage because of fear that it will end in divorce (Glick & Lin, 1986b). Postponement makes sense, since, as we'll see, the younger people are when they first marry, the likelier they are to split up. By and large, singles like their status (Austrom & Hanel, 1985). Most are not lonely (Cargan, 1981; Spurlock, 1990); they are busy and active and feel secure about themselves.

Gay and Lesbian Relationships

Guidepost
4.
How do homosexuals deal with "coming out," and what is the nature of gay and lesbian relationships?

Adults are more likely than adolescents to identify themselves as homosexual (refer back to Chapter 12). Still, fewer than 3 percent of U.S. men and $1\frac{1}{2}$ percent of women call themselves homosexual or bisexual. Slightly more—5 percent of men and 4 percent of women—report at least one homosexual encounter in adulthood. Gay or lesbian identification is more common in big cities—9 percent for men and 3 percent for women (Laumann et al., 1994; Michael et al., 1994).

Because of strong societal disapproval of homosexuality, **coming out**—the process of openly disclosing a homosexual orientation—is often slow and painful. Coming out generally occurs in four stages, which may never be fully achieved (King, 1996):

coming out
Process of openly disclosing one's homosexual orientation.

1. *Recognition of being homosexual.* This may take place early in childhood or not until adolescence or later. It can be a lonely, painful, confusing experience.

Most gays and lesbians, like most heterosexuals, seek love, companionship, and sexual fulfillment in a committed relationship.

2. *Getting to know other homosexuals* and establishing sexual and romantic relationships. This may not happen until adulthood. Contact with other homosexuals can diminish feelings of isolation and improve self-image.
3. *Telling family and friends.* Many homosexuals cannot bring themselves to do this for a long time—if ever. The revelation can bring disapproval, conflict, and rejection; or it may deepen family solidarity and support. Disclosure is often limited to the immediate family, usually mothers and sisters (Mays, Chatters, Cochran, & Mackness, 1998).
4. *Complete openness.* This includes telling colleagues, employers, and anyone else a person comes in contact with. Homosexuals who reach this stage have achieved healthy acceptance of their sexuality as part of who they are.

Gay and lesbian relationships take many forms, but most homosexuals (like most heterosexuals) seek love, companionship, and sexual fulfillment through a relationship with one person. Such relationships are more common in societies that tolerate, accept, or support them (Gardiner et al., 1998). The ingredients of long-term satisfaction are very similar in homosexual and heterosexual relationships (Patterson, 1995b).

Lesbians are more likely than gay men to have stable, monogamous relationships. Since the AIDS epidemic, however, gay men have become more interested in long-term relationships. Gay and lesbian partners who live together tend to be as committed as married couples (Kurdek, 1995), but gay partners tend to be less like each other in age, income, and education than heterosexual or lesbian partners (Kurdek & Schmitt, 1987). The notion that partners in homosexual relationships typically play "masculine" and "feminine" roles has been thoroughly discredited by research (Berger, 1984; Berger & Kelly, 1986; King, 1996).

Today, gays and lesbians in the United States are struggling to obtain the legal recognition of their unions that already exists in some countries (Kottak, 1994; Kristen, 1999) and now in the state of Vermont, and the right to adopt children or raise their own. (Many homosexuals who have been married and had children before coming out have been unable to gain or keep custody.) They also are pressing for an end to discrimination in employment and housing. A current issue is whether unmarried domestic partners—homosexual or heterosexual—should be entitled to coverage under each other's health insurance and pension plans, should be able to file joint tax returns, and should receive bereavement leave and other customary benefits of marriage. Such provisions already are in effect in France, Sweden, Norway, Denmark, and the Netherlands (Trueheart, 1999).

Consider this . . .

- Should homosexuals be allowed to marry? Adopt children? Be covered by a partner's health care plan?

Cohabitation

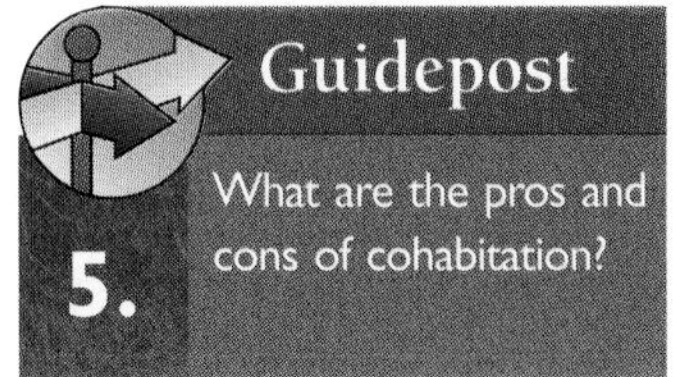

5. What are the pros and cons of cohabitation?

cohabitation
Status of a couple who live together and maintain a sexual relationship without being legally married.

Cohabitation is a lifestyle in which an unmarried couple involved in a sexual relationship live together in what is sometimes called a *consensual* or *informal union.* Such unions have become the norm in many countries, such as Sweden and Denmark, where cohabiting couples have practically the same legal rights as married ones (Popenoe & Whitehead, 1999). In Canada, 12 percent of couples were cohabiting in 1996, twice as many as in 1981 (Wu, 1999).

More than half of all U.S. couples who marry have lived together first, as did Ingrid Bergman and Roberto Rossellini (Popenoe & Whitehead, 1999). However, about 4 out of 10 cohabiting couples do *not* marry; they break up within two to five years, and each party looks for a new partner. As a result, many adults have two or more live-in partners before marriage (Michael et al., 1994; Popenoe & Whitehead, 1999).

A contributing factor to the rise in cohabitation may be the secular trend toward earlier sexual maturation (see Chapter 11). This, together with the increased number of young people pursuing advanced education, creates a longer span between physiological maturity and social maturity. Many young adults want close romantic and sexual relationships but are not ready for marriage—and may never be. Then, too, with the increase in divorce, many place less faith in marriage than in the past. An underlying factor is the shift from a strongly religious society, in which sex outside marriage was considered a sin, to a secular society in which individual autonomy and self-fulfillment are primary goals (Popenoe & Whitehead, 1999). Socioeconomic pressures and cultural factors also play a role. Cohabitation is especially common among African Americans, Puerto Ricans, and disadvantaged white women, for whom it tends to be an alternative rather than a prelude to marriage (Manning & Landale, 1996; Popenoe & Whitehead, 1999).

Still, the widespread acceptance of cohabitation is remarkable, considering that until about 1970 it was against the law, and still is in some states. Cohabitation can be a sort of trial marriage, and, according to national surveys, most young people think it is a good idea. Yet research shows that couples who live together before marriage tend to have unhappier marriages, less commitment to marriage, more risk of domestic violence and physical and sexual abuse of children, and greater likelihood of divorce (Popenoe & Whitehead, 1999).

In part, these findings may reflect the kinds of people who choose cohabitation rather than effects of cohabitation itself. Cohabitants tend to have unconventional attitudes about family life, and they are less likely than most other people to select partners like themselves in age and previous marital status. They are more likely to have divorced parents and stepchildren. All these factors tend to predict unstable marriages (D. R. Hall & Zhao, 1995; Popenoe & Whitehead, 1999).

Cohabitation also has direct effects on marriage. An analysis of data from a Canadian national survey shows that cohabition tends to delay marriage. It is easy for a cohabiting couple to keep extending the "trial period" before making a long-term commitment (Wu, 1999). Of more concern is that cohabitation—particularly a series of cohabitations—contributes to eventual marital instability, perhaps by undermining the commitment to the institution of marriage (Popenoe & Whitehead, 1999).

Cohabiting relationships themselves are less stable and, for the most part, less satisfying than marriages. Cohabitants miss out on some of the economic, psychological, and health benefits of marriage, which come from the security of a long-term commitment, greater sharing of economic and social resources, and a stronger community connection. Men and women tend to look at cohabitation differently: men as an opportunity to have a steady sex partner without being tied down, women as a step toward marriage (Popenoe & Whitehead, 1999).

Consider this . . .

- From your experience or observation, is it a good idea to live with a lover before marriage? Why or why not? Does it make a difference whether children are involved?

CHECKPOINT

Can you . . .

✔ State reasons why people remain single?

✔ List four stages of "coming out" for homosexuals and describe typical characteristics of gay and lesbian relationships?

✔ Give reasons for the rise in cohabitation and point out its disadvantages?

Marriage

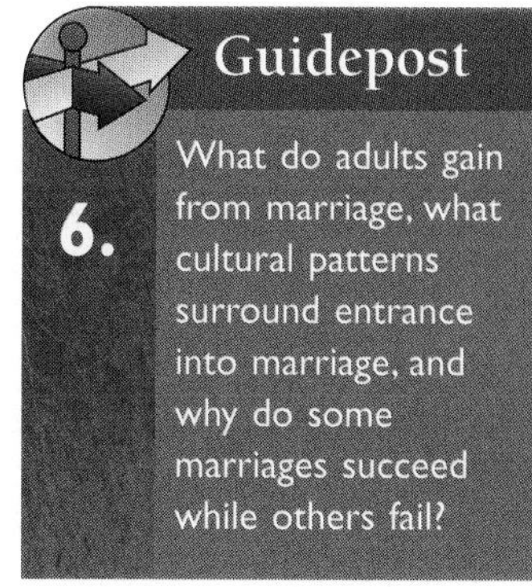

Guidepost
6.
What do adults gain from marriage, what cultural patterns surround entrance into marriage, and why do some marriages succeed while others fail?

In Tibet, a man and his father have the same wife. In Zaire, it's just the opposite: a woman shares her husband with her mother (World Features Syndicate, 1996). In many African societies, a woman—often one who is married to a man but is infertile—may take a "wife" to bear and care for her children (Cadigan, 1998). *Polygyny*—a man's marriage to more than one woman at a time—is common in Islamic countries, African societies, and parts of Asia. In *polyandrous* societies, where women generally wield more economic power, a woman may take several husbands—in some Himalayan regions, a set of brothers (Gardiner et al., 1998; Kottak, 1994). Marriage customs vary widely, but the universality of some form of marriage throughout history and around the world shows that it meets fundamental needs.

In most societies, marriage is considered the best way to ensure orderly raising of children. It allows for a division of labor within a consuming and working unit. Ideally, it offers intimacy, friendship, affection, sexual fulfillment, companionship, and an opportunity for emotional growth. In certain Eastern philosophical traditions, the harmonious union of male and female is considered essential to spiritual fulfillment and the survival of the species (Gardiner et al., 1998).

Today some benefits of marriage, such as sex, intimacy, and economic security, are not confined to wedlock. Still, among a national sample of more than 2,000 adults ages 18 to 90, married people tended to be happier than unmarried people. Contrary to earlier studies, men and women were found to benefit equally from a marital attachment, but in different ways—women from economic support and men from emotional support (Ross, 1995).

Entering Matrimony

Historically and across cultures, the most common way of selecting a mate has been through arrangement, either by the parents or by professional matchmakers. Among the chief considerations in arranged marriages are the wealth and social status of the families to be joined by the marriage. Sometimes betrothal takes place in childhood. The bride and groom may not even meet until their wedding day. Since the Renaissance, with the evolution of the nuclear family, free choice of mates on the basis of love has become the norm in the western world (Broude, 1994; Ingoldsby, 1995; refer back to Box 14-1); but in Japan, 25 to 30 percent of marriages still are arranged (Applbaum, 1995).

The typical "marrying age" varies across cultures. In eastern Europe, people tend to marry in or before their early twenties, as Ingrid Bergman did. But industrialized nations such as her native Sweden are seeing a trend toward later marriage as young adults take time to pursue educational and career goals or to explore relationships (Bianchi & Spain, 1986). In Canada, the average age of first marriage has risen from about 23 to 27 since 1961 (Wu, 1999). In the United States, the median age of first-time bridegrooms is nearly 27, and of first-time brides, 25—a rise of more than three years since 1975 (U.S. Bureau of the Census, 1999d).

The transition to married life brings major changes in sexual functioning, living arrangements, rights and responsibilities, attachments, and loyalties. Among other things, marriage partners need to redefine the connection with their original families, balance intimacy with

Marriage is universal in all cultures, though dress, celebratory customs, and even the number of partners, vary. This Indian couple in Durban, South Africa, may have been introduced by a matchmaker—worldwide, the most common way of selecting a mate.

autonomy, and establish a fulfilling sexual relationship (Wallerstein & Blakeslee, 1995). To help newlyweds adjust, some traditional societies give them extra privacy; in other societies, their sexual and other activities are subject to prescribed rules and supervision. In some cultures, newlyweds set up their own household; in other cultures, they live with parents, temporarily or permanently. In some societies, such as the Rajputs of Khalapur, India, husband and wife live, eat, and sleep apart (Broude, 1994). In contrast to Anglo-American cultures, where the chief purpose of marriage is seen as love and companionship (T. Smith, 1999), the sole purpose of marriage in Rajput society is reproduction; emotional and social support come from same-sex relatives and friends (Broude, 1994).

Sexual Activity After Marriage

Americans apparently have sex less often than media images suggest, and married people do so more often than singles, though not as often as cohabitors. Face-to-face interviews with a random sample of 3,432 men and women ages 18 to 59 found that only about one-third, including 40 percent of married couples, have intercourse two or more times a week (Laumann et al., 1994; Michael et al., 1994).

Frequency of sexual relations in marriage drops sharply after the early months, apparently due to loss of novelty, and then declines gradually as time goes on. Satisfaction with the marriage is the second most important factor after age—though it is unclear whether satisfaction influences frequency of sex or the other way around (Call, Sprecher, & Schwartz, 1995).

Some married people seek sexual intimacy outside of marriage, especially after the first few years, when the excitement of sex with the spouse wears off or problems in the relationship surface. It is hard to know just how common extramarital sex is, because there is no way to tell how truthful people are about their sexual practices, but surveys suggest that it is much less common than is generally assumed. In one survey, only about 21 percent of men and 11.5 percent of women who were ever married reported having had extramarital relations. Extramarital activity was more prevalent among younger cohorts than among those born before 1940 (T. W. Smith, 1994). Fear of AIDS and other sexually transmitted diseases may have curtailed extramarital sex since its reported peak in the late 1960s and early 1970s. In one nationwide survey, only about 2 percent of married respondents admitted to having been unfaithful during the previous year (Choi, Catania, & Dolcini, 1994).

Factors in Marital Success or Failure

One of the most important factors in marital success is a sense of commitment. Among a national sample of 2,331 married people, the partners' dependence on each other played a part in commitment to marriage, but the strongest factor was a feeling of obligation to the spouse (Nock, 1995).

Success in marriage is closely associated with how partners communicate, make decisions, and deal with conflict (Brubaker, 1983, 1993). Arguing and openly expressing anger seem to be good for a marriage; whining, defensiveness, stubbornness, and withdrawal are signs of trouble (Gottman & Krokoff, 1989). Among 150 couples who were followed through the first 10 years of marriage, those who learned to "fight fair" were 50 percent less likely to divorce (Markman, Renick, Floyd, Stanley, & Clements, 1993).

Age at marriage is a major predictor of whether a union will last. Teenagers have high divorce rates; people who wait at least until their late twenties to marry have the best chance of success. Also more likely to divorce are women who drop out of high school or college (Norton & Miller, 1992). As we have noted, cohabitation before marriage and having divorced parents are predictive of divorce; so are bearing a child before marriage, having no children, and having stepchildren in the home (Schoen, 1992; White, 1990). When there are children, the likelihood of a breakup increases if the husband is unemployed or under age 30, the family is living in poverty, or both parents work full time (U.S. Bureau of the Census, 1992c).

Economic hardship can put severe emotional stress on a marriage, increasing the likelihood of conflict. In a four-year longitudinal study of more than 400 married couples, those who were most resilient when faced with economic pressures were those who showed mutual supportiveness—who listened to each other's concerns, tried to help, were sensitive to each other's point of view, and expressed approval of each other's qualities. Those best able to resolve conflicts were those who worked together to devise effective, realistic problem-solving strategies (Conger, Rueter, & Elder, 1999).

Looking back on their marriages, 130 divorced women who had been married an average of eight years showed remarkable agreement on the reasons for the failure of their marriages. Regardless of their current income, or how long they had been divorced, the most frequently cited reasons were incompatibility and lack of emotional support; for more recently divorced, presumably younger women, this included lack of career support. Spousal abuse was third, suggesting that domestic violence may be more frequent than is generally realized (Dolan & Hoffman, 1998; see Box 14-2).

A subtle factor underlying marital conflict and marital failure may be a difference in what the two sexes expect from marriage. To many women, marital intimacy entails sharing of feelings and confidences; men tend to express intimacy through sex, practical help, companionship, and shared activities (Thompson & Walker, 1989). The mismatch between what women expect of their husbands and the way men look at themselves may be promoted by the media. The headlines, text, and pictures in men's magazines continue to reinforce the traditional masculine role as breadwinner, while women's magazines show men in nurturing roles (Vigorito & Curry, 1998).

CHECKPOINT

Can you . . .

- ✔ Identify several benefits of marriage?
- ✔ Note cultural differences in methods of mate selection, marrying age, and household arrangements?
- ✔ Discuss how sexual relations change after marriage?
- ✔ Identify factors in marital success or failure?

Family Life

Guidepost 7. When do most adults become parents, and how does parenthood affect a marriage?

Although the institution of the family is universal (Kottak, 1994), the "traditional" family—a husband, a wife, and their biological children—is not. As we pointed out in Chapter 1, in many African, Asian, and Latin American cultures the extended-family household is the traditional form. In western industrialized countries, family size, composition, structure, and living arrangements have changed dramatically. People are having smaller families and starting them later. In addition to the option of adoption (refer back to Chapter 10), infertile couples can acquire children by technological means unheard of a generation ago (refer back to Chapter 13). Most mothers now work for pay, in or outside the home, and a small but growing number of fathers are primary caregivers. More single women and cohabiting couples are having children and raising them. Millions of children live with gay or lesbian parents or with stepparents. On the other hand, an increasing number of couples remain childless by choice (Seccombe, 1991).

Becoming Parents

At one time, a blessing offered to newlyweds in the Asian country of Nepal was, "May you have enough sons to cover the hillsides!" Today, Nepali couples are wished, "May you have a very bright son" (B. P. Arjyal, personal communication, February 12, 1993). While sons still are preferred over daughters, even boys are not wished for in such numbers as in the past.

Practically Speaking Box 14-2
Dealing with Domestic Violence

Domestic violence, or *partner abuse*, is the physical, sexual, or psychological maltreatment of a spouse, a former spouse, or an intimate partner so as to gain or maintain power or control. Its full extent is unknown, both in the United States and around the world (Walker, 1999); it generally takes place in private, and victims often do not report it because they are ashamed or afraid (Bachman, 1994). Wife beating is common in many traditional societies, even some in which it is officially condemned. It is most prevalent in societies marked by aggressive behavior, restrictive sexual practices, inferior status of women, and use of physical force to resolve disputes. It is fairly rare in societies based on extended-family households (Broude, 1994).

Most victims of domestic violence are women, and they are more likely to be seriously hurt. Men who abuse their partners often seek to control or dominate and often were brought up in violent homes themselves.

The vast majority of known victims—more than 9 out of 10 in the United States—are women, and they are more likely than men to be seriously harmed. Once a woman has been abused, she is likely to be abused again (Holtzworth-Munroe & Stuart, 1994; U.S. Bureau of Justice Statistics, 1994).

Partner abuse occurs at every level of society, in all income groups; but the women at greatest risk are young, poor, uneducated, and divorced or separated (U.S. Bureau of Justice Statistics, 1994; Walker, 1999). Men who intentionally injure women tend to have less than a high school education, to be unemployed or intermittently employed, to have low incomes and alcohol or other drug problems, and to be the former or estranged husbands or former boyfriends of their victims (Heyman, O'Leary, & Jouriles, 1995; Kyriacou et al., 1999; McKenry, Julian, & Gavazzi, 1995). There is no appreciable difference in domestic violence against black and white women (Bachman, 1994).

Pushing, shoving, and slapping often begin even before marriage. Among 625 newlywed couples, 36 percent reported premarital violence (McLaughlin, Leonard, & Senchak, 1992). If nothing is done about it, the violence tends to increase (Holtzworth-Munroe & Stuart, 1994; O'Leary et al., 1989). Men who are seriously aggressive before marriage generally continue to be aggressive after marriage, and such marriages are likely to deteriorate and fail (Heyman, O'Leary, & Jouriles, 1995).

Spousal abuse is more frequent in marriages in which the man seeks to control or dominate (Yllo, 1984, 1993). Such relationships may be products of a socialization process in which boys are taught by example to prevail through aggression and physical force. Eight out of 10 men who physically assault their wives saw their fathers

In preindustrial farming societies, large families were a necessity: children helped with the family's work and would eventually care for aging parents. The death rate in childhood was high, and having many children made it more likely that some would reach maturity. Today, infant and child mortality rates have improved greatly (refer back to Chapters 4 and 7), and, in industrial societies, large families are no longer an economic asset. In developing countries, too, where overpopulation and hunger are major problems, there is recognition of the need to limit family size and to space children further apart.

Not only do people typically have fewer children today, but they also start having them later in life (refer back to Figure 14-2), often because they spend their early adult years getting an education and establishing a career. (Ingrid Bergman, like most women in her generation, did not wait to establish her career before becoming a mother; she had her first child at 23, just before coming to Hollywood.) Between 1975 and 1997, the percentage of women who gave birth in their thirties and after 40 increased steadily. Better-educated women tend to have babies later (Ventura, Martin, Curtin, & Mathews, 1999; see Figure 14-4).

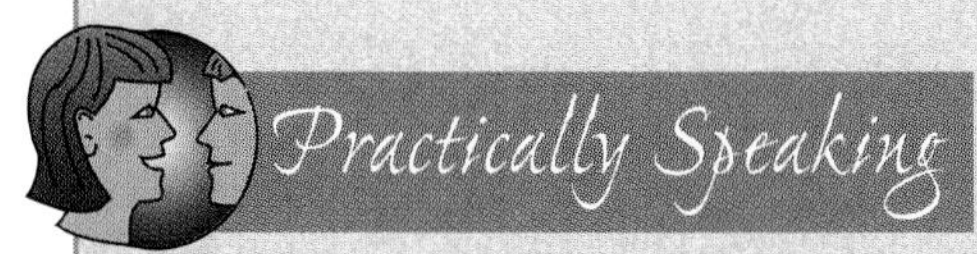

Practically Speaking —*Continued*

beat their mothers (Reiss & Roth, 1994). Men brought up in violent homes tend not to have learned to deal with conflict, frustration, and anger (Holtzworth-Munroe & Stuart, 1994).

The effects of domestic violence often extend beyond the couple. The children, especially sons, are likely to be abused by both parents (Jouriles & Norwood, 1995), and boys exposed to abuse are likely to grow up to be abusers themselves. Violence in the family is directly related to violence in the community (Walker, 1999).

Why do women stay with men who abuse them? Some cannot bring themselves to face and admit what is happening. Some have low self-esteem and feel they deserve to be beaten. Constant ridicule, criticism, threats, punishment, and psychological manipulation may destroy their self-confidence and overwhelm them with self-doubt (Fawcett, Heise, Isita-Espejel, & Pick, 1999; NOW Legal Defense and Education Fund & Chernow-O'Leary, 1987). Some minimize the extent of the abuse or hold themselves responsible for not living up to their marital obligations. Many see abuse as a private issue to be resolved within the family (Fawcett et al., 1999). Some women feel they have nowhere to turn. Their abusive partners isolate them from family and friends. They are often financially dependent and lack outside social support (Kalmuss & Straus, 1982; McKenry, Julian, & Gavazzi, 1995; Strube & Barbour, 1984).

Often the risks of acting seem to outweigh the benefits (Fawcett et al., 1999). If the woman tries to end the relationship or call the police, she gets more abuse (Geller, 1992). Some women are afraid to leave—a realistic fear, since some abusive husbands later track down, harass, and beat or even kill their estranged wives (Reiss & Roth, 1994; Walker, 1999). Women who are victims of severe violence they did not initiate, or of coercive sex, are the most fearful, perhaps because they feel the least control over what happens to them (DeMaris & Swinford, 1996).

In some cases, marital or family therapy may stop mild to moderate abuse before it escalates (Gelles & Maynard, 1987; Holtzworth-Munroe & Stuart, 1994; Walker, 1999). Evidence suggests that men who are arrested for family violence are less likely to repeat the abuse, and communities are increasingly adopting this approach (Bouza, 1990; L. W. Sherman & Berk, 1984; L. W. Sherman & Cohn, 1989; Walker, 1999). Sometimes, however, especially when the perpetrator has antisocial tendencies, arrest only worsens the abuse afterward (Walker, 1999).

In the United States, the Violence Against Women Act, adopted in 1994, provides for tougher law enforcement, funding for shelters, a national domestic violence hotline, and educating judges and court personnel, as well as young people, about domestic violence. Canada has similar programs to help battered women. Efforts to protect women and eliminate gender-based violence also are under way in various European and Latin American countries. In England and Brazil, police are being trained to understand gender-based violence and to help women feel comfortable in reporting it (Walker, 1999).

In the long run, the best hope for eliminating partner abuse is to "change men's socialization patterns so that power over women will no longer be a necessary part of the definition of what it means to be a man" and to "renegotiat[e] the balance of power between women and men at all levels of society" (Walker, 1999, pp. 25, 26).

Babies of older mothers may benefit from their mothers' greater ease with parenthood. When 105 new mothers ages 16 to 38 were interviewed and observed with their infants, the older mothers reported more satisfaction with parenting and spent more time at it. They were more affectionate and sensitive to their babies and more effective in encouraging desired behavior (Ragozin, Basham, Crnic, Greenberg, & Robinson, 1982). And, among a large, nationally representative sample, a subsample of 47 men who became fathers after their 35th birthdays spent more leisure time with their children, had higher expectations for the children's behavior, and were more nurturing than a

Couples today tend to have fewer children than in past generations, and to have them later in life. Infants may benefit from mature parents' ease with parenthood and willingness to invest more time in it.

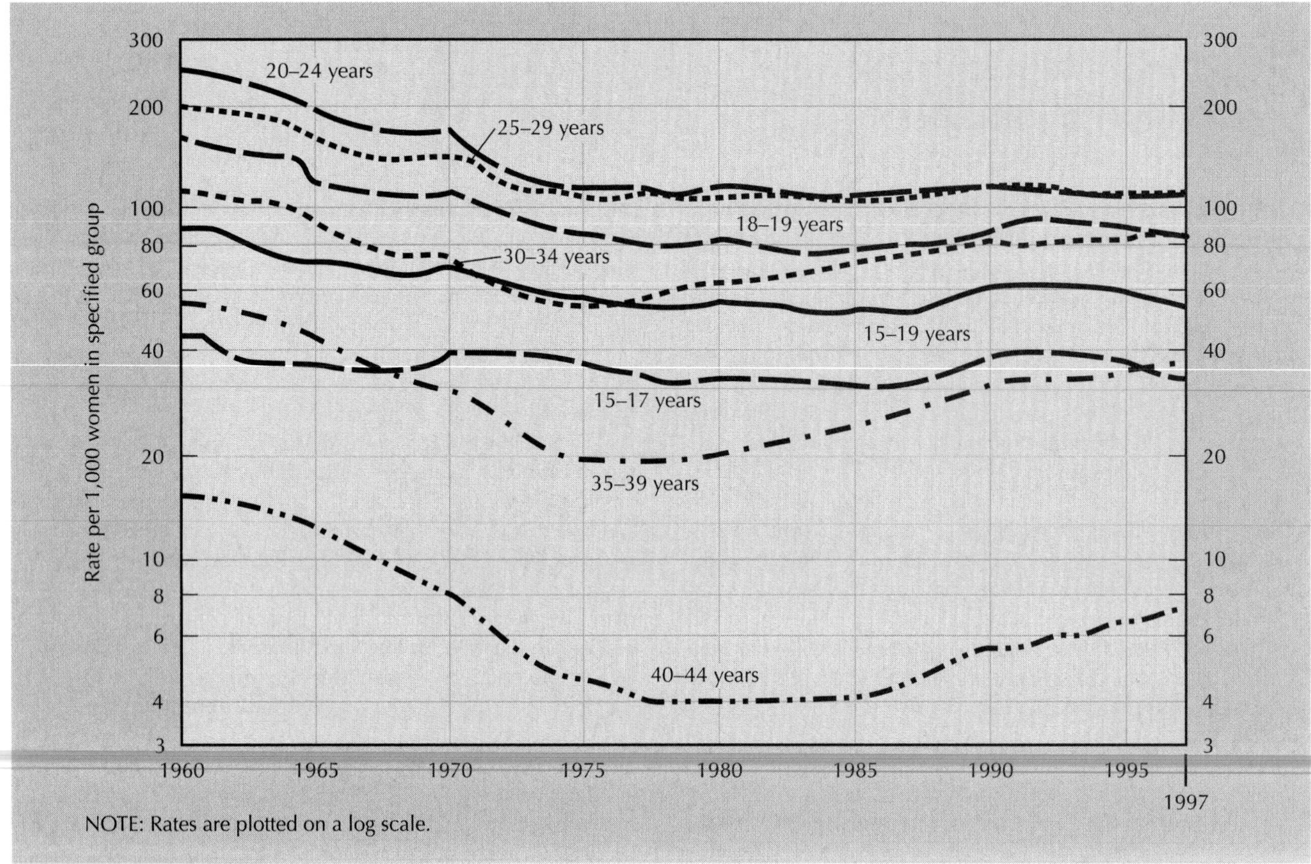

Figure 14-4
Birthrates by age of mother, 1960 to 1997.
(Source: Ventura et al., 1999, Figure 2.)

comparison group who became fathers before age 35 (Heath, 1994). On the other hand, looking far down the road, older parents are more likely to become a burden when their children reach middle age (see Chapters 16 and 18).

Parenthood as a Developmental Experience

A first baby marks a major transition in parents' lives. This totally dependent new person changes individuals and changes relationships. As children develop, parents do, too.

Men's and Women's Attitudes Toward Parenthood

Both women and men often have mixed feelings about becoming parents. Along with excitement, they may feel anxiety about the responsibility of caring for a child and the commitment of time and energy it entails. Among couples who do not have children, husbands consider having them more important and are more apt to want them than wives are (Seccombe, 1991); but once children come, fathers enjoy looking after them less than mothers do. Although fathers generally believe they should be involved in their children's lives, most are not nearly as involved as mothers are (Backett, 1987; W. T. Bailey, 1994; Boulton, 1983; LaRossa, 1988).

Apparently fathers think they are contributing more than they actually are. That finding comes from a study of parents of 4-year-olds in 10 European, Asian, and African countries and the United States. Internationally, fathers average less than 1 hour a day in sole charge of their children during the work week; and when men do supervise their children, it is usually with the mother. U.S. fathers spend only 1 hour a day in such shared child care, while U.S. mothers spend an average of nearly 11 hours each weekday caring for preschoolers—more than mothers in any of the other 10 countries (Olmsted & Weikart, 1994).

How Parenthood Affects Marital Satisfaction

Marital satisfaction typically declines during the childraising years (see Chapter 16). In a ten-year longitudinal study of predominantly white couples who married in their late twenties, both husbands and wives reported a sharp decline in satisfaction during the first 4 years, followed by a plateau and then another decline. Spouses who had children, especially those who became parents early in their marriage and those who had many children, showed a steeper decline. Although there was a high attrition rate—429 out of the original 522 couples divorced or separated during the course of the study or did not complete it—the presumably greater dissatisfaction of the couples who ultimately left the study did not seriously skew the findings while they were in it. The pattern of decline held true, though less strongly, even when this factor was controlled (Kurdek, 1999).

Of course, this statistical pattern is an average; it is not necessarily true of all couples. One research team followed 128 middle- and working-class couples in their late twenties from the first pregnancy until the child's third birthday. Some marriages got stronger, while others deteriorated, especially in the eyes of the wives. Many spouses loved each other less, became more ambivalent about their relationship, argued more, and communicated less. In these marriages, the partners tended to be younger and less well educated, to earn less money, and to have been married a shorter time. One or both partners tended to have low self-esteem, and husbands were likely to be less sensitive. The mothers who had the hardest time were those whose babies had difficult temperaments. Surprisingly, couples who were most romantic "pre-baby" had more problems "post-baby," perhaps because they had unrealistic expectations. Also, women who had planned their pregnancies were unhappier, possibly because they had expected life with a baby to be better than it turned out to be (Belsky & Rovine, 1990).

If a couple share household tasks fairly equally before becoming parents, and then, after the birth, the burden shifts to the wife, marital happiness tends to decline, especially for nontraditional wives (Belsky, Lang, & Huston, 1986). Among young Israeli first-time parents, fathers who saw themselves as caring, nurturing, and protecting experienced less decline in marital satisfaction than other fathers and felt better about parenthood. Men who were less involved with their babies, and whose wives were more involved, tended to be more dissatisfied. The mothers who became most dissatisfied with their marriages were those who saw themselves as disorganized and unable to cope with the demands of motherhood (Levy-Shiff, 1994).

Remaining Childless by Choice

"When are you going to have a baby?" This question is heard less often these days, as societal attitudes have moved away from the belief that all married couples who *can* have children *should* have them.

Some couples decide before marriage never to have children. Others keep postponing conception, waiting for the "right time," until they decide that the right time will never come. Some of these couples want to concentrate on careers or social causes. Some feel more comfortable with adults or think they would not make good parents. Some want to retain the intimacy of the honeymoon. Some enjoy an adult lifestyle, with freedom to travel or to make spur-of-the-moment decisions. Some women worry that pregnancy will make them less attractive and that parenthood will change their relationship with their spouse (Callan, 1986).

In one study, 36 voluntarily childless wives and 42 single women who planned to remain childless filled out questionnaires about what they imagined the impact of a first child on their lives would be. Their answers were compared with those of married mothers and singles who wanted children. All the groups had similar perceptions about the psychological advantages and disadvantages of having a child, but the voluntarily childless women, both married and single, gave more weight to the disadvantages (Callan, 1986)

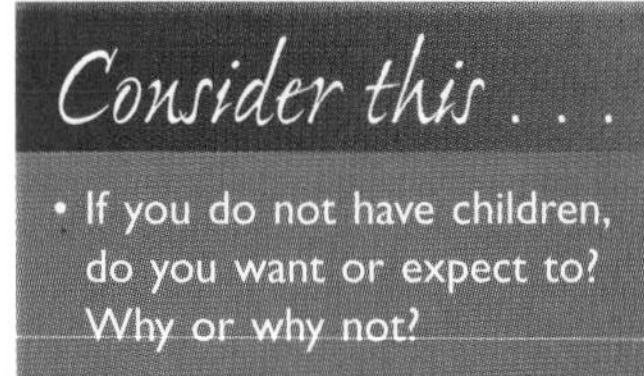

Consider this . . .
• If you do not have children, do you want or expect to? Why or why not?

Some people may be discouraged by the financial burdens of parenthood and the difficulty of combining parenthood with employment. The estimated total expenditures to support a child born in 1998 in a middle-income two-parent, two-child family for 17 years are $156,690—and this does not include the cost of summer camps or savings for college education (Lino, 1999). Better child care and other support services might help couples make truly voluntary decisions.

How Dual-Earner Couples Cope

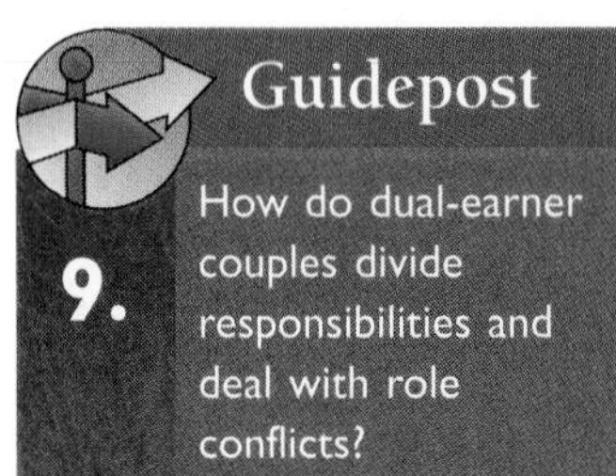

Guidepost
9.
How do dual-earner couples divide responsibilities and deal with role conflicts?

In almost all known societies, women—even if they work full time—have primary responsibility for housework and child raising (Gardiner et al., 1998). However, the ways couples divide breadwinning and household work, and the psychological effects of those decisions, vary.

Benefits and Drawbacks of a Dual-Earner Lifestyle

In the United States, nearly 2 out of 3 families consisting of a married couple with children under 18 are dual-earner families (Bureau of Labor Statistics, 1999a). Marriages in which both husband and wife are gainfully employed present both opportunities and challenges. On the positive side, a second income raises some families from poverty to middle-income status and makes others affluent. It makes women more independent and gives them a greater share of economic power, and it reduces the pressure on men to be providers; 47 percent of working wives contribute half or more of family income (Louis Harris & Associates, 1995). Less tangible benefits may include a more equal relationship between husband and wife, better health for both, greater self-esteem for the woman, and a closer relationship between a father and his children (Gilbert, 1994).

On the downside, working couples face extra demands on time and energy, conflicts between work and family, possible rivalry between spouses, and anxiety and guilt about meeting children's needs. The family is most demanding, especially for women who are employed full time, when there are young children (Milkie & Peltola, 1999; Warren & Johnson, 1995). Careers are especially demanding when a worker is getting established or being promoted. Both kinds of demands frequently occur in young adulthood.

Working men and women seem equally affected by physical and psychological stress, whether due to work interfering with family life or the other way around (Frone, Russell, & Barnes, 1996), and they tend to feel equally successful in maintaining a satisfactory balance (Milkie & Peltola, 1999). However, men and women may be stressed by different aspects of the work-family situation. Among 314 spouses with relatively high income and education, husbands were more likely to suffer from overload (perhaps because they had not been socialized to deal with domestic as well as occupational responsibilities). Women were more likely to feel the strain of conflicting role expectations—the need to be aggressive and competitive at work but compassionate and nurturing at home (Paden & Buehler, 1995).

Division of Domestic Work and Effects on the Marriage

The division of labor among dual-income couples tends to be different from that in one-paycheck families. The father is likely to do more housework and child care than the husband of a full-time homemaker (Almeida, Maggs, &

Galambos, 1993; Demo, 1991; Parke & Buriel, 1998) and to do more monitoring of older children's activities, especially in summer, when school is not in session (Crouter, Helms-Erikson, Updegraff, & McHale, in press; Crouter & McHale, 1993).

Nevertheless, the burdens of the dual-earner lifestyle generally fall most heavily on the woman. In 1997, employed married men spent nearly one hour more on household chores and one-half hour more with their children on workdays than in 1977; yet the husbands still did only about two-thirds as much domestic work and child care as employed married women (Bond & Galinsky, 1998).

The effects of a dual-earner lifestyle on a marriage may depend largely on how husband and wife view their roles. Unequal roles are not necessarily seen as inequitable, and it may be a *perception* of unfairness that contributes most to marital instability. A national longitudinal survey of 3,284 women in two-income families found greater likelihood of divorce the more hours the woman worked—*if* she had a nontraditional view of marital roles. Given that men generally do less household work than women, an employed woman who believes in an equal division of labor is likely to perceive as unfair the greater burden she carries in comparison with her husband; and this perception of unfairness will probably be magnified the more hours she puts in on the job (Greenstein, 1995).

What spouses perceive as fair may depend on the size of the wife's financial contribution, whether she thinks of herself as a coprovider or merely as supplementing her husband's income, and the meaning and importance she and her husband place on her work. Whatever the actual division of labor, couples who agree on their assessment of it and who enjoy a harmonious, caring, involved family life are more satisfied than those who do not (Gilbert, 1994).

Family-friendly policies in the workplace can help alleviate the strains experienced by dual-earner families. Parents in a supportive, flexible work environment with family-oriented benefits tend to feel less stress (Warren & Johnson, 1995). Such benefits can include more part-time, flex-time, and shared jobs; more at-home work (without loss of fringe benefits); more affordable high-quality child care; and tax credits or other assistance to let new parents postpone returning to work. One encouraging change is the Family and Medical Leave Act of 1993, which requires businesses with 50 or more workers to offer 12 weeks of unpaid leave for the birth or adoption of a child—though this still falls far short of (for example) the 6-month paid leave offered to new parents in Sweden.

CHECKPOINT

Can you . . .

- ✔ Describe trends in family size and age of parenthood?
- ✔ Compare men's and women's attitudes toward parenthood and parental responsibilities?
- ✔ Discuss how parenthood affects marital satisfaction?
- ✔ Give reasons why some couples choose not to become parents?
- ✔ Identify sources of stress in dual-earner families, and discuss how division of labor can affect the stability of the marriage?

Consider this . . .

- What advice would you give a dual-earner couple on how to handle family responsibilities?

When Marriage Ends

A popular play in the 1950s was *The Seven-Year Itch* by George Axelrod. The title still reflects reality: the average marriage in the United States lasts seven years (Amato & Booth, 1997). The high divorce rate shows how hard it is to attain the goals for which people marry, but the high remarriage rate shows that people keep trying, as Ingrid Bergman did. Divorce, more often than not, leads to remarriage with a new partner and the formation of a **blended family,** which includes children born to or adopted by one or both partners before the current marriage.

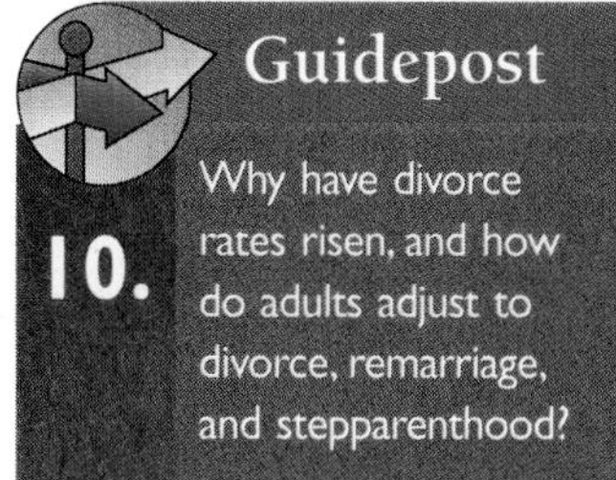

Guidepost
10.
Why have divorce rates risen, and how do adults adjust to divorce, remarriage, and stepparenthood?

Divorce

The United States has one of the highest divorce rates in the world: in 1998, according to provisional data, about 4 divorces a year per 1,000 population (National Center for Health Statistics [NCHS], 1999b). The number of divorces—more than 1.1 million a year—has tripled since 1960 (Amato & Booth, 1997; NCHS, 1999b). The divorce rate peaked in 1979 and now has leveled off (Singh, Mathews, Clarke, Yannicos, & Smith, 1995). Divorce also has skyrocketed in many other developed countries (see Figure 14-5).

blended family
Family consisting of a married couple, at least one of whom is remarried, which includes children born to or adopted by one or both partners before the current marriage.

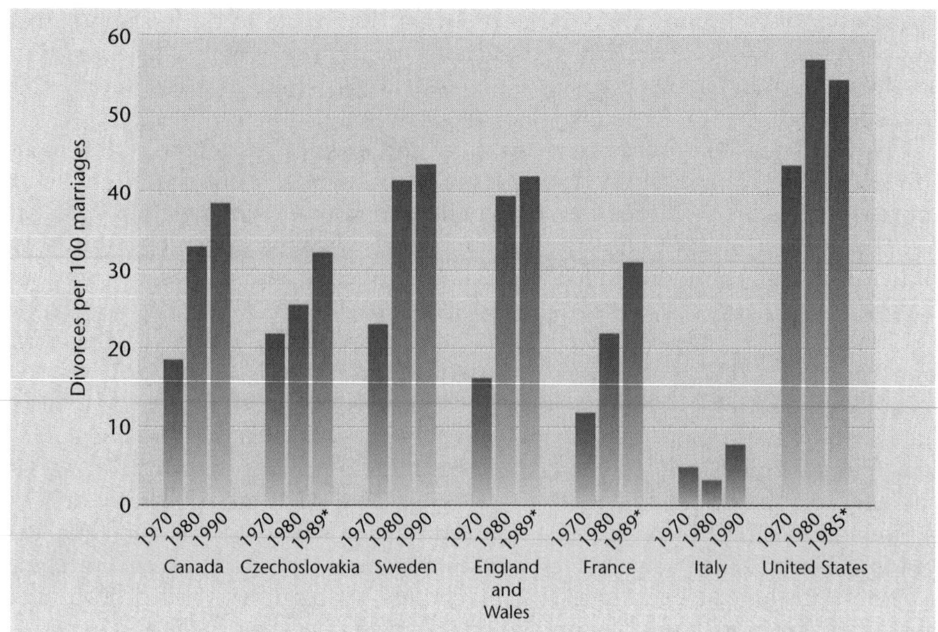

*Latest year a comparable figure was calculated

Figure 14-5
Divorce rates before and after the passage of more lenient divorce laws in the United States and many European countries. Divorce has risen since 1970 in many industrial societies, but rates remain relatively low in Italy, where religious opposition has prevented liberalization of divorce.
(Source: Burns, 1992.)

Why Has Divorce Increased?

The increase in divorce has accompanied the passage of more liberal divorce laws, which eliminate the need to find one partner at fault. No-fault laws were a response to societal developments that prompted a greater demand for divorce (Nakonezny, Shull, & Rodgers, 1995). A woman who is financially independent is less likely to remain in a bad marriage; and women today are more likely than men to initiate a divorce (Braver & O'Connell, 1998; Crane, Soderquist, & Gardner, 1995). Instead of staying together "for the sake of the children," many embattled spouses conclude that exposing children to continued parental conflict does greater damage—though research suggests that that is not always true (refer back to Box 10-1 in Chapter 10). And, for the increasing number of childless couples, it's easier to return to a single state (Berscheid & Campbell, 1981; Eisenberg, 1995). Perhaps most important, while most people today hope their marriages will endure, fewer *expect* them to last. Indeed, so expectable has divorce become that some sociologists refer to "starter marriages"—first marriages without children, from which a person moves on as from a first house (Amato & Booth, 1997).

Consider this . . .

- Has divorce become too easy to obtain in the United States?

On the other hand, in some ways young people today may expect *too much* from marriage. Young adults who live far from their families of origin may expect their spouses to take the place of parents and friends, as well as being confidantes and lovers—an impossibly tall order. Conflicts between men's and women's expectations may produce tension.

Adjusting to Divorce

Divorce is not a single event. It is a *process* with an indefinite beginning and ending—"a sequence of potentially stressful experiences that begin before physical separation and continue after it" (Morrison & Cherlin, 1995, p. 801). Ending even an unhappy marriage can be extremely painful, especially when there are children. (Issues concerning children's adjustment to divorce are discussed in Chapter 10.)

For the former spouses, divorce can bring feelings of failure, blame, hostility, and self-recrimination, as well as high rates of illness and death (Kitson & Morgan, 1990). Depression and disorganized thinking and functioning are common after divorce. So are relief and hope for a fresh start (J. B. Kelly, 1982; Kitson & Roach, 1989; Thabes, 1997).

Adjustment depends partly on how the ex-partners feel about themselves and each other and on how the divorce is handled. The person who takes the first step to end a marriage often feels a mixture of relief, sadness, guilt, apprehension, and anger. Nonetheless, the initiating partner is usually in better emotional shape in the early months of separation than the other partner, who has the additional pain of rejection, loss of control, and feelings of powerlessness (J. B. Kelly, 1982; Pettit & Bloom, 1984). Among 272 divorced women surveyed an average of fourteen years after divorce, about half had initiated the breakup but about 80 percent of the whole sample said it had taken them three years or more to feel comfortable being unattached. Older women, those without young children, those who had not been abused during their marriage, those with higher incomes, and those who had had good legal representation during the divorce tended to adjust better (Thabes, 1997).

An important factor in adjustment is emotional detachment from the former spouse. People who argue with their ex-mates or have not found a new lover or spouse experience more distress. An active social life, both at the time of divorce and afterward, helps (Thabes, 1997; Tschann, Johnston, & Wallerstein, 1989).

Among 290 divorced parents, most of them white and well educated, those who made the best adjustment had more personal resources before the separation: higher socioeconomic status for men and better psychological functioning for women. Those whose income dropped less adjusted better (Tschann et al., 1989). Divorced people in less advantaged circumstances tend to have more difficulties: a lower standard of living, increased work hours, and continued struggles with an ex-spouse who may default on child support (Kitson & Morgan, 1990). According to government figures, only 52 percent of custodial mothers and 43 percent of custodial fathers receive full child support payments; about one-fourth of women (24 percent) and more than one-third (37 percent) of men with support awards receive no payments at all (U.S. Bureau of the Census, 1996a). The lower a man's income, the less likely he is to come up with support money (Meyer & Bartfeld, 1996). However, the "deadbeat dad" problem may have been exaggerated by official reliance on mothers' reports (Braver & O'Connell, 1998; refer back to Chapter 10).

Remarriage and Stepparenthood

Remarriage, said the essayist Samuel Johnson, "is the triumph of hope over experience." The high divorce rate is not a sign that people do not want to be married. Instead, it often reflects a desire to be *happily* married and a belief that divorce is like surgery—painful and traumatic, but necessary for a better life. In a survey of 272 divorced women, reported in the preceding section, while more than 50 percent said they did not miss marriage, more than 90 percent said they would consider marrying again if they met the right person (Thabes, 1997).

An estimated three-quarters of divorced women in the United States remarry, and men are even likelier to remarry than women. Thus in 1998 only about 1 in 10 adults were currently divorced (U.S. Bureau of the Census, 1998). A woman is more likely to remarry if her first marriage was brief, if she was young when it ended, if she has no children, if she is non-Hispanic white, if she has a high school education, or if she lives in the west. Remarriages tend to be less stable than first marriages (Parke & Buriel, 1998).

Remarriage often brings a transition to stepparenthood. Becoming a stepparent presents special problems and concerns, and this may be especially true for stepmothers (refer back to Chapter 10). Interviews with 138 married or cohabiting stepparents who also had biological children in the home found that women had more trouble than men did in raising stepchildren, as compared with raising

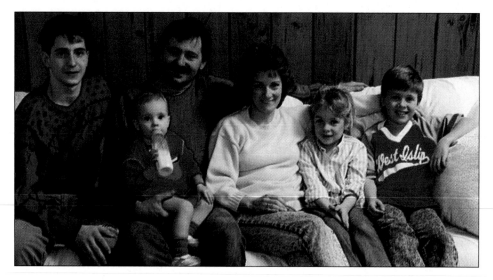

This "blended" family consists of a couple and three sets of children: a teenager from the husband's first marriage, two children from the wife's first marriage, and a toddler from the present marriage. Life is more complex in such families and presents special problems for stepparents, but most children in blended families adjust and thrive.

biological children. This may be because women generally spend more time with the children than men do. It does not seem to matter whether the biological children are from a previous marriage or the present one. The more recent the current marriage and the older the stepchildren, the harder stepparenting seems to be (MacDonald & DeMaris, 1996).

When stepparents rate their marriage and their relationships with their children, they seem less able to separate their feelings about the marriage from their feelings about their success as stepparents than they can with regard to their relationships with their biological children (Fine & Kurdek, 1995). The connection between satisfaction with stepparenting and with the marriage may have to do with the fact that both begin at the same time and are inextricably linked. When problems arise in raising stepchildren, the stepparent is likely to blame the biological parent (for example, for taking the child's side in an argument). The biological parent, whose relationship with the child is more secure, is less likely to blame the stepparent for trouble involving the child.

Challenging as stepparenting can be, one study found that blended families are no more likely than intact families to experience marital conflict (MacDonald & DeMaris, 1995). Findings differ as to whether a new baby increases or decreases tension in a blended family. Some researchers suggest that the impact of the birth may depend on what progress the reconstituted family has made toward becoming a real family unit.

For people who have been bruised by loss, the blended family has the potential to provide a warm, nurturing atmosphere, as does any family that cares about all its members. Successful, research-based strategies for building a blended family include the following (Visher & Visher, 1983; 1989, 1991):

- *Have realistic expectations:* Stepparents need to remember that a blended family is different from a biological family. Children may act out feelings of loss and insecurity. It takes time for new, loving relationships to develop.
- *Recognize divided loyalties:* A child who rejects a warm, loving stepparent may feel caught in a conflict of loyalties. Such conflict can be diminished by maintaining a courteous relationship with the absent parent. Children adjust best when they have close ties with both parents, are not used as weapons by angry parents to hurt each other, and do not have to hear a parent or stepparent insult the other parent.

- *Develop new customs and relationships within the stepfamily:* Blended families need to build new traditions and develop new ways of doing things. They need to see what is positive about their differences and how to make the most of diverse resources and experiences. Children need time alone with the biological parent, time alone with the stepparent, and time with both parents. The couple also need time alone.
- *Seek social support:* Sharing feelings, frustrations, and triumphs with other stepparents and stepchildren can help the whole family see their own situation more realistically and benefit from the experiences of others.

The bonds forged in young adulthood with friends, lovers, spouses, and children often endure throughout life and influence development in middle and late adulthood. The changes people experience in their more mature years also affect their relationships, as we'll see in Parts Seven and Eight.

CHECKPOINT

Can you . . .

✔ Explain why divorce has increased?

✔ Discuss factors in adjustment to divorce?

✔ Summarize findings about the prevalence and success of remarriage after divorce?

✔ Identify special challenges of stepparenting and recommendations for dealing with them?

Summary

Psychosocial Development: Four Approaches

Guidepost 1. Does personality change during adulthood, and if so, how?

- Whether and how personality changes during adulthood is an important issue among developmental theorists. Four important perspectives on adult personality are offered by **trait models, typological models, normative-crisis models,** and the **timing-of-events model.**
- The **five-factor model** of Costa and McCrae is organized around five groupings of related traits: neuroticism, extraversion, openness to experience, conscientiousness, and agreeableness. Studies find that people change very little in these respects after age 30.
- Typological research, pioneered by Jack Block, has identified personality types that differ in **ego-resiliency** and **ego-control.** These types seem to persist from childhood through adulthood.
- Normative-crisis models hold that age-related social and emotional change emerges in successive periods marked by crises. In Erikson's theory, the crisis of young adulthood is **intimacy versus isolation.** In Levinson's theory, transitions or crises lead to reevaluation and modification of the **life structure.** In the Grant Study, mature **adaptive mechanisms** were associated with greater well-being.
- The timing-of-events model, advocated by Neugarten, proposes that adult psychosocial development is influenced by the occurrence and timing of **normative life events.** As society becomes less age-conscious, however, this **social clock** has less meaning.
- Recently there have been attempts to synthesize various approaches to adult psychosocial development.

Foundations of Intimate Relationships

Guidepost 2. What is intimacy, and how is it expressed in friendship, sexuality, and love?

- Self-disclosure and a sense of belonging are important aspects of intimacy. Intimate relationships are associated with physical and mental health.
- Most young adults have friends but have increasingly limited time to spend with them. Women's friendships tend to be more intimate than men's.
- According to Sternberg's **triangular theory of love,** love has three aspects: intimacy, passion, and commitment. These combine into eight types of love relationships.
- People tend to choose partners like themselves. According to evolutionary psychology, males and females choose partners likely to help perpetuate their genetic legacy.
- Although attitudes toward premarital sex have been greatly liberalized, disapproval of homosexuality and extramarital sex remain strong.

Nonmarital and Marital Lifestyles

Guidepost 3. Why do some people remain single?

- Today more adults postpone marriage or never marry. Reasons for staying single include career opportunities, travel, sexual and lifestyle freedom, a desire for self-fulfillment, women's greater self-sufficiency, reduced social pressure to marry, fear of divorce, and difficulty in finding a suitable mate.

Guidepost 4. How do homosexuals deal with "coming out," and what is the nature of gay and lesbian relationships?

- For homosexuals, the process of **coming out** may last well into adulthood, and complete openness about their sexual orientation may never be fully achieved. Both gay men and women form enduring sexual and romantic relationships. Homosexuals in the United States are fighting for rights married people enjoy.

Guidepost 5. What are the pros and cons of cohabitation?

- **Cohabitation** has become common and is the norm in many countries. Cohabitation can be a "trial marriage" or a way of having an intimate relationship for couples not ready for marriage. Couples who cohabit before marriage tend to have weaker marriages.

Guidepost 6. What do adults gain from marriage, what cultural patterns surround entrance into marriage, and why do some marriages succeed while others fail?

- Marriage (in a variety of forms) is universal and meets basic economic, emotional, sexual, social, and childraising needs.
- Mate selection and marrying age vary across cultures. People in industrialized nations have been marrying later than in past generations.
- Frequency of sexual relations in marriage declines with age and loss of novelty. Fewer people appear to be having extramarital sexual relationships than in the past.
- Success in marriage may depend on strength of commitment and patterns of interaction set in young adulthood. Age at marriage is a major predictor of whether a marriage will last. Resilience in facing economic hardship, compatibility, emotional support, and men's and women's differing expectations may be important factors.

Family Life

Guidepost 7. When do most adults become parents, and how does parenthood affect a marriage?

- Family patterns vary across cultures and have changed greatly in western societies. Today women, especially educated ones, are having fewer children and having them later in life.
- Men tend to want children more than women do, but fathers are usually less involved in child raising than mothers.
- Marital satisfaction typically declines during the childbearing years. Expectations and sharing of tasks can contribute to a marriage's deterioration or improvement.

Guidepost 8. Why do some couples choose to remain childless?

- An increasing number of couples remain childless by choice. Reasons include a desire to concentrate on careers or an adult lifestyle or to retain greater marital intimacy, feelings of inadequacy for parenthood, and unwillingness to take on its financial burdens.

Guidepost 9. How do dual-earner couples divide responsibilities and deal with role conflicts?

- Women and men are equally affected by the stress of a dual-earner lifestyle, but they may be affected in different ways.
- In most cases, the burdens of a dual-earner lifestyle fall most heavily on the woman. Whether an unequal division of labor contributes to marital distress may depend on how the spouses perceive their roles.
- Family-friendly workplace policies can help alleviate stress in dual-earner families.

When Marriage Ends

Guidepost 10. Why have divorce rates risen, and how do adults adjust to divorce, remarriage, and stepparenthood?

- The United States has one of the highest divorce rates in the world. Among the reasons for the rise in divorce are women's greater financial independence, reluctance to expose children to parental conflict, and the greater "expectability" of divorce.
- Divorce usually entails a painful period of adjustment. Adjustment may depend on the way the divorce is handled, people's feelings about themselves and their ex-partners, emotional detachment from the former spouse, social support, and personal resources.
- Most divorced people remarry, but remarriages tend to be less stable than first marriages.
- In **blended families,** stepmothers, who are usually more involved in the raising of stepchildren than are stepfathers, tend to have more difficulty being stepparents.

Key Terms

trait models (523)
typological models (523)
normative-crisis models (523)
timing-of-events model (523)
five-factor model (524)
ego-resiliency (525)
ego-control (525)
intimacy versus isolation (526)
adaptive mechanisms (527)
life structure (527)
normative life events (529)
social clock (529)
triangular theory of love (534)
coming out (536)
cohabitation (538)
blended family (547)

Middle Adulthood

When does middle age begin? Is it at the birthday party when you see your cake ablaze with forty candles? Is it the day your "baby" leaves home and you now have time to pursue those activities you've put on hold for so long? Is it the day when you notice that police officers seem to be getting younger?

When does middle age end? Is it at your retirement party? Is it the day you get your Medicare card? Is it the first time someone younger gets up to give you a seat on the bus?

Middle adulthood has many markers, and they are not the same for everyone. The middle years are the central years of the adult life span, but their content varies greatly. At 40, some people become parents for the first time, while others become grandparents. At 50, some people are starting new careers, while others are taking early retirement.

As in earlier years, all aspects of development are interrelated. In Chapters 15 and 16, we note, for example, the psychological impact of menopause (and debunk some myths about it!), and we see how mature thinkers combine logic and emotion.

Linkups to Look For

- Some physical skills improve with age, due to practice, experience, and judgment.
- Physical symptoms associated with menopause seem to be affected by attitudes toward aging.
- Stressful experiences often lead to illness.
- Postformal thinking is especially useful with regard to social problems.
- Personality characteristics play an important role in creative performance.
- Modifications in men's and women's personalities at midlife have been attributed both to hormonal changes and to cultural shifts in gender roles.
- Responsibility for aging parents can affect physical and mental health.

Middle Adulthood: *A Preview*

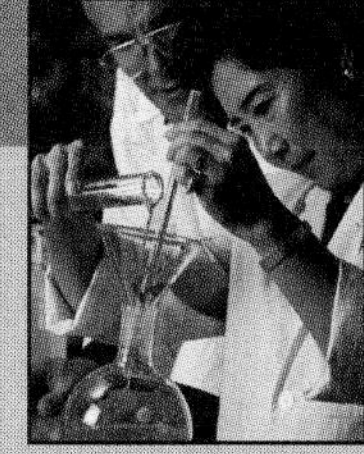

Chapter 15

Physical and Cognitive Development in Middle Adulthood

Some deterioration of sensory abilities, health, stamina, and prowess may take place.

Women experience menopause.

Most basic mental abilities peak; expertise and practical problem-solving skills are high.

Creative output may decline but improve in quality.

For some, career success and earning powers peak; for others, burnout or career change may occur.

Chapter 16

Psychosocial Development in Middle Adulthood

Sense of identity continues to develop; midlife transition may occur.

Double responsibilities of caring for children and elderly parents may cause stress.

Launching of children leaves empty nest.

Chapter 15

Physical and Cognitive Development in Middle Adulthood

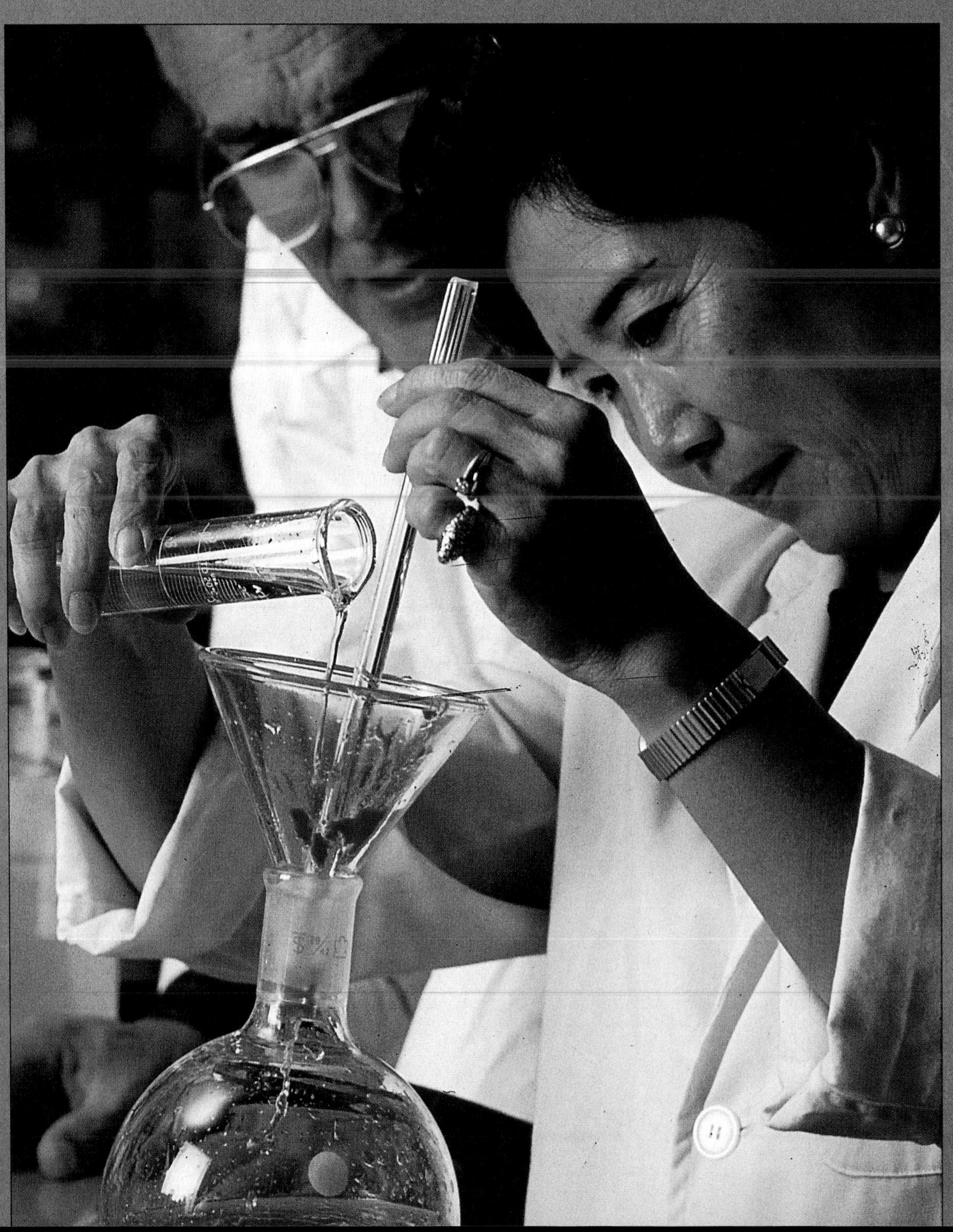

The primitive, physical, functional pattern of the morning of life, the active years before forty or fifty, is outlived. But there is still the afternoon opening up, which one can spend not in the feverish pace of the morning but in having time at last for those intellectual, cultural, and spiritual activities that were pushed aside in the heat of the race.

Anne Morrow Lindbergh, *Gift from the Sea*, 1955

OUTLINE

Mahatma Gandhi

Focus: Mahatma Gandhi, Father of a Nation

Mohandas Karamchand Gandhi (1869–1948)* was called *Mahatma* (Great Soul) by the people of his native India, whom he led to freedom from British colonial rule through a decades-long campaign of nonviolent resistance. His revolutionary ideas and practices profoundly influenced other world leaders, notably Nelson Mandela and Martin Luther King, Jr. He is considered one of the greatest moral exemplars of all time.

The son of an uneducated merchant, Ghandi admitted to less than average intellectual ability, but his linguistic and interpersonal skills were strong. He had a keen moral

*Sources of biographical information about Gandhi included J. M. Brown (1989), Gandhi (1948), Gardner (1997), and Kumar & Puri (1983).

sense and was a lifelong seeker of truth. He had the courage to challenge authority and take risks for a worthy goal.

As a young lawyer in South Africa, another British colony, he saw and experienced the discrimination the Indian minority suffered. It was in South Africa that Gandhi began to develop his philosophy of *satyagraha,* nonviolent social action. He organized civil disobedience campaigns and peaceful marches. Time and again, he invited arrest; in 1908, approaching his fortieth year, he was jailed for the first time. Eventually he would spend a total of seven years in prison.

Gandhi "felt he could not proceed as an ethical agent, seeking a better life for his people, unless he had himself attained and come to embody moral authority. He had to purify himself before he could make demands of others" (Gardner, 1997, p. 115). He moved with his wife and four sons from the South African capital, Johannesburg, to a farm outside Durban. He did daily exercises, prepared his own food, and gave up western dress for simple Indian garb. He founded a collective farm based on ascetic and cooperative principles.

Returning to India, Gandhi became the acknowledged leader of a nationalist movement. He taught his people to show forbearance. When a street mob in a small town rioted and killed police, he called off political actions throughout India. When mill owners were unbending and strikers became restive, he put his own physical well-being on the line by fasting until a satisfactory settlement was reached.

In 1930, to protest a tax on manufactured salt, Ghandi, now 60, led a 200-mile march to the sea, where hundreds of followers illegally extracted salt from seawater. The event, reminiscent of the Boston Tea Party, triggered protests all over India. When British police attacked and beat a line of peaceful marchers, their brutality made headlines around the world. It was the beginning of the end for British domination.

Gandhi's influence was the product of a seamless web of body, mind, and spirit. By living out his ideals, he was effective in solving real, almost intractable problems that affected millions of people. In his efforts to defuse conflict and inspire cooperation, he showed wisdom grounded in moral vision.

Few of us reach the heights of intelligence and creativity or achieve the moral and spiritual heights Gandhi did, and few of us have such influential careers. But caring and concern for others, including the generations to follow, are important in any adult, as is the work to which one chooses to devote one's life. As with Gandhi, these features tend to intensify or come to fruition in middle age.

In this chapter, we examine physical changes common in middle adulthood. We discuss how health problems may be worsened by poverty, racial discrimination, and other stresses. We consider how intelligence changes, how thought processes mature, what underlies creative performance and moral leadership such as Gandhi's, and how careers develop.

After you have read and studied this chapter, you should be able to answer the following questions:

Guideposts *for* **Study**

1. What are the distinguishing features of middle age?
2. What physical changes generally occur during the middle years, and what is their psychological impact?
3. What factors affect health at midlife?
4. What cognitive gains and losses occur during middle age?
5. Do mature adults think differently than younger people?
6. What accounts for creative achievement, and how does it change with age?
7. How have work patterns changed, and how does work contribute to cognitive development?
8. What is the value of education for mature learners?

Middle Age: A Cultural Construct

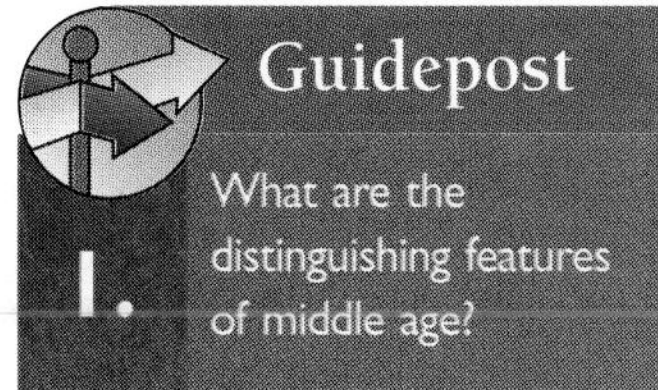

Guidepost

1. What are the distinguishing features of middle age?

Until recently, middle adulthood has been the least studied part of the life span. With the exception of the now largely discredited idea of the "midlife crisis" (see Chapter 16), the middle years were considered a relatively uneventful hiatus between the more dramatic changes of young adulthood and old age. Now that the "baby boom" generation is in middle age, research on that period is booming (Lachman & James, 1997; Moen & Wethington, 1999). In the United States, between 1990 and 2015, the 45- to 64-year-old population is expected to increase by 72 percent, from 47 to 80 million. This is the best educated and most affluent cohort ever to reach middle age anywhere, and it is changing our perspective on the importance and meaning of that time of life (Willis & Reid, 1999).

The concept of middle age is relatively new; the term came into use in Europe and the United States around the turn of the twentieth century. Today people in industrial societies are living far longer than in earlier times (see Figure 17-2 in Chapter 17), well past the years of active parenting, and middle adulthood has become a distinct stage of life with its own societal norms, roles, opportunities, and challenges. Thus some scholars describe "middle age" as a socially constructed concept, with culturally ascribed meaning (Gullette, 1998; Moen & Wethington, 1999). Indeed, some traditional societies, such as the Gusii in Kenya, do not recognize a middle stage of adulthood at all (see Box 16-1 in Chapter 16).

Ironically, as medical and nutritional advances have opened up an unprecedented second half of life in more developed societies, anxiety about physical and other losses has become a major theme in popular descriptions of middle age. In a youth-oriented culture, adults' expectations for these years may be influenced more by images in literature and the media than by what is going on in their own bodies and minds (Gullette, 1998). A life-span developmental perspective (refer back to Chapter 1) presents a more balanced, more complex picture. Middle age can be a time, not primarily of decline, but of personal growth (Lock, 1998; Moen & Wethington, 1999).

As life continues to lengthen and diversify, it is increasingly difficult to generalize about the middle years (Lachman & James, 1997). It is even difficult to say when they begin and end. With improvements in health and length of life, the upper limits of middle age are rising (Stewart & Ostrove, 1998). In one study, young adults in their twenties defined middle age as lasting from about 30 to 55, but older adults in their sixties and seventies saw the middle years as beginning at 40 and extending into the seventies (Lachman, Lewkowicz, Marcus, & Peng, 1994).

In this book, we define *middle adulthood,* in chronological terms, as the years between ages 40 and 65, but this definition is arbitrary. Middle age also can be defined contextually, and the two definitions may differ. One context is the family: a middle-aged person is sometimes described as one with grown children and/or elderly parents. Yet today some people in their forties and beyond are still raising young children; and some adults at any age have no children at all. Those with grown children may find the nest emptying—or filling up again. Age also has a biological aspect: a 50-year-old who has exercised regularly is likely to be biologically younger than a 35-year-old whose most strenuous exercise is clicking the remote control.

The meaning of middle age varies with health, gender, ethnicity, socioeconomic status, cohort, and culture (Helson, 1997; Moen & Wethington, 1999). Most middle-aged people in the United States today are in good physical, cognitive, and emotional shape—more so than in any previous generation—and feel good about the quality of their lives (see Figure 15-1). But earlier deprivation and disadvantage can limit opportunities and options at midlife (Moen & Wethington, 1999). The middle years are marked by growing individual differences based on prior choices and experiences, as well as on genetic makeup (Lachman & James, 1997). Some middle-aged people can run a marathon; others get winded climbing a steep stairway. Some have sharper memory than ever; others feel their memory beginning to slip. Some, like Gandhi, are at the height of creativity or careers; others have gotten a slow start or have reached dead ends. Still others dust off mothballed dreams or pursue new goals.

Middle age generally is a busy, sometimes a stressful time. Often it is filled with heavy responsibilities and multiple, demanding roles—responsibilities and roles that most adults feel competent to handle: running households, departments, or enterprises; launching children; and perhaps caring for aging parents or starting new midlife careers (Gallagher, 1993; Lachman et al., 1994; Merrill & Verbrugge, 1999). Many middle-aged people experience a heightened sense of success and control in work and social relationships, along with a more realistic awareness of their limitations and of outside forces they *cannot* control (Clark-Plaskie & Lachman, 1999).

Midlife is a time to look both backward and forward, at the years already lived and the years yet to live. This can be a time of taking stock, of reevaluating goals and aspirations and how well they have been fulfilled, and deciding how best to use the remaining part of the lifespan (Lachman & James, 1997).

Consider this . . .

- When would you say middle age begins and ends?
- Think of people you know who call themselves middle-aged. How old are they? Do they seem to be in good health? How involved are they in work or other activities?

CHECKPOINT

Can you . . .

✔ Explain why middle age is considered a cultural construct and why it has been relatively unstudied until recently?

✔ Differentiate between chronological, contextual, and biological meanings of middle age?

✔ Identify factors that contribute to individual differences in adjustment in middle adulthood?

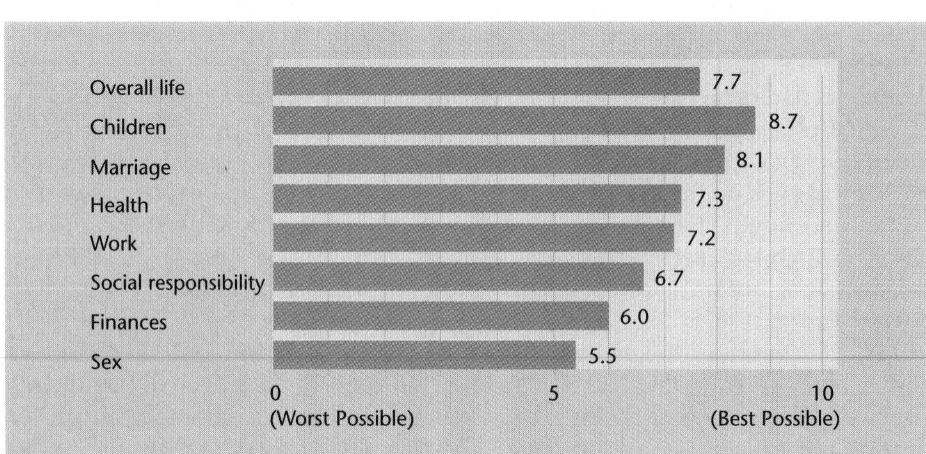

Figure 15-1

How middle-aged adults rate aspects of their quality of life.

(Source: Goode, 1999; data from MacArthur Foundation Research Network on Successful Midlife Development.)

Physical Development

Physical Changes

"Use it or lose it" is the motto of many middle-aged people who have taken up jogging, racquetball, tennis, aerobic dancing, and other forms of physical activity. Research bears out the wisdom of that creed. Some physiological changes are direct results of biological aging and genetic makeup; but an accumulation of behavioral factors and lifestyle, dating from youth, affect the likelihood, timing, and extent of physical change. By the same token, health and lifestyle habits in the middle years influence what happens in the years beyond (Merrill & Verbrugge, 1999). People who limit their exposure to the sun can minimize wrinkling and avoid skin cancer; and people who are physically active can retain muscle strength—a powerful predictor of physical condition in old age. In a longitudinal study of 6,089 Japanese American men, ages 45 to 68, in Oahu, Hawaii, strength of hand grip predicted which men were likely to have functional limitations and disabilities twenty-five years later (Rantanen et al., 1999).

Guidepost

2. What physical changes generally occur during the middle years, and what is their psychological impact?

The more people do, the more they *can* do. People who become active early in life reap the benefits of more stamina and more resilience after age 60 (Spirduso & MacRae, 1990). People who lead sedentary lives lose muscle tone and energy and become even less inclined to exert themselves physically. Still, as Gandhi realized, it is never too late to adopt a healthier lifestyle. Middle-aged people who had unhealthful habits in their youth can improve their physical well-being by changing their behavior (Merrill & Verbrugge, 1999).

The mind and the body have ways of compensating for changes that do occur. Most middle-aged people are realistic enough to take in stride alterations in appearance, in sensory, motor, and systemic functioning, and in reproductive and sexual capacities; and some experience a sexual renaissance.

Sensory and Psychomotor Functioning

From young adulthood through the middle years, sensory and motor changes are small, gradual, and almost imperceptible (Merrill & Verbrugge, 1999)—until one

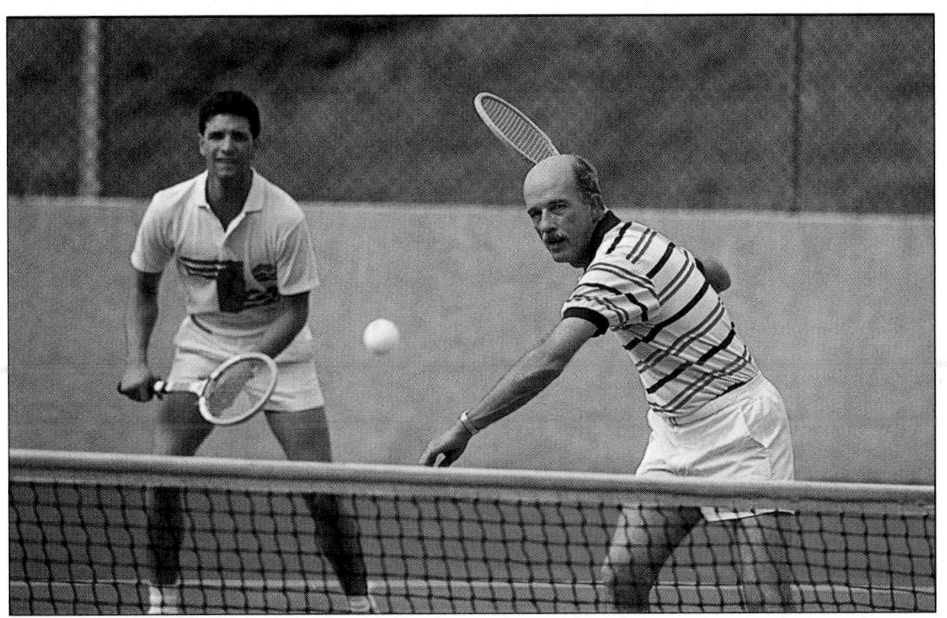

Many middle-aged people find that their improved ability to use strategies in a sport, as a result of experience and better judgment, outweigh the changes in strength, coordination, and reaction time that are common in midlife. A consistent exercise program beginning in young adulthood, such as playing tennis regularly, can help build muscles and maintain stamina and resilience in middle and old age.

day a 45-year-old man realizes that he cannot read the telephone directory without eyeglasses, or a 60-year-old woman has to admit that she is not as quick on her feet as she was.

Age-related visual problems occur mainly in five areas: *near vision, dynamic vision* (reading moving signs), *sensitivity to light, visual search* (for example, locating a sign), and *speed of processing* visual information (Kline et al., 1992; Kline & Scialfa, 1996; Kosnik, Winslow, Kline, Rasinski, & Sekuler, 1988). Also common is a slight loss in *visual acuity,* or sharpness of vision. Because of changes in the pupil of the eye, middle-aged people may need about one-third more brightness to compensate for the loss of light reaching the retina (Belbin, 1967; Troll, 1985).

presbyopia
Farsightedness associated with aging, resulting when the lens of the eye becomes less elastic.

myopia
Nearsightedness.

presbycusis
Gradual loss of hearing, which accelerates after age 55, especially with regard to sounds at the upper frequencies.

Because the lens of the eye becomes progressively less flexible, its ability to shift focus diminishes; this change usually becomes noticeable in early middle age and is practically complete by age 60 (Kline & Scialfa, 1996). Many people age 40 and older need reading glasses for **presbyopia,** a lessened ability to focus on near objects—a condition associated with aging. (The prefix *presby-* means "with age.") The incidence of **myopia** (nearsightedness) also increases through middle age (Merrill & Verbrugge, 1999). Bifocals and trifocals—eyeglasses in which lenses for reading are combined with lenses for distant vision—aid the eye in adjusting between near and far objects.

A gradual hearing loss, rarely noticed earlier in life, speeds up in the fifties (Merrill & Verbrugge, 1999). This condition, **presbycusis,** normally is limited to higher-pitched sounds than those used in speech (Kline & Scialfa, 1996). By the end of middle age, 1 in 4 people has significant hearing loss (Horvath & Davis, 1990). In some men, a decline in sensitivity to high-frequency sounds may be detected as early as age 30; and hearing loss proceeds twice as quickly in men as in women, even among people who do not work in noisy places (Pearson et al., 1995). Today, a preventable increase in hearing loss is occurring among 45- to 64-year-olds due to continuous or sudden exposure to noise at work, at loud concerts, through earphones, and elsewhere (Wallhagen, Strawbridge, Cohen, & Kaplan, 1997). Hearing losses due to environmental noise can be avoided by wearing hearing protectors, such as earplugs or special earmuffs.

Sensitivity to taste and smell generally begins to decline in midlife (Cain, Reid, & Stevens, 1990; Stevens, Cain, Demarque, & Ruthruff, 1991), especially in people who take medication or undergo medical treatment (Ship & Weiffenbach, 1993). As the taste buds become less sensitive and the number of olfactory cells diminishes, foods may seem more bland (Merrill & Verbrugge, 1999; Troll, 1985). Women tend to retain these senses longer than men. Adults begin to lose sensitivity to touch after age 45, and to pain after age 50. However, pain's protective function remains: although people feel pain less, they become less able to tolerate it (Katchadourian, 1987).

Strength and coordination decline gradually from their peak during the twenties. Some loss of muscle strength is usually noticeable by age 45; 10 to 15 percent of maximum strength may be gone by 60. Most people notice a weakening first in the back and leg muscles and then in the arm and shoulder—the latter, not until well into the sixties. The reason for this loss of strength is a loss of muscle mass, which is replaced by fat. By middle age, body fat, which comprised only 10 percent of body weight during adolescence, typically reaches at least 20 percent (Katchadourian, 1987; Merrill & Verbrugge, 1999; Spence, 1989). However, exercise and good nutrition can increase muscular bulk and density (Katchadourian, 1987; Nelson et al., 1994).

basal metabolism
Use of energy to maintain vital functions.

Endurance often holds up much better than strength (Spirduso & MacRae, 1990). Loss of endurance results from a gradual decrease in the rate of **basal metabolism** (use of energy to maintain vital functions) after age 40 (Merrill & Verbrugge, 1999). "Overpracticed" skills are more resistant to effects of age than those that are used less; thus athletes show a smaller-than-average loss in endurance (Stones & Kozma, 1996).

Simple reaction time, which involves a single response to a single stimulus (such as pressing a button when a light flashes) slows by about 20 percent, on average, between ages 20 and 60 (Birren, Woods, & Williams, 1980), depending on the amount and kind of information to be processed and the kind of response required. When a vocal rather than a manual response is called for, age differences in simple reaction time are substantially less (S. J. Johnson & Rybash, 1993).

Tasks that involve a choice of responses (such as hitting one button when a light flashes and another button when a tone is heard) and complex motor skills involving many stimuli, responses, and decisions (as in driving a car) decline more; but the decline does not necessarily result in poorer performance. Typically, middle-aged adults are better drivers than younger ones (McFarland, Tune, & Welford, 1964); and 60-year-old typists are as efficient as 20-year-olds (Spirduso & MacRae, 1990), apparently because they anticipate the keystrokes that are coming up (Salthouse, 1984).

In these and other activities, knowledge based on experience may more than make up for physical changes. Skilled industrial workers in their forties and fifties are often more productive than ever, partly because they tend to be more conscientious and careful. Middle-aged workers are less likely than younger workers to suffer disabling injuries on the job (Salthouse & Maurer, 1996)—a likely result of experience and good judgment, which compensate for any lessening of coordination and motor skills.

Structural and Systemic Changes

Some structural and systemic changes may become noticeable during the middle years. By the fifth or sixth decade, the skin may become less taut and smooth as the tissues just below the surface lose fat and collagen. Hair may become thinner, due to a slowed replacement rate, and grayer as production of melanin, the pigmenting agent, declines. People perspire less as the number of sweat glands decreases. They tend to gain weight, due to accumulation of body fat, and lose height due to shrinkage of the intervertebral disks (Merrill & Verbrugge, 1999).

Bone density normally peaks in the mid-to late thirties. From then on, people typically experience some net loss of bone as more calcium is absorbed than replaced, causing bones to become thinner and more brittle. Bone loss accelerates in the fifties; it occurs twice as rapidly in women as in men, sometimes leading to osteoporosis (discussed later in this chapter) (Merrill & Verbrugge, 1999). Joints may become stiffer, particularly on waking in the morning, as tendons and ligaments become less efficient (Katchadourian, 1987; Merrill & Verbrugge, 1999; Spence, 1989).

vital capacity
Amount of air that can be drawn in with a deep breath and expelled; may be a biological marker of aging.

Large proportions of middle-aged and even older adults show little or no decline in organ functioning (Gallagher, 1993). In some, however, the heart begins to pump more slowly and irregularly in the midfifties; by 65, it may lose up to 40 percent of its aerobic power. Arterial walls may become thicker and more rigid. Heart disease becomes more common beginning in the late forties or early fifties, especially among men. **Vital capacity**—the maximum volume of air the lungs can draw in and expel—may begin to diminish at about age 40 and may drop by as much as 40 percent by age 70. Temperature regulation and immune response may begin to weaken, and sleep may become less deep (Merrill & Verbrugge, 1999).

CHECKPOINT

Can you . . .

✔ Summarize changes in sensory and motor functioning and body structure and systems that may begin during middle age?

Sexuality and Reproductive Functioning

Sexuality is not just a hallmark of youth. Although both sexes experience losses in reproductive capacity sometime during middle adulthood—women become unable to bear children and men's fertility begins to decline—sexual enjoyment can continue throughout adult life. (Changes in the male and female reproductive systems are summarized in Table 15-1.)

Table 15-1 Changes in Human Reproductive Systems During Middle Age

	Female	Male
Hormonal change	Drop in estrogen and progesterone	Drop in testosterone
Symptoms	Hot flashes, vaginal dryness urinary dysfunction	Undetermined
Sexual changes	Less intense arousal, less frequent and quicker orgasms	Loss of psychological arousal, less frequent erections, slower organisms, longer recovery between ejaculations, increased risk of erectile dysfunction
Reproductive capacity	Ends	Continues; some decrease in fertility may occur

Still, many middle-aged people have concerns related to sexuality and reproductive functioning. Let's look at these.

Menopause and Its Meanings

menopause
Cessation of menstruation and of ability to bear children, typically around age 50.

perimenopause
Period of several years during which a woman experiences physiological changes that bring on menopause; also called *climacteric*.

Menopause takes place when a woman permanently stops ovulating and menstruating and can no longer conceive a child; it is generally considered to have occurred one year after the last menstrual period. In 4 out of 5 women, this happens between ages 45 and 55; on average, at about 51 (Avis, 1999; Merrill & Verbrugge, 1999). Some women, however, experience menstrual changes in their thirties; others, not until their sixties.

The period of several years during which a woman experiences physiological changes that bring on menopause is called **perimenopause,** also known as the *climacteric,* or "change of life." Beginning in her thirties, a woman's production of ova begins to decline imperceptibly. Then, as she nears her fiftieth birthday, the ovaries produce less of the female hormone estrogen. (Small amounts of estrogen continue to be secreted, even after menopause, by the adrenal and other glands.) Menstruation becomes irregular, with less flow than before and a longer time between menstrual periods. In women who have hysterectomies, menopause comes on abruptly, without preparation.

Attitudes Toward Menopause At one time, in rural Ireland, women who no longer menstruated would retire to their beds and stay there, often for years, until they died (U.S. Office of Technology Assessment, 1992). This traditional custom may seem extreme, but the attitude it expressed—that a woman's usefulness ends with her ability to reproduce—was typical in western societies until fairly recently (Avis, 1999; Crowley, 1994). During the early nineteenth century, the term *climacteric* came to mean the "period of life . . . at which the vital forces begin to decline" (Lock, 1998, p. 48). Menopause was seen as a disease, a failure of the ovaries to perform their natural function (Lock, 1998). One twentieth-century psychoanalyst called the loss of reproductive capacity a psychological death (Deutsch, 1945).

By contrast, in some cultures, such as that of the southwestern Papago Indians, menopause seems to be virtually ignored. In other cultures, such as those found in India and South Asia, it is a welcome event; women's status and freedom of movement increase once they are free of taboos connected with menstruation and fertility (Avis, 1999; Lock, 1994).

In the United States today, most women who have gone through menopause view it positively—more so than younger women do (Avis, 1999). For many women, menopause is a sign of a transition into the second half of adult life—a time of role changes, greater independence, and personal growth.

How a woman views menopause may depend on the value she places on being young and attractive, her attitudes toward women's roles, and her own circumstances. A childless woman may see menopause as closing off the possibility of motherhood; a woman who has had and raised children may see it as an opportunity for greater sexual freedom and enjoyment (Avis, 1999).

Symptoms and Myths Most women experience little or no physical discomfort during the perimenopausal period (NIA, 1993). Most common are "hot flashes" (sudden sensations of heat that flash through the body due to expansion and contraction of blood vessels); but many women never have them, while others have them continually (Avis, 1999). Administration of artificial estrogen, discussed later in this chapter, can alleviate hot flashes.

Physical symptoms that affect a small minority of women include vaginal dryness, burning, and itching; vaginal and urinary infections; and urinary dysfunction caused by tissue shrinkage. Some women do not become sexually aroused as readily as before, and some find intercourse painful because of thinning vaginal tissues and inadequate lubrication. Small doses of the male hormone testosterone may solve the first problem, and use of water-soluble gels can prevent or relieve the second. The more sexually active a woman is, the less likely she is to experience such changes (Katchadourian, 1987; King, 1996; Spence, 1989; M. E. Williams, 1995). Other physical problems sometimes reported by menopausal women include joint or muscle pain, headache, insomnia, fatigue, dizziness, weight gain, and constipation; but such symptoms seem to be only indirectly related to menopause, if at all (Avis, 1999; te Velde & van Leusden, 1994).

Such psychological problems as irritability, nervousness, anxiety, depression, memory loss, and even insanity have been blamed on the climacteric, but research shows no reason to attribute mental disturbances to this normal biological change. The myth that menopause produces depression may derive from the fact that women at this time are undergoing changes in roles, relationships, and responsibilities. These changes may be stressful, and the way a woman perceives them can affect her view of menopause. Still, in one study, most women reported *less* stress after menopause than before (Matthews, 1992) Women who are depressed during menopause are likely to have been depressed previously. They also are likely to be among the subgroup of women who report hot flashes, night sweats, or menstrual problems (Avis, 1999).

Taken together, the research suggests that "so-called menopausal syndrome may be related more to personal characteristics or past experiences than to menopause per se" (Avis, 1999, p. 129), as well as to societal views of women and of aging (see Box 15-1). In cultures in which older women acquire social, religious, or political power after menopause, few problems are associated with this natural event (Avis, 1999; Dan & Bernhard, 1989).

Changes in Male Sexuality

Men have no experience comparable to menopause (Sternbach, 1998). They do not undergo a sudden drop in hormone production at midlife, as women do; instead, testosterone levels decrease gradually from the late teens onward, adding up to a 30 to 40 percent reduction by age 70 (King, 1996).

The term *male climacteric* is sometimes used to refer to a period of physiological, emotional, and psychological change involving a man's reproductive system and other body systems. Symptoms supposedly associated with the climacteric include depression, anxiety, irritability, insomnia, fatigue, weakness, lower sexual drive, erectile failure, memory loss, and reduced muscle and bone mass and body hair (Henker, 1981; Sternbach, 1998; Weg, 1989), but it is not clear that these often vaguely defined complaints are related to testosterone levels. Men's psychological adjustments, like women's, may stem from such events as illness, worries about work, children's leaving home, or the death of parents, as well as from negative cultural attitudes toward aging (King, 1996).

Box 15-1
Japanese Women's Experience of Menopause

Many women accept hot flashes and night sweats as normal accompaniments of menopause. However, that apparently is not true everywhere.

Margaret Lock (1994) surveyed 1,316 Japanese women ages 45 to 55—factory workers, farm workers, and homemakers—and compared the results with information from 9,376 women in Massachusetts and Manitoba, Canada. Japanese women's experience of menopause turned out to be quite different from the experience of western women.

Fewer than 10 percent of Japanese women whose menstruation was becoming irregular reported having had hot flashes during the previous two weeks, compared with about 40 percent of the Canadian sample and 35 percent of the U.S. sample. In fact, fewer than 20 percent of Japanese women had *ever* experienced hot flashes, compared with 65 percent of Canadian women, and most of the Japanese women who had experienced hot flashes reported little or no physical or psychological discomfort. (Indeed, so little importance is given in Japan to what in western cultures is considered the chief symptom of menopause that there is no specific Japanese term for "hot flash," even though the Japanese language makes many subtle distinctions about body states.) Furthermore, only about 3 percent of the Japanese women said they experienced night sweats, and Japanese women were far less likely than western women to suffer from insomnia, depression, irritability, or lack of energy (Lock, 1994).

The Japanese women were more likely to report stiffness in the shoulders, headaches, lumbago, constipation, and other complaints that, in western eyes, do not appear directly related to the hormonal changes of menopause (Lock, 1994). Japanese physicians link such symptoms with the decline of the female reproductive cycle, which they believe is associated with changes in the autonomic nervous system (Lock, 1998).

The symptoms physicians noted were quite similar to those the women reported. Hot flashes were not at the top of the doctors' lists and in some cases did not appear at all. However, very few Japanese women consult doctors about menopause or its symptoms, and few physicians prescribe hormone therapy (Lock, 1994).

In Japan, menopause is regarded as a normal event in women's lives, not as a medical condition requiring treatment. The end of menstruation has far less significance than it does for western women; the closest term for it, *kônenki,* refers not specifically to what westerners call menopause, but to a considerably longer period comparable to the perimenopause or climacteric (Lock, 1994, 1998).

Traditional Japanese society focuses on a strict system of stages that each cohort experiences simultaneously, from birth to marriage to parenthood to death. Aging is a social process; individual biological changes are incidental. Even birthday celebrations are a recent innovation! *Kônenki* is just another process connected with aging (Lock, 1998).

Aging itself is less feared than in the west. Passage through most of adulthood is a matter of growing responsibility and status. Not until old age can women and men alike escape the daily round of duty and do as they please. Aging brings not only respect for wisdom, but newfound freedom—as does menopause. Today, Japanese culture is becoming somewhat westernized, and there is a growing tendency to medicalize *kônenki;* but so far, the traditional view prevails (Lock, 1998).

Cultural attitudes, then, may affect how women interpret their physical sensations, and these interpretations may be linked to their feelings about menopause. Hot flashes have been found to be rare or infrequent among Mayan women, North African women in Israel, Navajo women, and some Indonesian women (Beyene, 1986, 1989; Flint & Samil, 1990; Walfish, Antonovsky, & Maoz, 1984; Wright, 1983). For example, Mayan women, who are constantly pregnant or nursing babies, tend to regard childbearing as a burden and to look forward to its end (Beyene, 1986, 1989).

Nutritional practices also may influence the experience of menopause. Some plants, such as soybeans—a staple of Far Eastern diets—contain relatively high amounts of compounds known as *phytoestrogens,* which have a weak estrogen-like effect. A diet high in foods made with these plants, such as tofu and soy flour, may influence hormone levels in the blood. When natural estrogen levels fall during the climacteric, phytoestrogens may act like estrogen and inhibit symptoms of menopause. This, then, might help explain why middle-aged Japanese women do not experience the dramatic effects of a precipitous decline in estrogen levels, as many western women do (Margo N. Woods, M.D., Department of Family Medicine and Community Health, Tufts University School of Medicine, personal communication, November, 1996).

Interestingly, Japanese women, who, as a group, are the longest-lived in the world, have a much lower incidence of osteoporosis than American white women (despite lower average bone mass) and are about one-fourth as likely as American women to die of coronary heart disease. These ailments, in North America, become more common after menopause; their lower incidence before menopause has been attributed to estrogen's protective effect. Might phytoestrogens mimic this effect in postmenopausal Japanese women? Conclusions about the influence of diet on women's health during and after menopause must await the completion of controlled longitudinal studies (Margo N. Woods, personal communication, November, 1996). Meanwhile, the findings about Japanese women's experience of menopause show that even this universal biological event has major cultural variations, once again affirming the importance of cross-cultural research.

Men do show some changes in sexual functioning. Although a man can continue to reproduce until quite late in life, his sperm count begins to decline in the late forties or fifties, making it less likely that he will father a child (Merrill & Verbrugge, 1999). Erections tend to become slower and less firm, orgasms less frequent, and ejaculations less forceful; and it takes longer to recover and ejaculate again (Bremner, Vitiello, & Prinz, 1983; Katchadourian, 1987; King, 1996; Masters & Johnson, 1966). Still, sexual excitation and sexual activity can remain a normal, vital part of life.

An estimated 39 percent of 40-year-old men and 67 percent of 70-year-old men experience **erectile dysfunction** (popularly called *impotence*): persistent inability to achieve or maintain an erect enough penis for satisfactory sexual performance (Feldman, Goldstein, Hatzichristou, Krane, & McKinlay, 1994; Goldstein et al., 1998). According to the Massachusetts Male Aging Study, about 5 percent of 40-year-old and 15 percent of 70-year-old men are completely impotent (Feldman et al., 1994). Diabetes, hypertension, high cholesterol, kidney failure, depression, neurological disorders, and many chronic diseases are associated with erectile dysfunction (Utiger, 1998). Alcohol, drugs, smoking, poor sexual techniques, lack of knowledge, unsatisfying relationships, anxiety, and stress can be contributing factors.

erectile dysfunction
Inability of a man to achieve or maintain an erect penis sufficient for satisfactory sexual performance.

Some men suffering erectile dysfunction can be helped by treating the underlying causes or by adjusting medications ("Effective Solutions for Impotence," 1994; NIH, 1992). Sildenafil (known as Viagra), taken in the form of pills, has been found safe and effective (Goldstein et al., 1998; Utiger, 1998). Other treatments, each of which has both benefits and drawbacks, include a wraparound vacuum constrictive device, which draws blood into the penis; injections of prostaglandin E1 (a drug found in semen, which widens the arteries); and penile implant surgery. Still being tested are a topical cream and a suppository, both based on prostaglandin E1 ("Effective Solutions for Impotence," 1994; NIH, 1992) and another oral medication, Vasomax (Jordan & Schellhammer, 1998). If there is no apparent physical problem, psychotherapy or sex therapy (with the support and involvement of the partner) may help (NIH, 1992).

Sexual Activity

"My parents don't have sex. They have other things to do." (King, 1996, p. 258)

Many children of middle-aged parents are vastly ignorant of their parents' sexual activity. Myths about sexuality in midlife—for example, the idea that satisfying sex ends at menopause—have even been believed by middle-aged people themselves and have sometimes become self-fulfilling prophecies. Now, advances in health care and more liberal attitudes toward sex are making people more aware that sex can be a vital part of life during these and even later years.

Surveys suggest that sexual activity tends to diminish only slightly and gradually during the forties and fifties (King, 1996). Often a decline in frequency has nonphysiological causes: monotony in a relationship, preoccupation with business or financial worries, mental or physical fatigue, depression, failure to make sex a high priority, fear of failure to attain an erection, or lack of a partner. Possible physical causes include chronic disease, surgery, medications, and too much food or alcohol (King, 1996; Masters & Johnson, 1966; Weg, 1989).

Freed from worries about pregnancy, and having more uninterrupted time to spend with their partners, many people find their sexual relationship better than it has been in years. In a major survey introduced in Chapter 13, women in their fifties were only one-third as likely as younger women to experience pain during sex, and half as likely to report lack of pleasure or anxiety (Laumann, Paik, & Rosen, 1999). Women that age may know their own sexual needs and desires better, feel freer to take the initiative, and have more interest in sex. Because of men's slowed response, middle-aged lovers may enjoy longer, more leisurely periods of

CHECKPOINT

Can you . . .

- ✔ Tell the chief difference between men's and women's reproductive changes at midlife?
- ✔ Identify factors that can affect women's experience of menopause?
- ✔ Discuss the prevalence and treatment of erectile dysfunction?
- ✔ Describe changes in sexual activity during middle age?

Consider this . . .

- How often, and in what ways, do you imagine your parents express their sexuality? When you are their age, do you expect to be more or less sexually active than they seem to be?
- In your experience, do middle-aged women show more concern about appearance than middle-aged men? If so, in what ways, specifically?

sexual activity. Women may find their partner's longer period of arousal helpful in reaching their own orgasm—often by means other than intercourse. Couples who hold and caress each other, with or without genital sex, can experience heightened sexuality as part of an intimate relationship (Weg, 1989).

Concern with Appearance and Attractiveness

In a youth-oriented society, visible signs of aging such as wrinkles, sags, "age spots," and "middle-aged spread" can be distressing. Middle-aged people spend a great deal of time, effort, and money trying to look young.

Until recently, it was mostly women who fell prey to the relentless pursuit of youth. As long ago as medieval times, a mature man was considered wise, whereas a mature woman was considered "cold" and "dry" (Lock, 1998). In men, gray hair, coarsened skin, and "crow's feet" have been seen as indicators of experience and mastery; in women, signs of being "over the hill."

Changes in appearance are more likely to affect a husband's sexual responsiveness to his wife than vice versa (Margolin & White, 1987). According to evolutionary psychology, this double standard of aging goes back to the universal drive to perpetuate the species. Since women lose their reproductive capacity earlier than men do, loss of youthful appearance may have warned a man that a woman might no longer be a desirable (that is, fertile) mate (Katchadourian, 1987). Although attractiveness is no longer measured only by the biological mandate to reproduce, a societal standard "that regards beauty as the exclusive preserve of the young . . . makes women especially vulnerable to the fear of aging. . . . The relentless social pressures to retain a slim 'girlish' figure make women self-conscious about their bodies . . . [and] can be detrimental to the midlife woman's personal growth and sense of self-worth" (Lenz, 1993, pp. 26, 28).

Today the double standard of aging is waning (Gullette, 1998); men, too, suffer from the premium placed on youth. This is particularly true in the job market and the business world. It's no coincidence that "anti-aging" treatments for men have boomed in an era of corporate downsizing (Spindler, 1996). Men now spend as much as women on cosmetic products (Gullette, 1998) and are turning to cosmetic surgery in greater numbers.

Wrinkles and graying hair often imply that a woman is "over the hill" but that a man is "in the prime of life." This double standard of aging, which downgrades the attractiveness of middle-aged women but not of their husbands, can affect a couple's sexual adjustment.

Self-esteem suffers when people devalue their physical being. On the other hand, an effort to maintain youth and vigor can be positive if it is not obsessive and reflects concern with health and fitness (Gallagher, 1993). Men and women who can stay as fit as possible while accepting realistically the changes taking place in themselves, and who can appreciate maturity as a positive achievement for both sexes, are better able to make the most of middle adulthood—a time when both physical and cognitive functioning are likely to be at an impressively high level.

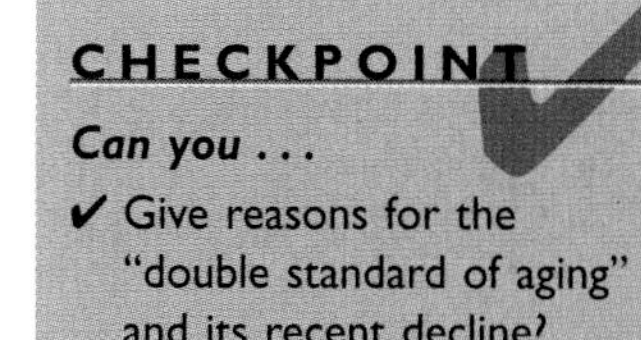

CHECKPOINT
Can you . . .
✔ Give reasons for the "double standard of aging" and its recent decline?

Health 

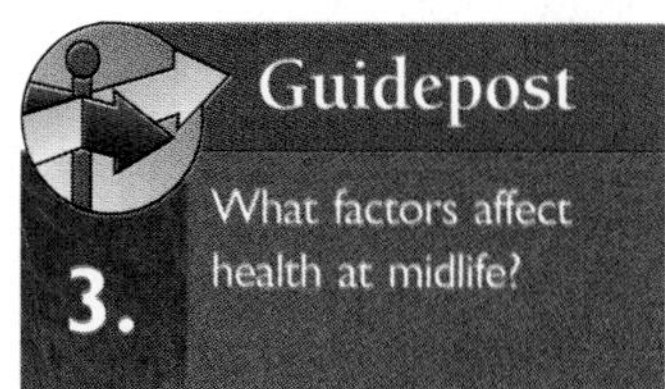

Guidepost
3.
What factors affect health at midlife?

Overall, middle-aged Americans—like middle-aged people in other industrialized countries—are quite healthy. Less than 17 percent of 45- to 64-year-olds consider themselves in fair or poor health. More than 3 out of 4 people in this age range have no functional limitations, and only 1 in 10 is unable to carry out important activities for health reasons. Men are more likely to have restrictions on major activities, women on secondary or minor ones (NCHS, 1998a). Activity limitations are generally caused by chronic ailments, such as back problems, arthritis, and rheumatism, and increase with age (Merrill & Verbrugge, 1999). Personality affects the way people judge their own health; those high in the personality dimension called *neuroticism* (refer back to Chapter 14) are less likely to report excellent health than people rated as extraverted, agreeable, or conscientious (Siegler, 1997).

Health Concerns

Despite their generally good health, many people in midlife are concerned about signs of potential decline. They may have less energy than in their youth and are likely to experience occasional or chronic pains and fatigue. They can no longer "burn the midnight oil" with ease, they are more likely to contract certain diseases, and they take longer to recover from illness or extreme exertion (Merrill & Verbrugge, 1999; Siegler, 1997).

People over 40 account for about one-third of recorded cases of AIDS in adults (NCHS, 1998a). Many patients in this age group contracted the disease, as Arthur Ashe apparently did (refer back to Chapter 13), through contaminated blood transfusions before routine screening began in 1985. The disease seems to be more severe and to progress more rapidly in middle-aged and older people, whose immune systems may be weakened (Brozan, 1990; USDHHS, 1992).

Hypertension (chronically high blood pressure) is an increasingly important concern from midlife on. It can lead to heart attack or stroke, or to cognitive impairment in late life (Launer, Masaki, Petrovitch, Foley, & Havlik, 1995). Blood pressure screening, low-salt diets, and medication have reduced the prevalence of hypertension, but it still affects about 34 percent of men and about 25 percent of women ages 45 to 54, and more than 40 percent of both men and women ages 55 to 64 (NCHS, 1998a).

hypertension
Chronically high blood pressure.

The leading causes of death between ages 45 and 64 are cancer, heart disease, accidents, and stroke. Between 1979 and 1997, mortality rates declined sharply for people in this age bracket (Hoyert, Kochanek, & Murphy, 1999) because of a decline in deaths from coronary heart disease (Siegler, 1997). This decline in coronary mortality seems largely due to improvements in treatment of heart attack patients (Rosamond et al., 1998).

Indirect Influences on Health: Poverty, Gender, and Ethnicity

People with low incomes are at increased risk of activity limitation and poor health (NCHS, 1998a). In a longitudinal study of 8,355 British civil servants ages 39 to 63, those in the lower ranks had poorer health than those in higher classifications, despite equal access to Britain's national health care system (Hemingway, Nicholson, Stafford, Roberts, & Marmot, 1997).

As in young adulthood, death rates in middle age are higher for men than for women and higher for African Americans than for white, Hispanic, Asian, and Native Americans (Hoyert et al., 1999; NCHS, 1998a). However, women are at increased risk after menopause, particularly for heart disease and osteoporosis. Let's look more closely at women's health and then at health hazards for African Americans, which are, in part, related to poverty.

Women's Health after Menopause

After age 50, women's risk of heart disease begins to catch up with men's (Avis, 1999). This happens faster after a hysterectomy. Furthermore, women younger than 74 have less chance than men of surviving a heart attack (Vaccarino et al., 1999). Regular exercise or brisk walking can lower the risk of heart disease, even for formerly sedentary women who do not become active until middle age (Manson et al., 1999; Owens, Matthews, Wing, & Kuller, 1992). A diet high in fiber, especially from cereals, also reduces the risk (Wolk et al., 1999).

As we have mentioned, gradual loss of bone density is a normal accompaniment of aging. In women, bone loss rapidly accelerates at menopause (Avis, 1999; Levinson & Altkorn, 1998). One in 4 postmenopausal women over age 60 has **osteoporosis** ("porous bones"), a condition in which the bones become thin and brittle as a result of calcium depletion associated with loss of estrogen ("Should You Take," 1994). Affected women may lose up to 50 percent of their bone mass between ages 40 and 70 (Spence, 1989). Frequent signs of osteoporosis are marked loss in height and a "hunchbacked" posture that results from compression and collapse of weakened bones. Osteoporosis is a major cause of broken bones in old age and can greatly affect quality of life and even survival (Levinson & Altkorn, 1998).

osteoporosis
Condition in which the bones become thin and brittle as a result of rapid calcium depletion.

Four out of 5 cases of osteoporosis occur in women, most often in white women with fair skin or a small frame, those with a family history of the condition, and those whose ovaries were surgically removed before menopause (NIA, 1993; "Should You Take," 1994). Since a predisposition to osteoporosis seems to have a genetic basis, measurement of bone density is an especially wise precaution for women with affected family members (Prockop, 1998; Uitterlinden et al., 1998).

hormone replacement therapy (HRT)
Treatment with artificial estrogen, sometimes in combination with the hormone progesterone, to relieve or prevent symptoms caused by decline in estrogen levels after menopause.

Bone loss can be slowed or even reversed with proper nutrition and exercise and avoidance of smoking (Eastell, 1998). Women over age 40 should get 1,000 to 1,500 milligrams of dietary calcium a day, along with recommended daily amounts of vitamin D, which helps the body absorb calcium (NIA, 1993). Studies have found value in calcium and vitamin D supplements (Dawson-Hughes, Harris, Krall, & Dallal, 1997; Eastell, 1998). Weight-bearing exercise, such as walking, jogging, and aerobic dancing, can increase bone density (Krall & Dawson-Hughes, 1994; NIA, 1993).

Since the most troublesome physical effects of menopause are linked to reduced levels of estrogen, **hormone replacement therapy (HRT)** in the form of artificial estrogen is often prescribed. Because estrogen

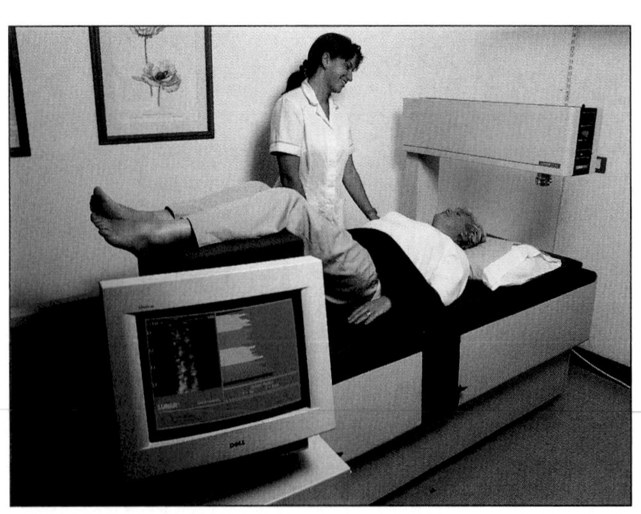

A bone density scan is a simple, painless X-ray procedure to measure bone density so as to determine whether osteoporosis is present. Osteoporosis, or thinning of the bones, is most common in women after menopause. The procedure is especially advisable for women with a family history of osteoporosis. Here, the monitor shows an image of this woman's spinal column.

taken alone increases the risk of uterine cancer, women whose uterus has not been surgically removed are usually given estrogen in combination with progestin, a form of the female hormone progesterone.

Besides relieving hot flashes and night sweats, HRT is the best-known treatment to prevent or stop bone loss after menopause, reducing the risk of osteoporosis and fractures (Davidson, 1995; Eastell, 1998; Levinson & Altkorn, 1998). HRT seems most effective when started at menopause and continued for at least five years. It may promote bone formation even when begun in later life, but findings on this point are mixed (Eastell, 1998; Felson et al., 1993; Levinson & Altkorn, 1998; Prestwood et al., 1994).

In a number of correlational studies, estrogen, alone or combined with progestin, dramatically cut the risk of heart disease (Davidson, 1995; Ettinger, Friedman, Bush, & Quesenberry, 1996; Grodstein, 1996) and improved the balance between HDL ("good") and LDL ("bad") cholesterol (The Writing Group of PEPI Trial, 1995), However, the validity of these findings has been questioned because estrogen users tend to have better health habits than nonusers (Avis, 1999). More recently, in an ongoing controlled study of 25,000 healthy postmenopausal women, those taking estrogen—with or without progestin—had slightly *more* heart attacks, strokes, and blood clots than those who took a placebo (Kolata, 2000).

Some studies of HRT have found protective effects against Alzheimer's disease (Mayeux, 1996; Paganini-Hill & Henderson, 1994; Tang et al., 1996) and improvements in cognitive functioning, particularly memory; but this research has had conflicting results and it, too, has been criticized on methodological grounds (Avis, 1999; Shaywitz et al., 1999; Yaffe, Sawaya, Lieberburg, & Grady, 1998). In one randomized, controlled study, magnetic resonance imaging (MRI) showed that estrogen altered brain activation in specific regions involved in memory; however, its use did not affect performance on simple memory tasks (Shaywitz et al., 1999). In another randomized, controlled study, estrogen therapy brought no improvement in cognitive functioning in women with mild to moderate Alzheimer's (Mulnard et al., 2000).

Estrogen treatment has risks as well as benefits (see Table 15-2). Much research has focused on a possible increased risk of breast cancer. Again, however, findings conflict (Avis, 1999; Colditz et al., 1995; Henrich, 1992; Steinberg, Smith, Thacker, & Stroup, 1994). Heightened risk seems to be mainly among current or recent estrogen users and increases with length of use (Willett, Colditz, & Stampfer, 2000). One recent study found no link between HRT and the most common types

Table 15-2 Estrogen: Benefits and Risks

Estrogen's Benefits	Estrogen's Risks
▶ Relief from the classic symptoms of menopause: hot flashes, mood swings, vaginal dryness, thinning skin	▶ An increased risk of endometrial cancer, which may be countered by adding progesterone to a regimen of estrogen
▶ Proven reduced bone loss (osteoporosis) associated with menopause, including a probable reduction in hip fractures	▶ Symptoms similar to premenstrual ones (swelling, bloating, breast tenderness, mood swings, headaches)
▶ Possible reduced risk of heart disease by improving cholesterol levels and the flexibility of blood vessels	▶ A menstrual discharge (when progesterone is taken with estrogen)
▶ Possible lowered risk of colon cancer	▶ Probable increased risk of breast cancer
	▶ Stimulation of the growth of uterine fibroids and endometriosis
	▶ Probable increased risk of gallstones and blood clots
	▶ Possible weight gain

Source: Adapted from "Hormone Therapy," 1997, p. 2.

of breast cancer, though the therapy did increase the risk of less common types that have a favorable prognosis (Gapstur, Morrow, & Sellers, 1999). Another large-scale study found greater risk from estrogen combined with progestin than from estrogen alone (Schairer et al., 2000).

About 10 percent of women taking hormones experience such side effects as headaches, nausea, fluid retention, swollen breasts, and vaginal discharge. There is also some risk of abnormal vaginal bleeding ("Alternatives to hormone replacement," 1994; NIA, 1993). Some women see HRT as based on a view of menopause as a disease or deficiency that needs to be treated with daily medication, rather than as a natural process that should be allowed to take its course (Lock, 1998; te Velde & van Leusden, 1994).

CHECKPOINT

Can you . . .

- ✔ Describe the typical health status in middle age, and identify health concerns that become more prevalent at this age?
- ✔ Tell how women's risk of heart disease and osteoporosis increases after menopause, and weigh the risks and benefits of, and alternatives to, hormone replacement therapy?

The safety of long-term hormone treatment is still unknown (Avis, 1999), and other treatments are being tested. A new group of nonhormonal chemicals called *selective estrogen receptor modulators,* chiefly tamoxifen and raloxifene (sometimes called "designer estrogens"), seem to have favorable effects on bone density and possibly on cholesterol levels without increasing the risk of breast cancer; but tamoxifen may stimulate uterine cancer (Avis, 1999; Eastell, 1998). Furthermore, the long-term effects of these drugs—positive or negative—have yet to be documented. Another nonhormonal drug, alendronate, one of a class called *bisphosponates,* has fewer adverse effects than estrogen but has proven less effective in preventing bone loss; it is not recommended for women with gastrointestinal problems (Eastell, 1998; Levinson & Altkorn, 1998).

More accurate evaluation of the effects of estrogen and alternative treatments must await completion of large, randomized, controlled studies. Meanwhile, women need to make the decision on hormone replacement on the basis of their particular situations, including their feelings about menopause and their family health history.

Risk Factors for African Americans

The death rate for middle-aged African Americans is nearly twice that for white Americans. Almost twice as many black people as white people ages 45 to 64 die of heart disease, close to one and a half times as many of cancer, and more than three times as many of stroke (Hoyert et al., 1999). Almost one-third of the excessive mortality of middle-aged black people can be traced to six risk factors: high blood pressure, high cholesterol, excess weight, diabetes, smoking, and alcohol intake. The first four may be partly attributable to heredity, but lifestyle plays a role in all six. Probably the largest single underlying factor is poverty, which is related to poor nutrition, substandard housing, inadequate prenatal care, and poor access to health care throughout life (Otten, Teutsch, Williamson, & Marks, 1990). Still, poverty cannot be the sole explanation, since the death rate for middle-aged Hispanic Americans, who also are disproportionately poor, is lower than that of white Americans (Hoyert et al., 1999).

About 1 in 3 African American adults has hypertension, as compared with fewer than 1 in 4 white Americans (NCHS, 1998a). Hypertension accounts for 1 in 5 deaths among black people—twice as many as among whites. The reasons cannot be entirely genetic, since people of African descent in Caribbean islands and Africans in Cameroon and Nigeria have markedly lower rates of hypertension than African Americans. Overweight, lack of exercise, and diet seem to explain 40 to 50 percent of the increased risk African Americans face as compared with rural Nigerians. Since only 7 percent of the latter have high blood pressure, hypertension may be largely a hazard of life in modern industrial societies (Cooper, Rotimi, & Ward, 1999).

Black women have been called "a minority within a minority" (Miller, quoted in Eastman, 1995). Besides being at higher risk for hypertension, they are more likely than white women to be overweight. They get less exercise and see doctors less often (Eastman, 1995). African American women are four times as likely as white women to die of heart disease or stroke before age 60; educational status makes little difference (Mosca et al., 1998). Black women also are more than twice as likely to die of breast cancer within five years of diagnosis, probably because they are less likely to get mammograms and their cancers tend to be diagnosed later (Eley et al., 1994).

Some observers attribute the health gap between black and white Americans in part to stress caused by prejudice (Chissell, 1989; Lawler, 1990, in Goleman, 1990). In parts of the Caribbean, where race relations may be smoother than in the United States, blacks' average blood pressure is about the same as that of other ethnic groups (Cooper et al., 1999).

CHECKPOINT

Can you . . .

✔ Cite factors in African Americans' excessive mortality in middle age?

Health and Lifestyle: The Influence of Stress

The health problems of African Americans, just discussed, underline the influence of lifestyle on health. Nutrition, smoking, alcohol and drug use, physical activity, and other influences discussed in Chapter 13 continue to affect health in middle age (see Table 15-3). People who do not smoke, are not overweight, and exercise regularly not only live longer but have shorter periods of disability at the end of life (Vita, Terry, Hubert, & Fries, 1998). Middle-aged men and women who stop smoking reduce their risk of heart disease and stroke (AHA, 1995; Kawachi et al., 1993; Stamler et al., 1993; Wannamethee, Shaper, Whincup, & Walker, 1995). Another important influence is stress, whose cumulative effects often show up in middle age.

Stress: Causes and Effects

The more stressful the changes that take place in a person's life, the greater the likelihood of illness within the next year or two. That was the finding of a classic study in which two psychiatrists, on the basis of interviews with 5,000 hospital patients, ranked the stressfulness of life events that had preceded illness (Holmes & Rahe, 1976; see Table 15-4). About half the people with between 150 and 300 "life change units" (LCUs) in a single year, and about 70 percent of those with 300 or more LCUs, became ill.

Change—even positive change—can be stressful, and some people react to stress by getting sick. However, these findings do not tell us *how* stress produces illness or why some people's bodies handle stress better than others. Furthermore, there are different kinds of **stressors** (stress-producing experiences). Hassles of day-to-day living are associated with minor physical ills such as colds and may have a stronger effect on mental health than major life events or transitions, or chronic or long-lasting problems (Chiriboga, 1997).

stressors
Stress-producing experiences.

Today, stress is under increasing scrutiny as a factor in such diseases as hypertension, heart ailments, stroke, peptic ulcers, and cancer (Levenstein, Ackerman, Kiecolt-Glaser, & Dubois, 1999; Light et al., 1999; Sapolsky, 1992). The most frequently reported physical symptoms of stress are headaches, stomachaches, muscle aches or muscle tension, and fatigue. The most common psychological symptoms are nervousness, anxiety, tenseness, anger, irritability, and depression.

Consider this . . .

- How do you handle stress? What methods have you found most successful? What are the main sources of stress in your life?

Psychological reactions to stress may increase vulnerability to illness. So, it seems, can the effort to cope with stress itself. People who experience stressful events are more likely to catch colds, whether or not they see themselves as under stress and regardless of their emotional reactions to it (Cohen, 1996; Cohen, Tyrell, & Smith, 1991, 1993). Intense or prolonged stress seems to weaken the immune system (Kiecolt-Glaser et al., 1984; Kiecolt-Glaser, Fisher, et al., 1987; Kiecolt-Glaser & Glaser, 1995; Kiecolt-Glaser, Glaser, et al., 1987).

Stress also seems to cause blockage of the arteries, which leads to cardiovascular disease (Baum, Cacioppo, Melamed, Gallant, & Travis, 1995). Middle-aged men with high levels of anxiety or tension are more likely to develop high blood pressure later in life (Markovitz, Matthews, Kannel, Cobb, & D'Agostino, 1993)

Table 15-3 Lifestyle Factors in Selected Diseases

Risk factor	Coronary Heart Disease	Stroke	Diabetes (non-insulin dependent)	Breast Cancer	Lung Cancer	Prostate Cancer	Colorectal Cancer	Melanoma (skin cancer)	Osteoporosis	Osteoarthritis
Cigarette smoking	X	X	X	X	X	X	X	X	X	X
Alcohol	?		?	?					X	
Dietary factors										
Cholesterol	X	X								
Calories			X							
Fat intake	X	X	?	?		X	?			
Salt intake		X								
Fiber			O							
Calcium									O	
Potassium	O									
Overweight	X	X	X						X	?
Physical inactivity	O	O	O						O	O
Exposure to toxins				X	X	X	X			
Exposure to ultraviolet rays								X		

Note: X= increases risk of disease; O = decreases risk of disease; ? = may increase risk of disease.

Source: Adapted from Merrill & Verbrugge, 1999, Table IV, p. 87.

and are four to six times more likely than less anxious men to die of sudden heart failure (Kawachi, Colditz, et al., 1994; Kawachi, Sparrow, Vokonas, & Weiss, 1994). Female nurses who work rotating night shifts (which tend to upset the body's natural rhythms) for more than six years are much more likely than coworkers to have heart attacks (Kawachi et al., 1995).

Of course, to some degree, stress is normal throughout adulthood (Siegler, 1997). However, in some people, response to stress becomes impaired with age. Long-term oversecretion of stress hormones may play a part in a number of age-related disorders, from mature-onset diabetes to osteoporosis (Krieger, 1982; Munck, Guyre, & Holbrook, 1984).

Stress can harm health indirectly, through other lifestyle factors. People under stress may sleep less, smoke and drink more, eat poorly, and pay too little attention to their health. Conversely, regular exercise, good nutrition, at least seven hours of sleep a night, and frequent socializing are associated with lower stress (Baum et al., 1995). Some adults drink under economic, marital, or job stress. But while low doses of alcohol may reduce stress response and improve performance, higher doses may actually induce stress by stimulating release of adrenaline and other hormones (NIAAA, 1996a).

One route by which stress leads to illness may have to do with loss of a sense of mastery or control. When people feel they can control stressful events, they are less likely to get sick. When expectations of control are violated, as in a nuclear

Table 15-4 Life Events in Order of Diminishing Stressfulness

Life Event	Value	Life Event	Value
Death of spouse	100	Son or daughter leaving home	29
Divorce	73	Trouble with in-laws	29
Marital separation	65	Outstanding personal achievement	28
Jail term	63	Wife beginning or stopping work	26
Death of close family member	63	Beginning or ending school	26
Personal injury or illness	53	Revision of habits	24
Marriage	50	Trouble with boss	23
Being fired at work	47	Change in work hours	20
Marital reconciliation	45	Change in residence	20
Retirement	45	Change in schools	20
Change in health of family	44	Change in recreation	19
Pregnancy	40	Change in social activity	18
Sex difficulties	39	Change in sleeping habits	16
Gain of new family member	39	Change in number of family get-togethers	15
Change in financial state	38	Change in eating habits	15
Death of close friend	37	Vacation	13
Change of work	36	Minor violations of law	11
Change in number of arguments with spouse	35		
Foreclosure of mortgage	30		
Change of responsibility at work	29		

Sources: Adapted from Holmes & Rahe, 1967, p. 213.

plant accident caused by human error, chronic stress-related problems tend to compound the physiological effects (Baum & Fleming, 1993).

Stress management workshops teach people to control their reactions through relaxation, meditation, and biofeedback. Men infected with the AIDS virus who learn such techniques are slower to develop symptoms of the disease; and women with breast cancer who participate in group therapy live longer than those who do not participate (Sleek, 1995). In one experiment, asthma and rheumatoid arthritis patients who wrote down their most stressful experiences improved their physical condition as compared with a control group of patients who wrote about emotionally neutral topics (Smyth, Stone, Hurewitz, & Kaell, 1999).

Work-Related Stress

Workplaces are generally designed for efficiency and profit, not for workers' well-being; but human costs can hurt the bottom line. When people feel they are in the wrong jobs, or when efforts to meet job demands are out of proportion to job satisfaction and other rewards, stress can result. And, as we have just shown, stress—intense, frequent, and prolonged—can play havoc with physical and mental health (Levi, 1990; Siegrist, 1996).

Today many U.S. workers are working harder and longer to maintain their standard of living. Some middle-income workers hold two jobs to make ends meet (McGuire, 1999). Employees who feel overworked, or who believe that their skills are not adequately recognized, or who do not have clear goals, tend to show high stress and low morale and productivity (Veninga, 1998). Another cause of stress on the job is conflict with supervisors, subordinates, and coworkers. Violence in the workplace, as a response to fear, uncertainty, or a perception of unfairness, is an increasing problem (Clay, 1995; Freiberg, 1998).

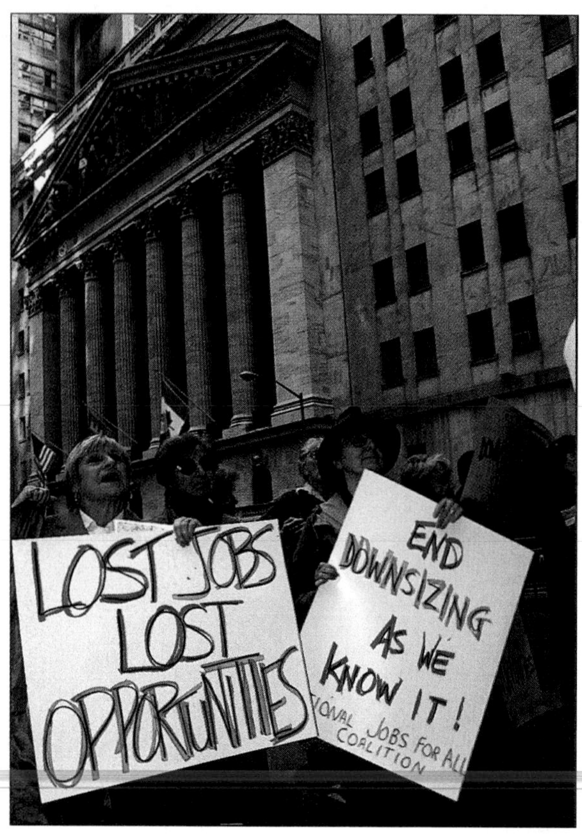

Corporate downsizing has forced many formerly well-paid middle-aged executives into the ranks of the unemployed. These members of the Jobs for All Coalition are demonstrating for full employment and decent benefits. Both men and women cope with unemployment better when they can draw on financial, psychological, and social resources and can see this forced change as an opportunity to do something new or as a challenge for growth.

In interviews with nearly 3,000 wage and salaried workers, 68 percent complained of having to work very fast, and 88 percent very hard. Nearly 1 in 4 said they often or very often felt nervous or stressed or emotionally drained by their work, and more than 1 in 3 said they felt used up at the end of the workday. At the same time, 6 out of 10 rated their chances for advancement as only fair or poor (Bond & Galinsky, 1998).

High levels of work-related stress have been reported in many other parts of the world (Veninga, 1998). A combination of high job demands with low autonomy or control and little pride in the product is a common stress-producing pattern (United Nations International Labor Organization [UNILO], 1993; G. Williams, 1991), which increases the risk of high blood pressure and heart disease (Schnall et al., 1990; Siegrist, 1996). Among 10,308 British civil servants ages 35 to 55, low job control and an imbalance between effort and reward were strongly associated with increased coronary risk during the next five years (Bosma, Peter, Siegrist, & Marmot, 1998).

Many women, in addition to juggling work and family, are under special pressure in the workplace, especially in corporations, where their superiors often are men. Some women complain that an invisible but inflexible "glass ceiling" inhibits their advancement to the highest ranks (Federal Glass Ceiling Commission, 1995). Another frequent source of stress is **sexual harassment:** psychological pressure created by unwelcome sexual overtures, particularly from a superior, which create a hostile or abusive environment.

sexual harassment
Unwelcome sexual overtures, particularly from a superior at work, which create a hostile or abusive environment, causing psychological pressure.

burnout
Syndrome of emotional exhaustion and a sense that one can no longer accomplish anything on the job.

Burnout **Burnout** involves emotional exhaustion, a feeling of being unable to accomplish anything on the job, and a sense of helplessness and loss of control. It is especially common among people in the helping professions (such as teaching, medicine, therapy, social work, and police work) who feel frustrated by their inability to help people as much as they would like to. Burnout is usually a response to continual stress rather than to an immediate crisis. Its symptoms include fatigue, insomnia, headaches, persistent colds, stomach disorders, abuse of alcohol or drugs, and trouble getting along with people. A burned-out worker may quit suddenly, pull away from family and friends, and sink into depression (Briley, 1980; Maslach & Jackson, 1985).

Measures that seem to help burned-out workers include cutting down on working hours and taking breaks, including long weekends and vacations. Other standard stress-reducing techniques—exercise, music, and meditation—also may help. However, the most effective way to relieve stress and burnout may be to change the conditions that cause it by seeing that employees have opportunities to do work that is meaningful to them, uses their skills and knowledge, and gives them a sense of achievement and self-esteem (Knoop, 1994).

Unemployment Perhaps the greatest work-related stressor is the loss of a job. Although unemployment in the late 1990s was low, in 1998 more than 6 percent of U.S. families—including about twice as many African American and Hispanic families as white families—reported having a member out of work (Bureau of Labor Statistics, 1999a).

Corporate downsizing has added a substantial number of middle-aged middle management executives to the unemployment rolls (Kuttner, 1994). Since employers generally prefer to hire younger workers, whose skills they believe to be more transferable, many of these longtime employees are forced into early retirement or lower-paid jobs (Forteza & Prieto, 1994). Survivors often feel demoralized, overworked, and fearful for their own jobs (Veninga, 1998). In one study, mentioned earlier, about 3 out of 10 employees considered it somewhat or very likely that they would lose their jobs in the next few years (Bond & Galinsky, 1998).

Research on unemployment has linked it to headaches, stomach trouble, and high blood pressure; to physical and mental illness, including heart attack, stroke, anxiety, and depression; to marital and family problems; to health, psychological, and behavior problems in children; and to suicide, homicide, and other crimes (Brenner, 1991; Merva & Fowles, 1992; Perrucci, Perrucci, & Targ, 1988; Voydanoff, 1990). In a study of 90 Canadian families that had undergone job loss, psychological problems were 55 to 75 percent greater among the unemployed than among those with steady work (Veninga, 1998).

Stress comes not only from loss of income and the resulting financial hardships, but also from the effects of this loss on the self-concept and on family relationships. Men who define manhood as supporting a family, and workers of both sexes who derive their identity from their work and define their worth in terms of its dollar value, lose more than their paychecks when they lose their jobs. They lose a piece of themselves and their self-esteem and feel less in control of their lives (Forteza & Prieto, 1994; Perrucci et al., 1988; Voydanoff, 1987, 1990).

Those who cope best with unemployment have financial resources (savings or earnings of other family members). Rather than blaming themselves or seeing themselves as failures, they assess their situation objectively. They have the support of understanding, adaptable families, and friends (Voydanoff, 1990). A sense of control is crucial. Among 190 unemployed workers, those who believed they had some influence on their circumstances were less anxious and depressed, had fewer physical symptoms, and had higher self-esteem and life satisfaction than those who believed external forces were in control (Cvetanovski & Jex, 1994).

Consider this . . .

- What would you do if you were told that the job you had been doing for ten years was obsolete or that you were being let go because of corporate downsizing?

CHECKPOINT

Can you . . .

✔ Tell how stress can affect health?

✔ Identify sources of work stress and burnout?

✔ Summarize physical and psychological effects of losing a job?

Cognitive Development

What happens to cognitive abilities in middle age? Do they improve or decline, or both? Do people develop distinctive ways of thinking at this time of life? How does age affect the ability to solve problems, to learn, to create, and to perform on the job?

Measuring Cognitive Abilities in Middle Age

Cognitively speaking, middle-aged people are in their prime. The life of Gandhi amply supports this conclusion. So does the Seattle Longitudinal Study of Adult Intelligence, conducted by K. Warner Schaie and his colleagues (Schaie, 1979, 1983, 1988a, 1988b, 1990, 1994, 1996a, 1996b; Schaie & Herzog, 1983, 1986; Schaie & Strother, 1968; Willis & Schaie, 1999).

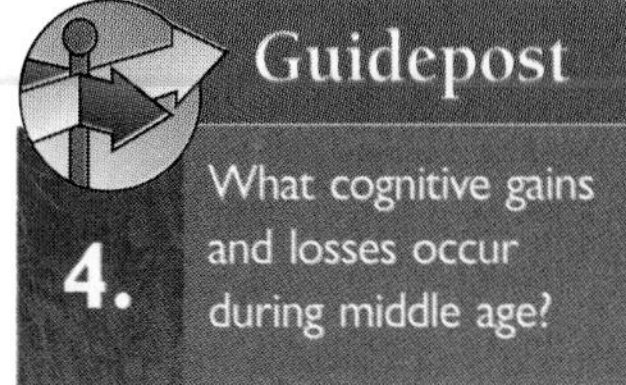

Guidepost
4.
What cognitive gains and losses occur during middle age?

Although this ongoing study is called longitudinal, it uses sequential methods (refer back to Chapter 2). The study began in 1956 with 500 randomly chosen participants: 25 men and 25 women in each five-year age bracket from 22 to 67. Participants took timed tests of six primary mental abilities based on those identified by Thurstone (1938). (Table 15-5 gives definitions and sample tasks for each ability.) Every seven years, the original participants were retested and new participants were added. By 1994, about 5,000 people, forming a broadly diverse socioeconomic sample from young adulthood to old age, had been tested.

The researchers found "no uniform pattern of age-related changes . . . [for] all intellectual abilities" (Schaie, 1994, p. 306). Apparently, cognitive development is uneven during adulthood, involving gains and losses in different abilities at different times. Although perceptual speed declines steadily beginning at age 25, and numerical ability begins to decline around 40, peak performance in four of the six abilities—inductive reasoning, spatial orientation, vocabulary, and verbal memory—occurs about halfway through middle adulthood (see Figure 15-2). In all four of these abilities—middle-aged people, especially women, score higher on average than they did at 25. Men's spatial orientation, vocabulary, and verbal memory peak in the fifties; women's, not until the early sixties. On the other hand, women's perceptual speed declines faster than men's (Willis & Schaie, 1999).

Despite wide individual differences, most participants in the Seattle study showed no significant reduction in most abilities until after age 60, and then not in all or even most areas. Virtually no one declined on all fronts, and many people improved in some areas (Schaie, 1994). Consistent with previous research, successive generations scored progressively higher at the same ages on reasoning, spatial orientation, and verbal abilities. However, among baby boomers currently in middle age, vocabulary has shown less improvement than in previous cohorts, and (as in earlier studies) numerical ability has declined (Willis & Schaie, 1999; see Figure 15-3). These cohort trends suggest that U.S. society may be approaching a limit on improvements in basic cognitive abilities attributable to education and healthy lifestyles (Schaie, 1990).

fluid intelligence
Type of intelligence, proposed by Horn and Cattell, which is applied to novel problems and is relatively independent of educational and cultural influences. Compare with *crystallized intelligence.*

Earlier research (Cattell, 1965; Horn, 1967, 1968, 1970, 1982a, 1982b; Horn & Hofer, 1992) distinguished between two aspects of intelligence: *fluid* and *crystallized.* **Fluid intelligence** is the ability to apply mental powers to novel problems that require little or no previous knowledge. It involves perceiving relations, forming concepts, and drawing inferences. These abilities, which are largely

Table 15-5 Tests of Primary Mental Abilities Given in Seattle Longitudinal Study of Adult Intelligence

Test	Ability Measured	Task	Type of Intelligence
Vocabulary	Recognition and understanding of words	Find synonym by matching stimulus word with another word from multiple-choice list	Crystallized
Verbal memory	Retrieving words from long-term memory	Think of as many words as possible beginning with a given letter, in a set time period	Part crystallized, part fluid
Number	Performing computations	Do simple addition problems	Crystallized
Spatial orientation	Manipulating objects mentally in two-dimensional space	Select rotated examples of figure to match stimulus figure	Fluid
Inductive reasoning	Identifying patterns and inferring principles and rules for solving logical problems	Complete a letter series	Fluid
Perceptual speed	Making quick, accurate discriminations between visual stimuli	Identify matching and nonmatching images flashed on a computer screen	Fluid

Sources: Schaie, 1989;, Willis & Schaie, 1999.

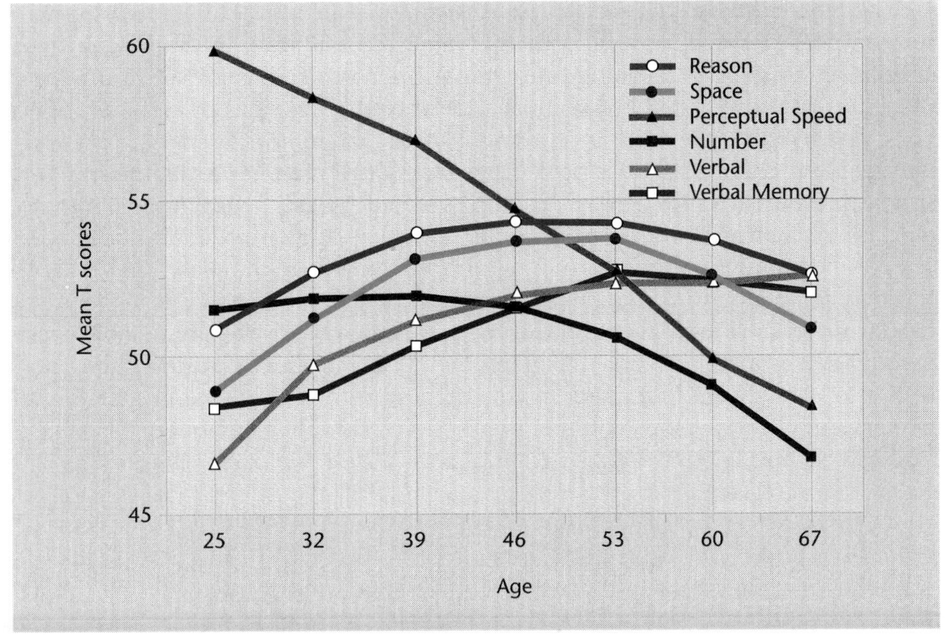

Figure 15-2
Longitudinal change in six basic mental abilities, ages 25 to 67.
(Source: Schaie, 1994; reprinted in Willis & Schaie, 1999, p. 237.)

determined by neurological status, tend to decline with age. **Crystallized intelligence** is the ability to remember and use information acquired over a lifetime. It is measured by tests of vocabulary, general information, and responses to social situations and dilemmas. These abilities, which depend largely on education and cultural experience, hold their own or even improve with age.

crystallized intelligence
Type of intelligence, proposed by Horn and Cattell, involving the ability to remember and use learned information; it is largely dependent on education and cultural background. Compare with *fluid intelligence*.

Typically, fluid intelligence has been found to peak during young adulthood, whereas crystallized intelligence improves through middle age and often until near the end of life (Horn, 1982a, 1982b; Horn & Donaldson, 1980). However, much of this research was cross-sectional and thus may at least partly reflect generational differences rather than changes with age.

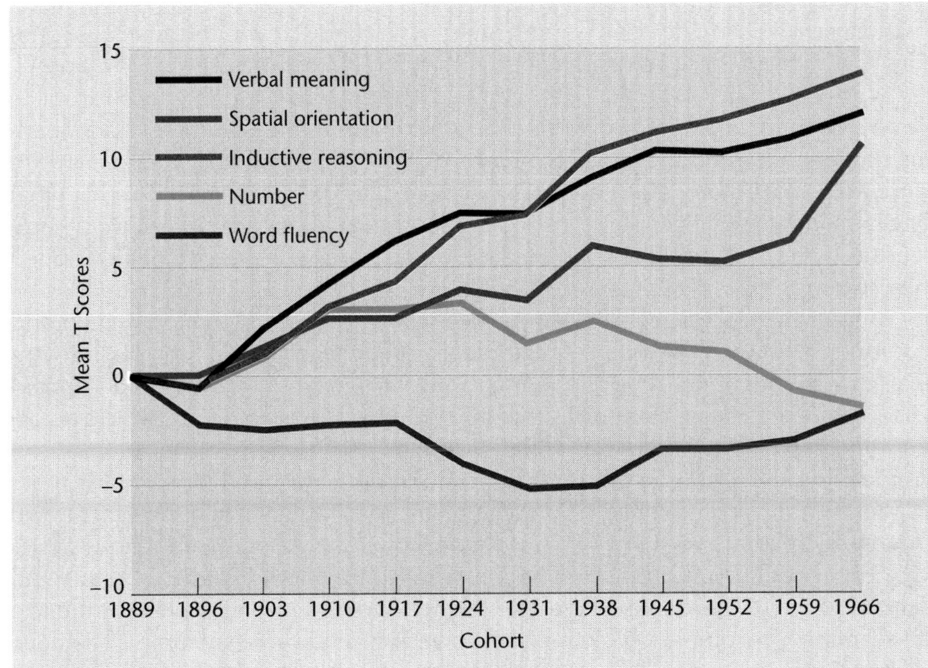

Figure 15-3
Cohort differences in scores on intelligence tests. In a group with mean birth years from 1889 to 1966, more recent cohorts scored higher on inductive reasoning, verbal meaning, and spatial orientation. Ability with numbers showed a decline.
(Source: Schaie, 1994.)

The Seattle study's sequential findings were somewhat different. Although fluid abilities did decline earlier than crystallized abilities, losses in such fluid abilities as inductive reasoning and spatial orientation did not set in until the midsixties, and in crystallized abilities, not until the seventies or eighties (Willis & Schaie, 1999).

One fluid ability that does peak quite early, beginning in the twenties, is perceptual speed. Adults may make up for losses in this basic neurological ability by gains in areas affected by learning and experience—higher-order abilities necessary for independent, productive living. Improvements in these crystallized abilities may be related to career development and the exercise of adult responsibilities. Advances in verbal memory during middle age are especially notable, since memory loss is a major worry for many people at midlife. Given the strong performance of most middle-agers in this area, objective evidence of substantial memory deficits in persons younger than 60 may indicate a neurological problem (Willis & Schaie, 1999).

CHECKPOINT

Can you . . .

- ✔ Summarize results of the Seattle Longitudinal Study concerning changes in basic mental abilities in middle age?
- ✔ Distinguish between fluid and crystallized intelligence and how they are affected by age?

The Distinctiveness of Adult Cognition

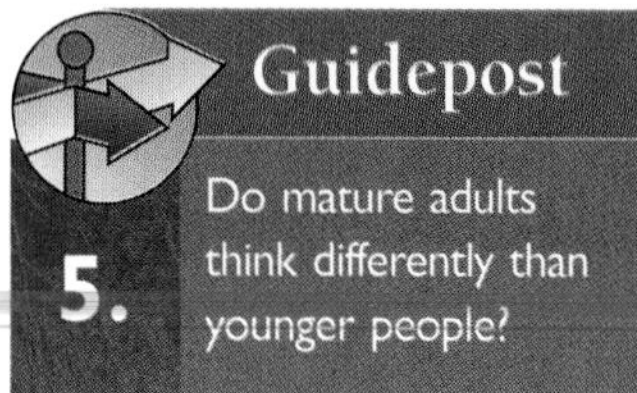

Guidepost
5.
Do mature adults think differently than younger people?

Instead of measuring the same cognitive abilities at different ages, some developmentalists find distinctive qualities in the thinking of mature adults. Some, working within the psychometric tradition, claim that accumulated knowledge changes the way fluid intelligence operates. Others, as we noted in Chapter 13, maintain that mature thought represents a new stage of cognitive development—a "special form of intelligence" (Sinnott, 1996, p. 361), which may underlie mature interpersonal skills and contribute to practical problem solving.

The Role of Expertise

Two young resident physicians in a hospital radiology laboratory examine a chest X ray. They study an unusual white blotch on the left side. "Looks like a large tumor," one of them says finally. The other nods. Just then, a longtime staff radiologist walks by and looks over their shoulders at the X ray. "That patient has a collapsed lung and needs immediate surgery," he declares (Lesgold, 1983).

Why do mature adults show increasing competence in solving problems in their chosen fields? The answer, according to William Hoyer and his colleagues (Hoyer & Rybash, 1994; Rybash, Hoyer, & Roodin, 1986), lies in specialized knowledge, a form of crystallized intelligence. Advances in expertise, according to Hoyer, continue at least through middle adulthood and are relatively independent of general intelligence and of any declines in the brain's information-processing machinery. Thus, although middle-aged people may take somewhat longer than younger people to process new information, they more than compensate when solving problems in their own fields with judgment developed from experience.

In one study (Ceci & Liker, 1986), researchers identified 30 middle-aged and older men who were avid horse racing fans. On the basis of skill in picking winners, the investigators divided the men into two groups: "expert" and "nonexpert." The experts used a more sophisticated method of reasoning, incorporating interpretations of much interrelated information, whereas nonexperts used simpler, less successful methods. Superior reasoning was not related to IQ; there was no significant difference in average measured intelligence between the two groups, and experts with low IQs used more complex reasoning than nonexperts with higher IQs. Similarly, on a much weightier plane, Gandhi, a man who claimed to have less than average intelligence, worked out an expert solution to the seemingly insoluble problem of empowering a powerless people to achieve independence.

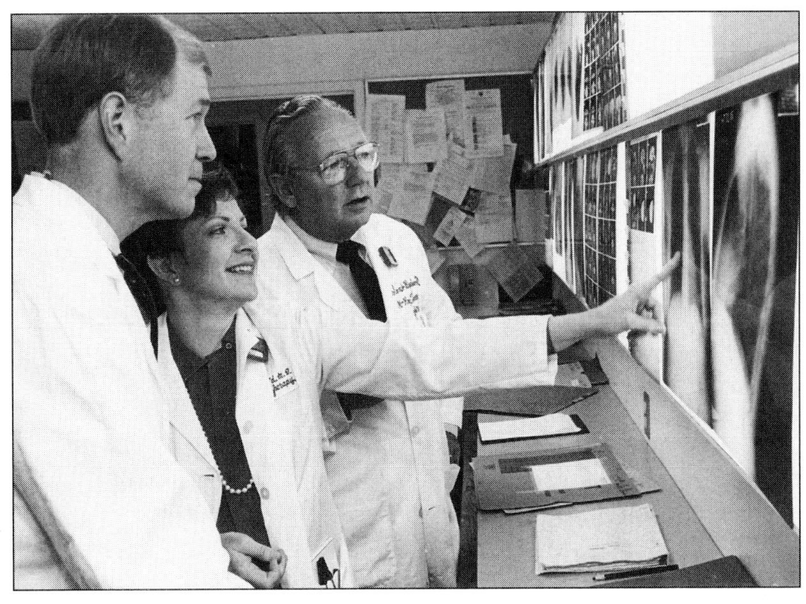

Expertise in interpreting x-rays, as in many other fields, depends on accumulated, specialized knowledge, which continues to increase with age. Experts often appear to be guided by intuition and cannot explain how they arrive at conclusions.

Hoyer explains such paradoxes through the concept of **encapsulation.** With experience, Hoyer suggests, information processing and fluid abilities become *encapsulated,* or dedicated to specific kinds of knowledge, making that knowledge easier to access, add to, and use. In other words, encapsulation "captures" fluid abilities for expert problem solving.

Expert thinking, like that of the experienced radiologist in our opening example, often seems automatic and intuitive. Experts generally are not aware of the thought processes that lie behind their decisions (Dreyfus, 1993–1994; Rybash et al., 1986). They cannot readily explain how they arrive at a conclusion or where a nonexpert has gone wrong: the experienced radiologist could not see why the residents would even consider diagnosing a collapsed lung as a tumor. Such intuitive, experience-based thinking is characteristic of what has been called postformal thought.

encapsulation
In Hoyer's terminology, progressive dedication of information processing and fluid thinking to specific knowledge systems, making knowledge more readily accessible.

The Integrative Nature of Postformal Thought

Postformal thought, introduced in Chapter 13, goes beyond abstract, formal reasoning, which Piaget considered the supreme achievement of adolescence. It is subjective and relativistic. It personalizes thinking by drawing on concrete experience. Although not limited to any particular period of adulthood, postformal thought seems well suited to the complex tasks, multiple roles, and perplexing choices and challenges of midlife (Sinnott, 1998).

An important feature of postformal thought is its *integrative* nature. Mature adults integrate logic with intuition and emotion; they integrate conflicting facts and ideas; and they integrate new information with what they already know. They interpret what they read, see, or hear in terms of its meaning for them. Instead of accepting something at face value, they filter it through their life experience and previous learning.

In one study (C. Adams, 1991), early and late adolescents and middle-aged and older adults were asked to summarize a Sufi teaching tale. In the story, a stream was unable to cross a desert until a voice told it to let the wind carry it; the stream was dubious but finally agreed and was blown across. Adolescents recalled more details of the story than adults did, but their summaries were largely limited to repeating the story line. Adults, especially women, gave summaries that were rich in interpretation, integrating what was in the text with its psychological and metaphorical meaning for them, as in this response of a 39-year-old:

> I believe what this story was trying to say was that there are times when everyone needs help and must sometimes make changes to reach their goals. Some people may resist change for a long time until they realize that certain things are beyond their control and they need assistance. When this is finally achieved and they can accept help and trust from someone, they can master things even as large as a desert. (p. 333)

Consider this . . .

- If you needed surgery, would you rather go to a middle-aged doctor or one who is considerably older or younger? Why?

Society benefits from this integrative feature of adult thought. Generally it is mature adults who, like Gandhi, become moral and spiritual leaders (see Box 15-2) and who translate their knowledge about the human condition into inspirational stories to which younger generations can turn for guidance. Postformal thought also may help in solving practical problems.

Digging Deeper

Box 15-2
Moral Leadership in Middle and Late Adulthood

What makes a single mother of four young children, with no money and a tenth-grade education, dedicate her life to religious missionary work on behalf of her equally poor neighbors? What leads a pediatrician to devote much of his practice to the care of poor children instead of to patients whose parents could provide him with a lucrative income?

In the mid-1980s, two psychologists, Anne Colby and William Damon, sought answers to questions like these. They embarked on a two-year search for people who showed unusual moral excellence in their day-to-day lives. The researchers eventually identified 23 "moral exemplars," interviewed them in depth, and studied how they had become moral leaders (Colby & Damon, 1992).

To find moral exemplars, Colby and Damon worked with a panel of 22 "expert nominators," people who in their professional lives regularly think about moral ideas: philosophers, historians, religious thinkers, and so forth. The researchers drew up five criteria: sustained commitment to principles that show respect for humanity; behavior consistent with one's ideals; willingness to risk self-interest; inspiring others to moral action; and humility, or lack of concern for one's ego.

The chosen exemplars varied widely in age, education, occupation, and ethnicity. There were 10 men and 13 women, ages 35 to 86, of white, African American, and Hispanic backgrounds. Education ranged from eighth grade up through M.D.s, Ph.D.s, and law degrees; and occupations included religious callings, business, teaching, and social leadership. Areas of concern involved poverty, civil rights, education, ethics, the environment, peace, and religious freedom.

The research yielded a number of surprises, not least of which was this group's showing on Kohlberg's classic measure of moral judgment. Each exemplar was asked about "Heinz's dilemma" (refer back to Chapter 11) and about a follow-up dilemma: how the man should be punished if he steals the drug. Of 22 exemplars (one response was not scorable), only half scored at the postconventional level; the other half scored at the conventional level. The major difference between the two groups was level of education: those with college and advanced degrees were much more likely to score at the higher level, and no one with only a high school diploma scored above the conventional level. Clearly, it is not necessary to score at Kohlberg's highest stages to live an exemplary moral life.

How does a person become morally committed? The 23 moral exemplars did not develop in isolation, but responded to social influences. Some of these influences, such as those of parents, were important from childhood on. Many other influences became significant in later years, helping these people evaluate their capacities, form moral goals, and develop strategies to achieve them.

These moral exemplars had a lifelong commitment to change: they focused their energy on changing society and people's lives for the better. But they remained stable in their moral commitments. At the same time, they kept growing throughout life, remained open to new ideas, and continued to learn from others.

The processes responsible for stability in moral commitments were gradual, taking many years to build up. They were also collaborative: leaders took advice from supporters, and people noted for independent judgment drew heavily on feedback from those close to them—both those people who shared their goals and those who had different perspectives.

Along with their enduring moral commitments, certain personality characteristics seemed to remain with the moral exemplars throughout middle and late adulthood: enjoyment of life, ability to make the best of a bad situation, solidarity with others, absorption in work, a sense of humor, and humility. They tended to believe that change was possible, and this optimism helped them battle what often seemed like overwhelming odds and to persist in the face of defeat.

While their actions often meant risk and hardship, these people did not see themselves as courageous. Nor did they agonize over decisions. Since their personal and moral goals coincided, they just did what they believed needed to be done, not calculating personal consequences to themselves or their families and not feeling that they were sacrificing or martyring themselves.

Of course, there is no "blueprint" for creating a moral giant, just as it does not seem possible to write directions to produce a genius in any field. What studying the lives of such people can bring is the knowledge that ordinary people can rise to greatness and that openness to change and new ideas can persist throughout adulthood.

Practical Problem Solving

Does deciding what to do about a flooded basement take the same kind of intelligence as playing word games? Is the ability to solve practical problems affected by age? Much research on practical problem solving has not found the declines sometimes seen in measures of fluid intelligence, and some research has found marked improvement, at least through middle age (Berg & Klaczynski, 1996).

In a number of studies, the quality of practical decisions (such as what car to buy, what kind of treatment to get for breast cancer, how much money to put away in a pension plan, or how to compare insurance policies) bore only a modest relationship, if any, to performance on tasks like those on intelligence tests (M. M. S. Johnson, Schmitt, & Everard, 1994; Meyer, Russo, & Talbot, 1995) and, often, no relationship to age (Capon, Kuhn, & Carretero, 1989; M. M. S. Johnson, 1990; Meyer et al., 1995; Walsh & Hershey, 1993). In other studies, problem solving improved with age (Cornelius & Caspi, 1987; Perlmutter, Kaplan, & Nyquist, 1990).

In one study (Denney & Palmer, 1981), 84 adults ages 20 to 79 were given two kinds of problems. One kind was like the game Twenty Questions. Participants were shown pictures of common objects and were told to figure out which one the examiner was thinking of, by asking questions that could be answered "yes" or "no." The older the participants were, the worse they did on this part of the test. The second kind of problem involved situations like the following: *Your basement is flooding;* or, *You are stranded in a car during a blizzard;* or, *Your 8-year-old child is $1\frac{1}{2}$ hours late coming home from school.* High scores were given for responses that showed self-reliance and recognition of a number of possible causes and solutions. According to these criteria, the best practical problem solvers were people in their forties and fifties, who based their answers on everyday experience.

A follow-up study posed problems with which elderly people would be especially familiar (concerning retirement, widowhood, and ill health), yet people in their forties still came up with better solutions (Denney & Pearce, 1989). However, in other studies in which problems were real rather than hypothetical and were brought up by the participants themselves, and in which solutions were rated by quality rather than quantity, practical problem-solving ability did *not* seem to decline after middle age (Camp, Doherty, Moody-Thomas, & Denney, 1989; Cornelius & Caspi, 1987).

What explains these inconsistencies? As we have seen, there are differences in the kinds of problems various researchers study, in the relevance of these problems to real life, and in the criteria used to rate the solutions. Also, individual differences—for example, in educational level—may affect how people perceive and solve problems (Berg & Klaczynski, 1996; Blanchard-Fields, Chen, & Norris, 1997).

Some studies focus on *instrumental* problems, or activities of daily living, such as reading a map or a medicine label. These abilities are highly related to fluid intelligence and show age-related decline (see Chapter 17). Declines may occur sooner in people with especially slow perceptual speed (Willis & Schaie, 1999; Willis et al., 1998).

By contrast, studies such as those just described deal mainly with *social* problems. These studies suggest that people of different ages interpret problems differently and see different kinds of solutions as effective. When problems are relevant to older adults' lives and feelings, the participants show more complex thought (Berg & Klaczynski, 1996). On this type of problem, both middle-aged and older adults tend to do better than younger ones; they have more extensive and varied repertoires of strategies to apply to different situations (Blanchard-Fields et al., 1997).

One thing seems clear: middle-aged people tend to be effective practical problem solvers. If the function of intelligence is to deal with real-life problems, as Gandhi did, the strengths of mature thought in midlife are plain.

CHECKPOINT

Can you . . .

- ✔ Discuss the relationship between expertise and fluid and crystallized intelligence?
- ✔ Explain why postformal thought seems especially suited to solving social problems typically encountered in middle age?
- ✔ Give an example of integrative thinking?
- ✔ Identify two types of practical problem solving, and tell how they are affected by age?

Creativity

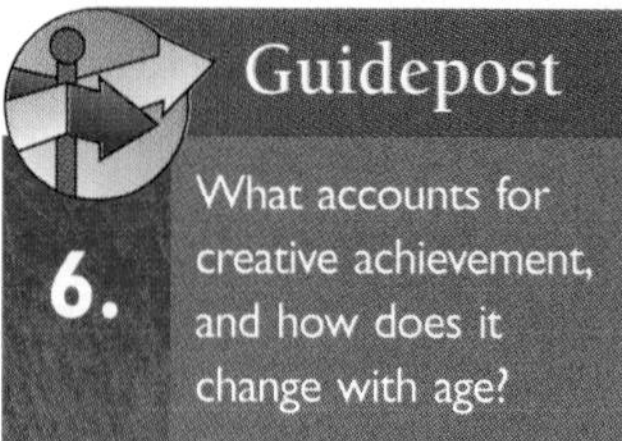

What accounts for creative achievement, and how does it change with age?

At about age 40, Frank Lloyd Wright designed Robie House in Chicago, Agnes deMille choreographed the Broadway musical *Carousel,* and Louis Pasteur developed the germ theory of disease. Charles Darwin was 50 when he presented his theory of evolution. Toni Morrison won the Pulitzer Prize for *Beloved,* a novel she wrote at about 55.

Creativity begins with talent, but talent is not enough. Children may show *creative potential;* but in adults, what counts is *creative performance*: what, and how much, a creative mind produces (Sternberg & Lubart, 1995). Creative performance, says Howard Gardner (1986, 1988), is the product of a web of biological, personal, social, and cultural forces, and the cognitive abilities and processes that contribute to it are hard to pin down. We can observe *what* creative achievers do, but just *how* they do it remains, in large part, a mystery.

Extraordinary creative achievement, according to one analysis (Keegan, 1996), results from deep, highly organized knowledge of a subject; intrinsic motivation to work hard for the sake of the work, not for external rewards; and a strong emotional attachment to the work, which spurs the creator to persevere in the face of obstacles. What carries such creative giants as Einstein and Picasso "over the threshold from competent but ordinary thinker to extraordinary and creative thinker" (p. 63) is the acquisition of expert knowledge—a process that takes many years. A person must first be thoroughly grounded in a field before she or he can see its limitations, envision radical departures, and develop a new and unique point of view.

Consider this . . .

- Think of an adult you know who is a creative achiever. To what combination of personal qualities and environmental forces would you attribute her or his creative performance?

Of course, not all experts are brilliant creators. Highly creative people are self-starters (Torrance, 1988). They have a strong sense of purpose and direction, and they can juggle several ideas or projects at a time (Gardner, 1981). Their thinking processes are often unconscious and offbeat, leading to sudden moments of illumination (Torrance, 1988). Like Gandhi, they look at a problem more deeply than other people do and come up with solutions that do not occur to others (Sternberg & Horvath, 1998).

Creativity and Intelligence

Creativity is not limited to the Darwins and deMilles; we can see it, for example, in an inventor who comes up with a better mousetrap, or a promoter who finds an innovative way to sell it. According to Robert Sternberg (Sternberg & Lubart, 1995), each of three aspects of intelligence (see Chapters 9 and 13) plays a role in creative performance.

The *insightful* component helps to define a problem or to see it in a new light. Creative people show special insight in three ways: (1) they pick out information relevant to the problem—often information that no one else thought to consider; (2) they "put two and two together," seeing relationships between apparently unrelated pieces of information; and (3) they see analogies between a new problem and one they have already encountered. These abilities do not emerge full-grown; they become more efficient with experi-

Creativity begins with talent, but talent is not enough. The author Toni Morrison, 1993 winner of the Nobel Prize in Literature, worked long, hard hours throughout her prolific career. Her achievements are examples of the creative productivity possible in middle age. *(Ulf Andersen/Gamma-Liaison)*

ence and knowledge (Sternberg & Horvath, 1998). In a classic longitudinal study of art students (Getzels & Csikszentmihalyi, 1968, 1975, 1976), those who, by selection and arrangement of objects for a still life, set up the most unusual and complex artistic problems for themselves to solve were the ones whose works were judged by art experts as best and most original and who later proved most successful in the field.

The *analytic* component of intelligence can evaluate an idea and decide whether it is worth pursuing. James D. Watson, a molecular biologist who won the Nobel Prize for the discovery of the structure of DNA, was described by one of his graduate students at Harvard University as having "an uncanny instinct for the important problem, the thing that leads to big-time results. He seems to . . . pluck it out of thin air" (Edson, 1968, pp. 29–31).

The *practical* aspect of intelligence comes into play in "selling" an idea—getting it accepted. Thomas Edison held more than 1,000 patents for his inventions, created several companies to market them, and had a knack for getting his name and picture in the newspapers. This practical aspect may well be strongest in middle age.

Creativity and Age

Is there a relationship between creative performance and age? On psychometric tests of divergent thinking (refer back to Chapter 9), age differences consistently show up. Whether data are cross-sectional or longitudinal, scores peak, on average, around the late thirties. A similar age curve emerges when creativity is measured by variations in output (number of publications, paintings, or compositions). A person in the last decade of a creative career typically produces only about half as much as during the late thirties or early forties, though somewhat more than in the twenties (Simonton, 1990).

However, the age curve varies depending on the field. Poets, mathematicians, and theoretical physicists tend to be most prolific in their late twenties or early thirties. Psychologists reach a peak around age 40, followed by a moderate decline. Novelists, historians, philosophers, and scholars become increasingly productive through their late forties or fifties and then level off. These patterns hold true across cultures and historical periods (Simonton, 1990).

Losses in productivity may be offset by gains in quality; maturity changes the tone and content of creative work. Age-related analyses of themes of ancient Greek and Shakespearean plays show a shift from youthful preoccupation with love and romance to more spiritual concerns (Simonton, 1983, 1986). And a study of the "swan songs" of 172 composers found that their last works—usually fairly short and melodically simple—were among their richest, most important, and most successful (Simonton, 1989).

CHECKPOINT

Can you . . .

- ✔ Discuss the relationship between creative potential and creative performance, and name several qualities of creative achievers?
- ✔ Tell how Sternberg's three aspects of intelligence apply to creative performance?
- ✔ Summarize the relationship between creative performance and age?

Work and Education: Are Age-Based Roles Obsolete?

The traditional life structure in industrialized societies is **age-differentiated:** roles are based on age (as in the left side of Figure 15-4). Young people are students; young and middle-aged adults are workers; older adults organize their lives around retirement and leisure. Yet, as the gerontologist Matilda White Riley (1994) has observed:

> . . . these structures fail to accommodate many of the changes in people's lives. After all, does it make sense to spend nearly one-third of adult lifetime in retirement? Or to crowd most work into the harried middle years? Or to label as "too old" those as young as 55 who want to work? Does it make sense to

age-differentiated
Life structure in which primary roles—learning, working, and leisure—are based on age; typical in industrialized societies. Compare *age-integrated.*

assume that . . . physically capable older people—an estimated 40 million of them in the next century—should expect greater support from society than they contribute to society? . . . Surely, something will have to change! (p. 445)

According to Riley, age-differentiated roles are a holdover from a time when life was shorter and social institutions less diverse. By devoting themselves to one aspect of life at a time, people do not enjoy each period as much as they might and may not prepare adequately for the next phase. By concentrating on work, adults may forget how to play; then, when they retire, they may not know what to do with a sudden abundance of leisure time. Increasing numbers of older adults (like Gandhi in his later years) are able to contribute to society (see Chapters 17 and 18), but opportunities to use and reward their abilities are inadequate.

age-integrated
Life structure in which primary roles—learning, working, and leisure—are open to adults of all ages and can be interspersed throughout the life span. Compare *age-differentiated.*

In an **age-integrated** society (as in the right side of Figure 15-4), all kinds of roles—learning, working, and playing—would be open to adults of all ages (Riley, 1994). They could intersperse periods of education, work, and leisure throughout the lifespan. Things seem to be moving in that direction. College students take work-study programs or "stop out" for a while before resuming their education. Mature adults take evening classes or take time off work to pursue a special interest. A person may have several careers in succession, each requiring additional education or training. People retire earlier or later than in the past, or not at all. Retirees devote time to study or to a new line of work.

Much of the existing research on education, work, leisure, and retirement reflects the old, age-differentiated model of social roles and the cohorts whose lives it describes. As "age integration" emerges, future cohorts may have very different experiences and attitudes. With that reservation in mind, let's look at work and education in middle adulthood.

Occupational Patterns and Paths: Stable or Shifting

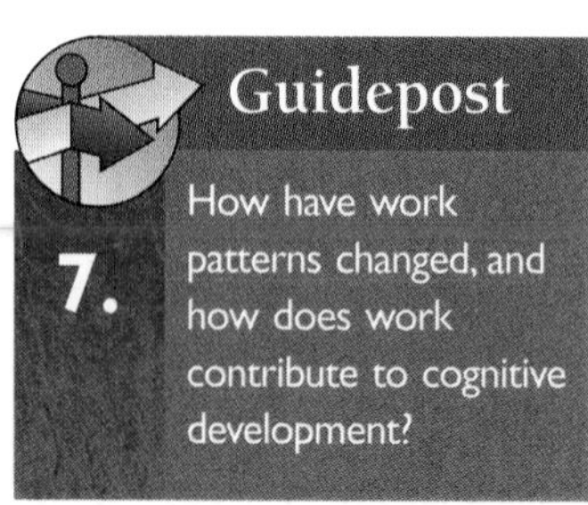

Guidepost
7.
How have work patterns changed, and how does work contribute to cognitive development?

Early theories of career development reflected a stable, mostly middle-class pattern. Donald Super's (1957, 1985) influential theory described an orderly progression of stages, from trying out entry-level jobs in the early twenties to commitment to a career goal in the late twenties, consolidation and maintenance of one's position in the thirties and forties, and preparing for and entering retirement in the fifties and sixties.

Super developed his theory at a time when relatively few women worked outside the home, and decisions made in young adulthood generally shaped a man's entire working life. Today, most women are in the labor force, and technological change and economic dislocations have resulted in layoffs, job obsolescence, and frequent job or career changes. Occupations that engaged millions of people no longer exist; occupations that may engage millions of people in the future have yet to be imagined. Even in Japan, where a worker used to be guaranteed the same job for life, only 1 in 5 is now covered by such a guarantee (Desmond, 1996).

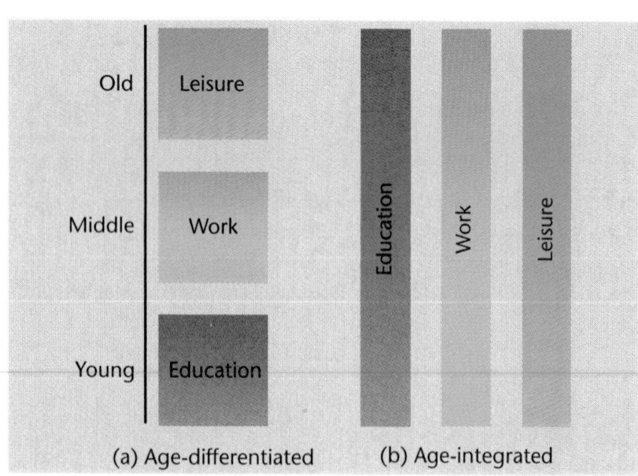

Figure 15-4
Contrasting social structures.
(a) Traditional age-differentiated structure, typical of industrialized societies. Education, work, and leisure roles are largely "assigned" to different phases of life.
(b) Age-integrated structure, which would spread all three kinds of roles throughout the adult life span and help break down social barriers between generations
(Source: M. W. Riley, 1994, p. 445.)

Mandatory retirement has been virtually eliminated, but downsizing, company pension plans, and other incentives have sparked a trend toward early retirement in the forties or fifties. On the other hand, many of today's middle-aged and older workers—caught between inadequate savings or pensions and a strained social security system, or simply unwilling to give up the stimulation of work—are choosing not to retire or to try a new line of work (see Chapter 18).

In a society undergoing dramatic change, career decisions are often open-ended. A theory that seeks to capture the dynamic character of vocational development is that of Eli Ginzberg (1972). After examining the occupational histories of women and men from a wide variety of backgrounds, Ginzberg concluded that career paths fall into one of two patterns: *stable* or *shifting*.

People with *stable* career patterns stay with a single vocation and, by midlife, often reach positions of power and responsibility. Middle-aged men with stable careers tend to be either "workaholics" or "mellowed" (Tamir, 1989). Workaholics work at a frenzied pace, either in a last-ditch effort to reach financial security before they retire or because they find it hard to relinquish authority. "Mellowed" people have come to terms with their level of achievement, even if they have not gone as far as they had hoped. The best adjusted among them have a sense of relaxation rather than failure. They are often happier, less cynical, and steadier in temperament than their more successful counterparts. Although they want to do challenging work, they do not pin their emotional well-being on their jobs as they used to (Bray & Howard, 1983).

Rather than settle for their initial occupational choice, people who follow the *shifting* pattern try to achieve a better match between what they can do, what they want and expect from their work, and what they are getting out of it. This reevaluation can lead to career change, as it did with Gandhi when he gave up a busy urban law practice for collective farming to prepare for moral and political leadership.

People may shift careers anytime during adulthood, but middle age, with its altered family responsibilities and financial needs, is a typical time to do it. Because fewer middle-aged and older women have worked throughout adulthood, they are less likely than men to exhibit the stable pattern; and, if they do, they may reach the traditional stages of career development later than men typically do (Avolio & Sosik, 1999).

Work and Cognitive Development

"Use it or lose it" applies to the mind as well as the body. Work can influence future cognitive functioning. Middle-aged architects, for example, tend to retain the ability to visualize spatial relationships longer than people in other fields (Salthouse, Babcock, Mitchell, Skrovronek, & Palmon, 1990).

Certain kinds of work strengthen cognitive skills. As we discussed in Chapter 13, people with substantively complex work—work requiring thought and independent judgment, such as writing new software programs—tend to become more flexible thinkers; and flexible thinking increases the ability to do complex work (Kohn, 1980). Thanks to this cumulative cycle of experience—and the knowledge that comes with it—people who are deeply engaged in complex

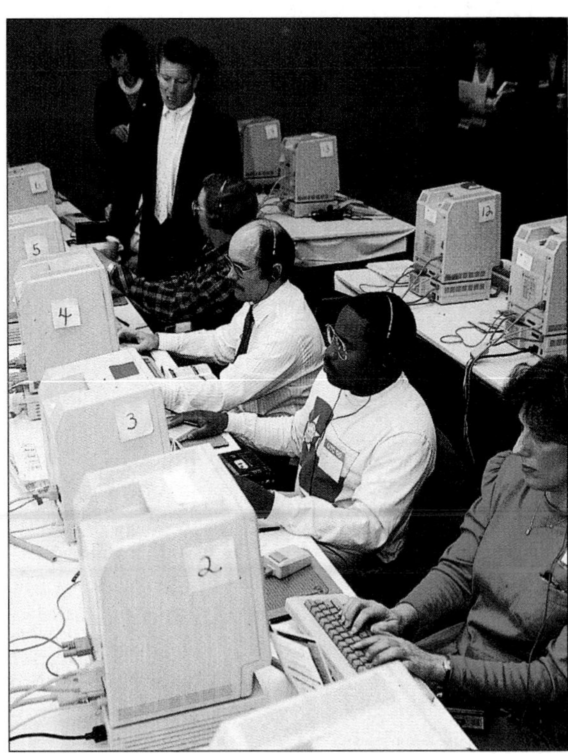

These government workers improving their computer skills are among the approximately 50 percent of adults in the United States who participate in continuing education. Most mature adults who take part-time classes do so for job-related reasons, and they tend to be more motivated than younger students.

work tend to show stronger cognitive performance in comparison with their peers as they age (Avolio & Sosik, 1999; Kohn & Schooler, 1983; Schaie, 1984; Schooler, 1984, 1990). Indeed, it has been estimated that as much as one-third of the individual variance in changes in cognitive ability with age may be attributable to such factors as education, occupation, and socioeconomic status (Schaie, 1990). Thus, if work could be made more meaningful and challenging, more adults might retain or improve their cognitive abilities (Avolio & Sosik, 1999).

This seems to be happening already. The gains in most cognitive abilities found in recent middle-aged and older cohorts in the Seattle Longitudinal Study may well reflect workplace changes that emphasize self-managed, multifunctional teams and put a premium on adaptability, initiative, and decentralized decision making. In such a climate, workers who expand their skills, knowledge, and competencies may reap rewards (Avolio & Sosik, 1999).

CHECKPOINT

Can you . . .

- ✔ Explain how an age-integrated society would differ from an age-differentiated society and give examples?
- ✔ Compare Super's and Ginzberg's theories of career development, and describe societal changes that correspond to the differences?
- ✔ Explain how work can affect future cognitive functioning?

Unfortunately, older workers are less likely than younger workers to be offered, or to volunteer for, training, education, and challenging job assignments, in the mistaken belief that older people cannot handle such opportunities. Yet the Seattle study found that declines in cognitive ability generally do not occur until very late in life, well after the working years (see Chapter 17). Indeed, work performance shows greater variability *within* age groups than between them (Avolio & Sosik, 1999).

Adults can actively affect their future cognitive development by the occupational choices they make. Those who constantly seek more stimulating opportunities—for example, in new or expanding fields such as Internet development and other electronic-and computer-based industries—are likely to remain mentally sharp (Avolio & Sosik, 1999).

The Mature Learner

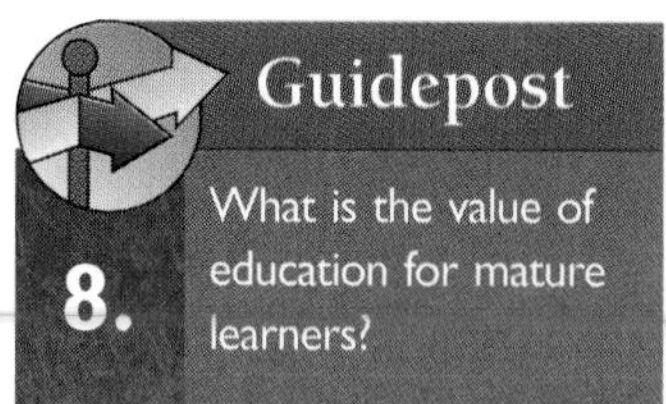

Guidepost
8.
What is the value of education for mature learners?

Changes in the workplace often entail a need for more training or education. A college degree earned in the early twenties will not suffice for most people in the future. Even now, many workers and retirees go back to school. Expanding technology and shifting job markets require a life-span approach to learning. For many adults, formal learning is an important way to develop their cognitive potential and to keep up with the changing world of work. In 1995, nearly 1 in 5 college and university students was 35 or older (Snyder et al., 1997).

To accommodate the practical needs of students of nontraditional age, most colleges grant credit for life experience and previous learning. They also offer part-time matriculation, Saturday and night classes, independent study, child care, financial aid, free or reduced-tuition courses, and **distance learning** via computers or closed-circuit broadcasts.

distance learning Arrangement for taking courses at a distant location via computer or closed-circuit radio broadcasts.

About 40 percent of all adults participate in continuing education, the fastest-growing part of the American educational system. About half of those who take part-time classes do so for job-related reasons (Snyder et al., 1997). Some seek training to update their knowledge and skills—to keep up with new developments in their fields and to understand and cope with technological change. Some train for new occupations when their old ones become obsolete or when their needs and interests change. Some want to move up the career ladder or to go into business for themselves. Some women who have devoted their young adult years to homemaking and parenting are taking the first steps toward reentering the job market. People close to retirement often want to expand their minds and skills to make more productive and interesting use of leisure. Some adults simply enjoy learning and want to keep doing it throughout life.

Consider this . . .

- From what you have seen, do students of nontraditional age seem to do better or worse in college than younger students? How would you explain your observation?

Unfortunately, many learning institutions are not structured to meet mature adults' educational and psychological needs or to take advantage of their cognitive strengths. Adult learners have their own motives, goals, developmental tasks, and experiences. Educational institutions, such as universities, typically are built around the way younger people in Schaie's (1977–1978; Schaie & Willis, 2000) *acquisitive stage* (refer back to Chapter 13) are expected to learn. Fact-laden lectures by authority figures, competitive grading systems, and an emphasis on memorization are not well suited to mature learners in the *responsible* or *executive* stages, who come with their own expertise and, often, with postformal thinking skills, and who need knowledge they can apply to specific problems. Cooperative study built around self-generated problems or projects is more appropriate to a mature adult. Also, there is danger in overemphasis on learning directed toward occupational preparation, which may quickly become obsolete. Learning for its own sake, to develop a person's human potential, may be a more practical investment in the long run (Sinnott, 1998).

CHECKPOINT

Can you . . .

✔ Give reasons why mature adults return to the classroom, and tell some ways in which educational institutions may not be suited to their needs?

Research about education and work—as well as about problem solving, creativity, and moral choices—shows that the mind continues to develop during adulthood. Such research also illustrates the links between the cognitive side of development and its social and emotional aspects, to which we turn again in Chapter 16.

Summary

Middle Age: A Cultural Construct

Guidepost 1. What are the distinguishing features of middle age?

- The concept of middle age is socially constructed. It came into use as an increasing life span led to new roles at midlife.
- The span of middle adulthood can be defined chronologically, contextually, or biologically.
- Most middle-aged people are in good physical, cognitive, and emotional condition. They have heavy responsibilities and multiple roles and feel competent to handle them.
- Middle age is a time for taking stock and making decisions about the remaining years.

PHYSICAL DEVELOPMENT

Physical Changes

Guidepost 2. What physical changes generally occur during the middle years, and what is their psychological impact?

- Although some physiological changes result from aging and genetic makeup, behavior and lifestyle can affect their timing and extent.
- Most middle-aged adults compensate well for gradual, minor declines in sensory and psychomotor abilities, including such age-related conditions as **presbyopia** and **presbycusis,** increases in **myopia,** and loss of endurance due to slowing of **basal metabolism.** Losses in bone density and **vital capacity** are common.
- **Menopause** occurs, on average, at about age 51, following the physiological changes of **perimenopause.** Attitudes toward menopause, and symptoms experienced, may depend on personal characteristics, past experiences, and cultural attitudes.
- Although men can continue to father children until late in life, many middle-aged men experience a decline in fertility and in frequency of orgasm and an increase in **erectile dysfunction.**
- Sexual activity generally diminishes only slightly and gradually, and the quality of sexual relations may improve.
- The "double standard of aging" causes women to seem less desirable as they lose their youthful appearance. For both sexes, anxiety about getting older is heightened in a society that places a premium on youth.

Health

Guidepost 3. What factors affect health at midlife

- Most middle-aged people are healthy and have no functional limitations.
- **Hypertension** is a major health problem beginning in midlife. AIDS tends to be more severe in older people becaused of weakened immune functioning.
- Low income is associated with poorer health. Death rates are higher for males than for females and higher for black people than for white people.
- Postmenopausal women become more susceptible to heart disease and **osteoporosis** and may take **hormone replacement therapy (HRT)** or an alternative treatment.
- African Americans' elevated health risks may be due to a combination of hereditary factors, lifestyle factors, poverty, and stress caused by racial prejudice.
- Diet, alcohol use, and smoking affect present and future health.
- Stress is related to a variety of physical and psychological problems. An accumulation of minor, everyday **stressors** can be more harmful than major life changes.
- Causes of occupational stress include work overload, interpersonal conflict, **sexual harassment** and a combination of high pressure and low control. Continual stress may lead to **burnout.**

- Unemployment creates stress. Physical and psychological effects may depend on coping resources.

COGNITIVE DEVELOPMENT

Measuring Cognitive Abilities in Middle Age

Guidepost 4. What cognitive gains and losses occur during middle age?

- The Seattle Longitudinal Study found most basic mental abilities peak during middle age. **Fluid intelligence** declines earlier than **crystallized intelligence.**

The Distinctiveness of Adult Cognition

Guidepost 5. Do mature adults think differently from younger people?

- Some developmentalists maintain that cognition takes distinctive forms at midlife. According to Hoyer and his colleagues, expertise, or specialized knowledge, can be explained by **encapsulation** of fluid abilities within a person's chosen field.
- Postformal thought seems especially useful in situations calling for integrative thinking.
- The ability to solve practical problems is strong, and may peak, at midlife.

Creativity

Guidepost 6. What accounts for creative achievement, and how does it change with age?

- Creative performance depends on personal attributes and environmental forces, as well as cognitive abilities.
- According to Sternberg, the insightful, analytic, and practical aspects of intelligence all play a part in creative performance.
- An age-related decline appears in both psychometric tests of divergent thinking and actual creative output, but peak ages for output vary by occupation.

Work and Education: Are Age-Based Roles Obsolete?

Guidepost 7. How have work patterns changed, and how does work contribute to cognitive development?

- A shift from **age-differentiated** to **age-integrated** roles appears to be occurring in response to longer life and social change.
- Early theories of career development, such as Super's, describe an orderly progression of stages along a single track. Ginzberg's theory, based on more recent changes in work life, describes two basic career paths: stability and change.
- Complex work helps maintain cognitive functioning. Changes in the workplace may make work more meaningful and cognitively challenging for many people.

Guidepost 8. What is the value of education for mature learners?

- Many adults go to college at a nontraditional age or participate in continuing education through regular classes or **distance learning.** Adults go to school chiefly to improve work-related skills and knowledge or to prepare for a change of career.
- Many learning institutions are not structured to meet mature adults' needs.

Key Terms

presbyopia (562)
myopia (562)
presbycusis (562)
basal metabolism (562)
vital capacity (563)
menopause (564)
perimenopause (564)
erectile dysfunction (567)
hypertension (569)
osteoporosis (570)
hormone replacement therapy (HRT) (570)
stressors (573)
sexual harassment (576)
burnout (576)
fluid intelligence (578)
crystallized intelligence (579)
encapsulation (581)
age-differentiated (585)
age-integrated (586)
distance learning (588)

Chapter 16

Psychosocial Development in Middle Adulthood

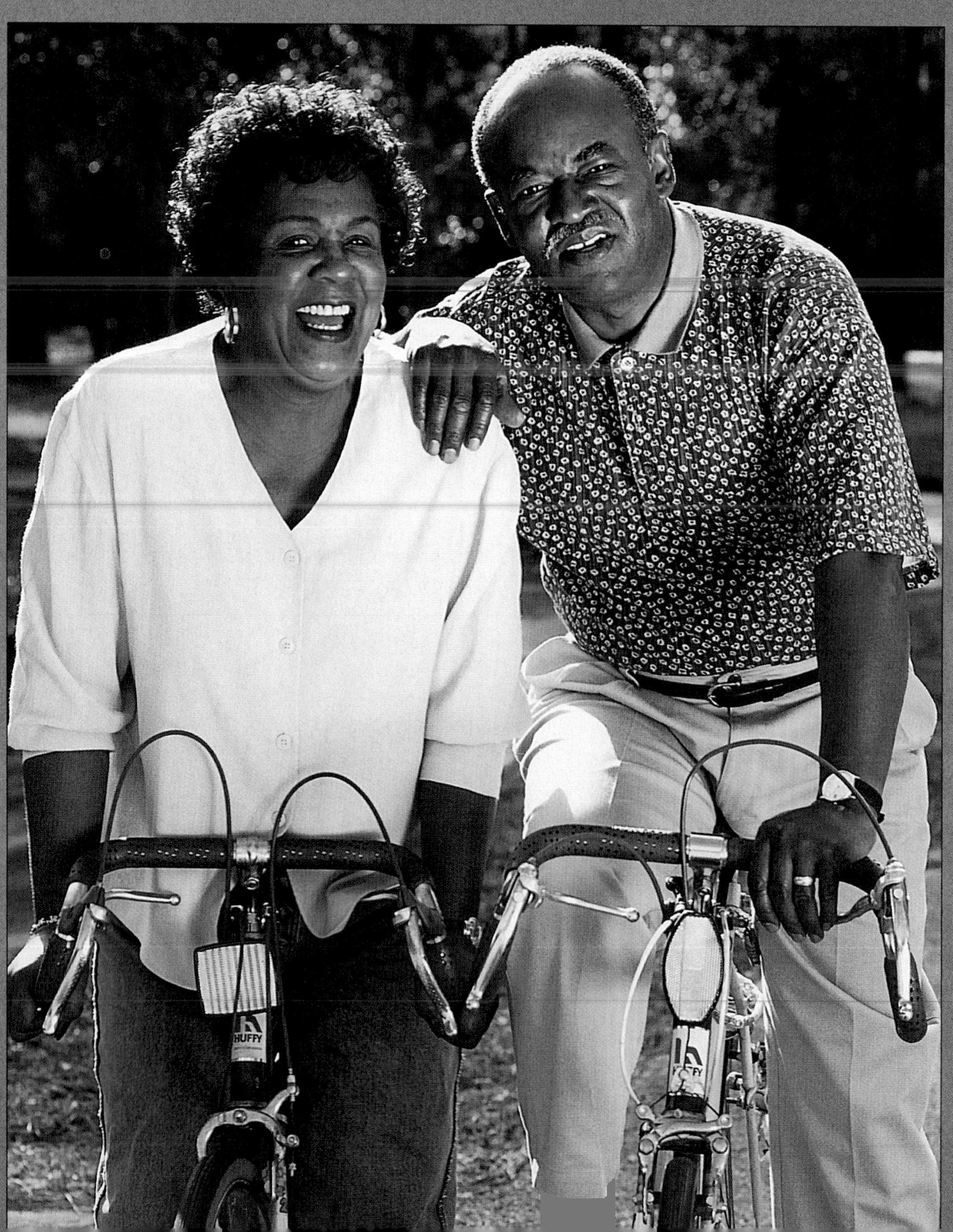

OUTLINE

To accept all experience as raw material out of which the human spirits distill meanings and values is a part of the meaning of maturity.

Howard Thurman, *Meditations of the Heart,* 1953

Madeleine Albright

Focus: Madeleine Albright, Top-Ranking Diplomat

On January 23, 1997, four months before her sixtieth birthday, Madeleine Korbel Albright* (b. 1937) was sworn in as Secretary of State, the highest rank ever achieved by a woman in the U.S. government. It was a heady moment for a woman who had arrived at age 11 with her family as refugees from Communist Czechoslovakia.

Albright's life is the story of "someone who has again and again reinvented herself" (Heilbrunn, 1998, p. 12). First there was the journey from her childhood as the daughter of a diplomat in war-torn Europe to her adolescence as a scholarship student at a private school in Denver. Then came a scholarship to Wellesley College and, three days after commencement, a "Cinderella marriage" to Joseph Medill Patterson Albright, heir to a prominent publishing family, followed by the birth of twin girls. Thirteen years and a third daughter later, she obtained a Ph.D. in political science at Columbia University as she entered middle age. As the women's movement gathered steam, President Jimmy Carter's national security adviser, Zbigniew Brzezinski, tapped Albright, his former student at Columbia, as congressional liaison for the National Security Council.

Less than a year after the Carter presidency and Albright's White House stint ended, her husband of twenty-three years announced that he was in love with a younger woman. The divorce was a turning point in her life. At 45, she was a single mother, "aching

*Sources of biographical material about Madeleine Albright were Blackman (1998) and Blood (1997).

to chart a new path" (Blackman, 1998, p. 187). She joined the faculty of Georgetown University's School of Foreign Service and became a "regular" on public television talk shows. The woman whom colleagues had seen as shy and self-effacing, whose self-esteem had been shattered by her divorce, developed confidence and self-assurance as she honed her crisp, succinct speaking style.

Albright broke into the national limelight as foreign policy adviser to vice-presidential candidate Geraldine Ferraro in 1984 and to presidential candidate Michael Dukakis in 1988. It was in the Dukakis campaign that Albright, now over 50, met Bill Clinton, who, in 1992, as president-elect, appointed her ambassador to the United Nations and four years later chose her to head the State Department.

As her middle years come to an end, Albright's life is full and fulfilling. Her bonds with her married daughters and her grandchildren are strong. So are her ties with the many friends who have supported her throughout her career.

One more twist in the "reinvention" of Madeleine Albright came as she was just settling in at the State Department. Press reports revealed that Albright, who was raised Catholic, had been born Jewish and that several close relatives had perished in the Holocaust. In 1941, in the dangerous climate of World War II, her parents had converted to Catholicism and had had themselves and "Madlenka," then barely 4, baptized.

Her now-deceased parents had never told her of her Jewish heritage. At 59, she had to come to a new understanding of her identity and her family history—an understanding brought home when she walked through the Old Jewish Cemetery in Prague and came face-to-face with the synagogue wall on which the names of her grandparents were inscribed along with nearly eighty thousand other victims of Naziism. As she stood there, silent, she thought about her parents and the "excruciating decision" they had made (Blackman, 1998, p. 293). "I'm very proud of what my parents did for me and my [then unborn] brother and sister," Albright said. "I have always been very proud of my heritage. And as I find out more about it, I am even more proud" (Blood, 1997, p. 226).

Although the specifics of Madeleine Albright's story are unusual, its main thrust is similar to the adult experience of many other women her age: marriage and motherhood, followed by a midlife career, sometimes a midlife divorce, and a blossoming of possibilities that comes with the emptying of the nest.

One of Albright's greatest assets is adaptability. Again and again, she has adjusted to new environments, learned new languages, mastered new challenges, and reshaped her identity. As she did, she grew in personal strength. Much of that mastery and growth occurred during middle age.

Midlife is a special time. Middle-aged people are not only in the middle of the adult life span, in a position to look back and ahead in their own lives; they also bridge older and younger generations. Very often, they are the ones who hold families together and, like Madeleine Albright, make societal institutions and enterprises work. Much can happen during the twenty-five-year span we call *middle adulthood;* and these experiences affect the way people look, feel, and act as they enter old age.

In this chapter we look at theoretical perspectives and research on psychosocial issues and themes at midlife. We then focus on intimate relationships, which shape the occurrence and timing of life events. As we examine marriage and divorce, gay and lesbian relationships, and friendship, as well as relationships with maturing children, aging parents, siblings, and grandchildren, we see how richly textured are these middle years.

After you have read and studied this chapter, you should be able to answer the following questions:

Guideposts *for* **Study**

1. How do developmental scientists approach the study of psychosocial development in middle adulthood?
2. What do classic theorists have to say about psychosocial change in middle age?
3. What issues concerning the self come to the fore during middle adulthood?
4. How does midlife development differ for women and men?
5. What role do social relationships play in the lives of middle-aged people?
6. Do marriages become happier or unhappier during the middle years?
7. How common is divorce at this time of life?
8. How do gay and lesbian relationships compare with heterosexual ones?
9. How do friendships fare during middle age?
10. How do parent-child relationships change as children approach and reach adulthood?
11. How do middle-aged people get along with parents and siblings?
12. How has grandparenthood changed, and what roles do grandparents play?

Looking at the Life Course in Middle Age

Developmentalists view the course of midlife psychosocial development in several ways. *Objectively,* they look at trajectories or pathways, such as Madeleine Albright's evolution from a wife and mother with a passion for politics to the most powerful woman in the country. But continuities and changes in roles and relationships also have a *subjective* side: people actively construct their sense of self and the structure of their lives. Thus it is important to consider how a person like Albright defines herself and how satisfied she is with her life (Moen & Wethington, 1999).

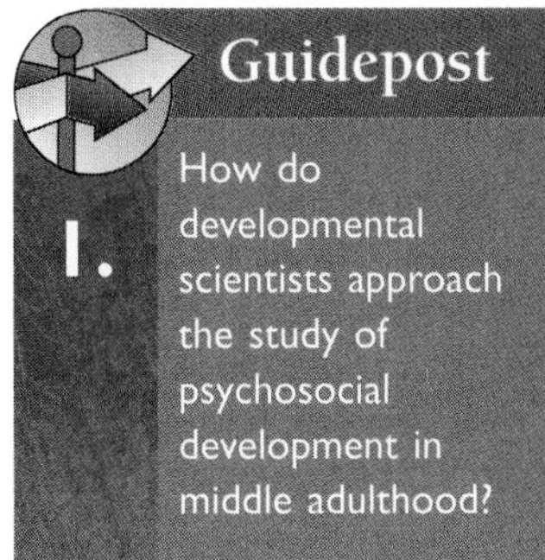

Guidepost

1. How do developmental scientists approach the study of psychosocial development in middle adulthood?

Change and continuity in middle age must be seen in the perspective of the entire life span. Albright's midlife career built on her childhood experiences and youthful strivings. But early patterns are not necessarily blueprints for later ones (Lachman & James, 1997); nor are the concerns of early middle age the same as those of late middle age (Helson, 1997). Just think of the difference between Albright's life at 40 and her life at 60!

Furthermore, lives do not progress in isolation. Individual pathways intersect or collide with those of family members, friends and acquaintances, and strangers. Work and personal roles are interdependent, as exemplified by Albright's career change after her divorce; and those roles are affected by trends in the larger society, as Albright's opportunities were enhanced by the changing status of women (Moen & Wethington, 1999).

CHECKPOINT

Can you . . .

- ✔ Distinguish between objective and subjective views of the life course?
- ✔ Name several factors that affect the life course at middle age?

Cohort, gender, and socioeconomic status profoundly affect the life course (Helson, 1997; Moen & Wethington, 1999). Madeleine Albright's path was very different from that of her mother, who made her family her total life's work. Unusual as Albright was for her time, her course also was different from that of most educated young women today, who embark on careers before marriage and motherhood. We can speculate on what Albright's expectations and trajectory would have been had she been a man, rather than a woman seeking to use her capabilities in a society based on male dominance. Albright's path also would have been different had she not married into a wealthy family, affording her the means to hire housekeepers while her children were young and she was working toward her doctorate. All these factors, and more, enter into the study of psychosocial development in middle adulthood.

Change at Midlife: Classic Theoretical Approaches

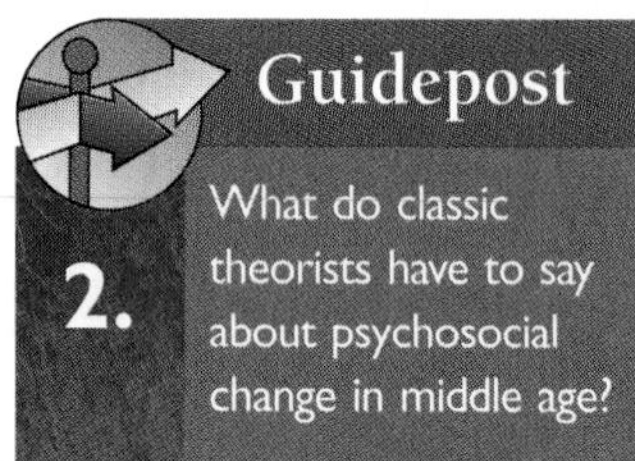

Guidepost
2.
What do classic theorists have to say about psychosocial change in middle age?

In psychosocial terms, middle adulthood once was considered a relatively settled period (Whitbourne & Connolly, 1999). Freud (1906/1942) saw no point in psychotherapy for people over 50 because he believed personality is permanently formed by that age and mental processes are too inflexible. Costa and McCrae (1994a), whose trait model we introduced in Chapter 14, also describe middle age as a time of essential stability in personality.

By contrast, humanistic theorists such as Abraham Maslow and Carl Rogers looked on middle age as an opportunity for positive change. According to Maslow (1968), self-actualization (refer back to Chapter 2) can come only with maturity. Rogers (1961) held that full human functioning requires a constant, lifelong process of bringing the self in harmony with experience.

As we noted in Chapter 14, developmental research today has moved beyond the debate over stability versus change. A number of longitudinal studies show that psychosocial development involves both (Franz, 1997; Helson, 1997). The question is, what *kinds* of changes occur and what brings them about?

Researchers study three types of developmental change (Franz, 1997): change related to maturational needs or tasks that all human beings experience at particular times of life; change related to culturally endorsed roles or historical events that affect a particular population; and change related to unusual experiences or the unusual timing of life events. Classic theories that deal with these three types of change are normative-crisis models and the timing-of-events model (both introduced in Chapter 14). Normative-crisis theories generally propose maturational stages of development, but these stages may be limited to the particular cohorts and cultures the theorists studied. The timing-of-events model focuses on unusual, or nonnormative, change.

CHECKPOINT

Can you . . .

✔ Identify three types of developmental change that researchers study, and give an example of each?

Normative-Crisis Models

Two early normative-crisis theorists whose work continues to provide a frame of reference for much developmental theory and research on middle adulthood are Carl C. Jung and Erik Erikson.

Carl G. Jung: Individuation and Transcendence

The Swiss psychologist Carl Jung (1933, 1953, 1969, 1971), the first major theorist about adult development, held that healthy midlife development calls for **individuation,** the emergence of the true self through balancing or integrating conflicting parts of the personality, including those parts that previously have been neglected. Until about age 40, said Jung, adults concentrate on obligations to family and society and develop those aspects of personality that will help them reach external goals. Women emphasize expressiveness and nurturance; men are primarily oriented toward achievement. At midlife, people shift their preoccupation to their inner, spiritual selves. Both men and women seek a "union of opposites" by expressing their previously "disowned" aspects.

individuation
In Jung's terminology, emergence of the true self through balancing or integration of conflicting parts of the personality.

Two necessary but difficult tasks of midlife are giving up the image of youth and acknowledging mortality. According to Jung (1966), the need to acknowledge mortality requires a search for meaning within the self. This inward turn may be unsettling; as people question their commitments, they may temporarily lose their moorings. But people who avoid this transition and do not reorient their lives appropriately will miss the chance for psychological growth.

Erik Erikson: Generativity versus Stagnation

In contrast to Jung, who saw midlife as a time of turning inward, Erikson described an outward turn. Erikson saw the years around age 40 as the time when people go through their seventh normative "crisis," **generativity versus stagnation. Generativity,** as Erikson defined it, is the concern of mature adults for establishing and guiding the next generation, perpetuating oneself through one's influence on those to follow. Looking ahead to the waning of their lives, people feel a need to leave a legacy—to participate in life's continuation. People who do not find an outlet for generativity become self-absorbed, self-indulgent, or stagnant (inactive or lifeless).

generativity versus stagnation
In Erikson's theory, the seventh critical alternative of psychosocial development, in which the middle-aged adult develops a concern with establishing, guiding, and influencing the next generation or else experiences stagnation (a sense of inactivity or lifelessness).

generativity
In Erikson's terminology, concern of mature adults for establishing, guiding, and influencing the next generation.

Generativity can be expressed not only through parenting and grandparenting, but through teaching or mentorship, productivity or creativity, and "self-generation," or self-development. It can extend to the world of work, to politics, art, music, and other spheres. The "virtue" of this period is *care:* "a widening commitment to *take care of* the persons, the products, and the ideas one has learned *to care for*" (Erikson, 1985, p. 67).

Jung's and Erikson's Legacy: Vaillant and Levinson

Jung and Erikson left a rich legacy. Their ideas and observations have influenced many other investigators, among them George Vaillant (1977) and Daniel Levinson (1978).

Vaillant's and Levinson's longitudinal studies of men (introduced in Chapter 14) described major midlife shifts—from occupational striving in the thirties to reevaluation and often drastic restructuring of lives in the forties to mellowing and relative stability in the fifties.* For Levinson's men, this transition was stressful enough to be called a crisis.

Vaillant, like Jung, reported a lessening of gender differentiation at midlife and a tendency for men to become more nurturant and expressive. Likewise, Levinson's men at midlife became less obsessed with personal achievement and more concerned with relationships; and they showed generativity by becoming mentors to younger men. As we will discuss later in this chapter, Vaillant has studied the relationship between generativity and psychosocial adjustment, or mental health.

Vaillant also echoed Jung's concept of turning inward. In the forties, many of his sample of Harvard graduates abandoned the "compulsive, unreflective busywork of their occupational apprenticeships and once more [became] explorers of the world within" (1977, p. 220). Bernice Neugarten (1977) noted a similar introspective tendency at midlife, which she called **interiority.**

interiority
In Neugarten's terminology, a concern with inner life (introversion or introspection), which usually appears in middle age.

As we pointed out in Chapter 14, these classic studies, insightful as they may have been, had serious weaknesses of sampling and methodology. Despite Levinson's recent posthumous publication of a small study of women, his model and that of Vaillant were built on research on mostly middle-class or upper middle-class men, whose experiences were taken as norms. Furthermore, their findings reflected the experiences of particular members of a particular cohort in a particular culture. They may not apply in a society in which masculinity and femininity no longer have such distinct meanings, and in which career development and life choices for both men and women have become more varied and more flexible. These findings also may not apply to people for whom economic survival is a pressing issue, or to cultures that have very different patterns of life course development (see Box 16-1). Finally, these studies dealt exclusively with heterosexuals, and the patterns may not apply to gays and lesbians (Kimmel & Sang, 1995).

*Levinson's description of the fifties was only projected.

Window on the World

Box 16-1
A Society without Middle Age

The universality of the midlife crisis is questionable even in the United States. What, then, happens in non-western cultures, some of which do not even have a clear concept of middle age? One such culture is that of the Gusii, a rural society of more than 1 million people in southwestern Kenya (Levine, 1980; LeVine & LeVine, 1998). The Gusii have a "life plan" with well-defined expectations for each stage, but this plan is very different from that in western societies. It is a hierarchy of stages based largely on the anticipation and achievement of reproductive capacity and its extension through the next generation (see table).

Many Gusii in western Kenya become ritual practitioners after their children are grown, seeking spiritual powers to compensate for their waning physical strength. For women like the diviner shown here, ritual practice may be a way to wield power in a male-dominated society.

Gusii Life Stages

Female	Male
Infant	Infant
Uncircumcised girl	Uncircumcised boy
Circumcised girl	Circumcised boy, warrior
Young married woman	
Female elder	Male elder

Source: Adapted from LeVine & LeVine, 1998, Table 2, p. 200.

The Gusii have no words for "adolescent," "young adult," or "middle-aged." A boy or girl is circumcised sometime between ages 9 and 11 and becomes an elder when his or her first child marries. Between these two events, a man goes through only one recognized stage of life: *omomura,* or "warrior." The *omomura* phase may last anywhere from twenty-five to forty years, or even longer. Because of the greater importance of marriage in a woman's life, women have an additional stage: *omosubaati,* or "young married woman."

Childbearing is not confined to early adulthood. As in other preindustrial societies where many hands are needed to raise crops, and death in infancy or early childhood is common, fertility is highly valued. Today, even though babies are much more likely to survive than in the past, people continue to reproduce as long as they are physiologically able. The average woman bears ten children. When a woman reaches menopause, her husband may take a younger wife and breed another family.

In Gusii society, then, transitions depend on life events. Status is linked to circumcision, marriage (for women), having children, and finally, becoming a parent of a married child and thus a prospective grandparent and respected elder. The Gusii have a "social clock," a set of expectations for the ages at which these events should normally occur. People who marry late or do not marry at all, men who become impotent or sterile, and women who fail to conceive, have their first child late, bear no sons, or have few children are ridiculed and ostracized and may undergo rituals to correct the situation.

Although the Gusii have no recognized midlife transition, some of them do reassess their lives around the time they are old enough to be grandparents. Awareness of mortality and of waning physical powers, especially among women, may lead to a midlife career as a ritual healer. The quest for spiritual powers has a generative purpose, too: elders are responsible for ritually protecting their children and grandchildren from death or illness. Many older women who become ritual practitioners or witches seek power either to help people or to harm them, perhaps to compensate for their lack of personal and economic power in a male-dominated society.

Gusii society has undergone change, particularly since the 1970s, as a result of British colonial rule and its aftermath. With infant mortality curtailed, rapid population growth is straining the supply of food and other resources; and a life plan organized around maximizing reproduction is no longer adaptive. Growing acceptance of birth limitation among younger Gusii suggest that "conceptions of adult maturity less centered on fertility will eventually become dominant in the Gusii culture" (LeVine & LeVine, 1998, p. 207).

Table 16-1 A Self-Report Test for Generativity

- I try to pass along the knowledge I have gained through my experiences.
- I do not feel that other people need me.
- I think I would like the work of a teacher.
- I feel as though I have made a difference to many people.
- I do not volunteer to work for a charity.
- I have made and created things that have had an impact on other people.
- I try to be creative in most things that I do.
- I think that I will be remembered for a long time after I die.
- I believe that society cannot be responsible for providing food and shelter for all homeless people.
- Others would say that I have made unique contributions to society.
- If I were unable to have children of my own, I would like to adopt children.
- I have important skills that I try to teach others.
- I feel that I have done nothing that will survive after I die.
- In general, my actions do not have a positive effect on others.
- I feel as though I have done nothing of worth to contribute to others.
- I have made many commitments to many different kinds of people, groups, and activities in my life.
- Other people say that I am a very productive person.
- I have a responsibility to improve the neighborhood in which I live.
- People come to me for advice.
- I feel as though my contributions will exist after I die.

Source: Loyola Generativity Scale. Reprinted from McAdams & de St. Aubin, 1992.

More recent research on midlife psychosocial development is more broadly based, uses more diverse samples and research designs, and covers more dimensions of personality and experience (Lachman & James, 1997). Still, the fundamental insights of the classic normative-crisis theorists continue to stimulate inquiry and refinement.

For example, instruments—behavioral checklists, Q-sorts, and self-reports (see Table 16-1)—have been devised to measure Erikson's concept of generativity. Using such techniques, researchers have found that middle-aged men and women tend to score higher on generativity than younger and older adults (McAdams, de St. Aubin, & Logan, 1993) and that there is no overall difference in generativity between men and women. However, men who have been parents are more generative than men who have not; this is less true of women (McAdams & de St. Aubin, 1992). Later in this chapter we'll discuss additional findings on generativity, as well as research based on Jung's insights on changes in gender roles at midlife.

CHECKPOINT

Can you . . .

✔ Summarize important changes that occur at midlife, according to Jung and Erikson, and tell how these ideas influenced other normative-crisis research?

Timing of Events: The Social Clock

According to the timing-of-events model (introduced in Chapter 14), adult personality development hinges less on age than on important life events. For the cohorts represented by the early normative-crisis studies, the occurrence and timing of such major events as marriage, retirement, and the birth of children and grandchildren were fairly predictable. Today lifestyles are more diverse, people's "social clocks" tick at different rates, and a "fluid life cycle" has blurred the boundaries of middle adulthood (Neugarten & Neugarten, 1987).

When women's lives revolved around bearing and rearing children, the end of the reproductive years meant something different from what it means now, when so many middle-aged women (like Madeleine Albright) have entered the workforce. When occupational patterns were more stable and retirement at age

Consider this . . .

- On the basis of your own observations, do you believe that adults' personalities change significantly during middle age? If so, do such changes seem to be related to maturation, or do they accompany important events, such as divorce or grandparenthood?

65 was almost universal, the meaning of work at midlife may have been different from its current meaning in a period of frequent job changes, downsizing, and early or delayed retirement. When people died earlier, middle-aged survivors felt old, realizing that they too were nearing the end of their lives. Many middle-aged people now find themselves busier and more involved than ever—some still raising young children while others redefine their roles as parents to adolescents and young adults and often as caregivers to aging parents.

CHECKPOINT

Can you . . .

✔ Contrast the views of Freud and of Costa and McCrae with those of humanistic, normative-crisis, and timing-of-events theorists?

✔ Tell how historical and cultural changes have affected the social clock for middle age?

However, the social clock has not stopped altogether, at least in some societies. In one study done in Berlin, Germany (Krueger, Heckhausen, & Hundertmark, 1995), adults of all ages were asked their impressions of hypothetical 45-year-old adults of their own sex whose family or work situations violated normal expectations for that age. Participants, regardless of their own age, expressed surprise about these "off-time" conditions and called them atypical. Reactions were stronger and more negative when development seemed late (as, for example, when a 45-year-old woman was described as having a 1-year-old child). Reactions were positive when development seemed early or on time (as, for example, when a 45-year-old man was said to be branch director of a bank). Society, apparently, is not yet age-blind; "people are sensitive to social clocks and . . . use them to understand and judge others" (Krueger et al., 1995, p. P91).

The Self at Midlife: Issues and Themes

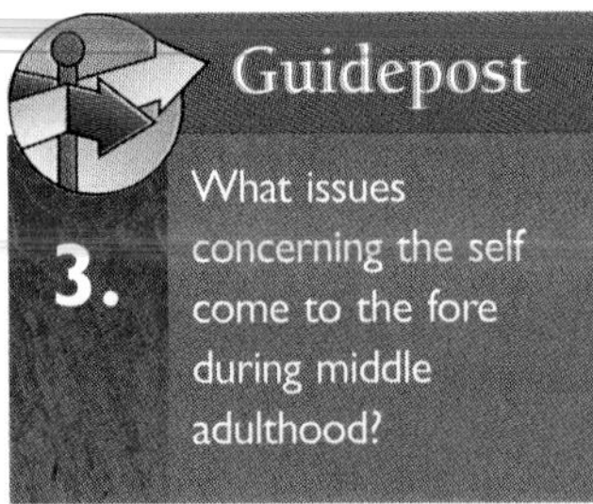

Guidepost
3.
What issues concerning the self come to the fore during middle adulthood?

"I'm a completely different person now from the one I was twenty years ago," said a 47-year-old architect as six friends, all in their forties and fifties, nodded vigorously in agreement. Many people feel and observe personality change occurring at midlife. Whether we look at middle-aged people objectively, in terms of their outward behavior, or subjectively, in terms of how they describe themselves, certain issues and themes emerge. Is there such a thing as a "midlife crisis"? How does identity develop in middle age? What contributes to psychological well-being? Do men and women change in different ways? All of these questions revolve around the self.

Is There A Midlife Crisis?

midlife crisis
In some normative-crisis models, stressful life period precipitated by the review and reevaluation of one's past, typically occurring in the early to middle forties.

Changes in personality and lifestyle during the early to middle forties are often attributed to the **midlife crisis,** a supposedly stressful period triggered by review and reevaluation of one's life. The term was coined by the psychoanalyst Elliott Jacques (1967). It burst into public consciousness in the 1970s—a period of rapid social change, alternative lifestyles, and widespread pursuit of personal growth—with the popularization of the normative-crisis theories of Erikson, Jung, and Levinson.

The midlife crisis was conceptualized as a crisis of identity; indeed, it has been called a second adolescence. What brings it on, said Jacques, is awareness of mortality. Many people now realize that they will not be able to fulfill the dreams of their youth, or that fulfillment of their dreams has not brought the satisfaction they expected. They know that if they want to change direction, they must act quickly. Levinson (1978, 1980, 1986, 1996) maintained that midlife turmoil is inevitable as people struggle with the need to restructure their lives.

Today, the reality of the midlife crisis as a normative developmental experience is greatly in doubt. While the concept is somewhat fuzzy and hard to test, extensive research—including findings in Hong Kong (Shek, 1996) as well as in western industrialized countries—fails to support its universality (Chiriboga, 1989, 1997; Costa et al., 1986; Farrell & Rosenberg, 1981; Klohnen, Vandewater, & Young, 1996; Rosenberg, Rosenberg, & Farrell, 1999), at least as a source of psychological disturbance (Helson, 1997).

Table 16-2 Characteristics of Ego-Resilient Adults

Most Characteristic	Most Uncharacteristic
Has insight into own motives and behavior	Has brittle ego-defense; maladaptive under stress
Has warmth; capacity for close relationships	Is self-defeating
Has social poise and presence	Is uncomfortable with uncertainty and complexities
Is productive; gets things done	Overreacts to minor frustrations; is irritable
Is calm, relaxed in manner	Denies unpleasant thoughts and experiences
Is skilled in social techniques of imaginary play	Does not vary roles; relates to all in same way
Is socially perceptive of interpersonal cues	Is basically anxious
Can see to the heart of important problems	Gives up and withdraws from frustration or adversity
Is genuinely dependable and responsible person	Is emotionally bland
Responds to humor	Is vulnerable to real or fancied threat; fearful
Values own independence and autonomy	Tends to ruminate and have preoccupying thoughts
Tends to arouse liking and acceptance	Feels cheated and victimized by life
Initiates humor	Feels a lack of personal meaning in life

Note: These items are used as criteria for rating ego-resiliency, using the California Adult Q-Set.

Source: Adapted from Block, 1991, as reprinted in Klohnen, 1996.

The onset of middle age may be stressful, but no more so than some events of young adulthood (Chiriboga, 1997). Apparently, midlife is just one of life's transitions, a transition typically involving an introspective review and reappraisal of values and priorities (Helson, 1997; Reid & Willis, 1999). This **midlife review** can be a psychological turning point, a time of stocktaking yielding new insights into the self and spurring midcourse corrections in the design and trajectory of one's life (Moen & Wethington, 1999; Stewart & Ostrove, 1998; Stewart & Vandewater, 1999).

midlife review
Introspective examination that often occurs in middle age, leading to reappraisal and revision of values and priorities.

Whether a transition turns into a crisis may depend less on age than on individual circumstances and personal resources. People with *ego-resiliency*—the ability to adapt flexibly and resourcefully to potential sources of stress—are more likely to navigate the midlife crossing successfully (Klohnen et al., 1996). (Table 16-2 outlines qualities considered most and least characteristic of ego-resilient persons.) For people with resilient personalities, like Madeleine Albright, even negative events, such as an unwanted divorce, can become springboards for positive growth (Klohnen et al., 1996; Moen & Wethington, 1999).

Consider this . . .

- As far as you know, did one or both of your parents go through what appeared to be a midlife crisis? If you are middle-aged, did you go through such a crisis? If so, what issues made it a crisis? Did it seem more serious than transitions at other times of life?

Identity Development

Although Erikson defined identity formation as the main concern of adolescence, he noted that identity continues to develop. Indeed, some developmentalists view identity formation as the central issue of adulthood (McAdams & de St. Aubin, 1992). Identity may consist, not just of one self, but of multiple "possible selves," including the self a person hopes to become and the self a person is afraid of becoming (Markus & Nurius, 1986). Turning points such as the midlife transition often involve changes in the way people see themselves.

As Erikson observed, identity is closely tied to social roles and commitments ("I am a mother," "I am a teacher," "I am a citizen"). Since midlife is a time of stocktaking with regard to roles and relationships, it may bring to the surface unresolved identity issues.

Generativity can be viewed as an aspect of identity formation. As Erikson wrote, "I am what survives me" (1968, p. 141). Research based on Erikson's theory supports the link between identity and generativity (DeHaan & MacDermid, 1994). The researchers tested 40 middle-class female bank employees in their early forties, who were mothers of school-age children, for James Marcia's identity statuses (refer back to Chapter 12). Women who had achieved identity after a period of conscious decision making and had come out with strong commitments were the most satisfied and the most psychologically healthy and felt the most in control of their lives. They also expressed the greatest degree of generativity, bearing out Erikson's view that successful achievement of identity paves the way for other tasks.

Susan Krauss Whitbourne: Identity Styles

The theoretical model of Susan Krauss Whitbourne (1987, 1996; Whitbourne & Connolly, 1999) draws on Erikson, Marcia, and Piaget. Whitbourne views identity as "an organizing schema through which the individual's experiences are interpreted" (Whitbourne & Connolly, 1999, p. 28). Identity is made up of accumulated perceptions of the self, both conscious and unconscious. Perceived personality traits ("I am sensitive" or "I am stubborn"), physical characteristics, and cognitive abilities are incorporated into the identity schema. These self-perceptions are continually confirmed or revised in response to incoming information, which can come from intimate relationships, work-related situations, community activities, and other experiences.

People interpret their interactions with the environment by means of two ongoing processes, similar to those Piaget described for children's cognitive development (refer back to Chapter 2): *identity assimilation* and *identity accommodation.* **Identity assimilation** is an attempt to fit new experience into an existing schema; **identity accommodation** is adjustment of the schema to fit the new experience. Identity assimilation tends to maintain continuity of the self; identity accommodation tends to bring about needed change. Most people use both processes to some extent. Madeleine Albright, when confronted with proof of her Jewish birth, accommodated her identity schema to include her Jewishness but also assimilated her new knowledge to her image of herself as the daughter of loving parents who had done their utmost to protect her. People often resist accommodation (as Albright apparently did for a while) until events (in this case, the imminence of press reports) force them to recognize the need.

identity assimilation
In Whitbourne's terminology, effort to fit new experience into an existing self-concept. Compare *identity accommodation.*

identity accommodation
In Whitbourne's terminology, adjusting the self-concept to fit new experience. Compare *identity assimilation.*

identity style
In Whitbourne's terminology, characteristic ways of confronting, interpreting, and responding to experience.

The equilibrium a person customarily reaches between assimilation and accommodation determines his or her **identity style.** A person who uses assimilation more than accommodation has an *assimilative identity style.* A person who uses accommodation more has an *accommodative identity style.* Overuse of either assimilation or accommodation is unhealthy, says Whitbourne. People who constantly *assimilate* are self-deluding and do not learn from experience; they see only what they are looking for. They may go to great lengths to avoid recognizing their inadequacies. People who constantly *accommodate* are weak, easily swayed, and highly vulnerable to criticism; their identity is easily undermined. Most healthy is a *balanced identity style,* seen in the most mature individuals, in which "identity is flexible enough to change when warranted but not unstructured to the point that every new experience causes the person to question fundamental assumptions about the self" (Whitbourne & Connolly, 1999, p. 29). Whitbourne sees identity styles as related to Marcia's identity statuses; for example, a person who has achieved identity would be expected to have a balanced identity style, whereas a person in foreclosure would most likely have an assimilative style.

According to Whitbourne, people deal with physical, mental, and emotional changes associated with the onset of aging much as they deal with other experiences that challenge the identity schema. Assimilative people seek to maintain a youthful self-image at all costs. Accommodative people may see themselves—perhaps prematurely—as old and may become preoccupied with symptoms of aging and disease. People with a balanced style realistically recognize changes that are occurring and seek to control what can be controlled and accept what cannot. However, identity styles can shift in the face of highly unsettling events, such as loss of a longtime job to a younger person. Thus a midlife crisis may be "an extreme accommodative reaction to a set of experiences that no longer can be processed through identity assimilation" (Whitbourne & Connolly, 1999, p. 30).

With or without the presence of a crisis, Whitbourne's model is a comprehensive attempt to account for both stability and change in the self. However, it is in need of more research support.

Narrative Psychology: Identity as a Life Story

The relatively new field of *narrative psychology* views the development of the self as a continuous process of constructing one's own life story—a dramatic narrative to help make sense of one's life. Indeed, some narrative psychologists view identity itself as this internalized story, or "script." People follow the "script" they have created as they act out their identity (McAdams, Diamond, de St. Aubin, & Mansfield, 1997).

Midlife often is a time for revision of the life story (McAdams, 1993). A "midlife crisis" may be experienced as an unsettling break in the continuity and coherence of the story line (Rosenberg et al., 1999).

The themes of identity narratives reflect culture and cohort. In in-depth interviews with 20 New England men who came of age during the 1940s and 1950s, a critical break in their stories tended to occur in their fifties in conjunction with loss of an active fathering role. For these men, whose formative years had been focused on family and security, the "organizing axis of their . . . narrative identities" was suddenly gone (Rosenberg et al., 1999, p. 61).

A younger group of men who came of age during the Vietnam era told very different narratives. Many of these baby boomers had been skeptics or rebels from adolescence on, alienated from traditional roles. Their midlife shift was toward a search for meaning and fulfillment and more stable families and careers. Their break with the past reflected a belated quest for an adult identity (Rosenberg et al., 1999).

As people grow older, generativity may become an important theme of the life story. A *generativity script* can give the life story a happy ending. It makes people feel needed and gives them a sense of "symbolic immortality." It is built on the conviction that generative acts make a difference (McAdams & de St. Aubin, 1992).

Highly generative adults often tell a *commitment story* (McAdams et al., 1997). Typically such people have enjoyed privileged lives and want to alleviate the suffering of others. They dedicate their lives to social improvement and do not swerve from that mission despite grievous obstacles, which eventually have positive outcomes. Moral exemplars organize their lives around such commitment stories (Colby & Damon, 1992; refer back to Box 15-2 in Chapter 15).

CHECKPOINT

Can you . . .

- ✔ Cite evidence against the existence of a universal midlife crisis?
- ✔ Discuss typical concerns of the midlife transition and factors that affect how successfully people come through it?
- ✔ Summarize Whitbourne's model of identity, and describe how people with each of the three identity styles might deal with signs of aging?
- ✔ Explain the concept of identity as a life story, and how it applies to the midlife transition and to generativity?

Psychological Well-Being and Positive Mental Health

Mental health is not just the absence of mental illness. *Positive* mental health involves a sense of psychological well-being, which goes hand in hand with a healthy sense of self (Ryff & Singer, 1998). But well-being is hard to define. How have theorists and researchers dealt with this elusive concept?

Generativity and Other Factors in Psychosocial Adjustment

For Erikson, as we have mentioned, healthy psychological functioning at midlife depends on successful resolution of the crisis of generativity versus stagnation. This resolution generally takes place in the context of social relationships and role involvements. Research has supported and expanded on Erikson's view.

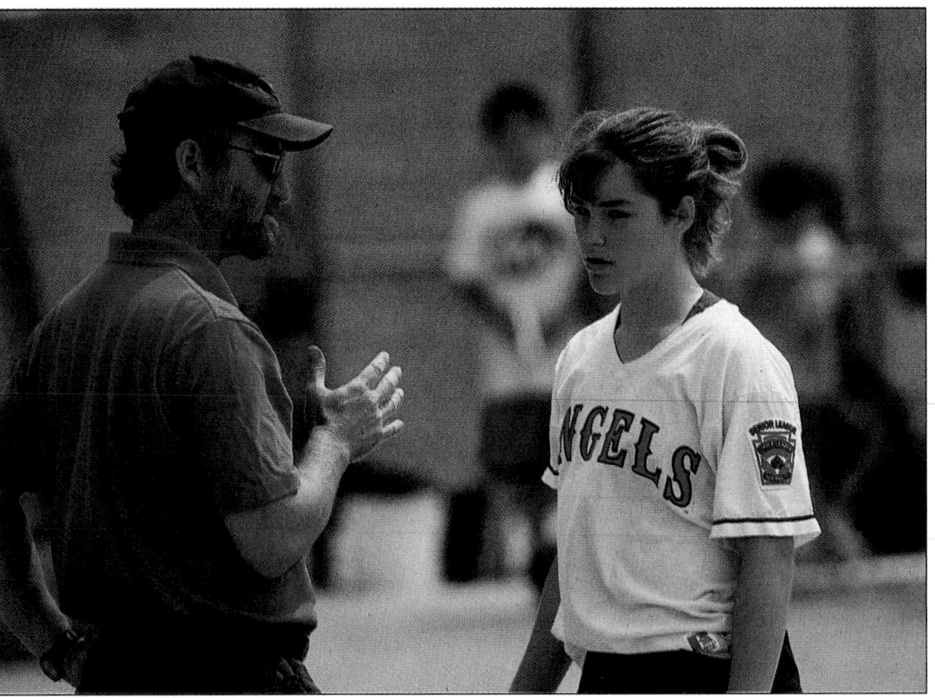

What Erikson called generativity—a concern for guiding the next generation—can be expressed through coaching or mentoring. Generativity may be a key to well-being at midlife.

Vaillant (Vaillant & Milofsky, 1980) found generativity to be a key to successful psychosocial adjustment in midlife. In their fifties, the best-adjusted men in Vaillant's (1989) sample of Harvard alumni were the most generative, as measured by their responsibility for other people at work, their gifts to charity, and the accomplishments of their children. These men were four times more likely to use mature ways of coping, such as altruism and humor, than to use immature ways, such as drinking or becoming hypochondriacs (Vaillant, 1989). Similarly, in a longitudinal study of 306 inner-city men, those who at age 47 used mature coping techniques had the best health and psychosocial functioning. Those who used immature coping techniques, such as projection (attributing one's own negative thoughts and feelings to others) and fantasy, were the worst adjusted (Soldz & Vaillant, 1998).

In other research on generativity and mental health, a 32-year longitudinal study followed 87 young men who were students at George Williams College, a training institution for social service work. Most of these men were initially in good physical and mental health and remained so in their fifties. By that time, according to Erikson's and Vaillant's criteria, more than half of the group had achieved generativity, defined as the highest stage of positive mental health. They had been successful in their work, taken responsibility for others, and achieved intimacy, typically through a longtime happy marriage. Less generative men met one or two of these criteria, but not all three. Satisfactory social relationships with peers and mentors in young adulthood were strong predictors of mental health at midlife, and men who had the benefit of mentoring relationships became mentors themselves later on (Westermeyer, 1998, 1999).

Generativity, apparently, is not necessarily across-the-board; a person may be generative as a parent but less so as a worker or spouse, or vice versa, and generativity in each of these roles may affect well-being differently. Cohort also may be a factor. One study compared two groups of 45 employed mothers with varied levels of occupational prestige. Each group had been in the same age range—35 to 55—when questioned, one group in 1978–79 and the other in 1991. For the earlier cohort, the major factor in well-being (as indicated by self-esteem, satisfaction with life, a sense of control over one's life, and lack of depression) was generativity as a parent; for the later cohort, well-being was linked primarily with generativity as a spouse. These contrasting findings may reflect changes in social expectations. In the late 1970s, women—even those in high-status occupations—were expected to find their primary identity in motherhood. By the early 1990s, women were marrying later and having fewer children, and the spousal role may have taken on more importance (MacDermid, Heilbrun, & DeHaan, 1997).

Carol Ryff: Multiple Dimensions of Well-Being

Well-being has many facets, and different researchers have used different criteria to measure it, making it difficult to compare results. Now Carol Ryff and her colleagues (Keyes & Ryff, 1999; Ryff, 1995; Ryff & Singer, 1998), drawing on a range of theorists from Erikson to Maslow, have developed a multifaceted model that includes six dimensions of well-being and a self-report scale to measure them. The six dimensions are: *self-acceptance, positive relations with others, autonomy, environmental mastery, purpose in life,* and *personal growth* (see Table 16-3). According to Ryff, psychologically healthy people have positive attitudes toward themselves

Table 16-3 Dimensions of Well-Being Used in Ryff's Scale

Self-Acceptance

High scorer: possesses a positive attitude toward the self; acknowledges and accepts multiple aspects of self including good and bad qualities; feels positive about past life.

Low scorer: feels dissatisfied with self; is disappointed with what has occurred in past life; is troubled about certain personal qualities; wishes to be different [from] what he or she is.

Positive Relations with Others

High scorer: has warm, satisfying, trusting relationships with others; is concerned about the welfare of others; [is] capable of strong empathy, affection, and intimacy; understands give and take of human relationships.

Low scorer: has few close, trusting relationships with others; finds it difficult to be warm, open, and concerned about others; is isolated and frustrated in interpersonal relationships; [is] not willing to make compromises to sustain important ties with others.

Autonomy

High scorer: is self-determining and independent; [is] able to resist social pressures to think and act in certain ways; regulates behavior from within; evaluates self by personal standards.

Low scorer: is concerned about the expectations and evaluations of others; relies on judgments of others to make important decisions; conforms to social pressures to think and act in certain ways.

Environmental Mastery

High scorer: has a sense of mastery and competence in managing the environment; controls complex array of external activities; makes effective use of surrounding opportunities; [is] able to choose or create contexts suitable to personal needs and values.

Low scorer: has difficulty managing everyday affairs; feels unable to change or improve surrounding context; is unaware of surrounding opportunities; lacks sense of control over external world.

Purpose in Life

High scorer: has goals in life and a sense of directedness; feels there is meaning to present and past life; holds beliefs that give life purpose; has aims and objectives for living.

Low scorer: lacks a sense of meaning in life; has few goals or aims, lacks sense of direction; does not see purpose in past life; has no outlooks or beliefs that give life meaning.

Personal Growth

High scorer: has a feeling of continued development; sees self as growing and expanding; is open to new experiences; has sense of realizing his or her potential; sees improvement in self and behavior over time; is changing in ways that reflect more self-knowledge and effectiveness.

Low scorer: has a sense of personal stagnation; lacks sense of improvement or expansion over time; feels bored [with] and uninterested [in] life; feels unable to develop new attitudes or behaviors.

Source: Adapted from Keyes & Ryff, 1999, Table 1, p. 163.

and others. They make their own decisions and regulate their own behavior, and they choose or shape environments compatible with their needs. They have goals that make their lives meaningful, and they strive to explore and develop themselves as fully as possible.

A series of cross-sectional studies based on Ryff's scale show midlife to be a period of generally positive mental health (Ryff & Singer, 1998). Middle-aged people expressed greater well-being than older and younger adults in some areas but not in others. They were more autonomous than younger adults but somewhat less purposeful and less focused on personal growth—future-oriented dimensions that declined even more sharply in late adulthood. Environmental mastery, on the other hand, increased between middle and late adulthood. Self-acceptance was relatively stable for all age groups. Of course, since this research was cross-sectional, we do not know whether the differences were due to maturation, aging, or cohort factors.

The studies also looked at influences of gender and class. Overall, men's and women's well-being was quite similar, but women had more positive social relationships. Well-being was greater for men and women with more education and better jobs (Ryff & Singer, 1998).

Indeed, paid work—long seen as central to men's well-being—is today being recognized as an important source of well-being for women as well, providing a sense of independence and competence apart from family duties. Despite the potential for stress, many middle-aged women seem to flourish best in multiple roles (Antonucci & Akiyama, 1997; Barnett, 1997).

Is Middle Age a Woman's Prime of Life?

For many women, like Madeleine Albright, late middle age may be the prime of life, as the early normative-crisis studies suggested it is for men. Among a cross-sectional sample of nearly 700 Mills College alumnae ages 26 to 80, women in their early fifties most often described their lives as "first-rate" (Mitchell & Helson, 1990). They were young enough to be in good health and old enough to have launched their children and to be financially secure. Life at home was simpler; the energy that had gone into child rearing was redirected to partners, work, community, or themselves. They tended to be caring for others, showing generativity. They had developed greater confidence, involvement, security, and breadth of personality.

Similarly, most of the women in Ravenna Helson's longitudinal study of Mills graduates found their early forties their time of greatest turmoil but by the early fifties rated their quality of life as high. They were more self-confident, independent, decisive, dominant, and self-affirming and less self-critical than they had been earlier in life. They became more comfortable with themselves, partly because they were adhering to their own standards (Helson & Wink, 1992; see Table 16-4). Whereas in their early forties these women had been keenly aware of the social clock, by the early fifties they were no longer concerned about meeting outside expectations (Helson, 1997; Helson & McCabe, 1993).

In line with Jung's theory, enhanced well-being for women may be the outcome of a midlife review that leads to pursuit of previously submerged aspirations. In a longitudinal study of the Radcliffe College class of 1964, the consequences of a midlife review seemed most substantial for women who wished they had explored educational or work options more fully before assuming traditional family roles. About two-thirds of the women in the class made major life changes between ages 37 and 43. Women who had midlife regrets and changed their lives accordingly had greater well-being and better psychological adjustment in the late forties than those who had regrets but did *not* make desired changes (Stewart & Ostrove, 1998; Stewart & Vandewater, 1999).

Table 16-4 Selected Feelings about Life Reported by Women in Their Early Fifties

	More True Now Than in Early Forties	Less True Now Than in Early Forties
Identity questioning and turmoil:		
Excitement, turmoil about my impulses and potential	21	56
Searching for a sense of who I am	28	47
Anxious that I won't live up to my potential	25	47
Coming near the end of one road and not finding another	27	45
Assurance of status:		
Feeling established	78	11
Influence in my community or field of interest	63	24
A new level of productivity	70	11
Feeling selective in what I do	91	2
A sense of being my own person	90	3
Cognitive breadth and complexity:		
Bringing both feeling and rationality into decisions	76	1
Realizing larger patterns of meaning and relationship	72	7
Appreciating my complexity	69	10
Discovering new parts of myself	72	11
Present rather than future orientation:		
Focus on reality—meeting the needs of the day and not being too emotional about them	76	6
More satisfied with what I have; less worried about what I won't get	76	11
Feeling the importance of time's passing	76	10
Adjustment and relational smoothness:		
Feeling secure and committed	71	12
Feeling my life is moving well	74	15
Feeling optimistic about the future	58	20
A new level of intimacy	53	30
Doing things for others and then feeling exploited	14	56
Feeling very much alone	26	45
Feelings of competition with other women	7	63
Feeling angry at men and masculinity	14	52
Awareness of aging and reduced vitality:		
Looking old	70	15
Being treated as an older person	64	14
Reducing the intensity of my achievement efforts	44	26
Liking an active social life	27	52
Being very interested in sex	19	64

Note: The women judged whether each item was more applicable to them now than in their early forties, less applicable now than then, or about the same.

Source: Helson & Wink, 1992.

The college-educated women in these studies are not, of course, representative of the whole population. Furthermore, the changes they went through are not necessarily maturational changes, which would occur regardless of class, cohort, and culture. The women in these studies were members of the first generation of American middle-class women to experience a shift between traditional and nontraditional female roles. Socialized to be homemakers and mothers, they matured at a time when large numbers of women began to take advantage of expanding educational and vocational opportunities. Their midlife pattern was not characteristic of their mothers' generation, who generally accepted the traditional woman's role (Stewart & Ostrove, 1998; Stewart & Vandewater, 1999). Nor may this pattern apply to more recent cohorts who have started careers earlier and put off motherhood longer, or to women of other socioeconomic groups (Stewart & Ostrove, 1998; Stewart & Vandewater, 1999).

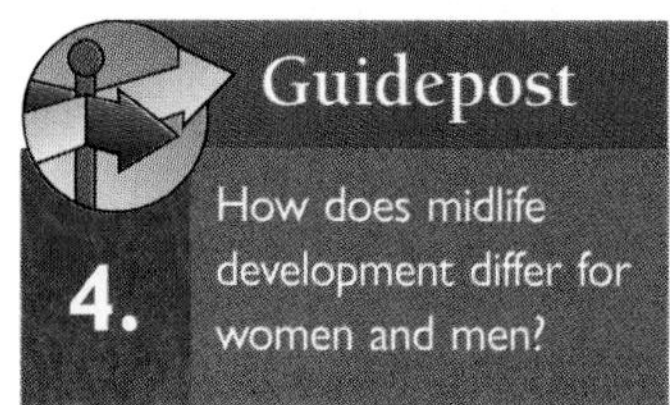

4. How does midlife development differ for women and men?

Gender Identity

In theory and research on personality, issues related to gender have been among the most provocative. In many studies during the 1960s, 1970s, and 1980s, middle-aged men were more open about feelings, more interested in intimate relationships, and more nurturing (characteristics traditionally labeled as feminine) than at earlier ages, whereas middle-aged women were more assertive, self-confident, and achievement-oriented (characteristics traditionally labeled as masculine) (Cooper & Gutmann, 1987; Cytrynbaum et al., 1980; Helson & Moane, 1987; Huyck, 1990; Neugarten, 1968).

Some social scientists attribute this development to hormonal changes at midlife (Rossi, 1980). Jung saw it as part of the process of individuation, or balancing the personality. The psychologist David Gutmann (1975, 1977, 1985, 1987) offers an explanation that goes further than Jung's.

gender crossover In Gutmann's terminology, reversal of gender roles after the end of active parenting.

Traditional gender roles, according to Gutmann, evolved to ensure the security and well-being of growing children. The mother must be the caregiver, the father the provider. Once active parenting is over, there is not just a balancing but a reversal of roles—a **gender crossover.** Men, now free to explore their previously repressed "feminine" side, become more passive; women become more dominant and independent.

These changes may have been normative in the preliterate agricultural societies Gutmann studied, which had very distinct gender roles, but they are not necessarily universal (Franz, 1997). In U.S. society today, men's and women's roles are becoming less distinct. Women spend more time on paid work and less on housework than in the past; for men the reverse is true (Verbrugge, Gruber-Baldini, & Fozard, 1996). In an era in which most young women combine employment with child rearing, when many men take an active part in parenting, and when childbearing may not even begin until midlife, gender crossover in middle age seems less likely. Indeed, the very use of the terms "masculine" and "feminine" to describe personality traits such as "dominant" and "submissive" has become questionable (Antonucci & Akiyama, 1997; James & Lewkowicz, 1997).

Consider this . . .

- From what you have observed, do men and women face similar or different kinds of challenges at midlife?

How well, then, has Gutmann's "gender-crossover" theory held up? In studies, such as those just noted, that have found increasing "masculinization" of women and "feminization" of men across adulthood, the amount and pattern of change varies. One factor seems to be methodology. Some studies (including Gutmann's) have used instruments that measure values, goals, interests, or motivations (for example, the relative priority men and women give to career and family). Other studies have measured personality traits, such as competitiveness ("masculine") and compliance ("feminine"). Some studies are longitudinal and others are cross-sectional. Most do not take possible cohort differences into account (Parker & Aldwin, 1997).

A sequential analysis of data from two longitudinal studies that together followed 20-, 30-, and 40-year-old, mostly well-educated men and women for more than two decades (1969–1991) was designed to deal with these methodological issues (Parker & Aldwin, 1997). The studies used both personality measures and values-oriented measures.

The personality measures did show age-related change: both men and women became increasingly "masculine" (or decreasingly "feminine") during their twenties. However, this trend leveled off by the forties. Contrary to Gutmann's model, there was *no* gender crossover. Nor was there evidence of increasing androgyny (refer back to Chapter 8) in successive cohorts. Regardless of age or cohort, men remained more "masculine" than women.

The values-oriented measures showed what at first appeared to be change but turned out to be cohort differences. For example, men and women in one cohort became less family-oriented and more career-oriented between their twenties and thirties (1969–1979), and then more family-oriented between their thirties and forties (1979–1991). However, this could not have been a developmental change, since a younger cohort who were in their twenties during the second time period (the 1980s) followed the same career-to-family shift during that time as the older cohort did, but at an earlier age. Thus the shift in values was probably due to sociocultural or historical influences affecting both cohorts at the same time.

Socioeconomic status may make a difference. In a 12-year values-oriented longitudinal study during the 1970s, researchers periodically interviewed 216 mostly white working-class to middle-class young and middle-aged adults about their needs for power and affiliation (intimacy). True to conventional standards, women at all ages showed greater need for affiliation than men; and while men's need for intimacy increased as they got older, they remained as power-centered as ever. The younger women, who were in their late fifties at the end of the study, did show an increased need for power, and younger men showed more affiliative concerns than older men, but, as in the Parker-Aldwin study, these seem to have been cohort effects unrelated to the end of active parenting (James & Lewkowicz, 1997).

One personality-oriented study that did show opposite change in men and women was the Mills longitudinal study. Between the beginning and the end of active parenting, the Mills women increased more than their male partners in competence, confidence, and independence, while the men increased more in affiliative traits. The women changed more dramatically than the men, perhaps because women's lives in the United States changed more than men's between the 1970s and the 1990s, when these couples' children were growing up (Helson, 1997). However, these changes did not amount to a gender crossover. Indeed, in line with Jung's view, the highest quality of life for women in their fifties was associated with a *balance* between autonomy and involvement in an intimate relationship (Helson, 1993).

Further research using sophisticated methods and diverse samples undoubtedly will sharpen our understanding of change and continuity in men's and women's personalities and attitudes at midlife. Two things seem clear: (1) development of gender identity during adulthood is far more complex than a simple gender crossover; and (2) influences of cohort and culture and of the individual life course need to be factored in.

CHECKPOINT

Can you . . .

- ✔ Discuss the relationship between generativity, mental health, and well-being?
- ✔ Explain the importance of a multifaceted measure of well-being, and name and describe the six dimensions in Ryff's model?
- ✔ Explain how a midlife review can affect well-being?
- ✔ Compare Jung's and Gutmann's concepts of changes in gender identity at midlife, and assess their research support?

Changes in Relationships at Midlife

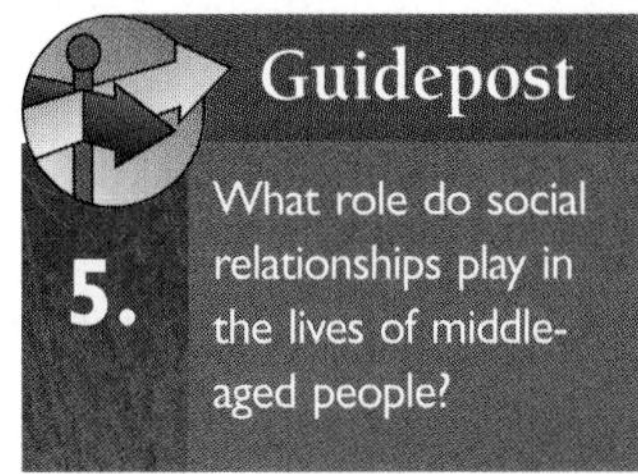

Guidepost
5.
What role do social relationships play in the lives of middle-aged people?

It is hard to generalize about the meaning of relationships in middle age today. Not only does that period cover a quarter-century of development; it also embraces a greater multiplicity of life paths than ever before. One 45-year-old may be happily married and raising children; another may be contemplating marriage or, like Madeline Albright, on the brink of divorce. One 60-year-old may have a large network of friends, relatives, and colleagues; another may have no known living relatives and only a few intimate friendships. For most middle-aged people, however, relationships with others are very important—perhaps in a different way than earlier in life.

Theories of Social Contact

According to **social convoy theory,** people move through life surrounded by *social convoys:* circles of close friends and family members on whom they can rely for assistance, well-being, and social support, and to whom they in turn also offer care, concern, and support (Antonucci & Akiyama, 1997; Kahn & Antonucci, 1980). Although convoys usually show long-term stability, their composition can change. At one time, bonds with siblings may be more significant; at another time, ties with friends (Paul, 1997).

social convoy theory
Theory of aging, proposed by Kahn and Antonucci, which holds that people move through life surrounded by concentric circles of intimate relationships of varying degrees of closeness, on which people rely for assistance, well-being, and social support.

In one study, people of a wide range of ages, from 8 to 93, identified three concentric circles of social convoys, with the inner circle containing the people closest and most important to them—typically a spouse, children, and parents. Middle-aged respondents had the largest convoys, averaging about ten to eleven persons and diminishing slightly after age 50 (a trend that, as we'll see in Chapter 18, continues during late adulthood). Women's convoys, particularly the inner circle, were larger than men's (Antonucci & Akiyama, 1997).

socioemotional selectivity theory
Theory, proposed by Carstensen, that people select social contacts throughout life on the basis of the changing relative importance of social interaction as a source of information, as an aid in developing and maintaining a self-concept, and as a source of emotional well-being.

Laura Carstensen's (1991, 1995, 1996) **socioemotional selectivity theory** offers a life-span perspective on the role of social convoys in middle age. According to Carstensen, social interaction has three main goals: (1) it is a source of information; (2) it helps people develop and maintain a sense of self; and (3) it is a source of pleasure and comfort, or emotional well-being. In infancy, the need for emotional support is paramount. From childhood through young adulthood, information-seeking comes to the fore. As young people strive to learn about their society and their place in it, strangers may well be the best sources of knowledge. By middle age, other methods of information gathering (such as reading) become more efficient, and the emotion-regulating function of social contacts again becomes central. People become more selective about these contacts, choosing to spend time with their "social convoys"—people who can be counted on in time of need.

Relationships and Quality of Life

Most middle-aged and older adults are optimistic about the quality of their lives as they age, according to a mail survey of 1,384 adults ages 45 and older (NFO Research, Inc., 1999). Although they consider satisfying sexual relationships important to that quality of life, social relationships are even more important. About 9 out of 10 men and women say a good relationship with a spouse or partner is important to their quality of life, and so are close ties to friends and family.

As in young adulthood, relationships seem to be good for physical as well as mental health. In a longitudinal study of 32,624 healthy U.S. men between ages 42 and 77, socially isolated men—those who were not married, had fewer than six friends and relatives, and did not belong to religious or community groups—were more likely to die of cardiovascular disease, accidents, or suicide during the next four years than men with larger social networks (Kawachi et al., 1996).

CHECKPOINT

Can you . . .

✔ Summarize two theoretical models of the selection of social contacts?

On the other hand, midlife relationships also present demands that can be stressful and restrictive. These demands, and their psychological repercussions, tend to fall most heavily on women. A sense of responsibility and concern for others may impair a woman's well-being when problems or misfortunes beset her mate, children, parents, friends, or coworkers. This "vicarious stress" may help explain why middle-aged women are especially susceptible to depression and other mental health problems and why they tend to be unhappier with their marriages than men (Antonucci & Akiyama, 1997; Thomas, 1997).

Consider this . . .

- Does either the social convoy model or socioemotional selectivity theory ring true to you according to your own experience and that of people you know well?

In studying midlife social relationships, then, we need to keep in mind that their effects can be both positive and negative. "More" does not necessarily mean "better"; the quality of a relationship and its impact on well-being are what counts, and these attributes can shift from time to time (Paul, 1997).

In the remaining sections of this chapter, we'll examine how intimate relationships develop during the middle years. We'll look first at relationships with spouses, homosexual partners, and friends; next at bonds with maturing children; and then at ties with aging parents, siblings, and grandchildren.

Consensual Relationships

Marriages, homosexual unions, and friendships typically involve two people of the same generation and involve mutual choice. How do these relationships fare in middle age?

Marriage

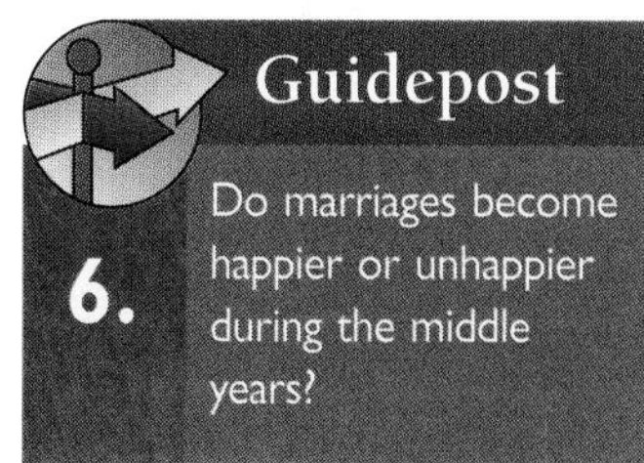

Guidepost

6. Do marriages become happier or unhappier during the middle years?

Midlife marriage today is very different from what it used to be. When life expectancies were shorter, couples who remained together for 25, 30, or 40 years were rare. The most common pattern was for marriages to be broken by death and for survivors to remarry. People had many children and expected them to live at home until they married. It was unusual for a middle-aged husband and wife to be alone together. Today, more marriages end in divorce, but couples who stay together can often look forward to twenty or more years of married life after the last child leaves home.

What happens to the quality of a longtime marriage? Marital satisfaction, in almost all studies, follows a U-shaped curve: after the first few years of marriage, satisfaction appears to decline and then, sometime in middle age, to rise again through the first part of late adulthood (S. A. Anderson, Russell, & Schumm, 1983; Gilford, 1984; Glenn, 1991; Gruber & Schaie, 1986; Hiedemann, Suhomlinova, & O'Rand, 1998; Lavee, Sharlin, & Katz, 1996; Orbuch, House, Mero, & Webster, 1996).

Although the U-shaped pattern is well established, the research has been criticized for its methodology. Many of the early studies dealt with only the husband's or wife's satisfaction, not with both. Also, most studies are cross-sectional: they show differences among couples of different cohorts rather than changes in the *same* couples, and they focus on age, not length of marriage. Furthermore, reports of rising marital satisfaction in late life may in part reflect the fact that older samples do not include couples who have divorced along the way (Blieszner, 1986; Lavee et al., 1996).

An analysis of data from two surveys of individuals in first marriages, conducted in 1986 and 1987–88 (Orbuch et al., 1996), sought to ascertain just when the dip and rise in satisfaction occur, and why. The samples were, of necessity, cross-sectional (there are no comparable longitudinal data covering the entire span of adulthood); but they were large (a total of 8,929), and one was nationally representative. Both women and men were included, and marital satisfaction was measured against the duration of a marriage. To control for any skewing of data due to termination of unsatisfactory marriages, statistical techniques simulated the inclusion of such couples, attributing to them low marital quality.

Consider this . . .

- How many longtime happily married couples do you know? Are the qualities that seem to characterize these marriages similar to those mentioned in the text?

The picture that emerged is a clear affirmation of the U-shaped pattern. During the first 20 to 24 years of marriage, the longer a couple have been married, the less satisfied they tend to be. Then the association between marital satisfaction and length of marriage begins to turn positive. At 35 to 44 years of marriage, a couple tend to be even more satisfied than during the first 4 years.

The years of marital decline are those in which parental and work responsibilities tend to be greatest (Orbuch et al., 1996). Two important factors in the demands on parents are family finances and the number of children still at home. The pressure of too little income and too many mouths to feed burdens a relationship, especially if the burdens are not equally shared (Lavee et al., 1996).

The U-shaped curve generally hits bottom during middle age, when many couples have teenage children and are heavily involved in careers. Satisfaction usually reaches a height when children are grown; many people are entering or are in retirement, and a lifetime accumulation of assets helps ease financial worries (Orbuch et al., 1996).

How a marriage fares in midlife may depend largely on its quality until then. Among 300 couples who had been happily married for at least fifteen years, both men and women credited a positive attitude toward the spouse as a friend and as a person, commitment to

The launching of a son or daughter may give a midlife marriage a new lease on life. Marital satisfaction generally improves when children are grown.

marriage and belief in its sanctity, and agreement on aims and goals. Happily married couples spent much time together and shared many activities (Lauer & Lauer, 1985).

Midlife Divorce

Guidepost
7.
How common is divorce at this time of life?

Most divorces occur during the first 10 years of marriage (Clarke, 1995). Thus, for people who, like Madeline Albright, go through a divorce at midlife when they may have assumed their lives were settled, the breakup can be traumatic. This may be particularly true of women, who are more negatively affected by divorce at any age than men are (Marks & Lambert, 1998).

The sense of violated expectations may be diminishing as midlife divorce becomes more common (Marks & Lambert, 1998; Norton & Moorman, 1987). Although divorce rates in general peaked in 1979–80, rates continued to increase for long-term marriages (National Center for Health Statistics [NCHS], 1992). This change appears to be due largely to women's growing economic independence. However, socioeconomic status and the timing of departure of children affect the equation, as was found in a 20-year longitudinal study of 2,484 mothers in their first marriages, taken from a nationally representative sample of women who were between ages 30 and 44 when the study began (Hiedemann et al., 1998).

marital capital Financial and emotional benefits built up during a long-standing marriage, which tend to hold a couple together.

Long-standing marriages may be less likely to break up than more recent ones, the researchers suggested, because as couples stay together they build up **marital capital,** financial and emotional benefits of marriage that become difficult to give up (Becker, 1991; Jones, Tepperman, & Wilson, 1995). College education decreases the risk of separation or divorce after the first decade of marriage, perhaps because college-educated women and their husbands tend to have accumulated more marital assets and may have more to lose from divorce than less-educated couples (Hiedemann et al., 1998). For less-educated women with less marital capital at stake, financial independence may be more of a spur to divorce (Hiedemann et al., 1998).

empty nest Transitional phase of parenting following the last child's leaving the parents' home.

The effects of the **empty nest**—the transition that occurs when the youngest child leaves home—depend on the quality and length of the marriage. In a good marriage, the departure of grown children may usher in a second honeymoon (Robinson & Blanton, 1993). In a shaky marriage, if a couple have stayed together for the sake of the children, they may now see no reason to prolong the bond. The less time the couple have been married, the greater the risk of a breakup. A thirty-year marriage may enable a couple to accumulate more protective marital capital than a twenty-year marriage, apart from the investment in their children (Hiedemann et al., 1998).

Divorce rates among aging baby boomers now in their fifties, many of whom married later and had fewer children than in previous generations, are projected to continue to rise (Hiedemann et al., 1998; Uhlenberg, Cooney, & Boyd, 1990). Even in long marriages, the increasing number of years that people can expect to live in good health after child rearing ends may make the dissolution of a marginal marriage and the prospect of possible remarriage a more practical and attractive option (Hiedemann et al., 1998).

Furthermore, divorce today may be *less* a threat to well-being in middle age than in young adulthood. That conclusion comes from a 5-year longitudinal study that compared the reactions of 6,948 young and middle-aged adults taken from a nationally representative sample (Marks & Lambert, 1998). The researchers used Ryff's six-dimensional measure of psychological well-being, as well as other criteria. In almost all respects, middle-aged people showed more adaptability than younger people in the face of separation or divorce, despite their more limited prospects for remarriage. Their greater maturity and expertise in handling life's problems may have given them an advantage in coping with the loss of a spouse. Middle-aged women in that position reported better social relations and greater personal mastery than younger women, as well as less depression and hostility. After remaining separated or divorced for five years, they also had a greater sense of autonomy. Middle-aged men facing termination of marriage were more self-accepting than younger men. Those who remained separated or divorced for five years reported less depression and hostility, but also less personal growth (Marks & Lambert, 1998).

Gay and Lesbian Relationships*

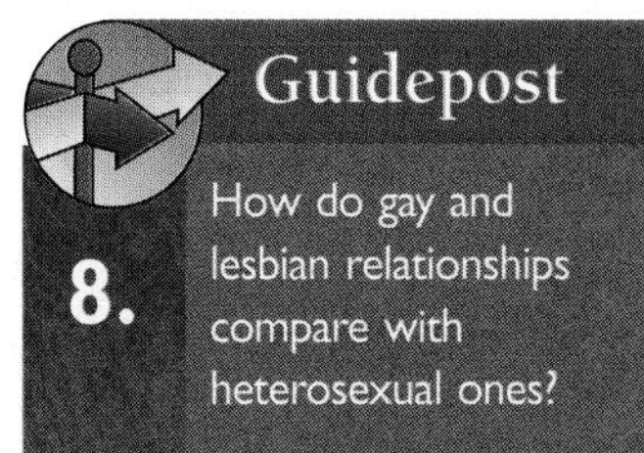

Guidepost
8.
How do gay and lesbian relationships compare with heterosexual ones?

Gays and lesbians now in middle age grew up at a time when homosexuality was considered a mental illness, and homosexuals tended to be isolated not only from the larger community but from each other. Today this pioneer generation is just beginning to explore the opportunities inherent in the growing acceptance of homosexuality as a way of life.

Since many homosexuals still do not come out until well into adulthood, the timing of this crucial event can affect other aspects of development. Middle-aged gays and lesbians may be associating openly for the first time and establishing relationships. Many are still working out conflicts with parents and other family members (sometimes including spouses) or hiding their homosexuality from them.

Because of the secrecy and stigma that have surrounded homosexuality, studies of gays and lesbians tend to have sampling problems. What little research exists on gay men has focused mostly on urban white men with above-average income and education. Yet, in a 1985 American Broadcasting Company-*Washington Post* poll, a disproportionate number of self-identified homosexual and bisexual men were low-income African Americans or Hispanic Americans, and more than half lived in small towns. Furthermore, 42 percent were in heterosexual marriages and thus easily overlooked.

Lesbians studied so far also tend to be mostly white, professional, and middle or upper class. In one study, more than 25 percent of middle-aged lesbians lived alone, even if they were in intimate relationships (Bradford & Ryan, 1991). This may in part be a cohort effect; lesbians who grew up in the 1950s may be uncomfortable about living openly with a partner, as many younger lesbians do now.

Gay men who do not come out until midlife often go through a prolonged search for identity, marked by guilt, secrecy, heterosexual marriage, and conflicted relationships with both sexes. By contrast, those who recognize and accept their sexual orientation early in life often cross racial, socioeconomic, and age barriers within the gay community. Some move to cities with large gay communities where they can more easily seek out and form relationships.

For the most part, the principles that apply to sustaining a heterosexual marriage also apply to maintaining gay and lesbian partnerships. Gay and lesbian relationships tend to be stronger if known as such to family and friends, and if the couple seek out supportive gay and lesbian environments (Haas & Stafford, 1998). Coming out to parents is often difficult but need not necessarily have an adverse impact on the couple's relationship (LaSala, 1998). When family and friends are supportive and validate the relationship, its quality tends to be higher (R. B. Smith & Brown, 1997).

Gay and lesbian couples tend to be more egalitarian than heterosexual couples (see Chapter 14), but, as with many heterosexual couples, balancing commitments to careers and relationship can be difficult. What happens, for example, if one partner has an opportunity for advancement that requires relocating to another city? Gay couples in which one partner is less career-oriented than the other have an easier time, but couples in which both partners are relationship-centered tend to be happiest.

CHECKPOINT

Can you . . .

- ✔ Describe the U-shaped curve of marital satisfaction, and cite factors that may help explain it?
- ✔ Give reasons for the tendency for divorce to occur early in a marriage, and cite factors that may increase the risk of divorce in midlife?
- ✔ Compare the formation and maintenance of homosexual relationships and heterosexual ones?

*Unless otherwise referenced, this discussion is based on Kimmel & Sang, 1995.

Friendships

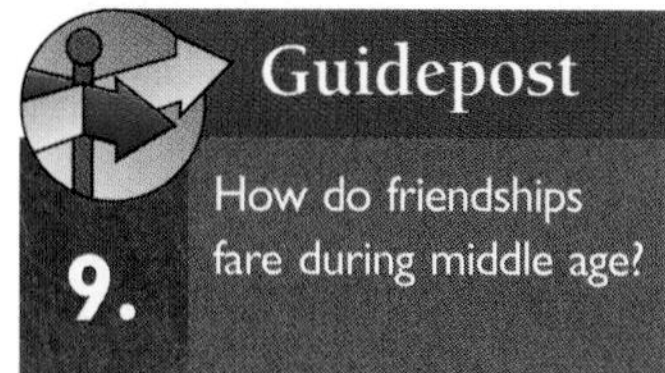

Guidepost
9.
How do friendships fare during middle age?

There has been little research on friendship in middle age. As compared with younger people, many middle-aged people have little time and energy to devote to friends; they are too busy with family and work and with building up security for retirement. Still, friendships do persist and, as with Madeline Albright, are a strong source of emotional support and well-being. Many of these friendships revolve around work and parenting (Baruch, Barnett, & Rivers, 1983; Hartup & Stevens, 1999; House, Landis, & Umberson, 1988). Many of the friends of midlife are old friends. Age is less a factor in making new friends than are such commonalities as length of marriage, age of children, and occupational status (Troll, 1975).

The quality of midlife friendships often makes up for what they lack in quantity of time spent. Especially during a crisis, such as a divorce or a problem with an aging parent, adults turn to friends for emotional support, practical guidance, comfort, companionship, and talk (Antonucci & Akiyama, 1997; Hartup & Stevens, 1999; Suitor & Pillemer, 1993). Conflicts with friends often center on differences in values, beliefs, and lifestyles; friends usually can "talk out" these conflicts while maintaining mutual dignity and respect (Hartup & Stevens, 1999).

As at earlier ages, women tend to have fewer but more intimate friends than men do. However, both sexes generally include two close friends in their social convoys (Antonucci & Akiyama, 1997). The importance of friendships can vary from time to time. In a longitudinal study of 155 mostly white men and women from middle-and lower-class backgrounds, friends were more important to women's well-being in early middle age, but to men's well-being in late middle age (Paul, 1997).

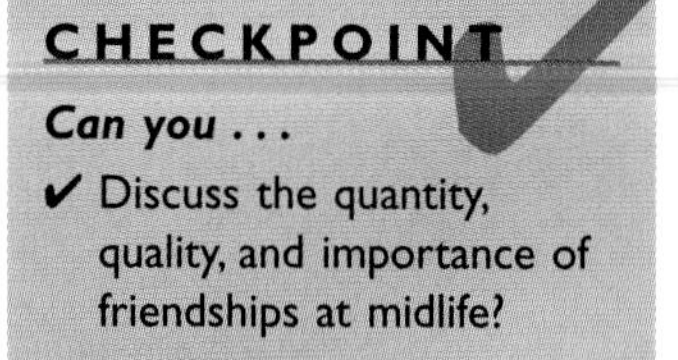

Can you . . .

✔ Discuss the quantity, quality, and importance of friendships at midlife?

Friendships often have a special importance for homosexuals. Lesbians are more likely to get emotional support from lesbian friends, lovers, and even exlovers than from relatives. Gay men, too, rely on friendship networks, which they actively create and maintain. Friendship networks provide solidarity and contact with younger people, which middle-aged heterosexuals normally get through family. Loss of friends to the scourge of AIDS has been traumatic for many gay men (Kimmel & Sang, 1995).

Relationships with Maturing Children

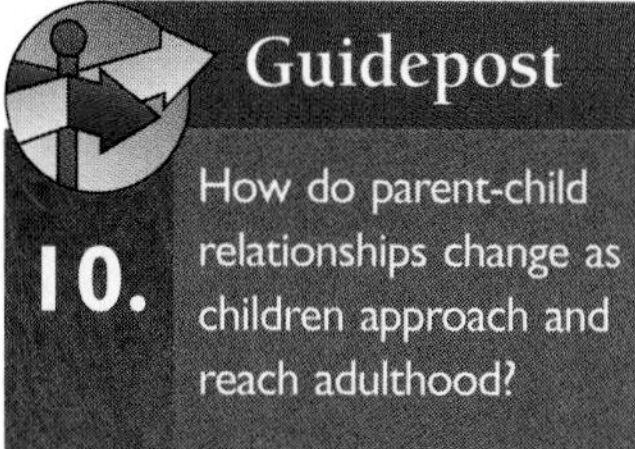

Guidepost
10.
How do parent-child relationships change as children approach and reach adulthood?

Parenthood is a process of letting go. This process usually reaches its climax during the parents' middle age. It is true that, with modern trends toward delaying marriage and parenthood, an increasing number of middle-aged people now face such issues as finding a good day care or kindergarten program and screening the content of Saturday morning cartoons. Still, most parents in the early part of middle age must cope with a different set of issues, which arise from living with children who will soon be leaving the nest. Once children become adults, parent-child ties usually recede in importance; but these ties normally last as long as parent and child live.

Adolescent Children: Issues for Parents

It is ironic that the people at the two times of life popularly linked with emotional crises—adolescence and midlife—often live in the same household. It is usually middle-aged adults who are the parents of adolescent children. While dealing with their own special concerns, parents have to cope daily with young people who are undergoing great physical, emotional, and social changes.

Although research contradicts the stereotype of adolescence as a time of inevitable turmoil and rebellion (refer back to Chapter 12), some rejection of parental authority is necessary for the maturing youngster. An important task for parents is to accept children as they are, not as what the parents had hoped they would be.

Theorists from a variety of perspectives have described this period as one of questioning, reappraisal, or diminished well-being for parents. However, this too is not inevitable, according to a questionnaire survey of 129 two-parent, intact, mostly white, socioeconomically diverse families with a firstborn son or daughter between ages 10 and 15. Most vulnerable were mothers who were not heavily invested in paid work; apparently work can bolster a parent's self-worth despite the challenges of having a teenage child. For some other parents, especially white-collar and professional men with sons, their children's adolescence brought increased satisfaction, well-being, and even pride. For most parents, the normative changes of adolescence elicited a mixture of positive and negative emotions. This was particularly true of mothers with early adolescent daughters, whose relationships generally tend to be both close and conflict-filled (Silverberg, 1996).

When Children Leave: The Empty Nest

Research is also challenging popular ideas about the empty nest, a supposedly difficult transition, especially for women. Although some women, heavily invested in mothering, do have problems at this time, they are far outnumbered by those who, like Madeline Albright, find the departure liberating (Antonucci & Akiyama, 1997; Barnett, 1985; Chiriboga, 1997; Helson, 1997; Mitchell & Helson, 1990). Today, the refilling of the nest by grown children returning home (discussed in the next section) is far more stressful (Thomas, 1997).

The empty nest does not signal the end of parenthood. It is a transition to a new stage: the relationship between parents and adult children. For many women, this transition brings relief from what Gutmann called the "chronic emergency of parenthood" (Cooper & Gutmann, 1987, p. 347). They can now pursue their own interests as they bask in their grown children's accomplishments. The empty nest does appear to be hard on women who have not prepared for it by reorganizing their lives (Targ, 1979). This phase also may be hard on fathers who regret that they did not spend more time with their children (L. B. Rubin, 1979).

In a longitudinal study of employed married women with multiple roles, the empty nest had *no* effect on psychological health, but cutting back on employment *increased* distress, whereas going to work full-time *decreased* it (Wethington & Kessler, 1989). On the other hand, in a comparison of stress at various stages of life, men in the empty nest stage were most likely to report health-related stress (Chiriboga, 1997).

CHECKPOINT

Can you . . .

- ✔ Explain why, and under what circumstances, parents of adolescent children tend to go through a process of reappraisal or lessened well-being?
- ✔ Tell how most women and men respond to the empty nest?

When Children Return: The Revolving Door Syndrome*

What happens if the nest does not empty when it normally should, or if it unexpectedly refills? In recent decades, more and more adult children have delayed leaving home. Furthermore, the **revolving door syndrome** (sometimes called the *boomerang phenomenon)* has become more common, as increasing numbers of young adults, especially men, return to their parents' home, sometimes more than once. The family home can be a convenient, supportive, and affordable haven while young adults are getting on their feet or regaining their balance in times of financial, marital, or other trouble.

revolving door syndrome Tendency for young adults to return to their parents' home while getting on their feet or in times of financial, marital, or other trouble.

According to the National Survey of Families and Households, at any given moment 45 percent of parents ages 45 to 54 with children over age 18 have an

*Unless otherwise referenced, this discussion is based on Aquilino (1996).

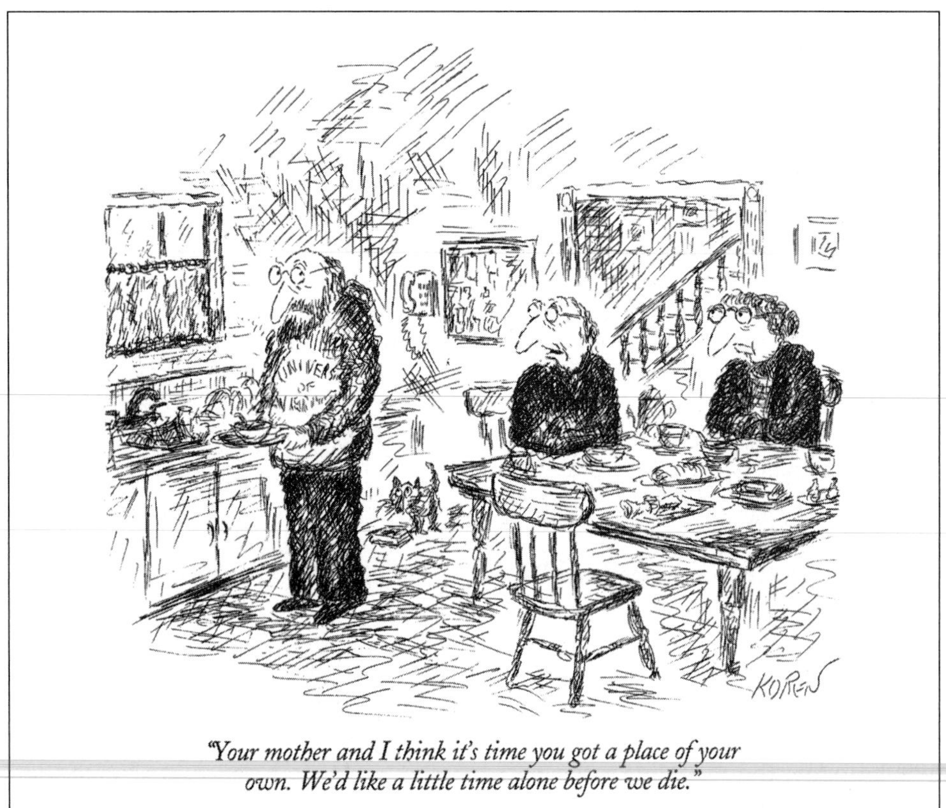

"Your mother and I think it's time you got a place of your own. We'd like a little time alone before we die."

Financial or marital problems induce an increasing number of adult children to return to the "nest," or not to leave at all. This nonnormative situation can create stress for middle-aged parents, especially when it is not temporary.

adult child living at home; and three out of four 19- to 34-year-olds have lived in the parental home at some time after turning 19 (in four out of ten cases, more than once). Thus this "nonnormative" experience is becoming quite normative, especially for parents with more than one child. Rather than an abrupt leave-taking, the empty nest transition may be seen as a more prolonged process of separation, often lasting several years.

The way this transition plays out for parents is "strongly related to children's progress through the transition to adulthood" (Aquilino, 1996, pp. 435–436). Most likely to come home are single, divorced, or separated children and those who end a cohabiting relationship. Leaving school and ending military service increase the chances of returning; having a child decreases them.

As common as it has become, the revolving door syndrome contradicts most parents' expectations for young adults. As children move from adolescence to young adulthood, parents expect them to become independent. Their autonomy is a sign of parental success. As the timing-of-events model would predict, then, an unanticipated return to the nest may lead to tension. Serious conflicts or open hostility may arise when a young adult child is unemployed and financially dependent or has returned after the failure of a marriage. Relations are smoother when the parents see the adult child moving toward autonomy, for example by enrolling in college.

Disagreements may center on household responsibilities and the adult child's lifestyle. The young adult is likely to feel isolated from peers, while the parents may feel hampered in renewing their intimacy, exploring personal interests, and resolving marital issues (Aquilino & Supple, 1991). The return of an adult child works best when parents and child negotiate roles and responsibilities, acknowledging the child's adult status and the parents' right to privacy.

Consider this . . .

- Do you think it is a good idea for adult children to live with their parents? If so, under what circumstances? What "house rules" do you think should apply?

Parenting Grown Children

Elliott Roosevelt, a son of President Franklin Delano Roosevelt, used to tell this story about his mother, Eleanor Roosevelt: At a state dinner, Eleanor, who was seated next to him, leaned over and whispered in his ear. A friend later asked Elliott, then in his forties, what she had said. "She told me to eat my peas," he answered.

Even after the years of active parenting are over and children have left home for good, parents are still parents. The midlife role of parent to young adults raises new issues and calls for new attitudes and behaviors on the part of both generations. Some parents have difficulty treating their offspring as adults, and many young adults have difficulty accepting their parents' continuing concern about them.

Still, young adults and their parents generally enjoy each other's company and get along well. Young newlyweds (especially women) tend to maintain close ties with their parents, who often help them with money, baby-sitting, and setting up their first homes. Parents and adult children visit frequently, and young couples spend a great deal of time talking with and about their parents. Parents generally give their children more than they get from them (Troll, 1989). Their continuing support probably reflects the relative strength of middle-aged adults and the continuing needs of young adults as they establish careers and families (Pearlin, 1980).

Most parents of grown children express satisfaction with their parenting role and with the way their children turned out (Umberson, 1992). Parents who believe that their children have turned out well tend to feel good about themselves. In one study, researchers interviewed 215 mothers and fathers (average age, about 54) on their grown children's attainments and personal and social adjustment. Parents who saw their children as successful and, especially, as well adjusted scored higher on all dimensions of well-being (except autonomy) than those who did not. They also were less likely to be depressed. Interestingly, however, well-being was *lower* when parents believed their children had turned out better than themselves. In such cases, children's success may be a bittersweet reminder of parents' own disappointments and regrets (Ryff, Lee, Essex, & Schmutte, 1994).

CHECKPOINT

Can you . . .

- ✔ Give reasons for the revolving door syndrome, and discuss parents' reactions to it?
- ✔ Describe typical features of relationships between parents and grown children?

Other Kinship Ties

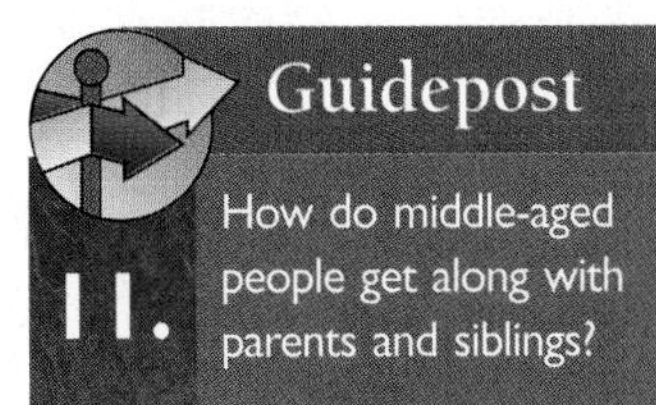

Guidepost
11.
How do middle-aged people get along with parents and siblings?

Except in times of need, ties with the family of origin—parents and siblings—recede in importance during young adulthood, when work, spouses or partners, and children take precedence. At midlife, these earliest kinship ties may reassert themselves in a new way, as the responsibility for care and support of aging parents begins to shift to their middle-aged children. In addition, a new relationship and role typically begins at this time of life: grandparenthood.

Relationships with Aging Parents

The bond between middle-aged children and their elderly parents is strong, growing out of earlier attachment and continuing as long as both generations live (Cicirelli, 1980, 1989b; Rossi & Rossi, 1990). Seven out of 10 people enter middle age with two living parents and leave middle age with none (Bumpass & Aquilino, 1993). The years in between often bring dramatic, though gradual, changes in filial relationships. Many middle-aged people look at their parents more objectively than before, seeing them as individuals with both strengths and weaknesses. Something else happens during these years: one day a son or daughter looks at a mother or father and sees an old person, and that realization may be distressing (Troll & Fingerman, 1996).

Contact and Mutual Help

Most middle-aged adults and their parents have close relationships based on frequent contact and mutual help (Antonucci & Akiyama, 1997). Many live near each other and see each other at least once a week (American Association of Retired Persons [AARP], 1995; Lin & Rogerson, 1995; Umberson, 1992). Mothers and daughters are especially likely to stay in close contact (G. R. Lee, Dwyer, & Coward, 1993; Troll, 1986).

Many older adults resume a more active parenting role when a child needs help (Aldous, 1987). And when they themselves need help, their children are the first people they turn to and the ones likely to do the most (Field & Minkler, 1988).

Although most older adults are physically fit, vigorous, and independent, some seek their children's assistance in making decisions and may depend on them for daily tasks and financial help. Most middle-aged people are conscious of their obligations to their parents and often expect more of themselves than the parents do of them. Among 144 parent-child pairs, both generations gave top ranking to the same three filial responsibilities: helping parents understand their resources, providing emotional support, and talking over matters of importance. Both generations gave less weight to adjusting work or family schedules to help parents. The children felt that they should give money to their parents, but most of the parents did not. More children than parents considered it important to make room for a parent in their homes in an emergency, to care for parents when they were sick, and to sacrifice personal freedom (Hamon & Blieszner, 1990).

filial maturity
Stage of life, proposed by Marcoen and others, in which middle-aged children, as the outcome of a filial crisis, learn to accept and meet their parents' need to depend on them.

filial crisis
In Marcoen's terminology, normative development of middle age, in which adults learn to balance love and duty to their parents with autonomy within a two-way relationship.

Becoming a Caregiver for Aging Parents

The need to care for elderly parents is a relatively recent phenomenon. In 1900, a middle-aged couple had only a 10 percent chance of having at least two parents alive; by 1976, the probability had risen to 47 percent (Cutler & Devlin, 1996). With the lengthening of the life span, some developmentalists have proposed a new life stage called **filial maturity**, when middle-aged children "learn to accept and to meet their parents' dependency needs" (Marcoen, 1995, p. 125). This normative development is seen as the healthy outcome of a **filial crisis**, in which adults learn to balance love and duty to their parents with autonomy within a two-way relationship.

Only 1 out of 5 older people who need care are in institutions (Center on Elderly People Living Alone, 1995b). With the high cost of nursing homes and most older people's reluctance to enter and stay in them, many dependent elders receive care in their own home or in a caregiver's. Middle-aged daughters are the ones most likely to take on this responsibility—usually for aging, ailing mothers (Matthews, 1995; Troll, 1986). Often the need arises when a mother is widowed, or when a

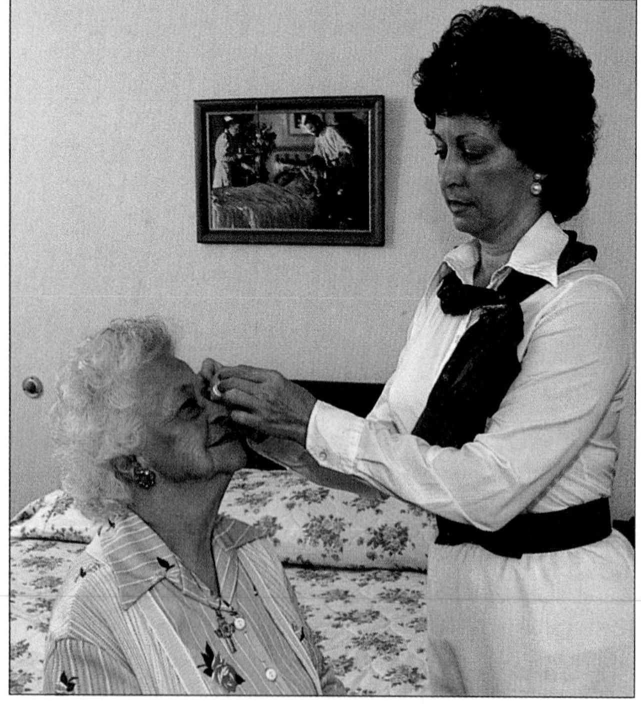

By middle age, many people can look at their parents objectively, neither idealizing them nor exaggerating their shortcomings. This middle-aged daughter putting drops in her mother's eyes realizes that her mother is no longer a tower of strength but instead is beginning to lean on *her.* Mothers and daughters usually remain closer than any other combination of family members.

woman divorced years before can no longer manage alone. Only or oldest children, or those who live nearby, are most likely to become caregivers (Marks, 1996).

Cultural assumptions that caregiving is a female function make it likely that a daughter will assume the role (Matthews, 1995). Also, perhaps because of the intimate nature of the contact and the strength of the mother-daughter bond, mothers may prefer a daughter's care (Lee et al., 1993). Sons do contribute, more than is often recognized, but they are less likely to provide primary, personal care (Marks, 1996; Matthews, 1995).

The chances of becoming a caregiver are greater than ever before, and the likelihood increases through middle age. Longer life means more risk of chronic diseases and disabilities; and families are smaller than in the past, with fewer siblings to share in a parent's care. The **parent-support ratio**—the number of people 85 and over for every 100 people ages 50 to 64—tripled (from 3 to 10) between 1950 and 1993; it may triple again by 2053 (U.S. Bureau of the Census, 1995). Worldwide, the elderly support burden will be 50 percent larger in 2025 than it was in 1998 (U.S. Bureau of the Census, 1999b).

parent-support ratio
In a given population, number of people age 85 and over for every 100 people ages 50 to 64, who may need to provide care and support for them.

At the same time, with more women working outside the home, it is harder for them to assume an added caregiving role (Marks, 1996). About one-third of caregivers also work for pay, and more than one-fourth have had to quit jobs to meet caregiving obligations (Noelker & Whitlatch, 1995). Flexible work schedules can help alleviate this problem. The Family and Medical Leave Act, adopted in 1993, guarantees family caregivers some unpaid leave, and some large corporations provide time off for caregiving. (Long-term care is discussed further in Chapter 18.)

Strains of Caregiving: The Sandwich Generation

The generations get along best while parents are healthy and vigorous. When older people become infirm—especially if they undergo mental deterioration or personality changes—the burden of caring for them may strain the relationship (Cicirelli, 1983; Marcoen, 1995). Caring for a person with physical impairments is hard. It can be even harder to care for someone with dementia, who, in addition to being unable to carry on basic functions of daily living, may be incontinent, suspicious, agitated, subject to hallucinations, likely to wander about at night, dangerous to self and others, and in need of constant supervision (Biegel, 1995). Many caregivers find the task a physical, emotional, and financial burden, especially if they work full time, are raising children, lack support and assistance, or have limited financial resources (Lund, 1993a).

Consider this . . .

- What would you do if one or both of your parents required long-term care? To what extent should children or other relatives be responsible for such care? To what extent, and in what ways, should society help?

Strain comes not only from caregiving itself but from its interference with other aspects of a caregiver's life. The need to care for elderly parents often comes at a time when middle-aged adults are trying to launch their own children or, if parenthood was delayed, to raise them. Members of this "generation in the middle," sometimes called the **sandwich generation,** are caught in a squeeze between these competing needs and their limited resources of time, money, and energy. Also troubling are conflicts between caregiving duties and personal interests, social activities, or travel plans (Mui, 1992). Caregiving can put strains on a marriage and may even lead to divorce (Lund, 1993a). All of these strains can contribute to **caregiver burnout,** a physical, mental, and emotional exhaustion that affects many adults who care for aged relatives (Barnhart, 1992).

sandwich generation
Middle-aged adults squeezed by competing needs to raise or launch children and to care for elderly parents.

caregiver burnout
Condition of physical, mental, and emotional exhaustion affecting adults who care for aged persons.

For many adults, the needs of aging parents seem to represent nonnormative, unanticipated demands. Adults expect to assume the physical, financial, and emotional care of their children. Most do *not* expect to have to care for their parents. When parents' dependency becomes undeniable, many adult children find it hard to cope (Barnhart, 1992).

If the eventual decision is to place a parent in a nursing home—as does happen in 1 out of 4 cases—the caregiver's role and stress may diminish but not end.

The burden now involves finding a good facility, working out financing, dealing with the staff, monitoring care, and facing anxiety, guilt, or other emotional consequences of the decision (Noelker & Whitlatch, 1995).

Still, 95 percent of caregivers accept their filial responsibility; they do not abandon their parents (Noelker & Whitlatch, 1995). Caregiving can be an opportunity for growth if a caregiver feels deeply about a parent and about family solidarity, looks at caregiving as a challenge, and has adequate personal, family, and community resources to meet that challenge (Bengtson, Rosenthal, & Burton, 1996; Biegel, 1995; Lund, 1993a). (Box 16-2 discusses sources of assistance to help prevent caregiver burnout.)

Relationships with Siblings

Relationships with siblings are the longest-lasting in most people's lives. About 85 percent of middle-aged Americans, like Madeleine Albright, have living siblings, and most siblings remain in contact. Sisters, especially, stay in touch and stand ready to help each other (Cicirelli, 1980, 1995; H. G. Ross, Dalton, & Milgram, 1980; Scott & Roberto, 1981).

In some cross-sectional research, sibling relationships over the life span appear to take the form of an hourglass, with the most contact at the two ends—childhood and middle to late adulthood—and the least contact during the childraising years. After establishing careers and families, siblings may renew ties (Bedford, 1995; Cicirelli, 1995).

Other studies indicate a decline in frequency of contact throughout adulthood. Regardless of how often siblings see or talk with each other, however, their relationship generally remains as close or closer than ever (Cicirelli, 1995). In a retrospective study, 35- to 65-year-olds rated the quality of their sibling relationships throughout the life span. For sisters, positive aspects of the relationship, such as trust and enjoyment, increased throughout adulthood; brothers reported no change. But for both brothers and sisters, negative aspects, such as rivalry and competition, declined continuously from adolescence to late life (Cicirelli, 1994, 1995).

Life events may have a positive or negative influence on sibling relationships. Marriage brings some siblings closer, while others drift apart (Cicirelli, 1995). The arrival of children may tighten the sibling bond, as do such unhappy events as divorce, widowhood, and the death of a family member (Connidis, 1992).

Relationships with siblings are important to psychological well-being in midlife, though their importance relative to other relationships, such as friendships, may rise and fall from time to time. Sibling relationships seem to serve somewhat different purposes for men and women. For women, positive feelings toward siblings are linked with a favorable self-concept; for men, with high morale. The more contact both men and women have with their siblings, the less likely they are to show symptoms of psychological problems (Paul, 1997).

Dealing with the care of aging parents brings some siblings closer together but causes resentment among others (Bedford, 1995; Bengtson et al., 1996). The quality of a sibling relationship during the early years—cooperative or conflictual—may affect the way adult siblings handle such issues (Bedford, 1995). Disagreements may arise over the division of care (Lerner, Somers, Reid, Chiriboga, & Tierney, 1991; Strawbridge & Wallhagen, 1991) or over an inheritance, especially if the sibling relationship has not been good. Among 95 married daughters caring for parents with dementia, siblings were a strong source of support, but also the most important source of interpersonal stress (Suitor & Pillemer, 1993).

CHECKPOINT

Can you . . .

- ✔ Describe the change in the balance of filial relationships that often occurs between middle-aged children and elderly parents, and how both parties tend to view the change?
- ✔ Cite several sources of strains on caregivers for elderly parents, and describe programs designed to alleviate those strains?
- ✔ Discuss the nature and importance of sibling relationships in middle age as compared with other parts of the life span?

Practically Speaking

Box 16-2
Preventing Caregiver Burnout

Even the most patient, loving caregiver may become frustrated, anxious, or resentful under the constant strain of meeting an older person's seemingly endless needs. Almost one-third of caregivers get no help with caregiving duties (Biegel, 1995). Sometimes the strains created by incessant, heavy demands are so great as to lead to abuse, neglect, or even abandonment of the dependent elderly person (see Chapter 18).

Often families and friends fail to recognize that caregivers have a right to feel discouraged, frustrated, and put upon. Caregivers need a life of their own, beyond the loved one's disability or disease (J. Evans, 1994).

Community support programs can reduce the strains and burdens of caregiving, prevent burnout, and postpone the need for institutionalization of the dependent person. Support services may include meals and housekeeping; transportation and escort services; and adult day care centers, which provide supervised activities and care while caregivers work or attend to personal needs. *Respite care* (substitute supervised care by visiting nurses or home health aides) gives regular caregivers some time off, whether for a few hours, a day, a weekend, or a week. Temporary admission to a nursing home is another alternative.

Although there is some dispute about their effectiveness, some research suggests that such programs do improve caregivers' morale and reduce stress (Gallagher-Thompson, 1995). In one longitudinal study, caregivers with adequate community support reported many dimensions of personal growth. Some had become more empathic, caring, understanding, patient, and compassionate, closer to the person they were caring for, and more appreciative of their own good health. Others felt good about having fulfilled their responsibilities (Lund, 1993a).

Behavioral training and psychotherapy can help caregivers deal with a patient's difficult behavior and their own tendency toward depression (Gallagher-Thompson, 1995). One behavioral training program at the University of Chicago had considerable success in getting patients to handle some self-care and to be more sociable and less verbally abusive. Caregivers learned such techniques as contingency contracting ("If you do this, the consequence will be . . .), modeling desired behaviors, rehearsal, and giving feedback (Gallagher-Thompson, 1995).

Through counseling, support, and self-help groups, caregivers can share problems, gain information about community resources, and improve skills. One such program helped daughters recognize the limits of their ability to meet their mothers' needs, and the value of encouraging their mothers' self-reliance. This understanding lightened the daughters' burden and improved their relationship with their mothers; as a result, the mothers became less lonely (Scharlach, 1987). In one longitudinal study, caregivers with adequate community support reported many dimensions of personal growth. Some had become more empathic, caring, understanding, patient, and compassionate, closer to the person they were caring for, and more appreciative of their own good health. Others felt good about having fulfilled their responsibilities. Some had "learned to value life more and to take one day at a time," and a few had learned to "laugh at situations and events" (Lund, 1993a).

A "Caregiver's Bill of Rights" (Home, 1985) can help caregivers keep a positive perspective and remind them that their needs count too:

A Caregiver's Bill of Rights

I have the right

- to take care of myself. This is not an act of selfishness. It will give me the capability of taking better care of my relative.
- to seek help from others even though my relative may object. I recognize the limits of my own endurance and strength.
- to maintain facets of my own life that do not include the person I care for, just as I would if he or she were healthy. I know that I do everything that I reasonably can for this person, and I have the right to do some things just for myself.
- to get angry, be depressed and express other difficult feelings occasionally.
- to reject any attempt by my relative (either conscious or unconscious) to manipulate me through guilt, anger or depression.
- to receive consideration, affection, forgiveness and acceptance for what I do from my loved ones for as long as I offer these qualities in return.
- to take pride in what I am accomplishing and to applaud the courage it has sometimes taken to meet the needs of my relative.
- to protect my individuality and my right to make a life for myself that will sustain me in the time when my relative no longer needs my full-time help.
- to expect and demand that as new strides are made in finding resources to aid physically and mentally impaired older persons in our country, similar strides will be made toward aiding and supporting caregivers.
- to (add your own statements of rights to this list. Read this list to yourself every day).

Grandparenthood

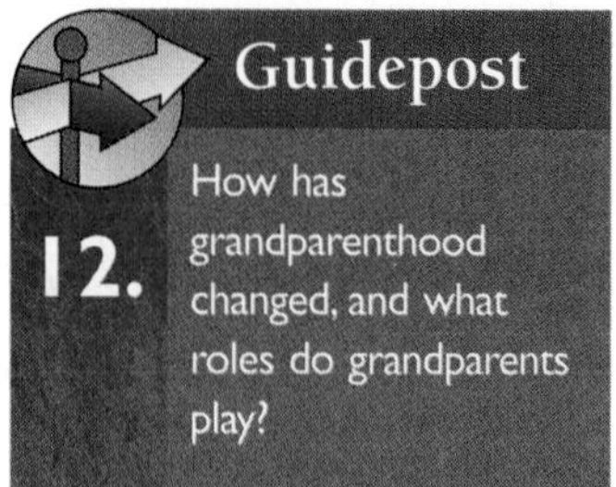

Guidepost
12.
How has grandparenthood changed, and what roles do grandparents play?

In some African communities, grandparents are called "noble." In Japan, grandmothers have traditionally worn red as a sign of their status (Kornhaber, 1986). In western societies, too, becoming a grandparent is an important event in a person's life; but its timing and meaning vary.

Adults in the United States usually become grandparents in their forties or fifties, often before the end of active parenting. With today's lengthening life spans, many adults spend several decades as grandparents. Since women tend to live longer than men (see Chapter 17), grandmothers typically live to see at least the oldest grandchild become an adult and to become great-grandmothers (Szinovacz, 1998).

Grandparenthood today is different in several ways from grandparenthood in the past. The average grandparent has 5 or 6 grandchildren, compared with 12 to 15 around the turn of the century (Szinovacz, 1998; Uhlenberg, 1988). With the rising incidence of midlife divorce, more grandparents are divorced or remarried, and many children have stepgrandparents. Grandmothers of younger children are more likely to be in the workforce (and thus less available to help out). On the other hand, trends toward early retirement free more grandparents to spend time with older grandchildren. Many grandparents still have living parents, whose care they must balance with grandchildren's needs. And an increasing number of grandparents assume primary responsibility for grandchildren at some point (Szinovacz, 1998).

The Grandparent's Role

In many traditional societies, such as those in Latin America and Asia, extended-family households are common (refer back to Chapter 1); and grandparents play an integral role in child raising and family decisions. In the United States today, the extended family remains important in Hispanic, African American, and some other minority communities. Still, the dominant household pattern is the nuclear

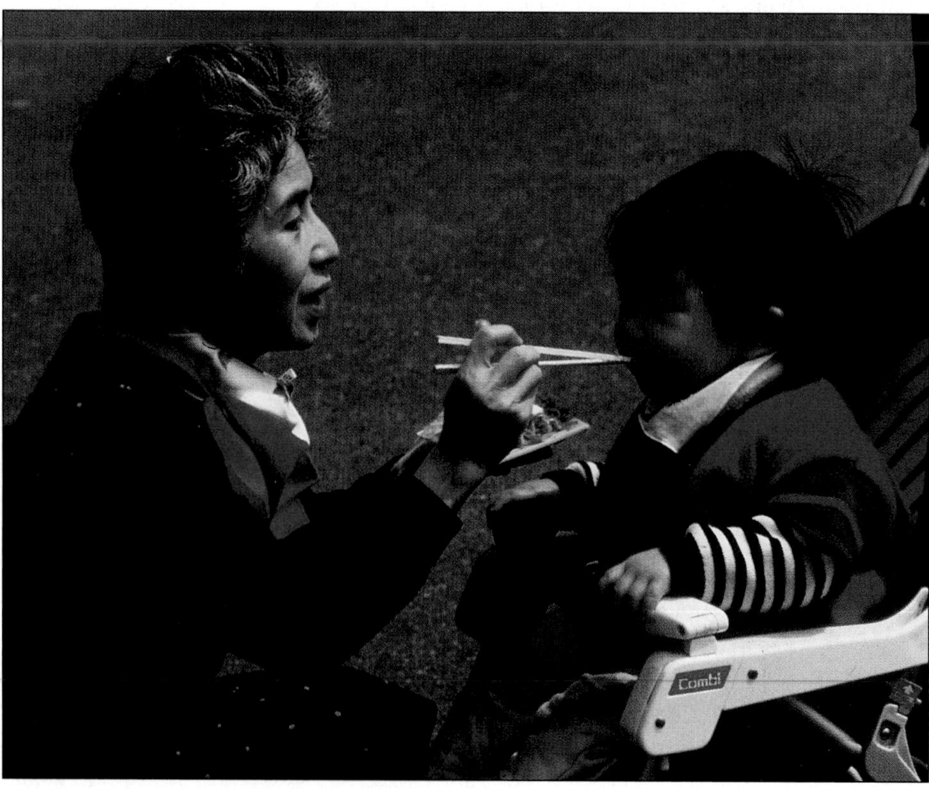

In Japan, grandmothers like this one traditionally wear red as a sign of their noble status. Grandparenthood is an important milestone in western societies as well.

family. When children grow up, they typically leave home and establish new, autonomous nuclear families wherever their inclinations and aspirations take them. It is not surprising, then, that, according to one study of 300 grandchildren ages 5 to 18, and 300 grandparents, only 15 percent of U.S. children have a "vital connection" with one or more grandparents (Kornhaber, 1986; Kornhaber & Woodward, 1981).

Other research puts contemporary grandparenthood in a more positive light. A major study of a nationally representative three-generation sample found that "grandparents play a limited but important role in family dynamics," and many have strong emotional ties to their grandchildren (Cherlin & Furstenberg, 1986a, p. 26). (Figure 16-1 shows the most frequent grandparent-grandchild activities.) According to one survey, about 1 in 3 grandparents provides occasional child care or supervision, and nearly 1 in 10 does so for 20 or more hours a week (Bass & Caro, 1996).

Consider this . . .

- Have you had a close relationship with a grandparent? If so, in what specific ways did that relationship influence your development?

Gender and Ethnic Differences

Men and women tend to have different expectations about grandparenthood, according to interviews with 152 white 40- to 73-year-olds before their first grandchild's birth (Somary & Strickler, 1998). Women expected to derive more satisfaction from grandparenting, and they expected the new baby to play a central role in their lives. Men expected to feel more comfortable about speaking their mind to the child's parents and being involved in advising and caretaking.

How well were those expectations fulfilled? Quite well in some respects, according to questionnaires filled out by 103 of the participants a year or two after the birth. Grandmothers were more satisfied with their role than grandfathers,

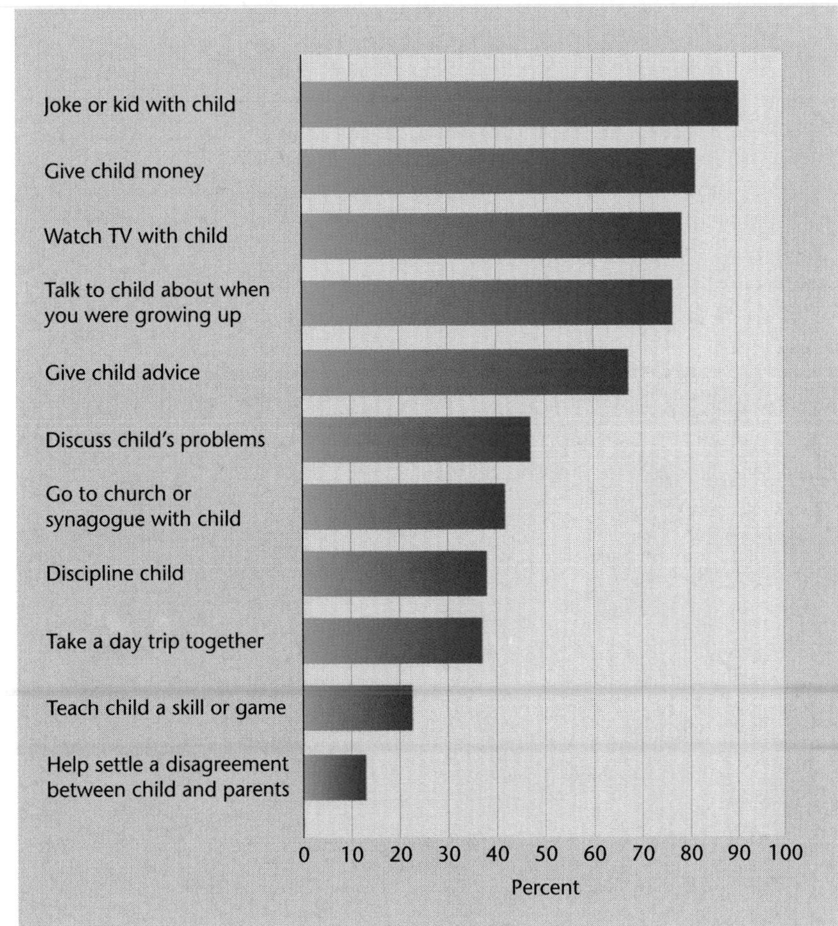

Figure 16-1
What grandparents do with their grandchildren: proportions of grandparents in a nationally representative sample who had engaged in various activities with their grandchildren in the previous 12 months.
(Source: Cherlin & Furstenberg, 1986b, p. 74.)

even though they spent no more time with their grandchildren than the grandfathers did. Grandfathers, as expected, tended to offer advice more openly to the new parents, whereas grandmothers refrained from giving advice so as to avoid tension. Both grandfathers and grandmothers, especially on the mother's side, reaped more satisfaction than they expected and were more involved in caregiving; and grandfathers were as likely as grandmothers to see the grandchild as playing a central role in their lives.

Other studies have found that grandmothers tend to have closer, warmer relationships with their grandchildren than grandfathers do, and to serve more often as surrogate parents. The mother's parents are likely to be closer to the children than are the father's parents and are more likely to become involved during a crisis (Cherlin & Furstenberg, 1986a, 1986b; Hagestad, 1978, 1982; B. Kahana & Kahana, 1970). However, this may be because the maternal grandparents tend to live closer by (Somary & Strickler, 1998).

African American grandparents are more likely than white grandparents to become involved in raising their grandchildren (Cherlin & Furstenberg, 1986a, 1986b; Strom, Collinsworth, Strom, & Griswold, 1992–1993). In one study, 2 out of 3 black teenage mothers named their mothers as their children's primary caregivers. In another study, 3 out of 4 children of teenage mothers lived in a grandmother's household during their first 3 years (Bengtson et al., 1996). Also, grandfatherhood may be more central for black men than for white men (Kivett, 1991).

Grandparenting After Divorce and Remarriage

One result of the rise in divorce and remarriage is a growing number of grandparents and grandchildren whose relationships are endangered or severed. Another result is the creation of large numbers of stepgrandparents.

After a divorce, since the mother usually has custody, her parents tend to have more contact and stronger relationships with their grandchildren, and the paternal grandparents tend to have less (Cherlin & Furstenberg, 1986b; Myers & Perrin, 1993). A divorced mother's remarriage typically reduces her need for support from her parents, but not their contact with their grandchildren. For paternal grandparents, however, the new marriage increases the likelihood that they will be displaced or that the family will move away, making contact more difficult (Cherlin & Furstenberg, 1986b).

Because ties with grandparents are important to children's development, every state in the Union has given grandparents (and in some states, great-

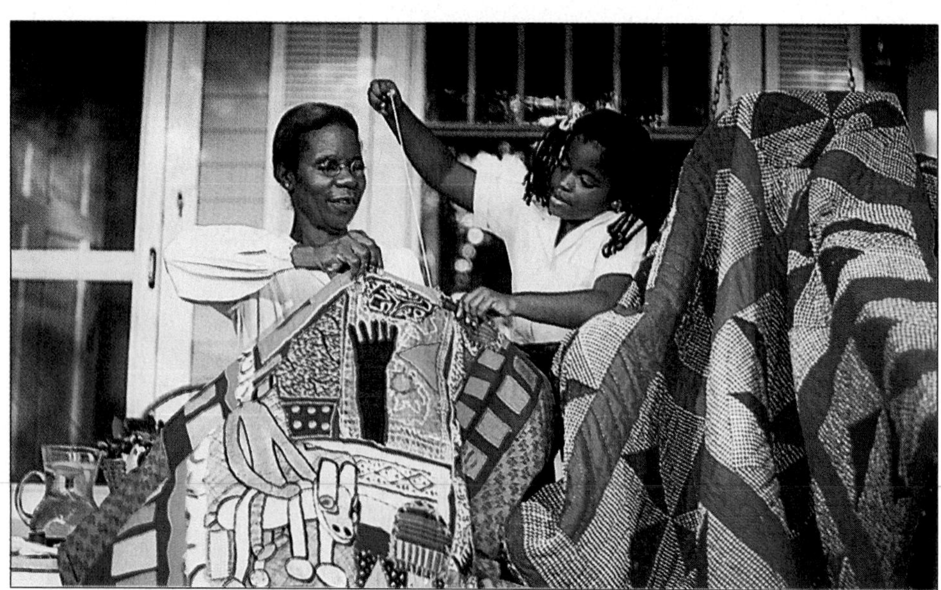

Grandparents, like this grandmother teaching her granddaughter to make a quilt, can have an important influence on their grandchildren's development. Grandmothers tend to have closer, warmer relationships with their grandchildren than grandfathers. Black grandparents, although often less educated than white grandparents, tend to be especially successful in teaching their grandchildren values, perhaps because they generally spend more time with them.

grandparents, siblings, and others) the right to visitation after a divorce or the death of a parent, if a judge finds it in the best interests of the child. A few state courts, however, have struck down such laws, and some legislatures have restricted grandparents' visitation rights. The Supreme Court in June 2000 invalidated an application of Washington state's "grandparents' rights" law as too broad an intrusion on parental rights (Greenhouse, 2000).

The remarriage of either parent often brings a new set of grandparents into the picture, and often stepgrandchildren as well. Stepgrandparents may find it hard to become close to their new stepgrandchildren, especially older children and those who do not live with the grandparent's adult child (Cherlin & Furstenberg, 1986b; Longino & Earle, 1996; Myers & Perrin, 1993). Such issues as birthday and Christmas presents for a "real" grandchild's half- or stepsiblings, or which grandparents are visited or included at holidays, can generate tension. Creating new family traditions; including *all* the grandchildren, step and otherwise, in trips, outings, and other activities; offering a safe haven for the children when they are unhappy or upset; and being understanding and supportive of all members of the new stepfamily are ways in which stepgrandparents can build bridges, not walls (T. S. Kaufman, 1993; Visher & Visher, 1991).

CHECKPOINT

Can you . . .

- ✔ Tell ways in which grandparenthood has changed in recent generations?
- ✔ Describe the role grandparents usually play in family life, and point out differences related to gender and ethnicity?
- ✔ Tell how parents' divorce and remarriage can affect grandparents' relationships with grandchildren?

Raising Grandchildren

An increasing number of grandparents are serving as "parents by default" for children whose parents are unable to care for them—often as a result of teenage pregnancy or substance abuse (Casper & Bryson, 1998; Chalfie, 1994; Minkler & Roe, 1996). In 1997, nearly 7 percent of households with children under 18 were maintained by grandparents—a 19 percent increase since 1990—and about one-third of these households had no parents present, the fastest-growing household type (Casper & Bryson, 1998). In some low-income urban areas, an estimated 30 to 50 percent of children are in **kinship care,** living in homes of grandparents or other relatives without their parents (Minkler & Roe, 1996).

kinship care
Care of children living without parents in the home of grandparents or other relatives, with or without a change of legal custody.

Unplanned surrogate parenthood can be a physical, emotional, and financial drain on middle-aged or older adults. They may have to quit their jobs, shelve their retirement plans, drastically reduce their leisure pursuits and social life, and endanger their health (Burton, 1992; Chalfie, 1994; Minkler & Roe, 1992, 1996). Most grandparents do not have as much energy, patience, or stamina as they once had, and respite care is generally unavailable (Crowley, 1993). Many of these families are in dire financial straits (Casper & Bryson, 1998).

Consider this . . .

- Did you ever live with a grandparent? If so, what advantages and difficulties did you experience? If not, what advantages and difficulties do you think there might have been if you had done so?

Most grandparents who take on the responsibility to raise their grandchildren do it because they love the children and do not want them placed in a stranger's foster home. According to one study, two-thirds of custodial grandparents report a greater sense of purpose in life (Jendrek, 1994). However, the age difference between grandparent and grandchild can become a barrier, and both generations may feel cheated out of their traditional roles. At the same time, grandparents often have to deal not only with a sense of guilt because the adult children they raised have failed their own children, but with the rancor they feel toward this adult child. For some caregiver couples, the strains produce tension in their own relationship. If one or both parents later resume their normal roles, it may be emotionally wrenching to return the child (Crowley, 1993; Larsen, 1990–1991).

Grandparents who do not become foster parents or gain custody have no legal status and no more rights than unpaid baby-sitters. They may face many practical problems, from enrolling the child in school and gaining access to academic records to obtaining medical insurance for the child. Grandchildren are usually not eligible for coverage under employer-provided health insurance even if the grandparent has custody (Chalfie, 1994; Simon-Rusinowitz, Krach, Marks, Piktialis, & Wilson, 1996). However, children in the poorest grandparent-headed families may be eligible for Medicaid (Casper & Bryson, 1998).

June Sands of Los Angeles hugs her 5-year-old daughter, Victoria, as her mother—Victoria's guardian, Elaine Sands—smiles fondly. Elaine and her husband, Don Sands, are among a growing number of grandparents raising grandchildren, temporarily or permanently. Elaine and Don took over Victoria's care while June was overcoming a 20-year drug addiction. June Sands had been in jail and in withdrawal when her daughter was born, but she had been drug-free for a year when this picture was taken. She lived near her parents, worked as a baby-sitter in a health club, and visited her daughter regularly.

CHECKPOINT

Can you . . .

✔ Discuss the challenges involved in raising grandchildren?

Like working parents, working grandparents need good, affordable child care and family-friendly workplace policies, such as time off to care for a sick child or go to a school conference (Simon-Rusinowitz et al., 1996). The federal Family and Medical Leave Act of 1993 does cover grandparents who are raising grandchildren, but many do not realize it.

Grandparents can be sources of guidance, companions in play, links to the past, and symbols of family continuity. They express generativity, a longing to transcend mortality by investing themselves in the lives of future generations. Men and women who do not become grandparents may fulfill generative needs by becoming foster grandparents or volunteering in schools or hospitals (Porcino, 1983, 1991). By finding ways to develop the "virtue" of care, adults prepare themselves to enter the culminating period of adult development and to discover the wisdom of old age.

Summary

Looking at the Life Course in Middle Age

Guidepost 1. How do developmental scientists approach the study of psychosocial development in middle adulthood?

- Developmental scientists view midlife psychosocial development both objectively, in terms of trajectories or pathways, and subjectively, in terms of people's sense of self and the way they actively construct their lives.

Change at Midlife: Classic Theoretical Approaches

Guidepost 2. What do classic theorists have to say about psychosocial change in middle age?

- Although some theorists, such as Freud and Costa and McCrae, held that personality is essentially formed by midlife, there is a growing consensus that midlife development shows change as well as stability.
- Carl Jung held that men and women at midlife undergo a process of **individuation,** in which they express previously suppressed aspects of personality. Two necessary tasks are giving up the image of youth and acknowledging mortality, which prompts introspection and questioning—or what Neugarten called **interiority.**
- Erikson's seventh psychosocial crisis is **generativity versus stagnation. Generativity** can be expressed through parenting and grandparenting, teaching or mentorship, productivity or creativity, and "self-generation," or self-development. The "virtue" of this period is care.
- Vaillant and Levinson found major midlife shifts in men's lives. Their findings echo Jung's and Erikson's theories in several ways.
- Despite the greater fluidity of the life cycle today, people still tend to expect and assess important events in their lives by a "social clock."

The Self at Midlife: Issues and Themes

Guidepost 3. What issues concerning the self come to the fore during middle adulthood?

- Key psychosocial issues and themes during middle adulthood concern the existence of a **midlife crisis,** identity development, psychological well-being, and gender identity.
- Research does not support a normative midlife crisis. It is more accurate to refer to a transition that often involves a **midlife review.**
- According to Whitbourne's model of identity development, people confirm or revise their self-perceptions through **identity assimilation** or **identity accommodation. Identity style** can predict adaptation to the onset of aging.
- According to narrative psychology, identity development is a continuous process of constructing a life story.
- Generativity is related to psychological well-being in middle age.
- Research based on Ryff's model has found that midlife is generally a period of positive mental health and well-being.
- Much research suggests that for women the fifties are a "prime time" of life.

Guidepost 4. How does midlife development differ for women and men?

- Research has found increasing "masculinization" of women and "feminization" of men at midlife, but this may be largely a cohort effect and may reflect the types of measures used. Research generally does *not* support Gutmann's proposed **gender crossover.**

Changes in Relationships at Midlife

Guidepost 5. What role do social relationships play in the lives of middle-aged people?

- Two theories of the changing importance of relationships are Kahn and Antonucci's **social convoy theory** and Laura Carstensen's **socioemotional selectivity theory.** According to both theories, social-emotional support is an important element in social interaction at midlife and beyond.
- Relationships at midlife are important to physical and mental health but also can present stressful demands.

Consensual Relationships

Guidepost 6. Do marriages become happier or unhappier during the middle years?

- Research on the quality of marriage suggests a dip in marital satisfaction during the years of child rearing, followed by an improved relationship after the children leave home.

Guidepost 7. How common is divorce at this time of life?

- Divorce at midlife is relatively uncommon, perhaps due in part to the buildup of **marital capital.** However, midlife divorce is increasing. Socioeconomic status and the timing and effects of the **empty nest** play a part.

Guidepost 8. How do gay and lesbian relationships compare with heterosexual ones?

- Because many homosexuals delay coming out, at midlife they are often just establishing intimate relationships.
- Gay and lesbian couples tend to be more egalitarian than heterosexual couples but experience similar problems in balancing family and career commitments.

Guidepost 9. How do friendships fare during middle age?

- Middle-aged people tend to invest less time and energy in friendships than younger adults do, but depend on friends for emotional support and practical guidance.

Relationships with Children

Guidepost 10. How do parent-child relationships change as children approach and reach adulthood?

- Parents of adolescents have to come to terms with a loss of control over their children's lives.
- The years when children have left home are often among the happiest. The "emptying of the nest" may be stressful, however, for fathers who have not been involved with child rearing, for mothers who have failed to prepare for the event, and for parents whose children have not become independent when expected.
- Today, more young adults are returning to live with parents (the **revolving door syndrome**). The situation is smoother if the parents see the adult child as moving toward autonomy.
- Middle-aged parents tend to remain involved with their adult children, and most are generally happy with the way their children turned out. Conflict may arise over grown children's need to be treated as adults and parents' continuing concern about them.

Other Kinship Ties

Guidepost 11. How do middle-aged people get along with parents and siblings?

- Relationships between middle-aged adults and their parents are usually characterized by a strong bond of affection. The two generations generally maintain frequent contact and offer and receive assistance.
- As life lengthens, more and more aging parents become dependent on their middle-aged children. Acceptance of these dependency needs is the mark of **filial maturity** and may be the outcome of a **filial crisis.** The chances of becoming a caregiver to an aging parent increase, especially for women, as the societal **parent-support ratio** grows. Caregiving can be a source of considerable stress for the **sandwich generation,** in part because they do not anticipate it. Community support programs can help prevent **caregiver burnout.**
- Most middle-aged people remain in contact with siblings, and sibling relationships are important to well-being.

Grandparenthood

Guidepost 12. How has grandparenthood changed, and what roles do grandparents play?

- Although most American grandparents today are less intimately involved in grandchildren's lives than in the past, they often play an important role.
- Divorce and remarriage of an adult child can affect grandparent-grandchild relationships and create new stepgrandparenting roles.
- An increasing number of children are in **kinship care.** For grandparents, raising grandchildren can create physical, emotional, and financial strains.

Key Terms

individuation (596)
generativity versus stagnation (597)
generativity (597)
interiority (597)
midlife crisis (600)
midlife review (601)
identity assimilation (602)
identity accommodation (602)
identity style (602)
gender crossover (608)
social convoy theory (609)
socioemotional selectivity theory (610)
marital capital (612)
empty nest (612)
revolving door syndrome (615)
filial maturity (618)
filial crisis (618)
parent-support ratio (619)
sandwich generation (619)
caregiver burnout (619)
kinship care (625)

Late Adulthood

Age 65 is the traditional entrance point for late adulthood, the last phase of life. Yet many adults at 65—or even 75 or 85—do not feel or act "old."

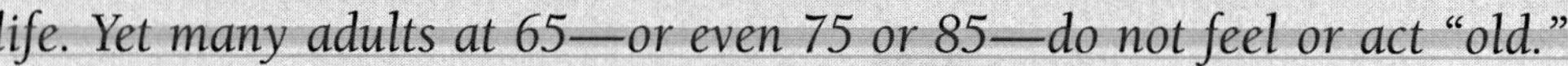

Individual differences become more pronounced in the later years, and "use it or lose it" becomes an urgent mandate. Most older adults enjoy good physical and mental health; people who keep physically and intellectually active can hold their own in most respects and even grow in competence. Physical and cognitive functioning have psychosocial effects, often determining an older person's emotional state and whether she or he can live independently.

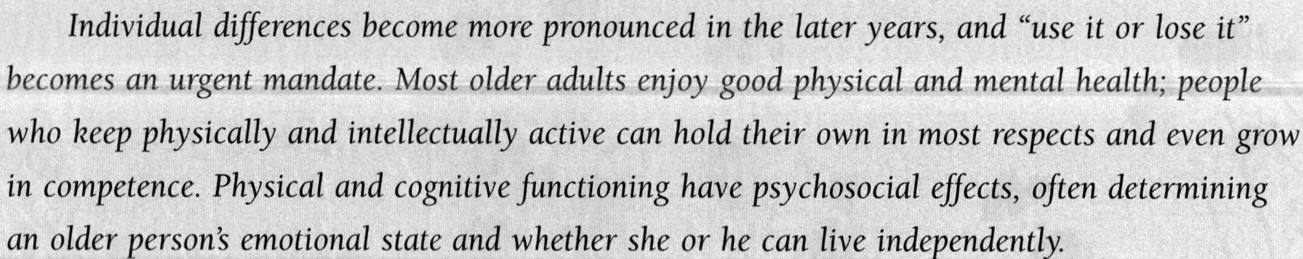

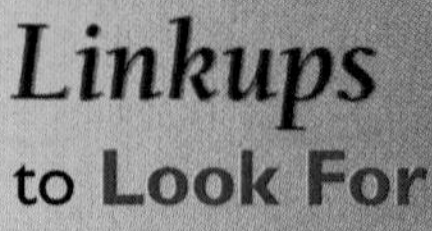

Linkups to **Look For**

- One reason that women tend to live longer than men may be their greater social support.
- Slowing of neurological responses can diminish the abilities to learn and remember.
- Poor comprehension of health-related information can limit effective access to appropriate care.
- Exercise may improve mental alertness and morale.
- High blood pressure can affect blood flow to the brain and interfere with cognitive performance.
- Older people often do poorly on intelligence tests because of lack of confidence, interest, or motivation.
- Conscientiousness and marital stability tend to predict long life.
- Cognitive appraisal of emotion-laden problems may help people develop strategies to cope with them.
- Men who continue to work after age 65 tend to be in better health and better educated than those who retire, and are more likely to view paid work as necessary to self-fulfillment.
- Both physical limitations and cultural patterns affect older people's choice of living arrangements.
- People who can confide in friends about their physical ills and worries tend to live longer.

Late Adulthood: A *Preview*

Chapter 17

Physical and Cognitive Development in Late Adulthood

Most people are healthy and active, although health and physical abilities decline somewhat.

Slowing of reaction time affects some aspects of functioning.

Most people are mentally alert.

Although intelligence and memory may deteriorate in some areas, most people find ways to compensate.

Chapter 18

Psychosocial Development in Late Adulthood

Retirement may offer new options for exploration of interests and activities.

People need to cope with personal losses and impending death as they seek to understand the meaning and purpose of their lives.

Relationships with family and close friends can provide important support.

Search for meaning in life assumes central importance.

Chapter 17

Physical and Cognitive Development in Late Adulthood

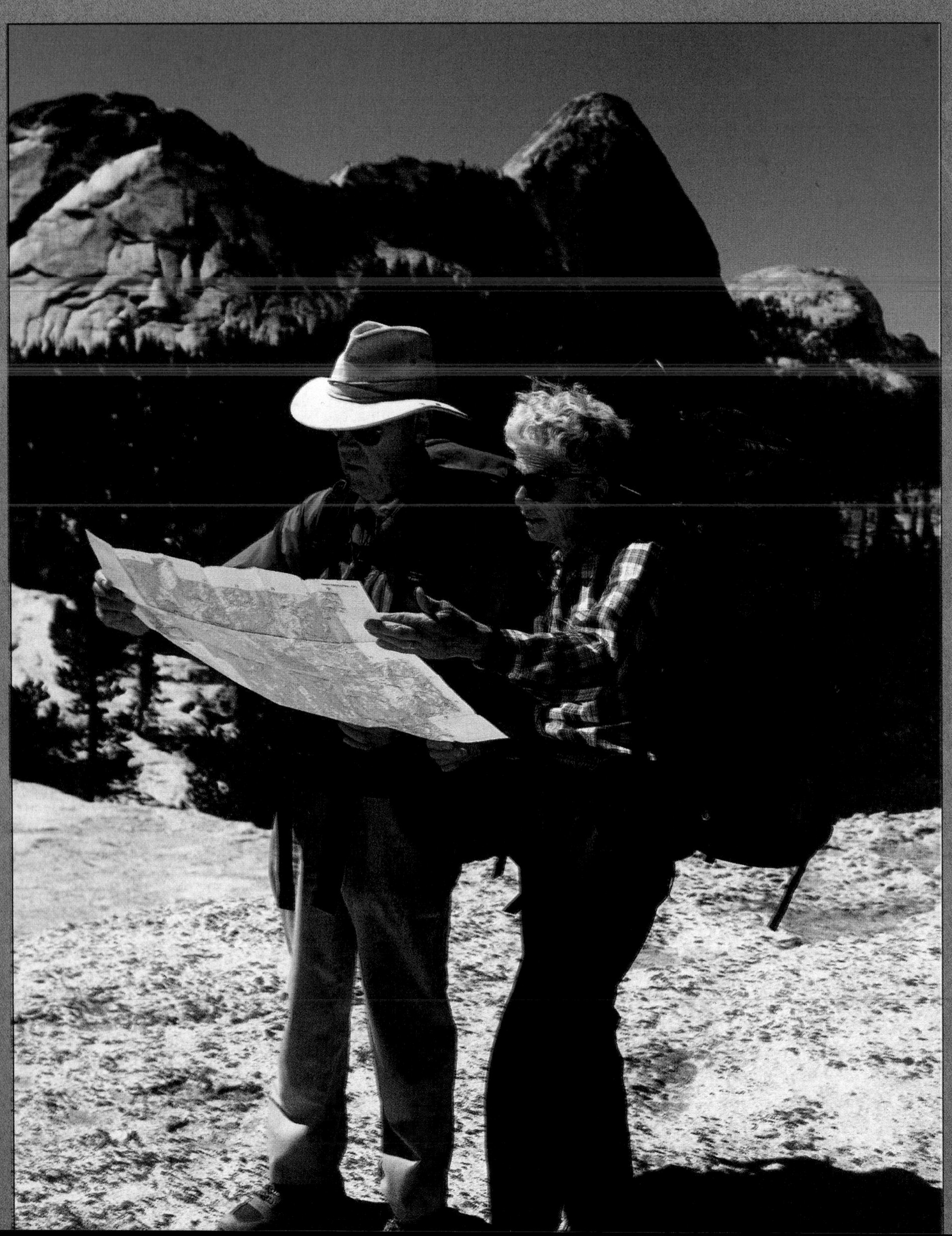

Why not look at these new years of life in terms of continued or new roles in society, another stage in personal or even spiritual growth and development?

Betty Friedan, *The Fountain of Age,* 1993

John Glenn

Focus: John Glenn, Space Pioneer

When John H. Glenn, Jr.* (b. 1921) blasted off from the Kennedy Space Center at Cape Canaveral on October 29, 1998, as a payload specialist on the shuttle *Discovery,* he became a space pioneer for the second time. In 1962, at the age of 40, Glenn had been the first American to orbit the earth. What made him a pioneer in 1998, when he next donned the orange jumpsuit, was that he was 77 years old—the oldest person ever to go into outer space.

Throughout his adult life, Glenn has won medals and set records. As a fighter pilot during the Korean War, he earned five Distinguished Flying Crosses. In 1957 he made the first cross-country supersonic jet flight. In 1962, when his *Friendship* 7 one-man space capsule circled the globe three times in less than five hours, he instantly became a national hero.

Glenn was elected a U.S. senator from Ohio in 1974 and served four terms. As a member of the Senate Special Committee on Aging and a grandfather of two, his interest in the subject of aging prompted him to offer himself as a human guinea pig on the nine-day *Discovery* mission.

As Glenn discovered while browsing through a medical textbook, the zero gravity conditions of space flight mimic at accelerated speed what normally happens to the body as it ages. Thus, Glenn reasoned, sending an older man into space might give scientists a thumbnail glimpse of processes of aging. By studying how weightlessness affected Glenn's

*Sources of information about John Glenn were Cutler, 1998, Eastman, 1965, and articles from the *New York Times* and other newspapers.

OUTLINE

bones, muscles, blood pressure, heart rates, balance, immune system, and sleep cycles, as well as his ability to bounce back after the flight as compared with younger astronauts, medical researchers could obtain information that might ultimately have broader applications. The data would not, of course, provide conclusive findings; but, as in any good case study, the findings could generate hypotheses to be tested by further research with larger groups of participants. The flight also would have an important side effect: to demolish common stereotypes about aging.

Space travel is a challenge even for the youngest and most physically fit adults. Not everyone can be an astronaut; candidates have to pass stringent physical and mental tests. Because of his age, Glenn was held to even tougher physical standards. An avid weight-lifter and power-walker, he was in superb physical condition. He passed the examinations with flying colors and then spent nearly 500 hours in training.

It was a clear, cloudless October day when, after two suspenseful delays, the shuttle *Discovery* lifted off with what the countdown commentator called "a crew of six astronaut heroes and one American legend." Three hours and ten minutes later, 342 miles above Hawaii, a beaming Glenn repeated his own historic words broadcast thirty-six years before: "Zero G, and I feel fine." On November 7, *Discovery* touched down at Cape Canaveral, and John Glenn, though weak and wobbly, walked out of the shuttle on his own two feet. Within four days he had fully recovered his balance and was completely back to normal.

Glenn's achievement proved that, at 77, he still had "the right stuff." His heroic exploit captured public imagination around the world. As Stephen J. Cutler, president of the Gerontological Society of America, put it, ". . . it's hard to imagine a better demonstration of the capabilities of older persons and of the productive contributions they can make" (1998, p. 1).

John Glenn epitomizes a new view of aging, challenging the formerly pervasive picture of old age as a time of inevitable physical and mental decline. On the whole, people today are living longer and better than at any time in history. In the United States, older adults as a group are healthier, more numerous, and younger at heart than ever before. With improved health habits and medical care, it is becoming harder to draw the line between the end of middle adulthood and the beginning of late adulthood. Many 70-year-olds act, think, and feel much as 50-year-olds did a decade or two ago.

Of course, not all older adults are models of vigor and zest. Indeed, Glenn's achievement is impressive precisely because it is unusual. As we will see in this chapter and the next, older adults vary greatly in health, education, income, occupation, and living arrangements. Like people of all ages, they are individuals with differing needs, desires, abilities, lifestyles, and cultural backgrounds.

In this chapter we begin by "debunking" negative images of aging and sketching trends among today's older population. We look at the increasing length and quality of life in late adulthood and at theories and research on causes of biological aging. We examine physical changes and health. We then turn to cognitive development: changes in intelligence and memory, the emergence of wisdom, and the prevalence of continuing education in late life. In Chapter 18, we look at adjustment to aging and at changes in lifestyles and relationships. What emerges is a picture not of "the elderly" but of individual human beings—some needy and frail, but most of them independent, healthy, and involved.

After you have read and studied this chapter, you should be able to answer the following questions:

17

1. What is ageism, and what harm can it do?
2. How is today's older population changing?
3. Why has life expectancy increased, and how does it vary?
4. What theories have been advanced for causes of aging, and what does research suggest about the possibilities for extending the life span?
5. What physical changes occur during old age, and how do these changes vary among individuals?
6. What health problems are common in late adulthood, and what factors influence health at that time?
7. What mental and behavioral disorders do some older people experience?
8. What gains and losses in cognitive abilities tend to occur in late adulthood, and are there ways to improve older people's cognitive performance?
9. What educational opportunities can older adults pursue?

Old Age Today

Traditional images of aging are quite different from the reality of aging today. Let's look at both.

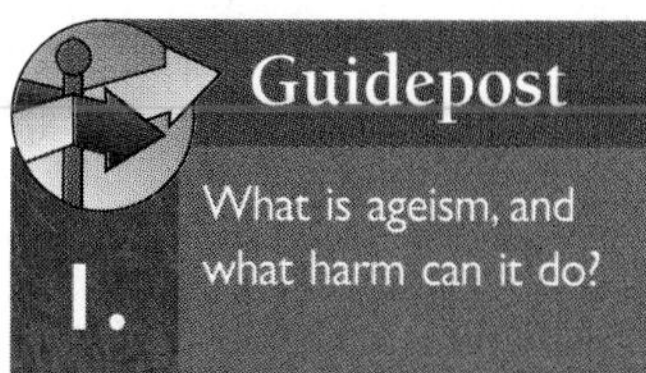

Guidepost
1.
What is ageism, and what harm can it do?

Images of Aging

In Japan, old age is a mark of status. There—in contrast to most western countries, where it is considered rude to ask a person's age—travelers checking into hotels are often asked their age to ensure that they will receive proper deference.

In the United States, aging is generally seen as undesirable. Stereotypes about aging reflect widespread misconceptions: that older people are usually tired, poorly coordinated, and prone to infections and accidents; that most of them live in institutions; that they can neither remember nor learn; that they have no interest in sexual activity; that they are isolated from others; that they do not use their time productively; and that they are grouchy, self-pitying, and cranky.

These negative stereotypes do real harm. A physician who does not bring up sexual issues with a 75-year-old heart patient may deny the patient an important source of fulfillment. An overprotective adult child may encourage an aging parent to become childlike. A social worker who considers depression "to be expected" may in effect abandon an elderly client. Positive stereotypes, which picture a golden age of peace and relaxation or a carefree second childhood spent idly on the golf course, are no more accurate or helpful.

Efforts to combat **ageism**—prejudice or discrimination (usually against older persons) based on age—are making headway, thanks to the visibility of a growing cadre of active, healthy older adults, epitomized by John Glenn. Articles with such titles as "Achievers after the Age of 90" (Wallechinsky & Wallace, 1993) appear in newspapers and magazines. On television, older people are less often portrayed as "comical, stubborn, eccentric, and foolish" and more often as "powerful, affluent, healthy, active, admired, and sexy" (Bell, 1992, p. 305). Meanwhile, "the media continue to bombard us with advertising for cosmetic surgery, hair coloring, anti-wrinkle creams, pills, potions, tonics and diet programs that, they assure us, will make it possible to maintain our youthful attractiveness forever" (Lenz, 1993, p. 26).

ageism
Prejudice or discrimination against a person (most commonly an older person) based on age.

We need to look beyond distorted images of age to its true, multifaceted reality, gazing through neither rose-colored glasses nor dark ones. Late adulthood is neither the climax of life nor an anticlimax. It is a normal period of the life span, with its own challenges and opportunities.

The Graying of the Population

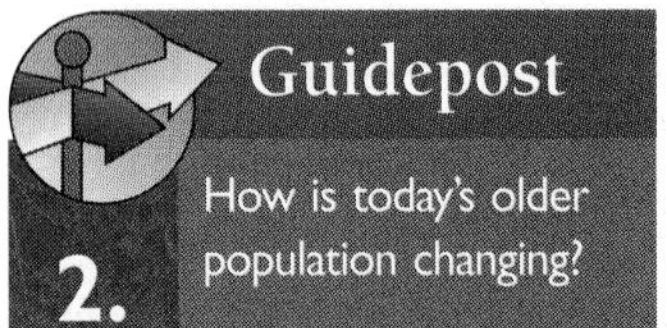

Since 1900, the proportion of Americans over the age of 65 has grown from 4 to 13 percent. By the year 2030, fully 20 percent of the U.S. population is likely to be in that age group (Abeles, 1998; Kramarow, Lentzner, Rooks, Weeks, & Saydah, 1999; see Figure 17-1).

Furthermore, the aged population itself is aging. Its fastest-growing segment consists of people 85 and older, and by 2030 their number could more than double (Kramarow et al., 1999). According to census estimates, the number of centenarians, people past their one-hundredth birthday, nearly doubled during the 1990s to more than 70,000. If this rate of growth continues, there may be close to 850,000 centenarians by the middle of the twenty-first century (Krach & Velkoff, 1999; see Box 17-1).

Ethnic diversity is increasing among the elderly, as in other age groups. In 1998, about 16 percent of older Americans were members of minority groups; by 2030, 25 percent will be. The proportion of older Hispanic Americans is likely to more than triple from 5.1 percent to 17.4 percent, exceeding the older African American population (AARP, 1999).

The graying of the population has several causes: chiefly, high birthrates and high immigration rates during the early to mid–twentieth century and longer life due to medical progress and healthier lifestyles. At the same time, the trend toward smaller families has reduced the relative size of younger age groups. The rate of growth of the older population will surge during the first third of the twenty-first century as the "baby boom" generation (born between 1946 and the early 1960s) enters old age (refer back to Figure 17-1).

The global population also is aging, thanks to an economic boom, increases in food supply, improved control of infectious disease, and better access to safe water, sanitation facilities, and health care. Worldwide, the elderly population is expected to more than double by 2025 (U.S. Bureau of the Census, 1999c). By

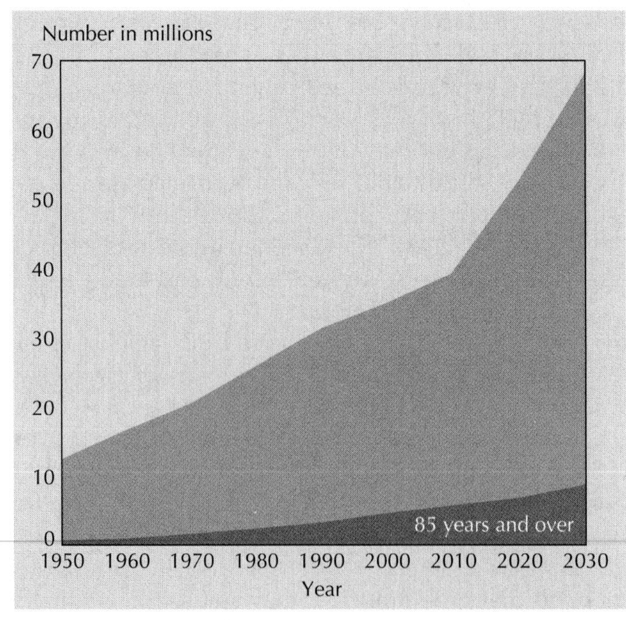

Figure 17-1
U.S. population age 65 and over, 1950–2030 (projected).
(Source: Kramarow et al., 1999, Figure 1, p. 23.)

Box 17-1
Centenarians

At 98, Ella May Stumpe of Frederick, Maryland, taught herself to use Microsoft software. Five years later, by 103, she had written several books on her computer, one of them entitled *My Life at 100*. Stumpe credits her longevity to a moderate way of life, including the nonacidic diet she adopted after having an ulcer at 30 (Ho, 1999).

Stumpe is one of the estimated 70,000-plus centenarians in the United States, a rapidly growing group whose characteristics are just beginning to be studied closely. The United States may have the largest proportion of centenarians among developed countries—120 centenarians for every 10,000 people ages 85 and older (Krach & Velkoff, 1999).

Given women's longer life expectancy, it is not surprising that 4 out of 5 U.S. centenarians are women, and most are widows. As of the 1990 census, only half of the then 37,306 centenarians had had some high school education, and one-fourth were living in poverty. About 15 percent lived alone, and nearly 20 percent were free of disability limitations. Close to half lived in nursing homes (Krach & Velkoff, 1999).

Research on the exploding centenarian population is shattering long-established beliefs about health and aging and about the limits of human life. As mentioned in the text, survival curves for human beings and other species have supported the idea of a biological limit to the life span, with more and more members of a species dying each year as they approach it. However, it now appears that the pattern changes after age 100: mortality rates begin to *decrease*. People at 110 are no more likely to die in a given year than people in their eighties. The same thing is true of fruit flies, wasps, and parasitic worms: at a certain point late in the life span, death rates peak and then drop (Vaupel et al., 1998). In other words, individuals hardy enough to reach a certain age are likely to go on living a while longer.

Furthermore, new findings are challenging the belief that a longer life span would mean a growing number of people with chronic disease. Actually, as a group, people who pass their nineties may be healthier than people ten or fifteen years younger. A study of all 460,000 inhabitants of six Massachusetts towns found that, of the 169 people who had reached their one hundredth birthdays, only 3 had had cancer, and about 1 in 4 had no dementia.

At 104, Anna Grupe of Sherburn, Minnesota, continued to write stories about her life and her family. The United States may have the largest proportion of centenarians among developed countries. Most are women, and a surprising number are healthy and active.

Medical expenses were lower than at 85 (Hilts, 1999; Silver, Jilinskaia, & Perls, in press; Silver, Newell, et al., 1998).

What might explain this picture? One possibility is exceptional genes, which may offer protection against dread diseases of old age, such as cancer and Alzheimer's. Evidence for this hypothesis comes from the finding, in the Massachusetts study, that large numbers of centenarians tend to run in families. The Massachusetts researchers also looked at lifestyle factors. A disproportionate number of the centenarians in the study were never-married women; among the women who were mothers, a disproportionate number had had children after age 40. No particular pattern of diet and exercise emerged. Some of the cententarians were vegetarians, while others ate a lot of red meat. Some were athletes and some did no strenuous activity. The only shared personality trait was the ability to manage stress (Perls, Alpert, & Fretts, 1997; Perls, Hutter-Silver, & Lauerman, 1999; Silver, Bubrick, Jilinskaia, & Perls, 1998).

Perhaps this quality is exemplified by Anna Morgan of Rehoboth, Massachusetts. Before her death at 101, she made her own funeral arrangements. "I don't want my children to be burdened with all this," she explained to the researchers. "They're old, you know" (Hilts, 1999, p. D7).

then, there will be more than 800 million people over 65 in the world, two-thirds of them in developing countries. In France, where there were only 200 centenarians in 1950, their number is expected to reach 150,000 in 2050, a 750-fold increase in 100 years (World Health Organization [WHO], 1998).

CHECKPOINT

Can you . . .

- ✔ Give examples of negative and positive stereotypes about aging?
- ✔ Discuss the causes and impact of the aging population?

This "aging avalanche" will change the physical, social, economic, and political environment (see Box 17-2), as the older population becomes more influential at the polls and in the marketplace. World leaders worry about the cost of supporting and providing health care for a growing contingent of older adults (Holden, 1996; WHO, 1998). A key question is whether national economies can grow fast enough to meet these challenges without placing an insupportable burden on a shrinking number of working adults (Binstock, 1993; Crown, 1993; WHO, 1998).

"Young Old," "Old Old," and "Oldest Old"

primary aging
Gradual, inevitable process of bodily deterioration throughout the life span. Compare with *secondary aging.*

An important factor in the economic impact of a graying population is the proportion of that population which is healthy and able-bodied. Here the trend is encouraging. Many problems that used to be considered part of old age are now understood to be due, not to aging itself, but to lifestyle factors or diseases. **Primary aging** is a gradual, inevitable process of bodily deterioration that begins

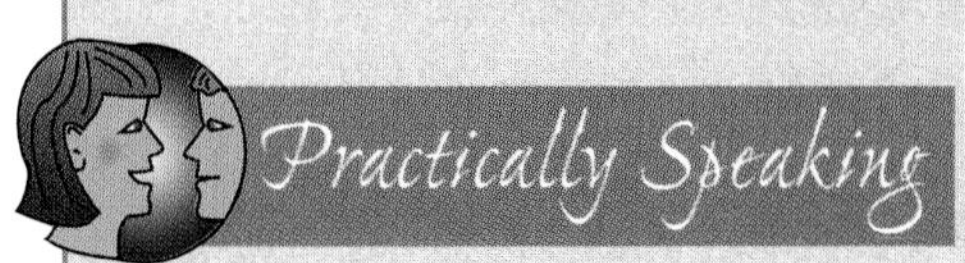

Box 17-2
New Environments for an Aging Population

As the population ages, we can expect many changes in our physical environment and in the products we use. Already, pain relievers, previously packaged in childproof bottles that stymied arthritic adults, are being repackaged in easier-to-open containers.

The gerontologist Ken Dychtwald, in *Age Wave* (Dychtwald & Flower, 1990), predicts ways in which the environment of the twenty-first century will be redesigned to accommodate physical changes that often accompany aging. Here are examples, some already in place.

Aids to Vision

Signals now given visually will be spoken as well. There will be talking exit signs, talking clocks, talking appliances that tell you when they get hot, talking cameras that warn you when the light is too low, and talking automobiles that caution you when you're about to collide with something. Windshields will adjust their tint automatically to varying weather and light conditions and will be equipped with large, liquid-crystal displays of speed and other information (so that older drivers need not take their eyes off the road and readjust their focus). Reading lights will be brighter, and books will have larger print. Floors will be carpeted or textured, not waxed to a smooth, glaring gloss.

Aids to Hearing

Public address systems and recordings will be engineered to an older adult's auditory range. Park benches and couches will be replaced by angled or clustered seating so that older adults can communicate face-to-face.

Aids to Manual Dexterity

To compensate for stiff, aging joints, it will become increasingly common to find such items as comb and brush extenders, stretchable shoelaces, Velcro tabs instead of buttons, lightweight motorized pot-and-pan scrubbers and garden tools, tap turners on faucets, foot mops that eliminate bending, voice-activated telephone dialers, long-handled easy-grip zippers, and contoured eating utensils.

Aids to Mobility and Safety

Ramps will become more common, levers will replace knobs, street lights will change more slowly, and traffic islands will let slow walkers pause and rest. Closet shelves and bus platforms will be lower, as will windows, for people who sit a lot. Regulators will keep tap water from scalding. "Soft tubs" will prevent slips, add comfort, and keep bath water from cooling too fast. Automobiles will be programmed to operate windows, radio, heater, lights, wipers, and even the ignition by verbal commands.

Temperature Adjustments

Because older bodies take longer to adjust to temperature changes and have more trouble keeping warm, homes and hotels will have heated furniture and thermostats in each room. Some people will wear heated clothing and eat heat-producing foods.

Such innovations will make life easier and more convenient for everyone. An environment designed for older rather than younger adults can be more user-friendly for all age groups.

early in life and continues through the years. **Secondary aging** consists of results of disease, abuse, and disuse—factors that are often avoidable and within people's control (Busse, 1987; J. C. Horn & Meer, 1987). By eating sensibly and keeping physically fit, many older adults can and do stave off secondary effects of aging.

secondary aging
Aging processes that result from disease and bodily abuse and disuse and are often preventable. Compare with *primary aging.*

Today, social scientists who specialize in the study of aging refer to three groups of older adults: the "young old," "old old," and "oldest old." Chronologically, *young old* generally refers to people ages 65 to 74, who are usually active, vital, and vigorous. The *old old,* ages 75 to 84, and the *oldest old,* age 85 and above, are more likely to be frail and infirm and to have difficulty managing some activities of daily living.

functional age
Measure of ability to function in physical and social environment in comparison with others of the same chronological age.

A more meaningful classification is by **functional age:** how well a person functions in a physical and social environment in comparison with others of the same chronological age. A person of 90 who is still in good health may be functionally younger than a person of 65 who is not. Some gerontologists, therefore, prefer to use the term *young old* for the healthy, active majority of older adults (such as John Glenn), and *old old* for the frail, infirm minority, regardless of chronological age (Neugarten & Neugarten, 1987).

CHECKPOINT
Can you . . .
✔ State two criteria for differentiating among the young old, old old, and oldest old?

Physical Development

Longevity and Aging

How long will you live? Why do you have to grow old? Would you want to live forever? Human beings have been wondering about these questions for thousands of years.

The first question involves two different but related concepts: **life expectancy,** the age to which a person born at a certain time and place is statistically likely to live, given his or her current age and health status; and **longevity,** how long a person actually does live. Life expectancy is based on the average longevity of members of a population. The second question expresses an age-old theme: a yearning for a fountain or potion of youth. Behind this yearning is a fear, not so much of chronological age as of biological aging: loss of health and physical powers. The third question expresses a concern not just with length but with quality of life.

life expectancy
Age to which a person in a particular cohort is statistically likely to live (given his or her current age and health status), on the basis of average longevity of a population.

longevity
Length of an individual's life.

Trends and Factors in Life Expectancy and Mortality

Today, most people can expect to grow old, even very old. A baby born in the United States in 1998 could expect to live 76.5 years, about 29 years longer than a baby born in 1900 (AARP, 1999; R. N. Anderson, 1999). Worldwide, average life expectancy has risen 37 percent since 1955, from 48 years to 66 years, and is projected to reach 73 years by 2025 (WHO, 1998).

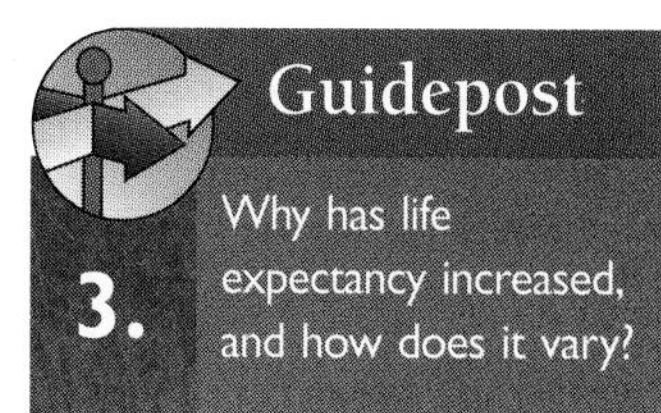

Guidepost
3.
Why has life expectancy increased, and how does it vary?

Such longevity—unprecedented in the history of humankind (see Figure 17-2)—is directly related to the graying of the population. It reflects a sharp decline in *mortality rates,* or death rates (the proportions of a total population or of certain age groups who die in a given year). Today's longer life spans stem largely from a dramatic reduction in deaths during infancy and childhood; fewer deaths in young adulthood, particularly in childbirth; new treatments for many once-fatal illnesses; and a better-educated, more health-conscious population.

In the United States, death rates from heart disease, the leading cause of death in late adulthood, have been cut in half since 1970 among 65- to 84-year-olds and have dropped 21 percent among those ages 85 and over (NCHS, 1999a). The other leading causes of death in late life, in descending order, are cancer, stroke, lung disease, pneumonia and influenza, diabetes, accidents, kidney disease, Alzheimer's disease, and septicemia (blood poisoning from bacterial infection) (Martin, Smith, Mathews, & Ventura, 1999).

The longer people live, the longer they are likely to live. Americans who made it to age 65 in 1998 could expect to reach nearly 83—six years more than the life expectancy of an infant born in that year (R. N. Anderson, 1999). Life expectancy at birth is lower in the United States than in many other industrialized countries that have lower infant mortality rates, but the gap closes by very old age, possibly because of more education or greater expenditures on health care (Manton & Vaupel, 1995). Less-educated people tend to have more severe diseases and disabilities, and therefore high mortality rates (Amaducci et al., 1998). Research in **gerontology,** the study of the aged and aging processes and **geriatrics,** the branch of medicine concerned with aging, has underlined the need for support services, especially for the oldest old, many of whom have outlived their savings and cannot pay for their own care.

gerontology
Study of the aged and the process of aging.

geriatrics
Branch of medicine concerned with processes of aging and age-related medical conditions.

Regional and Ethnic Differences

Globally, life expectancies vary widely. In sub-Saharan Africa, a child born in 1998 could expect to live to age 49 (U.S. Bureau of the Census, 1999c). In Japan, in the same year, life expectancy was 80 years (U.S. Bureau of the Census, 1998). In sixteen countries, life expectancy actually *decreased* between 1975 and 1995 (WHO, 1998)—in some, quite rapidly. For example, life expectancy in Russia declined by

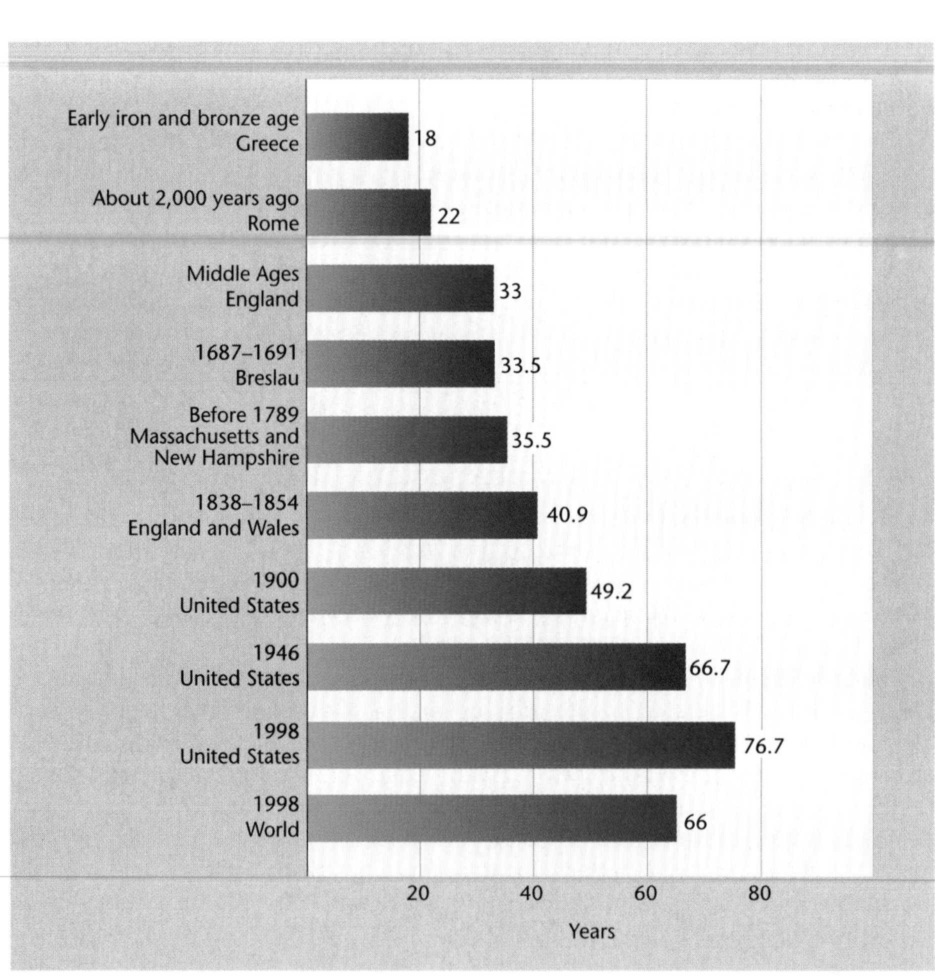

Figure 17-2
Changes in life expectancy from ancient to modern times.
(Source: Adapted from Katchadourian, 1987; 1998 data from Martin et al., 1999, and WHO, 1998.)

Table 17-1 Life Expectancy at Birth in Years, by Sex and Race, 1998, in the United States

	All Races	White	Black
Males	73.6	74.6	67.8
Females	79.4	79.9	75.0

Source: Martin et al., 1999 (preliminary data).

about five years between 1990 and 1994, due largely to economic and social instability, high rates of alcohol and tobacco use, poor nutrition, depression, and deterioration of the health care system (Notzon et al., 1998).

Wide disparities in length of life also exist within the United States. American Indian men in South Dakota have a life expectancy of only 56.5 years, and African American men in Washington, D. C., can expect to live only to about 58, no longer than in parts of Africa. Meanwhile, Asian American men in affluent regions of New York and Massachusetts survive to nearly 90 (Murray, Michaud, McKenna, & Marks, 1998). These radical disparities may be due in part to differences in income, education, and lifestyle and possibly to genetic factors as well.

On average, white Americans live about six years longer than African Americans, and women live about five to six years longer than men (Martin et al., 1999; see Table 17-1). As discussed in previous chapters, African Americans, especially men, are more vulnerable than white Americans to illness and death from infancy through middle adulthood. However, the gap begins to close in older adulthood, and by age 85 African Americans can expect slightly more remaining years than whites. It may be that black people who have managed to live that long are especially fit. It also has been suggested that this statistical "black-white crossover" effect may be due to inaccurate data on ages of older black adults, many of whom do not have birth certificates (Kramarow et al., 1999; Treas, 1995). Overall, the gap between black and white life expectancies has narrowed in recent years; men and women of both races are living longer than ever before (Martin et al., 1999).

Gender Differences

Women's longer life has been attributed to several factors: their greater tendency to take care of themselves and to seek medical care (refer back to Chapter 13); the higher level of social support that women, particularly older women, enjoy (see Chapter 18); and the greater biological vulnerability of males throughout life. Boys are more likely than girls to die in infancy; teenage boys and young men are more likely to die from AIDS or accidents; and middle-aged and older men are more likely than women to die of heart disease or other ailments. The health problems of older women are likely to be long-term, chronic, disabling conditions; men tend to develop short-term, fatal diseases.

Women in the United States benefited more than men from the gains in life expectancy during the twentieth century, particularly the reduction in deaths from childbirth. In 1900, there was only a two-year difference in life expectancy between the sexes. The gap widened to nearly eight years in 1979; since then, it has narrowed to about five and a half years, largely because more men than before are surviving heart attacks (Martin et al., 1999; Treas, 1995).

The gender difference in life expectancy means that older women outnumber older men by 3 to 2, and this disparity increases with advancing age. By age 80, the ratio of women to men is about 2 to 1 (Kramarow et al., 1999; U.S. Bureau of the Census, 1999a; see Figure 17-3).

Older women are more likely than older men to be widowed, to remain unmarried afterward, and to have more years of poor health and fewer years of

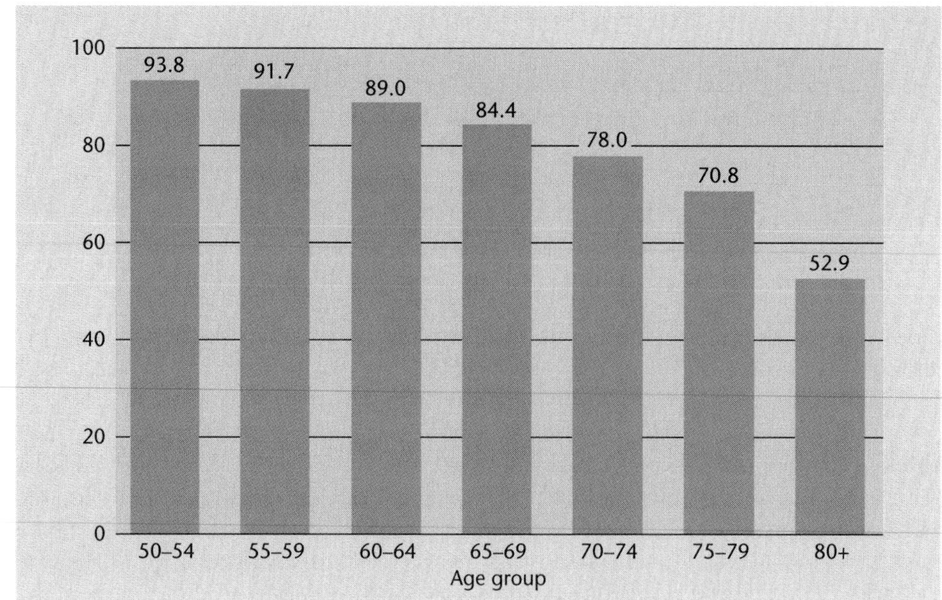

Figure 17-3
Number of men per 100 women in the Western Hemisphere by age, 1997. With age, the ratio of men to women declines. Because there are more older women, they are more likely than older men to live alone and to need help from their families and from society.
(Source: U.S. Bureau of the Census, 1999a.)

CHECKPOINT

Can you . . .

✔ Tell how life expectancy is related to mortality rates?

✔ Summarize trends in life expectancy, including regional, ethnic, and gender differences, and explain their significance?

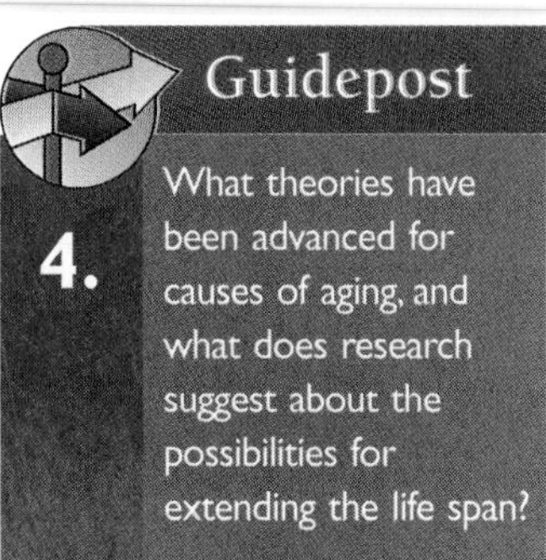

Guidepost

4. What theories have been advanced for causes of aging, and what does research suggest about the possibilities for extending the life span?

senescence
Period of the life span marked by changes in physical functioning associated with aging; begins at different ages for different people.

genetic-programming theories
Theories that explain biological aging as resulting from a genetically determined developmental timetable; compare *variable-rate theories*.

active life and independence (Katz et al., 1983; Longino, 1987; O'Bryant, 1990–1991; U.S. Bureau of the Census, 1992b, 1995). They are much more likely to be poor and to live alone. They are also more likely, at some point, to need help with eating, dressing, bathing, preparing meals, managing money, and going outside. Ultimately, they are more likely to live in nursing homes (AARP, 1999; Kramarow et al., 1999; Treas, 1995; U.S. Bureau of the Census, 1995, 1996c). The major reason for older women's impoverishment is the death of a husband and the resulting loss of financial support (U.S. Bureau of the Census, 1996c).

Why People Age

With the dramatic lengthening of the life span, scientists are focusing increasing attention on what happens to the human body with the passage of time. Early in adulthood, physical losses are typically so small and so gradual as to be barely noticed. With age, individual differences increase. One 80-year-old man can hear every word of a whispered conversation; another cannot hear the doorbell. One 70-year-old woman runs marathons; another cannot walk around the block. The onset of **senescence,** a period marked by obvious declines in body functioning sometimes associated with aging, varies greatly. Why? For that matter, why do people age at all? Most theories about biological aging fall into two categories: *genetic-programming theories* and *variable-rate theories* (summarized in Table 17-2).*

Genetic-Programming Theories

Genetic-programming theories hold that bodies age according to a normal developmental timetable built into the genes. Such a timetable implies a genetically decreed maximum life span. As we discussed in Chapter 3, cells in the body are constantly multiplying through cell division; this process is essential to balance the programmed death of useless or potentially dangerous cells and to keep organs and systems functioning properly (Golstein, 1998; Raff, 1998). Leonard Hayflick (1974) found that human cells will divide in the laboratory no more than

*This summary of theories of aging is indebted to NIH/NIA, 1993.

Table 17-2 Theories of Biological Aging

Genetic-Programming Theories	Variable-Rate Theories
Programmed senescence theory. Aging is the result of the sequential switching on and off of certain genes. Senescence is the time when the resulting age-associated deficits become evident.	*Wear-and-tear theory.* Cells and tissues have vital parts that wear out.
Endocrine theory. Biological clocks act through hormones to control the pace of aging.	*Free-radical theory.* Accumulated damage from oxygen radicals causes cells and eventually organs to stop functioning.
Immunological theory. A programmed decline in immune system functions leads to increased vulnerability to infectious disease and thus to aging and death.	*Rate-of-living theory.* The greater an organism's rate of metabolism, the shorter its life span.
	Autoimmune theory. Immune system becomes confused and attacks its own body cells.

Source: Adapted from NIH/NIA, 1993, p. 2.

fifty times; this is called the **Hayflick limit,** and it has been shown to be genetically controlled (Schneider, 1992). This suggests that there may be a biological limit to the life span of human cells, and therefore of human life—a limit Hayflick estimated at 110 years. If, as Hayflick (1981) suggested, cells go through the same aging process in the body as in a laboratory culture—a hypothesis that has not yet been proved—then environmental influences should play little or no role (Gerhard & Cristofalo, 1992). The human body, like a machine, would be biologically programmed to fail at a certain point.

Hayflick limit Genetically controlled limit, proposed by Hayflick, on the number of times cells can divide in members of a species.

Failure might come through *programmed senescence*: specific genes "switching off" before age-related losses (for example, in vision, hearing, and motor control) become evident. Or the biological clock might act through genes that control *hormonal changes* or cause problems in the *immune system,* leaving the body vulnerable to infectious disease. There is evidence that some age-related physical changes, such as loss of muscle strength, accumulation of fat, and atrophy of organs, may be related to declines in hormonal activity (Lamberts, van den Beld, & van der Lely, 1997; Rudman et al., 1990). And levels of immune cell production can predict two-year survival rates among the oldest old (R. A. Miller, 1996).

Still another hypothesis is that the biological clock is regulated by a gradual shortening of the *telomeres,* the protective tips of chromosomes, each time cells divide. This programmed erosion eventually progresses to the point where cell division stops (de Lange, 1998). Supporting evidence for this hypothesis comes from a study in which the gene for *telomerase*—an enzyme that enables sex chromosomes to repair their telomeres—was introduced into human body cells in a laboratory culture, along with a mechanism to activate the gene. The cells continued to divide well beyond their normal life span, without apparent abnormalities (Bodnar et al., 1998; see Figure 17-4). If telomere lengthening can reset the clock of biological aging, scientists may someday be able to prevent or treat atherosclerosis, dementia, skin wrinkling, stiff joints, and other diseases and disabilities of old age.

Clearly, genes "exert strong controls on life-span and patterns of aging" (Finch & Tanzi, 1997, p. 407). However, genetic programming alone cannot be the whole story; otherwise all human beings would die at the same age. Environmental and experiential factors interact with genetic ones (Finch & Tanzi, 1997).

variable-rate theories Theories explaining biological aging as a result of processes that vary from person to person and are influenced by both the internal and the external environment; sometimes called *error theories.* Compare *genetic-programming theories.*

Variable-Rate Theories

Variable-rate theories, sometimes called *error theories,* view aging as a result of processes that vary from person to person. These processes may be influenced by

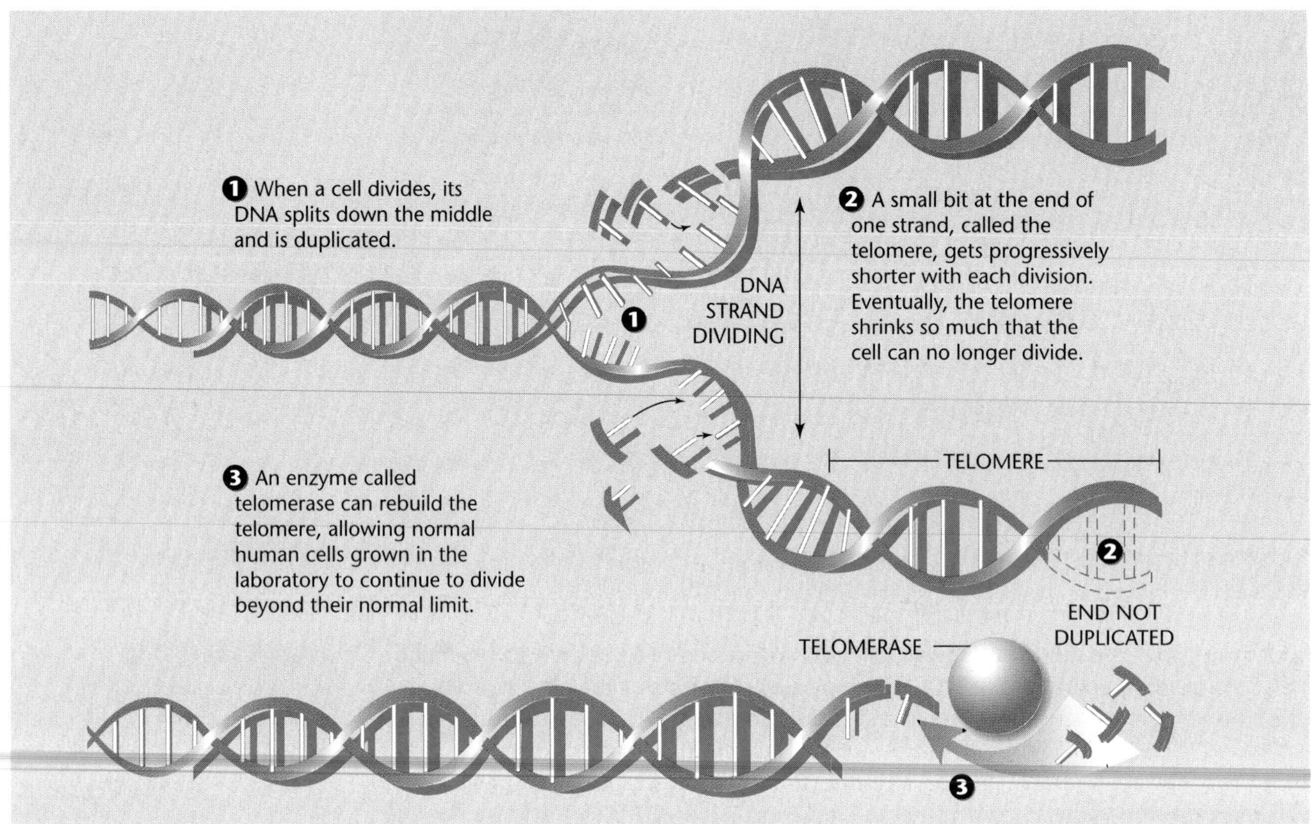

1 When a cell divides, its DNA splits down the middle and is duplicated.
2 A small bit at the end of one strand, called the telomere, gets progressively shorter with each division. Eventually, the telomere shrinks so much that the cell can no longer divide.
DNA STRAND DIVIDING
3 An enzyme called telomerase can rebuild the telomere, allowing normal human cells grown in the laboratory to continue to divide beyond their normal limit.
TELOMERE
END NOT DUPLICATED
TELOMERASE

Figure 17-4

How telomere loss affects cell division.

(Source: Letola, 1998.)

both internal and external factors. In most variable-rate theories, aging involves damage due to chance errors in, or environmental assaults on, people's biological systems. Other variable-rate theories focus on internal processes such as metabolism (the process by which the body turns food and oxygen into energy), which may more directly and continuously influence the rate of aging (NIA, 1993; Schneider, 1992).

Wear-and-tear theory holds that the body ages as a result of accumulated damage to the system. As cells grow older, they are believed to be less able to repair or replace damaged components. Internal and external stressors (including the accumulation of harmful materials, such as chemical by-products of metabolism) may aggravate the wearing-down process.

free radicals
Unstable, highly reactive atoms or molecules formed during metabolism, which can cause internal bodily damage.

Free-radical theory focuses on harmful effects of **free radicals:** highly unstable atoms or molecules formed during *metabolism* (conversion of oxygen into energy), which react with and can damage cell membranes, cell proteins, fats, carbohydrates, and even DNA. Damage from free radicals accumulates with age; it has been associated with arthritis, muscular dystrophy, cataracts, cancer, late-onset diabetes, and neurological disorders such as Parkinson's disease (Stadtman, 1992; Wallace, 1992).

Dramatic support for this theory comes from research in which fruit flies were given extra copies of genes that eliminate free radicals. Their life spans were extended by as much as one-third (Orr & Sohal, 1994). There also is evidence that mutations in the DNA of aging *mitochondria*, the "power generators" of human cells, cause them to produce free radicals (Michikawa, Mazzucchelli, Bresolin, Scarlato, & Attardi, 1999). In humans, research on the effects of antioxidant supplements, which are believed to counteract free radical activity, is inconclusive; but in one study, high intake of vitamin C and of vegetables high in beta-carotene did seem to protect against early death, particularly from heart disease (Sahyoun, Jacques, & Russell, 1996).

Rate-of-living theory suggests that the body can do just so much work, and that's all; the faster it works, the faster it wears out. Thus, speed of metabolism determines length of life. Evidence for this theory is that fish whose metabolism is lowered by putting them in cooler water live longer than they would in warm water (Schneider, 1992).

Autoimmune theory suggests that the immune system can become "confused" in old age and release antibodies that attack the body's own cells. This malfunction, called **autoimmunity,** is thought to be responsible for some aging-related diseases.

autoimmunity
Tendency of an aging body to mistake its own tissues for foreign invaders and to attack and destroy them.

An important part of the picture seems to be how cell death is regulated. Normally, this process is genetically programmed. However, when mechanisms that normally cause unneeded cells to destroy themselves malfunction, this breakdown in cell clean-out can lead to stroke damage, Alzheimer's disease, cancer, and autoimmune disease. Sometimes malfunction is triggered by exposure to environmental "insults," such as exposure to ultraviolet rays, X rays, and chemotherapy (Miller & Marx, 1998). On the other hand, problems may be caused by the death of *needed* cells. The growing sensitivity of T cells—white cells that destroy invading substances—to signals to self-destruct may help account for the weakening of the aging immune system (Aggarwal, Gollapudi, & Gupta, 1999).

Genetic-programming and variable-rate theories have practical consequences. If human beings are programmed to age at a certain rate, they can do little to retard the process except to try to alter the appropriate genes. Already scientists have begun to identify alleles that occur with unusual frequency in centenarians (Finch & Tanzi, 1997). Also, laboratory research on genetic modifications in animals (discussed in the next section) holds promise. If, on the other hand, aging is variable, as evidence presented in the following sections seems to suggest, then everyday lifestyle and health practices (like John Glenn's exercise regimen) may influence it.

It seems likely that each of these perspectives offers part of the truth. Genetic programming may limit the maximum length of life, but environmental and lifestyle factors may affect how closely a person approaches the maximum and in what condition.

Consider this . . .

- If you could live as long as you wanted to, how long would you choose to live? What factors would affect your answer?
- Which would you rather do: live a long life, or live a shorter time with a higher quality of life?

How Far Can the Life Span Be Extended?

When Jeanne Calment of France died in 1997 at the age of 122, hers was the longest human life span ever documented. Is it possible for human beings to live even longer—to 130, 150, or even 200?

Many gerontologists have maintained that 110 to 120 years is the upper limit of the human life span—the potential length of life for members of the human species—just as the upper limit for dogs is about 20 and for tortoises, 150 (NIA, 1993). The Hayflick limit predicts that, even if all diseases and causes of death were eliminated, humans would live only until about 110 years of age; then the cellular clock would run out and they would die. Until recently, historical changes in **survival curves**—percentages of people who live to various ages—supported the idea of a limit to human life. Although many people were living longer than in the past, the curves still ended around age 100; this suggested that, regardless of health and fitness, the maximum life span is not much higher. Now, however, data on centenarians seem to contradict that view (refer back to Box 17-1).

survival curves
Curves, plotted on a graph, showing percentages of a population that survive at each age level.

Jeanne Calment of Arles, France, is one of the only two human beings known to have lived to age 120, believed by some scientists to be the limit of the human life span. (The other was Shigechiyo Izumi of Japan, who died in 1986.) Calment is shown here shortly before her 120th birthday in March 1995, holding up her family photo album open to a picture of herself at age 40.

Today, animal research is challenging the idea of a genetically unalterable limit for each species. Scientists have extended the healthy life spans of worms, fruit flies, and mice through slight genetic mutations (Ishii et al., 1998; T. E. Johnson, 1990; Kolata, 1999; Lin, Seroude, & Benzer, 1998; Parkes et al., 1998; Pennisi, 1998). In human beings, however, genetic control of a biological process may be far more complex. Approximately 200 genes seem to be involved in regulating human aging (Schneider, 1992), with specific genes controlling different processes. It may well be that no single gene or process is responsible for senescence and the end of life. Thus gene therapy seems unlikely to change the maximum human life span, though it may increase average longevity (Gerhard & Cristofalo, 1992).

A promising line of nongenetic research is on dietary restriction. Rats fed 35 to 40 percent fewer calories than usual, with all necessary nutrients, live as much as 50 percent longer than other laboratory rodents (about 1,500 days as compared with 1,000 days). A spartan diet also has been found to extend life in worms and fish—in fact, in virtually all species on which it has been tried (Weindruch & Walford, 1988). These findings fit in with theories that view the rate of metabolism, or energy use, as the crucial determinant of aging (Masoro, 1985, 1988, 1992; Sohal & Weindruch, 1996). Caloric restriction also seems to reduce production of free radicals, facilitate DNA repair, and preserve the immune system's ability to fight disease (Walford, quoted in Couzin, 1998).

Although systematic life-extension studies have not yet been done on human beings, the potential implications of this research are staggering. These studies have raised hopes for eventual realization of the age-old dream of a "fountain of youth"; but they also raise ethical questions about the propriety of "tinkering" with human life and worries about the costs of supporting an elderly population far more numerous than currently projected.

A key question is whether increased longevity would be accompanied by the prevention or postponement of age-related diseases (Banks & Fossel, 1997). Some gerontologists—in line with the motto of the Gerontological Society of America, "To add life to years, not just years to life"—fear that eradicating the biggest killers, cancer and heart disease, would merely increase the number of people living long enough to cope with such disabling infirmities as arthritis and dementia (Cassel, 1992; Treas, 1995).

CHECKPOINT

Can you . . .

- ✔ Compare two kinds of theories of biological aging, their implicatons, and supporting evidence?
- ✔ Describe two lines of research on extension of life and discuss the import of their findings?

Some changes typically associated with aging are obvious even to a casual observer. Older skin tends to become paler, splotchier, and less elastic; as some fat and muscle disappear, the skin may wrinkle. Varicose veins of the legs become more common. The hair on the head turns white and becomes thinner, and body hair becomes sparser. Changes that are less visible affect internal organs and body systems, the brain, and sensory, motor, and sexual functioning.

Guidepost

5. What physical changes occur during old age, and how do these changes vary among individuals?

Organic and Systemic Changes

How does aging affect physical functioning and health? John Glenn's *Discovery* space mission was intended to shed light on this question.

Physiological changes in late adulthood are highly variable; many of the declines commonly associated with aging may actually be *effects* of disease rather than causes (T. F. Williams, 1992). Some body systems decline more rapidly than others (see Figure 17-5). The digestive system, including the liver and gallbladder, remains relatively efficient. Among the most serious changes are those affecting the heart. Its rhythm tends to become slower and more irregular, deposits of fat accumulate around it and may interfere with functioning, and blood pressure often rises. However, as Baltes's life-span developmental approach (refer back to Chapter 1) suggests, gains may compensate for losses. Although a healthy heart's ability to pump more rapidly during exercise tends to lessen with age, blood flow diminishes very little because the heart pumps more blood with each stroke (NIH/NIA, 1993; Rodehoffer et al., 1984).

Height shrinks from young adulthood to old age—on average, slightly more than one inch for men and as much as two inches for women (Whitbourne, 1985). Older adults become shorter as the disks between their spinal vertebrae atrophy; they may look even smaller because of stooped posture. Thinning of the bones may cause a "dowager's hump" at the back of the neck, especially in women with osteoporosis (refer back to Chapter 15). The chemical composition of the bones changes in osteoporosis, creating a greater risk of fractures. Although women in the United States are four times as likely to develop osteoporosis as men, an estimated one-third of hip fractures worldwide occur in men. Men tend to get osteoporosis ten years later than women because of greater bone mass and more gradual hormonal losses (USDHHS, 1999d).

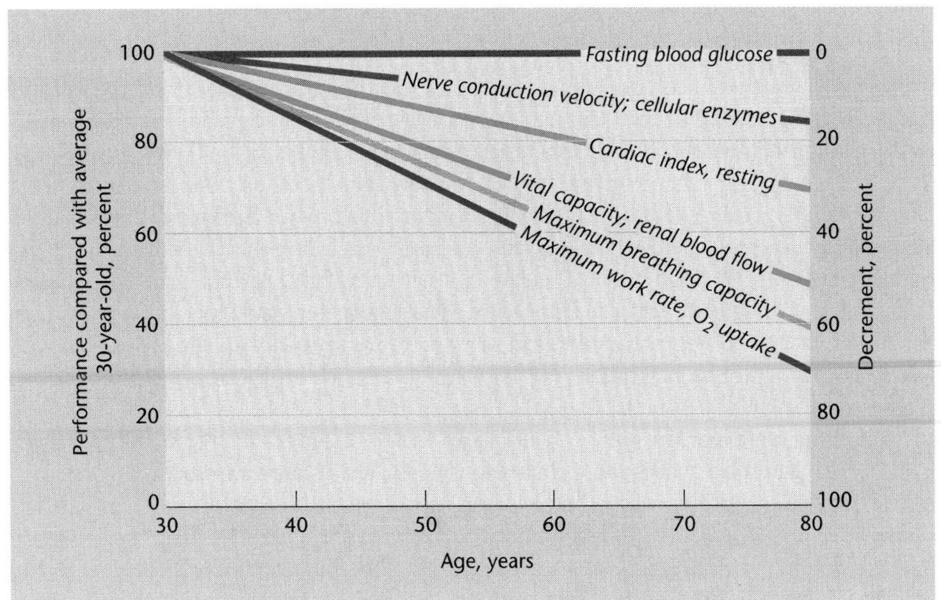

Figure 17-5
Declines in organ functioning. Differences in functional efficiency of various internal body systems are typically very slight in young adulthood but widen by old age.
(Source: Katchadourian, 1987.)

While estrogen therapy can protect women against osteoporosis, and possibly against heart disease and some other conditions, older women tend to be skeptical about its benefits. This skepticism seems to be related not only to concern about harmful effects (refer back to Chapter 15), but to the belief that they don't need it (Salamone, Pressman, Seeley, & Cauley, 1996).

People tend to sleep less and dream less in their later years. However, this does not mean older people *need* less sleep. Older people have the same circadian "clock," or internal regulator of sleep, as younger people do; but their hours of deep sleep are more restricted, and they may awaken more easily because of physical problems or exposure to light (Czeisler et al., 1999; Lamberg, 1997; Webb, 1987; Woodruff, 1985). The myth that sleep problems are normal in old age can be dangerous, since chronic *insomnia,* or sleeplessness, can be a symptom or, if untreated, a forerunner of depression. Cognitive-behavioral therapy (consisting of staying in bed only when asleep, getting up at the same time each morning, and learning about false beliefs pertaining to sleep needs) has produced long-term improvement with or without drug treatment, whereas drugs alone have not (Morin, Colecchi, Stone, Sood, & Brink, 1999; Reynolds, Buysse, & Kupfer, 1999).

reserve capacity
Ability of body organs and systems to put forth four to ten times as much effort as usual under stress; also called *organ reserve.*

Another important change that may affect health is a decline in **reserve capacity** (or *organ reserve*), a backup capacity that helps body systems function in times of stress. Normally, people do not use their organs and body systems to the limit. Extra capacity is available for extraordinary circumstances, allowing each organ to put forth four to ten times as much effort as usual. Reserve capacity helps preserve *homeostasis,* the maintenance of vital functions within their optimum range.

With age, reserve levels tend to drop. Although the decline is not usually noticeable in everyday life, older people generally cannot respond to the physical demands of stressful situations as quickly or efficiently as before. A person who used to be able to shovel snow and then go skiing afterward may now exhaust the heart's capacity just by shoveling. Young people almost always can survive pneumonia; older people often succumb to it or, if not, are at high risk of dying within the next few years (Koivula, Sten, & Makela, 1999). For that reason, influenza and pneumonia vaccines are especially important for the elderly.

Still, many normal, healthy older adults like John Glenn barely notice changes in systemic functioning. Many activities do not require peak performance levels to be enjoyable and productive. By pacing themselves, most older adults can do just about anything they need and want to do.

The Aging Brain

In normal, healthy older people, changes in the brain are generally modest and make little difference in functioning (Kemper, 1994). After age 30, the brain loses weight, at first slightly, then more and more rapidly. By age 90, the brain may have lost up to 10 percent of its weight. This weight loss has been attributed to a loss of *neurons* (nerve cells) in the *cerebral cortex,* the part of the brain that handles most cognitive tasks. However, newer research suggests that the cause is not a widespread loss of neurons, but rather a shrinkage in neuronal size due to loss of connective tissue: *axons, dendrites,* and *synapses* (refer back to Chapter 4). This shrinkage seems to begin earliest and advance most rapidly in the frontal cortex, which is important to memory and high-level cognitive functioning (West, 1996; Wickelgren, 1996).

Changes in the brain vary considerably from one person to another (Selkoe, 1991, 1992). Magnetic resonance imaging has shown that certain brain structures, including the cerebral cortex, shrink more rapidly in men than in women (Coffey et al., 1998). Cortical atrophy also occurs more rapidly in less-educated people (Coffey, Saxton, Ratcliff, Bryan, & Lucke, 1999). This finding is consistent with the hypothesis that education (or related factors, such as high income or decreased likelihood of disability) may increase the brain's reserve capacity—its ability to tolerate potentially injurious effects of aging (Friedland, 1993; Satz, 1993).

Along with loss of brain matter may come a gradual slowing of responses, beginning in middle age. Many adults over 70 no longer show the knee jerk; by 90, all such reflexes typically are gone (Spence, 1989). As we discuss later in this chapter, a slowdown of the central nervous system may affect not only physical coordination, but cognition as well.

Not all changes in the brain are destructive; some enhance brain functioning. Additional dendrites sprout between middle age and early old age. This "resprouting" may help compensate for any loss or shrinkage of neurons by adding new connections among nerve cells (NIH/NIA, 1993; Sapolsky, 1992; Selkoe, 1992).

Recently researchers have discovered that older brains can grow new nerve cells—something once thought impossible. Autopsies on five cancer patients, ages 55 to 70, whose veins had been injected with a chemical tracer, revealed cell division in a section of the hippocampus, a portion of the brain involved in memory (refer back to Chapter 5). Thus, even late in life, some regeneration of the human brain is possible (Eriksson et al., 1998). Researchers using a similar tracing technique on adult macaque monkeys found substantial neuronal replenishment in the cerebral cortex (Gould, Reeves, Graziano, & Gross, 1999). These discoveries hold out hope that scientists may eventually find ways to use the brain's own restorative potential to cure such brain disorders as Alzheimer's disease.

CHECKPOINT

Can you . . .

- ✔ Summarize common changes and variations in systemic functioning during late life?
- ✔ Identify a likely source of loss of brain weight, and cite two kinds of regenerative changes in the brain?

Sensory and Psychomotor Functioning

Although some older people experience sharp declines in sensory and psychomotor functioning, others find their daily lives virtually unchanged. Among the "old old," impairments tend to be more severe and may deprive them of activities, social life, and independence. New technologies, such as corrective surgery for cataracts and improved hearing aids or cochlear implants to correct hearing loss, help many older adults avoid these limitations.

Vision

With the help of glasses or contact lenses, most older people can see fairly well. However, many older adults have no better than 20/70 vision and have trouble perceiving depth or color or doing such things as reading, sewing, shopping, and cooking. Losses in visual contrast sensitivity can cause difficulty reading very small or very light print (Akutsu, Legge, Ross, & Schuebel, 1991; Kline & Scialfa, 1996).

More than half of people over 65 develop **cataracts,** cloudy or opaque areas in the lens of the eye that cause blurred vision (USDHHS, 1993). Surgery to remove cataracts is usually very successful and is one of the most common operations among older Americans (NIA, 1995a). **Age-related macular degeneration,** in which the center of the retina gradually loses the ability to sharply distinguish fine details, is the leading cause of functional blindness in older adults (Research to Prevent Blindness, 1994). More moderate visual problems often can be helped by corrective lenses, medical or surgical treatment, or changes in the environment (refer back to Box 16-2).

cataracts
Cloudy or opaque areas in the lens of the eye, which cause blurred vision.

age-related macular degeneration
Condition in which the center of the retina gradually loses its ability to discern fine details; leading cause of functional blindness in older adults.

Vision problems can cause accidents. Older eyes need more light to see, are more sensitive to glare, and may have trouble locating and reading signs. Driving may become hazardous, especially at night (D. W. Kline et al., 1992; D. W. Kline & Scialfa, 1996; Kosnik et al., 1988). Older drivers' higher collision risk may be related not so much to loss of visual acuity (sharpness of vision) as to impaired visual attentiveness and slowed visual processing, which can reduce the useful field of view by 40 percent or more (Owsley et al., 1998). When combined with slowed reaction time and less efficient coordination, these visual deficits can make driving risky (Wiseman & Souder, 1996).

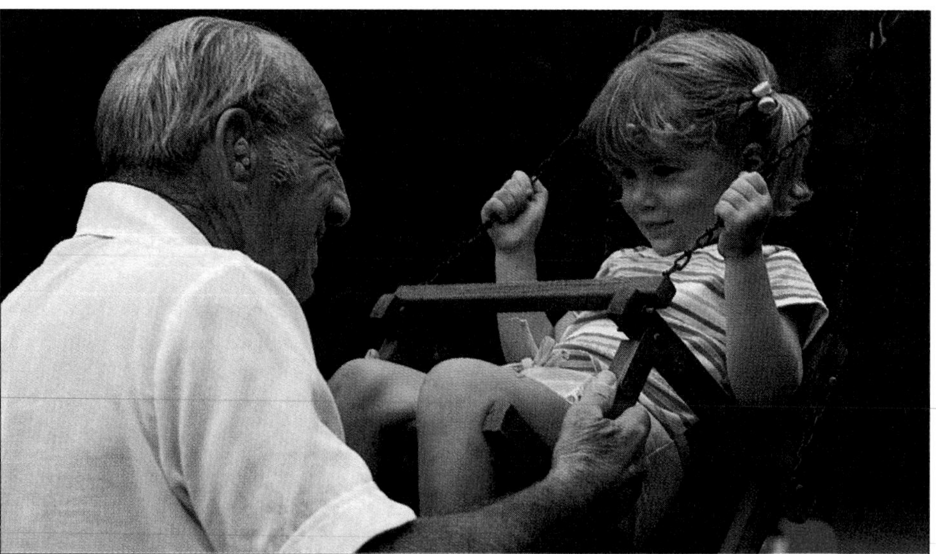

The hearing aid in this man's ear makes it easier for him to understand his young granddaughter's high-pitched speech. About one-third of 65- to 74-year-olds and one-half of those 85 and older have some degree of hearing loss that interferes with everyday activities, but only about 1 in 5 has a hearing aid, and many of those who do own one do not use it regularly.

Hearing

About 1 in 3 people ages 65 to 74, and about half of those 85 and older, have hearing loss that interferes with daily life (NIA, 1995c). Men, especially, lose sensitivity to high frequencies (D. W. Kline & Scialfa, 1996). Difficulty in hearing high-pitched sounds makes it hard to hear what other people are saying, especially when there is competing noise from radio or television or a buzz of several people talking at once. Hearing loss may contribute to the perception that older people are distractible, absentminded, and irritable.

Hearing aids can help; but no more than 1 in 5 older adults who need a hearing aid owns one, and fewer than half of those over 75 who do own one use it regularly (Jerger, Chmiel, Wilson, & Luchi, 1995). Hearing aids can be hard to adjust to, since they magnify background noises as well as the sounds a person wants to hear. In addition, many people feel that wearing a hearing aid is like wearing a sign saying "I'm getting old."

Taste and Smell

What you taste very often depends on what you can smell. Losses in both these senses can be a normal part of aging, but also may be caused by a wide variety of diseases and medications, by surgery, or by exposure to noxious substances in the environment. When older people complain that their food does not taste good anymore, it may be because they have fewer taste buds in the tongue, or because the taste receptors are not working properly. It also may be because the olfactory bulb—the organ in the brain that is responsible for the sense of smell—or other related brain structures are damaged (Schiffman, 1997). Sensitivity to sour, salty, and bitter flavors may be affected more than sensitivity to sweetness (Spitzer, 1988). Women seem to retain the senses of taste and smell better than men do (Ship & Weiffenbach, 1993).

Strength, Endurance, Balance, and Reaction Time

Older people can do most of the things younger ones can, but more slowly. They have less strength than they once had and are limited in activities requiring endurance or the ability to carry heavy loads. Adults generally lose about 10 to 20 percent of their strength up to age 70, especially in the muscles of the lower body, and more after that. Some people in their seventies or eighties have only half the strength they had at 30 (Spence, 1989; Spirduso & MacRae, 1990). Walking endurance declines more consistently with age, especially among women, than some other aspects of fitness, such as flexibility (Van Heuvelen, Kempen, Ormel, & Rispens, 1998).

Such losses may be reversible, however. In controlled studies with people in their sixties to nineties, weight training and resistance training programs lasting eight weeks to two years increased muscle strength, size, and mobility and also improved speed and endurance (Ades, Ballor, Ashikaga, Utton, & Nair, 1996; Fiatarone et al., 1990; Fiatarone, O'Neill, & Ryan, 1994; McCartney, Hicks, Martin, & Webber, 1996). In another study, low-impact, moderate-intensity aerobic dance and exercise training led to gains in peak oxygen uptake, leg muscle strength, and vigor (Engels, Drouin, Zhu, & Kazmierski, 1998). This evidence of *plasticity,* or modifiability of performance, is important because people whose muscles have atrophied are more likely to suffer falls and fractures and to need help with tasks of day-to-day living.

According to a Finnish study, the risk of injury from falls has more than doubled among older adults since 1970 (Kannus et al., 1999). Many of these falls are preventable by eliminating hazards commonly found in the home (Gill, Williams, Robison, & Tinetti, 1999). (Table 17-3 is a checklist for eliminating home hazards.)

Older adults are particularly susceptible to falls because of reduced sensitivity of the receptor cells that give the brain information about the body's position in space—information needed to maintain balance. Slower reflexes, decreased muscle strength, and loss of eyesight and depth perception also contribute to loss of balance (Neporent, 1999). Older adults may find it harder than younger adults to recover when they lose their balance (L. A. Brown, Shumway-Cook, & Wollacott, 1999), much as John Glenn was a bit slower than younger crewmates to recover his "sea legs" after floating weightless for nine days.

Exercises designed to improve balance can restore body control and postural stability. The traditional Chinese practice of *tai chi* is especially effective in maintaining balance, strength, and aerobic capacity (Baer, 1997; Kutner, Barnhart, Wolf, McNeely, & Xu, 1997; Lai, Lan, Wong, & Teng, 1995; Wolf et al., 1996; Wolfson et al., 1996).

Response time, which is generally related to neurological changes, also can respond to training. Older people who played video games for eleven weeks, using "joy sticks" and "trigger buttons," had faster reaction times after the training

Table 17-3 Safety Checklist for Preventing Falls in the Home

Stairways, hallways, and pathways	Free of clutter Good lighting, especially at top of stairs Light switches at top and bottom of stairs Tightly fastened handrails on both sides and full length of stairs Carpets firmly attached and not frayed; rough-textured or abrasive strips to secure footing
Bathrooms	Grab bars conveniently located inside and outside of tubs and showers and near toilets Nonskid mats, abrasive strips, or carpet on all surfaces that may get wet Night lights
Bedrooms	Telephones and night lights or light switches within easy reach of beds
All living areas	Electrical cords and telephone wires out of walking paths Rugs and carpets well secured to floor Inspect for hazards, such as exposed nails and loose threshold trim Furniture and other objects in familiar places and not in the way; rounded or padded table edges Couches and chairs proper height to get into and out of easily

Source: Adapted from NIA, 1993.

than did a sedentary control group (Dustman, Emmerson, Steinhaus, Shearer, & Dustman, 1992). Although training may not make older adults as quick as young ones who receive the same training, it can enable older adults to work and do everyday activities faster than they otherwise would (D. C. Park, 1992). Perhaps, with many young people today playing rapid-response computer games, we will not see such extensive declines in motor skills when this young adult generation gets older.

Sexual Functioning

The most important factor in maintaining sexual functioning in later life is consistent sexual activity over the years. A healthy man who has been sexually active usually can continue some form of active sexual expression into his seventies or eighties. Women are physiologically able to be sexually active as long as they live; the main barrier to a fulfilling sexual life for them is likely to be lack of a partner (Masters & Johnson, 1966, 1981; NIA, 1994; NFO Research Inc., 1999).

Sex is different in late adulthood from what it was earlier. Men normally take longer to develop an erection and to ejaculate, may need more manual stimulation, and may experience longer intervals between erections. Erectile dysfunction may increase, but it is often treatable (Bremner, Vitiello, & Prinz, 1983; NIA, 1994; refer back to Chapter 15). Women's breast engorgement and other signs of sexual arousal are less intense than before. The vagina may become less flexible and may need artificial lubrication.

Still, most older men and women can enjoy sexual expression (Bortz, Wallace, & Wiley, 1999). In a mail survey of a national sample of 1,384 middle-aged and older adults, two-thirds of those with sexual partners said they were satisfied with their sex lives. Sexual activity was more important to men than to women; among those ages 75 and older, 35 percent of men but only 13 percent of women called it important to their quality of life. Although reported sexual activity declined with age, overall about 3 out of 4 men and women with partners said they had intercourse at least once a month; among those 75 and over, about 1 in 4 reported engaging in it at least once a week (NFO Research, Inc., 1999).

Sexual expression can be more satisfying for older people if both young and old recognize it as normal and healthy. Housing arrangements and care providers should consider the sexual needs of elderly people. Physicians should avoid prescribing drugs that interfere with sexual functioning and, when such a drug must be taken, should alert the patient to its effects.

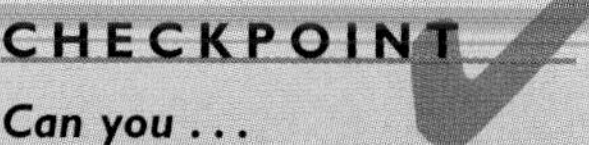

Can you . . .

- ✔ Describe typical changes in sensory and motor functioning, and tell how they can affect everyday living?
- ✔ Summarize changes in sexual functioning and attitudes toward sexual activity in late life?

Physical and Mental Health

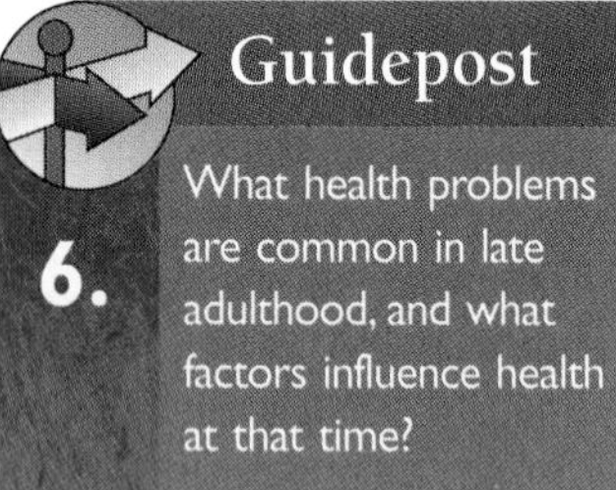

What health problems are common in late adulthood, and what factors influence health at that time?

Older adults in the United States and many other industrialized countries have a higher standard of living and more knowledge about their bodies than ever before. Better sanitation and the widespread use of antibiotics have contributed to better health. However, along with these positive changes have come negative ones: more cancer-causing agents in foods, in the workplace, and in the air we breathe; and a faster pace of life, which contributes to hypertension and heart disease. Also, longer life increases the likelihood of physical and mental disorders that tend to occur in old age. The chances of being reasonably healthy and fit in late life often depend on lifestyle, especially exercise and diet.

Health Status and Health Care

Most older adults are in good general health, but not as good, on average, as younger and middle-aged adults. The proportion in fair or poor health increases with age and is greater for black and Hispanic persons than for non-Hispanic whites (Kramarow et al., 1999). As people get older they tend to experience more persistent and potentially incapacitating health problems. In the presence of chronic conditions and loss of reserve capacity, even a minor illness or injury may have serious repercussions.

Most older people have one or more chronic physical conditions. By their own report, more than half of noninstitutionalized persons ages 70 and older have arthritis, about one-third have hypertension, more than one-fourth have heart disease or cataracts, and about one-tenth have diabetes (Kramarow et al., 1999). Since elevated cholesterol levels are a major risk factor for heart disease, lowering cholesterol through diet or drugs is particularly important in this age group (Grundy, Cleeman, Rifkind, & Kuller, 1999).

About 1 in 10 older adults reportedly suffers from asthma and other respiratory illnesses (NCHS, 1998a). Other common conditions include cancer, sinusitis, and visual, hearing, and orthopedic impairments (AARP, 1999; Kramarow et al., 1999). Such conditions become more frequent with age; but when a condition is not severe, it can usually be managed so that it does not interfere with daily life.

Arthritis—a group of disorders that cause pain and loss of movement, most often involving inflammation of the joints—is the most common chronic health problem of older adults (AARP, 1999; Kramarow et al., 1999). Its chief forms are *osteoarthritis,* or degenerative joint disease, which most often affects weight-bearing joints, such as the hips and knees, and *rheumatoid arthritis,* a crippling disease that progressively destroys joint tissue.

arthritis
Group of disorders affecting the joints, causing pain and loss of movement.

Treatment usually involves a combination of medication (usually anti-inflammatory drugs), rest, physical therapy, application of heat or cold, protecting the joints from stress, and sometimes replacing a joint, especially the hip. Withdrawal of fluid that may form in the joint cavity can relieve osteoarthritis. So can cortisone injections (especially in the knee). Dietary supplements containing glucosamine and chondroitin sulfate, which stimulate cartilage formation, have had good anecdotal results and are under study.

Older people need more medical care than younger ones. Medicare, Medicaid, and other government programs cover only about two-thirds of the cost; 70 percent of people on Medicare buy additional private insurance (AARP, 1998; Kramarow et al., 1999; Treas, 1995). Medicare beneficiaries who are 75 or older, disabled, in poor or fair health, or severely limited in activities of daily living, who have supplemental insurance but lack drug coverage, spend an average of 21 to 30 percent of their income on health care, and 4 to 7 percent on drugs alone (Gibson, Brangan, Gross, & Caplan, 1999).

The proportion of older adults with physical disabilities has declined since the mid-1980s—evidence of the trend toward healthy aging (Kramarow et al., 1999). All but about 9 percent of adults age 70 and older who are not in institutions can perform all essential activities of daily living, such as walking, eating, dressing, bathing, or toileting. However, 20 percent perform at least one such activity with difficulty, and about one-third receive help from a caregiver. Limitations on activity increase sharply with age (Kramarow et al., 1999) and are more common among women, African Americans, and people with low incomes (Kramarow et al., 1999; NCHS, 1998a). On the other hand, women are more likely than men to be able to walk without help, climb stairs, and do other physical activities.

Although only about 4 percent of all elderly people are in nursing homes, the proportion reaches almost 20 percent of those 85 and older. More than 50 percent of noninstitutionalized women and more than 40 percent of men in this "oldest old" group need assistance with everyday self-care activities (Kramarow et al., 1999). (We discuss issues pertaining to living arrangements and long-term care in Chapter 18.)

Influences on Health

Physical activity, nutrition, and other lifestyle factors influence health and disease. Obesity, for example, affects the circulatory system, the kidneys, and sugar metabolism; contributes to degenerative disorders; and tends to shorten life. Healthier lifestyles may enable an increasing number of today's young and middle-aged adults to maintain a high level of physical functioning well into old age.

Physical Activity

No one is too old to exercise. Physical activity—walking, jogging, bicycling, or weight lifting, as John Glenn does—is just as valuable in late adulthood as earlier in the life span. More than two-thirds of nondisabled older adults participate in some kind of exercise, such as walking, gardening, or stretching, at least once in two weeks; but only about one-third of those who exercise do so for 30 minutes at a time, the recommended level (Kramarow et al., 1999).

A lifelong program of exercise may prevent many physical changes formerly associated with "normal aging." Regular exercise prolongs life and can help prevent or reduce aging-related declines (Mazzeo et al., 1998; Rakowski & Mor, 1992). It can strengthen the heart and lungs and decrease stress. It can protect against hypertension, hardening of the arteries, heart disease, osteoporosis, and adult-onset diabetes. It helps maintain speed, stamina, strength, and endurance, and such basic functions as circulation and breathing. It reduces the chance of injuries by making joints and muscles stronger and more flexible, and it helps prevent or relieve lower-back pain and symptoms of arthritis. It may improve mental alertness and cognitive performance, may help relieve anxiety and mild depression, and often improves morale (Blumenthal et al., 1991; Clarkson-Smith & Hartley, 1989; H. L. Hawkins, Kramer, & Capaldi, 1992; Hill, Storandt, & Malley, 1993; Kramer et al., 1999; NIA, 1995b; Rall, Meydani, Kehayias, Dawson-Hughes, & Roubenoff, 1996; Shay & Roth, 1992).

Consider this . . .

- Do you engage regularly in physical exercise? How many of the older people you know do so? What kinds of physical activity do you think you will be able to maintain as you get older?

Nutrition

Many older people do not eat as well as they should, whether because of diminished senses of taste and smell, dental problems, difficulty in shopping and preparing food, or inadequate income. Then too, many older people live by themselves and may not feel like fixing nourishing meals for one. Studies have found

These enthusiastic cross-country skiers are deriving the benefits of regular physical exercise in old age, along with having fun. Exercise may well help them extend their lives and avoid some of the physical changes commonly—and apparently mistakenly—associated with "normal aging."

evidence of malnutrition or specific dietary deficiencies in the diets of elderly people (Lamy, 1994; Ryan, Craig, & Finn, 1992), especially in zinc, vitamin E, magnesium, calcium, and overconsumption of fats (Voelker, 1997).

Nutrition plays a part in susceptibility to such chronic illnesses as atherosclerosis, heart disease, and diabetes (Mohs, 1994). Vitamin deficiencies have been implicated in some mental illnesses. One study found that taking vitamin B-6 can improve memory performance (Riggs, Spiro, Tucker, & Rush, 1996). Vitamin D deficiency increases the risk of hip fracture (LeBoff et al., 1999). Eating fruits and vegetables—especially those rich in vitamin C, citrus fruits and juices, green leafy vegetables, broccoli, cabbage, cauliflower, and brussels sprouts—lowers the risk of stroke (Joshipura et al., 1999).

Loss of teeth due to decay or **periodontitis** (gum disease), often attributable to infrequent dental care (NCHS, 1998a), can have serious implications for nutrition. Because people with poor or missing teeth find many foods hard to chew, they tend to eat less and to choose softer, sometimes less nutritious foods (Wayler, Kapur, Feldman, & Chauncey, 1982).

CHECKPOINT

Can you . . .

✔ Summarize the health status of older adults, and identify several common chronic conditions in late life?

✔ Give evidence of the influences of exercise and nutrition on health?

periodontitis
Gum disease.

Mental and Behavioral Problems

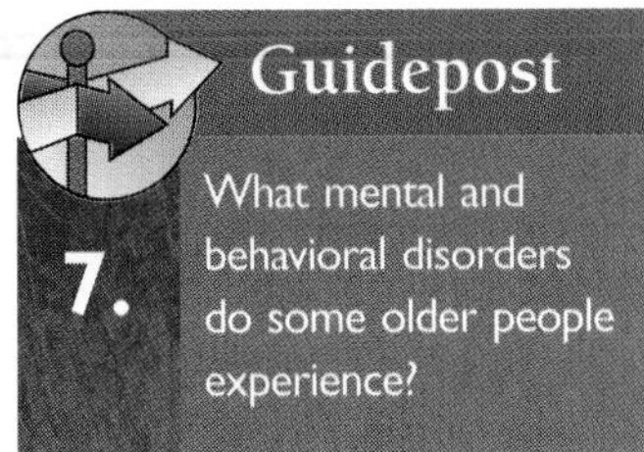

Guidepost
7.
What mental and behavioral disorders do some older people experience?

Decline in mental health is not typical in late life; in fact, mental illness is less common among older adults than among younger ones (Wykle & Musil, 1993). However, mental and behavioral disturbances that do occur in older adults can be devastating.

Dementia is the general term for physiologically caused cognitive and behavioral decline sufficient to affect daily life (American Psychiatric Association [APA], 1994). Contrary to stereotype, dementia is not an inevitable part of aging. Most dementias are irreversible, but some can be reversed with early diagnosis and treatment (Alzheimer's Association, 1998b; APA, 1994; NIA, 1993).

About two-thirds of cases of dementia may be caused by **Alzheimer's disease (AD),** a progressive, degenerative brain disorder, discussed in the next section (Small et al., 1997). **Parkinson's disease,** the second most common disorder involving progressive neurological degeneration, is characterized by tremor, stiffness, slowed movement, and unstable posture (Nussbaum, 1998). Medications that replenish the brain's supply of the chemical neurotransmitter *dopamine* can alleviate Parkinson's symptoms (Alzheimer's Association, 1998b). These two diseases, together with **multi-infarct dementia (MD),** which is caused by a series of small strokes, account for at least 8 out of 10 cases of dementia, all irreversible. Other causes of dementia include brain injuries or tumors, hemorrhages, cardiovascular problems, Huntington's disease (see Chapter 3), hydrocephalus (an abnormal accumulation of fluid causing pressure on the brain), thyroid disorders, liver or kidney failure, nutritional deficiencies (especially in vitamin B_{12} and folic acid), and infectious diseases, including AIDS and meningitis (Alzheimer's Association, 1998b; "Alzheimer's Disease, Part I," 1998; Selkoe, 1992).

dementia
Deterioration in cognitive and behavioral functioning due to physiological causes.

Alzheimer's disease
Progressive, degenerative brain disorder characterized by irreversible deterioration in memory, intelligence, awareness, and control of bodily functions, eventually leading to death.

Parkinson's disease
Progressive, irreversible degenerative neurological disorder, characterized by tremor, stiffness, slowed movement, and unstable posture.

multi-infarct dementia
Irreversible dementia caused by a series of small strokes.

Alzheimer's Disease

Alzheimer's disease "threatens to become the major health problem of the twenty-first century" ("Alzheimer's Disease, Part I," 1998). The most common and most feared irreversible dementia, it gradually robs people of intelligence, awareness, and even the ability to control their bodily functions—and finally kills them.

The disease was barely known a generation ago. Today an estimated 4 million people in the United States have been diagnosed with AD, and there may be as many as 14 million by 2040 unless a cure is found ("Alzheimer's Disease, Part I," 1998; Small et al., 1997).

The main reason more cases are diagnosed now than in the past is that far more people now reach an age when they are likely to show signs of it. Alzheimer's disease generally begins after age 60, and the risk rises dramatically with age.

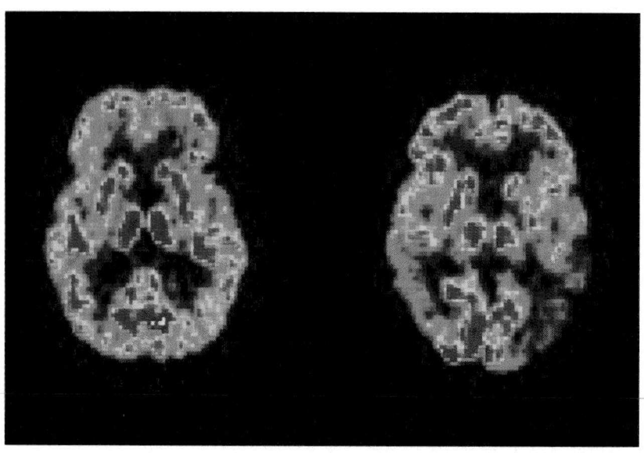

This PET (positron emission tomography) scan shows dramatic deterioration in the brain of an Alzheimer's patient (right) as compared with a normal brain (left). The red and yellow areas represent high brain activity; the blue and black areas, low activity. The scan on the right shows reduction of both function and blood flow in both sides of the brain, a change often seen in Alzheimer's disease. To obtain the PET scans, a radioactive tracer is injected into the blood to reveal metabolic activity in the brain.

Estimates of prevalence vary from 6 to 10 percent of adults over 65 and 30 to 50 percent of those 85 and older. Women, who are longer-lived than men, are more at risk (Hoyert & Rosenberg, 1999; Launer et al., 1999; Small et al., 1997; Truschke, 1998). It has been estimated that a ten-year delay in the average age of onset of the disease could mean a 75 percent reduction in the number of cases (Banner, 1992).

Symptoms and Diagnosis First signs of the disease are often overlooked because they look like ordinary forgetfulness or may be interpreted as signs of normal aging. (Table 17-4 compares early warning signs of Alzheimer's disease with normal mental lapses.) The most prominent early symptom is inability to recall recent events or take in new information. A person may repeat questions that were just answered or leave an everyday task unfinished. More symptoms follow: irritability, anxiety, depression, and, later, delusions, delirium, and wandering. Long-term memory, judgment, concentration, orientation, and speech all become impaired, and patients have trouble handling activities of daily life. Skills are lost in about the same order they were originally acquired; by the end, the patient, like an infant, cannot understand or use language, does not recognize family members, cannot eat without help, cannot control the bowels and bladder, and loses the ability to walk, sit up, and swallow solid food. Death usually comes within eight to ten years, but may be as long as twenty years, after symptoms appear ("Alzheimer's Disease, Part I," 1998; Hoyert & Rosenberg, 1999; Small et al., 1997).

So far, the only sure diagnosis depends on analysis of brain tissue, which can be done with certainty only by autopsy after death. The brain of a person with

Table 17-4 Alzheimer's Disease versus Normal Behavior

Normal Behavior	Symptoms of Disease
Temporarily forgetting things	Permanently forgetting recent events; asking the same questions repeatedly
Inability to do some challenging tasks	Inability to do routine tasks with many steps, such as making and serving a meal
Forgetting unusual or complex words	Forgetting simple words
Getting lost in a strange city	Getting lost on one's own block
Becoming momentarily distracted and failing to watch a child	Forgetting that a child is in one's care and leaving the house
Making mistakes in balancing a checkbook	Forgetting what the numbers in a checkbook mean and what to do with them
Misplacing everyday items	Putting things in inappropriate places where one cannot usefully retrieve them (e.g., a wristwatch in a fishbowl)
Occasional mood changes	Rapid, dramatic mood swings and personality changes; loss of initiative

Source: Adapted from Alzheimer's Association (undated).

Alzheimer's disease shows excessive amounts of **neurofibrillary tangles,** twisted masses of collapsed protein fibers, and large waxy chunks of **amyloid plaque,** insoluble tissue formed by a protein called *beta amyloid* and surrounded by fragments of dead neurons. These changes probably occur to some extent in all aging brains but are more pronounced in people with AD (Alzheimer's Association, 1998a; "Alzheimer's Disease, Part I," 1998; Haroutunian et al., 1999).

Doctors usually diagnose Alzheimer's disease in a living person through physical, neurological, and memory tests, as well as detailed interviews with patients and caregivers or close family members. Diagnoses made in this way can be about 85 percent accurate (Alzheimer's Association, 1998a; "Alzheimer's Disease, Part I, 1998; Cullum & Rosenberg, 1998). Researchers are constantly coming up with new "high-tech" tools to aid in early diagnosis or prediction: magnetic resonance imaging that measures changes in the size of brain structures associated with the disease (Bobinski et al., 1999; Jack et al., 1998, 1999); brain scans that can show atrophy and diminished rates of blood flow and energy consumption ("Alzheimer's Disease, Part I," 1998); and analysis of beta amyloid levels in cerebrospinal fluid (Andreasen et al., 1999). One research team developed a seven-minute neurocognitive screening test that can make reliable initial distinctions between patients experiencing cognitive changes related to normal aging and those in early stages of dementia (Solomon et al., 1998). Accurate diagnosis is important, not only for persons with AD, but for those with depression or reversible dementias, which are sometimes misdiagnosed as AD (Small et al., 1997).

neurofibrillary tangles
Twisted masses of protein fibers found in brains of persons with Alzheimer's disease.

amyloid plaque
Waxy chunks of insoluble tissue found in brains of persons with Alzheimer's disease.

Causes and Risk Factors So far, the causes of most cases of Alzheimer's disease are uncertain. Does formation of plaques and tangles produce dementia or result from it? If the former, what causes the plaques and tangles, and why do they develop earlier and faster in some brains than in others?

A study of adult monkeys suggests some answers. This research found that beta amyloid *does* cause brain cell death in aging rhesus monkeys, but not in younger ones. It may be that a protective agent against beta amyloid, present in young adults, dissipates or becomes inoperative with age (Geula et al., 1998)

However, not everyone with extensive plaques and tangles shows signs of dementia. A postmortem examination of 102 elderly nuns found that those who had exhibited poorer cognitive functioning and dementia before death were the ones whose brains showed evidence of strokes as well as plaques and tangles. Thus strokes may contribute to the presence and severity of symptoms of AD (Snowdon et al., 1996, 1997).

Alzheimer's disease is strongly heritable. Virtually all known sufferers have a family history of the disease. At least four alleles that increase production or reduce clearance of beta amyloid have been linked to AD ("Alzheimer's Disease, Part II," 1998).

An early-onset form of the disease, which appears in middle age, is related to dominant genetic mutations on chromosomes 1, 14, and 21 (Corliss, 1996; Karlinsky, Lennox, & Rossor, 1994; Post et al., 1997; Schellenberg et al., 1992; Small et al., 1997; St. George-Hyslop et al., 1987). *ApoE-4,* a variant of a gene on chromosome 19, is an important risk factor for the more common late-onset type, which appears after age 65 (Bondi, Salmon, Galasko, Thomas, & Thal, 1999; Corder et al., 1993; Farrer et al., 1997; Lennox et al., 1994; Reiman et al., 1996; Roses, 1994; Small et al., 1997). African Americans and Hispanic Americans have a higher risk of AD than whites, regardless of their ApoE genotype, suggesting that other genes or risk factors may be involved (Tang et al., 1998). While genetic testing for the three dominant chromosomal mutations mentioned is highly predictive of the relatively rare early-onset form, the presence of the ApoE-4 gene alone is not enough for prediction or diagnosis of late-onset AD (Post et al., 1997), though it may be useful in combination with clinical evidence of symptoms (Mayeux et al., 1998).

Lifestyle factors may play a part in AD. Education significantly decreases the risk ("Alzheimer's Disease, Part II," 1998; Launer et al., 1999; Small et al., 1997). Smoking greatly increases it (Launer et al., 1999; Ott et al., 1998).

Treatment and Prevention Tacrine (sold under the name Cognex) and donepezil (Aricept) are specific medications for Alzheimer's relief that can be prescribed at early stages. They may control symptoms but do not stop the underlying deterioration. Although some patients respond well, others show little effect; and any gains are lost when use is discontinued ("Alzheimer's Disease, Part II," 1998; Small et al., 1997).

Behavioral therapies can slow the deterioration in capabilities, improve communication, and reduce disruptive behavior. As patients regress in basic skills of everyday living, training linked to their current developmental level may delay further losses (Barinaga, 1998).

Drugs can relieve patients' agitation, lighten depression, and help them sleep. Proper nourishment and fluid intake, together with exercise, physical therapy, and social interaction may be helpful. In the early stages, memory training and memory aids may improve cognitive functioning (Camp et al., 1993; Camp & McKitrick, 1992; McKitrick, Camp, & Black, 1992). In ongoing trials, estrogen replacement therapy, anti-inflammatory drugs, the herbal remedy gingko biloba, and antioxidants, such as vitamin E, show some promise of protection against Alzheimer's or at least of modestly slowing its progress ("Alzheimer's Disease, Part II," 1998; Baldereschi et al., 1998; Le Bars et al., 1997; Marx, 1996; Small et al., 1997; Stewart, Kawas, Corrada, & Metter, 1997; Tang et al., 1996).

The discovery of a brain enzyme believed to be responsible for formation of amyloid plaque may eventually enable researchers to develop a drug to block the enzyme's action and prevent or slow the disease (Vassar et al., 1999). Also promising is a potential vaccine, which enabled young mice to grow up without developing plaques. In diseased mice, the treatment destroyed plaques, ameliorated neuron damage, and reduced inflammation (Novak, 1999).

CHECKPOINT

Can you . . .

- ✔ Name the three main causes of dementia in older adults?
- ✔ Summarize what is known about the prevalence, symptoms, diagnosis, causes, risk factors, treatment, and prevention of Alzheimer's disease?

Reversible Conditions

Many older people and their families mistakenly believe that they can do nothing about mental and behavioral problems, even though close to 100 such conditions, including about 10 percent of dementia cases, can be cured or alleviated. Sometimes apparent dementia turns out to be a side effect of drug intoxication. Because physicians do not always ask what other medicines a patient is taking, they may prescribe drugs that interact harmfully. Also, because of age-related changes in the body's metabolism, a dosage that would be right for a 40-year-old may be an overdose for an 80-year-old.

Besides drug intoxication, other common reversible conditions include delirium, metabolic or infectious disorders, malnutrition, anemia, alcoholism, low thyroid functioning, minor head injuries, and depression (NIA, 1980, 1993; Wykle & Musil, 1993). Let's look at alcohol use and depression.

Alcohol and Aging Surveys suggest that older adults drink less and are less likely to abuse alcohol than younger ones (National Institute on Alcohol Abuse and Alcoholism [NIAAA], 1998). As in other age groups, older men are more likely to be regular drinkers than older women, but women who drink regularly are as likely as men to drink too much (Wattis & Seymour, 1994).

In addition to the damage alcohol can do at any age (see Chapter 13), it poses special dangers for older adults. Sensitivity to alcohol and susceptibility to intoxication seem to increase with age; thus older people may no longer be able to tolerate amounts of liquor they were accustomed to consume. Alcohol can have harmful interactions with medications. It increases the risks of depression and suicide and also increases older drivers' risk of collisions. Heavy alcohol use may speed up normal effects of aging and may cause premature loss or shrinkage of brain tissue. Alcohol-related changes in the cerebellum may contribute to unsteady balance. Alcohol also can increase the risk of falls and hip fractures by lowering bone density (NIAAA, 1998). Older adults with alcohol problems respond to treatment at least as well as younger adults, especially if the problem drinking began late in life (Atkinson, Ganzini, & Bernstein, 1992; Horton & Fogelman, 1991; Lichtenberg, 1994; NIAAA, 1998).

Depression The serious clinical syndrome called **major depressive disorder** is extreme and persistent and can interfere significantly with ability to function (APA, 1994; American Association for Geriatric Psychiatry [AAGP], 1996; National Institute of Mental Health [NIMH], 1999b). Less severe forms of depression are either more transient or milder but can lead to major depression. Nearly 2 million older Americans—about 6 percent—are known to suffer from some form of depression, but the illness often goes unrecognized and untreated (NIMH, 1999b).

major depressive disorder Mental disorder lasting at least two weeks, in which a person shows extreme sadness, loss of pleasure or interest in life, and other symptoms such as weight changes, insomnia, feelings of worthlessness or inappropriate guilt, loss of memory, inability to concentrate, and thoughts of death or suicide.

Contrary to popular belief, depression is diagnosed less often in late life, even though *symptoms* of depression are *more* common among older adults than among younger ones. Many older people suffer from aches and pains or chronic illness; have lost close family and friends; take mood-altering medicines; and feel that they have little or no control over their lives. Any of these conditions can trigger depression (AAGP, 1996; Blazer, 1989; Jefferson & Greist, 1993; Wolfe, Morrow, & Fredrickson, 1996).

Why is depression underdiagnosed in older adults? It may be mistaken for dementia, or it may be wrongly seen as a natural accompaniment of aging (AAGP, 1996; "Alzheimer's Disease, Part I," 1998; George, 1993; Jefferson & Greist, 1993). It may be masked by physical illness. Or older people may simply be less likely to *say* they feel depressed—perhaps because of a belief that depression is a sign of weakness or that it will lift by itself (Gallo, Anthony, & Muthen, 1994; Wolfe et al., 1996). One indication that depression is often overlooked in older adults is the high prevalence of suicide in this age group (NIMH, 1999b; see Chapter 19).

Depression that is not properly diagnosed and treated may worsen. Sometimes depression may indicate a "silent" stroke caused by blockage or rupture of small blood vessels in the brain (Steffens, Helms, Krishnan, & Burke, 1999). Since depression can speed physical declines of aging, accurate diagnosis, prevention, and treatment could help many older people live longer and remain more active (Penninx et al., 1998).

Vulnerability to depression seems to result from the influence of multiple genes interacting with environmental factors (NIMH, 1999b), such as lack of exercise. Stressful events, loneliness, or the use of certain medications may trigger it (Jefferson & Greist, 1993; "Listening to Depression," 1995). Brain imaging of depressed patients reveals a chemical imbalance of critical neurotransmitters and a malfunctioning of neural circuits that regulate moods, thinking, sleep, appetite, and behavior (NIMH, 1999b).

CHECKPOINT

Can you . . .

- ✔ Explain why alcohol use poses special dangers for older adults?
- ✔ Tell why late-life depression may be more common than is generally realized?

A strong network of family and friends can help older people ward off depression or cope with it. Cognitive-behavioral psychotherapy and interpersonal therapy have had good results. Antidepressant drugs can restore the chemical balance in the brain; *selective serotonin reuptake inhibitors (SSRIs)*, such as Prozac, have fewer side effects than older drugs. More than 8 out of 10 people with depression improve when given appropriate treatment with medication, psychotherapy, or both; the combination treatment also can reduce recurrence (NIMH, 1999b). Electroconvulsive therapy (ECT), also called shock therapy, may be administered in severe cases.

Symptoms of depression are common in older adults but are often overlooked because they are wrongly thought to be a natural accompaniment of aging. Some older people become depressed as a result of physical and emotional losses, and some apparent "brain disorders" are actually due to depression. But depression often can be relieved if older people seek help.

Aspects of Cognitive Development

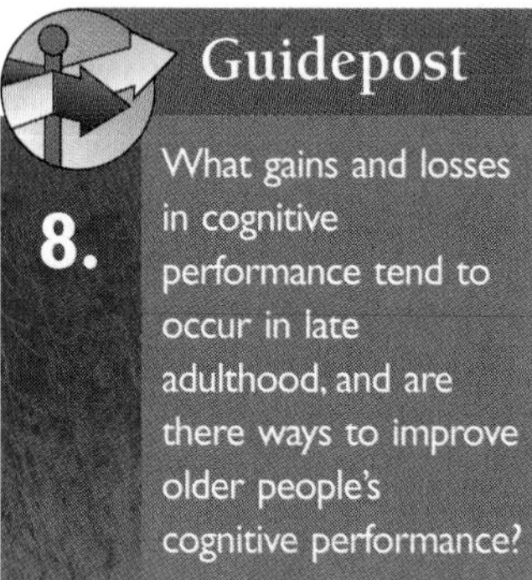

Guidepost
8.
What gains and losses in cognitive performance tend to occur in late adulthood, and are there ways to improve older people's cognitive performance?

Old age "adds as it takes away," said the poet William Carlos Williams in one of three books of verse written between his first stroke at the age of 68 and his death at 79. This comment seems to sum up current findings about cognitive functioning in late adulthood. As Baltes's life-span developmental approach suggests, age brings gains as well as losses. Let's look first at intelligence and processing abilities; then at memory; and then at wisdom, which is popularly associated with the later years. Then we'll examine education in late life.

Intelligence and Processing Abilities

Does intelligence diminish in late adulthood? The answer depends on what abilities are being measured, and how. Cognitive performance is uneven during adulthood; different abilities peak at different times. Whereas some abilities may decline in later years, others remain stable or even improve throughout most of adult life. Although changes in processing abilities may reflect neurological deterioration, there is much individual variation, suggesting that declines in functioning are not inevitable and may be preventable.

Measuring Older Adults' Intelligence

Measuring older adults' intelligence is complicated. A number of physical and psychological factors may lower their test scores and lead to underestimation of their intelligence. Older adults, like younger ones, do their best on tests when they are physically fit and well rested. Neurophysiological problems, high blood pressure, or other cardiovascular problems, which can affect blood flow to the brain, can interfere with cognitive performance (Sands & Meredith, 1992; Schaie, 1990). Vision and hearing problems may cause trouble in understanding test instructions. The time limits on most intelligence tests are particularly hard on older people. Since both physical and psychological processes, including perceptual abilities, tend to slow with age, older adults do better when they are allowed as much time as they need (Hertzog, 1989; Schaie & Hertzog, 1983).

Test anxiety is common among older adults. They may expect to do poorly, and this expectation may become a self-fulfilling prophecy (Schaie, 1996b). They may lack interest and motivation unless they are taking the test to qualify for a job or for some other important purpose.

Wechsler Adult Intelligence Scale (WAIS) Intelligence test for adults, which yields verbal and performance scores as well as a combined score.

To measure the intelligence of older adults, researchers often use the **Wechsler Adult Intelligence Scale (WAIS).** Like the Wechsler tests for children, the WAIS has subtests that yield separate scores. These scores are combined into a verbal IQ and a performance IQ, and, finally, a total IQ. Items are not graduated by age.

Older adults, as a group, do not perform as well as younger adults on the WAIS, but the difference is primarily in nonverbal performance. On the five subtests in the performance scale (such as identifying the missing part of a picture, copying a design, and mastering a maze), scores drop with age; but on the six tests making up the verbal scale—particularly tests of vocabulary, information, and comprehension—scores fall only slightly and very gradually (see Figure 17-6). This is called the *classic aging pattern* (Botwinick, 1984).

What might account for this pattern? For one thing, the verbal items that hold up with age are based on knowledge; unlike the performance tests, they do not require the test taker to figure out or do anything new. The performance tasks,

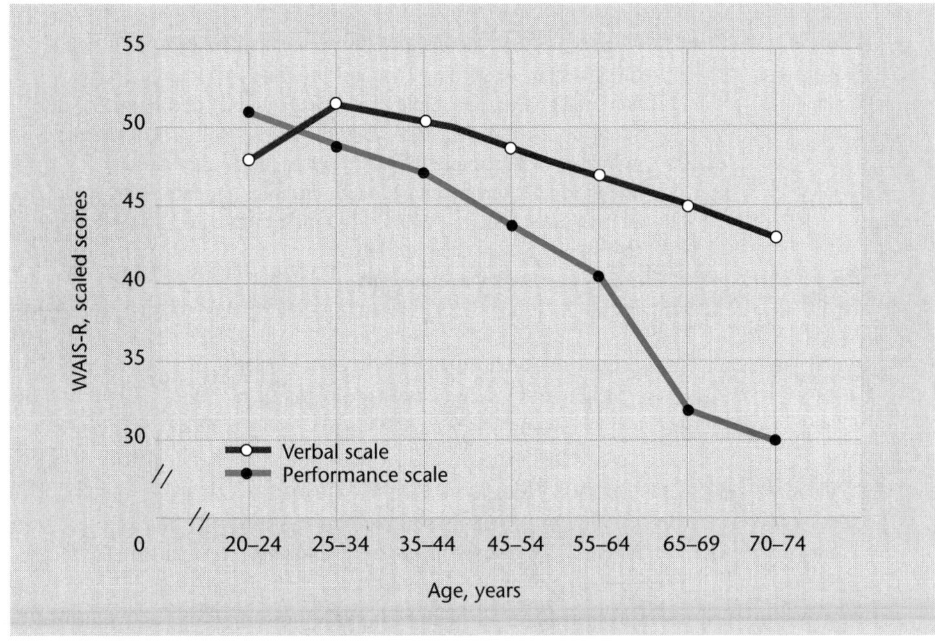

Figure 17-6
Classic aging pattern on the revised version of the Wechsler Adult Intelligence Scale (WAIS-R). Scores on the performance subtests decline far more rapidly with age than scores on the verbal subtests.
(Source: Botwinick, 1984.)

which involve the processing of new information, require perceptual speed and motor skills, which can reflect muscular and neurological slowing.

Another line of research, introduced in Chapter 15, has made a similar distinction between two kinds of abilities, *fluid* and *crystallized*, the former depending largely on neurological status and the latter on accumulated knowledge. As in the classic aging pattern on the WAIS, these two kinds of intelligence follow different paths. In the classic aging pattern, however, the trend in both verbal and performance scores is downward throughout most of adulthood; the difference, though substantial, is one of degree. Far more encouraging is the pattern of crystallized intelligence, which improves until fairly late in life, even though fluid intelligence declines earlier (see Figure 17-7).

In line with such findings, Baltes and his colleagues have proposed a **dual-process model,** which identifies and seeks to measure aspects of intelligence that may continue to advance as well as aspects that are more likely to deteriorate. In this model, **mechanics of intelligence** consist of content-free functions of information processing and problem solving. This dimension, like fluid intelligence, is physiologically based and often declines with age. **Pragmatics of intelligence** include such potential growth areas as practical thinking, application of accumulated knowledge and skills, specialized expertise, professional productivity, and wisdom (discussed later in this chapter). This domain, which often continues to develop in late adulthood, is similar to, but broader than, crystallized intelligence and includes information and know-how garnered from education, work, and life experience. Through **selective optimization with compensation** older people may use their pragmatic strengths to compensate for weakened mechanical abilities (Baltes, 1993; Baltes, Lindenberger, & Staudinger, 1998; Marsiske, Lange, Baltes, & Baltes, 1995).

dual-process model
Model of cognitive functioning in late adulthood, proposed by Baltes, which identifies and seeks to measure two dimensions of intelligence: mechanics and pragmatics.

mechanics of intelligence
In Baltes's dual-process model, the abilities to process information and solve problems, irrespective of content; the area of cognition in which there is often an age-related decline. Compare with *pragmatics of intelligence*.

pragmatics of intelligence
In Baltes's dual-process model, the dimension of intelligence that tends to grow with age and includes practical thinking, application of accumulated knowledge and skills, specialized expertise, professional productivity, and wisdom. Compare with *mechanics of intelligence*.

selective optimization with compensation
In Baltes's dual-process model, strategy for maintaining or enhancing overall cognitive functioning by using stronger abilities to compensate for those that have weakened.

Changes in Processing Abilities

Just what happens to the "mechanics" of intelligence in late adulthood? How does aging affect the machinery of the mind?

A general slowdown in central nervous system functioning, as measured by reaction time, is widely believed to be a major contributor to changes in cognitive abilities and efficiency of information processing. It can worsen performance on intelligence tests, especially timed tests, and can interfere with the abilities to

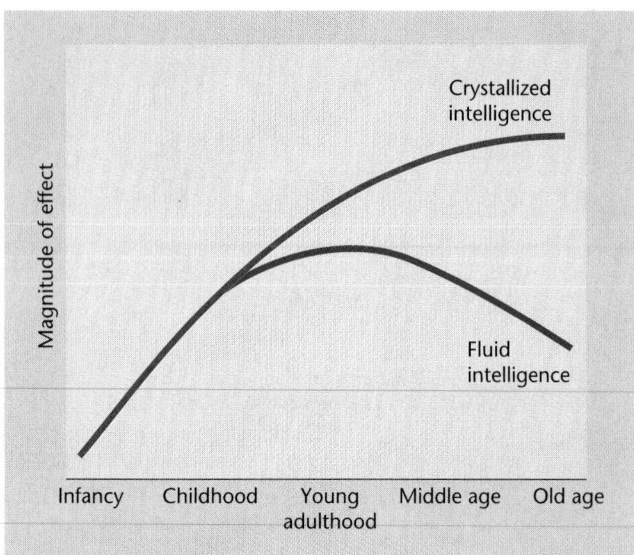

Figure 17-7

Changes in fluid intelligence and crystallized intelligence across the life span. According to classic studies by Horn and Cattell, fluid abilities (largely biologically determined) decline after young adulthood, but crystallized abilities (largely culturally influenced) increase until late adulthood. More recently, the Seattle Longitudinal Study found a more complex pattern, with some fluid abilities holding their own until late middle age (refer back to Figure 15-2 in Chapter 15).

(Source: J. L. Horn & Donaldson, 1980.)

learn and remember (Birren, Woods, & Williams, 1980; Salthouse, 1985; Spence, 1989). Slowed information processing may cause older people to ask others to repeat information that has been presented too quickly or not clearly enough. The more complex a task, the more evident this slowdown seems to become (Birren et al., 1980), at least with regard to nonverbal functioning.

The prevalent view has been that all components of processing slow equally. Now scientists can test that view directly, by observing the complex steps in stimulus-and-response processing that enter into reaction time. *Event-related potentials (ERPs)* are fluctuations in the direction of the brain's electrical activity that can be measured with electrodes attached to the scalp (Ridderinkhof & Bashore, 1995). In one study, researchers measured ERPs in young and older adults in three versions of a reaction-time task. Participants were asked to press a button when they located a particular word amid a jumbled mass of characters. The older adults were slower only in the final step of processing, the pressing of the button—perhaps because, at their age, the time it takes to identify a stimulus and to select a response may overlap. In addition, patterns of response differed with variations in the conditions of the task. These findings suggest that the brain's slowing is *not* global, but specific to certain tasks and operations (Bashore, Ridderinkhof, & van der Molen, 1998).

One ability that appears to slow with age and is linked with measures of cognitive functioning is ease in switching from one task or function to another (Salthouse, Fristoe, McGuthry, & Hambrick, 1998). This may help explain, for example, why older adults tend to have difficulties driving a car, which requires rapid switching among such skills as watching other vehicles and pedestrians, reading signs, and ignoring irrelevant information, as well as the specific skills required in operating the vehicle.

CHECKPOINT

Can you . . .

- ✔ Give several reasons why older adults' intelligence tends to be underestimated?
- ✔ Compare the classic aging pattern on the WAIS with the trajectories of fluid and crystallized intelligence?
- ✔ Discuss findings on the slowdown in neural processing and its relationship to cognitive decline?

Although losses in processing speed are related to cognitive performance, they do not tell the whole story. Specific cognitive abilities, such as reasoning, spatial abilities, and memory, do not seem to decline as rapidly as processing speed (Verhaeghen & Salthouse, 1997). Furthermore, the evidence for the role of processing speed in cognitive performance—like the evidence for cognitive decline itself—comes almost entirely from cross-sectional studies, which may confound cohort with age. Younger adults may have done better than older adults because they were healthier and better nourished, had more or better schooling, had gained more information from television, had jobs that depended on thinking rather than on physical labor, or had more—and more recent—experience taking tests. Longitudinal studies do not show the marked declines reported in cross-sectional studies. However, this research design may favor an older sample because of attrition and practice effects. People who score poorly are more likely to drop out of a study, and those who remain benefit from having taken the tests before.

One study measured links between age, speed, and cognition longitudinally as well as cross-sectionally among 302 adults with an average age of 77. Speed of processing accounted for most of the cross-sectional age differences in cognitive abilities, but far less of the longitudinal changes. The longitudinal results highlighted more strongly the role of individual differences (Sliwinski & Buschke, 1999).

The Seattle Longitudinal Study

The Seattle Longitudinal Study of Adult Intelligence, introduced in Chapter 15, sought to overcome drawbacks of cross-sectional and longitudinal research by combining both in a sequential design. The researchers measured six primary mental abilities: verbal meaning (vocabulary), verbal memory, number (computational ability), spatial orientation, inductive reasoning, and perceptual speed.

An encouraging finding is that cognitive decline is slow and not across-the-board. If they live long enough, most people's functioning will flag at some point; but very few weaken in all or even most abilities, and many improve in some areas. Most fairly healthy older adults show only small losses until the seventies. Not until the eighties do they fall below the average performance of younger adults (Schaie, 1996b).

As we might expect, there were substantial differences between the cross-sectional and longitudinal findings, due in large part to cohort effects. Cohort differences have been flattening out in recent years, suggesting that we may in the future see less significant declines in late life (Schaie, 1996b).

The most striking feature of the Seattle findings is the tremendous variation among individuals. Some participants showed declines during their thirties or forties, but a few maintained full functioning very late in life. Even in their late eighties, virtually all retained their competence in one or more of the abilities tested (Schaie, 1996b). Some people remained relatively strong in one area, others in another.

What accounts for these differences? The genetic endowment undoubtedly plays a part. So do physical and neurological status and environmental opportunities. People with higher scores tended to be healthier and better educated and to have higher incomes. High scorers also were more likely to have stable marriages, intelligent spouses, cognitively complex occupations, and active, stimulating lives. When measured in midlife, they tended to have flexible personality styles and to be relatively satisfied with their accomplishments (Gruber-Baldini, 1991; Schaie, 1990, 1994, 1996b; Schaie & Willis, 1996).

These findings gave rise to the **engagement hypothesis.** According to this hypothesis—somewhat similar to Kohn's concept of substantive complexity of work, discussed in Chapter 13—people who show high intellectual ability early in life and receive favorable educational and environmental opportunities tend, as adults, to have an "engaged" lifestyle marked by complex, intellectually demanding occupational and social activities. Engaging in activities that challenge cognitive skills in turn promotes the retention or growth of those skills in later life (Schaie, 1983).

engagement hypothesis
Proposal that an active, engaged lifestyle that challenges cognitive skills predicts retention or growth of those skills in later life.

Several longitudinal studies provide at least partial support for this "use-it-or-lose-it" hypothesis. A 45-year study of 132 Canadian World War II army veterans (Arbuckle, Maag, Pushkar, & Chaikelson, 1998; Gold et al., 1995) found considerable stability in individual differences in intelligence from young adulthood to late middle and old age. Participants with higher intelligence, education, and childhood socioeconomic status tended to have more engaged adult lifestyles, as measured by SES, intellectual involvement, and a sense of control over their lives. High engagement, in turn, predicted better maintenance of verbal (but not nonverbal) intelligence.

Another study, in which researchers tested 250 middle-aged and older adults three times over a six-year period, gives limited support to the engagement hypothesis (Hultsch, Hertzog, Small, & Dixon, 1999). Intellectually engaging activities—but not social or physical ones—were related to cognitive change, suggesting that such activities may act as buffers against cognitive decline. On the other hand, the findings could support an alternative hypothesis: that "high-ability individuals lead intellectually active lives until cognitive decline sets in" (Hultsch et al., 1999, p. 245). In other words, decline might occur regardless of what people do. Further research is needed to clarify the direction of causation.

Competence in Everyday Tasks and Problem Solving

The purpose of intelligence, of course, is not to take tests but to deal with the challenges of daily life. Research has found a strong relationship between fluid intelligence and certain practical skills that tend to decline with age, such as the ability to read a map or a newspaper or to perform everyday tasks (Diehl, Willis, & Schaie, 1994; Schaie, 1996a; Willis & Schaie, 1986a).

instrumental activities of daily living (IADLs) Everyday activities, competence in which is considered a measure of the ability to live independently; these activities include managing finances, shopping for necessities, using the telephone, obtaining transportation, preparing meals, taking medication, and housekeeping.

As people get older, an important test of cognitive competence is the ability to live independently, as measured by seven **instrumental activities of daily living (IADLs):** managing finances, shopping for necessities, using the telephone, obtaining transportation, preparing meals, taking medication, and housekeeping. Schaie and his colleagues gave older adults tasks in each of these areas: for example, filling out a Medicare form; filling out a mail-order catalog form; looking up an emergency telephone number; figuring out a bus schedule; reading a nutrition label on a food package; reading a medicine bottle label; and reading instructions for using a household appliance. Fluid intelligence and, to a lesser extent, crystallized intelligence accounted for more than half of the variance in performance. Home observations produced similar correlations. Health and educational background affected the results through their effects on cognitive ability. As we have pointed out before, this relationship may be bidirectional. Not only may poor health and lack of education limit cognition, but people with higher cognitive ability tend to get better educations and take care of their health (Schaie & Willis, 1996).

Although instrumental abilities, which depend heavily on information-processing skills, generally decline with age, that is not necessarily true of the ability to solve interpersonal problems, which tend to have strong emotional overtones and solutions that are less cut and dried. The effectiveness of older adults' responses to such problems often depends on how meaningful the problem is to them (Blanchard-Fields, Chen, & Norris, 1997).

The way older adults, like people of any age, deal with a problem depends on what kind of problem it is. In one study, when presented with consumer or home management problems, for which they could draw on a great deal of accumulated experience, older adults tended to use cognitive analysis of the situation and direct action, whereas adolescents and younger adults tended to avoid or deny the problem or depend on others to solve it. When a problem involved an emotionally charged situation, such as conflict with friends, older adults tended to call on a wider repertoire of strategies than younger ones, including both action and withdrawal (Blanchard-Fields et al., 1997).

Can Older People Improve Their Cognitive Performance?

A key issue separating psychologists with a relatively optimistic view of cognitive development in late adulthood from those with a less positive view is *plasticity:* can cognitive performance be improved with training and practice?

Plasticity is a key feature of Baltes's life-span developmental approach, and he and his colleagues have been in the forefront of research on effects of training. Several of these studies have been based on the Adult Development and Enrichment Project (ADEPT), originated at Pennsylvania State University (Baltes & Willis, 1982; Blieszner, Willis, & Baltes, 1981; Plemons, Willis, & Baltes, 1978; Willis, Blieszner, & Baltes, 1981). A seven-year follow-up of ADEPT found that participants who received training declined significantly less than a control group (Willis, 1990; Willis & Nesselroade, 1990). In one study, adults with an average age of 70 who received training in figural relations (rules for determining the next figure in a series), a measure of fluid intelligence, improved more than a control group who received no training. A third group who worked with the same training materials and problems without formal instruction also did better than the

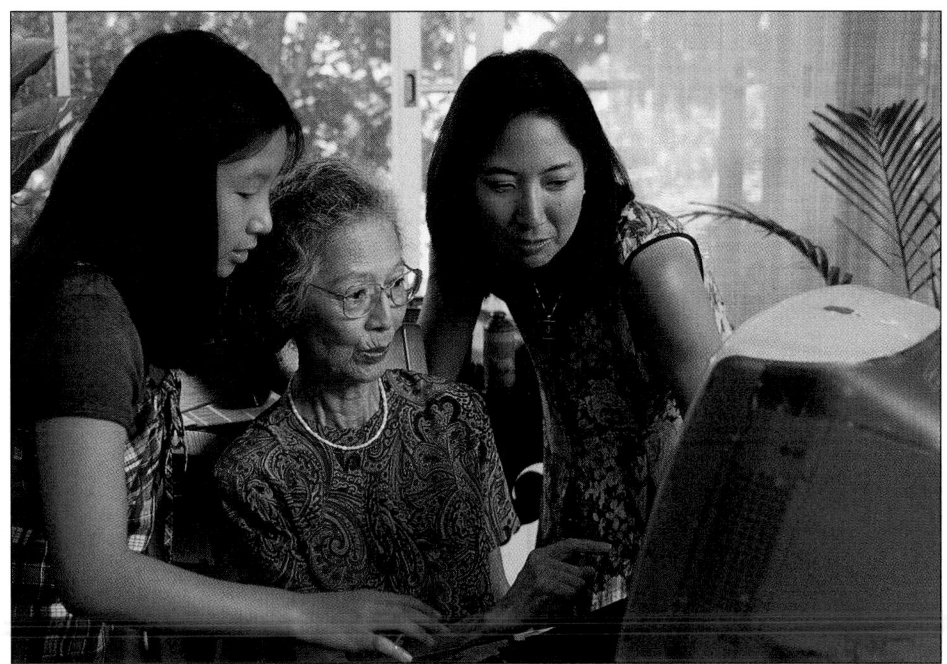

Young people are not the only ones becoming computer-literate these days. Many older people are joining the computer age and learning useful new skills. Research has found that older adults can expand their cognitive performance with training and practice.

control group, and this self-taught group maintained their gains better after one month (Blackburn, Papalia-Finlay, Foye, & Serlin, 1988). Apparently the opportunity to work out their own solutions fostered more lasting learning.

In training connected with the Seattle Longitudinal Study (Schaie, 1990, 1994, 1996b; Schaie & Willis, 1986; Willis & Schaie, 1986b), older people who already had shown declines in intelligence gained significantly in two fluid abilities: spatial orientation and, especially, inductive reasoning. In fact, about 4 out of 10 participants regained levels of proficiency they had shown 14 years earlier. Gains measured in the laboratory showed substantial correlations with objective measures of everyday functioning (Schaie, 1994; Willis, Jay, Diehl, & Marsiske, 1992).

In both the ADEPT and Seattle studies, trained participants retained an edge over an untrained control group, even after seven years (Schaie, 1994, 1996a, 1996b). Longitudinal findings suggest that training may enable older adults not only to recover lost competence but even to surpass their previous attainments (Schaie & Willis, 1996). (In the next section, we discuss results of memory training.)

Cognitive deterioration, then, often may be related to disuse (Schaie, 1994, 1996b). Much as many aging athletes can call on physical reserves, older people who get training, practice, and social support seem to be able to draw on mental reserves. Adults may be able to maintain or expand this reserve capacity and avoid cognitive decline by engaging in a lifelong program of mental exercise (Dixon & Baltes, 1986).

CHECKPOINT

Can you . . .

- ✔ Summarize findings of the Seattle Longitudinal Study with regard to cognitive changes in old age?
- ✔ Compare how older adults deal with instrumental and social problems?
- ✔ Cite evidence for the plasticity of cognitive abilities in late adulthood?

Memory: How Does It Change?

Failing memory is often considered a sign of aging. The man who always kept his schedule in his head now has to write it in a calendar; the woman who takes several medicines now measures out each day's dosages and puts them where she is sure to see them. Yet in memory, as in other cognitive abilities, older people's functioning varies greatly. To understand why, we need to look more closely at how memory works, as described in Chapter 9 and elsewhere in this text.*

*This discussion is largely indebted to Smith and Earles, 1996.

Short-Term Memory

Researchers assess short-term memory by asking a person to repeat a sequence of numbers, either in the order in which they were presented (*digit span forward*) or in reverse order (*digit span backward*). Digit span forward ability holds up well with advancing age (Craik & Jennings, 1992; Poon, 1985; Wingfield & Stine, 1989), but digit span backward performance does not (Craik & Jennings, 1992; Lovelace, 1990). Why? A widely accepted explanation is that immediate forward repetition requires only *sensory memory,* which retains efficiency throughout life, whereas backward repetition requires the manipulation of information in *working memory,* which gradually shrinks in capacity after about age 45 (Swanson, 1999).

A key factor is the complexity of the task (Kausler, 1990; Wingfield & Stine, 1989). As we have just seen, tasks that require only *rehearsal,* or repetition, show very little decline. Tasks that require *reorganization* or *elaboration* show greater falloff (Craik & Jennings, 1992). If you are asked to verbally rearrange a series of items (such as "Band-Aid, elephant, newspaper") in order of increasing size ("Band-Aid, newspaper, elephant"), you must call to mind your previous knowledge of Band-Aids, newspapers, and elephants (Cherry & Park, 1993). More mental effort is needed to keep this additional information in mind, using more of the limited capacity of working memory.

Long-Term Memory

Researchers divide long-term memory into three main components: *episodic memory, semantic memory,* and *procedural memory.*

Do you remember what you had for breakfast this morning? Did you lock your car when you parked it? Such information is stored in *episodic memory* (see Chapter 7), the component of long-term memory most likely to deteriorate with age. The ability to recall newly encountered information, especially, seems to drop off (Poon, 1985; A. D. Smith & Earles, 1996).

Because episodic memory is linked to specific events, you retrieve an item from this mental "diary" by reconstructing the original experience in your mind. Older adults are less able to do this, perhaps because they focus less on context (where something happened, who was there) and so have fewer connections to jog their memory (Kausler, 1990; Lovelace, 1990). Also, older people have had many similar experiences that tend to run together. When older people perceive an event as distinctive, they can remember it as well as younger ones (Camp, 1989; Cavanaugh, Kramer, Sinnott, Camp, & Markley, 1985; Kausler, 1990).

semantic memory
Long-term memory of general factual knowledge, social customs, and language.

Semantic memory is like a mental encyclopedia; it holds stored knowledge of historical facts, geographic locations, social customs, meanings of words, and the like. Semantic memory does not depend on remembering when and where something was learned, and it shows little decline with age (Camp, 1989; Horn, 1982b; Lachman & Lachman, 1980). In fact, vocabulary and knowledge of rules of language may even increase (Camp, 1989; Horn, 1982b). On a test that calls for definitions of words, older adults often do better than younger ones, but they have more trouble coming up with a word when given its meaning (A. D. Smith & Earles, 1996). Such "tip-of-the-tongue" experiences may relate to problems in working memory (Heller & Dobbs, 1993; Light, 1990; Schonfield, 1974; Schonfield & Robertson, 1960, cited in Horn, 1982b).

procedural memory
Long-term memory of motor skills, habits, and ways of doing things, which often can be recalled without conscious effort; sometimes called *implicit memory.*

priming
Increase in ease of doing a task or remembering information as a result of a previous encounter with the task or information.

Remembering how to ride a bicycle is an example of the third component of long-term memory: **procedural memory,** sometimes called *implicit memory* (Squire, 1992, 1994; see Chapter 7). This includes motor skills, habits, and ways of doing things that often can be recalled without conscious effort. A special use of unconscious memory that holds up with age is **priming,** which makes it easier to solve a puzzle, answer a question, or do a task that a person has previously encountered (A. D. Smith & Earles, 1996). Much as priming a surface prepares it for paint, perceptual priming prepares you to answer a test question you have seen in a list for review, or to do a math problem involving the same process as one you did in class. Priming explains why older adults are about as likely as younger ones to recall a familiar word association (for example, *dragon* and *fire*) but not an unfamiliar one (*dragon* and *fudge*).

Why Do Some Aspects of Memory Decline?

What explains older adults' losses, especially in working memory and episodic memory? Investigators have offered several hypotheses. One approach focuses on problems with the three steps required to process information in memory: *encoding, storage,* and *retrieval* (refer back to Chapter 9). Another approach focuses on the biological structures that make memory work.

Problems in Encoding, Storage, and Retrieval In general, older adults seem less efficient and precise than younger ones in *encoding* new information to make it easier to remember—for example, by arranging material alphabetically or creating mental associations (Craik & Byrd, 1982). Most studies have found that older and younger adults are about equally knowledgeable as to effective encoding strategies (Salthouse, 1991). Yet in laboratory experiments, older adults are less likely to *use* such strategies unless trained—or at least prompted or reminded—to do so (Craik & Jennings, 1992; Salthouse, 1991).

However, when younger and older adults were briefly instructed in an effective memory strategy (visual imagery) for recalling associated word pairs (such as *king* and *crown*), age differences in frequency of use of the strategy were fairly small and did not adequately account for age differences in recall. This finding suggests that older adults may use the same strategy less effectively than younger adults (Dunlosky & Hertzog, 1998).

Another hypothesis is that material in *storage* may deteriorate to the point where retrieval becomes difficult or impossible. Some research suggests that a small increase in "storage failure" may occur with age (Camp & McKitrick, 1989; Giambra & Arenberg, 1993). However, traces of decayed memories are likely to remain, and it may be possible to reconstruct them, or at least to relearn the material speedily (Camp & McKitrick, 1989; Chafetz, 1992).

Older adults have more trouble with recall than younger adults but do about as well with recognition, since recall puts greater demands on the *retrieval* system (Hultsch, 1971; Lovelace, 1990). Even then, it takes older people longer than younger ones to search their memories (Lovelace, 1990). Recall of details of a recent event can be enhanced by seeing photographs or reading descriptions of it (Koutstaal, Schacter, Johnson, Angell, & Gross, 1998). Individual differences in recall may reflect changes in other cognitive abilities. In a 16-year longitudinal study of 82 adults ages 55 to 81, vocabulary losses were linked with declines in the ability to recall a list of words, whereas deterioration of reasoning ability predicted declines in recall of textual passages (Zelinksi & Stewart, 1998).

Of course, we must keep in mind that most research on encoding, storage, and retrieval has been done in the laboratory. Those functions may operate somewhat differently in the real world.

Neurological Change Biological hypotheses point to neurological change: the more the brain deteriorates physically, the more loss of memory will take place. The decline in processing speed described earlier seems to be a fundamental contributor to age-related memory loss (Luszcz & Bryan, 1999). It is associated with most aspects of memory decline, including changes in the capacity of working memory. In a number of studies, controlling for perceptual speed eliminated virtually the entire age-related drop in performance (A. D. Smith & Earles, 1996).

The *hippocampus,* which seems critical to the ability to store new information in long-term memory (Squire, 1992), loses an estimated 20 percent of its nerve cells with advancing age (Ivy, MacLeod, Petit, & Markus, 1992) and is vulnerable to injury as blood pressure rises (Horn, 1982b). High levels of stress hormones in the bloodstream may shrink it and reduce its performance (Lupien et al., 1998; Sapolsky, 1992). Unconscious learning—apparently independent of the hippocampus—is less affected (Moscovitch & Winocur, 1992). So is recall of prior learning, which may improve as a result of the growing complexity of neural connections in the cortex (Squire, 1992).

Early decline in the *prefrontal cortex* may underlie such common memory problems of late adulthood as forgetting to keep appointments and thinking that imagined events actually happened (West, 1996). The latter tendency is attributed to a failure of *source monitoring* (awareness of where memories originated).

The likelihood that neurological deterioration underlies the weakening of certain abilities does *not* mean that nothing can be done. Older adults can improve source judgments by paying attention to factual, rather than emotional, aspects of a situation (who? what? when? where? how?) and by being more careful and critical in evaluating where a "memory" came from (Henkel, Johnson, & De Leonardis, 1998).

CHECKPOINT

Can you . . .

- ✔ Identify two aspects of memory that tend to decline with age, and give reasons for this decline?
- ✔ Explain how problems in encoding, storage, and retrieval may affect memory in late adulthood?
- ✔ Point out several neurological changes related to memory?

The brain often compensates for age-related declines in specialized regions by tapping other regions to help. In one study, researchers used positron-emission tomography (PET) to compare brain activity of college students with that of older adults during two memory tasks. When asked to remember sets of letters on a computer screen, the students used only the left hemisphere; when asked to remember the location of points on the screen, they used only the right hemisphere. The older adults, who did just as well as the students, used *both* the right and left frontal lobes for both tasks (Reuter-Lorenz, Stanczak, & Miller, 1999; Reuter-Lorenz et al., 2000). The brain's ability to compensate in this way may help explain why symptoms of Alzheimer's disease often do not appear until the disease is well advanced, and previously unaffected regions of the brain, which have taken over for impaired regions, also lose working capacity ("Alzheimer's Disease, Part I," 1998).

Metamemory: The View from Within

"I'm less efficient at remembering things now than I used to be."
"I have little control over my memory."
"I am just as good at remembering as I ever was."

When adults answer a questionnaire that asks them to agree or disagree with a list of statements like these, they are tapping *metamemory,* beliefs or knowledge about how memory works. These questions come from **Metamemory in Adulthood (MIA),** a questionnaire designed to measure metamemory in adults. The questions deal with several aspects of metamemory, including beliefs about one's own memory and selection and use of memory strategies.

Metamemory in Adulthood (MIA)
Questionnaire designed to measure various aspects of adults' metamemory, including beliefs about their own memory and selection and use of strategies for remembering.

Older adults taking the MIA report more perceived change in memory, less memory capacity, and less control over their memory than young adults do (Dixon, Hultsch, & Hertzog, 1988). However, these perceptions may, at least in part, reflect stereotyped expectations of memory loss in old age (Hertzog, Dixon, & Hultsch, 1990; Poon, 1985). When asked for a blanket assessment of their own memory, older adults are likely to claim that it has deteriorated; but when it comes to specific items or tasks, older adults are about as accurate as younger adults in judging their "feeling of knowing" or estimating how well they have done (Hertzog & Dixon, 1994; Hertzog, Saylor, Fleece, & Dixon, 1994; Salthouse, 1991).

This and other research suggests that older adults' complaints about their memory are unrelated to their objective performance. However, this conclusion does not consider individual differences. An older person who once had an outstanding memory may well be aware of a loss not detectable by comparison with the norm. A study that did take account of this factor found a modest link between memory complaints and objective performance (Levy-Cushman & Abeles, 1998).

Improving Memory in Older Adults

Some investigators have offered training programs in *mnemonics*: techniques designed to help people remember (refer back to Chapter 9), such as visualizing a list of items, making associations between a face and a name, or transforming the elements in a story into mental images. Programs also may include training in attention and relaxation, as well as information about memory and aging, including effects of mood on memory (Levy-Cushman & Abeles, 1998). An analysis of thirty-three studies found that older people do benefit from memory training. The particular kind of mnemonic made little difference (Verhaeghen, Marcoen, & Goossens, 1992). Other studies have reported specific gains in remembering names, in episodic memory, in memory span, and in perceptual speed (Schaie & Willis, 1996).

There is, then, considerable plasticity of memory performance for older people, but it may diminish with advancing age. Some research found that long-term effects of memory training for older adults are minimal (Anschutz, Camp, Markley, & Kramer, 1987). However, other studies suggest that such training can be transferred to everyday tasks and can be maintained (Levy-Cushman & Abeles, 1998; Lewinsohn, Antonuccio, Breckenridge, & Teri, 1984; Neeley & Bäckman, 1993, 1995).

An experiment with mice has raised hopes that genetic manipulation may eventually be able to counteract memory loss. The gene involved controls a unit of a neural signal receptor that normally becomes less active with age. A strain of mice bred with extra copies of this gene performed better than normal mice on a series of memory tests (Tang et al., 1999).

CHECKPOINT

Can you . . .

✔ Discuss how well older adults judge their memory capacities, and cite ways in which their memory can be improved?

Wisdom

With the graying of the planet, wisdom has become an important topic of psychological research. Erikson (as we'll see in Chapter 18) viewed wisdom as an aspect of late-life personality development. Other investigators define wisdom as an extension of postformal thought, a synthesis of reason and emotion. Another approach, rooted in eastern philosophy, focuses on the spiritual domain.

Robert Sternberg classifies wisdom as a *cognitive* ability that can be studied and tested. According to Sternberg (1998), wisdom is a special form of practical intelligence. It draws on *tacit knowledge* (refer back to Chapter 13)—generally based on experience or on observing role models—and is aimed at achieving a common good through the balancing of multiple, often conflicting interests. Unlike other forms of intelligence, which can be used for any purpose, wisdom involves value judgments about what ends are good and how best to reach them. An example might be John Glenn's decision to return to space, which balanced the potential benefits to medical science and his own sense of fulfillment against the bodily danger and his family's anxiety.

The most extensive research on wisdom has been done by Baltes and his colleagues. In Baltes's dual-process model, wisdom is an aspect of the pragmatics of intelligence. It is expert knowledge of the *fundamental pragmatics of life,* "permitting excellent judgment and advice about important and uncertain matters" (Baltes, 1993, p. 586). These "fundamental pragmatics" consist of knowledge and skills having to do with the conduct, interpretation, and meaning of life. Although wisdom is related to crystallized intelligence, creativity, a judicious style of thinking, and such personality dimensions as openness to experience and interest in psychological needs and motives, research suggests that it is a separate, unique quality (Staudinger, Lopez, & Baltes, 1997).

Wisdom may be fairly rare. Favorable conditions for its growth, according to Baltes, include general mental ability, education or training, practice in using the requisite skills, guidance from mentors, leadership experience, and professional specialization.

Consider this . . .

- Do your observations of older adults' cognitive functioning agree with the results of the Seattle Longitudinal Study and the memory research reported in this chapter? In what ways? Can you account for any differences?
- Given the importance of sustaining a high level of intellectual activity, what are some good ways to do this? Do you think you need to develop new or broader interests that you will want to pursue as you age?
- Think of the wisest person you know. Do the criteria that either Sternberg or Baltes and his colleagues established for wisdom seem to describe this person? If not, how would you define and measure wisdom?

To test the relationship between age and wisdom, Baltes and his associates asked adults of various ages and occupations to think aloud about hypothetical dilemmas. Responses were rated according to criteria drawn up by the researchers. The basic criteria were expert factual and procedural knowledge about the human condition and about strategies for life planning, life management, and solving life problems. Other criteria included awareness that life is unpredictable, that circumstances vary greatly, and that people differ in values, goals, and priorities, so that no one solution is best for everyone.

In one study (J. Smith & Baltes, 1990), 60 well-educated German professionals ages 25 to 81 were given four dilemmas involving such issues as weighing career against family needs and deciding whether to accept early retirement. Of 240 solutions, only 5 percent were rated wise, and these responses were distributed nearly evenly among young, middle-aged, and older adults. Participants showed more wisdom about decisions applicable to their own stage of life. For example, the oldest group gave its best answers to the problem of a 60-year-old widow who, having just started her own business, learns that her son has been left with two young children and wants her to help care for them.

Do certain kinds of life experience lend themselves to the development of wisdom? Researchers assembled 14 middle-aged and older adults (average age, 67) who had been identified by others as wise. When presented with two dilemmas—the one about the 60-year-old widow and another about a phone call from a friend who intends to commit suicide—these "wisdom nominees" equaled the performance of elderly clinical psychologists (the best performers in the previous study), who were trained to deal with the kinds of problems presented. Both of these groups gave wiser answers than control groups of older and younger adults with similar education and professional standing (Baltes, Staudinger, Maercker, & Smith, 1995).

Wisdom has an interactive aspect. In one experiment, both younger and older adults gave wiser responses to hypothetical dilemmas when told to think about what someone whose opinion they valued would say. When given extra time to think about a problem after discussing it with a spouse, domestic partner, relative, or friend, older adults gave wiser answers than younger ones (Staudinger & Baltes, 1996).

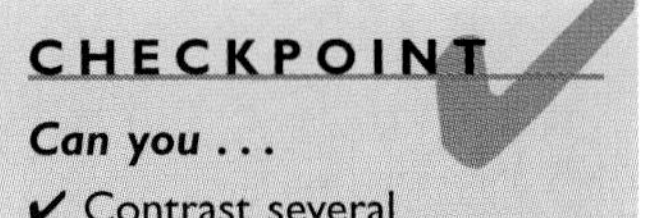
CHECKPOINT

Can you . . .

✔ Contrast several approaches to the study of wisdom?

✔ Summarize findings from Baltes's studies of wisdom?

Perhaps the most significant contribution of this line of research to the study of wisdom is the attempt to measure it systematically and scientifically. The key finding is that wisdom, though not exclusively the province of old age, is one area in which older people, especially those who have had certain kinds of experiences, can hold their own or better.

Lifelong Learning

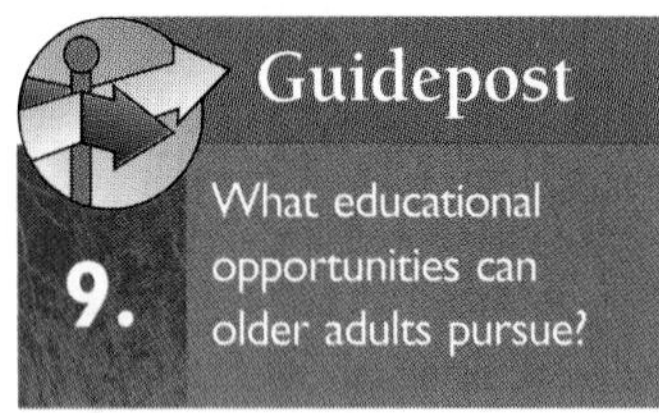
Guidepost
9.
What educational opportunities can older adults pursue?

lifelong learning
Organized, sustained study by adults of all ages.

Qian Likun, a star student who walks to his classes on health care and ancient Chinese poetry, took part in a 2.3-mile foot race. This might not seem unusual until you learn that Qian is 102 years old, one of thousands of students in China's network of "universities for the aged." More than 800 of these schools have been founded since the 1980s, showing China's commitment to its elderly population and demonstrating older people's willingness and ability to learn (Kristof, 1990). China's program exemplifies a trend toward **lifelong learning:** organized, sustained study by adults of all ages.

In today's complex society, the need for education is never over. Continuing mental activity helps keep performance high, whether this activity involves reading, conversation, crossword puzzles, bridge, or chess, or going back to school, as more and more older adults are doing.

Older people learn best when the materials and methods take into account physiological, psychological, and cognitive changes they may be experiencing. They do best when material is presented slowly over a fairly long period of time with intervals in between, rather than in concentrated doses.

Ruth Michael of Weslaco, Texas, graduated from college with honors at the age of 83, and now, as a volunteer, administers psychology tests to hospitalized patients. Educational opportunities for older adults have greatly expanded, enabling many older people to obtain the education they couldn't afford or didn't have time for earlier in life.

Educational programs specifically designed for mature adults are booming in many parts of the world. In one category are free or low-cost classes, taught by professionals or volunteers, at neighborhood senior centers, community centers, religious institutions, or storefronts. These classes generally have a practical or social focus (Moskow-McKenzie & Manheimer, 1994). In Japan, for example, *kominkans* (community educational centers) offer classes in child care, health, traditional arts and crafts, hobbies, exercise, and sports (Nojima, 1994). A second category consists of college- and university-based programs with education as the primary goal (Moskow-McKenzie & Manheimer, 1994). Elderhostel is an international network of 1,800 colleges and other educational institutions in forty-seven countries, which offers college-level, non-credit, week-long residential courses for adults age 55 and over and their spouses.

In the United States, today's older adults are better educated than their predecessors, and this trend will continue as younger cohorts age (AARP, 1999; Treas, 1995). Continuing education courses for older people have mushroomed since the mid-1970s (Moskow-McKenzie & Manheimer, 1994). Many regional community colleges and state universities, as well as a few private universities, offer special programs for the elderly. Some vocational programs give special attention to the needs of older women who have never worked for pay but now must do so. One of the most popular offerings is computer training.

Why do so many older adults want to learn to use computers? Some are just curious. Some need to acquire new job skills or update old ones. Some want to keep up with the latest technology: to talk with children and grandchildren who are computer-literate, to send and receive e-mail, or to explore the Internet.

CHECKPOINT

Can you . . .

✔ Identify conditions conducive to older adults' learning?

✔ Differentiate between two types of educational programs for older adults?

The trend toward continuing education in late life illustrates how each stage of life could be made more satisfying by restructuring the course of life (refer back to Chapter 15). Today, young adults usually plunge into education and careers, middle-aged people use most of their energy earning money, and some older people who have retired from work cast about for ways to fill time. If people wove work, leisure, and study into their lives in a more balanced way at all ages, young adults would feel less pressure to establish themselves early, middle-aged people would feel less burdened, and older people would be more stimulated and would feel—and be—more useful. Such a pattern might make an important contribution to emotional well-being in old age, as we discuss in Chapter 18.

Summary

Old Age Today

Guidepost 1. What is ageism, and what harm can it do?

- Attitudes toward older adults in the United States tend to reflect **ageism.** Stereotypes about aging perpetuate widespread misconceptions about older adults' physical, cognitive, and personality characteristics and affect the way they are treated.
- Efforts to combat ageism are making headway, thanks to the visibility of a growing number of active, healthy older adults.

Guidepost 2. How is today's older population changing?

- The proportion of older people in the United States and world populations is greater than ever before and is expected to continue to grow, straining social services. People over 85 are the fastest-growing age group.

- Today, many older people are healthy, vigorous, and active. Although effects of **primary aging** may be beyond people's control, they often can avoid effects of **secondary aging.**
- Specialists in **gerontology** and **geriatrics** sometimes refer to people between ages 65 and 74 as the *young old,* those over 75 as the *old old,* and those over 85 as the *oldest old.* However, these terms may be more useful when used to refer to **functional age.**

PHYSICAL DEVELOPMENT

Longevity and Aging

Guidepost 3. Why has life expectancy increased, and how does it vary?

- **Life expectancy** has increased dramatically since 1900. White people tend to have greater **longevity** than black people, and women longer than men; thus older women outnumber older men 3 to 2.
- Mortality rates have declined. Heart disease, cancer, and stroke are the three leading causes of death for people over age 65.

Guidepost 4. What theories have been advanced for causes of aging, and what does research suggest about the possibilities for extending the life span?

- **Senescence,** the period of the life span marked by physical changes associated with aging, begins at different ages for different people.
- Theories of biological aging fall into two categories: **genetic-programming theories,** suggested by the **Hayflick limit,** and **variable-rate theories,** or error theories, such as those that point to effects of **free radicals** and **autoimmunity.**
- **Survival curves** support the idea of a definite limit to the human life span, but research on extension of the life span through genetic manipulation or caloric restriction has challenged that idea.

Physical Changes

Guidepost 5. What physical changes occur during old age, and how do these changes vary among individuals?

- Changes in body systems and organs with age are highly variable and may be results of disease, which in turn is affected by lifestyle.
- Common physical changes include some loss of skin coloring, texture, and elasticity; thinning and whitening of hair; shrinkage of body size; thinning of bones; and a tendency to sleep less. Most body systems generally continue to function fairly well, but the heart becomes more susceptible to disease. **Reserve capacity** of the heart and other organs declines.
- Although the brain changes with age, the changes vary considerably and are usually modest. They include loss or shrinkage of nerve cells and a general slowing of responses. However, the brain also seems able to grow new neurons and build new connections late in life.
- Visual and hearing problems may interfere with daily life but often can be corrected. Common visual disorders include **cataracts** and **age-related macular degeneration.** Losses in taste and smell may lead to poor nutrition. Training can improve muscular strength, balance, and reaction time.
- Many older people are sexually active, though the frequency and intensity of sexual experience are generally lower than for younger adults.

Physical and Mental Health

Guidepost 6. What health problems are common in late adulthood, and what factors influence health at that time?

- Most older people are reasonably healthy, especially if they follow a healthy lifestyle. Most older people have chronic conditions, most commonly **arthritis,** but these usually do not greatly limit activities or interfere with daily life.
- Exercise and diet are important influences on health. Loss of teeth due to **periodontitis** can seriously affect nutrition.

Guidepost 7. What mental and behavioral disorders do some older people experience?

- Most older people are in good mental health. Depression, alcoholism, and many other conditions, including some forms of **dementia,** can be reversed with proper treatment; others, such as those brought on by **Alzheimer's disease, Parkinson's disease,** or **multi-infarct dementia,** are irreversible.
- Alzheimer's disease becomes more prevalent with age. It is characterized by the presence of **neurofibrillary tangles** and **amyloid plaque** in the brain. Its causes have not been definitively established, but research points to genetic factors. Behavioral and drug therapies can slow deterioration.
- **Major depressive disorder** tends to be underdiagnosed in older adults.

COGNITIVE DEVELOPMENT

Aspects of Cognitive Development

Guidepost 8. What gains and losses in cognitive abilities tend to occur in late adulthood, and are there ways to improve older people's cognitive performance?

- Physical and psychological factors that influence older people's performance on intelligence tests may lead to underestimation of intelligence. Cross-sectional research showing declines on the **Wechsler Adult Intelligence Scale (WAIS)** may reflect cohort differences.
- Measures of fluid and crystallized intelligence show a more encouraging pattern, with crystallized abilities increasing into old age. Baltes proposes a **dual-process model:** the **mechanics of intelligence** often decline, but the **pragmatics of intelligence** may continue to grow.
- A general slowdown in central nervous system functioning may affect the speed of information processing. However, this slowdown may be limited to certain processing tasks and may vary among individuals.

- The Seattle Longitudinal Study found that cognitive functioning in late adulthood is highly variable. Few people decline in all or most areas, and many people improve in some. The **engagement hypothesis** may help explain these differences.
- Although ability to perform **instrumental activities of daily living (IADLs)** generally declines with age, ability to solve interpersonal or emotionally charged problems does not.
- Older people show considerable plasticity in cognitive performance and can benefit from training.
- Some aspects of memory, such as sensory memory, **semantic memory, procedural memory,** and **priming** appear nearly as efficient in older adults as in younger people. Other aspects, mainly the capacity of working memory and the ability to recall specific events or recently learned information, are often less efficient.
- Neurological changes, as well as declines in perceptual speed, may account for much of the decline in memory functioning in older adults. However, the brain can compensate for some age-related declines.
- According to studies using **Metamory in Adulthood (MIA),** some older adults may overestimate their memory loss, perhaps because of stereotypes about aging.
- Older adults can benefit from memory training.
- According to Baltes's studies, older adults show as much or more wisdom than younger adults. People of all ages give wiser responses to problems affecting their own age group.

Guidepost 9. What educational opportunities can older adults pursue?

- **Lifelong learning** can keep older people mentally alert. Older adults learn better when material and methods are geared to the needs of this age group.
- Educational programs for older adults are proliferating. Most of these programs have either a practical-social focus or a more serious educational one.

Key Terms

ageism (635)
primary aging (638)
secondary aging (639)
functional age (639)
life expectancy (639)
longevity (639)
gerontology (640)
geriatrics (640)
senescence (642)
genetic-programming theories (642)
Hayflick limit (643)
variable-rate theories (643)
free radicals (644)
autoimmunity (645)
survival curves (645)
reserve capacity (648)
cataracts (649)
age-related macular degeneration (649)
arthritis (653)
periodontitis (655)
dementia (655)
Alzheimer's disease (655)
Parkinson's disease (655)
multi-infarct dementia (655)
neurofibrillary tangles (657)
amyloid plaque (657)
major depressive disorder (659)
Wechsler Adult Intelligence Scale (WAIS) (660)
dual-process model (661)
mechanics of intelligence (661)
pragmatics of intelligence (661)
selective optimization with compensation (661)
engagement hypothesis (663)
instrumental activities of daily living (IADLs) (664)
semantic memory (666)
procedural memory (666)
priming (666)
Metamemory in Adulthood (MIA) (668)
lifelong learning (670)

Chapter 18

Psychosocial Development in Late Adulthood

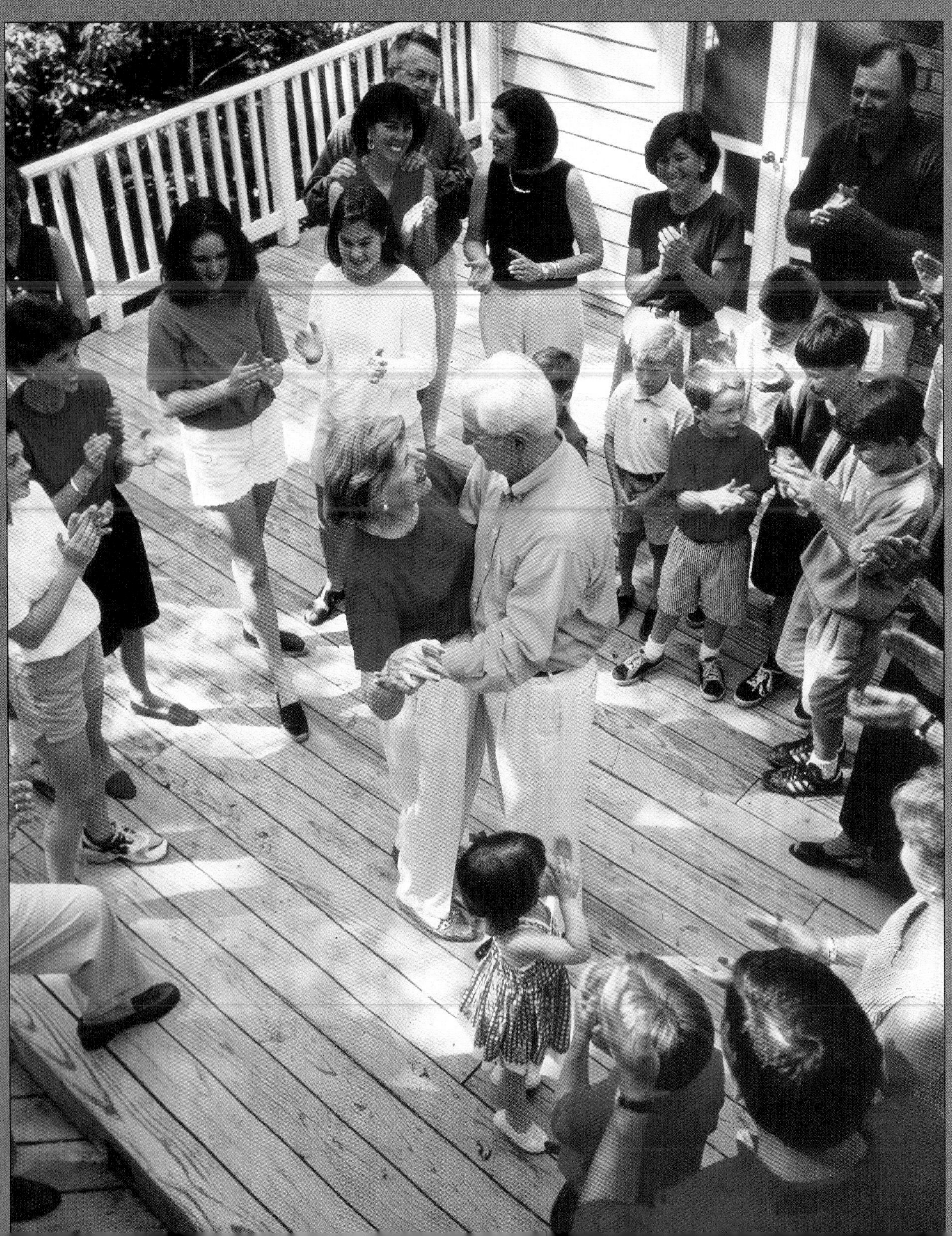

There is still today

And tomorrow fresh with dreams:

Life never grows old

Rita Duskin, "Haiku," *Sound and Light,* 1987

OUTLINE

Jimmy Carter

Focus: Jimmy Carter, "Retired" President

James Earl ("Jimmy") Carter, Jr. (b. 1924)* was one of the most unpopular presidents of the United States in the twentieth century. Yet two decades after having been turned out of office, he is one of the most active and admired ex-presidents in American history, "pursuing lost and neglected causes with a missionary's zeal"—and amazing success (Nelson, 1994).

In 1976, in the wake of the Watergate scandal, Carter, a peanut farmer who had completed a term as governor of Georgia, became the first southerner in the twentieth century to be elected president. His appeal was as an outsider who would clean up government and restore a moral tone. But despite such historic achievements as peace between Israel and Egypt, he became bogged down in the interminable Iranian hostage crisis and was blamed for high fuel prices and a sagging economy. After a devastating defeat in 1980, he retired from political life at the age of 56.

Carter and his wife and longtime helpmate, Rosalynn, faced a devastating crisis. His farm and warehouse business were deeply in debt, and he had no immediate prospects for work. "We thought the best of our life was over," he recalls. "And we went through a very difficult time with each other" (Beyette, 1998, p. 6A). Finally, determined to take charge of the remaining part of their lives, they took stock of their situation. They asked themselves what experiences they could build on for the future, what interests they had had too little time to pursue, and what talents they had not been able to fully develop.

*Sources of biographical information on Jimmy Carter were Beyette (1998), Bird (1990), Carter (1975, 1998), Carter Center (1995), J. Nelson (1994), Spalding (1977), Wooten (1995), and various news articles.

What has Carter, now in his late seventies, done since then? He is a professor at Emory University and teaches Sunday school at a Baptist church. He helps build and renovate houses for low-income families through the nonprofit Habitat for Humanity. He established the Carter Center, which sponsors international programs in human rights, education, preventive health care, agricultural techniques, and conflict resolution and has secured the release of hundreds of political prisoners.

As a roving peacemaker and guardian of freedom, Carter oversaw the Nicaraguan elections that ousted the Sandanistas. He brokered a cease-fire between Bosnian Muslims and Serbs. He pressed China to release prisoners taken during the 1989 protest in Tiananmen Square. He has been nominated several times for the Nobel Peace Prize.

It has been said that Carter "used his presidency as a stepping stone to higher things" (Bird, 1990, p. 564). Freed from the pressures of politics, he has risen to the role of elder statesman.

Carter has written fourteen books, most recently *The Virtues of Aging*. In it, he talks about how he and Rosalynn have learned to "give each other some space"; how becoming grandparents deepened their relationship; how the active lives of close friends and acquaintances have served as examples and inspiration; how he handled the loss of his mother, brother, and two sisters; and how his religious faith helps him face the prospect of his own death without fear.

What does Carter see as the virtues of aging? "We have an unprecedented degree of freedom to choose what we want to do. . . . We have a chance to heal wounds. . . . We have an opportunity to expand the ties of understanding with the people we love most." And there are still new worlds to conquer. "Our primary purpose" says Carter, "is not just to stay alive. . . , but to savor every opportunity for pleasure, excitement, adventure and fulfillment" (Beyette, 1998, pp. 6A–7A).

Although few adults have the resources and opportunities of an ex-president, Jimmy Carter is far from unique in using his retirement years productively. He is one of many older adults whose activism is creating a new view of life in old age.

In the early 1980s, shortly after Carter left office, the writer Betty Friedan was asked to organize a seminar at Harvard University on "Growth in Aging." The distinguished behaviorist B. F. Skinner declined to participate. Age and growth, he said, were "a contradiction in terms" (Friedan, 1993, p. 23). Skinner was far from alone in that belief. Yet, less than two decades later, late adulthood is increasingly recognized as a time of potential growth.

Today, such terms as *successful aging* and *optimal aging* appear frequently in the theoretical and research literature. These terms are controversial because they seem to imply that there is a "right" or "best" way to age. Still, some older adults do seem to get more out of life than others. Older people can adapt to the challenge of aging if they are flexible and realistic—if they can conserve their strength, adjust to change and loss, and use time wisely. "Growth in aging" *is* possible; and many older adults, who feel healthy, competent, and in control of their lives, experience this last stage of life as a positive one.

In this chapter, we look at theory and research on psychosocial development in late adulthood. We discuss such late-life options as work, retirement, and living arrangements, and their impact on society's ability to support an aging population and to care for the frail and infirm. Finally, we look at relationships with families and friends, which greatly affect the quality of these last years.

After you have read and studied this chapter, you should be able to answer the following questions:

Guideposts *for* **Study**

1. What happens to personality in old age?
2. What special issues or tasks do older people need to deal with?
3. How do older adults cope?
4. Is there such a thing as successful aging? If so, how can it be defined and measured?
5. What are some issues regarding work and retirement in late life, and how do older adults handle time and money?
6. What options for living arrangements do older adults have?
7. How do personal relationships change in old age, and what is their effect on well-being?
8. What are the characteristics of long-term marriages in late life, and what impact do divorce and remarriage have at this time?
9. How do unmarried older people and those in gay and lesbian relationships fare?
10. How does friendship change in old age?
11. How do older adults get along with—or without—grown children and with siblings, and how do they adjust to great-grandparenthood?

Theory and Research on Psychosocial Development

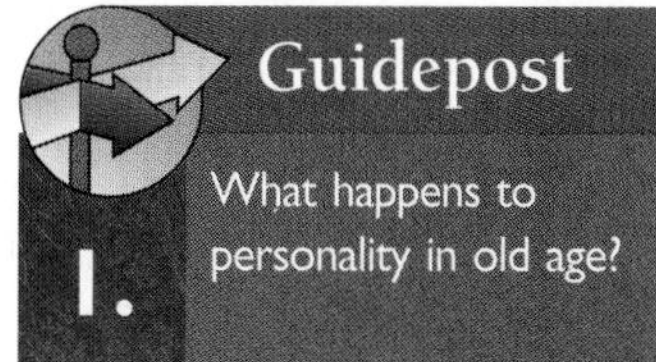
Guidepost
1.
What happens to personality in old age?

How much does personality change in late life? Not much, according to some research. Still, the experience of people like Jimmy Carter leads some theorists to view late adulthood as a developmental stage with its own special issues and tasks. Many older people reexamine their lives, complete unfinished business, and decide how best to channel their energies and spend their remaining days, months, or years. Acutely aware of the passage of time, some wish to leave a legacy to their children or to the world, pass on the fruits of their experience, and validate the meaning of their lives. Others simply want to take this last chance to enjoy favorite pastimes or to do things they never had enough time for when they were younger.

Let's see what theory and research on psychosocial development can tell us about this final phase of the lifespan, about ways older people cope with stress and loss, and what constitutes "successful," or "optimal" aging.

Stability of Personality Traits

Although some research has found late-life change in certain of the "Big Five" personality dimensions, such as increases in agreeableness and decreases in extraversion (D. Field & Millsap, 1991), Costa and McCrae's (1994a, 1994b, 1996) work has made an impressive case for the essential stability of personality traits (refer back to Chapter 14). Hostile people are unlikely to mellow much with age, unless they get psychotherapeutic treatment; and optimistic people are likely to remain their hopeful selves. Certain persistent trait patterns contribute to adaptation to aging and may even predict health and longevity (Baltes, Lindenberger, & Staudinger, 1998; see Box 18-1).

A common but mistaken belief is that older adults tend to become withdrawn or depressed. Actually, depression (unless associated with dementia) is strongly

Box 18-1
Does Personality Predict Health and Longevity?

In the Terman study of gifted children, childhood personality characteristics and family environment played an important part in adult success. Now it appears that such factors may influence how long people live.

Most of the approximately 1,500 California schoolchildren chosen for the study at about age 11 on the basis of high IQ have been followed periodically since 1921. Between 1986 and 1991, when the survivors were approaching age 80, a group of researchers (Friedman et al., 1993; Friedman, Tucker, Schwartz, Martin, et al., 1995; Friedman, Tucker, Schwartz, Tomlinson-Keasey, et al., 1995; Tucker & Friedman, 1996) decided to find out how many had died and at what ages, so as to spot predictors of longevity. Since the "Termites" as a group were bright and well educated, the results were not likely to be confounded by poor nutrition, poverty, or inadequate medical care.

Surprisingly, neither childhood self-confidence, energy, nor sociability turned out to be related to longevity. Nor was optimism or a sense of humor in childhood associated with long life. In fact, the reverse was true: cheerful children were more likely to die young. What *did* strongly predict longevity was the personality dimension called *conscientiousness*, or dependability—sometimes described as orderliness, prudence, or self-control.

What might explain these findings?

One possibility is that while a carefree, optimistic approach to life may be helpful in coping with short-term situations, such as recovery from illness, in the long run it may be unhealthy if it leads a person to ignore warnings and engage in risky behaviors. Just as optimistic people may be inclined to be risk takers, conscientious people may be less so. They may be less likely to smoke, to drink, to be injured, and to overeat and become obese. Conscientious people may be more likely to cultivate good health habits, follow sound advice, and cooperate with doctors. They may avoid stress by thinking ahead, steeling themselves for the worst that might happen, staying out of situations they can't handle, and preparing for contingencies—for example, by carrying extra car keys and plenty of insurance. Then too, their qualities may enable them to achieve career success and to have greater financial, informational, and social resources to deal with medical and other problems. They also may be more likely to have stable marriages and reliable, supportive friendship networks.

Conscientiousness (but not cheerfulness) was related to a variety of variables that have positive influences on longevity. By midlife, conscientious children tended to have finished more years of education than less conscientious children and were less likely to have shown mental problems. They also were less likely to have been divorced or to have experienced parental divorce in their childhood.

Apparently it is not marriage itself but marital *stability* that can lead to long life. "Termites" who, at age 40, were in their first marriages tended to live significantly longer than those who had been divorced, whether or not the latter had remarried. By contrast, "Termites" who had *never* married had only slightly increased risk of early death.

Marital instability in the childhood home also was a threat to longevity. People who, before the age of 21, had experienced the divorce of their parents—13 percent of the sample—lived, on average, four years less than those whose parents had stayed together. Early death of a parent, on the other hand, made little difference.

The findings about marital stability and personality are interrelated. Children rated as impulsive were more likely to grow into adults with unstable marital histories and were more likely to die young. Also, children of divorce were more likely to go through divorce themselves—explaining part of the influence of parental divorce on longevity.

It seems, then, that people who are dependable, trustworthy, and diligent both in taking good care of themselves and in preserving their marriages—and who are fortunate enough to have had parents who stayed married—may be rewarded with more years of life.

related to the "Big Five" personality dimension called *neuroticism*, an "enduring disposition" that is a far more powerful predictor of moods and mood disorders than such life circumstances as age, race, gender, income, education, and marital status (Costa & McCrae, 1996).

Another common belief is that personality becomes more rigid in old age. Early cross-sectional research seemed to support that view. However, McCrae and Costa (1994), in large longitudinal studies using a variety of samples and measures, have shown that this is *not* true for most people. Likewise, personality tests of 3,442 participants in the Seattle Longitudinal Study (refer back to Chapters 15 and 17) found only modest longitudinal declines in flexibility between ages 60 and 81 but much larger cohort differences (Schaie & Willis, 1991).

As a group, people in more recent cohorts seem to be more flexible (that is, less rigid) than previous cohorts. These findings suggest that "increases" in rigidity found in early cross-sectional studies may actually have been tied, not to age, but to the culturally influenced "baggage" of life experience that a particular generation carries throughout adulthood. If flexibility is becoming more characteristic of today's young adults, and if they carry that flexibility into late life, then future generations of older adults may be able to adapt more readily than their predecessors to the challenges of aging.

Normative Issues and Tasks

Whereas trait models emphasize the fundamental stability of the personality structure, other models, such as Baltes's life-span developmental approach, look at factors that may contribute to growth within that basic framework. According to normative-crisis theorists, growth depends on carrying out the psychological tasks of each stage of life in an emotionally healthy way.

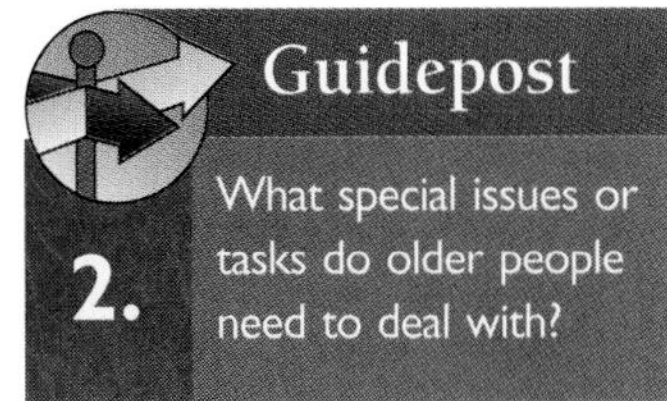

Guidepost
2.
What special issues or tasks do older people need to deal with?

Erik Erikson: Ego Integrity versus Despair

For Erikson, the crowning achievement of late adulthood is a sense of *ego integrity,* or integrity of the self, an achievement based on reflection about one's life. In the eighth and final crisis of the life span, **ego integrity versus despair,** older adults need to evaluate, sum up, and accept their lives so as to accept the approach of death. Building on the outcomes of the seven previous crises, they struggle to achieve a sense of coherence and wholeness, rather than give way to despair over their inability to relive the past differently (Erikson, Erikson, & Kivnick, 1986). People who succeed in this final, integrative task gain a sense of the order and meaning of their lives within the larger social order, past, present, and future. The "virtue" that may develop during this stage is *wisdom,* an "informed and detached concern with life itself in the face of death itself" (Erikson, 1985, p. 61).

ego integrity versus despair According to Erikson, the eighth and final critical alternative of psychosocial development, in which people in late adulthood either achieve a sense of integrity of the self by accepting the lives they have lived, and thus accept death, or yield to despair that their lives cannot be relived.

Wisdom, said Erikson, means accepting the life one has lived, without major regrets: without dwelling on "should-have-dones" or "might-have-beens." It involves accepting one's parents as people who did the best they could and thus deserve love, even though they were not perfect. It implies accepting one's death as the inevitable end of a life lived as well as one knew how to live it. In sum, it means accepting imperfection in the self, in parents, and in life. (This definition of *wisdom* as an important psychological resource differs from the largely cognitive definitions explored in Chapter 17.)

People who do not achieve acceptance are overwhelmed by despair, realizing that time is too short to seek other roads to ego integrity. Although integrity must outweigh despair if this crisis is to be resolved successfully, Erikson maintained that some despair is inevitable. People need to mourn—not only for their own misfortunes and lost chances but for the vulnerability and transience of the human condition.

Yet, Erikson believed, even as the body's functions weaken, people must maintain a "vital involvement" in society. On the basis of studies of life histories of people in their eighties, he concluded that ego integrity comes not just from reflecting on the past but, as with Jimmy Carter, from continued stimulation and challenge—whether through political activity, fitness programs,

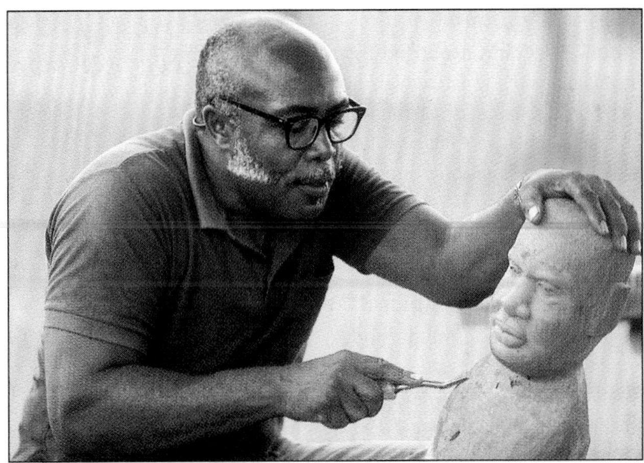

According to Erikson, ego integrity in late adulthood requires continuing stimulation and challenge, which, for this elderly sculptor, come from creative work. Sources of ego integrity vary widely, from political activity to fitness programs to building relationships with grandchildren.

creative work, or relationships with grandchildren (Erikson et al., 1986). Research inspired by Erikson's theory supports the importance men and women place on striving for ego integrity in late adulthood (Ryff, 1982; Ryff & Baltes, 1976; Ryff & Heincke, 1983).

George Vaillant: Factors in Emotional Health

In a follow-up to the Grant Study of Harvard men (Vaillant, 1993; Vaillant & Vaillant, 1990; refer back to Chapters 14 and 16), researchers examined 173 of the men at age 65 to identify personality attributes that make for healthy adaptation to aging. Probably the most significant factor in good emotional adjustment was the ability to use *mature adaptive mechanisms*—to handle problems without blame, bitterness, or passivity. The men who, over the years, had not collected injustices, complained, pretended nothing was wrong, or become embittered or prejudiced—and could thus respond appropriately to crises—were the best adjusted at age 65.

Surprisingly, a satisfying marriage, a successful career, and a childhood free of major problems (such as poverty or the death or divorce of parents) were unimportant in predicting good adjustment late in life. More influential was closeness to siblings at college age, suggesting a long-lasting source of emotional support. Factors predictive of poor adjustment at age 65 included major emotional problems in childhood and, before age 50, poor physical health, severe depression, alcoholism, and heavy use of tranquilizers.

While Erikson stressed growth through the achievement of ego integrity, Vaillant's work, like Costa and McCrae's, suggests that people adapt in late adulthood much as they have all along. Let's look more closely at how people do this.

CHECKPOINT

Can you . . .

- ✔ Summarize what is known about stability of personality in old age?
- ✔ Describe Erikson's crisis of ego integrity versus despair, and tell what Erikson meant by wisdom?
- ✔ Identify factors in healthy adaptation to aging, according to Vaillant's research?

Ways of Coping

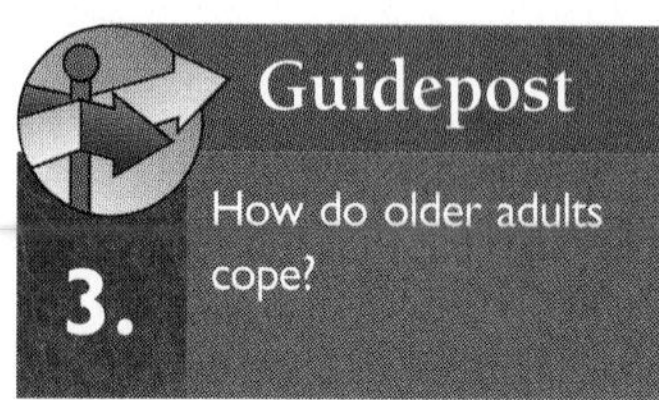
Guidepost
How do older adults cope?
3.

Their health may not be what it was, they've lost old friends and family members—often spouses—and they probably don't earn the money they once did. Their lives keep changing in countless stressful ways. Yet in general, older adults have fewer mental disorders and are more satisfied with life than younger ones (Mroczek & Kolarz, 1998; Wykle & Musil, 1993). What accounts for this remarkable ability to cope?

Coping is adaptive thinking or behavior aimed at reducing or relieving stress that arises from harmful, threatening, or challenging conditions. It is an important aspect of mental health, especially in old age. Let's examine a current approach to the study of coping: the cognitive-appraisal model. Then we'll look at a support system to which many older adults turn: religion.

coping Adaptive thinking or behavior aimed at reducing or relieving stress that arises from harmful, threatening, or challenging conditions.

cognitive-appraisal model Model of coping, proposed by Lazarus and Folkman, which holds that, on the basis of continuous appraisal of their relationship with the environment, people choose appropriate coping strategies to deal with situations that tax their normal resources.

problem-focused coping In the cognitive-appraisal model, coping strategy directed toward eliminating, managing, or improving a stressful situation. Compare *emotion-focused coping*.

Cognitive-Appraisal Model

In the **cognitive-appraisal model** (Lazarus & Folkman, 1984), people choose coping strategies on the basis of the way they perceive and analyze a situation. Coping occurs when a person perceives a situation as taxing or exceeding his or her resources and thus demanding unusual effort. Coping includes anything an individual thinks or does in trying to adapt to stress, regardless of how well it works. Because the situation is constantly changing, coping is a dynamic, evolving process; choosing the most appropriate strategy requires continuous reappraisal of the relationship between person and environment (see Figure 18-1).

Coping strategies may be either *problem-focused* or *emotion-focused*. **Problem-focused coping** aims at eliminating, managing, or improving a stressful condition. It generally predominates when a person sees a realistic chance of changing the situation, as Jimmy Carter and his wife did when together they looked at their

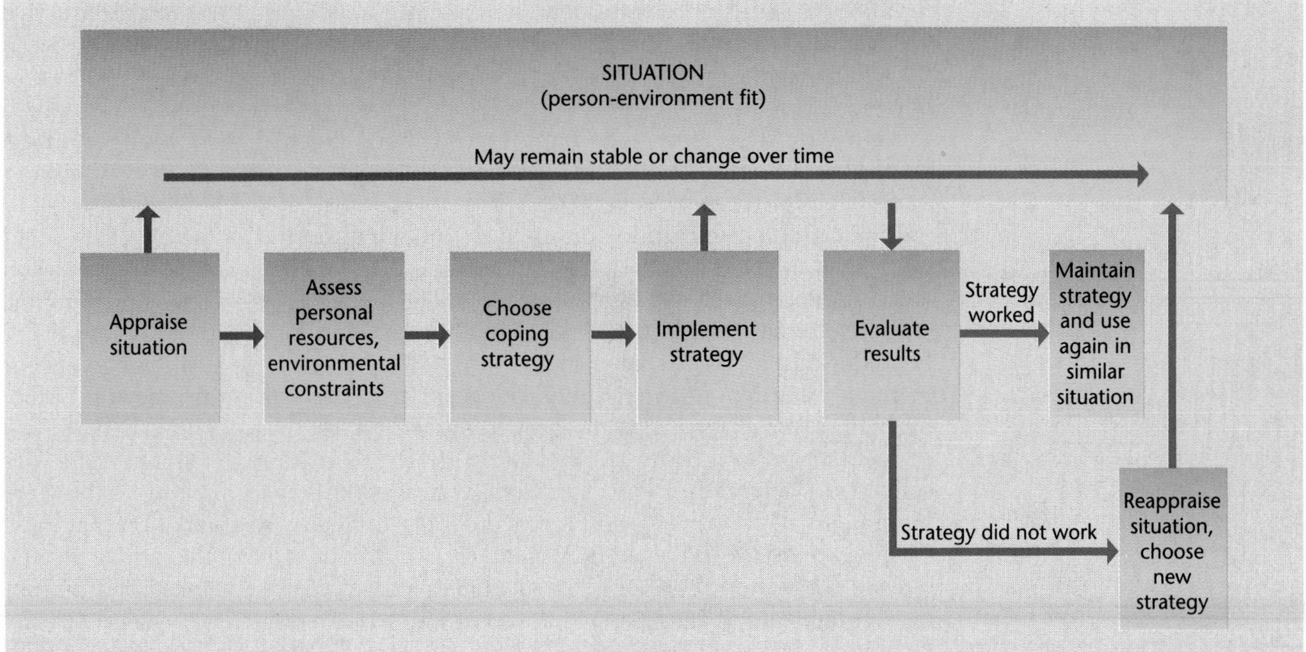

Figure 18-1

Cognitive-appraisal model of coping.

(Source: Based on Lazarus & Folkman, 1984.)

options after he lost his reelection bid. **Emotion-focused coping,** sometimes called *palliative coping,* is directed toward "feeling better": managing, or regulating, the emotional response to a stressful situation to relieve its physical or psychological impact. This form of coping is likely to predominate when a person concludes that little or nothing can be done about the situation itself. One emotion-focused strategy is to divert attention away from a problem; another is to give in; still another is to deny that the problem exists. Problem-focused responses to a series of harsh reprimands from an employer might be to work harder, seek ways to improve one's work skills, or look for another job. Emotion-focused responses might be to refuse to think about the reprimands or to convince oneself that the boss didn't really mean to be so critical.

emotion-focused coping In the cognitive-appraisal model, coping strategy directed toward managing the emotional response to a stressful situation so as to lessen its physical or psychological impact; sometimes called *palliative coping*. Compare *problem-focused coping*.

In general, older adults do more emotion-focused coping than younger people (Folkman, Lazarus, Pimley, & Novacek, 1987; Prohaska, Leventhal, Leventhal, & Keller, 1985). Is that because they are less able to focus on problems, or because they are better able to control their emotions?

Consider this . . .

- Which kind of coping do you tend to use more: problem-focused or emotion-focused? Which kind do your parents use more? your grandparents? In what kinds of situations is each type of coping most effective?

In one study (Blanchard-Fields, Jahnke, & Camp, 1995), 70 adolescents, 69 young adults, 74 middle-aged adults, and 74 older adults wrote essays on how to handle each of 15 problems. The participants, regardless of age, most often picked problem-focused strategies (either direct action or analyzing the problem so as to understand it better). This was especially true in situations that were not highly emotional, such as what to do about defective merchandise. The largest age differences appeared in problems with highly emotional implications, such as that of a divorced man who is allowed to see his child only on weekends but wants to see the child more often. Both young and old were more likely to use emotion regulation in such situations, but older adults chose emotion-regulating strategies (such as doing nothing, waiting until the child is older, or trying not to worry about it) more often than younger adults did.

Apparently, with age, people develop a more flexible repertoire of coping strategies. Older people *can* do problem-focused coping, but they also may be more able than younger people to use emotion regulation when a situation seems to call for it—when problem-focused action might be futile or counterproductive (Blanchard-Fields & Camp, 1990; Blanchard-Fields, Chen, & Norris, 1997; Blanchard-Fields & Irion, 1987; Folkman & Lazarus, 1980; Labouvie-Vief, Hakim-Larson, & Hobart, 1987). Older adults' ability to regulate their emotions may help explain why they tend to be happier and more cheerful than younger adults (Mroczek & Kolarz, 1998) and to experience negative emotions less often and more fleetingly (Carstensen, 1999).

Still, problem-focused coping tends to have a more positive effect on older people's well-being, according to a comparative analysis of two longitudinal studies involving 449 women with an average age of about 70. The women in one study were moving from their longtime homes to an independent living facility for older adults. The women in the other study were long-term caregivers for mentally retarded adult children. The women in the first group reported more problem-focused coping and, eight months after the move, showed more improvement in well-being (as measured by Ryff's multidimensional scale, described in Chapter 16). The caregivers, who were followed for nine years, were more likely to choose emotion-focused coping to deal with a situation that most of them apparently believed they could do little about. Among the caregivers who did use problem-focused coping, that strategy was more closely linked with a sense of environmental mastery and purpose in life; while for the larger group of caregivers who used emotion-focused coping, its use was more clearly associated with a decline in environmental mastery and self-acceptance and an increased incidence of depression (Kling, Seltzer, & Ryff, 1997).

Sometimes emotion-focused coping can be quite adaptive, and its flexible use in appropriate situations can be a mature coping strategy. It can be especially useful in coping with what the psychotherapist Pauline Boss (1999) calls *ambiguous loss*: the loss of a still-living loved one to Alzheimer's disease; the loss of a child to drug addiction; the loss of a homeland, which elderly immigrants may feel as long as they live. In one study (Diehl, Coyle, & Labouvie-Vief, 1996), adolescents and young adults tended to respond aggressively to conflict, whereas older adults were less confrontational and less impulsive. Older people also were more likely to withdraw from a conflict or to see its bright side. Perhaps experience had taught them to accept what they could not change—a lesson often reinforced by religion.

CHECKPOINT

Can you . . .

✔ Describe the cognitive-appraisal model of coping, and discuss the relationship between age and choice of coping strategies?

Religion and Emotional Well-Being in Late Life

Interviewers asked 100 well-educated white men and women, ages 55 to 80—about evenly divided between working class and upper middle class, and 90 percent Protestant—to describe how they had dealt with the worst events in their lives. The top strategies, cited by 58 percent of the women and 32 percent of the men, were behaviors associated with religion (Koenig, George, & Siegler, 1988; see Table 18-1). Other research echoes the supportive role religion plays for many elderly people, such as Jimmy Carter. Possible explanations include social support, the perception of a measure of control over life through prayer, and faith in God as a way of interpreting misfortunes.

Among 836 older adults from two secular and three religiously oriented groups, morale was positively associated with three kinds of religious activity: *organized* (church or synagogue attendance and participation), *informal* (praying or reading the Bible), and *spiritual* (personal commitment to religious beliefs). People who were high on any of these dimensions had higher morale and a better attitude toward aging and were more satisfied and less lonely (Koenig, Kvale, & Ferrel, 1988).

Elderly African Americans are more involved in religious activity than elderly white people, and women are more involved than men (Levin & Taylor, 1993; Levin, Taylor, & Chatters, 1994). Elderly black people who feel supported by their church tend to report high levels of well-being; the more actively religious they are, the more satisfied they are with their lives (Coke, 1992; Walls & Zarit, 1991).

Table 18-1 Spontaneously Reported Emotion-Regulating Coping Strategies Used by Older Adults

Rank Order	Frequency of Mention	
	Number	%
Religious	97	17.4
Kept busy	84	15.1
Accepted it	63	11.3
Support from family or friends	62	11.1
Help from professional	34	6.1
Positive attitude	31	5.6
Took one day at a time	29	5.2
Became involved in social activities	19	3.4
Planning and preparing beforehand	15	2.7
Optimized communication	13	2.3
Limited activities; didn't overcommit	11	2.0
Sought information	8	1.4
Exercised	8	1.4
Helped others more needy	7	1.3
Realized that time heals all wounds	7	1.3
Avoided situation	6	1.1
Experience of prior hardships	5	.9
Carried on for others' sake	5	.9
Ingested alcohol, tranquilizers	5	.9
Carried on as usual	4	.7
Took a vacation	3	.5
Realized others in same situation or worse	3	.5
Released emotion (cried or cursed)	3	.5
Lowered expectations or devaluated	3	.5
Miscellaneous	31	5.6
Totals	556	100.6

Note: 100 older adults reported 556 coping behaviors for 289 stressful experiences. Percentages add up to more than 100 because of rounding.

Source: Koenig, George, & Siegler, 1988, p. 306.

Religious involvement of virtually any kind has a positive impact on physical and mental health and longevity. This is true regardless of gender, race, ethnicity, education, and health status and may be related in part to availability of social support in time of need (Ellison & Levin, 1998; Koenig, George, & Peterson, 1998; McFadden & Levin, 1996; Mitka, 1998).

People with the most *or the least* religious commitment tend to have the highest self-esteem (Krause, 1995). It may be, as Fowler (1981) suggested (refer back to Chapter 13), that the emotional benefits nonreligious people derive from strong commitment to secular values are similar to the benefits religious people derive from a strong faith in God. Or it may be that people's self-esteem is highest when their behavior is consistent with their beliefs, whatever those beliefs may be.

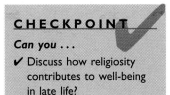

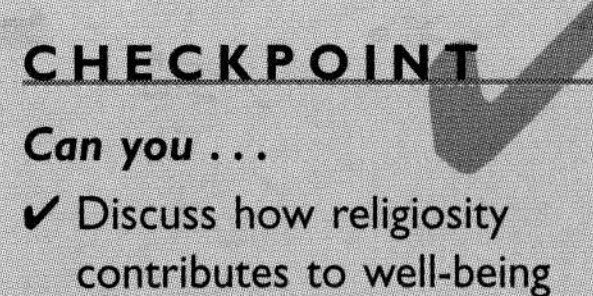

CHECKPOINT

Can you . . .

✔ Discuss how religiosity contributes to well-being in late life?

Models of "Successful" or "Optimal" Aging

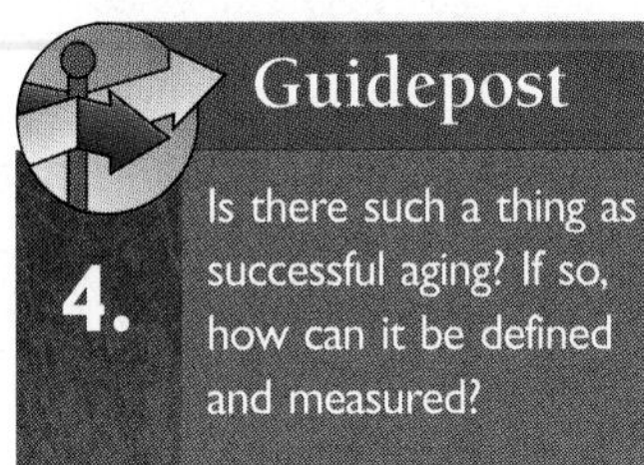

Guidepost

4. Is there such a thing as successful aging? If so, how can it be defined and measured?

Researchers disagree on how to define and measure *successful,* or *optimal, aging.* Some investigators focus on such criteria as cardiovascular functioning, cognitive performance, and mental health, about which there is consensus as to desirable outcomes. However, the whole may not be the same as the sum of its parts: a strong heart, a large vocabulary, and absence of depression do not necessarily add up to success in living. Other researchers view productivity, economic or otherwise, as an important criterion for a meaningful or healthful life. Still others look at longevity, which can be a sign of physical and mental health.

Another approach is to examine subjective experience: how well individuals attain their goals and how satisfied they are with their lives. One model, for example, emphasizes the degree of control people retain: their ability to shape their lives to fit their needs and optimize their development (Schulz & Heckhausen, 1996). In one study, people reported greater feelings of control over their work, finances, and marriages as they aged, but less control over their sex lives and relationships with children (Lachman & Weaver, 1998). The trouble with such criteria is that they do not lend themselves to accurate measurement. Furthermore, such research may tell us little that can be generalized beyond the individual.

All definitions of *successful,* or *optimal, aging* are value-laden—unavoidably so. Keeping this problem in mind, then, let's look at theory and research about aging well.

Disengagement Theory versus Activity Theory

disengagement theory Theory of aging, proposed by Cumming and Henry, which holds that successful aging is characterized by mutual withdrawal between the older person and society. Compare with *activity theory.*

activity theory Theory of aging, proposed by Neugarten and others, which holds that in order to age successfully a person must remain as active as possible. Compare with *disengagement theory.*

Who is making a healthier adjustment: a person who tranquilly watches the world go by from a rocking chair or one who keeps busy from morning till night? According to **disengagement theory,** aging normally brings a gradual reduction in social involvement and greater preoccupation with the self. According to **activity theory,** the more active people remain, the better they age.

Disengagement theory was one of the first influential theories in gerontology. Its proponents (Cumming & Henry, 1961) saw disengagement as a universal condition of aging. They maintained that declines in physical functioning and awareness of the approach of death result in a gradual, inevitable withdrawal from social roles (worker, spouse, parent); and, since society stops providing useful roles for the older adult, the disengagement is mutual. Disengagement is thought to be accompanied (as Jung suggested) by introspection and a quieting of the emotions.

After nearly four decades, disengagement theory has received little independent research support and has "largely disappeared from the empirical literature" (Achenbaum & Bengtson, 1994, p. 756). David Gutmann (1974, 1977, 1992) has argued that what *looks* like disengagement in traditional cultures is only a transition between the active roles of middle age and the more passive, spiritual roles of late adulthood, and that true disengagement occurs only in societies in which elderly people have no established roles appropriate to their stage of life. The result may be less-than-optimal satisfaction with life and underuse of human potential.

According to *activity theory,* an adult's roles are major sources of satisfaction; the greater the loss of roles through retirement, widowhood, distance from children, or infirmity, the less satisfied a person will be. People who are aging well keep up as many activities as possible and find substitutes for lost roles (Neugarten, Havighurst, & Tobin, 1968). For some older adults, even such a mundane activity as mall walking, if done as a regular routine, can serve, not simply as a form of exercise, but as a substitute for the sense of purpose, belonging, social contact, and self-discipline previously derived from paid

The author Betty Friedan, whose 1963 book, *The Feminine Mystique,* is credited with launching the women's movement in the United States, exemplifies successful aging as described by activity theory. At age 60, she went on the first Outward Bound survival expedition for people over 55. In her seventies she was teaching at universities in California and New York and, in 1993, published another best-seller, *The Fountain of Age.*

work (Duncan, Travis, & McAuley, 1995). Research on the *engagement hypothesis* (refer back to Chapter 17) suggests that involvement in challenging activities and social roles promotes retention of cognitive abilities and may have positive effects on health and social adjustment as well.

Activity theory has been influential, but, at least as originally framed, it is generally regarded as oversimplistic. In early research (Neugarten et al., 1968), activity generally was associated with satisfaction. However, some disengaged people also were well adjusted. This finding suggests that while activity may work best for most people, disengagement may be appropriate for some, and that generalizations about a particular pattern of "successful aging" may be risky. For some people, in some circumstances, accumulated roles can enhance health and well-being; for others, the result may be role strain and ill health (Moen, Dempster-McClain, & Williams, 1992; Musick, Herzog, & House, 1999).

Furthermore, most of the research on activity theory has been, of necessity, correlational. If a relationship between activity levels and successful aging were found, it would not reveal whether people age well because they are active or whether people remain active because they are aging well (Musick et al., 1999).

Much research has found that healthy older people *do* tend to cut down on social contacts and that activity in and of itself bears little relationship to psychological well-being or satisfaction with life (Carstensen, 1995, 1996; Lemon, Bengtson, & Peterson, 1972). However, activity theory has not, so far, been discarded (Marshall, 1994). A new view is that activities do affect well-being—not so much through social roles as through their impact on the sense of self-efficacy, mastery, and control (Herzog, Franks, Markus, & Holmberg, 1998). Some gerontologists have sought to refine activity theory by comparing past and present activity levels. Others maintain that the kind or content of the activity makes a difference.

Continuity Theory

Continuity theory, as described by the gerontologist Robert Atchley (1989), emphasizes people's need to maintain a connection between past and present. In this view, activity is important not for its own sake, but to the extent that it represents the continuation of a lifestyle. For older adults who always have been active and involved, it may be important to continue a high level of activity. Many retired people are happiest pursuing work or leisure activities similar to those they have enjoyed in the past (J. R. Kelly, 1994). Women who have been involved in multiple roles (such as wife, mother, worker, and volunteer) tend to continue to have multiple roles, and to reap the benefits, as they age (Moen et al., 1992). On the other hand, people who have been less active may do better in the proverbial rocking chair.

continuity theory
Theory of aging, described by Atchley, which holds that in order to age successfully people must maintain a balance of continuity and change in both the internal and external structures of their lives.

When aging brings marked physical or cognitive changes, a person may become dependent on caregivers or may have to make new living arrangements. Support from family, friends, or community services can help minimize discontinuity. Continuity theory, then, offers a reason to keep older adults out of institutions and in the community, and to help them live as independently as possible.

The Role of Productivity

Some researchers focus on productive activity, either paid or unpaid, as a key to aging well. One study (Glass, Seeman, Herzog, Kahn, & Berkman, 1995) compared nearly 1,200 men and women ages 70 to 79, who showed high physical and cognitive functioning ("successful agers"), with 162 medium- and low-functioning adults in the same age group ("usual agers"). Nearly all "successful" agers and more than 9 out of 10 "usual" agers engaged in some form of productive activity, but "successful" agers were far more productive. On average, they did one-third more housework than "usual" agers, more than twice as much yard work, more than three times as much paid work, and almost four times as much volunteer work.

Three years later, when interviewed again, 15 percent of the "successful" agers had become less productive, but 13 percent had become more so. People who originally had been more satisfied with their lives were more likely to have increased in productivity; so were people who showed gains in personal mastery. This research supports the idea that productive activity plays an important part in "successful" aging, and that older people not only can continue to be productive but can become even more so.

On the other hand, frequent participation in *leisure* activities can be as beneficial to health and well-being as frequent participation in productive ones. It may be that *any* regular activity that expresses and enhances some aspect of the self can contribute to "successful" aging (Herzog et al., 1998). Among 2,761 older residents of New Haven, both productive activity and sedentary social activity were as effective as physical exercise in reducing mortality (Glass, de Leon, Marottoli, & Berkman, 1999).

CHECKPOINT

Can you . . .

- ✔ Compare two ways in which researchers try to measure successful or optimal aging, and point out drawbacks of each method?
- ✔ Compare disengagement theory, activity theory, continuity theory, and productive aging?
- ✔ Give examples of how Baltes's concept of selective optimization with compensation applies to successful aging in the psychosocial realm?

Selective Optimization with Compensation

According to Baltes and his colleagues (Marsiske, Lange, Baltes, & Baltes, 1995), "successful" aging depends on having goals to guide development and resources that make those goals potentially achievable. In old age—indeed, throughout life, say these investigators—this occurs through *selective optimization with compensation.*

According to this concept, introduced in Chapter 17, the aging brain compensates for losses in certain areas by selectively "optimizing," or making the most of other abilities. For example, the celebrated concert pianist Arthur Rubinstein, who gave his farewell concert at 89, compensated for memory and motor losses by keeping up a smaller repertoire, practicing longer each day, and playing more slowly before fast movements (which he could no longer play at top speed) to heighten the contrast (Baltes & Baltes, 1990).

The same principle applies to psychosocial development. As we have seen, older adults often can be more flexible than younger ones in selecting coping strategies, and thus can optimize well-being in the face of overwhelming, intractable problems. Their greater ability to avail themselves of emotion-focusing strategies may compensate for loss of control over certain areas of their lives. Also, as Laura Carstensen's (1991, 1995, 1996) *socioemotional selectivity theory* (discussed in Chapter 16) suggests, people become more selective about social contacts as they age, maintaining contact with people who can best meet their current needs for emotional satisfaction. Such meaningful contacts may help older people compensate for the narrowing of possibilities in their lives. As in cognitive-appraisal theory, assessment of available resources is important to these and other adaptations (Baltes et al., 1998).

Consider this . . .

- Are you satisfied with any of the definitions of "successful" (or "optimal") aging presented in this section? Why or why not?

The argument about what constitutes "successful" or "optimal" aging is far from settled, and may never be. One thing is clear: people differ greatly in the ways they can and do live—and want to live—the later years of life.

Lifestyle and Social Issues Related to Aging

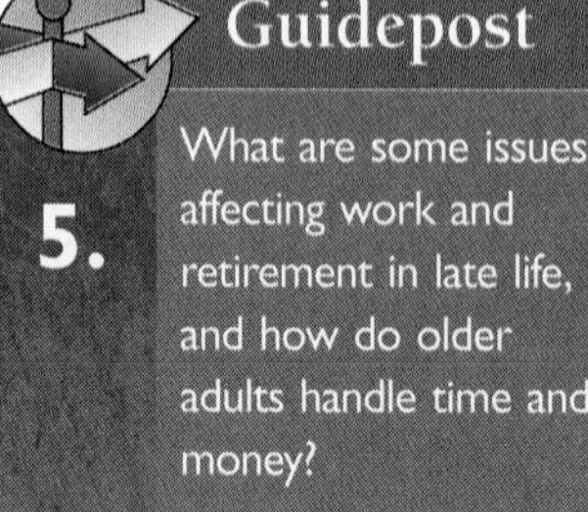

Guidepost
5.
What are some issues affecting work and retirement in late life, and how do older adults handle time and money?

"I—will—never—retire!" wrote the comedian George Burns (1983, p. 138) at age 87. Burns, who continued performing until two years before his death at the age of 100, was one of many late-life achievers who have kept their minds and bodies active doing the work they love.

Whether and when to retire are among the most crucial lifestyle decisions people make as they approach late adulthood. These decisions affect their financial situation and emotional state, as well as the ways they spend their waking hours and the ways they relate to family and friends. The problem of providing financial support for large numbers of retired older people also has serious implications for society, especially as the "baby boom" generation nears old age. A related problem is the need for appropriate living arrangements and care for older people who can no longer manage on their own. (Box 18-2 reports on issues related to support of the aging in Asian countries.)

Window on the World

Box 18-2
Aging in Japan

Since the 1940s Asia has been the most successful region of the world in reducing fertility. At the same time, higher standards of living, better sanitation, and immunization programs have extended the adult life span (Martin, 1988). The result: fewer young people to care for the old.

In Japan, the most rapidly aging industrial society, 1 person in 6 is now older than 65, accounting for close to half of the nation's total government-sponsored health care spending. By 2025 Japan will have twice as many older adults as children, pension reserves will likely be exhausted, and the social welfare burden—largely for retirement and health care costs for the elderly—may consume nearly three-fourths of the national income (WuDunn, 1997).

The Japanese pension sysem is a pay-as-you-go system like social security in the United States, and it has similar problems. Everyone is required to join and to pay a basic minimum into the fund. But many self-employed people do not make their required contributions because they no longer trust the system. Many people also belong to supplementary corporate plans, but with the stock market collapse in the early 1990s, many of those plans went bankrupt or are underfunded. Today's retirees, many of whom joined pension plans late in their working lives but collect full benefits, are doing well. The crunch will come when younger workers, who now are subsidizing the elderly, are ready to retire. As in the United States, the Japanese government plans to gradually raise the retirement age (now 60 in Japan). There also is talk of cutting benefits by one-fifth. Middle-aged workers worry that they cannot count on adequate pensions when they retire (WuDunn, 1997).

Throughout Asia, a large proportion of older people live with their children, but this pattern is less common than it used to be. In Japan, only 55 percent of the aged lived with adult children in 1994, as compared with more than 80 percent in 1957. Along with the shifting balance between old and young, such trends as urbanization, migration, and a larger proportion of women in the workforce make home care of elderly relatives less feasible. To halt the erosion in family care, Japan has made it a legal obligation to care for elderly relatives and has provided tax relief to those who give older relatives financial help (Martin, 1988; Oshima, 1996).

Institutionalization is seen as a last resort for those who are destitute or without families. But eventually Japan's exploding older population will outgrow family-based care. Already, since 1990, there has been a tenfold rise in nursing homes, infirmaries, and other institutions serving remote areas (Nishio, 1994), but the nation's 3,000 nursing homes can take only the bedridden or people with dementia, and 60,000 people are on waiting lists (Oshima, 1996). At the same time, a program to expand home services and institutional care through local governments is foundering for lack of funds (Oshima, 1996).

Most Japanese, like most other Asians, want to help elderly people remain independent and productive as long as possible and, when they do need assistance, to help their families care for them. Meeting these goals is a difficult challenge.

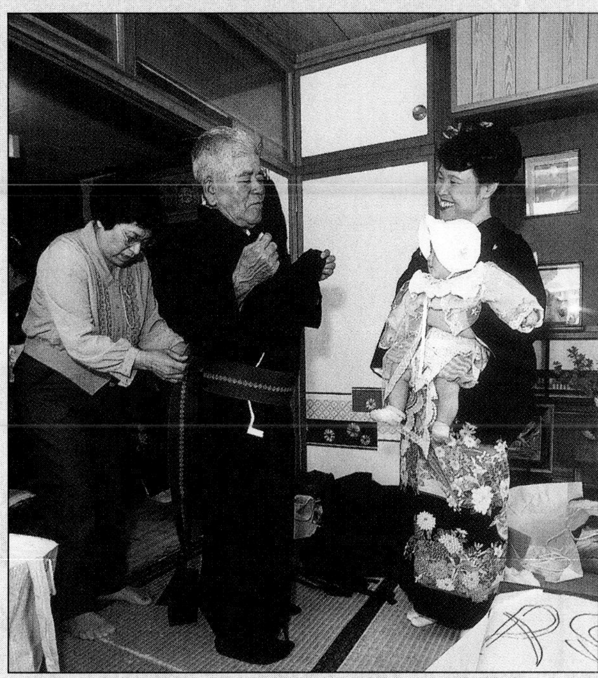

Multigenerational households like this one are becoming less common in Japan. There, as in the west, migration to cities and the movement of women into the workforce make home care of elderly relatives more difficult than in the past.

Work, Retirement, and Leisure

Retirement is a relatively new idea; it took hold in many industrialized countries during the late nineteenth and early twentieth centuries as life expectancy increased. In the United States, the economic depression of the 1930s was the impetus for the social security system, which, together with company-sponsored pension plans negotiated by labor unions, made it possible for many older workers to retire with financial security. Eventually, mandatory retirement at age 65 became almost universal.

Today compulsory retirement has been virtually outlawed as a form of age discrimination. Adults have many choices, among them early retirement, retiring from one career or job to start another, working part time to keep busy or to supplement income, going back to school, doing volunteer work, pursuing other leisure interests—or not retiring at all.

Does Age Affect Job Performance?

Older workers are often more productive than younger workers. Although they may work more slowly than younger people, they are more accurate (Czaja & Sharit, 1998; Salthouse & Maurer, 1996; Treas, 1995). Older workers tend to be more dependable, careful, responsible, and frugal with time and materials than younger workers; and their suggestions are more likely to be accepted (Forteza & Prieto, 1994; Warr, 1994).

The Age Discrimination in Employment Act (ADEA) protects most workers age 40 and older from being denied a job, fired, paid less, or forced to retire because of age. The ADEA, which applies to firms with twenty or more employees, has eliminated some blatant practices, such as help-wanted ads that specify "age 25 to 35." Still, many employers exert subtle pressures on older employees (Landy, 1994).

Powerful ammunition for older workers fighting age stereotypes came from a comprehensive study by an interdisciplinary task force commissioned by the United States Congress (Landy, 1992, 1994). The study found that age, in and of itself, does not predict job performance. The task force spent almost two years combing more than 5,000 research articles and collecting data from more than 500 cities. The chief findings were that (1) physical fitness and mental abilities vary increasingly with age and differ more within age groups than between age groups, and (2) tests of specific psychological, physical, and perceptual-motor abilities can predict job performance far better than age can.

CHECKPOINT

Can you . . .

✔ Cite findings on the relationship between aging and work skills?

Trends in Late-Life Work and Retirement

Even without mandatory retirement, most adults who *can* retire *do* retire; and, with increasing longevity, they spend more time in retirement than in the past (Kinsella & Gist, 1995). In industrialized countries, the working elderly range from only 3 percent of all older adults in Germany to 28 percent in Japan (Commonwealth Fund, 1992). In the United States, about 16 percent of older men and 8 percent of older women were in the workforce in 1998 (AARP, 1999). The pattern is quite different in most of the developing world, where large numbers of older adults continue to work for income (Ferraro & Su, 1999; Kaiser, 1993).

Despite a general decline in workforce participation by older people in industrialized societies, older women's participation has remained stable or even expanded. Thus, although older men still form a much larger proportion of the labor force, the proportion of older workers who are women is growing; and this is happening in many developing countries as well. Since many older women throughout the world serve as caregivers for frail, old-old parents, this trend has serious social consequences (Kinsella & Gist, 1995).

Public and private pension programs and other inducements to make way for younger workers, such as the availability of social security benefits (at a reduced level) at age 62, have contributed to a trend toward early retirement in the United

States, as in many industrialized countries (Kinsella & Gist, 1995). For people born after 1937, the age of eligibility for full social security benefits is scheduled to rise gradually from 65 to 67. This change was predicated on the rise in life expectancy, decreases in mortality, and improvements in health among older adults (Crimmins, Reynolds, & Saito, 1999).

Men who continue to work after age 65 tend to be better educated than those who retire. They are more likely to be in good health, and they may have wives who are still working. Usually they strongly want to work, in contrast to retired men, who generally do not view paid work as necessary to self-fulfillment (Parnes & Sommers, 1994). Older black men are less likely to remain in the workforce than older white men, often because of health problems that force them to stop working before normal retirement age. However, those who do remain healthy tend to continue working longer than white men (Gendell & Siegel, 1996; Hayward, Friedman, & Chen, 1996).

The line between work and retirement is not as clear as it used to be. Many people are retiring into "bridge jobs," new part-time or full-time jobs that may serve as bridges to eventual complete retirement. Some are semiretired; they keep doing what they were doing before but cut down on their hours and responsibilities. A poll of 803 men and women ages 50 to 75 found that 40 percent were working for pay in retirement or planned to do so (Peter D. Hart Research Associates, 1999).

How Do Older Adults Fare Financially?

Even Jimmy and Rosalynn Carter had to face financial issues after retirement. So do most older adults.

More than 9 out of 10 older Americans receive social security benefits, and about 2 out of 3 report income from assets. Other sources of income include pensions, earnings from work, and public assistance (AARP, 1999; see Figure 18-2).

Social security and other government programs, such as Medicare, which covers basic health insurance for people 65 and over, have enabled today's older adults, as a group, to be about as well off financially as younger and middle-aged adults, and their median net worth is well above the national average (AARP, 1995, 1999). Between 1959 and 1997, the proportion of older Americans living in poverty dropped from 35 percent to less than 11 percent. Older women are more likely than older men to live in poverty, and older African Americans and Hispanic Americans are nearly three times as likely as older white Americans to have incomes below the poverty line (Kramarow et al., 1999).

Although fewer older people live in poverty today, many face poverty some time during old age. An estimated 30 percent of 60-year-olds will spend at least a year below the poverty line (Rank & Hirschl, 1999). Older women who are single, widowed, or divorced are at greater risk of becoming poor during retirement than married women, who often can rely on a husband's pension (Burkhauser, Holden, & Feaster, 1988; Kinsella & Gist, 1995; Treas, 1995). Once poor, older adults are likely to stay poor (Treas, 1995). They may no longer be able to work, and inflation may have eroded their savings and pensions. Infirm or disabled people often outlive their savings at a time when their medical bills are soaring. Some people living in poverty get help from such public assistance programs as Supplemental Security Income,

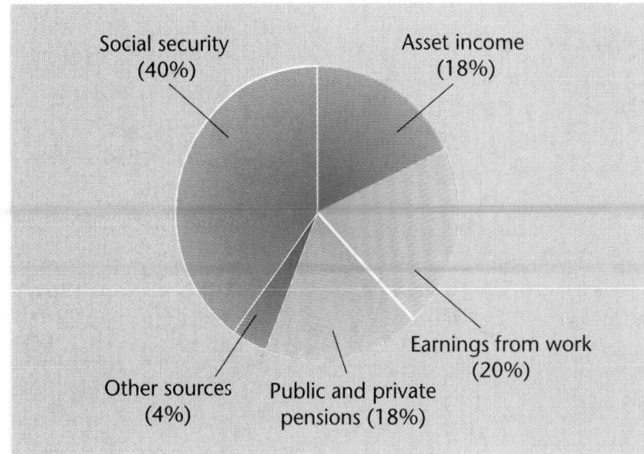

Figure 18-2
Sources of income of Americans ages 65 and older.
(Source: Based on data from AARP, 1999.)

subsidized housing, Medicaid, and food stamps. Others either are not eligible or do not take part in these programs, often because they do not know what the programs offer or how to apply.

How will today's middle-aged adults fare financially during retirement? With a growing elderly population and proportionately fewer workers contributing to the social security system, it seems likely that benefits (in real dollars) will not continue to rise and may even decline. As for private pensions, a shift from defined benefit plans that guarantee a fixed retirement income to riskier defined contribution plans, in which benefits depend on returns from invested funds, is making the financial future less certain for many workers (Rix, 1994; Treas, 1995). Still, among a nationally representative sample of 2,001 men and women ages 33 to 52 (AARP, 2000), about 60 percent—chiefly those with higher current income—expressed confidence in their ability to prepare financially for the future. Fewer than half (48 percent) were counting on social security as a source of retirement income. About 60 percent were counting on savings and investments, and 68 percent on self-directed retirement plans, such as IRAs and 401(k)s. The vast majority (84 percent) planned to work at least part time. Thirty-five percent expected to have to scale back their lifestyle, and 23 percent thought they would have to struggle to make ends meet.

CHECKPOINT

Can you . . .

✔ Describe current trends in late-life work and retirement?

✔ Identify factors in the economic status of older adults?

Life After Retirement

Retirement not only alters household income but also can bring changes in division of household work, marital quality, and distribution of power and decision making. There may now be more time for contact with extended family and friends and for caring for grandchildren. Not all these impacts can be fully anticipated. Changes in the family situation, such as an unexpected illness or disability or marital troubles of adult children, can affect the retirement experience (Szinovacz & Ekerdt, 1995).

During the first few years after retirement, people may have a special need for emotional support to make them feel they are still valued and to cope with the changes in their lives. In one longitudinal study, researchers interviewed 253 workers over the age of 50, drawn from a nationally representative sample, and then interviewed them again four years later. Of the 100 who had retired in the interim, 25 percent were more satisfied with their lives than before retirement, but 34 percent were less so. The most powerful predictor of satisfaction was the size of a retiree's social support network (Tarnowski & Antonucci, 1998).

Consider this . . .

- At what age, if ever, do you expect to retire? Why? How would you like to spend your time if and when you retire?

How do retired people use their time? Socioeconomic status may make a difference. One common pattern, the **family-focused lifestyle,** consists largely of accessible, low-cost activities that revolve around family, home, and companions: conversation, watching television, visiting with family and friends, informal entertaining, playing cards, or just doing "what comes along." The second pattern, **balanced investment,** is typical of more educated people, who allocate their time more equally among family, work, and leisure (J. R. Kelly, 1987, 1994). These patterns may change with age. In one study, younger retirees who were most satisfied with their quality of life were those who traveled regularly and went to cultural events; but after age 75, family- and home-based activity yielded the most satisfaction (J. R. Kelly, Steinkamp, & Kelly, 1986).

family-focused lifestyle
Pattern of retirement activity that revolves around family, home, and companions. Compare *balanced investment.*

balanced investment
Pattern of retirement activity allocated among family, work, and leisure. Compare *family-focused lifestyle.*

Sunday painters, amateur carpenters, and others who have made the effort to master a craft or pursue an intense interest often make that passion central to their lives during retirement (Mannell, 1993). This third lifestyle pattern, **serious leisure,** is dominated by activity that "demands skill, attention, and commitment" (J. R. Kelly, 1994, p. 502). Retirees who engage in this pattern tend to be extraordinarily satisfied with their lives.

serious leisure
Leisure activity requiring skill, attention, and commitment.

Since the late 1960s the proportion of older adults doing volunteer work (like Jimmy and Rosalynn Carter) has increased greatly (Chambre, 1993). Retired executives advise small businesses; retired accountants help fill out tax returns;

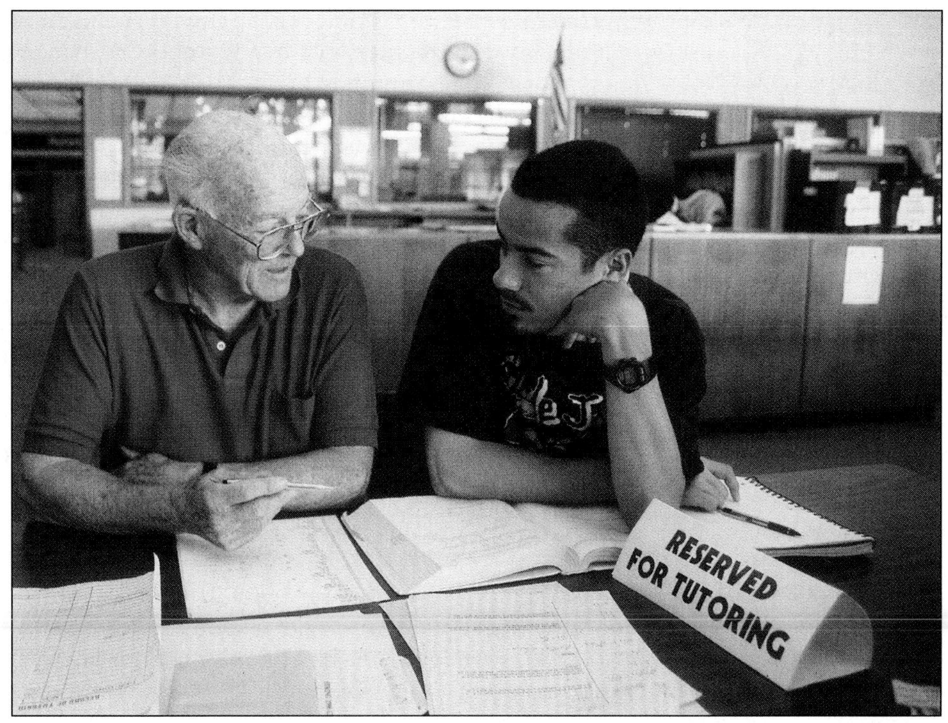

By using his leisure time to work as a volunteer tutoring a community college student, this retiree is helping not only the young man and the community but also himself. The self-esteem gained from using hard-won skills and from continuing to be a useful, contributing member of society is a valuable by-product of volunteer service.

senior companions visit frail elderly people in their homes; and foster grandparents, for a small stipend, provide social and emotional support to neglected children, teenage parents, or substance abusers. In one poll, 57 percent of retirees said they had done volunteer or community service work during the past year (Peter D. Hart Research Associates, 1999). One reason for the increase in volunteerism is a growing recognition that older people can be active, healthy, contributing members of a community. Volunteer work itself has taken on higher status, and today's better-educated older population has more to contribute and more interest in contributing (Chambre, 1993).

The many paths to a meaningful, enjoyable retirement have two things in common: doing satisfying things and having satisfying relationships. For most older people, both "are an extension of histories that have developed throughout the life course" (J. R. Kelly, 1994, p. 501).

CHECKPOINT

Can you . . .

- ✔ Discuss how retirement can affect family life, satisfaction with life, and use of time, and describe three common lifestyle patterns after retirement?
- ✔ Summarize trends in volunteerism after retirement?

Living Arrangements

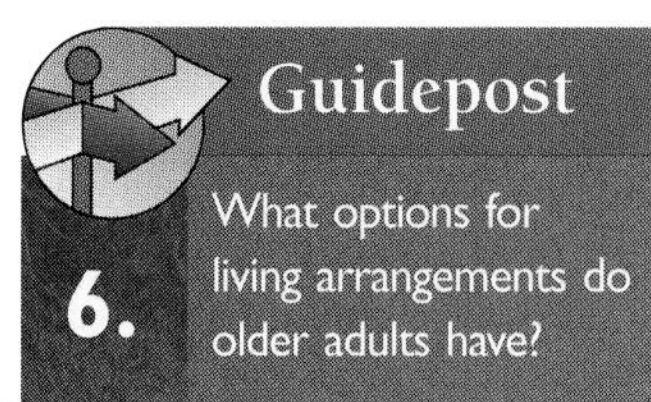

Guidepost
6.
What options for living arrangements do older adults have?

A growing number of aging Americans—more than 80 percent of those in their fifties or older, according to surveys—say they want to remain where they are indefinitely (AARP, 1993b, 1996). About 8 out of 10 older heads of households own their homes, and most prefer to stay there; many, even after they are widowed (AARP, 1999; Treas, 1995).

"Aging in place" makes sense for those who can manage on their own or with minimal help, have an adequate income or a paid-up mortgage, can handle the upkeep, are happy in the neighborhood, and want to be independent, to have privacy, and to be near friends, adult children, or grandchildren (Gonyea, Hudson, & Seltzer, 1990). A *reverse mortgage* can allow homeowners to live off their home's equity. For older people with impairments that make it hard to get along entirely on their own, minor support—such as meals, transportation, and home health aides—often can help them stay put. So can ramps, grab bars, and other modifications within the home. Older adults who cannot or do not want to maintain a house, do not have family nearby, prefer a different locale or climate, or want to travel may move into low-maintenance or maintenance-free townhouses, condominiums, cooperative or rental apartments, or mobile homes.

For some people, though—especially the old old—living arrangements can become a problem. Three flights of stairs may be too much to manage. A neighborhood may deteriorate, and helpless-looking older people may become prey to young thugs. Mental or physical disability may make living alone impractical. Older people in suburban areas, if they can no longer drive, may be isolated and unable to obtain necessities on their own.

Most older people do not need much help; and those who do can often remain in the community if they have at least one person to depend on. The single most important factor keeping people out of institutions is being married. As long as a couple are in relatively good health, they can usually live fairly independently and care for each other. The issue of living arrangements becomes more pressing when one or both become frail, infirm, or disabled, or when one spouse dies. People who are not living with a spouse most often get help from a child, usually a daughter. Those who cannot call on a spouse or child usually turn to friends (Chappell, 1991).

In 1997, 96 percent of Americans age 65 and older lived in the community, about one-third of them alone and almost all the rest with a spouse or other family members (Kramarow et al., 1999; see Figure 18-3). Although health, physical limitations, and other practical considerations affect the choice of living arrangements, cultural patterns also play a part. Minority elders, in keeping with their traditions, are more likely than white elders to live with relatives in extended-family households. Since marriage is less common among African Americans, fewer black elders live with a spouse (Kramarow et al., 1999).

Let's look more closely at the two most common living arrangements for older adults without spouses—living alone and living with adult children—and

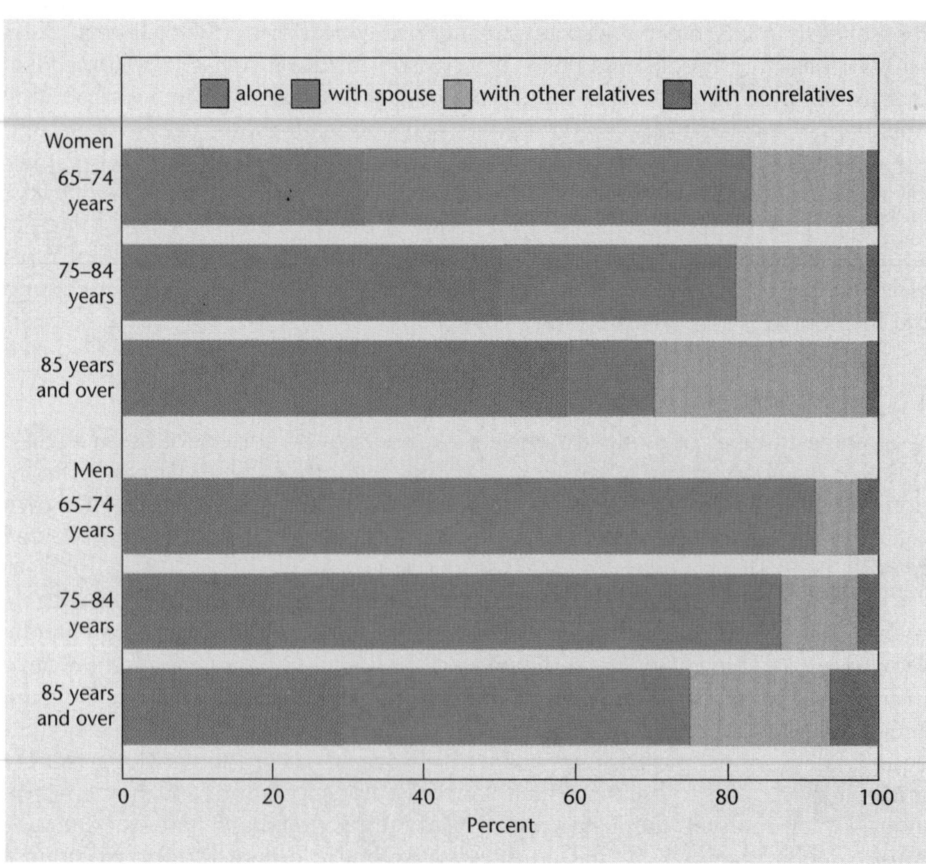

Figure 18-3

Living arrangements of noninstitutionalized persons age 65 and over, United States, 1997. As compared with men and women ages 65 to 74, fewer of those age 75 and over live with spouses, and more live alone or with children or other relatives. In all age groups over 65, women are more likely than men to live alone; men are more likely to live with spouses.

(Source: Kramarow et al., 1999, Figure 2, p. 25. Based on Lugaila, 1997.)

then at living in institutions and alternative forms of group housing. Finally, we'll discuss a serious problem for dependent older adults: abuse by caregivers.

Living Alone

About 4 out of 5 older adults who live alone are widowed, and almost half have no children or none living nearby. They are older and poorer on the average than elderly people who live with someone else. However, they are generally in better health than older people without spouses who have other living arrangements. The overwhelming majority value their independence and prefer to be on their own (Commonwealth Fund, 1986; Kramarow et al., 1999; U.S. Bureau of the Census, 1992a).

Because women live longer than men and are more likely to be widowed, older women are at least twice as likely as older men to live alone, and the likelihood increases with age. Among the oldest old (those 85 and over), nearly 6 out of 10 women and 3 out of 10 men live alone (Kramarow et al., 1999).

It may seem that older people who live alone, particularly the oldest old, would be lonely. However, other factors, such as personality, cognitive abilities, physical health, and a depleted social network may play a more significant role in vulnerability to loneliness (P. Martin, Hagberg, & Poon, 1997). Social activities, such as going to church or temple or a senior center, or doing volunteer work, can help an older person stay connected to the community (Steinbach, 1992).

Living with Adult Children

Unlike older people in many African, Asian, and Latin American societies, who can expect to live and be cared for in their children's homes, most older people in the United States, even those in difficult circumstances, do not wish to do so. They are reluctant to burden their families and to give up their own freedom. It can be inconvenient to absorb an extra person into a household, and everyone's privacy—and relationships—may suffer. The elderly parent may feel useless, bored, and isolated from friends. If the adult child is married and parent and spouse do not get along well, or caregiving duties become too burdensome, the marriage may be threatened (Lund, 1993a; Shapiro, 1994).

Despite these concerns, many older Americans, with advancing age, do live with adult children. The success of such an arrangement depends largely on the quality of the relationship that has existed in the past and on the ability of both generations to communicate fully and frankly. The decision to move a parent into an adult child's home should be mutual and needs to be thought through carefully and thoroughly. Parents and children need to respect each other's dignity and autonomy and accept their differences (Shapiro, 1994).

Consider this . . .

- Were you surprised to read that a large number of older adults like living alone, and that few want to live with their children? Why do you think this is so?

Living in Institutions

Most older people do not want to live in institutions, and most family members do not want them to. Older people often feel that placement in an institution is a sign of rejection; and children usually place their parents reluctantly, apologetically, and with great guilt. Sometimes, though, because of an older person's needs or a family's circumstances, such placement seems to be the only solution.

At any given time, only about 4 percent of people over 65 in the United States live in institutions, but the lifetime probability of spending time in a nursing home, even if only briefly to convalesce, is higher. About half of the women and one-third of the men who were 60 years old in 1990 will eventually stay in a nursing home at least once (AARP, 1999; Center on Elderly People Living Alone, 1995a; Treas, 1995). The likelihood of living in a nursing home increases with age—from about 1 percent at ages 65 to 74 to 19 percent at age 85 and over (Kramarow et al., 1999).

At highest risk of institutionalization are those living alone, those who do not take part in social activities, those whose daily activities are limited by poor health or disability, and those whose caregivers are overburdened (McFall & Miller, 1992; Steinbach, 1992). Institutionalization is twice as common among white and black people as among Hispanic and Asian Americans (Himes, Hogan, & Eggebeen, 1996), and it is more common among African Americans than among whites (Kramarow et al., 1999).

Three-fourths of the 1.5 million nursing home residents are women, mostly widows in their eighties. About 60 percent are mentally impaired. Nearly all (96 percent) need help with bathing, and nearly half (45 percent) with eating (AARP, 1995; Center on Elderly People Living Alone, 1995a; Kramarow et al., 1999; Strahan, 1997).

The difference between good and inferior nursing home care can be very great. A good nursing home has an experienced professional staff, an adequate government insurance program, and a coordinated structure that can provide various levels of care). It is lively, safe, clean, and attractive. It offers stimulating activities and opportunities to spend time with people of both sexes and all ages. It provides privacy—among other reasons, so that residents can be sexually active and so they can visit undisturbed with family members. A good nursing home also offers a full range of social, therapeutic, and rehabilitative services.

One essential element of good care is the opportunity for residents to make decisions and exert some control over their lives. Such measures may be important, not only for psychological well-being, but for physical health and life itself. Among 129 intermediate-care nursing home residents, those who had higher self-esteem, less depression, and a greater sense of satisfaction and meaning in life were less likely to die within four years—perhaps because their psychological adjustment motivated them to want to live and to take better care of themselves (O'Connor & Vallerand, 1998).

Federal law (the Omnibus Budget Reconciliation Act of 1987 and 1990) sets tough requirements for nursing homes and gives residents the right to choose their own doctors; to be fully informed about their care and treatment; and to be free from physical or mental abuse, corporal punishment, involuntary seclusion, and physical or chemical restraints. Some states train volunteer ombudsmen to act as advocates for nursing home residents, to explain their rights, and to resolve their complaints about such matters as privacy, treatment, food, and financial issues.

Because of gaps in private and governmental health insurance, nearly one-third of the cost of nursing home care falls directly on patients and their families. Privately purchased long-term care insurance, for those who can afford it, can cover part or all of this cost. Medicare pays for less than 9 percent of all expenditures on skilled nursing facilities. Although Medicaid covers nearly half of such expenditures, it is available only to people who have virtually exhausted their own resources (NCHS, 1999a). With the emergence of less expensive home health care services and group housing alternatives, utilization of nursing home beds has fallen (Strahan, 1997).

Alternative Housing Options

If and when they cannot manage entirely on their own, nearly 60 percent of adults over 50 say they would prefer to move to a residential facility that provides some care and assistance; only 26 percent would prefer to move in with relatives or friends (AARP, 1996). Today an emerging array of group housing options (see Table 18-2) makes it possible to remain in the community and to obtain needed services or care without sacrificing independence and dignity (Laquatra & Chi, 1998; Porcino, 1993).

One popular option is *assisted living,* the fastest growing form of housing for the elderly in the United States. Assisted-living facilities enable tenants to main-

Table 18-2 Group Living Arrangements for Older Adults

Facility	Description
Retirement hotel	Hotel or apartment building remodeled to meet the needs of independent older adults. Typical hotel services (switchboard, maid service, message center) are provided.
Retirement community	Large, self-contained development with owned or rental units or both. Support services and recreational facilities are often available.
Shared housing	Housing can be shared informally by adult parents and children or by friends. Sometimes social agencies match people who need a place to live with people who have houses or apartments with extra rooms. The older person usually has a private room but shares living, eating, and cooking areas and may exchange services such as light housekeeping for rent.
Accessory apartment or ECHO (elder cottage housing opportunity) housing	An independent unit created so that an older person can live in a remodeled single-family home or in a portable unit on the grounds of a single-family home—often, but not necessarily, that of an adult child. Units offer privacy, proximity to caregivers, and security.
Congregate housing	Private or government-subsidized rental apartment complexes or mobile home parks designed for older adults provide meals, housekeeping, transportation, social and recreational activities, and sometimes health care. One type of congregate housing is called a group home. A social agency that owns or rents a house brings together a small number of elderly residents and hires helpers to shop, cook, do heavy cleaning, drive, and give counseling. Residents take care of their own personal needs and take some responsibility for day-to-day tasks.
Assisted-living facility	Semi-independent living in one's own room or apartment. Similar to congregate housing, but residents receive personal care (bathing, dressing, and grooming) and protective supervision according to their needs and desires. Board-and-care homes are similar but smaller and offer more personal care and supervision.
Foster-care home	Owners of a single-family residence take in an unrelated older adult and provide meals, housekeeping, and personal care.
Continuing care retirement community	Long-term housing planned to provide a full range of accommodations and services for affluent elderly people as their needs change. A resident may start out in an independent apartment; then move into congregate housing with such services as cleaning, laundry, and meals; then into an assisted-living facility; and finally into a nursing home. Life-care communities are similar but guarantee housing and medical or nursing care for a specified period or for life; they require a substantial entry fee in addition to monthly payments.

Source: Laquatra & Chi, 1998; Porcino, 1993.

Assisted living in a homelike facility with easy access to medical and personal care is an increasingly popular alternative to nursing homes. These residents in an assisted-living facility can maintain a large degree of autonomy, as well as dignity, privacy, and companionship.

tain privacy, dignity, autonomy, and a sense of control over their own homelike space, while giving them easy access to needed personal and health care services (Citro & Hermanson, 1999).

Consider this . . .

- If you ever become incapacitated, what type of living arrangement would you prefer?

Currently less than 1 percent of older adults live in group housing, but if more such residences were available, up to 50 percent of people who would otherwise go into nursing homes might be able to stay in the community at lower cost (Laquatra & Chi, 1998). With a graying population, the need for all kinds of long-term care facilities is expected to grow rapidly by 2040, when the "baby boomers" will be in their eighties and nineties.

Mistreatment of the Elderly

A middle-aged woman drives up to a hospital emergency room in a middle-sized American city. She lifts a frail, elderly woman (who appears somewhat confused) out of the car and into a wheelchair, wheels her into the emergency room, and quietly walks out and drives away, leaving no identification (Barnhart, 1992).

elder abuse
Maltreatment or neglect of dependent older persons, or violation of their personal rights.

"Granny dumping" is one form of **elder abuse:** maltreatment or neglect of dependent older persons or violation of their personal rights. Each year, an estimated 100,000 to 200,000 geriatric patients are abandoned in emergency rooms throughout the United States by caregivers who feel they have reached the end of their rope (Lund, 1993a).

Studies in the United States, Canada, and Great Britain suggest that about 3 percent of older people are maltreated, and the number of reported cases appears to be rising (Lachs & Pillemer, 1995). There may be 2 million victims in the United States each year, according to one estimate (AARP, 1993b).

Mistreatment of the elderly may fall under any of four categories: (1) *physical violence* intended to cause injury; (2) *psychological or emotional abuse*, which may include insults and threats (such as the threat of abandonment or institutionalization); (3) *material exploitation*, or misappropriation of money or property; and (4) *neglect*—intentional or unintentional failure to meet a dependent older person's needs (Lachs & Pillemer, 1995). Physical violence may be less common than is generally believed; financial exploitation is probably more so (Bengtson, Rosenthal, & Burton, 1996). The American Medical Association (1992) has added a fifth category: *violating personal rights,* for example, the older person's right to privacy and to make her or his own personal and health decisions.

Contrary to popular belief, most elder abuse does *not* occur in institutions, where there are laws and regulations to prevent it. It most often happens to frail or demented elderly people living with spouses or children. The abuser is more likely to be a spouse, since more older people live with spouses (Lachs & Pillemer, 1995; Paveza et al, 1992; Pillemer & Finkelhor, 1988). Often, abuse of an elderly wife is a continuation of abuse that went on throughout the marriage (Bengtson et al., 1996). Neglect by family caregivers is usually unintentional; many don't know how to give proper care or are in poor health themselves.

Elder abuse should be recognized as a type of domestic violence. Most physical abuse can be resolved by counseling or other services (AARP, 1993a). Abusers need treatment to recognize what they are doing and assistance to reduce the stress of caregiving. Self-help groups may help victims acknowledge what is happening, recognize that they do not have to put up with mistreatment, and find out how to stop it or get away from it.

CHECKPOINT

Can you . . .

- ✔ Compare various kinds of living arrangements for older adults, their relative prevalence, and their advantages and disadvantages?
- ✔ Identify five types of elder abuse, give examples of each, and tell where and by whom abuse is most likely to occur?
- ✔ List several internationally adopted principles regarding the rights and needs of older adults?

Because the needs and human rights of older adults have become an international concern, the United Nations General Assembly in 1991 adopted a set of Principles for Older Persons. They cover rights to independence, participation in society, care, and opportunities for self-fulfillment (see Table 18-3). The General Assembly declared 1999 the International Year of Older Persons, with emphasis on implementing these principles.

Table 18-3 United Nations Principles for Older Persons

Independence	Participation
Older persons should have access to adequate food, water, shelter, clothing, and health care through the provision of income, family and community support, and self-help. Older persons should have the opportunity to work or to have access to other income-generating opportunities. Older persons should be able to participate in determining when and at what pace withdrawal from the labor force takes place. Older persons should have access to appropriate educational and training programs. Older persons should be able to live in environments that are safe and adaptable to personal preferences and changing capacities. Older persons should be able to reside at home for as long as possible.	Older persons should remain integrated in society, participate actively in the formulation and implementation of policies that directly affect their well-being, and share their knowledge and skills with younger generations. Older persons should be able to seek and develop opportunities for service to the community and to serve as volunteers in positions appropriate to their interests and capabilities. Older persons should be able to form movements or associations of older persons.
Care	**Self-fulfilment**
Older persons should benefit from family and community care and protection in accordance with each society's system of cultural values. Older persons should have access to health care to help them to maintain or regain the optimum level of physical, mental, and emotional well-being and to prevent or delay the onset of illness. Older persons should have access to social and legal services to enhance their autonomy, protection and care. Older persons should be able to utilize appropriate levels of institutional care providing protection, rehabilitation, and social and mental stimulation in a humane and secure environment. Older persons should be able to enjoy human rights and fundamental freedoms when residing in any shelter, care, or treatment facility, including full respect for their dignity, beliefs, needs, and privacy and for the right to make decisions about their care and the quality of their lives.	Older persons should be able to pursue opportunities for the full development of their potential. Older persons should have access to the educational, cultural, spiritual, and recreational resources of society. **Dignity** Older persons should be able to live in dignity and security and be free of exploitation and physical or mental abuse. Older persons should be treated fairly regardless of age, gender, racial or ethnic background, disability or other status, and be valued independently of their economic contribution.

Personal Relationships in Late Life

Most older people's lives are enriched by the presence of longtime friends and family members who play a major part in their lives. Although older adults may see people less often, personal relationships continue to be important—perhaps even more so than before (Antonucci & Akiyama, 1995; Carstensen, 1995; C. L. Johnson & Troll, 1992).

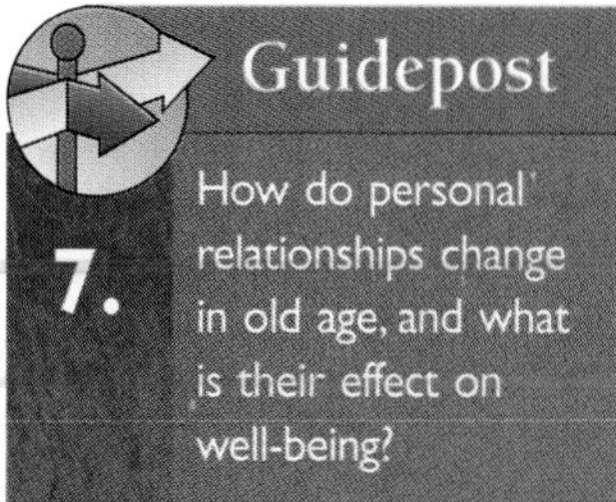

Guidepost
7.
How do personal relationships change in old age, and what is their effect on well-being?

Social Contact

As people age, they tend to spend less time with others (Carstensen, 1996). For most adults, work is a convenient source of social contact; thus longtime retirees have fewer social contacts than more recent retirees or those who continue to work. For some older adults, infirmities make it harder and harder to get out and see people. Studies also show that older people often bypass opportunities for increased social contact and are more likely than younger adults to be satisfied with smaller social networks. Yet the social contacts older adults *do* have are more important to their well-being than ever (Lansford, Sherman, & Antonucci, 1998).

Why is this? According to *social convoy theory* (introduced in Chapter 16), changes in social contact typically affect only a person's outer, less intimate social circles. After retirement, as coworkers and other casual friends drop away, most older adults retain a stable inner circle of social convoys: close friends and family members on whom they can rely for continued social support and who strongly affect their well-being for better or worse (Antonucci & Akiyama, 1995; Kahn & Antonucci, 1980).

According to *socioemotional selectivity theory* (Carstensen, 1991, 1995, 1996), older adults become increasingly selective about the people with whom they spend their time. When people perceive their remaining time as short, immediate emotional needs take precedence over long-range goals. A college student may be willing to put up with a disliked teacher for the sake of gaining knowledge to get into graduate school; an older adult may be less willing to spend precious time with a friend who gets on her nerves. Young adults with a free half hour and no urgent commitments may choose to spend the time with someone they would like to get to know better; older adults tend to choose someone they know well.

Even though older people may have fewer close relationships than younger people do, they tend to be more satisfied with those they have (Antonucci & Akiyama, 1995). While the size of the social network and the frequency of contacts declines, the quality of social support apparently does not (Bossé, Aldwin, Levenson, Spiro, & Mroczek, 1993).

Relationships and Health

As is true earlier in life, social relationships and health go hand-in-hand (Bosworth & Schaie, 1997). When Vaillant and his colleagues looked at 223 aging men from the Grant Study, social support during the previous 20 years—from friends more than from spouses and children—was a powerful predictor of physical health at age 70. However, the effect was much weaker when the researchers controlled for prior alcohol abuse, smoking, and depression—all of which can undermine both social relationships and health (Vaillant, Meyer, Mukamal, & Soldz, 1998).

What is the connection between social interaction and mortality? Among 2,575 men and women ages 65 to 102, in rural Iowa, those who reported regular contact with no more than two people during a three-year period were much more likely to die than those with larger social networks. This was true regardless of age, education, smoking history, symptoms of depression, or changes in physical health (Cerhan & Wallace, 1997).

As we reported in Box 18-1, a stable marriage seems to predict long life. But the relationship between marriage and health may be different for husbands than for wives. Whereas being married *itself* seems to have health benefits for men, women's health is linked to the *quality* of the marriage. Women are less likely to withdraw from emotionally charged conflicts; and, in a longtime marriage, an accumulation of such episodes may take a toll on women's health (Carstensen, Graff, Levenson, & Gottman, 1996).

Roles of Family and Friends

Family relationships and friendships play differing roles for older adults, as for younger ones. Friendships have the greatest positive effect on older people's well-being. As earlier in life, friendships revolve around pleasure and leisure, whereas family relationships tend to involve everyday needs and tasks. The family, however, is the primary source of emotional support. When that support is lacking, or family relationships are poor or absent, the negative effects can be profound (Antonucci & Akiyama, 1995).

The late-life family has special characteristics (Brubaker, 1983, 1990; C. L. Johnson, 1995). Many families now span four or even five generations, making it possible for a person to be both a grandparent and a grandchild at the same time. The presence of so many family members can be enriching but also can create special pressures. Increasing numbers of families are likely to have at least one member who has lived long enough to have several chronic illnesses and whose care may be physically and emotionally draining (C. L. Johnson, 1995). Many women today spend more of their lives caring for parents than for children (Abel, 1991). Now that the fastest-growing group in the population is age 85 and over, many people in their late sixties or beyond, whose own health and energy may be faltering, find themselves serving as caregivers.

The ways families deal with these issues often have cultural roots. The nuclear family, and the desire of older adults to live apart from their children whenever possible, reflect dominant American values of individualism, autonomy, and self-reliance. Hispanic and Asian American cultures traditionally emphasize *lineal,* or intergenerational obligations as seen in the multigenerational household, with power and authority lodged in the older generation. However, this pattern is being modified through assimilation into U.S. culture. African Americans and Irish Americans, whose cultures have been heavily impacted by poverty, stress *collateral,* egalitarian relationships; household structures may be highly flexible, often taking in siblings, aunts, uncles, cousins, or friends who need a place to stay. These varied cultural patterns affect family relationships and responsibilities toward the older generation (C. L. Johnson, 1995).

In the rest of this chapter we'll look more closely at older people's relationships with family and friends. We'll also examine the lives of older adults who are divorced or remarried, those who have never married, and those who are childless. (We discuss widowhood in the Epilogue.) Finally we'll consider the importance of a new role: that of great-grandparent.

Consider this . . .

- Have you ever lived in a multigenerational household? Do you think you ever might? What aspects of this lifestyle do or do not appeal to you?

CHECKPOINT

Can you . . .

✔ Tell how social contact changes in late life, and discuss theoretical explanations of this change?

✔ Cite evidence for a relationship between social interaction and health?

✔ Contrast the influences of friends and family on well-being?

✔ Compare cultural patterns that affect the position of older adults in a family?

Consensual Relationships 

Unlike other family relationships, marriage—at least in contemporary western cultures—is generally formed by mutual consent. Thus, in its effect on well-being, it has characteristics of both friendship and kinship ties (Antonucci & Akiyama, 1995). It can provide both the highest emotional highs and the lowest lows a person experiences (Carstensen et al., 1996). What happens to marital satisfaction in late life?

Guidepost

8. What are the characteristics of long-term marriages in late life, and what impact do divorce and remarriage have at this time?

Long-Term Marriage

The long-term marriage is a relatively new phenomenon; most marriages, like most people, used to have a shorter life span. Today, about 1 marriage in 5, like Jimmy and Rosalynn Carter's, lasts fifty or more years (Brubaker, 1983, 1993). Because women usually marry older men and outlive them, and because men are more likely to remarry after divorce or widowhood, many more men than women are married in late life (AARP, 1999; see Figure 18-4). The imbalance is especially striking among African Americans, since black men have a lower life expectancy than white men, and older black men, when they marry, tend to choose much younger women (Tucker, Taylor, & Mitchell-Kernan, 1993). Perhaps for this reason, most studies of long-term marriages have focused on white middle-class samples.

Married couples who are still together in late adulthood are more likely than middle-aged couples to report their marriage as satisfying, and many say it has

Many couples who are still together late in life, especially in the middle to late sixties, say that they are happier in marriage now than they were in their younger years. Important benefits of marriage, which may help older couples face the ups and downs of late life, include intimacy, sharing, and a sense of belonging to one another. Romance, fun, and sensuality have their place, too, as this couple in a hot tub demonstrate.

improved (Carstensen et al., 1996; Gilford, 1986). Since divorce has been easier to obtain for some years, spouses who are still together late in life are likely to have worked out their differences and to have arrived at mutually satisfying accommodations (Huyck, 1995). With the end of child rearing, children tend to become a source of shared pleasure and pride instead of a source of conflict (Carstensen et al., 1996).

How couples resolve conflicts is a key to marital satisfaction throughout adulthood. Patterns of conflict resolution tend to remain fairly constant throughout a marriage, but older couples' greater ability to regulate their emotions may make their conflicts less severe. In one study, happily and unhappily married middle-aged and older couples were videotaped discussing mutually chosen pleasant and conflictual topics. Later the spouses separately viewed the tapes while pressing a rating dial to record the degree of positive or negative emotion they had experienced during each conversation. In conflict situations, older couples showed less anger, disgust, belligerence, and whining, as well as more affection, than middle-aged couples; and they also derived more pleasure from talking about pleasant topics, such as mutual activities, children and grandchildren, dreams, and vacations (Carstensen et al., 1996).

In dual-career couples, when employment and retirement patterns conflict with role expectations, trouble may ensue. Because many middle-aged divorced men marry much younger women, a second wife may be at the peak of her career when her husband retires. If the husband has traditional attitudes about gender roles, he may object to her continuing to work and may feel threatened by loss of his status as provider. Arguments may arise if the wife expects him, as the at-home partner, to do more housework (Szinovacz, 1996).

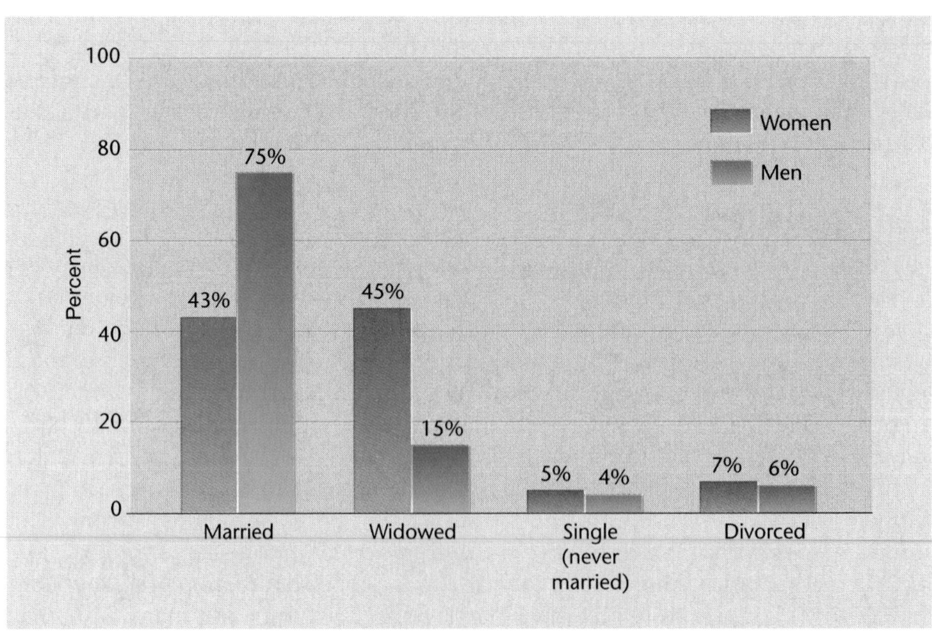

Figure 18-4
Marital status of noninstitutionalized persons age 65 and over, 1998.
(Source: American Association of Retired People [AARP], 1999; based on data from U.S. Bureau of the Census.)

Late-life marriage can be severely tested by advancing age and physical ills. Spouses who must care for disabled partners may feel isolated, angry, and frustrated, especially when they are in poor health themselves. Such couples may be caught in a "vicious cycle": the illness puts strains on the marriage, and these strains may aggravate the illness, stretching coping capacity to the breaking point (Karney & Bradbury, 1995) and putting the caregiver's life at heightened risk (Kiecolt-Glaser & Glaser, 1999; Schulz & Beach, 1999). Caregiving spouses who are optimistic and well adjusted to begin with, and who stay in touch with friends, usually cope best (Hooker, Monahan, Shifren, & Hutchinson, 1992; Skaff & Pearlin, 1992).

Divorce and Remarriage

Divorce in late life is rare; couples who take this step usually do it much earlier. Only about 7 percent of adults over age 65 are divorced and not remarried (refer back to Figure 18-4). However, since 1990 their numbers have increased five times as fast as the older population as a whole (AARP, 1999). Given the high divorce rates among younger cohorts, the proportion of older people who are divorced is likely to rise in the future; and given the greater opportunities for men to remarry, the gap between the sexes probably will widen (Norton & Miller, 1992; Uhlenberg, Cooney, & Boyd, 1990).

Divorce can be especially difficult for older people. Older divorced and separated men are less satisfied with friendships and leisure activities than married men. For both sexes, rates of mental illness and death are higher than average, perhaps in part because of inadequate social support (Uhlenberg & Myers, 1981).

Remarriage in late life may have a special character. Among 125 well-educated, fairly affluent men and women, those in late-life remarriages seemed more trusting and accepting, and less in need of deep sharing of personal feelings. Men, but not women, tended to be more satisfied in late-life remarriages than in midlife ones (Bograd & Spilka, 1996).

Remarriage has societal benefits, since older married people are less likely than those living alone to need help from the community. Remarriage could be encouraged by letting people keep pension and social security benefits derived from a previous marriage and by greater availability of shared living quarters, such as group housing.

Single Life

Only 4 percent of U.S. men and women 65 years and older have never married (AARP, 1998; refer back to Figure 18-4). This percentage is likely to increase as today's middle-aged adults grow old, since larger proportions of that cohort, especially African Americans, have remained single (U.S. Bureau of the Census, 1991a, 1991b, 1992a, 1993a). Since 1970 this has been a worldwide trend (United Nations, 1991).

Guidepost
9.
How do unmarried older people and those in gay and lesbian relationships fare?

Older never-married people are more likely than older divorced or widowed people to prefer single life and less likely to be lonely (Dykstra, 1995). However, women who have remained single do feel lonely if they lose their health. Poor health undermines their sense of self-reliance and may force them into dependence on relatives they would rather not be with (Essex & Nam, 1987).

Never-married, childless women in one study rated three kinds of roles or relationships as important: bonds with blood relatives, such as siblings and aunts; parent-surrogate ties with younger people; and same-generation, same-sex friendships (Rubinstein, Alexander, Goodman, & Luborsky, 1991).

Previously married older men are much more likely to date than older women, probably because of the greater availability of women in this age group. Most elderly daters are sexually active but do not expect to marry. Among both whites

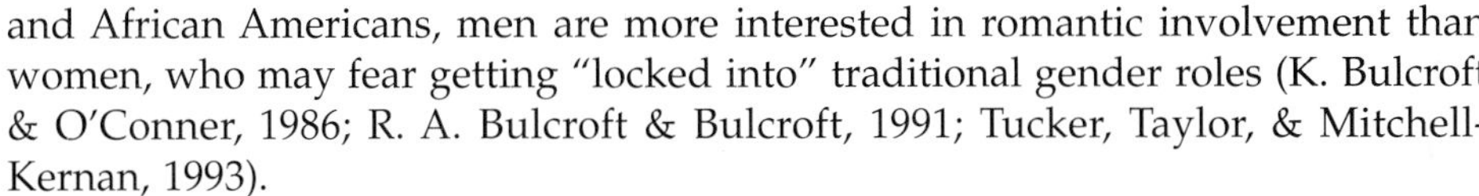

CHECKPOINT

Can you . . .

- ✔ Explain the difference in marital satisfaction between middle and late adulthood?
- ✔ Tell how divorce, remarriage, and single life differ in earlier and late adulthood?

and African Americans, men are more interested in romantic involvement than women, who may fear getting "locked into" traditional gender roles (K. Bulcroft & O'Conner, 1986; R. A. Bulcroft & Bulcroft, 1991; Tucker, Taylor, & Mitchell-Kernan, 1993).

As black women age, they are increasingly less likely than black men to be married, romantically involved, or interested in a romantic relationship—perhaps for practical reasons, as unmarried black women tend to be better off financially than married ones (Tucker et al., 1993). Yet a single state entails risk: a black woman living alone in late life is three times as likely to be poor as a white woman in that situation (U.S. Bureau of the Census, 1991b). Furthermore, women living alone are more likely to end up in institutions (Tucker et al., 1993).

Gay and Lesbian Relationships

There is little research on homosexual relationships in old age. This is largely because the current cohort of older adults grew up at a time when homosexuality was considered a perversion, and living openly as a homosexual was rare (Huyck, 1995). An important distinction is between elderly homosexuals who recognized themselves as gay or lesbian before the rise of the gay liberation movement in the late 1960s and those who did not do so until that movement (and the shift in public discourse it brought about) was in full swing. Whereas the self-concept of the first group was shaped by the prevailing stigma against homosexuality, the second group tend to view their homosexuality simply as a *status*: a characteristic of the self, like any other (Rosenfeld, 1999).

Older homosexual adults, like older heterosexual adults, have strong needs for intimacy, social contact, and generativity. Contrary to stereotypes about the lonely, isolated aging homosexual, gays' and lesbians' relationships in late life tend to be strong, supportive, and diverse. Many homosexuals have children from earlier marriages; others have adopted children. Friendship networks or support groups may substitute for the traditional family (Reid, 1995).

Many gays and lesbians—especially those who have maintained close relationships and strong involvement in the homosexual community—adapt to aging with relative ease. Having had practice in dealing with one kind of stigma, gays and lesbians who have achieved a comfortable sexual identity may be better prepared to cope with the stigma of aging. Their main problems grow out of societal attitudes: strained relationships with the family of origin, discrimination, lack of medical or social services and social support, insensitive policies of social agencies, and dealing with health care providers or bereavement and inheritance issues when a partner falls ill or dies (Berger & Kelly, 1986; Kimmel, 1990; Reid, 1995).

Intimacy is important to older lesbians and gays, as it is to older heterosexual adults. Contrary to stereotype, homosexual relationships in late life are generally strong and supportive.

According to some research, living openly as a gay man or lesbian may ease the adjustment to aging (Friend, 1991). Coming out—whenever it occurs—is an important developmental transition, which can enhance mental health, life satisfaction, self-acceptance, and self-respect (Reid, 1995). On the other hand, a study of 47 elderly Canadian gay men suggests that avoiding stress—including the stress of coming out—can contribute to well-being in old age (J. A. Lee, 1987). Because of the greater stigma attached to homosexuality when these men were younger, many did not publicly acknowledge their homosexuality until late life, if at all; and such a course may well have been adaptive, given the circumstances (Reid, 1995).

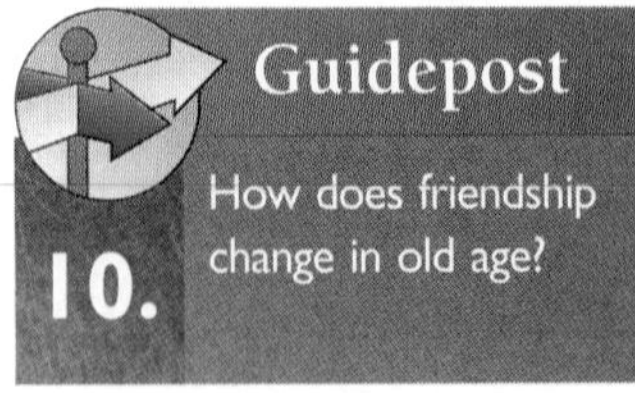

Guidepost
10.
How does friendship change in old age?

Friendships

The meaning of friendship—a relationship involving mutual give-and-take—changes little over the life span, but its context and content change. Among older adults, friendships typically are no longer linked to work and parenting, as in earlier periods of adulthood. Instead, they focus on companionship and support (Hartup & Stevens, 1999).

Most older people have close friends, and those with an active circle of friends are healthier and happier (Antonucci & Akiyama, 1995; Babchuk, 1978–1979; Lemon et al., 1972; Steinbach, 1992). Friends soften the impact of stress on physical and mental health (Cutrona, Russell, & Rose, 1986). People who can confide their feelings and thoughts and can talk about their worries and pain with friends deal better with the changes and crises of aging (Genevay, 1986; Lowenthal & Haven, 1968). They also seem to extend their lives (Steinbach, 1992).

The element of choice in friendship may be especially important to older people, who may feel their control over their lives slipping away (R. G. Adams, 1986). Intimacy is another important benefit of friendship for older adults, who need to know that they are still valued and wanted despite physical and other losses (Essex & Nam, 1987). It may be that women's greater comfort with self-disclosure and expression of feelings contributes to their greater life expectancy (Weg, 1987).

Older people enjoy time spent with their friends more than time spent with their families (Antonucci & Akiyama, 1995). In one study, 92 retired adults between ages 55 and 88 wore beepers for one week. At about two-hour intervals, when paged, they filled out reports on what they were doing and with whom, and what they were thinking and feeling (Larson, Mannell, & Zuzanek, 1986). These people were generally more alert, excited, and emotionally aroused with friends than with family members, including their spouses. One reason may be that older people spend more active, enjoyable leisure time with friends but do household tasks or watch television with family. Older people feel a reciprocal sense of openness with their friends, and the lightheartedness and spontaneity of friendships help them rise above daily concerns.

Still, spending time with friends does not result in higher overall life satisfaction, whereas spending more time with a spouse does. It may be the very brevity and infrequency of the time spent with friends that give it its special flavor. Friends are a powerful source of *immediate* enjoyment; the family provides greater emotional security and support (Antonucci & Akiyama, 1995).

People usually rely on neighbors in emergencies and on relatives for long-term commitments, such as caregiving; but friends may, on occasion, fulfill both these functions. Friends and neighbors often take the place of family members who are far away. And, although friends cannot replace a spouse or partner, they can help compensate for the lack of one (Hartup & Stevens, 1999). Among 131

Older people often enjoy the time they spend with friends more than the time they spend with family members. The openness and excitement of relationships between friends help them rise above worries and problems. Intimate friendships give older people a sense of being valued and wanted and help them deal with the changes and crises of aging.

older adults in the Netherlands who were never-married, divorced, or widowed, those who received high levels of emotional and practical support from friends were less likely to be lonely (Dykstra, 1995).

CHECKPOINT

Can you . . .

- ✔ Give reasons for the diversity of gay and lesbian relationships in late life and identify factors that influence homosexuals' adaption to aging?
- ✔ Cite special benefits of friendship in old age and tell in what ways friendships tend to change?

In line with social convoy and socioemotional selectivity theories, casual friends may fall by the wayside, but longtime friendships often persist into very old age (Hartup & Stevens, 1999). Sometimes, however, relocation, illness, or disability make it hard to keep up with old friends. Although many older people do make new friends, even after age 85 (C. L. Johnson & Troll, 1994), older adults are more likely than younger ones to ascribe the benefits of friendship (such as affection and loyalty) to specific individuals, who cannot easily be replaced if they die, go into a nursing home, or move away (de Vries, 1996).

Ethnicity may influence the nature of friendship and the size of perceived friendship networks. French Canadians, for example, name fewer friends than British Canadians, and they also live closer to the people they call friends and see them more often (de Vries, 1996).

Nonmarital Kinship Ties

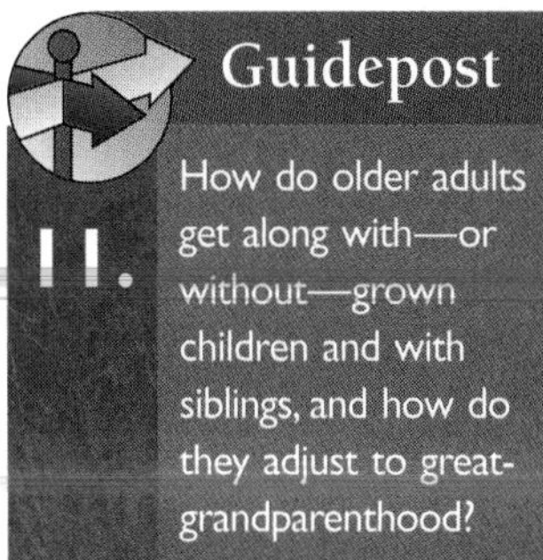

Guidepost
11.
How do older adults get along with—or without—grown children and with siblings, and how do they adjust to great-grandparenthood?

Some of the the most lasting and important relationships in late life are the ones that come, not from mutual choice (as marriages, homosexual partnerships, and friendships do), but from kinship bonds. Let's look at these.

Relationships with Adult Children—or Their Absence

As socioemotional selectivity theory predicts, aging adults seek to spend more of their time with the people who mean the most to them, such as their children (Troll & Fingerman, 1996). Four out of 5 older adults have living children, 6 out of 10 see their children at least once a week, and 3 out of 4 talk on the phone that often (AARP, 1995). Most older people live within ten miles of at least one adult child, and (if they have more than one child) within thirty miles of another (Lin & Rogerson, 1995).

Children provide a link with other family members—especially, of course, with grandchildren. In one group of 150 "old-old" people in diverse socioeconomic circumstances, those who were parents were more actively in touch with other relatives than were childless people (C. L. Johnson & Troll, 1992). Older people in better health have more contact with their families than those in poorer health and report feeling closer to them (Field, Minkler, Falk, & Leino, 1993).

The balance of mutual aid that flows between parents and their adult children tends to shift as parents age, with children providing a greater share of support (Bengtson et al., 1990; 1996). Institutional supports such as social security, Medicare, and Medicaid have lifted some responsibilities for the elderly from family members; but many adult children do provide significant assistance and care to aged parents (refer back to Chapter 16). Older adults are likely to be depressed if they need help from their children, whether or not they actually get it. In a society in which both generations value their independence, the prospect of dependency can be demoralizing. Parents do not want to be a burden on their children or deplete their children's resources. Yet parents may also be depressed if they fear that their children will *not* take care of them (G. R. Lee, Netzer, & Coward, 1995).

Older parents continue to show strong concern about their children, think about them often, and help them when needed. Especially in disadvantaged communities beset by unemployment, poverty, homelessness, unwed pregnancy, and drug abuse, family networks represent not only sources of help *for* elderly members but also, potentially, demands for help *from* them (Bengtson et al., 1996). Elderly parents tend to be distressed or become depressed if their children have serious problems, for example, with drugs or financial dependency; parents may consider such problems a sign of their own failure (Greenberg & Becker, 1988; G. R. Lee et al., 1995; Pillemer & Suitor, 1991; Suitor, Pillemer, Keeton, & Robison, 1995; Troll & Fingerman, 1996).

Many elderly people whose adult children are mentally ill, retarded, physically disabled, or stricken with AIDS or other serious illnesses serve as primary caregivers for as long as both parent and child live (Brabant, 1994; Greenberg & Becker, 1988; Ryff & Seltzer, 1995). And a growing number of grandparents, and even great-grandparents, particularly African Americans, raise or help raise children.

As we discussed in Chapter 15, nonnormative caregivers, who are pressed into active parenting at a time when such a role is unexpected, frequently feel strain. This may be even more true of elderly caregivers than of middle-aged ones. Often ill-prepared physically, emotionally, and financially for the task, they may not know where to turn for help and support. They worry about who will take over for them when they become sick or die—as well as who will take care of *them* (Abramson, 1995).

What about the 1 in 5 older adults without living children? Studies suggest that they are no lonelier, no more negative about their lives, and no more afraid of death than those with children (C. L. Johnson & Catalano, 1981; Keith, 1983; Rempel, 1985). However, some older women who never had children express regret, and that feeling becomes more intense the older they get (Alexander, Rubinstein, Goodman, & Luborsky, 1992).

Widows without grown children may lack an important source of solace (O'Bryant, 1988; Suitor et al., 1995). Childless people also may lack a ready source of care and support if they become infirm. Since almost 17 percent of the baby-boom women who were in their early forties in 1996 had not yet had children, and most of them probably will not do so, providing for their care may become a growing problem (NCHS, 1998a).

Relationships with Siblings

Elizabeth ("Bessie") and Sarah ("Sadie") Delany both lived to be over 100. Their father was a freed slave who became an Episcopal bishop. Bessie overcame racial and gender discrimination to become a dentist, and Sadie was a high school teacher. The sisters never married; for three decades they lived together in Mount Vernon, New York. Although their personalities were as different as sugar and spice, the two women were best friends, sharing a sense of fun and the values their parents had instilled in them (Delany, Delany, & Hearth, 1993).

More than 3 out of 4 Americans age 60 and older have at least one living sibling, and those in the "young-old" bracket average 2 or 3 (Cicirelli, 1995). Brothers and sisters play important roles in the support networks of older people. Siblings, more than other family members, provide companionship, as friends do; but siblings, more than friends, also provide emotional support (Bedford, 1995).

Most older adult siblings say they stand ready to provide tangible help and would turn to a sibling for such help if needed, but relatively few actually do so except in emergencies such as illness (when they may become caregivers) or the death of a spouse (Cicirelli, 1995). Siblings in developing countries are more likely to furnish economic aid (Bedford, 1995). Regardless of how much help they actually give, siblings' *readiness* to help is a source of comfort and security in late life (Cicirelli, 1995). For people who are unmarried or have only one or two children, or none, relationships with siblings and their children in late life may become increasingly significant (Bedford, 1995; Rubinstein et al., 1991).

The nearer older people live to their siblings and the more siblings they have, the more likely they are to confide in them (Connidis & Davies, 1992). Reminiscing about shared early experiences becomes more frequent in old age; it may help in reviewing a life and putting the significance of family relationships into perspective (Cicirelli, 1995).

Bessie and Sadie Delany, daughters of a freed slave, were best friends all their lives—more than 100 years—and wrote two books together about the values they grew up with and the story of their long, active lives. Elderly siblings are an important part of each other's support network, and sisters are especially vital in maintaining family relationships.

Sisters are especially vital in maintaining family relationships and well-being, perhaps because of women's emotional expressiveness and traditional role as nurterers (Bedford, 1995; Cicirelli, 1989a, 1995). Older people who are close to their sisters feel better about life and worry less about aging than those without sisters, or without close ties to them (Cicirelli, 1977, 1989a). Among a national sample of bereaved adults in the Netherlands, those coping with the death of a sister experienced more difficulty than those who had lost a spouse or a parent (Cleiren, Diekstra, Kerkhof, & van der Wal, 1994).

Conflict and overt rivalry generally decrease by old age, and some siblings try to resolve earlier conflicts. However, underlying feelings of rivalry may remain, especially between brothers (Cicirelli, 1995). In one study 80 percent of older siblings had positive relationships—intimate, congenial, or loyal—while 10 percent were apathetic and 10 percent were hostile (Gold, 1987).

CHECKPOINT

Can you . . .

- ✔ Tell how contact and mutual aid between parents and grown children changes during late adulthood, and how childlessness can affect older people?
- ✔ Discuss the importance of sibling relationships in late life?

The death of a sibling in old age may be understood as a normative part of that stage of life, but still, survivors may grieve intensely and become lonely or depressed. The loss of a sibling represents not only a loss of someone to lean on and a shift in the family constellation, but perhaps even a partial loss of identity. To mourn for a sibling is to mourn for the lost completeness of the original family within which one came to know oneself. It also can bring home one's own nearness to death (Cicirelli, 1995).

Becoming Great-Grandparents

As grandchildren grow up, grandparents generally see them less often (see the discussion of grandparenthood in Chapter 16). Then, when grandchildren become parents, grandparents move into a new role: great-grandparenthood.

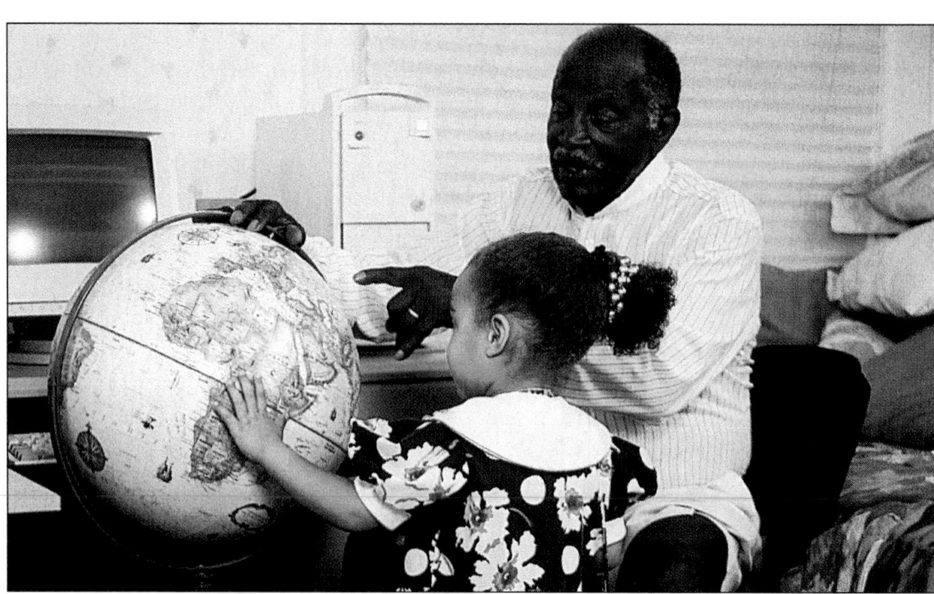

Grandparents and great-grandparents are an important source of wisdom and companionship, a link to the past, and a symbol of the continuity of family life. This African American great-grandfather points out to his great-granddaughter where her ancestors came from.

Because of age, declining health, and the scattering of families, great-grandparents tend to be less involved than grandparents in a child's life. And because four- or five-generation families are relatively new, there are few generally accepted guidelines for what great-grandparents are supposed to do (Cherlin & Furstenberg, 1986b). Still, most great-grandparents find the role fulfilling (Pruchno & Johnson, 1996). Great-grandparenthood offers a sense of personal and family renewal, a source of diversion, and a mark of longevity. When 40 great-grandfathers and great-grandmothers, ages 71 to 90, were interviewed, 93 percent made such comments as "Life is starting again in my family," "Seeing them grow keeps me young," and "I never thought I'd live to see it" (Doka & Mertz, 1988, pp. 193–194). More than one-third of the sample (mostly women) were close to their great-grandchildren. The ones with the most intimate connections were likely to live nearby and to be close to the children's parents and grandparents as well, often helping out with loans, gifts, and baby-sitting.

Grandparents and great-grandparents are important to their families. They are sources of wisdom, companions in play, links to the past, and symbols of the continuity of family life. They are engaged in the ultimate generative function: expressing the human longing to transcend mortality by investing themselves in the lives of future generations.

CHECKPOINT

Can you . . .

✔ Identify values great-grandparents find in their role?

Consider this . . .

• Which theories of psychosocial development in late life seem best supported by the information in this chapter on work, retirement, living arrangements, and relationships? Why?

Summary

Theory and Research on Psychosocial Development

Guidepost 1. What happens to personality in old age?

- Personality traits tend to remain stable in late adulthood, but cohort differences have been found.

Guidepost 2. What special issues or tasks do older people need to deal with?

- Erik Erikson's final crisis is **ego integrity versus despair,** culminating in the "virtue" of wisdom, or acceptance of one's life and impending death.
- George Vaillant found that the use of mature adaptive mechanisms was the most significant factor in emotional adjustment at age 65.

Guidepost 3. How do older adults cope?

- A current approach to the study of **coping** is the **cognitive-appraisal model.** Adults of all ages generally prefer **problem-focused coping,** but older adults do more **emotion-focused coping** than younger adults when the situation calls for it.
- Religion is an important source of emotion-focused coping for many older adults.

Guidepost 4. Is there such a thing as successful aging? If so, how can it be defined and measured?

- Two contrasting early models of "successful" or "optimal" aging are **disengagement theory** and **activity theory.** Disengagement theory has little support, and findings on activity theory are mixed. Newer refinements of activity theory are **continuity theory** and a distinction between productive and leisure activity.
- Baltes and his colleagues suggest that successful aging may depend on selective optimization with compensation, in the psychosocial as well as cognitive realm.

Lifestyle and Social Issues Related to Aging

Guidepost 5. What are some issues regarding work and retirement in late life, and how do older adults handle time and money?

- Some older people continue to work for pay, but the vast majority are retired. However, many retired people start new careers or do part-time paid or volunteer work.
- Age has both positive and negative effects on job performance, and individual differences are more significant than age differences. With appropriate training, older adults can learn new skills.
- The financial situation of older people has improved, but still about 30 percent can expect to live in poverty at some point. Many, especially widows and the infirm, become poor for the first time after retirement.
- Common lifestyle patterns after retirement include a **family-focused lifestyle, balanced investment,** and **serious leisure.**

Guidepost 6. What options for living arrangements do older adults have?

- Most older people live with family, usually with a spouse. Minority elders are more likely than white elders to live with extended family members. Most older people do not want to live with their children.
- About 1 in 3 uninstitutionalized older adults lives alone. Most of those are widowed women. Most older people prefer to remain in their own homes.
- Only 4 percent of the older population are institutionalized at a given time, but the proportion increases greatly with age. Fast-growing alternatives to

institutionalization include assisted-living facilities and other kinds of group housing.
- **Elder abuse** is most often suffered by a frail or demented older person living with a spouse or child.

Personal Relationships in Late Life

Guidepost 7. How do personal relationships change in old age, and what is their effect on well-being?

- Relationships are very important to older people, even though frequency of social contact declines in old age.
- According to social convoy theory, reductions or changes in social contact in late life do not impair well-being because a stable inner circle of social support is maintained. According to socioemotional selectivity theory, older people prefer to spend time with people who enhance their emotional well-being.
- Social support is associated with good health, and isolation is a risk factor for mortality.
- Friendships have the greatest positive effect on older people's well-being, but family relationships, or their absence, can have the greatest negative effects.
- The way multigenerational late-life families function often has cultural roots.

Consensual Relationships

Guidepost 8. What are the characteristics of long-term marriages in late life, and what impact do divorce and remarriage have at this time?

- As life expectancy increases, so does the potential longevity of marriage. More men than women are married in late life. Marriages that last into late adulthood tend to be relatively satisfying.
- Divorce is relatively uncommon among older people, and few divorced older adults do not remarry. Divorce can be especially difficult for older people. Remarriages may be more relaxed in late life.
- A small but increasing percentage of adults, especially African Americans, now reach old age without marrying. Never-married adults are less likely to be lonely than divorced or widowed ones.

Guidepost 9. How do unmarried older people and those in gay and lesbian relationships fare?

- Older homosexuals, like heterosexuals, have needs for intimacy, social contact, and generativity. Many gays and lesbians adapt to aging with relative ease. Adjustment may be influenced by coming-out status.

Guidepost 10. How does friendship change in old age?

- Friendships in old age focus on companionship and support, not work and parenting. Most older adults have close friends, and those who do are healthier and happier. Longtime friendships tend to persist.

Nonmarital Kinship Ties

Guidepost 11. How do older adults get along with—or without—grown children and with siblings, and how do they adjust to great-grandparenthood?

- Elderly parents and their adult children frequently see or contact each other, are concerned about each other, and offer each other assistance. An increasing number of elderly parents are caregivers for adult children, grandchildren, or great-grandchildren.
- In some respects, childlessness does not seem to be an important disadvantage in old age, but providing care for infirm elderly people without children can be a problem.
- Often siblings offer each other emotional support, and sometimes more tangible support as well. Sisters in particular maintain sibling ties.
- Great-grandparents are less involved in children's lives than grandparents, but most find the role fulfilling.

Key Terms

ego integrity versus despair (679)
coping (680)
cognitive-appraisal model (680)
problem-focused coping (680)
emotion-focused coping (681)
disengagement theory (684)
activity theory (684)
continuity theory (685)
family-focused lifestyle (690)
balanced investment (690)
serious leisure (690)
elder abuse (696)

Epilogue
The End of Life

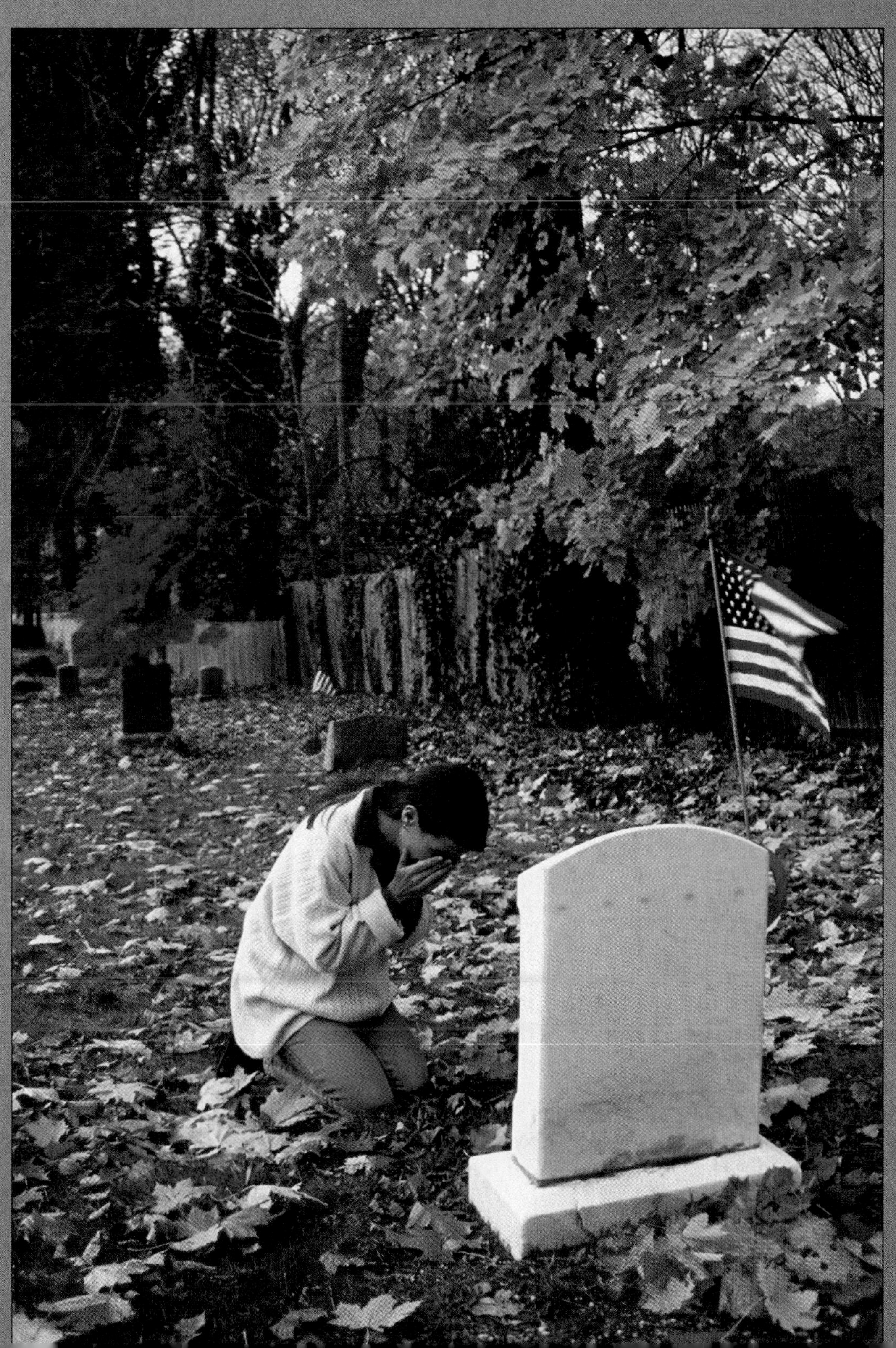

The key to the question of death unlocks the door of life.

Elisabeth Kübler-Ross, *Death: The Final Stage of Growth,* 1975

All the while I thought I was learning how to live, I have been learning how to die.

Notebooks of Leonardo da Vinci

Human beings are individuals; they undergo different experiences and react to them in different ways. Yet one unavoidable part of everyone's life is its end. The better we understand this inevitable event and the more wisely we approach it, the more fully we can live until it comes.

Death is a *biological* fact; but it also has *social, cultural, historical, religious, legal, psychological, developmental, medical,* and *ethical* aspects, and often these are closely intertwined. Customs and attitudes surrounding death are shaped by the time and place in which people live. Cultural aspects of death include care of and behavior toward the dying and the dead, the setting where death usually takes place, and mourning customs and rituals—from the all-night Irish wake, at which friends and family toast the memory of the dead person, to the weeklong Jewish *shiva,* at which mourners vent their feelings and share memories of the deceased. Some cultural conventions, such as flying a flag at half-mast after the death of a public figure, are codified in law.

Cultural and religious attitudes toward death and dying affect psychological and developmental aspects of death: how people of various ages face their own death and the deaths of those close to them. Death may mean one thing to an elderly Japanese Buddhist, imbued with teachings of accepting the inevitable, and another to a third-generation Japanese American youth who has grown up with a belief in directing one's own destiny.

Although death is inescapable, its timing may be, to some extent, under human control. Efforts to postpone or hasten death have medical, legal, and ethical ramifications. Although death is generally considered to be the cessation of bodily processes, criteria for death have become more complex with the development of medical apparatus that can prolong basic signs of life. These medical developments have raised questions about whether or when life supports may be withheld or removed and whose judgment should prevail. In some places, the claim of a "right to die" has led to laws either permitting or forbidding physicians to help a terminally ill person end a life that has become a burden.

The stark biological fact of death, then, is far from the whole story. Let's look at the many interwoven aspects of death, dying, and bereavement.

Death and Bereavement: The Social-Cultural-Historical Context

Although death and bereavement are universal experiences, they have a cultural context. Customs concerning disposal and remembrance of the dead, transfer of possessions, and even expression of grief vary greatly from culture to culture and often are governed by religious or legal prescriptions that reflect a society's view of what death is and what happens afterward.

In Malayan society, as in many other preliterate societies, death was seen as a gradual transition. A body was at first given only provisional burial. Survivors continued to perform mourning rites until the body decayed to the point where the soul was believed to have left it and to have been admitted into the spiritual realm.

In ancient Greece, bodies of heroes were publicly burned as a sign of honor; public cremation still is practiced by Hindus in India and Nepal. By contrast, cremation is prohibited under Orthodox Jewish law in the belief that the dead will rise again for a Last Judgment and the chance for eternal life (Ausubel, 1964).

In Japan, religious rituals encourage survivors to maintain contact with the deceased. Families keep an altar in the home dedicated to their ancestors; they talk to their dead loved ones and offer them food or cigars. In Gambia the dead are considered part of the community; among Native Americans, the Hopi fear the spirits of the dead and try to forget a deceased person as quickly as possible. Muslims in Egypt show grief through expressions of deep sorrow; Muslims in Bali are encouraged to suppress sadness, to laugh, and to be joyful (Stroebe, Gergen, Gergen, & Stroebe, 1992). All these varied customs and practices help people deal with death and bereavement through well-understood cultural meanings that provide a stable anchor amid the turbulence of loss.

Some modern social customs have evolved from ancient ones. Embalming goes back to a practice common in ancient Egypt and China: *mummification,* preserving a body so the soul can return to it. A traditional Jewish custom is never to leave a dying person alone. Anthropologists suggest that the original reason for this may have been a belief that evil spirits hover around, trying to enter the dying body (Ausubel, 1964). Such rituals give people facing a loss something predictable and important to do at a time when they otherwise might feel confused and helpless.

Facing Death and Loss: Social and Psychological Issues

One of the most moving parts of the classic nineteenth-century novel *Little Women* by Louisa May Alcott (1868–1929) is the chapter recounting the last year in the life of gentle, home-loving Beth—an account based on the death of Alcott's sister Lizzie at age 23 (Myerson, Shealy, & Stern, 1987). In Alcott's time, death was a frequent, normal, expected event, sometimes welcomed as a peaceful end to suffering. Caring for a dying person at home, as the Alcott family did, was a common experience (as it still is in many contemporary rural cultures). Looking death in the eye day by day, both adults and children absorbed an important truth: that dying is part of living, and confronting the end of life can give deeper meaning to the whole of life.

Advances in medicine and sanitation during the twentieth century have brought about a "mortality revolution," especially in developed countries. Women today are less likely to die in childbirth, infants are more likely to survive their first year, children are more likely to reach adulthood, adults are more likely to reach old age, and older people often can overcome illnesses they grew up regarding as fatal.

As death increasingly became a phenomenon of late adulthood, it became "invisible and abstract" (Fulton & Owen, 1987–1988, p. 380). Many older people lived and died in retirement communities. Care of the dying and the dead became largely a task for professionals. Such social conventions as isolation of the dying person in a hospital or nursing home and refusal to openly discuss his or her condition reflected and perpetuated attitudes of avoidance and denial of death. Death—even of the very old—came to be regarded as a failure of medical treatment rather than as a natural end to life (McCue, 1995).

Today, societal violence, drug abuse, poverty, and the spread of AIDS make it harder to deny the reality of death. Issues of quality versus quantity of life and the "right to die" are constantly in the news. *Thanatology,* the study of death and dying, is arousing interest, and educational programs have been established to help people deal with death. Because of the prohibitive cost of extended hospital care that cannot save the terminally ill, many more deaths are occurring at home (Techner, 1994).

Along with the growing tendency to face death more honestly, movements have arisen to make dying more humane. These include hospice care and self-help support groups for dying people and their families. *Hospice care* is personal, patient- and family-centered care for the terminally ill. Its focus is on *palliative care:* relief of pain and suffering, control of symptoms, maintaining a satisfactory quality of life, and allowing the patient to die in peace and dignity. Hospice care usually takes place at home; but such care can be given in a hospital or another institution, at a hospice center, or through a combination of home and institutional care. Family members often take an active part. In 1996 about 1,800 hospice programs and home health care agencies in the United States provided hospice care to an estimated 59,400 patients, most of whom had cancer or heart disease (Haupt, 1998).

"Stages" of Dying

How do people deal with imminent death? According to the psychiatrist Elisabeth Kübler-Ross, most dying people welcome an opportunity to talk openly about their condition and are aware of being close to death, even when they have not been told. After speaking with some 500 terminally ill patients, Kübler-Ross (1969, 1970) outlined five stages in coming to terms with death: (1) *denial* (refusal to accept the reality of what is happening); (2) *anger;* (3) *bargaining for extra time;* (4) *depression;* and ultimately (5) *acceptance.* She also proposed a similar progression in the feelings of people facing imminent bereavement (Kübler-Ross, 1975).

Kübler-Ross's model has been criticized. Although the emotions she described are common, not everyone goes through all five stages, and not necessarily in the same sequence. A person may go back and forth between anger and depression, for example, or may feel both at once. Unfortunately, some health professionals assume that these stages are inevitable and universal, and others feel that they have failed if they cannot bring a patient to the final stage of acceptance. Dying, like living, is an individual experience. For some people, denial or anger may be a healthier way to face death than calm acceptance. Kübler-Ross's description, then, should not be considered a universal model or a criterion for a "good death."

Patterns of Grieving

Grief, like dying, is a highly personal experience. Today research has challenged earlier notions of a single, "normal" pattern of grieving and a "normal" timetable for recovery. A widow talking to her late husband might once have been considered emotionally disturbed; now this is recognized as a common and helpful behavior (Lund, 1993b). Although some people recover fairly quickly after bereavement, others never do.

Perhaps the most widely studied pattern of grief is a three-stage one, in which the bereaved person accepts the painful reality of the loss, gradually lets go of the bond with the dead person, and readjusts to life by developing new interests and relationships. This process of *grief work,* the working out of psychological issues connected with grief, generally takes the following path—though, as with Kübler-Ross's stages, it may vary (J. T. Brown & Stoudemire, 1983; R. Schulz, 1978).

1. *Shock and disbelief.* Immediately following a death, survivors often feel lost and confused. As awareness of the loss sinks in, the initial numbness gives way to overwhelming feelings of sadness and frequent crying. This first stage may last several weeks, especially after a sudden or unexpected death.
2. *Preoccupation with the memory of the dead person.* In the second stage, which may last six months or longer, the survivor tries to come to terms with the death but cannot yet accept it. A widow may relive her husband's death and their entire relationship. From time to time, she may be seized by a feeling that her dead husband is present. These experiences diminish with time, though they may recur—perhaps for years—on such occasions as the anniversary of the marriage or of the death.
3. *Resolution.* The final stage has arrived when the bereaved person renews interest in everyday activities. Memories of the dead person bring fond feelings mingled with sadness, rather than sharp pain and longing.

Although the pattern of grief work just described is common, grieving does not necessarily follow a straight line from shock to resolution. One team of psychologists (Wortman & Silver, 1989) reviewed studies of reactions to major losses: the death of a loved one or the loss of mobility due to spinal injury. These researchers found some common assumptions to be more myth than fact.

First, depression is far from universal. From three weeks to two years after their loss, only 15 to 35 percent of widows, widowers, and victims of spinal cord injury showed signs of depression. *Second,* failure to show distress at the outset does not necessarily lead to problems; the people who were most upset immediately after a loss or injury were likely to be most troubled up to two years later. *Third,* not everyone needs to "work through" a loss or will benefit from doing so; some of the people who did the most intense grief work had more problems later. *Fourth,* not everyone returns to normal quickly. More than 40 percent of widows and widowers show moderate to severe anxiety up to four years after the spouse's death, especially if it was sudden. *Fifth,* people cannot always resolve their grief and accept their loss. Parents and spouses of people who die in car accidents often have painful memories of the loved one even after many years (Wortman & Silver, 1989).

Rather than a single three-stage pattern, this research found three main patterns of grieving. In the generally expected pattern, the mourner goes from high to low distress. In a second pattern, the mourner does not experience intense distress immediately or later. In a third pattern, the mourner remains distressed for a long time (Wortman & Silver, 1989).

The finding that grief takes varied forms and patterns has important implications for helping people deal with loss. It may be unnecessary and even harmful to urge or lead mourners to "work through" a loss, or to expect them to follow a set pattern of emotional reactions—just as it may be unnecessary and harmful to expect all dying patients to experience Kübler-Ross's stages. Respect for different ways of showing grief can help the bereaved deal with loss without making them feel that their reactions are abnormal.

Most bereaved people eventually are able, often with the help of family and friends, to come to terms with their loss and resume normal lives. For some, however, *grief therapy* is indicated. Professional grief therapists help survivors express sorrow, guilt, hostility, and anger. They encourage clients to review the relationship with the deceased and to integrate the fact of the death into their lives. In helping people handle grief, counselors need to take into account ethnic and family traditions and individual differences.

Death and Bereavement across the Life Span

There is no single way of viewing death at any age; people's attitudes toward it reflect their personality and experience, as well as how close they believe they are to dying. Still, broad developmental differences apply. As the timing-of-events model suggests, death probably does not mean the same thing to an 85-year-old man with excruciatingly painful arthritis, a 56-year-old woman at the height of a brilliant legal career who discovers she has breast cancer, and a 15-year-old who dies of an overdose of drugs. Typical changes in attitudes toward death across the life span depend both on cognitive development and on the normative or non-normative timing of the event.

Childhood

Not until sometime between the ages of 5 and 7 do most children understand that death is *irreversible*—that a dead person, animal, or flower cannot come to life again. At about the same age, children realize two other important concepts about death: first, that it is *universal* (all living things die); and second, that a dead person is *nonfunctional* (all life functions end at death). Before then, children may believe that certain groups of people (say, teachers, parents, and children) do not die, that a person who is smart enough or lucky enough can avoid death, and that they themselves will be able to live forever. They also may believe that a dead person still can think and feel. The concepts of irreversibility, universality, and cessation of functions usually develop at the time when, according to Piaget, children move from preoperational to concrete operational thinking (Speece & Brent, 1984).

Children can be helped to understand death if they are introduced to the concept at an early age and are encouraged to talk about it. The death of a pet may provide a natural opportunity. If another child dies, teachers and parents need to try to allay the surviving children's anxieties.

Six percent of American children under age 10 have lost at least one parent. More have lost grandparents, many of whom played an important role in their lives. Some mourn the deaths of siblings, other relatives, or friends (AAP Committee on Psychosocial Aspects of Child and Family Health, 1992).

The way children show grief depends on cognitive and emotional development. Children sometimes express grief through anger, acting out, or refusal to acknowledge a death, as if the pretense that a person is still alive will make it so. They may be confused by adults' euphemisms: that someone "expired" or that the family "lost" someone or that someone is "asleep" and will never awaken. A loss is more difficult if the child had a troubled relationship with the person who died; if a troubled surviving parent depends too much on the child; if the death was unexpected, especially if it was a murder or suicide; if the child has had previous behavioral or emotional problems; or if family and community support are lacking (AAP Committee on Psychosocial Aspects of Child and Family Health, 1992).

Parents or other caregivers can help children deal with bereavement by helping them understand that death is final and that they did not cause the death by their misbehavior or thoughts. Children need reassurance that they will continue to receive care from loving adults. It is usually helpful to make as few changes as possible in a child's environment, relationships, and daily activities; to answer questions simply and honestly; and to encourage the child to talk about the person who died.

Adolescence

Death is not something adolescents normally think much about unless they are faced with it. Still, in many communities in which adolescents (and even younger children) live, violence and the threat of death are inescapable facts of daily life. Many adolescents take heedless risks. They hitchhike, drive recklessly, and experiment with drugs and sex—often with tragic results. In their urge to discover and express their identity, they may be more concerned with *how* they live than with how *long* they will live.

Suicide is the third leading cause of death among 15- to 24-year-olds; and the leading cause is accidents, some of which may actually be suicides (NCHS, 1998a). Adolescent boys are five times as likely as adolescent girls to take their lives (NIMH, 1999a, 1999b).

Young people who attempt suicide tend to have histories of emotional illness: depression, drug or alcohol abuse, antisocial or aggressive behavior, or unstable personality. They also tend to have attempted suicide before, or to have friends or family members who did (Garland & Zigler, 1993; NIMH, 1999a, 1999b; Slap, Vorters, Chaudhuri, & Centor, 1989; "Suicide—Part I," 1996).

Suicidal teenagers tend to think poorly of themselves, to feel hopeless, and to have poor impulse control and low tolerance for frustration and stress. These young people are often alienated from their parents and have no one outside the family to turn to. Many come from troubled or broken families—often with a history of unemployment, imprisonment, or suicidal behavior—and a high proportion have been abused or neglected (Deykin, Alpert, & McNamara, 1985; Garland & Zigler, 1993; Slap et al., 1989; "Suicide—Part I," 1996; Swedo et al., 1991). Homosexual and bisexual boys are at high risk (Remafedi, French, Story, Resnick, & Blum, 1998).

Ready availability of guns in the home is a major factor in the increase in teenage suicide (Rivara & Grossman, 1996). Although most young people who *attempt* suicide do it by taking pills or ingesting other substances, those who *succeed* are most likely to use firearms (Garland & Zigler, 1993).

Some suicide prevention programs may do harm by exaggerating the extent of teenage suicide and painting it as a reaction to normal stresses of adolescence rather than as a pathological act. Instead, programs should identify and treat young people at high risk of suicide, including those who already have attempted it. Equally important is to attack risk factors through programs to reduce substance abuse and strengthen families (Garland & Zigler, 1993; NIMH, 1999a, 1999b).

Adulthood

Young adults who have finished their education and have embarked on careers, marriage, or parenthood are generally eager to live the lives they have been preparing for. If they are suddenly struck by a potentially fatal illness or injury, they are likely to be extremely frustrated. Frustration may turn to rage, which can make them difficult hospital patients.

Today, many people who develop AIDS in their twenties or thirties—often gay men—must face issues of death and dying at an age when they normally would be dealing with such issues of young adulthood as establishing an intimate relationship. Rather than having a long lifetime of losses as gradual preparation for the final loss of life, "the gay man may find his own health, the health of his friends, and the fabric of his community all collapsing at once" (Cadwell, 1994, p. 4).

In middle age, most people realize more keenly than before that they are indeed going to die. Their bodies send them signals that they are not as young, agile, and hearty as they once were. More and more they think about how many years they may have left and of how to make the most of those years (Neugarten, 1967). Often—especially after the death of both parents—there is a new awareness of being the older generation next in line to die (Scharlach & Fredriksen, 1993).

Older adults may have mixed feelings about the prospect of dying. Physical losses and other problems and losses of old age may diminish their pleasure in living and their will to live (McCue, 1995). On the other hand, when 414 hospitalized patients in their eighties and nineties were asked how much time they would be willing to trade for excellent health, about 2 out of 3 were unwilling to give up more than one month of life (Tsevat et al., 1998). According to Erikson, older adults who resolve the final crisis of *integrity versus despair* (refer back to Chapter 18) achieve acceptance both of what they have done with their lives and of their impending death. One way to accomplish this resolution is through a *life review,* discussed later in this chapter. People who feel that their lives have been meaningful and who have adjusted to their losses may be better able to face death.

Three especially difficult losses that may occur during adulthood are the deaths of a spouse, a parent, and a child.

Surviving a Spouse

Widowhood is one of the greatest emotional challenges that can face a human being. Because women tend to live longer than men and to be younger than their husbands, they are more likely to be widowed.

There is a strong likelihood that a widowed person will soon follow the spouse to the grave. In a large-scale Finnish study, a woman or, especially, a man was highly likely to die within five years after the death of a spouse. The risk was greatest for young adults and for those whose loss was still fresh (Martikainen & Valkonen, 1996).

Many studies have found older adults to adjust better to widowhood than younger adults (DiGiulio, 1992). In general, though, age is not a major factor in the grieving process; coping skills are. People who have had practice in coping with loss and have developed effective coping resources—self-esteem and competence in meeting the demands of everyday life—are better able to deal with bereavement (Lund, 1993b).

The survivor of a long marriage is likely to face many emotional and practical problems. A good marriage can leave a gaping emotional void. Even if the marriage was a troubled one, the widowed person is likely to feel a loss. This loss may be especially hard for a woman who has structured her life and her identity around caring for her husband. Widowed women have elevated rates of depression, at least during the first five years after the death (Marks & Lambert, 1998).

Economic hardship can be a major problem. When the husband has been the main breadwinner, his widow is deprived of his income; when the husband is widowed, he has to buy many of the services his wife provided. When both spouses have been employed, the loss of one income can be a blow.

Social life changes, too. Friends and family usually rally to the mourner's side immediately after the death but then may go back to their own lives (Brubaker, 1990). Still, widows and widowers see friends more often than married people do (Field & Minkler, 1988).

Although it takes time for the pain to heal, most bereaved spouses eventually rebuild their lives. Loneliness, sadness, and depression give way to confidence in the ability to manage on their own. People who adjust best are those who keep busy, take on new roles (such as new paid or volunteer work), or become more deeply involved in ongoing activities. They see friends often, and they may join support or self-help groups (Lund, 1989, 1993b). Adult children can be an important source of assistance and emotional support (Suitor, Pillemer, Keeton, & Robison, 1995). The ability to talk openly about their experience can help some people find meaning and coherence in the transition to widowhood (van den Hoonard, 1999).

Elderly widowers are four times as likely to remarry as elderly widows (Carstensen & Pasupathi, 1993), in part because available women greatly outnumber available men. The need for intimacy also may be a factor. If a husband has a confidant, it is likely to be his wife, whereas wives (who generally have more intimate friendships) are more likely to confide in someone outside the marriage (Tower & Kasl, 1996). Many widows are not interested in remarriage (Talbott, 1998). Women usually can handle their household needs and may be reluctant to give up survivors' pension benefits or the freedom of living alone, or to face the prospect of caring for an infirm husband, perhaps for the second time.

Losing a Parent

Little attention has been paid to the impact of the death of a parent on an adult child. Today, with longer life expectancies, this loss often occurs in middle age (Umberson & Chen, 1994).

In-depth interviews with 83 volunteers ages 35 to 60 found a majority of bereaved adult children still experiencing emotional distress—ranging from sadness and crying to depression and thoughts of suicide—after one to five years, especially following loss of a mother (Scharlach & Fredriksen, 1993). Still, the death of a parent can be a maturing experience. It can push adults into resolving important developmental issues: achieving a stronger sense of self and a more pressing, realistic awareness of their own mortality, along with a greater sense of responsibility, commitment, and attachment to others (M. S. Moss & Moss, 1989; Scharlach & Fredriksen, 1993).

The death of a parent often brings changes in other relationships (M. S. Moss & Moss, 1989; Scharlach & Fredriksen, 1993). A bereaved adult child may assume more responsibility for the surviving parent and for keeping the family together. The intense emotions of bereavement may draw siblings closer, or they may become alienated over differences that arose during the parent's final illness. A parent's death may free an adult child to spend more time and energy on relationships that were temporarily neglected to meet demands of caregiving. Or the death may free an adult child to shed a relationship that was being maintained to meet the parent's expectations.

Recognition of the finality of death and the impossibility of saying anything more to the deceased parent motivate some people to resolve disturbances in their ties to the living while there is still time. Some people are moved to reconcile with their own adult children. Sometimes estranged siblings, realizing that the parent who provided a link between them is no longer there, try to mend the rift.

Losing a Child

In earlier times, it was not unusual for a parent to bury a child. Today, with medical advances and the increase in life expectancy in industrialized countries, infant mortality has reached record lows, and a child who survives the first year of life is far more likely to live to old age.

A parent is rarely prepared emotionally for the death of a child. Such a death, no matter at what age, comes as a cruel, unnatural shock, an untimely event that, in the normal course of things, should not have happened. The parents may feel they have failed, no matter how much they loved and cared for the child, and they may find it hard to let go.

If a marriage is strong, the couple may draw closer together, supporting each other in their shared loss. But in other cases, the loss weakens and destroys the marriage. Unresolved issues stemming from a child's death often lead to divorce, even years later (Brandt, 1989).

Although each bereaved parent must cope with grief in his or her own way, some have found that plunging into work, interests, and other relationships or joining a support group eases the pain. Some well-meaning friends tell parents not to dwell on their loss, but remembering the child in a meaningful way may be exactly what they need to do.

Medical, Legal, and Ethical Issues: The "Right to Die"

Do people have a right to die? If so, under what circumstances? Should a terminally ill person who wants to commit suicide be allowed or helped to do so? Should a doctor prescribe medicine that will relieve pain but may shorten the patient's life? What about giving a lethal injection to end a patient's suffering? Who decides that a life is not worth prolonging? These are some of the thorny moral, ethical, and legal questions that face individuals, families, physicians, and society—questions involving the quality of life and the nature and circumstances of death.

Suicide

Although suicide is no longer a crime in modern societies, there is still a stigma against it, based in part on religious prohibitions and on society's interest in preserving life. A person who expresses suicidal thoughts may be considered—often with good reason—mentally ill. On the other hand, as longevity increases and, with it, the risk of long-term degenerative illness, a growing number of people consider a mature adult's deliberate choice of a time to end his or her life a rational decision and a right to be defended.

In 1998, according to preliminary data, more than 29,000 people in the United States committed suicide, making it the eighth leading cause of death. Furthermore, the yearly suicide rate in the United States—10.8 deaths per 100,000 population (Martin et al., 1999)—is moderate compared with rates in some other industrial countries (McIntosh, 1992; "Suicide—Part I," 1996). Suicide rates rise markedly after natural disasters, such as floods, hurricanes, and earthquakes, which can cause injuries and heavy financial loss (Krug et al., 1998).

Statistics probably understate the number of suicides, since many go unreported and some (such as traffic "accidents" and "accidental" medicinal overdoses) are not recognized as such. Also, the figures on suicides often do not include suicide *attempts*; an estimated 10 to 40 percent of people who commit suicide have tried before (Meehan, 1990; "Suicide—Part II," 1996). U.S. men end their own lives more than four times as often as women, though twice as many women as men attempt suicide (NIMH, 1999a, 1999b). White Americans are almost twice as likely to commit suicide as African Americans, Hispanic Americans, and Asian Americans or Pacific Islanders, but a little less likely than American Indians (NCHS, 1998a).

In most nations, suicide is most prevalent among older men (McIntosh, 1992). In the United States, by far the highest rate of suicide throughout the life span is among elderly white men, particularly those 85 and older (NCHS, 1998a;

NIMH, 1999b). Older African Americans are much less likely to commit suicide (NCHS, 1998a), perhaps in part because of religion and in part because they may be used to coping with hard knocks. Suicide among the elderly often occurs in conjunction with depression, alcohol abuse, and social isolation. Older adults who attempt suicide are more likely than younger ones to complete it, perhaps because they tend to use more lethal methods, especially firearms (CDC, 1996).

Although some people intent on suicide carefully conceal their plans, there often are warning signs. These may include withdrawing from family or friends; talking about death, the hereafter, or suicide; giving away prized possessions; abusing drugs or alcohol; and personality changes, such as unusual anger, boredom, or apathy. People who are about to kill themselves may neglect their appearance, stay away from work or other customary activities, complain of physical problems when nothing is organically wrong, or sleep or eat much more or much less than usual. They often show signs of depression, such as unusual difficulty concentrating, loss of self-esteem, and feelings of helplessness, hopelessness, extreme anxiety, or panic. Indeed, 9 out of 10 people who kill themselves have depression or another mental or substance use disorder (NIMH, 1999a).

Euthanasia and Assisted Suicide

In Milwaukee, Wisconsin, a 79-year-old man visited his 62-year-old wife in a nursing home. Once successful in business, the wife, now suffering from advanced Alzheimer's disease, screamed constantly and was unable or unwilling to speak. The man pushed his wife's wheelchair into a stairwell, where he killed her with a pistol shot. The district attorney who prosecuted the husband called his action "classic first-degree murder," but the grand jury refused to indict, and he went free (Malcolm, 1984).

This husband claimed to be practicing euthanasia ("good death"). If so, his act was an example of *active euthanasia* (sometimes called *mercy killing*), action taken deliberately to shorten a life in order to end suffering or allow a terminally ill person to die with dignity. *Passive euthanasia* is deliberately withholding or discontinuing treatment that might extend the life of a terminally ill patient, such as medication, life-support systems, or feeding tubes. Active euthanasia is generally illegal; passive euthanasia, in some circumstances, is not. An important question regarding either form of euthanasia is whether it is *voluntary*; that is, whether it is done at the direct request, or to carry out the expressed wishes, of the person whose death results.

Assisted suicide—in which a physician or someone else helps a person bring about a self-inflicted death by, for example, prescribing or obtaining drugs or enabling a patient to inhale a deadly gas—is illegal in most places but recently has come to the forefront of public debate. Assisted suicide is similar in principle to voluntary active euthanasia, in which, for example, a patient asks for, and receives, a lethal injection. The main difference is that in assisted suicide the person who wants to die performs the actual deed. All of these are varying forms of what is sometimes called *aid in dying.*

Advance Directives

Changing attitudes toward aid in dying can be attributed largely to revulsion against technologies that keep patients alive against their will despite intense suffering, and sometimes even after the brain has, for all practical purposes, stopped functioning. The U.S. Supreme Court has held that a person whose wishes are clearly known has a constitutional right to refuse or discontinue life-sustaining treatment (Cruzan v. Director, Missouri Department of Health, 1990; Gostin, 1997). A person's wishes can be spelled out in advance in a document called a *living will.*

Some "living will" legislation applies only to terminally ill patients, not to those who are incapacitated by illness or injury but may live many years in severe pain. Nor do living wills help many patients in comas or in a *persistent vegetative state,* in which, while technically alive, they have no awareness and only rudimentary brain functioning. Such situations can be covered by a *durable power of attorney,* which appoints another person to make decisions if the maker of the document becomes incompetent to do so. A number of states have adopted a simple form known as a *medical durable power of attorney,* expressly for decisions about health care.

Even with advance directives, however, many people die in pain after protracted, fruitless treatment. Concern about peer review, the press of a perceived medical emergency, or a philosophical commitment to sustaining life may lead physicians and nurses to continue "heroic" measures despite patients' wishes (M. Solomon, 1993).

In a five-year study of some 9,000 critically ill patients at five U.S. teaching hospitals, doctors were frequently unaware of patients' request not to be resuscitated in the event of cardiac arrest (The SUPPORT Principal Investigators, 1995). According to family members of patients who died, 1 in 10 of these patients disagreed with the care they received. Clear doctor-patient communication about preferences and prognoses was uncommon (Lynn et al., 1997).

Such findings have led the American Medical Association to form a Task Force on Quality Care at the End of Life. Many hospitals now have ethics committees that create guidelines, review cases, and help doctors, patients, and their families with decisions about end-of-life care (Simpson, 1996).

Physician Aid in Dying

In September 1996, an Australian man in his sixties with advanced prostate cancer was the first person to die legally by assisted suicide. Under a law passed in the Northern Territories, he pressed a computer key that administered a lethal dose of barbiturates ("Australian Man," 1996). Shortly afterward, the law was repealed (Ryan & Kaye, 1996).

In the United States, assisted suicide is illegal in almost all states. However, such activity often goes on covertly, without regulation. The American Medical Association opposes physician aid in dying as contrary to a practitioner's oath to "do no harm." But doctors can give drugs that may shorten a life if the purpose is to relieve pain—even though that distinction may be unclear (Gostin, 1997; Quill, Lo, & Brock, 1997). As public pressure builds for a "right to die" for the terminally ill, some legal scholars and physicians question the meaningfulness of a distinction between withholding care and helping a person take his or her own life (Orentlicher, 1996).

With national polls favoring aid in dying by as much as 3 to 1, some physicians are acceding to patients' requests (Castaneda, 1996; Lee et al., 1996; Quill, 1991; "Suicide—Part II," 1996; Taylor, 1995). A nationwide survey of 1,902 physicians whose specialties involve care of dying patients found that, of those who had received requests for help with suicide (18 percent) or lethal injections (11 percent), about 6 percent had complied at least once (Meier et al., 1998). In a poll of 352 doctors (Larson, 1995–1996), nearly 3 out of 4 said they should be allowed to help terminally ill patients die with dignity; of these, 95 percent favored withholding life support, 37 percent approved of providing the means for suicide, and nearly 13 percent said they would administer a lethal medication.

Despite changing attitudes, a unanimous U.S. Supreme Court in 1997 rebuffed challenges to state bans on assisted suicide. The court held that physician aid in dying is not a constitutionally protected liberty and thus is subject to state regulation. Measures to legalize assisted suicide for the terminally ill have been introduced in several states, but so far Oregon is the only state to pass such a law.

Some legal scholars and ethicists advocate legalizing all forms of voluntary euthanasia and assisted suicide, with safeguards to protect against involuntary euthanasia. They argue that the key issue is not how death occurs but who makes the decision; that there is no difference in principle between pulling the plug on a respirator and giving a lethal injection or prescribing an overdose of pills; and that a person sufficiently competent to control his or her own life should have the right to exercise that control. They maintain that aid in dying, if openly available, would reduce fear and helplessness by enabling patients to control their fate (Brock, 1992; R. A. Epstein, 1989).

Opponents maintain a distinction between passive euthanasia, in which nature is allowed to take its course, and directly causing a death. They contend that physician-assisted suicide would inevitably lead to voluntary active euthanasia, since self-administered pills do not always work (Groenwoud et al., 2000). The next step on the "slippery slope," they warn, would be involuntary euthanasia, especially for patients unable to express their wishes. They claim that people who want to die are often temporarily depressed and might change their minds with treatment or palliative care (Butler, 1996; Hendin, 1994; Latimer, 1992; Quill et al., 1997; Simpson, 1996; Singer, 1988; Singer & Siegler, 1990).

The limited experience under the Oregon Death with Dignity Act may help allay some of these concerns. In its first two years of operation, only 43 terminally ill people used it to end their lives. Less than half the patients who sought assisted suicide changed their minds after palliative interventions (Ganzini et al., 2000).

Still, one salutary result of the aid-in-dying controversy has been to call attention to the need for better palliative care and closer attention to patients' state of mind. A request for aid in dying can provide an opening to explore the reasons behind it. Sometimes a psychiatric consultation may discover an underlying disturbance masked by a seemingly rational request (Muskin, 1998). In terminally ill patients, the will to live can fluctuate greatly, so it is essential to ensure that such a request is not just a passing one (Chochinov, Tataryn, Clinch, & Dudgeon, 1999). If lethal measures *are* taken, it is important that a physician be present to ensure that the death is as merciful and pain-free as possible (Nuland, 2000).

The issue of aid in dying will become more pressing as the population ages. Much of the debate turns on whether it is possible to write laws permitting some forms of aid with adequate protections against abuse (Baron et al., 1996; Callahan & White, 1996). In years to come, both the courts and the public will be forced to come to terms with that question, as increasing numbers of people claim a right to die with dignity and with help.

Finding Meaning and Purpose in Life and Death

The central character in Leo Tolstoy's *The Death of Ivan Ilyich* is wracked by a fatal illness. Even greater than his physical suffering is his mental torment. He asks himself over and over what meaning there is to his agony, and he becomes convinced that his life has been without purpose and his death will be equally pointless. At the last minute, though, he experiences a spiritual revelation, a concern for his wife and son, which gives him a final moment of integrity and enables him to conquer his terror.

What Tolstoy dramatized in literature is being confirmed by research. In one study of 39 women whose average age was 76, those who saw the most purpose in life had the least fear of death (Durlak, 1973). Conversely, according to Kübler-Ross (1975), facing the reality of death is a key to living a meaningful life:

> It is the denial of death that is partially responsible for [people's] living empty, purposeless lives; for when you live as if you'll live forever, it becomes too easy to postpone the things you know that you must do. In contrast, when you fully understand that each day you awaken could be the last you have, you take the time that day to grow, to become more of who you really are, to reach out to other human beings. (p. 164)

Reviewing a Life

In Charles Dickens's *A Christmas Carol,* Scrooge changes his greedy, heartless ways after seeing ghostly visions of his past, his present, and his future death. In Akira Kurosawa's film *Ikiru* ("To Live"), a petty bureaucrat who discovers that he is dying of cancer looks back over the emptiness of his life and, in a final burst of energy, creates a meaningful legacy by pushing through a project for a children's park, which he has previously blocked. These fictional characters make their remaining time more purposeful through *life review,* a process of reminiscence that enables a person to see the significance of his or her life.

Life review can, of course, occur at any time. However, it may have special meaning in old age, when it can foster ego integrity—according to Erikson, the final critical task of the life span. As the end of their journey approaches, people may look back over their accomplishments and failures and ask themselves what their lives have meant. Awareness of mortality may be an impetus for reexamining values and seeing one's experiences and actions in a new light. Some people find the will to complete unfinished tasks, such as reconciling with estranged family members or friends, and thus to achieve a satisfying sense of closure.

Not all memories are equally conducive to mental health and growth. Older people who use reminiscence for self-understanding show the strongest ego integrity, while those who entertain only pleasurable memories show less. Most poorly adjusted are those who keep recalling negative events and are obsessed with regret, hopelessness, and fear of death; their ego integrity has given way to despair (Sherman, 1993; Walasky, Whitbourne, & Nehrke, 1983–1984).

Life-review therapy can help focus the natural process of life review and make it more conscious, purposeful, and efficient (Butler, 1961; M. I. Lewis & Butler, 1974). Methods often used for uncovering memories in life-review therapy (which also may be used by individuals on their own) include writing or taping one's autobiography; constructing a family tree; talking about scrapbooks, photo albums, old letters, and other memorabilia; making a trip back to scenes of childhood and young adulthood; reunions with former classmates or colleagues or distant family members; describing ethnic traditions; and summing up one's life's work.

Development: A Lifelong Process

In his late seventies, the artist Pierre-Auguste Renoir had crippling arthritis and chronic bronchitis and had lost his wife. He spent his days in a wheelchair, and his pain was so great that he could not sleep through the night. He was unable to hold a palette or grip a brush: his brush had to be tied to his right hand. Yet he continued to produce brilliant paintings, full of color and vibrant life. Finally, stricken by pneumonia, he lay in bed, gazing at some anemones his attendant had picked. He gathered enough strength to sketch the form of these beautiful flowers, and then—just before he died—lay back and whispered, "I think I am beginning to understand something about it" (L. Hanson, 1968).

Even dying can be a developmental experience. As one health practitioner put it, " . . . there are things to be gained, accomplished in dying. Time with and for those whom we are close to, achieving a final and enduring sense of self-worth, and a readiness to let go are priceless elements of a good death" (Weinberger, 1999 p. F3).

Within a limited life span, no person can realize all capabilities, gratify all desires, explore all interests, or experience all the richness that life has to offer. The tension between possibilities for growth and a finite time in which to do the growing defines human life. By choosing which possibilities to pursue and by continuing to follow them as far as possible, even up to the very end, each person contributes to the unfinished story of human development.

Glossary

A, not-B, error Tendency, noted by Piaget, for 8- to 12-month-old infants to search for a hidden object in a place where they previously found it, rather than in the place where they most recently saw it being hidden. (164)

acceleration Approach to educating the gifted, which moves them through the curriculum, or part of it, at an unusually rapid pace. (361)

accommodation In Piaget's terminology, changes in an existing cognitive structure to include new information. (38)

achievement tests Tests that assess how much children know in various subject areas. (341)

achieving stage Second of Schaie's seven cognitive stages, in which young adults use knowledge to gain competence and independence. (503)

acquired immune deficiency syndrome (AIDS) Viral disease that undermines effective functioning of the immune system. (97)

acquisitive stage First of Schaie's seven cognitive stages, in which children and adolescents learn information and skills largely for their own sake or as preparation for participation in society. (503)

activity theory Theory of aging, proposed by Neugarten and others, which holds that in order to age successfully a person must remain as active as possible. Compare with *disengagement theory.* (684)

acute medical conditions Occasional illnesses that last a short time. (329)

adaptation In Piaget's terminology, adjustment to new information about the environment through the complementary processes of assimilation and accommodation. (38)

adaptive mechanisms Vaillant's term to describe four characteristic ways people adapt to life circumstances: mature, immature, psychotic, and neurotic. (527)

adolescence Developmental transition between childhood and adulthood entailing major physical, cognitive, and psychosocial changes. (410)

adolescent growth spurt Sharp increase in height and weight that precedes sexual maturity. (413)

adolescent rebellion Pattern of emotional turmoil, characteristic of a minority of adolescents, which may involve conflict with family, alienation from adult society, reckless behavior, and rejection of adults' values. (463)

Adult Attachment Interview (AAI) Instrument for measuring the clarity, coherence, and consistency of an adult's memories of attachment to her or his parents. (215)

age-differentiated Life structure in which primary roles—learning, working, and leisure—are based on age; typical in industrialized societies. Compare *age-integrated.* (585)

age-integrated Life structure in which primary roles - learning, working, and leisure - are open to adults of all ages and can be interspersed throughout the life span. Compare *age-differentiated.* (586)

ageism Prejudice or discrimination against a person (most commonly an older person) based on age. (635)

age-related macular degeneration Condition in which the center of the retina gradually loses its ability to discern fine details; leading cause of functional blindness in older adults. (649)

alcoholism Chronic disease involving dependence on use of alcohol, causing interference with normal functioning and fulfillment of obligations. (493)

alleles Paired genes (alike or different) that affect a particular trait. (69)

altruism, or prosocial behavior Behavior intended to help others without external reward. (302)

Alzheimer's disease Progressive, degenerative brain disorder characterized by irreversible deterioration in memory, intelligence, awareness, and control of bodily functions, eventually leading to death. (655)

ambivalent (resistant) attachment Attachment pattern in which an infant becomes anxious before the primary caregiver leaves, is extremely upset during his or her absence, and both seeks and resists contact on his or her return. (212)

amniocentesis Prenatal diagnostic procedure in which a sample of amniotic fluid is withdrawn and analyzed to determine whether any of certain genetic defects are present. (100)

amyloid plaque Waxy chunks of insoluble tissue found in brains of persons with Alzheimer's disease. (657)

animism Tendency to attribute life to objects that are not alive. (253)

anorexia nervosa Eating disorder characterized by self-starvation. (420)

anoxia Lack of oxygen, which may cause brain damage. (115)

Apgar scale Standard measurement of a newborn's condition; it assesses appearance, pulse, grimace, activity, and respiration. (117)

aptitude tests Tests that measure children's general intelligence, or capacity to learn. (341)

arthritis Group of disorders affecting the joints, causing pain and loss of movement. (653)

assimilation In Piaget's terminology, incorporation of new information into an existing cognitive structure. (38)

attachment Reciprocal, enduring tie between infant and caregiver, each of whom contributes to the quality of the relationship. (211)

attention-deficit/hyperactivity disorder (ADHD) Syndrome characterized by persistent inattention and distractibility, impulsivity, low tolerance for frustration, and inappropriate overactivity. (358)

authoritarian In Baumrind's terminology, parenting style emphasizing control and obedience. Compare *authoritative* and *permissive.* (300)

authoritative In Baumrind's terminology, parenting style blending respect for a child's individuality with an effort to instill social values. Compare *authoritarian* and *permissive.* (300)

autism Pervasive developmental disorder characterized by lack of normal sociability, impaired communication, and repetitive, obsessive behaviors. (86)

autobiographical memory Memory of specific events in one's own life. (267)

autoimmunity Tendency of an aging body to mistake its own tissues for foreign invaders and to attack and destroy them. (645)

autonomy versus shame and doubt In Erikson's theory, the second crisis in psychosocial development, occurring between about 18 months and 3 years, in which children achieve a balance between self-determination and control by others. (222)

autosomes The 22 pairs of chromosomes not related to sexual expression. (68)

avoidant attachment Attachment pattern in which an infant rarely cries when separated from the primary caregiver and avoids contact upon his or her return. (212)

balanced investment Pattern of retirement activity allocated among family, work, and leisure. Compare family-focused lifestyle. (690)

basal metabolism Use of energy to maintain vital functions. (562)

basic trust versus basic mistrust In Erikson's theory, the first crisis in psychosocial development, occurring between birth and about 18 months, in which infants develop a sense of the reliability of people and objects in their world. (210)

Bayley Scales of Infant Development Standardized test of infants' mental and motor development. (157)

behavior therapy Therapeutic approach using principles of learning theory to encourage desired behaviors or eliminate undesired ones; also called *behavior modification.* (397)

behavioral genetics Quantitative study of relative hereditary and environmental influences. (78)

behaviorism Learning theory that emphasizes the study of observable behaviors and events and the predictable role of environment in causing behavior. (34)

behaviorist approach Approach to the study of cognitive development based on learning theory, which is concerned with the basic mechanics of learning. (153)

bilingual Fluent in two languages. (355)

bilingual education A system of teaching foreign-speaking children in two languages—their native language and English—and later switching to all-English instruction after the children develop enough fluency in English. (355)

bioecological theory Bronfenbrenner's approach to understanding processes and contexts of development. (41)

birth trauma Injury sustained at the time of birth due to oxygen deprivation, mechanical injury, infection, or disease. (118)

bisexual Describing a person whose sexual orientation is toward both the same sex and the other sex. (453)

blended family Family consisting of a married couple, at least one of whom is remarried, which includes children born to or adopted by one or both partners before the current marriage. (547)

body image Descriptive and evaluative beliefs about one's appearance. (325)

brain growth spurts Periods of rapid brain growth and development. (131)

Brazelton Neonatal Behavioral Assessment Scale Neurological and behavioral test to measure neonate's response to the environment. (117)

bulimia nervosa Eating disorder in which a person regularly eats huge quantities of food and then purges the body by laxatives, induced vomiting, fasting, or excessive exercise. (420)

bullying Aggression deliberately and persistently directed against a particular target, or victim, typically one who is weak, vulnerable, and defenseless. (393)

burnout Syndrome of emotional exhaustion and a sense that one can no longer accomplish anything on the job. (576)

canalization Limitation on variance of expression of certain inherited characteristics. (81)

caregiver burnout Condition of physical, mental, and emotional exhaustion affecting adults who care for aged persons. (619)

case study Scientific study covering a single case or life. (48)

cataracts Cloudy or opaque areas in the lens of the eye, which cause blurred vision. (649)

cell death Elimination of excess brain cells to achieve more efficient functioning. (133)

central executive In Baddeley's model, element of working memory that controls the processing of information. (338)

central nervous system Brain and spinal cord. (130)

centration In Piaget's theory, a limitation of preoperational thought that leads the child to focus on one aspect of a situation and neglect others, often leading to illogical conclusions. (254)

cephalocaudal principle Principle that development proceeds in a head-to-tail direction; that is, that upper parts of the body develop before lower parts. (87)

cesarean delivery Delivery of a baby by surgical removal from the uterus. (111)

child-directed speech (CDS) Form of speech often used in talking to babies or toddlers; includes slow, simplified speech, a high-pitched tone, exaggerated vowel sounds, short words and sentences, and much repetition. Also called *parentese.* (187)

childhood depression Affective disorder characterized by such symptoms as a prolonged sense of friendlessness, inability to have fun or concentrate, fatigue, extreme activity or apathy, feelings of worthlessness, weight change, physical complaints, and thoughts of death or suicide. (396)

chorionic villus sampling Prenatal diagnostic procedure in which tissue from villi (hairlike projections of the membrane surrounding the fetus) is analyzed for birth defects. (100)

chromosome One of 46 rod-shaped structures that carry the genes. (67)

chronic medical conditions Physical, developmental, behavioral, and/or emotional disorders or impairments requiring special health services. (329)

chronosystem In Bronfenbrenner's terminology, a system that shows effects of time on the microsystem, mesosystem, exosystem, and macrosystem. (44)

circular reactions In Piaget's terminology, processes by which an infant learns to reproduce desired occurrences originally discovered by chance. (161)

class inclusion Understanding of the relationship between a whole and its parts. (333)

classical conditioning Kind of learning in which a previously neutral stimulus (one that does not originally elicit a particular response) acquires the power to elicit the response after the stimulus is repeatedly associated with another stimulus that ordinarily does elicit the response. (34)

classical conditioning Kind of learning in which a previously neutral stimulus (one that does not originally elicit a particular response) acquires the power to elicit the response after the stimulus is repeatedly associated with another stimulus that ordinarily does elicit the response. (154)

clone (verb) To make a genetic copy of an individual; (noun) a genetic copy of an individual. (65)

code mixing Use of elements of two languages, sometimes in the same utterance, by young children in households where both languages are spoken. (187)

code switching Process of changing one's speech to match the situation, as in people who are bilingual. (187)

cognitive neuroscience approach Approach to the study of cognitive development that links brain processes with cognitive ones. (40)

cognitive neuroscience approach Approach to the study of cognitive development by examining brain structures and measuring neurological activity. (168)

cognitive perspective View of development that is concerned with thought processes and the behavior that reflects those processes. (37)

cognitive-appraisal model Model of coping, proposed by Lazarus and Folkman, which holds that, on the basis of continuous appraisal of their relationship with the environment, people choose appropriate coping strategies to deal with situations that tax their normal resources. (680)

cohabitation Status of a couple who live together and maintain a sexual relationship without being legally married. (538)

cohort Group of people who share a similar experience, such as growing up at the same time and in the same place. (20)

coming out Process of openly disclosing one's homosexual orientation. (536)

commitment In Marcia's terminology, personal investment in an occupation or system of beliefs. (449)

committed compliance In Kochanska's terminology, a toddler's wholehearted obedience of a parent's orders without reminders or lapses. (224)

componential element In Sternberg's triarchic theory, term for the analytic aspect of intelligence, which determines how efficiently people process information and solve problems. (343)

concordant Term describing twins who share the same trait or disorder. (80)

concrete operations Third stage of Piagetian cognitive development (approximately from ages 7 to 12), during which children develop logical but not abstract thinking. (331)

conduct disorder (CD) Repetitive, persistent pattern of aggressive, antisocial behavior violating societal norms or the rights of others. (395)

conscience Internal standards of behavior, which usually control one's conduct and produce emotional discomfort when violated. (223)

conservation In Piaget's terminology, awareness that two objects that are equal according to a certain measure (such as length, weight, or quantity) remain equal in the face of perceptual alteration (for example, a change in shape) so long as nothing has been added to or taken away from either object. (255)

constructive play In Piaget's and Smilansky's terminology, the second cognitive level of play, involving use of objects or materials to make something. (294)

contextual element In Sternberg's triarchic theory, term for the practical aspect of intelligence, which determines how effectively people deal with their environment. (343)

contextual perspective View of development that sees the individual as inseparable from the social context. (41)

continuity theory Theory of aging, described by Atchley, which holds that in order to age successfully people must maintain a balance of continuity and change in both the internal and external structures of their lives. (685)

control group In an experiment, a group of people who are similar to the people in the experimental group but who do not receive the treatment whose effects are to be measured; the results obtained with this group are compared with the results obtained with the experimental group. (51)

conventional morality (or morality of conventional role conformity) Second level in Kohlberg's theory of moral reasoning, in which the standards of authority figures are internalized. (431)

convergent thinking Thinking aimed at finding the one "right" answer to a problem. Compare *divergent thinking.* (361)

coping Adaptive thinking or behavior aimed at reducing or relieving stress that arises from harmful, threatening, or challenging conditions. (680)

coregulation Transitional stage in the control of behavior in which parents exercise general supervision and children exercise moment-to-moment self-regulation. (373)

correlational study Research design intended to discover whether a statistical relationship between variables exists, either in direction or in magnitude. (50)

crisis In Marcia's terminology, period of conscious decision making related to identity formation. (449)

critical period Specific time when a given event, or its absence, has the greatest impact on development. (21)

cross-modal transfer Ability to use information gained by one sense to guide another. (170)

cross-sectional study Study design in which people of different ages are assessed on one occasion, providing comparative information about different age cohorts. (54)

cross-sequential study Study design that combines cross-sectional and longitudinal techniques by assessing people in a cross-sectional sample more than once. (55)

crystallized intelligence Type of intelligence, proposed by Horn and Cattell, involving the ability to remember and use learned information; it is largely dependent on education and cultural background. Compare with *fluid intelligence.* (579)

cultural bias Tendency of intelligence tests to include items calling for knowledge or skills more familiar or meaningful to some cultural groups than to others, thus placing some test-takers at an advantage or disadvantage due to their cultural background. (342)

culture A society's or group's total way of life, including customs, traditions, beliefs, values, language, and physical products—all learned behavior passed on from parents to children. (19)

culture-fair Describing an intelligence test that deals with experiences common to various cultures, in an attempt to avoid cultural bias. Compare *culture-free.* (342)

culture-free Describing an intelligence test that, if it were possible to design, would have no culturally linked content. Compare *culture-fair.* (342)

decenter In Piaget's terminology, to think simultaneously about several aspects of a situation; characteristic of operational thought. (255)

deductive reasoning Type of logical reasoning that moves from a general premise about a class to a conclusion about a particular member or members of the class. (333)

deferred imitation In Piaget's terminology, reproduction of an observed behavior after the passage of time by calling up a stored symbol of it. (163)

dementia Deterioration in cognitive and behavioral functioning due to physiological causes. (655)

Denver Developmental Screening Test Screening test given to children 1 month to 6 years old to determine whether they are, developing normally; it assesses gross motor skills, fine motor skills, language development, and personality and social development. (141)

deoxyribonucleic acid (DNA) Chemical of which genes are composed, which controls the functions of body cells. (67)

dependent variable In an experiment, the condition that may or may not change as a result of changes in the independent variable. (52)

depth perception Ability to perceive objects and surfaces three-dimensionally. (145)

developmental priming mechanisms Preparatory aspects of the home environment that seem to be necessary for normal cognitive and psychosocial development to occur. (160)

differentiation Process by which neurons acquire specialized structure and function. (133)

difficult children Children with irritable temperament, irregular biological rhythms, and intense emotional responses. (203)

discipline Tool of socialization, which includes methods of molding children's character and of teaching them to exercise self-control and engage in acceptable behavior. (297)

disengagement theory Theory of aging, proposed by Cumming and Henry, which holds that successful aging is characterized by mutual withdrawal between the older person and society. Compare with *activity theory.* (684)

dishabituation Increase in responsiveness after presentation of a new stimulus. Compare *habituation.* (168)

disorganized-disoriented attachment Attachment pattern in which an infant, after being separated from the primary caregiver, shows contradictory behaviors upon his or her return. (212)

distance learning Arrangement for taking courses at a distant location via computer or closed-circuit radio broadcasts. (588)

divergent thinking Thinking that produces a variety of fresh, diverse possibilities. Compare *convergent thinking.* (361)

dizygotic (two-egg) twins Twins conceived by the union of two different ova (or a single ovum that has split) with two different sperm cells within a brief period of time; also called *fraternal twins.* (66)

dominant inheritance Pattern of inheritance in which, when an individual receives contradictory alleles for a trait, only the dominant one is expressed. (69)

Down syndrome Chromosomal disorder characterized by moderate-to-severe mental retardation and by such physical signs as a downward-sloping skin fold at the inner corners of the eyes. (76)

drug therapy Administration of drugs to treat emotional disorders. (397)

dual representation hypothesis Proposal that children under the age of 3 have difficulty grasping spatial relationships because of the need to keep more than one mental representation in mind at the same time. (252)

dual-process model Model of cognitive functioning in late adulthood, proposed by Baltes, which identifies and seeks to measure two dimensions of intelligence: mechanics and pragmatics. (661)

dyslexia Developmental disorder in which reading achievement is substantially lower than predicted by IQ or age. (357)

early intervention Systematic process of planning and providing therapeutic and educational services to families that need help in meeting infants', toddlers', and preschool children's developmental needs. (160)

easy children Children with a generally happy temperament, regular biological rhythms, and a readiness to accept new experiences. (203)

ecological validity Characteristic of adult intelligence tests that indicate competence in dealing with real problems or challenges faced by adults. (504)

ego integrity versus despair According to Erikson, the eighth and final critical alternative of psychosocial development, in which people in late adulthood either achieve a sense of integrity of the self by accepting the lives they have lived, and thus accept death, or yield to despair that their lives cannot be relived. (679)

egocentrism In Piaget's terminology, inability to consider another person's point of view; a characteristic of preoperational thought. (256)

ego-control Self-control. (525)

ego-resiliency Adaptability under potential sources of stress. (525)

elaboration Mnemonic strategy of making mental associations involving items to be remembered. (340)

elder abuse Maltreatment or neglect of dependent older persons, or violation of their personal rights. (696

electronic fetal monitoring Mechanical monitoring of fetal heartbeat during labor and delivery. (110)

embryonic stage Second stage of gestation (2 to 8 weeks), characterized by rapid growth and development of major body systems and organs. (90)

embryoscopy Prenatal medical procedure in which a scope is inserted in the abdomen of a pregnant woman to permit viewing of the embryo for diagnosis and treatment of abnormalities. (101)

emergent literacy Preschoolers' development of skills, knowledge, and attitudes that underlie reading and writing. (264)

emotional intelligence In Salovey's and Mayer's terminology, ability to understand and regulate emotions; an important component of effective, intelligent behavior. (506)

emotional maltreatment Action or inaction that may cause behavioral, cognitive, emotional, or mental disorders. (306)

emotion-focused coping In the cognitive-appraisal model, coping strategy directed toward managing the emotional response to a stressful situation so as to lessen its physical or psychological impact; sometimes called *palliative coping.* Compare *problem-focused coping.* (681)

emotions Subjective reactions to experience that are associated with physiological and behavioral changes. (197)

empathy Ability to put oneself in another person's place and feel what that person feels. (256)

empty nest Transitional phase of parenting following the last child's leaving the parents' home. (612)

encapsulation In Hoyer's terminology, progressive dedication of information processing and fluid thinking to specific knowledge systems, making knowledge more readily accessible. (581)

encoding Process by which information is prepared for long-term storage and later retrieval. (338)

engagement hypothesis Proposal that an active, engaged lifestyle that challenges cognitive skills predicts retention or growth of those skills in later life. (663)

English-immersion Approach to teaching English as a second language in which instruction is presented only in English from the outset of formal education. (355)

enrichment Approach to educating the gifted, which broadens and deepens knowledge and skills through extra activities, projects, field trips, or mentoring. (361)

enuresis Repeated urination in clothing or in bed. (241)

environment Totality of nongenetic influences on development, external to the self. (16)

episodic memory Long-term memory of specific experiences or events, linked to time and place. (266)

equilibration In Piaget's terminology, the tendency to strive for equilibrium (balance) among cognitive elements within the organism and between the organism and the outside world. (38)

erectile dysfunction Inability of a man to achieve or maintain an erect penis sufficient for satisfactory sexual performance. (567)

ethnic group Group united by ancestry, race, religion, language, and/or national origins, which contribute to a sense of shared identity. (19)

ethnographic study In-depth study of a culture, which uses a combination of methods including participant observation. (49)

ethological perspective View of development that focuses on the biological and evolutionary bases of behavior. (40)

executive stage Fourth of Schaie's seven cognitive stages, in which middle-aged people responsible for societal systems deal with complex relationships on several levels. (503)

exosystem In Bronfenbrenner's terminology, a system of linkages between two or more settings, one of which does not contain the developing person. (43)

experiential element In Sternberg's triarchic theory, term for the insightful aspect of intelligence, which determines how effectively people approach both novel and familiar tasks. (343)

experiment Rigorously controlled, replicable (repeatable) procedure in which the researcher manipulates variables to assess the effect of one on the other. (51)

experimental group In an experiment, the group receiving the treatment under study; any changes in these people are compared with changes in the control group. (51)

explicit memory Memory, generally of facts, names, and events, which is intentional and conscious. Compare implicit memory. (175)

extended family Multigenerational kinship network of parents, children, and more distant relatives, sometimes living together in an extended-family household. (18)

external memory aids Mnemonic strategies using something outside the person. (339)

family therapy Psychological treatment in which a therapist sees the whole family together to analyze patterns of family functioning. (397)

family-focused lifestyle Pattern of retirement activity that revolves around family, home, and companions. Compare balanced investment. (690)

fast mapping Process by which a child absorbs the meaning of a new word after hearing it once or twice in conversation. (261)

fertilization Union of sperm and ovum fuse to produce a zygote; also called conception. (65)

fetal alcohol syndrome (FAS) Combination of mental, motor, and developmental abnormalities affecting the offspring of some women who drink heavily during pregnancy. (94)

fetal stage Final stage of gestation (from 8 weeks to birth), characterized by increased detail of body parts and greatly enlarged body size. (91)

filial crisis In Marcoen's terminology, normative development of middle age, in which adults learn to balance love and duty to their parents with autonomy within a two-way relationship. (618)

filial maturity Stage of life, proposed by Marcoen and others, in which middle-aged children, as the outcome of a filial crisis, learn to accept and meet their parents' need to depend on them. (618)

fine motor skills Abilities such as buttoning and copying figures, which involve the small muscles and eye-hand coordination. (141)

fine motor skills Physical skills that involve the small muscles and eye-hand coordination. (242)

five-factor model Theoretical model, developed and tested by Costa and McCrae, based on the "Big Five" factors underlying clusters of related personality traits: neuroticism, extraversion, openness to experience, conscientiousness, and agreeableness. (524)

fluid intelligence Type of intelligence, proposed by Horn and Cattell, which is applied to novel problems and is relatively independent of educational and cultural influences. Compare with *crystallized intelligence.* (578)

fontanels Soft spots on head of young infant. (115)

foreclosure Identity status, described by Marcia, in which a person who has not spent time considering alternatives (that is, has not been in crisis) is committed to other people's plans for his or her life. (450)

formal operations In Piaget's theory, the final stage of cognitive development, characterized by the ability to think abstractly. (425)

free radicals Unstable, highly reactive atoms or molecules formed during metabolism, which can cause internal bodily damage. (644)

functional age Measure of ability to function in physical and social environment in comparison with others of the same chronological age. (639)

functional play In Piaget's and Smilansky's terminology, the lowest cognitive level of play, involving repetitive muscular movements. (294)

gateway drugs Drugs such as alcohol, tobacco, and marijuana, the use of which tends to lead to use of more addictive drugs. (423)

gender Significance of being male or female. (210)

gender constancy Awareness that one will always be male or female. Also called *sex-category constancy.* (290)

gender crossover In Gutmann's terminology, reversal of gender roles after the end of active parenting. (608)

gender identity Awareness, developed in early childhood, that one is male or female. (286)

gender roles Behaviors, interests, attitudes, skills, and traits that a culture considers appropriate for males or for females. (287)

gender stereotypes Preconceived generalizations about male or female role behavior. (287)

gender-schema theory Theory, proposed by Bem, that children socialize themselves in their gender roles by developing a mentally organized network of information about what it means to be male or female in a particular culture. (290)

gender-typing Socialization process by which children, at an early age, learn appropriate gender roles. (210, 287)

gene Basic functional unit of heredity, which contains all inherited material passed from biological parents to children. (67)

generativity In Erikson's terminology, concern of mature adults for establishing, guiding, and influencing the next generation. (597)

generativity versus stagnation In Erikson's theory, the seventh critical alternative of psychosocial development, in which the middle-aged adult develops a concern with establishing, guiding, and influencing the next generation or else experiences stagnation (a sense of inactivity or lifelessness. (597)

generic memory Memory that produces a script of familiar routines to guide behavior. (266)

genetic counseling Clinical service that advises couples of their probable risk of having children with particular hereditary defects. (77)

genetic testing Procedure for ascertaining a person's genetic makeup for purposes of identifying predispositions to specific hereditary diseases or disorders. (78)

genetic-programming theories Theories that explain biological aging as resulting from a genetically determined developmental timetable; compare *variable-rate theories.* (642)

genome imprinting Process by which genes that temporarily have been chemically altered in the mother or father have differing effects when transmitted to offspring. (77)

genotype Genetic makeup of a person, containing both expressed and unexpressed characteristics. (69)

genotype-environment correlation Tendency of certain genetic and environmental influences to reinforce each other; may be passive, reactive (evocative), or active. Also called *genotype-environment covariance.* (82)

genotype-environment interaction The portion of phenotypic variation that results from the reactions of genetically different individuals to similar environmental conditions. (82)

geriatrics Branch of medicine concerned with processes of aging and age-related medical conditions. (640)

germinal stage First 2 weeks of prenatal development, characterized by rapid cell division, increasing complexity and differentiation, and implantation in the wall of the uterus. (87)

gerontology Study of the aged and the process of aging. (640)

goodness of fit Appropriateness of environmental demands and constraints to a child's temperament. (203)

gross motor skills Physical skills such as jumping and running, which involve the large muscles. (141, 242)

guided participation Participation of an adult in a child's activity in a manner that helps to structure the activity and to bring the child's understanding of it closer to that of the adult. (176)

habituation Simple type of learning in which familiarity with a stimulus reduces, slows, or stops a response. Compare *dishabituation.* (168)

handedness Preference for using a particular hand. (243)

Hayflick limit Genetically controlled limit, proposed by Hayflick, on the number of times cells can divide in members of a species. (643)

heredity Inborn influences on development, carried on the genes inherited from the biological parents. (16)

heritability Statistical estimate of contribution of heredity to individual differences in a specific trait within a given population. (78)

heterosexual Describing a person whose sexual orientation is toward the other sex. (453)

heterozygous Possessing differing alleles for a trait. (69)

hierarchy of needs In Maslow's terminology, a rank-order of needs that motivate human behavior. (36)

holophrase Single word that conveys a complete thought. (180)

Home Observation for Measurement of the Environment (HOME) Instrument to measure the influence of the home environment on children's cognitive growth. (159)

homosexual Describing a person whose sexual orientation is toward the same sex. (453)

homozygous Possessing two identical alleles for a trait. (69)

horizontal décalage In Piaget's terminology, a child's inability to transfer learning about one type of conservation to other types, because of which the child masters different types of conservation tasks at different ages. (334)

hormone replacement therapy (HRT) Treatment with artificial estrogen, sometimes in combination with the hormone progesterone, to relieve or prevent symptoms caused by decline in estrogen levels after menopause. (570)

hostile aggression Aggressive behavior intended to hurt another person. (304)

human development Scientific study of change and continuity throughout the human life span. (9)

humanistic perspective View of personality development that sees people as having the ability to foster their own positive, healthy development through the distinctively human capacities for choice, creativity, and self-realization. (36)

hypertension Chronically high blood pressure. (569)

hypotheses Possible explanations for phenomena, used to predict the outcome of research. (27)

hypothetical-deductive reasoning Ability, believed by Piaget to accompany the state of formal operations, to develop, consider, and test hypotheses. (426)

ideal self The self one would like to be. Compare real self. (282)

identification In Freudian theory, the process by which a young child adopts characteristics, beliefs, attitudes, values, and behaviors of the parent of the same sex. (289)

identity accommodation In Whitbourne's terminology, adjusting the self-concept to fit new experience. Compare *identity assimilation.* (602)

identity achievement Identity status, described by Marcia, that is characterized by commitment to choices made following a crisis, a period spent in exploring alternatives. (450)

identity assimilation In Whitbourne's terminology, effort to fit new experience into an existing self-concept. Compare *identity accommodation.* (602)

identity diffusion Identity status, described by Marcia, which is characterized by absence of commitment and lack of serious consideration of alternatives. (451)

identity statuses In Marcia's terminology, states of ego development that depend on the presence or absence of crisis and commitment. (449)

identity style In Whitbourne's terminology, characteristic ways of confronting, interpreting, and responding to experience. (602)

identity versus identity confusion In Erikson's theory, the fifth crisis of psychosocial development, in which an adolescent seeks to develop a coherent sense of self, including the role she or he is to play in society. Also called *identity versus role confusion.* (447)

imaginary audience In Elkind's terminology, an observer who exists only in an adolescent's mind and is as concerned with the adolescent's thoughts and actions as the adolescent is. (429)

implicit memory Memory, generally of habits and skills, which does not require conscious recall; sometimes called *procedural memory.* Compare *explicit memory.* (175)

imprinting Instinctive form of learning in which, during a critical period in early development, a young animal forms an attachment to the first moving object it sees, usually the mother. (208)

independent variable In an experiment, the condition over which the experimenter has direct control. (52)

individual differences Variations in characteristics or developmental outcomes between one child and another. (16)

individual psychotherapy Psychological treatment in which a therapist sees a troubled person one-on-one, to help the patient gain insight into his or her personality, relationships, feelings, and behavior. (396)

individuation In Jung's terminology, emergence of the true self through balancing or integration of conflicting parts of the personality. (596)

inductive reasoning Type of logical reasoning that moves from particular observations about members of a class to a general conclusion about that class. (333)

inductive techniques Disciplinary techniques designed to induce desirable behavior by appealing to a child's sense of reason and fairness. Compare *power assertion* and *withdrawal of love.* (298)

industry versus inferiority In Erikson's theory, the fourth critical alternative of psychosocial development, occurring during middle childhood, in which children must learn the productive skills their culture requires or else face feelings of inferiority. (370)

infant mortality rate Proportion of babies born alive who die within the first year. (123)

infertility Inability to conceive after 12 to 18 months of trying. (499)

information-processing approach Approach to the study of cognitive development by observing and analyzing the mental processes involved in perceiving and handling information. (39)

information-processing approach Approach to the study of cognitive development by observing and analyzing the mental processes involved in perceiving and handling information. (168)

initiative versus guilt In Erikson's theory, the third crisis in psychosocial development, occurring between the ages of 3 and 6, in which children must balance the urge to pursue goals with the moral reservations that may prevent carrying them out. (284)

instrumental activities of daily living (IADLs) Everyday activities, competence in which is considered a measure of the ability to live independently; these activities include managing finances, shopping for necessities, using the telephone, obtaining transportation, preparing meals, taking medication, and housekeeping. (664)

instrumental aggression Aggressive behavior used as a means of achieving a goal. (303)

integration Process by which neurons coordinate the activities of muscle groups. (133)

intelligent behavior Behavior that is goal-oriented (conscious and deliberate) and adaptive to circumstances and conditions of life. (153)

interiority In Neugarten's terminology, a concern with inner life (introversion or introspection), which usually appears in middle age. (597)

internalization Process by which children accept societal standards of conduct as their own; fundamental to socialization. (222)

intimacy versus isolation According to Erikson, the sixth critical alternative of psychosocial development, in which young adults either make commitments to others or face a possible sense of isolation and consequent self-absorption. (526)

invisible imitation Imitation with parts of one's body that one cannot see; e.g., the mouth. (166)

IQ (intelligence quotient) tests Psychometric tests that seek to measure how much intelligence a person has by comparing her or his performance with standardized norms. (157)

irreversibility In Piaget's terminology, a limitation on preoperational thinking consisting of failure to understand that an operation can go in two or more directions. (255)

Kaufman Assessment Battery for Children (K-ABC) Nontraditional individual intelligence test for children ages $2^1/_2$ to $12^1/_2$, which seeks to provide fair assessments of minority children and children with disabilities. (344)

kinship care Care of children living without parents in the home of grandparents or other relatives, with or without a change of legal custody. (625)

laboratory observation Research method in which the behavior of all participants is noted and recorded in the same situation, under controlled conditions. (48)

language Communication system based on words and grammar. (177)

language acquisition device (LAD) In Chomsky's terminology, an inborn mechanism that enables children to infer linguistic rules from the language they hear. (184)

lanugo Fuzzy prenatal body hair, which drops off within a few days after birth. (115)

lateralization Tendency of each of the brain's hemispheres to have specialized functions. (131)

learning Long-lasting change in behavior that occurs as a result of experience. (34)

learning disabilities (LDs) Disorders that interfere with specific aspects of learning and school achievement. (357)

learning perspective View of development that holds that changes in behavior result from experience, or adaptation to the environment; the two major branches are behaviorism and social-learning theory. (34)

legacy creating stage Seventh of Schaie's seven cognitive stages, in which very old people prepare for death by recording their life stories, distributing possessions, and the like. (504)

life expectancy Age to which a person in a particular cohort is statistically likely to live (given his or her current age and health status), on the basis of average longevity of a population. (639)

life structure In Levinson's theory, the underlying pattern of a person's life at a given time, built on whatever aspects of life the person finds most important. (527)

lifelong learning Organized, sustained study by adults of all ages. (670)

life-span development Concept of development as a lifelong process, which can be studied scientifically. (10)

linguistic speech Verbal expression designed to convey meaning. (180)

literacy Ability to read and write. (177)

literacy In an adult, ability to use printed and written information to function in society, achieve goals, and develop knowledge and potential. (515)

longevity Length of an individual's life. (639)

longitudinal study Study design in which data are collected about the same people over a period of time, to assess developmental changes that occur with age. (53)

long-term memory Storage of virtually unlimited capacity, which holds information for very long periods. (338)

low birthweight Weight of less than $5^1/_2$ pounds at birth because of prematurity or being small for date. (118)

macrosystem In Bronfenbrenner's terminology, the system of overall cultural patterns that embraces all of a society's microsystems, mesosystems, and exosystems. (44)

major depressive disorder Mental disorder lasting at least two weeks, in which a person shows extreme sadness, loss of pleasure or interest in life, and other symptoms such as weight changes, insomnia, feelings of worthlessness or inappropriate guilt, loss of memory, inability to concentrate, and thoughts of death or suicide. (659)

marital capital Financial and emotional benefits built up during a long-standing marriage, which tend to hold a couple together. (612)

maternal blood test Prenatal diagnostic procedure to detect the presence of fetal abnormalities, used particularly when the fetus is at risk of defects in the central nervous system. (101)

maturation Unfolding of a genetically influenced, often age-related, sequence of physical changes and behavior patterns, including the readiness to master new abilities. (16)

mechanics of intelligence In Baltes's dual-process model, the abilities to process information and solve problems, irrespective of content; the area of cognition in which there is often an age-related decline. Compare with *pragmatics of intelligence.* (661)

mechanistic model Model, based on the machine as a metaphor, that views development as a passive, predictable response to internal and external stimuli; focuses on quantitative development; and studies phenomena by analyzing the operation of their component parts. (28)

meconium Fetal waste matter, excreted during the first few days after birth. (115)

menarche Girl's first menstruation. (415)

menopause Cessation of menstruation and of ability to bear children, typically around age 50. (564)

mental retardation Significantly subnormal cognitive functioning. (356)

mesosystem In Bronfenbrenner's terminology, a system of linkages of two or more microsystems of which a person is a part. (43)

metacognition Awareness of a person's own mental processes. (347)

metamemory Understanding of processes of memory. (339)

Metamemory in Adulthood (MIA) Questionnaire designed to measure various aspects of adults' metamemory, including beliefs about their own memory and selection and use of strategies for remembering. (668)

microgenetic study Study design that allows researchers to directly observe change by exposing participants to stimuli repeatedly over a short period of time. (55)

microsystem In Bronfenbrenner's terminology, a setting in which a person interacts bidirectionally with others on an everyday, face-to-face basis. (43)

midlife crisis In some normative-crisis models, stressful life period precipitated by the review and reevaluation of one's past, typically occurring in the early to middle forties. (600)

midlife review Introspective examination that often occurs in middle age, leading to reappraisal and revision of values and priorities. (601)

mnemonic strategies Techniques to aid memory. (339)

monozygotic (one-egg) twins Twins resulting from the division of a single zygote after fertilization; also called identical twins. (66)

morality of constraint First of Piaget's two stages of moral development, characterized by rigid, egocentric judgments. (336)

morality of cooperation Second of Piaget's two stages of moral development, characterized by flexible, subtle judgments and formulation of one's own moral code. (336)

moratorium Identity status, described by Marcia, in which a person is currently considering alternatives (in crisis) and seems headed for commitment. (451)

mother-infant bond Close, caring connection between mother and newborn. (208)

multifactorial transmission Combination of genetic and environmental factors to produce certain complex traits. (69)

multi-infarct dementia Irreversible dementia caused by a series of small strokes. (655)

mutual regulation Process by which infant and caregiver communicate emotional states to each other and respond appropriately. (217)

myelination Process of coating neurons with a fatty substance (myelin) that enables faster communication between cells. (134)

myopia Nearsightedness. (562)

nativism Theory that human beings have an inborn capacity for language acquisition. (184)

natural childbirth Method of childbirth, developed by Dr. Grantly Dick-Read, that seeks to prevent pain by eliminating the mother's fear of childbirth through education about the physiology of reproduction and training in methods of breathing and relaxation during delivery. (112)

naturalistic observation Research method in which behavior is studied in natural settings without the observer's intervention or manipulation. (48)

negativism Behavior characteristic of toddlers, in which they express their desire for independence by resisting authority. (222)

neglect Failure to meet a child's basic needs. (306)

neonatal jaundice Condition, in many newborn babies, caused by immaturity of liver and evidenced by yellowish appearance; can cause brain damage if not treated promptly. (115)

neonatal period First 4 weeks of life, a time of transition from intrauterine dependency to independent existence. (114)

neonate Newborn baby, up to 4 weeks old. (114)

neurofibrillary tangles Twisted masses of protein fibers found in brains of persons with Alzheimer's disease. (657)

neurons Nerve cells. (132)

niche-picking Tendency of a person, especially after early childhood, to seek out environments compatible with his or her genotype. (83)

nonshared environmental effects The unique environment in which each child grows up, consisting of distinctive influences or influences that affect one child differently than another. (83)

normative Characteristic of an event that occurs in a similar way for most people in a group. (20)

normative life events In the timing-of-events model, commonly expected life experiences that occur at customary times. (529)

normative-crisis models Theoretical models that describe psychosocial development in terms of a definite sequence of age-related changes. (523)

nuclear family Two-generational economic, kinship, and living unit made up of parents and their biological or adopted children. (17)

obesity Extreme overweight in relation to age, sex, height, and body type; sometimes defined as having a body mass index (weight-for-height) at or above the 85th or 95th percentile of growth curves for children of the same age and sex. (84)

object permanence In Piaget's terminology, the understanding that a person or object still exists when out of sight. (164)

observational learning In social-learning theory, learning that occurs through watching the behavior of others. (36)

open adoption Adoption in which the birth parents and adoptive parents know each other's identities and share information or have direct contact. (378)

operant conditioning Form of learning in which a person tends to repeat a behavior that has been reinforced or to cease a behavior that has been punished. (154)

operant conditioning Kind of learning in which a person tends to repeat a behavior that has been reinforced or to cease a behavior that has been punished. (35)

oppositional defiant disorder (ODD) Pattern of behavior, persisting into middle childhood, marked by negativity, hostility, and defiance. (395)

organismic model Model that views development as internally initiated by an active person, or organism, and as occurring in a universal sequence of qualitatively different stages of maturation. (28)

organization In Piaget's terminology, integration of knowledge into a system to make sense of the environment. (38)

organization Mnemonic strategy of categorizing material to be remembered. (340)

osteoporosis Condition in which the bones become thin and brittle as a result of rapid calcium depletion. (570)

Otis-Lennon School Ability Test Group intelligence test for kindergarten through twelfth grade. (341)

overt aggression Aggression that is openly directed at its target. (304)

parent-support ratio In a given population, number of people age 85 and over for every 100 people ages 50 to 64, who may need to provide care and support for them. (619)

Parkinson's disease Progressive, irreversible degenerative neurological disorder, characterized by tremor, stiffness, slowed movement, and unstable posture. (655)

participant observation Research method in which the observer lives with the people or participates in the activity under observation. (49)

parturition Process of uterine, cervical, and other changes, usually lasting about two weeks, preceding childbirth. (110)

patchwork self In Elkind's terminology, a sense of identity constructed by substituting other people's attitudes, beliefs, and commitments for one's own. (453)

perimenopause Period of several years during which a woman experiences physiological changes that bring on menopause; also called *climacteric.* (564)

periodontitis Gum disease. (655)

permissive In Baumrind's terminology, parenting style emphasizing self-expression and self-regulation. Compare *authoritarian* and *authoritative.* (300)

personal fable In Elkind's terminology, conviction that one is special, unique, and not subject to the rules that govern the rest of the world. (429)

phenotype Observable characteristics of a person. (69)

physical abuse Action taken to endanger a child involving potential bodily injury. (306)

Piagetian approach Approach to the study of cognitive development based on Piaget's theory, which describes qualitative stages, or typical changes, in children's and adolescents' cognitive functioning. (153)

plasticity Modifiability of performance. (11) Modifiability, or "molding," of the brain through experience. (137)

postconventional morality (or morality of autonomous moral principles) Third level in Kohlberg's theory of moral reasoning, in which people follow internally held moral principles of right, fairness, and justice, and can decide among conflicting moral standards. (431)

postformal thought Mature type of thinking, which relies on subjective experience and intuition as well as logic and is useful in dealing with ambiguity, uncertainty, inconsistency, contradiction, imperfection, and compromise. (502)

postmature Referring to a fetus not yet born as of 2 weeks after the due date or 42 weeks after the mother's last menstrual period. (121)

power assertion Disciplinary strategy designed to discourage undesirable behavior through physical or verbal enforcement of parental control. Compare *inductive techniques* and *withdrawal of love.* (298)

pragmatics Set of linguistic rules that govern the use of language for communication. (347)

pragmatics The practical knowledge needed to use language for communicative purposes. (262)

pragmatics of intelligence In Baltes's dual-process model, the dimension of intelligence that tends to grow with age and includes practical thinking, application of accumulated knowledge and skills, specialized expertise, professional productivity, and wisdom. Compare with *mechanics of intelligence.* (661)

preconventional morality First level of Kohlberg's theory of moral reasoning, in which control is external and rules are obeyed in order to gain rewards, or avoid punishment, or out of self-interest. (430)

preimplatation genetic diagnosis Medical procedure in which cells from an embryo conceived by in vitro fertilization are analyzed for genetic defects prior to implantation of the embryo in the mother's uterus. (101)

prejudice Unfavorable attitude toward members of certain groups outside one's own, especially racial or ethnic groups. (387)

prelinguistic speech Forerunner of linguistic speech; utterance of sounds that are not words. Includes crying, cooing, babbling, and accidental and deliberate imitation of sounds without understanding their meaning. (178)

premenstrual syndrome (PMS) Disorder producing symptoms of physical discomfort and emotional tension during the one to two weeks before a menstrual period. (498)

preoperational stage In Piaget's theory, the second major stage of cognitive development (approximately from age 2 to age 7), in which children become more sophisticated in their use of symbolic thought but are not yet able to use logic. (250)

prepared childbirth Method of childbirth, developed by Dr. Ferdinand Lamaze, that uses instruction, breathing exercises, and social support to induce controlled physical responses to uterine contractions and reduce fear and pain. (112)

presbycusis Gradual loss of hearing, which accelerates after age 55, especially with regard to sounds at the upper frequencies. (562)

presbyopia Farsightedness associated with aging, resulting when the lens of the eye becomes less elastic. (562)

pretend play In Piaget's and Smilansky's terminology, the third cognitive level of play, involving imaginary people or situations; also called fantasy play, dramatic play, or imaginative play. (295)

preterm (premature) infants Infants born before completing the thirty-seventh week of gestation. (118)

primary aging Gradual, inevitable process of bodily deterioration throughout the life span. Compare with *secondary aging.* (638)

primary sex characteristics Organs directly related to reproduction, which enlarge and mature during adolescence. Compare *secondary sex characteristics.* (414)

priming Increase in ease of doing a task or remembering information as a result of a previous encounter with the task or information. (666)

private speech Talking aloud to oneself with no intent to communicate. (262)

problem-focused coping In the cognitive-appraisal model, coping strategy directed toward eliminating, managing, or improving a stressful situation.

Compare *emotion-focused coping.* (680)

procedural memory Long-term memory of motor skills, habits, and ways of doing things, which often can be recalled without conscious effort; sometimes called *implicit memory.* (666)

protective factors Influences that reduce the impact of early stress and tend to predict positive outcomes. (123, 399)

proximodistal principle Principle that development proceeds from within to without; that is, that parts of the body near the center develop before the extremities. (87)

psychoanalytic perspective View of development concerned with unconscious forces motivating behavior. (29)

psychometric approach Approach to the study of cognitive development that seeks to measure the quantity of intelligence a person possesses. (153)

psychosexual development In Freudian theory, an unvarying sequence of stages of personality development during infancy, childhood, and adolescence, in which gratification shifts from the mouth to the anus and then to the genitals. (29)

psychosocial development In Erikson's theory, the socially and culturally influenced process of development of the ego, or self; it consists of eight stages throughout the life span, each revolving around a crisis that can be resolved by achieving a healthy balance between alternative positive and negative traits. (33)

puberty Process by which a person attains sexual maturity and the ability to reproduce. (410)

punishment In operant conditioning, a stimulus experienced following a behavior, which decreases the probability that the behavior will be repeated. (35)

qualitative change Change in kind, structure, or organization, such as the change from nonverbal to verbal communication. (12)

quantitative change Change in number or amount, such as in height, weight, or size of vocabulary. (12)

quantitative trait loci (QTL) Interaction of multiple genes, each with effects of varying size, to produce a complex trait. (69)

random assignment Technique used in assigning members of a study sample to experimental and control groups, in which each member of the sample has an equal chance to be assigned to each group and to receive or not receive the treatment. (52)

random selection Sampling method that ensures representativeness because each member of the population has an equal and independent chance to be selected. (46)

reaction range Potential variability, depending on environmental conditions, in the expression of a hereditary trait. (81)

real self The self one actually is. Compare *ideal self.* (282)

recall Ability to reproduce material from memory. Compare *recognition.* (265)

recessive inheritance Pattern of inheritance in which an individual receives identical recessive alleles from both parents, resulting in expression of a recessive (nondominant) trait. (69)

recognition Ability to identify a previously encountered stimulus. Compare *recall.* (265)

reflex behaviors Automatic, involuntary, innate responses to stimulation. (134)

rehearsal Mnemonic strategy to keep an item in working memory through conscious repetition. (339)

reinforcement In operant conditioning, a stimulus experienced following a behavior, which increases the probability that the behavior will be repeated. (35)

reintegrative stage Sixth of Schaie's seven cognitive stages, in which older adults choose to focus limited energy on tasks that have meaning to them. (504)

relational aggression Aggression aimed at damaging or interfering with another person's relationships, reputation, or psychological well-being; also called *covert, indirect,* or *psychological aggression.* (304)

reliability Consistency of a test in measuring performance. (157)

reorganizational stage Fifth of Schaie's seven cognitive stages, in which adults entering retirement reorganize their lives around nonwork-related activities. (504)

representational ability In Piaget's terminology, capacity to mentally represent objects and experiences, largely through the use of symbols. (163)

representational mappings In neo-Piagetian terminology, the second stage in development of self-definition, in which a child makes logical connections between aspects of the self but still sees these characteristics in all-or-nothing terms. (282)

representational systems In neo-Piagetian terminology, third stage in development of self-definition, characterized by breadth, balance, and the integration and assessment of various aspects of the self. (370)

reserve capacity Ability of body organs and systems to put forth four to ten times as much effort as usual under stress; also called *organ reserve.* (648)

resilient children Children who weather adverse circumstances, function well despite challenges or threats, or bounce back from traumatic events that would have a highly negative impact on the emotional development of most children. (399)

responsible stage Third of Schaie's seven cognitive stages, in which middle-aged people are concerned with long-range goals and practical problems related to their responsibility for others. (503)

retrieval Process by which information is accessed or recalled from memory storage. (338)

revolving door syndrome Tendency for young adults to return to their parents' home while getting on their feet or in times of financial, marital, or other trouble. (615)

risk factors Conditions that increase the likelihood of a negative developmental outcome. (19)

rough-and-tumble play Vigorous play involving wrestling, tumbling, kicking, grappling, and sometimes chasing, often accompanied by laughing and screaming. (327)

sample Group of participants chosen to represent the entire population under study. (46)

sandwich generation Middle-aged adults squeezed by competing needs to raise or launch children and to care for elderly parents. (619)

scaffolding Temporary support given to a child who is mastering a task. (45)

schemes In Piaget's terminology, basic cognitive structures consisting of organized patterns of behavior used in different kinds of situations. (38)

schemes In Piaget's terminology, basic cognitive structures consisting of organized patterns of behavior used in different kinds of situations. (161)

schizophrenia Mental disorder marked by loss of contact with reality; symptoms include hallucinations and delusions. (86)

school phobia Unrealistic fear of going to school; may be a form of separation anxiety disorder or social phobia. (395)

scientific method System of scientific inquiry, including identification of a problem, formulation and testing of alternative hypotheses, collection and analysis of data, and public dissemination of findings. (45)

script General remembered outline of a familiar, repeated event, used to guide behavior. (266)

secondary aging Aging processes that result from disease and bodily abuse and disuse and are often preventable. Compare with *primary aging.* (639)

secondary sex characteristics Physiological signs of sexual maturation (such as breast development and growth of body hair) that do not involve the sex organs. Compare *primary sex characteristics.* (414)

secular trend Trend that can be seen only by observing several generations, such as the trend toward earlier attainment of adult height and sexual maturity, which began a century ago. (412)

secure attachment Attachment pattern in which an infant cries or protests when the primary caregiver leaves and actively seeks out the caregiver upon the caregiver's return. (212)

selective optimization with compensation In Baltes's dual-process model, strategy for maintaining or enhancing overall cognitive functioning by using stronger abilities to compensate for those that have weakened. (661)

self-actualization In Maslow's terminology, the highest in the hierarchy of human needs (which can be achieved only after other needs are met): the need to fully realize one's potential. (36)

self-awareness Realization that one's existence and functioning are separate from those of other people and things. (200)

self-concept Sense of self; descriptive and evaluative mental picture of one's abilities and traits. (221, 281)

self-definition Cluster of characteristics used to describe oneself. (281)

self-efficacy Sense of capability to master challenges and achieve goals. (310, 434)

self-esteem The judgment a person makes about his or her self-worth. (285)

self-fulfilling prophecy False expectation or prediction of behavior that tends to come true because it leads people to act as if it already were true. (351)

self-regulation Child's independent control of behavior to conform to understood social expectations. (222)

semantic memory Long-term memory of general factual knowledge, social customs, and language. (666)

senescence Period of the life span marked by changes in physical functioning associated with aging; begins at different ages for different people. (642)

sensorimotor stage In Piaget's theory, the first stage in cognitive development, during which infants (from birth to approximately 2 years) learn through their developing senses and motor activity. (161)

sensory memory Initial, brief, temporary storage of sensory information. (338)

separation anxiety Distress shown by an infant when a familiar caregiver leaves. (215)

separation anxiety disorder Condition involving excessive, prolonged anxiety concerning separation from home or from people to whom a child is attached. (395)

seriation Ability to order items along a dimension. (333)

serious leisure Leisure activity requiring skill, attention, and commitment. (690)

sex chromosomes Pair of chromosomes that determines sex: XX in the normal female, XY in the normal male. (68)

sex-linked inheritance Pattern of inheritance in which certain characteristics carried on the X chromosome inherited from the mother are transmitted differently to her male and female offspring. (75)

sexual abuse Sexual activity involving a child and an older person responsible for the child's care. (306)

sexual dysfunction Persistent disturbance in sexual desire or sexual response. (497)

sexual harassment Unwelcome sexual overtures, particularly from a superior at work, which create a hostile or abusive environment, causing psychological pressure. (576)

sexual orientation Focus of consistent sexual, romantic, and affectionate interest, either heterosexual, homosexual, or bisexual. (453)

sexually transmitted diseases (STDs) Diseases spread by sexual contact. (455)

single representations In neo-Piagetian terminology, first stage in development of self-definition, in which children describe themselves in terms of individual, unconnected characteristics and in all-or-nothing terms. (282)

situational compliance In Kochanska's terminology, a toddler's obedience of a parent's orders only in the presence of prompting or other signs of ongoing parental control. (224)

slow-to-warm-up children Children whose temperament is generally mild but who are hesitant about accepting new experiences. (203)

small-for-date (small-for-gestational age) infants Infants whose birthweight is less than that of 90 percent of babies of the same gestational age, as a result of slow fetal growth. (118)

social capital Family and community resources upon which a person can draw. (438)

social clock Set of cultural norms or expectations for the times of life when certain important events, such as marriage, parenthood, entry into work, and retirement, should occur. (529)

social construction Concept about the nature of reality, based on societally shared subjective perceptions or assumptions. (13)

social convoy theory Theory of aging, proposed by Kahn and Antonucci, which holds that people move through life surrounded by concentric circles of intimate relationships of varying degrees of closeness, on which people rely for assistance, well-being, and social support. (609)

social interaction model Model, based on Vygotsky's sociocultural theory, which proposes that children construct autobiographical memories through conversation with adults about shared events. (268)

social phobia Extreme fear and/or avoidance of social situations. (395)

social promotion Policy in which children are automatically promoted from one grade to another even if they do not meet academic standards for the grade they are completing. (353)

social referencing Understanding an ambiguous situation by seeking out another person's perception of it. (220)

social speech Speech intended to be understood by a listener. (262)

social-contextual approach Approach to the study of cognitive development by focusing on the influence of environmental aspects of the learning process, particularly parents and other caregivers. (168)

socialization Process of developing the habits, skills, values, and motives shared by responsible, productive members of a particular society. (222)

social-learning theory Theory, proposed by Bandura, that behaviors are learned by observing and imitating models. Also called *social cognitive theory.* (35)

sociocultural theory Vygotsky's theory, which analyzes how specific cultural practices, particularly social interaction with adults, affect children's development. (44)

socioeconomic status (SES) Combination of economic and social factors describing an individual or family, including income, education, and occupation. (18)

socioemotional selectivity theory Theory, proposed by Carstensen, that people select social contacts throughout life on the basis of the changing relative importance of social interaction as a source of information, as an aid in developing and maintaining a self-concept, and as a source of emotional well-being. (610)

spermarche Boy's first ejaculation. (415)

spillover hypothesis Hypothesis that there is a positive correlation between intellectuality of work and of leisure activities because of a carryover of learning from work to leisure. (514)

spontaneous abortion Natural expulsion from the uterus of a conceptus that cannot survive outside the womb; also called *miscarriage.* (90)

standardized norms Standards for evaluating performance of persons who take an intelligence test, obtained from scores of a large, representative sample who took the test while it was in preparation. (157)

Stanford-Binet Intelligence Scale Individual intelligence test used to measure memory, spatial orientation, and practical judgment. (270)

state of arousal An infant's degree of alertness; his or her condition, at a given moment, in the periodic daily cycle of wakefulness, sleep, and activity. (116)

Sternberg Triarchic Abilities Test (STAT) Test that seeks to measure componential, experiential, and contextual intelligence in verbal, quantitative, and figural (spatial) domains. (344)

"still-face" paradigm Research method used to measure mutual regulation in infants 2 to 9 months old. (218)

storage Retention of memories for future use. (338)

Strange Situation Laboratory technique used to study attachment. (212)

stranger anxiety Wariness of strange people and places, shown by some infants during the second half of the first year. (215)

stress Response to physical or psychological demands. (246)

stressors Stress-producing experiences. (573)

substance abuse Repeated, harmful use of a substance, usually alcohol or other drugs. (422)

substance dependence Addiction (physical or psychological, or both) to a harmful substance. (422)

substantive complexity Degree to which a person's work requires thought and independent judgment. (514)

sudden infant death syndrome (SIDS) Sudden and unexplained death of an apparently healthy infant. (125)

survival curves Curves, plotted on a graph, showing percentages of a population that survive at each age level. (645)

symbolic function In Piaget's terminology, ability to use mental representations (words, numbers, or images) to which a child has attached meaning. (250)

syntax Rules for forming sentences in a particular language. (181)

systems of action Increasingly complex combinations of simpler, previously acquired skills, which permit a wider or more precise range of movement and more control of the environment. (140) Combinations of motor skills that permit increasingly complex activities. (242)

tacit knowledge In Sternberg's terminology, information that is not formally taught or openly expressed but is necessary to get ahead. (505)

telegraphic speech Early form of sentence consisting of only a few essential words. (181)

temperament Person's characteristic disposition, or style of approaching and reacting to people and situations. (66, 202)

teratogenic Capable of causing birth defects. (92)

theory Coherent set of logically related concepts that seeks to organize, explain, and predict data. (27)

theory of mind Awareness and understanding of mental processes. (257)

theory of multiple intelligences Gardner's theory that distinct, multiple forms of intelligence exist in each person. (342)

time window Limited period of time following an event, during which an infant can integrate new information with the memory of it. (156)

timing-of-events model Theoretical model that describes adult psychosocial development as a response to the expected or unexpected occurrence and timing of important life events. (523)

traditional (intact) families Families that include a married couple and their biological children, or children adopted in infancy. (376)

trait models Theoretical models that focus on mental, emotional, temperamental, and behavioral traits, or attributes. (523)

transduction In Piaget's terminology, a preoperational child's tendency to mentally link particular experiences, whether or not there is logically a causal relationship. (253)

transitional objects Objects used repeatedly by a child as bedtime companions. (241)

transitive inference Understanding of the relationship between two objects by knowing the relationship of each to a third object. (333)

triangular theory of love Sternberg's theory that patterns of love hinge on the balance among three elements: intimacy, passion, and commitment. (534)

triarchic theory of intelligence Sternberg's theory describing three types of intelligence: componential (analytical ability), experiential (insight and originality), and contextual (practical thinking). (343)

two-way (dual-language) learning Approach to second-language education in which English speakers and foreign speakers learn together in their own and each other's languages. (356)

typological models Theoretical models that identify broad personality types, or styles. (523)

ultrasound Prenatal medical procedure using high-frequency sound waves to detect the outline of a fetus and its movements, so as to determine whether a pregnancy is progressing normally. (91)

umbilical cord sampling Prenatal medical procedure in which samples of a fetus's blood are taken from the umbilical cord to assess body functioning; also called *fetal blood sampling.* (101)

validity Capacity of a test to measure what it is intended to measure. (157)

variable-rate theories Theories explaining biological aging as a result of processes that vary from person to person and are influenced by both the internal and the external environment; sometimes called *error theories.* Compare genetic-programming theories. (643)

vernix caseosa Oily substance on a neonate's skin that protects against infection. (115)

violation-of-expectations Research method in which dishabituation to a stimulus that conflicts with previous experience is taken as evidence that an infant recognizes the new stimulus as surprising. (171)

visible imitation Imitation with parts of one's body that one can see, such as the hands and the feet. (166)

visual cliff Apparatus designed to give an illusion of depth and used to assess depth perception in infants. (145)

visual preference Tendency of infants to spend more time looking at one sight than another. (169)

visual-recognition memory Ability to distinguish a familiar visual stimulus from an unfamiliar one when shown both at the same time. (170)

vital capacity Amount of air that can be drawn in with a deep breath and expelled; may be a biological marker of aging. (563)

Wechsler Adult Intelligence Scale (WAIS) Intelligence test for adults, which yields verbal and performance scores as well as a combined score. (660)

Wechsler Intelligence Scale for Children (WISC-III) Individual intelligence test for schoolchildren, which yields verbal and performance scores as well as a combined score. (341)

Wechsler Preschool and Primary Scale of Intelligence, Revised (WPPSI-R) Individual intelligence test for children ages 3 to 7, which yields verbal and performance scores as well as a combined score. (270)

withdrawal of love Disciplinary strategy that may involve ignoring, isolating, or showing dislike for a child. Compare *power assertion* and *inductive techniques.* (299)

working memory Short-term storage of information being actively processed. (176, 338)

zone of proximal development (ZPD) Vygotsky's term for the difference between what a child can do alone and what the child can do with help. (44)

zygote One-celled organism resulting from fertilization. (65)

Bibliography

The ***New! Interactive Bibliography*** to accompany Papalia, *Human Development*, Eighth Edition.

Announcing the first truly interactive text bibliography, giving you and your students the opportunity to learn more about this text's references and researchers. This comprehensive bibliography has been greatly enhanced and expanded to offer the most up-to-date listing of reference citations in developmental psychology. Now located on the text's Online Learning Center, this interactive resource for instructors and students of *Human Development,* Eighth Edition, contains website links to many important sites highlighting key researchers, research organizations, and groups (both government and independent) actively supporting issues related to human development. Instructors can supplement their lectures by quickly researching additional information for further in-depth study or for gathering topical and interesting ideas for classroom discussion. Students can use this resource for investigating key topics and people for research projects, exams, or for career or personal interest. We invite you to try this exciting new resource at http://www.mhhe.com/papaliah8

Printed copies of the bibliography are available upon request.

Acknowledgments

Textual Credits

Chapter 2

From MOTIVATION AND PERSONALITY by Maslow, © 1971. Reprinted by Permission of Prentice-Hall, Inc., Upper Saddle River, NJ.

Chapter 3

Figure 3-8: From *A Child's World, 8th edition* by Diane E. Papalia, Sally Wendkos Olds, Ruth Duskin Feldman. Copyright © 1998. Reproduced with permission of The McGraw-Hill Companies.

Table 3-2: From *Choices, Not Chances* by Aubrey Milunsky, M.D. Copyright © 1977, 1989 by Aubrey Milunsky, M.D. By permission of Little, Brown and Company (Inc.).

Figure 3-10: From Brody, J., "Preventing birth defects even before pregnancy," *The New York Times,* June 28, 1995, p. C10. Copyright © 1995 by The New York Times Co. Reprinted by permission.

Chapter 4

Figure 4-1: From Lagercrantz, H. and T. A. Slotkin, "The 'stress' of being born," *Scientific American,* 254(4), 1986, pp.100–107. Reprinted by permission of Patricia J. Wynne.

Table 4-2: Adapted from V. Apgar, "A proposal for a new method of evaluation of the newborn infant," pp. 260–267, *Current Research in Anesthesia and Analgesia,* 32, 1953. Reprinted by permission of Williams & Wilkins.

Figure 4-5: From *The Brain* by Richard Restak, M.D., copyright © 1984 by Educational Broadcasting Corporation and Richard M. Restak, M.D. Used by permission of Bantam Books, a division of Random House, Inc. and Sterling Lord Literistic Inc. Copyright 1988 by Richard M. Restak.

Figure 4-6: Lach, J. (1997) From Lach, J., "Cultivating the mind" from *Newsweek,* Special Issue, Spring/Summer, 1997, pp. 38–39. © 1997, Newsweek, Inc. All rights reserved. Reprinted by permission.

Figure 4-7: Reprinted by permission of the publisher from *The Postnatal Development Of The Human Cerebral Cortex*, Vol. I–VIII by Jesse LeRoy Conel, Cambridge, Mass.: Harvard University Press, Copyright © 1939–1975 by the President and Fellows of Harvard College.

Figure 4-8: From "Fertile Lands" by J.M. Nash, *Time*, February 3, 1997. Copyright © 1997 Time Inc. Reprinted by permission.

Table 4-5: From W.K. Frankenburg, et al, *Denver II Training Manual*, 1992, Denver Developmental Materials Inc., Denver, CO. Reprinted by permission of Dr. Wm. K. Frankenburg.

Chapter 5

Figure 5-2: From Rovee-Collier-Collier, C. & Boller, K. (1995). Current theory and research on infant learning and memory: Application to early intervention. *Infants and Young Children,* 7(3), 1–12. Copyright © 1995 Aspen Publishers, Inc. Reprinted by permission of Aspen Publishers, Inc.

Table 5-1: From Bayley, N., *Bayley Scales of Infant Development: Second Edition.* Copyright © 1993 by The Psychological Corporation, a Harcourt Assessment Company. Reproduced by permission. All rights reserved.

Figure 5-4: From R. Baillargeon and J. DeVos, "Object permanence in young infants: Further evidence," pp. 1227–1246 in *Child Development*, Vol. 62, 1991. Reprinted by permission of the Society for Research in Child Development.

Figure 5-5: Figure from K. Wynn, "Evidence against empiricist accounts of the origins of numerical knowledge", *Mind and Language*, 7, pp. 315–322, 1992. Reprinted by permission of Blackwell Publishers.

Figure 5-6: From R. Baillargeon, "How do infants learn about the physical world?", pp. 133–139, *Current Directions in Psychological Science*, Vol. 3, No. 5, 1994. Reprinted by permission of Blackwell Publishers.

Chapter 6

Lyrics 6-2: From Hartford, J., "Life Prayer." Copyright © 1968 by Ensign Music Corporation.

Table 6-1: From Sroufe, L.A., adapted from "Socioemotional development" in J. Osofsky, *Handbook of Infant Development.* Copyright © 1979. Reprinted by permission of John Wiley & Sons, Inc.

Figure 6-1: Adaptation from Lewis, M. (1997), The self in self-conscious emotions. In S.G. Snodgrass & R.L. Thompson (eds.) The self across psychology: Self-recognition, self-awareness, and the self-concept. *Annals of the New York Academy of Sciences*, Vol. 818. Reprinted by permission of the New York Academy of Sciences and Professor Michael Lewis.

Table 6-2: From Thomas, A., and S. Chess, "Genesis and evolution of behavioral disorders: From infancy to early adult life", *American Journal of Psychiatry*, 141(1), pp. 1–9. Copyright 1984 American Psychiatric Association. Adapted by permission.

Table 6-4: Robin Peth-Pierce. "The NICHD Study of Early Child Care", 1998, www.nichd.nih.gov.

Table 6-4 "Summary Table of Findings, Child Care and Children's Development" from "The NICHD Study of Early Child Care," prepared by Robin Peth-Pierce, 1998, p. 15. http://www.nichd.nih.gov/publications/pubs/early_child_care.htm.

Chapter 7

Table 7-1: Adapted with permission from Charles B. Corbin, *A Textbook of Motor Development.* Copyright © 1973 Wm. C. Brown Publishers, Dubuque, Iowa.

Figure 7-1: From *Analyzing Children's Art* by Rhoda Kellogg. Copyright © 1969, 1970 by Rhoda Kellogg. Reprinted by permission of Mayfield Publishing Company.

Figure 7-2: Used with permission of the American Academy of Pediatrics, from Wegman, M.E. (1999). Foreign aid, international organizations, and the world's children. *Pediatrics*, 103, 646–654, 1999.

Figure 7-3: Source: Luxembourg Income Study; reprinted in *Children's Defense Fund*, 1996, p. 6.

Chapter 8

Table 8-2: Table adapted from M.B. Parten, "Social play among preschool children" in *Journal of Abnormal and Social Psychology*, 27, 1932, pp. 243–269.

Table 8-3: From R.J. Morris and T.R. Kratochwill, "Childhood Fears," *Treating Children's Fears and Phobias: A Behavioral Approach*. Copyright © 1983 by Allyn & Bacon. Reprinted by permission.

Table 8-4: From K.A. Kendall-Tackett, L. M. Williams and D. Finkelhor, "Impact of sexual abuse on children: A review and synthesis of recent empirical studies," in *Psychological Bulletin*, 113, 1993, pp. 164–180. Copyright © 1993 by the American Psychological Association. Reprinted with permission of American Psychological Association and the author.

Chapter 9

Table 9-1: From Bryant J. Cratty, *Perceptual and Motor Development in Infants and Children, 3e*. Copyright © 1986 by Allyn & Bacon. Adapted by permission.

Table 9-3: From Hoffman, M.L., "Moral development" in *Carmichael's Manual of Child Psychology*, Vol 2, edited by P. H. Mussen, pp. 261–360. Copyright © 1970. Reprinted by permission of John Wiley & Sons, Inc.

Chapter 10

Figure 10-2: Source: Casper, L.M., & Bryson, K.R. (1998). Co-resident grandparents and their grandchildren: Grandparent-maintained families (Population Division Working Paper No. 26). Washington, DC: U.S. Bureau of the Census.)

Table 10-2: From J. Garbarino, N. Dobrow, K. Kostelny, and C. Pardo in *Children in Danger: Coping with the Consequences of Community Violence*. Copyright © 1992. Reprinted by permission of Jossey-Bass, Inc., a Subsidiary Rights Department.

Table 10-3: Table from Masten & Coatsworth, "Characteristics of Resilient Children and Adolescents", *American Psychologist* 53, 205–220, 1998, p. 212. Copyright © 1998 by the American Psychological Association. Reprinted with permission.

Chapter 11

Figure 11-1: From *Promoting the Health of Adolescents: New Directions For The Twenty-First Century*, edited by Susan G. Millstein, et al, copyright © 1994 by Oxford University Press, Inc. Used by permission of Oxford University Press Inc.

Figure 11-2: Source: Mathias, R. (1999). Tracking trends in teen drug abuse over the years. *NIDA Notes* (National Institute on Drug Abuse) 14 (1), p. 58.)

Figure 11-3: Figures from Cognitive Development by Melinda Y. Small and Jerome Kagan, copyright © 1990 by Harcourt, Inc., reproduced by permission of the publisher.

Table 11-2a: From Kohlberg, L. "Stage and sequence: The cognitive-development approach to socialization," in *Handbook of Socialization Theory and Research* by David A. Goslin, Rand McNally, 1969. Reprinted by permission of David A. Goslin.

Table 11-2b: From Lickona, Thomas, *Moral Development and Behavior*. Holt, Rinehart and Winston, 1976. Reprinted by permission of Dr. Thomas Lickona.

Table 11-3: From Zimmerman and Bandura, "Self-motivation for academic attainment", *American Educational Research Journal*, 29, 663–676. Copyright © 1992 by the American Educational Research Association. Adapted by permission of the publisher.

Table 11-4: From F. F. Furstenberg and M. E. Hughes, "Social capital in successful development," pp. 580–592 in *Journal of Marriage and the Family*, 57, 1995. Copyrighted 1995 by the National Council on Family Relations, 3989 Central Ave., NE, Suite 550, Minneapolis, MN 55421. Reprinted by permission.

Chapter 12

Poem 12-2: Merriam, Eve. "Conversation with Myself" from *A Sky Full of Poems* by Eve Merriam. Copyright © 1964, 1970, 1973 Eve Merriam. Used by permission of Marian Reiner.

Table 12-3: From J. Kroger, "Ego identity: An overview," *Discussions on Ego and Identity*, edited by J. Kroger, 1993. Reprinted by permission of Lawrence Erlbaum Associates Inc. and Dr. Jane Kroger.

Table 12-1: From J.E. Marcia, "Development and validation of ego identity status," pp. 551–558, *Journal of Personality and Social Psychology*, 3(5), 1966. Copyright 1966 by the American Psychological Association. Adapted by permission.

Table 12-2: From Marcia, J.E. from "Identity in adolescence" in *Handbook of Adolescent Psychology*, 1980. Reprinted by permission of John Wiley & Sons, Inc.

Figure 12-1: From *A Child's World, 8th edition* by Diane E. Papalia, Sally Wendkos Olds, Ruth Duskin Feldman. Copyright © 1998. Reproduced with permission of The McGraw-Hill Companies.

Chapter 13

Figure 13-1: From R. Stamler, J. Stamler, and D. Garside. Reprinted with permission from *The 20-year Story of the Chicago Heart Association Detection Project in Industry*, American Heart Association, Midwest Affiliate.

Figure 13-2: Source: Hoyert, D.L., Kochanek, K.D., & Murphy, S.L. (1999), Deaths: Final data for 1997. *National Vital Statistics Reports*, 47 (19). Hyattsville, MD: National Center for Health Statistics, p. 7, Fig. 3.

Figure 13-3: From "Toward A Stage Theory of Adult Cognitive Development," *International Journal of Aging and Human Development*, Vol. 8(2), pp. 129–138. Reprinted by permission of Baywood Publishing Company, Inc.

Table 13-1: Reprinted by permission of the publishers from *In A Different Voice: Psychological Theory And Women's Development* by Carol Gilligan, Cambridge, Mass.: Harvard University Press, Copyright © 1980 by the President and Fellows of Harvard College.

Chapter 14

Figure 14-1: Figure from P.T. Costa, Jr. and R.R. McCraie, "Still stable after all these years: Personality as a key to some issues in adulthood and old age," *Life-Span Development and Behavior*, Vol. 3, edited by P.B. Baltes, Jr. and O.G. Brim, pp. 65–102, copyright © 1980 by Academic Press, reproduced by permission of publisher. All rights reserved.

Figure 14-3: R. Helson, "Women's Difficult Times and the Rewriting of the Life Story," *Psychology of Women Quarterly*, Vol. 16, No. 3 (September 1992), p. 342. Copyright © 1992 by Division 35, American Psychological Association. Reprinted with the permission of Cambridge University Press.

Table 14-1: From R.J. Sternberg, "A Triangular Theory of Love," in *Psychological Review*, 93, 1986, pp. 119–135. Copyright © 1986 by the American Psychological Association. Reprinted with permission.

Figure 14-4: Source: Ventura, S.J., Martin, J.A., Curtin, S.C. & Mathews, T.J. (1999). Births: Final data for 1997. *National Vital Statistics Reports*, 47 (18). Hyattsville, MD: National Center for Health Statistics, p. 5, Fig. 2.

Figure 14-5: From A. Burns, "Mother-headed families: An international perspective and the case of Australia", *Social Policy Report of the Society for Research in Child Development*, VI(1), Spring 1992. Reprinted by permission of the author.

Chapter 15

Figure 15-1: From "New study finds middle age is prime of life" by E. Goode in *The New York Times*, Feb. 16, 1999. Reprinted by permission of the New York Times.

Table 15-2: From "Hormone Therapy: When and for how long?", p. 1–2 from *HealthNews*, March 25, 1997, 3 (4). Copyright © 1997 Massachusetts Medical Society. All rights reserved. Reprinted by permission of the publisher.

Table 15-3: Table from Merrill and Verbrugge, "Health & Disease in Midlife," in S.L. Willis & J.D. Reid (Eds) *Life in the Middle; Psychological & Social Development in Middle Age*. p. 87, copyright © 1999 by Academic Press, reproduced by permission of the publisher.

Table 15-4: Reprinted from *Journal of Psychosomatic Research*, Vol. 11, 1967, Holmes et al, "The Social Readjustment Rating Scale", with permission from Elsevier Science.

Figure 15-2: From K.W. Schaie, "The course of adult intellectual development," in *American Psychologist*, 49 (4), 1994, pp. 303–313. Copyright © 1994 by the American Psychological Association. Reprinted with permission.

Figure 15-3: From K.W. Schaie, "The course of adult intellectual development," in *American Psychologist*, 49 (4), 1994, pp. 303–313. Copyright © 1994 by the American Psychological Association. Reprinted with permission.

Figure 15-4: Republished with permission of The Gerontologist, from M.W. Riley, "Aging and society: Past, present, and future," pp. 436–445, *The Gerontologist*, 34, 1994; permission conveyed through Copyright Clearance Center Inc.

Chapter 16

Table 16-1: From LeVine & Levine, "Fertility and Maturity in America," RA Schweder (Ed) *Welcome to Middle Age!* 1998. Reprinted by permission of The University of Chicago Press.

Table 16-1: From McAdams and de St. Aubin, "Loyola Generativity Scale," *Journal of Personality & Social Psychology* 62, 1003–1015, 1992. Copyright © 1992 by the American Psychological Association. Reprinted with permission.

Table 16-2: Table from Klohnen, Vandewater & Young, "Negotiating the middle years; Ego resiliency and successful midlife adjustment in women", *Psychology and Aging*, 11, pp. 431–442, 1996. Copyright © 1996 by the American Psychological Association. Reprinted with permission of American Psychological Association and Jack Block.

Table 16-3: Table from Keyes & Ryff, "Psychological Well Being in Mid-life," in S.L. Willis & J.D. Reid (Eds) *Life in the Middle; Psychological & Social Development in Middle Age*. p. 87, copyright © 1999 by Academic Press, reproduced by permission of the publisher and the author.

Table 16-4: From R. Helson and P. Wink, "Personality change in women from the early 40s to the early 50s," *Psychology and Aging*, 7(1), 1992, pp. 46–55. Copyright © 1992 by the American Psychological Association. Reprinted with permission.

Table 16-5: Table from Hamon, R.R., and R. Blieszner, "Filial responsibility expectations among adult child-older parent pairs," *Journal of Gerontology*, Vol. 45, pp. 110–112, 1990. Copyright © The Gerontological Society of America. Reprinted by permission.

Box 16-2: Home, Jo, "A Caregiver's Bill of Rights," *Caregiving: Helping an Aging Loved Ones*, 1995, p. 299. © 1995, AARP. Reprinted with the permission of the American Association of Retired Persons.

Figure 16-1: From *The New American Grandparent* by A. Cherlin and F. F. Furstenberg, Jr., Basic Books, 1986, p. 74. Reprinted by permission of the authors.

Chapter 17

Figure 17-1: Source: Kramarow, E., Lentzner, H., Rooks, R., Weeks, J., & Saydah, S. (1999). *Health and Aging Chartbook from Health, United States, 1999.* Hyattsville, MD: National Center for Health Statistics, Figure 1, p. 23.

Figure 17-3: Source: U.S. Bureau of the Census. (1999c). *Aging in the Americas into the XXI Century*. Available online: http://www.census.gov/80/ipc/www/agingam.html.

Figure 17-4: From "Giving cells longer life" by J. Letola, *Time*, January 26, 1998. Copyright © 1998 Time Inc. Reprinted by permission.

Figure 17-5: From *Fifty: Midlife In Perspective* by H. Katchadourian © 1987 by W.H. Freeman and Company. Used with permission.

Table 17-3: Source: Adapted from NIA, 1993.

Table 17-4: Adapted from *Is It Alzheimer's? Warning Signs You Should Know*, 1993. Adapted with permission from the Alzheimer's Association.

Figure 17-6: From Botwinick, J. from *Aging and Behavior, 3rd ed.*, 1984. Used by permission of Springer Publishing Company, Inc, New York 10012.

Figure 17-7: Reprinted by permission of the publishers from *Constancy And Change In Human Development* edited by O.G. Brim and J. Kagan, Cambridge., Mass.: Harvard University Press, Copyright © 1980 by the President and Fellows of Harvard College.

Chapter 18

Table 18-1: From Koenig, H.G., L.K. George, and I.C. Siegler, "The use of religion and other emotion-regulating coping strategies among older adults," *Gerontologist*, Vol. 28, pp. 303–310, 1988. Copyright © The Gerontological Society of America.

Figure 18-3: Source: Kramarow, E. Lentzner, H., Rooks, R., Weeks, J., & Saydah, S. (1999). *Health and Aging Chartbook from Health, United States, 1999.* Hyattsville, MD: National Center for Health Statistics, Figure 2, p. 25.

Table 18-3: United Nations Principles for Older Persons. Reprinted by permission of United Nations.

Photo Credits

Part Openers

1: © Nilo Lima/Photo Researchers; **2:** © J.M. Trois/Explorer/Photo Researchers; **3:** © David Young-Wolff/PhotoEdit; **4:** © Lauren Lantos/Index Stock Imagery; **5:** © Bob Daemmrich/The Image Works; **6:** © L. Koolvoord/The Image Works; **7:** John Eastcott & Yva Momatiuk/The Image Works; **8:** © Wayne Hoy/Index Stock Imagery.

Chapter 1

Opener: © Richard Hutchings/PhotoEdit; **p. 7:** Contemporary portrait of Victor of Aveyron from DE L'EDUCATION D'UN HOMME. Reproduced by kind permission of The British Library; **p. 10:** John Vachon/Library of Congress; **p. 17:** © Blair Seitz/Photo Researchers; **p. 21:** © Erika Stone.

Chapter 2

Opener: © Kenneth Gabrielsen/Liaison Agency; **p. 25:** Bettmann/Corbis; **p. 28:** © Adam Butler/Topham/The Image Works; **p. 32:** Mary Evans/Sigmund Freud Copyrights; **p. 34:** UPI/Corbis; **p. 35:** © Linda Cicero/Stanford University News Service; **p. 38:** © Yves DeBraine/Black Star; **p. 41:** © Richard Hutchings/Photo Researchers; **p. 44:** Ria-Novosti/Sovfoto; **p. 48:** © Laura Dwight/PhotoEdit; **p. 52:** © James Wilson/Woodfin Camp & Associates.

Chapter 3

Opener: © P. Wysocki/Explorer/Photo Researchers; **p. 65:** © Petit Format/Science Source/Photo Researchers; **p. 76:** © Ellen Senisi/The Image Works; **p. 80:** © T.K. Wanstal/The Image Works; **p. 83:** © Jalandoni/Monkmeyer; **p. 88 (top to bottom):** (1 month) Petit Format/Nestle/Science Source/Photo Researchers; (7 weeks) Petit Format/Nestle/Science Source/Photo

Researchers; (3 months) Lennart Nilsson, from A CHILD IS BORN. English translation © 1966, 1977 by Dell Publishing Co. Inc. (4 months) © J.S. Allen/Daily Telegraph/International Stock; (5 months) © James Stevenson/Photo Researchers; **p. 89 (top to bottom):** (6 months) © Lennart Nilsson, from BEING BORN; (7 months) Petit Format/Nestle/Science Source/Photo Researchers; (8 months) Petit Format/Nestle/Science Source/Photo Researchers; (9 months) Ronn Maratea/International Stock Photo; **p. 95:** © George Steinmetz; **p. 97:** Fred R. Conrad/NYT Pictures; **p. 100:** © Billy E. Barnes/PhotoEdit.

Chapter 4

Opener: © Ariel Skelley/The Stock Market; **p. 107:** Bettmann/Corbis; **p. 112:** © Mark Richards/PhotoEdit; **p. 113:** © J.T. Miller; **p. 115:** © Joseph Nettis/Stock, Boston; **p. 119:** © Hank Morgan/Science Source/Photo Researchers; **p. 122:** © Mike Teruya/Free Spirit Photography; **p. 129:** © Myrleen Ferguson Cate/PhotoEdit; **p. 136 (top row, left to right):** © Mimi Forsyth/Monkmeyer; © Lew Merrim/Monkmeyer; © Laura Dwight/Black Star; **(bottom row, left to right):** © Mimi Forsyth/Monkmeyer; © Elizabeth Crews; © Elizabeth Crews; **p. 141 (above left):** © Erika Stone; **(above right):** © Elizabeth Crews; **(below):** © Margaret Miller/Photo Researchers; **p. 144:** © Innervisions; **p. 145:** © Steve Maines/Stock, Boston.

Chapter 5

Opener: PhotoDisc/Volume 41, Education 2; **p. 151:** Neg. No. 326799 Courtesy Department Library Services/American Museum of Natural History; **p. 154:** © Mary Ellen Mark; **p. 156:** © Michael Newman/PhotoEdit; **p. 169:** © James Kilkelly; **p. 171:** © Doug Goodman/Monkmeyer; **p. 174:** © Peter Southwick/Stock, Boston; **p. 180:** PhotoDisc/Volume 28, Vacation; **p. 184:** © Jose Pelaez/The Stock Market; **p. 188:** © Tony Freeman/PhotoEdit; **p. 189:** © Anthony Wood/Stock, Boston.

Chapter 6

Opener: © Nancy Sheehan/Index Stock Photography; **p. 195:** Library of Congress; **p. 199 (top):** Digital Stock, Babies and Children; **(bottom):** © Laura Dwight; **p. 203:** © Ruth Duskin Feldman; **p. 207:** Harry Harlow Primate Laboratory, University of Wisconsin; **p. 208 (above):** Thomas McAvoy/Life Magazine © Time Inc.; (below) © Ellen B. Senisi/Photo Researchers; **p. 211:** Real Life Medicine/Corbis CD; **p. 214:** Jonathan Finlay; **p. 216:** © Kathy McLaughlin/The Image Works; **p. 218:** © Sybil Shackman/Monkmeyer; **p. 221:** © Rick Kopstein/Monkmeyer; **p. 226:** © Eastcott/The Image Works; **p. 228:** © Joseph Schuyler/Stock, Boston.

Chapter 7

Opener: Bob Daemmrich/Stock, Boston; **p. 237:** Cynthia Johnson/Liaison Agency; **p. 243 (top row, left to right):** © Laura Dwight; PhotoDisc/Volume 28, People, Lifestyles, and Vacations; © Miro Vintoniv/Stock, Boston; below: Tom McCarthy/The Image Bank; **p. 246:** © Elliot Varner-Smith/International Stock Photo; **p. 249:** © Lester Sloan/Newsweek/Liaison Agency; **p. 253:** © Erika Stone; **p. 260:** The Photo Works/Monkmeyer; **p. 261:** © Newman Brown/Monkmeyer; **p. 266:** © Elizabeth Crews/The Image Works; **p. 270:** © Erika Stone/Photo Researchers; **p. 272:** © David Young-Wolff/PhotoEdit.

Chapter 8

Opener: © CLEO Photo/Index Stock Imagery; **p. 279:** Bettmann/Corbis; **p. 282:** © Laura Dwight/PhotoEdit; **p. 285** © Nancy Richmond/The Image Works; **p. 286:** © Network Pro/The Image Works; **p. 290:** Courtesy of Sandra Lipsitz Bem; **p. 293:** © Stephen McBrady/PhotoEdit; **p. 295:** © Zabala/Monkmeyer; **p. 302:** © Margaret Miller/Photo Researchers; **p. 303:** © Sybil Shackman/Monkmeyer; **p. 310:** © Janet Fries; **p. 313:** © Nita Winter

Chapter 9

Opener: © Bill Bachman/PhotoEdit; **p. 321:** National Archives; **p. 329:** PhotoDisc/Volume 18, Medicine; **p. 331:** © Bob Daemmrich/Stock, Boston; **p. 334** © Laura Dwight; **p. 339** © David Lassman/The Image Works; **p. 342:** PhotoDisc/Volume 24, Education; **p. 349:** PhotoDisc/Volume 41, Education 2; **p. 351:** © Laura Dwight/PhotoEdit; **p. 354:** © Peter Dublin/Stock, Boston; **p. 355:** © Bob Daemmrich/The Image Works; **p. 357:** © Richard S. Orton; **p. 360:** © Ken Kerbs/Monkmeyer.

Chapter 10

Opener: © Tom McCarthy/The Stock Market; **p. 367:** UPI-Bettmann/Corbis; **p. 371:** © M. Justice/The Image Works; **p. 373:** © Laura Dwight/PhotoEdit; **p. 378:** © Myrleen Ferguson/PhotoEdit; **p. 379:** © C. Boretz/The Image Works; **p. 383:** © Deborah Davis/PhotoEdit; **p. 385:** © James R. Holland/Stock, Boston; **p. 387:** © Mindy E. Klarman/Photo Researchers; **p. 389:** © Dallas & John Heaton/Stock, Boston; **p. 390:** © Erika Stone; **p. 392:** © Bob Daemmrich/The Image Works; **p. 396:** © Michal Heron/Monkmeyer.

Chapter 11

Opener: © Bob Daemmrich/The Image Works; **p. 407:** Culver Pictures; **p. 409:** © Bill Gillette/Stock, Boston; **p. 414:** © Mary Kate Denny/PhotoEdit; **p. 416:** © Robert Brenner/PhotoEdit; **p. 420:** © Kelley Chin/The Kansas City Star/AP/Wide World Photos; **p. 424:** PhotoDisc/Volume 45 Lifestyles Today; **p. 426:** © Mimi Forsyth/Monkmeyer; **p. 435:** © Erika Stone.

Chapter 12

Opener: © Paula Lerner/Index Stock Imagery; **p. 445:** AP/Wide World Photos; **p. 448:** © Miro Vintoniv/Stock, Boston; **p. 452:** © Bob Daemmrich/The Image Works; **p. 455:** © Ellen Skye/Monkmeyer; **p. 458:** The Children's Defense Fund; **p. 462:** © Tim Greenway/AP/Wide World Photos; **p. 466:** © Ruth Duskin Feldman; **p. 470:** © Tom McCarthy/PhotoEdit; **p. 473:** © Laura Rauch/AP/Wide World Photos; **p. 478:** © A. Ramey/Stock, Boston.

Chapter 13

Opener: Bob Daemmrich/The Image Works; **p. 485:** © Rob Straus/ Woodfin Camp & Associates; **p. 487:** PhotoDisc/Volume 27, International Sports; **p. 490:** PhotoDisc/Volume 45 Lifestyles Today; **p. 494:** © Mark Ludak/Impact Visuals; **p. 500:** © Mehau Kulyk/Science Photo Library/Photo Researchers; **p. 505:** © David Young-Wolff/PhotoEdit; **p. 511:** © Keith Carter Photography; **p. 513:** © Charles Gupton/Stock, Boston; **p. 517:** © Frank Niemeir/The Atlanta Constitution.

Chapter 14

Opener: © Adam G. Sylvester/Photo Researcher; **p. 521:** AP/Wide World Photos; **p. 526:** © Jeffrey Dunn/Stock, Boston; **p. 532:** © Michael Dwyer/Stock, Boston; **p. 537 (left):** PhotoDisc/Volume 45 Lifestyles Today; **(right):** PhotoDisc/Signature Series 17; **p. 539:** © Andy Bernhauf/Photo Researchers; **p. 542:** PhotoDisc/Volume 25 Government and Social Issues; **p. 543:** PhotoDisc/Volume 46 Beauty and Health; **p. 550:** © Erika Stone.

Chapter 15

Opener: USDA/Science Source/Photo Researchers; **p. 557:** Kanu Ghandi/Library of Congress; **p. 561:** David Lawrence/The Stock Market; **p. 568:** © Brian Yarvin/The Image Works; **p. 570:** © Science Photo Library/Photo Researchers; **p. 576:** © Michael Kaufman/Impact Visuals; **p. 581:** © Tim Davis/Photo Researchers; **p. 584:** © Ulf

Andersen/Liaison Agency; **p. 587:** © Bob Daemmrich/The Image Works.

Chapter 16

Opener: © Bill Bachmann/Photo Researchers; **p. 593:** © Doug Mills/AP/Wide World Photos; **p. 598:** © Levine/Anthro-Photo; **p. 604:** © David Young-Wolff/PhotoEdit; **p. 611:** © A. Ramey/Woodfin Camp & Associates; **p. 618:** © Parke/Liaison Agency; **p. 622:** © Cameramann/The Image Works; **p. 624:** © Tom McCarthy/Index Stock Imagery; **p. 626:** © Eugene Richards/Magnum Photos.

Chapter 17

Opener: © David Young-Wolff/PhotoEdit; **p. 633:** NASA; **p. 637:** © Lori Peters/AP/Wide World Photos; **p. 646:** © Robert Ricci/Liaison Agency; **p. 650:** © Barbara Kirk/The Stock Market; **p. 654:** © Boiffin-Viviere/Explorer/Photo Researchers; **p. 656:** © Dr. Robert Friedlan/SPLibrary/Photo Researchers; **p. 659:** © Oscar Burriel/Latin Stock/Science Photo Library/Photo Researchers; **p. 665:** © Joe Carini/The Image Works; **p. 671:** Courtesy of Ruth Michael/© Dennis Wells.

Chapter 18

Opener: © Scott Barrow/International Stock; **p. 675:** © Evan Agostini/Liaison Agency; **p. 679:** © Skip O'Rourke/The Image Works; **p. 684:** © Shelley Gazin/Corbis; **p. 687:** © Dave Bartriff/The Image Works; **p. 691:** Spencer Grant/Stock, Boston; **p. 695:** © Blair Seitz/Photo Researchers; **p. 700:** © Paul Fusco/Magnum Photos; **p. 702:** © Bill Aron/PhotoEdit; **p. 703:** © Cary Wolinsky/Stock, Boston; **p. 706:** © Matthew Jordan Smith/Liaison Agency; **p. 706:** © CLEO Photo/Index Stock Imagery.

Epilogue

Opener: © Armed Forces/Corbis CD; **E-2:** © Bob Daemmrich/Stock, Boston.

Name Index

Subject Index

Boldface terms indicate key terms; **boldface** page numbers indicate the pages on which they are defined.